CRIMINAL AND FORENSIC EVIDENCE:
Cases, Materials, Problems

CRIMINAL AND FORENSIC EVIDENCE:

Cases, Materials, Problems
Third Edition

Robert J. Goodwin
J. Russell McElroy Professor of Law
Samford University Cumberland School of Law

Jimmy Gurulé
Professor of Law
Notre Dame Law School

2009

 LexisNexis

Library of Congress Cataloging-in-Publication Data

Goodwin, Robert J., 1949-
    Criminal and forensic evidence : cases, materials, problems / Robert J. Goodwin,
Jimmy Gurulé. — 3d ed.
    p. cm.
        Rev. ed. of: Criminal and scientific evidence. 2nd ed. c2002.
    Includes index.
    ISBN 978-1-4224-7033-6 (hardbound)
    1. Evidence, Criminal — United States — Cases. 2. Evidence, Expert — United States — Cases. I. Gurulé, Jimmy. II.
Goodwin, Robert J., 1949- Criminal and scientific evidence. III. Title.
    KF9660.G66 2009
        345.73'06--dc22   2009024844

Editorial Offices
121 Chanlon Rd., New Providence, NJ 07974 (908) 464-6800
201 Mission St., San Francisco, CA 94105-1831 (415) 908-3200
www.lexisnexis.com

MATTHEW◆BENDER

(2009–Pub.3030)

DEDICATION

Professor Goodwin dedicates his work on this project to
his son Andrew.

Professor Gurulé dedicates this book to his loving parents,
Rita and Mauro Franco.

PREFACE TO THE THIRD EDITION

A. Text Orientation

We are pleased to publish the Third Edition. At the outset, we should note that we have changed the title of our casebook. Although previous editions were titled, CRIMINAL AND SCIENTIFIC EVIDENCE, the Third Edition is titled, CRIMINAL AND FORENSIC EVIDENCE. We feel that this change more accurately reflects the scope of the casebook, which covers the admissibility of *both* scientific and non-scientific expert testimony in criminal cases. In addition, the change seems appropriate because "forensic" has become closely associated with crime laboratories and criminal cases.

The change in title does not, however, reflect a change in the casebook's orientation. The focus of the Third Edition is the same as its predecessors; to explore how the rules of evidence are applied in criminal cases. As with previous editions, we have divided materials into two parts. Part One examines scientific and expert evidence issues, while Part Two addresses more "traditional" evidentiary issues (character evidence, hearsay, impeachment, etc.). Either part could be used independently to teach an evidence course related solely to the issues discussed in that part, or, if desired, an instructor could combine chapters from parts one and two to present a comprehensive evidence course that covers both forensic and traditional evidentiary issues in criminal cases.

We tried to avoid making substantive changes unless a corresponding change in the law made such changes necessary. Major revisions were required, however, to address the transformation of Confrontation Clause jurisprudence resulting from the United States Supreme Court's decisions in *Crawford v. Washington* and *Davis v. Washington*. Accordingly, this third edition includes a significant amount of new material covering the high Court's decisions in *Crawford* and *Davis*, as well as lower court applications of the constitutional and evidentiary principles announced in those cases. Other than changes related to the new Confrontation Clause standard, previous adopters should find the third edition updated but familiar. As with the earlier editions, the authors encourage and welcome comments and criticisms.

B. Procedural Matters

Short form citations have been used for two excellent treatises that are heavily cited. First, the two-volume treatise by Paul C. Giannelli and Edward J. Imwinkelried, SCIENTIFIC EVIDENCE (Matthew Bender & Co., 4th ed. 2007) is cited as "SCIENTIFIC EVIDENCE." Second, the two-volume treatise by Edward J. Imwinkelried, Paul C. Giannelli, Francis A. Gilligan, & Frederic I. Lederer, entitled COURTROOM CRIMINAL EVIDENCE, (Matthew Bender & Co. 4th ed. 2005) is cited as "COURTROOM CRIMINAL EVIDENCE."

To save space and make for smoother reading of judicial opinions and excerpts from law review articles, most internal citations have been eliminated. These deletions are not noted. Deletions from the text of judicial opinions and law review articles are noted. Also, for readability, many footnotes have been omitted. Footnotes within judicial opinions that are included retain their original numbers, but are enclosed in brackets. This same treatment (original number enclosed in brackets) has been given to footnotes contained in law review articles and excerpts from secondary sources. Footnotes by the authors of this text are numbered without brackets.

C. Acknowledgments

Professor Goodwin would like to recognize the invaluable assistance provided by several individuals. Mrs. Tracy Luke assisted with the tireless task of proofreading, and provided critical technical assistance. Ms. Stephanie Whatley (Cumberland '09) provided valuable and timely assistance with research, cite checking, and proofreading. Finally, Professor Edward J. Imwinkelried deserves special mention for his scholarship and related contributions in the field of Evidence. This text relies heavily upon his research, and would not have been possible without his encouragement and support.

Professor Gurulé would like to compliment Christopher O'Byrne, Notre Dame Law School research librarian, whose competence, professionalism, and timely response to research requests greatly contributed to the Third Edition. Additionally, Daniel Hebel's (Class of 2009) dedicated hard work researching book chapters is sincerely appreciated. Finally, Carlo Rolando (Class of 2009) deserves special recognition. Mr. Rolando provided invaluable research assistance. He further worked tirelessly cite-checking cases and other legal sources, as well as editing and proofreading early drafts of book chapters. There is no doubt that upon entering the practice of law, Mr. Rolando will be an outstanding lawyer.

Table of Contents

Table of Contents

Table of Contents

Table of Contents

Table of Contents

Table of Contents

Table of Contents

Table of Contents

Table of Contents

Table of Contents

Table of Contents

Table of Contents

Table of Contents

Table of Contents

Table of Contents

Part 1

Scientific Evidence and Techniques

Chapter 1

FORENSIC SCIENCE AND THE CRIMINAL JUSTICE SYSTEM

A. THE NATURE OF FORENSIC SCIENCE AND ITS "CORRUPTION" IN THE COURTROOM

[1]   Introduction

Clearly, the use of scientific evidence in criminal trials is here to stay. Techniques such as fingerprinting, firearms identification, hair analysis, and blood typing — to name just a few — have produced valuable evidence for years, and their utility in resolving questions of guilt or innocence has rarely been questioned. Furthermore, science is not static, and the criminal justice system has demonstrated a willingness to embrace evidence derived from a newly developed scientific technique, such as DNA analysis, once the technique has been shown to be reliable. In fact, some observers have argued that jurors have become so enamored with scientific evidence that they expect the prosecution to present it in every case, and are reluctant to convict in its absence. To combat this so-called, "CSI effect," some prosecutors contend that the presentation of scientific evidence is necessary and relevant to achieve a conviction even when it does not connect the accused to the crime being tried.[1]

Nonetheless, the reliance on science evidence in criminal trials has not escaped controversy. Critics argue that courts too readily accept evidence based on unproven scientific methodologies and techniques.[2] On the other hand, not all scientific techniques have been warmly received by the courts. For example, evidence based upon the results of testing performed on the polygraph machine is rarely admitted. The question, therefore, is not whether scientific evidence should, or should not, be used in the courtroom; rather, the question is *which scientific principles, methods, and techniques* will courts accept, and what *conditions*, if any, will be placed on the admissibility and use of evidence derived from science.

To illustrate the ambivalence that the criminal justice system displays toward scientific evidence, consider that courts appear to prefer questionable and uncertain eyewitness testimony over evidence that is more certain, but which is based upon the application of a scientific technique. If (as will be seen) courts are primarily concerned with "reliability" when they decide whether to admit scientific evidence, why is it that unreliable eyewitness testimony is routinely admitted?[3] Put another way, what

---

[1] *See, e.g.*, State v. Cooke, 914 A.2d 1078, 1082–88, 1093–95 (Del. Super. Ct. 2007) (discussing "CSI effect" at length, and holding prosecution may present results of hair and fingerprint analysis that did not connect defendant to murder he was charged with committing).

[2] *See* Committee on Identifying the Needs of the Forensic Sciences Community, National Research Council, *Strengthening Forensic Science in the United States: A Path Forward* 3-1 (prepublication copy, Feb. 2009). The Report also found that the rules governing the admissibility of forensic evidence were "inadequate to the task of curing the documented ills of the forensic science system." *Id.*

[3] The reliability of eyewitness identifications is examined in Chapter 5.

characteristics of scientific evidence make its admission in criminal cases particularly troublesome even though it may be just as reliable (if not more so) as eyewitness testimony on the same topic? To fully comprehend the difficulty the law has experienced with evidence generated by science, one must understand the nature of *forensic* science, its ability to produce accurate evidence, and — most critically — the ability of the jury to perceive the strengths and weaknesses of forensic evidence.

To begin with, consider the possibility of a jury overestimating the objectivity of scientific evidence in a criminal trial. A jury may, understandably, view science and the scientific method as objective and impartial — a quest for truth — and assume that when a scientist offers an opinion based upon the results of a scientific technique or procedure, that such testimony should be accepted at face value. Although objectivity may exist when scientific research is conducted outside the legal setting, a forensic scientists' conclusions are developed for — and presented by — an advocate (usually the prosecution) in the courtroom. In this regard consider the difference between a "scientist" and a "*forensic* scientist." While virtually any scientific discipline may find its way, on occasion, into a courtroom, there is a distinct professional identity for the scientist who assists the legal system and routinely appears in court. Such a person is referred to as a "*forensic* scientist." Providing expert testimony in the courtroom is part of the forensic scientist's profession and job description. Consider also that while forensic science could be a part of civil as well as criminal cases, forensic scientists are closely identified with criminal investigations and trials and typically apply their talents in aid of the police and the prosecution. This close identification with the legal system, and with the prosecution in particular, has led some to question the objectivity of forensic science.

Second, consider the related problem of a jury overestimating the accuracy of scientific evidence. Scientific evidence encompasses a wide range of scientific disciplines that can produce evidence on diverse topics. For example, science can provide data on how fast a car was traveling as indicated by a radar gun; whether a person is telling the truth based upon the administration of a polygraph test; the manner of death as determined by a pathologist after an autopsy, and identity based upon a variety of techniques, such as, fingerprint analysis, bitemark analysis, hair analysis, DNA typing, etc. Accompanying this diversity of disciplines, however, is diversity of reliability. Quite simply, different scientific techniques have different error rates. Error, for example, could occur because the technique itself is not 100% accurate; because data produced by the technique requires subjective interpretation; or because of a simple human error in conducting a test. The problem here is not that conclusions derived from scientific testing are wrong most of the time — indeed, the opposite is true — the concern is whether the jury possesses the background and experience necessary to assess and assign appropriate weight to scientific evidence.

This chapter examines the nature of forensic science, its potential to erroneously alter the outcome of a criminal case, and the ability of the legal system to recognize and correct such errors. We begin with excerpts from two articles and a Bureau of Justice Statistics Census. The first article, by John I. Thornton, highlights the differences between "science" and "forensic science," and describes how crime laboratories came to be established in this country. The second article, by Joseph L. Peterson, Steven Mihajlovic and Joanna L. Bedrosian, reports on the control and use of crime laboratories. Following the second article are excerpts from a report issued in July of 2008 by the Department of Justice's, Bureau of Justice Statistics, titled, *Census of Publicly Funded Forensic Crime Laboratories*, 2005.

[2]   The Nature of Forensic Science

JOHN I. THORNTON, USES AND ABUSES OF FORENSIC SCIENCE
69 A.B.A.J. 288, 289–91 (March, 1983)[4]

[I]n the broadest sense, forensic science is any science used in the resolution of legal conflicts. . . . [F]orensic science has come to mean the study and practice of applying natural and physical sciences to the just resolution of social and legal issues. What distinguishes it from other sciences is its use by the legal system; what distinguishes a forensic scientist from other scientists is the expectation of routine appearances in a court of law.

Forensic science exists at the confluence of law and science. The two frequently work in harmony, but at best there is an uneasy truce between them. I have a fairly cynical view concerning the amalgamation of these two forces, a view that will not comport in all respects to the perceptions of others but that might prompt reflections on the practical interrelationships of law and science.

Although forensic science historically has been identified closely with the criminal justice system, the forensic scientist now plays an increasingly active role in civil litigation and in regulatory matters. Virtually no limitation exists to the scope of physical evidence that is the grist for all forensic scientists. Physical evidence may range in size from the microscopic (for example, a pollen grain) to the macroscopic (for example, a diesel truck). It may be as appalling as the lifeless body of a battered child, as intangible as the fleeting vapors of gasoline following a suspected arson fire, or as obscure as the composition of dyes in the ink of a contested will.

Various disciplines within forensic science have emerged in response to this diversity in evidence and in recognition of the need for expertise either within or beyond the bounds of general knowledge. These needs have been voiced clearly by the legal profession. Forensic science is one of the windows through which the law may view the scientific and technological advances of our age.

. . . .

A number of disciplines exist within the rubric of forensic science. . . . The American Academy of Forensic Sciences, the largest professional forensic society in the world, recognizes the following scientific disciplines: forensic pathology, forensic toxicology, forensic anthropology, forensic odontology, forensic psychiatry, questioned documents, forensic engineering, and criminalistics. . . .

Pathology is the study of disease, and forensic pathology is a subspecialty dealing with the investigation of death or injury as a result of violence, or with the cause of unexpected and unexplained death. In addition to determining the cause of death, the inquiry includes, to the extent possible, any extrinsic factual circumstances affecting the body of the deceased at the time of death. For example, a forensic pathologist may determine that the cause of death was a gunshot wound and then consider whether the death was homicidal, suicidal, or accidental, based on factors including the position of the weapon, the location of the wound, and the bullet pathway through the body. Without exception, forensic pathologists are medical doctors.

Forensic psychiatry, as the name suggests, concerns the practice of psychiatry in its special medicolegal context. . . . The principal function of the forensic psychiatrist is to determine the mental state of a person at the time of a past action. Because this is done retrospectively, the results are necessarily subjective. Because criminal responsibility and mental competency are emotionally charged issues, forensic psychiatry can be controversial, and the opinions of forensic psychiatrists often are strongly contested.

Forensic odontology is the branch of dentistry dealing with dental evidence, usually involving an examination of dental remains for identification of the victim, injuries to the teeth or jaw, or bite marks for comparison with those of a suspect. Although the forensic odontologist might play a critical role in a criminal investigation, most of the work concerns the identification of victims after mass disasters — airplane crashes, for example. Forensic odontologists frequently co-operate with forensic anthropologists.

Forensic anthropology deals with the identification of skeletal remains through the application of standard anthropological techniques. The forensic anthropologist might in many instances determine from this evidence the sex, race, physical stature, and age at death of a victim. Less frequently, the remains might provide insight into the physique, injuries, diseases, or facial features of the deceased. . . .

Toxicology is the study of effects of harmful substances on living systems, and forensic toxicology is the practice of this science in the legal setting. Forensic toxicologists study the analyses of tissues and fluids from deceased persons to identify toxic substances that might have caused the death. They are concerned otherwise with a broad range of matters, including blood analyses in cases involving driving under the influence of drugs. In some urban areas where a high percentage of all crime is thought to be drug related, forensic toxicologists are given a formidable role in the administration of justice. . . .

Questioned documents is the discipline within forensic science that attempts to resolve various legal questions through the examination of handwriting, typewriting, paper, ink, and other factors.

Forensic engineering is a relatively new discipline; forensic engineers frequently are called on to assist with the reconstruction of automobile accidents, to assess evidence in product liability cases, and to conduct failure analyses on a wide variety of manufactured items.

Criminalistics may be described in either a subtractive or an additive manner. In the former sense it represents what remains other than pathology, odontology, toxicology, and the other forensic subspecialties. In the additive sense, criminalistics is concerned with the analysis, identification, and interpretation of hairs and fibers; bloodstains and seminal stains; firearms evidence; soil, glass, and paint classifications; toolmarks; arson accelerants; explosives; serial number restoration; and virtually anything else that does not fit tidily into one of the other disciplines. . . .

. . . .

Forensic science is essentially a 20th century innovation. Various attempts were made earlier to use scientific evidence of one sort or another, but the results were less than satisfactory. . . . The first operational crime laboratory in the country was not established until 1923 in Los Angeles, followed by the Scientific Crime Detection Laboratory at Northwestern University in 1929, and the Federal Bureau of Investigation laboratory in 1932. . . . Forensic science is still suffering from some teething problems and has yet to fulfill its inherent promise as a profession.

Although one might suppose that the inception of forensic science resulted from progressive attitudes of pathologists, lawyers, police administrators, or scientists, this rarely was the case. . . . In fact, many of the nation's crime laboratories owe their existence not to enlightened attitudes of police administrators or other public officials but to adverse publicity or the threat of it. Police tended to view other forensic laboratories as a public relations ploy rather than a legitimate means of providing objective information useful in the conduct of police affairs.

To be fair, there undoubtedly were some law enforcement officials who saw in forensic science the opportunity to incorporate objective scientific data into the resolution of social and legal questions, but condescension was the prevailing attitude. The intrinsic intellectual appeal of science is every bit as much responsible for developing forensic science as is the felt need of investigative agencies. Some forensic laboratories are still within administrative organizations that are tightly governed by their police function, and the laboratories consequently are unable to give free expression to the scientific method or to the maintenance of an atmosphere conducive to the proper exercise of professional functions. Forensic science, however, is used extensively in our contemporary legal processes and shows every indication of being used to an even greater extent.

It is clear that in a complex society many facets of human endeavor fall outside the experiences of the general public, the bar, and the judiciary. Indeed issues may fall outside the comprehension of these groups. Specific provisions therefore are made in the law for scientific witnesses to explain the scientific underpinnings of those issues. There are many experts in the world, but many of them avoid the agony of participating in trials. Forensic scientists expect to defend their positions in a court of law, accepting the adversarial proceedings (which may include being labeled as a "trained seal" by the opposing side) as something that "goes with the territory." The forensic scientist, then, is a person with a twofold purpose: to conduct examinations of the physical evidence as necessary in accordance with generally accepted professional standards, and to convey the results to the trier of fact and defend professional opinions if called upon to do so.

In a criminal case the forensic scientist may assist in establishing an essential element of the crime, identifying the suspect, determining the factual circumstances, and ascertaining the guilt or innocence of the accused, although this last function is only incidental to the others. . . .

NOTE

American Academy of Forensic Sciences. By 1995 the American Academy of Forensic Sciences (AAFS) had expanded its forensic pathology section to include biology, and its forensic psychiatry section to include behavioral sciences. On February 28, 2008, the AAFS created a new forensic section, the Digital and Multimedia Sciences (DMS) section. On that date the AAFS had nine scientific sections: Criminalistics, Digital & Multimedia Sciences, Engineering Sciences, Odontology, Pathology and Biology, Physical Anthropology, Psychiatry and Behavioral Sciences, Questioned Documents, and Toxicology. In addition, the AAFS has a Jurisprudence section that studies legal issues associated with the forensic sciences.

The next two excerpts report, primarily, on the nature of services provided by crime laboratories. The first excerpt contains results from a survey conducted in 1983 with the assistance of a grant from the National Institute of Justice. The second excerpt is from a Bureau of Justice Statistics census conducted 22 years later, in 2005.

JOSEPH L. PETERSON, STEVEN MIHAJLOVIC & JOANNE L. BEDROSIAN, THE CAPABILITIES, USES AND EFFECTS OF THE NATION'S CRIMINALISTICS LABORATORIES
30 J. Forensic Sci. 10, 10–16 & 22 (Jan. 1985)[5]

Method

Our goal was to survey all bona fide crime laboratories within the United States. The first task was to compile a listing of all crime laboratories (public and private) that regularly examine physical evidence in criminal cases and offer reports and expert testimony to courts of law. . . . What resulted was a compilation of 319 federal, state, and local crime laboratories, each of which was mailed a copy of an eight-page questionnaire. . . . The response rate was 82% (260/319). . . .

Origin and Placement of Laboratories

The oldest crime laboratory in the United States was established in 1923 and the most recent one in 1982. Fifty-five percent of all laboratories were established in the ten year period from 1968 to 1978. During this period, Supreme Court decisions restricting police interrogation practices, the President's Crime Commission Report and advice to police to place greater reliance on physical evidence, the creation of the Law Enforcement Assistance Administration (LEAA) and the availability of federal monies, the drug abuse explosion, and the upsurge in violent crime were all factors that stimulated the growth of laboratories.

Seventy-nine percent of all laboratories responding to our survey are located within law enforcement/public safety agencies. The remaining laboratories were distributed throughout such agencies as medical examiner's offices, prosecutor's offices, scientific/public health agencies, and other public or private institutions.

. . . .

Laboratories were asked to report the type of jurisdiction they *primarily* served. Apart from the federal laboratories (9% of respondents) and the independent laboratories (3%), the remaining laboratories were almost evenly divided between state facilities (46%) and local operations (42%). Within the state category, we found twice as many satellite laboratories (30%) as main facilities (16%). At the local level the number was almost evenly divided among municipal (14%), county (15%), and regional (13%) operations.

. . . .

---

[5] Extracted, with permission from the *Journal of Forensic Sciences*, Vol. 30, No. 1 copyright ASTM, 100 Barr Drive, West Conshohocken, PA 19428.

Availability of Services to Various Users

. . . .

Fifty-seven percent of the responding laboratories would *only* examine evidence submitted by law enforcement officials. . . . [S]tate and federal laboratories examined evidence for users who are not law enforcement officials at a significantly lower rate than other types of laboratories.

. . . .

Case Examination Practices

. . . Almost all of the laboratories surveyed examined drug evidence (93%). More than three-fourths of the laboratories examined semen, bloodstains, fibers, hairs, accelerants, paint, and toolmarks. More than half the laboratories examined firearms, glass, alcohol, explosives, and fingerprints. Less than half the laboratories examined documents, gunshot residues, voiceprints, or toxicological samples or have responsibility for polygraph examinations.

. . . .

Scientific Examiners and Their Involvement in Court

It was reported that on the average, crime laboratory examiners testified in 8% of drug cases (the percentage ranged from 0 to 86%) and 10% of criminalistic cases (the percentage ranged from 0 to 87%) where evidence was examined. Laboratory directors were asked to estimate the fraction of time their examiners spent conferring beforehand with prosecutors and defense attorneys before testifying in court. On the average, examiners conferred with prosecutors in 57% of cases, but with defense attorneys only 13% of the time. . . .

. . . .

Conclusion

. . . .

Crime laboratories were customarily positioned within police agencies and usually restrict their services to law enforcement clients. They did little casework for private individuals, and only about one-third would analyze noncriminal samples. Overall, approximately two-thirds of the caseloads of laboratories were in the offense areas of drugs and driving while intoxicated: accordingly, only about one-third were in the personal and property crime area.

. . . .

. . . [L]aboratory directors believed that jurors and police administrators had the poorest understanding of [forensic science] evidence, while prosecutors and police investigators had the best understanding. Judges and defense attorneys were ranked in between these groups.

MATTHEW R. DUROSE, CENSUS OF PUBLICLY FUNDED FORENSIC CRIME LABORATORIES, 2005, U.S. DEPARTMENT OF JUSTICE, BUREAU OF JUSTICE STATISTICS, (July 2008)[6]

Overview

In 2005 the nation's forensic crime laboratories received evidence from an estimated 2.7 million criminal investigations. These cases included requests for a variety of forensic services, such as DNA analysis, controlled substance identification, and latent fingerprint examination. A case not completed within 30 days was classified as backlogged. An estimated 359,000 cases were backlogged at the end of 2005 — a 24% increase from the estimated 287,000 cases backlogged at yearend 2002. Other major findings on publicly funded forensic crime laboratories in 2005 included —

- Controlled substance identification accounted for about half of all requests backlogged at yearend.

- DNA testing was performed by about half of the laboratories.

- About half of the public laboratories outsourced one or more types of forensic services to private laboratories.

- Eight in 10 laboratories were accredited by the American Society of Crime Laboratory Directors/Laboratory Accreditation Board.

About 80% of forensic requests backlogged from 2004 and new requests received in 2005 were completed by the end of 2005. The remaining requests were backlogged at yearend. To achieve a 30-day turnaround on all 2005 requests, the different forensic disciplines would have needed varying increases in the number of full-time examiners performing that work — ranging from an estimated 73% increase in DNA examiners to an estimated 6% increase in examiners conducting toxicology analysis.

The average backlog rose for a wide range of forensic analyses during 2005. A typical laboratory performing DNA testing began 2005 with 86 backlogged requests for DNA analysis and finished the year with a backlog of 152 requests.

These findings are based on data from the Bureau of Justice Statistics' (BJS) Census of Publicly Funded Forensic Crime Laboratories. Forensic crime laboratories are responsible for examining and reporting on physical evidence collected during criminal investigations for federal, state, and local jurisdictions. This report provides a comprehensive look at forensic services across the nation and the resources devoted to completing the work.

. . . [This] census obtained data from 351 of the 389 laboratories operating in 2005, including at least 1 lab from every state. State-operated laboratories, which can serve the entire state or regional areas, accounted for more than half of all forensic crime laboratories in 2005. More than 80% of state laboratories were part of a multiple laboratory system.

. . . .

---

[6] Available at www.ojp.usdoj.gov/bjs/pub/pdf/cpffcl05.pdf.

More laboratories were accredited in 2005

In 2005 more than three-quarters of laboratories (78%) were accredited by the American Society of Crime Laboratory Directors/Laboratory Accreditation Board (ASCLD/LAB). Another 3% were accredited by some other professional organization, such as the International Organization for Standardization. State-operated laboratories (91%) were more likely to be accredited than laboratories serving county (67%) or municipal (62%) jurisdictions.

. . . .

Crime laboratories provided an average of 6 different forensic services

Crime laboratories are typically responsible for several analytical services. They receive evidence from criminal investigations submitted by a variety of sources, including law enforcement officials, prosecutors, and medical examiners. In 2005 laboratories provided a median number of six functions. Controlled substance identification was the analysis performed by the largest percentage (89%) of the 351 laboratories responding to the census (table 6). Forensic work for computer crime investigations was the function reported to be performed by the smallest percentage of laboratories (12%).

Table 6. Forensic functions performed by crime laboratories in 2005, by type of jurisdiction

Forensic function	Total*	State	County	Municipal
Controlled substances	89%	88%	94%	85%
Firearms/toolmarks	59	60	59	56
Biology screening	57	58	61	51
Latent prints	55	50	51	76
Trace evidence	55	57	59	44
DNA analysis	53%	55%	61%	42%
Toxicology	53	57	49	47
Impressions	52	50	53	56
Crime scene	40	36	46	56
Questioned documents	20	18	22	24
Computer crimes	12	9	16	15
Number of labs reporting	351	207	79	55

Note: Detail sums to more than 100% because some laboratories reported performing more than one function. See *Methodology* for definitions of individual forensic functions.

*Includes federal labs, not shown separately.

About 6 in 10 crime labs examined firearms or toolmarks in 2005. Labs that performed this function were asked about their use of the Bureau of Alcohol, Tobacco, Firearms and Explosives' National Integrated Ballistic Information Network (NIBIN). Using this electronic system, forensic examiners can compare evidence (such as fired bullets and cartridges) from crime scenes to firearm evidence from other criminal investigations for matches (or hits). Seventy-six laboratories reported making about 95,000 NIBIN entries and searches in 2005. Almost 2,000 hits that year were reported by 56 laboratories.

More than half (55%) of crime laboratories analyzed latent (or hidden) fingerprints recovered from crime scenes. These laboratories were asked to report on their use of the FBI's Integrated Automated Fingerprint Identification System (IAFIS) in 2005. More than 100 laboratories reported making about 328,000 searches and finding 33,000 hits using IAFIS in 2005.

NOTES

1. *Numbers of Publicly Funded Crime Laboratories in 2005*. As noted in the Bureau of Justice Statistics (BJS) census, there were 389 publicly funded forensic science crime laboratories in operation in 2005. The census reported that there were 210 state or regional laboratories, 84 county laboratories, 62 municipal laboratories, and 33 federal laboratories.

2. *Services Provided*. With the exception of DNA analysis and computer crimes, the services provided by crime laboratories did not change significantly in the 22-year period between the 1983 survey and the 2005 BJS census.

[3]   The "Corruption" of Forensic Science

This section examines how scientific evidence is used by the legal system in general — and the criminal justice system in particular. We begin with a second excerpt from Professor Thornton's 1983 American Bar Association Journal article in which he suggests that the marriage of law and science can be an abusive relationship — with science being the abused partner. As you read through this article, note that the problem Professor Thornton describes is inherent in the relationship. That is, the abuse he describes is systemic in nature and exists regardless of how accurately and professionally a scientist performs his or her job.

JOHN I. THORNTON, USES AND ABUSES OF FORENSIC SCIENCE
69 A.B.A.J. 288, 291–92 (March, 1983)[7]

The ways in which forensic science can be abused also deserve attention. Basic conflicts that influence the practice of forensic science become apparent at the interface of law and science. Law and science on occasion have conflicting goals, each having developed in response to different social and intellectual needs. The goal of law is the just resolution of human conflict, while the goal of science traditionally has been cast, although perhaps too smugly, as the search for "truth." Certainly there is nothing intrinsically dichotomous in the pursuit of these goals; the court or jury strives in good faith to determine the truth in a given situation as a way to resolve conflicts. But proof is viewed somewhat differently by law and science, as is the application of logic and the perception of societal values.

. . . .

Jacques Barzun illustrates the point in *Science — The Glorious Entertainment* (1964): "Perhaps the shortest way to mark the difference between the legal outlook and the scientific is to point to two characteristics of the English criminal law: first, it sets its hand against statistical living, for it prefers to see a guilty person escape to having an innocent wrongly punished. That is why it protects the accused and even the known criminal. This is not 'reasonable' but it is civilized — if by civilization is meant the social recognition of individual rights. In the second place, the law excludes certain kinds of evidence. Knowing that life is full of incommensurables, knowing the difficulty of so understanding a complex situation as to leave no reasonable doubt, knowing the impressionability of the human mind, even the experienced and well-trained, the law will not allow all ascertained facts to be presented in court — for example, the fact that the prisoner has been previously convicted of crime."

How, then, do these differences between law and science lead to abuse of forensic science? They do simply because all the players want to win and are likely to use any ethical means at their disposal to do so. The attorneys in a case are aligned with only one side, and it is entirely appropriate under the adversary system for them to advocate a particular point of view, even without full and fair disclosure of all relevant facts. Subject only to the rules of evidence, the rules of procedure, and the Code of Professional Responsibility, attorneys are free to manipulate scientific evidence to maximize the opportunity for their side to prevail. Not only is behavior of this sort countenanced by the law, it is the ethical responsibility of counsel to attempt to do so.

Despite the near reverence frequently ascribed to science by the general public and the emphatic mandate for increased use of scientific evidence enunciated by members of the bench and bar, the law is just not much enamored with science. In short, despite lip service to the contrary, lawyers frequently perceive forensic scientists as strictly utilitarian tools of the lawyers trade.

The law views forensic science as its handmaiden, and conflicts almost invariably are resolved in favor of the mistress. . . . Forensic science is not prepared to withstand this abuse. If conflicts are invariably resolved in favor of the law at the expense of science, it makes the forensic scientist somewhat less of a scientist and removes much of the justification for his being in the courtroom.

Next consider the distinction between the introduction of evidence and the introduction of an interpretation of that evidence. The two are by no means synonymous. Not infrequently, the side wishing to introduce its particular interpretation will treat itself to a scientific "smorgasbord," selecting this or that morsel for examination by the forensic scientist. The evidence will be selected or rejected with only those items that conform to the arguments of one side being actually submitted for examination. A distinct possibility exists that the results of the examination by the forensic scientist will be skewed. This also is an abuse of science because the scientist is not allowed to consider all alternative interpretations of the evidence. As a result, the ethical standards of the scientist may be challenged by cogent cross examination.

These situations represent potential sources of mischief. There is nothing necessarily unethical or mendacious about these practices, and they even might not be unfair because opposing counsel is presumed to be equally astute in reviewing the potential evidence to be introduced. Attorneys orchestrate the presentation of physical evidence and bear the responsibility for the conduct of the case in general, and it is understandable that they will wish the evidence to support the best possible case. The danger is that conflicts easily arise between the scientist and the lawyer — the former attempts to describe the evidence as it actually is, while the latter attempts to describe it in the most favorable light.

These abuses of science might be subtle, but they are not trivial. Too many members of our society, including lawyers, view science as a product rather than a process. But the key to sound science is sound process, which cannot be disregarded for long without regrettable consequences. Both science and law would benefit from a concerted effort to mitigate the aggravations.

NOTES

1. *Abused Science — Attorneys "Manipulate" the Presentation of Scientific Evidence.* In the excerpt above, Professor Thornton suggests that an abuse of science can result from the way attorneys "manipulate scientific evidence to maximize the opportunity for their side to prevail." As expressed in the article, the forensic scientist "attempts to describe the evidence as it actually is," while the attorney "attempts to describe it in the most favorable light." Note that, as a general proposition, there is nothing unusual or unethical in an attorney presenting only evidence that supports his or her case (and presenting such evidence in a "favorable light"), and leaving it to one's opponent to bring out contradictory inferences and evidence.

In an adversarial system, however, is it possible that an attorney may feel compelled to "push the envelope," and pressure a forensic scientist to enhance his or her testimony? *See, e.g., Troedel v. Wainwright*, 667 F. Supp. 1456, 1459 (S.D. Fla. 1986) ("[A]s Mr. Riley [the expert] candidly admitted in his deposition, he was 'pushed' further in his analysis at Troedel's trial than at Hawkins' [Troedel's co-defendant] trial. Furthermore, at the. . . . evidentiary hearing held before this Court, one of the prosecutors testified that, . . . after Mr. Riley had rendered his opinion which was contained in his written report, the prosecutor *pushed* to 'see if more could have been gotten out of this witness.' ") (emphasis in original); *McCarty v. State*, 765 P.2d 1215, 1219 (Okla. Crim. App. 1988) ("[T]he Oklahoma County District Attorney's Office may have placed undue pressure upon Ms. Gilchrist [the expert] to give a so-called expert opinion, which was beyond scientific capabilities[.]"). *See also* Paul C. Giannelli, *Wrongful Convictions and Forensic Science: The Need to Regulate Crime Labs*, 86 N.C.L.REV. 163, 225–28 (2007) (discussing the *Troedel* and *McCarty* cases and labeling the problem as, "Testifying Beyond the Report").

2. *Another Reason for Abused Science — Law Enforcement Control of Crime Laboratories.* Roughly 80% of publicly funded crime laboratories are controlled by law enforcement agencies, such as police departments. Lack of independence over administrative matters and budget, and the close working relationship that develops between forensic scientists and law enforcement has been cited as a factor that may lead to bias in interpreting test results, and in presenting those results in court. *See generally* Committee on Identifying the Needs of the Forensic Sciences Community, National Research Council, *Strengthening Forensic Science in the United States: A Path Forward* 6–7 (prepublication copy, Feb. 2009) (*NRC Report*) (recommending removal of "all public forensic laboratories and facilities from the administrative control of law enforcement agencies or prosecutor's offices").

In addition, law enforcement control over the investigation of the crime scene and the collection of evidence may taint forensic evidence. As noted in the second excerpt from Professor Thornton's article, police investigators may come to a hasty conclusion about a suspect's guilt, and then limit evidence brought to forensic scientists for analysis to only "this or that morsel" that conforms to the police theory of guilt. *See also id.* at 6-2 (noting that evidence collection and crime scene investigation are normally not within the control of forensic scientists).

The concern examined here is not one of fraud. The concern is that scientific objectivity is compromised when forensic scientists are under the control of law enforcement and operate in a legal system that promotes advocacy. The materials below provide examples.

(A) Pro-Prosecution and "Contextual" Bias. Many observers have argued that forensic scientists should not be told what results police favor or anticipate prior to performing forensic testing. Problems of overt bias, and a more subtle, "contextual bias," have been encountered.

> [The] biggest problem with crime labs is the personal element, the relationship that develops between police officers and forensics experts. "It often works like this," says defense attorney [Ben] Sudderth. "A policeman comes into the lab and says, 'Look, we're sure we've got the guy who did this, and it's just a matter of proving our case. I sure hope you can help us nail this murdering bastard.'" In Sudderth's opinion, forensic scientists should not be allowed to discuss or have any knowledge of a case while they perform their tests, and conversely, law enforcement agencies should also be forbidden to have any personal contact with forensic scientists. "DNA tests may not lie," he says, "but in my experience, lawmen often do."

Audrey Duff, *Trial and Error*, TEX. MONTHLY 32, 40 (Oct. 1994).[8] *See also* Paul C. Giannelli, *The Abuse Of Scientific Evidence In Criminal Cases: The Need For Independent Crime Laboratories*, 4 VA. J. SOC. POL'Y & L. 439, 470 (1997) ("Considering the professional relationship between crime labs and police departments, pro-prosecution bias in forensic science is not surprising. . . . In short, 'forensic scientists who run with the hounds cannot be expected to give a savaged fox the kiss of life.' "); Andre A. Moenssens, *Symposium On Scientific Evidence: Forward: Novel Scientific Evidence In Criminal Cases: Some Words Of Caution*, 84 J. CRIM. L. & CRIMINOLOGY 1, 6 (Spring 1993) ("[E]ven where crime laboratories do employ qualified scientists, these individuals may be so imbued with a pro-police bias that they are willing to circumvent true scientific investigation methods for the sake of 'making their point.' "); Paul Wilson, *Lessons from the Antipodes: Successes and Failures of Forensic Science*, 67 FORENSIC SCI. INT'L 79, 83 (1994) ("Strong links between police and forensic science are a serious source of potential bias. Some scientists . . . see the police as their customers, while . . . police officers believe the scientist's job is to find evidence which will contribute to their inquiries.").

A more subtle form of bias termed "contextual bias" has also been documented. A study conducted by British researchers appears to confirm that, as a general proposition, forensic scientists should not be given information about the results that are expected, prior to conducting a forensic test. In the British study, researchers asked five fingerprint examiners to compare a crime scene fingerprint with a fingerprint from a known suspect. The five examiners were told that the pair of prints were from a high-profile case involving a terrorist bombing, and that the FBI — after initially declaring the pair to match — publicly acknowledged that their initial conclusions were wrong, and that the pair of prints did not match. The five examiners were then told to ignore the fact that the FBI concluded that the pair of prints did not match, and to focus

---

[8] Copyright © 1994 by *Texas Monthly*. Reprinted with permission.

only on the prints in making their own, independent assessment. However, unknown to the five fingerprint examiners, the prints that they were given to compare were not from the FBI's terrorist bombing case. The prints were actually from criminal cases each examiner had worked five years earlier — and which each had judged to be clear and definite matches. Remarkably, only one of the examiners judged the prints to match; the other four changed their identification decision from the one they themselves had made five years earlier. The information the examiners were given about the FBI's conclusion appeared to bias the analysis. *See* Itiel E. Dror et al., *Contextual Information Renders Expert Vulnerable to Making Erroneous Identifications*, 156 FORENSIC SCI. INT'L 74, 75–76 (2006). *See also NRC Report, supra.* at 6-2; D. Michael Risinger, et al., *The Daubert/Kumho Implications of Observer Effects in Forensic Science: Hidden Problems of Expectations and Suggestion*, 90 CAL. L. REV. 1 (2002).

Finally, consider the following comments made by a forensic scientist who worked for the Los Angeles County Sheriff's Department:

> Defense attorneys see us as extensions of the police and prosecution. I once gave a talk to a group of public defenders in Los Angeles. You may know these publicly funded defense lawyers as "legal aid lawyers." In my address to them I explained how I saw our role as an independent, scientific evaluator of the physical evidence. The lawyers in that group laughed at me. They saw me and all government employed forensic scientists as being on the side of the prosecution and not at all unbiased.

Barry A.J. Fischer, *Developing a Forensic Science Laboratory Operating Strategy*, 31 J. FORENSIC SCI. 1177, 1178 (1986).[9]

(B) Police Investigatory Techniques. Consider also how police investigatory techniques, and control over what items of evidence are presented for analysis, can corrupt good science.

> . . . [O]ver 80 percent of the crime laboratories in this country are controlled by police agencies, and not all of their crime-scene technicians — persons who gather the evidence — adhere to the standards of the forensic scientists. Police investigators use a variety of methods to procure information from witnesses and suspects, sometimes resorting to trickery or coercion to gain what is desired. This is understandable and not always undesirable. Nevertheless we must recognize that these methods influence the types of evidence examined by the police laboratories and ultimately the results of those examinations.

> Police officers collect the evidence to be tested and often become advocates in convincing prosecutors and judges that a particular suspect committed the crime. Much potential evidence is overlooked in this screening process or, if not overlooked, simply is not submitted for analysis. And even if the evidence is submitted, the results might not be used if they do not support the police investigator's theory concerning the crime. And, of course, personnel of the crime laboratory determine which tests to conduct. It is important to recognize that the police agency controls the formal and informal system of rewards and sanctions for laboratory examiners. Many of these laboratories make their services available only to law enforcement agencies. All of these factors raise a legitimate issue regarding the objectivity of laboratory personnel.

---

[9] Extracted, with permission from the *Journal of Forensic Sciences*, Vol. 31, No.4, copyright ASTM, 100 Barr harbor Drive, West Conshohocken, PA 19428.

Symposium on Science and the Rules of Procedure, 101 F.R.D. 599, 642 (1983) (remarks of Dr. Joseph L. Peterson).

Last, consider the following criticism of what the author terms, "the prevalent police philosophy of obtaining a confession at all costs."

> The crime scene is often not properly searched and evaluated. The significance and meaning of blood splatters and patterns are not considered or photographed. All the relevant physical evidence is not retrieved, and the proper experts are not consulted. Finally the numerous theories suggested by the physical evidence are not explored. For instance, a cigarette butt left by a secretor, if properly analyzed, might exclude a number of suspects and form a circumstantial link of evidence as to a particular suspect. Yet this type of evidence is often overlooked, seldom analyzed, or even considered.

> The problem is made worse by the prevalent police philosophy of obtaining a confession at all costs, leaving the prosecutor to determine how to enter the confession or admission into evidence. Thus, police efforts are expended on duress, deception, fraud and trickery to get a confession that may or may not be admissible in a subsequent trial. These activities are often coupled with extensive subterfuges and fictions to avoid constitutional and statutory safeguards and are performed by the police to accomplish the intended result: a confession at any cost. Once the confession or admission is obtained, the investigation either ceases entirely or focuses on the *one* suspect to the exclusion of all other suspects and evidence. The effect of this approach is to ignore or relegate as insignificant any evidence that is not consistent with the police's theory of a particular suspect's involvement in the crime under investigation.

Joseph F. Keefe, *Forensic Sciences Services and the Criminal Justice System as Viewed by the Defense*, 24 J. FORENSIC SCI. 673, 674–75 (July 1979).[10]

QUESTIONS

1. What does Thornton see as the goals, respectively, of science and law? What factors or conflicts between law and science does Thornton identify as leading to the "abuse" of science in the courtroom? How is science abused by these conflicts? Is the prosecution or the defense more likely to "abuse" science in the manner Thornton suggests?

2. Do you accept the criticisms of forensic science as not being objective because of the close working relationship that exists between most crime laboratories and the police? If so, should a rule of evidence address the potential for bias that may (or may not) exist in such a situation? Does it already?

On the other hand, isn't there less reason to question scientific evidence when the evidence is presented by a forensic scientist who is a public employee, and is not an "outside" expert hired by the prosecution or the defense?

3. How much of a threat to a fair trial are the "abuses" mentioned in the article by Professor Thornton, and in the Notes that followed? That is, do you feel juries

---

[10] Extracted, with permission from the *Journal of Forensic Sciences*, Vol. 24, No. 3, copyright ASTM, 100 Barr Harbor Drive, West Conshohocken, PA 19428.

appreciate that, because of its association with the legal system in general, and with law enforcement in particular, there is a possibility that some evidence generated by crime laboratories may be either biased, or at least presented in court in a biased manner?

4. If you represented a defendant in a criminal case, would you want to know what scientific tests were conducted on evidence associated with your case even if the test results were not going to be used against your client? Why, or why not? *See* Fed. R. Crim. Proc. 16; *Symposium on Science and the Rules of Legal Procedure*, 101 F.R.D. 599, 630–34 (1983).

B.   THE RELIABILITY OF FORENSIC SCIENCE

[1]   The Problem of Inaccuracy: Testing Errors and Irregularities

Put aside, for the moment, problems of manipulation and bias associated with the way the legal system utilizes forensic science, and which can lead to a "skewed" presentation of scientific findings. In this section we examine the possibility of error, and the impact erroneous scientific evidence can have on the outcome of a case. We begin with the opinion of the United States Supreme Court in the case of *Miller v. Pate*.

In *Miller v. Pate* a forensic scientist assisted in identifying the accused, Miller, as a rapist and a murderer by connecting the victim's blood type with blood found on clothing, alleged to belong to Miller, that was found near the crime scene. The scientist was wrong. The "blood" on the clothing was paint. Any witness can be wrong. For example, an eyewitness can report what he or she honestly thought they saw but be wrong. As you read through the *Miller* case, consider whether there is any reason for courts to be more cautious about admitting opinions offered by forensic scientists as opposed to opinions offered by lay witnesses. If you believe that there is reason for increased caution, what safeguards, if any, should be employed?

MILLER v. PATE
386 U.S. 1 (1967)

Mr. Justice Stewart delivered the opinion of the Court.

On November 26, 1955, in Canton, Illinois, an eight-year-old girl died as the result of a brutal sexual attack. The petitioner was charged with her murder.

Prior to his trial in an Illinois court, his counsel filed a motion for an order permitting a scientific inspection of the physical evidence the prosecution intended to introduce. The motion was resisted by the prosecution and denied by the court. The jury trial ended in a verdict of guilty and a sentence of death. On appeal the judgment was affirmed by the Supreme Court of Illinois. On the basis of leads developed at a subsequent unsuccessful state clemency hearing, the petitioner applied to a federal district court for a writ of habeas corpus. After a hearing, the court granted the writ and ordered the petitioner's release or prompt retrial. The Court of Appeals reversed, and we granted certiorari to consider whether the trial that led to the petitioner's conviction was constitutionally valid. We have concluded that it was not.

There were no eyewitnesses to the brutal crime which the petitioner was charged with perpetrating. A vital component of the case against him was a pair of men's underwear shorts covered with large, dark, reddish-brown stains — People's Exhibit 3 in the trial record. These shorts had been found by a Canton policeman in a place known as the Van Buren Flats three days after the murder. The Van Buren Flats were about a mile from the scene of the crime. It was the prosecution's theory that the petitioner had been wearing these shorts when he committed the murder, and that he had afterwards removed and discarded them at the Van Buren Flats.

During the presentation of the prosecution's case, People's Exhibit 3 was variously described by witnesses in such terms as the "bloody shorts" and "a pair of jockey shorts stained with blood." Early in the trial the victim's mother testified that her daughter "had type 'A' positive blood." Evidence was later introduced to show that the petitioner's blood "was of group 'O'."

Against this background the jury heard the testimony of a chemist for the State Bureau of Crime Identification. The prosecution established his qualifications as an expert, whose "duties include blood identification, grouping and typing both dry and fresh stains," and who had "made approximately one thousand blood typing analyses while at the State Bureau." His crucial testimony was as follows:

> "I examined and tested 'People's Exhibit 3' to determine the nature of the staining material upon it. The result of the first test was that this material upon the shorts is blood. I made a second examination which disclosed that the blood is of human origin. I made a further examination which disclosed that the blood is of group 'A'."

The petitioner, testifying in his own behalf, denied that he had ever owned or worn the shorts in evidence as People's Exhibit 3. He himself referred to the shorts as having "dried blood on them."

In argument to the jury the prosecutor made the most of People's Exhibit 3:

> "Those shorts were found in the Van Buren Flats, with blood. What type blood? Not 'O' blood as the defendant has, but 'A' — type 'A.'"

And later in his argument he said to the jury:

> "And, if you will recall, it has never been contradicted the blood type of Janice May was blood type 'A' positive. Blood type 'A'. Blood type 'A' on these shorts. It wasn't 'O' type as the defendant has. It is 'A' type, what the little girl had."

Such was the state of the evidence with respect to People's Exhibit 3 as the case went to the jury. And such was the state of the record as the judgment of conviction was reviewed by the Supreme Court of Illinois. The "blood stained shorts" clearly played a vital part in the case for the prosecution. They were an important link in the chain of circumstantial evidence against the petitioner,[11] [8] and, in the context of the revolting crime with which he was charged, their gruesomely emotional impact upon the jury was incalculable.

So matters stood with respect to People's Exhibit 3, until the present habeas corpus proceeding in the Federal District Court. In this proceeding the State was ordered to produce the stained shorts, and they were admitted in evidence. It was established that

---

[11] [n.8] In affirming the petitioner's conviction, the Supreme Court of Illinois stated that "it was determined" that the shorts "were stained with human blood from group A," and referred to the petitioner's "bloody shorts."

their appearance was the same as when they had been introduced at the trial as People's Exhibit 3. The petitioner was permitted to have the shorts examined by a chemical microanalyst. What the microanalyst found cast an extraordinary new light on People's Exhibit 3. The reddish-brown stains on the shorts were not blood, but paint.

The witness said that he had tested threads from each of the 10 reddish-brown stained areas on the shorts, and that he had found that all of them were encrusted with mineral pigments ". . . which one commonly uses in the preparation of paints." He found "no traces of human blood." The State did not dispute this testimony, its counsel contenting himself with prevailing upon the witness to concede on cross-examination that he could not swear that there had never been any blood on the shorts.[12] [12]

It was further established that counsel for the prosecution had known at the time of the trial that the shorts were stained with paint. The prosecutor even admitted that the Canton police had prepared a memorandum attempting to explain "how this exhibit contains all the paint on it."

In argument at the close of the habeas corpus hearing counsel for the State contended that "(e)verybody" at the trial had known that the shorts were stained with paint.[13] [13] That contention is totally belied by the record. The microanalyst correctly described the appearance of the shorts when he said, "I assumed I was dealing . . . with a pair of shorts which was heavily stained with blood. . . . (I)t would appear to a layman . . . that what I see before me is a garment heavily stained with blood." The record of the petitioner's trial reflects the prosecution's consistent and repeated misrepresentation that People's Exhibit 3 was, indeed, "a garment heavily stained with blood." The prosecution's whole theory with respect to the exhibit depended upon that misrepresentation. For the theory was that the victim's assailant had discarded the shorts *because* they were stained with blood. A pair of paint-stained shorts, found in an abandoned building a mile away from the scene of the crime, was virtually valueless as evidence against the petitioner.[14] [15] The prosecution deliberately misrepresented the truth.

More than 30 years ago this Court held that the Fourteenth Amendment cannot tolerate a state criminal conviction obtained by the knowing use of false evidence. There has been no deviation from that established principle. There can be no retreat from that principle here.

The judgment of the Court of Appeals is reversed and the case is remanded for further proceedings consistent with this opinion. It is so ordered.

---

[12] [n.12] The witness pointed out, however, that "blood substances are detectable over prolonged periods. That is, there are records of researches in which substances extracted from Egyptian mummies have been identified as blood."

[13] [n.13] "Now, then, concerning the paint on the shorts, the petitioner yesterday introduced scientific evidence to prove that there was paint on the shorts, a fact that they knew without scientific evidence. Everybody knew, in connection with the case, whoever looked at the shorts, and I think that the Court can look at them now and know there is paint on them. This is not anything that was not disclosed to anybody. It is very obvious by merely looking at them. . . ."

[14] [n.15] The petitioner was not a painter but a taxi driver.

NOTES

1. *Aftermath of Miller.* Miller spent more than 10 years on death row and received 10 stays of execution before the United States Supreme Court ordered that he receive a new trial in 1967. One of the stays occurred just seven hours before he was to be put to death. Following the Supreme Court decision in *Miller v. Pate* it was determined that a confession he had given was coerced, and the key prosecution witness admitted that she had lied in implicating Miller in the murder. Thereafter Miller was released. CHICAGO TRIBUNE, Dec. 23, 1985, at 1. The *Chicago Tribune* reported that Miller left the country after his release and in 1985 was thought to be living in Mexico. *Id.*

Approximately two months after the United States Supreme Court rendered its opinion in *Miller*, the Grievance Committee of the Illinois State Bar Association began an investigation to determine if the prosecutor in *Miller* ought to be disciplined for concealing the existence of paint on the shorts. On May 14, 1968, the Committee issued a report that vindicated the prosecutor and stated that "the United States Supreme Court had misapprehended the facts of the case." The Committee accepted the testimony of the chemist in Miller's trial and concluded that there "was no reason to doubt" that there was blood (as well as paint) on the shorts at the time of the trial. Therefore, according to the Committee, the question was whether it was unethical for the prosecutor to conceal the existence of paint from the defense. The Committee found that the existence of paint (as well as blood) on the shorts was not a material question in Miller's case and recommended no disciplinary action against Miller's prosecutor. *See The Vindication of a Prosecutor*, 59 J. CRIM. L., C. & P.S. 335, 335–37 (1968).

2. *Defense Discovery.* Miller was tried in 1956. Even though Miller's counsel formally requested that he be permitted to conduct his own scientific inspection of the stained undershorts, his request was denied and his expert was not allowed to examine the shorts until 1963, during preparation for the habeas corpus hearing. Such defense discovery requests are now routinely granted. The modern right to discovery in criminal cases emanates, primarily, from two sources; a 1963 Supreme Court decision and the Federal Rules of Criminal Procedure.

First, the prosecution has a constitutional duty to disclose *exculpatory* evidence. In 1963, several years after Miller's trial, the United States Supreme Court held that suppression of evidence favorable to the defense violated due process. *Brady v. Maryland*, 373 U.S. 83 (1963).

A second and more comprehensive right to discover prosecution evidence is embodied in Rule 16 of the Federal Rules of Criminal Procedure.

Rule 16. Discovery and Inspection

(a) Government's Disclosure.

(1) Information Subject to Disclosure.

. . . .

(E) Documents and Objects. Upon a defendant's request, the government must permit the defendant to inspect and to copy or photograph books, papers, documents, data, photographs, tangible objects, . . . or copies or portions of any of these items, if the item is within the government's possession, custody or control and:

(i) the item is material to preparing the defense;

(ii) the government intends to use the item in its case-in-chief at trial; or

(iii) the item was obtained from or belongs to the defendant.

(F) Reports of Examinations and Tests. Upon a defendant's request, the government must permit a defendant to inspect and to copy or photograph the results or reports of any physical or mental examination and of scientific test or experiment if:

(i) the item is within the government's possession, custody or control;

(ii) the attorney for the government knows — or through due diligence could know — that the item exists; and

(iii) the item is material to preparing the defense or the government intends to use the item in its case-in-chief at trial.

Unlike the constitutional right to discovery articulated in *Brady*, Rule 16 is not limited to disclosure of evidence that is favorable to the defense. Further, there also is a provision in subsection (b) of Rule 16 that permits prosecution discovery of defense evidence, including reports by defense experts. By utilizing both a *Brady* request for discovery of exculpatory evidence, and a Rule 16 request for tangible objects and reports, a defendant should be able to gain access to evidence that has been scientifically analyzed as well as the resultant forensic reports.

3. *Defense Retesting.* Note that Rule 16 does not explicitly provide for scientific testing or retesting of prosecution evidence by the defense. There is, however, authority for the proposition that the rule includes the right of defense retesting. *See, e.g., United States v. Dukes,* 139 F.3d 469, 477 (5th Cir. 1998) (not disputing Dukes's right to inspect and retest pursuant to Fed. R. Crim. P. 16(a)(1)(C) [now (E)]). State procedural rules governing defense retesting vary. *See* 1 SCIENTIFIC EVIDENCE, § 3.07, at 168–73 (4th ed. 2007). There also is authority indicating that retesting physical evidence is part of the concept of fundamental fairness found in the Due Process Clause of the Fifth Amendment of the United States Constitution. *Barnard v. Henderson,* 514 F.2d 744 (5th Cir. 1975); *but see Frias v. State,* 547 N.E.2d 809 (Ind. 1989) (defendant's right to cross-examine is sufficient protection and independent retesting is not required).

A related issue involves the defendant's rights when the state's testing of physical evidence consumes the entire sample of physical evidence and thereby makes retesting impossible. The preferred procedure is for the defendant's expert to be present when such tests are conducted. *See People v. Garries,* 645 P.2d 1306, 1309 (Colo. 1982) (when blood samples are to be completely consumed by state testing, defendant must be contacted before testing to determine if he or she wishes to have a defense expert present at testing). This procedure is required by statute in some jurisdictions. *See, e.g.,* OHIO REV. CODE ANN. § 2925.51(E) (Baldwin 1991). *See also* 1 SCIENTIFIC EVIDENCE, § 3.08, at 172–73 (4th ed. 2007).

QUESTIONS

1. What was the constitutional violation in *Miller*: a conviction obtained as a result of inaccurate scientific evidence or the *knowing* use of such false and inaccurate evidence? Put another way, if, at the time of Miller's trial, neither the prosecutor nor the chemist were aware that the shorts contained paint and not blood, would the Supreme Court have reversed Miller's conviction? *See Herrera v. Collins,* 506 U.S. 390, 400–01 (1993); *Napue v. Illinois,* 360 U.S. 264, 269 (1959); *In the Matter of an Investigation of the*

West Virginia State Police Crime Laboratory, Serology Division, 438 S.E.2d 501, 504–06 (W.Va. 1993).

2. How is the error that the chemist made in *Miller* different from an error made by an eyewitness who mistakenly swears that it was the defendant who committed a crime?

———

Just how rare are errors in forensic testing? The following excerpt from an article by Professor Paul C. Giannelli, and the Notes that follow, discuss the prevalence of error in scientific testing, and the related problem of unreliable and misleading laboratory reports.

PAUL C. GIANNELLI, THE ADMISSIBILITY OF LABORATORY REPORTS IN CRIMINAL TRIALS: THE RELIABILITY OF SCIENTIFIC PROOF,
49 Ohio St. L.J. 671, 688–95 (1988)[15]

B. *Reliability of Laboratory Reports*

Reliability issues involve two different but related problems — the first concerns the reliability of the scientific test itself; the second involves the way in which the test results are reported.

1. *Reliability of the Test*

There is little question that laboratory examinations may result in incorrect findings. Indeed, the Supreme Court has recognized that "the results of laboratory tests may be contrived,"[16] [148] and in one instance an FBI analyst "reported results of lab tests that he did not in fact conduct."[17] [149] Moreover, erroneous conclusions have been reported even with well-accepted scientific techniques. In one case, a court wrote: "The fingerprint expert's testimony was damning — and it was false."[18] [150] Similarly, a firearms identification expert in a different case "negligently presented false demonstrative evidence in support of his ballistics testimony."[19] [151]

. . . .

Unfortunately, the examples cited above cannot be dismissed as isolated instances. In 1978 the results of a Laboratory Proficiency Testing Program sponsored by the Law

———

[15] Originally published in 49 Ohio St. L.J. 671, 688–95 (1988). Copyright © 1988 by Ohio State Law Journal. Reprinted with permission.

[16] [n.148] *United States v. Ash*, 413 U.S. 300, 320 (1973).

[17] [n.149] *State v. Ruybal*, 408 A.2d 1284, 1285 (Me. 1979). *See also State v. DeFronzo*, 59 Ohio Misc. 113, 118, 394 N.E.2d 1027, 1031 (C.P. 1978) (Expert represented that certain laboratory tests were conducted, when "no such tests were ever conducted."); Annotation, *Perjury or Wilfully False Testimony of Expert Witness as Basis for New Trial on Ground of Newly Discovered Evidence*, 38 A.L.R.3d 812 (1971).

[18] [n.150] *State v. Caldwell*, 322 N.W.2d 574, 586 (Minn. 1982). This case is discussed in Starrs, *A Miscue in Fingerprint Identification: Causes and Concerns*, 12 J. Police Sci. & Admin. 287 (1984).

[19] [n.151] *In re Kirschke*, 53 Cal. App. 3d 405, 408, 125 Cal. Rptr. 680, 682 (1975). For a discussion of this case as well as other illustrations of erroneous expert testimony, *see* Starrs, *In the Land of Agog: An Allegory for the Expert Witness*, 30 J. Forensic Sci. 289 (1985).

Enforcement Assistance Administration were reported.[20] [152] Over 200 crime laboratories participated in this program, which involved such common forensic examinations as firearms, blood, drug, and trace evidence analyses. The Report concluded: "A wide range of proficiency levels among the nation's laboratories exists, with several evidence types posing serious difficulties for the laboratories. . . ."[21] [153] Thus, although some laboratories performed exceptionally well, the performance of others was disturbing: "65 percent of the laboratories had 80 percent or more of their results fall into the acceptable category. At the other end of the spectrum, 3 percent of laboratories had less than 50 percent of their responses considered acceptable."[22] [154] Similarly, certain types of examinations caused few problems, whereas others produced very high rates of "unacceptable proficiency."[23] [155] Unacceptable proficiency was most often attributed to: (1) misinterpretation of test results due to carelessness or inexperience; (2) failure to employ adequate or appropriate methodology; (3) mislabeling or contamination of primary standards; and (4) inadequate data bases or standard spectra.[24] [156] One of the report's authors later commented: "In spite of being a firm advocate of forensic science, I must acknowledge that a disturbingly high

---

[20] [n.152] J. PETERSON, E. FABRICANT & K. FIELD, CRIME LABORATORY PROFICIENCY TESTING RESEARCH PROGRAM (L.E.A.A. Oct. 1978).

[21] [n.153] *Id.* at 3.

[22] [n.154] Peterson, *The Crime Lab*, in THINKING ABOUT POLICE 184, 195 (c). Klockars ed. 1983) [hereinafter *The Crime Lab*].

[23] [n.155] Unacceptable response rates for the various test samples were as follows:

Test Sample	Evidence Type	Rate	Test Sample	Evidence Type	Rate
1	Controlled		14	Arson	28.8%
	substance	7.8%	15	Drugs	18.2%
2	Firearms	28.2%	16	Paint	34.0%
3	Blood	3.8%	17	Metal	22.1%
4	Glass	4.8%	18	Hair	
5	Paint	20.5%		(A) [dog]	50.0%
6	Drugs	1.7%		(B) [cat]	27.8%
7	Firearms	5.3%		(C) [deer]	54.4%
8	Blood	71.3%		(D) [cow]	67.8%
9	Glass	31.3%		(E) [mink]	35.6%
10	Paint	51.4%	19	Wood	21.5%
11	Soil	35.5%	20	Questioned	
12	Fibers	1.7%		Documents (A)	5.4%
				(B)	18.9%
13	Physiological			Firearms	13.6%
	Fluids (A)	2.3%	21		
	(B)	1.6%			

The number of laboratories responding ranged from a low of 65 to a high of 205. An unacceptable response did not necessarily mean an incorrect response. Other reasons for an unacceptable designation included a correct response for the wrong reason, an unsupported, inclusive response, multiple responses, and incomplete responses. *Id.* at 188–91.

[24] [n. 156] J. PETERSON, E. FABRICANT & K. FIELD, *supra* note 152, at 258.

percentage of laboratories are not performing routine tests competently, as shown by our proficiency testing."[25] [157]

Perhaps as troubling as the results of this study are the reasons that may underlie them. In 1967 the President's Crime Commission commented that "the great majority of police department laboratories have only minimal equipment and lack highly skilled personnel able to use the modern equipment now being developed and produced by the instrumentation industry."[26] [158] A later commission concluded: Too many police crime laboratories have been set up on budgets that preclude the recruitment of qualified, professional personnel."[27] [159] Since the time these reports were issued, the number of crime laboratories has increased dramatically, from about 100 in 1968, to more than 300 in 1983. Problems, however, remain.[28] [161] In particular, national standards to ensure the competency of examiners have not been developed. As explained by Professor Peterson:

> [T]here are no minimum standards or certification requirements that must be satisfied before these examiners become responsible for analyzing the evidence and testifying in court. Nor are standard laboratory procedures available that the examiners are expected to follow when analyzing typical forms of evidence.[29] [162]

In addition, quality control procedures, such as independent proficiency testing, are not required by the majority of laboratories, although attempts to change this situation have been undertaken. Other problems, such as high caseload volume, have also been cited. The picture that emerges is one of inconsistency, with some very good laboratories at one end of the spectrum and some very poor ones at the other end.

Even when competent analysts use valid procedure, error may occur. The reason is that the conclusions drawn from many commonly employed procedures are based on subjective judgments, with the result that disagreement among experts is possible. Courts excluding scientific reports have noted this problem. Psychiatric evaluations and autopsy reports are perhaps the clearest examples. This problem, however, goes far beyond these illustrations. Even apparently routine and objective procedures involve an element of subjectivity. For example, a firearms identification examiner may conclude that two bullets had been fired from the same weapon. Although a positive identification is based on objective data — the striations on the bullet surfaces the examiner's conclusion rests on a subjective evaluation. There are no objective criteria used for this

---

[25] [n.157] *Symposium on Science and the Rules of Legal Procedure*, 101 F.R.D. 599, 645 (1984) (remarks of Professor Joseph Peterson).

Problems involving proficiency testing are not limited to crime laboratories. A proficiency testing program of laboratories engaged in urine analyses for drug detection reached the following conclusions: "Error rates for the 13 laboratories on samples containing barbiturates, amphetamines, methadone, cocaine, codeine, and morphine ranged from 11% to 94%, 19% to 100%, 0% to 33%, 0% to 100%, 0% to 100%, and 5% to 100%, respectively." Hansen, Caudill & Boone, *Crisis in Drug Testing: Results of CDC Blind Study*, 253 J. Am. Med. A. 2382, 2382 (1985).

[26] [n.158] President's Commission Law Enforcement and Administration of Justice, The Challenge of Crime in a Free Society 255 (1967).

[27] [n.159] National Advisory Commission on Criminal Justice Standards and Goals, Police 304 (1974).

[28] [n.161] "The newly formed laboratories and existing laboratories continued to suffer from the same old problems: lack of coordination, unqualified personnel, and the absence of uniform standards and procedures to guide the analysis and interpretation of evidence." Peterson, *The Crime Lab, supra* note 154, at 185.

[29] [n.162] *Symposium on Science and the Rules of Legal Procedure*, 101 F.R.D. 599, 642–43 (1984) (remarks by Professor Joseph Peterson).

determination: "In general, the texts on firearms identification take the position that each practitioner must develop his own intuitive criteria of identity gained through practical experience."[30] [169] In this sense, firearms identification is more of an art than a science. Thus, it is not surprising that two experts may disagree about whether there are sufficient points of identity to render a positive conclusion.[31] [171] Fingerprint evidence raises the same problem. Because there is no consensus on the number of points necessary for an identification, fingerprint identification is "an evaluative art."[32] [172] Again, disagreement among experts remains a possibility:

> In a murder case . . . state police fingerprint experts testified that a latent print lifted from the crime's scene was the defendant's by demonstrating 14 points of similarity. Defense was able to procure its own expert who proved three crucial points of dissimilarity. An acquittal followed.[33] [173]

Even where the scientific technique uses instrumentation, subjectivity may be a problem.

The point is not that most laboratory test results are erroneous or that examinations with a subjective element are unreliable. Indeed, the opposite is true. Rather, the point is that the risk of error is significant enough to preclude routine admission of test results without the opportunity to cross-examine the analyst.[34] [175]

2. *Reliability of the Report*

The laboratory report itself raises additional reliability concerns, mainly because of what it does *not* say. Typically, the report contains only the expert's conclusions. For instance, in a controlled substance prosecution the report may state only that the examined substance was "heroin." Other critical information is not disclosed.

First, the bases for the analyst's findings frequently are not revealed. In particular, the laboratory report will often not indicate the specific test employed. For example, a gunshot residue report indicating that a person recently fired a weapon may be based on the paraffin test, neutron activation analysis, atomic absorption, scanning electron

---

[30] [n.169] Biasotti, *The Principles of Evidence Evaluation as Applied to Firearms and Tool Mark Identification*, 9 J. Forensic Sci. 428, 429 (1964). *See also* J. Peterson, E. Fabricant & K. Field, *supra* note 152, at 207 ("Ultimately, unless other issues are involved, it remains for the examiner to determine for himself the modicum of proof necessary to arrive at a definitive opinion.").

[31] [n.171] *See In re Kirschke*, 53 Cal. App. 3d 405, 411, 125 Cal. Rptr. 680, 684 (1975) (One firearms identification expert made a conclusive identification, whereas other experts "were not able to make a positive identification. . . ."); *State v. Nemeth*, 182 Conn. 403, 408, 438 A.2d 120, 123 (1980) (One expert testified "that he was unable to determine whether the bullets had been fired from the same gun," whereas another "testified that both bullets had been fired from the same gun."); *Commonwealth v. Ellis*, 373 Mass. 1, 5, 364 N.E.2d 808, 812 (1977) ("The Commonwealth's two [firearms identification] experts did not fully agree.").

[32] [n.172] P. Giannelli & E. Imwinkelried, Scientific Evidence 539 (1986).

[33] [n.173] Note, *The Indigent's Right to an Adequate Defense: Expert and Investigational Assistance in Criminal Proceedings*, 55 Cornell L. Rev. 632, 638 n.38 (1970) (citation omitted). *See also* Osborn, *Proof of Finger-Prints*, 26 J. Crim. L. & Criminology 587, 588 (1936) ("[E]rrors in [fingerprint] identification are not only possible but have been made.").

[34] [n.175] "Only a small percentage of the cases in any jurisdiction go to trial, so the technicians or scientists in the crime laboratories seldom are called upon to justify their procedures or conclusions under rigorous cross-examination. I think the realization that their work will not be reviewed — either by independent scientist or by opposing counsel and expert in court — decreases the care and completeness with which examiners process evidence." *Symposium on Science and the Rules of Legal Procedure*, 101 F.R.D. 599, 643 (1984) (remarks of Professor Joseph Peterson).

microscopy, or some other procedure. Some of these tests are valid, while others are suspect. Similarly, a laboratory report identifying a substance as marijuana might not specify whether this conclusion is based upon a visual examination, the Duquenois-Levine test, thin-layer chromatography, or some other procedure. Many of these tests are not specific.

. . . .

Second, even if a valid procedure is used, there is no way to determine, without the testimony of the analyst, if it was properly employed at the time of the examination. One court has noted:

> Since most laboratory reports only state general conclusions, they may be given far more significance in court than they rightfully deserve. Inquiry during examination of the chemist may reveal the possibility of laboratory error due to the carelessness of the chemist sharing a limited area with others and due to the large number of samples being tested. The defense may further wish to ask what other substances were in the sample and how these would affect a true test reaction.[35] [188]

Similarly, admission of the laboratory report may cover up gaps in the chain of custody. . . .

Third, information about the analyst is not reported. Only the name and position of the examiner usually appear. Academic degrees, years of experience, specialized training, and number of analyses performed cannot be determined. Nor can it be assumed that all analysts are competent. An article on drug testing describes the cross-examination of a drug expert with 43 years of experience and more than 2500 court appearances as follows:

> [The expert] admitted that not only did he not have a college degree, but that he had never even finished high school. He claimed that heroin was an alkaloid, which it is, but did not remember what an alkaloid was. He could not draw the structure of heroin or benzene, one of the commonest and simplest organic molecules . . . In addition, he could not explain any single chemical reaction about which he had testified.[36] [190]

. . . .

In sum, there is nothing "scientific" about the way test results are typically reported. . . . In effect, the report masks critical reliability issues. Instead of a probing cross-examination of the expert, the jury receives an "official" report, prepared by someone with "unquestioned" expertise.

NOTES

1. *Catalog of Errors.* There is ample evidence to suggest that crime laboratory errors of the sort mentioned in Professor Giannelli's article and reported in the 1978 Laboratory Proficiency Testing Program remain a problem. First, a follow-up

---

[35] [n.188] *United States v. Davis*, 14 M.J. 847, 848 n.3 (A.C.M.R. 1982). *See also United States v. Ware*, 247 F.2d 698, 701 (7th Cir. 1957) (concurring opinion) ("[T]he defendant at trial was helpless because he had no way to determine whether proper methods of analysis were used and were free from error in their execution.").

[36] [n. 190] Stein, Laessig & Indriksons, *An Evaluation of Drug Testing Procedures Used by Forensic Laboratories and the Qualifications of Their Analysts*, 1973 WISC. L. REV. 727, 728 (footnote omitted).

proficiency testing program conducted over a 14-year period (1978 to 1991) found that crime laboratories had made little progress in correctly identifying and/or comparing fibers, paints, glass, animal hair, and human hair. Some improvement was noted in identifying drugs, and in identifying and comparing blood stains. *See* Joseph L. Peterson, et al., *Crime Laboratory Proficiency Testing Results, 1978–1991, II: Resolving Questions of Common Origin*, 40 J. FORENSIC SCI. 1009, 1026–29 (Nov. 1995).

Second, a study of the first 200 wrongfully convicted persons exonerated through DNA testing found that faulty forensic evidence supported erroneous convictions in 57% (113) of the cases. Brandon L. Garrett, *Judging Innocence*, 108 COLUM. L. REV. 55, 81 (2008). Faulty serological analysis of blood and semen appeared most often (79 cases), followed by: hair comparison (43 cases); soil comparison (5 cases); DNA tests (3 cases); bitemark evidence (3 cases); fingerprint evidence (2 cases); dog scent identification (2 cases), spectrographic voice evidence (1 case); shoe prints (1 case), and fiber comparison (1 case). *Id.* The study also noted that in many wrongful conviction cases forensic scientists improperly exaggerated the probative significance of forensic evidence in their testimony. *Id.* at 82 n.99 (preliminary review of 61 trial transcripts finds improper trial testimony in 57% of the cases).

Finally, there have been well-documented reports of crime laboratories failures in several cities and states, including Baltimore, Chicago, Cleveland, Houston, Los Angeles, Fort Worth, Oklahoma City, San Antonio, Seattle, Montana, Virginia, and West Virginia. *See* Paul C. Giannelli, *Wrongful Convictions and Forensic Science: The Need to Regulate Crime Labs*, 86 N.C.L.REV. 163, 172–95 (2007) (failures attributed to incompetence, sloppy procedures, and fraud; noting that it is often difficult to distinguish between malfeasance and misfeasance because of the lack of quality assurance protocols). *See also* Committee on Identifying the Needs of the Forensic Sciences Community, National Research Council, *Strengthening Forensic Science in the United States: A Path Forward* 1–8 to 1–10 (prepublication copy, Feb. 2009) ("In recent years, the integrity of crime laboratories increasingly has been called into question[.]" summarizing documented cases of laboratory error and fraud); Janine Arvizu, *Forensic Laboratories: Shattering The Myth*, THE CHAMPION 18, 19–20 & 20–21 (May 2000) (describing errors in the F.B.I. crime laboratory and several state crime laboratories). *Cf.* Pamela R. Metzger, *Cheating the Constitution*, 59 VAND. L. REV. 475, 491 (2006) ("The legal community now concedes . . . that our system produces erroneous convictions based on discredited forensics."); EDWARD J. IMWINKELRIED, THE METHODS OF ATTACKING SCIENTIFIC EVIDENCE, § 1-1[b], at 6–9 (4th ed. 2004) (summarizing several studies finding error in scientific evidence); Mark Hansen, *Body of Evidence*, 81 A.B.A.J. 60 (June 1995) (citing situations where coroners and medical examiners have testified concerning the cause of death in murder trials, but were unable to distinguish murders from suicides); D. Michael Risinger, Mark P. Denbeaux & Michael J. Saks, *Exorcism of Ignorance as a Proxy for Rational Knowledge: The Lessons of Handwriting Identification "Expertise,"* 137 U. PA. L. REV. 731, 743–48 (1989) (in five Forensic Science Foundation proficiency tests, handwriting experts were only able to reach the right conclusion in 45% of the cases); Edward J. Imwinkelried, *The Debate in the DNA Cases over the Foundation for the Admission of Scientific Evidence: The Importance of Human Error as a Cause of Forensic Misanalysis*, 69 WASH. U. L.Q. 19, 22–23 & 25–27 (1991) (citing several studies that "established impressive evidence of a substantial error margin in contemporary laboratory analysis"); Lawrence Mike & Maria Hewitt, *Accuracy and Reliability of Urine Drug Tests*, 36 U. KAN. L. REV. 641, 657 (1988) (error rates are high when laboratories conduct their usual business instead of performing under known scrutiny).

2. *The Reason for Errors by Crime Laboratories.* As important as recognizing that errors do occur, is discovering the *reasons* for the errors. If, for example, a defense attorney knows why a forensic scientist might have made an error, the attorney then knows areas to investigate and explore on cross-examination. Similarly, such knowledge should alert the prosecution to areas of potential attack from the defense.

(A) Honest Errors. Professor Giannelli discusses several reasons that underlie crime laboratory errors. He mentions such things as "minimal equipment," the lack of "highly skilled personnel," low budgets, no national standards to ensure competency of examiners, the lack of required independent proficiency testing, high caseloads, and the fact that many procedures involve subjective judgments on which experts could differ. Note that all the reasons listed in Professor Giannelli's article could exist in a situation where a forensic scientist is, in good faith, working to the best of his or her ability. *See generally*; Committee on Identifying the Needs of the Forensic Sciences Community, National Research Council, *Strengthening Forensic Science in the United States: A Path Forward* 1–8 to 1–9 (prepublication copy, Feb. 2009) (listing sources of error and observing that parts of the forensic science community resist acknowledging that there is a reliability problem); Paul C. Giannelli, *Wrongful Convictions and Forensic Science: The Need to Regulate Crime Labs*, 86 N.C.L.Rev. 163, 172–95 (2007) (failures attributed to incompetence, sloppy procedures, and fraud; noting that it is often difficult to distinguish between malfeasance and misfeasance because of the lack of quality assurance protocols); Pamela R. Metzger, *Cheating the Constitution*, 59 Vand. L. Rev. 475, 494–95 (2006) ("[L]aboratory error and operator error exist even with the most well-established or unassailable scientific method."); Andre A. Moenssens, *Symposium On Scientific Evidence: Forward: Novel Scientific Evidence In Criminal Cases: Some Words Of Caution*, 84 J. Crim. L. & Criminology 1, 12–13 (Spring 1993) (article describes difficulty crime labs have in attracting and training qualified individuals and asserts that "human error is a more important factor than previously suspected").

(B) Dishonest Errors. Another source of unreliability in forensic science must be mentioned — intentional wrongdoing.

> Sau Chan (Associated Press), *Police Chemist Charged with Faking Evidence*, Birmingham News, Aug. 7, 1994, at 5A:[37]
>
> Fred Zain, a police chemist whose expert testimony and lab tests helped put scores of rapists and murderers behind bars in two states over 13 years, now finds himself in the dock.
>
> Zain is charged with lying in court and tampering with evidence in his laboratories, compelling judges in West Virginia and Texas to release men sent to prison on the strength of blood and semen samples Zain verified.
>
> "I really have no idea why he did what he did," said Jack Buckalew, a former superintendent of the West Virginia State Police. "The only possible reason I can speculate on is to enhance his status with prosecutors by saying what he thought they wanted him to say."
>
> Zain, 43, surrendered on Thursday in Hondo, Texas, to answer charges of aggravated perjury, evidence tampering and fabrication connected to the 1990 rape conviction of Gilbert Alejandro.
>
> "I think there's no criminal intent," said attorney Sam Bayless.

---

[37] Copyright © 1994 by The Associated Press. Reprinted with permission.

Zain worked as a serologist for the West Virginia State Police from 1980 to 1989. He resigned to become chief of physical evidence for the medical examiner in Bexar County, Texas.

Texas has freed two men convicted on now-disproven blood tests done by Zain: Alejandro, who served four years of a 12-year sentence, and Jack W. Davis, convicted of murder in 1990.

Davis missed a death sentence by the vote of one juror and is suing Zain for $10 million. After Davis' conviction, Zain changed his testimony about blood at the scene of a teacher's mutilation-murder, acknowledging the blood came from the victim rather than Davis.

Zain's work or testimony figures in hundreds of other Texas cases, and authorities say they will review each one.

On Thursday, Zain goes to West Virginia to be arraigned on charges he lied about his credentials and about performing specific lab tests in a 1991 double-murder trial.

Seventy-one convictions, all but five of them for murder or rape, were granted reviews because of Zain's "long history of falsifying evidence in criminal prosecutions," according to a report presented to the West Virginia Supreme Court last year.

Also, consider the case of pathologist Ralph Erdmann. Erdmann was a freelance pathologist who worked for about 40 counties in the Texas panhandle. In 1993 Erdmann was sentenced to 10 years' probation and 200 hours of community service after he entered a plea of no contest to seven felony charges that arose out of his allegedly faking hundreds of autopsies. Richard L. Fricker, *Pathologist's Plea Adds to Turmoil*, 79 A.B.A.J. 24 (March 1993). Regrettably, there have been other documented cases involving forensic science fraud. *See generally* Paul C. Giannelli, *Wrongful Convictions and Forensic Science: The Need to Regulate Crime Labs*, 86 N.C.L.Rev. 163, 172–187 (2007); Pat A. Wertheim, *Latent Fingerprint Evidence: Fabrication, Not Error*, The Champion 16, 19–20 & 20–21 (Nov./Dec. 2008).

3. *Admitting Laboratory Reports in Lieu of Direct Testimony.* Professor Giannelli suggests that reliability problems may be hidden if a laboratory report containing test results and analyst conclusions is admitted into evidence in lieu of live testimony from the analyst who conducted the testing. The results of drug analyses, fingerprint comparisons, intoxication tests, and rape victim examinations, among other techniques, have been introduced in this fashion. *See generally*, 1 Scientific evidence § 6.01, at 339–42 (4th ed. 2007). The downside to this practice is that there is no one for the evidence's opponent to cross-examine on reliability issues such as analyst qualification, analyst bias, whether instrumentation used was in proper working order, and whether proper test procedure was followed.

On the other hand, often the most expedient way to place the results of scientific testing in evidence is through the laboratory report. The admission of just the laboratory report benefits the evidence's proponent (usually the prosecution) in that the test's results are placed before the trier of fact without subjecting the test's conductor to cross-examination. In addition, if the analyst does not have to appear in court, he or she does not have to lose time away from the laboratory. Proponents of this practice argue that there is little to be gained by cross-examining an analyst who performed a routine test.

> Federal courts have noted the practical reality that cross-examination of technicians who perform these tests is unlikely to yield meaningful information since the tests are routine and repeatedly performed, such that it is unlikely that a technician would specifically remember the performance of one among many identical tests performed months (if not years) before trial. *See Reardon v. Manson*, 806 F.2d 39, 41–42 (2d Cir. 1986); *United States v. Bell*, 785 F.2d 640, 643 (8th Cir. 1986) (stating that producing the technicians who perform such tests "rarely leads to any admissions helpful to the party challenging the evidence").

Baber v. State, 775 So. 2d 258, 261 n. 4 (Fla. 2001).

(A) Evidentiary Issues. When a laboratory report is used to present test results in lieu of testimony from the analyst who performed the test, problems of authentication and compliance with the original writing, or "best evidence" rule, must be considered. If the laboratory report is certified and prepared by a government laboratory (as is usually the case), it is likely to be self-authenticating under the Rules of Evidence. *See, e.g.* Fed. R. Evid. 902(4) (certified copy of official record or report is self-authenticating). Similarly, a copy of a public record, certified as correct in accordance with Rule 902, should satisfy the best evidence rule. *See* Fed. R. Evid. 1005 ("contents of an official record . . . may be proved by copy, certified as correct in accordance with Rule 902. . . ."). *See also* 1 Scientific Evidence § 6.01, at 340–41 (4th ed. 2007).

The rule against hearsay presents a more significant admissibility hurdle. Hearsay problems may be overcome, however, if the laboratory report fits the business records or official records exception to the hearsay rule. *See* Fed. R. Evid. 803(6) & (8). Courts are divided on whether those exceptions apply when laboratory reports are prepared by forensic scientists who are employed by a government agency. *See generally* 1 Scientific Evidence § 6.02[a]–[c], at 343–56 (4th ed. 2007).

(B) Statutory Admissibility:"Certificate of Analysis" Statutes. Admissibility hurdles imposed by the Rules of Evidence may be overcome if admissibility is authorized by statute. The overwhelming majority of states have enacted so-called "certificate of analysis" statutes that authorize the admission of a certified laboratory report containing the forensic conclusions of the analyst. Although the details of these statutes vary, they generally cover a variety of scientific tests, and contain little more than the analyst's conclusions.

As a general proposition, certificate of analysis statutes require the prosecution to provide notice that it intends to introduce a certified laboratory report. Once any required notice is given, the burden shifts to the defendant to demand that the analyst appear at trial for cross-examination. A few statutes — so-called "notice and demand" statutes — provide that the analyst must appear at trial if the defendant makes a timely demand. *See* Pamela R. Metzger, *Cheating the Constitution*, 59 Vand. L. Rev. 475, 482 (2006) (12 states have "notice and demand" statutes). Other statutes require the defendant to make a timely demand for the analyst's presence at trial, *and* to also make a prescribed factual showing, or to "show cause" in order to compel the analyst's presence at trial. *See id.* at 481–89 (2006) (describing 4 categories of statutes: "notice and demand"; "notice and demand-plus"; "anticipatory demand;" and "defense subpoena").

(C) Constitutional Issues: The Confrontation Clause.[38] Although certificate of analysis statutes may overcome evidentiary hurdles imposed by the Rules of Evidence, they cannot override constitutional requirements. The Sixth Amendment's Confrontation Clause provides that "[i]n all criminal prosecutions, the accused shall enjoy the right . . . to be confronted with the witnesses against him. . . ." In *Crawford v. Washington* the United States Supreme Court held that the Confrontation Clause applied to "*testimonial*" statements from an absent witness, and rendered such statements inadmissible *unless*: (1) the declarant is unavailable *and* (2) the defendant had a prior opportunity for cross-examination. *Crawford v. Washington*, 541 U.S. 36, 53–54 (2004). Five years later, in *Melendez-Diaz v. Massachusetts*, ___ U.S. ___, 2009 WL 1789468 (June 25, 2009), the Court ruled that the conclusions of a forensic analyst contained in a certificate of analysis were "testimonial" statements subject to exclusion under the Confrontation Clause. *Id.* at *4.

The *Melendez-Diaz* Court noted, however, that the admission of a laboratory report pursuant to a certificate of analysis statute would be constitutional if the statute contained a "notice and demand" provision. The Court explained:

> In their simplest form, notice-and-demand statutes require the prosecution to provide notice to the defendant of its intent to use an analyst's report as evidence at trial, after which the defendant is given a period of time in which he may object to the admission of the evidence absent the analyst's appearance live at trial. . . . [T]hese statutes shift no burden whatever. The defendant *always* has the burden of raising his Confrontation Clause objection; notice-and-demand statutes simply govern the *time* within which he must do so. States are free to adopt procedural rules governing objections. . . . There is no conceivable reason why [the defendant] cannot . . . be compelled to exercise his Confrontation Clause rights before trial. Today's decision will not disrupt criminal prosecutions in the many large States whose practice is already in accord with the Confrontation Clause.

Melendez-Diaz, supra, ___ U.S. at ___, 2009 WL 1789468 at *12 (emphasis in original). In a footnote to the above excerpt the Court added the following concerning which type of "notice and demand" statute might pass constitutional muster.

> As the dissent notes, *some* state statutes, "requir[e] defense counsel to subpoena the analyst, to show good cause for demanding the analyst's presence, or even to affirm under oath an intent to cross-examine the analyst." We have no occasion today to pass on the constitutionality of every variety of statute commonly given the notice-and-demand label. It suffices to say that what we have referred to as the "simplest form [of] notice-and-demand statutes," is constitutional [and] that such provisions are in place in a number of States. . . .

Melendez-Diaz, supra, ___ U.S. at ___ n.12, 2009 WL 1789468 at *12 n.12 (emphasis in original).

The Court referenced statutes in Georgia, Texas, and Ohio as examples of the "simplest form [of] notice-and-demand statutes" that would pass constitutional muster. These statutes require the accused to object in writing to the admission of a certificate of analysis within a prescribed time-frame, but do not require the accused to take any additional steps to prevent admission of the certificate of analysis. *See* Ga.Code Ann.

---

[38] The admissibility of out-of-court statements in compliance with the Confrontation Clause is examined at length in Chapter 8, *infra*.

§ 35-3-154.1 (2006) (object in writing at least 10 days prior to trial); Tex.Code Crim. Proc. Ann., Art. 38.41, § 4 (Vernon 2005) (object in writing no later than 10 days before trial begins); Ohio Rev.Code Ann. § 2925.51(c) (West 2006) (accused must demand testimony from the person signing the laboratory report within 7 days from receiving the report).

QUESTIONS

1. *The Practicality Of Retesting.* How likely is it that an error in forensic testing will be discovered? For example, if you were assigned today to represent an indigent defendant in a case like *Miller v. Pate*, and if you had limited resources available to hire experts, would you hire an expert to retest the stains on the shorts to confirm that they were blood? If not, what, if anything, would you do relative to the chemist's testimony?

2. *Reliability Of Laboratory Reports.* Why might a laboratory report be unreliable and/or misleading?

3. *Is There A Need For Evidentiary Hurdles?* If you accept that errors are made in scientific testing, should a rule of evidence be fashioned that assumes incompetency (or wrongdoing) on the part of forensic scientists or the police and makes admissibility of scientific evidence more difficult than other types of evidence? Is cross-examination and jury "common sense" sufficient to deal with such situations if and when they arise?

4. *Subpoenas.* Would a state statute violate the Confrontation Clause if it allowed the prosecution to introduce a laboratory report without calling the forensic analyst and did not contain an "notice and demand" provision, but instead provided that the accused had the right to subpoena and call the analyst as his or her own witness?

[2]   The Problem of Inaccuracy: Invalid Scientific Theory

Put aside, for the moment, allegations of bias and the problem of errors (honest and dishonest). Instead, focus upon problems that may exist if a scientific theory or technique is invalid.

State and federal courts have grappled for years with the problem of how to determine whether or when to allow experts to base opinions upon new and/or untested scientific theories or techniques. Because a scientist's opinion will only be as reliable as the scientific technique it is based upon, if the scientific technique is "junk," then the opinion will likely be "junk" as well. If, for example, the technique used to determine alcohol content in a person's blood was unreliable, an expert's testimony that an accused had.15% alcohol would be unreliable no matter how much the scientist who performed the test believed his or her testimony was accurate, and no matter how precisely the "invalid" test was conducted.

The fear, of course, is that the jury will not be able to assess the validity of the underlying scientific technique and, in ignorance, will accept the expert's opinions as valid.[39] Accordingly, many courts feel the need to stand between the jury and testimony that is based upon an untested or invalid scientific technique or theory.

But how can a court determine that a scientific technique is invalid or unreliable? Is it enough if a qualified expert explains the technique used and vouches for its reliability?

---

[39] The possibility of human error, bias, or fraud presents this same concern (jury inability to appreciate or weigh the possibility of inaccuracy) even if valid scientific theories are used.

As you might imagine, over the years the courts have employed more than one test for determining a technique's scientific validity. The various tests will be examined in some detail in Chapter 2. At this point do not be concerned with what test, if any, is preferable. Rather, focus on the nature of the problem and the wisdom of fashioning an evidentiary hurdle that examines the accuracy or reliability of the *scientific theory* and/ or *scientific technique* that expert testimony is based upon (as opposed to an evidentiary hurdle that is designed to uncover human bias and/or error in performing a specific scientific test). Finally, consider that what is, and what is not, reliable science may not be as obvious as you think.

The *Bullard* case that follows illustrates the problem just described. In *Bullard* a forensic anthropologist developed and, in good faith, applied an apparently invalid scientific technique. Unfortunately, the expert's testimony based upon this invalid technique helped convict Vonnie Ray Bullard of murder. As you read through the *Bullard* case and the article by Mark Hansen that follows it, contrast the reliability problem presented in *Bullard* with the reliability problem presented in *Miller v. Pate*.

STATE v. BULLARD
322 S.E.2d 370 (N.C. 1984)

FRYE, JUSTICE.

The defendant raises several assignments of error. Both parties agree, however, that the dispositive and crucial issue to this appeal is whether the trial court improperly allowed Dr. Louise Robbins, a physical anthropologist, to testify as an expert in the identification of a bloody bare footprint. This issue is one of first impression in this State. It is our conclusion, after carefully reviewing the entire record, the parties' arguments, and the relevant law, that the trial court correctly allowed Dr. Robbins to testify and render her opinion. . . .

The trial of Vonnie Ray Bullard was complicated. Eighty-one witnesses testified, and more than half of them possessed the surname Bullard. Exhibits in excess of 1000 were also introduced into evidence. The testimony revolved around the sequence of events during the evening of August 25, 1981. The majority of this testimony concerned the location of Pedro Hales (the decedent), Vonnie Ray Bullard (the defendant) and defendant's truck during various times on 25 and 26 August 1981. The evidence, which is mostly circumstantial, is summarized as follows:

> Pedro Hales and the defendant were neighbors. . . . In October of 1978, Pedro Hales had shot and wounded the defendant's son and had been found not guilty by a jury on the basis of self-defense. Since that time, Vonnie Ray Bullard had made threatening statements about Pedro Hales to several witnesses. . . .

At approximately 8:30 p.m. on August 1981, the defendant and Pedro were seen riding in Pedro's truck and talking at a local store. Several witnesses stated that they observed the defendant addressing Pedro in a loud and angry voice but could not determine what was being said. Later that evening, prior to Pedro's disappearance, the defendant was seen with a small pistol in his watch pocket. Defendant acknowledged that he owned a.22 caliber pistol, but claimed he had lost it several days before Pedro's death. The defendant was not wearing shoes when he was seen during this time.

Pedro was last seen alive without apparent injuries at approximately 11:00 p.m. on 25 August 1981. A local neighbor, who had seen Pedro on the side of the road and suspected he was drunk, went to Pedro's mother's house to tell Pedro's brother, Carson Hales, about Pedro. The neighbor and Carson both observed the defendant's red truck going by as they stood on Carson Hales' porch at approximately 11:05 p.m. Immediately thereafter, they went back to where Pedro had last been seen but could not find him. Fruitlessly, they began to search in the general area for Pedro. Carson Hales and his mother also went to defendant's home at approximately 11:30 p.m. to inquire whether the defendant had seen Pedro, since the defendant had driven earlier in the general direction where Pedro was last seen. However, no one was home and defendant's red truck was not there.

Meanwhile, at approximately the same time of 11:30 p.m., two witnesses observed a vehicle stopped on Melvin's Bridge, located approximately four miles from where Pedro was last seen. These witnesses pulled over on the side of the road as they approached the bridge. After about forty-five seconds, the vehicle drove away from the bridge, toward the two witnesses, who described the vehicle as the distinctive red truck owned by the defendant. The witnesses could not see who was driving the truck.

The defendant's truck was next observed at approximately 12 midnight, traveling at a rapid rate of speed. He was seen pulling his truck behind his house, which is not where he normally parks it. The defendant was observed turning his headlights off as soon as his truck entered the driveway. Approximately ten minutes later, the defendant spoke with several witnesses, who testified that defendant's hair was wet and freshly combed and that he looked as though he had just changed clothes and showered.

The following day, 26 August 1981, a large amount of blood, a.22 bullet, . . . bloody bare footprints, a bare footprint in sand, [and] tire tracks . . . were found on Melvin's Bridge. . . .

A detective from the Sampson County Sheriff's Department testified that he took a series of photographs with a 35mm camera at varying shutter speeds of a bloody bare footprint on the asphalt and another bare footprint in sand. He also testified that he had brushed some sand away from the bloody footprint before he photographed it. This same footprint was later sprayed with luminol reagent, which enhances the footprint and illuminates the bloody areas. Photographs of the luminol-enhanced footprint were also taken. Additionally, the detective testified that as he was trying to remove the piece of asphalt with the bloody footprint, the asphalt broke primarily in the heel region of the footprint.

A supervisor of the latent evidence section of the SBI laboratory testified that he took ink and latex paint impressions of the defendant's feet and that he gave the impressions and copies of the photographs of the unknown footprint (both natural light and luminol enhanced) to Dr. Louise Robbins. He also testified that he observed no ridge details on the unknown footprints found on the bridge and could not make a comparison with known footprints of the defendant. He also testified he would not make an identification of the footprints based on shape alone.

Dr. Louise Robbins, a physical anthropologist employed at the University of North Carolina at Greensboro, testified, over objection and after a lengthy *voir dire* hearing, about her background, qualifications, and independent studies in bare footprint comparisons. She explained her methodology for comparing known and unknown bare footprints by size and shape, without relying on ridge detail in the bare footprints. She testified that in her opinion a bloody bare footprint found on Melvin's Bridge was that of the defendant.

Pedro's body was found several days later in the South River. An autopsy revealed he had been stabbed seventeen times and shot three times. A.22 bullet was removed from his body. The first bullet had entered the left side of the head exiting at the center of the back. The second bullet had entered the right side of the back near the shoulder, and there was no exit wound. A.22 caliber bullet was found in this back wound. The third bullet entered in the left shoulder and exited a short distance later. Basically, the wounds were inflicted in a left to right direction.

. . . .

Defendant denied killing Pedro and stated that they were friends. Defendant admitted he was with Pedro earlier on the evening of 25 August 1981. He also stated that no one else used his truck during the entire evening. Evidence was presented that three people went over Melvin's Bridge earlier during the morning of 26 August 1981 and no blood was observed by these three people. A deputy with the Cumberland County Sheriff's Department did observe the blood on the north side of Melvin's Bridge at approximately 10:30 a.m. that same morning. Several character witnesses testified on behalf of the defendant. The defense also presented testimony of Professors Cartmill and Robertson of the Duke University Medical School, Department of Anatomy, who stated that Dr. Louise Robbins' method of footprint analysis was inaccurate and that the unknown footprints did not, in their opinion, belong to the defendant.

I.

EXPERT TESTIMONY

We first consider defendant's challenge to the introduction of the testimony of Dr. Louise Robbins, a physical anthropologist.[40] [1] The defendant's objection to Dr. Robbins' testimony is premised on the following specifically alleged errors by the trial court:

1. The trial court erred in allowing Dr. Robbins to testify as an expert in the field of footprint identification when, in fact, as shown by the evidence adduced in *voir dire* hearing prior to her testimony, there is no such area of such expertise recognized by our law.

2. The trial court erred in failing to exclude or suppress Dr. Robbins' testimony because it has no basis or recognition whatever in the scientific community and is not sufficiently reliable or acceptable by the court.

3. The trial court erred by failing to grant defendant's motion to strike the opinion testimony of Dr. Robbins because she was not properly qualified to give such an opinion, and her testimony was too speculative and had no basis in science or fact.

. . . .

The first three contentions by defendant primarily deal with the application of a technique utilized by Dr. Robbins which is allegedly unprecedented in North Carolina

---

[40] [n.1] Dr. Robbins testified that physical anthropology is a subdivision of anthropology in which the focus is on the biological makeup of people, namely, the similarities and differences in people around the world. More specifically, Dr. Robbins has been involved in forensic anthropology, which is the application of anthropological techniques and methods to problems pertaining to law enforcement.

and the United States[41] [2]. . . . Before beginning our analyses and conclusions . . . some attention to Dr. Robbins' professional background and her challenged methodology is in order.

Dr. Robbins testified during *voir dire* and on direct examination about her qualifications and achievements in the field of physical anthropology. During direct examination, she explained, by utilizing colored slides, how she examines unknown footprints for purposes of trying to determine if they are made by a particular individual.

The method of comparison employed by Dr. Robbins does not involve ridge detail as does traditional fingerprint analysis. Instead, she relies upon a technique of comparison pertaining to the size and shape of the footprint in four areas: namely, the heel, arch, ball, and toe regions. The footprint size and shape reflect the size and shape of the internal bone structure of the foot, so the bones indirectly play a major part in the analysis of the footprint, according to Dr. Robbins. Dr. Robbins explains that since each person's foot size and shape are unique, she can identify a footprint represented by a clearly definable print of whatever part of the foot touches the ground. By examining the sides, front, and rear ends of each region of the foot, Dr. Robbins explains that she can compare known footprints with unknown footprints and determine if they are made by the same person.

At the time of trial Dr. Robbins stated that she had testified as an expert in Oklahoma, California, Pennsylvania, and Florida.[42] [6] The only reported decisions from Florida did not refer to Dr. Robbins; however, her name did appear in the transcript as an expert.

B.

We will now discuss defendant's first three assignments of error, which can be condensed into one issue: Whether scientific evidence which tends to identify an accused by bare footprint comparison is admissible where the expert relies upon methods other than ridge detail in making such comparison. This is an issue of first impression in this jurisdiction. Counsel for the defense strenuously argues that to allow the expert testimony of Dr. Robbins would require the jury to make a "leap of faith," blindly accepting at face value the ultimate opinion of a person who professes to be the only one skilled in a particular subject area. Defendant argues that the fundamental differences between the method of identification used in existing case law and that which was propounded by the State in this case necessitates an independent determination by this Court that the method used by Dr. Robbins is itself reliable and sufficiently established to have gained general acceptance in its field.

---

[41] [n.2] Dr. Robbins testified that she is the only person in this country to attempt the kind of analysis undertaken to identify the footprints in question. She has been in contact with Owen Macey of Scotland Yard and Arly Claus of Germany who employ the same technique and analysis. Also there are several persons in India who engage in footprint analysis consistent with her analysis.

[42] [n.6]. . . The defendant vigorously attacked the State's assertion that there was legal authority reported in the national reporting system where Dr. Robbins' testimony had been considered. . . .

It is worth noting that Dr. Robbins testified in a trial court of North Carolina as an expert in the field of physical anthropology in the case of *State v. Maccia*, 316 S.E.2d 241 (1984). Shoes found at the crime scene contained imprints on the insole of footprints. Dr. Robbins prepared a cast of the imprints and compared them with footprints made in paint and ink by the defendant. She concluded that "the defendant's feet made the imprints inside the shoes found at the scene of the crime." *Id.* at 243. This is sometimes referred to as a "Cinderella analysis." The expert testimony by Dr. Robbins was not an issue on appeal.

The single fact that the application of the method employed by Dr. Robbins suffers a dearth of recognition does not *per se* prevent the admissibility of her testimony. . . .

. . . .

. . . [W]e have here the development of a scientific method that is in its infancy. Admittedly, the method utilized by Dr. Robbins has not been cited in any reported decision. . . . However, that fact alone [does] not prevent the . . . court from accepting the expert testimony.

In varying degrees all courts have sometimes been reluctant to admit unique scientific testimony. In fact, the use of fingerprinting as a means of identification, which existed prior to the time of Christ, was itself the subject of doubt and speculation. This form of scientific evidence, though universally accepted now, had to make its appearance for acceptance in some court. In *People v. Jennings*, 96 N.E. 1077 (1911), the admission of fingerprint evidence was a case of first impression, but the court accepted this novel and unique method. In *Jennings*, the court stated:

> When photography was first introduced, it was seriously questioned whether pictures thus created could properly be introduced into evidence, but this method of proof, as well as by means of x-rays and the microscope, is now admitted without question.

96 N.E. at 1082. As with most scientific phenomena, the passage of time can serve, as it has in fingerprinting, to demonstrate the reliability and acceptance of a once speculative and unproved premise. Thus, the novelty of a chosen technique does not justify rejecting its admissibility into evidence.

. . . The courts of this nation, including our own, have struggled to enunciate a formula for ruling on the admission of new and untested scientific principles. . . .

. . . .

In [*State v*]. *Temple*, [273 S.E.2d 273 (N.C. 1981)], however, the Court stated a general rule for admitting new scientific methods:

> This Court is of the opinion, that we should favor the adoption of scientific methods of crime detection, where the demonstrated accuracy and reliability has become established and recognized. Justice is truth in action, and any instrumentality, which aids justice in the ascertainment of truth, should be embraced without delay.

Id. at 280. A second general principle regarding admissibility of such evidence in this State is as follows:

> In general, when no specific precedent exists, scientifically accepted reliability justifies admission of the testimony of qualified witnesses, and such reliability may be found either by judicial notice or from the testimony of scientists who are expert in the subject matter, or by a combination of the two.

1 Brandis on North Carolina Evidence, § 86, at 323 (footnote citations omitted).

We will examine the law in this area . . . in an effort to synthesize the significant factors relied upon by the courts when evaluating whether a scientific method in its infancy is reliable and whether it should be adopted or rejected.

. . . .

In matching threads among the cases and analogizing them to the present one, we determine that the method employed by Dr. Robbins is reliable. . . . [Dr. Robbins] used scientifically established measurement techniques relied upon in the established field of physical anthropology to make her measurements. . . . Certainly, the extensive professional achievements and endeavors of Dr. Robbins should render her testimony reliable. . . . She did not ask the jury to sacrifice its independence by accepting her scientific hypotheses on faith. Rather, she explained in detail to the jury the basis of her measurements and the interrelationships of the various portions of the foot and how her visual comparisons enabled her to identify unknown footprints and compare them with known footprints.

She explained the number of footprints she had collected to justify why she believed each footprint is unique. . . . All of the foregoing factors relative to an expert's testimony based on a novel scientific method have been accepted by this Court as cogent to its determination that the expert's method was reliable and his testimony admissible. We also have determined that Dr. Robbins' unique scientific method is reliable because of her explanatory testimony, professional background, independent research, and use of established procedures to make her visual comparisons of bare footprints.

. . . .

C.

After determining that this evidence is sufficiently reliable, the next question is whether it is also relevant. Relevant evidence is admissible if it "has any logical tendency however slight to prove a fact at issue in the case.". . . .

[I]n this case . . . defendant introduced the testimony of two witnesses who contradicted the testimony of Dr. Robbins by stating that they did not agree that defendant's footprint matched the footprint at he crime scene. This rebuttal testimony goes to the weight of the evidence, not to its admissibility. "What the evidence proves or fails to proves is a question of fact for the jury." The differing views of the experts concerning the comparisons of the footprints were properly submitted to the jury for their determination. The reliability and credibility of Dr. Robbins' opinion were subject to refutation, and the weight of her testimony was fairly presented to the jury.

. . . .

. . . In the defendant's trial, we find NO ERROR.

MARK HANSEN, BELIEVE IT OR NOT,
79 A.B.A.J. 64, 64–67 (June 1993)[43]

Louise Robbins had but one claim to fame: She could see things in a footprint that nobody else could see.

Give her a ski boot and a sneaker, for instance, and Robbins contended that she could tell whether the two shoes had ever been worn by the same person.

Show her even a portion of a shoeprint on any surface, Robbins maintained, and she could identify the person who made it.

---

[43] Copyright © 1993. Printed in the U.S.A. American Bar Association. Reprinted by permission of the *ABA Journal*.

It might sound amusing, coming as it did from an anthropology professor who once astounded her colleagues by describing a 3.5 million-year-old fossilized footprint in Tanzania as that of a prehistoric woman who was 5½ months pregnant.

It might also be considered harmless, had it remained a subject of academic speculation at the University of North Carolina at Greensboro, where Robbins taught anthropology courses and collected footprints from her students for comparison.

By 1976, however, Robbins had taken her quirky ideas out of the classroom and into the courtroom, where her amazing feet-reading abilities seemed to dazzle juries and made her something of a celebrity on the criminal trial circuit. Newspapers called her a female "Quincy." She was profiled in the *ABA Journal*. Her techniques were even touted in the pages of *Time* magazine.

By her own account, Robbins appeared as an expert, mostly for the prosecution, in more than 20 criminal cases in 11 states and Canada over the next 10 years until a losing battle with brain cancer finally forced her off the witness stand. She died in 1987 at the age of 58. By then, her testimony had helped send at least a dozen people to prison. And it may have put one man on death row.

There's just one catch. Robbins was the only person in the world who claimed to do what she said she did. And her claims have now been thoroughly debunked by the rest of the scientific community.

Melvin Lewis, a John Marshall Law School professor who keeps track of more than 5,000 expert witnesses, dismisses Robbins' work as "complete hogwash."

"It barely rises to the dignity of nonsense," he said.

And FBI agent William Bodziak, one of the world's leading authorities on footprints, said that Robbins' theories were totally unfounded.

"Nobody else has ever dreamed of saying the kinds of things she said," he explained.

Robbins' story, as reported last year by the CBS news program "48 Hours," provides a graphic illustration of how far some prosecutors and defense lawyers are willing to go to find an expert witness to bolster a case. It also shows how easily one self-proclaimed expert with little or no credence in the scientific community can make a mockery out of the criminal justice system.

"It's frightening to me that something like that could go as far as it did," said Lewis, who runs a school-sponsored referral service that puts lawyers in touch with qualified experts. "Her so-called evidence was so grotesquely ridiculous, it's necessary to say to yourself, if that can get in, what can't?"

Today, nearly six years after her death, some of the legal ramifications of Robbins' testimony are still being felt.

Stephen Buckley, who spent three years in an Illinois jail awaiting trial for the 1983 murder of a 10-year-old Chicago-area girl, is suing prosecutors for allegedly violating his civil rights.

Buckley's first trial, in 1985, ended in a hung jury, despite Robbins' testimony that a bootprint left on the victim's kicked-in front door had been made by him. He was freed in 1987, but only because Robbins was then too sick to testify at his retrial.

. . . .

Yet Buckley . . . might consider [himself] lucky, in light of what has happened to Vonnie Ray Bullard.

Bullard is still serving a life sentence in a North Carolina prison for the 1981 murder of another man after Robbins testified that a bare footprint outlined in the victim's blood was his. Having exhausted his appeals, based largely on Robbins' testimony, Bullard won't be eligible for parole until the year 2001.

Other experts can match feet with footprints or shoes with shoeprints, provided that the two samples being compared share enough of the same ridge details or random characteristics. But Robbins was alone in claiming that she could tell whether a person made a particular print by examining any other shoes belonging to that individual.

Robbins built her reputation on the theory that footprints, like fingerprints, are unique. It was her contention that, because of individual variations in the way people stand and walk, everyone's foot will leave a distinct impression on any surface, including the inside sole of his or her shoe. Those impressions, she contended, show up as "wear patterns" on the bottom of every shoe.

. . . .

Robbins' claims were hotly contested from the moment she first set foot in a courtroom. Shortly before her death, a panel of more than 100 forensic experts concluded that her footprint identification techniques didn't work. In hindsight, her theories may seem patently absurd.

In fact, many of her colleagues have been saying as much since 1978, when Robbins joined a scientific expedition at Laetoli, Tanzania, then the site of one of the most important archaeological discoveries ever made. During that expedition, according to her colleagues, Robbins misidentified one set of prehistoric human footprints as belonging to an antelope and concluded that another set of footprints had been made by the prehistoric woman who was 5½ months pregnant. . . .

Tim White, an anthropology professor at the University of California at Berkeley who was also a member of the expedition, said it was hard enough to determine that the footprints they found were indeed human. But it was impossible to tell if any of the prints had been made by a woman, let alone one who was 5½ months pregnant, he said.

"Her observations were unreliable, she was overly imaginative and she was incredibly suggestive regarding the interpretation of evidence," White said. "She kept saying things that could not be documented, and for very good reason, it was all in her mind."

"It truly reveals her as someone who was willing to go to any extremes to come up with an interesting story," said University of Chicago anthropology professor Russell Tuttle, who has studied Robbins' work and appeared opposite her in court. "She'd say anything anybody wanted her to say."

But that didn't keep Robbins from being qualified as an expert, with no known exceptions, from the time she first testified for the prosecution in the arson trial of a Pennsylvania man in 1976, until her last known appearance in court, once again as a prosecution witness, at the 1986 murder trial of a Chicago man.

In some cases, like Bullard's, her testimony may have been cumulative. In other cases, like Buckley's. . . , it constituted the only physical evidence linking the defendant to the crime.

Prosecutors usually succeeded in getting her testimony admitted by portraying Robbins as a pioneer in a new field of science and by putting on testimonials as to her character and credentials from one or two of her peers. One prosecutor noted that it took 400 years for Galileo's theories to win acceptance. Another pointed out that fingerprint evidence also was considered a new science just 80 years ago.

Since Robbins had no competition, her testimony was difficult to refute. But defense lawyers depicted her variously as a fraud, a charlatan, an opportunist and a hired gun. And they presented other experts who testified that there was no scientific basis for any of the claims she made.

By her own admission, Robbins never took or taught a course on shoeprint identification techniques or the wear patterns of shoes. She never conducted a blind test of her abilities, published her findings in a scientific journal or submitted her work to peer review. And she never accounted for such things as manufacturing differences in shoewear construction, dynamic changes in a person's foot or the effect of various surfaces on the quality of a shoeprint.

"She may well have believed what she was saying," said C. Owen Lovejoy, an anthropology professor at Kent State University, "but the scientific basis for her conclusions was completely fraudulent."

Tuttle said he concluded after hearing her testify at a 1983 murder trial in Winnipeg that Robbins was "either a crook or a self-deluded quack."

. . . .

Bullard's conviction . . . was affirmed in 1984 by the North Carolina Supreme Court. It held that new scientific methods are admissible if they are reliable, which it said was the case with respect to Robbins' techniques. Any rebuttal testimony, the court said, goes to the weight of the evidence, not its admissibility.

Under that standard, which remains in effect, Robbins could still testify in North Carolina if she were alive today, according to Carl Barrington, Jr., Bullard's defense lawyer.

NOTES

1. *Comparative Bullet Lead Analysis.* Comparative Bullet Lead Analysis (CBLA) is a process that compares trace chemicals found in bullets at a crime scene with ammunition found in the possession of a suspect. It was used by the FBI for more than 30 years to link suspects to crimes in cases where bullets had fragments to the point where traditional firearms tracing (based on gun-barrel groove markings) would not work. The assumption was that bullets made from the same batch of lead would have the same chemical composition. Unfortunately, very few studies were ever published on the technique. In 2004 a National Research Council study concluded that the data did not support any statement that a crime bullet came from a particular box of ammunition. The FBI stopped CBLA testing in 2005. *See* Paul C. Giannelli, *Wrongful Convictions and Forensic Science: The Need to Regulate Crime Labs*, 86 N.C.L.Rev. 163, 200–202 (2007); William A. Tobin & William C. Thompson, Evaluating and Challenging Forensic Identification Evidence, The Champion 12, (July 2006).

2. *Other Controversial Scientific Theories.* *Bullard* is not unique. In other cases litigants have offered expert testimony based upon a scientific device, instrument, or procedure that rests upon a questionable theory or technique. *See, e.g., State v. Kunze,*

988 P.2d 977, 987 & 991 (Wash. App. 1999) (expert testifies that he is "100% confident" that defendant's left ear was the source of a latent earprint found at the crime scene based upon comparison of earprints; appellate court reverses conviction because latent earprint identification is not generally accepted in the forensic science community); *Gentry v. State*, 443 S.E.2d 667, 668–69 (Ga. Ct. App. 1994) (expert testifies that defendant not normally aroused by adult women based upon results of a "penile plethysmograph" test); *Commonwealth v. Graves*, 456 A.2d 561, 565 (Pa. Super. Ct. 1983) (forensic odontologists testify they can connect scratches on murder victim's back with defendant's fingernails); *Fisher v. State*, 361 So. 2d 203, 204 (Fla. Dist. Ct. App. 1978) (medical examiner testifies that stab wounds were "more characteristic of those made by a woman" in a female defendant's murder trial); *Commonwealth v. Crawford*, 364 A.2d 660, 662–64 (Pa. 1976) (prosecution's expert testifies that palm print belonging to defendant, and found on car next to murder victim's body, was made "at the time of the killing" — even though such prints cannot be dated); Mark Hansen, *Out of the Blue*, 82 A.B.A.J. 50 (Feb. 1996) (discussing the testimony and forensic abilities of forensic dentist Michael H. West, who, among other things, developed an ultraviolet light technique that purportedly allowed him to see markings on the skin that are invisible to the naked eye and which cannot be photographed).

3. *Buckley v. Fitzsimmons*. The preceding article by Mark Hansen mentions the case of Stephen Buckley. As the article indicates, Buckley was charged with murder, and Dr. Louise Robbins testified at Buckley's trial that a bootprint on the murder victim's front door had been made by Buckley. Buckley's first trial resulted in a hung jury, and Buckley was released from custody when Dr. Robbins became too ill to testify in his second trial. After being released from custody Buckley filed a civil suit for damages against the prosecutors who brought criminal charges against him. Among other things, Buckley claimed that the prosecutors "manufactured" evidence against him by "shopping among potential expert witnesses for favorable testimony." *Buckley v. Fitzsimmons*, 20 F.3d 789, 795 (7th Cir. 1994). The Seventh Circuit held that "[n]either shopping for a favorable witness nor hiring a practitioner of junk science is actionable, although it may lead to devastating cross-examination if the judge permits the witness to testify." *Id.* at 796.

QUESTIONS

1. *Reliability Factors*. What factors does the North Carolina Supreme Court cite as indicating the reliability of Dr. Robbins's technique? Once the court determines admissibility, what safeguards or "checks" are there (according to the North Carolina Supreme Court) to prevent a decision from being reached upon an invalid scientific technique?

2. *The Jury's Ability to Weigh the Evidence*. Are you comfortable with the North Carolina Supreme Court's position that once the technique is accepted by the trial court as reliable, any opposing party's criticism of the technique or the expert's credibility goes to weight rather than admissibility? How comfortable are you with the ability of the jury to assign weight to the reliability and credibility of Dr. Robbins and her technique? When you read the excerpt below from Dr. Robbins' testimony, does her scientific technique seem as absurd as the Hansen article makes it appear?

Dr. Robbins testified on direct as follows:

Q: Can you point out to the jurors what, if any, features you observed when you were making the comparison?

A: The particular features that I was observing in the photograph pertaining to the left footprint and the acetate tracings of the left footprint was with the footprint of the left foot on the brown paper here. Again, I was looking at the toe region, the ball, the arch region and the heel region. The most noticeable features were the inner balls on the inside of the big toe pads, the absence of the stem or [sic] the big toe and the absence of the inside ball of the left footprint. Also, the position relative to one another of toes two, three and four; toe four's position, in turn, relative to where toe five is placed, noting that toe five is placed very close to the front margin of the ball and there being a notable space between toe four and the little toe next to it. The other side of the ball was examined, was compared, again noting that only the outer part of the ball is impressed on the paper in many of the left footprints. The outer part of the arch, a rather narrow arch was impressed on the paper; but yet, we get the inside part of the heel as well as the outer part of the heel impressed on the paper.

Q: Any of the other features that you observed on both the rolls that are up there and the photographs?

A: Looking at the right footprint, using the acetate tracing that had been made of the right footprint, and the photograph, I compared the heel region. It has a long, oval shape to it. The narrow to moderately wide arch. You will notice that there is some variation in width of the arch region in the different footprints on the brown paper. Also, the outer margin along the arch and the ball showing a rather long, slightly bulging margin up to a rather sharp point behind toe five where the outer margin meets with the front margin of the ball. The front margin has this long, kind of indenting contour here behind the little toe. The little toe is positioned very close to the front edge of the ball. It is separated a little bit from toe four, which is more full in some right footprints than in others. And toes three and four cluster together along with toe two. But, three and four, in particular, show up in front of this peaking part that is in the front margin of the ball.

State v. Bullard, 322 S.E.2d 370, 377 (N.C. 1984).

Is it possible that the jury assumed her technique was reliable because Dr. Robbins made a good presentation and the court let the jury hear her testimony over defendant's objection?

3. Miller, Bullard, *and Evidentiary Hurdles.* If you accept the criticism of Dr. Robbins's expertise contained in the article by Mark Hansen, Dr. Robbins's testimony was very likely inaccurate because it was based upon an invalid scientific theory or technique. If so, how is Dr. Robbins's inaccurate testimony in *Bullard* different from the chemist's inaccurate testimony (concerning the existence of blood on a pair of shorts) in the *Miller* case? More importantly, what safeguard or safeguards, if any, would protect against both type of errors?

[3]   The Problem of Inaccuracy: Identifying, Exposing, and Correcting Untrustworthy Forensic Science Evidence

If problems of bias, error, fraud, and invalid scientific theory were easy to detect and correct, they would be troubling but not particularly significant. Unfortunately, there are numerous examples of inaccurate scientific evidence contributing to the conviction of a defendant, and discovered only after a defendant was convicted and sentenced. *See generally*, EDWARD CONNORS, THOMAS LUNDREGAN, NEAL MILLER, & TOM MCEWEN, CONVICTED BY JURIES, EXONERATED BY SCIENCE: CASE STUDIES IN THE USE OF DNA EVIDENCE TO ESTABLISH INNOCENCE AFTER TRIAL, 15 (June 1996). One of the most egregious (and well-documented) examples of false forensic evidence in the criminal justice system involves a forensic scientist named Fred Zain. Fred Zain's misconduct was so extensive that the West Virginia Supreme Court of Appeals held that as a matter of law any testimonial or documentary evidence offered by Zain should be deemed "invalid, unreliable and inadmissible in determining whether to award a new trial in any subsequent habeas corpus proceeding."[44]

If there is a positive side to the Fred Zain fiasco, it is the lesson that can be learned from studying how so much untrustworthy scientific evidence was admitted into evidence. The article by George Castelle that follows recounts the misconduct of Fred Zain and suggests that four "lessons" can be learned from the Fred Zain affair. The first three lessons constitute warnings (or reminders) about the unreliability of forensic science. The fourth lesson boldly asserts that "untrustworthy forensic science can be caught and corrected," and provides a 10-step approach to identifying such evidence. As you read through the article pay particular attention to the 10 steps. Specifically, do you think that an attorney employing the 10 steps would be successful in *preventing the admission* of untrustworthy forensic evidence? If not, what other benefits might flow from utilizing the 10 steps?

GEORGE CASTELLE, LAB FRAUD: LESSONS LEARNED,
23 The Champion 12, 13–16 & 52–57 (May 1999)[45]

Lab Fraud History

During his career as a forensic scientist, Fred Zain tested physical evidence and testified to the results in hundreds of murder and rape trials. Although his work primarily involved cases in state courts in West Virginia and Texas, during later portions of his career he also accepted referrals from across the country. . . .

State Trooper Zain was a forensic science superstar, capable of finding flecks of blood and smudges of semen where his colleagues found nothing. In addition to remarkable vision, he also possessed phenomenal lab techniques — a unique ability to detect genetic markers in crime scene stains that turned otherwise hopeless cases into prosecution dreams.

Unfortunately for the criminal justice system, it was a massive fraud. In 1993, the West Virginia Supreme Court of Appeals appointed a retired judge to preside over a Special Investigation into Trooper Zain's work. The investigation focused on the serology division of the West Virginia State Police Crime Laboratory. Zain worked in the serology division from 1977 until 1989. . . .

As part of the 1993 state Supreme Court investigation, independent experts selected by the American [Society] of Crime Laboratory Directors (ASCLD) reviewed the raw data from the lab — the original records of the actual test results — and compared that data to the written reports prepared by Fred Zain. The ASCLD experts then compared

---

[44] In the Matter of an INVESTIGATION OF the WEST VIRGINIA STATE POLICE CRIME LABORATORY, SEROLOGY DIVISION, 438 S.E.2d 501, 506 (W.Va. 1993). [The opinion of the West Virginia Supreme Court in the Fred Zain matter is included in the appendix to this text.]

[45] Copyright © 1999 by THE CHAMPION. Reprinted with permission.

the raw data to Fred Zain's trial testimony. The ASCLD team reached a startling conclusion. In virtually every case where there was sufficient evidence to review, the ASCLD experts found fraud.

. . . .

. . .In addressing what may be the most egregious case of forensic science fraud in the history of American jurisprudence, the West Virginia Supreme Court of Appeals concluded:

> as a matter of law, any testimonial or documentary evidence offered by Zain at any time in any criminal prosecution should be deemed invalid, unreliable, and inadmissible in determining whether to award a new trial in any subsequent *habeas corpus* proceeding.

Although individual cases of fraud have been uncovered at various times in crime labs throughout the country, the *Zain* case appears to be the first time that an appellate court has discredited a forensic scientist's entire career and authorized the reopening, in *habeas corpus* proceedings, of every case that the forensic scientist handled.

Lessons Learned from the Zain Fiasco

. . . .

Although the "Fred Zain" *habeas* proceedings are not yet complete, the five years of effort is long enough to pause and reflect on the lessons learned, lessons that may be helpful to criminal defense lawyers in other settings where questionable lab practices, if not outright fraud, continue to plague the criminal justice system.

Lesson 1: Fraudulent Forensic Science Is Endemic

. . . .

. . . Because it is safe to assume that most of the forensic science fraud that occurs goes undetected, the amount of fraud that has been revealed bears disturbing implications for any estimate of the amount of fraud that passes without notice.

Lesson 2: Inadvertent Error, Sloppiness, Exaggeration, and Biased Forensic Science Are Equally Pervasive

Wholly apart from the problems associated with fraud, the trustworthiness of forensic science is also impaired by problems of innocent error, sloppiness, exaggeration and bias. Even the most respected labs, with presumably rigorous safeguards, still experience problems of inadvertent mislabeling or switching of samples, loss of evidence, misreading of results, mistaken recording of data, and mis-transcribing of results.

. . . .

Lesson 3: Untrustworthy Forensic Science Contaminates the Seemingly Independent Non-Scientific Evidence

One of the unexpected revelations in the Fred Zain cases is the degree to which faulty forensic science contaminates the seemingly independent *non-scientific* evidence in many cases.

One of the disturbing examples is provided by the case of William Harris, a talented and respected high school senior, a state champion athlete with college scholarships and a bright future ahead of him. His promising life collapsed in 1984 when a woman who lived nearby was sexually assaulted by a person she described as a young, athletic black male. Although Harris did not fit many of the details of the victim's description, he was ultimately arrested and tried for the crime.

At trial, besides the fraudulent scientific testimony of Fred Zain, the victim unhesitatingly identified Harris as the assailant, testifying that there was "no doubt" in her mind that he was the person who committed the crime. . . .

Based on this "overwhelming" evidence of guilt, Harris was convicted and sentenced to a 10 to 20-year term in the maximum security West Virginia Penitentiary. In 1995, after seven years of imprisonment, he was released when, despite the eyewitness testimony, the results of DNA testing confirmed his innocence.

Was the eyewitness testimony simply mistaken? The answer lies in the original police report, disclosed in the ensuing civil suit — a police report that had been concealed for over a decade. In stark contrast to the testimony at trial, the concealed report stated:

> Suspect [William Harris] eliminated with photo lineup on March 6, 1985. Victim said she knew him and it wasn't him.

What occurred between the victim's *elimination* of Harris as a suspect and the testimony in the 1987 trial that stated with dramatic confidence precisely the opposite? Among other influences, the faulty scientific "evidence" was shared with the non-scientific witnesses, including the investigating deputies and the victim. The exposure to faulty scientific evidence reinforced their belief that the eyewitness elimination of William Harris must be wrong, and they were willing to commit *Brady* violations and perhaps perjury to prove it.

Every "Fred Zain prisoner" who was falsely convicted who later established his innocence was convicted not solely on the fraudulent testimony of Zain. Instead, like William Harris, each was convicted by tainted "independent" non-scientific evidence of guilt, non-scientific evidence that was bolstered, exaggerated, or — as in the case of Harris — manufactured, following exposure of the witness to the fraudulent scientific evidence.

Consequently, it is important for criminal defense lawyers to realize that faulty forensic science contaminates more than the scientific portion of the evidence — it is capable of contaminating the entire case. As a result, the dismantling of a wrongful conviction can be a particularly difficult task. Even when the erroneous forensic science is exposed, the prosecution will be likely to assert that the error is harmless, based on the "strength" of the non-scientific evidence. The defense lawyer is then faced with the doubly difficult task of establishing the contaminating effect of the erroneous science on the seemingly independent non-scientific evidence. . . .

Lesson 4: Untrustworthy Forensic Science Can Be Caught and Corrected: 10 Steps To Identifying and Addressing Untrustworthy Forensic Science

The final, most valuable lesson learned from the Fred Zain fiasco is that, through diligent effort, untrustworthy forensic science often can be caught and corrected. Through five years of efforts in unraveling Fred Zain cases, the following ten-step procedure has evolved — ten steps that should assist in the seemingly formidable task of identifying and correcting untrustworthy forensic science in a wide variety of settings.

Step 1: Obtain the Underlying Raw Data

As part of pretrial discovery in criminal cases, the defense will ordinarily receive written reports from prosecution experts reciting the tests that were performed and stating, in conclusory terms, the results achieved. These conclusory reports are rarely adequate for independent review.

For the defense to challenge a questionable scientific result by a prosecution expert, it is essential for the defense to do what lawyers in the Fred Zain cases failed to do for 16 years: obtain the underlying raw data — the actual test results, bench notes, worksheets, photographs, autorads, computer printouts, spectrographs, questions and answers in psychological and psychiatric testing — whatever underlying records were used to reach the conclusion set forth in the expert's written report or proposed testimony.

In pre-trial stages, the underlying data should be discoverable in all jurisdictions under either Rule 16(a)(1)(C) and (D) of the Federal Rules of Criminal Procedure and Rule 705 of the Federal Rules of Evidence or their corollaries in state courts. . . .

. . . .

Additionally, when the raw data is eventually provided in discovery, it is often incomplete. Consultation with an independent expert (*Step Three*) is often necessary to determine the complete set of records that should exist, which records are missing, and the significance of the missing records. Needless to say, the discovery that underlying records are missing can greatly affect the trustworthiness — and the admissibility — of the prosecution's purported results.

. . . .

Step 2: Obtain the Written Correspondence and Notes of Telephone Communications Between the Investigating Officers and the Lab

In assessing the trustworthiness of scientific results, beyond obtaining the raw data it is often valuable to obtain the written correspondence and notes of telephone communications between the investigating officers and the lab. These communications can reveal significant weaknesses in the collection and testing of evidence.

In the work of even the most respected laboratories, the communications between the lab and the police or prosecutors can provide helpful points for cross-examination and impeachment. In cases of more glaring misconduct, disclosure of these communications can lead to the ultimate exposure of the wrongdoing.

. . . .

Step 3: Submit the Underlying Data for Review by an Independent Expert

The raw data from scientific testing is rarely comprehensible to anyone unschooled in the details of the particular scientific procedure. For an accurate assessment of most scientific data, it is imperative that an independent expert review the data.

. . . .

. . . Had even a single defense lawyer pursued an independent review of the raw data obtained by Fred Zain early in his career, much of the history of fraud and the resulting imprisonment of innocent people may have been avoided.

Step 4: Obtain Independent Retesting of any Questionable Results

In addition to obtaining independent review of the underlying raw data in tests performed by prosecution experts, for any questionable result it is also critical to obtain independent testing, repeating the tests that the prosecution expert purported to perform, as well as any further testing that the independent expert recommends.

. . . .

Step 5: Consult Relevant Forensic Science Manuals

Although much of the review and retesting of questionable forensic science can be performed only by an expert in the field, significant challenges to untrustworthy forensic science can be mounted at little or no cost, without an expert, simply by reviewing applicable forensic science literature.

. . .

Step 6: Subject Absolute Statements to Particular Scrutiny

Legitimate scientists acknowledge the shortcomings and uncertainties that exist in their fields. Similarly, responsible scientists will forthrightly acknowledge error rates, and allow for the possibilities of erroneous conclusions. By contrast, it is a perverse irony of forensic fraud that the more erroneous the data, the more extreme is the scientist's claim of accuracy.

Fred Zain, for example, comfortably testified that "the tests used for the identification of semen are specific and 100 percent accurate. The testing for the blood characteristics are also the same."

Consequently, absolute statements by forensic scientists should be subjected to particular scrutiny. A scientist's claim of perfection is a nearly certain warning that the testimony is ripe for withering cross-examination and rebuttal.

Step 7: Subject Enhanced Trial Testimony to Particular Scrutiny

Fred Zain routinely embellished his testimony at trial, testifying to data and to percentages that were particularly damning to the defense but that appeared nowhere in the written reports that were presented to the defense pre-trial.

. . . .

In such instances, defense counsel should consider a variety of options, including (in descending order) moving for a mistrial based on the discovery violations, moving for a recess to consult independent experts to prepare for cross-examination and rebuttal of the surprise testimony, and moving to strike the surprise testimony with an instruction to the jury to disregard the testimony because it is not reliable. . . .

Step 8: Be Suspicious of Crime Evidence That Was 'Overlooked' the First Time, That Appears in Unexpected Locations, or That is Found in Amounts 'Just Large Enough To Be Testable'

Fred Zain frequently reported results when his colleagues had previously examined the evidence and found nothing. In the case of Paul Walker, for example, after Fred Zain left West Virginia, the state police lab examined a cloth patch on the defendant's jacket and found no trace of the victim's blood nor anything else to incriminate the defendant. In hopes that Fred Zain could see what was invisible to everyone else, the investigating officer then sent the defendant's jacket, along with a vial of the victim's blood, to Fred Zain in his new position in San Antonio. When the blood-free jacket was examined by Zain, a bloodstain suddenly appeared, in an amount just large enough to be testable, consistent with the blood of the victim.

. . . .

. . . Fred Zain's colleagues repeatedly observed him reporting results that no one else could detect. In other instances, when challenged, Zain sometimes sought refuge in the claim that the small amount of evidence was consumed by his testing, leaving nothing remaining for independent review or examination.

Consequently, it is important that defense counsel vigorously challenge such claims. . . .

Step 9: Develop a Professional Working Relationship With the Reputable Forensic Scientists in the Field

Reputable, forthright forensic scientists are probably the most valuable source of information regarding the strengths and weaknesses in their own fields and in their own work within that field. Of course, a hallmark of legitimate science is unbiased honesty, and reputable scientists should willingly, if reluctantly, acknowledge the history of errors, mislabeling of samples, failure of equipment, misreading of results, mis-transcribing of data, false positives, false negatives, and outright fraud that diminishes the certainty of scientific results.

In perhaps every instance where forensic science fraud has been exposed, the exposure resulted from the work of respected and courageous forensic scientists who were unwilling to tolerate fraud among colleagues. Innocent prisoners are free today because experts from the American Society of Crime Laboratory Directors were willing to investigate the West Virginia State Police Crime Laboratory and document the fraud.

. . . .

Step 10: Schedule a Pre-Trial Hearing To Challenge the Admissibility of Question-able Prosecution Science, Based on Daubert, Rule 403, or Rule 702

In *Daubert v. Merrell Dow Pharmaceuticals*, the United States Supreme Court acknowledged the "gatekeeping" role of the trial judge in preventing unreliable forensic science from reaching the jury.[46] A reliability assessment, as authorized by *Daubert*, is also appropriate under Rule 403 of the Rules of Evidence (exclusion of evidence on grounds of unfair prejudice, confusion of the issues, or misleading the jury) and under Rule 702 of the Rules of Evidence (permitting scientific opinion testimony only if it will

---

[46] The *Daubert* case and its progeny will be discussed at length in Chapter 2 of this text.

assist the trier of fact to understand the evidence or to determine a fact in issue).

. . . .

NOTES

1. *Untrustworthy Forensic Science at the Trial Stage.* If Castelle's 10 steps are utilized before (and during) trial they may (in an extreme case) produce enough doubt about the reliability of forensic evidence to persuade a trial court to grant a motion to exclude. On the other hand, if the suspect scientific evidence is admitted, information discovered via the 10 steps can be used to mount an attack on the weight the jury gives such evidence, by focusing and enhancing cross-examination, and by facilitating the presentation of opposing forensic expert evidence.

Reorganizing the 10 steps within the context of a pretrial and a trial strategy demonstrates one way an attorney could organize an assessment of his or her opponent's forensic evidence.

Before Trial Obtain:

    (a) Raw Data (Step 1)

    (b) Written Correspondence Between Investigators and the Lab (Step 2)

Before Trial Conduct Research And Fact-Finding:

    (a) Submit Data to Your Own Independent Expert for Review (Step 3)

    (b) Research Relevant Forensic Science Manuals (Step 5)

    (c) Study Raw Data and Expert Reports Looking For:

        "*Absolute Statements*" (Step 6)

        "*Suspicious . . . Crime Evidence . . . 'Overlooked' the First Time . . .*" (Step 8)

        "*Suspect Communications*" Between Investigators and the Lab (Step 2)

        "*Questionable Results,*" Given Your Expert's (and Your) Review (Step 3)

    (d) Independently Retest Results Your Expert Questions (Step 4)

    (e) Determine if the Theory and Technique Underlying the Evidence is Scientifically Valid — If Not Request a *Daubert* Hearing (Step 10)

At Trial:

    (a) Be Alert for "Enhanced" Trial Testimony (Step 7)

    (b) Be Alert for "Absolute Statements" (Step 6)

    (c) Conduct Cross-Examination on All Weaknesses Discovered Pretrial

2. *Untrustworthy Forensic Science After Conviction — The Problem of Limited Remedies.* What if scientific evidence is used to assist in convicting a defendant and it is discovered years later (after all state appeals have been exhausted) that the scientific evidence was fraudulent (as in the case of Fred Zain), or, if not fraudulent, simply wrong? In such a situation the prisoner would have newly discovered evidence showing that the forensic evidence admitted at his or her trial was inaccurate and should not have been admitted. The question concerns what post-conviction remedy exists in this situation.

(A) Motion for a New Trial Based on Newly Discovered Evidence. First, the defendant could request a new trial based upon newly discovered evidence. The new evidence in this scenario is the evidence that demonstrates the inaccuracy of expert scientific testimony admitted at trial. One problem with this remedy from the prisoner's point of view is that most jurisdictions have deadlines on presenting newly discovered evidence, and if too much time has passed a motion for a new trial may be barred regardless of its merits. *See* EDWARD CONNORS, THOMAS LUNDREGAN, NEAL MILLER & TOM McEWEN, CONVICTED BY JURIES, EXONERATED BY SCIENCE: CASE STUDIES IN THE USE OF DNA EVIDENCE TO ESTABLISH INNOCENCE AFTER TRIAL, 28–29 (June 1996) ("Most States have a time limit on presenting evidence newly discovered after trial, conviction, and sentencing. The reason for limiting the time to file appeals based on new evidence is to ensure the integrity of the trial process, and jury verdicts. . . . [M]any State procedures may preclude consideration of new exculpatory DNA evidence at postconviction stages."); Vivian Berger, Herrera v. Collins: *The Gateway of Innocence for Death-Sentenced Prisoners Leads Nowhere,* 35 WM & MARY L. REV. 943, 947 n.24 (1994) [hereinafter *The Gateway of Innocence*] ("All jurisdictions provide for such motions, but just 15 permit their filing more than three years after conviction, Of these, six have waivable bars; only nine have no limitation."). For example, Rule 33 of the Federal Rules of Criminal Procedure states that such a motion shall be filed within three years after the verdict or finding of guilty.

A second problem with utilizing a new trial motion in this situation is that the standards for establishing a right to a new trial based upon newly discovered evidence are demanding and typically include showing that the result at trial would have been different had the new evidence been available at trial. *See The Gateway of Innocence, supra* , 35 WM & MARY L. REV. at 957–61. If one accepts "Lesson 3" from the article by George Castelle (that inaccurate scientific evidence "contaminates . . . seemingly independent non-scientific evidence"), it may be difficult to demonstrate that the result would have been different without the tainted scientific evidence.

The standards vary somewhat from jurisdiction to jurisdiction; however, the so-called "*Berry* standard" is typical. West Virginia utilizes a slightly modified *Berry* standard in evaluating requests for a new trial based upon newly discovered evidence.

> "A new trial will not be granted on the ground of newly-discovered evidence unless the case comes within the following rules: (1) The evidence must appear to have been discovered since the trial. . . . (2) It must appear . . . that the new evidence is such that due diligence would not have secured it before the verdict. (3) Such evidence must be new and material, and not merely cumulative. . . . (4) The evidence must be such as ought to produce an opposite result at a second trial on the merits. (5) And the new trial will generally be refused when the sole object of the new evidence is to discredit or impeach a witness on the opposite side."

In the Matter of an INVESTIGATION OF the WEST VIRGINIA STATE POLICE CRIME LABORATORY, SEROLOGY DIVISION, 438 S.E.2d 501, 504 (W.Va. 1993). *See also, United States v. Lee,* 68 F.3d 1267, 1273–74 (11th Cir. 1995) ("A new trial is warranted upon circumstances coming to light after trial only if the . . . five part test is satisfied.").

(B) Habeas Relief. Assume that a prisoner's motion for a new trial is barred because of stringent state time deadlines, or is denied for failure to satisfy the *Berry* standards. At this point federal habeas relief may be considered. If the scientific evidence was false and *known to be false* by the prosecution, then the conviction would likely be invalid as a violation of the Constitution. *Napue v. Illinois*, 360 U.S. 264, 269 (1959) ("a conviction obtained through use of false evidence, known to be such by representatives of the State, must fall under the Fourteenth Amendment. . . ."). Of course, the prisoner would still have to show that this constitutional error was material, and not a "harmless error."

On the other hand, the admission of scientific evidence that is factually incorrect, but was admitted in good faith (that is, neither the prosecutor nor the expert witness believed the evidence was inaccurate), may not violate the Constitution and thus may not provide a basis for habeas relief — even if the prisoner is innocent. In *Herrera v. Collins*, 506 U.S. 390 (1993), the United States Supreme Court made clear that federal courts do not sit to correct errors of fact that occurred in a state criminal trial.

> Claims of actual innocence based on newly discovered evidence have never been held to state a ground for federal habeas relief absent an independent constitutional violation occurring in the underlying state criminal proceeding. Chief Justice Warren made this clear in *Townsend v. Sain*, 372 U.S. 293, 317 (1963) (emphasis added):
>
> > "Where newly discovered evidence is alleged in a habeas application, evidence which could not reasonably have been presented to the state trier of facts, the federal court must grant an evidentiary hearing. Of course, such evidence must bear upon the constitutionality of the applicant's detention; *the existence merely of newly discovered evidence relevant to the guilt of a state prisoner is not a ground for relief on federal habeas corpus.*"
>
> This rule is grounded in the principle that federal habeas courts sit to ensure that individuals are not imprisoned in violation of the Constitution — not to correct errors of fact. *See, e.g., Moore v. Dempsey*, 261 U.S. 86, 87–88 (1923) (Holmes, J.) ("[W]hat we have to deal with [on habeas review] is not the petitioners' innocence or guilt but solely the question whether their constitutional rights have been preserved"); . . . *Ex parte Terry*, 128 U.S. 289, 305 (1888) ("As the writ of *habeas corpus* does not perform the office of a writ of error or an appeal, [the facts establishing guilt] cannot be re-examined or reviewed in this collateral proceeding").

Herrera, 506 U.S. at 400–01. *See also* Brandon L. Garrett, *Claiming Innocence*, 92 Minn. L. Rev. 1629, 1684 (2008) (traditional habeas corpus review provides conduit for procedural constitutional claims pertaining to trial's fundamental fairness, but not the defendant's innocence).

(C) Seek Executive Clemency. If efforts to secure a new trial and habeas relief are not successful, the prisoner may seek clemency from the Governor. In fact, clemency may be the only avenue open to a prisoner who claims innocence, but who is too late to prevail on a motion for a new trial based upon newly discovered evidence and who cannot point to a constitutional violation in the admission of erroneous scientific evidence. *See Herrera v. Collins*, 506 U.S. 390, 417 (1993) ("History shows that the traditional remedy for claims of innocence based on new evidence, discovered too late in the day to file a new trial motion, has been executive clemency."); Vivian Berger, Herrera v. Collins: *The Gateway of Innocence for Death-Sentenced Prisoners Leads Nowhere*, 35 Wm & Mary L. Rev. 943, 966–69 (1994).

QUESTIONS

1. Which of the "10 steps" listed in the Castelle article can be routinely followed in any criminal case without the assistance of a forensic expert?

2. Which, if any, of the "10 steps" listed in the Castelle article could realistically be characterized as an "evidentiary hurdle" that the proponent of scientific evidence must overcome to achieve admissibility?

PROBLEM

Problem 1-1. Assume you represented Vonnie Ray Bullard at the trial stage (*See State v. Bullard, supra*).

(A) Go back over the 10 steps for identifying and addressing untrustworthy scientific evidence contained in the Castelle article. What steps would you take as you prepare for trial to address what may reasonably be viewed as untrustworthy or inaccurate scientific evidence from Dr. Robbins?

(B) Review the facts of the *Bullard* case. From the information given, does it appear as though there was anything that Bullard's defense counsel could have done to expose the untrustworthy scientific evidence of Dr. Robbins?

(C) Finally, assume that you represent Vonnie Ray Bullard *today* and that Bullard is still in prison. Assume that you can now prove conclusively that Dr. Robbins' expert testimony was scientifically invalid, but you have no evidence of *intentional* wrongdoing by Dr. Robbins, the prosecution, or anyone else. That is, it appears that Dr. Robbins and the prosecution had reason to believe that her opinions were scientifically valid at the time she testified.

In sum, you have *additional, new evidence* that shows expert testimony from Dr. Robbins was inaccurate (recall that at trial the defense offered the testimony of two experts — Professors Cartmill and Robertson of Duke University Medical Center — who stated that Dr. Robbins's methods were inaccurate), but inaccurate scientific evidence is the *only* error you can establish with your new evidence.

(1) What are your chances of prevailing on a motion for new trial based upon newly discovered evidence in a state that follows the *Berry* standard?

(2) What are your chances of prevailing in federal court on a habeas corpus petition?

Chapter 2

INSURING RELIABILITY OF SCIENTIFIC THEORY AND TECHNIQUE

A. INTRODUCTION

Inextricably intertwined with concerns about lack of objectivity, mistakes (honest and fraudulent), and invalid scientific theory is the concern that the jury may not be able to perceive weaknesses in scientific evidence because of its inherently technical and specialized nature. One court described this troubling aspect of scientific proof as its ability to "assume a posture of mystic infallibility in the eyes of a jury of laymen." *United States v. Addison*, 498 F.2d 741, 744 (D.C. Cir. 1974).

While all human endeavors present the possibility of error, scientific evidence presents the possibility of error that is not capable of being discovered or, if discovered, not fully appreciated. Indeed, would there be any need to concern ourselves with questions of bias, error, fraud, or unreliability if such matters were so apparent to a jury that they could be assessed and discounted where appropriate?

To illustrate, consider that a jury may be able to evaluate the truthfulness or accuracy of eyewitness observation testimony from a lay person because the lay witness speaks in familiar terms about familiar subjects. When an expert in a subject like DNA profiling testifies, however, the jury often has no basis in their experience or education to assess the underlying data that forms the foundation for the expert opinion.

The fear that inaccurate scientific evidence will mislead an unsuspecting jury has led courts to erect a variety of evidentiary hurdles designed to ensure that such evidence is reliable. There are several hurdles because more than one factor is perceived as contributing to the potential for inaccurate scientific evidence. For example, as seen in Chapter 1, forensic science can be inaccurate either because the theory underlying the technique is invalid, or because the scientist applying an admittedly valid technique made an error on a particular occasion. Moreover, even if a reliable scientific technique is properly applied there is the possibility of a biased expert overstating the significance of test results to an unsuspecting jury.

As a general proposition, to gain admissibility, most jurisdictions require the proponent of scientific evidence to establish: (1) the authenticity of any samples or specimens that were subjected to scientific analysis or testing; (2) the validity[1] of the scientific theory and technique applying the theory, and (3) proper application of the technique on *this* particular occasion. In addition, courts sometimes express a concern

---

[1] Courts often use the terms "validity" and "reliability" interchangeably. In *Daubert v. Merrell Dow Pharmaceuticals, Inc.*, 509 U.S. 579, 590 n.9 (1993), the United States Supreme Court acknowledged that scientists distinguish between "validity" (does the principle support what it purports to show?) and "reliability" (does application of the principle produce consistent results?), but stated that its concern was "*evidentiary* reliability — that is, trustworthiness," and added that in a case involving scientific evidence, "*evidentiary reliability* will be based on *scientific validity*." (Emphasis in original).

that scientific evidence might be excluded — even if reliable — when it is not needed by the trier of fact, or when its probative value is outweighed by its potential to mislead.

This chapter will examine the second requirement listed above — establishing the validity of the scientific theory and the technique applying the theory.[2] At the outset, it is important to keep in mind the difference between the underlying scientific theory or principle at issue, and the technique that applies the theory or principle.

> One could accept the validity of the premise underlying DNA profiling — every person's DNA is unique except for identical twins — but still question whether the Short Tandem Repeat (STR) technique can identify that uniqueness. Similarly, the underlying psychological and physiological principles of polygraph testing could be acknowledged without endorsing the proposition that a polygraph examiner can detect deception by means of the polygraph technique.

1 COURTROOM CRIMINAL EVIDENCE § 601, at 190 (4th ed. 2005).

The validity of a scientific theory and technique may be established by: (1) the presentation of evidence to satisfy an admissibility test; (2) judicial notice; (3) legislative recognition; or (4) stipulation. The method that generates the most controversy is the presentation of evidence to satisfy an evidentiary test. This is because presenting evidence is typically only used with novel theories and techniques whose validity and admissibility is in doubt. As stated by the Oregon Supreme Court in *State v. O'Key*, 899 P.2d 663, 672–73 (Or. 1995):

> . . . [I]n the absence of a clear case, a case for judicial notice, or a case of *prima facia* legislative recognition, trial courts have an obligation to ensure that proffered expert scientific testimony that a court finds possesses significantly increased potential to influence the trier of fact as "scientific" assertions is scientifically valid. This is especially true in cases where the proffered expert scientific testimony is innovative, nontraditional, unconventional, controversial, or close to the frontier of understanding.

This chapter will explore the four methods courts use to guard against the admission of scientific evidence that is inaccurate or misleading because it was derived from an invalid scientific theory or technique. The examination begins with admissibility tests.

B. ESTABLISHING RELIABILITY OF THE THEORY AND TECHNIQUE

[1] Admissibility Tests

[a] The *Frye* Test: Scientific General Acceptance

A new or novel scientific technique is unlikely to have gained sufficient recognition to make its reliability a candidate for judicial notice or legislative recognition. In this situation courts receive evidence, including testimony from experts, on the issue of the technique's reliability. The question then becomes what is the standard? That is, what must the evidence establish in order to demonstrate that opinions based upon a new scientific technique are reliable, and not likely to unfairly prejudice a case or mislead a jury? One test for demonstrating the validity of a novel scientific theory or technique

---

[2] Chapter 3 examines the other admissibility requirements.

was dominant in both federal and state courts for 70 years. This test, the *Frye*, or "general acceptance test," remains an important and viable standard in many state courts notwithstanding the fact that it is no longer the majority rule.[3]

The general acceptance test had its genesis in the 1923 case of *Frye v. United States*, 293 F. 1013 (D.C. 1923). In *Frye* the defendant, James Alphonzo Frye, appealed a conviction for second degree murder. Prior to Frye's trial, he had been given a "systolic blood pressure deception test." This test, the precursor of the modern polygraph, or "lie detector" test, measured a person's blood pressure as he or she was being questioned. The theory asserted was that conscious deception — coupled with the fear of being detected — would cause a person's blood pressure to rise, and by monitoring blood pressure during questioning any deception would be noted.

Frye took and passed such a test before his trial, and offered the expert who conducted the test to testify as to the results obtained. The trial court refused to allow the expert to testify. Frye then asked for a systolic blood pressure deception test to be conducted in the presence of the jury. This request was also denied. Frye was convicted and argued on appeal that the trial court's refusal to allow expert testimony on the results of his systolic blood pressure deception test was error. The D.C. Court of Appeals upheld Frye's conviction, and the exclusion of his expert testimony. In a passage that became the basis for the "*Frye* test of general acceptance," the D.C. Court of Appeals stated:

> . . . Just when a scientific principle or discovery crosses the line between the experimental and demonstrable stages is difficult to define. Somewhere in this twilight zone the evidential force of the principle must be recognized, and while courts will go a long way in admitting expert testimony deduced from a well-recognized scientific principle or discovery, the thing from which the deduction is made must be sufficiently established to have gained general acceptance in the particular field in which it belongs.

> We think the systolic blood pressure deception test has not yet gained such standing and scientific recognition among physiological and psychological authorities as would justify the courts in admitting expert testimony deduced from the discovery, development, and experiments thus far made.

Frye v. United States, 293 F. 1013, 1014 (D.C. 1923).

The *Frye* test raised as many questions as it answered. For example, what is the "thing" which must be generally accepted — the underlying theory, the technique applying the theory, or both? How does a trial court determine the "particular field" (or "fields") within which a scientific principle "belongs"? What percentage of experts in a particular field must accept a scientific principle or discovery before it can be considered as having achieved "*general*" acceptance? (If 51% of the experts in a field accept a technique, is it generally accepted? If not 51%, how about 60%?) What is a "*scientific principle*"? The *Kelly, Stoll,* and *Hasan* cases that follow illustrate how courts have attempted to answer (or avoid) such questions.

---

[3] Since 1993 all federal courts (and many state courts) have employed an alternative test adopted by the United States Supreme Court in *Daubert v. Merrell Dow Pharmaceuticals, Inc.*, 509 U.S. 579 (1993). The "*Daubert* test" will be examined later in this chapter.

PEOPLE v. KELLY

549 P.2d 1240 (Cal. 1976)

RICHARDSON, JUSTICE.

In this case we examine the new and emerging technique of speaker identification by spectrographic analysis, commonly described as "voiceprint." Particularly we inquire whether it has achieved that degree of general scientific acceptance as a reliable identification device which will permit the introduction of voiceprint evidence in California courts.

We have concluded that, on the record before us, the People's showing on this important issue was insufficient, and that since the voiceprint evidence at issue herein was the primary evidence of defendant's guilt, the judgment of conviction must be reversed. Although voiceprint analysis may indeed constitute a reliable and valuable tool in either identifying or eliminating suspects in criminal cases, that fact was not satisfactorily demonstrated in this case.

Defendant was convicted of extortion arising out of a series of anonymous, threatening telephone calls to Terry Waskin. The police, acting with Waskin's consent, tape recorded two of these calls (the extortion tapes). An informant familiar with defendant's voice subsequently listened to these tapes and tentatively identified defendant as the caller. Thereafter, the officers obtained a tape recording of defendant's voice during a telephone call (the control tape). Copies of the extortion tapes and the control tape were then sent to Lieutenant Ernest Nash of the Michigan State Police for spectrographic analysis. On the basis of his examination, Nash concluded that the voices on these tapes were those of the same person.

Defendant was indicted by the grand jury and brought to trial. The case was submitted to the trial court, sitting without a jury, on the grand jury transcript and the testimony at a pretrial hearing on the issue of the admissibility of the voiceprint evidence. The People had sought to introduce Nash's testimony, and had asked the trial court to order that an evidentiary hearing be held to determine the admissibility of this evidence. . . . Accordingly, Nash was called and testified that among those who were familiar with and used voice identification analysis the technique was considered reliable. No other expert testimony was presented by either side.

Considering Nash's testimony . . . the trial court ruled that voiceprint analysis had attained sufficient scientific approval, and that Nash's testimony identifying defendant as the extortionist was properly admissible.

Defendant attacks his conviction arguing that (1) the People failed to establish that voiceprint techniques have reached the requisite degree of general acceptance in the scientific community, (2) Nash was not qualified to express an expert opinion regarding the judgment of scholars and experts and (3) the testing procedures employed in identifying defendant's voice were not conducted in a fair and impartial manner. Finding ourselves in general agreement with defendant's first two contentions, we do not reach the third.

1. The Voiceprint Technique

Voiceprint analysis is a method of identification based on the comparison of graphic representations or "spectrograms" made of human voices. The method utilizes a machine known as a spectrograph which separates the sounds of human voices into the three component elements of time, frequency and intensity. Using a series of lines or bars, the machine plots these variables across electronically sensitive paper. The result is a spectrogram of the acoustical signal of the speaker, with the horizontal axis representing time lapse, the vertical axis indicating frequency, and the thickness of the lines disclosing the intensity of the voice. Spectrograms are taken of certain cue words, such as "the," "me," "on," "is," "I," and "it," spoken by a known voice and an unknown voice. An examiner then visually compares the spectrograms of the same words, as spoken, and also listens to the two voices. Based upon these visual and aural comparisons, the examiner states his opinion whether or not the voices, known and unknown, are the same. Since the identification process is essentially an exercise in pattern matching, the examiner's opinion is to a large extent a subjective one based upon the relative aural similarity or dissimilarity of the two voices and visual comparison of their spectrograms. In some instances, the examiner is unable to declare positively either that there is a match or nonmatch of the sample tests, in which event no opinion is rendered.

2. General Principles of Admissibility

The parties agree generally that admissibility of expert testimony based upon the application of a new scientific technique traditionally involves a two-step process: (1) the *reliability of the method* must be established, usually by expert testimony, and (2) the witness furnishing such testimony must be properly *qualified as an expert to give an opinion* on the subject. Additionally, the proponent of the evidence must demonstrate that correct scientific procedures were used in the particular case.

The test for determining the underlying reliability of a new scientific technique was described in the germinal case of *Frye v. United States*, involving the admissibility of polygraph tests:

> "Just when a scientific principle or discovery crosses the line between the experimental and demonstrable stages is difficult to define. Somewhere in this twilight zone the evidential force of the principle must be recognized, and while courts will go a long way in admitting expert testimony deduced from a well-recognized scientific principle or discovery, the thing from which the deduction is made must be *sufficiently established to have gained general acceptance in the particular field in which it belongs*." (Italics added.)

We have expressly adopted the foregoing *Frye* test and California courts, when faced with a novel method of proof, have required a preliminary showing of general acceptance of the new technique in the relevant scientific community. Some criticism has been directed at the *Frye* standard, primarily on the ground that the test is too conservative, often resulting in the prevention of the admission of relevant evidence. As indicated below, we are satisfied that there is ample justification for the exercise of considerable judicial caution in the acceptance of evidence developed by new scientific techniques.

Arguably, the admission of such evidence could be left, in the first instance, to the sound discretion of the trial court, in which event objections, if any, to the reliability of the evidence (or of the underlying scientific technique on which it is based) might lessen the weight of the evidence but would not necessarily prevent its admissibility. This has not been the direction taken by the California courts or by those of most states. *Frye*, and the decisions which have followed it, rather than turning to the trial judge have assigned the task of determining reliability of the evolving technique to members of the scientific community from which the new method emerges. As stated in a recent voiceprint case, *United States v. Addison*, 498 F.2d 741, 743–744 [(D.C. Cir. 1974)].

"The requirement of general acceptance in the scientific community assures that *those most qualified to assess the general validity of a scientific method will have the determinative voice*. Additionally, the *Frye* test protects prosecution and defense alike by assuring that a minimal reserve of experts exists who can critically examine the validity of a scientific determination in a particular case." (Italics added.)

Moreover, a beneficial consequence of the *Frye* test is that it may well promote a degree of uniformity of decision. Individual judges whose particular conclusions may differ regarding the reliability of particular scientific evidence, may discover substantial agreement and consensus in the scientific community.

The primary advantage, however, of the *Frye* test lies in its essentially conservative nature. For a variety of reasons, *Frye* was deliberately intended to interpose a substantial obstacle to the unrestrained admission of evidence based upon new scientific principles. Several reasons founded in logic and common sense support a posture of judicial caution in this area. Lay jurors tend to give considerable weight to "scientific" evidence when presented by "experts" with impressive credentials. We have acknowledged the existence of a ". . . misleading aura of certainty which often envelops a new scientific process, obscuring its currently experimental nature." As stated in *Addison, supra*, in the course of rejecting the admissibility of voiceprint testimony, "scientific proof may in some instances assume a posture of mystic infallibility in the eyes of a jury. . . ." (*United States v. Addison, supra*, 498 F.2d at p. 744.)

Exercise of restraint is especially warranted when the identification technique is offered to identify the perpetrator of a crime. . . . Moreover, once a trial court has admitted evidence based upon a new scientific technique, and that decision is affirmed on appeal by a published appellate decision, the precedent so established may control subsequent trials, at least until new evidence is presented reflecting a change in the attitude of the scientific community.

For all the foregoing reasons, we are persuaded by the wisdom of, and reaffirm our allegiance to, the *Frye* decision and the "general acceptance" rule which that case mandates. In the matter before us, the People attempted to satisfy the *Frye* test by reliance upon prior decisions of the courts of this state and sister states, and upon Lieutenant Nash's testimony. Yet, as discussed below, none of these sources provide satisfactory proof of the reliability of voiceprint evidence.

3. *The Voiceprint Cases*

Our review of the applicable authorities reveals no uniform or established trend either for or against the admissibility of voiceprint evidence. Cases outside California have reached varying conclusions on the matter.

. . . .

The California cases likewise have reached varying conclusions. . . .

. . . .

The . . . review of cases from California and other jurisdictions satisfies us that the admissibility of voiceprint testimony remains unresolved. Certainly these cases do not establish, as a matter of law, the reliability of the voiceprint technique. Moreover, amici have cited a number of scientific and legal articles containing differing forms of opposition to the admissibility of voiceprint evidence. Such writings may be considered by courts in evaluating the reliability of new scientific methodology. . . .

4. *Lieutenant Nash's Testimony*

Finding the case authority on the issue before us conflicting and inconclusive, we turn to the record in the present case to determine whether, as the trial court concluded, the prosecution established the reliability of the voiceprint technique. . . .

As indicated, Lieutenant Nash was *the sole witness* testifying on the reliability issue. The record discloses that Nash has been associated with the voiceprint technique since 1967, having been trained in voiceprint analysis by Kersta, the pioneer in this field. At the time of trial, Nash was employed by the Michigan State Police as head of its voice identification unit. Nash studied audiology and speech sciences at Michigan State University, and completed courses in anatomy and the physiology of speech. Although Nash had received approximately 50 hours of college credit in these subjects, he had not attained a formal degree.

Lieutenant Nash testified that since 1967 he has prepared or reviewed 180,000 voice spectrograms. [H]e worked with Dr. [Oscar] Tosi [a professor of audiology, speech sciences and physics,] in preparing the design for [a] 1968–1970 Michigan State University study which Dr. Tosi conducted, and he assisted Tosi in drafting the final report of the study. According to Nash, the Tosi study demonstrated a high degree of reliability. It was a "controlled experimental situation" based on examination and identification of the voices of students and other nonsuspect persons, rather that a forensic, in-the-field study of the reliability of voiceprint analysis in identifying criminals.

Lieutenant Nash stated that among members of the scientific community involved in voiceprint analysis there is general acceptance of the technique as "extremely" reliable. Nash admitted, however, that those persons who are actually involved in voiceprint work are primarily voiceprint examiners "connected with a government agency of some kind," i.e., law enforcement officers such as Nash himself.

Our analysis of Nash's testimony discloses at least three infirmities which, in combination, are fatal to the People's claim that they established that voiceprint analysis is generally accepted as reliable by the scientific community. First, we think it questionable whether the testimony of a single witness alone is ever sufficient to represent, or attest to, the views of an entire scientific community regarding the reliability of a new technique. Ideally, resolution of the general acceptance issue would require consideration of the views of a typical cross-section of the scientific community, including representatives, if there are such, of those who oppose or question the new technique. Several courts have thus concluded that, before evidence based upon a new scientific method may be introduced, "*something more than the bare opinion of one man, however qualified, is required.*" (*People v. King*, 72 Cal. Rptr. 478, 488 (Cal. App. 1968)). In *King*, for example, the trial court heard the views of three prosecution experts and seven defense experts on the issue of general acceptance.

One commentator has suggested that in an appropriate case trial courts should take affirmative steps to assure that an accurate description of the views of the scientific community is placed before the court.

After deciding which are the relevant fields, the court must see that the appropriate experts testify. Where only proponents of a technique appear, the court should *sua sponte* take the responsibility of inquiring not just whether the experts believe the scientific community is generally in agreement, but whether they are in fact aware of any opposing sentiment in the relevant scientific community. *The court should then make an effort to ascertain the extent of any opposition so identified, calling its spokesmen as court appointed experts if necessary.* (Comment, [*The Voiceprint Dilemma: Should Voices be Seen and not Heard?* (1975)] 35 Md.L.Rev. 267, at p. 293; fn. omitted, italics added).

In California the trial court's authority to appoint an expert is set forth in [the] Evidence Code. . . . As the scientific literature . . . makes clear, in the area of voiceprint analysis there exists several persons whose qualifications would enable them to testify knowledgeably and critically.

We are troubled by a second feature of the evidentiary record before us. In addition to the trial court's reliance solely upon Nash's testimony to the exclusion of other, possibly adverse, expert witnesses, a serious question existed regarding Nash's ability fairly and impartially to assess the position of the scientific community. Nash has had a long association with the development and promotion of voiceprint analysis. His qualifications in this somewhat limited area cannot be doubted. In addition to his work with Dr. Tosi, Nash was the chief of the Michigan State Police Voice Identification Unit, a position which led him to testify as a voiceprint expert in numerous cases throughout the country. Further, Nash is either a founder or member of four other organizations which promote the use of voiceprint analysis.

Nash's background thus discloses that he is one of the leading proponents of voice-print analysis; he has virtually built his career on the reliability of the technique. This situation is closely akin to that in *People v. King, supra,* in which Kersta, a pioneer in the field, was the chief prosecution witness supporting the admissibility of voiceprint evidence. The court in *King* rejected Kersta's testimony regarding the scientific basis of voiceprint analysis and warned that "(b)efore a technique or process is generally accepted in the scientific community, self-serving opinions should not be received which invade the province of the trier of fact." (*Id.,* at p. 491.) Likewise, Nash, a strong advocate of the voiceprint technique, may be too closely identified with the endorsement of voiceprint analysis to assess fairly and impartially the nature and extent of any opposing scientific views. A more detached and neutral observer might more fairly do so. In the absence of additional and impartial evidence regarding general acceptance, the trial court was in a similar position to that presented in *King,* in which "a court could only receive Kersta's opinion on faith." (*People v. King, supra,* 72 Cal. Rptr. at p. 490.)

A third objection to Nash's testimony pertains to his qualifications as an expert in the field of voiceprint analysis. Substantial doubt exists whether Nash possessed the necessary academic qualifications which would have enabled him to express a competent opinion on the issue of the general acceptance of the voiceprint technique in the scientific community.

. . . .

The record in the instant case reveals that Nash has an impressive list of credentials in the field of voiceprint analysis. However, these qualifications are those of *a technician and law enforcement officer, not a scientist.* Neither his training under Kersta, his association with the Tosi study, his limited college study in certain speech sciences, his membership in organizations promoting the use of voiceprints, nor his former position as head of the Michigan State Police Voice Identification Unit, necessarily qualifies Nash to express an informed opinion on the view of the scientific community toward voiceprint analysis. This area may be one in which only another scientist, in regular communication with other colleagues in the field, is competent to express such an opinion.

Nash was allowed to testify in a dual role, both as a technician and a scientist, in order to show both that the voiceprint technique is reliable and that it has gained general acceptance in the scientific community. From the demonstrably wide technical experience of Nash, it does not necessarily follow that academic and scientific knowledge are present as well. As expressed in *King*: "Kersta's engineering abilities must not be confused with or made a substitute for learning and training in the fields of anatomy, medicine, physiology, psychology[,] phonetics or linguistics." (*People v. King, supra*, 72 Cal. Rptr. at p. 491.) In considering the position of the scientific community, a court is found [*sic*] to let scientists speak for themselves. Nash's undoubted qualifications as a technician, like Kersta's, do not necessarily qualify him as a scientist to express an opinion on the question of general scientific acceptance.

Indeed, it is both noteworthy and commendable that Nash was careful and fair in not claiming that he represented the views of the general scientific community on the subject of the reliability of the voiceprint technique. Instead, he expressed the opinion of those persons engaged in the actual use of the spectrogram, persons who were primarily engaged in law enforcement activities. Although the *Frye* test may be satisfied by a showing of general acceptance by those scientists who are most familiar with the use of a new technique, such a showing, ordinarily, should be presented by those who are engaged in the scientific fields.

. . . .

6. *Conclusion*

We conclude that the People failed to carry their burden of establishing the reliability of voiceprint evidence. We emphasize, however, that our decision is not intended in any way to foreclose the introduction of voiceprint evidence in future cases. We simply circumscribe, carefully and deliberately, the admission of evidence born of new techniques until the time when there is demonstrated solid scientific approval and support of the new methods. The *Frye* test was not designed to eliminate reliance upon scientific evidence, but to retard its admissibility until the scientific community has had ample opportunity to study, evaluate and accept its reliability. Although the present record is insufficient to justify the admissibility of voiceprint evidence, the future proponent of such evidence may well be able to demonstrate in a satisfactory manner that the voiceprint technique has achieved that required general acceptance in the scientific community.

The judgment is reversed.

NOTES

1. ***Admissibility of "Voiceprint" Evidence.*** Admissibility of expert opinion connecting an unknown recorded voice with that of a known person based upon the results of the voice spectrograph has not been warmly received. Courts are split on admissibility, and studies by professional groups have been critical of the technique's reliability. *See United States v. Drones*, 218 F.3d 496, 503 (5th Cir. 2000) (court states "spectrographic analysis is . . . of questionable scientific validity," noting that under

the *Frye* standard four circuits found voice spectrographic evidence admissible and one circuit found it inadmissible); *United States v. Bahena*, 223 F.3d 797, 809 (8th Cir. 2000) (upholding trial court exclusion of voiceprint evidence under the *Daubert* test, but observing that, "We assume for present purposes that spectrographic voice analysis, as such, would not necessarily be inadmissible in every case."); *State v. Coon*, 974 P.2d 386, 402–03 (Alaska 1999) (abandoning the *Frye* test and admitting voice spectrograph evidence under the *Daubert* test; noting, however, that courts were split on both admissibility and general acceptance). *See generally* ANDRE A. MOENSSENS, CAROL E. HENDERSON & SHARON G. PORTWOOD, SCIENTIFIC EVIDENCE IN CIVIL AND CRIMINAL CASES § 12.07 (5th ed. 2007) (dividing voiceprint cases into four time periods, beginning prior to 1976, for purposes of assessing precedent value); 1 SCIENTIFIC EVIDENCE § 10.05 1.06[d], at 580–89 (4th ed. 2007) (summarizing the scientific research).

2. *Jurisdictions That Follow Frye.* At one point the *Frye* test had been adopted by a majority of state and federal courts. Support for the *Frye* standard had been eroding when, in 1993, the United States Supreme Court held that the *Frye* test had not been incorporated into the Federal Rules of Evidence, and that a "reliability" test based, primarily, on Federal Rule of Evidence 702 was the test that federal courts should use in determining the admissibility of scientific evidence. *See Daubert v. Merrell Dow Pharmaceuticals, Inc.*, 509 U.S. 579, 589 (1993).

In *Daubert* the United States Supreme Court was interpreting the Federal Rules of Evidence. Accordingly, *Daubert's* rejection of the *Frye* test is binding on federal courts but not state courts. Nonetheless, several *Frye* states (with evidence codes modeled after the Federal Rules of Evidence) found *Daubert's* reasoning persuasive, and abandoned the *Frye* test for *Daubert*, or a "*Daubert*-like" test. *See, e.g., State v. Coon*, 974 P.2d 386, 389–391 (Alaska 1999) ("Although we are not bound by the Supreme Court's conclusion [in *Daubert*], its analysis of the corresponding federal rules is helpful and, moreover has triggered a wealth of useful critical comment."). On the other hand, other *Frye* states reexamined and reaffirmed their allegiance to *Frye* after the *Daubert* decision. *See, e.g., People v. Leahy*, 882 P.2d 321, 325–31 (Cal. 1994); *Logerquist v. McVey*, 1 P.3d 113, 124–34 (Ariz. 2000).

Despite being a numerical minority, *Frye* jurisdictions include the most populous states (excepting Texas and Ohio), and almost one-half of the American population. *See* David E. Bernstein, Frye, Frye *Again: The Past, Present, and Future of the General Acceptance Test*, 41 JURIMETRICS J. 385, 386–87 (2001). States that follow *Frye* include: Alabama, *Turner v. State*, 746 So. 2d 355, 361 n.7 (Ala. 1998) (by statute, however, the *Daubert* test is used to determine the admissibility of DNA evidence); Arizona, *Logerquist v. McVey*, 1 P.3d 113, 124–34 (Ariz. 2000); California, *People v. Leahy*, 882 P.2d 321, 324–31 (Cal. 1994); District of Columbia, *Nixon v. United States*, 728 A.2d 582, 588 (D.C.1999); Florida, *Hildwin v. State*, 951 So. 2d 784, 792 (Fla. 2006); Illinois, *People v. McKown*, 875 N.E.2d 1029, 1034 (Ill. 2007); Kansas, *State v. Shively*, 999 P.2d 952, 955 (Kan. 2000); Maryland, *State v. Baby*, 946 A.2d 463, 491 (Md. 2008); Minnesota, *State v. MacLennan*, 702 N.W.2d 219, 230 (Minn. 2005); Missouri, *State v. Funke*, 903 S.W.2d 240, 244 (Mo. App. 1995); New Jersey, *State v. Williams*, 599 A.2d 960, 963 (N.J. Super. L. Div. 1991); New York, *People v. LeGrand*, 867 N.E.2d 374, 379–80 (N.Y. 2007); Pennsylvania, *Commonwealth v. Puksar*, 951 A.2d 267, 272 (Pa. 2008); and Washington, *State v. Russell*, 882 P.2d 747, 761 (Wash. 1994). *See generally* 1 SCIENTIFIC EVIDENCE § 1.16, at 85–88 (4th ed. 2007).

3. *Policy Rationales Favoring Frye.* In *Kelly* the California Supreme Court noted several justifications for using the *Frye* test. The New Hampshire Supreme Court noted similar policy justifications favoring *Frye*.

> [A]dherence to [*Frye*]: (1) permits disputes concerning scientific validity to be resolved by the relevant scientific community, (2) ensures that a minimal reserve of experts exist who can critically examine the validity of a scientific determination in a particular case, (3) spares courts from the time-consuming and difficult task of repeatedly assessing the validity of innovative scientific techniques, and (4) promotes a degree of uniformity of decisions.

State v. Vandebogart, 616 A.2d 483, 489 (N.H. 1992).

4. *Procedural Issues.*

(A) The Frye Hearing — Burden of Establishing General Acceptance on the Proponent. Under *Frye*, the proponent of the scientific evidence has the burden of establishing by a preponderance of the evidence that the scientific principle and the technique applying that principle are generally accepted. *Ramirez v. State*, 651 So. 2d 1164, 1168 (Fla. 1995) ("burden is on the proponent of the evidence to prove the general acceptance of both the underlying scientific principle and the testing procedures used to apply that principle to the facts of the case at hand"); *Commonwealth v. Blasioli*, 713 A.2d 1117, 1119 (Pa. 1998) (theory and technique must be generally accepted). This is usually done in a hearing held outside the presence of the jury before the trial starts; however, the hearing may be held during the trial if the jury is excused. *Ramirez, supra,* 651 So. 2d at 1168 n.4.

(B) Trial Court Determinations. At the *Frye* hearing it is the trial court's task to make two determinations. First, the trial court must decide the field or fields in which the underlying principle falls. Second, the trial court must determine whether the principle and technique in question have been generally accepted by scientists in the identified field or fields. *See* 1 SCIENTIFIC EVIDENCE § 1.06[b], at 19–21 (4th ed. 2007).

(C) Evidence Used to Establish General Acceptance. Typically, experts are called to testify to a scientific technique's validity and general acceptance in the pertinent field. In addition to — or in lieu of — expert testimony, the trial court may receive or take judicial notice of relevant scientific and legal publications. *See, e.g., People v. Leahy*, 882 P.2d 321, 336 (Cal. 1994) (considerations of judicial economy would permit a trial court to scrutinize published writings in lieu of live testimony); *People v. Wallace*, 17 Cal. Rptr. 2d 721, 724 (Cal. App. 1993) (trial court admits scientific publications into evidence on issue of general acceptance). Many courts also consider judicial decisions in other jurisdictions. *People v. McKown*, 875 N.E.2d 1029, 1034 (Ill. 2007) (court may determine general acceptance based on the results of a *Frye* hearing, or by taking judicial notice of "unequivocal and undisputed prior judicial decisions or technical writings on the subject"); *State v. Coon*, 974 P.2d 386, 402 (Alaska 1999) ("In determining whether evidence is generally accepted within the scientific community, courts have generally looked to three sources for guidance: (a) judicial opinions; (b) scientific literature; and (c) expert testimony presented at an evidentiary hearing."). Because *Frye* is an attempt to discern whether *scientists* accept the theory and technique under consideration, the appropriate use of judicial opinions would be to ascertain the testimony of experts in other cases on the general acceptance issue — not to ascertain whether a court did, or did not, generally accept a particular theory or technique. *See* 1 SCIENTIFIC EVIDENCE § 1.06[d], at 27 (4th ed. 2007).

Finally, the opponent of scientific evidence has the right to present evidence indicating that the theory and application are *not* generally accepted. *Ramirez, supra,*

651 So. 2d at 1168.

(D) Appeal. Courts are divided over the proper standard to use when reviewing a trial court's general acceptance determination. Many courts, perhaps a majority, review such decisions de novo. *See, e.g., State v. Bible*, 858 P.2d 1152, 1181 (Ariz. 1993) (de novo); *In re Commitment of Simons*, 821 N.E.2d 1184, 1189–90 (Ill. 2004) (de novo); *State v. Shively*, 999 P.2d 952, 955 (Kan. 2000) (de novo); *Hadden v. State*, 690 So.2d 573, 579 (Fla. 1997) (de novo); *State v. Cauthron*, 846 P.2d 502, 505 (Wash. 1993) (de novo); *But see Commonwealth v. Dengler*, 890 A.2d 372, 379 (Pa. 2005) (abuse of discretion standard).

There are several arguments to support de novo review of a trial court's general acceptance decision. First, general acceptance of a scientific theory and technique does not vary from case to case with the facts of the case, i.e., it is not a case-specific determination. Second, an appellate court's ruling on general acceptance will have precedential value and be, in essence, a ruling establishing the law of the jurisdiction. Accordingly, a decision on general acceptance could be viewed as more a legal question than a factual question. Furthermore, diverse trial court rulings on the admissibility of a scientific technique within a jurisdiction would create confusion. *See generally In re Commitment of Simons*, 821 N.E.2d 1184, 1189–90 (Ill. 2004) (reviewing arguments favoring de novo review and listing de novo review jurisdictions); 1 Scientific Evidence § 1.06[e], at 28–29 (4th ed. 2007).

Under de novo review an appellate court is not confined to a review of the record developed in the trial court's *Frye* hearing:

> We specifically note that the appropriate standard of review of a *Frye* issue is de novo. Thus, an appellate court reviews a trial court's ruling as a matter of law rather than under an abuse-of-discretion standard. When undertaking such a review, an appellate court should consider the issue of general acceptance at the time of appeal rather than at the time of trial. An appellate court may examine expert testimony, scientific and legal writings, and judicial opinions in making its determination.

Hadden v. State, 690 So.2d 573, 579 (Fla. 1997). *See also Brim v. State*, 695 So.2d 268, 270–74 (Fla. 1997) (report issued during pendency of appeal should be considered in determining whether novel scientific evidence is admissible); *People v. Watson*, 629 N.E.2d 634, 640 (Ill. App. 1994) (in reviewing trial court's decision under *Frye*, appellate court may look not only at expert evidence presented to trial court, but also at judicial opinions from other jurisdictions and pertinent legal and scientific commentaries); *State v. Copeland*, 922 P.2d 1304, 1312–13 (Wash. 1996) (review of a *Frye* decision is de novo, and the reviewing court will undertake a searching review which may extend beyond the record and include materials not available until after the *Frye* hearing).

5. *The Proper Field(s).* To satisfy *Frye* the new scientific principle must be generally accepted *"in the particular field in which it belongs."* Selecting the field or fields to which a particular technique belongs could have a significant impact upon whether the technique is found to be generally accepted.

For example, in *Reed v. State*, 391 A.2d 364 (Md. 1978), the Maryland Court of Appeals reviewed a trial court decision finding that the voiceprint technique had achieved general acceptance. In *Reed* the trial court had defined the field that must generally accept the voiceprint technique to be "the group actually engaged in the use of this technique and in the experimentation with this technique." *Id.* at 377. The court of appeals reversed, stating:

> [W]e find that the trial court's formulation is inconsistent with the proper
> acceptance necessary for admissibility. The circumstances of the instant case
> suggest no basis for restricting the relevant field of experts to those who have
> performed voiceprint experiments, and eliminating from consideration the
> opinions of those scientists in the fields of speech and hearing, as well as related
> fields, who by training and education are competent to make professional
> judgments concerning experiments undertaken by others. The purpose of *Frye*
> is defeated by an approach which allows a court to ignore the informed opinions
> of a substantial segment of the scientific community which stands in opposition
> to the process in question.

Id.

It is not unusual for courts to require general acceptance in more than one scientific
field. *See United States v. Alexander*, 526 F.2d 161, 164 (8th Cir. 1975) (polygraph
machine and technique must attain scientific acceptance among experts in polygraphy,
psychiatry, physiology, psychophysiology, neurophysiology, and other related disciplines — not just among polygraph operators); *People v. LeGrand*, 867 N.E.2d 374, 380
(N.Y. 2007) (principles underlying expert testimony on the reliability of eyewitness
identifications was generally accepted by social scientists and psychologists working in
the field); *People v. King*, 72 Cal. Rptr. 478, 490 (Cal. App. 1968) (assessing general
acceptance of the voiceprint and observing that communication by speech does not fall
into any one established category of science, but rather requires an understanding of
anatomy, physiology, physics, psychology, and linguistics).

6. General Acceptance.

(A) The Trial Court's Role. It is important to note that under the *Frye* test the court
does not make a determination that a particular scientific theory or technique is reliable,
or that claims of validity or invalidity made by one group of scientists are more
meritorious than the claims made by another group. Rather, the court's role under *Frye*
is to determine whether a significant number of *scientists* in the relevant field oppose the
principle or technique as unreliable. The scientific community — not the trial court —
determines reliability under the *Frye* test. The California Supreme Court discussed the
court's role under *Frye* in a case involving the admissibility of posthypnotic testimony:

> It is not our function, however, to resolve . . . disputes within the scientific
> community, any more than it is our task to determine whether posthypnotic
> testimony is reliable as a matter of scientific fact. The courts view the
> professional literature on hypnosis as evidence not of the actual reliability of the
> new scientific technique, but of its acceptance *vel non* in the scientific commu-
> nity. That is all the *Frye* test requires. . . .

People v. Guerra, 690 P.2d 635, 656 (Cal. 1984). *See also People v. LeGrand*, 867 N.E.2d
374, 379 (N.Y. 2007) ("[T]his test emphasizes counting scientists' votes, rather than . . .
verifying the soundness of a scientific conclusion."); *State v. Carlson*, 906 P.2d 999, 1003
n.22 (Wash. App. 1995) ("Under *Frye*, scientists decide, and the court recognizes their
decision if and when it is generally accepted in their community."); *People v. Barney*, 10
Cal. Rptr. 2d 731, 743 (Cal. App. 1992) ("The point is not whether there are more
supporters than detractors, or whether . . . the supporters are right and the detractors
are wrong. The point is that there is disagreement between two groups, each significant
in both number and expertise."); *Reed v. State*, 391 A.2d 364, 376 (Md. 1978) (under *Frye*,

the court is not to determine the merits of various scientists' claims). In defending this aspect of *Frye*, the Florida Supreme Court stated:

> The underlying theory for [*Frye*] is that a courtroom is not a laboratory, and as such it is not the place to conduct scientific experiments. If the scientific community considers a procedure or process unreliable for its own purposes, then the procedure must be considered less reliable for courtroom use.

Stokes v. State, 548 So.2d 188, 193–94 (Fla. 1989).

(B) What Degree of Acceptance Constitutes "General Acceptance"? Unfortunately, there is no precise answer as to what amount, or what degree, of acceptance constitutes *general* acceptance. Unanimity, however, is not required.

> The *Frye* test does not demand the impossible — proof of an absolute unanimity of views in the scientific community before a new technique will be considered reliable; any such unanimity would be highly unusual, especially in the field of behavioral sciences. Rather the test is met if use of the technique is supported by a *clear majority* of the members of that community.

People v. Guerra, 690 P.2d 635, 656 (Cal. 1984). *See also Commonwealth v. Lykus*, 327 N.E.2d 671, 678 n.6 (Mass. 1975) (there need not be uniform and total acceptance; *Frye* does not require unanimity); John William Strong, *Questions Affecting the Admissibility of Scientific Evidence*, 1970 U. ILL. L.F. 1, 11 ("something greater than acceptance by the expert himself but less than all experts in the field").

(C) The Quality of the Scientific Support or Opposition Matters. In determining whether a "clear majority" exists the trial court must do more than "count heads." There is a qualitative as well as a quantitative aspect to "general acceptance." That is, general acceptance requires more than just "counting heads."

> [T]he *Frye* test [calls] for "substantial agreement and consensus in the scientific field." Of course, the trial courts, in determining the general acceptance issue, must consider the quality, as well as the quantity, of the evidence supporting or opposing a new scientific technique. Mere numerical majority support or opposition by persons minimally qualified to state an authoritative opinion is of little value. . . .

People v. Leahy, 882 P.2d 321, 336–37 (Cal. 1994). *See also Ramirez v. State*, 810 So. 2d 836, 844 (Fla. 2002) (court not required to accept a "nose count" of experts); *Hadden v. State*, 690 So.2d 573, 576 n.2 (Fla. 1997) (general acceptance means acceptance by a clear majority of the members of the relevant scientific community with consideration by the trial court of both the quality and quantity of those opinions.").

Similarly, as indicated in the *Kelly* case, the bald assertion by the testifying expert that his or her deduction is based on well-recognized scientific principles should not be enough to justify a finding of *general* acceptance. This is particularly true if the expert has a personal stake in the new theory of technique at issue. *Ramirez v. State*, 810 So. 2d 836, 844 n.13 (Fla. 2002).

QUESTIONS

1. Did the California Supreme Court find that identifying a speaker by spectrographic analysis ("voiceprint") was unreliable? If so, why? If there was no finding of unreliability, then why was Kelly's conviction reversed?

2. Prior to assessing the testimony of Lt. Nash, to what sources did the California Supreme Court in *Kelly* refer to assist it in determining if the voiceprint technique was generally accepted?

Once the court turned to the testimony of Lt. Nash, what factors made his testimony unsuitable for establishing general acceptance?

3. According to the court in *Kelly*, what is the field or fields in which the voiceprint technique must gain general acceptance? Why couldn't Lt. Nash's testimony establish general acceptance in that field or fields?

4. If a trial court takes judicial notice of an article in a scientific journal that takes the position that a particular technique is valid, what is it the court takes notice of — the validity of the technique or the existence of a scientific article with a point of view? *See* 1 SCIENTIFIC EVIDENCE § 1.06[d], at 25–27 (4th ed. 2007).

5. If the party who opposes the admission of novel scientific evidence offers no witnesses in opposition, must the proponent of the evidence call hostile witnesses to afford the court a typical cross-section of the scientific community? If not, what, if anything, should the trial court do before ruling on the admissibility of challenged scientific evidence?

PROBLEMS

Problem 2-1. Assume you are the trial judge trying to decide if a new scientific technique is generally accepted. Expert testimony and scientific articles offered into evidence at the *Frye* hearing by the parties establish that 80% of the scientists in the appropriate field(s) accept the technique, but 20% do not. You (the trial judge), however, believe that the 20% who do not accept the technique make the more persuasive argument.

(A) Do you rule against admissibility? *See People v. Guerra*, 690 P.2d 635, 656 (Cal. 1984); *People v. Barney*, 10 Cal. Rptr. 2d 731, 743 (Cal. App. 1992).

(B) Does it make any difference *who* the 20% are that do not accept the new technique? *See People v. Leahy*, 882 P.2d 321, 336–37 (Cal. 1994).

Problem 2-2. Assume that after the *Kelly* case Lt. Nash returns to Michigan State University and conducts an additional empirical study of the reliability of spectrographic analysis. Assume that the study is not published.

(A) If, in a subsequent case in California, Lt. Nash's testimony is the same *except* that now he can present his own empirical study that supports the reliability of spectrographic analysis, what result? *See* 1 SCIENTIFIC EVIDENCE § 1.06[b], at 22–23 (4th ed. 2007).

(B) What difference, if any, would it make if the person who conducted the empirical study and who came to court to testify as to the reliability of spectrographic analysis were Dr. Tosi, the professor of audiology, speech sciences and physics at Michigan State University? *See* 1 SCIENTIFIC EVIDENCE § 1.06[b], at 22–23 (4th ed. 2007).

Recall that *Frye* applies to "*new scientific principles.*" What is a "*new* scientific principle"? Just how "new" or novel must a scientific principle be to warrant scrutiny under *Frye*? Are there certain forms of novel expert opinion testimony that do not involve a "*scientific*" principle. If so, what are the characteristics of such non-scientific expert testimony? The next two cases, *People v. Stoll* and *State v. Hasan*, discuss when the *Frye* test is — and is not — applied to expert opinion testimony. In reading these cases and the Notes that follow pay particular attention to the rationale for applying *Frye*.

The first case, *People v. Stoll*, involved charges of child sexual abuse in which a defense psychologist was prepared to offer expert opinion testimony (based, in part, upon standardized personality tests) that the defendant displayed no signs of "deviance" or "abnormality." The prosecution asserted that such evidence was new or experimental scientific evidence that must satisfy *Frye* before it could be admitted.

PEOPLE v. STOLL
783 P.2d 698 (Cal. 1989)

EAGLESON, JUSTICE.

. . . .

FACTS

Four defendants — John Stoll, Grant Self, Margie Grafton, and Timothy Palomo — were jointly tried and convicted in the aggregate of thirty-six counts of lewd and lascivious conduct against a total of seven young boys. The crimes . . . occurred in Bakersfield, California, between June 1983 and June 1984.

Evidence adduced at trial in late 1984 and early 1985 indicated that defendants sometimes acted together and sometimes acted apart in committing the crimes. Since we granted review only as to defendants Grafton and Palomo, we will focus on evidence offered by and against them.[4] [1]

A. *Evidence Admitted at Trial*

Defendants [Margie] Grafton and [Timothy] Palomo were romantically involved and lived together during the pertinent time period. . . .

Five children testified against Grafton . . . [including] a neighbor boy who lived near Stoll's house on Center Street, Victor. Except for Victor, the same children also testified against Palomo. [Grafton and Palomo testified and denied all charges].

. . . .

B. *Excluded Testimony of Defense Psychologist*

Grafton called Dr. [Roger M.] Mitchell [, a psychologist,] in her case-in-chief. The prosecutor successfully requested an offer of proof on the nature of the proposed testimony. Outside the jury's presence, Grafton's counsel explained that, based upon professional experience, interviews, and the administration of certain psychological tests, Dr. Mitchell would give an expert opinion as to whether Grafton possesses any "pathology" in the nature of "sexual deviation." Counsel insisted that the testimony was

---

[4] [n.1] Stoll did not petition for review. Self's petition was denied.

admissible as "character evidence," because it tended to show that Grafton has no predisposition to commit lewd or incestuous acts.

Relying on [*People v.*] *Kelly*, 549 P.2d 1240 (1976), the prosecutor essentially replied that a defendant must first show that a psychological "profile" of a child molester exists, and that its absence in a particular person is generally accepted by other experts to mean that the person has not molested children. Defense counsel countered that the proffered testimony need only meet, and did meet, the requirements for expert opinion testimony, . . . i.e., it would "assist" the trier of fact, and was based on "matter" upon which experts may "reasonably rel[y]." . . .

The trial court ruled that a *Kelly/Frye* "reliability" showing of an unspecified nature must be made before the jury would be allowed to hear Dr. Mitchell's testimony. In the ensuing hearing . . . Dr. Mitchell first listed his expert qualifications — an issue which has never been in serious dispute.

Grafton's counsel then elicited the following testimony on direct voir dire examination: approximately one week earlier, Grafton was administered two "standardized" measures of "personality function," the Minnesota Multiphasic Personality Inventory (MMPI), and the Millon Clinical Multiaxial Inventory (MCMI). The MMPI — the "primary" test — was copyrighted in 1943 and, following several revisions, is still "the most widely used psychological test" on both a local and national level.

. . . .

After reviewing Grafton's test results, Dr. Mitchell interviewed her for two hours in jail, discussing the charges against all defendants. Based on his "*individual interpretation*" of the test and interview results, Dr. Mitchell was of the "*professional opinion*" that Grafton "has a *normal personality function*, likely has [had] throughout her lifetime, and . . . is falsely charged[5] [13] in this matter." He immediately clarified this last phrase to mean that Grafton has "*[not] engaged in the past in sexual deviancy* of any kind . . . [and] shows *no indications of deviancy in any other personality function. . . . Especially [in light of] a low indication for antisocial or aggressive behavior*, I must conclude that it is *unlikely . . . she would be involved in the events she's been charged with*." He added that his opinion was based also on the results of similar examinations of Palomo, and his knowledge of the Grafton-Palomo relationship.

On cross-examination by the prosecutor, Dr. Mitchell testified: neither he nor other qualified experts use the two tests as a "lie detector" to reach an absolute determination as to whether an individual is guilty of charged crimes. Rather, his opinion of Grafton was based upon a "*diagnostic process*" combining "*many, many pieces of data*," including professional experience with other individuals in other situations, knowledge of Grafton's and Palomo's test results, knowledge about the charges against them, and his personal assessment of them. Dr. Mitchell said his examination of Grafton was "extensive," such that the MMPI and MCMI were "*not by any means the sole*

---

[5] [n.13] A psychologist, called to testify as an expert on the existence of certain personality traits and likelihood of certain behavior is generally not competent to testify as to the "truth" or "falsity" of criminal charges. Although opinion testimony is not made inadmissible solely because "it embraces the ultimate issue to be decided by the trier of fact," an expert giving such an opinion must be otherwise qualified to do so. Here, of course, nothing in the voir dire testimony suggested that Dr. Mitchell was qualified to render a *legal* opinion as to whether all elements of the charged crimes could be proven beyond a reasonable doubt against Grafton and Palomo. However, since Dr. Mitchell immediately retracted his assessment of the charges, we need not explore this issue further.

determinor" of his opinion. Rather, it reflects, in many respects, a *"subjective judgment"* that is not based on *"an absolute cut and dried scientific approach."*

. . . .

At one point during cross-examination, defense counsel objected when the prosecutor characterized Dr. Mitchell as having testified that Grafton "did not fit within the profile of a child molester." The court overruled the objection. Dr. Mitchell corrected the prosecutor's characterization, saying his actual opinion was that Grafton showed no *"possibility for sexual deviancy in her personality profile."*

Following redirect examination and further argument by both counsel, the trial court excluded the proffered testimony. Adopting the prosecutor's terminology, the court reasoned that the defense had not met its burden, under *Kelly*, of establishing that a profile of a child molester is generally accepted in the scientific community, or that a person who does not fit the profile has not actually molested children.

Grafton's counsel immediately urged the court to reconsider on grounds that Dr. Mitchell did not refer to, or rely upon, any "profile." Counsel also insisted that if Dr. Mitchell were allowed to testify, he would eliminate all references to the truth or falsity of the charges and focus only on the lack of "sexual deviation." The court denied Grafton's request.

Palomo's counsel then stated that he too intended to call Dr. Mitchell for the purpose of testifying that Palomo had tested "within the range of normal heterosexuality." The court refused to allow the testimony on grounds that its exclusionary ruling applied to Palomo as well.

C. *Verdict and Appeal*

[The] jury entered guilty verdicts against Grafton on five counts and against Palomo on four counts. In a consolidated appeal, the Court of Appeal affirmed the judgment as to all defendants in three separate opinions. . . .

DISCUSSION

The Attorney General argues that Dr. Mitchell's use of tests and an asserted "profile" constitutes a new scientific technique subject to *Kelly/Frye*. He insists that defendants have failed to show that this technique is generally accepted in the psychiatric or psychological community for the purpose offered here — to uncover personality traits that are linked to noncommission of the charged criminal acts.

Grafton and Palomo insist that a close reading of this record reveals that testimony on only one narrow trait was offered. Referring variously to that trait as lack of sexual deviance, homosexuality, incestuous desires, or pedophilia, defendants argue that expert opinion as to its existence has always been admissible, without reference to *Kelly/Frye*, to show that a defendant is not likely to commit criminal sexual misconduct. As we will discuss, defendants provide a more accurate picture of the law and facts.

At the outset, defendant's claim that the testimony is relevant character evidence must be sustained. . . .

[The California Evidence Code] allows an accused to present expert opinion testimony of this kind to indicate his nondisposition to commit a charged sex offense.[6] [17]. . . .

The Attorney General argues that even if the proffered testimony [is relevant character evidence], it also must meet California's version of the rule first announced in *Frye* for the admissibility of "new scientific technique[s]." We disagree.

. . . .

While the standards imposed by the *Kelly/Frye* rule are clear, the definition of a "new scientific technique" is not. In *Kelly*, for example, the parties did not dispute that the *Frye* test applied to an identification process in which an expert analyst compares "voiceprints," or graphs of human voices, produced by a "spectrograph" machine. Because the inventions and discoveries which could be considered "scientific" have become virtually limitless in the near-70 years since *Frye* was decided, application of its principle has often been determined by reference to its narrow "common sense" purpose, i.e., to protect the jury from techniques which, though "new," novel, or " 'experimental,' " convey a " 'misleading aura of certainty.' "

This approach has produced two discernible themes. First, *Kelly/Frye* only applies to that limited class of expert testimony which is based, in whole or part, on a technique, process, or theory which is *new* to science and, even more so, the law. The courts are willing to forego admission of such techniques completely until reasonably certain that the pertinent scientific community no longer views them as experimental or of dubious validity. This all-or-nothing approach was adopted in full recognition that there would be a " 'considerable lag' " between scientific advances and their admission as evidence in a court proceeding.

The second theme in cases applying *Kelly/Frye* is that the unproven technique or procedure appears in both name and description to provide some definitive truth which the expert need only accurately recognize and relay to the jury. The most obvious examples are machines or procedures which analyze physical data. Lay minds might easily, but erroneously, assume that such procedures are objective and infallible. (*See e.g., People v. Coleman* (1988) 759 P.2d 1260 ["hemostick" method of presumptive testing for presence of blood]; *People v. Brown* (1985) 726 P.2d 516 [electrophoretic testing of body fluid and blood stains to identify donor]; *see also People v. Shirley* (1982) 723 P.2d 1354 [listing cases which have applied the *Frye* test to polygraph examinations, "truth serum," Nalline testing, human bite marks, and microscopic identification of gunshot residue particles].)

Kelly/Frye also has been applied to less tangible new procedures which carry an equally undeserved aura of certainty. In *People v. Shirley, supra,* 723 P.2d 1354, we applied the *Kelly/Frye* rule to, and barred admission of, "post-hypnotic" testimony of a rape complainant. We explicitly rejected the Attorney General's claim in that case that the *Kelly/Frye* rule was limited to techniques analyzing "physical evidence." We noted that, given the rule's prophylactic purpose, nothing precludes its application to "a new scientific process operating on purely psychological evidence." As thoroughly explained

---

[6] [n.17] Section 1102 provides: "In a criminal action, evidence of the defendant's character or a trait of his character in the form of an opinion or evidence of his reputation is not made inadmissible by Section 1101 if such evidence is: ¶ (a) Offered by the defendant to prove his conduct in conformity with such other character or trait of character[:] [¶] (b) Offered by the prosecution to rebut evidence adduced by the defendant under subdivision (a).

in Justice Mosk's majority opinion, the danger of hypnotically refreshed testimony lies in the tendency of the process to "actively contribute [] to the formation of pseudomemories, to the witness' abiding belief in their veracity, and to the inability of the witness (or anyone else) to distinguish between the two."

However, absent some special feature which effectively blindsides the jury, expert opinion testimony is not subject to *Kelly/Frye*. This distinction was recently confirmed in our unanimous decision in *People v. McDonald*, 690 P.2d 709 (Cal. 1984). There we found prejudicial error in the exclusion of defense expert testimony on the psychological factors undermining the accuracy of eyewitness identification. In dispensing with any need for a *Kelly/Frye* showing in that case, Justice Mosk noted that

> [w]hen a witness gives his personal opinion on the stand — even if he qualifies as an expert — the jurors may temper their acceptance of his testimony with a healthy skepticism born of their knowledge that all human beings are fallible. . . .

> . . . We have never applied the *Kelly/Frye* rule to expert medical testimony, even when the witness is a psychiatrist and the subject matter is as esoteric as the reconstitution of a past state of mind or the prediction of future dangerousness, or even the diagnosis of an unusual form of mental illness not listed in the diagnostic manual of the American Psychiatric Association.

(*McDonald, supra,* 690 P.2d 709).

The psychological testimony proffered here raises none of the concerns addressed by *Kelly/Frye*. The methods employed are not *new* to psychology or the law, and they carry no misleading aura of scientific infallibility.

California courts have routinely admitted defense expert opinion analogous to the one offered here, with no suggestion that *Kelly/Frye* applies. In some of these cases, expert testimony of the defendant's personality was admitted to prove that defendant was not likely to commit certain acts in the future.

In other cases the testimony was introduced as circumstantial evidence that the defendant did not harbor the requisite criminal intent or mental state at the time he committed the charged act.

Moreover, as Dr. Mitchell testified, diagnostic use of written personality inventories such as the MMPI and MCMI has been established for decades. Modern courts have not resisted reference to these tests. [D]efense expert opinion on an impressive range of psychiatric diagnoses has been admitted without reference to *Kelly/Frye* where the expert made known at trial that he relied, in part, on the MMPI or analogous tests.

We see no reason to depart from this settled approach. As discussed, criminal defendants are authorized to use character evidence, including expert opinion, to prove "*conduct* in conformity." This principle applies where lack of deviance is offered as circumstantial evidence that a defendant is unlikely to have committed charged acts of molestation.

. . . [E]xpert reliance on the MMPI and MCMI for this particular purpose is *not* a "revolutionary" development. [S]tandardized personality tests previously have been used in forming expert opinion admitted to show that an accused did not harbor the requisite "*mental state* at the time the alleged acts were committed." Here, defendants offered similar expert testimony to suggest that they did not commit the requisite *act*.

In either case, the fundamental purpose of the testimony is the same — to raise a reasonable doubt as to guilt of charged crimes. [There is] no legal or logical basis for conditioning application of the *Kelly/Frye* rule upon the particular *theory* by which the accused seeks "to exclude [himself] from the relevant class of offenders." It would be anomalous to view the MMPI and similar tests as a "new" technique at this late date.

We also are persuaded that no reasonable juror would mistake an expert's reliance on standardized tests as a source of infallible "truth" on issues of personality, predisposition, or criminal guilt. Here, for example, Dr. Mitchell stated that the MMPI was essentially 70 percent accurate in diagnosing some patients, but "completely invalid" as to others. Although the witness expressed faith in his own methods, he recounted one instance in which an "admitted" child sex offender had tested "normal" on the MMPI. Thus, despite testimony regarding "validity scales," the test results — which were never actually described below — were not made to appear "foolproof."

More importantly, the MMPI and MCMI are obviously a springboard for a far more normative and subjective diagnostic process. That this process is a learned professional *art*, rather than the purported exact "science" with which *Kelly/Frye* is concerned, is well illustrated by the witness's guarded testimony here. Dr. Mitchell left no doubt that he *also* relied heavily upon patient interviews, case history, and past experience in forming his educated, but debatable, opinion.

Along these lines, we reiterate that issues of test reliability and validity may be thoroughly explored on cross-examination at trial. The prosecution also may call, in rebuttal, another expert of comparable background to challenge defense expert methods. . . .

. . . .

Faced with the question here, we are persuaded that *Kelly/Frye* did not preclude admission of Dr. Mitchell's proffered testimony. Expert opinion that defendants show no obvious psychological or sexual problem is circumstantial evidence which bears upon whether they committed sexual acts upon children, and is admissible "character" evidence on their behalf. The testimony and the matter upon which it is based also meet traditional standards for competent expert opinion, without need for additional screening procedures applicable to new, novel, or experimental "scientific" evidence not previously accepted in court. We conclude the trial court erred in using *Kelly/Frye* to exclude the testimony proffered by Grafton and Palomo.

. . . .

Insofar as it upholds the convictions against defendants Grafton and Palomo, the judgment of the Court of Appeal is reversed.

NOTE

1. ***"Themes" — Not a Definition of "New Scientific Principle" — For Determining Whether Expert Opinion Testimony Should Be Subjected to* Frye."** *Frye* jurisdictions do not apply its general acceptance test to all expert testimony. In determining when to apply *Frye* most courts have been guided by whether the evidence is beyond the understanding of the ordinary juror, rather than by a technical definition of what is, or is not, a "scientific principle" or a "scientific technique." In the language of the *Stoll* case, "absent some special feature which . . . blindsides the jury, expert opinion testimony is not subject to [*Frye*]." *Stoll, supra*, 783 P.2d at 710. To put it

simply, the purpose of *Frye* is to protect the jury, and, generally, *Frye* is only applied when the court feels the jury needs protection.

Certain techniques are, therefore, *deemed* "scientific," and others are *deemed* "not scientific" for the purpose of determining whether the testimony is based upon a "new scientific technique," — thereby implicating the *Frye* test. The California Supreme Court commented on this aspect of *Frye* in a 1994 case.

> In *Stoll*, we . . . observed that, by reason of the potential breadth of the term "scientific" in the *Kelly/Frye* doctrine, the courts often refer "to its narrow 'common sense' purpose, i.e., to protect the jury from techniques which, though 'new,' novel, or 'experimental,' convey a 'misleading aura of certainty.'" According to *Stoll*, a technique may be deemed "scientific" for purposes of *Kelly/Frye* if the unproven technique or process appears *in both name and description* to provide some definitive truth which the expert need only accurately recognize and relay to the jury.

People v. Leahy, 882 P.2d 321, 333 (Cal. 1994) (emphasis in original).

Stoll offers two "themes" to guide a court in deciding whether the proffered expert testimony is to be subjected to *Frye*. First, the technique must be "new;" that is, new to science and the law. Second, even if "new," the technique will not be "deemed scientific" for *Frye* purposes unless it "appears in both name and description to provide some definitive truth."

QUESTIONS

1. In *Stoll* the California Supreme Court states that, "[w]hile the standards imposed by the *Kelly/Frye* rule are clear, the "definition of a 'new scientific technique' is not." Does the Court define "new scientific technique"?

2. What factors does the court identify in *Stoll* as indicating that Dr. Mitchell's expert testimony does not present "infallible truth"?

3. What is it that distinguishes expert scientific opinion (to which *Frye* applies) from expert personal opinion (to which *Frye* does *not* apply)?

4. In *Stoll* the California Supreme Court made the following findings concerning the methodology underlying Dr. Mitchell's opinions: "The methods employed are not *new* to psychology or the law, and they carry no misleading aura of scientific infallibility. California courts have routinely admitted defense expert opinion analogous to the one offered here, with no suggestion that *Kelly/Frye* applies." *Stoll, supra*, 738 P.2d at 711.

(A) Does this mean that an expert's methodology can escape scrutiny under *Frye* simply because it has been used by the courts for years?

(B) If not, what indication is there that scientists generally accept the personality tests (MMPI and the MCMI) as reliable for *any* purpose? See *Stoll, supra*, 783 P.2d at 718 (Lucas, C.J., dissenting) (no case has found the MMPI or similar standardized psychological tests generally accepted by the scientific community).

5. In *Stoll* the California Supreme Court also found that the personality tests used by Dr. Mitchell were not new to science or the law. Isn't the *way* he used them significantly different? Isn't using a personality test to *exclude* [someone] from a relevant class of offenders, different from using such tests as evidence of the defendant's mental state at the time the acts were committed? See *Stoll, supra*, 783

P.2d at 718 (Lucas, C.J., dissenting) ("[N]o cases exist which sanction such a revolutionary application of standardized test procedures as was attempted in this case.").

6. Assume the *prosecution* calls a psychologist to the witness stand in a child abuse case during the prosecution's case-in-chief. Would the prosecution's psychologist be permitted to testify that, based on the administration of standardized tests, interviews, personal experience, and training, the defendant does *not* possess a normal personality function, and was likely to be involved in the events charged?

PROBLEMS

Problem 2-3. Assume that law enforcement officers have used a technique called the horizontal gaze nystagmus test for more than 30 years to determine if someone is intoxicated. Nystagmus is involuntary, rapid eye movement. Horizontal gaze nystagmus, or HGN, is the inability of the eyes to remain visually fixed upon an object as the object is moved from in front of a person horizontally to an acute angle. The HGN *test* involves a police officer requiring a person to cover one eye and track an object, such as a pen light, with the other eye as the object is moved from directly in front of them to an acute angle toward the ear. The officer observes the angle at which nystagmus occurs. The theory is that alcohol intoxication hastens the onset of nystagmus and a police officer can determine if someone is intoxicated by noting when nystagmus occurs. If an HGN test indicates intoxication, the individual being tested may be taken to the police station and given a breath test.

Assume that the defendant is charged with driving while intoxicated in a state where the results of an HGN test have never been offered into evidence. The prosecution wishes to offer expert opinion, from a police officer trained in administering the HGN test (and who administered the HGN test to the defendant on this occasion), that the defendant was intoxicated based *solely* upon a police officer's observations when she administered the HGN test to the defendant in the field.

(A) Is the HGN test "new"? Must the court hold a *Frye* hearing?

(B) Specifically, what impact, if any, does long-standing use by police officers in the field (30 years) have on whether or not the HGN test is new and whether a *Frye* hearing ought to be held? *See People v. Leahy*, 882 P.2d 321, 331–32 (Cal. 1994).

Problem 2-4. Assume that a court believes that the HGN test described above is new. Assume further that at trial the police officer who used the HGN test in this case is prepared to testify that she has "always been right" whenever she checked her conclusions from an HGN test with subsequent blood alcohol tests.

(A) Does the HGN test involve "definitive truth" as that phrase is defined in *Stoll?*

(B) Specifically, what impact, if any, does the police officer's testimony about "always [being] right" have on the HGN test being considered as "definitive truth" which the expert need "recognize and relay to the jury"? *See People v. Leahy*, 882 P.2d 321, 333 (Cal. 1994); *State v. Witte*, 836 P.2d 1110, 1115–17 (Kan. 1992); *City of Fargo v. McLaughlin*, 512 N.W.2d 700, 705–07 (N.D. 1994).

As indicated in the *Stoll* case, the *Frye* test is not applied every time an expert testifies, even if the testimony is based upon a scientific principle. *Frye's* application in a particular case is determined by *Frye's* purpose — to protect jurors with little or no scientific expertise from being misled by unproven scientific techniques that appear infallible, i.e., techniques that "convey a misleading aura of certainty." The two themes discussed in *Stoll* are there to assist a court in determining if *Frye's* purpose is implicated.

In terms of *Frye's* actual application, expert testimony can be placed into categories and some generalizations can be made. *Stoll* provides two such categories. First, if expert opinion is nothing more than relaying to the jury as accurate the results produced by a machine or process-particularly if the machine or process analyzes physical evidence — *Frye* applies and the machine or process must be shown to be generally accepted as reliable by the relevant scientific community. On the other hand, if an expert's opinion can be categorized as "personal opinion" based upon the experience and trained observation of the expert, the testimony will not be subjected to *Frye*.

In the next case, *State v. Hasan*, the Connecticut Supreme Court was confronted with the question of whether *Frye* should be applied to an opinion from a podiatrist that connected the defendant to a pair of sneakers that were, in turn, linked to a crime scene. In the course of its opinion the court describes additional categories of expert opinion testimony that are not generally subjected to *Frye's* general acceptance test.

STATE v. HASAN
534 A.2d 877 (Conn. 1987)

HULL, ASSOCIATE JUSTICE.

The sole issue in this appeal is whether the trial court erred in admitting the testimony of a podiatrist identifying as the defendant's a pair of sneakers linked to the scene of the crimes with which he was charged.

After a jury trial, the defendant, Wendell Hasan, was found guilty of felony murder and burglary in the first degree. This appeal followed.

. . . On July 2, 1985, the police were called to the home of George and Rachel Tyler to investigate a possible homicide. The police found George Tyler dead in the kitchen, Rachel Tyler injured, and the premises apparently ransacked. The Tylers' son and daughter-in-law determined that George Tyler's wallet was missing as was some of Rachel Tyler's jewelry. Among the evidence secured by the police were broken glass and linoleum bearing a bloody footprint made by a sneaker. Police suspicion turned to the defendant when, on July 5, 1985, a plumber repairing a clogged toilet in a South Norwalk apartment found two credit cards belonging to George Tyler to be the cause of the clog. The plumber turned the cards over to the owner of the apartment, who reported the find to the police. The police obtained a warrant to search the apartment.

The defendant had been living at the South Norwalk apartment intermittently; it was also occupied by his mother, stepfather, his brother, James Singleton, two sisters and James' girlfriend. Pursuant to the warrant, the police seized several pairs of shoes, including a pair of size ten Puma low cut sneakers which they found at the foot of the bed in which James and his girlfriend slept. The bedroom was actually the defendant's and most of the belongings there were his. James told the police that the sneakers were the defendant's and that his own shoe size was thirteen. During custodial interrogation, the defendant stated that the apartment was his primary residence and that he owned a pair of Puma sneakers like the ones seized.

The conviction depended in large measure on circumstantial evidence. Glass shards and linoleum fibers found in the sole of one of the sneakers, were similar to the mass produced glass and linoleum located at the crime scene, but could not be positively identified as having come from there. Similarly, human blood detected on the sneakers was consistent with the victims' blood, but could not be positively identified as theirs. During trial, a forensic expert from the Connecticut state police forensic laboratory identified the Puma sneakers as those that made the footprints on the Tylers' kitchen floor. . . .

In addition to the foregoing, the jury heard the testimony of Dr. Robert Rinaldi, a podiatrist called by the state as an expert witness, who concluded "within reasonable podiatric certainty" that based on his examination of the sneakers and the defendant's feet, the sneakers belonged to the defendant. The defendant excepted to the admission of this testimony and appeals on this ground.

. . . .

Many jurisdictions have adopted a special rule for admissibility of scientific evidence, in accordance with *Frye v. United States.* . . .

The *Frye* "general acceptance" test has been employed to assess the admissibility of spectographic analysis; ion microscopic analysis of hair samples; and hypnotically refreshed recollection. We have acknowledged that *Frye* sets forth the prevailing standard for evaluating the admissibility of evidence derived from innovative scientific techniques. We have expressly applied it to polygraph testing; and to human leukocyte antigen testing for paternity.

The defendant argues that the evidence elicited from Rinaldi was scientific evidence subject to the standard for admissibility articulated in *Frye*. We disagree.

. . . *Frye* contemplates those situations in which the evidence sought to be admitted is beyond the understanding of the ordinary juror who must sacrifice his independent judgment in deference to the expert. Among the dangers created by such scientific evidence is its potential to mislead lay jurors "awed by an 'aura of mystic infallibility' surrounding 'scientific techniques,' 'experts' and the 'fancy devices' employed." *United States v. Williams*, 583 F.2d 1194, 1199 (2d Cir. 1978). The fact that a technique or method has gained general acceptance in the scientific community to which it belongs tends to ensure that the jury will not accord undue weight to theories whose validity has not been adequately tested.

Such infirmities do not inhere in all types of expert evidence. Accordingly, the *Frye* test has been either ignored or rejected in cases in which the method used by the expert was a matter of physical comparison rather than scientific test or experiment; *Ex parte Dolvin*, 391 So. 2d 677 (Ala. 1980) (identification of skeletal remains by comparing teeth and facial structure with photographs of victim; *Frye* inapplicable); the basic data upon which the expert relied was verifiable by the factfinder; *People v. Marx*, [126 Cal. Rptr. 350 (1975)] (bite mark identification; trier shown models, photographs, X-rays and slides of victim's wounds and defendant's teeth; *Frye* inapplicable); or where established techniques were applied to the solution of novel problems. *State v. Temple*, 273 S.E.2d 273 ([N.C.]1981) (bite mark identification by application of dentistry and photography; *Frye* ignored). Many of these cases have involved identification of bite marks by comparison of the defendant's dental impressions to bite marks found on a victim's body; and identification of footprints by comparing shoes found at the crime scene with shoes worn by the defendant. In such cases, the jury is in a position to weigh the probative value of the testimony without abandoning common sense and sacrificing independent judgment to the expert's assertions based on his special skill or knowledge. Furthermore, where understanding of the method is accessible to the jury, and not dependent on familiarity with highly technical or obscure scientific theories, the expert's qualifications, and the logical bases of his opinions and conclusions can be effectively challenged by cross-examination and rebuttal evidence. Rinaldi's testimony falls within this category.

. . . .

. . . Rinaldi testified that, with wear, shoes conform to the contours of the foot and that the foot's characteristics are manifested in the outline of the shoe. He explained that, in order to determine the proper fit of a shoe, he observes the foot, feels the foot inside the shoe and measures the foot with a Brannick device.[7] [6] He then detailed his method for matching the Puma sneakers to the defendant's feet, illustrating his testimony with the sneakers. He explained that before he saw the defendant, he examined the shoes, concluding that the wearer was flatfooted, was on the heavy side and had prominences on two of his toes. His subsequent examination of the defendant's feet confirmed his hypothesis. He measured the defendant's feet with a Brannick device and felt the feet, both with and without socks, in the sneakers and out, walking, standing and sitting. He noted that when the defendant put the shoes on, he slipped his feet into them, unlacing them only "a very, very little bit," confirming the podiatrist's personal observation that when a shoe has been molded to a foot, the foot slides easily in and out of it. He observed that the defendant was flatfooted and that the shape of his heel was consistent with that condition. Furthermore, he felt the protruberances on the defendant's toes and the molding of the shoe around them. On the basis of these observations, Rinaldi concluded, with reasonable podiatric certainty, that the sneakers had been worn by and belonged to the defendant.

On cross-examination, Rinaldi conceded that there is no science, within the profession of podiatry, of matching sneakers to people, that he had never before testified in court on the subject, that he had never performed any blind studies or conducted research in the area, and that if given several pairs of sneakers, he could not definitely match them with their owners. Furthermore, he testified that the features of the defendant's feet from which he drew his conclusions are very common.

The fact that there is no science of matching shoes to people or that Rinaldi was not qualified as an expert practitioner in that narrow field forms no barrier to the admissibility of his testimony. We consider this case one in which the established techniques in Rinaldi's uncontested area of expertise have been applied to the solution of a novel problem that is well within the capability of those techniques.

We conclude that the admissibility of Rinaldi's testimony did not depend on general acceptance of his theories in the scientific community. His conclusions relied on no advanced technology, nor did he employ scientifically sophisticated methods, the understanding of which lies beyond the intellectual powers of the ordinary layperson. The jury was not required to accept blindly the merit of his conclusions or methods. It had before it the same sneakers which had been examined by the podiatrist and, during the course of the trial, had seen the defendant try them on and walk in them. The value of Rinaldi's expertise lay in its assistance to the jury in viewing and evaluating the

---

[7] [n.6] Rinaldi explained that a Brannick device measures the length and width of the foot and is considered by the shoe industry to provide the most accurate measurement of the foot.

evidence. Cross-examination exposed the jury to the lack of literature pertaining to matching shoes to feet, and to the absence of studies or research in this area by Rinaldi or others. His credentials and methodology were before the jurors, who were competent to assess the reliability of the evidence and who could freely accept or reject his conclusions. We hold, therefore, that the trial court did not abuse its discretion in admitting Rinaldi's testimony.

There is no error.

NOTES

1. *Scientific Theories and Methodologies That are Not Generally Subjected to the* Frye *Standard.*

(A) The Application of Established Techniques to Solve a Novel Problem, Verifiable Data, and Physical Comparisons. The *Hasan* court considered the methodology employed by the podiatrist, Rinaldi, to be exempt from scrutiny under *Frye* because, "established techniques in Rinaldi's uncontested area of expertise have been applied to the solution of a novel problem. . . ." *Hasan, supra,* 534 A.2d at 881. Many courts do not apply the *Frye* test when an expert bases his or her conclusions on a *new application or use* of an existing, generally accepted scientific technique. This is particularly true when the jury is shown the data the expert relied upon in arriving at his or her conclusion, or when the opinion is based on a physical comparison that is shown to the jury. As noted in *Hasan,* such cases often involve an expert who compares bitemarks, shoe impressions, or footprints. *Frye* is not considered necessary for two reasons. First, the measuring devices and other instruments used to make the comparisons are already generally accepted. Second, when jurors can see and independently verify the accuracy of the expert's conclusions, there is little danger of the jurors being misled.

People v. Marx, 126 Cal. Rptr. 350 (Cal. App. 1975), a bitemark case, illustrates this concept. In *Marx,* the California Court of Appeal was asked to apply the *Frye* test to a procedure in which experts compared casts of teeth marks, taken from the nose of a murder victim, to casts of the defendant's teeth. *Id.* at 352. Bitemark experts concluded that the bitemarks on the victim's nose were made by the defendant's teeth. The jury was shown photos of the bitemarks on the deceased's nose and the cast that was made of the defendant's teeth. Comparing teeth to dental records and X-rays was (and is) an accepted way of identifying a person. Identifying a person from bitemarks left by teeth in a crime victim's flesh was, however, new to the California courts at the time of *Marx.* *Id.* at 353–55. Nonetheless, the California Court of Appeal declined to apply *Frye* and admitted the expert opinion, reasoning that the concerns that dictate the use of *Frye* were not present. The court stated:

> What is significantly different about the evidence in this case is this: the trier of fact . . . was shown models, photographs, X-rays, and dozens of slides of the victim's wounds and defendant's teeth. It could see what we have seen in reviewing the exhibits. . . . First . . . the extent to which the appearance of the wounds changed between the time that the autopsy was performed and time the body was exhumed. . . . Second, the extent to which the purported bite marks appear to conform generally to obvious irregularities in defendant's teeth. Thus the basic data on which the experts based their conclusions were verifiable by the [trier of fact]. Further, in making their painstaking comparisons and reaching their conclusions, the experts did not rely on untested

methods, unproven hypotheses, intuition or revelation. Rather they applied scientifically and professionally established techniques — X-rays, models, microscopy, photography — to the solution of a particular problem which, though novel, was well within the capability of those techniques. In short, . . . [the trier of fact] did not have to sacrifice its independence and common sense in evaluating [the evidence].

People v. Marx, 126 Cal. Rptr. 350, 356 (Cal. App. 1975). *See also People v. Webb*, 862 P.2d 779, 798 (Cal. 1993) (*Kelly/Frye* does not apply to fingerprint evidence produced by new chemical and laser process because the process merely isolated physical evidence whose existence, appearance, nature, and meaning are obvious to the senses of a layperson); *People v. Clark*, 857 P.2d 1099, 1142 (Cal. 1993) (*Kelly/Frye* does not apply to blood spatter evidence because "methods employed are *not* new to [science] or the law, and they carry no misleading aura of scientific infallibility. . . . Rather it is a matter of common knowledge, readily understood by the jury, that blood will be expelled from the human body if it is hit with sufficient force" and that inferences can be drawn based upon where it lands); *Bundy v. State*, 455 So. 2d 330, 348–49 (Fla. 1984) (bitemark comparison differs from other scientific techniques; with bitemarks the jury is able to make comparison for itself and need not totally rely on scientific interpretation).

(B) Expert Personal Opinion Based Upon Experience and Observation. The *Stoll* court noted that the *Frye* test does not apply when an expert's "personal opinion" is based upon the expert's training and experience, and not the application of a scientific procedure. The two excerpts below explain when an expert's opinion might be considered as being based purely upon experience and observation. First, in *State v. Roscoe*, 700 P.2d 1312 (Ariz. 1984), the Arizona Supreme Court discussed whether the opinion of a dog handler named Preston — concerning the ability of his tracking dog to identify scent — was subject to *Frye*.

> The evidence here was not bottomed on any scientific theory. In fact, it appears that no one knows exactly how or why some dogs are able to track or scent, or the degree to which they are able to do so. No attempt was made to impress the jury with the infallibility of some general scientific technique or theory. Rather, this evidence was offered on the basis that it is common knowledge that some dogs, when properly trained and handled, can discriminate between human odors. Preston's testimony was premised upon this simple idea and was not offered as a product of the application of some accepted scientific process, principle, technique or device. It was offered as *Preston's opinion* of the meaning of his dog's reaction; that opinion was based upon *Preston's* training of and experience with the dog. The weight of the evidence did not hinge upon the validity or accuracy of some scientific principle; rather, it hinged on Preston's credibility, the accuracy of his past observation of the dog's performance, the extent of the training he had given the dog, and the reliability of his interpretations of the dog's reactions. It was not the theories of Newton, Einstein or Freud which gave the evidence weight; if so, the *Frye* test should have been applied. It was, rather, Preston's knowledge, experience and integrity which would give the evidence weight and it was Preston who was available for cross-examination. His credentials, his experience, his motives and his integrity were effectively probed and tested. Determination of these issues does not depend on science; it is the exclusive province of the jury.

Roscoe, supra, 700 P.2d at 1319–20.

Second, in *Hadden v. State*, 690 So.2d 573 (Fla. 1997), the Florida Supreme Court explained how a opinion from a mental health counselor diagnosing a child as suffering "child sexual abuse accommodation syndrome" differed from pure opinion testimony, for purposes of determining whether or not to apply the *Frye* test.

> [T]he *Frye* standard for admissibility of scientific evidence is not applicable to an expert's *pure opinion testimony which is based solely on the expert's training and experience*. While an expert's pure opinion testimony comes cloaked with the expert's credibility, the jury can evaluate this testimony in the same way that it evaluates other opinion or factual testimony. When determining the admissibility of this kind of expert-opinion testimony which is personally developed through clinical experience, the trial court must determine admissibility on the qualifications of the expert and the applicable provisions of the evidence code. We differentiate pure opinion testimony from profile and syndrome evidence because profile and syndrome evidence rely on conclusions based on studies and tests.

Hadden, supra, 690 So. 2d at 578–79.

(C) Expert Medical Opinion. Courts generally do not apply *Frye* to expert medical opinions, including those given by a psychiatrist, on "traditional" issues such cause of an injury or a person's sanity or state of mind. As a general proposition, such opinions are not considered "new" to either science or the law, and so long as the opinion is based, primarily, on the expert's training and experience, admissibility is not controversial. *See Wilson v. Phillips*, 86 Cal. Rptr. 2d 204, 208 (Cal. App. 1999) (expert medical opinion, unlike scientific evidence, does not require proof of reliability by way of general acceptance.). *Logerquist v. McVey*, 1 P.3d 113, 123 (Ariz. 2000) ("*Frye* is inapplicable when a qualified witness offers relevant testimony or conclusions based on experience and observation about human behavior for the purpose of explaining that behavior. . . . This does *not* mean, as the dissenters argue, that we believe the practice of medicine, including psychiatry, is not based on science. Rather it means that expert evidence based on a qualified witness' own experience, observation, and study is treated differently from opinion evidence based on novel scientific principles advanced by others. As in the past, *Frye* continues to apply only to the latter.").

2. Scientific Theories and Methodologies Generally Subjected to the Frye Standard.

(A) Devices and Procedures That Manipulate Physical Evidence. The *Stoll* case provides a concrete example of when an expert's opinion might mislead or "blindside" the jury. If the expert's opinion testimony is based upon the results of testing that was conducted on a "machine or procedure which analyze[s] physical data," *Frye* will apply. *Stoll, supra*, 783 P.2d at 710. In *People v. McDonald* the California Supreme Court explained why the *Frye* test would apply to such evidence by contrasting it with expert opinion based upon the expert's own observations and personal experience.

> . . . It is important to distinguish . . . between expert testimony and scientific evidence. When a witness gives his personal opinion on the stand — even if he qualifies as an expert — the jurors may temper their acceptance of his testimony with a healthy skepticism born of their knowledge that all human beings are fallible. But the opposite may be true when the evidence is produced by a machine: like many laypersons, jurors tend to ascribe an inordinately high degree of certainty to proof derived from an apparently "scientific" mechanism, instrument or procedure. Yet the aura of infallibility that often surrounds such

evidence may well conceal the fact that it remains experimental and tentative. For this reason, courts have invoked the *Kelly/Frye* rule primarily in cases involving novel devices or processes such as lie detectors, "truth serum," Nalline testing, experimental systems of blood typing, "voiceprints," identification by human bite marks, microscopic analysis of gunshot residue, and hypnosis. . . .

People v. McDonald, 690 P.2d 709, 723–24 (Cal. 1984). *See also, People v. Hampton*, 746 P.2d 947, 950–51 (Colo. 1987) (emphasis added) (*Frye* should be applied to "novel scientific *devices and processes involving the manipulation of physical evidence* including lie detectors, experimental systems of blood typing, voiceprints, identification of human bite marks, and microscopic analysis of gunshot residue.").

(B) Social Science Research Used as a Basis for Diagnosing a Profile or Syndrome. When an expert's opinion is based upon research conducted in the social sciences, some courts distinguish between whether the expert is using such research as a basis for a diagnosis, or merely to explain unusual behavior. As a general proposition, these courts hold that the *Frye* standard governs admissibility when such research is used as a basis for testimony *diagnosing* a person as fitting a particular "profile" or as having a particular "syndrome," but *Frye* does not apply to opinions that use such research to explain why a person behaved a certain way. *See, e.g., State v. MacLennan*, 702 N.W.2d 219, 234 (Minn. 2005) (*Frye* standard does not govern the admissibility of expert testimony explaining the phenomenon of the battered child syndrome; expert may not, however, testify that defendant suffers from the syndrome); *Logerquist v. McVey*, 1 P.3d 113, 123 (Ariz. 2000) (*Frye* not applicable to expert testimony on repressed memory; "To put it simply, *Frye* is inapplicable when a qualified witness offers relevant testimony or conclusions based upon experiences and observations about human behavior for the purpose of explaining that behavior."); *Hadden v. State*, 690 So. 2d 573, 575 (Fla. 1997) (*Frye* test applies to expert opinion that child has symptoms consistent with child sexual abuse accommodation syndrome because the opinion is based on diagnostic standards). Some courts, however, have applied *Frye* to expert opinions derived from social science research without addressing whether the research is being used as the basis for a diagnosis or to explain behavior. *See State v. Baby*, 946 A.2d 463, 493 (Md. 2008) (rape trauma syndrome evidence must satisfy *Frye* standard); *State v. Janes*, 850 P.2d 495, 501–03 (Wash. 1993) (child abuse syndrome testimony satisfies *Frye* standard).

QUESTIONS

1. If the *Frye* test is applied to the expert testimony of Dr. Rinaldi, what are the chances of the testimony satisfying *Frye*?

2. What three categories of expert testimony does *Hasan* describe as not being subject to a *Frye* hearing? Why are these three categories of expert testimony exempt from *Frye*?

3. If *Frye* does not apply, what is the standard or test for the admissibility of expert opinion testimony? Put another way, if the trial court in the *Hasan* case felt that Dr. Rinaldi's testimony should not be admitted, what would be the basis for such a ruling? Would the ruling likely be upheld on appeal?

4. Think back to the "narrow common sense purpose" of *Frye* (as articulated in the *Stoll* case) "to protect the jury from techniques which . . . convey a misleading aura of certainty." Given *Frye's* purpose, was the court correct in *Hasan* in concluding that

Frye should not be applied to Dr. Rinaldi's testimony? Why or why not?

5. Recall the voiceprint technique discussed in *People v. Kelly*. Should the voiceprint technique be required to meet the *Frye* test for admissibility? What arguments could you make that *Frye* does, or, does not, apply to the voiceprint technique?

PROBLEMS

Problem 2-5. The body of Ellen Sherman was found at 1:00 p.m. on Sunday, August 4, 2000. She had been strangled in her bedroom. The bedroom was locked and the air conditioner was running. The next-door neighbor who found Ellen Sherman's body commented to police that the room felt "noticeably cold" and "very cold, like a refrigerator," from the running of the air conditioner. The victim's husband was out of town when the body was discovered. He was on a sailing trip with four friends and could account for every minute of his time from 6:00 p.m. Friday evening, August 2, until the time the body was found at 1:00 p.m. on, Sunday, August 4th — a 43-hour period.

The state medical examiner was not at the crime scene, but did examine the body during the autopsy of Ellen Sherman conducted at the morgue that Sunday evening (August 4, 2000). The medical examiner initially determined that Mrs. Sherman died between 24 and 36 hours prior to her body being discovered (early Saturday morning). Her estimate was based upon the degree of rigidity observed in Mrs. Sherman's body (rigidity was just beginning to subside during the autopsy) and the accepted fact (taught in forensic pathology classes) that under average room temperatures (68–70 degrees) rigidity is fully developed 12 hours after death and persists for another 12 to 24 hours before beginning to subside. This original estimate as to the time of death provided Mrs. Sherman's husband a complete alibi.

The next day, after being informed that the temperature of the bedroom where the body was discovered was "very cold, like a refrigerator," the medical examiner revised her estimation of the time of death and concluded that Mrs. Sherman had died between 48 and 96 hours prior to her body being discovered — making it possible for Mr. Sherman to have murdered his wife *before* he left on his fishing trip.

After the medical examiner revised her estimation as to the time of death, Ellen Sherman's husband was charged with murder. Mr. Sherman filed a motion in limine to challenge the admissibility of the medical examiner's second opinion as to the time of death. The defendant, Mr. Sherman, contended that the medical examiner's opinion was not admissible unless it satisfied *Frye*; the state contended that the medical examiner's opinion was admissible and that *Frye* did not apply.

Before trial a hearing was held to determine whether the medical examiner's opinion should be subjected to *Frye*. At this hearing, the medical examiner testified that both of her opinions as to time of death were based on the degree of rigidity observed in the body during autopsy. She explained that she changed her estimate as to the time of death after learning that the room was "very cold" based upon her application of the generally accepted principle that colder temperatures slow the rate of rigidity. Under cross-examination she admitted that while it is an understood fact in the field of forensic pathology that colder temperatures retard the rate of rigidity, there is no established scale (such as exists for the rate of rigidity at normal room temperatures) for just how much coldness slows the onset of rigidity. Consequently, she developed her own hypothesis as to how the cold bedroom effected the onset of rigidity in this case. Based on the generally accepted principle that colder temperatures slow the rate of rigidity, her personal observations of the rate of rigidity of bodies stored in her morgue refrigerator, her assumption that "very cold, like a refrigerator" meant between 40 and 45 degrees, and her general expertise she arrived at the second estimated time of death in this case.

(A) Should the court conduct a *Frye* hearing to determine if the medical examiner's opinion is generally accepted? Why or why not? *See State v. Sherman*, 662 A.2d 767, 785–88 (Conn. App. 1995).

(B) Assume that the trial court decides that a *Frye* hearing is not necessary on these facts. Is the expert's testimony admissible?

[b]   The *Daubert* Test: Reliability and Relevancy

Although the *Frye* test was widely adopted (and remains the standard in several states), it has not escaped criticism. Opponents point out that the test is inconsistently applied because of uncertainty over what is, and is not, "new science." Critics also contend that the *Frye* standard is difficult to apply because of uncertainty over what degree of acceptance constitutes "general" acceptance, and how to determine in which scientific field a principle belongs. *See generally* Paul C. Giannelli, *The Admissibility of Novel Scientific Evidence:* Frye v. United States, *A Half Century Later*, 80 Colum. L. Rev. 1197, 1208–23 (1987); 1 Scientific Evidence § 1.06[f], at 30–32 (4th ed. 2007).

Even if the *Frye* test were consistently and easily applied, criticism has been directed at the *wisdom* of a test that requires "general acceptance" as a precondition for the admission of evidence based upon a new scientific principle or technique. Critics assert that *Frye's* conservative nature and singular focus on general acceptance precludes admission of reliable, but new, scientific evidence. They point out that it takes considerable time for a new technique to become known and reviewed by a scientific community, and the *Frye* test — by design — excludes new scientific evidence during this period of peer review. *See, e.g., Coppolino v. State*, 223 So. 2d 68, 75 (Fla. Dist. Ct. App. 1969) (Mann, J. concurring) ("Society need not tolerate homicide until there develops a body of medical literature about some lethal agent"). Further exacerbating this concern is the fear that *Frye* may retard the admission of reliable evidence even if no one in the scientific community has raised an objection to a technique's validity; *Frye* requires scientific *acceptance*, not scientific ambivalence.

The primary alternative to the *Frye* test is the reliability test adopted by the United States Supreme Court in *Daubert v. Merrell Dow Pharmaceuticals, Inc.*, 509 U.S. 579 (1993). The "*Daubert* test" imposes a "gatekeeper" duty on the trial court. That is, the trial court is required to make an independent determination as to whether scientific evidence is both *reliable* and relevant. The *Daubert* test used in federal courts today incorporates the holdings of three Supreme Court opinions. The three opinions, collectively, are referred to as the "*Daubert* trilogy." Although all cases in the *Daubert* trilogy are civil cases, the test they define clearly applies in criminal cases. Nonetheless, whether the *Daubert* test is applied with the same rigor in criminal cases has been the subject of some debate. The application of the *Daubert* test in criminal cases is examined in the next section.

DAUBERT v. MERRELL DOW PHARMACEUTICALS, INC.
509 U.S. 579 (1993)

JUSTICE BLACKMUN delivered the opinion of the Court.

In this case we are called upon to determine the standard for admitting expert scientific testimony in a federal trial.

I.

Petitioners Jason Daubert and Eric Schuller are minor children born with serious birth defects. They and their parents sued respondent in California state court, alleging that the birth defects had been caused by the mothers' ingestion of Bendectin, a prescription anti-nausea drug marketed by respondent. Respondent removed the suits to federal court on diversity grounds.

After extensive discovery, respondent moved for summary judgment, contending that Bendectin does not cause birth defects in humans and that petitioners would be unable to come forward with any admissible evidence that it does. In support of its motion, respondent submitted an affidavit of Steven H. Lamm, physician and epidemiologist, who is a well-credentialed expert on the risks from exposure to various chemical substances. Doctor Lamm stated that he had reviewed all the literature on Bendectin and human birth defects — more than 30 published studies involving over 130,000 patients. No study had found Bendectin to be a human teratogen (*i.e.*, a substance capable of causing malformations in fetuses). On the basis of this review, Doctor Lamm concluded that maternal use of Bendectin during the first trimester of pregnancy has not been shown to be a risk factor for human birth defects.

Petitioners did not (and do not) contest this characterization of the published record regarding Bendectin. Instead, they responded to respondent's motion with the testimony of eight experts of their own, each of whom also possessed impressive credentials. These experts had concluded that Bendectin can cause birth defects. Their conclusions were based upon "in vitro" (test tube) and "in vivo" (live) animal studies that found a link between Bendectin and malformations; pharmacological studies of the chemical structure of Bendectin that purported to show similarities between the structure of the drug and that of other substances known to cause birth defects; and the "reanalysis" of previously published epidemiological (human statistical) studies.

The District Court granted respondent's motion for summary judgment. The court stated that scientific evidence is admissible only if the principle upon which it is based is " 'sufficiently established to have general acceptance in the field to which it belongs.' " The court concluded that petitioners' evidence did not meet this standard. Given the vast body of epidemiological data concerning Bendectin, the court held, expert opinion which is not based on epidemiological evidence is not admissible to establish causation. Thus, the animal-cell studies, live-animal studies, and chemical-structure analyses on which petitioners had relied could not raise by themselves a reasonably disputable jury issue regarding causation. Petitioners' epidemiological analyses, based as they were on recalculations of data in previously published studies that had found no causal link between the drug and birth defects, were ruled to be inadmissible because they had not been published or subjected to peer review.

The United States Court of Appeals for the Ninth Circuit affirmed. Citing *Frye v. United States*, 293 F. 1013, 1014 (1923), the court stated that expert opinion based on a scientific technique is inadmissible unless the technique is "generally accepted" as reliable in the relevant scientific community. The court declared that expert opinion based on a methodology that diverges "significantly from the procedures accepted by recognized authorities in the field . . . cannot be shown to be 'generally accepted as a reliable technique.' "

The court emphasized that other Courts of Appeals considering the risks of Bendectin had refused to admit reanalyses of epidemiological studies that had been neither published nor subjected to peer review. . . . Contending that reanalysis is generally accepted by the scientific community only when it is subjected to verification and scrutiny by others in the field, the Court of Appeals rejected petitioners' reanalyses as "unpublished, not subjected to the normal peer review process and generated solely for use in litigation." The court concluded that petitioners' evidence provided an insufficient foundation to allow admission of expert testimony that Bendectin caused their injuries and, accordingly, that petitioners could not satisfy their burden of proving causation at trial.

We granted certiorari, in light of sharp divisions among the courts regarding the proper standard for the admission of expert testimony.

II.

A.

In the 70 years since its formulation in the *Frye* case, the "general acceptance" test has been the dominant standard for determining admissibility of novel scientific evidence at trial. Although under increasing attack of late, the rule continues to be followed by a majority of courts, including the Ninth Circuit.

. . . .

The merits of the *Frye* test have been much debated, and scholarship on its proper scope and application is legion. Petitioners' primary attack, however, is not on the content but on the continuing authority of the rule. They contend that the *Frye* test was superseded by the adoption of the Federal Rules of Evidence. We agree.

We interpret the legislatively enacted Federal Rules of Evidence as we would any statute. Rule 402 provides the baseline:

> "All relevant evidence is admissible, except as otherwise provided by the Constitution of the United States, by Act of Congress, by these rules, or by other rules prescribed by the Supreme Court pursuant to statutory authority. Evidence which is not relevant is not admissible."

"Relevant evidence" is defined as that which has "any tendency to make the existence of any fact that is of consequence to the determination of the action more probable or less probable than it would be without the evidence." Rule 401. The Rule's basic standard of relevance thus is a liberal one.

. . . .

Here there is a specific Rule that speaks to the contested issue. Rule 702, governing expert testimony, provides:

"If scientific, technical, or other specialized knowledge will assist the trier of fact to understand the evidence or to determine a fact in issue, a witness qualified as an expert by knowledge, skill, experience, training, or education, may testify thereto in the form of an opinion or otherwise."

Nothing in the text of this Rule establishes "general acceptance" as an absolute prerequisite to admissibility. Nor does respondent present any clear indication that Rule 702 or the Rules as a whole were intended to incorporate a "general acceptance" standard. The drafting history makes no mention of *Frye*, and a rigid "general acceptance" requirement would be at odds with the "liberal thrust" of the Federal Rules and their "general approach of relaxing the traditional barriers to 'opinion' testimony." Given the Rules' permissive backdrop and their inclusion of a specific rule on expert testimony that does not mention "general acceptance," the assertion that the Rules somehow assimilated *Frye* is unconvincing. *Frye* made "general acceptance" the exclusive test for admitting expert scientific testimony. That austere standard, absent from and incompatible with the Federal Rules of Evidence, should not be applied in federal trials.

B.

That the *Frye* test was displaced by the Rules of Evidence does not mean, however, that the Rules themselves place no limits on the admissibility of purportedly scientific evidence. Nor is the trial judge disabled from screening such evidence. To the contrary, under the Rules the trial judge must ensure that any and all scientific testimony or evidence admitted is not only relevant, but reliable.

The primary focus of this obligation is Rule 702, which clearly contemplates some degree of regulation of the subjects and theories about which an expert may testify. *"If scientific, technical, or other specialized knowledge will assist the trier of fact* to understand the evidence or to determine a fact in issue" an expert "may testify *thereto."* (Emphasis added.) The subject of an expert's testimony must be "scientific . . . knowledge."[8] [8]

The adjective "scientific" implies a grounding in the methods and procedures of science. Similarly, the word "knowledge" connotes more than subjective belief or unsupported speculation. The term "applies to any body of known facts or to any body of ideas inferred from such facts or accepted as truths on good grounds." Webster's Third New International Dictionary 1252 (1986). Of course, it would be unreasonable to conclude that the subject of scientific testimony must be "known" to a certainty; arguably, there are no certainties in science. But, in order to qualify as "scientific knowledge," an inference or assertion must be derived by the scientific method. Proposed testimony must be supported by appropriate validation — *i.e.,* "good grounds," based on what is known. In short, the requirement that an expert's testimony pertain to "scientific knowledge" establishes a standard of evidentiary reliability.[9] [9]

---

[8] [n.8] Rule 702 also applies to "technical, or other specialized knowledge." Our discussion is limited to the scientific context because that is the nature of the expertise offered here.

[9] [n.9] We note that scientists typically distinguish between "validity" (does the principle support what it purports to show?) and "reliability" (does application of the principle produce consistent results?). Although "the difference between accuracy, validity, and reliability may be such that each is distinct from the other by no more than a hen's kick," our reference here is to evidentiary reliability — that is, trustworthiness. In a case involving scientific evidence, *evidentiary reliability* will be based upon *scientific validity*.

Rule 702 further requires that the evidence or testimony "assist the trier of fact to understand the evidence or to determine a fact in issue." This condition goes primarily to relevance. *See . . . United States v. Downing*, 753 F.2d 1224, 1242 (CA3 1985) ("An additional consideration under Rule 702 — and another aspect of relevancy — is whether expert testimony proffered in the case is sufficiently tied to the facts of the case that it will aid the jury in resolving a factual dispute"). The consideration has been aptly described . . . as one of "fit." "Fit" is not always obvious, and scientific validity for one purpose is not necessarily scientific validity for other, unrelated purposes. The study of the phases of the moon, for example, may provide valid scientific "knowledge" about whether a certain night was dark, and if darkness is a fact in issue, the knowledge will assist the trier of fact. However (absent creditable grounds supporting such a link), evidence that the moon was full on a certain night will not assist the trier of fact in determining whether an individual was unusually likely to have behaved irrationally on that night. Rule 702's "helpfulness" standard requires a valid scientific connection to the pertinent inquiry as a precondition to admissibility.

That these requirements are embodied in Rule 702 is not surprising. Unlike an ordinary witness, see Rule 701, an expert is permitted wide latitude to offer opinions, including those that are not based on first hand knowledge or observation. See Rules 702 and 703. Presumably, this relaxation of the usual requirement of firsthand knowledge . . . is premised on an assumption that the expert's opinion will have a reliable basis in the knowledge and experience of his discipline.

C.

Faced with a proffer of expert scientific testimony, then, the trial judge must determine at the outset, pursuant to Rule 104(a), whether the expert is proposing to testify to (1) scientific knowledge that (2) will assist the trier of fact to understand or determine a fact in issue.[10] [11] This entails a preliminary assessment of whether the reasoning or methodology underlying the testimony is scientifically valid and of whether that reasoning or methodology properly can be applied to the facts in issue. We are confident that federal judges possess the capacity to undertake this review. Many factors will bear on the inquiry, and we do not presume to set out a definitive checklist or test. But some general observations are appropriate.

Ordinarily, a key question to be answered in determining whether a theory or technique is scientific knowledge that will assist the trier of fact will be whether it can be (and has been) tested. "Scientific methodology today is based on generating hypotheses and testing them to see if they can be falsified; indeed, this methodology is what distinguishes science from other fields of human inquiry." Green, [*Expert Witnesses and Sufficiency of Evidence in Litigation: The Legacy of Agent Orange and Bendectin Litigation*, 86 Nw. U. L. Rev. 643,] 645 [(1992)]. See also C. Hempel, Philosophy of Natural Science 49 (1966) ("[T]he statements constituting a scientific explanation must be capable of empirical test"); K. Popper, Conjectures and Refutations: The Growth of Scientific Knowledge 37 (5th ed. 1989) ("[T]he criterion of the scientific status of a theory is its falsifiability, or refutability, or testability").

---

[10] [n.11] Although the *Frye* decision itself focused exclusively on "novel" scientific techniques, we do not read the requirements of Rule 702 to apply specially or exclusively to unconventional evidence. Of course, well-established propositions are less likely to be challenged than those that are novel, and they are more handily defended. Indeed, theories that are so firmly established as to have attained the status of scientific law, such as the laws of thermodynamics, properly are subject to judicial notice under Fed. Rule Evid. 201.

Another pertinent consideration is whether the theory or technique has been subjected to peer review and publication. Publication (which is but one element of peer review) is not a *sine qua non* of admissibility; it does not necessarily correlate with reliability, and in some instances well-grounded but innovative theories will not have been published. Some propositions, moreover, are too particular, too new, or of too limited interest to be published. But submission to the scrutiny of the scientific community is a component of "good science," in part because it increases the likelihood that substantive flaws in methodology will be detected. The fact of publication (or lack thereof) in a peer-reviewed journal thus will be a relevant, though not dispositive, consideration in assessing the scientific validity of a particular technique or methodology on which an opinion is premised.

Additionally, in the case of a particular scientific technique, the court ordinarily should consider the known or potential rate of error, see, *e.g.*, *United States v. Smith*, 869 F.2d 348, 353–354 (CA7 1989) (surveying studies of the error rate of spectrographic voice identification technique), and the existence and maintenance of standards controlling the technique's operation, see *United States v. Williams*, 583 F.2d 1194, 1198 (CA2 1978) (noting professional organization's standard governing spectrographic analysis).

Finally, "general acceptance" can yet have a bearing on the inquiry. A "reliability assessment does not require, although it does permit, explicit identification of a relevant scientific community and an express determination of a particular degree of acceptance within that community." *United States v. Downing*, 753 F.2d, at 1238. Widespread acceptance can be an important factor in ruling particular evidence admissible, and "a known technique that has been able to attract only minimal support within the community," *Downing*, 753 F.2d at 1238, may properly be viewed with skepticism.

The inquiry envisioned by Rule 702 is, we emphasize, a flexible one.[11] [12] Its overarching subject is the scientific validity — and thus the evidentiary relevance and reliability — of the principles that underlie a proposed submission. The focus, of course, must be solely on principles and methodology, not on the conclusions that they generate.

Throughout, a judge assessing a proffer of expert scientific testimony under Rule 702 should also be mindful of other applicable rules. Rule 703 provides that expert opinions based on otherwise inadmissible hearsay are to be admitted only if the facts or data are "of a type reasonably relied upon by experts in the particular field in forming opinions or inferences upon the subject." Rule 706 allows the court at its discretion to procure the assistance of an expert of its own choosing. Finally, Rule 403 permits the exclusion of relevant evidence "if its probative value is substantially outweighed by the danger of unfair prejudice, confusion of the issues, or misleading the jury. . . ." Judge Weinstein has explained: "Expert evidence can be both powerful and quite misleading because of the difficulty in evaluating it. Because of this risk, the judge in weighing possible prejudice against probative force under Rule 403 of the present rules exercises more control over experts than over lay witnesses."

---

[11] [n.12] A number of authorities have presented variations on the reliability approach, each with its own slightly different set of factors. To the extent that they focus on the reliability of evidence as ensured by the scientific validity of its underlying principles, all these versions may well have merit, although we express no opinion regarding any of their particular details.

III.

We conclude by briefly addressing what appear to be two underlying concerns of the parties and *amici* in this case. Respondent expresses apprehension that abandonment of "general acceptance" as the exclusive requirement for admission will result in a "free-for-all" in which befuddled juries are confounded by absurd and irrational pseudoscientific assertions. In this regard respondent seems to us to be overly pessimistic about the capabilities of the jury, and of the adversary system generally. Vigorous cross-examination, presentation of contrary evidence, and careful instruction on the burden of proof are the traditional and appropriate means of attacking shaky but admissible evidence. Additionally, in the event the trial court concludes that the scintilla of evidence presented supporting a position is insufficient to allow a reasonable juror to conclude that the position more likely than not is true, the court remains free to direct a judgment, and likewise to grant summary judgment. These conventional devices, rather than wholesale exclusion under an uncompromising "general acceptance" test, are the appropriate safeguards where the basis of scientific testimony meets the standards of Rule 702.

Petitioners and, to a greater extent, their *amici* exhibit a different concern. They suggest that recognition of a screening role for the judge that allows for the exclusion of "invalid" evidence will sanction a stifling and repressive scientific orthodoxy and will be inimical to the search for truth. It is true that open debate is an essential part of both legal and scientific analyses. Yet there are important differences between the quest for truth in the courtroom and the quest for truth in the laboratory. Scientific conclusions are subject to perpetual revision. Law, on the other hand, must resolve disputes finally and quickly. The scientific project is advanced by broad and wide-ranging consideration of a multitude of hypotheses, for those that are incorrect will eventually be shown to be so, and that in itself is an advance. Conjectures that are probably wrong are of little use, however, in the project of reaching a quick, final, and binding legal judgment — often of great consequence — about a particular set of events in the past. We recognize that in practice, a gatekeeping role for the judge, no matter how flexible, inevitably on occasion will prevent the jury from learning of authentic insights and innovations. That, nevertheless, is the balance that is struck by Rules of Evidence designed not for the exhaustive search for cosmic understanding but for the particularized resolution of legal disputes.

IV.

To summarize: "general acceptance" is not a necessary precondition to the admissibility of scientific evidence under the Federal Rules of Evidence, but the Rules of Evidence — especially Rule 702 — do assign to the trial judge the task of ensuring that an expert's testimony both rests on a reliable foundation and is relevant to the task at hand. Pertinent evidence based on scientifically valid principles will satisfy those demands.

The inquiries of the District Court and the Court of Appeals focused almost exclusively on "general acceptance," as gauged by publication and the decisions of other courts. Accordingly, the judgment of the Court of Appeals is vacated and the case is remanded for further proceedings consistent with this opinion.

It is so ordered.

CHIEF JUSTICE REHNQUIST, with whom JUSTICE STEVENS joins, concurring in part and dissenting in part.

The petition for certiorari in this case presents two questions: first, whether the rule of *Frye v. United States*, 293 F. 1013 (1923), remains good law after the enactment of the Federal Rules of Evidence; and second, if *Frye* remains valid, whether it requires expert scientific testimony to have been subjected to a peer review process in order to be admissible. The Court concludes, correctly in my view, that the *Frye* rule did not survive the enactment of the Federal Rules of Evidence, and I therefore join Parts I and II-A of its opinion. The second question presented in the petition for certiorari necessarily is mooted by this holding, but the Court nonetheless proceeds to construe Rules 702 and 703 very much in the abstract, and then offers some "general observations."

. . . .

[E]ven if it were desirable to make "general observations" not necessary to decide the questions presented, I cannot subscribe to some of the observations made by the Court. In Part II-B, the Court concludes that reliability and relevancy are the touchstones of the admissibility of expert testimony. Federal Rule of Evidence 402 provides, as the Court points out, that "[e]vidence which is not relevant is not admissible." But there is no similar reference in the Rule to "reliability." The Court constructs its argument by parsing the language "[i]f scientific, technical, or other specialized knowledge will assist the trier of fact to understand the evidence or to determine a fact in issue, . . . an expert . . . may testify thereto. . . ." Fed.Rule Evid. 702. It stresses that the subject of the expert's testimony must be "scientific . . . knowledge," and points out that "scientific" "implies a grounding in the methods and procedures of science" and that the word "knowledge" "connotes more than subjective belief or unsupported speculation." From this it concludes that "scientific knowledge" must be "derived by the scientific method." Proposed testimony, we are told, must be supported by "appropriate validation." Indeed, in footnote 9, the Court decides that "[i]n a case involving scientific evidence, *evidentiary reliability* will be based upon *scientific validity*." (emphasis in original).

Questions arise simply from reading this part of the Court's opinion, and countless more questions will surely arise when hundreds of district judges try to apply its teaching to particular offers of expert testimony. Does all of this *dicta* apply to an expert seeking to testify on the basis of "technical or other specialized knowledge" — the other types of expert knowledge to which Rule 702 applies — or are the "general observations" limited only to "scientific knowledge"? What is the difference between scientific knowledge and technical knowledge; does Rule 702 actually contemplate that the phrase "scientific, technical, or other specialized knowledge" be broken down into numerous subspecies of expertise, or did its authors simply pick general descriptive language covering the sort of expert testimony which courts have customarily received? The Court speaks of its confidence that federal judges can make a "preliminary assessment of whether the reasoning or methodology underlying the testimony is scientifically valid and of whether that reasoning or methodology properly can be applied to the facts in issue." The Court then states that a "key question" to be answered in deciding whether something is "scientific knowledge" "will be whether it can be (and has been) tested." Following this sentence are three quotations from treatises, which not only speak of empirical testing, but one of which states that the " 'criterion of the scientific status of a theory is its falsifiability, or refutability, or testability.' "

I defer to no one in my confidence in federal judges; but I am at a loss to know what is meant when it is said that the scientific status of a theory depends on its "falsifiability," and I suspect some of them will be, too.

I do not doubt that Rule 702 confides to the judge some gatekeeping responsibility in deciding questions of the admissibility of proffered expert testimony. But I do not think it imposes on them either the obligation or the authority to become amateur scientists in order to perform that role. I think the Court would be far better advised in this case to decide only the questions presented, and to leave the further development of this important area of the law to future cases.

NOTES

1. *The "Relevancy Plus Reliability" Test Compared to the "General Acceptance" Test.* The *Frye* and *Daubert* tests are both concerned with reliability. *Frye* looks solely to "general acceptance" among scientists in the pertinent scientific community to ensure reliability. On this point, as compared to *Frye*, the significance of *Daubert's* approach is that *Daubert* requires the *trial court* — not scientists — to determine whether a scientific principle is scientifically valid (and thus has evidentiary reliability), and permits scientific validity to be demonstrated by a variety of factors that may, or may not, include general acceptance within the scientific community.

2. *The Relevance or "Fit" Requirement.* In *Daubert* the United States Supreme Court construed Rule 702's requirement that evidence must "assist the trier of fact to understand the evidence or to determine a fact in issue" to be, primarily, a relevance requirement. The Court borrowed the term "fit" from the Third Circuit's opinion in *United States v. Downing*, 753 F.2d 1224, 1242 (3d Cir. 1985).

In *Downing* the Third Circuit considered the admissibility of expert testimony on the fallibility of eyewitness identifications. Researchers had found impaired accuracy in identifications that were cross-racial and stressful (among others). The Third Circuit stated that in the absence of a detailed offer of proof establishing that *in the case before the court* the eyewitness identifications were cross-racial or made under stressful conditions, expert opinion was not tied to the facts of the case and did not "fit." *Id.*

The problem of "fit," therefore, appears to be one of establishing that the proffered expert opinion relates to facts or data that exist in the case before the court. *See* Margaret A. Berger, *Evidentiary Framework, in* REFERENCE MANUAL ON SCIENTIFIC EVIDENCE, 37, 47–48 (Federal Judicial Center 1994) ("Even if an expert testifies that Substance X can cause plaintiff's injury, this testimony will not suffice if the plaintiff failed to produce evidence that he or she was exposed to Substance X."). No matter how valid an expert opinion may be in the abstract, it will not assist the trier of fact if it does not "fit" the case before the court. *See* G. Michael Fenner, *The* Daubert *Handbook: The Case, Its Essential Dilemma, and Its Progeny*, 29 CREIGHTON L. REV. 939, 1005 (1996).

3. *Jurisdictions That Follow Daubert or a "Daubert-like" Test.* The United States Supreme Court's rejection of *Frye* and its delineation of the *Daubert* test is, of course, binding upon federal courts. It is not, however, binding upon state courts. Nonetheless, most states have evidence codes modeled on the Federal Rules of Evidence, and a majority of them have adopted the *Daubert* test, or a "reliability" test similar to that discussed in *Daubert.* Some of these states had adopted a relevancy plus reliability standard *prior* to the Court's decision in *Daubert* while others found the *Daubert* reasoning persuasive, and abandoned *Frye* after the Supreme Court's decision in *Daubert.*

States that embrace *Daubert's* relevant and reliable test — or employ a reliability test and "gatekeeping" requirement similar to that described in *Daubert* — include: Alabama, *Turner v. State*, 746 So. 2d 355, 361 & 361 n.7 (Ala. 1998) (Alabama, by statute, uses the *Daubert* test to determine the admissibility of DNA evidence, but uses the *Frye* test for all other scientific subjects); Alaska, *State v. Coon*, 974 P.2d 386, 399 (Alaska 1999) (abandons *Frye* and adopts *Daubert*; *Daubert* standard gives courts "greater flexibility . . . to keep pace with science as it evolves"); Arkansas, *Jones v. State*, 862 S.W.2d 242, 245 (Ark. 1993) (Court indicates it has no criticism of *Daubert* and had reached "the same conclusion" as *Daubert* previously); Colorado, *People v. Shreck*, 22 P.3d 68, 70 (Colo. 2001) (Colorado Rule 702, not *Frye*, governs the admissibility of expert and scientific evidence); Connecticut, *State v. Porter*, 698 A.2d 739, 751 (Conn. 1997) (abandons *Frye* for *Daubert*); Delaware, *Nelson v. State*, 628 A.2d 69, 74 (Del. 1993) (*Daubert* persuasive; scientific evidence must meet standards of rules of evidence, not *Frye*); Hawaii, *State v. Maelega*, 907 P.2d 758, 766 n.11, 767 (Haw. 1995) (Hawaii's Rule 702 incorporates a reliability factor); Idaho, *State v. Parkinson*, 909 P.2d 647, 652 (Idaho App. 1996) (*Daubert* provides guidance in applying state's version of Rule 702 to determine scientific reliability); Indiana, *Steward v. State*, 652 N.E.2d 490, 498 (Ind. 1995) (*Daubert's* concerns coincides with requirements of Indiana Evidence Rule 702(b)); Iowa, *Leaf v. Goodyear Tire & Rubber Co.*, 590 N.W.2d 525, 531–33 (Iowa 1999) (Iowa's Rule 702 consistent with *Daubert*; *Daubert* is not controlling but trial courts may find its considerations helpful); Kentucky, *Mitchell v. Commonwealth*, 908 S.W.2d 100, 101 (Ky. 1995) (Court adopts *Daubert* and abandons *Frye*); Louisiana, *State v. Foret*, 628 So. 2d 1116, 1123 (La. 1993) (adopting *Daubert's* reliability requirement for scientific testimony for Louisiana's Rule 702); Massachusetts, *Commonwealth v. Lanigan*, 641 N.E.2d 1342, 1348–49 (Mass. 1994) (*Daubert's* reasoning persuasive; rejecting general acceptance as the only means for demonstrating reliability); Mississippi, *Mississippi Transp. Comm'n v. McLemore*, 863 So. 2d 31, 39 (Miss. 2003) (Mississippi's Rule 702 recognizes *Daubert*); Montana, *State v. Weeks*, 891 P.2d 477, 489 (Mont. 1995) (cites *Daubert* and states Montana rejected *Frye* in 1983); Nebraska, *Schafersman v. Agland Coop.*, 631 N.W.2d 862, 867 (Neb. 2001) (framework for evaluating expert opinion testimony should be guided by criteria set forth in *Daubert*, not *Frye*); New Hampshire, *State v. Whittey*, 821 A.2d 1086, 1092 (N.H. 2003) (adopting *Daubert* test); New Mexico, *State v. Alberico*, 861 P.2d 192, 202–04 (N.M. 1993) (rejects *Frye* and adopts *Daubert*-like validity factors in applying its version of Rule 702); Ohio, *State v. Nemeth*, 694 N.E.2d 1332, 1337–39 (Ohio 1998) (rejects *Frye* and uses *Daubert* factors to determine reliability under Ohio's Rule 702); Oklahoma, *Taylor v. State*, 889 P.2d 319, 328 (Okla. Crim. App. 1995) (abandons *Frye* and adopts *Daubert*); Oregon, *State v. O'Key*, 899 P.2d 663, 680 (Or. 1995) (uses *Daubert* analysis and finds it instructive); Rhode Island, *DiPetrillo v. Dow Chemical Co.*, 729 A.2d 677, 689 (R.I. 1999) (citing *Daubert* and holds proffering party must prove reliability and relevance of expert scientific evidence); South Carolina, *State v. Council*, 515 S.E.2d 508, 517–18 (S.C. 1999) (Court never adopted *Frye* and does not adopt *Daubert*, however, trial court must determine reliability under state's Rule 702 using factors similar to *Daubert's*); South Dakota, *State v. Schweitzer*, 533 N.W.2d 156, 159 (S.D. 1995) (South Dakota recognized *Daubert* in 1994); Tennessee, *McDaniel v. CSX Transportation, Inc.*, 955 S.W.2d 257, 265 (Tenn. 1997) (*Daubert* not expressly adopted; Tennessee's adoption of Rules 702 and 703 supersedes the *Frye* test and requires trial court to determine reliability; trial court may consider *Daubert* reliability factors); Texas, *E.I. Du Pont de Nemours & Co. v. Robinson*, 923 S.W.2d 549, 556 (Tex. 1995) (under Texas' Rule 702 scientific evidence must be "relevant and reliable"); Vermont, *State v. Streich*, 658 A.2d 38, 46 (Vt. 1995) (Vermont follows *Daubert's* principles in scientific evidence cases);

West Virginia, *Wilt v. Burbacker*, 443 S.E.2d 196, 203 (W.Va. 1993) (*Frye* supplanted by adoption of Rule 702 of West Virginia Rules of Evidence; *Daubert's* analysis of Rule 702 should be followed); Wyoming, *Springfield v. State*, 860 P.2d 435, 442–43 (Wyo. 1993) (citing *Daubert* in holding that Wyoming Rules of Evidence, not *Frye*, govern admissibility and Wyoming's approach parallels *Daubert*). *See generally* David E. Bernstein and Jeffrey D. Jackson, *The* Daubert *Trilogy In The States*, 44 Jurimetrics 351, 356–57. 361–63 (Spring 2004) (by mid-2003, 27 states had adopted a test consistent with *Daubert*, five states found *Daubert* instructive and utilized its factors in interpreting their own test, but only nine states had adopted the full holdings of all three cases in the *Daubert* trilogy); 1 SCIENTIFIC EVIDENCE § 1.14–15, at 79–85 (4th ed. 2007) (listing, respectively, states considered "*Daubert* jurisdictions" and states considered "other reliability test jurisdictions").

4. *States That Have Not Embraced* Daubert. Some states have expressly refused to abandon *Frye* even though their evidence code is modeled on the Federal Rules of Evidence. Several arguments have been advanced to support the proposition that a state's version of the *Frye* test survived the adoption of an evidence code patterned after the Federal Rules of Evidence.

(A) Evidence Rules Judicially Enacted. Recall that the Federal Rules of Evidence are legislatively enacted. Accordingly, as the Court indicated in *Daubert*, the Federal Rules of Evidence are interpreted like any other statute, and congressional intent must be given due deference. Some state evidence codes, however, are judicially enacted. In such jurisdictions a construing court looks at the text of the code and the intent of the enacting *court* in interpreting evidence rules. *See State v. Alt*, 504 N.W.2d 38, 46 (Minn. App. 1993) (Minnesota's rules of evidence were promulgated by the Minnesota Supreme Court, not the legislature, and the Court reserved the common law power to refine evidentiary standards through case law); *Logerquist v. McVey*, 1 P.3d 113, 128 (Ariz. 2000) (Nothing in Arizona's Rule 702, or in the court or committee comments to Rule 702, indicated that a reliability standard was contemplated when Rule 702 was adopted. Given the Rule's text and interpreting cases no such standard can be found.).

(B) Legislative Inaction and Stare Decisis. California confirmed its adherence to the *Frye* standard the year after *Daubert*. In *People v. Leahy*, 882 P.2d 321 (Cal. 1994) the California Supreme Court noted that it had declared *Frye* the test to use for determining the admissibility of scientific evidence in 1976–11 years after California had legislatively enacted an evidence code similar to the Federal Rules of Evidence. Accordingly, the decision to adopt *Frye* was considered compatible with California's evidence code at that time. Having used the *Frye* standard for almost 20 years, the California Supreme Court stated that principle of *stare decisis* supported its decision to stay with *Frye*. *Id.* at 328. Further, since the state legislature had taken no action to abrogate or modify the general acceptance standard since 1976, the Court presumed that there was legislative acquiescence in adhering to the *Frye* standard. *Id.* at 331.

QUESTIONS

1. According to *Daubert*, what two things is a trial court to determine when faced with a proffer of expert scientific testimony?

2. What is "reliable" scientific evidence? That is, what is it a trial court is looking for when presented with a challenge to scientific evidence?

3. The Supreme Court notes that "[m]any factors will bear on the inquiry." Specifically, to what inquiry is the Court referring, and what are the factors (the so-called "*Daubert* factors")?

4. If a scientist pursues proper methodology but reasons to "absurd and irrational pseudoscientific" conclusions, will such conclusions be admitted under *Daubert*? (This question will be reposed after you read the next case in the *Daubert* trilogy, *General Electric Co. v. Joiner*).

On the other hand, if a brilliant scientist fails (or refuses) to use orthodox methodology, but arrives at "authentic insights," will such insights be available to the jury under *Daubert*? *See* Michael H. Gottesman, *Admissibility of Expert Testimony After* Daubert: *The Prestige Factor*, 43 EMORY L.J. 867, 870–72 (Summer 1994); David L. Faigman, Elise Porter & Michael J. Saks, *Check Your Crystal Ball at the Courthouse Door, Please: Exploring the Past, Understanding the Present, and Worrying About the Future of Scientific Evidence*, 15 CARDOZO L. REV. 1799, 1833 (April 1994) [hereinafter, *The Future of Scientific Evidence*].

5. Do forensic techniques that have been admitted by courts for years, like fingerprinting, have to satisfy *Daubert* to be admissible?

6. If only a minority of scientists accept a particular scientific technique as reliable is it still possible for an expert opinion based upon that methodology to be admitted consistent with *Daubert*?

7. Under the *Daubert* test, is a trial court to decide if there is enough evidence for a jury to find the methodology reliable, or is the court to actually make a finding as to the soundness and reliability of a scientist's methodology?

PROBLEM

Problem 2-6. Under *Daubert* the trial court, pursuant to its "gatekeeping" function, not the jury, determines if an expert is testifying about "scientific knowledge," i.e., whether the reasoning or methodology underlying the testimony is scientifically valid. *Daubert, supra*, 509 U.S. at 592–93. The Supreme Court's opinion in *Daubert* is quite clear that the trial court's "focus . . . must be solely on principles and methodology, not on the conclusions that they generate." *Id.* at 595.

Assume that a forensic scientist's conclusions are based upon valid methodology, but the trial court believes that the jury will assign too much weight to the expert's testimony because of the expert's solid methodology and the complexity of the scientific principle at issue. Is there any ruling a court could make — consistent with *Daubert* — to exclude such expert opinion? *See The Future of Scientific Evidence, supra*, at 1833–44; DAVID L. FAIGMAN, MICHAEL J. SAKS, JOSEPH SANDERS & EDWARD K. CHENG, 1 MODERN SCIENTIFIC EVIDENCE: THE LAW AND SCIENCE OF EXPERT TESTIMONY § 1:36, at 108–10 (2008).

[i]   *Daubert* Refined — The *Joiner* Case: Examining Expert Conclusions, And Establishing "Abuse of Discretion" as the Standard of Review

Like *Frye* 70 years before, *Daubert* left questions unanswered. If the focus must be "*solely* on principles and methodology," does that mean a trial court should ignore *altogether* the expert's conclusions? If "[m]any factors will bear on the [reliability] inquiry," what are these other factors? Does the *Daubert* test apply to nonscientific experts, or — as with *Frye* — are opinions by nonscientific experts excluded from scrutiny?

Beyond this, serious questions were raised concerning the ability of trial courts to determine the "scientific validity." Recall Justice Rehnquist's dissenting opinion in *Daubert* in which he wrote that he was at a loss to know what the majority meant when it said the "scientific status of a theory depends on its 'falsifiability,' " and that he did not think a trial court should have to become an "amateur scientist" in order to carry out their gatekeeping responsibilities. *Daubert, supra,* 509 U.S. at 600–01 (Rehnquist, C.J. concurring in part, and dissenting in part). The Ninth Circuit in its opinion in *Daubert II* (the *Daubert* case on remand from the Supreme Court), expressed similar concerns.

A. *Brave New World*

Federal judges ruling on the admissibility of expert scientific testimony face a far more complex and daunting task in a post-*Daubert* world than before. . . .

[T]hough we are largely untrained in science and certainly no match for any of the witnesses whose testimony we are reviewing, it is our responsibility to determine whether those experts' proposed testimony amounts to "scientific knowledge," constitutes "good science," and was "derived by the scientific method. . . ."

Our responsibility, . . . unless we badly misread the Supreme Court's opinion, is to resolve disputes among respected, well-credentialed scientists about matters squarely within their expertise, in areas where there is no scientific consensus as to what is and what is not "good science," and occasionally to reject such expert testimony because it was not "derived by the scientific method." Mindful of our position in the hierarchy of the federal judiciary, we take a deep breath and proceed with this heady task.

Daubert v. Merrell Dow Pharmaceuticals, Inc., 43 F.3d 1311, 1315–16 (9th Cir. 1995). *See also* Barry C. Scheck, *DNA and Daubert,* 15 Cardozo L. Rev. 1959, 1961 (1994) ("*Daubert* could easily degenerate into a . . . superficial four-factor exercise in labeling where courts . . . resolve complicated scientific disputes between experts as matters of weight, not admissibility, . . . because it is too difficult to 'come to grips' with the science.").

Accordingly, it was clear from the outset that *Daubert* was a work in progress. In the next six years the United States Supreme Court issued two more opinions dealing with the application of the *Daubert* test. In the second case, *General Electric Co. v. Joiner,* 522 U.S. 136 (1997), the Court discussed the applicable standard for appellate review, and restated its view on when a trial court could properly consider an expert's *conclusions* when determining the scientific validity of the principles and methodology underlying scientific evidence. The third case — *Kumho Tire v. Carmichael,* 526 U.S. 137 (1999) — resolved the question of whether *Daubert* applied to nonscientific experts, and set out a procedural framework that made the trial court's gatekeeping obligation a less "complex and daunting task." As noted above, these three cases, *Daubert, Joiner,* and *Kumho Tire,* constitute the "*Daubert* trilogy," and, collectively, define the *Daubert* test used in federal court.

GENERAL ELECTRIC CO. v. JOINER
522 U.S. 136 (1997)

CHIEF JUSTICE REHNQUIST delivered the opinion of the Court.

We granted certiorari in this case to determine what standard an appellate court should apply in reviewing a trial court's decision to admit or exclude expert testimony under *Daubert v. Merrell Dow Pharmaceuticals, Inc.*, 509 U.S. 579 (1993). We hold that abuse of discretion is the appropriate standard. We apply this standard and conclude that the District Court in this case did not abuse its discretion when it excluded certain proffered expert testimony.

I.

Respondent Robert Joiner began work as an electrician in the Water & Light Department of Thomasville, Georgia (City) in 1973. This job required him to work with and around the City's electrical transformers, which used a mineral-based dielectric fluid as a coolant. Joiner often had to stick his hands and arms into the fluid to make repairs. The fluid would sometimes splash onto him, occasionally getting into his eyes and mouth. In 1983 the City discovered that the fluid in some of the transformers was contaminated with polychlorinated biphenyls (PCBs). PCBs are widely considered to be hazardous to human health. Congress, with limited exceptions, banned the production and sale of PCBs in 1978.

Joiner was diagnosed with small cell lung cancer in 1991. He sued petitioners in Georgia state court the following year. . . . Joiner had been a smoker for approximately eight years, his parents had both been smokers, and there was a history of lung cancer in his family. He was thus perhaps already at a heightened risk of developing lung cancer eventually. The suit alleged that his exposure to PCBs "promoted" his cancer; had it not been for his exposure to these substances, his cancer would not have developed for many years, if at all.

Petitioners removed the case to federal court. Once there, they moved for summary judgment. They contended that . . . there was no admissible scientific evidence that PCBs promoted Joiner's cancer. [Joiner] . . . relied largely on the testimony of expert witnesses. In depositions, his experts had testified that PCBs alone can promote cancer. . . .

[The District Court] granted summary judgment for petitioners because . . . the testimony of Joiner's experts had failed to show that there was a link between exposure to PCBs and small cell lung cancer. The court believed that the testimony of respondent's experts to the contrary did not rise above "subjective belief or unsupported speculation." Their testimony was therefore inadmissible.

The Court of Appeals for the Eleventh Circuit reversed. 78 F.3d 524 (1996). It held that "[b]ecause the Federal Rules of Evidence governing expert testimony display a preference for admissibility, we apply a particularly stringent standard of review to the trial judge's exclusion of expert testimony." *Id.* at 529. Applying that standard, the Court of Appeals held that the District Court had erred in excluding the testimony of Joiner's expert witnesses. . . . [I]t excluded the experts' testimony because it "drew different conclusions from the research than did each of the experts." The Court of Appeals opined that a district court should limit its role to determining the "legal reliability of proffered expert testimony, leaving the jury to decide the correctness of competing expert opinions." *Id.* at 533. . . .

We granted petitioners' petition for a writ of certiorari, and we now reverse.

II.

Petitioners challenge the standard applied by the Court of Appeals in reviewing the District Court's decision to exclude respondent's experts' proffered testimony. They argue that that court should have applied traditional "abuse of discretion" review. Respondent agrees that abuse of discretion is the correct standard of review. He contends, however, that the Court of Appeals applied an abuse of discretion standard in this case. As he reads it, the phrase "particularly stringent" announced no new standard of review. It was simply an acknowledgement that an appellate court can and will devote more resources to analyzing district court decisions that are dispositive of the entire litigation. All evidentiary decisions are reviewed under an abuse of discretion standard. He argues, however, that it is perfectly reasonable for appellate courts to give particular attention to those decisions that are outcome-determinative.

. . . .

[W]hile the Federal Rules of Evidence allow district courts to admit a somewhat broader range of scientific testimony than would have been admissible under *Frye*, they leave in place the "gatekeeper" role of the trial judge in screening such evidence. A court of appeals applying "abuse of discretion" review to such rulings may not categorically distinguish between rulings allowing expert testimony and rulings which disallow it. We . . . reject respondent's argument that because the granting of summary judgment in this case was "outcome determinative," it should have been subjected to a more searching standard of review. On a motion for summary judgment, disputed issues of fact are resolved against the moving party — here, petitioners. But the question of admissibility of expert testimony is not such an issue of fact, and is reviewable under the abuse of discretion standard.

We hold that the Court of Appeals erred in its review of the exclusion of Joiner's experts' testimony. In applying an overly "stringent" review to that ruling, it failed to give the trial court the deference that is the hallmark of abuse of discretion review.

III.

We believe that a proper application of the correct standard of review here indicates that the District Court did not abuse its discretion. Joiner's theory of liability was that his exposure to PCBs and their derivatives "promoted" his development of small cell lung cancer. In support of that theory he proffered the deposition testimony of expert witnesses. . . .

Petitioners contended that the statements of Joiner's experts regarding causation were nothing more than speculation. Petitioners criticized the testimony of the experts in that it was "not supported by epidemiological studies . . . [and was] based exclusively on isolated studies of laboratory animals." Joiner responded by claiming that his experts had identified "relevant animal studies which support their opinions." He also directed the court's attention to four epidemiological studies[12] [2] on which his experts had relied.

---

[12] [n.2] Epidemiological studies examine the pattern of disease in human populations.

The District Court agreed with petitioners that the animal studies on which respondent's experts relied did not support his contention that exposure to PCBs had contributed to his cancer. The studies involved infant mice that had developed cancer after being exposed to PCBs. The infant mice in the studies had had massive doses of PCBs injected directly into their peritoneums or stomachs. Joiner was an adult human being whose alleged exposure to PCBs was far less than the exposure in the animal studies. The PCBs were injected into the mice in a highly concentrated form. The fluid with which Joiner had come into contact generally had a much smaller PCB concentration of between 0-500 parts per million. The cancer that these mice developed was alveologenic adenomas; Joiner had developed small-cell carcinomas. No study demonstrated that adult mice developed cancer after being exposed to PCBs. One of the experts admitted that no study had demonstrated that PCBs lead to cancer in any other species.

Respondent failed to reply to this criticism. Rather than explaining how and why the experts could have extrapolated their opinions from these seemingly far-removed animal studies, respondent chose "to proceed as if the only issue [was] whether animal studies can ever be a proper foundation for an expert's opinion." Of course, whether animal studies can ever be a proper foundation for an expert's opinion was not the issue. The issue was whether *these* experts' opinions were sufficiently supported by the animal studies on which they purported to rely. The studies were so dissimilar to the facts presented in this litigation that it was not an abuse of discretion for the District Court to have rejected the experts' reliance on them.

The District Court also concluded that the four epidemiological studies on which respondent relied were not a sufficient basis for the experts' opinions. The first such study involved workers at an Italian capacitor[13] [4] plant who had been exposed to PCBs. The authors noted that lung cancer deaths among ex-employees at the plant were higher than might have been expected, but concluded that "there were apparently no grounds for associating lung cancer deaths (although increased above expectations) and exposure in the plant." Given that [the authors of the Italian study] were unwilling to say that PCB exposure had caused cancer among the workers they examined, their study did not support the experts' conclusion that Joiner's exposure to PCBs caused his cancer.

The second study followed employees who had worked at Monsanto's PCB production plant. The authors of this study found that the incidence of lung cancer deaths among these workers was somewhat higher than would ordinarily be expected. The increase, however, was not statistically significant and the authors of the study did not suggest a link between the increase in lung cancer deaths and the exposure to PCBs.

The third and fourth studies were likewise of no help. The third involved workers at a Norwegian cable manufacturing company who had been exposed to mineral oil. A statistically significant increase in lung cancer deaths had been observed in these workers. The study, however, (1) made no mention of PCBs and (2) was expressly limited to the type of mineral oil involved in that study, and thus did not support these experts' opinions. The fourth and final study involved a PCB-exposed group in Japan that had seen a statistically significant increase in lung cancer deaths. The subjects of this study, however, had been exposed to numerous potential carcinogens, including toxic rice oil that they had ingested.

---

[13] [n.4] A capacitor is an electrical component that stores an electric charge.

Respondent points to *Daubert*'s language that the "focus, of course, must be solely on principles and methodology, not on the conclusions that they generate." 509 U.S. at 595. He claims that because the District Court's disagreement was with the conclusion that the experts drew from the studies, the District Court committed legal error and was properly reversed by the Court of Appeals. But conclusions and methodology are not entirely distinct from one another. Trained experts commonly extrapolate from existing data. But nothing in either *Daubert* or the Federal Rules of Evidence requires a district court to admit opinion evidence which is connected to existing data only by the *ipse dixit* of the expert. A court may conclude that there is simply too great an analytical gap between the data and the opinion proffered. That is what the District Court did here, and we hold that it did not abuse its discretion in so doing.

We hold, therefore, that abuse of discretion is the proper standard by which to review a district court's decision to admit or exclude scientific evidence. We further hold that, because it was within the District Court's discretion to conclude that the studies upon which the experts relied were not sufficient, whether individually or in combination, to support their conclusions that Joiner's exposure to PCBs contributed to his cancer, the District Court did not abuse its discretion in excluding their testimony. . . .

. . . We accordingly reverse the judgment of the Court of Appeals. . . .

It is so ordered

JUSTICE BREYER, concurring.

The Court's opinion, which I join, emphasizes *Daubert*'s statement that a trial judge, acting as "gatekeeper," must " 'ensure that any and all scientific testimony or evidence admitted is not only relevant, but reliable.' " This requirement will sometimes ask judges to make subtle and sophisticated determinations about scientific methodology and its relation to the conclusions an expert witness seeks to offer — particularly when a case arises in an area where the science itself is tentative or uncertain, or where testimony about general risk levels in human beings or animals is offered to prove individual causation. Yet, as *amici* have pointed out, judges are not scientists and do not have the scientific training that can facilitate the making of such decisions.

Of course, neither the difficulty of the task nor any comparative lack of expertise can excuse the judge from exercising the "gatekeeper" duties that the Federal Rules impose — determining, for example, whether particular expert testimony is reliable and "will assist the trier of fact," Fed. Rule Evid. 702, or whether the "probative value" of testimony is substantially outweighed by risks of prejudice, confusion or waste of time. Fed. Rule Evid. 403. To the contrary, when law and science intersect, those duties often must be exercised with special care.

Today's toxic tort case provides an example. The plaintiff in today's case says that a chemical substance caused, or promoted, his lung cancer. His concern, and that of others, about the causes of cancer is understandable, for cancer kills over one in five Americans. Moreover, scientific evidence implicates some chemicals as potential causes of some cancers. Yet modern life, including good health as well as economic well-being, depends upon the use of artificial or manufactured substances, such as chemicals. And it may, therefore, prove particularly important to see that judges fulfill their *Daubert* gatekeeping function, so that they help assure that the powerful engine of tort liability, which can generate strong financial incentives to reduce, or to eliminate, production, points towards the right substances and does not destroy the wrong ones. It is, thus, essential in this science-related area that the courts administer the Federal Rules of Evidence in order to achieve the "ends" that the Rules themselves set forth, not only so that proceedings may be "justly determined," but also so "that the truth may be ascertained." Fed. Rule Evid. 102.

I therefore want specially to note that, as cases presenting significant science-related issues have increased in number, judges have increasingly found in the Rules of Evidence and Civil Procedure ways to help them overcome the inherent difficulty of making determinations about complicated scientific or otherwise technical evidence. Among these techniques are an increased use of Rule 16's pretrial conference authority to narrow the scientific issues in dispute, pretrial hearings where potential experts are subject to examination by the court, and the appointment of special masters and specially trained law clerks.

NOTES AND QUESTIONS

1. *Policy Rationales: Tort Reform.* In *Logerquist v. McVey*, 1 P.3d 113 (Ariz. 2000), the Arizona Supreme Court discussed (and rejected) a rationale for adopting the *Daubert* test, not mentioned in *Daubert* or *Joiner*, that appears to combine *Frye's* concern that a jury might be "blindsided" by expert testimony with concerns over improper jury verdicts in tort cases.

> One of the arguments for adopting *Daubert* is to allow trial judges to put a halt to improper verdicts from jurors misled by junk science and experts ready at the drop of a hat (or a dollar) to say anything for any party. This, of course, is a two-edged sword-plaintiffs' lawyers do not have a monopoly on venal or inaccurate experts. But we do not believe that *Daubert* . . . will provide a good antidote. Implicit in *Joiner* . . . is the assumption that trial judges as a group will be more able than jurors to tell good science from junk, true scientists from charlatans, truthful experts from liars, and venal from objective experts. But most judges, like most jurors, have little or no technical training "and are not known for expertise in science," let alone in the precise discipline involved in a particular case.

Logerquist, supra, 1 P.3d at 129. Is "improper verdicts from jurors misled by junk science" what Justice Breyer was talking about in his concurring opinion in *Joiner*?

2. *The Abuse of Discretion Standard.* The abuse of discretion standard for appellate review is, of course, a deferential standard. In describing this standard to a group of Certified Public Accountants Judge Alex Kozinski of the Ninth Circuit (the judge who authored the Ninth Circuit's opinions in the *Daubert* case) said;

> The Supreme Court made it quite clear the standard we appellate judges use is the abuse of discretion standard, which basically asks, "Would the trial judge have to have been drunk or crazy to make this decision?" If we think a sober person could come to that conclusion, then we have to let it stand.

Alex Kozinski, *Expert Testimony After Daubert*, Journal of Accountancy 59, 60 (July 2000). *See also United States v. Coleman*, 179 F.3d 1056, 1061 (7th Cir. 1999) ("We review the district court's determination for abuse of discretion, noting that '[a]ppellants who challenge evidentiary rulings of the district court are like rich men who wish to enter the Kingdom: their prospects compare with those of camels who wish to pass through the eye of the needle.' ").

3. *Methodology and Conclusions.* The *Daubert* Court stated that in determining the scientific validity of the principles and methodology underlying scientific evidence, "[t]he "focus of course, must be solely on principles and methodology, not on the conclusions that they generate." *Daubert, supra,* 509 U.S. at 595. In *Joiner,* the Court adds the following:

> [C]onclusions and methodology are not entirely distinct from one another. Trained experts commonly extrapolate from existing data. But nothing in either *Daubert* or the Federal Rules of Evidence requires a district court to admit opinion evidence that is connected to existing data only by the *ipse dixit* of the expert. A court may conclude that there is simply too great an analytical gap between the data and the opinion proffered. That is what the District Court did here, and we hold that it did not abuse its discretion in so doing.

Joiner, supra, 522 U.S. at 146. If a scientist uses a scientifically valid procedure or methodology to produce data, and then extrapolates from the data to a conclusion that the trial court believes is an "absurd and irrational pseudoscientific assertion," will such conclusions be admitted under *Daubert/Joiner*? Does *Joiner* represent a change from the way *Daubert* taught that trial courts should view methodology and conclusions? *See In re Paoli R.R. PCB Litigation,* 35 F.3d 717, 746 (3d Cir. 1994) (pre-*Joiner* decision stating, "This distinction [between methodology and conclusions] has only limited practical import. When a judge disagrees with the conclusions of an expert, it will generally be because he or she thinks that there is a mistake at some step in the investigative or reasoning process of that expert.").

4. *Methodology, Conclusions, and the Abuse of Discretion Standard.* How "great" an "analytical gap" was there between the existing data produced by the four epidemiological studies, and the conclusion Joiner's experts drew from that data (that PCB's promoted Joiner's lung cancer)? Note that all four epidemiological studies found increased lung cancer deaths among workers, and in three of the four studies the workers had been exposed to PCBs. Put another way, if the situation in *Joiner* had been reversed (i.e., the district court had *admitted* the testimony of plaintiff's experts, would the district court's decision to *admit* the expert testimony be an abuse of discretion?

Do you agree with the Arizona Supreme Court in *Logerquist* (*see* Note 1 above) that judges as a group are no better equipped than jurors to tell "good science from junk"? If so, how does this impact the ability of the trial court to decide whether an expert's conclusions are, or are not, sufficiently connected to existing data when making a *Daubert* reliability ruling?

PROBLEM

Problem 2-7. Assume that a key issue in a criminal trial is whether hair found at the crime scene belonged to the defendant. Assume also that both prosecution and defense experts examine the hair in question using precisely the same methodology and standards.

(A) If the prosecution expert concludes that the crime scene hair matches the defendant's, but the defense expert concludes that the crime scene hair does not match the defendant, may the trial court, based upon *Joiner,* exclude one of the experts from offering his or her opinion? Put another way, both opinions cannot be correct, and if an opinion is not correct can it be "reliable"? *See Lust v. Merrell Dow Pharmaceuticals, Inc.,* 89 F.3d 594, 598 (9th Cir. 1996).

(B) On the other hand, would it be an abuse of discretion for the trial court to find both opinions "reliable," and to allow both experts to testify? *See* Fed. R. Evid. 702 advisory committee's note to 2000 amendment; *Lust v. Merrell Dow Pharmaceuticals, Inc.*, 89 F.3d 594, 598 (9th Cir. 1996); *Logerquist v. McVey*, 1 P.3d 113, 130 (Ariz. 2000) (under state constitution the jury decides questions of fact by determining credibility of witnesses and weight of conflicting evidence).

[ii]   *Daubert* Refined — The *Kumho Tire* Case: Extending *Daubert* to Nonscientific Expert Testimony, and Granting Trial Courts "Broad Latitude" in Deciding *How* to Determine Reliability

The *Kumho Tire* case is the third case in the "*Daubert* trilogy." Recall that *Daubert* was only concerned with "scientific" expert testimony because scientific testimony was the type of expertise proffered by the parties. After *Daubert*, a split developed within the Circuits over whether the trial judge's gatekeeping obligations extended to nonscientific experts. In *Kumho Tire* the Supreme Court discussed how the *Daubert* test and reliability factors apply to engineers, social scientists, and other nonscientific experts. Beyond this, the Supreme Court used *Kumho Tire* to provide some much needed guidance on *Daubert*-related procedural issues that had been perplexing the lower courts.

KUMHO TIRE COMPANY v. CARMICHAEL
526 U.S.137 (1999)

JUSTICE BREYER delivered the opinion of the Court.

In *Daubert v. Merrell Dow Pharmaceuticals, Inc.*, 509 U.S. 579 (1993), this Court focused upon the admissibility of scientific expert testimony. It pointed out that such testimony is admissible only if it is both relevant and reliable. And it held that the Federal Rules of Evidence "assign to the trial judge the task of ensuring that an expert's testimony both rests on a reliable foundation and is relevant to the task at hand." The Court also discussed certain more specific factors, such as testing, peer review, error rates, and "acceptability" in the relevant scientific community, some or all of which might prove helpful in determining the reliability of a particular scientific "theory or technique."

This case requires us to decide how *Daubert* applies to the testimony of engineers and other experts who are not scientists. We conclude that *Daubert's* general holding — setting forth the trial judge's general "gatekeeping" obligation — applies not only to testimony based on "scientific" knowledge, but also to testimony based on "technical" and "other specialized" knowledge. See Fed. Rule Evid. 702. We also conclude that a trial court *may* consider one or more of the more specific factors that *Daubert* mentioned when doing so will help determine that testimony's reliability. But, as the Court stated in *Daubert*, the test of reliability is "flexible," and *Daubert's* list of specific factors neither necessarily nor exclusively applies to all experts or in every case. Rather, the law grants a district court the same broad latitude when it decides *how* to determine reliability as it enjoys in respect to its ultimate reliability determination. See *General Electric Co. v. Joiner*, 522 U.S. 136 (1997) (courts of appeals are to apply "abuse of discretion" standard when reviewing district court's reliability determination). Applying these standards, we determine that the District Court's decision in this case — not to admit certain expert testimony — was within its discretion and therefore lawful.

I.

On July 6, 1993, the right rear tire of a minivan driven by Patrick Carmichael blew out. In the accident that followed, one of the passengers died, and others were severely injured. In October 1993, the Carmichaels brought this diversity suit against the tire's maker and its distributor, whom we refer to collectively as Kumho Tire, claiming that the tire was defective. The plaintiffs rested their case in significant part upon deposition testimony provided by an expert in tire failure analysis, Dennis Carlson, Jr., who intended to testify in support of their conclusion.

. . . .

Carlson's testimony . . . accepted certain background facts about the tire in question. He assumed that before the blowout the tire had traveled far. (The tire was made in 1988 and had been installed some time before the Carmichaels bought the used minivan in March 1993; the Carmichaels had driven the van approximately 7,000 additional miles in the two months they had owned it.) Carlson noted that the tire's tread depth, which was 11/32 of an inch when new had been worn down to depths that ranged from 3/32 of an inch along some parts of the tire, to nothing at all along others. He conceded that the tire tread had at least two punctures which had been inadequately repaired.

Despite the tire's age and history, Carlson concluded that a defect in its manufacture or design caused the blow-out. He rested this conclusion in part upon three premises which, for present purposes, we must assume are not in dispute: First, a tire's carcass should stay bound to the inner side of the tread for a significant period of time after its tread depth has worn away. Second, the tread of the tire at issue had separated from its inner steel-belted carcass prior to the accident. Third, this "separation" caused the blowout.

Carlson's conclusion that a defect caused the separation, however, rested upon certain other propositions, several of which the defendants strongly dispute. First, Carlson said that if a separation is *not* caused by a certain kind of tire misuse called "overdeflection" (which consists of underinflating the tire or causing it to carry too much weight, thereby generating heat that can undo the chemical tread/carcass bond), then, ordinarily, its cause is a tire defect. Second, he said that if a tire has been subject to sufficient overdeflection to cause a separation, it should reveal certain physical symptoms. . . . Third, Carlson said that where he does not find *at least two* of the four physical signs [of overdeflection] he concludes that a manufacturing or design defect caused the separation.

Carlson . . . inspected the tire in question. He conceded that the tire to a limited degree showed [physical symptoms of overdeflection such as] greater wear on the [tire's] shoulder than in the center, . . . some discoloration, . . . and inadequately filled puncture holes (which can also cause heat that might lead to separation). But, in each instance, he testified that the symptoms were not significant, and he explained why he believed that they did not reveal overdeflection. For example, the extra shoulder wear, he said, appeared primarily on one shoulder, whereas an overdeflected tire would reveal equally abnormal wear on both shoulders. Carlson concluded that the tire did not bear at least two of the four overdeflection symptoms, nor was there any less obvious cause of separation; and since neither overdeflection nor the punctures caused the blowout, a defect must have done so.

Kumho Tire moved the District Court to exclude Carlson's testimony on the ground that his methodology failed Rule 702's reliability requirement. The court agreed with Kumho that it should act as a *Daubert*-type reliability "gatekeeper," even though one might consider Carlson's testimony as "technical," rather than "scientific." The court then examined Carlson's methodology in light of the reliability-related factors that *Daubert* mentioned, such as a theory's testability, whether it "has been a subject of peer review or publication," the "known or potential rate of error," and the "degree of acceptance . . . within the relevant scientific community." The District Court found that all those factors argued against the reliability of Carlson's methods, and it granted the motion to exclude the testimony (as well as the defendants' accompanying motion for summary judgment).

[The court] conceded that there may be widespread acceptance of a "visual-inspection method" for some relevant purposes. But the court found insufficient indications of the reliability of

> "the component of Carlson's tire failure analysis which most concerned the Court, namely, the methodology employed by the expert in analyzing the data obtained in the visual inspection, and the scientific basis, if any, for such an analysis. . . ."

The Eleventh Circuit reversed. . . . It noted that . . . "a *Daubert* analysis" applies only where an expert relies "on the application of scientific principles," rather than "on skill- or experience-based observation." It concluded that Carlson's testimony, which it viewed as relying on experience, "falls outside the scope of *Daubert*," that "the district court erred as a matter of law by applying *Daubert* in this case," and that the case must be remanded for further (non-*Daubert*-type) consideration under Rule 702.

. . . We granted certiorari in light of uncertainty among the lower courts about whether, or how, *Daubert* applies to expert testimony that might be characterized as based not upon "scientific" knowledge, but rather upon "technical" or "other specialized" knowledge.

II.

A.

In *Daubert*, this Court held that Federal Rule of Evidence 702 imposes a special obligation upon a trial judge to "ensure that any and all scientific testimony . . . is not only relevant, but reliable." 509 U.S., at 589. The initial question before us is whether this basic gatekeeping obligation applies only to "scientific" testimony or to all expert testimony. We, like the parties, believe that it applies to all expert testimony.

For one thing, Rule 702 itself says:

> "If scientific, technical, or other specialized knowledge will assist the trier of fact to understand the evidence or to determine a fact in issue, a witness qualified as an expert by knowledge, skill, experience, training, or education, may testify thereto in the form of an opinion or otherwise."

This language makes no relevant distinction between "scientific" knowledge and "technical" or "other specialized" knowledge. It makes clear that any such knowledge might become the subject of expert testimony. In *Daubert*, the Court specified that it is the Rule's word "knowledge," not the words (like "scientific") that modify that word, that "establishes a standard of evidentiary reliability." Hence, as a matter of language, the Rule applies its reliability standard to all "scientific," "technical," or "other specialized" matters within its scope. We concede that the Court in *Daubert* referred only to "scientific" knowledge. But as the Court there said, it referred to "scientific" testimony "because that [wa]s the nature of the expertise" at issue. *Id.*, at 590, n. 8.

. . . .

We conclude that *Daubert's* general principles apply to the expert matters described in Rule 702. The Rule, in respect to all such matters, "establishes a standard of evidentiary reliability." [*Id.*], at 590. It "requires a valid . . . connection to the pertinent inquiry as a precondition to admissibility." *Id.*, at 592. And where such testimony's factual basis, data, principles, methods, or their application are called sufficiently into question, see Part III, *infra*, the trial judge must determine whether the testimony has "a reliable basis in the knowledge and experience of [the relevant] discipline." [*Id.*], at 592.

B.

The petitioners ask more specifically whether a trial judge determining the "admissibility of an engineering expert's testimony" *may* consider several more specific factors that *Daubert* said might "bear on" a judge's gate-keeping determination. These factors include:

— Whether a "theory or technique . . . can be (and has been) tested";

— Whether it "has been subjected to peer review and publication";

— Whether, in respect to a particular technique, there is a high "known or potential rate of error" and whether there are "standards controlling the technique's operation"; and

— Whether the theory or technique enjoys "general acceptance" within a "relevant scientific community." 509 U.S., at 592–594.

Emphasizing the word "may"in the question, we answer that question yes.

Engineering testimony rests upon scientific foundations, the reliability of which will be at issue in some cases. In other cases, the relevant reliability concerns may focus upon personal knowledge or experience. As the Solicitor General points out, there are many different kinds of experts, and many different kinds of expertise. See Brief for United States as *Amicus Curiae* 18–19, and n. 5 (citing cases involving experts in drug terms, handwriting analysis, criminal *modus operandi*, land valuation, agricultural practices, railroad procedures, attorney's fee valuation, and others). Our emphasis on the word "may" thus reflects *Daubert's* description of the Rule 702 inquiry as "a flexible one." *Daubert* makes clear that the factors it mentions do not constitute a "definitive checklist or test." And *Daubert* adds that the gatekeeping inquiry must be " 'tied to the facts' " of a particular "case." We agree with the Solicitor General that "[t]he factors identified in *Daubert* may or may not be pertinent in assessing reliability, depending on the nature of the issue, the expert's particular expertise, and the subject of his testimony." The conclusion, in our view, is that we can neither rule out, nor rule in, for all cases and for all time the applicability of the factors mentioned in *Daubert*, nor can we now do so for subsets of cases categorized by category of expert or by kind of evidence. Too much depends upon the particular circumstances of the particular case at issue.

Daubert itself is not to the contrary. It made clear that its list of factors was meant to be helpful, not definitive. Indeed, those factors do not all necessarily apply even in every instance in which the reliability of scientific testimony is challenged. It might not be surprising in a particular case, for example, that a claim made by a scientific witness has never been the subject of peer review, for the particular application at issue may never previously have interested any scientist. Nor, on the other hand, does the presence of *Daubert's* general acceptance factor help show that an expert's testimony is reliable where the discipline itself lacks reliability, as, for example, do theories grounded in any so-called generally accepted principles of astrology or necromancy.

At the same time, and contrary to the Court of Appeals' view, some of *Daubert's* questions can help to evaluate the reliability even of experience-based testimony. In certain cases, it will be appropriate for the trial judge to ask, for example, how often an engineering expert's experience-based methodology has produced erroneous results, or whether such a method is generally accepted in the relevant engineering community. Likewise, it will at times be useful to ask even of a witness whose expertise is based purely on experience, say, a perfume tester able to distinguish among 140 odors at a sniff, whether his preparation is of a kind that others in the field would recognize as acceptable.

We must therefore disagree with the Eleventh Circuit's holding that a trial judge may ask questions of the sort *Daubert* mentioned only where an expert "relies on the application of scientific principles," but not where an expert relies "on skill- or experience-based observation." 131 F.3d, at 1435. We do not believe that Rule 702 creates a schematism that segregates expertise by type while mapping certain kinds of questions to certain kinds of experts. Life and the legal cases that it generates are too complex to warrant so definitive a match.

To say this is not to deny the importance of *Daubert's* gatekeeping requirement. The objective of that requirement is to ensure the reliability and relevancy of expert testimony. It is to make certain that an expert, whether basing testimony upon professional studies or personal experience, employs in the courtroom the same level of intellectual rigor that characterizes the practice of an expert in the relevant field. Nor do we deny that, as stated in *Daubert*, the particular questions that it mentioned will often be appropriate for use in determining the reliability of challenged expert testimony. Rather, we conclude that the trial judge must have considerable leeway in deciding in a particular case how to go about determining whether particular expert testimony is reliable. That is to say, a trial court should consider the specific factors identified in *Daubert* where they are reasonable measures of the reliability of expert testimony.

C.

The trial court must have the same kind of latitude in deciding *how* to test an expert's reliability, and to decide *whether* or when special briefing or other proceedings are needed to investigate reliability, as it enjoys when it decides whether or not that expert's relevant testimony is reliable. Our opinion in *Joiner* makes clear that a court of appeals is to apply an abuse-of-discretion standard when it "review[s] a trial court's decision to admit or exclude expert testimony." That standard applies as much to the trial court's decisions about how to determine reliability as to its ultimate conclusion. Otherwise, the trial judge would lack the discretionary authority needed both to avoid unnecessary "reliability" proceedings in ordinary cases where the reliability of an expert's methods is properly taken for granted, and to require appropriate proceedings in the less usual or more complex cases where cause for questioning the expert's reliability arises. Indeed, the Rules seek to avoid "unjustifiable expense and delay" as part of their search for "truth" and the "jus[t] determin[ation]" of proceedings. Fed. Rule Evid. 102. Thus, whether *Daubert's* specific factors are, or are not, reasonable measures of reliability in a particular case is a matter that the law grants the trial judge broad latitude to determine. And the Eleventh Circuit erred insofar as it held to the contrary.

III.

We further explain the way in which a trial judge "may" consider *Daubert's* factors by applying these considerations to the case at hand. . . . The District Court did not doubt Carlson's qualifications. . . . Rather, it excluded the testimony because, despite those qualifications, it initially doubted, and then found unreliable, "the methodology employed by the expert in analyzing the data obtained in the visual inspection, and the scientific basis, if any, for such an analysis." [T]he District Court determined that Carlson's testimony . . . fell outside the range where experts might reasonably differ, and where the jury must decide among the conflicting views of different experts, even though the evidence is "shaky." In our view, the doubts that triggered the District Court's initial inquiry here were reasonable, as was the court's ultimate conclusion.

For one thing, and contrary to respondents' suggestion, the specific issue before the court was not the reasonableness *in general* of a tire expert's use of a visual and tactile inspection to determine whether overdeflection had caused the tire's tread to separate from its steel-belted carcass. Rather, it was the reasonableness of using such an approach, along with Carlson's particular method of analyzing the data thereby obtained, to draw a conclusion regarding *the particular matter to which the expert testimony was directly relevant*. That matter concerned the likelihood that a defect in the tire at issue caused its tread to separate from its carcass. The tire in question, the expert conceded, had traveled far enough so that some of the tread had been worn bald; it should have been taken out of service; it had been repaired (inadequately) for punctures; and it bore some of the very marks that the expert said indicated, not a defect, but abuse through overdeflection. The relevant issue was whether the expert could reliably determine the cause of *this* tire's separation.

. . . .

For another thing, the transcripts of Carlson's depositions support both the trial court's initial uncertainty and its final conclusion. . . . The court could reasonably have wondered about the reliability of a method of visual and tactile inspection sufficiently precise to ascertain with some certainty the abuse-related significance of minute shoulder/center relative tread wear differences, but insufficiently precise to tell "with any certainty" from the tread wear whether a tire had traveled less than 10,000 or more than 50,000 miles. And these concerns might have been augmented by Carlson's repeated reliance on the "subjective[ness]" of his mode of analysis in response to questions seeking specific information regarding how he could differentiate between a tire that actually had been overdeflected and a tire that merely looked as though it had been. . . .

. . . .

Respondents now argue to us, as they did to the District Court, that a method of tire failure analysis that employs a visual/tactile inspection is a reliable method, and they point both to its use by other experts and to Carlson's long experience working for Michelin as sufficient indication that that is so. But no one denies that an expert might draw a conclusion from a set of observations based on extensive and specialized experience. Nor does anyone deny that, as a general matter, tire abuse may often be identified by qualified experts through visual or tactile inspection of the tire. As we said before, the question before the trial court was specific, not general. The trial court had to decide whether this particular expert had sufficient specialized knowledge to assist the jurors "in deciding the particular issues in the case."

The particular issue in this case concerned the use of Carlson's two-factor test and his related use of visual/tactile inspection to draw conclusions on the basis of what seemed small observational differences. We have found no indication in the record that other experts in the industry use Carlson's two-factor test or that tire experts such as Carlson normally make the very fine distinctions about, say, the symmetry of comparatively greater shoulder tread wear that were necessary, on Carlson's own theory, to support his conclusions. Nor, despite the prevalence of tire testing, does anyone refer to any articles or papers that validate Carlson's approach. Indeed, no one has argued that Carlson himself, were he still working for Michelin, would have concluded in a report to his employer that a similar tire was similarly defective on grounds identical to those upon which he rested his conclusion here. Of course, Carlson himself claimed that his method was accurate, but, as we pointed out in *Joiner*, "nothing in either *Daubert* or the Federal Rules of Evidence requires a district court to admit opinion evidence that is connected to existing data only by the *ipse dixit* of the expert."

. . . .

In sum, Rule 702 grants the district judge the discretionary authority, reviewable for its abuse, to determine reliability in light of the particular facts and circumstances of the particular case. The District Court did not abuse its discretionary authority in this case. Hence, the judgment of the Court of Appeals is *Reversed*.

NOTES

1. ***Revisions to the Federal Rules of Evidence.*** Rules 701 and 702 of The Federal Rules of Evidence were amended (effective December 1, 2000) in response to the Supreme Court's decisions in the "*Daubert* trilogy."

(A) Rule 701. Rule 701, which regulates opinion testimony by *lay witnesses*, was revised to make it clear that lay opinion testimony could "not [be] based on scientific, technical, or other specialized knowledge within the scope of Rule 702." The Advisory Committee Note accompanying Rule 701's 2000 amendment explained the rationale behind this amendment.

> Rule 701 has been amended to eliminate the risk that the reliability require-ments set forth in Rule 702 will be evaded through the simple expedient of proffering an expert in lay witness clothing. Under the amendment, a witness' testimony must be scrutinized under the rules regulating expert opinion to the extent that the witness is providing testimony based upon scientific, technical, or other specialized knowledge within the scope of Rule 702.

To illustrate, consider a trial where the defendant is charged with drug trafficking. If a police officer offers an opinion that the defendant's conduct was consistent with that of a drug trafficker, the police officer could not be offered to the court as a Rule 701 lay opinion witness to avoid the rigors of Rule 702 and scrutiny under the "*Daubert* trilogy." *See United States v. Peoples*, 250 F.3d 630, 641 n.3 (8th Cir. 2001) ("[T]he 2000 revisions to Rules 701 and 702 emphasize [the] distinction between lay and opinion testimony.").

(B) Rule 702. Rule 702 itself was also amended in 2000. In the words of the advisory committee, Rule 702 was amended "in response to *Daubert v. Merrell Dow Pharmaceuticals, Inc.* . . . and to the many cases applying *Daubert*, including *Kumho Tire Co. v. Carmichael*." The "response" entailed adding three requirements at the end of the previous version of Rule 702.

Rule 702. Testimony by Experts

If scientific, technical, or other specialized knowledge will assist the trier of fact to understand the evidence or to determine a fact in issue, a witness qualified as an expert by knowledge, skill, experience, training, or education, may testify thereto in the form of an opinion or otherwise, *if (1) the testimony is based upon sufficient facts or data, (2) the testimony is the product of reliable principles and methods, and (3) the witness has applied the principles and methods reliably to the facts of the case.*

Fed. R. Evid. 702 (emphasis added). In *Nelson v. Tennessee Gas Pipeline Company*, 243 F.3d 244 (6th Cir. 2001), the Sixth Circuit stated that the "amendment [to Rule 702] is consistent with the gatekeeping function articulated in *Daubert* and *Kumho*," and "does not alter the standard for evaluating the admissibility of the experts' opinions in this case." *Id.* at 250 n. 4.

2. *State Courts Application of* Daubert *(or a "* Daubert-*like") Test to Nonscientific Experts.* The Supreme Court's opinion in *Kumho Tire* brought an end to the controversy that had developed among federal circuits over whether *Daubert's* reliability test should be applied to nonscientific experts. Note, however, that *Kumho Tire* involved an interpretation of the Federal Rules of Evidence and is not binding on state courts. Even if a state has an evidence code modeled after the Federal Rules of Evidence and employs a relevancy plus reliability test identical to *Daubert*, it might not apply its Rule 702's gatekeeping requirements to nonscientific experts. *See e.g. State v. Sanchez-Cruz*, 33 P.3d 1037, 1040 n.4 (Or. App. 2001) (noting law is unclear but cases suggest only scientific evidence is subject to the trial court's gatekeeping role); *State v. Kelley*, 1 P.3d 546, 551 (Utah 2000) (expert testimony not subject to Utah's "inherent reliability standard" because it was not "based on novel scientific principles or techniques"); *West Virginia Div. Of Highways v. Butler*, 516 S.E.2d 769, 774 n.4 (W. Va. 1999) ("We decline to adopt the *Kumho [Tire]* analysis in this case."). *See also*, David E. Bernstein and Jeffrey D. Jackson, *The* Daubert *Trilogy in the States*, 44 Jurimetrics 351, 357–61 (Spring 2004) (only nine states had adopted the full holdings of all three cases in the *Daubert* trilogy, and seven states that adopted *Daubert's* reasoning had not adopted the holdings of *Kumho Tire* or *Joiner*).

3. *Reliability Factors.* The heart of the trial court's reliability (and, hence, admissibility) determination lies in the court's choice of reliability factors. In *Daubert* the Supreme Court identified the five factors,[14] listed below as bearing on the reliability

---

[14] Courts and commentators sometimes refer to *four Daubert* reliability factors. The difference comes from whether "the known or potential rate of error, and the existence and maintenance of standards controlling the

inquiry.

(1) *Testing and Testability*. Has the expert's theory or technique been tested, or can it be tested? That is, can the expert's technique or theory be challenged in some objective sense, or is it simply a subjective, conclusory approach that cannot be assessed for reliability? *See* Fed. R. Evid 702 advisory committee's note 2000 amendment. The *Daubert* Court considered this a "key question." *Daubert, supra*, 509 U.S. at 593.

(2) *Peer Review and Publication*. Has the theory or technique been subjected to peer review and publication? The *Daubert* Court referred to this as "a relevant, though not dispositive, consideration in assessing scientific validity." *Daubert, supra*, 509 U.S. at 594.

(3) *Error Rate*. The known or potential error rate of the theory or technique when applied.

(4) *Existence and Maintenance of Standards and Controls*. Are there standards controlling the technique's operation such as a certifying procedure adopted by a professional association? *See* 1 SCIENTIFIC EVIDENCE § 1.08[b], at 47–48 (4th ed. 2007).

(5) *General Acceptance*. Is the theory or technique generally accepted in the scientific community?

In *Kumho Tire* the Court emphasized that the factors identified in *Daubert* were not definitive, and "do not necessarily apply in every instance" even when scientific evidence is challenged. *Kumho Tire, supra*, 526 U.S. at 151. Rather, the Court stressed that *it is the trial court's task* to determine whether one or more of the *Daubert* factors is reasonable to use in a particular case. *Id.* at 152–53. When Rule 702 was amended in 2000, five additional reliability factors were listed in the amendment's accompanying advisory committee's note.

(1) *Research Independent of the Litigation*. Is the expert's testimony based upon research conducted independent of the litigation? On remand in *Daubert*, the Ninth Circuit stated that "[o]ne very significant fact to be considered is *whether the experts are proposing to testify about matters growing naturally and directly out of research they have conducted independent of litigation, or whether they have developed their opinions expressly for the purposes of testifying*." *Daubert v. Merrell Dow Pharmaceuticals, Inc.*, 43 F.3d 1311, 1317 (9th Cir. 1995) (emphasis added). The Ninth Circuit commented in a footnote that, "There are, of course, exceptions. Fingerprint analysis, voice recognition, DNA fingerprinting and a variety of other scientific endeavors closely tied to law enforcement may indeed have the courtroom as a principal theater of operations. As to such disciplines, the fact that the expert has developed an expertise principally for purposes of litigation will obviously not be a substantial consideration." *Id.* at 1317 n. 5.

(2) *Whether the Expert Has Unjustifiably Extrapolated from an Accepted Premise to an Unfounded Conclusion*. That is, whether the expert's opinion is connected to the data only by the *Ipse Dixit* of the expert. This factor was described by the Supreme Court in its *Joiner* decision. "A court may conclude that there is simply too great an analytical gap between the data and the opinion proffered." *Joiner, supra*, 522 U.S. at 146. *See U.S. v. $141,770 in U.S. Currency*, 157 F.3d 600, 605–606 (8th Cir. 1998) (defense expert's broad assertion that 99% of all U.S. currency is contaminated with drug residue properly

---

technique's operation," *Daubert, supra*, 509 U.S. at 594, is considered as one or two factors. In this text they are considered as two different factors. This is consistent with the listing of factors in the advisory committee's note to Fed. R. Evid 702.

excluded, in part, because all bills except five that the expert examined were brought to him by the narcotics unit of a police department).

(3) *Alternative Explanations* — *Whether the expert has accounted for obvious alternative explanations. See Claar v. Burlington Northern R. Co.*, 29 F.3d 499 (9th Cir. 1994) (testimony excluded where physician fails to rule out alternative explanations for medical conditions or explain basis for proffered opinion).

(4) *Same Level of Intellectual Rigor* — *Whether the expert "is being as careful as he or she would be in their regular professional work outside their paid litigation consulting.* This factor — mentioned and applied in *Kumho Tire* — asks whether the expert "employs in the courtroom the same level of intellectual rigor that characterizes the practice of an expert in the relevant field." *Kumho Tire, supra*, 526 U.S. at 152.

(5) *Unreliable Field of Expertise* — *Whether the field of expertise claimed by the expert is known to reach reliable results for the type of opinion the expert would give.* This factor was also mentioned by the Supreme Court in *Kumho Tire. Kumho Tire, supra*, 526 U.S. at 151 (*Daubert's* general acceptance factor does not "help show that an expert's testimony is reliable where the discipline itself lacks reliability, as for example, do theories grounded in any so-called generally accepted principles of astrology or necromancy.").

By asserting that the reliability determination was "a flexible one," and that "many factors will bear on the inquiry," *Daubert, supra*, 509 U.S. at 594, 595, the Supreme Court did not foreclose a court from identifying additional reliability factors. *See, e.g., Elcock v. Kmart Corporation*, 233 F.3d 734, 745–46 (3d Cir. 2000) (Court lists the five original *Daubert* factors and three additional factors, stating that "[w]e will henceforth refer to these factors as the *Daubert* factors."); *Prater v. State*, 820 S.W.2d 429, 431–32 (Ark. 1991) (court mentions novelty of the technique, relationship of the technique to established modes of scientific analysis, existence of specialized literature, use of the correct protocol, and nonjudicial uses of the technique as appropriate factors to use in determining reliability); *State v. Anderson*, 881 P.2d 29, 36 (N.M. 1994) (whether the scientific technique is based upon "well-recognized" scientific principles and is capable of supporting opinions based upon "reasonable probability rather than conjecture."); *State v. O'Key*, 899 P.2d 663, 676 & 676 n.15 (Or. 1995) (Oregon Supreme Court identifies a total of 18 reliability factors).

4. ***Appeal: One Standard for All Determinations.*** Abuse of discretion is the proper standard for reviewing a trial court's decision to admit or exclude scientific and other expert evidence, and for reviewing *all decisions* a trial court makes in the process of ruling on the admissibility of expert testimony. Decisions left to the trial court's discretion include: (1) whether reliability is "called sufficiently into question," (2) what sort of proceedings are needed to investigate reliability; (3) which reliability factors to apply; and (4) the ultimate decision on reliability.

Review under the abuse of discretion standard provides the trial court with flexibility and makes the gatekeeping task less onerous. On the other hand, isn't it possible that broad trial court discretion might result in inconsistent rulings and encourage forum shopping? *See* 1 Scientific Evidence § 1.08[g], at 61–62 (4th ed. 2007) ("The problem with the abuse-of-discretion approach is the inevitable lack of consistency, one court finding polygraph evidence reliable and another finding the exact opposite."); David L. Faigman, Michael J. Saks, Joseph Sanders, & Edward K. Cheng, 1 Modern Scientific Evidence: The Law and Science of Expert Testimony § 1.25, at 67–68 (2008) ("[A]ppellate deference to the factors used to assess the different categories of expertise is a possible Achilles' heel in an other wise solidly reasoned opinion. If taken literally, it would allow different judges in the same district to apply different factors to similar kinds of expert testimony."); Robert J. Goodwin, *Roadblocks to Achieving "Reliability" for Non-Scientific Expert Testimony: A Response to Professor Edward J. Imwinkelried*, 30 Cumb. L. Rev. 215, 220 (2000) ("The unintended result of . . . broad discretion . . . may be that the court where expert testimony is proffered will be as important a consideration as the reliability of the opinion.").

Not all state courts that have adopted *Daubert*, or a *Daubert*-like reliability test, use the abuse of discretion standard to review all trial court decisions related to the reliability inquiry. *See State v. Torres*, 976 P.2d 20, 29 (N.M. 1999) ("threshold question of whether the trial court applied the correct evidentiary rule or standard is subject to de novo review on appeal"); *State v. O'Key*, 899 P.2d 663, 688 n.45 (Or. 1995) ("[I]f evidentiary rulings as to the admissibility of scientific evidence are reviewed with deference to trial court discretion, inconsistent decisions concerning the admissibility of scientific evidence may go unchecked from one trial court to another.").

QUESTIONS

1. May a trial judge consider one or more of the five reliability factors listed in *Daubert* when determining whether a nonscientific expert's testimony is reliable? If so, how is a trial court to determine *which ones are applicable* in a particular case?

2. Is the *"Daubert* trilogy" a more liberal or a more conservative test for admissibility of *scientific* evidence than *Frye*? *See* 1 Scientific Evidence § 1.08, at 36–37 (4th ed. 2007). What about *nonscientific* evidence? For example, which test is more likely to admit an expert's conclusions based upon psychology and sociology? *See Weisgram v. Marley Co.*, 528 U.S. 440, 455 (2000) ("Since *Daubert*, . . . parties relying on expert evidence have had notice of the exacting standards of reliability such evidence must meet.").

3. In *Kumho Tire* does the Supreme Court suggest any reliability factors that would be reasonable measures of the reliability of an experienced-based expert's testimony? If so, what are they?

4. In *Kumho Tire* the plaintiff's expert used a "visual/tactile inspection" method. In Part III of its *Kumho Tire* opinion Justice Breyer writes that,

> [N]o one denies that an expert might draw a conclusion from a set of observations based upon extensive and specialized experience. Nor does anyone deny that, as a general matter, tire abuse may often be identified by qualified experts through visual or tactile inspection of the tire.

Given the above statement, why did the Supreme Court affirm the district court's exclusion of the plaintiffs' expert testimony? What reliability factors does the Supreme Court cite in Part III of its *Kumho Tire* opinion to justify its rejection of the plaintiffs' expert's testimony?

PROBLEM

Problem 2-8. Recall that a primitive version of today's polygraph machine was the scientific device discussed in 1923 in the *Frye* case. Since 1923, the polygraph machine has been significantly improved, and its accuracy and reliability has been subjected to numerous studies.

Assume that there have been hundreds of studies conducted on the reliability of the polygraph machine in the last 20 years. The results of several of the studies have been published in the *Journal of Forensic Science*, a peer-reviewed professional journal. The studies show that the polygraph can detect deception 90% of the time if the person conducting the test is adequately trained. Further, licensing regulations for polygraph examiners (that include training requirements) exist in only 20 states. The amount and type of a training varies from state to state. Finally, two surveys of psychophysiologists (the scientific discipline that involves the relationship between psychological processes and bodily reactions) have been conducted; one in 1996 and the other in 2006. Of those psychophysiologists surveyed, 62% and 60%, respectively, believed the polygraph was an accurate tool for assessing truth or deception if the polygraph examiner was adequately trained. Among psychophysiologists suveyed in 2006 who considered themselves to be "well-informed on the literature related to the polygraph," 80% believed the polygraph was an accurate tool for assessing truth or deception if the polygraph examiner was adequately trained. The results of each survey were published in a professional journal.

On the other hand, other studies conclude that 10% of the population are able to fool the test and the test examiner without being detected. Further, reliability of these results is directly related to the ability of the examiner to correctly read the test results. Finally, the use of drugs and countermeasures by the person being tested has been found to make test results inaccurate.

Defendant is on trial for income tax evasion. An element of the crime that the government must establish is that the defendant *knowingly* failed to report certain income. Defendant took a lie detector test before trial. When asked by the polygrapher, "did you knowingly fail to report your income?," the defendant answered "no." The polygrapher is prepared to testify that in her (the test examiner's) opinion the defendant answered truthfully when he denied that he knowingly failed to report income.

The polygrapher in this case is a psychophysiologist and a professor of psychology at the University of Utah, whose primary area of study and research is focused on the polygraph technique. The polygrapher has received training in administering polygraph exams, but was not licensed because there were no licensing requirements in her state. The polygrapher is prepared to testify that she conducted and interpreted the polygraph exam in this case pursuant to guidelines established by the F.B.I.

(A) Put yourself in the role of trial judge. Select reliability factors that are reasonable measures of reliability in this circumstance, and decide how they impact scientific validity and admissibility. *See United States v. Galbreth*, 908 F. Supp. 877, 891–93 (D.N.M. 1995).

(B) If the scientific community is split, with only 62% of the psychophysiologists in the field accepting the polygraph as an accurate method for detecting deception, can expert opinion testimony based upon the technique be admitted in a jurisdiction that follows *Daubert*? In a jurisdiction that follows *Frye*? *See United States v. Galbreth*, 908 F. Supp. 877, 892–93 (D.N.M. 1995).

(C) Does *Daubert* require that a scientific technique or test be *conducted* in a certain manner by a person with specified credentials to be admissible? Specifically, can a *Daubert* court condition admissibility on the test procedures used on a specific occasion and the training received by the specific test examiner, or is that a question of weight for the jury? *See Galbreth, supra*, at 880–82; *Daubert v. Merrell Dow Pharmaceuticals*,

Inc., 43 F.3d 1311, 1318 n.10 (9th Cir. 1995). How does revised Rule 702 address this issue?

[c]   The *Daubert* Trilogy Applied in Criminal Cases

The *Daubert* test — as defined in the "*Daubert* trilogy" — is used in all federal courts, and a majority of state courts use either the *Daubert* test or a *Daubert*-like reliability test that imposes gatekeeper obligations on the trial court. Although the *Daubert* test does not distinguish between civil and criminal cases, critics contend that courts generally do not apply the *Daubert* test with the same rigor to forensic evidence in criminal cases, as they do to scientific evidence in civil cases. *See* Committee on Identifying the Needs of the Forensic Sciences Community, National Research Council, *Strengthening Forensic Science in the United States: A Path Forward* 3-17 (prepublication copy, Feb. 2009). Indeed, one study concluded that civil defendants win their *Daubert* reliability challenges most of the time, but criminal defendants virtually always lose their challenges to government proffers. *See* D. Michael Risinger, *Navigating Expert Reliability: Are Criminal Standards of Certainty Being Left on the Dock?*, 64 Albany L. Rev. 99 (2000).

On the other hand, *Daubert* — by design — grants trial courts a great deal of latitude in determining how to test the reliability of scientific evidence, and their judgments are reviewed under the highly deferential abuse-of-discretion standard. If certain forensic techniques enjoy widespread acceptance, and their reliability has not been called into doubt, how demanding should courts be?

[i]   The *Daubert* Trilogy Applied in Criminal Cases — Forensic Science Techniques That Have Been Routinely Used for Years

In 1911 the Illinois Supreme Court became the first appellate court to admit fingerprint evidence. *People v. Jennings*, 96 N.E. 1077 (1911). Since 1911, fingerprints have been routinely used to "match" a questioned crime scene fingerprint to a known, inked fingerprint. It would be fair to describe fingerprinting as a "generally accepted" forensic technique that is not "novel," or new to the legal system. Note, however, that the *Jennings* case was decided in 1911, 12 years before *Frye*. Accordingly, fingerprinting was admitted in criminal trials without being subjected to scrutiny under the *Frye* standard.

Regardless of how fingerprinting has been received under the *Frye* standard, recall that in *Daubert* the Supreme Court stated that, "[a]lthough the *Frye* decision itself focused exclusively on "novel" scientific techniques, we do not read the requirements of Rule 702 to apply specially or exclusively to unconventional evidence." *Daubert, supra,* 509 U.S. at 592 n.11. Therefore, familiar forensic techniques like fingerprinting should be required to demonstrate their reliability under the *Daubert* test as a precondition for admissibility, shouldn't they? On the other hand, in the *Kumho Tire* case the Court stated that a trial court had "discretionary authority . . . to avoid unnecessary 'reliability' proceedings in ordinary cases where the *reliability of an expert's methods is properly taken for granted. . . .*" *Kumho Tire, supra,* 526 U.S. at 152 (emphasis added). Does this passage from *Kumho Tire* mean that a trial court may take the reliability of fingerprint identification "for granted" and not subject it to scrutiny under *Daubert*?

In the next case, *United States v. Crisp*, the accused argued that fingerprint identification and handwriting analysis fail the *Daubert* test because no empirical research had been conducted to establish the validity of either technique (among other arguments). As you read the Fourth Circuit's opinion in the *Crisp* case, consider how its application of the *Daubert* test compares with the application of the *Daubert* test in the *Joiner* and *Kumho Tire* cases.

UNITED STATES v. CRISP
324 F.3d 261 (4th Cir. 2003)

KING, CIRCUIT JUDGE:

Patrick Leroy Crisp appeals multiple convictions arising from an armed bank robbery carried out in Durham, North Carolina, on June 13, 2001. Crisp maintains that his trial was tainted by the Government's presentation of inadmissible expert testimony. His appeal presents a single question: whether the disciplines of forensic fingerprint analysis and forensic handwriting analysis satisfy the criteria for expert opinion testimony under *Daubert v. Merrell Dow Pharmaceuticals, Inc.*, 509 U.S. 579 (1993). As explained below, the prosecution's fingerprint and handwriting evidence was properly admitted, and we affirm the convictions.

I.

At approximately 12:25 p.m. on June 13, 2001, a lone male, wearing a mask and surgical gloves, and carrying a handgun, entered the Central Carolina Bank in Durham, North Carolina. He approached . . . a teller, threw a bag on the counter, and instructed her to "fill up the . . . bag." [The teller] gave the gunman the sum of $7,854 in cash. . . . Then, a horn sounded twice from the parking lot outside, and the robber . . . made his getaway in a purple Ford Probe automobile.

. . . .

The next day, June 14, 2001, the authorities received a call on its Crimestoppers telephone line from an individual who claimed to have information about the robbery. . . . [L]ater that day the police met the caller, Michael Mitchell, at a local restaurant. Mitchell informed the officers that Patrick Crisp and Lamont Torain had robbed the bank. He further attested that Crisp and Torain had attempted to recruit him to participate in the robbery, but that he had declined. . . . On the basis of Mitchell's information, the police [arrested] Crisp.

. . . .

Torain was also arrested, and he was incarcerated in the same jail as Crisp. On June 20, 2001, as he [Torain] walked past Crisp's cell, a handwritten note (the "Note") was slid out from under Crisp's door. The Note, the last line of which was allegedly crossed out when delivered, stated:

Lamont.

You know if you don't help me I am going to get life in prison, and you ain't going to get nothing. Really it's over for me if you don't change what you told them.

Tell them I picked you up down the street in Kathy's car. Tell them that I don't drive the Probe. Tell them Mike drove the Probe. He is the one that told on us. Tell them the gun and all that shit was Mike's. That is what I am going to tell them tommorow [sic].

Tell the Feds Mike drove you away from the bank.

Patrick.

[In the course of the investigation, [police] officers obtained palmprints and handwriting exemplars from Crisp, and learned that Crisp's had a girlfriend named Katherine Bell]

. . . .

At [Crisp's] trial, Mary Katherine Brannan, a fingerprint expert with the North Carolina State Bureau of Investigation ("SBI"), testified that Crisp's right palm had produced a latent print that had subsequently been recovered from the Note. Furthermore, a handwriting expert, Special Agent Thomas Currin, a "questioned document analyst" with the SBI, testified that Crisp had authored the Note. [The jury found Crisp guilty. He received a sentence of 356 months in prison and five years supervised release.]

. . . .

II.

Fingerprint and handwriting analysis have long been recognized by the courts as sound methods for making reliable identifications. *See, e.g., Piquett v. United States*, 81 F.2d 75, 81 (7th Cir.1936) (fingerprints); *Robinson v. Mandell*, 20 F. Cas. 1027 (D.Mass.1868) (handwriting). Today, however, Crisp challenges the district court's decisions to permit experts in those fields to testify on behalf of the prosecution. The fingerprinting expert, Brannan, gave her opinion that a palm print lifted from the Note was that of Crisp; the handwriting expert, Currin, testified that, in his judgment, the handwriting on the Note matched Crisp's handwriting. We review for abuse of discretion a district court's decision to admit or reject expert testimony. *General Elec. Co. v. Joiner*, 522 U.S. 136 (1997); *see also Kumho Tire Co., Ltd. v. Carmichael*, 526 U.S. 137 (1999) ("[T]he trial judge must have considerable leeway in deciding in a particular case how to go about determining whether particular expert testimony is reliable.").

The Federal Rules of Evidence provide that "[i]f scientific, technical, or other specialized knowledge will assist the trier of fact to understand the evidence or to determine a fact in issue, a witness qualified as an expert by knowledge, skill, experience, training, or education, may testify thereto in the form of an opinion or otherwise. . . ." Fed. R. Evid. 702. The Supreme Court has made clear that it is the trial court's duty to play a gatekeeping function in deciding whether to admit expert testimony: "[T]he trial judge must ensure that any and all scientific testimony or evidence admitted is not only relevant, but reliable." *Daubert v. Merrell Dow Pharms., Inc.*, 509 U.S. 579 (1993).

In *Daubert*, the Court announced five factors that may be used in assessing the relevancy and reliability of expert testimony: (1) whether the particular scientific theory "can be (and has been) tested"; (2) whether the theory "has been subjected to peer review and publication"; (3) the "known or potential rate of error"; (4) the "existence and maintenance of standards controlling the technique's operation"; and (5) whether the technique has achieved "general acceptance" in the relevant scientific or expert community. *Id.* at 593–94. Rather than providing a definitive or exhaustive list, *Daubert* merely illustrates the types of factors that will "bear on the inquiry." *Id.* As *Daubert* emphasized, the analysis must be "a flexible one." *Id.; see also Kumho*, 526 U.S. at 141–42 (concluding that testing of reliability should be flexible and that *Daubert*'s five factors neither necessarily nor exclusively apply to every expert).

A.

We turn first to whether the fingerprint evidence was properly admitted against Crisp. Crisp has challenged the admission of this evidence on several grounds: His primary contention is that the premises underlying fingerprinting evidence have not been adequately tested. Crisp also maintains that there is no known rate of error for latent fingerprint identifications, that fingerprint examiners operate without a uniform threshold of certainty required for a positive identification, and that fingerprint evidence has not achieved general acceptance in the relevant scientific community.

1.

Fingerprint identification has been admissible as reliable evidence in criminal trials in this country since at least 1911. *See People v. Jennings*, 96 N.E. 1077 (1911). While we have not definitively assessed the admissibility of expert fingerprint identifications in the post — *Daubert* era, every Circuit that has done so has found such evidence admissible. *See United States v. Hernandez*, 299 F.3d 984 (8th Cir. 2002) (concluding that fingerprint identification satisfies *Daubert*); *United States v. Havvard*, 260 F.3d 597, 601 (7th Cir. 2001) (same); *United States v. Sherwood*, 98 F.3d 402, 408 (9th Cir. 1996) (noting defendant's acknowledgment that "fingerprint comparison has been subjected to peer review and publication," and holding that trial court did not commit clear error where it admitted fingerprint evidence without performing *Daubert* analysis); *see also United States v. Llera Plaza*, 188 F. Supp. 2d 549, 572–73 (E.D. Pa. 2002) (discussing long history of latent fingerprint evidence in criminal proceedings, and citing lack of proof of its unreliability, to hold such evidence admissible).

. . . .

2.

In his challenge to the admissibility of the fingerprint evidence, Crisp begins with the contention that the basic premises underlying fingerprint identification have not been subjected to adequate testing. The two premises that he singles out as requiring more searching scrutiny are: (1) that no two persons share the same fingerprint; and (2) that fingerprint examiners are able to make reliable identifications on the basis of small, distorted latent fingerprint fragments. In support of his assertions, Crisp notes that the expert in this case, Brannan, was unable to reference any study establishing that no two persons share the same fingerprint; she was able only to testify that no study had ever proven this premise false. In addition, Crisp contends that the Government itself seems unsure of the reliability of fingerprint evidence: in particular, Crisp notes that the National Institute of Justice, an arm of the Department of Justice, issued a solicitation for fingerprint validation studies in March of 2000. This solicitation calls for "basic research to determine the scientific validity of individuality in friction ridge examination," and also seeks the development of standard procedures for fingerprint comparisons and for the testing of those procedures once adopted. National Institute of Justice,

Forensic Friction Ridge (Fingerprint) Examination Validation Studies 4 (Mar. 2000). Finally, though Crisp cites no studies demonstrating the unreliability of fingerprinting analysis, he brings to our attention two law review articles discussing the paucity of research into the fingerprint identification process.[15] [3]

Crisp next maintains that, because the basic premises behind fingerprint analysis have not been properly tested, there can be no established error rates. He also asserts that fingerprint examiners operate without uniform, objective standards, noting that Brannan herself testified that there is no generally accepted standard regarding the number of points of identification necessary to make a positive identification. Finally, Crisp contends that, while fingerprint analysis has gained general acceptance among fingerprint examiners themselves, this factor should be discounted because, according to Crisp, the relevant community "is devoid of financially disinterested parties such as academics." *United States v. Starzecpyzel*, 880 F. Supp. 1027, 1038 (S.D.N.Y. 1995).

3.

Crisp today advocates the wholesale exclusion of a long — accepted form of expert evidence. Such a drastic step is not required of us under *Daubert*, however, and we decline to take it. The *Daubert* decision, in adding four new factors to the traditional "general acceptance" standard for expert testimony, effectively opened the courts to a broader range of opinion evidence than was previously admissible. Although *Daubert* attempted to ensure that courts screen out "junk science," it also enabled the courts to entertain new and less conventional forms of expertise. As the Court explained, the addition of the new factors would put an end to the "wholesale exclusion [of expert testimony based on scientific innovations] under an uncompromising 'general acceptance' test." *Daubert*, 509 U.S. at 596.

The touchstones for admissibility under *Daubert* are two: reliability and relevancy. Under *Daubert*, a trial judge need not expend scarce judicial resources reexamining a familiar form of expertise every time opinion evidence is offered. In fact, if a given theory or technique is "so firmly established as to have attained the status of scientific law," then it need not be examined at all, but instead may properly be subject to judicial notice. *Daubert*, 509 U.S. at 592 n. 11.

While the principles underlying fingerprint identification have not attained the status of scientific law, they nonetheless bear the imprimatur of a strong general acceptance, not only in the expert community, but in the courts as well. *See Havvard*, 260 F.3d at 601 (noting lower court's observation that fingerprint analysis has enjoyed "100 years of successful use in criminal trials"); *Jennings*, 96 N.E. at 1083 (upholding admissibility of fingerprint identification evidence ninety — two years ago). Put simply, Crisp has provided us no reason today to believe that this general acceptance of the principles underlying fingerprint identification has, for decades, been misplaced. Accordingly, the

---

[15] [n.3] *See* Margaret A. Berger, *Procedural Paradigms for Applying the Daubert Test*, 78 Minn. L.Rev. 1345, 1353 (1994) ("Considerable forensic evidence [such as fingerprinting] made its way into the courtroom without empirical validation of the underlying theory and/or its particular application."); Michael J. Saks, *Merlin and Solomon: Lessons from the Law's Formative Encounters With Forensic Identification Science*, 49 Hastings L.J. 1069, 1105–06 (1998) (noting that the first courts to recognize the validity of fingerprint analysis "invested little effort assessing the merits of the proffered scientific evidence" and observing that: "Fingerprint evidence may present courts applying *Daubert* with their most extreme dilemma. By conventional scientific standards, any serious search for evidence of the validity of fingerprint identification is going to be disappointing. Yet the intuitions that underlie fingerprint examination, and the subjective judgments on which specific case opinions are based, are powerful.").

district court was well within its discretion in accepting at face value the consensus of the expert and judicial communities that the fingerprint identification technique is reliable.

In addition to a strong expert and judicial consensus regarding the reliability of fingerprint identification, there exist the requisite "standards controlling the technique's operation." *Daubert*, 509 U.S. at 593. As Brannan testified, while different agencies may require different degrees of correlation before permitting a positive identification, fingerprint analysts are held to a consistent "points and characteristics" approach to identification. Analysts are also consistently subjected to testing and proficiency requirements. Brannan's testimony is entirely in keeping with the conclusions of the post — *Daubert* courts that uniform standards have been established "through professional training, peer review, presentation of conflicting evidence and double checking." *Cf. Havvard*, 260 F.3d at 599 (holding that, while uniform standards may not exist, "the unique nature of fingerprints is counterintuitive to the establishment of such a standard").

Furthermore, in *Havvard*, the Seventh Circuit determined that *Daubert*'s "known error rate" factor was satisfied because the expert had testified that the error rate for fingerprint comparison was "essentially zero." 260 F.3d at 599. Similarly, and significantly, Brannan testified here to a negligible error rate in fingerprint identifications.

In sum, the district court heard testimony to the effect that the expert community has consistently vouched for the reliability of the fingerprinting identification technique over the course of decades. That evidence is consistent with the findings of our sister circuits, and Crisp offers us no reason to believe that the court abused its discretion in crediting it. The district court also heard evidence from which it was entitled to find the existence of professional standards controlling the technique's operation. Those standards provide adequate assurance of consistency among fingerprint analyses. Finally, the court heard testimony that fingerprint identification has an exceedingly low rate of error, and the court was likewise within its discretion in crediting that evidence. While Crisp may be correct that further research, more searching scholarly review, and the development of even more consistent professional standards is desirable, he has offered us no reason to reject outright a form of evidence that has so ably withstood the test of time.

Finally, even if we had a more concrete cause for concern as to the reliability of fingerprint identification, the Supreme Court emphasized in *Daubert* that "[v]igorous cross — examination, presentation of contrary evidence, and careful instruction on the burden of proof are the traditional and appropriate means of attacking shaky but admissible evidence." *Daubert*, 509 U.S. at 596. Ultimately, we conclude that while further research into fingerprint analysis would be welcome, "to postpone present in — court utilization of this bedrock forensic identifier pending such research would be to make the best the enemy of the good." *Llera Plaza*, 188 F. Supp.2d at 573.

B.

In seeking to have his convictions vacated, Crisp also challenges the admissibility of the opinions of Currin, the handwriting expert, on grounds that are essentially identical to those on which he relied to make his case against fingerprint evidence. Crisp contends that, like fingerprinting identifications, the basic premise behind handwriting analysis is that no two persons write alike, and thus that forensic document examiners can reliably determine authorship of a particular document by comparing it with known samples. He maintains that these basic premises have not been tested, nor has an error rate been established. In addition, he asserts that handwriting experts have no numerical standards to govern their analyses and that they have not subjected themselves and their science to critical self — examination and study.

1.

While the admissibility of handwriting evidence in the post — *Daubert* world appears to be a matter of first impression for our Court, every circuit to have addressed the issue has concluded, as on the fingerprint issue, that such evidence is properly admissible. *See United States v. Jolivet*, 224 F.3d 902, 906 (8th Cir. 2000) (citing Eleventh Circuit's *Paul* decision and upholding admission of expert handwriting testimony); *United States v. Paul*, 175 F.3d 906, 911 (11th Cir.1999) (emphasizing "flexible" nature of district court's gatekeeping function, and noting that "the ability of the jury to perform the same visual comparisons as the experts cuts against the danger of undue prejudice from the mystique attached to experts" (internal quotation omitted)); *United States v. Jones*, 107 F.3d 1147, 1161 (6th Cir.1997) (upholding admission of expert handwriting testimony and observing that "just because the threshold for admissibility [of expert testimony] under Rule 702 has been crossed, a party is not prevented from challenging the reliability of the admitted evidence"); *United States v. Velasquez*, 64 F.3d 844 (3rd Cir.1995) (discussing standard methodology applied by handwriting analysts, and upholding admission of expert handwriting testimony).[16] [5]

2.

The Government's handwriting expert, Thomas Currin, had twenty — four years of experience at the North Carolina SBI. On voir dire, and then on direct examination, he explained that all questioned documents that come into the SBI are analyzed first by a "questioned document examiner"; and that the initial analysis is then reviewed by another examiner. Currin discussed several studies showing the ability of qualified document examiners to identify questioned handwriting.[17] [6] In addition, he had passed numerous proficiency tests, consistently receiving perfect scores. Currin testified to a consistent methodology of handwriting examination and identification, and he stated that the methodology "has been used not only at the level of state crime laboratories, but [also in] federal and international crime laboratories around the world." When he was questioned regarding the standards employed in questioned document examination, Currin explained that every determination of authorship "is based on the uniqueness of [certain] similarities, and it's based on the quality and the skill and the training of the document examiner."

At trial, Currin drew the jury's attention to similarities between Crisp's known handwriting exemplars and the writing on the Note. . . . He went on to testify that, in his opinion, Crisp had authored the Note.

---

[16] [n.5] Certain district courts, however, have recently determined that handwriting analysis does not meet the *Daubert* standards. *See, e.g., United States v. Lewis*, 220 F. Supp.2d 548, 554 (S.D.W.Va. 2002) (finding proficiency tests and peer review meaningless where the evidence showed that handwriting experts "*always* passed their proficiency tests, . . . [and that] peers *always* agreed with each others' results" (emphasis in original)); *United States v. Brewer*, 2002 WL 596365 (N.D.Ill. 2002); *United States v. Saelee*, 162 F. Supp.2d 1097 (D.Alaska 2001); *United States v. Hines*, 55 F. Supp.2d 62 (D.Mass. 1999).

[17] [n.6] Rather than analyzing the ability of document examiners to correctly identify authorship, the studies to which Currin referred examined whether document examiners were more likely than lay people to identify authorship correctly. In one study, lay participants had a 38% error rate, while qualified document examiners had a 6% error rate.

3.

Our analysis of *Daubert* in the context of fingerprint identification applies with equal force here: like fingerprint analysis, handwriting comparison testimony has a long history of admissibility in the courts of this country. *See, e.g., Robinson v. Mandell*, 20 F. Cas. 1027 (D.Mass. 1868). The fact that handwriting comparison analysis has achieved widespread and lasting acceptance in the expert community gives us the assurance of reliability that *Daubert* requires. Furthermore, as with expert testimony on fingerprints, the role of the handwriting expert is primarily to draw the jury's attention to similarities between a known exemplar and a contested sample. Here, Currin merely pointed out certain unique characteristics shared by the two writings. Though he opined that Crisp authored the Note in question, the jury was nonetheless left to examine the Note and decide for itself whether it agreed with the expert.

To the extent that a given handwriting analysis is flawed or flimsy, an able defense lawyer will bring that fact to the jury's attention, both through skillful cross — examination and by presenting expert testimony of his own. But in light of Crisp's failure to offer us any reason today to doubt the reliability of handwriting analysis evidence in general, we must decline to deny our courts and juries such insights as it can offer.

III.

For the foregoing reasons, we affirm the district court's evidentiary rulings, and thus we affirm the convictions of Patrick Leroy Crisp.

Affirmed.

NOTES

1. *Fingerprint Identification.* Courts confronted with a *Daubert* challenge to the admissibility of fingerprint identification testimony have not felt the need to scrutinize its reliability rigorously. In fact, some courts have not felt it was necessary to conduct a pretrial *Daubert* hearing on the admissibility of such evidence. In the *Havvard* case, the Seventh Circuit observed:

> The issue of the reliability of fingerprint evidence after *Daubert* appears to be one of first impression in this circuit, and few other courts have addressed this question. Those discussing the issue have not excluded fingerprint evidence; instead, they have declined to conduct a pretrial *Daubert* hearing on the admissibility of fingerprint evidence, *see United States v. Martinez-Cintron*, 136 F. Supp.2d 17 (D.P.R. 2001) (relying on the district court's order in this case); *United States v. Cooper*, 91 F. Supp.2d 79, 82–83 (D.D.C. 2000), or have issued brief opinions asserting that the reliability of fingerprint comparisons cannot be questioned, *see United States v. Sherwood*, 98 F.3d 402, 408 (9th Cir.1996); *United States v. Joseph*, 2001 WL 515213 (E.D.La. May 14, 2001).

United States v. Havvard, 260 F.3d 597, 600 (7th Cir. 2001). *Cf. United States v. Llera Plaza*, 188 F. Supp. 2d 549, 571–72 (E.D. Pa. 2002) (vacating court's previous order excluding expert testimony on fingerprint identification although acknowledging *Daubert*'s "testing" factor is unsatisfied; "[t]here is no evidence that certified FBI fingerprint examiners present erroneous identification testimony, . . . no evidence that the rate of error of certified FBI fingerprint examiners is unacceptably high" and that it is "not persuaded that courts should defer admission of testimony with respect to fingerprinting . . . until academic investigators . . . make substantial headway on a research agenda."). *See also* DAVID L. FAIGMAN, MICHAEL J. SAKS, JOSEPH SANDERS & EDWARD K. CHENG, 4 MODERN SCIENTIFIC EVIDENCE: THE LAW AND SCIENCE OF EXPERT TESTIMONY § 32:3, at 294 (2008) ("With few exceptions, recent judicial opinions reacting to challenges to asserted fingerprint identification expertise are united by their failure — typically, their refusal — to conduct any thoughtful analysis under *Daubert* and *Kumho Tire*.").

QUESTIONS

1. Does the court in *Crisp* take judicial notice of the reliability of fingerprint and handwriting identification? If not, what reliability factors does the court use in determining these techniques are reliable?

2. In *Crisp* the court stated, "While the principles underlying fingerprint identification have not attained the status of scientific law, they nonetheless bear the imprimatur of a strong general acceptance. . . ." *Crisp*, *supra*, 324 F.3d at 268. To whom is the court referring? That is, who generally accepts fingerprint identification? Would there be any question as to the admissibility of such evidence in a *Frye* jurisdiction?

3. In *Crisp* the court also stated, "Fingerprint identification has been admissible as reliable evidence in criminal trials in this country since at least 1911." *Crisp*, *supra*, 324 F.3d at 266. If fingerprint identification has not been tested, how does the court know it is reliable?

4. Finally, note that in *Crisp* the court wrote, "the district court was well within its discretion in accepting at face value the consensus of the expert and judicial communities that the fingerprint identification technique is reliable." *Crisp*, *supra*, 324 F.3d at 269. Isn't this just admitting the expert's opinion based on the *ipse dixit* of the expert? Is this consistent with *Daubert*? Is it consistent with *Kumho Tire*?

[ii]   The *Daubert* Trilogy Applied in Criminal Cases — Nonscientific Experts; Personal Knowledge and Experience as Reliability Factors

In *Kumho Tire* the Court wrote, "[e]ngineering testimony rests upon scientific foundations, the reliability of which will be at issue in some cases. In other cases, the relevant reliability concerns may focus upon *personal knowledge or experience*." *Kumho Tire*, *supra*, 526 U.S. at 150 (emphasis added). Personal knowledge and experience, of course, are qualities that *qualify* a person to be an expert pursuant to Fed. R. Evid 702. Could the Supreme Court be saying that the opinions of certain nonscientific experts could be deemed reliable based upon the expert's qualifications? If so, isn't that perilously close to finding an opinion is reliable just because a qualified expert said so? As you read through the *Brumley* and *Hankey* cases that follow, ask yourself if the expert's opinion is considered reliable and admissible simply because the expert is qualified and experienced, or if there is something more the trial court is looking for. If so, what is that "something more"?

UNITED STATES v. BRUMLEY
217 F.3d 905 (7th Cir. 2000)

ILANA DIAMOND ROVNER, CIRCUIT JUDGE

[A search of Brumley's home led to recovery of methamphetamine, scales, cash and two handguns. Following a jury trial defendant was convicted of conspiracy to possess with intent to distribute methamphetamine. Brumley (who was a user of methamphetamine) challenged his conviction on a number of grounds, contending, among other things, that a DEA agent named Dan Schmidt was erroneously allowed to give expert testimony on the issue of what quantities of methamphetamine constituted user and dealer amounts.]

B.

Brumley . . . objected to the admission of DEA Agent Dan Schmidt's testimony regarding what amounts of methamphetamine constituted user quantities and what amounts were dealer quantities. Specifically, Brumley disputed the agent's conclusion that any amounts in excess of one ounce were distribution as opposed to personal use amounts. Brumley raises [several] objections to the admission of this testimony. First, the agent's opinion was based on his subjective belief or unsupported speculation. Second, the agent's opinion was not based on any professionally sound or reliable underlying methodology. . . . [Third], the agent's opinion testimony was highly prejudicial but did not assist the trier of fact in understanding the evidence or determining a fact in issue.

The government sought to qualify Agent Schmidt as an expert in the area of drug trafficking, including packaging quantities, distribution methods, and user quantities versus distribution quantities. Agent Schmidt had approximately seven years of law enforcement experience, much of it involving investigations relating to narcotics and other drugs, including methamphetamine. He had, in the course of those investigations, interviewed people he arrested who decided to cooperate with the government. He testified that through his investigations and experience, he became familiar with how methamphetamine is packaged and sold, including prices and quantities. He testified that as a result of the approximately one hundred methamphetamine investigations in which he had participated, he knew what quantities of methamphetamine were for personal use and what quantities were dealer amounts. On the basis of this testimony, the district court allowed Agent Schmidt to testify that, in his opinion, an ounce or more of methamphetamine constituted a dealer quantity. Because Brumley was charged with possession with intent to distribute, possession of dealer quantities was probative as to Brumley's intent, and the government indeed sought to use this testimony to prove Brumley's intent to distribute.

The admission of expert testimony from technical fields is governed by the same concerns and criteria as the admission of scientific expert testimony. *See Kumho Tire Co., Ltd. v. Carmichael*, 526 U.S. 137 (1999). . . . [W]e review the district court's decision to admit or exclude expert testimony only for an abuse of discretion. The Supreme Court in *Kumho Tire* explained that the *Daubert* "gatekeeper" factors had to be adjusted to fit the facts of the particular case at issue, with the goal of testing the reliability of the expert opinion. For example, engineering testimony rests on scientific foundations, but "[i]n other cases, the relevant reliability concerns may focus upon personal knowledge or experience." The reason for this needed flexibility is that there are many different kinds of experts and many different kinds of expertise, including experts in drug terminology, handwriting analysis, land valuation, agricultural practices, railroad procedures, and so forth.

The district court applied this flexible approach by determining the extent and type of experience that Agent Schmidt had in the area of methamphetamine distribution. The court carefully limited both the questioning and the agent's testimony to reflect only those areas in which the agent had extensive experience and training, and in which the jury would be aided by his testimony. The district court therefore applied the *Daubert* gatekeeping tests for relevance and reliability and we will review the court's decision to admit this evidence for abuse of discretion only. Addressing Brumley's objections *seriatim*, the record reveals that the agent's testimony was based not on his subjective belief or unsupported speculation but rather on his extensive experience investigating methamphetamine distribution crimes. For example, the agent testified that in his experience, methamphetamine was sold on the streets of Indiana during the relevant time frame for $100 per gram, and that there are approximately 28 grams in an ounce. From his experience, the agent testified that an ounce or more of methamphetamine constituted a dealer quantity. As the district court pointed out, another expert might disagree with this opinion, but the disagreement does not render the opinion inadmissable. Rather, Brumley was entitled to cross-examine Agent Schmidt and to put on his own expert to offer a counter opinion. That addresses Brumley's second objection as well, that Agent Schmidt's opinion was not based on any professionally sound or reliable underlying methodology. The opinion was based on his extensive investigative experience, and *Kumho Tire* explains that the reliability of different kinds of expertise may be shown in different ways.

. . . .

Finally, Brumley complains that the evidence was highly prejudicial and did not aid the jury. . . . Brumley [states] that his objection is . . . based on the fact none of Agent's Schmidt's experience of training was related to distinguishing user quantities from dealer quantities. However the argument is framed, the result is the same. The district court properly determined that Agent Schmidt had expertise in the matter of distinguishing user from dealer quantities, expertise gained through his extensive experience investigating crimes of this very nature. Brumley's argument goes not to the admissibility of this evidence but rather to its weight, and he was free to cross-examine the agent about the basis for his opinion. Through cross-examination and testimony from his own witness, Brumley was free to reveal any weaknesses or errors in the agent's opinion. Because the district court carried out the gatekeeper function appropriately and limited the evidence to those areas in which the agent had expertise gained through experience and training, we affirm the admission of Agent Schmidt's expert testimony.

Affirmed.

UNITED STATES v. HANKEY, aka Poo
203 F.3d 1160 (9th Cir. 2000)

Jones, District Judge:

Lavern Hankey appeals his conviction and sentence for distributing and conspiring to possess with intent to distribute phencylidine ("PCP"). At trial, after Hankey's co-defendant testified that Hankey was not involved in the transactions, the district court admitted rebuttal testimony from a police gang expert that gang members who testify against one of their own are customarily beaten or killed by other members of their gang. . . .

FACTS AND PROCEDURAL BACKGROUND

In 1996, the Drug Enforcement Administration (DEA) began an investigation of suspected PCP distributor James Anthony Welch.[18] [3] On August 14, 1996, a confidential informant arranged with Welch to purchase a quart of PCP for $1,500. Under DEA surveillance, the informant met Welch and drove with him to the 400 block of Spruce Street in Compton, California, where they met with an individual who identified himself as "Poo." . . . Poo and Welch poured PCP into [a] juice bottle and gave it to the informant.

Law enforcement later identified "Poo" as Lavern Hankey, who lived in his mother's home on the 400 block of Spruce Street-the site of the PCP transactions in question.

. . . .

[After additional incidents involving undercover informants and the sale of PCP, the government charged Hankey and Welch with distribution of PCP and conspiracy to possess with intent to distribute PCP. Hankey and Welch were tried together]

Hankey's defense was that he was not the "Poo" who engaged in the transactions. . . . Welch, while testifying on his own behalf, . . . claimed that the "Poo" who supplied the PCP was a rapper named Marcus Prea. Welch explained the proximity of the drug deals to Hankey's house by the fact that the house next door was vacant and being used as a local drug hangout.

In rebuttal, the government sought to discredit the exculpatory testimony of . . . Welch by offering the expert testimony of Mark Anderson, Compton Police Department Officer and member of an FBI anti-gang task force. Anderson testified at a motion in limine Federal Rule of Evidence 104 hearing, outside the presence of the jury, that . . . Welch and Hankey were members of affiliated street gangs, and that these gangs enforce a code of silence among their members that any affiliated gang member would be subject to violent retribution if one gang member testified against another.

[T]he court allowed [Anderson] to testify before the jury regarding the gang affiliation of Welch and Hankey. Further, the court permitted Anderson to express his opinion that if a member of one of the affiliated gangs in the area testified against another member, the witness would be beaten or killed. At the trial, the court gave a limiting instruction regarding this testimony, telling the jury that it could consider Anderson's opinions as they related to Welch's testimony about Hankey's misidentification, and that it "ought not be a factor in your determination as to whether the government has proved the charges in this case. . . ."

. . . .

The jury convicted Hankey on both charged counts, but acquitted Welch, apparently accepting Welch's argument that he was entrapped by the DEA informants.

---

[18] [n.3] Welch was tried with Hankey as a codefendant.

. . . [O]n appeal Hankey challenges the admission of the gang expert testimony. . . .

. . . .

DISCUSSION

A. *Testimony of Police Gang Expert*

Hankey . . . argues that the district court abused its discretion in admitting the opinion testimony of Officer Anderson regarding the gang affiliations of the co-defendants and the consequences Welch would suffer if he were to testify against Hankey. Specifically, he contends that the district court failed to properly discharge its gatekeeping function for the admission of testimony offered under FRE 702 as set forth in *Kumho Tire* and *Daubert*. . . .

In *Daubert*, the Supreme Court, in addressing admissibility of "scientific expert evidence," held that FRE 702 imposes a "gatekeeping" obligation on the trial judge to "ensure that any and all scientific testimony . . . is not only relevant, but reliable." While holding that the trial court has substantial discretion in discharging its gatekeeping obligation, it suggested a number of factors that the court might consider: 1) whether a theory or technique can be tested; 2) whether it has been subjected to peer review and publication; 3) the known or potential error rate of the theory or technique; and 4) whether the theory or technique enjoys general acceptance within the relevant scientific community.

In *Kumho Tire*, the Court clarified that the gatekeeping function is not limited to "scientific" expert testimony, but applies to all expert testimony, ruling that the district court did not abuse its discretion in excluding the testimony of a tire failure analyst on the grounds that the expert's methodology was unreliable. . . .

Hankey invokes *Kumho Tire* to argue that the district court failed properly to assess the reliability of Officer Anderson's "non-scientific" testimony. He mistakenly implies that the court should have assessed this testimony in the same way that the district court reviewed the methodology used by the tire defect expert in *Kumho Tire*. However, far from requiring trial judges to mechanically apply the *Daubert* factors — or something like them — to both scientific and non-scientific testimony, *Kumho Tire* heavily emphasizes that judges are entitled to broad discretion when discharging their gatekeeping function. Indeed, not only must the trial court be given broad discretion to decide *whether* to admit expert testimony, it "must have the same kind of latitude in deciding *how* to test an expert's reliability."

The *Daubert* factors were not intended to be exhaustive nor to apply in every case. However, a trial court may consider the specific factors identified in *Daubert* where they are reasonable measures of the reliability of proffered expert testimony.

Likewise, in considering the admissibility of testimony based on some "other specialized knowledge," Rule 702 generally is construed liberally.

Thus, admissibility of expert opinion testimony generally turns on the following preliminary question of law determinations by the trial judge under FRE 104(a).

- Whether the opinion is based on scientific, technical, or other specialized knowledge;

- Whether the expert's opinion would assist the trier of fact in understanding the evidence or determining a fact in issue;

- Whether the expert has appropriate qualifications — i.e., some special knowledge, skill, experience, training or education on that subject matter;

- Whether the testimony is relevant and reliable;

- Whether the methodology or technique the expert uses "fits" the conclusions (the expert's credibility is for the jury);

- Whether its probative value is substantially outweighed by the risk of unfair prejudice, confusion of issues, or undue consumption of time.

Here, the district court conducted extensive voir dire to assess the basis for and the relevance and reliability of Officer Anderson's testimony. Anderson stated that he had been with the Compton Police Department for 21 years; he had been working undercover with gang members in the thousands since 1989; he had received formal training in gang structure and organization; and he taught classes about gangs. He stated that he had extensive personal knowledge regarding the two affiliated gangs of which Hankey [and] Welch . . . were members. Further, he testified he personally knew Hankey and Welch for 10 or 11 years each and that in the early 1990's Hankey and Welch told him they were members of these affiliated gangs during the late 1980's and early 1990's. He testified he believed that, because they continued to live in the neighborhood and associate with gang members, they were still members themselves because those who become unaffiliated leave town. Further, he based his opinion about Hankey's current gang membership on the criminal activity and observations he made in the field prior to the arrest for the current offenses. Upon further questioning by the court, Officer Anderson stated that he had personally seen Hankey and Welch together in 1996. . . . On this basis the court . . . allowed testimony regarding the membership of Welch and Hankey, as well as the "code of silence" and retaliation that prevented members of affiliated gangs from testifying against one another. Anderson based his testimony as to the "code of silence" and retaliation upon his current and past communications with gang members and gang officers.

Given the type of expert testimony proffered by the government, it is difficult to imagine that the court could have been more diligent in assessing relevance and reliability. The *Daubert* factors (peer review, publication, potential error rate, etc.) simply are not applicable to this kind of testimony, whose reliability depends heavily on the knowledge and experience of the expert, rather than the methodology or theory behind it. *See Kumho Tire*, 119 S.Ct. at 1175 ("Engineering testimony rests upon scientific foundations, the reliability of which will be at issue in some cases. . . . In other cases, the relevant reliability concerns may focus upon personal knowledge or experience.").[19] [7] The district court probed the extent of this knowledge and experience during the motion in limine-FRE 104 hearing, and therefore did not abuse its discretion in determining how best to conduct an assessment of the expert testimony.

---

[19] [n.7] A number of Ninth Circuit cases have held that *Daubert* does not apply to "non-scientific" testimony at all. *See United States v. Plunk*, 153 F.3d 1011, 1017 (9th Cir.1998); *McKendall v. Crown Control Corp.*, 122 F.3d 803, 806 (9th Cir.1997); *United States v. Webb*, 115 F.3d 711, 716 (9th Cir.1997). To this extent, these cases are no longer good law after *Kumho Tire*, which eliminated the analytical distinction between "scientific" and "non-scientific" testimony. However, these cases are still good law to the extent that they permit the admission of expert testimony on the basis of the expert's "knowledge, skill, experience, training, or education," which is consistent with *Kumho Tire*.

Here, the witness had devoted years working with gangs, knew their "colors," signs, and activities. He heard the admissions of the specific gang members involved. He had communicated and worked undercover with thousands of other gang members. This type of street intelligence might be misunderstood as either remote (some dating back to the late 1980's) or hearsay (based upon current communications about "retaliation" and "code of silence."), but FRE 702 works well for this type of data gathered from years of experience and special knowledge.

Certainly the officer relied on "street intelligence" for his opinions about gang membership and tenets. How else can one obtain this encyclopedic knowledge of identifiable gangs? Gangs such as involved here do not have by-laws, organizational minutes, or any other normal means of identification-although as Anderson testified, some wear colors, give signs, bear tattoos, etc. Anderson was repeatedly asked the basis for his opinions and fully articulated the basis, demonstrating that the information upon which he relied is of the type normally obtained in his day-to-day police activity.

. . . .

After the motion in limine, the trial judge, pursuant to FRE 104(a), made findings that the foundation for Anderson's opinions was relevant and reliable. The background information for the "code of silence" and "retaliation" testimony was current and not subject to attack on remoteness grounds. Nor did the court abuse its discretion in making its ultimate decision to admit the evidence. The testimony was certainly helpful to the jury. Welch claimed on the stand that Hankey was not involved in drug transactions. Officer Anderson countered this claim by providing the jury with an explanation for why Welch would lie on Hankey's behalf. . . .

. . . .

CONCLUSION

For the foregoing reasons, the district court did not abuse its discretion in admitting the testimony of a police gang expert to impeach co-defendant Welch's testimony that Hankey was not involved in the alleged drug transactions. . . .

Affirmed.

————

In the next case, *United States v. Mamah*, the reviewing court takes a much more detailed look at the research that supported the expert's opinion, and affirmed the trial court's exclusion of the expert's testimony. As you read the Court's opinion in *Mamah*, consider whether it is consistent with the court's opinion in *Hankey*. The expert in *Mamah* was proffered by the defendant. Did that make any difference?

UNITED STATES v. MAMAH
332 F.3d 475 (7th Cir. 2003)

KANNE, CIRCUIT JUDGE.

Abdul Mamah, a Ghanaian immigrant, was charged with one count of possession with intent to distribute in excess of 100 grams of heroin in violation of 21 U.S.C. § 841(a)(1). At trial Mamah sought to introduce testimony from two expert witnesses in support of his claim that the confession he gave to the FBI after his arrest was false. The district court ruled the testimony of both experts inadmissible, and a jury subsequently found Mamah guilty. On appeal Mamah argues that the court excluded his expert witnesses in violation of Federal Rule of Evidence 702. We affirm.

In May 2000 Mamah told Falilat Giwa that he planned to travel to Chicago, Illinois, to engage in a narcotics transaction. Unbeknownst to Mamah, Giwa was a confidential informant for the FBI and was taping their telephone conversation on instructions from Special Agent Thomas Wilson.

Mamah subsequently flew . . . to Chicago to meet Giwa and checked into a hotel. . . . When Giwa arrived at the hotel to buy narcotics from Mamah, she was accompanied by Agent Wilson and several other FBI Agents. . . . [Mamah was approached by one of the FBI agents who identified himself as an FBI agent and] obtained Mamah's consent to search his hotel room. During their search, agents discovered $5000 in currency wrapped in newspaper and a plastic bag containing 300 grams of heroin hidden behind the drapes.

Mamah was arrested and taken to the FBI office in downtown Chicago, where he received *Miranda* warnings and agreed to an interview. Mamah initially denied knowledge of the heroin recovered from his room but eventually admitted his guilt in a statement that [FBI] Agent Wilson transcribed and Mamah signed.

Part of Mamah's defense was his claim that he falsely confessed. Before trial Mamah had moved the court to admit the expert testimony of Dr. Deborah Pellow, an anthropologist[.] According to Mamah's filings, Dr. Pellow, a specialist in the culture of Ghana, would testify that behaviors adopted by Ghanaians in response to living under a military regime could lead them to make false confessions when confronted by law enforcement authorities. . . .

The district court concluded that the proposed testimony of . . . Dr. Pellow . . . was unreliable and thus inadmissible under Rule 702. The court reasoned that . . . Dr. Pellow was [not] a clinical psychologist qualified to assess Mamah's susceptibility to the interrogation techniques used by the FBI agents. The court had additional concerns about Dr. Pellow's testimony. First, the court noted that Mamah had been living in the United States since 1984, more than enough time to have learned the difference between Ghanaian and American law — enforcement practices. Further, since Mamah claimed that he had been detained and beaten while still living in Ghana, the court viewed the relevance of Dr. Pellow's testimony as dependent upon similarities between this incident and the FBI agents' interview of Mamah. But, the court noted, Mamah had not accused the FBI agents of engaging in tactics similar to those purportedly common in Ghana, and so any mention of Mamah's mistreatment at the hands of Ghanaian authorities would be overly prejudicial and confusing to the jury.

At trial Agent Wilson testified that Mamah had received *Miranda* warnings and then signed a waiver form before dictating his confession. Agent Wilson asserted that he went over the statement with Mamah line by line before Mamah signed it. Mamah testified that Agent Wilson had used abusive language during the interview and warned Mamah that he would get life imprisonment and never see his children again unless he cooperated. According to Mamah, his oral statement did not correspond to the written statement, which, at the agents' direction, he had signed without reading. Mamah testified that he had no idea how the heroin came to be in his hotel room.

Mamah's sole contention on appeal is that the district court erred in finding the expert testimony of Dr. Pellow . . . inadmissible under Rule 702 and *Daubert v.*

Merrell Dow Pharmaceuticals, 509 U.S. 579 (1993). We begin our analysis by looking at the actual text of Rule 702, which was amended in 2000 in response to *Daubert* and *Kumho Tire Co. v. Carmichael*, 526 U.S. 137 (1999). The new Rule 702 lists three criteria for courts to consider when determining the admissibility of expert testimony. The first of these is that the expert's opinions be "based upon sufficient facts or data," and Dr. Pellow's . . . proposed testimony [did not meet] this requirement.

Mamah argues that excluding the testimony of Dr. Pellow . . . was tantamount to a statement that social science can never form the basis of expert testimony. We acknowledge that social scientists frequently testify as experts, and their opinions are "an integral part of many cases." But whether social science studies can ever be a proper foundation for an expert's opinion is not the issue here. The issue is whether [*this*] social science study, the research of [*this*] expert, sufficiently supported the expert opinion Mamah wanted to present to the jury — and [it] did not. *Cf. Gen. Elec. Co. v. Joiner*, 522 U.S. 136, 144 (1997) ("[W]hether animal studies can ever be a proper foundation for an expert's opinion was not the issue. The issue was whether *these* experts' opinions were sufficiently supported by the animal studies on which they purported to rely.").

Mamah contends that the district court disregarded Dr. Pellow's . . . impressive educational backgrounds and professional accomplishments in ruling [her] testimony inadmissible. In doing so, Mamah is conflating subpart (1) of Rule 702, the requirement for "sufficient facts and data," with subpart (2) of Rule 702, the necessity for "a reliable foundation in principles and method." Whether or not Dr. Pellow . . . grounded [her] work in sound social science principles and methods, the court still needed to satisfy itself that [her] work yielded facts and data sufficient to support [her] proposed testimony. As we have observed, "experts' opinions are worthless without data and reasons."

It is critical under Rule 702 that there be a link between the facts or data the expert has worked with and the conclusion the expert's testimony is intended to support. *See Gen. Elec.*, 522 U.S. at 146, ("A court may conclude that there is simply too great an analytical gap between the data and the opinion proffered."). The court is not obligated to admit testimony just because it is given by an expert. *Id.* ("[N]othing in either *Daubert* or the Federal Rules of Evidence requires a district court to admit opinion evidence which is connected to existing data only by the *ipse dixit* of the expert."). The problem with the proposed testimony in this case does not lie in the quality of Dr. Pellow's . . . research. Rather the problem is the absence of an empirical link between that research and the opinion that Mamah likely gave a false confession.

Mamah argues that Dr. Pellow would have testified that what he experienced in Ghana predisposed him to manipulation and intimidation during his interrogation by FBI agents. Such an opinion, however, would fall outside the scope of Dr. Pellow's work, which concentrates upon Ghanaian culture. Dr. Pellow's testimony may have been useful in answering questions about how a repressive military regime shapes Ghanaian behavioral patterns, but those questions were not pertinent here because the interrogation in this case did not occur in Ghana and Mamah has not lived in Ghana since 1984.

Dr. Pellow's expertise is limited to the cultural practices of Ghanaian nationals living in Ghana; she has no basis for extrapolating this conclusion to Mamah, a Ghanaian expatriot. Had she offered an empirical study demonstrating that Ghanaian ex — patriots who have lived in the United States for more than ten years are unusually likely to give false confessions, then perhaps she could have established this link. But Dr. Pellow did not have at her disposal sufficient facts and data to support the proposition that Mamah's cultural background might have induced him to give a false confession.

. . . .

Affirmed.

NOTES

1. *The "Something More."* In footnote 7 to the Ninth Circuit's opinion in *Hankey*, the court writes that certain pre-*Kumho Tire* "cases are still good law to the extent that they permit the admission of expert testimony on the basis of an expert's 'knowledge, skill, experience, training, or education,' which is consistent with *Kumho Tire*." Knowledge, skill, experience, training, and education are what can *qualify* a person to be an expert pursuant to Rule 702. Doesn't a trial court's gatekeeping obligations require more than an assessment of the expert's qualifications? If so, what, in addition to qualifications, make an expert's experienced based opinions reliable? Put another way, if qualifications are all that are considered isn't it accurate to say that *Daubert* is not to be applied to experienced-based experts? What, if anything, does the gatekeeping obligation require a trial court to look for *in a particular case* in addition to the expert's qualifications?

The advisory committee's note to the 2000 amendment to Fed. R. Evid. 702 speaks to these questions. The note mentions three questions that must be addressed.

> Nothing in this amendment is intended to suggest that experience alone — or experience in conjunction with other knowledge, skill, training or education — may not provide a sufficient basis foundation for expert testimony. To the contrary the test of Rule 702 expressly contemplates that an expert may be qualified on the basis of experience. In certain fields, experience is the predominant, if not sole, basis for a great deal of reliable testimony. *See, e.g., United States v. Jones*, 107 F.3d 1147 (6th Cir. 1997) (no abuse of discretion in admitting the testimony of a handwriting examiner who had years of practical experience and extensive training, and who explained his methodology in detail). . . .

> If the witness is relying solely or primarily on experience, then the witness [1] *must explain* how the experience leads to conclusion reached, [2] why that experience is a sufficient basis, and [3] how that experience is reliably applied to the facts. *The trial court's gatekeeping function requires more than simply "taking the expert's word for it." Daubert v. Merrell Dow Pharmaceuticals, Inc.*, 43 F.3d 1311, 1319 (9th Cir. 1995) ("We've been presented with only the experts' qualifications, their conclusions and their assurances of reliability. Under *Daubert*, that's not enough."). *The more subjective and controversial the expert's inquiry, the more likely the testimony should be excluded as unreliable. See O'Conner v. Commonwealth Edison Co.*, 13 F.3d 1090 (7th Cir. 1994) (expert testimony based on a completely subjective methodology held properly excluded). *See also Kumho Tire Co. v. Carmichael*, 119 S.Ct. 1167, 1176 (1999) ("[I]t will at times be useful to ask even of a witness whose expertise is based purely on experience, say, a perfume tester able to distinguish among 140 odors

at a sniff, whether his preparation is of a kind that others in the field would recognize as acceptable.").

Fed. R. Evid. 702 advisory committee's note to 2000 amendment (emphasis added and bracketed numbers added).

2. *Law Enforcement Agents Opining on the Criminality of the Accused's Conduct or Intent.* *Brumley* and *Hankey* are representative of a number of cases that permit law enforcement personnel to offer expert opinions concerning the criminal nature of an accused's conduct (often offered as relevant to show the accused's criminal intent) based upon the expert's training and experience working with other similar cases. *See United States v. Taylor*, 239 F.3d 994, 998 (9th Cir. 2001) (academic expert on the relationship between prostitutes and pimps allowed to testify why a prostitute "might not have testified truthfully in previous proceedings about her relationship with her pimp"); *United States v. Alatorre*, 222 F.3d 1098, 1100 (9th Cir. 2000) (Customs Service special agent testifies to wholesale and retail value of marijuana based upon 12 years experience as a special agent, specialized training, reviewing reports from other agents, and consulting the various Narcotics Information Networks systems). *United States v. Campos*, 217 F.3d 707, 719 (9th Cir. 2000) (Pregerson, J., concurring in part and dissenting in part) (jury "properly heard [agent's] expert testimony that (1) the marijuana had a street value of $120,000; and (2) that 'marijuana drug trafficking organizations, . . . particular[ly those involved in] the smuggling or the transportation [of drugs] from Mexico to the United States,' often use human 'mules' whose only 'job is to drive the car, or the truck, or whatever the vehicle happens to be' across the border."); *United States v. Plunk*, 153 F.3d 1011, 1017 (9th Cir. 1998) (upholding admission of expert testimony from law enforcement officer regarding jargon of narcotics trade, on basis of expert's training, experience, and personal knowledge).

Criminal defense attorneys have been critical of the prosecution's use of law enforcement agents as experts. Courts almost universally admit such opinion evidence under the *Daubert* trilogy, finding that the opinion is reliable because the law enforcement officer is "experienced" and the testimony is relevant. For the defense attorney view on this practice, consider the following excerpt from an article that appeared in *The Champion*, a magazine published by the National Association of Criminal Defense Lawyers.

> Experienced criminal defense lawyers are acutely aware of how prosecutors have used Rule 702 as a vehicle for admitting "soft" expert testimony from law enforcement agents about the methods and techniques employed in drug distribution, telemarketing schemes, and other forms of organized or disorganized criminal activity. Indulgent appellate courts have upheld the admission of expert testimony which comes perilously close to a bald conclusion that the defendant is guilty. See, e.g., *United States v. Harris*, 192 F.3d 580 (6th Cir. 1999) (defendant was observed with his pants leg rolled up; no error in admitting police officer's expert testimony that a rolled up pants leg signifies that the individual in question has drugs for sale); *United States v. Webb*, 115 F.3d 711 (9th Cir. 1997) (police found a handgun wrapped in a shirt in the engine compartment of defendant's car; police expert's testimony that people typically conceal guns in that manner so that law enforcement officers will not find them, or the person can claim ignorance of the weapon if it is found, was relevant and admissible to prove the defendant's knowledge of the gun's presence. The author was fascinated by this concept, but since 1997 has been unable to find one defense lawyer who was aware of this modus operandi.). One significant

problem with these cases is that the appellate decisions are based on an abuse of discretion standard. The prosecution ignores this and argues in subsequent district court cases that this type of testimony has been approved by the court of appeals and should be admitted.

This kind of soft "expert testimony" will ensure a conviction in many cases. It is difficult, if not impossible, to rebut because virtually all of the available experts are affiliated with the prosecution and, unlike more traditional forms of expert testimony, there is no body of authoritative published work which can be used to test and evaluate the validity of the police expert's opinions. Cross-examination is risky and rarely successful because the "expert" is free to support his opinions with examples from dozens or hundreds of other supposedly similar incidents about which defense counsel will have little or no information.

Barry Tarlow, *RICO Report*, THE CHAMPION 39, 46 (May 2000).[20]

QUESTIONS

1. What reliability factors are used by the Seventh and Ninth Circuits in *Brumley* and *Hankey* to test the reliability of the government's experts? What reliability factors does the Seventh Circuit use in *Mamah*?

2. In *Kumho Tire* the Supreme Court wrote:

[S]ome of *Daubert's* questions can help evaluate the reliability of even experience-based testimony. In certain cases, it will be appropriate for the trial judge to ask, for example, how often an engineering expert's experience-based methodology has produced erroneous results, or whether such a method is generally accepted in the relevant engineering community. Likewise, it will at times be useful to ask even of a witness whose expertise is based purely on experience, say, a perfume tester able to distinguish among 140 odors at a sniff, whether his preparation is of a kind that others in the field would recognize as acceptable.

Kumho Tire, supra, 526 U.S. at 151. Are the opinions in *Brumley, Hankey*, and *Mamah* consistent with the above passage from *Kumho Tire*? Are they consistent with the advisory committee's note to amended Fed. R. Evid. 702 (*see* Note 1, *supra*, following the *Hankey* case)? If not, in what ways are they inconsistent?

PROBLEMS

Problem 2-11. For the purposes of determining what *Daubert/Kumho Tire* reliability factors should apply, what is the difference between a police officer's opinion that an individual was driving an automobile under the influence of alcohol based upon the administration of a breath test, and the same police officer offering the same opinion based upon the officer's firsthand observations of the accused and 15 years of work as a traffic officer arresting intoxicated drivers? What factors are "reasonable" measures of reliability for each opinion?

Problem 2-12. If Hankey's trial were held in a state that followed the *Frye* test for the admissibility of scientific evidence, should the trial court hold a hearing to determine if Anderson's (the gang expert) opinion is generally accepted? Put another way, does *Frye* apply to opinion testimony from experience-based experts?

[iii]   The *Daubert* Trilogy Applied in Criminal Cases — The Pretrial Hearing and Taking Reliability "For Granted"

The next case, *United States v. Alatorre*, illustrates how *Kumho Tire* altered the procedures trial courts utilize when making — or refusing to make — a *Daubert* reliability determination.

UNITED STATES v. ALATORRE
222 F.3d 1098 (9th Cir. 2000)

McKeown, Circuit Judge:

The question in this case is whether the district court must hold a separate hearing before trial, as opposed to making an evidentiary determination during trial, in order to fulfill the "gatekeeping" function outlined in the Supreme Court's trilogy of cases addressing the admissibility of expert testimony: *Daubert v. Merrell Dow Pharmaceuticals, Inc.*, 509 U.S. 579 (1993), *General Elec. Co. v. Joiner*, 522 U.S. 136 (1997), and *Kumho Tire Co. v. Carmichael*, 526 U.S. 137 (1999). Here the district court rejected appellant Jorge Alberto Alatorre's request for such a pretrial hearing but permitted him to question the government's proffered expert at trial, in the presence of the jury, via voir dire. Alatorre appeals the court's refusal to grant his request for a separate hearing. Although we believe that it may be appropriate, at least in some cases, to conduct a pretrial or other hearing outside the presence of the jury to assess preliminary questions of relevance and reliability relating to experts, we hold that a separate hearing is not required. Further, under the circumstances presented here, the district court did not abuse its discretion in denying Alatorre's request.

BACKGROUND

On February 7, 1999, Alatorre, accompanied by his two children, drove a car to the San Ysidro, California, port of entry near San Diego, where he drew the attention of a U.S. Customs Service inspector. While the inspector was questioning Alatorre, a dog alerted to the car he was driving, and upon further inspection, packages of marijuana weighing 68.8 pounds were found in a compartment above the rear tire well. A grand jury indicted Alatorre on charges of importing marijuana, and possessing marijuana with intent to distribute.

Prior to trial, the parties filed motions in limine regarding the government's proposed expert testimony. After a hearing on the motions, the district court ruled that the government could introduce expert testimony on the value of the marijuana seized and on whether it was a distributable quantity. . . .

During the in limine hearing, Alatorre requested that a separate "*Daubert* hearing" be held outside the presence of the jury to determine whether the government's proposed expert witness was qualified to testify about the value of the marijuana and to assess whether this testimony was relevant to the sole issue in the case: whether

Alatorre knew that the car he was driving contained drugs. The court denied this request but indicated that Alatorre could conduct voir dire of the proffered expert at trial, in the presence of the jury, and stated that if the expert's testimony raised any concerns, then further questioning would be permitted outside the jury's presence[21] [2]

. . . .

At trial, the government called Lee Jacobs, a senior special agent of the Customs Service, to testify as an expert about the issues of value [and] distributable quantity. . . . The government elicited background testimony that Jacobs was familiar with the relative prices of marijuana as a result of his activities "as the case agent, co-case agent, running undercover operations, being an undercover operative, reviewing reports from other agents, and consulting with the various Narcotics Information Network systems and intelligence systems" available to agents in San Diego. The government also elicited testimony that Jacobs had twelve years of experience as a special agent; that he had specialized training in the methods by which narcotics are used and sold; and that, based on his experience, he was familiar with the structure of marijuana smuggling operations.

During voir dire, Alatorre inquired at length into the basis for Jacobs's expertise on the value issue and established that he used the low-end figure cited by the Narcotics Information Network to estimate conservatively the wholesale value of the marijuana seized. When Alatorre renewed his objection to the value testimony . . . on *Daubert* grounds, the court overruled his objection. Jacobs then testified about the wholesale and retail value of the marijuana; he explained that the wholesale value increased when the marijuana crossed the border and that the marijuana's value increased again when it was broken down into retail quantities for sale in San Diego.

. . . .

The jury convicted Alatorre on both counts charged, and the district court sentenced him to 21 months imprisonment.

DISCUSSION

We review the district court's decision to admit expert testimony for an abuse of discretion, *see Joiner*, 522 U.S. at 139. . . .

The Supreme Court's trilogy of cases — *Daubert, Joiner,* and *Kumho Tire* — provides the backdrop for analysis of the issue presented here: whether a separate, pretrial hearing, outside the presence of the jury, is required before expert testimony may be admitted at trial. In light of the Supreme Court's emphasis on the broad discretion granted to trial courts in assessing the relevance and reliability of expert testimony, and in the absence of any authority mandating such a hearing, we conclude

---

[21] [n.2] The court explained: "I don't find that we need to have any evidentiary hearing outside the presence of the jury on the expertise on that. Unfortunately, I gather, all three of us have heard this so many times, but the reality is, is that their experts will testify it's based upon the seizures that they make, talking to the people bringing the drugs across, as well as undercover operatives and . . . confidential informants, that that's how they find out what the prices are at any one time for both wholesale and retail." The court further noted: "I'm going to let that be laid in front of the jury because I've seen it so many times. To me, that's just a fishing expedition. We know how they get it. And then if you want to take him on voir dire, fine. If there's something that happens during the expert's testimony that appears to open it up, then I will let that be done outside the jury. We'll just excuse them at that point."

that trial courts are not compelled to conduct pretrial hearings in order to discharge the gatekeeping function.

. . . .

Nowhere in *Daubert, Joiner*, or *Kumho Tire* does the Supreme Court mandate the form that the inquiry into relevance and reliability must take, nor have we previously spoken to this issue. Although the Court stated that the inquiry is a "preliminary" one, to be made "at the outset," *Daubert*, 509 U.S. at 592, this does not mean that it must be made in a separate, pretrial hearing, outside the presence of the jury. Indeed, *Kumho Tire* belies any such interpretation:

> The trial court must have the same kind of latitude in deciding how to test an expert's reliability, and to decide whether or when special briefing or other proceedings are needed to investigate reliability, as it enjoys when it decides whether or not that expert's relevant testimony is reliable. . . . Otherwise, the trial judge would lack the discretionary authority needed both to avoid unnecessary "reliability" proceedings in ordinary cases where the reliability of an expert's methods is properly taken for granted, and to require appropriate proceedings in the less usual or more complex cases where cause for question-ing the expert's reliability arises. Indeed, the Rules seek to avoid "unjustifiable expense and delay" as part of their search for "truth" and the "jus[t] determin[ation]" of proceedings.

Kumho Tire, 526 U.S. at 152–53. If a separate hearing were a prerequisite to admission of expert testimony, then the reference to avoiding "unnecessary 'reliability' proceedings in ordinary cases where the reliability of an expert's methods is *properly taken for granted*," *id.* at 152, (emphasis added), makes no sense. This example, especially when considered together with the Court's references to cases that may require "special briefing or other proceedings" and to concerns about avoiding unjustifiable delay and expense, indicates that the Court did not intend the imposition of any one method of discharging the gatekeeping duty.

Our conclusion that a pretrial hearing is not required finds further support in the Court's repeated assertion that the preliminary inquiry as to relevance and reliability is a flexible one, subject to no set list of factors. *See Kumho Tire*, 526 U.S. at 141–42 ("[T]he test of reliability is 'flexible,' and *Daubert*'s list of specific factors neither necessarily nor exclusively applies to all experts or in every case. Rather, the law grants a district court the same broad latitude when it decides how to determine reliability as it enjoys in respect to its ultimate reliability determination.").

. . . .

Other circuits agree that no pretrial hearing is required. . . . *See United States v. Nichols*, 169 F.3d 1255, 1262–63 (10th Cir.1999) (rejecting claim that defendant was entitled to a preliminary hearing on admissibility of expert testimony and concluding that court did not abuse its discretion in refusing such a hearing); *Kirstein v. Parks Corp.*, 159 F.3d 1065, 1067 (7th Cir.1998) (rejecting plaintiffs' claim that they were entitled to a hearing on the admissibility of expert opinion, holding that trial court "had a sufficient basis for her decision without holding a hearing" and further explaining that "[w]e have not required that the *Daubert* inquiry take any specific form and have, in fact, upheld a judge's sua sponte consideration of the admissibility of expert testimony").

. . . .

The Supreme Court's insistence on flexibility and the need for case-by-case analysis of the proffered expert testimony cannot be squared with Alatorre's insistence that a *Daubert* hearing must be conducted before trial. To hold otherwise would impermissibly narrow the trial court's discretion to decide what procedures are necessary to assess the reliability of challenged testimony. Here the court adopted a practical procedure, well within its discretion, when it allowed Alatorre to explore Jacobs's qualifications and the basis for his testimony at trial via voir dire and then, following voir dire, rejected his renewed objections to the testimony regarding wholesale and retail value. Notably, this case does not involve a trial court's refusal to permit any inquiry into an expert's qualifications or the basis for the proffered opinion, nor does it involve an attempt to duck these issues. On the contrary, the trial court permitted Alatorre to question Jacobs — and to question him extensively — and also indicated that it would allow further questioning outside the presence of the jury should that become necessary. Such a procedure is appropriate.

Of particular relevance is our decision in *[United States v.] Hankey*, [203 F.3d 1160 (9th Cir. 2000)]. Jacobs's background, as well as the experiential basis of his knowledge, is similar to that of the expert in *Hankey*, who testified on voir dire that he had: 1) twenty-one years of experience with the Compton police department; 2) experience with thousands of gang members in the past decade; 3) formal training in gang structure and organization; and 4) extensive personal knowledge of the two gangs at issue. We concluded that the district court did not abuse its discretion in admitting the gang expert's testimony given that the court "probed the extent of [the expert's] knowledge and experience" through voir dire during a "motion in limine-FRE 104 hearing," and "made findings that the foundation for [the expert's] opinions was relevant and reliable."

Here, as in *Hankey*, voir dire established that Jacobs was qualified to testify on both the value and structure issues. He had twelve years of experience as a special agent, specialized training in the methods by which narcotics are used and sold, and extensive knowledge of marijuana smuggling as a result of his work as a case agent and in other capacities. Although the voir dire in *Hankey* was pretrial, in terms of the trial court's "gatekeeping" responsibility as to admissibility of this type of experiential expert testimony, we see no significant difference between the two cases. The same type of background information was before both trial courts. Having found no abuse of discretion in the admission of expert testimony given the foundation established in *Hankey*, we find none here.

We further note that this case is distinguishable from *United States v. Velarde*, 214 F.3d 1204 (10th Cir. 2000), in which the Tenth Circuit reversed and remanded the case for a new trial because the district court failed to conduct *any* reliability determination with regard to the challenged expert testimony. Faced with requests for a *Daubert* hearing on the reliability of the proposed expert testimony of two government witnesses, the court denied both requests, apparently on the sole basis that it had "had this testimony before in trials, and it's not new and novel. . . ."

Here, although the trial court initially used similar language in denying Alatorre's request for a "*Daubert* hearing" prior to trial,[22] [9] it specified that he would have an opportunity — during voir dire, at trial — to explore the relevance and reliability of the proposed testimony. The court also stated that if voir dire turned up any issues, further questioning, outside the jury's presence, would be in order. Then, at trial, the court

---

[22] [n.9] Specifically, the court stated in part that "all three of us have heard this so many times before" and "I've seen that so many times. To me, that's just a fishing expedition."

permitted Alatorre to conduct a lengthy voir dire. Finally, after voir dire, in rejecting Alatorre's renewed objections, the court ruled on the relevance and reliability of Jacobs's testimony. This course of events shows that the court did not abandon its gatekeeping function. By overruling Alatorre's objections and permitting the testimony after hearing not only the government's foundational proffer but also extensive voir dire, the court fulfilled its duty to make a determination as to the reliability of the expert's testimony.

Having held that neither the Supreme Court's trilogy of cases nor any of our own compels trial courts to conduct separate, pretrial hearings to discharge their gatekeeping duties, we note that holding such hearings-or at least ensuring an opportunity for voir dire outside the presence of the jury-may be appropriate in certain cases. Trial courts should be mindful of the difficulties posed when counsel must explore an expert's qualifications and the basis for the expert's opinion in the presence of the jury and, depending on the circumstances of the case, should give due consideration to requests that questioning occur unconstrained by that presence. But, in the end, such a determination is a judgment call best left to the discretion of the trial court. That said, the trial court's decision to admit Jacobs's testimony is

Affirmed.

NOTES

1. ***Procedural Issues; "Broad Latitude" for Gatekeeping Decisions.*** *Daubert* held that the trial court's relevancy and reliability determination is to be made "at the outset" pursuant to Rule 104(a). Accordingly, it was clear from the outset that, under *Daubert*, the proponent of expert testimony would have the burden of demonstrating relevance and reliability by a preponderance of the evidence. Beyond this, however, *Daubert* was silent as to what procedures governed the Rule 104(a) reliability determination. Prior to *Kumho Tire* trial courts often erred on the side of caution; holding formal evidentiary hearings and applying the five *Daubert* factors in nearly every case that involved a challenge to expert testimony. *See* Robert J. Goodwin, *The Hidden Significance of* Kumho Tire Co. v. Carmichael: *A Compass for Problems of Definition and Procedure Created by* Daubert v. Merrell Dow Pharmaceuticals, Inc., 52 BAYLOR L. REV. 603, 617–21 (Summer 2000) [hereinafter *The Hidden Significance of Kumho Tire*].

Kumho Tire addressed this procedural uncertainty — but did not establish any procedural "hard and fast" rules. As indicated in *Alatorre*, specifics of when, how, and whether to make a Rule 104(a) determination are matters that *Kumho Tire* grants trial courts "broad latitude" to decide, with *all trial court decisions* reviewed by the most forgiving of standards — the abuse of discretion standard.

2. ***A Framework for Determining Reliability.*** Trial court discretion is broad, but not limitless. As stated by Justice Scalia in his *Kumho Tire* concurrence:

> I join the opinion of the Court, which makes clear that the discretion it endorses — trial-court discretion in choosing the manner of testing expert reliability — is not discretion to abandon the gatekeeping function. I think it worth adding that it is not discretion to perform the function inadequately. Rather it is discretion to choose among *reasonable* means of excluding expertise that is *fausse* and science that is junky. Though, as the Court makes clear today, the

Daubert factors are not holy writ, in a particular case the failure to apply one or another of them may be unreasonable, and hence an abuse of discretion.

Kumho Tire, supra, 526 U.S. at 158–59 (Scalia, J. concurring).

Despite *Kumho Tire's* emphasis on "broad latitude," and the flexible nature of the *Daubert* test, certain steps, or decisions, should be considered whenever there is a challenge to expert testimony.

(A) First Step: Determine Whether a Formal Reliability Inquiry Is Needed; What "Triggers" a Daubert/Kumho *Reliability Inquiry?* Recall that *Kumho Tire* states that a trial court's gatekeeping obligation is not triggered until the reliability of an expert's testimony is "called *sufficiently* into question."

> [W]here such testimony's factual basis, data, principles, methods, or their application are called sufficiently into question, . . . the trial court must determine whether the testimony has "a reliable basis in the knowledge and experience of [the relevant] discipline."

Kumho Tire, supra, 526 U.S. at 149 *quoting Daubert, supra,* 509 U.S. at 592.

Accordingly, the opponent of expert testimony should be prepared, in "ordinary cases," to show why the trial court should doubt or question the reliability of proffered expert testimony. In close cases, would it be appropriate to say that the burden of production has been placed on the opponent of expert testimony? *See Tanner v. Westbrook,* 174 F.3d 542, 546 (5th Cir. 1999) (opponent of expert testimony called testimony "sufficiently into question" by "providing conflicting medical literature and expert testimony" in their pretrial motion for a Rule 104(a) reliability hearing); *Padillas v. Stork-Gamco, Inc.,* 186 F.3d 412, 418 (3d Cir. 1999) (emphasis added) (*if* the ground's supporting an expert's opinion appear to be "insufficiently explained and the reasons and foundations for them inadequately and perhaps confusingly explicated" *then* the district court "should hold an in limine hearing to assess . . . admissibility. . . ."). *See also* Margaret A. Berger, *The Supreme Court's Trilogy on the Admissibility of Expert Testimony, in* REFERENCE MANUAL ON SCIENTIFIC EVIDENCE, SECOND EDITION, 9, 29 (Federal Judicial Center 2000) ("Although the burden of persuasion with regard to showing the admissibility of expert testimony is clearly on the proponent, shifting the burden of production to the party seeking to exclude the expert testimony may at times be expeditious and economical.").

The "trigger," however, may be a "hair trigger," and trial courts may find it prudent to conduct some sort of a *Daubert* reliability inquiry in all but the most obvious cases. There is authority for the proposition that, if a trial court is to take reliability "for granted," the court, at a minimum, must explain why. The Tenth Circuit discussed a situation where a trial court took the reliability of an expert's testimony "for granted," and was found to have abused its discretion by not conducting *any Daubert* reliability inquiry.

> While we recognize that the trial court is accorded great latitude in determining how to make *Daubert* reliability findings before admitting expert testimony, *Kumho* and *Daubert* make it clear that the court must, on the record, make *some* kind of reliability determination. "[T]rial-court discretion in choosing the manner of testing expert reliability [ ] is not discretion to abandon the gatekeeping function." *Kumho,* 526 U.S. at 158–59 (Scalia, J., concurring).

The record in this case reveals no such reliability determination. Even when *Kumho* was specifically called to the court's attention, thereby removing any question that the expert testimony to be offered by Dr. Ornelas was subject to *Daubert/Kumho* reliability standards, the court made no reliability findings. Rather, the court seemed to assume that Dr. Ornelas's proffered testimony fell within the category of testimony in "ordinary" cases where courts may "avoid unnecessary 'reliability' proceedings . . . where the reliability of an expert's methods is properly taken for granted." *Kumho*, 526 U.S. at 152. However, the court gave no indication why this case could be viewed as such an "ordinary" case, or why Dr. Ornelas's methods could be "properly taken for granted," *id.*, except for the court's remark that "I've had this testimony before in trials, and it's not new and novel."

Here, even with *Kumho* squarely before it, the district court made no reliability determination with respect to Dr. Ornelas's proposed testimony. We conclude that, having failed to do so, the court abused its discretion when it admitted that testimony.

United States v. Velarde, 214 F.3d 1204, 1209–10 & 1211 (10th Cir. 2000). *See also United States v. Smithers*, 212 F.3d 306, 315 (6th Cir. 2000) ("When a defendant's liberty is at stake, it is incumbent upon the trial court to apply the correct law, follow the appropriate decision-making steps and articulate the bases upon which its decision rests. Here the district court should have applied the analytical principles set forth in *Daubert*, but it did not.").

Similarly, the trial court should allow the *proponent* of challenged expert testimony some opportunity to be heard before excluding an expert witness. *See United States v. Nacchio*, 519 F.3d 1140, 1154 (10th Cir. 2008) ("at a minimum it is an abuse of discretion to exclude an expert witness because his methodology is unreliable without allowing the proponent to present any evidence of what the methodology would be"); *Smith v. Clement*, 983 So. 2d 285, 290 n.3 (Miss. 2008) (an actual hearing is not required to comply with *Daubert*, but the party sponsoring a challenged expert must be given a "fair opportunity to respond").

(B) Second Step: Determine the Format of the Rule 104(a) Determination. If the trial court determines that there is cause for questioning the expert's reliability, a Rule 104(a) reliability determination must be made. The format of this determination is within the trial court's sound discretion. While many trial courts have held pretrial evidentiary hearings to determine reliability, as pointed out in *Alatorre*, the trial court is not required to conduct such a formal hearing in every case. *See In re Scrap Metal Antitrust Litigation*, 527 F.3d 517, 532 (6th Cir. 2008) (not an abuse of discretion to fail to hold *Daubert* hearing because issues were fully briefed and the record was extensive); *Nelson v. Tennessee Gas Pipeline Company*, 243 F.3d 244, 249 (6th Cir. 2001) ("whether to hold a hearing is a question that falls within the trial court's discretion"); *Tanner v. Westbrook*, 174 F.3d 542, 546 (5th Cir. 1999) (trial court rules on admissibility at trial based upon arguments and scientific literature submitted with pretrial motions; trial court found to have "effectively conducted a *Daubert* inquiry even though an evidentiary hearing was not held); *United States v. Brumley*, 217 F.3d 905, 908 (7th Cir. 2000) (*voir dire* of expert during trial). *See generally, The Hidden Significance of Kumho Tire*, 52 BAYLOR L. REV. at 636–40.

In *Alatorre* the Ninth Circuit noted that even though separate pretrial hearings are not required, they may be "appropriate in certain cases." *Alatorre, supra,* 222 F.3d at

1105. *See United States v. Stork-Gamco, Inc.*, 186 F.3d 412, 418 (3d Cir. 1999) ("[W]hen the ruling on admissibility turns on factual issues, . . . at least in the summary judgment context, failure to hold such a hearing may be an abuse of discretion."). Cases requiring an evidentiary hearing might include complex civil litigation, or criminal cases where voir dire in front of the jury might unfairly prejudice the defendant. *See* Margaret A. Berger, *The Supreme Court's Trilogy on the Admissibility of Expert Testimony, in* REFERENCE MANUAL ON SCIENTIFIC EVIDENCE, SECOND EDITION 9, 29 (Federal Judicial Center 2000).

(C) Third Step: Determine Which Reliability Factors Are "Reasonable Measures" of Reliability in the Case at Issue. There is no checklist of factors to be applied to a particular type of expert or category of expertise.

> The conclusion, in our view, is that we can neither rule out, nor rule in, for all cases and for all time the applicability of the factors mentioned in *Daubert*, nor can we now do so for subsets of cases categorized by category of expert or by kind of evidence. Too much depends upon the particular circumstances of the particular case at issue.

Kumho Tire, supra, 526 U.S. at 150. Instead, the trial court is given "considerable leeway" to determine whether the factors listed in *Daubert* or some other factors are "reasonable measures" of reliability in the particular case before the court. *Kumho Tire, supra*, 526 U.S. at 152.

Unfortunately, the Court provided little guidance as to just how a trial court was to determine whether a particular factor, or factors, were reasonable measures of reliability in a given case, or when a trial court abused discretion for not choosing a particular factor. Presumably, certain factors will be settled upon as reasonable for particular categories of expert testimony over time. *See* DAVID L. FAIGMAN, MICHAEL J. SAKS, JOSEPH SANDERS & EDWARD K. CHENG, 1 MODERN SCIENTIFIC EVIDENCE: THE LAW AND SCIENCE OF EXPERT TESTIMONY § 1.25, at 68–69 (2008) ("Trial courts, of course, consistently see specific types of expert testimony. . . . Given the press of time, they are likely to seek factor-lists or tests, such as the one *Daubert* offered for traditional scientific evidence," for other categories of experts.).

(D) Fourth Step: Determine Whether the Proffered Opinion Is Reliable, Whether it "Fits," and Whether it is More Prejudical Than Probative." The trial court's ultimate determination of admissibility is, in reality, a three-pronged determination. First, the trial court must determine if the expert's opinion is reliable based upon an application of reliability factors that the court has chosen as appropriate in the circumstances of the particular case. Second, the trial court must determine if the proffered evidence or testimony will "assist the trier of fact." This raises the question of relevance, or, "fit." As described by the Supreme Court in *Daubert*, "fit" involves determining that the scientific knowledge is valid *for the purpose offered. Daubert, supra*, 509 U.S. at 591. Finally, the trial court must decide if the proffered evidence or opinion is more misleading than probative and, if so, determine whether Rule 403 mandates exclusion.

QUESTIONS

1. What is it that "triggers" the trial court's gatekeeping obligation? Must a trial court conduct some sort of reliability inquiry every time an objection to expert testimony is made?

Go back and review the first three paragraphs of Part III of the *Kumho Tire* decision. Specifically, what was it about Carlson's methodology that "triggered" the reliability inquiry in that case? Would it have been an abuse of discretion for the district court to not have made any formal *Daubert* reliability inquiry?

2. If the trial court is inclined to *admit* expert testimony without making a reliability inquiry because the court feels that it can properly take the expert's methods "for granted," what, if anything, must the court explain on the record?

3. Could two different trial courts use *different* reliability factors to assess the reliability of the same type of expertise (in different trials), and both trial courts be upheld on appeal? What if the two trial courts make different admissibility rulings; is it possible for both to be upheld on appeal?

PROBLEMS

Problem 2-9. Joe Markey owned a video rental store that was facing bankruptcy. In March of last year Markey took out additional fire insurance on his video rental store. Two months later, in early May, the building caught fire. The fire department responded and extinguished the fire before the building was extensively damaged. As a precaution, before the fire department left, they doused the building with 1100 gallons of water. About an hour after the firefighters returned to the station, they received a second alarm on Markey's video rental store. This time when they arrived at the video store it was totally engulfed in flames. The building burned to the foundation.

Joe Markey is charged with arson in a state that has adopted the *Daubert* test as delineated in the "*Daubert* trilogy." At his trial the prosecution calls Fire Chief Buck Pearson as an expert witness. On direct examination before the jury, Chief Pearson testifies that his qualifications as an expert include fighting fires for 29 years (including 10 years as fire chief); attending a state-sponsored, three-day arson investigation seminar for fire chiefs; and inspecting the fire scene in this case.

After Chief Pearson testifies as to his qualifications, education, and experience, but before he gives any expert opinions, Markey's attorney objects, asserting that prior to receiving expert opinion from an arson investigator the court must hold a *Daubert* hearing — outside the presence of the jury — and determine whether Chief Pearson's proffered testimony is reliable. The government responds by asserting that arson experts have been used for years in criminal trials and — prior to the adoption of *Daubert* — had been generally accepted in the state where Markey's trial is taking place. The prosecution asserts that a *Daubert* reliability determination is not necessary.

After the objection and outside the presence of the jury, the prosecution tells the trial judge that Chief Pearson is prepared to testify that he has seen fires rekindle but never as fast as this fire. Further, he is prepared to testify that a quick and devastating rekindling of a fire after being soaked with water is extremely rare. Finally, if allowed to testify, Chief Pearson will say that the second fire was a completely separate fire that was intentionally set and did not rekindle.

(A) Must the court make a *Daubert* reliability determination, or is this an "ordinary case" where the trial court may take the reliability of the expert's methods "for granted"? Is there anything the defense could, or should, do to enhance the probability of "triggering" a formal *Daubert* reliability determination?

(B) If the trial court determines that a reliability determination must be made, should the determination be made outside the hearing of the jury? If not, what procedure should the trial court utilize to make its Rule 104(a) reliability determination?

(C) If a reliability determination must be made, what reliability factors should the trial court use? *See United States v. Diaz*, 300 F.3d 68, 76–77 (1st Cir. 2002).

Problem 2-10. Assume that a child is reported to have been sexually abused. Police arrest one of the child's neighbors, a single man, age 28, and charge him with child molestation. The allegations of molestation involve fondling; there is no physical evidence of abuse. The defendant denies all allegations.

To support the allegations of molestation, the prosecution arranges for the child and her mother to be interviewed by a psychologist. The interviews reveal that since the alleged molestation the child has had nightmares, fears men, has had angry outbursts, has experienced bed-wetting, stays inside her room, and has not been communicative. Based upon these interviews, the psychologist is prepared to testify that the child is suffering from child sexual abuse accommodation syndrome (CSAAS), and has been sexually abused.

The defense files a motion in limine to preclude the psychologist's opinion testimony. The motion in limine asserts that the psychologist's opinions are not admissible expert testimony under the *Daubert* trilogy. The trial court overrules the motion without opinion before trial and allows the expert to testify at the defendant's trial. The defendant is convicted and appeals.

On appeal the defendant argues that the trial court must make "some kind of gatekeeping reliability determination" under *Daubert* and *Kumho Tire.*

(A) Did the trial court abuse discretion in not making a *Daubert* reliability determination?

(B) If so, should the determination have been made outside the hearing of the jury?

(C) If so, what reliability factors should the trial court have used? *See United States v. Velarde*, 214 F.3d 1204, 1208–12 (10th Cir. 2000); *United States v. Majors*, 196 F.3d 1206, 1215–16 (11th Cir. 1999).

[d]   The Simple Relevancy Test

We now leave establishing reliability by presenting evidence in satisfaction of either the *Frye* or *Daubert* standards. Should scientific evidence be treated like any other category of evidence? That is, should scientific evidence be admitted when it is relevant subject only to the trial court's balancing of the evidence's probative value against countervailing harms? If so, reliability becomes a weight consideration for the jury, and not an admissibility requirement. This standard — the simple relevancy test — is described in the *Peters* case below.

STATE v. PETERS
534 N.W.2d 867 (Wis. Ct. App. 1995)

MYSE, JUSTICE.

Sherideane Peters appeals a judgment of conviction for six crimes, including: one count of kidnapping; two counts of first-degree sexual assault; one count of armed robbery; one count of attempted first-degree intentional homicide while using a dangerous weapon; and one count of mayhem. Peters contends that his conviction should be reversed and the cause remanded because: (1) the evidence of the statistical probability that his DNA (deoxyribonucleic acid) matched the DNA of the perpetrator was unreliable . . . [among other claims]. We reject Peters' arguments and affirm the judgment.

FACTS

On April 20, 1992, Peters abducted fifteen-year-old Sarah B. at gunpoint from a DePere parking lot, placed her in the trunk of a vehicle and drove to a Brown County Park. Once at the park, Peters led Sarah to a wooded area, where he forced her to participate in acts of fellatio and penis-vagina intercourse. Peters then robbed Sarah of her jewelry, cut her eyelids with a knife and attempted to kill her by stabbing her repeatedly in the neck, chest and abdomen.

Peters was eventually apprehended and charged in a six-count information. Prior to trial, Peters filed a motion opposing the admission of DNA evidence. A hearing was subsequently held on the matter. At the hearing, Peters did not dispute that his DNA matched the DNA taken from Sarah's clothes and person.[23] [1] However, as a Native-American, Peters argued that the DNA evidence was not sufficiently reliable because the probability statistics were based on comparisons to population databases that did not include Native-Americans. Accordingly, Peters argued that the evidence should not be admissible at trial because the population databases may not adequately account for variances among his ethnic heritage.[24] [2]

The State conceded that there was no population database for Native-Americans. However, it argued that precautions were taken to increase the reliability of the probability calculation. . . . At the conclusion of the hearing, the trial court determined that the laboratory's probability calculations regarding Peters' DNA were sufficiently reliable and denied Peters' motion. The case then proceeded to trial.

At trial, the jury was presented with the results of the DNA testing. Doctor Lisa Forman, an expert in population genetics, testified that Peters' DNA was compared to the DNA taken from Sarah's cervical swabs, vaginal swabs and shorts. Based on this comparison . . . Forman testified that the likelihood that Peters' DNA would match the DNA of the perpetrator by chance was one in 7.6 million. Additionally, Forman testified that she compared Peters' DNA to each of the three population databases using a basic probability calculation to determine the likelihood of a chance match. Based on these

---

[23] [n.1] A DNA "match" means only that the defendant could be the source of the evidence in question. Once it is determined that the defendant's DNA matches the sample taken from the victim, a calculation must be performed to determine the probability that the match is merely a coincidence.

[24] [n.2] The three population databases to which Peters' DNA was compared were: (1) Hispanic; (2) African-American; and (3) Caucasian.

calculations, Forman testified that the likelihood of a chance match between Peters' DNA and that which was taken from Sarah's person and clothes was one in 340 million for the Caucasian population, one in 26 billion for the African-American population and one in 260 million for the Hispanic population.

. . . .

The jury ultimately found Peters guilty on all six counts of the information. The trial court . . . sentenced him to thirty-five years on the attempted homicide conviction and to consecutive thirty-year prison terms on the remaining five convictions. Peters appeals.

ADMISSIBILITY OF SCIENTIFIC EVIDENCE

The first issue is whether the trial court properly admitted the DNA evidence. We review a challenge to the admissibility of evidence deferentially under the erroneous exercise of discretion standard. We will uphold the trial court's discretionary decision if it "examined the relevant facts, applied a proper standard of law, and, using a demonstrated rational process, reached a conclusion that a reasonable judge could reach."

Peters contends that the statistical probability evidence, which was derived from the DNA tests, was unreliable because his DNA was compared to population databases that did not include Native-Americans. Accordingly, Peters argues that the trial court erred by admitting this evidence. We are not persuaded.

Traditionally, state courts have used one of two approaches to determine whether scientific evidence is admissible: the *Frye* test or the relevancy test. The *Frye* test, which was first articulated in *Frye v. United States*, 293 F. 1013 (D.C. Cir. 1923), conditions the admission of scientific evidence upon whether the underlying scientific principle has gained "general acceptance in the particular field to which it belongs." *Id.* at 1014. If the trial court determines that the scientific principle is generally accepted in the scientific community, the evidence is deemed to be sufficiently reliable to be admitted at trial.

In *Daubert v. Merrell Dow Pharmaceuticals*, however, the United States Supreme Court held that the *Frye* test was superseded by Fed. R. Evid. 702. . . .

When faced with a question regarding admissibility of scientific evidence under Rule 702, the trial court must determine whether the evidence will assist the trier of fact. While *Daubert* represents a shift away from *Frye*'s general acceptance test, the court noted that the reliability of the particular scientific evidence was still a prerequisite to admissibility. Specifically, the Court stated: "[U]nder the Rules the trial judge must ensure that any and all scientific evidence admitted is not only relevant but reliable." If the trial court does not conclude that the scientific evidence is both relevant and reliable, the evidence may not be admitted. Thus, under *Frye* and *Daubert*, reliability is a necessary condition to the admissibility of scientific evidence.

In Wisconsin, however, our supreme court expressly rejected the *Frye* test in favor of the relevancy test. Because Wisconsin rejected the *Frye* test and adopted a test unrelated to that used by the federal courts and many state courts, our standard for the admission of scientific evidence was unaffected by *Daubert*. Thus, the rule remains in Wisconsin that the admissibility of scientific evidence is not conditioned upon its reliability. Rather, scientific evidence is admissible if: (1) it is relevant,[25] [6] (2) the witness is qualified as an expert,[26] [7] and (3) the evidence will assist the trier of fact in determining an issue of fact, *State v. Walstad*, 351 N.W.2d 469, 486 (Wis. 1984). If these requirements are satisfied, the evidence will be admitted.

Moreover, scientific evidence is admissible under the relevancy test regardless of the scientific principle that underlies the evidence. As our supreme court noted in *Walstad*:

> The fundamental determination of admissibility comes at the time the witness is "qualified" as an expert. In a state such as Wisconsin, where substantially unlimited cross-examination is permitted, the underlying theory or principle on which admissibility is based can be attacked by cross-examination or by other types of impeachment. Whether a scientific witness whose testimony is relevant is believed is a question of credibility for the finder of fact, but it clearly is admissible.

Id.

However, while Wisconsin confines itself to a determination of relevancy, we are compelled to acknowledge that Wisconsin judges do serve a limited and indirect gatekeeping role in reviewing the admissibility of scientific evidence. Unlike judges in *Frye* and *Daubert* jurisdictions, this role is much more oblique and does not involve a direct determination as to the reliability of the scientific principle on which the evidence is based. For instance, in Wisconsin, judges may reject relevant evidence if they conclude: (1) the evidence is superfluous; (2) the evidence will involve a waste of judicial time and resources; (3) the probative value of the evidence is outweighed by its prejudice to the defendant; (4) the jury is able to draw its own conclusions without it; (5) the evidence is inherently improbable; or (6) the area of testimony is not suitable for expert opinion. The foregoing list is not an exhaustive inventory of those grounds upon which the trial court may rely in refusing to admit relevant evidence. However, it demonstrates that although Wisconsin judges do not evaluate the reliability of scientific evidence, they may restrict the admissibility of such evidence through their limited gatekeeping functions.

In this case, Peters contends that the trial court erred because it did not make a direct determination as to the reliability of the statistical evidence. This argument is without merit. Once the relevancy of the evidence is established and the witness is qualified as an expert, the reliability of the evidence is a weight and credibility issue for the fact finder and any reliability challenges must be made through cross-examination or by other means of impeachment. Thus, the trial court was not required to determine that the DNA evidence and the statistics derived therefrom were reliable. Rather, the trial court's obligation was to determine whether the testifying witness was qualified as an expert, whether the evidence was relevant and whether it would assist the trier of fact. That said, we will next determine whether the trial court properly exercised its discretion in admitting the statistical probability evidence.

---

[25] [n.6] "Relevant evidence" means evidence having any tendency to make the existence of any fact that is of consequence to the determination of the action more probable or less probable than it would be without the evidence. Section 904.01, Stats.

[26] [n.7] Section 907.02, Stats. states:

> If scientific, technical, or other specialized knowledge will assist the trier of fact to understand the evidence or to determine a fact in issue, a witness qualified as an expert by knowledge, skill, experience, training, or education, may testify thereto in the form of an opinion or otherwise.

There is no dispute that Forman, the State's primary DNA witness, was a qualified expert. Forman has a Ph.D. in human variation, anthropology and population genetics and has worked for Cellmark Diagnostics, a DNA identification company, since 1989. Additionally, Forman has testified as an expert in population genetics in approximately ninety criminal cases and has substantial experience in the area of molecular biology. Finally, Forman has acted as a contributing author on several papers in the area of population genetics. Based on her background, it is apparent that Forman was sufficiently qualified to testify as an expert in the area of DNA analysis.

Additionally, the evidence was relevant to an issue of fact at trial. Evidence is relevant if it makes a fact that is of consequence to the determination of the action more or less probable. Here, Forman testified that the . . . method of probability calculation [used] was an acceptable means of probability calculation in the absence of a Native-American database and that it adequately accounted for potential subpopulation variances in estimating DNA frequencies. Further, the statistical probability evidence derived from the DNA testing linked Peters' DNA to the DNA gathered from the victim's person and clothing. Accordingly, the statistical evidence was relevant because it made the existence of the fact that Peters perpetrated the crime more probable than it would have been without the evidence.

Further, the probability evidence was necessary to assist the jury in determining the significance of the match between Peters' DNA and the DNA found on the victim. As we previously recognized, the mere fact that a defendant's DNA matches a sample taken from the victim does not establish that the defendant perpetrated the crime. Statistical probability evidence is necessary to determine the likelihood of a coincidental match between the defendant's DNA and the sample taken from the victim's person and clothing. Without statistical evidence, the jury would have been unable to determine the significance of the DNA match. Accordingly, this evidence was of assistance to the jury.

. . . .

The trial court's decision to admit the DNA evidence was a proper exercise of discretion. The State's primary DNA witness was a qualified expert, the evidence was relevant and it assisted the jury in determining a fact in issue. . . . Having established this foundation, we conclude that the evidence was properly admitted.

. . . .

Judgment affirmed.

NOTE

Simple Relevancy as Minority View. Wisconsin may stand alone in not considering reliability of scientific evidence a factor in determining its admissibility. Sometimes a court will state that reliability is a weight question for the jury, and is not an admissibility consideration. This is usually a reference to the allegedly improper way a test was performed on a particular occasion and not a reference to the validity of the scientific theory and the technique that applies it. An example of this distinction can be found in *State v. Pierce*, 597 N.E.2d 107 (Ohio 1992). In *Pierce* the Ohio Supreme Court ruled that DNA evidence was admissible. The Court then observed:

On appeal, *Pierce does not challenge the underlying scientific principles involved in the testing procedures* used by [the laboratory performing the DNA testing] in this case. Rather, he attacks the reliability of the actual procedures used and analysis of the results of the DNA testing made by [the laboratory] here.

. . . .

. . . We hold that questions regarding the reliability of DNA evidence *in a given case* go to the weight of the evidence rather than its admissibility. No pretrial evidentiary hearing is necessary to determine the reliability of DNA evidence. The trier of fact . . . can determine whether DNA evidence is reliable based on the expert testimony and other evidence presented.

Id. at 113, 115 (emphasis added).

Whether using proper testing procedures on a particular occasion presents admissibility or weight questions is examined in Chapter 3, *infra*. It should be noted that some courts have considered the proper application of DNA testing procedures on a particular occasion to present admissibility issues, and refer to this standard for admissibility of DNA evidence as "*Frye*-plus," or "*Daubert*-plus," depending upon which test is used in the jurisdiction. The admissibility of DNA evidence is examined in Chapter 4, *infra*.

QUESTIONS

1. Under the "simple relevancy" approach described by the Wisconsin Court of Appeals in *Peters*, what factors (other than relevancy) does a court consider in determining admissibility?

2. If testimony based upon a new scientific principle is admitted under either *Daubert* or the "simple relevancy" test, may the party who opposes such testimony still offer evidence that indicates that the technique is not generally accepted?

3. In a *Frye* jurisdiction, if *Frye* is not applied to a particular category of expert testimony, how is admissibility determined?

4. Exactly what is the *court* to determine under:

(A)   the *Frye* test;

(B)   the *Daubert* test;

(C)   the simple relevancy test?

5. Exactly what is the *jury* to determine under:

(A)   the *Frye* test;

(B)   the *Daubert* test;

(C)   the simple relevancy test?

PROBLEM

Problem 2-13. Recall the case of *State v. Bullard* and the article by Mark Hansen that followed it, "Believe It or Not," *supra* Chapter 1. In *Bullard* the defendant was convicted of murder primarily on the strength of expert testimony provided by Dr. Louise Robbins that the defendant's foot matched a bloody footprint found at the scene of the crime. Dr. Robbins's expert testimony was based upon a scientific technique that has since been discredited, but which was admitted under a "relevancy plus reliability" test.

Knowing what we now know about Dr. Robbins' technique:

(A) Would Dr. Robbins's testimony be admissible under the *Frye* test? Would the *Frye* test be applied to a technique such as Dr. Robbins's footprint comparisons under standards discussed in *People v. Stoll*, and *State v. Hasan, supra* in this chapter?

(B) Would Dr. Robbins's testimony be admissible under the *Daubert* test? What reliability factors would apply to Dr. Robbins's methodology in a *Daubert* jurisdiction?

(C) Would Dr. Robbins's testimony be admissible under the simple relevancy test described in *Peters*?

[2]   Judicial Notice

The next two methods of establishing reliability of a scientific theory, or a technique applying that theory, do not rely on the presentation of testimony to the same extent as the *Frye* and "relevancy plus reliability" tests. As you might assume, for the most part, judicial notice and legislative recognition are not normally available when there is serious controversy over the reliability of the scientific technique at issue.

STATE v. INMAN
350 A.2d 582 (Me. 1976)

WEATHERBEE, JUSTICE.

A Penobscot County jury found the defendant guilty of . . . murder. The defendant has appealed. We deny his appeal.

The victim was Miss Charlotte Dunn, an elderly lady, who lived alone in an apartment in Bangor. Sometime about midnight on May 31, 1971, residents of other apartments in the building heard sounds of a struggle, a woman's screams and "growling noises" coming from the vicinity of the victim's apartment. None of them reported or made any effort to determine the nature of the woman's distress.

The next morning the victim's semi-nude, badly beaten body was found sprawled on the floor of her apartment. She had been strangled. It was evident that the victim had also been cruelly sexually mistreated. A latent palm print was found on the floor near her left shoulder.

The defendant had occupied an apartment in that building some seven or eight months before. His name was given to the police as a suspect soon after the discovery of the crime.

Lieutenant Bruton of the State Police assumed charge of the investigation and that evening he sent a State Police detective and another officer to the defendant's home in East Holden to ask the defendant to come with the officers to the Bangor Police Department for questioning. . . .

At the Police Department, Lieutenant Bruton noted what appeared to be scratches on the defendant's hands, face and neck and "floor burns" on his elbows. The defendant was not placed under arrest until a time several weeks later when the police obtained his palm print and were satisfied that it matched the latent print which had been found beside the body.

The defendant was indicted upon a charge of murder. . . . Trial . . . proceeded in the Superior Court and the defendant was found guilty. We will consider separately the several errors claimed by defendant on appeal.

. . . .

The Taking of Judicial Notice of the Reliability of Palm Prints and the [Trial Court's] Instruction Thereon

Midway in his instructions the [trial court] told the jury:

Now it may be that the Court will take judicial notice of certain facts. I believe before I am finished I will. . . .

At the conclusion of his instructions he said:

I indicated that I would ask you to take judicial notice of one thing. I now say that I have taken judicial notice that fingerprinting, which includes palmprinting, is the most accurate present means of identification, and that it is universally used in cases of this kind, but I also say to you that fingerprint and palmprint analysis requires greater skill than that which the ordinary witness has.

And in this connection, you are to assume that I have taken judicial notice and hand it to you that the fingerprint method of identification is accurate and no two sets of fingerprints or palmprints are exactly alike.

The defendant objected to the giving of this instruction. He now urges us that the reliability of the palm print method of identification is not subject to judicial notice and is a question of fact for jury determination upon adequate evidentiary proof.

We said in *State v. Rush*, Me., 324 A.2d 748, 750 (1974):

To be a proper subject of judicial notice, a fact must be a matter of common knowledge, which is generally accepted without qualification or contention.

. . . The modern trend has enlarged the concept to include matters which are of such verifiable certainty that they may be confirmed by reference to sources of indisputable accuracy. (Citations omitted.)

In *State v. Inman*, Me., 301 A.2d 348, 353 (1973), we recognized the absolute reliability of fingerprint identification, saying:

When one's fingerprints are found in a particular place such person cannot be heard to say he was not at that place at some time.

The infallibility of fingerprints as a method of identification is now too widely accepted to require citation of authority. We further acknowledged in *Inman* [that] the reliability of palm prints as evidence that a person was in the place where the palm print was found is now so well accepted that we know of no courts who hold such evidence to be incompetent. In fact, since the learned and comprehensive analysis of their attributes by the Nevada Court in *State v. Kuhl*, 175 P. 190, (1918), palm prints have been adjudged no less reliable than fingerprints in jurisdictions where the issue has arisen.

. . . .

[In] *Inman* we also said:

Experts in dactylography recognize that palm prints have the characteristic of uniqueness and that they contain reference points that enable accurate and conclusive comparisons *just as do fingerprints.*

(Emphasis added.) *State v. Inman, supra,* 301 A.2d at 353.

We are satisfied that this was a statement of a principle which is accepted without qualification or contention in fields of crime detection and medical jurisprudence and may be confirmed by reference to sources of indisputable accuracy. Moenssens, Moses and Inbau, Scientific Evidence in Criminal Cases, ch. 7, § 7.10. There was no error in the [trial court's] statement of this principle to the jury.

While the [trial court] took judicial notice of the scientific principle of the *capacity* for identification by comparison of two sets of palm prints, he properly left to the jury to decide what confidence they should place in the securing and preservation of the print on the floor and the defendant's prints which were used for comparison and the process of comparison *as conducted by these officers,* the competence and reliability of the expert witness and the credibility of the witnesses. He did not take from the jury the essential decision of whether the print on the floor near the victim's shoulder was or was not made by the defendant's palm. In language of undoubted clarity, the [court below] discussed the manner in which opinions of experts may be considered by the jury and concluded:

If you should decide that the opinion of an expert witness is not based upon sufficient education and experience, or if you should conclude that the reasons given in support of the opinion are not founded, or that the opinion is outweighed by other evidence in the case, you may disregard the opinion in whole or in part.

We are not satisfied that there was error.

. . . .

Appeal denied.

NOTES

1. Scope of Judicial Notice. Judicial notice of the validity of *certain* scientific techniques is not a controversial concept. Courts have taken judicial notice of the validity of the principles underlying established techniques such as radar, intoxication tests, fingerprinting, palm printing, bitemark evidence, firearms identification, and handwriting comparisons, among other things. *See generally* 1 COURTROOM CRIMINAL EVIDENCE § 602, at 191–93 (4th ed. 2005). Recently courts have taken judicial notice of the reliability of DNA testing. *See, e.g., United States v. Martinez,* 3 F.3d 1191, 1197 (8th Cir. 1993); *United States v. Jakobetz,* 955 F.2d 786, 799–800 (2d Cir. 1992).

Recall also that the United States Supreme Court acknowledged the appropriateness of taking judicial notice of "firmly established" scientific theories in *Daubert v. Merrell Dow Pharmaceuticals, Inc.,* 509 U.S. at 592 n.11:

[T]heories that are so firmly established as to have attained the status of scientific law, such as the laws of thermodynamics, properly are subject to judicial notice under Fed. R. Evid. 201.

Note that the validity of the technique *applying* the theory may or may not be judicially noticed. For example, a court could take judicial notice of the underlying principle of radar (the Doppler Effect) but not its application in a new type of device, such as moving radar. *See* 1 COURTROOM CRIMINAL EVIDENCE § 602, at 191 n.12 (4th ed. 2005).

Finally, be aware that just because a court takes judicial notice of the validity of a theory, and the technique applying that theory, does not mean that expert testimony will always be admitted. There remains the issue of whether the technique was properly applied *on this particular occasion*. *See United States v. Martinez, supra* at 1197–98 ("[T]he reliability inquiry in *Daubert* mandates that there be a preliminary showing that the expert properly performed a reliable methodology in arriving at his opinion."). Not all courts agree on whether proper test performance on a particular occasion is an admissibility (as opposed to weight) requirement. This problem is examined in more detail in Chapter 3, in the notes following *People v. Tobey*.

2. Offering Evidence Attacking the Reliability of a Theory or Technique That Has Been Judicially Noticed.

(A) Prior To Taking Judicial Notice. Prior to a court taking judicial notice, the party who opposes the taking of judicial notice is usually given an opportunity to demonstrate the impropriety of taking judicial notice. *See* Fed. R. Evid. 201(e); CHRISTOPHER B. MUELLER & LAIRD C. KIRKPATRICK, 1 FEDERAL EVIDENCE § 2:7, at 367–68 (3d ed. 2007). This is typically done in a hearing held outside the jury's presence. *Id.*

(B) After the Taking of Judicial Notice in a Criminal Case. Assume that a defendant in a criminal case opposes the taking of judicial notice of the validity of a scientific theory or technique such as palmprinting. Assume further that the trial court holds a hearing outside the jury's presence and determines that the court *will* take judicial notice of the theory and technique. May the defendant still call a witness to testify before the jury that the *theory* behind palmprinting is not valid and reliable? In other words, may the defendant in a criminal case attack the *weight* a jury gives scientific evidence by attacking the reliability of a scientific technique whose reliability has been judicially noticed?

The answer is, generally, "yes"; however, the rationale for permitting an attack on facts that a court has noticed as reliable may depend upon whether the facts that the court notices are viewed as Rule 201 "adjudicative facts" or facts that must be found by the court preliminary to the admission of evidence pursuant to Rule 104(a).

(i) Adjudicative Facts. Rule 201 of the Federal Rules of Evidence governs the taking of judicial notice. Rule 201, however, applies *only* to "*adjudicative*" facts. The Advisory Committee Note to Rule 201(a) describes "adjudicative" facts as "the facts of the particular case," and later, expands upon this description by adding that adjudicative facts indicate "who did what, where, when, how, and with what motive or intent."

Rule 201(g) makes judicially noticed adjudicative facts conclusive and not subject to rebuttal in a civil case *but not in a criminal case*. To allow rebuttal would undermine the purpose of taking judicial notice. In a criminal case, however, the court is *required* by Rule 201(g) to instruct the jury that it (the jury) may, but is not required, to accept as conclusive a judicially noticed fact. The Advisory Committee Note to Rule 201(g) indicates that the reason for this is the fear that instructing a jury that it must accept an adjudicative fact as established would amount to directing a verdict against the defendant (and arguably violating the defendant's Sixth Amendment right to trial by jury). *See* CHRISTOPHER B. MUELLER & LAIRD C. KIRKPATRICK, 1 FEDERAL EVIDENCE, § 2:9, at 374–75 (3d ed. 2007); *United States v. Garland*, 991 F.2d 328, 333 (6th Cir. 1993) (judicially noticed facts may be contested in criminal cases). Not all states adopt the federal approach; some states allow a court to judicially notice and make *conclusive* adjudicative facts in criminal cases. CHRISTOPHER B. MUELLER & LAIRD C. KIRKPATRICK, 1 FEDERAL EVIDENCE § 2:10, at 378 (3d ed. 2007).

Recall that we are examining facts that support the reliability of a scientific theory and the technique applying that theory. Such facts may simply not be *adjudicative facts* as that term is defined in Fed. R. Evid. 201. If, however, these facts are viewed as adjudicative facts (and if in a federal court), Rule 201 applies, and the court, pursuant to Rule 201(g), must instruct the jury that it need not accept the court's finding of the technique's reliability as conclusive. If reliability is not considered conclusive, then presumably the defendant may offer evidence to undermine the judicially noticed proposition before the jury.

(ii) Facts Preliminary to the Admission of Evidence. Consider, as an alternative, that the facts that establish the reliability and validity of scientific theories and techniques are not adjudicative facts and, therefore, are not regulated by Fed. R. Evid. 201. Instead, the existence of such facts can be viewed as preliminary questions that must be determined by the trial court regulated by Fed. R. Evid. 104. *See* CHRISTOPHER B. MUELLER & LAIRD C. KIRKPATRICK, 1 FEDERAL EVIDENCE § 2:12, at 398 (3d ed. 2007) (judicial notice of facts used in determining the reliability and acceptance of scientific principles and techniques governed by Rule 104(a), not Rule 201).

The pertinent part of Rule 104(a) states:

> Preliminary questions concerning . . . the admissibility of evidence shall be determined by the court. . . . In making its determination it is not bound by the rules of evidence except those with respect to privilege.

If a court takes judicial notice of the reliability of a scientific technique under Rule 104(a), then the court is *not* required to instruct the jury (consistent with Rule 201(g)) that it need not accept the judicially noticed fact as "conclusive" because the court is not "bound by the rules of evidence" when making a Rule 104(a) determination. Even though no Rule 201(g) instruction is required, the end result is the same since Rule 104(e) provides, "This rule does not limit the right of a party to introduce before the jury evidence relevant to weight or credibility." Accordingly, in federal courts a defendant should be able to contest the validity (but not the admissibility) of scientific techniques whose reliability has been judicially noticed regardless of whether the process is controlled by Rule 201or Rule 104.

(iii) Constitutional Considerations. The Constitution, arguably, requires that a defendant *in a criminal case* be allowed to attack the reliability of a scientific technique whose reliability has been judicially noticed. The Sixth Amendment right to trial by jury and the related concept of "jury nullification" are, allegedly, impediments to *conclusive* judicial notice. Such an attack would, of course, be an attack upon the weight the jury gives the evidence, and not an admissibility attack. The matter remains unsettled. *See* Edward J. Imwinkelried & Robert G. Scofield, *The Recognition of an Accused's Constitutional Right to Introduce Expert Testimony Attacking the Weight of Prosecution Scientific Evidence: The Antidote for the Supreme Court's Mistaken Assumption in* California v. Trombetta, 33 ARIZ. L. REV. 59 (1991); CHRISTOPHER B. MUELLER & LAIRD C. KIRKPATRICK, 1 FEDERAL EVIDENCE § 2:10, at 377–78 (3d ed. 2007); KENNETH S. BROUN, MCCORMICK ON EVIDENCE § 332, at 448–52 (6th ed. 2006).

QUESTIONS

1. Note that the court in *Inman* took judicial notice only of the validity of the underlying principle and the validity of the technique applying the principle. Whether the principle was correctly *applied* on the particular occasion before the jury is not a proper subject for judicial notice, and neither is the related conclusion that defendant's palm made the print. Why? *See United States v. Dreos*, 156 F. Supp. 200, 208 (D. Md. 1958); 1 Courtroom Criminal Evidence § 602, at 194 (4th ed. 2005).

2. Note that the defendant in *Inman* argued that the reliability of the palmprint technique was a question of fact for the jury. Which of the three methods for establishing reliability of a scientific technique does the defendant's request most closely resemble: general acceptance, relevance plus reliability, or simple relevance?

3. In *Inman*, after the trial court took judicial notice of the reliability of palmprinting and admitted palmprint evidence during the prosecution's case, could the defendant call an expert witness to testify that palmprint identification was not a reliable method of identification? If so, why would such evidence be relevant?

PROBLEM

Problem 2-14. Assume that a court takes judicial notice of the reliability of radar to determine the speed of a car. Assume further that the defendant is convicted of speeding and the only testimony offered against the defendant by the prosecution was that the radar machine indicated a speed of 70 m.p.h. in a 55 m.p.h. speed zone, that the radar machine was working properly, and that the person operating it was properly trained. If the defendant asserts on appeal that he was denied his Sixth Amendment right to confront his accusers when the court took judicial notice of the radar machine's reliability and thereby did not afford him the opportunity to cross-examine the experts who claim that radar is reliable, how should the court rule? *See State v. Finkle*, 319 A.2d 733, 738 (N.J. App. 1974).

[3]   Legislative Recognition

Sometimes a statute will recognize the validity of a scientific technique and/or provide that the results of a specific scientific test may be admitted into evidence. Usually, but not always, the techniques involved will be so firmly established that their reliability will also make them candidates for judicial notice. The case that follows, *Seewar v. Town of Summerdale*, involves an Alabama statute that generally accepted the validity of a breath test used to determine a person's blood alcohol content.

SEEWAR v. TOWN OF SUMMERDALE
601 So. 2d 198 (Ala. Crim. App. 1992)

Taylor, Judge.

The appellant, Debra Jean Brown Seewar, was convicted of driving under the influence of alcohol, a violation of § 32-5A-191(a)(2), Code of Alabama 1975. She was sentenced to pay a $250 fine and court costs and to attend DUI school.

The prosecution's evidence tended to show that on May 1, 1991, Officer Roy Nix of the Summerdale Police Department clocked the appellant driving 57 m.p.h. in a 45 m.p.h. zone as she drove north on Alabama Highway 59 in Baldwin County. When Nix pulled into a convenience store parking lot to turn around and pursue her, an off-duty officer with the Foley Police Department drove up next to him and told him that he had seen the appellant "driving all over the highway."

Nix then pursued the appellant and, after noticing that she was weaving as she drove, pulled her over just inside the Summerdale police jurisdiction. The appellant got out of her car and walked towards the police car and spoke with Nix. He noticed that the appellant swayed as she walked, that her speech was slurred, and that she smelled of alcohol. When Nix asked her if she had been drinking, the appellant replied that she had had "several drinks."

. . . An Intoxilyzer 5000 test was administered to the appellant at the Robertsdale Police Department. The test indicated that her blood alcohol content was .132, exceeding the legal limit by .032.

. . . .

I.

The appellant initially contends that the circuit court erred when it denied her pretrial motion to suppress the results of the . . . Intoxilyzer 5000 test. More specifically, she argues that the . . . Intoxilyzer 5000 test [is a] novel scientific test that under *Frye v. United States*, 293 F. 1013 (D.C. Cir. 1923), and *Prewitt v. State*, 460 So. 2d 296, 301 (Ala. Cr. App. 1984), require[s] experts to testify as to [its] reliability and general acceptance in the scientific community.

. . . .

The appellant . . . contends that the results of the Intoxilyzer 5000 test should not have been received into evidence because, under *Frye* and *Prewitt*, the state failed to establish the test's reliability and general acceptance in the particular scientific field in which it belongs.

. . . .

Because the Intoxilyzer 5000 has been generally accepted as a valid test under § 32-5A-194 . . . no *Frye* predicate is required for the admissibility of its results. "Despite [its] overall acceptance in the courts, however, a foundation must be laid to show that the particular test in question was conducted by an appropriate person and in a reliable way." C. Gamble, *McElroy's Alabama Evidence* § 490.01(2) (4th ed. 1991) (footnote omitted). In *Ex parte Bush*, 474 So. 2d 168 (Ala. 1985), the Alabama Supreme Court explained the requisite foundation for the admissibility of test results indicating one's blood alcohol content pursuant to § 32-5A-194(a)(1), Code of Alabama 1975:

> "This predicate may be established by showing, first, that the law enforcement agency has adopted the particular form of testing that was in fact used. Second, there must be a showing that the test was performed according to methods approved by the State Board of Health. This may be proved by the introduction of the rules and regulations the officer followed while administering the test and the officer's testimony that he did, in fact, follow those rules when he administered the test in question. Third, there must be a showing that the person administering the test has a valid permit issued by the State Board of Health for that purpose."

Bush, 474 So. 2d at 170 (citations omitted).

After applying the *Bush* predicate to the facts of this case, we find that the state met the requirements for the admissibility of the Intoxilyzer 5000 test results.

The circuit court did not err by failing to require the state to prove the general acceptance of the Intoxilyzer 5000 under *Frye* and *Prewitt* and by receiving its results into evidence.

The circuit court did not err in denying the appellant's motion to suppress.

Affirmed.

NOTES AND QUESTIONS

1. *Legislative Recognition.* The validity and admissibility of techniques such as radar, intoxication tests, and blood tests are often legislatively recognized. As indicated in the *Seewar* case, legislative recognition (like judicial notice) relieves the evidence's proponent from providing expert testimony of the technique's reliability but not, necessarily, from providing proof that the technique was applied properly on a given occasion. *See generally* 1 COURTROOM CRIMINAL EVIDENCE § 603, at 196 (4th ed. 2005).

Statutes recognizing the validity of such techniques often (but not always) specify that the results of the technique will be admissible *if* certain procedures are followed. In such cases legislative recognition does not relieve the evidence's proponent from establishing that the mandated procedures have been followed. *State v. Souza,* 732 P.2d 253, 257 (Haw. Ct. App. 1987). Adherence to legislatively mandated *procedures* as a precondition to admissibility are examined at greater length in Chapter 3, *infra*, at § A.1.b.

2. *Extending Legislative Recognition to Techniques Not Candidates for Judicial Notice.* Legislation recognizing the validity of certain techniques and mandating admission if certain procedures are followed is not controversial when the techniques are generally accepted and/or likely candidates for judicial notice. Some statutes, however, require the admission of evidence based upon scientific techniques that would not (in all probability) be judicially noticed as reliable or generally accepted. For example, Missouri has a statute that mandates the admission of expert testimony on the battered spouse syndrome that provides, in part:

> 1. Evidence that the actor was suffering from the battered spouse syndrome shall be admissible upon the issue of whether the actor lawfully acted in self-defense or defense of another.

Mo. ANN. STAT. § 563.033 (1994). As is often the case when scientific techniques are legislatively recognized, the Missouri statute specifies procedures that must be followed if the defendant proposes to offer evidence of the battered spouse syndrome.

Other examples of legislative recognition of scientific techniques that, arguably, would not qualify for judicial notice include the recognition of hypnosis, CAL. EVID. CODE § 795 (2005), and rape trauma syndrome, ILL. COMP. STAT. ANN. 725, § 5/115-7.2 (Smith-Hurd 1992), among others. *See* 1 SCIENTIFIC EVIDENCE § 1.03, at 8–9 (4th ed. 2007).

3. *Attacking the Reliability of a Technique That Is Legislatively Recognized.* There is some authority for the proposition that once a scientific technique has been recognized as reliable by legislative determination, general rebuttal testimony on the reliability issue is barred. *See State v. Vega*, 465 N.E.2d 1303, 1305, 1308 (Ohio 1984) (the accused is not denied his constitutional right to present a defense where the trial judge does not permit the defendant to attack the reliability of the intoxilyzer because of legislative recognition); Edward J. Imwinkelried & Robert G. Scofield, *The Recognition of an Accused's Constitutional Right to Introduce Expert Testimony Attacking the Weight of Prosecution Science Evidence: The Antidote for the Supreme Court's Mistaken Assumption in* California v. Trombetta, 33 ARIZ. L. REV. 59, 64–65 (1991) (Some courts that bar an attack on the reliability of scientific evidence that has been legislatively recognized take the position that the legislature has conclusively determined that the scientific technique is trustworthy and, accordingly, is "unassailable.").

The dominant (and more persuasive) position holds that a defendant in a criminal case should be able to offer evidence that undercuts the weight and credibility (as opposed to admissibility) of evidence that has been admitted pursuant to a legislative mandate. *See State v. Burling*, 400 N.W.2d 872, 876 (Neb. 1987) (defendant established unreliability of Intoxilyzer test results admitted pursuant to statute); *State v. Lowther*, 740 P.2d 1017, 1020 (Haw. Ct. App. 1987) (statute providing for admissibility of results of Intoxilyzer test relieves prosecution from providing testimony regarding general reliability of machine, but it does not make reliability an unquestioned fact); *Cooley v. Municipality*, 649 P.2d 251, 254 (Alaska Ct. App. 1982) ("even though breathalyzer test results may be admitted into evidence, that does not mean that those results are unassailable"); *Keel v. State*, 609 P.2d 555, 557 (Alaska 1980) (statute makes results of breathalyzer test admissible, not unassailable). To do otherwise would, arguably, compromise the defendant's rights to present a complete defense and to receive a trial by jury. *See generally Arizona v. Youngblood*, 488 U.S. 51, 56 (1988) (Court reaffirms its belief that a defendant can make a weight attack on the state's scientific evidence); *Crane v. Kentucky*, 476 U.S. 683, 690 (1986) (accused has constitutional right to present a complete defense and may challenge the reliability of a confession that has been ruled admissible by the trial court); *California v. Trombetta*, 467 U.S. 479, 490 (1984) (Court describes weight attacks as "alternative means" of attacking prosecution's scientific evidence).

The United States Supreme Court has not specifically declared a defendant's ability to attack the weight of the prosecution's scientific evidence a constitutionally protected right. *See* Edward J. Imwinkelried & Robert G. Scofield, *supra*, 33 ARIZ. L. REV. at 61–62 (Supreme Court mistakenly assumes in *Youngblood* and *Trombetta* that all courts permit a defendant the right to attack the weight of the state's scientific evidence). Accordingly, while most states permit a defendant to attack the weight to be given to scientific techniques that are legislatively recognized, not all states do so, and there apparently is no clearly articulated constitutional right that would compel a state to do so. *See State v. Vega*, 465 N.E.2d 1303, 1305, 1308 (Ohio 1984). The argument that a defendant's right to present a complete defense includes the right to make a weight attack on the reliability of scientific evidence that has been legislatively recognized as valid would seem particularly strong if the technique that is legislatively recognized is one that is controversial or not generally accepted in all jurisdictions, such as the battered woman syndrome or rape trauma syndrome.

[4]   Stipulations

Brief mention should be made of a fourth method used in some situations to deal with the problem of proving the validity of a particular scientific theory and/or the technique that applies that theory — stipulations. By stipulating, parties, in effect, waive any objection to the validity of the basic theory underlying a particular scientific technique.

In the case of *United States v. Piccinonna*, 885 F.2d 1529 (11th Cir. 1989), the Eleventh Circuit discussed the circumstances under which evidence of polygraph testing would be admitted:

> Polygraph expert testimony will be admissible in this circuit when both parties stipulate in advance as to the circumstances of the test and as to the scope of its admissibility. The stipulation as to circumstances must indicate that the parties agree on material matters such as the manner in which the test is conducted, the nature of the questions asked, and the identity of the examiner administering the test. The stipulation as to scope of admissibility must indicate the purpose or purposes for which the evidence will be introduced. Where the parties agree to both of these conditions in advance of the polygraph test, evidence of the test results is admissible.

Id. at 1536.

Of course, the stipulation does nothing to enhance the scientific validity or evidentiary reliability of the principle or technique at issue.[27]

---

[27] The admissibility of polygraph evidence in general, and pursuant to a stipulation, is examined in Chapter 4 of this text.

Chapter 3

INSURING PROPER APPLICATION AND INTERPRETATION OF THE SCIENTIFIC TECHNIQUE ON A PARTICULAR OCCASION

The last chapter examined methods of insuring the "validity" of a scientific theory and technique. Consider, however, that even if the theory and technique applying that theory are valid, errors can be made on a particular occasion. If, for example, a Breathalyzer is not properly cleaned and maintained, the results of a breath test will not be reliable. If a lab technician takes a "short cut" and fails to follow appropriate test protocol, test results may be compromised. If a test tube containing blood has been mislabeled — and does not contain blood from the person identified on the label — test results will be irrelevant. Finally, consider that even if scientific equipment is properly maintained and operating to accepted standards, and even if all test procedures are meticulously followed, the results of many forensic techniques, such as bitemark comparison, fingerprint analysis, handwriting analysis, etc., must be analyzed and interpreted by human beings. There is always the possibility of human error in the subjective interpretation of test results.

Recognizing that an improperly conducted scientific test or procedure may produce false or misleading evidence has led courts — and, occasionally, legislatures — to establish evidentiary hurdles designed to ensure proper test application and interpretation on a particular occasion. As a general proposition, the proponent of evidence derived from scientific testing must demonstrate three things: (1) that any machine, instrument, or chemicals used were in proper working order and/or condition; (2) that proper test procedures were followed; and (3) that the person (or persons) who conducted the test and interpreted test results was qualified. Courts are split over whether such a showing is an admissibility requirement, or goes only to the weight given scientific evidence.

In addition to demonstrating proper test application and interpretation, two related evidentiary hurdles may need to be satisfied in certain cases. First, if an expert intends to offer an opinion in the form of mathematical probabilities or percentages, courts express concern over the empirical foundation for such an opinion as well as the potential such an opinion has to mislead the jury into thinking that the uncertain has been mathematically proven. Second, if a scientific procedure was conducted upon an item with no visually unique identifying characteristics (e.g., blood, marijuana, semen, etc.) or upon an item that was subject to contamination or spoilage, the evidence's proponent will most likely be required to establish a "chain of custody." The chain must link the item tested with the parties before the court, and demonstrate that the item tested remained in the proper condition to produce accurate test results. Chain-of-custody requirements are imposed regardless of whether the scientific technique involved is valid. In fact, chain-of-custody requirements are often applied to scientific techniques like blood typing and drug testing that are judicially noticed as reliable by many courts.

In sum, the proponent of evidence derived from scientific testing must be concerned with establishing three things *in addition* to the validity of the scientific theory and/or technique: (1) proper application and interpretation of the technique by qualified individuals, (2) proper expression of the expert's ultimate opinion, and (3) a proper chain of custody. It is appropriate to characterize the focus of the last chapter on the validity of the scientific theory and technique as *substantive*, while the focus of this chapter is more aptly described as *procedural*. The procedural nature of the material covered in this chapter should not be taken as an indicator that the subject is not significant. Many (if not most) courtroom battles over the admissibility of and weight given to scientific evidence are about alleged procedural irregularities (such as irregular laboratory testing procedures, improper or sloppy collection of samples at the crime scene, contamination of evidence at the testing laboratory, broken chain of custody, poorly trained technicians, etc.) and not the validity of the scientific theory or technique. Bear in mind, however, that the overriding concern remains the same: ensuring the trustworthiness of evidence derived from science.

A.   PROPER APPLICATION AND INTERPRETATION

[1]   The Proper Procedures and Proper Working Order Requirements

[a]   Expert Testimony Establishing What Procedures and Maintenance Are Necessary

PEOPLE v. TOBEY
231 N.W.2d 403 (Mich. Ct. App. 1975)

McGREGOR, JUDGE

The defendant was convicted of two counts of illegal sale of heroin by a jury, on August 8, 1973, and sentenced to two concurrent terms of 10 to 20 years in prison.

On February 17, 1972, Officer VanTiem purchased ¼ ounce of heroin for $200 from the defendant. Officer VanTiem had been introduced to the defendant through Allen Lang and confidential informant I.L. 333, neither of whom testified at trial. On February 28, 1972, Officer VanTiem recorded two telephone conversations with a person he believed to be the defendant. The next day, VanTiem went to the defendant's apartment and purchased one ounce of heroin for $900.

Following the defendant's arrest, the trial judge granted the prosecutor's motion to compel the defendant to make voice exemplars into a recording device, using the identical words spoken in the telephone recordings, to enable the prosecution's experts to run a voiceprint test on the two tapes.

At trial, the prosecution called three expert witnesses on the subject of voiceprint identification: Dr. Oscar Tosi,[1] [1] Lt. Ernest Nash[2] [2] and Police Officer Lonnie

---

[1] [n.1] Dr. Tosi is Professor of the Department of Audiology and Speech Sciences and Physics at Michigan State University, holds two doctorates, one in Audiology and Speech Sciences and Electronics from Ohio State University, and the other in Engineering and Physics from Buenos Aires University. He is a member of a number of societies in the fields of speech, logopedics and phoniatrics. He has published two books and more

Leonard Smrkovski. Based on Dr. Tosi's testimony, the trial court ruled, over defendant's objection, that evidence of voiceprint identification tests made under proper conditions was admissible.

Lt. Nash testified that a voiceprint analysis had been run on the tape of the telephone recording made on February 28th, and the tape made by the defendant under court order. He stated that, in his opinion, the two voices were from the same person. The trial court then admitted the two tapes with a limiting instruction and allowed them to be placed before the jury.

Officer Smrkovski testified that he had conducted the voiceprint analysis on the two tapes. Based on this analysis, Officer Smrkovski opined that it was the defendant who had made the incriminating remarks in the telephone conversation with Officer VanTiem.

Defendant appeals as of right from the jury's verdict of guilty on both offenses.

. . . .

. . . [D]efendant claims that the court erred in admitting voiceprint identification information, since the prosecutor failed to lay a proper foundation for the admission of this testimony.[3] [3] We agree.

Before the evidence of spectrograph analysis can be admitted, the prosecutor must lay a proper foundation of proof of the accuracy of the scientific and mechanical instruments used in the test. The trial court's admission of the spectrograph comparison over the defendant's timely objection, based upon the prosecutor's failure to lay a proper foundation for this evidence, was reversible error.

The foundation laid in this case was insufficient in three ways. First, the samples which were compared for analysis were not similar. The unknown tape was recorded over the telephone, while the compelled exemplar was not. Dr. Tosi testified that direct versus telephonic obtaining of the sample is a variable which must be considered. Further, Officer Nash testified that the telephone eliminates high and low pitch sounds below 300 Hz. and above 3,500 Hz., and admitted that fully 8% of vocal range lies below 300 Hz. No compensation in the spectrograph was made for this variance; neither was the compelled voice exemplar played through a telephone in order to get similar samples for the comparison. We note, however, that Officer Nash did testify that research has indicated that this discrepancy is probably insignificant in voice identification.

---

than 35 papers in the fields of audiology and phonetics; he has qualified as an expert in these fields in the courts of almost a dozen states.

[2] [n.2] Ernest Nash is a Detective Lieutenant with the Michigan State Police and is the officer in charge of the Voice Identification Unit of the Scientific Crime Laboratory of the Michigan State Police. He has been in charge of that unit since 1967. Since 1968, he has been a student at Michigan State University, where he has majored in Audiology and Speech Sciences. He has had extensive experience in making sound spectrograms of individual voices as they relate to voice identification. He is a member of several societies in this field and has presented numerous papers on the subject of voiceprint identification. He has heretofore been qualified as an expert in the courts of 20 states. He has examined approximately 180,000 sound spectrograms of the human voice.

[3] [n.3] Since the prosecution failed to lay a proper foundation for the admission of the results of the spectrograph comparison, we need not decide the issue of whether voiceprint identification is admissible as scientific evidence under the test set forth in *Frye v. United States*, 293 F. 1013 (1923), and *People v. Morse*, 38 N.W.2d 322 (1949).

Secondly, the spectrograph itself lacked calibration and proper maintenance. Proof of a scientific or mechanical instrument's accuracy and proper use is a requisite for the admission of the results derived from such devices. In the case at bar, the voiceprint operators admitted that the machine used was never checked until "nothing came out." Neither was there a periodic maintenance or calibration of the machine. Thus, it cannot be known whether the spectrograms made here were in any way accurate.

The third and most important defect in the prosecution's foundation was the length of time between the taking of the unknown tape and the taking of the exemplar from the defendant. The unknown tape recording was made on February 28, 1972; the trial judge granted the prosecution's motion to compel the defendant to give a voice exemplar on December 6, 1972. No experiment has ever verified the use of samples taken more than one month apart. Further, the Michigan State University Voice Identification Project, performed under the direction of Dr. Tosi, demonstrates that if spectrograms were used from samples made a month apart, more errors were made than using samples made at the same time.

. . .

Admission of the spectrograph comparison of the tapes was prejudicial. Viewing the record in its entirety, we cannot say that the jury might not have reached a different result if the voiceprint identification had been properly excluded.

Reversed and remanded for a new trial.

NOTES AND QUESTIONS

1. *Determining What Procedures and Maintenance Are Proper.* The *Tobey* case illustrates that exactly what procedures are "proper" may vary from case to case — even when the same scientific technique is being utilized. According to *Tobey* there is, apparently, no one procedure that is always proper when making a voice exemplar. Rather, the voice exemplar must be recorded over the same device that recorded the sample to which it is being compared; in *Tobey* that device was the telephone.

In THE METHODS OF ATTACKING SCIENTIFIC EVIDENCE, Professor Imwinkelried suggests asking three questions when analyzing whether correct procedures or correct maintenance of a scientific device was employed:

> Is a particular test [or maintenance] procedure required? Did the witness comply with that procedure? If not, what effect does the noncompliance have on the testimony's admissibility?

EDWARD J. IMWINKELRIED, THE METHODS OF ATTACKING SCIENTIFIC EVIDENCE §§ 5-4 & 5-6, at 155–58 & 164–68 (4th ed. 2004).

In answering the first of Professor Imwinkelried's questions (i.e., what is correct test protocol or instrument maintenance), one can refer to expert testimony (as the court did in *Tobey*), learned treatises, or even the instruction manual that accompanies a scientific device or instrument. *See generally id.*, § 5-6[a], at 164–66.

The first part of the second question (was there compliance with required test procedures in this case?) can be answered several ways: by firsthand testimony, the use of business records, or even testimony of habit and custom. Establishing proper machine maintenance and working order can also be done in a number of ways; what could prove fatal to admissibility, however (as indicated in *Tobey*), is doing nothing. That is, even though a machine *appears* to be working properly and has not previously malfunctioned, the proponent of scientific evidence must show that the machine was regularly maintained.

2. *The Effect of Noncompliance: Weight or Admissibility?* The third of Professor Imwinkelried's three questions presents the problem of how a court should deal with noncompliance. If a forensic scientist departs from generally accepted procedures in conducting a test or in maintaining scientific equipment, but is prepared to defend both the procedures used and the results obtained, should the evidence be excluded? Put another way, if the theory and technique applying the theory are valid and the problem is one of "sloppy" procedures used on a specific occasion, why not admit the results and/or the expert opinion and let the opponent of the evidence attack the *weight* that the trier of fact should attach to the expert testimony?

(A) Courts Split. Surprisingly, the issue has been largely neglected by courts and commentators. *See* Edward J. Imwinkelried, *The Debate in the DNA Cases Over the Foundation for the Admission of Scientific Evidence: The Importance of Human Error as a Cause of Forensic Misanalysis*, 69 WASH. U. L.Q. 19, 23 (1991). Furthermore, the courts that have addressed the issue are split. *See* 1 SCIENTIFIC EVIDENCE § 1.12[a]-[b], at 70–73 (4th ed. 2007). Some courts hold that to gain admissibility of the results of forensic testing, the proponent of scientific evidence must make an affirmative showing both that the machine, instrument, chemicals, etc., used were in proper working order or condition *and* that the proper testing procedures were followed in the case before the court. *See, e.g., People v. Castro*, 545 N.Y.S.2d 945, 987 (N.Y. Sup. Ct. 1989) (in context of DNA evidence *Frye* has three prongs, the third being the proper performance of testing on a particular occasion); *People v. Lindsey*, 868 P.2d 1085, 1088 (Colo. App. 1993) (cites to *Castro* in applying three-prong *Frye* test in DNA cases); *Barna v. Commissioner of Pub. Safety*, 508 N.W.2d 220, 222 (Minn. Ct. App. 1993) (proponent of scientific evidence must establish that the test is reliable and that its administration conformed to the procedure necessary to ensure reliability); *Pruitt v. State*, 393 S.W.2d 747, 751 (Tenn. 1965) (State must show that measuring device is "scientifically acceptable and accurate" before results of intoxication test are admissible). *See also* EDWARD J. IMWINKELRIED, THE METHODS OF ATTACKING SCIENTIFIC EVIDENCE § 5-4[a], at 155 (4th ed. 2004) (prevailing view is that proponent must affirmatively show that any instrument used was in good operational condition).

The opposing view sees such issues as going to the weight, but not the admissibility, of the evidence. *See, e.g., State v. Russell*, 882 P.2d 747, 761 (Wash. 1994) (*Frye* does not require acceptance of testing procedures in the case before the court; concerns about errors or mistakes can be argued to the jury); *State v. Vandebogart*, 616 A.2d 483, 490 (N.H. 1992) (proper application not a part of the *Frye* analysis); *Taylor v. State*, 889 P.2d 319, 323 n.4 (Okla. Crim. App. 1995) (*Frye* is a two-part test; proper application of a scientific technique on a specific occasion is not a part of *Frye*).

(B) Distinguishing "Test Protocol" from "Carelessness." The California Supreme Court addressed this issue and distinguished between procedures that can be charac-terized as "test protocol" (procedures that are accepted by the scientific community as a part of the technique and that are essential in achieving an accurate result) and procedures that can be better characterized as "careless" or "sloppy," but that do not necessarily negate the accuracy of the test.

> The *Kelly* test's [correct scientific procedures] prong does not apply the *Frye* requirement of general scientific acceptance — it assumes the methodology and

technique in question has already met that requirement. Instead, it inquires into the matter of whether the procedures actually utilized in the case were in compliance with that methodology and technique, as generally accepted by the scientific community. The third prong is thus case specific[.]

. . . .

Our reference to "careless testing affect[ing] the weight of the evidence and not its admissibility" was intended to characterize shortcomings other than the failure to use correct, scientifically accepted procedures such as would preclude admissibility under the [correct scientific procedures] prong of the *Kelly* test.

. . . .

The *Kelly* test's third prong [correct scientific procedures] does not, of course, cover all derelictions in following the prescribed scientific procedures. Shortcomings such as mislabeling, mixing the wrong ingredients, or failing to follow routine precautions against contaminants may well be amenable to evaluation by jurors without the assistance of expert testimony. Such readily apparent missteps involve "the degree of professionalism" with which otherwise scientifically accepted methodologies are applied in a given case, and so amount only to "careless testing affect[ing] the weight of the evidence and not its admissibility."

People v. Venegas, 954 P.2d 525, 545–47(Cal. 1998).

Which view do you prefer — admissibility or weight? A middle ground would reflect the *Venegas* view: certain techniques can *only* give reliable results when performed in a certain way. A *Frye* state following this "middle ground" would say that such a technique is only "accepted" as reliable when its accompanying test protocol is observed, and procedural irregularities that do not implicate test protocol go to weight, not admissibility.

In determining which is the better approach, what is the likelihood that a machine, like those used to establish intoxication, might give an erroneous reading because it had not been maintained within the prescribed period or because an irregular test procedure had been used? On the other hand, if improper maintenance and/or test protocol is viewed as going only to weight, how is a defendant to get access to proof to show that on a particular occasion a machine was not working properly? *See generally* Edward J. Imwinkelried, *The Debate in the DNA Cases Over the Foundation for the Admission of Scientific Evidence: The Importance of Human Error as a Cause of Forensic Misanalysis*, 69 WASH. U. L.Q. 19, 24–33 (1991).

3. The "Daubert Trilogy" and the Application of Proper Procedures as an Admissibility Requirement. The 2000 amendment to Fed. R. Evid. 702 specifically refers to proper application as an admissibility requirement.

Rule 702. Testimony by Experts

If scientific, technical, or other specialized knowledge will assist the trier of fact to understand the evidence or to determine a fact in issue, a witness qualified as an expert by knowledge, skill, experience, training, or education, may testify thereto in the form of an opinion of otherwise, if (1) the testimony is based upon sufficient facts or data, (2) the testimony is the product of reliable principles and methods, and (3) *the witness has applied the principles and methods reliably to the facts of the case.*

Fed. R. Evid. 702 (emphasis added). The Advisory Committee's Note to the 2000 amendment adds that,

> Under the amendment, as under *Daubert*, when an expert purports to apply principles and methods in accordance with professional standards, and yet reaches a conclusion that other experts in the field would not reach, the trial court may fairly suspect that the principles and methods have not been faithfully applied. The amendment specifically provides that the trial court must scrutinize not only principles and methods used by the expert, but also whether those principles and methods have been properly applied to the facts of the case. As the court said in *In re Paoli R.R. Yard PCB Litig.*, 35 F.3d 717, 745 (3d Cir. 1994), "*any* step that renders analysis unreliable . . . renders the expert's testimony inadmissible. *This is true whether the step completely changes a reliable methodology or merely misapplies that methodology.*"

Fed. R. Evid. 702 advisory committee's note to 2000 amendment (emphasis in original).

In 1995, in the pre-*Kumho Tire* case of *United States v. Galbreth*, 908 F. Supp. 877 (D.N.M. 1995), the United States District Court for the District of New Mexico explained why proper application was an admissibility requirement in the context of determining the admissibility of the results of a polygraph examination.

> The issue at hand does not require the Court to determine whether, in the context of other forensic scientific techniques, a court must scrutinize the specific application of the scientific technique. . . . However, after reviewing the case law addressing this issue in the context of other forensic laboratory techniques and after careful consideration of the testimony presented at the hearing regarding the polygraph technique, the Court holds that in the context of polygraph evidence, such scrutiny is imperative to a faithful application of *Daubert*.

> Such scrutiny appears to be mandated by *Daubert*'s directive that trial courts determine whether the purportedly scientific evidence is "reliable. . . ." [T]he validity of polygraph results in a particular case is absolutely dependent on certain conditions such as a properly conducted examination by a competent examiner. Where the examination is not properly conducted by a competent examiner, the validity of the entire testing procedure, and hence the result of the procedure, is seriously called into question. Absent a showing that the examination was properly conducted by a competent examiner, the proponent simply cannot establish that the evidence is sufficiently trustworthy to be admissible in court.

> Further militating in favor of this Court's approach is *Daubert*'s more specific mandate that "proposed testimony be supported by appropriate valida-tion." As will be discussed below, field and laboratory studies have validated the hypothesis underlying the modern polygraph technique. However, certain essential conditions, such as the administration of the exam by a competent examiner and utilization of standard polygraph techniques, existed at the time of the studies. Unless these conditions are also present during the specific test at issue, testimony concerning the test is not "supported by appropriate validation." Absent such essential conditions, there is absolutely no guarantee of trustworthiness in the results of the particular test. In this way, the testimony regarding the test results lacks the requisite validation which the *Daubert* Court considered so essential to admissibility.

. . . .

Thus, for the aforementioned reasons, this Court holds that in addition to establishing the scientific validity of the polygraph technique in the abstract, the proponent of the proposed testimony must also prove that the specific examination was conducted properly by a competent examiner.

United States v. Galbreth, 908 F. Supp. 877, 880–82 (D.N.M. 1995). *See also United States v. Martinez*, 3 F.3d 1191, 1197–98 (8th Cir. 1993).

4. *Court Procedure.* In those jurisdictions that require the proponent of scientific evidence to establish proper procedures and working order to gain admissibility, the issue is governed by Fed. R. Evid. 104(a) (or its state counterpart). It is the trial court's job to determine what testing procedure and what maintenance is required, and whether or not those procedures were followed on the particular occasion before the court. The proponent of the evidence must make the required showing by a preponderance of the evidence, and the court is not bound by the rules of evidence in reaching its determination.

Of course, even if the court is satisfied that correct procedures were followed and admits the evidence, the opponent of the evidence may still present evidence of irregularities in an effort to diminish the weight the fact finder gives the evidence.

PROBLEMS

Problem 3-1. Assume that you are in a state that follows the majority rule and requires an affirmative showing of proper test procedures, machine maintenance, and proper working order of machines as a prerequisite to admission. Assume further, that in a prosecution for driving under the influence of alcohol the prosecutor seeks to have the results of defendant's Breathalyzer test admitted into evidence. If the police officer responsible for maintaining a Breathalyzer and administering Breathalyzer tests testifies honestly that she simply does not recall the test in question, how can the prosecutor establish that proper procedures were followed and that the machine was properly maintained? *See* FED. R. EVID. 406 & 803(6); EDWARD J. IMWINKELRIED, THE METHODS OF ATTACKING SCIENTIFIC EVIDENCE § 5-6[a], at 164–72 (4th ed. 2004).

Problem 3-2. If a Breathalyzer test given to a motorist arrested for driving under the influence of alcohol indicates that the motorist was *not* intoxicated, should the motorist be able to offer the test results into evidence as substantive evidence showing that the motorist was not intoxicated, without establishing that the officer who administered the test followed correct test protocol and that the machine was properly maintained?

[b]   Legislative Action: Mandated Admissibility and Prescribed Procedures and Maintenance

In the *Tobey* case the Michigan Court of Appeals considered the testimony of experts in voice analysis in determining what procedures were necessary for the technique to produce reliable results and (since a scientific device was used) what maintenance was required to ensure that the voice spectrograph was working properly. Obviously, if experts agree that certain procedures must be followed and that a scientific instrument or device must be properly maintained to achieve accurate results, failure to follow those procedures may compromise test results.

The next two cases, *State v. Krause* and *McDaniel v. State*, deal with a different situation. In both cases proper procedures and maintenance requirements were predetermined by an administrative agency authorized to promulgate such rules by the state legislature. As discussed in Chapter 2, legislative recognition is one of the ways scientific evidence gains admissibility and escapes scrutiny under *Frye* or *Daubert.* Routinely, as a precondition for statutory admissibility, such legislation also requires the evidence's proponent to demonstrate three things: (1) that *prescribed* procedures were followed, (2) that *prescribed* maintenance was performed, and (3) that the test was performed by a competent and qualified individual with *prescribed* training and/or certification.

STATE v. KRAUSE
405 So. 2d 832 (La. 1981)

DIXON, CHIEF JUSTICE.

Patrick A. Krause was charged by complaint-affidavit with operating a vehicle while intoxicated. . . . Following a bench trial, defendant was found guilty and sentenced to a $500.00 fine plus 115 days' imprisonment. . . . This court granted defendant's application for judicial review. . . .

On August 6, 1980 defendant was found on the 4-H Club Road near Denham Springs, Louisiana by Officer Lamar G. Tolbert. On direct examination, Officer Tolbert testified that defendant's truck had left the road at a bad curve and struck two trees, causing extensive damage to the vehicle and bodily injuries to Krause. Defendant was arrested and taken to the police station in Denham Springs. After several refusals, defendant submitted to a Photo Electric Intoximeter (PEI) test. The PEI reading revealed a.18% blood-alcohol level which was sufficient to create a statutory presumption of intoxication.[4] [1]

. . . .

Assignment of Error No. 3

In this assignment defendant objects to the trial court's admission into evidence of the PEI test results on the ground that the state did not prove compliance with the rules and regulations promulgated by the Department of Public Safety.[5] [2] Before the state may avail itself of the statutory presumption of a defendant's intoxication arising from a chemical analysis of his blood, it must show that (1) the state has officially promulgated detailed methods, procedures and techniques which will insure the integrity and reliability of the chemical tests, including specifically the standard quality of chemicals used; and (2) the state has strictly complied with the officially promulgated methods, procedures and techniques in the chemical analysis offered as evidence in the case on trial. *State v. Goetz*, 374 So. 2d 1219 (La. 1979).

---

[4] [n.1] R.S. 32:662 establishes the following presumption: "If there was . . . 0.10 per cent or more by weight of alcohol in the person's blood, it shall be presumed that the person was under the influence of alcoholic beverages."

[5] [n.2] R.S. 32:663 empowered the Department of Public Safety to approve satisfactory techniques for conducting chemical tests for intoxication, to ascertain the qualifications and competence of individuals to conduct such analyses, and to issue permits to those individuals.

The rationale behind requiring strict compliance with the regulations was clearly enunciated by this court in *State v. Goetz, supra*, at 1220:

Because an intoxication test conducted with chemicals of inferior quality could bring to bear a practically conclusive presumption of guilt against an innocent person, it is essential that the officially promulgated methods, procedures and techniques include a thorough analysis of the chemicals by a chemist under laboratory conditions to insure that they are of proper composition, strength and volume at the time a test is conducted. . . .

Pursuant to R.S. 32:663, the Department of Public Safety adopted certain regulations which require a maintenance check of all PEI machines at least once every four months accompanied by a spot check of the lot of ampuls used with each machine.[6] [3] This spot check is to be conducted by the Applied Technology Unit and a recertification form filled out. The recertification may be filed with the appropriate court in the parish where each device is located and it will serve as prima facie evidence of the chemical accuracy of the tests performed on that machine with chemicals taken from the lot of ampuls checked.[7] [4]

The trial court refused to allow introduction of the recertification of machine #168 dated June 30, 1980.[8] [5] The recertification contained a spot check of ampul lot #14, from which the chemicals used to test Krause were taken. In denying the introduction of the certificate the court referred to the fact that the inspecting technician, George

---

[6] [n.3] Regulation No. 4 provides in pertinent part:

"c. The Applied Technology Unit shall require manufacturers of ampuls to certify each lot of ampuls made, as to their standard of quality in reference to the chemical contents and tolerance. The Applied Technology Unit shall maintain these certificates on file from the manufacturer. The Applied Technology Unit shall then have the authority to spot check the ampuls with respect to their performance. The machine recertification form that is filed every four months with the clerks of court shall also state that the ampul lot numbers used at each agency were spot checked for performance.

d. Maintenance checks will be performed on a routine basis at least once every four months, by the Louisiana State Police Crime Laboratory, Applied Technology Unit. Items to be checked shall be, but are not limited to, the following: (1) Each lot of ampuls shall be spot checked for performance. (2) Clean instrument. (3) Calibration check of standard ampuls. (4) Running of a known alcohol solution in which results shall be within plus or minus.010% of the known alcohol value. (5) In the event any repair work is needed, it will be recorded in detail."

La. Register, vol. 4, No. 4, p. 391 (1978).

[7] [n.4] Regulation No. 1 states:

"1. After the Louisiana Department of Public Safety has approved a prototype breath testing device as an acceptable model for chemical analysis in breath alcohol testing it shall be necessary for each individual instrument of the approved model to be checked out and approved for use by the State Police Crime Laboratory, Applied Technology Unit, at least once every four months, and a machine recertification form shall be maintained for each machine in the State Police Crime Laboratory, Applied Technology Unit. A copy of this certificate may be filed with the clerk of the applicable court in the respective parishes in which each device is used for breath testing, and this copy shall be prima facie evidence as to the operating performance of the instruments and standard of quality of the ampuls."

La. Register, vol. 4, No. 1, p. 390 (1978).

[8] [n.5] The recertification form read as follows:

. . . .

"This is to certify that Instrument #168 Model 400 Photo-Electric Intoximeter is an approved instrument for use in Breath-alcohol Testing and is certified to be in proper functioning condition on this 30th day of June, 1980. Located at Denham Springs Police Department, Denham Springs, La. Ampul lot #14 spot checked for performance. This certificate is prima facie evidence of the proper functioning of the instrument."

The recertification is signed by George Dunn and Bailey D. Hughes II.

Dunn, was not present to testify. *See State v. Goetz, supra.* Hence, the sole proof of the chemical reliability of the ampuls utilized in the test conducted on defendant was the manufacturer's "Certificate of PEI Standard of Quality," dated November 6, 1979, introduced by the state;[9] [7] this certificate from the manufacturer was over nine months old when defendant was tested.

The issue presented by this assignment becomes whether the manufacturer's certificate remains prima facie proof of the chemical accuracy of the test after it is four months old. In *State v. Goetz, supra* , decided under the current regulations, this court held that the manufacturer's certificate of standard chemical quality is deemed prima facie evidence of the good quality of the test chemicals. However, where the manufacturer's certificate is over four months old, the regulations must be read to require a recertification by a local technician. As pointed out in *Goetz*, the present regulations constitute an apparent attempt by the Department of Public Safety to implement the preferred practice in other states whereby all chemicals are kept under the supervision of a local chemist who conducts periodic spot checks. In any event, we hold that although the manufacturer's certificate may be afforded prima facie weight during the initial four month period, the regulations demand that the Applied Technology Unit perform a maintenance check of all PEI machines at least once every four months accompanied by a spot check of the lot of ampuls used with each machine. The recertification by the Applied Technology Unit will replace the manufacturer's certificate as prima facie proof of the chemical accuracy of the tests.

The trial court based its decision to allow the introduction of the PEI test results upon the manufacturer's certificate as prima facie proof of standard chemical quality. Since we hold that the manufacturer's certificate is not entitled to prima facie weight, the introduction of the PEI results was improper. Without those results, there is no presumption of defendant's intoxication.

. . . .

The conviction and sentence are therefore reversed, and the defendant is ordered discharged.

McDANIEL v. STATE
706 So. 2d 1305 (Ala. Crim. App. 1997)

BROWN, JUDGE.

The appellant, Walter Todd McDaniel, was convicted in St. Clair District Court of several traffic offenses, including driving under the influence of alcohol, a violation of § 32-5A-191, *Code of Alabama* 1975. . . . On appeal the appellant challenges only his conviction for driving under the influence of alcohol. As required by Rule 30.2, Ala. R. Crim. P., the parties have stipulated to the facts. . . .

Following his arrest, the appellant submitted to chemical testing by the Intoxilyzer 5000 ("I-5000"). His first breath test resulted in a 0.10% blood-alcohol reading. The second test rendered an "invalid" result because the appellant was unable to provide a sufficient breath sample for analysis. Trooper Allen Vines, the arresting officer, deemed

---

[9] [n.7] Other documentary evidence introduced by the state included a rights form, a permit issued to George Dunn qualifying him as an operator, maintenance technician, and instructor, and the results of the test performed on defendant.

the appellant's unsuccessful attempt a "refusal." At trial, the state introduced the result of the first test over the appellant's objection.

The appellant contends that the trial court erred by admitting into evidence testimony concerning the results of the I-5000 blood-alcohol test administered to him by the arresting officer. Specifically, the appellant argues that because, he says, the state failed to establish the statutory predicate for admission of the test results, as required by § 32-5A-194(a)(1), *Code of Alabama* 1975, the test result was inadmissible.

[1] Section 32-5A-194(a)(1) provides:

"(a) Upon the trial of any civil, criminal or quasi-criminal action or proceeding arising out of acts alleged to have been committed by any person while driving or in actual control of a vehicle while under the influence of alcohol or controlled substance, evidence of the amount of alcohol or controlled substance in a person's blood at the alleged time, as determined by a chemical analysis of the person's blood, urine, breath or other bodily substance, shall be admissible. Where such a chemical test is made the following provisions shall apply:

"(1) Chemical analyses of the person's blood, urine, breath or other bodily substance to be considered valid under the provisions of this section shall have been performed according to methods approved by the Department of Forensic Sciences and by an individual possessing a valid permit issued by the Department of Forensic Sciences for this purpose. *The court trying the case may take judicial notice of the methods approved by the Department of Forensic Sciences.* The Department of Forensic Sciences is authorized to approve satisfactory techniques or methods, to ascertain the qualifications and competence of individuals to conduct such analyses, and to issue permits which shall be subject to termination or revocation at the discretion of the Department of Forensic Sciences. The Department of Forensic Sciences shall approve permits required in this section only for employees of state, county, municipal, and federal law enforcement agencies and for laboratory personnel employed by the Department of Forensic Sciences."

(Emphasis added.) Those "methods approved by the Department of Forensic Sciences" referred to in § 32-5A-194(a)(1) are found in the Alabama Administrative Code at Rule 370-1-1-.01(4)(a) and (b) of the rules of the Alabama Department of Forensic Sciences, entitled "Report of Breath Test Result":

"(a) Two (2) samples of breath shall be tested. Wait at least two (2) minutes, but not more than fifteen (15) minutes after the first test to do the second test.

"Report the lower test result. Maintain the record of each test result.

"(b) Any person directed to submit to the breath test procedure requiring two (2) breath samples and *fails* or refuses *to give two samples sufficient for analysis by the Intoxilyzer 5000 shall be deemed to have refused the entire test and such person shall be reported as having refused to submit to the chemical test.*"

(Emphasis added.) In order to lay a proper predicate for the admission of test results under § 32-5A-194(a)(1), the state must show that the test was administered in strict compliance with the aforementioned administrative code section.

McDaniel contends that because the state had the results from only one valid breath test, those results were inadmissible because, he says, the statutory predicate was not established. We agree that because the administrative rules adopted by the Department of Forensic Sciences require that two valid breath tests be administered, the state failed to satisfy the statutory requirement; however, the statutory predicate set out in § 32-5A-194(a)(1) is only one way by which the I-5000 test results can be admitted into evidence.

An alternative method is the establishment of a traditional evidentiary predicate, wherein the prosecution establishes "that the test was administered by a qualified officer in the usual manner and that the I-5000 in question passed inspection before and after the test." *Ex parte Mayo*, 652 So.2d 201, 211 (Ala.1994). In determining what constituted a proper evidentiary predicate, the Supreme Court, in *Mayo*, cited with approval the following language from [previous cases]:

> "To establish a predicate for admitting the test results, without reliance on the statute, there should be evidence that:
>
> "(1) the theory underlying the photoelectric intoximeter [now, the I-5000] test is valid and generally accepted as such;
>
> "(2) the intoximeter [I-5000] is a reliable instrument and generally accepted as such;
>
> "(3) the intoximeter [I-5000] test was administered by a qualified individual who could properly conduct the test and interpret the results; and
>
> "(4) the instrument used in conducting the test was in good working condition and the test was conducted in such a manner as to secure accurate results."

In *Gwarjanski v. State*, 700 So.2d 357 (Ala. Cr. App.1996), this court upheld the defendant's DUI conviction, determining that a traditional evidentiary predicate had been established through the testimony of the state trooper who had administered the I-5000 test. The trooper testified that he was qualified to administer the blood-alcohol test, and that he administered the test to the appellant in the usual manner. We further held that the admission into evidence of the I-5000 logbook was sufficient "substantive proof that the machine had passed inspection and was properly calibrated and operating at the time of the appellant's test." *Id.*, at 359.

In the present case, our review of the record convinces us that the state failed to lay a traditional evidentiary predicate. Indeed, the state concedes as much. The stipulation of fact does, at least arguably, acknowledge the validity of the I-5000 test and that the usual operating procedures were followed. However, the stipulation of fact contains no mention of Trooper Vines's qualifications to administer the I-5000 test, and it does not establish that the I-5000 used to test the appellant passed inspection before and after the test. Accordingly, because the state did not lay a sufficient traditional evidentiary predicate, the trial court erred in allowing Trooper Vines to testify concerning the results of the I-5000 test.

Moreover, . . . admission of the I-5000 test results was not harmless error. Although the stipulation of fact noted that Trooper Vines gave other testimony concerning the appellant's intoxicated condition at the time of his arrest, including the fact that he smelled the odor of alcohol on the appellant's breath, the evidence of intoxication in this case was conflicting. That portion of the stipulation of fact summarizing the appellant's testimony provided that he was suffering from a chronic, severe stomach disorder, and that he was taking numerous prescribed medications for the treatment of this condition. He maintained that his condition was not caused by intoxication, but rather, was the result of his having become severely ill while traveling to Pell City. "In light of the conflicting testimony and the great weight often given to results from sophisticated, technical machinery," *Ex parte Curtis*, 502 So.2d 833, 835 (Ala.1986), we are unable to say that admission of Trooper Vines's testimony concerning the I-5000 test results was harmless error.

The judgment of the trial court is reversed and this cause is remanded to that court for further proceedings consistent with this opinion.

Reversed and Remanded.

NOTES

1. *Statutory Presumptions and Statutory Procedures.*

(A) Strict Compliance with Statutory Procedures. Note that in *Krause* Louisiana statutes allowed PEI test results into evidence (without a showing that the technique was reliable) *and* created a statutory presumption of being under the influence of alcohol if two conditions were met: (1) the test results showed that the person tested had 0.10% alcohol or more in his or her blood, and (2) the prescribed procedures were followed. *Cf. Commonwealth v. Smith*, 624 N.E.2d 604, 607–08 (Mass. App. Ct. 1993) (Breathalyzer test results are admissible if regulations requiring police officer administering test to "test and prove the device every time it is used" are complied with). Such statutes are common with certain scientific techniques that are designed to detect if a person is under the influence of alcohol. ANDRE A. MOENSSENS, CAROL E. HENDERSON & SHARON G. PORTWOOD, SCIENTIFIC EVIDENCE IN CIVIL AND CRIMINAL CASES § 3.12, at 230 (5th ed. 2007) (all 50 states and the District of Columbia have statutes that either prescribe presumptions based upon blood alcohol content or create "per se" offenses for driving with a certain amount of alcohol in the blood).

A second area where one typically finds statutes mandating admissibility of the results of a scientific technique is speed detection. When it is a crime to drive above a certain speed, statutes that call for the admissibility of the reading from certain speed detection devices (e.g., radar) have the effect of establishing a prima facia case of speeding. *See id.*, § 4.10, at 265.

When a statute mandates admissibility for a scientific technique *and* creates a presumption of guilt based upon test results, courts typically require strict compliance with all statutory requirements, including prescribed maintenance, testing procedure, and operator qualification. *Ex parte Mayo*, 652 So. 2d 201, 209 (Ala. 1994) (due process requires the state to carefully control the tests it administers to supply proof of blood alcohol content when it is *per se* illegal to drive with a blood alcohol content of .10% or more); *Commonwealth v. Barbeau*, 585 N.E.2d 1392, 1394–95 (Mass. 1992) (state must establish compliance with statutorily required testing program to admit results of Breathalyzer test); *State v. Brayman*, 751 P.2d 294, 299 (Wash. 1988) (breath test alone not conclusive proof of driving under the influence of alcohol; state must also prove breath test machine to be in proper working order and test properly administered by a certified person); *State v. Souza*, 732 P.2d 253, 257 (Haw. Ct. App. 1987) ("foundational prerequisites for the admission of the Intoxilyzer test result [requires] a showing of strict compliance with those provisions of the Rules which have a direct bearing on the validity and accuracy of the test result.").

(B) Judicial Rationale for Strict Compliance. There is an aura of unfairness that may rise to a constitutional level and, arguably, result in depriving the defendant of due

process if a scientific test or instrument that "finds a defendant guilty" was not conducted pursuant to legislatively prescribed procedures. *Cf. State v. Lowther*, 740 P.2d 1017, 1019–21 (Haw. Ct. App. 1987) (due process guarantee of a fair trial may be violated if a defendant is not given the opportunity to attack the reliability of an intoxilyzer that has been legislatively recognized as reliable); Edward J. Imwinkelried & Robert G. Scofield, *The Recognition of an Accused's Constitutional Right to Introduce Expert Testimony Attacking the Weight of Prosecution Science Evidence: The Antidote for the Supreme Court's Mistaken Assumption in* California v. Trombetta, 33 ARIZ. L. REV. 59, 73 (1991) (defendant ought to have a constitutional right to offer rebuttal evidence challenging test results from scientific techniques recognized as valid by statute or judicial decision).

The difficulty in defending oneself when a scientific technique finds you "guilty" may not be the only reason for requiring strict compliance with statutes that mandate admissibility and create a presumption of guilt. Consideration should be given to the possibility that courts simply question the accuracy of results obtained from machines used to gauge intoxication and, as a result, require strict compliance with legislatively prescribed procedures. The following passage from *State v. Gerber*, 291 N.W.2d 403 (Neb. 1980), displays judicial skepticism toward the Breathalyzer as a device to measure alcohol in the blood:

> While perhaps not necessary to our decision, we nevertheless observe that the reliability of Breathalyzer test results is dependent on two basic assumptions: (1) That there is a direct correlation between alcohol content of air in the lungs and alcohol in the blood; and (2) That this relationship is equally true for all people. The first assumption may be true, but the measurement is subject to immense error due to such factors as the absence of recent vomiting or even burping and the cleanliness of the mouth, to name only a few. It is the second assumption, however, that is most fallacious. The scientific literature establishes that the correlative factor used is simply a mean or average. Significant percentages of persons would have alcohol content in the blood above or below the amount indicated by the Breathalyzer result. In a significant number of cases, where the measurement is at the minimum to establish illegality, persons can be convicted wrongly.

> While not raised in this appeal and therefore not now decided, many commentators have suggested that Breathalyzers should be limited to a corroborative role in the prosecution of the offense of driving while intoxicated. The use of a test which can, standing alone, result in conviction of a crime, when the test results can and do differ from individual to individual, offends our sense of justice and fair play.

Id. at 412.

2. *Alternative to Statutory Admissibility.* As indicated in the *McDaniel* case, not all courts follow the approach taken in *Krause* of automatically excluding scientific evidence when statutory procedures mandating admissibility are not strictly followed. Instead, "when the *statutory predicate* for admission is not established, the results of a chemical test for intoxication may still be admitted if the prosecution establishes a sufficient predicate under *traditional evidentiary rules for the admission of scientific test results.*" *Ex parte Mayo*, 652 So. 2d 201, 209 (Ala. 1994). *See also State v. Kennedy*, 657 A.2d 773, 774 (Me. 1995) ("Compliance with administrative requirements is not an absolute prerequisite to admission. The question . . . is whether the test results were . . . reliable. . . .").

Also, one should keep in mind that a conviction for an offense like driving under the influence of alcohol can be obtained without the admission of *any* scientific evidence.

> Even discarding the Intoxilyzer test result, the preliminary breath test result, and the "horizontal gaze test" result the remaining evidence that defendant had the odor of alcohol on his breath, slurred his speech, had bloodshot eyes, had trouble retrieving his license from his billfold, was disheveled, could not recite the alphabet, had difficulty in coordinating his movements, could not keep his balance, failed to stop at a stop sign, and crossed the centerline of the road four or five times overwhelmingly supports the conclusion that he had ingested alcohol in an amount sufficient to impair to an appreciable degree his ability to operate a motor vehicle in a prudent and cautious manner, thus establishing a violation of [driving while under the influence of alcohol]. Therefore, the error . . . in considering the Intoxilyzer test result was harmless. . . .

State v. Burling, 400 N.W.2d 872, 877 (Neb. 1987).

3. Certification Statutes. The procedures specified in a statute as preconditions to admissibility need not be as exacting as those discussed in the *Krause* and *McDaniel* cases. Recall the discussion in Chapter 1, *supra*, of state "certificate of analysis" statutes that authorize the admissibility of laboratory reports containing the results of forensic testing. Precisely *what* must be certified in such statutes varies from jurisdiction to jurisdiction, but, typically, the requirements are minimal when compared to requirements like those discussed in *Krause* and *McDaniel*. *See, e.g.*, ALA. CODE § 12-21-300(b) (1975) (certification must contain date evidence delivered to facility, name of persons delivering and receiving evidence, description of the evidence, type of examination requested, name of person analyzing evidence, date of analysis, results of analysis.).

QUESTIONS

1. In the *Krause* case, could the prosecution have obtained a conviction based upon Officer Tolbert's testimony that Krause appeared intoxicated?

2. In *Krause*, why isn't the recertification certificate admissible to establish compliance with statutory procedures without the testimony of inspecting technician Dunn? *See State v. Goetz*, 374 So. 2d 1219 (La. 1979); FED. R. EVID. 803(8)(B). *Compare United States v. Oates*, 560 F.2d 45, 78–89 (2d Cir. 1977) *with United States v. Orozco*, 590 F.2d 789, 793 (9th Cir. 1979).

3. In *McDaniel*, what was the problem with the foundation for *statutory admission* of the results of the Intoxilyzer 5000? What was the problem with the foundation for *traditional admission* of the results of the Intoxilyzer 5000?

PROBLEM

Problem 3-3. Assume that you represent the state in the *Krause* case at the trial court level. You are aware that there is a problem in complying with state regulations because the recertification of the PEI does not comply with state regulations, and you are aware that the manufacturer's certificate of quality is invalid because it is more than four months old.

What is your best strategy for getting the results of the PEI test into evidence? *See Ex parte Mayo*, 652 So. 2d 201, 209 (Ala. 1994); *State v. Krause*, 405 So. 2d 832, 836 (La. 1981) (Lemmon, J. dissenting).

[2]　　The Qualified Operators and Interpreters Requirement[10]

Up until now the focus has been primarily upon the scientific theory and the application of the theory. The requirement under examination in this subsection looks at the *people* who are involved in the process of conducting a scientific technique and laying a foundation for the admission of results or opinions based on the technique.

Consider that there are three types of experts needed to lay a proper foundation for admission of scientific evidence. The first witness will be called the "teaching witness." If the validity of a scientific theory is not judicially noticed or legislatively recognized, the teaching witness becomes essential. This witness testifies at a theoretical level about a theory's validity and, if a machine is involved, about the validity of an instrument or machine in applying the technique. Testimony from this type of witness may satisfy the requirements of *Frye* or *Daubert*, but such testimony, in and of itself, does not connect the theory or the instrument with the case being considered.

In addition to establishing a theory's general acceptance and/or reliability, someone must testify as to how the theory was *properly applied in the one particular case under consideration.* This person will be called the "application witness." (The teaching witness, of course, may also be the application witness.) The application witness is usually the person who conducted the test, and often is able to establish that proper procedures were followed. Similarly, unless technical expertise is required beyond mere physical ability to operate a machine or conduct a test, the application witness may also establish proper working order and maintenance of a machine or instrument. Finally, the application witness will usually be the witness who establishes the final link in the chain of custody by testifying to receipt of the item to be tested and safekeeping up until the time of testing.[11]

A third expert witness (or perhaps, *category* of expert testimony), the "interpreting witness," is sometimes required. This witness takes the results testified to by the "application witness" and explains the significance of the results to the jury. For example, unless a statute created a presumption of intoxication at a certain level of blood alcohol content, one witness, usually a police officer, would testify about how an intoxication test was administered and what the results of the test showed (the application witness). This witness would be followed by a medical doctor or toxicologist who would explain what the test results mean in terms of the suspect being intoxicated (the interpreting witness). In the example being used, the interpreting witness would tell the jury that the level of blood alcohol content found by the police officer administering the test would cause a person to be intoxicated.

The focus in this section is on the qualifications of the teaching witness, application witness, and interpreting witness, and the proper scope of their testimony.

---

[10] *See generally* EDWARD J. IMWINKELRIED, THE METHODS OF ATTACKING SCIENTIFIC EVIDENCE § 5-1, at 148–49 (4th ed. 2004).

[11] Chain of custody requirements will be examined in Section C of this chapter.

FRENCH v. STATE
484 S.W.2d 716 (Tex. Crim. App. 1972)

ONION, PRESIDING JUDGE.

The conviction out of which this appeal arises is for driving a motor vehicle upon a public highway while under the influence of intoxicating liquor. The punishment was assessed by the court following the jury's verdict of guilty at three days in the county jail and a $100.00 fine.

Appellant contends the court erred in admitting into evidence the results of a Breathalyzer test and permitting the jury to consider the same in its deliberations. He contends (a) the test was not shown to have been performed by an individual possessing a valid certificate issued by the Texas Department of Public Safety or according to methods approved by such agency, and (b) there is no evidence the chemicals used in such test were the correct chemicals or in the proper proportion to insure an accurate test, and (c) there is no evidence showing periodic inspection of the Breathalyzer, etc.

At appellant's trial on March 29, 1971, George Herbert, Texas Highway Patrolman, testified that he arrested the appellant for driving while intoxicated on the night of August 27, 1969, in Brazoria County after he stopped appellant's motor vehicle for speeding and for having no taillights. Herbert related he carried the appellant to Angleton for a Breathalyzer test. He expressed the opinion the appellant was intoxicated, but, also, testified that if the Breathalyzer test had shown less than ".10%" he would not have filed charges.

Tommy D. Orand, Texas Highway Patrolman, testified that on the night of August 27, 1969, he was "certified" as a Breathalyzer operator and that he administered the test to the appellant. The record fails to reflect by whom he was certified. He answered affirmatively to conclusory questions, over objections, that proper chemicals had been used and that the machine was in working order. He related that the result of such test showed ".16."

On cross examination, he testified as follows:

Q.   What was in the bottles that you used on the simulator test?

A.   As a solution, I don't know the content. It's some type of an acid, but I don't remember what type of acid.

Q.   What was the control number on the bottle?

A.   I don't remember. I'd have to look at the check-slip.

Q.   But you don't have the check-slip?

A.   No, sir.

Q.   So, we don't know what that machine was run with, do we? You don't know where the bottles came from or the number that was on the bottles?

A.   It was stuff that was locked up in the cabinet to be used when running tests.

Q.   But you can't say what was used for sure of your own knowledge?

A.   I don't know what the number was on the vial.

Q.   Sir?

A.   I don't know what the number was on the vial.

Q.   You don't know who prepared these vials?

A.   No, sir, I do not know who prepared them.

Q.   You don't know who put what in these vials, do you, of your own knowledge?

A.   No, sir.

Q.   In fact these vials are sealed, aren't they?

A.   Yes, sir.

Q.   So, whoever sealed these vials was the last that could say whether or not the vials were contaminated?

A.   Yes, sir.

On re-direct examination, he related he was not a chemist, but had "a week's training in Austin" but was not taught to analyze or prepare chemicals.

At the conclusion of Orand's testimony, appellant's counsel moved,

> to strike the testimony concerning the Breathalyzer test as this officer cannot testify what was used in the Breathalyzer test or what chemical solution was used in the Breathalyzer test. He cannot even testify as to where the vials came from or what the control number was on the vials, the control number being necessary to know what's in the vials, or who prepared the solution, and whether the proper solution was used or whether it was defective. . . .

The motion was overruled.

Robert Bauer, chemist-toxicologist with the Department of Public Safety, testified.16, the results of the test given, would indicate the amount of alcohol present in a certain percentage of appellant's blood, and the accepted standard for determining intoxication of the National Safety Council, American Medical Association, and the President's Committee on National Safety was.10%.

On cross examination, he acknowledged that if proper chemicals were not used, there would be an inaccurate reading on the Breathalyzer. He admitted he could not say whether the chemicals used in the test administered to the appellant were properly mixed and without the control numbers there would not be any way he could tell. He related that the Breathalyzer was a delicate instrument and could be easily damaged.

After both sides rested and closed, the appellant timely objected to the failure of the court to include in his charge an instruction to the jury to disregard the results of the Breathalyzer test.

. . . .

In *Hill v. State*, 256 S.W.2d 93 (1953), this court discussed the necessary predicate for the admissibility of an interpretation of the results of a breath test. There it was held that the State must show (1) the use of properly compounded chemicals; (2) the existence of periodic supervision over the machine and operation by one who understands the scientific theory of the machine; (3) proof of the result of the test by a witness or witnesses qualified to translate and interpret such result so as to eliminate hearsay.

In the instant case, Chemist Bauer was shown to be qualified to translate and interpret the results of a Breathalyzer test, thus satisfying the third prong of the *Hill* test.

Officer Orand, the testing officer, was not a chemist and had not been instructed in the analysis or preparation of chemicals. However, an officer may administer a breath test even though he is not otherwise qualified to interpret the results, and the standards required to qualify one to administer the test are far less than those qualifying to interpret the results.

Orand testified that he was "certified" as a Breathalyzer operator, but he did not testify by whom. Since the test was given prior the effective date of [the Texas statute establishing standards for the administration of such tests,] we do not deem this a disqualification. However, Orand testified that he did not have any instruction in chemistry; did not know what was contained in the vials he used to conduct the test; did not know the number on the vial nor who prepared the sealed vial. Bauer testified that, without the control number, he could not tell if the chemicals used were properly compounded and, if the proper chemicals were not used, an inaccurate reading would result. Thus, the first prong of the *Hill* test was not met.

Further, while Bauer testified he was a Supervisor, there was no showing he was assigned to the area in question or whether he or any one else periodically inspected or exercised supervision over the machine used to administer the test. The second prong of the *Hill* test was not met.

Therefore, we must conclude the court erred in allowing the jury to consider the results of the Breathalyzer test in their assessment of the evidence.

For the error noted, the judgment is reversed and the cause remanded.

NOTE

Distinguishing Between the Teaching and Application Witness. In *State v. Fuller*, 802 P.2d 599 (Kan. Ct. App. 1990), the defendant was convicted of selling marijuana. On appeal he challenged his conviction, asserting that a police officer, who admittedly was trained to conduct tests to determine if a substance was marijuana (i.e., was a qualified application witness), was not qualified to give an opinion as to the reliability or general acceptance of such test (i.e., was not qualified as a teaching witness). The Kansas Court of Appeals reversed the defendant's conviction, observing as follows:

> Lieutenant Harold Bonawitz testified that he had tested the contents of the bag [of marijuana] using techniques he learned at a four-day training session held by the Kansas Bureau of Investigation. At the time of trial, Bonawitz had tested over 200 marijuana samples and testified as an expert in marijuana identification between 100 and 150 times. Lieutenant Bonawitz testified about the marijuana testing procedures and positive test results in this case. At trial, the defendant objected to Bonawitz's qualifications to testify as to the reliability of the testing procedure he had used and the results of the tests.
>
> . . . .
>
> . . . *The fact that a person is qualified to testify as to the results of a test does not necessarily qualify that person to testify about the reliability of the test in general.*

. . . .

The State in this case failed to establish that Lieutenant Bonawitz was qualified to testify as an expert in the field of marijuana identification techniques or as to the general acceptance of the marijuana identification techniques used by him. The State did little more than introduce Bonawitz and then ask him whether the tests he used were generally recognized as the standard tests for the identification of marijuana. Bonawitz testified that he had 16 years' experience with the police department as a shift supervisor and as a firearms, handgun, and self-defense instructor, and does marijuana analysis for the department. Bonawitz took a four-day course in marijuana identification at the Kansas Bureau of Investigation and has examined over 250 samples and testified between 100 and 150 times as an expert in marijuana identification.

The defense correctly argues that Bonawitz was only qualified to testify as to the operation of the tests. Bonawitz is not qualified to testify that the tests he used were generally accepted as reliable in the scientific community as required by *Frye*. In his testimony, Bonawitz answered that the techniques he used were "standard." However, "standard" is not synonymous with "reliable." Under these circumstances, the State did not establish that Bonawitz had the background or knowledge on which he could have based an opinion as to the reliability of the test as required by *Frye*. . . . Accordingly, the trial court erred by allowing the test results into evidence.

Id. at 600–02 (emphasis added).

QUESTIONS

1. Assume that at the time the *French* case was decided Texas legislatively recognized the reliability of the Breathalyzer machine. If Patrolman Orand was properly trained to administer the test, and if Chemist Bauer was properly qualified to interpret the test results, would reversal of French's conviction still be proper?

2. In what situations would an interpretive witness be totally unnecessary? Or, must a witness be called in all cases to explain the significance of test results to a jury? *See* EDWARD J. IMWINKELRIED, THE METHODS OF ATTACKING SCIENTIFIC EVIDENCE § 6-1, at 186–87 (4th ed. 2004).

3. Must the interpretive witness be present when tests are conducted so that opinions offered by the interpretive witness are based upon first-hand knowledge? *See* Fed. R. Evid. 703.

B.   EXPERT CERTAINTY AND PREJUDICING THE JURY: ULTIMATE OPINIONS AND PROBABILITY TESTIMONY

Even if there is judicial confidence in both the underlying scientific theory and the application and interpretation of that theory on a particular occasion, concerns about the "mystic infallibility" of scientific evidence are exacerbated when expert opinion based upon a scientific technique is expressed in terms of mathematical probabilities. The problem is one of balancing the probative value of expert probability opinion with the potential the evidence has for misleading the jury into thinking that the uncertain has been mathematically proven. The concern is heightened when probabilities are used in criminal cases to identify the accused as the wrongdoer.

For example, a forensic scientist in a murder case may be able to testify (based upon an analysis of blood tests) that the odds of blood found at the crime scene belonging to anyone but the defendant are one in a million. On the other hand, the expert could refrain from any mention of odds and probabilities and simply testify that defendant's blood type is the "same" or "consistent with" blood found at the crime scene. Which form of the expert opinion is preferable?

Clearly testimony expressed in terms of mathematical probabilities is more probative of guilt and, at the same time, more prejudicial to the defendant. The critical question involves whether the testimony is *unfairly* prejudicial to the defendant.

[1]   The Constitutional Dimension

UNITED STATES ex rel. DiGIACOMO v. FRANZEN
680 F.2d 515 (7th Cir. 1982)

Before PELL, WOOD and ESCHBACH, CIRCUIT JUDGES.

PER CURIAM.

In this appeal from the denial of a petition for a writ of habeas corpus, petitioner James G. DiGiacomo claims that he was denied a fair trial when the state was allowed to use mathematical probability to identify him as the perpetrator of a crime. We hold that the admission of the challenged testimony violated no right guaranteed by the Constitution and affirm the district court's judgment denying the petition.

I.

In March 1977, James G. DiGiacomo was tried in an Illinois state court on charges of rape, deviate sexual assault, aggravated kidnapping, and battery. The principal witness against DiGiacomo was Patricia Marik, the victim of the assault. Marik testified that DiGiacomo abducted her at knife point from a tavern in Naperville, Illinois, on November 5, 1976, and ordered her to drive him to a cornfield in the country where, after a brief struggle, he forced her to have sexual intercourse with him.

In an effort to bolster Marik's identification of DiGiacomo as her assailant at trial, the state called an expert witness to testify concerning a number of hairs that had been recovered from Marik's automobile after the attack. Sally Dillon, the supervising criminologist at the Illinois Bureau of Identification, testified that she had compared the hairs found in Marik's car with a sample of DiGiacomo's hair and found them to be microscopically similar. She was then asked, over defense counsel's objection, whether she could testify as to the statistical probability of the hair found in Marik's car belonging to someone other than DiGiacomo. Dillon responded that based on a recent study she had read, "the chances of another person belonging to that hair would be one in 4,500."

Several hours after beginning their deliberations, the jury, apparently confused by Dillon's testimony, submitted the following question to the court in writing: "Has it been established by sampling of hair specimens that the defendant was positively proven to have been in the automobile?" After consulting with the parties, the trial judge sent a written response to the jury in which he instructed them that it was their duty to determine the facts from the evidence presented at trial and that he could therefore provide no answer to their question. Neither side objected.

The jury later returned guilty verdicts on each of the charges, and DiGiacomo was sentenced to three concurrent terms of eight to twenty-five years for the kidnapping, rape, and deviate sexual assault, and 364 days, also concurrent, for the battery. DiGiacomo appealed his conviction to the Illinois Appellate Court, claiming, *inter alia*, that the trial court had erred in permitting the state to use mathematical odds to identify him as the perpetrator of a crime. The Appellate Court held that Dillon's testimony was properly admissible and affirmed the conviction. Leave to appeal further was denied by the Illinois Supreme Court.

His state remedies thus exhausted, DiGiacomo filed a petition for habeas corpus in the United States District Court for the Northern District of Illinois in which he claimed that the admission of Dillon's testimony regarding the statistical likelihood of the hairs found in Marik's car belonging to him constituted a denial of due process. The district court denied the petition, and this appeal followed.

II.

Under 28 U.S.C. § 2254, a federal court is authorized to issue a writ of habeas corpus in behalf of a person in custody under the judgment of a state court "only on the ground that he is in custody in violation of the Constitution or laws or treaties of the United States." Because the admissibility of evidence in state courts is a matter of state law, evidentiary questions are not subject to federal review under § 2254 unless there is a resultant denial of fundamental fairness or the denial of a specific constitutional right.

In this case, DiGiacomo contends the admission of expert testimony as to the mathematical likelihood of hairs found in Marik's car belonging to him resulted in a denial of fundamental fairness in that it misled the jury into believing that the state had conclusively established that he was in the car.[12] [2] In support of his contention, DiGiacomo cites the Eighth Circuit's decision in *United States v. Massey*, 594 F.2d 676 (8th Cir. 1979).

In *Massey*, the court held that the trial judge's comments construing expert testimony with respect to comparison of hair samples in terms of mathematical probability of error, coupled with the prosecutor's emphasis upon the mathematical probabilities in his closing argument, constituted plain error under Rule 52(b), Fed. R. Crim. P., and required reversal of the defendant's bank robbery conviction even though no objection had been made at trial. The expert in that case had testified that three of five hairs found in a blue ski mask similar to one worn by one of the perpetrators of the robbery were microscopically similar to the defendant's hair. He was then asked by the trial judge how many people in the country might have similar hair that could not be distinguished. The expert responded that in his own experience there had been only a "couple" of cases out of over 2,000 in which he had been unable to distinguish hair from two different individuals. He added, however, that according to a recent study, apparently the same study on which Dillon had based her testimony, there was a one in 4,500 chance of another person having the same hair. In an attempt to clarify the

---

[12] [n.2] DiGiacomo does not claim that identification evidence based on microscopic analysis of hair samples is inadmissible by itself, but only that the conclusions reached from such analysis should not be expressed in terms of mathematical probability. . . . This court rejected a claim that expert testimony based on microscopic analysis of hair samples was not based upon a reasonable scientific certainty in *United States v. Cyphers*, 553 F.2d 1064, 1071–72 (7th Cir. 1977).

response, the trial judge asked the witness if this meant there was only a one in 4,500 or a one in 2,000 chance of his identification being wrong. Although the expert's response was somewhat confusing, the prosecutor later emphasized these numbers throughout his closing argument to the jury, concluding with the statement that by itself "the hair sample would be proof beyond a reasonable doubt because it is so convincing." 594 F.2d at 681.

In reversing the conviction, the Eighth Circuit held that not only had the Government failed to establish a proper foundation for these mathematical conclusions, but in his closing argument the prosecutor had confused the identification of the hair found in the ski cap with the identification of the perpetrator of the crime. Because of this confusion by the prosecutor and the potential for confusion already inherent in such evidence, the court concluded that plain error had been shown.

DiGiacomo contends that his case is even stronger because the record shows more than a mere possibility that the jury was confused. Here, he contends, it is apparent from the written question the jury submitted to the trial court shortly after beginning its deliberations that the jury was in fact confused by the expert testimony. The jury's confusion, which the trial judge's response wholly failed to remedy, he contends, clearly warrants the granting of federal habeas relief.

We agree that the interjection into the criminal trial process of sophisticated theories of mathematical probability raises a number of serious concerns. As one court has aptly stated, "(m)athematics, a veritable sorcerer in our computerized society, while assisting the trier of fact in the search for truth, must not cast a spell over him." *People v. Collins*, 438 P.2d 33 (1968). While perhaps the most serious danger in admitting evidence of statistical probability in a criminal trial is the possibility that it will be used improperly, *see People v. Collins*, 438 P.2d 33, 36, the possibility of prejudice also exists even when it is used in accordance with generally accepted principles. In a case involving the admissibility of virtually the same testimony with which we are faced here, the Supreme Court of Minnesota noted:

> Testimony expressing opinions or conclusions in terms of statistical probabilities can make the uncertain seem all but proven, and suggest, by quantification, satisfaction of the requirement that guilt be established "beyond a reasonable doubt." See Tribe, *Trial by Mathematics*, 84 Harv. L. Rev. 1329. Diligent cross-examination may in some cases minimize statistical manipulation and confine the scope of probability testimony. We are not convinced, however, that such rebuttal would dispel the psychological impact of the suggestion of mathematical precision, and we share the concern for "the substantial unfairness to a defendant which may result from ill conceived techniques with which the trier of fact is not technically equipped to cope." *People v. Collins*, 438 P.2d 41.

State v. Carlson, 267 N.W.2d 170, 176 (Minn. 1978) (footnote omitted). Because of the danger that such evidence could mislead or confuse the jury, the court concluded in *Carlson* that an expert's testimony regarding the mathematical probability of certain incriminating hairs belonging to someone other than the defendant was improperly received. . . .

Even though we share in the concern of these courts that the admission of evidence as to mathematical probability in a criminal trial may mislead and confuse the jury, we do not find on the facts before us that its admission here constituted a denial of due process. Unlike *Massey*, the prosecutor in this case did not suggest in his closing argument that the mathematical odds testified to by the expert witness made her identification of the hair specimen virtually certain. In fact, the prosecutor conceded during argument that "some people have hair like that." Furthermore, the prosecutor in this case did not confuse the issue of whether the hairs found in the car were DiGiacomo's with the issue of whether he in fact committed the crime, although DiGiacomo concedes that in this case the questions are one and the same.

Although it may be true, as the question submitted to the trial court would seem to indicate, that one or more members of the jury were nevertheless confused about the significance of the hair identification testimony, we cannot say that this confusion was caused by any error of constitutional magnitude. Generally, the admission of expert testimony is very much a matter within the broad discretion of the trial judge. The Constitution does not and, indeed, cannot guarantee that only completely reliable evidence will be placed before the jury. Although it does demand that a defendant be given a full and fair opportunity to challenge whatever evidence is admitted, DiGiacomo was afforded that opportunity here. Through his counsel, he was free to challenge Dillon's testimony if it was not true, or clarify it if it was misleading. He was also free to call his own expert if he thought Dillon's testimony was at odds with the established views of the scientific community. DiGiacomo in fact did none of these things. No attempt was made to cross-examine Dillon regarding her testimony that the hairs found in Marik's car belonged to the defendant.

Even now, DiGiacomo does not claim that Dillon was wrong in her conclusion as to the likelihood of the hair found in Marik's car belonging to someone other than him. His contention is only that she should not have been allowed to express that conclusion in terms of mathematical probability. Instead, he contends she should have stated only whether or not the hairs were similar. But to limit her testimony in this way would have robbed the state of the full probative value of its evidence. To say that the defendant's hair is merely similar to hair found in the victim's automobile is significantly different than saying that there's a one in 4,500 chance of it belonging to someone else. If the expert's testimony is the latter, we know of no constitutional principle by which its admission could be held improper. While the better practice may be for the court specifically to instruct the jury on the limitations of mathematical probability whenever such evidence is admitted, we have no authority to impose such a rule upon the Illinois courts. Thus, we are unable to say that DiGiacomo's conviction resulted from a denial of any right guaranteed by the Constitution.

Of course, jury confusion by itself, even when not the product of a constitutional violation, could justify the granting of habeas relief if it resulted in a verdict that no rational trier of fact could have reached on the basis of the evidence presented. *Jackson v. Virginia*, 443 U.S. 307, 319 (1979). But DiGiacomo does not argue that no rational trier of fact could have found him guilty and, even if he did, the record does not support such a claim. Marik's positive identification of him as the man who had assaulted her together with the other evidence introduced by the state was more than sufficient to support a rational jury's verdict of guilty.

The district court's judgment denying the petition is affirmed.

NOTE

Federal Court Review of State Court Evidentiary Rulings. State court evidentiary rulings are generally not overturned by a federal court unless the state court ruling in some way contravenes the United States Constitution. Furthermore, as the Seventh Circuit indicated in *DiGiacomo*, the United States Constitution is not offended simply because unreliable evidence is placed before the jury. *See also Herrera v. Collins*, 506 U.S. 390, 400, 113 S. Ct. 853, 860 (1993) (federal habeas courts sit to ensure that individuals are not imprisoned in violation of the Constitution — not to correct errors of fact); *Wedemann v. Solem*, 826 F.2d 766, 768 (8th Cir. 1987) (errors in the admission of evidence under state law are not grounds to grant a federal writ of habeas corpus); *Tatum v. Armontrout*, 669 F. Supp. 1496, 1501 (W.D. Mo. 1987) (state evidentiary error is not grounds to grant a federal writ of habeas corpus unless error denies due process of law); *but see Williamson v. Reynolds*, 904 F. Supp. 1529, 1554–58 & 1576 (E.D. Okla. 1995) (in addition to constitutional violations, court finds hair comparison to be unreliable and erroneously admitted in habeas petitioner's trial).

QUESTIONS

1. In *DiGiacomo* the Seventh Circuit expresses serious concern over an expert giving opinions in terms of mathematical probabilities. The concern is that it may "mislead and confuse the jury." If, as the court acknowledges in footnote 2 of its opinion, the scientific technique of microscopic analysis of hair is not being attacked, what is it about mathematical probabilities that may mislead and confuse the jury?

Put another way, why is saying that the defendant's hair is similar to the hair found in the car (which does not seem to trouble the court in *DiGiacomo*) "significantly different" from saying that there is a one in 4,500 chance of the hair found in the car belonging to someone other than the defendant?

2. In *DiGiacomo* what was the purpose for offering Sally Dillon's testimony: (1) to establish that the odds of DiGiacomo being innocent are one in 4,500; (2) to establish that there is a small pool of people in Naperville, Illinois, who, along with the defendant, could have committed the crime; or (3) to establish the likelihood of DiGiacomo's hair being in the victim's car? Is there some other purpose? Constitutionally, does the purpose for which the testimony is offered matter?

3. If the United States Constitution does not guarantee that only reliable evidence will be used, is there any scenario where a conviction based upon unreliable evidence would be found to violate the Constitution?

PROBLEM

Problem 3-4. Assume that the body of a 12-year-old girl is found. Investigation reveals that the girl had been sexually assaulted and then beaten to death. Clutched in the girl's hand were a small number of head hairs. The police arrest a teenager with whom the girl was seen earlier in the day at a shopping mall and who is a friend of the deceased girl's brother. The police take a sample of the teenager's hair and submit it for forensic analysis.

Assume that the teenager is charged with murder and that the *only* evidence of his guilt (other than being seen with the girl earlier in the day) is testimony from a criminologist who examined the hairs clutched in the girl's hand and compared them with those taken from the teenager. The criminologist testifies that "there is only a one in 4,500 chance that the hair in the girl's hand came from anyone other than the defendant teenager."

(A) If the teenager is convicted and challenges his conviction in a federal court habeas corpus proceeding, what result? *See Davis v. State*, 476 N.E.2d 127, 135 (Ind. App. 1985); *State v. Carlson*, 267 N.W.2d 170, 176 (Minn. 1978); *Roberson v. State*, 16 S.W.3d 156, 167 (Tex. App. 2000); EDWARD J. IMWINKELRIED, THE METHODS OF ATTACKING SCIENTIFIC EVIDENCE § 14-4[g], at 463–64 (4th ed. 2004).

(B) In the above problem assume that the jury sent a note to the judge several hours after beginning deliberations. The note asked, "Has it been established by sampling of hair specimens that the defendant was positively proven to have been with the victim before she died?" According to *DiGiacomo*, what effect does such a question from the jury have in this fact pattern?

[2]   The Admissibility of Probability Testimony

The two cases that follow represent different approaches to the problem of admitting statistical expert opinion. The first case, *Davis v. State*, represents the majority view in this area.

[a]   The Majority View

DAVIS v. STATE
476 N.E.2d 127 (Ind. Ct. App. 1985)

SHIELDS, JUDGE.

Defendants Reed Davis and Mary Davis (Davises) appeal their convictions for neglect of a dependent, [raising, the issue of]. . . . whether the trial court properly admitted evidence of parentage probabilities.

. . . .

On August 3, 1982, at approximately 12:30 p.m., a full-term male infant (Baby Lucky), estimated to be a few hours old, was found at the side of a gravel road near Warren, Indiana. An anonymous telephone call to the police implicated the Davises as the parents. After an investigation and blood tests to determine the probabilities of parentage, the Davises were indicted by the Huntington County grand jury for neglect of a dependent. After a jury trial, both were found guilty and sentenced to an executed term of two years.

. . . .

III. PARENTAGE

The Davises . . . allege the trial court erred in [admitting] expert testimony concerning the mathematical probability of the Davises' parentage of Baby Lucky based on the results of blood tests. Specifically, the Davises argue . . . the potentially exaggerated impact of probability evidence, [and] the misrepresentation of calculations as the probability of parentage rather than the probability of exclusion. . . .

The target of [these] objections was the expert testimony of Michael Conneally, a professor of medical genetics at Indiana University. Conneally based his testimony on the results of two separate series of standard tests: 1) HLA (Human Leucocyte Antigen) tissue-typing and 2) a series of blood tests for 20 separate genetic marker systems. The test results are not disputed; only the statistical presentation of the probability calculations based upon the results are the subject of argument.

Conneally first testified that the results of the tests "do not exclude the possibility that Mr. and Miss [sic] Davis are the father and mother are the parents [sic] of Infant Doe." Conneally then testified regarding the "probability of parentage" computed by multiplying the frequency of occurrence of each genetic marker in the caucasian population of Indiana. The frequencies were based on accepted scientific tables. Based on the 20 series test,[13] [7] Conneally concluded "the probability that — uh — Mr. and Miss [sic] Davis are the parents of Baby Lucky rather than another couple picked at random from the community is ninety-eight point three percent (98.3%)." Based on the Davises' rare HLA typing, Conneally testified:

> [T]he chance that they are the parents of this child versus a random set of parents in the community . . . comes out to be ninety nine point nine eight eight six seven percent (99.98867%) or just based on tissue typing alone odds of eight thousand eight hundred and twenty eight (8,828) to one that Mr. and Mrs. Davis are the parents of Baby Lucky rather than another couple taken from the community. . . ."

Conneally then combined the results of the HLA and 20 series test and concluded:

> "we have ninety-eight point seven percent (98.7%). . . . When we multiply these we get odds of five hundred and eighteen thousand (518,000) to one (1). . . . [T]he probability of ninety-nine point three nine eight 0 [sic] seven percent (99.398079%) that Mr. and Mrs. Davis are the father [sic] of Baby Lucky rather than another couple taken at random in the community."

Conneally converted the probability percentages into "real numbers" and concluded only one couple in half a million couples could have been the parents of Baby Lucky.

. . . .

Probability Testimony [exaggerated impact of probability evidence]

The Davises challenge the probability evidence as unduly prejudicial. They claim the jury was necessarily but "unlawfully impressed by the mystique of mathematical demonstrations." Consequently, they argue the probability evidence should have been excluded because of its "potentially exaggerated impact."

Courts and commentators have traditionally viewed mathematical probability testimony with extreme caution because of its need for foundational support and its need for sufficient explanation to the fact finder.

Foundational deficiencies are widespread. For example, in the leading case of *People v. Collins*, 438 P.2d 33 (1968), the California Supreme Court reversed a conviction for robbery based on the unduly prejudicial effect of mathematical probabilities introduced by the prosecutor. A mathematics instructor at a state college had calculated the probability that the couple charged committed the robbery based on the occurrence in the population of the couple's unusual physical characteristics.[14] [10] The prosecutor in

---

[13] [n.7] The blood tests identified different blood characteristics, or "genetic markers." Conneally tested for 20 different characteristics.

[14] [n.10] The crime was allegedly committed by a caucasian woman with a blond ponytail who left the scene accompanied by a black male with a beard and a mustache in a partly yellow automobile.

closing argument thereby arrived at a probability of one in 12 million that any randomly selected couple possessed the charged couples' combination of distinctive characteristics. However, the probabilities assigned to each individual characteristic were purely speculative. As emphasized by the court: "*Without presenting any statistical evidence whatsoever in support of the probabilities for the factors selected*, the prosecutor then proceeded to have the witnesses *assume* probability factors for the various characteristics which he deemed to be shared by the guilty couple and all other couples answering to such distinctive characteristics." *Id.* at 36–37 (emphasis in original). Moreover, even the testimony on which the calculations were based, describing the physical characteristics of the robbers, was conflicting. The court concluded that although "risks of error permeate the prosecution's circumstantial case, . . . few jurors could resist the temptation to accord disproportionate weight" to a "numerical index of probable guilt." *Id.* at 40.

Similarly inadequate statistical bases for probability calculations have been consistently rejected in criminal cases. . . . [T]he concern . . . focuses not on the calculations but upon the foundation for the calculations. When unsubstantiated estimates are used in probability calculations, speculation is presented to the jury clothed in scientific accuracy; the prejudicial impact clearly outweighs the probative value.

However, where probability testimony is based on empirical scientific data, rather than unsubstantiated estimates, the presentation and admission of probability testimony need not constitute error. . . .

There is no foundational error in the instant case. The probability calculations were not based upon speculation but upon accepted scientific tables reporting the frequency of each genetic marker in the caucasian population in Indiana. . . .

We are also unpersuaded by the Davises' claim of "exaggerated impact" due to the alleged ability of seemingly impressive numbers to mislead or confuse the jury. Nor are we persuaded that probability calculations are too difficult or complicated to explain.

. . . .

We recognize the need for caution in the admission and evaluation of probability testimony. The presentation of a percentage representing the probability of parentage may be deceptively attractive to the fact finder. Indeed, it may be well within the trial court's discretion to caution the fact finder against equating the probability of parentage with proven guilt. However, thorough preparation and cross-examination, as demonstrated in the instant case, are adequate opportunities for clarification. For example, if the probability of parentage is 99%, a full 1% of the relevant population, or 1 out of every 100 persons tested at random, would also exhibit the incriminating characteristics. In a relevant population of 1,000,000 persons, 10,000 persons would also have a probability of parentage of 99%. Again, based on the blood tests alone, the defendant is no more likely than any of the remaining 10,000 persons to be the true parent.[15] [13] In short, the defendant is entitled to explain he is merely one member of the relatively small population which exhibits the incriminating genetic markers. When explained in this manner, the fact finder need only further understand that the probability of parentage does not consider the nonquantitive evidence which the jury must evaluate together with the probability evidence.

---

[15] [n.13] Consequently, the similarity of blood types or the probability of paternity is as insufficient to support a finding of paternity as is mere presence at the scene of a crime insufficient to support a conviction for theft.

We agree with the Supreme Court of Utah in its evaluation of the jury's ability to evaluate this probability testimony: "This Court . . . [has] a higher opinion of a jury's ability to weigh the credibility of such figures when properly presented and challenged, and accord this type of testimony the weight it deserves." *State v. Clayton*, 646 P.2d 723, at n. 1 (Utah 1982). A jury which finds this presentation of this type of evidence in conjunction with the nonquantitive evidence to be highly persuasive is justified in its evaluation.

. . . .

Probability of Exclusion

Similarly, . . . [Conneally] represented the calculations as the probability of parentage rather than the probability of exclusion. The Davises cite to no testimony or authority which impeaches the characterization of the results as the "probability of parentage."[16] [15] Further, the evidence was that all couples who shared Baby Lucky's blood and tissue characteristics would have an equal probability of parentage.

. . . .

IV. SUFFICIENCY

Both Reed and Mary allege the evidence was insufficient to sustain their convictions. We find the evidence sufficient to sustain Mary's conviction but insufficient to convict Reed.

Mary

. . . .

Mary . . . alleges the evidence was insufficient to demonstrate she abandoned or placed Baby Lucky in a situation that endangered his health. Baby Lucky was born just a "few hours" before he was found between 12:30 p.m. and 1:00 p.m. on August 3rd. The uncontroverted evidence indicates Mary was home alone, accompanied only by her son Tyson, between the hours of 5:30 a.m. and 3:30 p.m. on the day Baby Lucky was born. Sometime shortly after birth, Baby Lucky was left alone by the side of a deserted country gravel road out of the view of passersby. The evidence of Mary's sole control over Baby Lucky supports a reasonable inference that she abandoned him or placed him in a situation that endangered his health. We must therefore affirm Mary's conviction.

Reed

The evidence is . . . sufficient to conclude Reed was Baby Lucky's father. However, [Indiana law] requires the endangerment or abandonment to have been either knowing or intentional. Although a parent need not possess a specific intent to commit neglect, he or she must at a minimum be "aware of facts that would alert a reasonable parent under the circumstances to take affirmative action to protect the child."

---

[16] [n.15] We recognize the probabilities were capable of alternative phrasing. For example, a 99% probability of parentage also indicates 1% of the population, or 1 out of 100 couples, could have parented Baby Lucky. This alternative view was properly and adequately explained to the jury through the expert testimony, as indicated, and affected the weight, rather than the admissibility, of the calculations.

Even assuming Reed was aware of Mary's pregnancy, the uncontradicted evidence placed Reed at his workplace when Baby Lucky was born, abandoned, and found. Reed's workplace was a twenty minute drive from his home. He clocked in at work at 6:08 a.m. and clocked out at 5:40 p.m. He took his lunch to work and was observed at his workplace throughout the day. We must therefore reverse Reed's conviction for insufficient evidence.

Judgment affirmed with respect to Mary and reversed with respect to Reed.

[b]   The Minnesota View

Recall that the *DiGiacomo* case referred to a 1978 Minnesota Supreme Court case, *State v. Carlson.* In the *Carlson* case the Minnesota Supreme Court held that it was improper for an expert in a criminal case to express an opinion in the form of mathematical probability. The Minnesota Supreme Court had occasion to reconsider that ruling in the 1987 case of *State v. Kim.*

STATE v. KIM
398 N.W.2d 544 (Minn. 1987)

WAHL, JUSTICE.

. . . Joon Kyu Kim is charged with accomplishing sexual penetration by use of force or coercion in violation of Minn. Stat. §§ 609.344(c) and 609.345(c) (1984). At a pretrial hearing, the state proffered scientific evidence in the form of blood test results linking Kim to semen found at the scene of the alleged rape and a statistical analysis of the frequency with which Kim's blood type occurred in the local male population. The trial court ruled that the blood test results and expert testimony that the test results were consistent with Kim having been the source of the semen could be admitted at trial, but ruled that the statistical population frequency evidence was to be excluded. The state appealed the portion of the order suppressing evidence. . . .

The facts in this case, as derived from police reports, indicate the complainant reported to police that on December 10, 1984, Joon Kyu Kim, her employer, had forcible, nonconsensual sexual intercourse with her. The complainant and her husband were employed as managers of a St. Paul apartment complex owned by Kim. On the evening of December 10, 1984, the complainant told police she was home alone. She and her husband had quarreled earlier in the evening and he had left the apartment. Her husband told police that after he left the apartment, he went to talk with Kim and they discussed, among other things, his marital problems. About 10 p.m., the complainant reported, Kim showed up at her apartment and began to talk about her marital relationship, telling her she wasn't having enough sex with her husband and that he would show her how. She said Kim then . . . grabbed her [and] forced her into the bedroom and onto the bed. . . . He removed his clothing and her clothing and then climbed on top of her, she stated, . . . penetrating her vagina with his penis until he ejaculated. She said that as he left, Kim gave her a twenty dollar bill and told her next time it would be thirty dollars. He also told her she wouldn't call the police because she "needed the job too much." The complainant contacted the police shortly after Kim left the apartment.

At the time the complainant reported the incident, she turned over to police the sheet from the bed where she alleged she had been raped, a pair of panties she was wearing, a sanitary pad, [and] a towel she had used to clean herself. . . . At the hospital, swab samples were taken of fluid present in the complainant's vagina. The Bureau of Criminal Apprehension Laboratory (BCA) found semen present on the bed sheet and on the vaginal swabs.

Kim was questioned by police the next day and denied having had sexual intercourse, consensual or nonconsensual, with the complainant. He admitted he had gone to her apartment that night, but stated he went there to fire her from her job as caretaker. He claimed her accusation was motivated by this firing. He pleaded not guilty to the criminal sexual conduct charges subsequently filed against him.

The trial court, on the state's motion, ordered samples of Kim's blood, saliva and hair taken for purposes of comparing his blood type with the semen found on the bed sheet and in the complainant's body.[17] [1] Comparison samples of blood were also taken from the complainant and from her husband. The samples were tested at the BCA Lab using blood type testing (ABO system) and electrophoresis testing, a procedure that identifies distinctive enzymatic genetic markers present in the blood and bodily fluids. The tests were repeated at the Minneapolis War Memorial Blood Bank and the BCA results were replicated. The BCA Lab analyst was prepared to offer testimony that the semen found in the complainant's body and on the bed sheet was consistent with Kim's blood type and PGM reading.[18] [2] Further, the analyst was prepared to testify that 96.4 percent of males in the Twin Cities metropolitan population, but not Kim, could be excluded on the basis of this combination of blood factors as possible sources of the semen found on the bed sheet.

Kim objected to all of the scientific evidence at the pretrial hearing. As to the statistical population frequency evidence, he argued that its prejudicial impact outweighed its probative value. The trial court excluded the statistical population frequency evidence under the rule of *State v. Boyd*, 331 N.W.2d 480 (Minn. 1983). This pretrial appeal followed.

. . . .

[T]he defendant in *Boyd* was prosecuted for criminal sexual conduct in the third degree, for having sexual intercourse with a 14-year-old girl, who became pregnant and gave birth as a result. We held that expert testimony that there was a 99.911 percent likelihood of paternity, based on population frequency statistics applied to interpret blood test results, must be excluded. "[T]here is a real danger," we stated, "that the jury will use the [statistical population frequency] evidence as a measure of the probability of the defendant's guilt or innocence, and that the evidence will thereby undermine the presumption of innocence, erode the values served by the reasonable doubt standard, and dehumanize our system of justice." *Id.* at 483.[19] [3]

The state argues in this appeal that the statistical evidence it seeks to introduce against Kim can be distinguished from that we disapproved in *Boyd*. The difference

---

[17] [n.1] The majority of people, including Kim, secrete their blood type in their body fluids, including semen, saliva, etc.

[18] [n.2] PGM is an enzyme. It is a genetic marker that may be detected in the blood by use of the electrophoresis testing process.

[19] [n.3] *Boyd* was preceded by *State v. Carlson*, 267 N.W.2d 170 (Minn. 1978) where we found it was error to admit expert testimony that there was a 1–800 chance that pubic hairs found on the victim were not those of the defendant and a 1–4,500 chance that head hairs found clutched in the victim's hand were not those of the defendant. *Id.* at 176. Because the testimony was found to be merely cumulative evidence, we held the error was nonprejudicial. *Id.*

between the evidence in *Boyd* — that 99.911 percent of the population, but not the defendant, could be excluded as donors — and the evidence it has proffered in this case — that 3.6 percent of the population, including the defendant, are possible donors — is the difference between inclusion and exclusion. The state contends that when statistics are stated as an exclusion figure, as in *Boyd*, the risk is greater that the jury will interpret the statistical percentage as a statement of the probability of the defendant's guilt. By contrast, when stated as an inclusion figure, the danger of such quantification is urged to be less.[20] [4]

The court of appeals correctly rejected this purported distinction, stating that *Boyd* "do[es] not focus on the nature of the statistics but rather on the impact of the statistics on the trier of fact." The danger we recognized in *Boyd* is that statistics on the frequency with which certain blood type combinations occur in a population will be understood by the jury to be a quantification of the likelihood that the defendant, who shares that unique combination of blood characteristics, is guilty. This danger exists as much in an inclusion as in an exclusion figure because, as the trial court noted, faced with an exclusion percentage, a jury will naturally convert it into an inclusion percentage. Because we cannot meaningfully distinguish the evidence offered in *Boyd* from that in the case now before us, we conclude that *Boyd* controls. We affirm the decision of the court of appeals and hold that the state has not clearly and unequivocally shown that the trial court order suppressing statistical population frequency evidence was erroneous.

The state next argues that if its proffered evidence cannot be distinguished from the evidence we disapproved in *Boyd*, we should modify or overrule *Boyd* but has presented no new or compelling argument. The state argues that the effect of *Boyd* is to exclude from the factfinding process reliable scientific evidence with great probative evidentiary value. The probative value of such evidence is, however, not of controlling significance in the analysis we adopted in *Boyd*. Under the Minnesota Rules of Evidence, relevant evidence may be excluded if its probative value is substantially outweighed by the danger of unfair prejudice. Minn. R. Evid. 403. In *Boyd*, we clearly determined that the danger of population frequency statistics used to analyze blood test results unfairly prejudicing a defendant due to its "potentially exaggerated impact on the trier of fact" outweighs any probative value. *Boyd*, 331 N.W.2d at 482 (citation omitted).

Boyd does not foreclose the use of expert interpretations of blood test results.[21] [6] As we stated in *Boyd*. . . , "subject to careful instruction, there may be occasions when the jury should be informed of the underlying statistical evidence." 331 N.W.2d at 482. We also stated:

> It does not follow from . . . the *Carlson* case . . . that the correct approach is to suppress the evidence entirely, as the trial court did. We believe that the

---

[20] [n.4] The state's inclusion-exclusion argument is somewhat confused in that the state has differently characterized the statistical evidence it seeks to introduce at different times. In first discussing the evidence before the trial court, the state argued in terms of an exclusion figure, i.e., that there would be testimony that 96.4 percent of the population could be excluded as possible sources of the semen. In briefs submitted in this appeal, the state characterizes the evidence in terms of the inclusion figure, i.e., that there would be testimony that 3.6 percent of the population could be included as possible sources.

[21] [n.6] The concern about the prejudicial effect of blood test evidence expressed in *Boyd* does not apply outside of the context of criminal prosecutions. Blood test results and expert explanations thereof are admissible in evidence, for example, in a paternity proceeding. *See, e.g., State ex rel. Kremin v. Graham*, 318 N.W.2d 853 (Minn. 1982); *Hennepin County Welfare Bd. v. Ayers*, 304 N.W.2d 879 (Minn. 1981).

trial court may appropriately limit [the expert's] testimony so as to omit reference to the degree of probability that defendant is the father of the child and to omit reference to the number of unrelated men one would have to randomly test before one would find another man who could have been the father of the child. On the other hand, [the expert] should be permitted to testify as to the basic theory underlying blood testing and should be permitted to testify that not one of the 15 tests excluded defendant as the father of the complainant's baby. We believe that his hypothetical opinion should be limited to the following: that the scientific evidence in the form of the test results is consistent with the view that defendant is the father of the baby.

331 N.W.2d at 483. As in *Boyd*, the expert called by the state in this case should not be permitted to express an opinion as to the probability that the semen is Kim's and should not be permitted to get around this by expressing the opinion in terms of the percentage of men in the general population with the same frequency of *combinations* of blood types. The expert should be permitted to testify, however, as to the basic theory underlying blood testing, to testify that not one of the individual tests excluded Kim as a source of the semen and to give the percentage of people in the general population with each of the *individual* blood types, and to express an opinion that scientific evidence is consistent with Kim having been the source of the semen.

. . . .

Affirmed.

KELLEY, JUSTICE (dissenting):

. . . .

In a criminal case, we are concerned that no conviction shall be upheld unless guilt has been established beyond a reasonable doubt. In any system of criminal justice, a convicted person will necessarily be convicted on something less than absolute proof. Indeed, because in almost every case some doubt does exist, the law uses the expression "beyond a reasonable doubt" instead of "beyond any doubt." Thus, jurors routinely use probabilities in assessing whether the state has met its evidentiary burden. . . . The question is whether it is preferable to submit to the jury properly established scientific and mathematical probabilities of the existence of a fact to bear on its decision-making process than to ignore reality by asserting people are convicted only when absolute proof is available when, in fact, absolute proof is rarely, if ever, at hand. . . .

I suggest that notwithstanding a recent consideration of the issue in *State v. Carlson* and *State v. Boyd*, the time may now have come for us to reconsider those holdings. Just a few years short of the 21st century, perhaps courts should utilize those kinds of empirical, mathematical, scientific and statistical analyses used by all sorts of professional people including those in science, industry, engineering, administration, education and planning.

. . . .

. . . In my view, not to permit this evidence evinces on our part a distrust of both the abilities of the bar to demonstrate any weaknesses in analysis as well as our distrust of the ability of the jury to consider empirical scientific and mathematical statistical evidence with the same discrimination that it has to use, for example, in considering the opinion of a psychiatrist that the accused is insane.

Accordingly, even though with reluctance, I would reverse the trial court and overrule *State v. Carlson* and *State v. Boyd*.

NOTES AND QUESTIONS

1. *Kim.* Kim's case was set for trial on June 16, 1987. After two jurors were selected, the prosecution and defense reached an agreement, and Kim pleaded guilty to the lesser of the two charges against him. The agreement called for Kim to receive a gross misdemeanor sentence even though he pleaded guilty to a felony. The more serious charge, criminal sexual conduct in the third degree, was dismissed. *See Kim v. State*, 434 N.W.2d 263, 264 (Minn. 1989). Kim received a sentence of six months and a $3,000 fine. He began serving his sentence on February 9, 1989. *See* St. Paul Pioneer Press Dispatch, Feb. 11, 1989, at 6A.

2. *The Rationale for the Minnesota Rule and Minnesota's DNA Exception.*

(A) Rationale. Note that even if one is satisfied that an adequate foundation for probability testimony is presented, there still remains the problem of such testimony unfairly prejudicing the jury. This is the problem that the Minnesota Supreme Court seems most concerned about.

> Our concern over this evidence is not with the adequacy of its foundation, but rather with its potentially exaggerated impact on the trier of fact. Testimony expressing opinions or conclusions in terms of statistical probabilities can make the uncertain seem all but proven, and suggest, by quantification, satisfaction of the requirement that guilt be established beyond a reasonable doubt. Diligent cross-examination may in some cases minimize statistical manipulation and confine the scope of probability testimony. We are not convinced, however, that such rebuttal would dispel the psychological impact of the suggestion of mathematical precision.

State v. Carlson, 267 N.W.2d 170, 176 (Minn. 1978). Further, in *State v. Boyd*, 331 N.W.2d 480 (Minn. 1983) the court added,

> [it] is not that it is necessarily wrong to inform the jury of the underlying statistical evidence but that there is a real danger that the jury will use the evidence as a measure of the probability of the defendant's guilt or innocence, and that the evidence will thereby undermine the presumption of innocence, erode the values served by the reasonable doubt standard, and dehumanize our system of justice.

Id. at 483. These concerns are the concerns that the *Davis* court dismissed by simply stating that it was "unpersuaded" that a jury would be misled or confused by "seemingly impressive numbers." *Davis v. State, supra*, 476 N.E. at 135.

How serious is the concern that the jury may be misled by statistical evidence?

(B) The DNA Exception in Minnesota. In *State v. Bloom*, 516 N.W.2d 159 (Minn. 1994), the Minnesota Supreme Court carved out an exception to the "*Kim* rule" applicable only to statistical probability evidence in DNA cases:

> [N]otwithstanding the fact that the intense debate continues concerning the most reliable, accurate way of estimating random match probability [in DNA cases] and the proper role of statistical evidence in criminal trials, we now conclude, based on all the circumstances, including the very conservative nature

of the probability figures obtained using the N[ational] R[esearch] C[ouncil]'s approach, that a DNA exception to the rule against admission of quantitative, statistical probability evidence in criminal prosecutions to prove identity is justified. Accordingly, any properly qualified prosecution or defense expert may, if evidentiary foundation is sufficient, give an opinion as to random match probability using the NRC's approach to computing that statistic.

We also conclude that, in an appropriate [DNA] case, where there is an underlying statistical foundation for such an opinion, a properly qualified expert should be allowed to say more than that the DNA test results merely are consistent with the defendant's being the source of the physical evidence left behind by the assailant. This modification of *Kim* does not stem from a belief that this court was wrong in limiting the expert to the use of the "consistent with" language in the *Carlson-Boyd-Kim* trilogy. Indeed, the state's own expert says that we were right. Rather, it stems from the belief that the reason for such a limitation, while present in those cases, is not always present in the DNA context and is not present in this case. The underlying probability figure in *Carlson* was 1 in 4,500; the figure in *Boyd* was 1 in 1,121; the corresponding figure in *Kim* was that 96.4% of men could be excluded but not defendant. In our opinion, given the underlying statistical evidence, the only fair way of verbally presenting this evidence in a qualitative rather than quantitative way was to say that the microscopic analysis evidence was "consistent with" the foreign hair being defendant's (*Carlson*), that the blood test evidence was "consistent with" defendant's being the father (*Boyd*), and that the blood test evidence was "consistent with" defendant's being the source of the semen (*Kim*).

. . . .

We have concluded that the DNA expert should be allowed to express the opinion that there is a "match" between the defendant's DNA profile and that left by the assailant at the scene or on the victim. The strength of the expert's opinion is something the jury should be told; it will depend in part on the degree of the expert's confidence in the opinion and in part on the underlying statistical foundation for the opinion. We also agree . . . that the expert should be allowed to phrase the opinion this way: that given a reliable multi-locus match, the probability that the match is random or coincidental is extremely low.

The expert should not, of course, be allowed to say that a particular profile is unique. Nor should the expert be allowed to say that defendant is the source to the exclusion of all others or to express an opinion as to the strength of the evidence. But should a properly qualified expert, assuming adequate foundation, be allowed to express an opinion that, to a reasonable scientific certainty, the defendant is (or is not) the source? We believe so. In reaching this conclusion, we merely are saying, as we intended all along, that the admissibility in a criminal trial of qualitative expert opinion testimony on DNA identification techniques be governed by the same basic rules of admissibility that historically have applied to qualitative expert opinion testimony based on other scientific identification techniques.

Id. at 167–68. *See also State v. Roman Nose*, 667 N.W.2d 386, 396 (Minn. 2003) (discussing the *Kim* case, Minnesota's rule against the admission of statistical probability evidence in criminal prosecutions to prove identity, and the exception the court created for DNA evidence in *State v. Bloom*).

3. *Davis as Majority View.* The *Davis* case represents the majority view. If an expert can demonstrate that probabilities are based upon empirical scientific data, the probability testimony is generally admitted. *Cf. Miller v. State*, 399 S.W.2d 268, 270 (Ark. 1966) (probabilities inadmissible in view of expert's use of estimates and assumptions and not empirical scientific data).

The Minnesota approach was discussed and rejected by the *Davis* court:

> The Davises brief and our independent research reveal only one case which found error in the admission of probability calculations which were unquestioningly based upon empirical scientific data. . . . In *State v. Boyd*, 331 N.W.2d 480 (Minn. 1983) . . . the Supreme Court of Minnesota excluded statistical probability evidence in paternity actions.

> The approach taken in Minnesota, however, has been rejected by an impressive myriad of courts and commentators. Indeed, blood test results have enjoyed increasing acceptance in the judicial forum because of the increased reliability of HLA testing procedures to exclude a significant portion of the population as possible fathers in paternity actions.

Davis v. State, 476 N.E.2d 127, 135 (Ind. Ct. App. 1985).

It is the exceptional case that finds error in the admission of computations that the court considers well founded. Indeed, one prominent commentator has noted that the Minnesota exclusionary rule, "and the argument that 'there is a real danger that the jury will use the evidence as a measure of defendant's guilt or innocence, and that the evidence will thereby undermine the presumption of innocence, erode the values served by the reasonable doubt standard and dehumanize our system of justice,' has been rejected by every other jurisdiction to face the question. . . ." KENNETH S. BROUN, 1 MCCORMICK ON EVIDENCE § 210, at 917 n.21 (6th ed. 2006).

In the 1989 case of *State v. Schwartz*, 447 N.W.2d 422 (Minn. 1989) (Kelley, J., concurring), the Minnesota Supreme Court reaffirmed its allegiance to *Kim*'s holding with respect to statistical evidence. *Id.* at 428–29 n.6. In a special concurrence Justice Kelley (the judge who dissented in *Kim*) called for a reexamination of *Kim* in light of the fact that 19 state appellate courts and three federal appellate courts declined to utilize *Kim*'s limitation on scientific population frequency statistics. *Id.* at 429.

4. *Must Expert Testimony on Probabilities Satisfy* Frye or Daubert? Consider the situation where a scientific technique has recently gained general acceptance, but scientists disagree on the mathematical probability of the technique producing an exclusive "match" with a specific individual. If in a *Frye* state, must experts generally agree on the accuracy of the underlying data and the methodology that produced the mathematical probability testimony? If in a *Daubert* jurisdiction, must the court be satisfied that the methodology and data used in computing the statistical probabilities is "reliable?"

This issue arose in DNA cases. For a period of time scientists generally agreed that the theory and techniques used in DNA testing were valid, but there was disagreement within the scientific community over the validity of the data base used to compute the statistical significance of a match between a known individual's DNA and DNA found at a crime scene.

Most courts examining this issue during the time the controversy raged considered that both the procedures used to obtain a match *and* the methodology used to calculate the statistical significance of a match must satisfy the jurisdiction's test for the admission of scientific evidence. *See Nelson v. State*, 628 A.2d 69, 76 (Del. 1993) (court surveys jurisdictions and states that "an overwhelming majority of courts have excluded the evidence of a match after finding the corresponding statistical calculation to be inadmissible because not scientifically valid"); *but see State v. Pierce*, 597 N.E.2d 107, 115 (Ohio 1992) (statistical calculations go to the weight, not the admissibility, of DNA evidence).

5. *Ultimate Opinion Rule.* Many jurisdictions allow expert opinion testimony on certain ultimate issues but not others. The fear appears to be that expert opinion *on certain topics* will prejudice the jury while expert opinions on other topics will not.

For example, Fed. R. Evid. 704(a) abolishes the "Ultimate Issue Rule" and allows expert (and lay) opinion testimony on the ultimate issue in a case, but with limitations. The Advisory Committee Note to Fed. R. Evid. 704(a) states:

> The abolition of the ultimate issue rule does not lower the bars so as to admit all opinions. Under Rules 701 and 702, opinions must be helpful to the trier of fact, and Rule 403 provides for exclusion of evidence which wastes time.

A more specific limitation on expert opinion was added to the Federal Rules of Evidence in 1984. Rule 704 was amended by adding a section (b) that prohibits expert opinion testimony, on the mental state of a defendant when the mental state is an element of the crime charged or of a defense to the crime charged. *See* Fed. R. Evid. 704(b) and accompanying Advisory Committee Note.

Another illustration of a specific limitation on expert opinion can be found in Alabama. In 1990 the Alabama Court of Criminal Appeals asserted, "the rule is now simply stated that even an expert may not testify as to the relative positions of the parties before a shot is fired." *Robinson v. State*, 574 So. 2d 910, 915 (Ala. Crim. App. 1990) (citation omitted).

PROBLEMS

Problem 3-5. Consider the following passage from the *Davis* case:

> [Recent] cases emphasize [the] distinction between an inadequate and an adequate foundation for probability testimony. . . . [In] *People v. DiGiacomo*, 388 N.E.2d 1281 (1979), a criminologist was allowed to testify that the chances a hair sample belonged to a person other than the defendant was "one in 4,500." In . . . [*DiGiacomo*] a sufficient foundation demonstrated the reliability of the probability calculations based upon scientific reports or tables rather than upon mere speculation."

Davis v. State, 476 N.E.2d 127, 135 (Ind. Ct. App. 1985). Recall that in *DiGiacomo* the expert criminologist based her probability opinion on "a recent study she had read." If you agree that probability calculations are appropriate when there is a proper foundation,

    (A) is reading a study sufficient foundation?

    (B) should the study itself be presented in court?

    (C) if you represented DiGiacomo and opposed the probability testimony offered in his case, how would you challenge its admissibility or, once admitted, the weight it is given by the trier of fact?

See State v. Scarlett, 426 A.2d 25, 28 (N.H. 1981); *State v. Clayton*, 646 P.2d 723, 725–27 (Utah 1982); KENNETH S. BROUN, 1 MCCORMICK ON EVIDENCE § 210, at 916 n.18 (6th ed. 2006); EDWARD J. IMWINKELRIED, THE METHODS OF ATTACKING SCIENTIFIC EVIDENCE § 6-6[d], at 215–16 (4th ed. 2004). *See generally* Annot., *Admissibility, in Criminal Case, of Statistical or Mathematical Evidence Offered for Purpose of Showing Probabilities*, 36 A.L.R.3D 1194 (1971).

Problem 3-6. Assume that a chemistry professor testifies that the reddish-brown soil found on defendant's clothing was of the same color, texture, and density as soil at the scene of a murder. Further, he testifies that the probability of two soil samples having the same color is one in 100; the same texture, one in 100; and the same density, one in 100; and the probability that two samples would match in all these characteristics was one in 1,000,000. When asked what he bases the probabilities on, the chemist states that they are his personal estimates and assumptions.

(A) Is the expert opinion admissible? *See Miller v. State*, 399 S.W.2d 268, 270 (Ark. 1966).

(B) Assume that the court rules the opinion to be admissible. Assume also that there is testimony that reddish-brown soil *always* has the density present in this case; that is, the two characteristics of color and density are not independent. Does this have any bearing on whether the chemist's opinion is admissible? *See* EDWARD J. IMWINKELRIED, THE METHODS OF ATTACKING SCIENTIFIC EVIDENCE § 6-6[d], at 219–20 (4th ed. 2004); *People v. Collins*, 438 P.2d 33, 39 (Cal. 1968).

C. INSURING RELIABILITY: CHAIN OF CUSTODY

Authentication in General

All *physical* evidence must be authenticated or identified.[22] This requirement is reflected in Fed. R. Evid. 901(a):

> The requirement of authentication or identification as a condition precedent to admissibility is satisfied by evidence sufficient to support a finding that the matter in question is what its proponent claims."

Authentication, therefore, simply requires that the proponent of physical evidence produce evidence showing that the item proffered is genuine; i.e., that it is what the proponent claims it to be.[23] For example, if a prosecuting attorney wishes to show a jury a pistol that the prosecutor claims was used in a murder, Rule 901(a) and its state counterparts require that some evidence be introduced to: (1) identify the gun produced in court as *the* gun used in the crime, and (2) show that its condition is substantially unchanged. Rule 902 of the Federal Rules of Evidence, and Rule 902's state counterparts, list situations where evidence is "self-authenticating" in the sense that no extrinsic evidence of authenticity is required. There are two principal methods of identifying physical evidence that is not self-authenticating.

---

[22] *See* United States v. Grant, 967 F.2d 81, 82–83 (2d Cir. 1992) ("no need to authenticate testimony of live witnesses"); CHRISTOPHER B. MUELLER & LAIRD C. KIRKPATRICK, 5 FEDERAL EVIDENCE § 9:2. at 327 (3d ed. 2007) (authentication requirement "applies to evidence in every form, except for live testimony").

[23] Just how much evidence must be produced to authenticate and gain admissibility is examined in Subsection [3] of this section, *infra.*

First, one may offer testimony from a person who can identify and connect the physical evidence with a crime. If an item of evidence is in some way unique, it will be "readily identifiable" and a person who saw the item at the crime scene will be able to give testimony at trial identifying the item as the one they previously saw and confirm that it is in substantially the same condition as when it was originally observed. A unique characteristic (color, size, shape, identifying marks, etc.) makes it possible for the witness to recall and identify the object.

Second, if the item that is offered is not unique and cannot, visually, be distinguished from other items of the same type (e.g., a bullet or a bag of cocaine), it will be impossible for any witness to testify credibly that he or she can identify the item displayed in court as *the* item involved in a crime. In such situations, proponents of evidence may identify the evidence and demonstrate that it is genuine by establishing a "chain of custody" of the item. An unbroken chain of possession of an item of real evidence, beginning with the point in time when the item was first connected with the crime, establishes that the nondescript item is indeed the item involved in *this* crime. Establishing a chain of custody should be viewed as an alternative method for identifying physical evidence that has no distinguishing or "readily identifiable" characteristics.

Scientific Evidence

The necessity of establishing a chain of custody to authenticate or identify can occur with any item of physical evidence, but occurs regularly with scientific evidence. This is due, partly, to the fungible nature of most items subjected to scientific analysis. Many items of real evidence that are subjected to scientific analysis have no unique characteristics that make it possible for a witness to identify them at trial. For example, items like hair, blood, semen, marijuana, cocaine, heroin, etc., are commonly encountered in a criminal case and are not distinguishable from other samples of hair, bodily fluids, or drugs that are linked to *other* criminal cases. Accordingly, if a prosecuting attorney wishes to offer into evidence cocaine seized at a crime scene, a "chain of custody" will have to be shown that links the cocaine produced at trial with the cocaine seized at the crime scene.

Fungibility is not the sole reason that the admission of scientific evidence often requires establishment of a chain of custody. Often the primary relevance of an item is not just that it was discovered at the crime scene, or seized from a crime suspect or victim. Frequently, the primary relevance of physical evidence is the *scientific analysis* of the item that occurred *after* the item was seized. For example, simply finding a drop of blood at the scene of a murder without more is not terribly probative. If, however, scientific analysis of the blood indicates that DNA in the drop of blood and the suspect's DNA match, the evidentiary value of the evidence is critical. In such a case the primary relevance of the crime scene blood is the result of the analysis.

Recall that authentication and identification require that the proponent of physical evidence demonstrate that the evidence's condition is substantially unchanged. With evidence that is analyzed, a "substantial" change in condition would be one that alters the results of the analysis. Because items of physical evidence that are scientifically analyzed are often of a delicate or perishable nature, demonstrating that physical evidence was in the proper *condition to be analyzed* is critical to making the results of analysis relevant. To illustrate, consider that in a case involving allegations of driving while intoxicated, analysis of the defendant's blood for alcohol content will be highly probative of the defendant's guilt or innocence. If blood taken from the defendant is placed in a container that is not properly sealed or is left in a place where the temperature may destroy the alcohol content in the blood, the results will be unreliable, of no evidentiary value, and, accordingly, irrelevant. Note that this will be true even though we can establish a chain of custody that *identifies* the blood as the blood taken from the defendant. In this situation, in order to show that the condition of the blood was substantially unchanged and achieve admissibility of the test results, the chain must *also* establish that the blood was properly handled and not tampered with or contaminated after being collected.

Furthermore, with the analysis of scientific evidence, identification must not only connect physical evidence with the crime but must also connect that same physical evidence with the laboratory analysis. To illustrate, consider that because one vial of blood looks just like any other vial of blood, there is always the possibility that a laboratory analyzed the wrong vial or, perhaps, that unknown to laboratory personnel the correct vial was tampered with prior to being delivered to the laboratory. Establishing that each person who handled a laboratory blood sample safeguarded the blood ensures that the vial of blood tested contains the same blood taken from the defendant and is not a vial of blood from some other case that was innocently or otherwise substituted.

In summary, authentication of scientific evidence requires a chain of custody because physical evidence that is scientifically analyzed is often not readily identifiable and is susceptible to alteration by tampering or contamination. The chain must establish two things: identity and condition. The chain must:

(1)   link the evidence with the crime,

(2)   link the evidence with analysis, and

(3)   demonstrate that the evidence was properly safeguarded and was not contaminated along the way.

The first two items listed above go to identity, and the third goes to condition.

The existence of a chain of custody is an indicator that scientific evidence is reliable; the absence of links in the chain is an indicator that the evidence may not be reliable. Potential problems in analyzing a chain of custody can occur with (1) recognizing when and why a chain is required; (2) recognizing which links are essential to the chain and what must be shown as to each link; (3) meeting the burden of proof and persuasion as to each link in the chain; and (4) recognizing when a chain ends and begins. Each of these four areas of potential problems will be examined in the materials that follow.

[1]   When is a Chain Required?

[a]   When the Item Is *Not* "Readily Identifiable"

LUCAS v. STATE
413 N.E.2d 578 (Ind. 1980)

PRENTICE, JUSTICE.

Defendant (Appellant) was indicted for Count I, Murder in the First Degree, and Count II, Kidnapping. After trial by jury he was convicted upon both counts and sentenced to life imprisonment. This direct appeal presents the [issue of] whether or not the trial court erred in admitting into evidence the defendant's clothing; no proper chain of custody having been established.

. . . .

[FACTS]

On August 8, 1977 at about 11:00 a.m., Captain Harold Trees of the Hancock County Sheriff's Department was dispatched to the scene of an automobile accident on Meridian Road just north of U.S. 40. At the scene he found a badly damaged Triumph sports car. He checked with headquarters to establish the ownership of the vehicle and learned that it belonged to Betty Dye. He saw a lady's brown handbag in the automobile. It contained credit cards and Betty Dye's driver's license. He requested the radio operator to check with the local hospital to determine if anyone had recently been admitted. Upon receiving a negative response, he proceeded towards Betty Dye's residence, which was nearby. En route, he passed a barnyard and observed a white Chevrolet automobile departing from that area.

The barns in the yard were known to Trees as the scene of an alleged battery and rape of Betty Dye, for which the defendant had been charged and released on bond.

As the Chevrolet departed Trees did not then recognize the driver. He followed the vehicle until it crossed State Road 13 in violation of a stop sign. Trees signaled the driver to stop, which he did.

The defendant got out of his automobile, whereupon Trees noticed that the vehicle's fender was damaged. He then recognized the defendant and suspected that he had been involved in an accident with Betty Dye. . . . Trees . . . said, . . . "[W]hat happened to your front fender? Did you run [Betty] off the road?" The defendant answered, "Yes."

Trees then asked the defendant what he was doing back at the barn, and he answered that he was watching to see if she [Betty Dye] got home all right. Trees said, "Betty's back at the barn, isn't she?" And, the defendant answered, "yes."

Trees told the defendant to lock his automobile and accompany him back to the barn to see how badly Betty Dye was hurt. . . .

Trees drove to one barn, and the defendant advised him to go to the other. He opened the door and saw the body of the victim lying in a pool of blood. Trees and the defendant approached the body, and the defendant kneeled, laid his head on the victim's shoulder, and cried, "Betty I'm sorry, I'm sorry I killed you."

. . . .

[CHAIN OF CUSTODY ISSUE]

Over objection of the defendant, the trial court admitted into evidence the white shirt and blue trousers which were taken from the defendant at the time he was booked at the police station. Both garments contained spots of blood. . . . The defendant contends that no proper chain of custody was shown.

The shirt and trousers were placed in a plastic bag and left in the booking room which was unattended for fifteen to twenty minutes while Officer Johnson placed the defendant in the cellblock. Officer Johnson had tied the bag in a knot and initialed it. The officer then placed the bag in an unlocked closet, where all the clothes of persons arrested were placed. The closet is located in a room not accessible to the public. The bag remained there unattended for up to two hours, while Officer Johnson took film to the scene of the crime. From there, he was sent back to the station to retrieve the bag, which he found in the same condition as it was when he had left it. He returned to the scene [with the plastic bag containing defendant's clothes] and turned the bag over to Officer Hollingsworth, who took it to Officer Kuhn [who performs blood type testing at the State Police Laboratory in Indianapolis] and requested that tests for blood type be performed, which he did.

The defendant recognizes that our rule requiring that the chain of custody be established before exhibits are admitted into evidence applies with diminishing strictness as the exhibits concerned become decreasingly susceptible to alteration, tampering or substitution. However, he apparently urges us to remove the blood spots from the clothing and treat them as a fungible commodity, in which event a more strict compliance would be required.

At trial the arresting officer, Captain Trees, identified the shirt and trousers as the garments that the defendant was wearing on the day of the crime. Additionally Officer Johnson testified that the bag containing the shirt and trousers appeared undisturbed when he retrieved it from the closet. The defendant made no claim that the exhibits had been tampered with.

Our decisions do not require a strict showing of the chain of custody, where as here, the exhibit is nonfungible, and a witness identifies it. That these garments contained blood spots made it all the easier to distinguish them from any other white shirt and blue trousers. We find no error in the admission of this evidence.

. . . .

[The] judgment of the trial court is affirmed.

QUESTIONS

1. How do we know that the blood of the victim did not get on the defendant's clothes when he "laid his head on the victim's shoulder" when he was with Captain Trees at the barn?

2. Where was the bag containing defendant's clothes after it was given to Officer Hollingsworth at the crime scene? How do we know that someone did not place drops of blood on defendant's clothes sometime after Officer Hollingsworth received the bag containing defendant's clothes, but before the clothes were brought to the courtroom during defendant's trial?

[b]   When the Condition of Real Evidence is Relevant: Problems of Alteration, Tampering, and Contamination

As the *Lucas* case indicates, there is no need to establish a chain of custody if the item of proffered evidence is readily identifiable and identity is the *only* relevant characteristic. In the next case, *Whaley v. Commonwealth*, the Virginia Supreme Court discusses the need to establish a chain of custody for physical evidence that has been subjected to scientific analysis, when an expert bases his or her opinion upon the results of the analysis.

WHALEY v. COMMONWEALTH
200 S.E.2d 556 (Va. 1973)

I'ANSON, JUSTICE.

Defendant, Nathaniel Whaley, was convicted by a jury of rape and statutory burglary and was sentenced to twenty years and five years, respectively, in the State penitentiary. We granted defendant a writ of error in each case.

Defendant contends that the trial court erred in . . . admitting into evidence a pair of undershorts. . . .

The evidence shows that shortly after midnight on September 7, 1970, defendant entered, without breaking, the home of Edward Lee Bell, in the City of Petersburg. Defendant aroused Bell, who was sleeping downstairs, and brandishing a pistol, demanded money. When Bell told him that he did not have any money, he was ordered by defendant to lead him upstairs to determine if anyone else was in the house.

Bell led the defendant to a room where Arleather Hill, a sixteen-year-old girl, was sleeping. Miss Hill was awakened, and was ordered by defendant to go outside with him to a wooded area where he forced her at gunpoint to undress and have sexual intercourse with him.

In response to a call, several Petersburg police officers went to the Bell home and found Miss Hill near the home in some bushes. She had lacerations on her body and a knot on her forehead. They also found at the scene blood spots, scuff marks on the ground and a billfold containing defendant's Selective Service card.

After taking Miss Hill to the hospital for a medical examination which revealed fresh and dried blood in and around her vaginal area and on one of her upper thighs, the police went to defendant's home where they found him in bed. While defendant was getting dressed the officers noticed some red smears on his undershorts.

When defendant was taken to police headquarters and was advised of his rights, he was told to undress. While defendant was disrobing, the police again noticed red smears on the front of his undershorts. He told the police that the smears were caused by recent sexual relations with his girl friend, not with the prosecutrix.

. . . .

Defendant says it was error for the court to admit into evidence the undershorts because no chain of possession was shown, [and] no connection was shown between the undershorts and the rape, and thus no proper foundation was laid for their introduction.

Robinson v. Commonwealth, 183 S.E.2d 179 (1971), relied upon by the defendant, is readily distinguishable from the present case. In *Robinson*, the trial court had admitted into evidence stained clothing and pubic hair, allegedly taken from a rape victim, and had also admitted the expert testimony of FBI agents concerning the results of their chemical and comparison analyses of the items. We found that the Commonwealth had failed to establish a vital link in the chain of possession of the items. We stated:

> "Without an unbroken chain of possession of the panties, blouse and pubic hair, they were not admissible as evidence *insofar as they supplied a basis for the opinion testimony of the FBI agents, who had examined them.* Thus, the opinions of the FBI agents were also not admissible." 183 S.E.2d at 181. (Emphasis added.)

We did not hold in *Robinson* that the Commonwealth is required in every case to establish an unbroken chain of possession before an item may be admitted into evidence. Rather, we held that where the results of a chemical or other technical analysis of an item are sought to be introduced into evidence, it must be shown with reasonable certainty that there has been no alteration or substitution of the item. And we said that in such a case the test of reasonable certainty is not met where there is missing a vital link in the chain of possession of the item. But our opinion in *Robinson* clearly limits its application to the particular situation there involved. This limitation is demonstrated by the underscored language in the quotation set out above and by the further statement in the opinion that if the articles of clothing there in question, having been identified by the victim, had been admitted into evidence only to establish what she was wearing when she was attacked, there would have been no error in their admission.

In this case, no chemical or other technical analysis of the defendant's undershorts was sought to be introduced into evidence. So rules different from those enunciated in *Robinson* apply here.

In McCormick's Handbook of the Law of Evidence, Demonstrative Evidence, § 212, at 527 (2d ed. 1972), it is said:

> If the offered item possesses characteristics which are fairly unique and readily identifiable, and if the substance of which the item is composed is relatively impervious to change, the trial court is viewed as having broad discretion to admit merely on the basis of testimony that the item is the one in question and is in a substantially unchanged condition. . . .

. . . .

In the present case, the undershorts taken from the defendant were placed with the custodian charged with the duty of safely keeping such property. The police officer who obtained the undershorts from the defendant identified them, when presented as evidence, as the same ones he had received from the defendant, and they were in a substantially unchanged condition. The undershorts were admitted in evidence to show that they were worn by defendant at the time the rape was committed and to permit the jury to consider whether the red smears on the undershorts had any connection with the rape, since the evidence shows that the prosecutrix did bleed when the rape was committed.

Hence we hold that the proper foundation was laid for admission of the undershorts in evidence.

. . . .

Reversed and remanded [on other grounds].

NOTES AND QUESTIONS

1. *When a "Chain" Is Needed to Authenticate or Identify Physical Evidence.*

(A) "Readily Identifiable" Items. If an item possesses characteristics that make it unique (or at least "readily identifiable"), laying a foundation for admission is relatively simple. The complete foundation consists of three steps: (1) establishing that the object has a unique feature, (2) establishing that the witness observed the unique feature, and (3) establishing that the witness can now, in court, recall that feature. *See* EDWARD J.

IMWINKELRIED, THE METHODS OF ATTACKING SCIENTIFIC EVIDENCE § 3-2[a], at 74–75 (4th ed. 2004).

Items may have characteristics that make them inherently unique, like a distinctive design or a serial number. On the other hand, many items that do not have inherently unique characteristics can be made to be unique. For example, a police officer investigating a crime scene may make a common pistol unique by scratching his or her initials and a date on the handle. *See United States v. Madril*, 445 F.2d 827, 828 (9th Cir. 1971) (not error to admit pistol that police officers identified from their markings placed on the grip). Alternatively, an item could be made unique by placing it in an evidence envelope, sealing the envelope, and writing one's initials across the seal. In the latter case, as long as the seal remains unbroken, the person who placed it in the envelope and sealed it will be able to identify the envelope and, by inference, the item inside. *See United States v. Santiago*, 534 F.2d 768, 770 (7th Cir. 1976) (Lock-seal envelopes with seals sufficient to identify fungible narcotics inside bag); 1 SCIENTIFIC EVIDENCE § 7.02, at 388–89 (4th ed. 2007).

It is only when one of the three foundational elements cited above is missing or when the item's evidentiary relevance depends on more than mere identification that a proponent of real evidence is required to establish a more stringent foundation, a "chain of custody," to establish the identity of the item proffered as the item connected with the case being litigated. *See United States v. Clounts*, 966 F.2d 1366, 1368 (10th Cir. 1992) ("If evidence is unique, readily identifiable and resistant to change, the foundation for admission need only be testimony that the evidence is what it purports to be."); *State v. Gaudet*, 638 So. 2d 1216, 1223 (La. App. 1994) ("To properly identify evidence at trial, the identification can be visual or by chain of custody of the object.").

(B) Chain of Custody: Items That Are Fungible or Whose Evidentiary Relevance Depends on More Than Identity. As the *Lucas* and *Whaley* cases indicate, two situations may require the proponent of evidence to establish a chain of custody. First, as discussed in the paragraph above, objects are not always readily identifiable. This most often occurs when the item of real evidence is fungible; however, it can occur whenever an item of real evidence cannot be identified, whether fungible or not. Because the lack of a unique feature precludes testimony identifying the item, courts require a chain of custody stretching back to the relevant historical incident to establish that the item proffered is the same one originally connected with the case being litigated (i.e., the item is "what its proponent claims").

Second, as indicated in *Whaley*, regardless of whether an object is unique, the object is sometimes offered into evidence not only because the object was connected to a crime, but also (or perhaps primarily) for the results of forensic testing performed on the object, or on a feature on the object, like a blood stain. When the results of scientific analysis on evidence collected at a crime scene are important, the fact that the evidence is readily identifiable by the person who collected the evidence at the crime scene may be sufficient to establish its identity as an item connected to the crime, but it does not identify the item as the item analyzed at a crime laboratory at some later point. Nor does it show the condition of the item when analyzed. *See United States v. Santiago*, 534 F.2d 768, 769 (7th Cir. 1976) ("Purpose of the chain of custody rule is to insure that the substance offered into evidence is in substantially the same condition as when it was seized.").

Accordingly, when an item subjected to analysis is offered into evidence at trial, the chain of custody must follow the item from the crime scene to laboratory, and then into the courtroom. This establishes that the item seized was the item analyzed *and* that the item analyzed is now the same item being produced in court. Furthermore, because contamination may, in some circumstances, alter the results of scientific testing, courts require that the chain of custody demonstrate not only that the item brought to court was the item analyzed, but also that the item was properly handled by each link in the chain to ensure that it was in the proper condition for analysis. *See* 1 SCIENTIFIC EVIDENCE § 7.03, at 391–93 (4th ed. 2007).

(C) Identity and Condition. Finally, you should be aware that often an item of real evidence is fungible *and* its condition may be susceptible to contamination or alteration. This would be true with items like drugs and body fluids. Such items are fungible and, even if they have been identified as connected with a particular case, the results of scientific analysis may become unreliable if the items are contaminated. In such situations the chain of custody must establish both the identity of the item as the item connected with the case and as the item analyzed, *and* also that the item was not tampered with, altered, or contaminated.

For example, a chain of custody for an expert opinion based upon an analysis of a blood sample taken from a defendant must establish three things: (1) the identity of the blood analyzed as the blood taken from the defendant in that particular case, (2) that the blood delivered to the laboratory for analysis was the same blood taken from the defendant, and (3) that the sample was not contaminated from the time seized until the time analyzed in the laboratory. *See Rodgers v. Commonwealth*, 90 S.E.2d 257, 260 (Va. 1955) (where substance analyzed has passed through several hands, evidence must show who had it and what was done with it between seizure and analysis); *Suttle v. State*, 565 So. 2d 1197, 1199 (Ala. Crim. App. 1990) (if specimen is taken from the human body, prosecution must show that the specimen analyzed was in fact the specimen taken from the defendant).

2. Connecting Evidence. In *Whaley*, in addition to raising alleged chain-of-possession problems, the defendant argued that "no connection was shown between the undershorts and the rape, and thus no foundation was laid for their introduction." What is the basis for this claim? Why are red-smeared undershorts relevant in *Whaley? Cf. United States v. Stabler*, 490 F.2d 345, 348–49 (8th Cir. 1974) (in murder case it was error to admit army jacket into evidence accompanied by testimony that jacket had a blood stain on the cuff without evidence linking the stain to the murder victim); CHRISTOPHER B. MUELLER & LAIRD C. KIRKPATRICK, 5 FEDERAL EVIDENCE § 9:11, at 414–17 (3d ed. 2007) (scientific analysis can connect an object with a case).

PROBLEMS

Problem 3-7. In the *Whaley* case recall that the police officer who obtained the defendant's undershorts identified them and testified that they were in "substantially unchanged condition." Assume that sometime after being seized by police the undershorts were accidentally torn. If all other facts of *Whaley* are the same, how does this affect admissibility? *See Duke v. State*, 58 So. 2d 764, 769 (Ala. 1952); 1 SCIENTIFIC EVIDENCE § 7.01, at 387–88 (4th ed. 2007).

Problem 3-8. Assume that a woman calls the police and reports that she has just been raped in her apartment. When police arrive at the woman's apartment, they find her quite upset. She tells police that she was physically attacked by a neighbor and forcibly raped. Further, she tells police that her dress was torn during the attack when she struggled with her attacker. She states that after her assailant left she showered and washed her clothes. She gives police the dress she says she was wearing at the time of the attack. It appears to have been freshly laundered and does indeed have a large tear on the front.

The police arrest the neighbor identified by the woman as her assailant, and he is charged with rape. He admits to having sexual intercourse with his accuser but claims that the victim consented. At trial the victim identifies the dress as the one she wore the night she was attacked. The prosecutor then offers the victim's torn dress into evidence. The defense objects.

(A) Is a chain of custody necessary? Has the prosecution laid a proper foundation for the admission of the dress?

(B) What objections, if any, could reasonably be made by the defense to the introduction of the dress into evidence?

(C) How should the court rule on the objections?

See United States v. Skelly, 501 F.2d 447 (7th Cir. 1974); *Davidson v. State*, 69 S.E.2d 757, 759 (Ga. 1952); 1 SCIENTIFIC EVIDENCE § 7.01, at 387–88 (4th ed. 2007).

Problem 3-9. In the problem described above, assume that rather than a torn dress the victim of the assault gives police a dress with a stain on it. The stain is analyzed, and a police serologist is prepared to testify that the stain on the dress is blood that matches the blood type of the defendant. The prosecution theory, supported by the victim's testimony, is that the sexual intercourse was not consensual and that the victim struck her attacker and bloodied his nose during the attack, resulting in his blood being found on her dress.

(A) The prosecution wants to offer the dress into evidence. If the victim washed the dress prior to giving it to the police but the stain is still prominent and visible, is a chain of custody necessary?

(B) The prosecution wants to offer testimony from the serologist that an analysis of the stain indicated that it was blood of the same type as the defendant. Is a chain of custody necessary? What must the prosecution establish, if anything, to lay a foundation for admitting the testimony of the police serologist?

See Bruce v. State, 375 N.E.2d 1042, 1073 (Ind. 1978).

[2]   The Adequacy of Proof of the Chain: "Missing Links" and "Weak Links"

[a]   Circumstantial Proof of a "Link"

A "link" in a chain of evidence is any individual who had physical custody of the item of evidence. To establish a chain of custody, must the evidence's proponent call each and every "link" to the witness stand? In the *Holton* case that follows, a police officer who took what later turned out to be cocaine to the forensic laboratory for analysis did not testify in the defendant's trial. However, the person who *gave* it to the police officer testified and the person who *received* it from the police officer testified. Can a chain of custody sufficient to gain admissibility be established in such a situation?

HOLTON v. STATE
590 So. 2d 918 (Ala. 1991)

Ingram, Justice.

Danny Ray Holton was convicted of selling cocaine and was sentenced to 21 years in prison. The Court of Criminal Appeals affirmed his conviction, 590 So. 2d 914, and Holton petitioned this Court for certiorari review. . . . We granted certiorari review to examine . . . whether the State sufficiently proved the chain of custody of the cocaine allegedly sold by Holton to Alcoholic Beverage Control Board Officer Yvonne Bedgood. . . .

I.

Holton argues that the State failed to prove a sufficient chain of custody in order [to] admit into evidence the cocaine allegedly sold to Bedgood by Holton. At trial, the State presented the following testimony: Bedgood testified that she had received the cocaine from Holton. She testified that she put the cocaine into a plastic bag, which, she said, she put into an envelope. She testified that she sealed the envelope and put her initials on it and then turned the envelope over to Governor Jackson, a narcotics investigator with the Dothan Police Department.

Jackson testified that he put tape over the seams of the envelope and that he also initialed the envelope. He further testified that he put the envelope in the police locker, to which only he had access. He testified that he later gave the envelope to Ray Owens, a Dothan police officer, to transport to the forensic laboratory. He stated that the envelope was in the same condition when he gave it to Owens as it was when he placed it in the locker.

The next person to testify was Joe Saloom, the director of the forensic laboratory in Enterprise. He testified that he had received the item from Owens and that when he received the envelope, it was sealed. Owens did not testify.

Holton argues that Owens's testimony is an essential link in the State's chain of custody and that, without such testimony, the cocaine was inadmissible. The State contends that the lack of testimony from Owens merely "weakens" the chain and creates a question of credibility, rather than one of admissibility.

This opinion sets forth an analysis to be followed in deciding whether a proper chain of custody has been shown. We have held that the State must establish a chain of custody without breaks in order to lay a sufficient predicate for admission of evidence. *Ex parte Williams*, 548 So. 2d 518, 520 (Ala. 1989). Proof of this unbroken chain of custody is required in order to establish sufficient identification of the item and continuity of possession, so as to assure the authenticity of the item. *Id.* In order to establish a proper chain, the State must show to a "reasonable probability that the object is in the same condition as, and not substantially different from, its condition at the commencement of the chain." *McCray v. State*, 548 So. 2d 573, 576 (Ala. Crim. App. 1988). Because the proponent of the item of demonstrative evidence has the burden of showing this reasonable probability, we require that the proof be shown on the record with regard to the various elements discussed below.

The chain of custody is composed of "links." A "link" is anyone who handled the item. The State must identify each link from the time the item was seized. In order to show a proper chain of custody, the record must show each link and also the following with regard to each link's possession of the item: "(1) [the] receipt of the item; (2) [the] ultimate disposition of the item, i.e., transfer, destruction, or retention; and (3) [the] safeguarding and handling of the item between receipt and disposition." Imwinkelried, *The Identification of Original, Real Evidence*, 61 Mil. L. Rev. 145, 159 (1973).

If the State, or any other proponent of demonstrative evidence, fails to identify a link or fails to show for the record any one of the three criteria as to each link, the result is a "missing" link, and the item is inadmissible. If, however, the State has shown each link and has shown all three criteria as to each link, but has done so with circumstantial evidence, as opposed to the direct testimony of the "link," as to one or more criteria or as to one or more links, the result is a "weak" link. When the link is "weak," a question of credibility and weight is presented, not one of admissibility.

In this case, Owens failed to testify as to his action regarding the envelope. However, the record reflects his receipt of the item; he received the item from Jackson, who testified that he had given the envelope to Owens. Also, Owens's ultimate disposition of the item appears in the record through the testimony of Saloom, who testified that he received the item from Owens. Therefore, the only criterion left to analyze is the handling and safeguarding by Owens. Again, Owens did not testify; thus, there is no direct evidence of his handling of the item. However, both Jackson and Saloom testified that the envelope was sealed when given to and when taken from Owens. A sealed envelope was adequate circumstantial evidence to establish the handling and safeguarding of the item by Owens to treat the item as authenticated. Although the lack of Owens's direct testimony "weakens" the chain, the testimony of Jackson and Saloom prevented a break in the chain. The cocaine was properly admitted by the trial court, and the jury could decide how much weight to give the evidence, given the lack of direct testimony from Owens.

This opinion has presented an approach for analyzing chain-of-custody problems. In this case, the chain of custody was sufficient to authenticate the item, allowing the envelope containing the cocaine to be entered into evidence. Circumstantial evidence is generally sufficient to authenticate the item sought to be entered into evidence, except when there appears to be evidence that the item of evidence was tampered with or that a substitution was made while the item was in the custody of the link who has failed to appear and testify. In this case, there is no suggestion that Owens tampered with or made a substitution as to the item he was to deliver. Thus, we hold that as to the envelope containing the cocaine the State established a chain of custody sufficient to authenticate that item. The Court of Criminal Appeals properly decided the issue regarding the chain of custody.

. . . .

Affirmed.

_____

The next two cases examine the significance of there being no direct testimony from one of the evidence's custodians. One case finds the chain-of-custody problem fatal, and the other case views the lack of testimony from a link as going to the weight of the evidence, not its admissibility. Are the cases consistent?

SUTTLE v. STATE
565 So. 2d 1197 (Ala. Crim. App. 1990)

BOWEN, JUDGE.

Julian R. ("Randy") Suttle was convicted of vehicular homicide arising out of the death of Howard Deavers and sentenced to five years' imprisonment. This conviction must be reversed because the prosecution failed to establish the proper chain of custody for the introduction of a blood sample allegedly taken from Suttle.

Shortly after 11:00 p.m. on April 8, 1987, Suttle's truck collided with a Toyota Corolla automobile in which Deavers was a passenger. Trooper Elizabeth Cobb later transported Suttle to the Selma Medical Center, arriving there around 12:25 a.m. After a cut on Suttle's face was sutured, Nurse Barbara Middleton took blood samples from him. Nurse Middleton testified that these samples were taken "after 1:00 a.m." on April 9, a Thursday, and that she used two vacuum-type vials to extract the samples. Nurse Middleton labelled the vials with Suttle's name and gave them to Trooper Cobb. The vials were not taped at this time.

Trooper Cobb was deceased at the time of trial and thus did not testify. Toxicologist Laura Shevlin testified that on Monday, April 13, 1987, she retrieved from the Department of Forensic Sciences' post office box in Auburn, Alabama, a gray cardboard mailing cylinder containing two vials of blood labelled "Randy Suttle, 4-9-87." The mailing cylinder "was sealed with white tape that was labelled 'E.S.C.' " Although not specifically so stated by Ms. Shevlin, it appears from the record that the two vials were also taped at the time she received them. Ms. Shevlin was unable to testify as to where the vials had been before she received them, when they were mailed or who mailed them. Nevertheless, over strenuous objection by Suttle, the vials were admitted and Ms. Shevlin was permitted to testify that she tested the blood sample in one of the vials and found it to have a blood alcohol level of.29%. She was further permitted to testify as to what effect a blood alcohol level of.29% has on a person.

. . . .

With regard to specimens taken from the human body, it is . . . incumbent upon the prosecution to show that the specimen analyzed was in fact the specimen taken from the defendant. In such cases, "[t]he 'chain of custody' involves 'the necessity of proving where and by whom the specimen was kept and through whose hands it passed'. . . ." "[W]here the substance analyzed has passed through several hands *the evidence must not leave it to conjecture as to who had it and what was done with it between the taking and the analysis.*" *Rodgers v. Commonwealth*, 90 S.E.2d 257, 260 (1955) (emphasis added).

. . . .

Here . . . there is a "missing link" in the chain of custody. We recognize the difficulty faced by the prosecution in establishing the chain of custody in view of the intervening death of Trooper Cobb. However, absolutely no effort was made by the prosecution to account for the whereabouts of the samples during the four days between the time they were taken by Nurse Middleton and the time they were received by Ms. Shevlin. Compare *People v. Porter*, 362 N.Y.S.2d 249 (1974) (where nurse gave blood sample to officer and officer delivered sample to chemist, from whom he obtained a receipt, and chemist's son testified as to results of test from the deceased chemist's log book). . . . Where a "vital link in the chain of possession is not accounted for," there can be no reasonable probability that "the evidence analyzed was the evidence originally received." *Robinson v. Commonwealth*, 183 S.E.2d 179, 180 (1971). Moreover, in view of Shevlin's testimony on the effect of the blood alcohol level on the body, the error in the admission of the samples cannot be deemed harmless.

. . . .

For the reasons stated above, the judgment of the circuit court is reversed and this cause is remanded for further proceedings not inconsistent with this opinion. . . .

Reversed and remanded.

QUESTIONS

1. Which of the four items of proof that must be shown for each chain of custody link is missing in the *Suttle* case?

2. If Trooper Cobb could have anticipated her unavailability at the time of trial, is there anything you would have advised her to do at the time she handled the blood to make her a "weak" rather than a "missing" link?

3. In *Suttle* the court commented that "absolutely no effort was made by the prosecution to account for the whereabouts of the samples during the four days between the time they were taken by Nurse Middleton and the time they were received by Ms. Shevlin." What, if anything, could or should the prosecution have done at trial?

4. In 1995 Alabama enacted the following statute:

> Physical evidence connected with or collected in the investigation of a crime shall not be excluded from consideration by a jury or court due to a failure to prove the chain of custody of the evidence. Whenever a witness in a criminal trial identifies a physical piece of evidence connected with or collected in the investigation of a crime, the evidence shall be submitted to the jury or court for whatever weight the jury or court may deem proper. The trial court in its charge to the jury shall explain any break in the chain of custody concerning the physical evidence.

ALA. CODE § 12-21-13 (1975). Since the above statute requires a witness to identify physical evidence, does it alter traditional concepts of authentication and identification as to readily identifiable physical evidence? If the above statute had been in effect at the time the *Suttle* case was decided, would it have changed the outcome? *See Lee v. State*, 748 So.2d 904, 912–13 (Ala. Crim. App. 1999).

UNITED STATES v. CARDENAS
864 F.2d 1528 (10th Cir. 1989)

BRORBY, CIRCUIT JUDGE.

Defendants Martin Cardenas and Julian Rivera-Chacon were tried jointly in the United States District Court for the District of New Mexico. A jury rendered guilty verdicts on all counts in the indictments . . . [including] conspiracy to distribute cocaine . . . [and] possession with intent to distribute cocaine. . . .

Defendant Cardenas seeks reversal of the cocaine convictions, alleging an inadequate foundation for the admission of the cocaine based on the incomplete chain of custody and material alteration of the cocaine. . . .

A. FACTS

On July 9, 1987, Martin Cardenas and Julian Rivera-Chacon were arrested in the underground parking lot in the area of the (then) Regent Hotel located in Albuquerque, New Mexico. . . .

. . . .

Officers Montoya, Gunter and Garcia of the Bernalillo Police Department, Officer Mares of the Socorro County Sheriff's Office, and Special Agent Ortiz of the United States Bureau of Alcohol, Firearms and Tobacco, were all present. . . . Officer Garcia, conduct[ed] a full inventory search of Cardenas' truck. . . . Under the front seat, Garcia found a brown paper bag containing a plastic sack with a white substance inside. Garcia handed the brown paper bag containing the plastic sack, . . . to Officer Gunter. From this moment, Officer Gunter had sole physical custody of this evidence.

Officer Mares testified that Gunter showed him a plastic sack containing a white substance. Mares was too busy to inspect the substance. He testified that he did not see a brown paper bag, nor did he see Garcia give the substance to Gunter. In addition, at trial Officer Mares could not absolutely identify the plastic sack containing the white substance as the plastic sack that Gunter displayed at the scene; however, he did state that the plastic sack exhibited at trial in every respect resembled the sack displayed to him at the arrest. No field test was performed on the substance. Officer Garcia accompanied Gunter to the station with the seized evidence. At the station, Mares assisted Gunter in tagging the evidence. Gunter then, unobserved, carried the sealed evidence bags to the evidence room on the third floor of the station. The evidence technician testified that no brown paper bag was submitted to her; that she is obligated to accept any evidence given her; and that ultimately the police officers decide what is evidence and what is not.

Since Officer Gunter committed suicide one month prior to the trial, he was not available to testify.

[Admission of Plastic Sack Containing Cocaine]

Defendant alleges that the plastic sack containing cocaine was improperly admitted into evidence on two bases: (1) the government failed to provide a sufficient chain of custody; and (2) there was a material alteration of the evidence. We disagree.

The standard of review of an appellate court when deciding the proper admission or exclusion of evidence at trial is abuse of discretion, defined in this circuit as an arbitrary, capricious, whimsical, or manifestly unreasonable judgment.

Controlling the admission or exclusion of real evidence at trial, Fed. R. Evid. Rule 901(a) provides that "[t]he requirement of authentication or identification as a condition precedent to admissibility is satisfied by evidence sufficient to support a finding that the matter in question is what its proponent claims." The rationale is that in the absence of showing that the evidence is what its proponent alleges, the evidence is simply irrelevant. The condition precedent to the admission of real evidence is met by providing the proper foundation. If the proffered evidence is unique, readily identifiable and relatively resistant to change, the foundation need only consist of testimony that the evidence is what its proponent claims. E. Cleary, McCormick on Evidence, § 212 at 667 (3d ed. 1984). However, when the evidence, as here, is not readily identifiable and is susceptible to alteration by tampering or contamination, the trial court requires a more stringent foundation "entailing a 'chain of custody' of the item with *sufficient completeness* to render it *improbable* that the original item has either been exchanged with another or been contaminated or tampered with." (Emphasis added.) *Id.* at 668.

This circuit's controlling test for the admission and exclusion of real evidence under Fed. R. Evid. Rule 901(a) was clearly enunciated in *Reed v. United States*, 377 F.2d 891, 893 (10th Cir. 1967). Before admitting or excluding real evidence, the trial court must consider the nature of the evidence, and the surrounding circumstances, including presentation, custody and probability of tampering or alteration. If, after considering these factors, the trial court determines that the evidence is substantially in the same condition as when the crime was committed, the court may admit it. *Reed*, 377 F.2d at 893.

The cocaine, not uniquely identifiable, requires a sufficient chain of custody to support its admission. However, the chain of custody need not be perfect for the evidence to be admissible. The well-established rule in this circuit is that deficiencies in the chain of custody go to the weight of the evidence, not its admissibility; once admitted, the jury evaluates the defects and, based on its evaluation, may accept or disregard the evidence.

On appeal, defendant alleges that there was an insufficient chain of custody to support the trial court's admission of the cocaine since Officer Gunter, who had custody of it from the time of its initial seizure until he delivered it to the evidence room, was unavailable to testify. Based on this, defendant contends that the cocaine should not have been admitted since there was a "substantial break in the chain."

From the moment Officer Garcia seized the cocaine from Cardenas' truck, its whereabouts were accounted for. Testimony at trial by Officers Garcia and Mares shows that there was no substantial break in the chain. Upon seizing the cocaine, Officer Garcia handed it to Officer Gunter who, in turn, displayed it to Officer Mares. Admittedly Officer Mares could not absolutely identify the plastic sack containing white powder offered at trial as that seized from the truck. However, given that the plastic sack was not uniquely identifiable and considering his testimony that the evidence at trial in every respect resembled the evidence seized from the truck, the lack of absolute identification does not amount to an insufficient chain of custody. *See United States v. Brewer*, 630 F.2d 795, 802 (10th Cir. 1980) (lack of positive identification went to weight of evidence). After the arrests, Officers Garcia and Gunter drove directly to the police station where Gunter, in the presence of Mares, tagged and sealed the evidence. Officer Gunter then walked up three flights to the evidence room, delivered the evidence, tagged and sealed, to the evidence technician who secured it for testing. This was the only moment Officer Gunter was alone with the evidence; however, considering the brevity of time, the fact that the evidence was already tagged and sealed, and defendant's lack of any evidence of tampering or alteration at this point in the chain of custody, we do not consider it a substantial break resulting in alteration. The trial court need not rule out every possibility that the evidence underwent alteration; it need only find that the reasonable probability is that the evidence has not been altered in any material aspect.

The fact that Officer Gunter was not available to testify is not determinative of the admissibility of the cocaine since the whereabouts of the cocaine was accounted for from its original seizure from Cardenas' truck until it was offered as evidence at trial. There is no rule that the prosecution must produce all persons who had custody of the evidence to testify at trial. Defendant's allegation as to the insufficiency of the chain of custody is unpersuasive.

Defendant also alleges that the evidence was "materially altered" and, as such, should not have been admitted. We disagree. The fact that the brown bag was not secured as evidence does not equate with material alteration.

Officer Garcia testified that when he found the plastic sack containing cocaine it was in a brown paper bag. (At trial, a brown paper bag was exhibited to demonstrate how it could conceal the identity of the cocaine. When Officer Gunter showed the cocaine to Officer Mares, the paper bag was gone. The reasonable inference is that the paper bag was inadvertently discarded, not that Officer Gunter tampered with the plastic sack of cocaine in the presence of four other law enforcement officers from three different departments. No evidence elicited at trial pointed to the alteration of the cocaine itself; and so long as the relevant features remain unaltered, the evidence is admissible. Here, defendants were charged with and convicted of possession of cocaine, not possession of the brown paper bag. The absence of the brown paper bag is irrelevant to the evidentiary value of the cocaine. Its absence does not give us reason to doubt that the powder was cocaine despite the lack of a field test. After all, the purpose of the undercover activity was the purchase of cocaine.

"Absent some showing by the defendant that the [evidence has] been tampered with, it will not be presumed that the investigators who had custody of [it] would do so." *United States v. Wood*, 695 F.2d 459, 462 (10th Cir. 1982).

The cocaine was properly admitted. Nothing in the record suggests that its admission was arbitrary, capricious, or unreasonable to warrant a finding of abuse of discretion.

. . . .

We affirm the conviction. . . .

NOTES

1. *"Weak Links" and Circumstantial Evidence.* The view that not all the links need *personally* testify so long as the evidence is circumstantially accounted for appears to be the majority view. Circumstantial evidence establishing a link goes to weight, not admissibility. Note, however, that some courts that follow this principle are not as precise in defining and distinguishing between "weak" and "missing" links as was the Alabama Supreme Court in *Holton*. For example, the Fourth Circuit in *United States v. Howard-Arias*, 679 F.2d 363 (4th Cir. 1982), termed a "missing link" what the Alabama Supreme Court would have called a "weak link." The results, however, appear consistent:

> [T]he ultimate question is whether the authentication testimony was sufficiently complete so as to convince the court that it is improbable that the original item had been exchanged with another or otherwise tampered with. Contrary to the appellant's assertion, precision in developing the "chain of custody" is not an iron-clad requirement, and the fact of a "missing link" does not prevent the

admission of real evidence, *so long as there is sufficient proof that the evidence is what it purports to be and has not been altered in any material aspect.*

Id. at 366 (emphasis added).

2. *Persons with Access to, But Not Custody of, Evidence; The Potential for Tampering And the "Presumption of Regularity."* Evidence is sometimes left in a location where it could be tampered with. For example, evidence may be left unattended in a room that many people have access to, or may be placed in an envelope or bag that is not sealed. Courts generally hold that the proponent of evidence for which a chain of custody must be established need not account for every person who had *access* to an item of evidence but who did not have actual custody. Instead, there exists a "presumption of regularity" — that is, a presumption that government officials properly discharge their official duties. Because of this presumption, the burden is on the party challenging the authenticity of the evidence to produce evidence of tampering.

> The defendant argues that the State failed to establish a proper chain of custody of the blood samples. Nurse Roberts drew the blood and handed two sealed samples to Officer Meadows. On Saturday morning, Meadows placed the tubes containing the blood samples, which had been sealed inside a styrofoam box (a "DUI evidence kit"), in a refrigerator at City Hall where the kit remained over the weekend. The refrigerator was in the hallway, was not locked or secured, and was accessible to any number of city employees. On Monday morning, Officer Meadows retrieved the still-sealed kit and delivered it to the forensics expert who tested the blood samples. The expert testified that there was nothing to indicate that the kit had been tampered with.

> Although the evidence indicates some carelessness in the storage of the blood samples, we find that the evidence of the test results was properly admitted. "[I]t is to be presumed that the integrity of evidence routinely handled by governmental officials was suitably preserved '[unless the accused makes] a minimal showing of ill will, bad faith, evil motivation, or some evidence of tampering.' "

United States v. Roberts, 844 F.2d 537, 549–50 (8th Cir. 1988). *See also United States v. Santiago*, 534 F.2d 768, 769 (7th Cir. 1976) (prosecution need not exclude all possibility of tampering); *United States v. Wood*, 695 F.2d 459, 462 (10th Cir. 1982) ("Absent showing by defendant that the [evidence has] been tampered with, it will not be presumed that the investigators who had custody of [it] would do so."); *Gallego v. United States*, 276 F.2d 914, 917 (9th Cir. 1960) ("In the absence of any evidence to the contrary, the trial judge was entitled to assume that this official would not tamper with the sack and can or their contents. When no evidence indicating otherwise is produced, the presumption of regularity supports the official acts of public officers, and courts presume that they have properly discharged their official duties.").

3. *"Sloppy" Crime Scene Procedures.* Carelessness in gathering evidence at the crime scene and/or in handling evidence by police officers typically results in a claim that the evidence has lost its evidentiary value. Courts treat sloppy handling of evidence the same way they treat allegations that there may have been tampering: the allegations go to weight — not admissibility.

To illustrate, consider the case of *United States v. Lane*, 591 F.2d 961 (D.C. Cir. 1979). In *Lane* the defendant was charged with making eight separate sales of heroin to an undercover police officer. The defendant claimed that because of sloppy handling of the heroin, primarily by the undercover officer, Velma N. Holmes, there was no way to ensure that the substance analyzed by a DEA chemist and identified as heroin was really the material given to Officer Holmes by the defendant. *Id.* at 963.

The testimony at trial by the police was that each time heroin was purchased by Officer Holmes she placed it in a manila envelope, sealed the envelope, and placed the defendant's name on the envelope. She then gave the envelope to a supervisor, who placed the envelope in a larger lock-seal envelope, sealed the larger lock-seal envelope, labeled it, and then placed it in the department's narcotics mailbox. From there it was transported to the DEA laboratory for chemical analysis.

The handling of the evidence that defendant claimed made it inadmissible, was as follows:

> Officer Holmes testified that she initialed the packets of heroin as she purchased them, yet on one of the eight she could not find her initials. Officer Holmes also testified that she sealed the manila envelopes containing the packets, yet a control officer testified that he could not recall whether one of the envelopes was sealed when he received it from her. Moreover, prior to meetings with her control officers, Officer Holmes kept the envelopes enclosing purchases from appellant together with envelopes of purchases from others. Transfers of the envelopes to control officers did not always occur on the dates of sale; on these occasions, she took the envelopes home for the night. One of the control officers testified also that he, too, might have kept transferred envelopes at home overnight when unable to deposit them in the Department's narcotics mailbox on days they were received from field officers. Appellant further notes that before being secured in lock-seal envelopes the drugs were handled in unlockable envelopes.
>
> . . . Officer Holmes undertook to account for the discrepancy between her statement that upon receipt she initialed all the packets of heroin and her inability to find any markings on one — a tinfoil packet — at trial. When confronted with the variance, she responded, "I guess I should have (pressed) down more on the tinfoil here than I did."

Id. at 964.

The court upheld admitting the evidence, stating that "[t]o be sure, the safeguards erected were not foolproof but, as a matter of reasonable probability, the substances purchased from appellant were protected against the risk of misidentification or adulteration." *Id.* at 966. The court added that a governing principle was that the government "need not rule out every conceivable chance that somehow the identity or character of the evidence underwent change." *Id.* at 962.

4. *More "Missing Links."* Another missing link case (i.e., no proof, not even circumstantial evidence, of the identity of a link and/or receipt, disposition or safeguarding of an item of evidence) is *Graham v. State*, 255 N.E.2d 652 (Ind. 1970). *Graham*, like *Suttle*, makes it clear that the burden on the proponent can be satisfied if circumstantial evidence is offered but that absence of *any* proof (direct or circumstantial) breaks the chain and is fatal:

> [T]he exhibit in question was deposited in the usual manner in the police custody room on the afternoon of November 22, 1966, within two hours after the "buy." The police property room records reflected receipt of same and no challenge to the evidence is made by appellant up to that point. *However on the next day,*

November 23, 1966, the record reveals that a Sergeant Elmore from the crime laboratory removed the exhibit from the police property room and that it was not returned until 6 days later when it was brought back by a Lieutenant Sullivan. The exhibit's whereabouts or disposition during this period was neither ascertainable from police records nor explained by any state's witnesses. Neither Sergeant Elmore nor Lieutenant Sullivan testified at the trial. What happened to the Juicy Fruit gum wrapper and its contents between November 23 and November 29 was not testimonially established. It would appear to be unreasonable and unrealistic to argue that the unaccounted-for absence of a police exhibit *of this nature* for six days and six nights is not a complete break in the chain of evidence.

Not until February 21, 1967, did the chemical examination take place which formed the basis for the expert testimony of the state's laboratory witness and the basis for the conviction. The fact that the chewing gum wrapper was identifiable as that acquired from appellant at the drugstore cannot cure the defective evidentiary chain of custody which preceded the laboratory experiments. Appellant was not convicted for possession of a chewing gum wrapper.

We think that the facts in this case insofar as they relate to the custody of the alleged heroin compel us to conclude that the evidence of the laboratory findings of February 21, 1967, should have been excluded. The added burden imposed upon the prosecution by this holding is not great. Had the state produced either Sergeant [Elmore] or Lt. Sullivan to account for the exhibit's whereabouts during the six-day period, or to explain any discrepancies in the police department's custody records, there likely would have been no grounds to challenge the continuity of custody. Ordinarily where the chain of evidence is challenged, production of the record books of the police custody room will suffice. The fact that an out-of-the-ordinary procedure was followed or that oral testimony was required to explain errors in the written police records would go to the weight rather than the admissibility of the evidence.

Id. at 655–56 (emphasis in original). *Cf. Smith v. United States*, 157 F.2d 705, 705–06 (D.C. Cir. 1946) (robbery conviction reversed where neither the victim nor the police officer who took allegedly stolen articles from the defendant was called as a witness to connect the defendant to the articles).

QUESTION

Are *Cardenas* and *Suttle* consistent? If so, what makes the chain "stronger" in *Cardenas* than it is in *Suttle*?

PROBLEMS

Problem 3-10. Assume that a rape victim is taken to a nearby hospital for a physical examination. At the hospital the victim and a nurse go into a private room where only the two of them are present. During the examination the nurse takes the victim's panties and places them in a clear plastic Ziplock bag. The panties are white and have no distinguishing features except for a small stain. After the examination the nurse emerges from the examination room and gives a waiting police officer a clear plastic bag with a white pair of panties inside. The police officer takes the bag to a police lab for

DNA analysis. The analysis reveals that the stain on the panties is semen containing defendant's DNA profile.

At trial a pair of panties in a clear plastic Ziplock bag is produced and shown to the victim. The victim says the clear plastic Ziplock bag is "like" the one used at the hospital. The victim says the panties are her panties — the pair she was wearing when attacked. The nurse who took the panties from the victim and placed them in a plastic bag does not testify, but the officer who received them from the nurse at the hospital does, as well as everyone else who handled them.

At trial the prosecution wants to offer the expert opinion of the forensic scientist who analyzed the panties and who will say she found defendant's DNA profile in the semen stain. The defense objects to testimony about the *analysis* of the stain, arguing that there is no chain of custody as to the panties. Is the testimony of the forensic scientist admissible? *See Robinson v. State*, 183 S.E.2d 179, 180–81 (Va. 1971); *Smith v. State*, 677 So. 2d 1240, 1245–46 (Ala. Crim. App. 1995).

Problem 3-11. Assume that police are called to investigate a burglary at a private residence early Friday evening. When police arrive, the homeowner tells them that he came home and surprised a burglar who was standing in his kitchen with the homeowner's wallet in his hand. The homeowner also states that when the burglar saw him he dropped the wallet and ran. The police find the wallet that the burglar was holding on the kitchen floor and take it to the police crime laboratory to be checked for fingerprints.

The next morning (Saturday) the police arrest a suspect in the burglary named Mo Martin. Martin is placed in jail where he spends the entire weekend before being released the following Monday.

Mo Martin is charged with the burglary. At Martin's trial a police fingerprint expert testifies that the wallet collected as evidence from the homeowner's kitchen was delivered to him the night of the burglary, Friday. He also testifies that he did not check the wallet for fingerprints until the following Monday, and that his analysis revealed that fingerprints on the wallet match those of Mo Martin, the defendant. On cross-examination the fingerprint expert admits that after receiving the wallet on Friday night, he left it sitting on top of his desk in the crime lab, unsecured, and out in the open all weekend. He also admits that all of the employees of the crime lab and two janitors have keys to the crime lab and could have been in the lab over the weekend.

If the defendant's attorney objects to the admission of any evidence about fingerprints on the wallet matching those of Mo Martin, how should the court rule? *See Wright v. State*, 420 S.W.2d 411, 413 (Tex. Crim. App. 1967).

Problem 3-12. Two men, Saturn and Smit, spent the evening of December 13, 1995, drinking and bar-hopping. Shortly after 11:00 p.m. the car that the two men were riding in crossed the center line of the highway and struck a car coming in the opposite direction head-on. The driver of the other car was killed, but Saturn and Smit survived with minor injuries. Saturn and Smit were standing beside the wreckage of the two cars when police arrived, and each claimed that the other was driving when the accident occurred. The police concluded that Saturn was driving and charged him with vehicular homicide.

To establish that Saturn, and not Smit, was driving, the prosecution wants to offer into evidence two strands of hair that were found imbedded in the windshield on the passenger side of the car that Saturn and Smit were driving. A forensic scientist is prepared to testify that one week after the accident she went to the county-owned lot where the vehicle was being held and recovered two hairs from a crack in the windshield on the passenger side. Laboratory tests indicated that the hair is human hair consistent with Smit's head hair and inconsistent with Saturn's. The defendant, Saturn, objects to the hair and testimony of its analysis being admitted. In support of his objection, Saturn offers uncontested evidence that proves that the car he and Smit were in was towed to a county-owned lot that was not secure, and that the car was vandalized prior to the recovery of head hair from the windshield by the state's forensic expert.

How should the court rule? *See State v. Satern*, 516 N.W.2d 839, 841–42 (Iowa 1994).

[b]   Links for Which No Proof is Required

Recall that the Alabama Court of Criminal Appeals in *Suttle* stated that when a *"vital link*" in the chain of possession is not accounted for, there can be no reasonable probability that the evidence analyzed was the evidence originally received." *Suttle v. State, supra*, 565 So. 2d at 1200 (emphasis added). By using the phrase "vital link," did the court mean to say that some links are not *"vital"*? If some links are not vital, can such links be missing and the item still be admissible?

SCHACHT v. STATE
50 N.W.2d 78 (Neb. 1951)

CARTER, JUSTICE.

The defendant was convicted in the district court for Pierce County for driving an automobile while under the influence of alcoholic liquor. The trial court sentenced the defendant to serve four days in the county jail, pay a fine of $40 and costs, and revoked the driver's license of defendant for a period of six months from the date of his discharge from the county jail. The defendant instituted error proceedings in this court, seeking a reversal of the judgment of the district court.

The evidence shows that defendant was driving his automobile on U.S. Highway No. 20 in Pierce County, Nebraska, on June 18, 1950, about 6:00 p.m., at which time he was arrested by officer Otis J. Knotwell of the Nebraska State Safety Patrol for driving while in an intoxicated condition. Officer Knotwell testified that defendant was driving his car from one side of the highway to the other, that there was a strong odor of intoxicating liquor on his breath, that his eyes were bloodshot, that he was unsteady on his feet, and that in his opinion he was intoxicated. . . .

The defendant attempted to excuse his bad driving by his testimony that he suffered a coughing and sneezing attack which caused him to expel his false teeth, and that any deficiency in his driving was due to his efforts to retrieve them. This raised an issue which the jury considered and determined. The evidence was ample to sustain the verdict of the jury.

The questions here raised go to the correctness of the court's rulings on the admission of certain exhibits. . . .

The record shows that Dr. Calvert, with the consent of the defendant, took samples of the defendant's blood for the purpose of having a chemical analysis made to determine if defendant was under the influence of intoxicating liquor. . . . The evidence shows that Dr. Calvert came to the jail and took the blood samples. He took the samples home with him and, it being Sunday, he placed them in a refrigerator until the next morning when he mailed them to the laboratory of the State Department of Health at Lincoln. They were received at the laboratory in due course of mail by A. E. Johnson, whose duty it was to open such packages and deliver them to the proper persons in the department. Defendant asserts that, as there is no evidence by the person who obtained the package at the post office and delivered it to Johnson, the foundation is insufficient to admit the result of the test into evidence. The evidence shows that Dr. Calvert placed the samples of blood in two vials and marked them with defendant's name and the time of taking. He wrapped them in an invoice requesting a blood examination and mailed them as heretofore stated. . . . The vials were marked and wrapped as described by Dr. Calvert when received at the laboratory. The foundation was sufficient. We think there is a presumption that articles transported by regular United States mail and delivered in the ordinary course of the mails are delivered in substantially the same condition in which they are sent. This presumption is a rebuttable one, but where there is no evidence tending to overcome the presumption it is sufficient to establish the identity of the article mailed and that it is in substantially the same condition as at the time of mailing. The rule for which the defendant contends would place a great burden upon addressee, such as the one here involved, to keep meticulous records of mail deliveries to protect against the mere possibility that articles so delivered might possibly become pertinent in a court proceeding. We think the objection as to foundation on this ground was properly overruled.

. . . .

Affirmed.

UNITED STATES v. JONES
486 F.2d 476 (8th Cir. 1973)

Per Curiam.

Clifford Jones was tried and convicted, by a jury, of violating the provisions of 21 U.S.C. § 841(a)(1) - intentional and knowing distribution of heroin. From that conviction Jones appeals. We affirm.

On appeal Jones asserts [that] the district court erred in admitting exhibits 1, 2 and 3, exhibits relating to the narcotics involved in the crime. . . .

. . . .

II. *Chain of Custody*

The lock seal envelope, Exhibit 1, containing narcotics, Exhibit 3, was received by a government "evidence technician" at the laboratory of the Bureau of Narcotics and Dangerous Drugs on November 22, 1972. The technician was not called as a witness. On December 13, 1972, Van Sickle, a government chemist, took these two exhibits from the evidence vault and conducted chemical tests to determine the nature of the substance. He then placed these exhibits in another lock seal envelope, Exhibit 2, and placed them in a vault. Van Sickle was called to testify at trial.

Objection is made to the introduction of this evidence because it is asserted that the "chain of custody" was not properly established because of the failure of the evidence technician to testify. This failure is said to render the admission of the evidence objectionable for lack of a proper foundation. We disagree.

As we have recently said:

> The criteria governing admission of exhibits into evidence is that there must be a showing that the physical exhibit being offered is in substantially the same condition as when the crime was committed. That determination is to be made by the trial judge, not the jury, and may not be overturned except for a clear abuse of discretion. Factors to be considered in making the determination of admissibility include the nature of the article, the circumstances surrounding its preservation and custody, and the likelihood of others tampering with it. If upon the consideration of such factors, the trial judge is satisfied that in reasonable probability the article has not been changed in any important respect, he may permit its introduction in evidence. *United States v. Brown*, 482 F.2d 1226, 1228 (8th Cir. 1973).

In sum, "[w]hile the government might have provided further information as to . . . the receiving and storing procedures at the laboratory. . . , we do not find these omissions significant." *United States v. Jackson*, 482 F.2d 1264, 1267 (8th Cir. 1973). In this case there was no evidence introduced to indicate that the exhibits had been tampered with. Both the chemist who examined the material and the agent who obtained the material testified. The agent testified that he obtained the material, transported it to Kansas City, Missouri, placed it in a lock seal envelope, mailed it, by registered mail, return receipt requested, to the laboratory. He testified that the material offered as evidence was in the same condition as when he received it. The chemist testified that the material was received at the laboratory, and was placed in the evidence vault. Thereafter it was examined and again placed in the evidence vault. We can find no error in the admission of this evidence.

. . . .

For the reasons hereinbefore expressed the judgment of conviction is affirmed.

NOTES

1. *The Post Office and "Minor Links."* As indicated by *Schacht*, even though the general rule is that any person who has possession of an item of evidence is a link in the chain, courts usually presume, without the admission of any evidence, proper handling by the United States Post Office. Note, however, that it may be important to establish that the item of evidence in question was actually delivered to a post office or a mail box — as opposed to merely being placed in a *departmental* "outgoing mail" box.

> The importance of the chain of custody of a blood sample was demonstrated by this court in *Miller v. State*, 484 So.2d 1203 (Ala. Crim. App. 1986). There a lab technician took a blood sample from the defendant, placing it in " 'a vacutainer type instrument' " which he then wrapped in tape and gave to a trooper. The trooper took the sample to the trooper post, " 'put it in an envelope, sealed it and initialed it,' " then placed it "in 'the mail,' " meaning the department's outgoing mail, *not* the United States mail. The toxicologist "received 'this container in the mail' " and determined the blood alcohol level of the sample. 484 So.2d at 1204.

> We held that the prosecution had failed to establish the requisite chain of custody because there was no showing of the use of the United States mail so

as to raise the presumption that " 'articles shipped by mail [United States Postal Service] are delivered in substantially the same condition as when placed in the mail box or post office.' " 484 So. 2d at 1205.

Suttle v. State, 565 So. 2d 1197, 1199 (Ala. Crim. App. 1990).

For so-called "minor" links — individuals who have possession for a brief period, and who merely pass the evidence along to another person — courts usually consider circumstantial evidence sufficient to make an initial showing of proper handling. For example, circumstantial evidence of proper handling is usually sufficient for laboratory personnel who receive evidence and then deliver it to the forensic scientist for testing. *See* 1 SCIENTIFIC EVIDENCE § 7.03[b], at 401–02 (4th ed. 2007) ("In short, 'accounting for' all the links in the chain of custody does not necessarily mean all the links need testify at trial.").

2. *Informants.* In addition to minor links, many courts do not require direct evidence of proper handling by government informants. The situation sometimes arises, typically in drug cases, where a government informant makes a drug buy outside of the presence of the police and then delivers the drugs to the police. If the informant does not testify at trial, testimony from a link is absent. For informants, testimony of an accompanying police officer with firsthand knowledge (i.e., who observed the drug buy) or circumstantial evidence may supply information about the link's (the informant's) safe handling and receipt in the absence of the link's presence and testimony. *See, e.g. United States v. Amaro*, 422 F.2d 1078, 1080 (9th Cir. 1970) (marked bills given to informant found in defendant's possession after alleged drug sale sufficient to establish that defendant possessed drugs given to police by the informant). *See also* 1 SCIENTIFIC EVIDENCE § 7.03[b], at 399 (4th ed. 2007).

PROBLEM

Problem 3-13. On a November afternoon in 1988 an automobile accident occurred that resulted in the death of a man driving one car and minor injuries to the driver of the other car. The injured driver was charged with vehicular homicide. Blood test results indicated that the defendant had a blood alcohol content of.298% a few minutes after the accident. At the defendant's trial the prosecution sought to admit the blood test evidence. The following testimony was offered:

> The injured driver was taken to a hospital. A registered nurse testified that she took three samples of his blood at 3:30 p.m. Each sample was placed in a separate tube with a different color top. The nurse sealed each tube and placed the man's name and the hospital's name on each tube. The nurse further testified that she then gave the tubes to the "unit secretary to be sent to the lab," and that, "somebody from the lab picked it up." Neither the unit secretary nor the person from the lab who picked up the sample testified.

> A hospital toxicologist testified that she tested the blood. She stated that she received the blood in a sealed condition with the defendant's name and the hospital's name written on it. She can only identify the person she received the blood from as "laboratory personnel." She does not remember what time she received the sample but does know that she performed the tests at 4:15 p.m.

Are the blood test results admissible without testimony from the unit secretary or the lab courier? *See Moorman v. State*, 574 So. 2d 953, 956 (Ala. Crim. App. 1990).

[3]   Burden of Proof and Standard of Proof

The following case, *United States v. Hon*, discusses how the Federal Rules of Evidence changed the standard of proof needed to establish a chain of custody.

UNITED STATES v. HON
904 F.2d 803 (2d Cir. 1990)

WALKER, CIRCUIT JUDGE.

Nam Ping Hon appeals from his conviction, after a jury trial in the United States District Court for the Southern District of New York on two counts of trafficking and attempting to traffic in wrist watches bearing prestige-brand counterfeit trademarks, in violation of 18 U.S.C. § 2320. . . .

BACKGROUND

In early 1988, undercover agents of the United States Customs Service, seeking to buy counterfeit watches, made contact with Nam Ping Hon and his wife Sandy Hon who had imitation Rolex, Gucci, Piaget and Movado watches for sale at prices ranging between $13 and $17. The watches generally bore a close resemblance to the genuine article and carried an identical or nearly identical trademark, but their quality of manufacture was poor.

On January 25, 1988, the agents purchased eight counterfeit watches at the Hons' place of business at 326 Canal Street in New York City and told the Hons that, if these were satisfactory, they would purchase a much larger quantity. Through the spring and summer, the agents kept sporadic contact with the Hons. On August 23, Sandy Hon agreed to sell Agent Bonnie Goldblatt 1,200 counterfeit watches at 8:00 a.m. on August 25. Sandy said that Nam Ping Hon would be with her and gave the agent a list of the styles and prices involved. The total price for the watches was $17,200, an average price of $14.33 per watch.

On the morning of August 25, 1988, Nam Ping Hon, accompanied by Sandy Hon and carrying two shopping bags he had taken from his car, met Agent Goldblatt outside his Canal Street address. Both Hons separately indicated that the watches were in the bags. Agent Goldblatt said that she had seen police nearby and suggested that they complete the transaction elsewhere. Sandy went in a car with Agent Goldblatt and Special Agent Blaise Piazza to the pre-arranged spot. Nam Ping left on foot with the two shopping bags. When the group reconvened, Sandy and Nam Ping conferred separately. Sandy returned alone to the agents and said that the deal was off. The agents arrested Sandy Hon and, shortly thereafter, Nam Ping Hon.

A surveillance agent found and seized Hon's car and took the two shopping bags — containing 889 counterfeit watches — from the trunk. Searches ensued at 326 Canal Street with a warrant, and at 325 Canal Street and Hon's home on consent. The agents seized a total of 2,600 counterfeit watches from these locations and found $68,000 in cash in a bedroom closet.

The Hons were charged with one count of conspiracy . . . and three counts of trafficking and attempting to traffic in counterfeit watches. . . . Sandy Hon pled guilty to all counts and was sentenced to 36 months' probation, a $6,000 fine and a $200 special assessment. A jury found Nam Ping Hon guilty of two of the counts of trafficking and attempting to traffic. Judge Sweet sentenced Hon to five months' imprisonment, five months in a community treatment center, a $3,000 fine and a $100 special assessment.

DISCUSSION

. . . .

III.

. . . Hon argues that the "chain of custody" proof was insufficient to warrant the district court's admission into evidence of certain watches.[24] [3] This argument is meritless.

As Hon concedes, Fed. R. Evid. 901 requires that to meet the admissibility threshold the government need only prove a rational basis for concluding that an exhibit is what it is claimed to be.[25] [4]

The government more than adequately demonstrated such a rational basis in this case. Although the government, with greater care in handling the exhibits, could have avoided the issue, any "weaknesses" in the government's chain of custody were insufficient to offset the ample evidence supporting admission of the watches. Once the exhibits were admitted into evidence, the alleged defects in the government's chain of custody proof were for the jury to evaluate in its consideration of the weight to be given to the evidence. *See United States v. Johnson*, 513 F.2d 819, 822 n.1 (2d Cir. 1975). *See also* Fed. R. Evid. 901, Advisory Committee's Note at [1]-(a) (authentication and identification represent a special aspect of relevancy, governed by the procedure of Fed. R. Evid. 104(b)).

Agent Goldblatt, who purchased the eight watches on January 25, 1988, testified that immediately after the purchase she and her partner brought the watches back to the Customs House, where she placed them in an evidence bag and sealed and labelled it, indicating date and time of purchase and a description of contents. She stored the bag in a locked cabinet in her office, removed it a week later so that the watches could be certified as counterfeit, and then placed the watches back into the bag and resealed it. Agent Piazza, who received the stapled evidence bag from Goldblatt, kept it in his desk, which contained no other evidence of any kind. He took it out on only one occasion when he broke the seal to examine the contents, and then returned the bag, albeit unsealed, to his desk. Goldblatt also testified at trial that she could identify the eight watches as those she purchased from the Hons by the watches themselves, the label on the bag, and the receipt she received at the time of purchase. The incorrect case number on the

---

[24] [n.3] Hon cites evidence that an evidence bag bore a label with an incorrect case number; that the watches in that bag were initially carried loose in the pockets of an agent who was not called as a witness; that the bag was left open for several months in an unlocked desk drawer; that certain other evidence bags and boxes when initially received from the seizing agent may have been left uncounted for several days in an office to which many agents had access; that these bags were never actually sealed when placed in an evidence room to which many persons had access; that no written records were kept of who had custody of various items in the evidence room or when various items entered or left the room.

[25] [n.4] Hon cites a Seventh Circuit case, *United States v. Lampson*, 627 F.2d 62, 65 (7th Cir. 1980), for the proposition that when the issue concerns the very identity of the evidence, rather than just possible changes in its condition, heightened scrutiny is appropriate for chain of custody claims. Even if this Circuit were to adopt such a principle, which we need not decide here, we do not believe that this case involves "the very identity of the evidence" as opposed to changes in its condition. Moreover, we believe that the evidence of authentication in this case would support admissibility of the watches even under a heightened standard.

label arose because Agent Goldblatt mistakenly wrote a "6" instead of a "2" for the ninth digit of the case number.

Regarding the watches seized from the trunk of the Hons' car on August 25, 1988, one agent testified that he and his partner physically handed the items to Agent Piazza on that day. Agent Piazza testified that he first locked the watches in his supervisor's office, then in one evidence room and then in a different evidence room, until he brought the exhibits to the U.S. Attorney's office for trial preparation. Although Piazza apparently sealed only the boxes and not the bags, Piazza stated that he covered the rolled-up bags with the boxes when he placed them in the two evidence rooms and found the bags in their original positions when he retrieved them from the rooms.

The prosecution is not required to "exclude all possibility that the article may have been tampered with." Given the ample evidence offered by the government to demonstrate that the exhibits were what they were claimed to be, we conclude that the district court did not abuse its discretion in admitting them into evidence.

Judgment affirmed.

NOTE

Burden of Proof. Prior to the adoption of the Federal Rules of Evidence, federal and state courts described the standard of proof in terms of "reasonable probability," *United States v. Brown*, 482 F.2d 1226, 1228 (8th Cir. 1973), or "reasonable certainty," *Robinson v. Commonwealth*, 183 S.E.2d 179, 180 (Va. 1971). Typically, under this standard the proponent of physical evidence must show both identity and unchanged condition to a "reasonable probability" or "reasonable certainty." This appears to be no more than the preponderance standard and, in fact, some courts have termed it that. *See State v. Williams*, 273 So. 2d 280, 281 (La. 1973) ("clear preponderance"). Under this standard the trial court determines whether the proof is adequate prior to admitting the proffered item of real evidence.

After adoption of the Federal Rules of Evidence, federal courts were confronted with Fed. R. Evid. 901(a), which requires the offering party to introduce *"evidence sufficient to support a finding* that the matter in question is what its proponent claims" (emphasis added). If Rule 901(a)'s standard is applied to chain-of-custody issues, the proponent of the evidence need only offer enough evidence from which a jury (not the court) could decide that the evidence is identified. Professors Giannelli and Imwinkelried describe Rule 901(a)'s requirement by saying, "[t]he offering party need make only a 'prima facie' showing of authenticity to gain admissibility, and the jury decides whether the evidence has been sufficiently identified. . . . Not only is the prima facie standard less stringent than the 'more probable than not' standard, but it also results in a different rule concerning the application of the rules of evidence." 1 SCIENTIFIC EVIDENCE § 7.04, at 403 (4th ed. 2007). The "different rule" referred to in the preceding excerpt from SCIENTIFIC EVIDENCE is Rule 104(b) (as opposed to Rule 104(a), which controls when the court makes the admissibility decision). If Rule 104(b) governs this situation, the rules of evidence apply since the jury is sharing in the authenticity decision with the trial court.

Many state courts — and some federal circuits — continue to apply the pre-Federal Rules "reasonable probability" standard to establishing a chain of custody. *See, e.g., United States v. Coombs*, 369 F.3d 925, 938 (6th Cir. 2004); *United States v. Beal*, 279 F.3d 567, 572 (8th Cir. 2002); *People v. Lucas*, 907 P.2d 373, 391 (Cal. 1995); *Ex parte*

Holton, 590 So. 2d 918, 919–20 (Ala. 1991). *See also* 1 Scientific Evidence § 7.04, at 402, 404–05 (4th ed. 2007) (citing cases from the Second, Fifth, Sixth, Seventh, Eighth, and Tenth Circuits). *See generally* Edward J. Imwinkelried, Comment, *The Identification of Original Real Evidence*," 61 Mil. L. Rev. 145, 158–59 (1973).

[4]   When Does the Chain Begin and End?

[a]   The Chain's Beginning

When a chain of custody is required, either to show the identity of an item or that its condition is unchanged (or both), it is necessary to determine when the chain begins and ends. Arguably, any unaccounted-for custodian (breaks or "missing links" in the chain) before or after the chain is considered to have begun or ended does not affect admissibility. Accordingly, it can be quite important to establish just when the chain begins and ends.

The next two cases discuss when the chain begins and present different views. One approach holds that the chain of possession begins with the incident that links the physical evidence to the case being tried. A second view holds that the chain of possession begins when the item comes into the possession of the police.

[i]   The Time of the Incident

UNITED STATES v. WHITE
569 F.2d 263 (5th Cir. 1978)

Thornberry, Circuit Judge.

Phillip . . . White . . . appeal[s] [his] convictions on heroin charges. [He was] convicted by a jury of . . . a substantive count of heroin possession with intent to distribute. . . . [among other things]. [He] received a . . . six-year sentence . . . for the substantive offense.

. . . Phillip . . . makes a "chain of custody" argument in challenging his substantive conviction. . . . [W]e affirm Phillip's conviction for the substantive offense.

I. FACTUAL BACKGROUND

These convictions were obtained largely through the efforts of two undercover agents for the Drug Enforcement Administration, Widener and Wendt, who worked closely with a confidential informant. . . .

. . . [O]n August 31, [1976] a confidential informant named Oatis Leeper was instructed by the agents to try to make a heroin buy. . . . On September 3 and 4, Leeper purchased small quantities of heroin from Phillip and discussed the possibility of selling for him.

. . . .

II. THE SUBSTANTIVE OFFENSE

The basis of this count [heroin possession with intent to distribute] against Phillip was Leeper's purchase on September 4. Phillip contends that there was not an adequate chain of custody regarding the heroin that the DEA agents took from Leeper after the buy had been made. He relies on the fact that the agents did not personally observe the transaction and that Leeper could possibly have obtained the heroin from another source.

This is not a routine chain of custody situation in which the chain is broken between seizure of the evidence from the accused and a subsequent trial. Rather, the alleged break occurred before the government came into possession of the heroin.

The more typical chain of custody cases make clear that the mere possibility of a break in the chain does not render the physical evidence inadmissible, but raises the question of the weight to be accorded by the jury to the sufficiency of the proof of a chain of custody. We apply the same rule in the instant case.

Here the alleged break is that government agents did not witness the deal's consummation. Moreover, there is nothing in the record indicating that marked bills supplied by the government were found in Phillip's possession after the sale. Nonetheless, Leeper's testimony supplies the missing link in the chain, since he testified that he purchased the drugs from Phillip. Leeper's credibility on this point is an issue for the jury, as would also be the case had an undercover government agent, rather than an informant, made the buy.

Allowing the informant's testimony to supply the missing link is no different than allowing connection of physical evidence with a defendant to be shown by circumstantial evidence. In [this] case proof of the connection goes to the weight of the physical evidence rather than its admissibility. We thus find Phillip's argument without merit and affirm his conviction for the substantive offense.

III. CONCLUSION

Phillip White's conviction for possession of heroin with intent to distribute is affirmed.

[ii]   When the Item Comes into the Possession of the Police

WASH v. STATE
408 N.E.2d 634 (Ind. Ct. App. 1980)

STATON, JUDGE.

A jury found Patrick Wash guilty of robbery while armed with a deadly weapon. Wash was sentenced to the Indiana Department of Correction for a period of ten years.

On appeal, Wash raises four issues for our review [including] . . . did the trial court err by admitting State's Exhibit "1," a stocking cap, into evidence? . . .

We affirm.

. . . .

The evidence most favorable to the State reveals that Wash entered Alyse LaMonte's apartment and hid in the closet of the bedroom while she was out of the apartment. When LaMonte returned to her apartment and entered the bedroom, Wash jumped out of the closet and placed a knife against LaMonte's back. LaMonte immediately fell on the bed. Wash stood over LaMonte with the knife in his hand and demanded that she remove her clothes. Wash then cut her right breast with the knife. As LaMonte stood up to remove her clothes, she ran from the apartment to her neighbor's apartment. While standing at her neighbor's door, LaMonte saw Wash leave the apartment with her purse which had been lying on the bed during the attack.

. . . .

II. Admissibility

Wash contends that the trial court erred by admitting into evidence a red and blue stocking cap which LaMonte identified as the cap worn by Wash during the attack. LaMonte returned to her apartment for the first time after the robbery on January 17, 1979 [approximately one week after the attack], and found the cap in the closet of her bedroom. She notified the police immediately of her finding, but the police did not pick up the cap until January 31, 1979. At trial, Wash objected to the admission of the cap into evidence because LaMonte "obviously didn't know where (the cap) was" for a week after the attack. Wash asserted that the one week lapse in time between the robbery and the finding of the cap was a fatal defect rendering the cap inadmissible because a realistic threat of tampering or substitution existed. In his brief, Wash characterized the alleged error in admitting the cap into evidence as the State's failure to establish a proper "chain of custody" foundation.

The error raised by Wash is not a chain of custody issue. A chain of custody foundation is not required for the period before the evidence came into the possession of the police. The State has an obligation to establish a proper chain of custody foundation only from the point in time when the police obtain possession of the challenged item to the moment the State seeks to introduce that item into evidence at trial.[26] [3] The admissibility of an item is predicated upon connecting the item to the defendant through direct testimony and demonstrating that the item is relevant to the issues of the case. An item that tends to connect the defendant to the commission of the crime is relevant and therefore admissible. The fact that the connection of the item to the defendant is inconclusive or slight only goes to the weight of the evidence and not to its admissibility. Positive proof of authentication of an item is not a prerequisite to its admissibility.

Based on the preceding cases, the State was not required to establish a chain of custody foundation for the period before the cap came into the possession of the police. A sufficient foundation was established when LaMonte positively identified the cap as that worn by her attacker. The cap was thus connected to Wash, and it was found relevant for the purpose of corroborating LaMonte's identification of her attacker. The delay in finding the cap was a matter for the jury to weigh with subsequent evidence

---

[26] [n.3] Recent cases have required a showing of a complete chain of custody "from the original receiver to the final custodian" of the item. *Williams v. State* (1979), Ind., 387 N.E.2d 1317, 1319; *Coker v. State* (1980), Ind. App., 399 N.E.2d 857, 858–59. "Original receiver" is limited to law enforcement personnel and should not be construed to include the first possessor of an item who is not affiliated with the police. Both *Williams* and *Coker* impose a chain of custody requirement only for "seized" items, which necessarily implies some form of police possession of the challenged items.

concerning the cap. The trial court did not abuse its discretion by admitting the stocking cap into evidence.

In his brief, Wash also contends that the State failed to properly establish a chain of custody of the stocking cap from the time it came into the possession of the police on January 31, 1979, to the day of trial. However, Wash waived any error that may have been committed by failing to object to the admission of the cap on that particular ground at trial and in his motion to correct errors. Grounds for objection to the admission of evidence asserted on appeal may not differ from those stated at trial.[27] [4]

. . . .

We find no error. The judgment of the trial court is affirmed.

NOTE

The "Police Accountability Theory." The view that the chain of custody does not begin until the police get possession of an item of evidence is applied in two types of cases: (1) where a third party possessed an object after a crime took place prior to turning it over to police, and (2) where an item of evidence is not discovered at the crime scene for a period of time after the commission of a crime. *See* 1 SCIENTIFIC EVIDENCE § 7.03[a], at 394–395 (4th ed. 2007). Cases in Alabama, Indiana, and Montana have all endorsed the view that the chain does not begin until the police receive possession. *Broadnax v. State*, 825 So. 2d 134, 171 (Ala. Crim. App. 2000) ("The chain of custody for an item of evidence does not begin at the time of the crime, but at the time the item comes into the state's possession."); *Burrell v. State*, 689 So.2d 992, 995 (Ala. Crim. App. 1996) ("Proper analysis of a chain of custody question . . . does not begin at the time of the offense; the chain of custody begins when the item is seized by the state."); *Watkins v. State*, 436 N.E.2d 83, 85 (Ind. 1982) ("The chain of custody showing is not required . . . for periods before the evidence comes into possession of law enforcement personnel."); *State v. Walton*, 722 P.2d 1145, 1147 (Mont. 1986) ("[T]he chain of custody rule . . . does not require the police or prosecutors to account for the possession of evidence before it comes into their hands.").

States that adhere to this view seem to be taking the position that the purpose of the chain of custody rule is to hold the police accountable for proper handling of evidence. *See e.g., Whitt v. State*, 733 So.2d 463, 473 (Ala. Crim. App. 1998) ("The purpose of establishing a chain of custody is to demonstrate with reasonable probability that the evidence has not been tampered with or altered."); *Arnold v. State*, 436 N.E.2d 288, 291 (Ind. 1982) ("The purpose of the rule requiring that the state show a continuous chain of custody . . . of fungible evidence is to prevent tampering, loss, substitution, or mistake with respect to the exhibit[;] the rule operates . . . only . . . after the evidence comes into the possession of law enforcement personnel."). Professors Giannelli and Imwinkelried argue that the police accountability theory "misconceives the purpose of the chain of custody rule," which is not to hold police accountable, but is to ensure that evidence is relevant. 1 SCIENTIFIC EVIDENCE § 7.03[a], at 395 (4th ed. 2007).

---

[27] [n.4] Assuming that Wash had properly raised a chain of custody objection at trial, Wash would still be precluded from contending that the trial court erred by admitting the cap without a chain of custody foundation. Such a foundation for the period after the police gained possession of a challenged item is not required where the item is hard, physical evidence whose characteristics are capable of eyewitness identification and not susceptible to tampering or substitution. The cap in the present case would fall under this exception to the chain of custody rule.

QUESTIONS

1. Is the purpose of the chain-of-custody rule to hold the police accountable for their handling of the evidence, or is it to ensure that the evidence is relevant? Are the two purposes mutually exclusive?

2. In states like Indiana that consider the chain to begin when the police come into possession of an item of physical evidence, is it possible that the prosecution could establish a complete chain and still not have an item of evidence be admissible? *See Williams v. State*, 379 N.E.2d 981, 984 (Ind. 1978) (chain of custody not required for periods before evidence comes into possession of law enforcement personnel, but relevancy and materiality of all evidence must be established as a precondition of its admission).

3. On the other hand, in a state adhering to the police accountability theory, could readily identifiable physical evidence be identified at trial and still be excluded from a case if police cannot establish a complete chain of custody from the time the evidence came into their possession?

4. According to the court in *White*, did the chain begin when the DEA agents received the heroin from Leeper, or when the transaction that the evidence was involved with (the drug sale) occurred? In that regard, is a police informant (e.g., Oatis Leeper) considered an agent of the police so that drugs can be considered to have come into police possession at the time of the alleged sale of the heroin? What difference would it make if Leeper was, or was not, considered an "agent" of the police anyway? Finally, what does the court consider Oatis Leeper a "missing link" or a "weak link"?

PROBLEMS

Problem 3-14. If a third party finds a knife (or some other piece of real evidence) that may have been used in a crime several hours or days after the crime has occurred and turns the knife over to the police, should the police be required to account for the knife's whereabouts and safe handling during the time after the crime but before the knife was found and turned over to them? During the time the knife was in the possession of the third party? *See Powell v. State*, 796 So. 2d 404, 420–21 (Ala. Crim. App. 1999); *Golden v. State*, 439 So. 2d 813, 815–16 (Ala. Crim. App. 1983); *Williams v. State*, 379 N.E.2d 981, 984 (Ind. 1978); *Zupp v. State*, 283 N.E.2d 540, 542–43 (Ind. 1972).

What if, rather than a third party finding a weapon and turning it over to the police, police simply find the weapon in some bushes several days later? *See People v. Brown*, 496 N.Y.S.2d 272 (N.Y. App. 1985).

Problem 3-15. Assume that an undercover police officer and an informant named Paz drive to a bar where the informant is supposed to introduce the police officer to drug dealers. The police officer stays in his car while Paz goes inside the bar. Paz comes out with a man named Watkins. Watkins tells the undercover police officer that he will sell the undercover officer heroin for $75, but that he would only give the heroin to Paz who could then give it to the undercover officer. The undercover police officer gives $75 to Paz, who leaves with Watkins and reenters the bar. Five minutes later, Paz returns with a white powder that is later analyzed and determined to be heroin. Paz no longer has the $75. Assume that Paz was searched before and after the drug sale by police and he did not have any drugs or money on his person (other than the drugs he gave police after the alleged sale).

Watkins is arrested and charged with selling heroin. At trial the state offers the white powder the undercover police officer was given by the informant, Paz, into evidence. Paz does not testify, but the police can establish a complete chain of custody for the powder from the time the undercover officer received it up until trial.

(A) Is the evidence admissible in a jurisdiction that follows *White*?

(B) Is the evidence admissible in a jurisdiction that follows *Wash? See Watkins v. State*, 436 N.E.2d 83, 85–86 (Ind. 1982).

[b]   The Chain's Ending

Must the proponent of fungible physical evidence establish receipt, safe handling, and disposition up until the time that the item is actually brought into court? If so, suppose that a bag containing what appeared to be cocaine was analyzed and a report prepared indicating that the bag contained cocaine. If the cocaine were subsequently lost or destroyed, would testimony about the analysis be inadmissible? Put another way, does the chain of custody end at the time of analysis or at trial?

The next two cases examine different views about when the chain ends.

STATE v. CONLEY
288 N.E.2d 296 (Ohio Ct. App. 1971)

COLE, JUDGE.

The indictment reads in part:

". . . [O]ne Charles Eddie Conley unlawfully then and there did sell an hallucinogen, to wit: LSD, said sale not being in accordance with sections 3719.40 to 3719.49, inclusive, of the Ohio Revised Code, contrary to Section 3719.44, D of the Ohio Revised Code. . . ."

. . . .

. . . The defendant contends the judgment of the trial court [resulting in his conviction for the unlawful sale of LSD] is against the weight of the evidence and contrary to law. . . .

The first [contention] concerns the admitting into evidence of [a] certain [exhibit] — Exhibit 1 being a brown envelope containing a cellophane sack (a cigarette container) and in which were 18 pills of an orange coloring. . . .

The problem here is essentially one of identity. If an exhibit is directly identified by a witness as the object which is involved in the case, then that direct identification is sufficient. Such is the case with many objects which have special identifying characteristics, such as a number or mark, or are made to have such identifying characteristics by special marks. However, where the objects are more or less interchangeable and have no special characteristics, the problem of establishing identity usually involves some evidence as to a chain of custody. One dollar bill, except as to its serial number, looks like any other dollar bill and positive identification is difficult. One white pill looks much like any other white pill and hence positive identification simply by observation is usually impossible. To identify a particular item of this type as being part of a pertinent incident in the past usually requires the showing of a continuous chain of custodians up to the material moment. When a chemical analysis is involved, as here, the material moment is the moment of analysis, since this provides the basis for the expert testimony and makes that testimony relevant to the case. In the case of many other items, the material moment occurs at the trial.

As to the pills, . . . [t]he important connection . . . is to establish that the pills sold by the defendant to Jenkins [the police informant] were the pills analyzed at the bureau of criminal identification and investigation (hereinafter referred to as BCI) and found to be LSD. The subsequent custody and presentation into evidence is not as important as the critical moment — the moment of the chemical analysis which formed the basis for the expert's subsequent testimony.

Jenkins testified that he bought the pills placed in a cellophane wrapper from a cigarette pack; that they were orange type; that Exhibit 1 was the same kind of wrapper and the same kind of pills (from which it can be inferred they were of the same size, shape and color). He further stated that he put the pills which were so enclosed in his helmet. These were later given to an officer.

The officer states he took the helmet from Jenkins, removed the pills contained therein and placed them in his jacket pocket; that Exhibit 1 looked like the pills and container; and that the pills and wrapper were turned over to a Capt. Severns. Severns put certain writing (that 20 orange sunshine pills were in a cellophane wrapper) on a property envelope (this was positively identified), and placed the pills and wrapper therein after having received them from Officer Tidd. It was taken by him to the BCI and given to a man in the laboratory.

Mr. Rector, the BCI chemist, testified that the envelope was obtained by him from a filing cabinet in the laboratory, that it then bore a BCI case number, and that he put his initials both on the outside envelope and on the cellophane wrapper. It then contained twenty orange tablets in the cellophane wrapper. He used up two pills in analysis. After the analysis, the remaining pills, the wrapper, and the envelope were placed in a sealed envelope and kept in a locked storage area. He then brought the sealed envelope to the trial.

It is immediately apparent that there is a complete chain of custody or other evidence of identity with the possible exception of the period between the delivery of the property envelope and its contents, by Severns, to an unidentified person in the BCI laboratory and the moment Rector took this envelope from a file drawer. There is no direct testimony by the person or persons who received the envelope with its contents and placed it in this drawer.

However, direct testimony as to custody is not the only way that identity may be established. It may also be established by inference. In this case the inferences of identity are very strong. They are as follows:

(1) The brown envelope composing the outside wrapper was positively identified by the writing upon it;

(2) The contents were identical in description in that,

(a) there were twenty pills of the same size and shape,

(b) all pills were orange in coloring, and

(c) the pills were in a cellophane wrapper of a cigarette pack;

(3) The pills and wrapper are stated by all witnesses to be similar to those received from defendant; and

(4) The uncontradicted testimony by Rector as to standard operating procedure states that when such material is brought in it is assigned a case number by an evidence coordinator and placed by him in the file of the appropriate section, and the chemist takes the material bearing the case number from the file and processes it.

From this it may be inferred that the pills examined by Rector were the same pills brought in by Severns and the chain of identity was thus established. We cannot say as a matter of law that a jury could not determine such identity beyond a reasonable doubt. The question involves the weight to be assigned the inferences and not their absolute inadequacy as a matter of law, which would preclude a reasonable doubt.

It is our conclusion that . . . this assignment of error is not well taken.

. . . .

Judgment affirmed.

NOTE

People v. Julian. In *People v. Julian*, 392 N.Y.S.2d 610 (N.Y. Sup. Ct. 1977), the prosecutor could not establish a complete chain of custody for the period of time *after* an analysis had indicated that certain evidence seized by police was illegal drugs. Prior to trial an unknown person took the drugs from police vaults as part of a reinventory and reanalysis of all drugs to determine if anyone was stealing drugs from police evidence vaults. The drugs were later returned to the police vault and were retrieved before Julian's trial. *Id.* at 611–12. The court found that the fact that the chain was broken after analysis was not a bar to admission:

> Defendant's better argument challenges whether the circumstances provide a reasonable assurance that the evidence had not been tampered with. Even though the evidence is adequately identified as the items initially seized, a further question is whether, during the gap in the chain of custody, some unknown party could have caused a material and prejudicial change in the condition or nature of the evidence. By the time the present gap occurred, however, the opportunity for creating such a prejudicial alteration no longer existed. It is undisputed that a chain of custody was adequately established from the time of seizure to the time of the first chemical analysis. Its finding that the packages contained illegal drugs could not be affected by any tampering that might have occurred after the analysis. Thus, there was no possibility that the gap could have permitted any *prejudicial* alteration of the contents of the drugs initially seized.

Id. at 613 (emphasis in original). *See also Congo v. State*, 409 So. 2d 475, 479 (Ala. Crim. App. 1981) ("any tampering with the evidence after it had already been tested and determined to be contraband would have been immaterial"); *Blanco v. State*, 485 So. 2d 1217, 1219 (Ala. Crim. App. 1986) ("alteration . . . after . . . analysis and comparison . . . immaterial").

PROBLEMS

Problem 3-16. Assume that Mr. Rector (the chemist who analyzed the pills in *Conley*) did not have the pills with him when he arrived at court. Assume that he can testify about his analysis and is prepared to state that the "orange pills" he took from the filing cabinet were in a property envelope that bore both the BCI case number and the writing that Captain Severns states he (Severns) put on them. Further, assume that when asked why he did not bring the pills with him he says that when he went to the locked storage room where he put them after analysis they were gone, and he has no idea what happened to them. Is testimony about the chemical analysis admissible?

Problem 3-17. Assume that in addition to the analysis of the "orange pills," the prosecuting attorney offers the *pills themselves* into evidence, asserting that these are *the* pills that were sold by the defendant to Jenkins. When does the chain end as to the pills in this situation? Is it necessary to actually offer the pills into evidence in this situation?

The *G.E.G.* case that follows presents a different view as to when the chain of custody ends. Compare the reasoning of the Florida Supreme Court in *G.E.G.* with that of the Ohio Supreme Court in the *Conley* case.

G.E.G. v. STATE
417 So. 2d 975 (Fla. 1982)

SUNBERG, JUSTICE.

The typical drug possession case finds the defendant contesting on appeal the admission into evidence of the substance allegedly possessed. This case presents the antipodal issue: petitioner challenges the nonintroduction of a substance marked for identification and about which there was testimony that it was marijuana, but which was not introduced into evidence.

Upon receiving a tip from petitioner's stepfather that a "pot party" was going on in a neighbor's house, police looked in a window and saw petitioner put in his pocket a plastic bag containing a brown substance. The officers asked petitioner to come onto the porch, searched him, found the plastic bag, and conducted a Voltex test which indicated the brown substance was marijuana. Petitioner, sixteen years old when he was arrested, received a juvenile adjudicatory hearing. . . . Up to a certain point the adjudicatory hearing proceeded normally, with the state presenting evidence of chain of custody, presumably as a predicate for chemical analysis testimony and the eventual introduction into evidence of the plastic bag containing the brown substance marked as an exhibit. . . . The hearing proceeded with the state continuing to establish chain of custody and introducing testimony of a chemist that the brown substance was marijuana. Then, surprisingly, the state rested its case without attempting to admit the much-discussed exhibit or any other item of physical evidence. The trial judge determined that petitioner violated section 893.13(1), Florida Statutes (1977), by unlawfully possessing less than five grams of cannabis. He adjudicated petitioner delinquent and committed him to the Division of Youth Services for an indeterminate period not to extend beyond his twenty-first birthday.

The District Court of Appeal, Fifth District, affirmed, expressly declining to follow a sibling court's holding that the failure to introduce the controlled substance in a drug possession case is a per se denial of a defendant's right of confrontation.[28] [1] We have jurisdiction to resolve this conflict. Our analysis must include an examination of the

---

[28] [n.1] *Alexander v. State*, 288 So. 2d 538 (Fla. 3d DCA 1974).

policy behind the introduction of physical evidence and the consequences of ruling either that physical evidence must always be introduced or that it need never be introduced. Taking a Solomonic rather than an absolute approach, we hold that when a defendant is charged with possession of a controlled substance, that substance, if available, must be introduced into evidence but that a defendant who fails to object to its nonintroduction may not be heard to complain of the error on appeal.[29] [2]

Sir William Blackstone would no doubt have found our present dilemma needless and the answer obvious.

> [T]he one general rule that runs through all the doctrine of trials is this — that the best evidence the nature of the case will admit of shall always be required, if possible to be had; but, if not possible, then the best evidence that can be had shall be allowed. For if it be found that there is any better evidence existing than is produced, the very not producing it is a presumption that in it would have been detected some falsehood that at present is concealed.

3 W. Blackstone, Commentaries 368 (footnote omitted). For us it is not so easy. In Florida the "best evidence rule" only applies to writings, recordings, and photographs. But the fact that we are no longer fettered by the letter of Blackstone's words hardly implies that we are not free to be persuaded by their spirit.

We use Blackstone's principle and the practicalities of modern trial practice to steer a course between two equally undesirable absolutes. An absolute rule that a substance may be introduced or not at the discretion of the prosecutor is practically undesirable because of its potential for abuse. For example, such prosecutorial discretion could deliberately or unwittingly be used to confuse defense counsel and thwart the ability to make certain objections, particularly objections to chain of custody. A defense attorney might wait for the proper moment for an objection, the moment when the state offers the substance into evidence, only to find that the moment never arrives because the state has exercised its discretion in favor of nonintroduction. Counsel's efforts to preserve the case for appellate review would therefore be frustrated.

In addition to infecting trials with tactical or fortuitous confusion, an absolute holding that a substance need never be introduced into evidence would have another undesirable consequence. The state's failure to introduce the substance in evidence against the defendant might put the defendant in the awkward position of introducing it himself should he wish to challenge its authenticity where there has been testimony of its existence as here. We are therefore all the more unwilling to give nonintroduction our absolute imprimatur.

For equally practical reasons we eschew the extreme posture of raising to the level of fundamental error the failure to introduce a substance. We therefore require a

---

[29] [n.2] We are mindful that in *Roberts v. State*, 164 So. 2d 817 (Fla. 1964), the only case in which this Court has addressed a similar issue, we found no error in the failure of the state to introduce a test bullet into evidence. *Roberts* is distinguishable and therefore unaffected by our decision today. *Roberts* was not trying to defend a charge of possessing the test bullet, nor was the test bullet actual physical evidence of the crime, such as the fatal bullet itself, which was introduced. Similarly unaffected by our decision are cases excusing the nonintroduction of evidence because of unavoidable destruction of the substance during testing. *See, e.g., State v. Atkins*, 369 So. 2d 389 (Fla. 2d DCA 1979). Unavoidable destruction prevents the defendant from conducting an independent analysis of the substance, [but is] not an issue in this case. More importantly, the state in petitioner's trial offered absolutely no excuse for its failure to introduce the substance. The substance was actually present during every moment of the trial and was handled, examined, and referred to by the prosecutor and the state's witnesses. Furthermore, we do not perceive this case as involving the defendant's right of confrontation, as did both the third district court in *Alexander* and the fifth district court in this case.

defense objection to the nonintroduction. Since the failure to introduce the substance would no doubt in most cases be the result of prosecutorial oversight, it is only fair that the defendant be required to put the trial court on notice that error has occurred. *Castor v. State*, 365 So. 2d 701 (Fla. 1978). The situation illustrated by the present case is a classic example of how it is both possible and desirable "to cure early that which must be cured eventually." *Id.* at 703. Upon objection by the defendant a trial court would undoubtedly permit the state to reopen its case to offer the contraband as evidence. If the substance is in no way faulty, its introduction into evidence can only help the state's case. If it is faulty, Blackstone's presumption is vindicated, and the state should not be allowed to rest its hopes for a conviction on the chance that the fault will go undiscovered.

Petitioner in this case failed to raise an objection which would put the trial court on notice of possible error and preserve the point for appellate review. Defense counsel's motion for judgment of acquittal contained two grounds: (1) defective chain of custody, and (2) absence of proof that the substance was marijuana. Petitioner urges that this second ground is tantamount to an objection to nonintroduction, but a review of the record reveals that defense counsel's argument to the trial judge was premised not upon the state's failure to introduce the substance but upon an erroneous belief that the chemist failed to testify that the substance was marijuana. We therefore agree with the District Court of Appeal, Fifth District, that petitioner is entitled to no relief, but we disagree with its reasons for so holding.

. . . .

In conclusion, we disapprove both the decision of the District Court of Appeal, Third District, in *Alexander* and the decision of the District Court of Appeal, Fifth District, in this case, to the extent they are inconsistent with our views as expressed above. The case is remanded to the district court with instructions to remand to the trial court for action consistent with our opinion.

It is so ordered.

BOYD, JUSTICE, concurring in part and dissenting in part.

. . . I dissent from the general rule requiring introduction of contraband evidence and requiring the defendant to point out a deficiency in the state's case.

Notwithstanding Blackstone's pronouncements on the subject, it has long been an established principle of American jurisprudence that the best evidence rule applies only to written documents and not to tangible objects. The distinction is based on the understanding that a person's ability to recall the appearance of an object is usually greater than his ability to recall all the words of a written document. Because variation of just a few words can totally change the effect of a written document, it is recognized that the document itself is the most accurate, and perhaps the only reliable, evidence of the contents.

This rationale for the best evidence rule does not apply to physical objects, not even contraband evidence like controlled substances. To prove that an object found in the possession of the accused is a controlled substance, the state must present the testimony of a qualified expert. The testimony of a non-expert, based on simple observation, will not be enough to establish whether an object is a controlled substance under section 893.03, Florida Statutes (1981). It is the testimony of the expert witness, and not the substance itself, that is the essential item of evidence proving the nature of the substance. With regard to substances that are not contraband, an expert's description is usually admissible without the introduction of the substance itself.

. . . .

I do not believe that the decision of this case requires the fashioning of such a general rule as the majority, in its Solomonic wisdom, attempts to develop. Here the judge who ruled on the admissibility of the evidence was also the trier of fact. He saw the physical evidence, heard testimony identifying it and establishing the chain of custody, and heard expert testimony establishing that it was cannabis. For all practical purposes, although not formally, the cannabis was in evidence in the sense that it was placed before the eyes of the trier of fact along with identifying and authenticating testimony. Thus we need not be concerned with fashioning a general rule. In cases tried to a jury, where the defense challenges the admissibility of tangible evidence, the jury, if defense counsel does his job correctly, will not see the evidence nor even hear it referred to unless and until it has been ruled admissible by the court.

The majority suggests as one reason for its general rule the right of the defendant to examine and challenge the substance offered as evidence of illegal possession. However, the defendant's interest in challenging the authenticity of the evidence is fully protected by the criminal rules governing discovery. See Fla. R. Crim. P. 3.220(a). Therefore there is no need, as far as the defendant is concerned, for a general rule requiring that the controlled substance itself be admitted into evidence.

The foregoing remarks indicate my reasons for disagreement with the majority's general rule requiring the presentation of the controlled substance as tangible evidence. If, however, there are cases where it must be held as a matter of law that the evidence of guilt is insufficient without the introduction of the actual physical substance possessed, then I am deeply troubled by the Court's holding that the defendant must point out the evidentiary insufficiency to the court and to the state. The Court's suggestion that upon objection, the trial court would allow the state to reopen its case to remedy the evidentiary deficiency embarks upon a new line of authority. This sets a precedent for allowing the state to reopen its case when a defendant's motion for judgment of acquittal points out the state's failure to present sufficient evidence. This newly imposed duty of defense counsel conflicts with the principle that the burden of proof is on the state and with the lawyer's duty to act in the best interest of his client. It is tantamount to asking defense counsel to perform the state's job.

In summary, I would simply hold that there was sufficient evidence to support the adjudication of delinquency and that petitioner was not prejudiced by the nonintroduction of the physical evidence. On this basis I would approve the decision of the district court of appeal.

NOTES

1. *Introduction of Real Evidence at Trial.* The prosecution is generally not required to introduce real evidence in order to prove its case even if such evidence is available. If physical evidence need not be introduced then, as a matter of establishing relevancy, the chain of custody need only extend to the point of analysis (if the results of an analysis are what makes an item of evidence relevant).

On the other hand, if a state follows the approach taken by the Florida Supreme Court in *G.E.G.*, and requires real evidence to be introduced at trial, identifying the item of evidence at trial is critical to admissibility. Accordingly, if such evidence is fungible, or has been subjected to analysis, the chain may extend to trial. *See generally*, 1 SCIENTIFIC EVIDENCE § 7.03[a], at 397 (4th ed. 2007).

2. *Forida G.E.G. Cases.* In subsequent cases Florida courts have both refined and extended *G.E.G.* First, G.E.G. has been extended to cases where the defendant is charged with "delivery of drugs." *Mack v. State*, 711 So. 2d 1154, 1154 (Fla. Dist. Ct. App. 1998) ("While *G.E.G.* involved a charge of possession of contraband, we see no reason that its holding would not apply equally to a charge of delivery of drugs.").

In *Marrisette v. State*, 780 So. 2d 1020 (Fla. Dist. Ct. App. 2001) a Florida appellate court discussed how the state should go about proving that there were no drugs to introduce into evidence in a drug possession case. In *Marrisette* the defendant was charged with possession of cocaine, and the state did not introduce the actual cocaine the defendant was charged with possessing. When the state rested, the defendant moved for acquittal, based upon *G.E.G.* The prosecutor argued to the trial court that there was no actual cocaine left to introduce into evidence because only residue was found in a glass pipe that was in the defendant's possession. The trial court denied the defendant's motion for acquittal, and the defendant appealed. Defendant's possession conviction was overturned on appeal.

> Because the state . . . failed to introduce the cocaine into evidence, under *G.E.G.* it had the burden of proving that the substance was unavoidably destroyed during testing. It did not meet this burden. Without some testimony, as opposed to the unsworn argument of the prosecutor, as to why the cocaine was unavailable at trial, the court should have granted Marrisette a judgment of acquittal on the cocaine possession charge.

Marrisette, supra, 780 So. 2d at 1021.

Finally, in *Morra v. State*, 467 So. 2d 742 (Fla. Dist. Ct. App. 1985) the defendant was convicted of trafficking in cocaine. At trial the state established a chain of custody from seizure to analysis and introduced expert testimony that the substance analyzed was, in fact, cocaine. The defendant then moved for the cocaine to be excluded because the post-analysis chain of custody was defective. The appeals court upheld the defendant's conviction, stating:

> *G.E.G.* is not controlling. In this case the substance was not left out as evidence by mistake, but was excluded on the defendant's own motion. The question here . . . is whether a conviction for possession of a controlled substance can stand where the evidence is excluded on defendant's motion because of a probability that the substance was tampered with after it had been analyzed by a State's chemist, but the chain of custody is established from the point of seizure through the time of analysis, and there is no challenge to the expert testimony that the substance is in fact contraband.

This conviction for possession of a controlled substance is reconcilable with G.E.G.'s requirement that the controlled substance be introduced into evidence if it is available. The court's finding in this case that the substance could not be traced after analysis was the functional equivalent of a finding that the substance actually seized became unavailable, which caused the chemist's testimony to become the next "best evidence-."Appellant could have, but did not, request production of the evidence or indicate a desire to inspect or examine evidence. . . .

Morra, supra, 467 So.2d at 743–44. *See also D.R.S. v. State*, 912 So. 2d 1280, 1281 (Fla. Dist. Ct. App. 2005) (reversing delinquency finding based on allegations of possession of marijuana where State did not offer marijuana into evidence; noting that, "State did not specifically ask to reopen its case in order to place the marijuana in evidence").

QUESTIONS

1. In *G.E.G.*, what charges were brought against the defendant? Because police testify that they searched defendant and found a plastic bag containing a "brown substance" in defendant's pocket, what else must be shown to make testimony at trial about a plastic bag containing a brown substance relevant and admissible?

2. As to the plastic bag containing the brown substance, what is the "material moment"?

3. According to the reasoning of the majority in *G.E.G.*, would the prosecution be required to offer into evidence items that were allegedly stolen in a prosecution for possession of stolen property? If you believe the answer is "yes" to the preceding question, would the state be required to offer into evidence an item like an automobile? *Cf. Holle v. State*, 337 A.2d 163, 166–67 (Md. 1975) (holding in prosecution involving stolen marked currency that it is not always necessary for tangible evidence to be physically offered at trial).

4. In *G.E.G.*, who has the better of the argument, the majority or the dissent? *See generally Holle v. State*, 337 A.2d 163, 166–67 (Md. 1975) (not always necessary to produce, as distinguished from prove, the object of a crime); Annot., *Proof of identity of person or thing where object, specimen, or part is taken from a human body, as a basis for admission of testimony or report of expert or officer based on such object, specimen, or part*, 21 A.L.R.2D 1216, 1235–36 (1952) (Annotation examines case law requiring a chain of custody to be established after analysis and until introduction at trial and concludes that "it is nowise customary to produce in court a specimen or part upon which an analysis has been made.").

PROBLEMS

Problem 3-18. Assume that the defendant is charged with murder in Florida and raises the defense of mistaken identity. In an effort to prove that defendant was actually the murderer, the state has DNA testing done on drops of blood found at the crime scene. At trial the state establishes a chain of custody for the drops of blood from the crime scene up until laboratory analysis. Based upon DNA testing, the state's expert testifies that the defendant's DNA and the DNA found at the crime scene "match."

If the trial takes place in Florida, must the state offer into evidence whatever remains from the crime scene blood drops?

Problem 3-19. Assume that a local church has discovered money missing from its safe. After each church service the money collected is counted and placed in the safe. In the last two weeks less money was in the safe on Monday morning than when counted immediately after being collected. Fearing that someone was stealing money from the safe before it could be deposited, church officials met with local police and arranged to have the money "marked" with an infrared light after counting but before being put in the safe. Defendant was arrested outside of the church the following Sunday evening. He had $712 in his pocket. At the police station the money was put under a fluorescent light and all of the bills showed the infrared marking.

Defendant was charged with stealing $712. At his trial, testimony from police officers establish all the above-listed facts. None of the marked money is brought into court or offered into evidence. Defendant is convicted and appeals. What result? *See Holle v. State*, 337 A.2d 163, 166–67 (Md. 1975).

Chapter 4

PROBLEMS OF ADMISSIBILITY AND USE ASSOCIATED WITH SPECIFIC SCIENTIFIC TECHNIQUES

A. INTRODUCTION

The preceding chapters examined evidentiary rules that govern the admissibility of scientific evidence, and the reason those rules were developed. The primary focus of chapters 1–3 is the "big picture" — that is, evidentiary rules and admissibility concerns applicable to scientific evidence generally, regardless of which scientific principle, technique, or procedure is employed. In this chapter the focus narrows to evidence derived from a select group of scientific techniques and procedures — the polygraph, hypnosis, "truth serums," and DNA.

The primary reason for devoting a chapter to a select group of scientific techniques is because some techniques have become so associated with the investigation and prosecution of criminal activity that no course addressing criminal evidence would be complete without examining admissibility issues related to those techniques. In addition, since it would be virtually impossible to examine all, or even a significant minority, of the scientific techniques that have been used in criminal cases, the alternative is to focus upon techniques that are commonly used, that illustrate issues commonly encountered with scientific evidence, or that have generated a significant amount of interest or controversy.

Admissibility questions for the techniques examined in this chapter have, for the most part, been addressed by the courts. For example, the polygraph machine and hypnosis have been available for most of the twentieth century, and expert opinion based upon these techniques has been repeatedly offered in criminal cases. Accordingly, it is possible to examine precedent and identify whether, or under what conditions, evidence based upon these techniques will be accepted in a particular jurisdiction.

Nonetheless, when considering the admissibility of evidence based upon "older" techniques with a judicial track record, two caveats should be noted. First, science is not static. Older techniques that were initially rejected may become acceptable if they are refined and subjected to additional testing. Recognizing this possibility, the Tenth Circuit commented "without a doubt matters of factual proof must keep pace with developing scientific standards." *United States v. Wainwright*, 413 F.2d 796, 803 (10th Cir. 1969). The polygraph machine, which is examined in the next section, is an example of a scientific device that has matured and increased in reliability over time.

Second, the effect of *Daubert v. Merrell Dow Pharmaceuticals, Inc.*, 509 U.S. 579 (1993), must be considered. The *Daubert* test has replaced the *Frye* "general acceptance" test in federal courts as the test used to assess the admissibility of expert testimony. Similarly, in the decade of the 1990s the *Daubert* test, or a "*Daubert*-like" "reliability" test, replaced the *Frye* standard in a majority of state jurisdictions.[1] Unlike

---

[1] The *Frye* and *Daubert* tests are examined in Chapter 2, *supra.*

the *Frye* test — which is only applied to novel scientific evidence — all federal courts (and many state courts) apply the *Daubert* test to all Rule 702 expert testimony. As a result of *Daubert's* general applicability some older, routinely employed techniques may have to be *shown* to be reliable. Simply because a technique has been used by the legal system for years, and has achieved the status of "generally accepted," may not be enough to gain admissibility under *Daubert*, or a *Daubert*-like reliability test. With every technique examined, the effects of maturation and the *Daubert* standard should be kept in mind.

B.   TRUTH-SEEKING DEVICES

[1]   A Scientific Device that Detects Truth: The Polygraph

The polygraph ("lie detector") is an example of an older technique that has undergone reconsideration due to the combined effects of maturation and *Daubert*. The materials that follow examine how the polygraph has matured since the 1920s, and how this maturation, coupled with the rejection of *Frye*, has altered the way some courts deal with the admissibility of expert opinion based upon the polygraph.

[a]   The Modern Polygraph Machine: Theory and Technique

In 1995 the District Court for the District of New Mexico was asked to admit polygraph evidence in a tax evasion trial. *United States v. Galbreth*, 908 F. Supp. 877, 878 (D.N.M. 1995). In making its ruling, the court examined the modern polygraph instrument, the theory underlying the polygraph technique (including questioning and scoring techniques), and challenges that are made to the technique's reliability. *Id.* at 883–90. In *Galbreth* the district court found that the polygraph passed the *Daubert* test and that the results of the test were admissible. *Id.* at 895–96. The charges against Galbreth were dismissed at the conclusion of the government's case, however, so no polygraph testimony was presented at trial, and no appeal was taken. *Id.* at 878 n.1. Nonetheless, the court's observations about the modern polygraph machine, the theory underlying the polygraph technique, questioning techniques, and criticisms of the polygraph are pertinent to an understanding of the materials that follow.

UNITED STATES v. GALBRETH
908 F. Supp. 877 (D.N.M. 1995)

VASQUEZ, DISTRICT JUDGE.

. . . .

IV. THE POLYGRAPH INSTRUMENT

. . . [T]he modern polygraph machine is a sophisticated instrument capable of continuously and simultaneously measuring and recording various autonomic responses.[2] [9] It measures respiration at two points on the body; on the upper chest, . . . and on the abdomen. The polygraph machine also measures skin conductance or

---

[2] [n.9] Autonomic responses are responses that one is generally unable to control, such as blood pressure and the sweating of the palms. The autonomic nervous system controls how the body adjusts to changes in conditions. Because the autonomic nervous system is relatively impervious to voluntary control, it is very

galvanic skin response. Electrodes attached to the subject's fingertip or palm of the hand indicate changes in the sweat gland activity in those areas. In addition, the polygraph measures increases in blood pressure and changes in the heart rate. This measurement, known as the cardiovascular measurement, is obtained by placing a standard blood pressure cuff on the subject's upper arm. Finally, the polygraph may also measure, by means of a *plethysmograph*, blood supply changes in the skin which occur as blood vessels in the skin of the finger constrict due to stimulation.

Even opponents of the polygraph technique readily concede that a quality polygraph machine can accurately measure and record these responses.

V. SCIENTIFIC THEORY UNDERLYING THE POLYGRAPH TECHNIQUE

. . . [T]he underlying scientific theory upon which the modern polygraph technique is based is derived from the notion that if a person is threatened or concerned about a stimulus or question, such as a question addressing the matter under investigation, that this concern will express itself in terms of measurable physiological reactions which the subject is unable to inhibit and which can be recorded on a polygraph instrument. A skilled examiner can then review the charts and determine whether the subject is practicing deception or is being truthful in answering the questions concerning the matter under investigation.

A. [Probable Lie] Control Question Technique

[T]he most widely used and accepted polygraph technique is the control question technique. This particular technique was designed to overcome the weaknesses of the relevant-irrelevant technique.[3] [10] The control question technique involves basically two types of questions; control or comparison questions and relevant questions that specifically concern the investigation at hand. The control questions are designed to arouse the concern of the innocent subject and it is expected that the subject will react more strongly to them than to the relevant questions. The control questions deal with acts that are similar to the issue of the investigation. However, they are more general, cover long periods of time in the life history of the subject, and are deliberately vague. During the pretest review of the control questions, the examiner carefully introduces the control questions to the subject so that in answering these questions on the test the subject is likely to be deceptive or uncertain as to the truthfulness of his answers. In this way, the innocent subject will react more strongly to the control questions than to

---

difficult for the subject of a polygraph exam to manipulate the outcome of a polygraph test.

[3] [n.10] [T]he relevant-irrelevant technique is premised on the notion that attempts to deceive will produce elevated physiological reactions to crime-relevant questions and that those reactions will differ qualitatively or quantitatively from reactions associated with truthful answers to irrelevant or relevant questions. Thus, if a person shows stronger physiological reactions to a relevant question, such as, "did you shoot X?" than to the irrelevant question, such as, "is your first name Y?" the examiner assumes that deception to the question about shooting provoked involuntary autonomic processes that caused the observed difference in the reactions. On the other hand, if the reactions to the two types of questions are not observably different, the examiner assumes that the subject did not lie when he answered the relevant question. However, a variety of factors other than deception might cause a subject to react more strongly to questions about crimes of which they are accused than to innocuous questions. Those reactions are indistinguishable from reactions that occur as a result of deception. Primarily for this reason, the technique has major deficiencies and the results of this technique are subject to a great deal of error, particularly false positive error. Although the relevant-irrelevant technique may accurately detect all the guilty subjects, it erroneously labels almost all the innocent subjects as deceptive.

the relevant questions. On the other hand, guilty subjects who answer the relevant questions deceptively will be more concerned about being detected in that deception than with the control questions. Thus, it is the comparative reactivity rather than the absolute reactivity to a particular question that forms the basis for determining truth or deception.

[T]he pretest interview is absolutely critical to the accuracy of the polygraph results. First, as explained above, the examiner must introduce the control questions in such a way as to carefully manipulate the subject such that his answer is deceptive or likely to be deceptive. Second, if the examiner does not review the questions in advance, they will come as a surprise and may elicit the same kinds of reactions that would arise if the subject is being deceptive. Under such circumstances it is impossible to distinguish between the two potential causes. Third, if a question is asked for the first time on the test, the subject may have to analyze the meaning of the question in order to formulate an answer. This process of cognitive appraisal can cause substantial reactions which may be indistinguishable from a reaction caused by deception. Fourth, there may be terms in the question that are ambiguous which if not clarified during the pretest interview may cause a reaction indistinguishable from a reaction caused by deception. It is extremely important that all of these potential problems by eliminated in advance of the test, otherwise the task of determining whether the subject's reactions are produced by deception or by some other factor is impossible.

The specific control question technique described above is known as the probable lie control question technique. The drawbacks of this technique are that it demands considerable manipulation of the subject, it can be very invasive and is cumbersome to use.

B. Directed Lie Control Question Technique

Another type of control question technique . . . is the directed lie control question technique. This is a refined version of the probable lie technique. . . . [T]here is no fundamental difference in the underlying scientific theories upon which the two tests are based. However, the directed lie test is more simplistic and straightforward to administer and is less intrusive than the probable lie technique.

The directed lie test includes questions to which the subject is instructed to lie. These directed lie questions are introduced after the administration of a number test during which the subject chooses a number and is then instructed to lie about the number chosen. The examiner tells the subject that the number test enables the examiner to determine the subject's characteristic response patterns when lying and when answering truthfully. The examiner then explains that the directed lie questions will ensure that the subject will be correctly classified as truthful or deceptive on the subsequent polygraph test. It is the expectation that the examiner sets that she can detect when the subject is practicing deception that causes the guilty person to be more concerned with the relevant questions than with the directed lie questions. As he answers the relevant questions, which are the questions that have put him in great jeopardy he will think to himself "oh, the examiner knows what my pattern looks like when I'm lying because she can see it on those questions to which she told me to lie and she's going to see that this is the same pattern and I am going to be in big trouble." On the other hand, the innocent subject's concern is focused on the directed lie questions and the subject often thinks very hard to make sure he has something in mind when he answers those questions falsely so that it produces an enhanced reaction.

As with the probable lie control question technique, it is the differential reactivity of physiological responses to the control and relevant questions respectively that enables the examiner to determine truth or deception. . . .

VI. LABORATORY AND FIELD STUDIES

. . . .

Laboratory and field studies have been conducted to test the scientific hypothesis underlying the probable lie control question technique. . . . [H]undreds of studies have been conducted and reported in the literature. Those of which are high quality studies number in the many dozens. On the whole, these high quality studies support the hypothesis underlying the control question technique. They indicate a slight difference in false positive as opposed to false negative errors. The error rate for the former is 10% and for the latter is 5%. Some of the methodologically weaker studies indicate a false positive error rate of 30–40%. Nonetheless, even the methodologically weaker studies indicate results in the predicted direction.

. . . .

. . . [Laboratory] studies have produced accuracy rates in excess of 90%. In this way, the laboratory tests tend to confirm with a very high degree of accuracy the underlying hypothesis of the polygraph technique. Specifically, the accuracy rate for detecting guilty subjects is approximately 95% and for detecting innocent subjects is approximately 90%. That is, there are slightly more false-positive errors than false-negative errors. Thus, when a person passes the test, the examiner has higher confidence in the accuracy of the result than if the person fails the test.

VII. SCORING TECHNIQUES

. . . [T]he earliest method for evaluating polygraph results was called the "global" method. This method continues to be used by some examiners. It is comprised of the examiner's overall impression of the charts plus other factors, including the examiner's "clinical impressions" of the subject during the pretest interview and examination. Thus, the examiner considers both the subject's demeanor as well as the physiological reactions recorded on the machine. The obvious drawback of this method is its subjectivity.

By contrast, the numerical method of evaluating polygraph results, introduced in 1960, helps to ensure a rigorous, semi-objective evaluation of the physiological information contained in the charts, thereby safeguarding against examiner bias. This method involves a systematic procedure of applying a set of scoring rules, writing down numbers and adding them up in order to reach a conclusion. The examiner inspects the relative size of reactions to the relevant and control questions for each of the physiological measurements and assigns a number to that comparison reflecting the amount of observed difference. If there is no noticeable difference, the examiner assigns a zero. If there is a noticeable difference, the examiner assigns a one, two or three depending on the degree of the difference. The examiner assigns a positive number if the reaction to the comparison question is greater than the reaction to the relevant question and a negative number if the reaction to the relevant question is greater. This method is the most widely used method and has been the subject of the most research.

Another method of quantitatively evaluating test results is by computer. The . . . computer scoring method . . . works by . . . using a standard computer program. The examiner simply runs the program and the computer makes tens of thousands of calculations within five to ten seconds. This scoring method is completely objective.

VIII. CHALLENGES TO THE POLYGRAPH TECHNIQUE

[S]everal challenges have been raised to the polygraph technique. . . .

A. Examiner Incompetence and Lack of Integrity

The competence of the examiner is crucial in arriving at reliable polygraph results. This is so because it is the examiner who determines the suitability of the subject for testing, formulates proper test questions, establishes the necessary rapport with the subject, stimulates the subject to react, and interprets the charts.

[O]ne of the major problems with polygraph evidence is the "sorry state of training for polygraph examiners." The American Psychological Association has . . . commented on the need for improved training of polygraph examiners noting that those administering polygraph tests often have limited training and expertise in psychology and in the interpretation of psychophysiological measures. . . .

Another challenge raised with respect to examiners is the ability of a polygraph examiner to manipulate the subject and the examination in such a way as to produce a desired result. [T]his is certainly a valid concern. . . .

B. Examiner Shopping

Another challenge raised is the problem of "examiner shopping." If enough tests are conducted, it is argued that a psychophysiological habituation to the relevant test questions or perhaps even chance may result in a guilty subject eventually passing the test. Thus, if only the final test, the one passed, is presented to the jury the result would be misleading. . . .

C. Certain Personality Types Can Defeat the Test

. . . [S]ome opponents of the polygraph technique have suggested that people with certain personality types, such as psychopaths, can beat the polygraph test. However, this hypothesis has been invalidated. . . . [S]everal studies [have been conducted] to determine whether psychopaths can beat the polygraph. [These] studies have indicated very clearly that psychopaths cannot beat a properly conducted test. . . .

D. Use of Drugs as a Countermeasure

Another frequently raised challenge to the polygraph technique . . . is that drugs may be used to defeat the test. It has never been demonstrated that drugs can be an effective countermeasure against the control question technique. [T]his is so because the control question technique requires differential reactivity between the control and the relevant questions and there is simply no drug that can selectively reduce the reaction to relevant questions while leaving the control questions unaffected. At worst, in theory the effect of the drug may make the result of the test inconclusive. However, . . . the studies indicate that the use of drugs does not interfere with the ability of the control question technique to accurately detect deception.

E. Friendly Polygrapher Hypothesis

A theory that has been posited against the admission of polygraph results by defendants is the "friendly polygrapher" theory. This theory, warmly embraced by many courts, was first suggested by Dr. Martin Orne, a psychiatrist-psychologist in Pennsylvania. Dr. Orne hypothesized that if a person takes a polygraph test on a confidential basis where the formal understanding is that if he passes the test it may be helpful to him, but if he fails the test it falls under attorney-client privilege and cannot be disclosed, such person unconcerned with failing the test would be able to beat the test. [T]his hypothesis has never been validated and, in fact, the only research bearing on it does not support it. [A]ll the accumulated experience of conducting confidential tests for defense attorneys shows that people who are guilty fail the test. Furthermore, . . . on a theoretical basis, Dr. Orne's hypothesis does not make sense because in order for it to work, the subject would still have to react to the control questions. If the subject is not worried or concerned about the outcome of the test, then the subject would not react anymore to the control questions than to the relevant questions.

F. Physical Countermeasures

[A]nother challenge raised to the polygraph technique is that a person can beat the test by engaging in physical countermeasures. [R]esearch indicates that if a person is given specific training by an expert on how to employ certain kinds of subtle, unobservable maneuvers, if the test process is explained to them, and if they practice the techniques while being observed by an expert, a substantial proportion of them, possibly up to 50%, can produce an erroneous result on the polygraph test in a mock crime situation. Such maneuvers include unobtrusively biting the tongue lightly to produce reactions on control questions, tensing muscles in the legs to produce reactions on control questions, or engaging in mental arithmetic by subtracting backwards by sevens implicitly on control questions. Under such circumstances . . . experts cannot even detect that the subject has been engaging in countermeasures. However, . . . merely providing a subject with extensive information about countermeasures does not enable a subject to effectively use them. Without specialized hands-on training from a sophisticated expert, attempts to defeat the test by engaging in countermeasures are invariably unsuccessful.

QUESTIONS

1. According to the district court in *Galbreth*, what physical responses does the modern polygraph measure? If there is little or no dispute that these body responses can be accurately measured and recorded, why is it that there is opposition to the admissibility of expert testimony based upon the polygraph?

2. What is the scientific theory that underlies the polygraph?

3. What is the difference between the "relevant-irrelevant technique" and the "control question technique" (CQT)?

4. What are the six criticisms or challenges that have been made to the reliability of polygraph tests cited in *Galbreth, supra* ?

5. What reasons, *apart from reliability concerns*, might there be to limit the use of the polygraph in criminal trials, or to exclude it from criminal trials altogether?

6. What does the *Galbreth* case report as error rates for polygraph exams using the probable lie control question technique?

[b]   The Admissibility of Polygraph Evidence

The polygraph has been the subject of judicial scrutiny since it was first declared inadmissible in *Frye v. United States*, 293 F. 1013 (1923). Occasionally, polygraph evidence has been admitted in both federal and state court trials. Nonetheless, it probably would be fair to describe most courts as hostile to the receipt of polygraph evidence. It should be noted, however, that the polygraph is used in a variety of settings other than in the guilt or innocence phase of criminal trials, and courts have not been nearly as averse to admitting the results of polygraph tests in these other settings. *See* 1 SCIENTIFIC EVIDENCE § 8.04, at 439, 472–75 (4th ed. 2007) (some courts that exclude polygraph evidence at trial admitted it in suppression hearings, sentencing hearings, and motions for new trial proceedings, among other settings); James R. McCall, *Misconceptions and Reevaluation-Polygraph Admissibility After* Rock *and* Daubert, 1996 U. ILL. L. REV. 363, 378 ("Outside of jury or bench trials, the admission of unstipulated polygraph test results in various types of judicial and nonjudicial hearings has become relatively commonplace.").

The primary focus of this section is the use of polygraph evidence in criminal trials. Three distinct admissibility approaches can be gleaned from the cases. First, the traditional and majority view taken by state courts is *per se inadmissibility* based upon the perception that the polygraph is unreliable and prejudicial. Second, *discretionary admissibility* is the approach taken by some state courts and most federal circuits. Under this approach questions of reliability and prejudice (and, hence, admissibility) are left to the sound *discretion* of the trial court. Third, some courts that routinely exclude polygraph evidence as unreliable will admit it if the parties *stipulate* to its admissibility and (typically) if certain procedural safeguards are followed. Each of these three approaches to the admissibility of polygraph evidence will be examined below. *See generally United States v. Scheffer*, 523 U.S. 303, 311–12 (1998) (discussing different approaches to admissibility of polygraph evidence taken in federal and state courts); *State v. Porter*, 698 A.2d 739, 773–77 (Conn. 1997) (same).

[i]   Per se exclusion

Overview. Per se exclusion is the majority view in state courts and, at one time, was the majority view in federal courts. The United States Supreme Court's decision in *Daubert v. Merrell Pharmaceuticals, Inc.* has, however, altered the way many federal courts assess the admissibility of polygraph evidence, and it would not be accurate to place most federal circuits in the per se exclusion camp post-*Daubert. Daubert's* impact in this area will be examined in the section that follows.

Courts that follow the per se exclusion approach express two concerns. First, there is concern over polygraph reliability. Per se exclusion jurisdictions view the polygraph as unreliable because of "the lack of empirical validation, the numerous uncontrollable factors involved in the examination, the subjective nature of the deception determination, and the absence of adequate standards for assessing the qualifications of examiners." 1 SCIENTIFIC EVIDENCE § 8.04[b], at 449–50 (4th ed. 2007). A Louisiana Appeals Court summarized its concerns about polygraph reliability stating,

[P]olygraph results, generally, are inadmissible in criminal trials. This hard line is understandable, as there, simply, is no consensus that polygraph evidence is reliable. In fact, the scientific community remains extremely polarized about polygraph techniques' reliability.

Furthermore, assuming that "the basic debate about the reliability of polygraph technology itself were resolved, however, there would still be controversy over the efficacy of countermeasures, or deliberately adopted strategies that a polygraph examinee can employ to provoke physiological responses that will obscure accurate readings and thus 'fool' the polygraph machine and examiner."

. . . .

While the machine appears to produce straightforward and reliable physiological measurements, the examiner's method of questioning, as well as his or her interpretation of the results, may not. Therein lies an acute danger. "[T]he individual skill and training of examiners . . . affects the reliability of a polygraph. Clearly, 'bells do not go off' at the moment someone tells a lie. Rather, the polygraph's ability to discern the truth rests in the skill of examiners. 'Although an adequate instrument is essential for proper testing, the role of the examiner in interviewing the examinee, designing test questions, and evaluating and interpreting the polygram is much more critical to an accurate diagnosis than is the mechanical function of the polygraph itself.' Thus, the skill of examiners fundamentally affects the ultimate reliability of the test."

Evans v. Deridder Municipal Fire & Police Civil Service Board, 789 So. 2d 752, 757 (La. Ct. App. 2001), *rev'd on other grounds*, 815 So. 2d 61 (La. 2002). *See also State v. Blank*, 955 So. 2d 90, 131 (La. 2007) ("This Court has long adhered to the view that lie detector or polygraph test results are inadmissible for any purpose at the trial of guilt or innocence in criminal cases. . . . The principle reasons such evidence is inadmissible are its lack of probative value, insufficient scientific reliability, and its potential for an unduly prejudicial effect on lay jurors.").

Second, — *even if reliable* — per se exclusion has been justified because of the danger that polygraph evidence would intrude too much into the jury's traditional function of assessing witness credibility. Additionally, courts adopting the per se exclusion rule have voiced concern over the possibility that the jury might overvalue polygraph evidence, and that the trial might degenerate into a trial of the polygraph instead of a trial of the accused. *See* 1 SCIENTIFIC EVIDENCE § 8.04[b], at 450–51 (4th ed. 2007).

For example, in upholding its per se exclusion rule, the Connecticut Supreme Court stated:

[W]e assume that polygraph evidence may have enough demonstrated validity to pass the *Daubert* threshold for admissibility.

We conclude, however, that admission of the polygraph test would be highly detrimental to the operation of Connecticut courts, both procedurally and substantively. Moreover, . . . the probative value of polygraph evidence is very low, even if it satisfies *Daubert.* Accordingly, we also conclude that any limited evidentiary value that polygraph evidence does have is substantially outweighed by its prejudicial effects. We therefore reaffirm our per se rule against the use of polygraph evidence in Connecticut courts.

. . . .

The most significant, and fundamental, problem with allowing polygraph evidence in court is that it would invade the fact-finding province of the jury. The jury has traditionally been the sole arbiter of witness credibility. . . .

*   *   *

Furthermore, admission of polygraph test results at trial would likely produce regular, and immensely time consuming, "battles of the experts."

State v. Porter, 698 A.2d 739, 768–69, 771 (Conn. 1997). *See also, State v. Shively*, 999 P.2d 952, 958 (Kan. 2000) ("Kansas appellate courts . . . disallow polygraph evidence in trials absent a stipulation of the parties. In so doing, we have noted the unreliability of the results in accurately measuring truthfulness and deceit, and that such evidence invades the unique role of the jury as truthfinder. We have continued to voice concern about the weight a jury might place on such evidence.").

States following the per se exclusion approach generally do not allow evidence that a person was willing to take, took, or refused to take a polygraph test. *See, e.g., State v. Blank*, 955 So. 2d 90, 131 (La. 2007) ("the rule excluding polygraph evidence 'also operates to prevent any reference during trial to the fact that a witness has taken a polygraph examination with respect to the subject matter of his testimony.' "); *Bennett v. Commonwealth*, 511 S.E.2d 439, 443–44 (Va. App. 1999) ("Because a polygraph examination has no proper evidentiary use, neither the results of a polygraph nor evidence of a person's willingness or unwillingness to submit to a polygraph is admissible in court.").

<u>*The Constitutionality of Per Se Exclusion*</u> : United States v. Scheffer. Sometimes a defendant in a criminal case will have taken and passed a polygraph test, or will have access to another person's test results that tend to exculpate the accused and incriminate the person who took the polygraph test. Sometimes in a per se exclusion jurisdiction the question arises whether the defendant's right to present a defense includes the right to offer such favorable polygraph test results.

In *United States v. Scheffer*, 523 U.S. 303 (1998), Scheffer, a member of the air force, was facing court martial on charges of using methamphetamine, among other things. Scheffer testified at his court martial and, relying on an "innocent ingestion" theory, denied that he *knowingly* used drugs. After being impeached during cross-examination, Scheffer tried to bolster his credibility by introducing evidence of a polygraph test he took that indicated "no deception" when he denied using drugs since joining the Air Force. His polygraph evidence was excluded based upon the per se rule of exclusion found in Military Rule of Evidence 707 (Rule 707). *Id.* at 306. Scheffer was convicted, and his case eventually made its way to the United States Supreme Court, where he argued that the per se rule of exclusion contained in Rule 707 was unconstitutional because it deprived him of his constitutional right to present a defense. *Id.* at 305.

Justice Thomas, writing for the majority, first acknowledged that defendants have a *qualified* right to present a defense.

A defendant's right to present relevant evidence is not unlimited, but rather is subject to reasonable restrictions. A defendant's interest in presenting such evidence may thus "bow to accommodate other *legitimate interests* in the criminal process." As a result, state and federal rulemakers have broad latitude under the Constitution to establish rules excluding evidence from criminal trials. Such rules do not abridge the accused's right to present a defense so long as they are not "arbitrary" or "disproportionate to the purposes they are designed to serve." Moreover, we have found the exclusion of evidence to be unconstitutionally arbitrary or disproportionate only where it has infringed upon a weighty interest of the accused.

Id. at 308 (emphasis added).

Justice Thomas found that state and federal governments "have a *legitimate interest* in ensuring that *reliable evidence* is presented to the trier of fact in a criminal trial," *Id.* at 309 (emphasis added), and then turned to the question of polygraph reliability.

> [T]here is simply no consensus that polygraph evidence is reliable. To this day, the scientific community remains extremely polarized about the reliability of polygraph techniques. Some studies have concluded that polygraph tests overall are accurate and reliable. See, *e.g.*, S. Abrams, The Complete Polygraph Handbook 190–191 (1989) (reporting the overall accuracy rate from laboratory studies involving the common "control question technique" polygraph to be "in the range of 87 percent"). Others have found that polygraph tests assess truthfulness significantly less accurately — that scientific field studies suggest the accuracy rate of the "control question technique" polygraph is "little better than could be obtained by the toss of a coin," that is, 50 percent.

Id. at 309–10. Justice Thomas noted that the lack of scientific consensus was reflected in court decisions. He observed that some federal and state courts have found polygraph evidence to be both reliable and admissible, while other courts have reached the opposite conclusion. He also noted that "[n]othing in *Daubert* foreclosed, as a constitutional matter, *per se* exclusionary rules for certain types of expert or scientific evidence." *Id.* at 311, n. 7.

Justice Thomas concluded his review of polygraph reliability and the defendant's right to present a defense by upholding the per se rule of exclusion found in Rule 707.

> The approach taken by the President in adopting Rule 707 — excluding polygraph evidence in all military trials — is a rational and proportional means of advancing the legitimate interest in barring all unreliable evidence. Although the degree of reliability of polygraph evidence may depend upon a variety of identifiable factors, there is simply no way to know in a particular case whether a polygraph examiner's conclusion is accurate, because certain doubts and uncertainties plague even the best polygraph exams. Individual jurisdictions therefore may reasonably reach differing conclusions as to whether polygraph evidence should be admitted. We cannot say, then, that presented with such widespread uncertainty, the President acted arbitrarily or disproportionately in promulgating a *per se* rule excluding all polygraph evidence.

Id. at 312.

Accordingly, *Scheffer* walks a fine line on reliability and per se exclusion; it upholds the constitutionality of per se exclusion rules while permitting state and federal courts to admit polygraph evidence if they reach different conclusions as to reliability. *Compare United States v. Benavidez-Benavidez*, 217 F.3d 720, 724 n. 2 (9th Cir. 2000) ("Thus, although the policy discussion in *Scheffer* is valuable, *Scheffer* did not impact our holding . . . that unstipulated polygraph testimony is potentially admissible under the Federal Rules of Evidence.") *with United States v. Ruhe*, 191 F.3d 376, 388 (4th Cir. 1999) (court refuses to reconsider its per se ban citing *Scheffer, supra* , holding "the Supreme Court has . . . held that such per se bans are permissible.").

NOTES

1. ***Castillo v. Johnson.*** The Fifth Circuit relied on *Scheffer, supra* , in holding that the exclusion of a capital murder defendant's polygraph evidence pursuant to a Texas per se exclusion rule did not violate the defendant's right to present a defense.

> Castillo first argues that the trial court violated his federal constitutional rights by excluding testimony relating to the results of a polygraph examination of Rudolfo Rodriguez, an early suspect in the Champion murder, at Castillo's trial. He urges that Texas' mechanistic rule of per se polygraph exclusion violates his right to due process and the fundamental right to present a defense. Castillo insists that he sought to introduce at trial evidence of a failed polygraph examination that inculpated Rodriguez. Castillo contends that such evidence was crucial to his defense as it directly contradicts the State's theory of the case.

> . . . .

> The shortcomings of Castillo's argument are . . . underscored by the Supreme Court's recent holding regarding the admission of polygraph evidence and federal constitutional rights. . . . The Supreme Court recently held in *[United States v.] Scheffer*, that a per se rule against admission of polygraph evidence did not violate the Fifth or Sixth Amendment rights of the accused to present a defense. . . .

> Under Texas law, "results of a polygraph test are inadmissible *for all purposes.*" *Nethery v. State*, 692 S.W.2d 686, 700 (Tex. Crim. App. 1985), (emphasis in original). The trial court excluded the evidence Castillo sought to introduce on this basis. As the *Scheffer* Court indicates, states are entitled to such latitude in establishing evidentiary rules. Castillo's claim challenging the exclusion of evidence based on state law thus does not afford a basis for federal habeas corpus relief. Federal habeas corpus review is limited to errors of constitutional dimension, and federal courts do not sit to review the mere admissibility of evidence under state law. As the *Scheffer* Court noted, "state and federal governments unquestionably have a legitimate interest in ensuring that reliable evidence is presented to the trier of fact in a criminal trial. Indeed, the exclusion of unreliable evidence is a principal objective of many evidentiary rules." We hold that the trial court's exclusion of polygraph evidence based on state law did not violate Castillo's federal constitutional rights."

Castillo v. Johnson, 141 F.3d 218, 221–22 (5th Cir. 1998).

2. ***The Polygraph and*** **Frye.** As mentioned above, the per se rule of exclusion is the dominant rule in state courts. In state courts that follow *Frye*, the lack of consensus on the reliability issue (referred to in the above excerpt from the *Scheffer* case) presents a serious (if not insurmountable) obstacle to admissibility. In addition, *Frye* jurisdictions must contend with determining which field, or fields, must generally accept the polygraph. In its decision in the *Frye* case the D.C. Circuit looked to the fields of psychology and physiology. More recently, courts have considered such fields as polygraphy, neurology, psychiatry, and "other related disciplines." *See United States v. Alexander*, 526 F.2d 161, 164 (8th Cir. 1975). In *United States v. Galbreth*, 908 F. Supp. 877 (D.N.M. 1995), the court looked to the field of psychophysiology for general acceptance. *Id.* at 892. According to *Galbreth*, "[p]sychophysiology is the scientific

discipline that involves the study of the relationship between psychological processes and bodily reactions [and] the polygraph is the primary instrument used in the field of psychophysiology." *Id.* at 882–83.

3. *Special Circumstances.* Sometimes the fact that a person took a polygraph test is admitted under a "special circumstances" exception. When the special circumstances exception is invoked, the evidence is admitted for a narrow purpose, and the primary relevance is not related to the inherent reliability of the polygraph. For example, the fact that a person took a polygraph test could be admitted because it establishes an alibi. *United States v. Crumby*, 895 F. Supp.1354, 1356 (D.Ariz. 1995) (admissible to show defendant could not have committed a crime because he was taking a polygraph examination at the time the crime was committed). *See also United States v. Hall*, 805 F.2d 1410, 1416–17 (10th Cir. 1986) (fact that defendant failed two polygraph examinations admitted for limited purpose of explaining why detective did not conduct a more complete investigation); *United States v. Bowen*, 857 F.2d 1337, 1341 (9th Cir. 1988) ("[I]f polygraph evidence is being introduced because it was relevant that a polygraph examination was given regardless of its results, then it may be admissible.").

4. *Proceedings Other Than Trial.* Courts have not been reluctant to approve the use of the polygraph *outside* the context of the trial to determine guilt or innocence. For example, in *People v. Barbara*, 255 N.W.2d 171, 197–98 (Mich. 1977), the Michigan Supreme Court held that results of a polygraph test could be used by the court in determining whether to grant a motion for a new trial even though it could not be used in the trial itself.

Similarly, polygraph tests have been used in grand jury proceedings, *In re Grand Jury Invest.*, 791 F. Supp. 192, 194 (S.D. Ohio 1992); in determining if a defendant violated a plea agreement by giving false information, *Hentz v. Hargett*, 71 F.3d 1169, 1175 (5th Cir. 1996); *United States v. Santiago-Gonzales*, 66 F.3d 3, 6 (1st Cir. 1995); in prison disciplinary hearings, *Toussaint v. McCarthy*, 926 F.2d 800, 803 (9th Cir. 1990); in determining probable cause, *Bennett v. Grand Prairie*, 883 F.2d 400, 405–06 (5th Cir. 1989); in evidence suppression hearings, *People v. McKinney*, 357 N.W.2d 825, 828 (Mich. 1984); as a condition of probation, *Cassamassima v. State*, 657 So. 2d 906 (Fla. App. 1995) (convicted child molester must submit to polygraph examination as a condition of probation), in sentencing hearings, *State v. Jones*, 521 P.2d 978, 983 (Ariz. 1974), and as mitigating evidence in the sentencing phase of capital cases, *Paxton v. Ward*, 199 F.3d 1197, 1214–15 (10th Cir. 1999), among other uses. *See generally* 1 Scientific Evidence § 8.06, at 472–75 (4th ed. 2007).

QUESTIONS

1. According to the excerpt from *Scheffer, supra* , what accuracy rates have studies placed upon the polygraph? Why might accuracy rates vary so much?

2. If polygraph reliability were increased to the point where studies indicated relatively consistent and acceptable accuracy rates (so that reliability of the polygraph could no longer be reasonably questioned), what is the probability that a per se exclusion jurisdiction would still refuse to admit unstipulated polygraph evidence? *See State v. Shively*, 999 P.2d 952, 961 (Kan. 2000).

3. In what situations, and in what sort of proceedings, might a per se inadmissible jurisdiction admit evidence of an unstipulated polygraph examination?

PROBLEMS

Problem 4-1. Ginger Mann shot and killed her husband as he slept in the couples' bedroom early one morning. She is charged with murder. Ginger Mann claims she shot her husband in self-defense and that she is a victim of the battered woman syndrome.

No one disputes that one month prior to the shooting her husband had been accused of molesting the couples' five-year-old daughter. Further, it is not disputed that, while in custody, Ginger Mann's husband took a lie detector test that indicated that he answered truthfully when he denied molesting his daughter, and that Ginger Mann was aware of this test. Nonetheless, her husband was charged with molesting their daughter. He was out of jail on bail and awaiting trial on his molestation charge at the time of his death.

Ginger Mann testifies at her trial. She asserts that initially, after her husband was charged with molesting their daughter, she kept him away from her and their daughter, but after he convinced her of his innocence she allowed him to move back into their home. Further, she testifies that, on the night of his death, her husband admitted having molested their daughter and that she tried to call the police but he threatened to kill her and her daughter if she did. She said that after her husband fell asleep she got her pistol and, as she recalled all the past instances when he had abused her, she shot him.

In rebuttal the prosecutor is prepared to call a police detective who will testify that Ginger Mann's husband had taken a lie detector test that indicated that he did not molest his daughter, and that the defendant, Ginger Mann, knew of this test. The defendant's attorney objects to this proffer, stating that the results of lie detector tests are unreliable and inadmissible.

Assume that you are in a jurisdiction that treats polygraph evidence as "per se inadmissible." If you represent the state, what is the strongest argument for admitting the challenged testimony? *See State v. Manning*, 598 N.E.2d 25, 29 (Ohio App. 1991).

Problem 4-2. The defendant is on trial for the murder of his wife and daughter. He testifies that he and his wife and daughter took a canoe trip in the Ozark National Scenic Riverways Park. They started their canoe trip down the Upper Jacks Fork River on a Saturday morning. They floated down the river until 3:00 that afternoon and then stopped to set up camp on a gravel bar across from a swimming hole eight to ten feet deep. The family swam for a while, ate dinner, and then went for another swim. Both mother and daughter were good swimmers.

The defendant states that his wife and daughter then decided to change out of their wet swim suits, and he went to look for firewood. When he returned his wife and daughter were gone. The defendant noticed that their swimsuits were hanging on the clothes line, and he changed clothes and waited for them to return. When it started to get dark, he built up a fire in case they returned, and walked three-fourths of a mile to find help.

Other testimony showed that park rangers started searching for the women that night. The next morning the defendant's wife's body was found fully clothed three-fourths of a mile downstream from the camp, caught on a root-wad. The defendant's daughter's body was found 250 yards downstream, but her glasses were found 25 yards from the camp. Both women had several scrapes and bruises on their bodies, and both died of drowning.

A week after the murders the defendant agreed to take a polygraph examination administered by the police but did not stipulate that the results could be used at trial. The polygraph examiner concluded that the defendant did not respond truthfully to relevant questions. At trial, no mention was made that the defendant took a polygraph test; rather, a police officer who was present during the examination testified that he was present during an "interrogation" of the defendant. The police officer testified that during the "interrogation" the defendant was asked three times, in slightly different ways, whether he had killed his wife and daughter. When the defendant was asked each of the three questions, the police officer testified, the defendant would hold his breath for five to 15 seconds, reply "no," and then pant like a dog. The police officer also stated that the defendant sweated profusely during the "interrogation."

The defendant claims that the trial court erred in allowing the police officer to testify about the polygraph examination responses because the jurisdiction follows the per se rule excluding evidence of polygraph examinations. Was the testimony admissible? *See Rothgeb v. United States*, 789 F.2d 647, 650–51 (8th Cir. 1986).

[ii]   Discretionary Admission: *Daubert's* Impact Upon Per Se Exclusion

As mentioned above, at one time per se exclusion of polygraph evidence was the dominant view in both federal and state courts. After the Supreme Court issued its decision in *Daubert v. Merrell Dow Pharmaceuticals, Inc.* several federal circuits reassessed their per se exclusion rules in light of *Daubert*. Discretionary admission jurisdictions acknowledge (unlike per se exclusion jurisdictions) that the polygraph has achieved a relatively high degree of reliability, and that it would be inconsistent with *Daubert's* focus upon reliability and trial court discretion to exclude such evidence out of hand. The Fifth Circuit was the first federal circuit to abandon its per se exclusion rule after *Daubert*. It observed that,

> [t]here can be no doubt that tremendous advances have been made in polygraph instrumentation and technique in the years since *Frye*. . . . Current research indicates that, when given under controlled conditions, the polygraph technique accurately predicts truth or deception between seventy and ninety percent of the time. Remaining controversy about test accuracy is almost unanimously attributed to variations in the integrity of testing environment and the qualifications of the examiner.

United States v. Posado, 57 F.3d 428, 434 (5th Cir. 1995). *See also, United States v. Cordoba*, 104 F.3d 225, 227 (9th Cir. 1997) ("*Cordoba I*") ("[t]he per se . . . rule excluding unstipulated polygraph evidence is inconsistent with the 'flexible inquiry' assigned to the trial judge by *Daubert*.").

Abolishing the per se exclusion rule, however, does not mean that polygraph evidence will, invariably, be admitted. When the Ninth Circuit abandoned its per se exclusion rule in *United States v. Cordoba ("Cordoba I")*, *supra* , it observed:

> With this holding, we are not expressing new enthusiasm for admission of unstipulated polygraph evidence. The inherent problematic nature of such evidence remains. [P]olygraph evidence has grave potential for interfering with the deliberative process. However, these matters are for determination by the trial judge, who must not only evaluate the evidence under Rule 702, but consider admission under Rule 403. [T]hese are matters which must be left to the sound discretion of the trial court, consistent with *Daubert* standards.

Id. at 228.

After abolishing their per se exclusion rule in *Cordoba I*, the Ninth Circuit returned Cordoba's case to the trial court to determine the admissibility of the polygraph evidence offered at Cordoba's trial. The trial judge held a *Daubert* hearing, examined the Rule 403 issues, and held the polygraph evidence inadmissible. *United States v. Cordoba*, 991 F. Supp. 1199, 1207–08 (C.D. Cal. 1998) ("*Cordoba II*"). The case that follows (referred to as *Cordoba III* by the Ninth Circuit) is the Ninth Circuit's review of the district court's rulings under the "discretionary admission" approach.

UNITED STATES v. CORDOBA ("CORDOBA III")
194 F.3d 1053 (9th Cir. 1999)

BRUNETTI, CIRCUIT JUDGE:

The issue of the admissibility of polygraph evidence has a long and controversial history in the courts. In the wake of the Supreme Court's decision in *Daubert v. Merrell Dow Pharmaceuticals, Inc.*, 509 U.S. 579 (1993), the question of whether polygraph evidence is reliable enough to be admissible in a trial has once again come into issue. On this, the second appeal in this matter, we must decide whether the district court abused its discretion in finding, after holding an evidentiary hearing, the results of an unstipulated polygraph examination inadmissible under both Federal Rules of Evidence 702 and 403. . . .

I.

Appellant Frank Javier Cordoba was arrested while driving a van which was found to contain 300 kilograms of cocaine and was charged with possession of cocaine with intent to distribute. At trial, Cordoba presented a defense of lack of knowledge. To bolster his credibility, Cordoba sought to admit the results of an unstipulated polygraph exam which supported his contention that he was not aware that the van he was driving contained cocaine. The district court excluded the evidence, finding that Ninth Circuit precedent made polygraph evidence per se inadmissible. The jury returned a guilty verdict.

On appeal, we reversed, holding that *Daubert*, 509 U.S. 579, overruled the " 'bright line rule' excluding all unstipulated polygraph evidence offered in civil or criminal trials." *United States v. Cordoba*, 104 F.3d 225, 227 (9th Cir.1996) ("*Cordoba I*"). We found that, under *Daubert*, a district court was required to make a particularized factual inquiry into the scientific validity of the proffered polygraph evidence under Rule 702 as well as weigh the probative value of the evidence against its prejudicial effect under Rule 403. *Id.* at 227–28. We remanded with instructions to the district court to "conduct individualized inquires under Rules 702 and 403 to determine whether Cordoba's unstipulated polygraph evidence is admissible." *Id.* at 230. We provided that "[i]f the district court conclude[d] that the unstipulated polygraph evidence [was] inadmissible under Rule 702 or 403, the district court [could] reinstate the judgment of conviction." *Id.*

Upon remand, the district court held a two day evidentiary hearing, received extensive briefing, and reviewed numerous affidavits and reports supplied by the parties. After considering this evidence, the district court found that the polygraph evidence was inadmissible under both Rules 702 and 403. *United States v. Cordoba*, 991

F. Supp. 1199 (C.D.Cal.1998) ("*Cordoba II*"). The district court found that polygraph evidence generally did not meet the reliability standard of *Daubert* and that, due to defects in the test given to Cordoba, "the questionable reliability of the Defendant's polygraph evidence undermines its relevance, and the potential prejudice substantially outweighs its probative value." *Id.* at 1208. The district court reinstated Cordoba's sentence and this appeal followed.

II.

We review a district court's decision to admit or exclude expert testimony for abuse of discretion. *General Electric Co. v. Joiner*, 522 U.S. 136 (1997). . . . "[I]t is very much a matter of discretion with the [trial] court whether to receive or exclude the evidence" and appellate courts should "not reverse in such a case unless the ruling is manifestly erroneous." *Joiner*, [522 U.S. at 142].

A. Admissibility of Polygraph Evidence Under Rule 702

1. Rule 702 Analysis

. . . .

The [*Daubert*] Court enumerated a series of general observations designed to aid trial judges in making initial admissibility determinations. In ascertaining whether proposed testimony is scientific knowledge, trial judges first must determine if the underlying theory or technique is based on a testable scientific hypothesis. The second element considers whether others in the scientific community have critiqued the proposed concept and whether such critiques have been published in peer-review journals. Third, the trial judge should consider the known or potential error rate. Fourth, courts are to consider whether standards to control the technique's operation exist. Lastly, the trial court is to appraise whether the relevant scientific community accepts the technique. The Court instructed that the presence or absence of any single *Daubert* criterion is not to be dispositive in determining the admissibility or inadmissibility of the evidence. To make the determination of whether the testimony would assist the trier of fact, the trial judge must evaluate the relevancy of the evidence.

2. Scientific Premises of the Polygraph

. . . A polygraph instrument consists of an assortment of instrumentalities that measure the following physiological functions: blood volume, heart rate, respiratory activity, and galvanic skin resistance (palmar sweating). After an examiner attaches the instruments to the subject, any changes in the physiological measurements are transmitted to pens which record them on moving chart paper.

The general hypothesis upon which the theory of polygraphy rests is the notion that when a person lies, the human aversion to lying causes a physiological response which in turn causes an involuntary physiological reaction. A lie is believed to precipitate an alteration in the rate and pattern of breathing, blood pressure, rate and volume of blood flow, and the moisture on the skin. Truthful responses do not precipitate these same reactions.

In the Controlled Question Technique ("CQT"), the test method used most often by polygraph examiners, an examiner asks three different types of questions: neutral, control and relevant. The neutral questions are asked to ascertain the subject's chart readings when answering honestly. The control questions, which are formulated by the examiner and the subject, are designed to be stress inducing. The control questions deal with issues similar to the incident in question, but which are more general. They are worded in such a vague manner that it is difficult for anyone to simply answer "no." The examiner asks the questions in a way that leads the subject to believe that an affirmative answer will affect the examiner's perception of the subject. The control questions are designed to elicit an untruthful answer.[4] [4]

Finally, the relevant, or incident-specific, questions deal specifically with the crime of which the subject has been accused.[5] [5]

The theoretical underpinning of the CQT is that a person who answers relevant questions truthfully will be more concerned about the broader control questions which they answer falsely. The truthful subject, therefore, will have greater physiological responses to the control questions than to the relevant questions. A deceptive subject, by contrast, will have stronger physical responses to the relevant questions. Thus, the examiner determines whether the subject is answering the relevant questions truthfully by comparing the subject's physiological changes to the relevant and control questions.

3. District Court Findings

After holding an evidentiary hearing . . . the district court made the following findings:

> The reliability of polygraph testing fundamentally depends on the reliability of the protocol followed during the examination. After considering the evidence and briefing, the court concludes the proposed polygraph evidence is not admissible under Fed. R. Evid. 702. Although capable of testing and subject to peer review, no reliable error rate conclusions are available for real-life polygraph testing. Additionally, there is no general acceptance in the scientific community for the courtroom fact-determinative use proposed here. Finally, there are no reliable and accepted standards controlling polygraphy. Without such standards, there is no way to ensure proper protocol, or measure the reliability of a polygraph examination. Without such standards, the proposed polygraph evidence is inadmissible because it is not based on reliable 'scientific knowledge.'

Cordoba II, 991 F. Supp. at 1201–02.

Cordoba claims that the district court abused its discretion in finding that polygraph evidence is inadmissible under Rule 702. He avers that the district court misapplied *Daubert* and that its conclusions rested on clearly erroneous findings of fact. Cordoba's

---

[4] [n.4] The control questions are usually related to the type of crime that the subject has been accused. Following are the control questions used during Cordoba's exam: "Before 1995, did you ever lie to anyone to benefit yourself?"; and,"Before 1995, did you ever do anything against the law?"

[5] [n.5] Cordoba was asked the following relevant questions: "Did you put boxes or anything containing cocaine in the van?"; "Did you know that any of the bags, boxes, or anything in the van contained cocaine?"; "In January 1995, did you agree to posses, distribute, or transport cocaine in the van?"; and, "Before your arrest this year did you know Robert Rodriguez was involved in drug trafficking?"

argument that the district court applied an erroneous legal standard is premised on the proposition that once a district court finds that a theory is capable of and has been tested and has been subject to peer review, the evidence is admissible as a matter of law under *Daubert*. This argument is without merit. Although the Supreme Court indicated in *Daubert* that these two factors were important to the determination of whether expert scientific testimony is admissible, the Court also stated that "[t]he inquiry envisioned by Rule 702 is, we emphasize, a flexible one." *Daubert*, 509 U.S. at 594. Because the district court, in making its determination, focused on "the reliability of [the polygraph] as ensured by the scientific validity of its underlying principles," *id.* at 594–95 n. 12, it applied the correct legal standard in evaluating the evidence.

Cordoba also avers that the record contains no competent evidence to support the district court's factual findings. We reject this argument as we find the record contains ample evidence to support each of the district court's factual findings.

a. Testing of the Scientific Hypothesis

The district court found that the scientific hypotheses underlying the polygraph have been subject to both field and laboratory testing. The district court noted that the reliability of both tests have been called into question by critics. Despite these criticisms, the district court found that the polygraph met this requirement. The record supports these findings.

b. Peer Review and Publication

The district court found that "[h]undreds of articles about polygraph have been published, many in peer-reviewed journals. The polygraph appears to meet the peer review factor of the *Daubert* analysis." The district court did not err in making this finding.

c. Known or Potential Error Rate

The district court found, based on the testimony of Cordoba's expert witness, Dr. Raskin, that studies indicate that a properly conducted, high quality CQT examination can have a 5–10% error rate. The district court determined, however, that the results of these tests were not transferable to real-life exams. Due to the number of variables which can impact the reliability of a particular exam including variations in the particular polygraph examiners' skills, the subjectiveness of the examiner, the susceptibility of the subject to the pressure of the exam, the ability of the subject to control the results of the exam by employing countermeasures, and the setting of the exam, the district court found that "the error rate of real-life polygraph tests is not known and is not particularly capable of analyzing."

Although Dr. Raskin testified at the evidentiary hearing that the results of field and laboratory studies establish a low error rate for real-life exams, the district court was not required to accept this testimony.[6] [6] In assessing the known error rate for polygraph exams, the district court properly relied on a study prepared by The United States Congressional Office of Technology Assessment ("OTA") in 1983 in which the

---

[6] [n.6] The district court noted that Dr. Raskin is one of the leading experts in the field of conducting scientific research on the polygraph technique.

OTA evaluated all then available studies on the reliability of polygraph tests. The OTA noted in its concluding comment:

> A major reason why scientific debate over polygraph validity yields conflicting conclusions is that the validity of such a complex procedure is difficult to assess and may vary widely from one application to another. The accuracy obtained in one situation or research study may not generalize to different situations or to different types of persons being tested.

. . . .

The reasonableness of the district court's conclusion that there is no known error rate for real-life polygraph exams is bolstered by the Supreme Court's recent assessment of the literature on the validity of polygraph exams [in] *United States v. Scheffer.* . . .

The district court did not err in basing its conclusions in part on the same learned treatises upon which the Supreme Court relied in *Scheffer* or in reaching the same conclusion as the Supreme Court.

d. General Acceptance in the Scientific Community

To demonstrate that the polygraph technique enjoys widespread acceptance in the relevant scientific community, Cordoba submitted to the district court three surveys which purport to show that two-thirds of the members of the Society of Psychophysiological Research view polygraph exams as reliable. The district court found that this evidence did not show that polygraph exams met the general acceptance test. The district court first noted that the surveys only sampled a small segment of the relevant scientific community. [S] ee . . . *United States v. Pitner*, 969 F. Supp. 1246, 1251 (W.D. Wash. 1997) (noting that polygraph expert admitted on cross examination that the relevant scientific community for the purpose of determining the general acceptance of polygraph to some degree includes psychiatrists, neuroscientists, and medical doctors). Second, and more importantly, the district court found that the survey results did not indicate that the individuals polled viewed the results of polygraph exams to be sufficiently reliable to be used as evidence in a trial. The surveys only show that sixty-two percent of the respondents indicated that they viewed the polygraph as "a useful diagnostic tool when considered with other available information."

In finding that the relevant scientific community did not generally accept polygraph exams as being sufficiently reliable to be used as evidence in a trial, the district court also relied on a scholarly treatise which found that "[s]cientific opinion about the validity of polygraph techniques is extremely polarized." *Id.* at 1205 (citing 1 D. Faigman, et al., Modern Scientific Evidence § 14-1.4, at 565). . . .

e. Controlling Standards

In response to a request from the district court, the parties submitted information regarding the existence of controlling standards for a CQT polygraph exam. To determine if adequate standards existed, the district court reviewed the following sources:

> the American Association of Police Polygraphists List of Generalized Terminology and Procedure ("AAPP List"), the American Polygraph Association Code of Ethics Standards and Principles of Practice ("APA Code"), the Federal Bureau of Investigations' Manual chapter on conducting polygraph exa mina-

tions ("FBI" Manual), the California Association of Polygraph Examiners Standards and Principles of Practice ("CAPE Standards"), New Mexico Evidence Code § 11-707, and Department of Defense Polygraph Institute ("DoDPI") Regulations.

Cordoba II, 991 F. Supp. at 1205.

The district court found that there are no standards which control the procedures used in the polygraph industry and that without such standards a court can not adequately evaluate the reliability of a particular polygraph exam. A review of the relevant literature supports the district court's findings. For example, under the DoDPI regulations, if a subject fails one question, the subject cannot pass the test. Dr. Raskin testified, however, that he does not follow the DoDPI's procedure in this regard. Under Dr. Raskin's procedure, a subject could pass an exam despite the fact that he failed one question. Similarly, although results from a polygraph are inadmissible under the New Mexico Rules of Evidence unless the exam is recorded, Dr. Raskin testified that in his view a recording is not required to ensure that a test is unbiased and that results from an unrecorded exam should be admissible. Dr. Raskin opined that a recording was only necessary if there were indicia that an exam was not properly conducted.

Cordoba's claim that there are standards which control the industry is significantly undercut by Dr. Raskin's evaluation at the evidentiary hearing of the exam given to Cordoba. The government offered persuasive evidence that Cordoba's exam was defective in that it deviated from the industry "standards" in several significant ways. Based on this evidence, the district court found:

> Defendant's test contained many factors which would be considered defects under various versions of the industry "standards." The duration and substance of the pre-test interview was not preserved. No tape or video was made of the pre-test interview or the polygraph exam. The examiner didn't calibrate the machine at the prison test site. Although the examiner asked four supposedly "relevant questions," only one was really relevant: two involved undisputed facts, one was marginally relevant, and the wording of the truly relevant question was arguably too ambiguous to be helpful. The examiner found deception in the marginally-relevant question's answer (while Dr. Raskin did not), but the examiner scored it as truthful after obtaining Defendant's explanation for the answer. The examiner's report was filled with errors and defects: the report was drafted before the test, it did not include a fingertip test, according to Dr. Raskin it lacked attention to detail, it omitted Defendant's response to whether he was under drugs or medication, it misstated the machine used, and it says the stimulation test was done after the first test when it was actually done first. Although there was movement on a response, the examiner scored the response. The examiner did not record a significant breath. The examiner did not ask if Defendant had proper sleep before the exam. The examiner acknowledged the exam was conducted in a poor setting with many distractions.

Cordoba II, 991 F. Supp. at 1207.

Despite the occurrence of all these deviations from the purportedly controlling standards, Dr. Raskin testified that the exam in question was sufficiently reliable to be admitted at trial. He acknowledged many of the irregularities delineated above but found that they were not significant. The district court found that Dr. Raskin's approval of this obviously defective test illustrated that the industry did not have sufficient controlling standards to allow for the admission of polygraph evidence into court. The district court concluded "[i]f pro-polygraph's best expert declines to find any fault with an obviously faulty examination, that is strong evidence that there are insufficient controlling standards." *Id.* As the record supports the district court's factual findings regarding Cordoba's exam, the district court did not err in concluding that the polygraph industry lacks controlling standards.

In view of the evidence offered by the government at the evidentiary hearing regarding the lack of a known error rate for real life polygraph exams, the controversy in the relevant scientific community regarding the validity of the theoretical basis for the polygraph, and the paucity of controlling standards, the district court did not abuse its discretion in finding that polygraph evidence is inadmissible under Rule 702 and *Daubert.*

B. Rule 403 Analysis

If polygraph evidence is found to generally meet the requirements of Rule 702, a district court may nevertheless exclude the results of a particular polygraph exam if it finds that the probative value of the evidence is "substantially outweighed by the danger of unfair prejudice, confusion of the issues, or misleading the jury." Fed. R. Evid. 403.

As discussed above, the district court found that the polygraph test administered to Cordoba was defective in several significant respects. It noted that the admission of Cordoba's defective polygraph evidence ran a substantial risk of unfairly prejudicing the jury because it was being offered to bolster Cordoba's credibility. It concluded that the risks associated with admitting evidence of a flawed exam greatly outweighed the probative value of such evidence and that therefore the evidence was inadmissible pursuant to Rule 403. The district court did not abuse its discretion in so finding. *See United States v. Kwong,* 69 F.3d 663, 668 (2d Cir.1995) (upholding a district court's determination that the results of a defective polygraph exam were inadmissible under Rule 403).

III.

The district court conducted a thorough and careful evaluation of all the proffered evidence regarding the reliability of polygraph evidence. On the basis of this evidence, the district court did not abuse its discretion in finding that "polygraph evidence does not presently satisfy the *Daubert* standards" and that Cordoba's polygraph evidence was therefore inadmissible under Rule 702. The district court also did not abuse its discretion in finding that the probative value of Cordoba's flawed polygraph exam did not outweigh the substantial risk of unfair prejudice that might result from admitting such evidence.

Affirmed.

QUESTIONS

1. In *Cordoba III* did the Ninth Circuit find polygraph evidence to be unreliable generally, or did it simply find that the polygraph evidence proffered by Cordoba was unreliable?

2. What, if anything could a litigant do in a subsequent case in the Ninth Circuit to enhance the prospect of admitting polygraph evidence? Put another way, what, specifically, was wrong with Cordoba's polygraph evidence, and were these problems with the polygraph technique in general, or with the way the specific polygraph test was administered to Cordoba?

In *Cordoba III* the Ninth Circuit found that the trial court had not abused discretion in finding that Cordoba's polygraph evidence failed *Daubert's* Rule 702 reliability standard. Note, however, that even if the evidence had been found reliable, Rule 403 still remained as a significant admissibility hurdle. The focal point of the next case, also out of the Ninth Circuit, is upon Rule 403 as an *independent reason* for excluding evidence based upon the polygraph. As you read through *Benavidez-Benavidez* ask yourself how the discretionary admissibility approach differs from the per se inadmissibility approach.

UNITED STATES v. BENAVIDEZ-BENAVIDEZ
217 F.3d 720 (9th Cir. 2000)

THOMAS, CIRCUIT JUDGE:

This appeal presents the question whether the district court properly excluded unstipulated polygraph evidence. We conclude that it did and affirm the judgment of conviction.

I.

Juan A. Benavidez-Benavidez ("Benavidez") was arrested . . . as he tried to enter the United States in a van at the Lukeville, Arizona port of entry. . . . When questioned by customs agents at the primary inspection area . . . [h]e denied that he was bringing anything into the country. An agent knocked on the side of the van and thought it sounded dense and solid. Upon opening the rear of the van, the agent noticed a sweet perfume or air freshener type smell. After further investigation, the agents discovered seventy-six bundles of marijuana, weighing approximately 169 pounds, in the doors and walls of the van.

A customs agent interviewed Benavidez. The interview was not tape recorded and the substance is a matter of dispute. The customs agent testified that Benavidez [initially denied knowledge of marijuana being in the van, but] . . . eventually admitted that he was aware that the marijuana was in the van and confessed that he had agreed to transport the marijuana to Phoenix for a third party in exchange for receiving ownership of the van. The defendant denied confessing the crime to the customs agent. He also denied telling the agent that he was to receive ownership of the van as compensation.

Prior to trial, Benavidez took a polygraph examination and sought to introduce the results of the examination at trial, specifically the measured responses of his negative answers to the following questions:

- Did you admit to Agent Cherry that you were knowingly transporting marijuana?

- Did you tell Agent Cherry that you knew there was marijuana in the van when you crossed the border?

- Did you know there was marijuana in the van when you crossed the border into the United States?

In response, pursuant to *Daubert v. Merrell Dow Pharmaceuticals, Inc.*, 509 U.S. 579,(1993), the district court held a hearing to consider the admissibility of the proffered evidence. At the hearing, . . . Dr. Charles Honts testified on behalf of Benavidez. The hearing took place on October 19–20, 1998.

Voluminous exhibits were offered at the hearing. Most of these exhibits consisted of scientific papers pertaining to such issues as the reliability of polygraphs, the use of countermeasures by persons taking polygraphs, and the relative merits of various techniques for both administering and studying polygraphs. The district court issued its ruling on December 18, 1998 and held the evidence inadmissible on three different grounds: Fed. R. Evid. 403, 702, and 704(b). Benavidez challenges each of these rulings. . . .

We review a district court's decision to exclude expert testimony for abuse of discretion. Under the abuse of discretion standard, we cannot reverse unless we have a definite and firm conviction that the district court committed a clear error of judgment.

II.

The question of admissibility of unstipulated polygraph evidence has had a long history in this circuit and around the country. . . .

Prior to 1986, evidence of the results of a polygraph examination was potentially admissible. However, we afforded district courts "wide discretion in refusing to admit the testimony." *United States v. Marshall*, 526 F.2d 1349, 1360 (9th Cir.1975). . . .

In 1986, we assessed the state of the law and polygraph science and adopted a *per se* rule that unstipulated polygraph evidence "was inadmissible as technical or scientific evidence under Fed. R. Evid. 702 because it 'does not assist the trier of fact to understand the evidence or to determine a fact in issue.'" *Brown v. Darcy*, 783 F.2d 1389, 1395 (9th Cir.1986). The rationale in *Brown* was founded in large part on "the questionable accuracy of polygraph examinations" and the lack of consensus on their reliability. *Id.*

. . . .

Following *Daubert*, [we held] . . . in *United States v. Cordoba*, 104 F.3d 225, 228 (9th Cir.1997) ("*Cordoba I*") . . . that *Daubert* had implicitly overruled *Brown*. . . . On remand, the district court excluded the evidence after conducting a *Daubert* hearing on the basis of both Fed. R. Evid. 702 and 403. *See United States v. Cordoba*, 991 F. Supp. 1199 (C.D.Cal.1998) ("*Cordoba II*"). We affirmed the district court in *United States v. Cordoba*, 194 F.3d 1053 (9th Cir.1999) ("*Cordoba III*"). After *Cordoba III*, we held that Rule 704(b) prohibits the admission of polygraph evidence offered for the purpose of proving the defendant's mental state. *See United States v. Campos*, 217 F.3d 707 (9th Cir.2000).

Thus, with the exception of exclusion of evidence under rule 704(b), our *Cordoba* decisions returned our jurisprudence to its pre-*Brown* state, affording the district court "wide discretion in refusing to admit the testimony." *Marshall*, 526 F.2d at 1360. In doing so, we did not mandate a new seriatim formalistic inquiry, requiring the district courts to conduct a *Daubert* hearing in each case. Indeed, to do so would have run contrary to our settled law that allows rejection *either* on the basis of foundation *or* prejudice. After *Cordoba I*, district courts are free to reject the admission of polygraph evidence on the basis of any applicable rule of evidence without analyzing all other potential bases of exclusion. Thus, for example, an exclusion based solely on Rule 403 affords us "ample authority for affirming the trial court." *Cordoba III*, 194 F.3d at 1064 (Goodwin, J., concurring). In short, although a district court may conduct a Rule 702, 403 or 704(b) examination, it is not required to undertake each of those inquiries before denying admission of the evidence. Of course, a court may choose to do so to provide alternative reasons for excluding the evidence, as the district court did in *Cordoba II*, and nothing in this opinion precludes counsel from objecting on alternative grounds.

III.

Our historical exegesis is prompted by defendant's claim of error in this case. In considering the admissibility of the defendant's proffered evidence, the district court held a searching and thorough hearing. At the conclusion, the court held that the *Daubert* factors had been met, except for "the requisite general acceptance in the relevant scientific community." Thus, the court denied admission of the evidence pursuant to Fed. R. Evid. 702.

The court also concluded that admission of the polygraph evidence would be unduly prejudicial and that its probative value was outweighed by the danger of unfair prejudice, citing the special risk that the jury might give excessive weight to the polygrapher's conclusions. Thus, the court held that the polygraph evidence was also inadmissible under Fed. R. Evid. 403. Additionally, the court made a passing reference to the evidence's inadmissibility under Rule 704(b).[7] [3]

Benavidez asserts that the district court had no choice but to admit the evidence because the defendant "won" the *Daubert* hearing and that the district court could not reject the evidence simply because it had not achieved acceptance in the scientific community. Despite defendant's argument that the district court's Rule 702 analysis was erroneous because it relied solely on a single *Daubert* factor, his argument is without merit.

The district court's exclusion of the polygraph evidence under Fed. R. Evid. 403 is, standing alone, sufficient. As we noted in discussing this very issue a quarter-century ago, "a trial court will rarely abuse its discretion by refusing to admit the evidence, even for a limited purpose and under limited conditions." *Marshall*, 526 F.2d at 1360. After careful examination of the record, we conclude that the district court did not do so in this instance. Certainly, as able defense counsel urged at oral argument, the courts should allow science to evolve in the courtroom. However, this evolution will not come at the expense of trial court discretion in assessing whether probative value exceeds the prejudicial effect on the jury.

Having found exclusion of the evidence proper under Rule 403, we need not reach the issue of whether the district court also properly excluded the evidence under Rules 702 or 704(b). . . . The reason for this is that, unlike other evidentiary exclusions which may bar evidence for one purpose only to have it admitted for another purpose, exclusion under Rule 403 is absolute. Once the probative value of a piece of evidence is

---

[7] [n.3] Only one aspect of the polygraph examination in this case was potentially impacted by Rule 704(b): "Did you know there was marijuana in the van when you crossed the border into the United States?" Thus, application of *Campos* would not have settled the admissibility of all the tendered polygraph evidence in this case.

found to be substantially outweighed by the danger of unfair prejudice, there is no other evidentiary rule that can operate to make that same evidence admissible. In this way, Rule 403 can be viewed as a gateway, albeit a very wide one, through which all evidence must pass prior to admission at trial. Although a trial court may choose to analyze evidence admissibility by assessing the effect of other rules of evidence first, it is under no compulsion to do so. It is equally acceptable to perform a Rule 403 analysis prior to undertaking any other evidentiary inquiry. In a case such as this one, where evidence has been ruled inadmissible under Rule 403, and the district court has not abused its discretion in so doing, there is no need to proceed with further evidentiary analysis.

Affirmed.

NOTES

1. ***Increased Reliability.*** The polygraph instrument and the examination technique have increased in reliability in the years since *Frye*, and since 1986 in particular. *See United States v. Posado*, 57 F.3d 428, 434 (5th Cir. 1995) ("There can be no doubt that tremendous advances have been made in polygraph instrumentation and technique in the years since *Frye*."); *United States v. Crumby*, 895 F. Supp. 1354, 1361 (D. Ariz. 1995) ("The science of polygraphy has made significant progress over the past decade."); William J. Yankee, *The Current Status of Research in Forensic Psychophysiology and Its Application in the Detection of Deception*, 40 J. FORENSIC SCI. 63 (1995) ("The period between 1986 and the present has been one of unparalleled advances in the psychophysiological detection of deception testing procedures and processes."). Advances in the testing technique or process refer to refined test questions and polygrapher training. *See, e.g., United States v. Galbreth*, 908 F. Supp. 877, 884–85, 888–90 (D.N.M. 1995). Advances in instrumentation refer to more sensitive equipment to detect physical reactions and the use of computers to evaluate test results. William J. Yankee, *supra*, 40 J. FORENSIC SCI. 63, 63–65 (1995).

In a dissenting opinion he authored in *Scheffer*, *supra*, Justice Stevens acknowledged the possibility of polygraph error in a particular case, but presented a relatively positive view of polygraph reliability.

> There are a host of studies that place the reliability of polygraph tests at 85% to 90%. While critics of the polygraph argue that accuracy is much lower, even the studies cited by the critics place polygraph accuracy at 70%. Moreover, to the extent that the polygraph errs, studies have repeatedly shown that the polygraph is more likely to find innocent people guilty than vice versa. Thus, exculpatory polygraphs-like the one in this case-are likely to be more reliable than inculpatory ones.

> Of course, within the broad category of lie detector evidence, there may be a wide variation in both the validity and the relevance of particular test results. Questions about the examiner's integrity, independence, choice of questions, or training in the detection of deliberate attempts to provoke misleading physiological responses may justify exclusion of specific evidence. But such questions are properly addressed in adversary proceedings; they fall far short of justifying a blanket exclusion of this type of expert testimony.

United States v. Scheffer, 523 U.S. 303, 333 (1998) (Stevens, J. dissenting).

2. *The Polygraph and* Daubert: *Shifting from Rule 702 to Rule 403.* The discretionary admissibility approach spawned by *Daubert* does not appear to have significantly increased how often polygraph evidence is admitted at trial. *See generally* 1 SCIENTIFIC EVIDENCE § 8.04[d], at 460–63 (4th ed. 2007). In part, this is because under the discretionary admissibility approach a trial court must contend with the same two issues that provide the rationale for the per se exclusion rule — reliability and Rule 403. In *Posado, supra* , the Fifth Circuit stated that "we do not now hold that polygraph examinations are scientifically valid or that they will always assist the trier of fact, in this or any other case. We merely remove the obstacle of the per se rule against admissibility. . . ." *Posado, supra*, 57 F.3d at 434. Nonetheless, discretionary admissibility does force a trial court to confront the enhanced reliability achieved by the polygraph since *Frye*, and leaves the door open for admissibility if reliability can be demonstrated in the case before the court.

(A) Reliability Under Daubert. Two cases that found polygraph evidence to be both reliable and admissible are *United States v. Crumby*, 895 F. Supp. 1354 (D.Ariz. 1995), and *United States v. Galbreth*, 908 F. Supp. 1365 (D. New Mexico 1995). Other cases are not inconsistent with *Crumby* and *Galbreth* insofar as they do not see Fed. R. Evid. 702's reliability requirement as the major hurdle in admitting evidence based upon a polygraph examination. *See, e.g., United States v. Gilliard*, 133 F.3d 809, 813 (11th Cir. 1998) (government concedes that the probable lie control question technique "if properly utilized, has been recognized in the scientific community as being 'good science.' "); *United States v. Posado*, 57 F.3d 428, 433, 435 (5th Cir. 1995) (a per se rule is not viable after *Daubert*; court assumes without deciding that polygraph may satisfy requirements of Rule 702); *United States v. Dominguez*, 902 F. Supp. 737, 739 (S.D. Tex. 1995) (court assumes polygraph reliable); *United States v. Lech*, 895 F. Supp. 582, 585 (S.D.N.Y. 1995) (court assumes polygraph results are admissible under Rule 702); *State v. Porter*, 698 A.2d 739, 769 (Conn. 1997) ("[W]e assume that polygraph evidence may have enough demonstrated validity to pass the *Daubert* threshold for admissibility").

On the other hand, opinions from other courts are consistent with *Cordoba III* in finding polygraph evidence to fail the reliability prong of *Daubert. See e.g., United States v. Orians*, 9 F. Supp. 2d 1168, 1174 (D. Ariz. 1998) (court finds four of five *Daubert* factors militate against admissibility; only peer review and publication favors admission).

(B) Rule 403. Note, however, that a finding of reliability under Fed. R. Evid. 702 does not mean automatic admissibility; the effects of Fed. R. Evid. 403 must also be taken into consideration. Several courts that have examined polygraph admissibility under the discretionary admissibility approach after *Daubert* see Rule 403 as the major obstacle to admissibility. *United States v. Lea*, 249 F.3d 632, 639 n.4 (7th Cir. 2001) (polygraph evidence admissible if Rule 403 complied with); *United States v. Waters*, 194 F.3d 926, 930 (8th Cir. 1999) (Rule 403 independent ground to exclude polygraph evidence; no need to hold a *Daubert* hearing); *United States v. Kwong*, 69 F.3d 663, 668 (2d Cir. 1995) (court assumes admissibility under Rule 702 but excludes evidence under Rule 403); *United States v. Sherlin*, 67 F.3d 1208, 1216 (6th Cir. 1995) (court excludes unilaterally obtained polygraph evidence as inadmissible under Rule 403); *United States v. Dominguez*, 902 F. Supp. 737, 739 (S.D. Tex. 1995) (court assumes Rule 702 is satisfied but finds Rule 403 a bar to admissibility because government not invited to be present at defendant's examination); *United States v. Lech*, 895 F. Supp. 582, 585 (S.D.N.Y. 1995) (court assumes polygraph results are admissible under Rule 702 but finds Rule 403 a bar to admissibility because of improper test questions); *State v. Porter*, 698 A.2d 739,

769–70 (Conn. 1997) ("We conclude . . . that admission of the polygraph test would be highly detrimental to the operation of Connecticut courts, both procedurally and substantively."). Accordingly, the key to admissibility after *Daubert* may lie in a close reading of what procedures produce "reliable" results, *and* what does and does not comport with Rule 403.

3. *Rule 403 Guidelines.* In *United States v. Dominguez*, 902 F. Supp. 737 (S.D. Tex. 1995), the defendant asked the trial court to admit the results of a polygraph examination taken by the defendant. The court assumed, without deciding, that the polygraph examination passed the reliability prong of *Daubert. Id.* at 739. Nonetheless, the court excluded the evidence because it was not "able to clear the Rule 403 hurdle." *Id.* Anticipating proffers of polygraph evidence in future cases, the court discussed what might avoid a Rule 403 "unfair prejudice" claim:

> The Court feels that there are other factors which should be considered before the Court determines that the probative value of the test is not substantially outweighed by the danger of unfair prejudice. Specifically, the Court feels the following suggestions are relevant factors:
>
> > 1) That all parties be present to observe the proceedings[, but only the examiner should be in the room with the defendant].
> >
> > 2) That there be a legal commitment irrevocably allowing the admission of the results by both sides.
> >
> > 3) That the subject commit to being examined by any polygraphic expert designated by the other side.
> >
> > 4) When more than one exam is contemplated, the choice of the first examiner take place by chance.
> >
> > 5) That the pre-test interview be allowed by all sides with all sides present.
> >
> > 6) That the post-test interview be allowed by all sides with all sides present.
> >
> > 7) That immediately prior to the test the subject be examined for any sedative or drugs in his body.
> >
> > 8) That the rules that do not admit character evidence for truthfulness be legally waived.
> >
> > 9) That no questions be permitted as to the mental state of the defendant at the time of the alleged commission of the event.
> >
> > 10) The failure of the defendant to make himself available to testify in the case should also be a consideration.
>
> The Court does not here today state that all of these factors need be met before polygraph test results be admitted. However, it is clear that this Court is confronted with a "legal Pandora's box" with the prospect of admitting future polygraph test results. Therefore, the Court will weigh and take into consideration the care and attention with which the parties adhere to these guidelines. [T]he Court feels that the previously mentioned guidelines are a necessity in mitigating the unfair prejudice that these tests can produce.

Id. at 740–41.

4. *Evidentiary Issues.*

(A) United States v. Campos: Rule 704(b) as an Independent Ground for Exclusion. In *Benavidez-Benavidez* the Ninth Circuit mentioned three potential grounds for excluding polygraph evidence; Rule 702 (*Daubert*), Rule 403, and Rule 704(b). Rule 704(b)'s exclusion becomes relevant if the defendant's polygraph evidence is "*offered for the purpose of proving the defendant's mental state.*" *Benavidez-Benavidez, supra,* 217 F.3d at 724 (emphasis added).

Rule 704(b) provides that,

> [n]o expert witness testifying with respect to the mental state or condition of a defendant in a criminal case may state an opinion or inference as to whether the defendant did or did not have the mental state or condition constituting an element if the crime charged or of a defense thereto. Such ultimate issues are matters for the trier of fact alone.

Fed. R. Evid. 704(b). In *United States v. Campos,* 217 F.3d 707 (9th Cir. 2000), an opinion issued the same day as *Benavidez-Benavidez,* the Ninth Circuit acknowledged that Rule 704(b) was "primarily targeted . . . toward limiting the use of psychiatric expert testimony" on the issue of whether a defendant was "sane or insane," *Campos, supra,* 217 F.3d at 711, but stated that it was clear that the rule's prohibition extended to "all expert witnesses" including "expert polygraph testimony on ultimate issues."

Accordingly, if a defendant is charged with an offense that requires the government to prove that the defendant acted "knowingly" and/or "intentionally," and the defendant denies having such criminal intent or knowledge, the defendant will not be able to offer the results of a polygraph test the defendant took and passed on the mens rea issue. Significantly, if polygraph evidence is precluded by operation of Rule 704(b), there will be no need to conduct a *Daubert* hearing. *See Campos, supra,* 217 F.3d at 712 ("If evidence is inadmissible by application of one evidentiary rule, there is no need for a court to determine whether it satisfies predicate evidentiary standards pertaining to another rule.").

(B) Admitting Polygraph Evidence ONLY for Corroboration or Impeachment Purposes. Some courts that fall into the discretionary admissibility camp have held that polygraph evidence is *only* admissible when offered to impeach or to corroborate the testimony of the individual who took the polygraph. *See, e.g., United States v. Gilliard,* 133 F.3d 809, 812 (11th Cir. 1998) (emphasis added) ("[A] district court can admit polygraph in two circumstances: (1) when the parties stipulate in advance as to the circumstances of the test and as to the scope of its admissibility; and (2) *to impeach or corroborate the testimony of the witness at trial.*"); *United States v. Crumby,* 895 F. Supp. 1354 (D.Ariz. 1995) ("The use of polygraph evidence at trial must be narrowly tailored to the circumstances for which it its relevant, and . . . so as to limit its potential prejudicial effect. . . . [T]he polygraph evidence may only be used to impeach or corroborate the *credibility* of the defendant [who took the test]."). Similarly, some courts that admit polygraph evidence upon stipulation of the parties hold that such evidence is admissible only to rehabilitate or corroborate. *See State v. Souel,* 372 N.E.2d 1318, 1323 (Ohio 1978) ("if such evidence is admitted the trial judge should instruct the jury that the examiner's testimony does not tend to prove or disprove any element of the crime with which a defendant is charged but at most tends only to indicate that at the time of the examination defendant was not telling the truth").

One concern voiced by courts that limit polygraph evidence to the issue of credibility is that the jury will confuse the expert's ability to determine a subject's truthfulness with the expert's ability to determine the ultimate issue in the case. *See Crumby, supra,* 895

F. Supp. at 1362–63. If only admissible for credibility purposes, the polygraph evidence would only be relevant and admissible if the person who took the polygraph testified. *But see*, Edward J. Imwinkelried & James R. McCall, *Issues Once Moot: The Evidentiary Objections to the Admission of Exculpatory Polygraph Examinations*, 32 WAKE FOREST L. REV. 1045, 1056–73 (1997) (arguing that polygraph evidence proffered by a non-testifying defendant in a criminal case ought to be considered relevant and admissible even in jurisdictions that have viewed the polygraph as only relevant on the issue of credibility.).

QUESTIONS

1. In what way is the Ninth Circuit's post-*Daubert* polygraph jurisprudence different from that found in per se exclusion jurisdictions?

2. In *Benavidez-Benavidez* did the district court abuse discretion in holding that the proposed polygraph evidence did not satisfy *Daubert*? What did the Ninth Circuit say about this aspect of the district court's ruling?

PROBLEMS

Problem 4-3. The defendant, Brent Malewski, is allegedly a James Bond "wannabe." He is charged with attempted murder of an Assistant United States Attorney. The government contends that Malewski sent the U.S. Attorney a briefcase containing a bomb. The only charge against Malewski is attempted murder. His trial takes place in federal court.

Before trial Malewski's attorney arranged for him to take a polygraph test. The test was conducted by a certified polygraph examiner that Malewski's attorney hired without notice to the government. Relevant questions posed to Malewski were:

1.   Did you conspire with anyone to send that package to the Assistant United States Attorney?

2.   Were you the one that sent that package to the Assistant United States Attorney?

Malewski answered "no" to both questions. At trial Malewski does not take the witness stand, but does offer the polygraph examiner as an expert witness. If allowed to testify, the polygraph examiner will testify to the questions asked during the test, Malewski's responses, and will offer the opinion that Malewski was truthful when he answered the questions.

Assume you are in federal court and bound by *Daubert*. If you represented the *government*, what arguments would you make to exclude the testimony of the polygraph examiner? *See United States v. Kwong*, 69 F.3d 663, 667–69 (2d Cir. 1995); *United States v. Dominguez*, 902 F. Supp. 737, 739–41 (S.D. Tex. 1995).

Problem 4-4. Assume that a man named Mo Jeter was robbed and beaten by a masked man at a local bar named the "Voodoo Lounge." Assume you represent, Don Defendant — the man authorities charge with robbery and assault in the case — and you arrange for Defendant to take a polygraph test. During the polygraph test, Defendant was asked; "Have you ever been in the Voodoo Lounge?"; "Did you beat Mo Jeter?"; and "Did you rob Mo Jeter?." The defendant answers "no" to all three questions. The polygraph examiner is prepared to testify that, in the polygrapher's opinion, the defendant answered all questions truthfully.

Assume further that you plan to offer evidence of the polygraph test at trial, and the trial takes place in a "discretionary admissibility" jurisdiction that has held that polygraph evidence, if admissible, is only relevant on the issue of credibility. The prosecution requests a *Daubert* hearing, and after the hearing, the trial court rules that the polygraph evidence you plan to offer is reliable, was properly administered, and that there are no Rule 403 obstacles to admissibility. Finally, assume that you do *not* plan to call your client as a witness to testify.

Based upon the belief that your client will *not testify* at trial the prosecution now raises evidentiary objections to your polygraph evidence in a pretrial motion. The prosecution's objections are listed below. How would you respond to each?

(A) PROSECUTION ARGUMENT: "The polygraph evidence is *irrelevant unless the defendant testifies.* Polygraph evidence is only admissible on the issue of credibility. If the defendant testifies at trial and is impeached then he may support his credibility with polygraph evidence. Since the defendant does not plan to testify, his credibility will not be an issue at trial and the polygraph evidence, therefore, is irrelevant."

How would you respond? Why is the polygraph examiner's opinion that the defendant answered truthfully relevant if the defendant does not testify?

(B) PROSECUTION ARGUMENT: "The polygraph evidence is *hearsay.* Even if relevant on an issue other than credibility, the polygraph evidence is hearsay since it contains out of court statements from a non-testifying witness who cannot be cross-examined. The defense is offering the defendant's out-of-court statements that he had never been in the Voodoo Lounge, and that did not beat or rob Mo Jeter, to prove the truth of the matter asserted."

How would you respond? Why isn't the testimony of the polygraph examiner concerning what Defendant said during the polygraph examination hearsay?

See Edward J. Imwinkelried & James R. McCall, *Issues Once Moot: The Evidentiary Objections To The Admission Of Exculpatory Polygraph Examinations,* 32 WAKE FOREST L. REV. 1045, 1056–73 (1997).

[iii]   Admissibility Pursuant to Stipulation.

Many federal and state courts hold that if the defendant and the state both agree, the results of a polygraph test may be admitted — even if the jurisdiction would otherwise exclude the polygraph evidence pursuant to a per se exclusion rule. The case that follows examines the enforceability of such agreements.

WYNN v. STATE
423 So. 2d 294 (Ala. Crim. App. 1982)

TYSON, JUDGE.

Henry Joe Wynn was indicted for robbery in the first degree. The jury found him guilty as charged, and the trial court set sentence at forty-five years in the penitentiary. A motion for a new trial was overruled and this appeal followed.

. . . .

I.

Appellant's primary argument urging reversal raises a question of first impression in Alabama: i.e., whether the results of a lie detector test taken by the accused, and not allowed in evidence, as a matter of law, are admissible upon stipulation of the parties.

Several days prior to trial, appellant, his counsel, and the assistant district attorney agreed in open court that appellant would voluntarily submit to a polygraph test, and all parties stipulated on the record that the "results," whether "favorable or unfavorable" to appellant, "would be admissible" at trial.

During the prosecution's case-in-chief, Investigator Cecil C. Holliday, polygraph examiner for the Etowah County Sheriff's department, testified for the State. He explained the operation of the polygraph machine and began to outline his qualifications for interpreting the test results, when appellant's counsel made the following objection:

"MR. HART: Your Honor — excuse me. Doc — your Honor, the Defendant, of course, is willing to stipulate the results of the test which Mr. Holliday gave.

"MR. MOORE: Your Honor, I —

"MR. HART: But our agreement, as I understand, we didn't go into this but we are merely willing to stipulate the results of the test. But as far as stipulating anything about Doc's background or past with the polygraph, we object to that as not being relevant to what our agreement was.

"THE COURT: Overruled."

After Holliday testified to his background and experience in polygraphy, he gave his opinion that polygraph examinations were "approximately 95% accurate." He then described the procedure used during his examination of appellant, and stated that appellant answered "no" to all four "relevant questions" asked during the test.[8] [1] Holliday analyzed appellant's responses to questions 1, 3, and 4 as "deception indicated." He interpreted appellant's answer to the second question to show "no deception indicated."

His pre-trial stipulation notwithstanding, appellant now maintains that the court should not have admitted any of the polygraph evidence. In the alternative, he claims that the trial judge should have disallowed the testimony of Investigator Holliday and read to the jury the following proposed "Defense Exhibit I":

STIPULATION

"In the opinion of C.C. Holliday, Polygraph Examiner for the Etowah County Sheriff's Department, based upon a polygraph test he gave, Henry Joe Wynn was not telling the truth when he denied being involved in the robbery of which he stands accused.

---

[8] [1] Holliday stated that a "relevant question" relates to the incident in dispute. The subject's responses to those inquiries are then compared to innocuous introductory questions and to "control questions," those for which the answer is known and the examinee is likely to give a truthful answer. The relevant questions were:

(1) Were you in that Quick Shop on November the 23rd, 1981?
(2) Did you take any part of that money from that Quick Shop?
(3) Did you have a gun in that Quick Shop on November the 23rd, 1981? and
(4) Did you receive any part of that money taken from that Quick Shop?

"You will be charged by me at the end of this trial as to the weight you shall give to this piece of evidence."

Thus, we must determine whether stipulated polygraph evidence is admissible at all, and, if so, whether the "results" stipulated in this case included all of the evidence later introduced.

We start with the recognition that Alabama, like most other jurisdictions,[9] [2] rejects evidence derived from lie detector tests. . . .

Although there have been numerous claims to the greater accuracy of the polygraph since the *Frye* court determined in 1923 that the testing device had not achieved general scientific acceptance, the apparatus still has its critics, and our Supreme Court aptly observed in 1980 that "[T]he lie detector test has not gained the required acceptance in the intervening fifty-seven years," *Ex parte Dolvin*, 391 So. 2d at 679.

Nevertheless, among the jurisdictions which have considered the question whether to allow polygraph evidence that has been stipulated to be admissible, there is a division of authority. The majority of courts have allowed the evidence, either upon a theory of waiver or estoppel, or upon the satisfaction of certain conditions. A sizeable minority of jurisdictions, on the other hand, have determined that polygraph evidence is inadmissible at trial under any circumstances.

After careful consideration of the reasoning underlying both positions, it is our judgment that stipulated polygraph evidence should be admitted under certain circumstances, as we will set out herein. . . .

D. The Stipulation

[C]ourts and commentators opposed to the admission of stipulated polygraph evidence question how a stipulation can alter the law so as to make unreliable evidence trustworthy and admissible.

One answer to the question is provided by the following synthesis of the cases:

> For the moment, the stipulation cases stand only for the proposition that the courts will permit the parties to take a reasonable gamble with an experimental device where all agree, but none will be forced to do so.

Comment, *The Truth About the Lie Detector in Federal Courts*, 51 Temple L.Q. 69, 90 (1978).

We believe the answer to the question derives not from the fact that the stipulation somehow imbues the evidence with reliability, but from the fact that the parties are estopped, by their stipulated waiver of the right to object, from asserting the unacceptability of the evidence. . . .

Furthermore, in view of the fact that an accused can waive certain constitutional rights, e.g., *Miranda v. Arizona*, 384 U.S. 436 (1966), and statutory guarantees, e.g., Ala. Code § 15-11-1 (preliminary hearing), we see no reason why he should be prevented from waiving the protection afforded him by the rule in question here. . . .

---

[9] [n.2] New Mexico and New York appear to be the only state court exceptions to the rule. There, the results of a lie detector test are admissible, even without a stipulation, provided the proponent of the evidence establishes the reliability of the procedure and the qualifications of the examiner. *See State v. Dorsey*, 539 P.2d 204 (1974); *People v. Daniels*, 422 N.Y.S.2d 832, 837 (N.Y. Sup. Ct. 1979).

With the . . . weaknesses of the polygraph method in mind, we hold that a pre-trial stipulation providing for a defendant's submission to the polygraph test and for subsequent admission of the results at trial is lawful and valid and should be given effect if the following conditions are met:

1. That the stipulation must be entered into by all parties — the district attorney, the defendant, and the defendant's counsel, and must be a matter of record, either by a filed written document signed by all parties, or by an oral agreement of the parties in open court.

2. That the stipulation, whether written or oral, should be preceded by the trial judge's informing the defendant of his right against self-incrimination, his right to refuse to submit to the test, and his right, under ordinary rules of evidence, to have the fact or outcome of a lie detector test excluded.

That the trial judge should not accept the stipulation unless he is satisfied that the defendant understands the foregoing rights and waives them intelligently and voluntarily. In addition, we adopt the following conditions almost verbatim from the opinion of the Arizona Supreme Court in *State v. Valdez*, 371 P.2d 894, 900–01 (1962):

3. "That notwithstanding the stipulation the admissibility of the test results is subject to the discretion of the trial judge, i.e., if the trial judge is not convinced that the examiner is qualified or that the test was conducted under proper conditions he may refuse to accept such evidence.

4. "That if the graphs [or] examiner's opinion are offered in evidence the opposing party shall have the right to cross-examine the examiner respecting:

a.   the examiner's qualifications and training;

b.   the conditions under which the test was administered;

c.   the limitations of and possibilities for error in the technique of polygraphic interrogation; and

d.   at the discretion of the trial judge, any other matter deemed pertinent to the inquiry.

5. "That if such evidence is admitted the trial judge should instruct the jury that the examiner's testimony does not tend to prove or disprove any element of the crime with which a defendant is charged but at most tends only to indicate that at the time of the examination defendant was not telling the truth. Further, the jury members should be instructed that it is for them to determine what corroborative weight and effect such testimony should be given."

In the instant case, all of the foregoing conditions were fully met. The trial judge properly advised appellant of his rights and ascertained that appellant had waived them knowingly and voluntarily. In addition, the court found that Investigator Holliday was qualified as a polygraph examiner.

. . . .

Finally, the trial court's charge to the jury covered the instruction we have outlined above. The remaining inquiry is whether the trial court erred by allowing the State to introduce the qualifications and further testimony of Investigator Holliday concerning the administration of the polygraph test.

While we believe that the stipulation in the case before us could have been more precisely drawn, . . . it is our judgment that the term "results" as used in the instant stipulation covered not only the examiner's final conclusion, but also certain background information necessary to an evaluation of his opinion.

In other words, we believe that the jury can properly assess the polygraph evidence only if they have the following necessary predicate information:

(1)   the qualifications of the examiner;

(2)   an explanation of how the polygraph works;

(3)   the conditions under which the test was conducted.

Therefore, in the absence of stipulated terms to the contrary, we hold that the "results" of a polygraph test encompass all the information given to the jury in the case before us, i.e., items (1)-(3) above.

. . . .

The possibilities of the jury's relying too heavily on the lie detector evidence . . . can, we believe, be overcome by cross-examination of the polygraph examiner and the trial court's careful instruction to the jury.

. . . .

Affirmed.

NOTES

1. *Courts That Reject Stipulated Polygraph Evidence.* Note that the stipulation of the parties, by itself, does little, if anything, to make the results of a polygraph test more reliable. *See State v. Dean*, 307 N.W.2d 628, 648–49 (Wis. 1981). Fearing that the integrity of the trial may be compromised, several jurisdictions have refused to allow the results of polygraph examinations into evidence even if the parties stipulate to the results being admissible. *See id.* at 646–48 (court discusses cases in other jurisdictions that refuse to admit stipulated polygraph evidence).

2. *Voice Stress Analysis.* Some experts theorize that a person's voice changes when that person is being deceptive, and that the emotional stress accompanying deception produces physiological responses that can be recorded and analyzed. Psychological Stress Evaluation (PSE) is the most widely known type of voice stress analysis. PSE has been referred to as a "voice lie detector." *See generally* 1 Scientific Evidence § 8.11, at 482-84 (4th ed. 2007).

PSE has not been well received by courts. *See United States v. Traficant*, 566 F. Supp. 1046 (N.D. Ohio 1983). The New Mexico Supreme Court, however, has ruled PSE admissible in a civil case at the discretion of the trial judge under the same terms that polygraph evidence is admissible in that jurisdiction. *Simon Neustadt Family Center, Inc. v. Bludworth*, 641 P.2d 531, 535 (N.M. Ct. App. 1982). The PSE test has also been used in investigations by police. *See Snead v. State*, 415 So. 2d 887, 889 (Fla. Dist. Ct. App. 1982).

QUESTIONS

1. In *Wynn, supra*, the Alabama Court of Appeals stated that stipulated evidence is admissible not because the "stipulation somehow imbues the evidence with reliability but [because] the parties are estopped, by their stipulated waiver of the right to object." *Wynn, supra*, 423 So. 2d at 299. If that is the case, have all objections been waived? For example, is the evidence admissible in the prosecution's case in chief or is it only admissible to impeach if the defendant takes the witness stand? If the stipulation concerns a non-party, have hearsay objections been waived as well as reliability objections?

2. If a defendant and the prosecuting authority agree that charges against the defendant should be dismissed if the defendant passes a polygraph test and the defendant passes the test, is the agreement enforceable? Can the prosecutor break the agreement? *See State v. Sanchell*, 216 N.W.2d 504, 508 (Neb. 1974) (agreement not enforceable since court approval for dismissal of charges was required and not obtained prior to the agreement); *Snead v. State*, 415 So. 2d 887, 889 (Fla. Dist. Ct. App. 1982) (defendant took "psychological stress test"; oral agreement with sheriff not enforceable); *cf. State v. Anderson*, 853 P.2d 135, 136 (N.M. Ct. App. 1993) (state must abide by bargain it made agreeing to allow defendant to plead *nolo contendere* and reserving the right to appeal on stipulated facts).

If, in answering questions posed by a polygraph examiner, a defendant is waiving his or her Fifth Amendment right to remain silent, is the argument for enforcing such agreements strengthened? *See People v. Stark*, 478 N.E.2d 350, 355–56 (Ill. 1985) (state must abide by agreement to dismiss charges).

PROBLEM

Problem 4-5. Assume that you are in a jurisdiction that follows a stipulation rule identical to that adopted by the Alabama Court of Appeals in *Wynn, supra*. Defendant is accused of robbery. The only evidence against him is that of the victim who identified him. However, the victim concedes that it was dark during the attack and that the entire incident was over very quickly.

Recognizing the importance of credibility in this case, the defendant's attorney contacts the prosecuting attorney and asks for a "*Wynn* stipulation" — to admit the results of a polygraph examination the defendant is willing to take. The prosecutor refuses, giving no reason for her refusal. At trial the only evidence against defendant is the shaky eyewitness testimony of the victim. The defendant testifies and denies all involvement in the crime. Defendant is convicted and appeals. After conviction he takes and passes a polygraph test.

On appeal the defendant challenges the prosecutor's refusal to stipulate to the admissibility of test results.

If stipulations are allowed in a jurisdiction, does a prosecutor have an absolute veto over whether or not to stipulate? *See McMorris v. Israel*, 643 F.2d 458, 463–66 (7th Cir. 1981); 1 Scientific Evidence § 8.05, at 467-68 (4th ed. 2007).

[2]   Scientific Techniques that Compel One to Tell The Truth

[a]   Hypnosis

[i]   Overview

Hypnosis is a controversial technique for acquiring admissible evidence. Nonetheless, the technique has been repeatedly used by law enforcement and in criminal trials. In 1987 the United States Supreme Court rendered a decision concerning the admissibility of testimony from a person who has had his or her recall "hypnotically refreshed."

This section will examine the two areas that have become the focus of most attention vis-a'-vis the admissibility of testimony generated by hypnosis: (1) the admissibility of statements made by a person while under hypnosis, and (2) the admissibility of testimony from a witness who has previously had his or her recollection "refreshed" by hypnosis.

Prior to turning to an examination of how courts have dealt with the proffer of hypnotically induced testimony, consider the following excerpt from SCIENTIFIC EVIDENCE that provides background on the history and technique involved with hypnosis. The excerpt is followed by a passage from a Second Circuit case, *Borawick v. Shay*, in which the Second Circuit summarizes the reliability concerns courts have expressed about hypnosis.

PAUL C. GIANNELLI & EDWARD J. IMWINKELRIED, 1 SCIENTIFIC EVIDENCE, §§ 12.01 & 12.02, at 619-24 (4th ed. 2007)[10]

§ 12.01. In General.

The courts rejected hypnotic evidence when first offered at trial. In 1897 the California Supreme Court wrote: "The law of the United States does not recognize hypnotism."[11] [1] The issue remained dormant until the 1970s when the use of hypnosis in criminal investigations increased dramatically. . . .

Several factors may have accounted for this trend. First, the seminal case permitting hypnotically refreshed testimony was decided in 1968. Second, by the 1960s professional organizations, such as the American Medical Association, had recognized the validity of hypnosis for therapeutic purposes. Third, hypnotic induction is easily learned: "A police officer can become a reasonably skilled hypnotist in a few hours of practice, with or without formal instruction."[12] [5] Fourth, a number of books and articles on hypnosis had advocated its use, often claiming that hypnosis provided valuable leads in many investigations: "In 77% of cases, important information was

---

[11] [n.1] *People v. Eubanks*, 117 Cal. 652, 665, 49 P. 1049, 1053 (1897). *See generally* Ladd, *Legal Aspects of Hypnotism*, 11 Yale L.J. 173 (1902).

[12] [n.5] Diamond, *Inherent Problems in the Use of Pretrial Hypnosis on a Prospective Witness*, 68 Calif. L. Rev. 313, 314 (1980).

elicited that had not been available by routine interrogation."[13] [6]

The increased use of hypnosis in criminal investigations sparked controversy. The Society for Clinical and Experimental Hypnosis and the International Society of Hypnosis passed resolutions "strongly opposing" the training of police officers as hypnotists. Moreover, some books were criticized for making "extravagant claims of the usefulness and reliability of hypnosis for criminal investigative purposes."[14] [9] Other commentators pointed out instances where hypnotically recalled information proved erroneous: "[I]n *State v. Mack* (1980), a hypnotized person remembered eating a pizza in a restaurant that did not serve pizza, seeing tattoos on someone who had none, and having been stabbed with scissors or a knife where there was no evidence that a weapon was involved."[15] [10] Finally, the lack of research was cited by some commentators: "[I]t is a provable fact that the law about forensic hypnosis developed before the science of forensic hypnosis was developed."

Chowchilla Case (1976)

The proponents of hypnosis often cite the Chowchilla, California, case in which a busload of school children and their driver were kidnapped. The kidnappers transported the children and driver 100 miles by car to a quarry and imprisoned them in a van that had been buried in the ground. They escaped sixteen hours later but could not provide meaningful leads to identify their kidnappers. Under hypnosis, the driver was able to recall all but one digit of the license number of the culprit's car.

. . . .

§ 12.02. Nature of Hypnosis.

Hypnosis has been defined in a variety of ways. One court has written: "Hypnosis is a state of heightened concentration with diminished awareness of peripheral events."[16] [17] Hypnosis has also been defined as "a special psychological state with certain physiological attributes, resembling sleep only superficially and marked by a functioning of the individual at a level of awareness other than the ordinary conscious state."[17] [18] The differences in definition reflect an underlying disagreement about the nature of hypnosis. According to the Council on Scientific Affairs of the American Medical Association, there "is no single, generally accepted theory of hypnosis, nor is there consensus about a single definition."[18] [20]

Although individuals differ in their ability to experience hypnosis, most people are able to experience some degree of hypnosis. . . .

---

[13] [n.6] Reiser & Nielson, *Investigation Hypnosis: A Developing Speciality*, 23 AM. J. CLINICAL HYNPOSIS 75, 76 (1980).

[14] [n. 9] Diamond, *supra* note 5, at 313 n.3.

[15] [n.10] Orne, Whitehouse, Dinges & Orne, *Reconstructing Memory Through Hypnosis: Forensic and Clinical Implications*, in HYPNOSIS AND MEMORY 21, 41 (H.M. Pettinati ed., 1988) (citing *State v. Mack*, 292 N.W.2d 764, 768 (Minn. 1980)).

[16] [n.17] *State v. Hurd*, 86 N.J. 525, 534, 432 A.2d 86, 90 (1981).

[17] [n.18] *"Hypnosis,"* 6 ENCYCLOPEDIA BRITANNICA 133 (15th ed. 1989) (Dr. Martin Orne & A. Gordon Hammer).

[18] [n.20] Council on Scientific Affairs, *Scientific Status of Refreshing Recollection by the Use of Hypnosis*, 253 J.A.M.A. 1918, 1919 (1985). . . .

The various techniques of hypnotic induction typically involve establishing rapport between the hypnotist and subject; inducing a passiveness that makes the subject receptive to suggestion, often by engendering eye fatigue through the focusing on a close object; and inducing a trance-like state through a series of suggestions. One widely employed procedure is hypnotic age regression, during which the subject relives an event which has occurred in the past, sometimes to the extent of behaving in a manner appropriate to the age the subject had been at the time of the event.

Another procedure that is used for refreshing memory is the "television technique." Once hypnotized, the subject is told to imagine a television screen on which he will see a documentary of the "to-be-remembered event." The subject is then directed to the event and asked to describe the documentary as he views it. The theory underlying this technique is that human memory functions much like a videotape recorder, receiving and storing all sensory impressions. Under this theory, these impressions can be retrieved through hypnosis. This theory of memory, however, has been challenged as "not consistent with research findings or with current theories of memory."[19] [25] The research indicates that neither perception nor memory functions like a videotape recorder; both are subject to numerous influences that may affect what impressions are perceived and the content of the memory retained. In particular, confabulation — the "filling in" of gaps in the memory with fantasies — is a significant problem with hypnotized subjects.

Hypnosis has been recognized as a legitimate subject of clinical and laboratory research. In addition, the American Medical Association has recognized hypnosis as an accepted medical technique for psychotherapy, treatment of psychosomatic illnesses, and amnesia. Nevertheless, distinguishing between the clinical and forensic uses of hypnosis is critical. In its forensic application, hypnosis is concerned with establishing past facts, and thus its reliability is paramount. The nonforensic uses of hypnosis are quite different. "Psychiatrists and psychologists use hypnosis in an effort to alleviate distress. . . . It can help the patient work out symptoms even though his or her beliefs about his or her illness are entirely erroneous. Dentists, obstetricians, and anesthesiologists use hypnosis entirely for the control of pain."[20] [28] Thus, hypnosis may be valid for therapeutic purposes and yet invalid for forensic purposes. As noted by one court, for hypnosis to be "therapeutically useful, it need not produce historically accurate memory."[21] [29]

The clinical and forensic uses of hypnosis also differ in another respect. If therapy hypnosis is unsuccessful, little harm may be done. If forensic hypnosis is invalid, an erroneous conviction may result.

BORAWICK v. SHAY
68 F.3d 597 (2d Cir. 1995)

. . . .

The courts have identified several problems with the reliability of hypnotically-refreshed recall. First, a person undergoing hypnosis becomes more susceptible to suggestion. The subject may be influenced by verbal and nonverbal cues, intentionally

---

[19] [n.25] *Id.* at 1920.

[20] [n.28] Levitt, *The Use of Hypnosis to "Freshen" the Memory of Witnesses or Victims*, 17 TRIAL 56, 58 (Apr. 1981).

[21] [n.29] *State v. Mack*, 292 N.W.2d 764, 768 (Minn. 1980).

or unintentionally planted by the hypnotist. This suggestibility may be enhanced by the perception that hypnosis will refresh one's memory and by a wish to please the hypnotist.

In addition, a hypnotized person may "confabulate," that is, fill in the gaps in her memory to make it comprehensible. The added details may be derived from irrelevant or unrelated facts or from pure fantasy. Like suggestibility, confabulation can occur as a result of the subject's desire to please the hypnotist by coming up with complete and coherent memories.

A third problem with hypnotically-refreshed recall is "memory hardening," a phenomenon which gives the subject enhanced confidence in the facts remembered, whether they be true or false. Even as inaccurate recollections increase, the subject's confidence is likely to remain constant or even to increase. . . . The lack of correlation between the accuracy of recall and the subject's confidence in the accuracy makes it more difficult for a jury or even an expert to judge the credibility of hypnotically-enhanced testimony and makes cross-examination difficult.

Finally, after undergoing hypnosis to refresh memory, individuals may lose the ability to assess their memory critically and be more prone to speculation than if they had relied only on normal memory recall. The subject becomes less able "to discriminate between accurate and inaccurate recollections." He or she may also experience "source amnesia," believing that a statement heard prior to hypnosis was a product of his or her own memory.

As a result of the foregoing phenomena, the "hypnotically recalled memory is apt to be a mosaic of (1) appropriate actual events, (2) entirely irrelevant actual events, (3) pure fantasy, and (4) fantasized details supplied to make a logical whole." In the worst case, someone who has undergone hypnosis might "inaccurately reconstruct the memory . . . and . . . then become convinced of the absolute accuracy of the reconstruction through memory hardening." The "constructionist" views, supported as they are in the scientific community, have considerable force. In our view, they cannot easily be discounted when the integrity of the judicial factfinding process is at stake, particularly when no study has shown that hypnosis used to refresh memory increases only accurate recall.

[ii]   The Admissibility of Statements Made While Under Hypnosis

Consider the situation where a person has witnessed a shocking event and has "blocked" all memory of that event. Under hypnosis the person "relives" the event and describes it in detail to the person who has placed the witness under hypnosis. When the person is brought out of the hypnotic trance, however, he or she still does not have a present memory of the events described under hypnosis. Should the hypnotist be allowed to testify to what the person said while hypnotized or to show a videotape containing the hypnotized person's statements?

In this regard, recall that Fed. R. Evid. 804(a) considers a declarant "unavailable" (for purposes of the "declarant unavailable" exceptions to the hearsay rule) if the declarant "testifies to a lack of memory of the subject matter of the declarant's statement." The admissibility of such statements is discussed in the case below.

GREENFIELD v. COMMONWEALTH
204 S.E.2d 414 (Va. 1974)

I'ANSON, JUSTICE.

Defendant, Ronald W. Greenfield, was tried by a jury for the murder of Mary Frances Jordan, found guilty of murder of the second degree, and his punishment was fixed at twenty years in the penitentiary. He was sentenced accordingly, and he is here on a writ of error.

Defendant contends that the trial court erred in refusing to allow a psychiatrist to state in detail the basis for his opinion that the defendant was unconscious at the time of the alleged crime. . . .

The evidence shows that on the night of November 7, 1972, the defendant and Mary Frances Jordan, the deceased, were employees of Poe's, a restaurant and beer parlor near the University of Virginia in Charlottesville. The deceased, a 21-year-old college student, was a waitress, and the defendant, 17 years of age, was a doorman at the establishment.

Defendant testified that it was raining quite heavily that night and Mary Frances offered him a ride home. About 12:30 on the morning of November 8, they left Poe's with Mary Frances using the defendant's green 'army-type' jacket to shield herself from the rain while going for her car. Defendant waited for her under an awning in front of Poe's. After Mary Frances picked him up, she drove to a parking lot near his apartment where they sat and talked for about fifteen minutes. She criticized him for his use of drugs, which he resented, but both were on friendly terms before he left the car. He had consumed heroin early in the evening and some psilocybin (a hallucinogenic drug) later that same night before leaving the restaurant. He said that as he was alighting from the car he felt a falling sensation, and the next thing he could remember was awaking and finding himself on the ground about fifteen feet away from the car on the driver's side. When he got up, he saw a person running from the scene, Mary Frances lying motionless in a pool of blood on the driver's side of the car, and his pocket knife on the car floor. He picked up the knife and put it in his pocket. He then noticed that his hand was cut and bleeding. He concluded that he must have 'freaked out' and that he had killed her. He fled from the scene and eventually got a ride to Richmond with a truck driver.

Around 12:25 a.m. a college student, who lived near the parking lot where the deceased and defendant had parked, thought he heard a woman screaming. Responding to those screams, he left his apartment, observed a man wearing an olive army coat running from the parking lot, and saw the victim lying beside the open door of her car on the driver's side. He carried her to his apartment, and called the rescue squad and the police. The victim died shortly thereafter at the University of Virginia Hospital. The cause of her death was multiple stab wounds.

During the daylight hours of November 8th, defendant was arrested at a hospital in Richmond where he had sought medical attention for his hand. After receiving his *Miranda* rights, the defendant freely and voluntarily made a statement to a Richmond detective who took it down in longhand. The statement, in part, contained an admission that he killed the deceased and that the knife taken from him by the police was the murder weapon.

. . . .

Dr. Kenneth R. Locke, a psychiatrist, testified that he had made a diagnosis of defendant's mental condition. He had two interviews with the defendant in the Charlottesville jail and put him under hypnosis for the purpose of trying to get him to recall what happened between the time he was leaving the automobile and when he found the victim had been stabbed. . . .

Dr. Locke stated that based on the interviews with the defendant (excluding what defendant had told him while under hypnosis), the information given him by members of defendant's family, a review and analysis of defendant's school and medical records, and after listening to defendant's testimony in his trial, it was his opinion that the defendant was unconscious at the time the homicide was committed. He said, however, that he had insufficient data to express an opinion on the cause of defendant's unconsciousness.

. . . .

[D]efendant's argument under his first assignment of error is that the trial court should have permitted Dr. Locke to state what he learned from the defendant while he was under hypnosis. Defendant concedes that there is no law in this Commonwealth to support his argument, but he says several other states have admitted hypnotic evidence under limited circumstances. He argues that the hypnotic evidence should have been admitted in the present case in order to fully develop his defense because there were no eyewitnesses to the crime, he had no memory of having committed the crime, and he was not identified as the man seen running from the scene of the crime.

It is true, as defendant says, that a few jurisdictions have permitted hypnotic evidence to be admitted under limited circumstances. In those jurisdictions where such evidence has been admitted, its admissibility has rested in the sound discretion of the trial judge. But even in those jurisdictions, the trial judge in exercising his discretion must weigh the probative value of defendant's statements under hypnosis as part of the expert's opinion against the risk of the jury considering it "as independent proof of the facts recited." *See People v. Modesto*, 382 P.2d 33 (Cal. 1963); *People v. Hiser*, 72 Cal. Rptr. 906 (1968); *State v. Harris*, 405 P.2d 492 (Or. 1965).

. . . .

Most experts agree that hypnotic evidence is unreliable because a person under hypnosis can manufacture or invent false statements. A person under a hypnotic trance is also subject to heightened suggestibility. McCormick, Law of Evidence § 208, at 510 (2d ed. 1972). There it is said: "Declarations made under hypnosis have been treated judicially in a manner similar to drug-induced statements. The hypnotized person is ultrasuggestible, and this manifestly endangers the reliability of his statements. The courts have recognized to some extent the usefulness of hypnosis, as an investigative technique and in diagnosis and therapy. However, they have rejected confessions induced thereby, statements made under hypnosis when offered by the subject in his own behalf, and opinion as to mental state based on hypnotic examination." (Footnotes omitted.)

In fact, we have held that "truth serum" test results were properly excluded by the trial court because they were unreliable and led to self-serving answers.

We agree with the vast majority of authorities which have concluded that hypnotic evidence, whether in the form of the subject testifying in court under hypnosis or through another's revelation of what the subject said while under a hypnotic trance, is not admissible.

. . . .

For the reasons stated, the judgment of conviction and sentence is Affirmed.

Greenfield represented himself in a federal court habeas corpus proceeding that was decided some two years later. Greenfield raised several claims that the Constitution was violated at his trial. Included were claims that his constitutional right to present a defense was violated by trial court rulings that denied him the opportunity to testify *while hypnotized* and that did not allow his expert to testify as to what Greenfield said while he was hypnotized. The court's opinion in that case follows.

GREENFIELD v. ROBINSON
413 F. Supp. 1113 (W.D. Va. 1976)

DALTON, DISTRICT JUDGE.

Ronald William Greenfield was convicted on June 16, 1973 of the second degree murder of Mary Frances Jordan by a jury in the Circuit Court of the City of Charlottesville. The conviction followed a highly publicized and somewhat bizarre trial in which Greenfield was ably represented. He was sentenced to serve twenty years in the Virginia State Penitentiary. He subsequently appealed this conviction to the Supreme Court of Virginia which affirmed it in a written opinion of the court.

He now has filed a petition for a writ of habeas corpus in this court pursuant to 28 U.S.C. § 2254. He makes the following arguments: . . . 4) The trial court should have allowed the defendant to testify while under hypnosis [and] 5) The trial court failed to allow a defense witness to testify as to matters related to him by the defendant while the defendant was under hypnosis. . . .

. . . .

FACTS

. . . .

At trial, the defendant relied on the defense of unconsciousness. He repeated that he had used heroin and a hallucinogenic drug on the night of November 7th. He also indicated that he had been sick for the entire week before that night. Dr. Kenneth R. Locke, a psychiatrist, testified that he had interviewed the defendant and attempted to diagnose his medical condition. He indicated that he had hypnotized the defendant in an effort to make him recapture his memory of events of the night in question. . . . Dr. Locke expressed his opinion that the defendant was unconscious at the time of the homicide but he did not express an opinion as to the cause of this unconsciousness.

While counsel were arguing out of the jury's presence over the admissibility of the statements made by the defendant to Dr. Locke, the defendant's attorney stated his intention to call the defendant to the stand while in a hypnotic trance and have him questioned by Dr. Locke for the purpose of extracting greater details from the defendant than he would normally be able to remember. The trial judge refused to permit this procedure. The trial judge also refused to permit Dr. Locke to state what the defendant had said to him while under hypnosis. . . . For the record, Dr. Locke revealed that while under hypnosis the defendant had recounted the series of events in a manner consistent with his previous statements, but in much greater detail. This account of the night in question included a clearer description of the conversation between Greenfield and Jordan in the church parking lot and a memory of having seen [a] man who yelled "Hey" at him [just after he became aware of Mary Frances Jordan's body] as being bigger than him and wearing a jacket that looked very much like his own. Dr. Locke also stated that the defendant told him that he chased after this man until he came to a junction where he decided for unknown reasons to give up the chase.

. . . .

. . . [T]he jury returned a second degree murder conviction and fixed the defendant's punishment at twenty years' imprisonment.

DISCUSSION OF LAW

. . . .

Defendant's . . . claims . . . concern evidentiary rulings. The trial judge refused to permit the defendant to testify while in a hypnotic trance or the defendant's expert witness to testify concerning statements the defendant made to him while in a hypnotic trance. This court must admit that these contentions present interesting and novel issues before this court. However within the scope of its review, this court cannot conclude that these rulings denied petitioner his constitutional rights.

Petitioner's argument at the State Supreme Court level was that hypnotic evidence ought to be permitted in limited situations. The defense argued that this was one such situation because there was no direct evidence concerning the night in question and the only witness who could tell the court about the incident had had a lapse of memory. Thus to permit the introduction of hypnotic evidence would merely have allowed the defendant to fully develop his defense. The defense cited *Chambers v. Mississippi*, [410 U.S. 284 (1973)] in support of their constitutional argument.

In *Chambers v. Mississippi, supra* , the U.S. Supreme Court found that Mississippi's application of the "voucher" and hearsay rules of evidence had combined to deny the defendant in a murder case an opportunity to cross-examine a man who had made prior oral and written confessions to the murder. The court specifically limited its holding to the facts and circumstances of the case at hand. An examination of these circumstances reveals that the defendant in *Chambers* had already taken some steps at trial towards demonstrating that this other man was in fact the murderer by attacking his alibi and by presenting an eyewitness who stated it was this man and not the defendant who committed the crime. Furthermore, there was every reason to believe the man's written confession was reliable as it was corroborated orally. In essence then the rules of evidence as strictly applied by the Mississippi courts did not serve the ends of justice.

This case does not have similar circumstances. Here there were no eyewitnesses and only minute evidence to suggest that the defendant did not commit the crime. Even more important, there is no reason to suggest that the excluded evidence is reliable. Indeed the very reason for excluding hypnotic evidence is due to its potential unreliability. . . . [T]here is a recognized majority of states that exclude statements made while under a trance. This court knows of no rule that requires a judge to accept evidence of uncertain value to go to a defense that is otherwise completely uncorroborated. The mere fact that a crime has no eyewitnesses or direct evidence does not warrant a court to accept evidence that may be able to tell the trier of fact something about the crime, but may also be of dubious quality. As a constitutional principle then, this court simply finds that petitioner's due process guarantees were not abrogated by the trial court's refusal to permit the defendant to relate his story under hypnosis or an expert witness to recount what the defendant told him while under hypnosis.

. . . .

Accordingly, this court is of the opinion that this petition for a writ of habeas corpus must be DENIED and DISMISSED. Judgment is herein awarded to the respondent.

NOTES AND QUESTIONS

1. *Hearsay Problems.* Courts have uniformly rejected statements made by a person while hypnotized. Paul C. Giannelli, *The Admissibility of Hypnotic Evidence in U.S. Courts*, XLIII INT'L J. CLIN. & EXPERIMENTAL HYPNOSIS 212, 214 (Apr. 1995).

Aside from reliability problems, statements made during an out of court hypnotic trance, are hearsay if offered for the truth of the matters asserted. When the hypnotized person has no *present* recollection of the matters stated while hypnotized (and, accordingly, cannot be cross-examined), the hearsay problems are significant. What hearsay exception(s) would apply to allow such testimony? Can or should the hypnotized person be considered as an unavailable declarant?

2. *Confabulation.* Would it make any difference if a witness were hypnotized in open court (as Greenfield had requested) and opposing counsel was given the opportunity to question the witness *while still hypnotized*? Would taking such testimony in open court mitigate any reliability or cross-examination concerns? In this regard recall the passage concerning confabulation in *Borawick v. Shay, supra* :

> [A] hypnotized person may "confabulate," that is, fill in the gaps in her memory to make it comprehensible. The added details may be derived from irrelevant or unrelated facts or from pure fantasy. [C]onfabulation can occur as a result of the subject's desire to please the hypnotist by coming up with complete and coherent memories.

Borawick v. Shay, supra, 68 F.3d at 603.

3. *Confessions Under Hypnosis — Incriminatory Statements.* Note that the rule of exclusion can work in favor of the accused. In *People v. Schreiner*, 573 N.E.2d 552, 556 (N.Y. 1991), the defendant, while hypnotized, indicated that he was involved in a murder that had taken place three years earlier. The statement was held inadmissible because of the inherent unreliability of recollections that are the result of hypnosis. *See also Leyra v. Denno*, 347 U.S. 556, 561 (1954) (confession obtained by a psychiatrist with "considerable knowledge of hypnosis" involuntary).

[iii]   In-Court Testimony That Has Been Hypnotically Refreshed

When an individual is prepared to testify, has a present recollection of past events, and is able to be cross-examined on those events in open court, should the testimony be disallowed simply because the witness had no recollection (or an incomplete recollection) of those events prior to being hypnotized? Note that this situation does not present the same hearsay problem encountered when we considered allowing a third party, the hypnotist, to testify to what his or her subject said while hypnotized. The reliability problems, however, would appear to be similar. Courts have adopted several different approaches when presented with hypnotically refreshed testimony. The case that follows discusses those approaches.

STATE v. HURD
432 A.2d 86 (N.J. 1981)

PASHMAN, J.

This case presents the question, previously undecided in this State, whether the testimony of a witness who has undergone hypnosis to refresh her recollection is admissible in a criminal trial and, if so, in what circumstances. Although we recognize the problems raised by this use of hypnosis, we hold that, subject to strict safeguards to ensure the reliability of the hypnotic procedure, such testimony is admissible. In this case, we find that the State has failed to demonstrate the reliability of the hypnotic procedures it used. Therefore, we affirm the order of the trial court suppressing the challenged testimony.

I.

At approximately 5:45 a.m. on June 22, 1978, Jane Sell was attacked and stabbed repeatedly while sleeping in the bedroom of her ground floor apartment. Her assailant apparently did not intend to rob her or commit a sexual assault. She ultimately escaped her attacker, but only after sustaining many knife wounds.

Mrs. Sell lived in the apartment with her husband, David Sell, and her three sons, two of whom are children from a previous marriage with the defendant, Paul Hurd. Although at the time of the assault she had been divorced from the defendant for seven years, they continued to disagree over the disposition of jointly owned property and visitation rights. . . .

The investigation by the police department and prosecutor's office centered on two suspects, David Sell and the defendant. Because Mrs. Sell stated that she was . . . unable to identify her attacker . . . the prosecutor's office suggested that she visit a psychiatrist who might be able to enhance her recollection of the incident through hypnosis. Mrs. Sell agreed. On July 14, 1978, two officers from the prosecutor's office, Detective Marilyn Pierangeli and Lt. Laurence VanWinkle, drove Mrs. Sell and her husband to the New York City office of Dr. Herbert Spiegel. Besides Dr. Spiegel and Mrs. Sell, the only people present during the hypnotic session were the two officers and a medical student; David Sell waited outside the room.

Dr. Spiegel first conducted some tests to determine whether Mrs. Sell was capable of undergoing hypnosis. Once the doctor was satisfied that Mrs. Sell was hypnotizable, a tape recorder was turned on and the interview began. Before subjecting her to hypnosis, Dr. Spiegel questioned Mrs. Sell concerning her memory of the event and learned that she had images of a person standing near the dresser in her bedroom and a person leaning in the window. She also knew the name of one of the suspects in the case, but did not reveal which one. Finally, Dr. Spiegel instructed Mrs. Sell that while she was in a trance she should respond to questions from the officers as well as to his questions.

After this brief interview, the doctor induced hypnosis. Mrs. Sell began to relive the attack. In response to Dr. Spiegel's questions she described various facial features of her assailant and his clothing. Suddenly she began to cry hysterically. At this point Detective Pierangeli continued the questioning: "Jane, I want you to think very, very hard of what you are seeing right now. It's up to you to help me. It is up to you now to describe for me what you see. Is it somebody that you know, Jane?" Mrs. Sell answered, "Yes." "Is it David, Jane?" "No," Mrs. Sell cried. "Is it Paul?" "Yes," Mrs. Sell responded emotionally.

After Mrs. Sell was brought out of the trance and into a post-hypnotic state, she expressed mistrust "about her thinking." Dr. Spiegel and Detective Pierangeli in effect encouraged her to accept the identification she had made. . . .

Six days later, on July 20, 1978, Jane Sell came to the North Plainfield Police Department and gave a statement identifying Paul Hurd as her attacker. On the basis of this statement, defendant was indicted and charged with assault with intent to kill, atrocious assault and battery, assault with a deadly weapon, possession of a dangerous knife, and breaking and entry with intent to assault. Before the jury selection, defendant moved to suppress the proposed in-court identification by Mrs. Sell. He argued that testimony refreshed through the use of hypnosis is *per se* inadmissible because hypnosis fails to satisfy the standard for the admissibility of scientific evidence, *see Frye v. United States*, 293 F. 1013 (D.C. Cir. 1923). . . . Even if such testimony is not *per se* inadmissible, he argued in the alternative, the hypnotic procedure in this case was so tainted by coercion and suggestion as to render the resulting identification inadmissible because it was likely to result in irreparable misidentification.

After hearing lengthy expert testimony concerning the reliability of hypnosis as a means of refreshing recollection and the likely effect of hypnosis on Mrs. Sell, the trial court suppressed the proposed identification.

. . . .

. . . The prosecutor . . . filed a motion in this Court seeking leave to appeal. . . . We granted this motion in order to address the novel questions raised in this case, and we now affirm the order of the trial court.

II.

. . . .

. . . The principal question in this case is whether the testimony of a witness who has undergone hypnosis to refresh her memory is admissible in a criminal trial and, if so, under what conditions. Courts in other jurisdictions have divided in their treatment of this issue.

A majority of the courts that have considered the question have held that hypnotically induced testimony is admissible. These cases have generally reasoned that testimony of a witness whose memory has been revived through hypnosis should be treated like any other present recollection refreshed. That the witness' memory may have been impaired by hypnosis or that suggestive material may have been used to refresh his recollection is considered to be a matter affecting credibility, not admissibility. It is assumed that skillful cross-examination will enable the jury to evaluate the effect of hypnosis on the witness and the credibility of his testimony.

Two recent cases have criticized the assumptions underlying this attitude toward hypnotically refreshed testimony. *State v. Mena*, 624 P.2d 1274 (Ariz. 1981); *State v. Mack*, 292 N.W.2d 764 (Minn. 1980). . . . Because hypnosis is a scientific procedure capable of irreparably contaminating a witness' memory, the Arizona and Minnesota courts held that the procedure must satisfy the standard for the admissibility of scientific evidence established in *Frye v. United States*, 293 F. 1013 (D.C. Cir. 1923). Applying the *Frye* test, both courts found that hypnosis has not "gained general acceptance in the particular field in which it belongs," *Frye, supra*, 293 F. at 1014, at least as a means of obtaining accurate recall of prior events. Therefore, they held that the testimony of a witness who has undergone hypnosis to refresh his recollection is *per se* inadmissible in a criminal trial.

We agree with the trial court below and those courts elsewhere that have held that hypnotically refreshed testimony must satisfy the standard of acceptability for scientific evidence before it is admissible in a criminal trial. . . . This standard has previously been applied only to the results of physical tests such as radar, the polygraph, and voiceprints. But we believe that the policy reasons embodied in the general acceptance standard are germane to hypnotically refreshed testimony as well.

Like the results of a polygraph examination or voiceprint analysis, the credibility of recall stimulated by hypnosis depends upon the reliability of the scientific procedure used. If the procedure is not capable of yielding reasonably reliable results, then its probative value may be outweighed by the risks entailed in its use in a criminal trial. These risks include prejudice, jury confusion, and consumption of time and trial resources. When hypnosis results in an eyewitness identification of the defendant, for example, the defendant is clearly prejudiced if there is not even a reasonable likelihood that the witness' memory was accurately revived. . . .

III.

. . . Unlike the courts in *Mena, supra* , and *Mack, supra* , the court below did not demand, as a precondition of admissibility, that hypnosis be generally accepted as a means of reviving truthful or historically accurate recall. We think this was correct. The purpose of using hypnosis is not to obtain truth, as a polygraph or "truth serum" is supposed to do. Instead, hypnosis is employed as a means of overcoming amnesia and restoring the memory of a witness. In light of this purpose, hypnosis can be considered reasonably reliable if it is able to yield recollections as accurate as those of an ordinary witness, which likewise are often historically inaccurate. Based on the evidence submitted at trial, we are satisfied that the use of hypnosis to refresh memory satisfies the *Frye* standard in certain instances. If it is conducted properly and used only in appropriate cases, hypnosis is generally accepted as a reasonably reliable method of restoring a person's memory. Consequently, hypnotically-induced testimony may be admissible if the proponent of the testimony can demonstrate that the use of hypnosis in the particular case was a reasonably reliable means of restoring memory comparable to normal recall in its accuracy.

. . . .

Several features of the hypnotic experience explain why hypnosis, unless carefully controlled, is not generally accepted as a reliable means of obtaining accurate recall. First, a person undergoing hypnosis is extremely vulnerable to suggestions. In describing the events he is reliving, he will tend to shape his "recall" in response to intentional or inadvertent cues from the questioner. These cues may be as obvious as leading questions or as subtle as the inflection of the questioner's voice or degree of apparent approval by the hypnotist. In addition, a subject often will incorporate into his response his notion of what is expected of him. Authorities note that there are particular problems of suggestibility when the subject is aware of a preferred response or when the examiner has a preconceived theory that is likely to influence his questioning. Because of the unpredictability of what will influence a subject, it is difficult even for an expert examining a videotape of a hypnotic session to identify possible cues.

A second aspect of hypnosis that contributes to its unreliability is the loss of critical judgment. A person under hypnosis is more willing to speculate and will respond to questions with a confidence he would not have as a waking person.

The third and perhaps most troubling phenomenon is the tendency to confound memories evoked under hypnosis with prior recall. Typically a subject is told that he will remember what he has recalled under hypnosis after he awakes from the trance. In response to this post-hypnotic suggestion, most subjects will indiscriminately mix their hypnotic recall together with their waking memory. Many experts believe that the subject is then unable to evaluate critically the resulting memory to determine what he himself believes is the accurate version. Furthermore, he will have strong subjective confidence in the validity of his new recall, which will make it difficult for an expert or a jury to judge the credibility of his memory.

The inherent limitations on hypnosis as a method for obtaining completely accurate recall have led the dissenting members of our Court and some other courts to conclude that the testimony of a witness whose memory has been enhanced through hypnosis is never admissible in a criminal trial. *Mena, supra ; Mack, supra.* The Supreme Court of Minnesota explained its conclusion as follows:

> However, the fact that a witness' memory results from hypnosis bears on the question of whether her testimony is sufficiently competent, relevant, and more probative than prejudicial, to merit admission at all. The crux of the problem is that hypnosis can create a memory of perceptions which neither were nor could have been made, and, therefore, can bring forth a "memory" from someone who cannot establish that she perceived the events she asserts to remember. Neither the person hypnotized nor the expert observer can distinguish between confabulation and accurate recall in any particular instance. After the hypnosis session, the hypnotically "retrieved" account differs in another way from ordinary human recall, to which the state seeks to liken it. Because the person hypnotized is subjectively convinced of the veracity of the "memory," this recall is not susceptible to attack by cross-examination. (*Mack, supra*, 292 N.W.2d at 769–70 (footnote omitted)).

Although we share the dissent's concern about the possible contamination of a witness' memory, we believe that a rule of *per se* inadmissibility is unnecessarily broad and will result in the exclusion of evidence that is as trustworthy as other eyewitness testimony. Without underestimating the seriousness of the problems associated with hypnosis, it should be recognized that psychological research concerning the reliability of ordinary eyewitnesses reveals similar shortcomings. Studies indicate that memory does not merely reproduce perceptions of an event; "memory, like perception, is an active, constructive process that often introduces inaccuracies by adding details not present in the initial representation or in the event itself. . . .

As the trial court found, the experts who testified at trial indicated that in appropriate cases and where properly conducted the use of hypnosis to refresh memory is comparable in reliability to ordinary recall. Therefore, we hold that testimony enhanced through hypnosis is admissible in a criminal trial if the trial court finds that the use of hypnosis in the particular case was reasonably likely to result in recall comparable in accuracy to normal human memory. If the testimony is admissible, the opponent may still challenge the reliability of the particular procedures followed in the individual case by introducing expert testimony at trial, but the opponent may not attempt to prove the general unreliability of hypnosis. The trier of fact must then decide how much weight to accord the hypnotically refreshed testimony.

IV.

Whenever a party in a criminal trial seeks to introduce a witness who has undergone hypnosis to refresh his memory, the party must inform his opponent of his intention and provide him with the recording of the session and other pertinent material.[22] [3] The trial court will then rule on the admissibility of the testimony either at a pretrial hearing or at a hearing out of the jury's presence. In reviewing the admissibility of hypnotically refreshed testimony, the trial court should evaluate both the kind of memory loss that hypnosis was used to restore and the specific technique employed, based on expert testimony presented by the parties. The object of this review is not to determine whether the proffered testimony is accurate, but instead whether the use of hypnosis and the procedure followed in the particular case was a reasonably reliable means of restoring the witness' memory.

The first question a court must consider is the appropriateness of using hypnosis for the kind of memory loss encountered. The reason for a subject's lack of memory is an important factor in evaluating the reliability of hypnosis in restoring recall. According to the defendant's expert . . . hypnosis often is reasonably reliable in reviving normal recall where there is a pathological reason, such as traumatic neurosis, for the witness' inability to remember.[23] [4]

Once it is determined that a case is of a kind likely to yield normal recall if hypnosis is properly administered, then it is necessary to determine whether the procedures followed were reasonably reliable. Of particular importance are the manner of questioning and the presence of cues or suggestions during the trance and the post-hypnotic period. . . . An additional factor affecting the reliability of the procedures is the amenability of the subject to hypnosis, since some experts believe that subjects capable of entering deeper trances are usually more suggestible. None of these factors should be considered absolute prerequisites to admissibility, nor are they exclusive. They are listed to illustrate the nature of the inquiry.

To provide an adequate record for evaluating the reliability of the hypnotic procedure, and to ensure a minimum level of reliability, we also adopt several procedural requirements. . . . Before it may introduce hypnotically refreshed testimony, a party must demonstrate compliance with these requirements.

First, a psychiatrist or psychologist experienced in the use of hypnosis must conduct the session. This professional should also be able to qualify as an expert in order to aid the court in evaluating the procedures followed. Although we recognize that there are

---

[22] [n.3] The defendant may be constitutionally entitled to this material. *United States v. Miller*, 411 F.2d 825 (2d Cir. 1969).

[23] [n.4] We do not mean to suggest that hypnosis is inappropriate for refreshing memory where there is no pathological reason for a subject's lack of recall. Hypnosis remains a valuable tool for developing leads in an investigation. However, the reliability of hypnosis in such cases is questionable. Therefore, its usefulness in eliciting admissible testimony should be especially carefully evaluated by the trial court in such cases.

many other people trained to administer hypnosis and skilled in its use for investigative purposes, we believe that a professional must administer hypnosis if the testimony revealed is to be used in a criminal trial. . . .

Second, the professional conducting the hypnotic session should be independent of and not regularly employed by the prosecutor, investigator or defense. This condition will safeguard against any bias on the part of the hypnotist that might translate into leading questions, unintentional cues, or other suggestive conduct.

Third, any information given to the hypnotist by law enforcement personnel or the defense prior to the hypnotic session must be recorded, either in writing or another suitable form. This requirement will help the court determine the extent of information the hypnotist could have communicated to the witness either directly or through suggestion.

Fourth, before inducing hypnosis the hypnotist should obtain from the subject a detailed description of the facts as the subject remembers them. The hypnotist should carefully avoid influencing the description by asking structured questions or adding new details.

Fifth, all contacts between the hypnotist and the subject must be recorded. This will establish a record of the pre-induction interview, the hypnotic session, and the post-hypnotic period, enabling a court to determine what information or suggestions the witness may have received during the session and what recall was first elicited through hypnosis. The use of videotape, the only effective record of visual cues, is strongly encouraged but not mandatory.

Sixth, only the hypnotist and the subject should be present during any phase of the hypnotic session, including the pre-hypnotic testing and the post-hypnotic interview. Although it may be easier for a person familiar with the investigation to conduct some of the questioning, the risk of undetectable, inadvertent suggestion is too great, as this case illustrates. Likewise, the mere presence of such a person may influence the response of the subject.

Once compliance with these safeguards is shown, the trial court can determine the reliability and therefore the admissibility of hypnotically refreshed testimony, according to the standard set forth above.

Concerning the burden of proof, . . . the party seeking to introduce hypnotically refreshed testimony has the burden of establishing admissibility by clear and convincing evidence. We recognize that this standard places a heavy burden upon the use of hypnosis for criminal trial purposes.[24] [6] This burden is justified by the potential for abuse of hypnosis, the genuine likelihood of suggestiveness and error, and the consequent risk of injustice. . . .

. . . .

---

[24] [n.6] Because the stakes are less in a civil proceeding, we do not decide whether a party must establish the reliability of hypnotically enhanced testimony by clear and convincing evidence as a condition for admissibility. Nor do we decide whether all of the procedural requirements set forth below would be necessary. As a minimum, however, we believe that a recording of the session is essential; otherwise the opponent will have no effective way to challenge the credibility of the testimony at trial.

VI.

Turning to the present case, we find, as did the trial court, that the State has failed to meet its burden of establishing the admissibility of the proffered identification by clear and convincing evidence. First, we note that the procedural requirements set forth above were not satisfied. In particular, there is no record of what Dr. Spiegel knew about the case before the session; there is no statement of what Mrs. Sell remembered prior to undergoing hypnosis; the pre-hypnotic session was not recorded; and law enforcement personnel were present during the session. If our only concern was the failure to observe these procedures, we might not require suppression of the testimony, because the State could not have anticipated the details of the required procedures. Furthermore, the purpose of creating a record of the session has been substantially satisfied. But, the procedures followed in this case raise grave doubts about the reliability of the hypnotically refreshed testimony obtained, which renders that testimony inadmissible.

The most troubling aspect of the session was the role played by Detective Pierangeli. Not only was she present during the session, but she asked specific questions, such as "Is it Paul?" This form of questioning, together with the pressure she exerted on Mrs. Sell to cooperate by making an identification, raises the real possibility of suggestiveness. . . . Moreover, Mrs. Sell's identification has not been corroborated by any other evidence. Based on these facts, we cannot find that the State has shown, by clear and convincing evidence, that hypnosis as performed in this case was a reasonably reliable means of yielding normally accurate recall. . . .

For the reasons stated above, we affirm the judgment of the trial court precluding the proposed in-court identification of defendant.

NOTES

1. *Hypnotically Refreshed Testimony.* The *Hurd* case discusses different approaches courts follow when presented with hypnotically refreshed trial testimony. At the time *Hurd* was decided, a majority of courts that had considered the question found hypnotically refreshed testimony to be admissible. This view has changed and most courts now consider such testimony to be per se inadmissible. The three approaches mentioned in *Hurd*, and a fourth, the "totality of the circumstances" approach, are discussed below. *See State v. Fertig*, 668 A.2d 1076, 1081–82 (N.J. 1996) (discussing approaches noting that "[t]wenty-six courts now conclude that hypnotically-refreshed testimony is per se inadmissible"). *See generally* 1 Scientific Evidence § 12.05, at 630 (4th ed. 2007).

(A) *Per Se Exclusion.* The majority of courts have adopted a per se rule of exclusion based upon the perception that hypnotically induced testimony is unreliable. *See People v. Shirley*, 723 P.2d 1354 (Cal. 1982). Supporters of per se exclusion argue that when a person is hypnotized for the purpose of memory enhancement there is danger of the person grafting onto his or her memory fantasies or suggestions that are deliberately or unwittingly communicated by the hypnotist. *See* Bernard L. Diamond, *Inherent Problems in the Use of Pretrial Hypnosis on a Prospective Witness*, 68 Calif. L. Rev. 313, 314 (1980) (author argues that the risk of contaminating recollections is so great that hypnosis by the police "is tantamount to the destruction or fabrication of evidence").

(B) *Per Se Admissible — The "Credibility Approach."* Second, some courts (a distinct minority) allow such testimony to be admitted without any particular procedural safeguards, holding that the fact that a witness was hypnotized affects the credibility, not the admissibility, of the refreshed testimony. *See e.g., State v. Brown*, 337 N.W.2d 138, 151 (N.D. 1983).

(C) Procedural Safeguards — New Jersey Rejects Hurd. Third, several courts follow the approach described by the New Jersey Supreme Court in *Hurd*, and admit hypnotically enhanced testimony if certain procedural safeguards are satisfied. The specific safeguards required and the degree of compliance with those safeguards varies. Oregon has adopted a statute that requires limited procedural safeguards when hypnosis has been used on a witness in a criminal trial. Or. Rev. Stat. § 136.675 (2006).

Fifteen years after *Hurd* the New Jersey Supreme Court reexamined the admissibility of hypnotically refreshed testimony in *State v. Fertig*, 668 A.2d 1076 (N.J. 1996). The court noted that since *Hurd* the "tide has run the other way" and that the majority view was now that of per se inadmissibility. *Id.* at 1081. Nonetheless, the court refused to adopt the per se inadmissible approach at that time absent a more complete record. *Id.* That changed 10 years later. In *State v. Moore*, 902 A.2d 1212 (N.J. 2006), the New Jersey Supreme Court overruled *Hurd* stating that, "[b]ecause we are no longer confident that procedural safeguards can guard effectively against the risks associated with hypnotically refreshed testimony, we reject the *Hurd* approach and hold [the] testimony inadmissible." *Id.* at 1229.

In *Rock v. Arkansas*, 483 U.S. 44 (1987), the United States Supreme Court discussed the variety of procedural safeguards some states use that allow hypnotically refreshed testimony to be introduced at trial and then listed some jurisdictions that follow the procedural safeguard approach:

> In some jurisdictions, courts have established procedural prerequisites for admissibility in order to reduce the risks associated with hypnosis. Perhaps the leading case in this line is *State v. Hurd*, 432 A.2d 86 (N.J. 1981). *See also Sprynczynatyk v. General Motors Corp.*, 771 F.2d 1112, 1122–1123 (CA8 1985); *United States v. Harrington*, 18 M.J. 797, 803 (A.C.M.R. 1984); *House v. State*, 445 So. 2d 815, 826–827 (Miss. 1984); *State v. Beachum*, 643 P.2d 246, 253–254 (N.M. App. 1981); *State v. Weston*, 475 N.E.2d 805, 813 (Ohio App. 1984); *State v. Armstrong*, 329 N.W.2d 386 (Wis. 1983).

Rock v. Arkansas, 483 U.S. 44, 59 n.16 (1987).

(D) Discretionary Admissibility Based on the Totality of the Circumstances. An approach that is similar to the procedural safeguards guidelines used in *Hurd, supra*, is the totality-of-the- circumstances approach, the one that is used by most federal courts. The primary distinction between this approach and the procedural-safeguard approach adopted in *Hurd, supra*, is that the totality-of-the-circumstances approach gives the trial court the discretion on a case-by-case basis to balance all factors (including procedural safeguards) and assess the reliability of the evidence. Under this approach the *Hurd* safeguards are relevant, but not determinative. The Fourth Circuit in *McQueen v. Garrison*, 814 F.2d 951 (4th Cir. 1987), described the difference between the two approaches:

> Even though all the *Hurd* safeguards might be employed, the defendant may still be able to demonstrate by expert testimony that a witness' memory has been irreparably distorted by hypnosis. On the other hand, even if the hypnosis procedures are flawed, a trial or appellate court might discern that a witness'

testimony was nonetheless independent of the dangers associated with hypnosis.

Id. at 958. *See also, Mersch v. City of Dallas*, 207 F.3d 732, 735 (5th Cir. 2000) (case-by-case approach); *Roark v. Commonwealth*, 90 S.W.3d 24, 36 (Ky. 2002) (totality of the circumstances); *People v. Romero*, 745 P.2d 1003, 1016–17 (Colo. 1987) (totality-of-circumstances approach).

2. *Prehypnotic Recollections as an Exception to the Per Se Exclusion Rule.* Note that for courts following a per se rule of exclusion for hypnotically refreshed testimony there is a problem of how to treat testimony about matters that were recalled *prior* to being hypnotized. For example, what if a witness is hypnotized and offers absolutely no new information that has not already been given to the police by that witness? Is the person disqualified as a witness? The prevailing view is contained in *State ex rel. Collins v. Superior Court*, 644 P.2d 1266, 1295 (Ariz. 1982):

> [A] witness will be permitted to testify with regard to those matters which he or she was able to recall *and* relate prior to hypnosis. Thus, for example, the rape victim would be free to testify to the occurrence of the crime, the lack of consent, the injury inflicted and the like, assuming that such matters were remembered and related to the authorities prior to the use of hypnosis.

See also Cal. Evid. Code § 795 (2006) (prehypnotic testimony admissible if procedural safeguards followed). *See generally*, 1 Scientific Evidence § 12.05[a], at 636–38 (4th ed. 2007).

3. *Test for Admissibility.*

(A) Frye *Jurisdictions.* State courts that use the *Frye* test for determining the admissibility of novel scientific evidence are not in agreement as to whether the *Frye* test should apply to hypnotically refreshed testimony. Some courts, like *Hurd*, apply *Frye* and hold that hypnosis is generally accepted for certain purposes. The real inquiry for these courts is whether correct procedures were followed in applying the hypnosis technique.

On the other hand, other jurisdictions apply *Frye* and hold that hypnosis is not generally accepted. Note that *what* must be considered generally accepted may have a significant impact on the admissibility of the testimony. For example, is the *Frye* inquiry whether hypnosis is generally accepted as a means of providing *accurate* recollection, or is it whether hypnosis is a generally accepted method of refreshing memory? The *Hurd* court thought the proper inquiry was the latter.

Finally, some *Frye* jurisdictions do not think that the general acceptance test is applicable to a technique like hypnosis.

> Even if this court applied the test set out in *Frye*, that test could not be used to determine the admissibility of hypnotically affected testimony. *Frye* applied to the admissibility of "expert testimony deduced from a well-recognized scientific principle." Here, it is not expert testimony that is challenged. Rather, it is the admissibility of an eyewitness' post-hypnosis identification which is in question.

> But it is not the reliability of hypnosis to put one in a hypnotic trance that is at issue when the witness testifies. It is the reliability of a specific human memory as affected by hypnosis that must be examined. There are no experts who can testify as to what specific effects hypnosis has had on the witness'

memory, just as there are no experts who can testify that a normal waking memory of an event is in fact a completely accurate representation of what actually occurred. The most a trial judge can do is review the hypnotic session to ensure that no impermissible suggestiveness has occurred. However, in such a review, it is not the reliability of hypnosis that is to be examined. Rather, it is the effect of a specific hypnotic session that is to be determined.

We conclude that the test set out in *Frye* is inapplicable to this case.

State v. Armstrong, 329 N.W.2d 386, 393 (Wis. 1983).

(B) Daubert *Jurisdictions.* Some courts take the position that the *Daubert* test does not apply to hypnotically refreshed testimony because no expert opinion is being presented. In *Borawick v. Shay* the Second Circuit took this position.

> We do not believe that *Daubert* is directly applicable to the issue here since *Daubert* concerns the admissibility of data derived from scientific techniques or expert opinions. The issue before us is whether Borawick is a competent witness, or whether her lay testimony is admissible. Under either characterization, the question does not concern the admissibility of experimental data or expert opinions.

> Even though *Daubert* does not provide direct guidance, our decision today is informed by the principles underlying the Supreme Court's holding. First, by loosening the strictures on scientific evidence set by *Frye, Daubert* reinforces the idea that there should be a presumption of admissibility of evidence. Second, it emphasizes the need for flexibility in assessing whether evidence is admissible. Rather than using rigid "safeguards" for determining whether testimony should be admitted, the Court's approach is to permit the trial judge to weigh the various considerations pertinent to the issue in question. Third, *Daubert* allows for the admissibility of scientific evidence, even if not generally accepted in the relevant scientific community, provided its reliability has independent support. Finally, the Court expressed its faith in the power of the adversary system to test "shaky but admissible" evidence, and advanced a bias in favor of admitting evidence short of that solidly and indisputably proven to be reliable. Finally, we note that, even if *Daubert* were of direct application, nothing in *Daubert* is inconsistent with our outlined approach.

Borawick v. Shay, 68 F.3d 597, 610 (2d Cir. 1995). Other courts have taken the view that *Daubert* applies because hypnotically refreshed testimony "is the product of scientific intervention." *State v. Tuttle*, 780 P.2d 1203, 1211(Utah 1989).

QUESTIONS

1. The court in *Hurd* expressed concern over "the possible contamination of a witness' memory." *Hurd, supra,* 432 A.2d at 94. Which of the *Hurd* procedural safeguards deals with the problems of overconfidence or confabulation?

2. Note that the court in *Hurd* states "the opponent [of hypnotically refreshed testimony] may not attempt to prove the general unreliability of hypnosis." Why not? *See People v. Guerra*, 690 P.2d 635, 656 (Cal. 1984).

[iv]   Constitutional Considerations: An Exception to the Per Se Exclusion Rule

If a state follows a *per se* rule of exclusion as to hypnotically induced testimony and applies such a rule to a *defendant* in a criminal case, are any constitutional rights implicated? In the following case the United States Supreme Court addressed per se exclusion of hypnotically refreshed testimony from the perspective of the defendant in a criminal case, and carved out an exception.

ROCK v. ARKANSAS
483 U.S. 44 (1987)

Justice Blackmun delivered the opinion of the Court.

The issue presented in this case is whether Arkansas' evidentiary rule prohibiting the admission of hypnotically refreshed testimony violated petitioner's constitutional right to testify on her own behalf as a defendant in a criminal case.

I.

Petitioner Vickie Lorene Rock was charged with manslaughter in the death of her husband, Frank Rock, on July 2, 1983. A dispute had been simmering about Frank's wish to move from the couple's small apartment adjacent to Vickie's beauty parlor to a trailer she owned outside town. That night a fight erupted when Frank refused to let petitioner eat some pizza and prevented her from leaving the apartment to get something else to eat. When police arrived on the scene they found Frank on the floor with a bullet wound in his chest. . . . According to the testimony of one of the investigating officers, petitioner told him that "she stood up to leave the room and [her husband] grabbed her by the throat and choked her and threw her against the wall and . . . at that time she walked over and picked up the weapon and pointed it toward the floor and he hit her again and she shot him."

Because petitioner could not remember the precise details of the shooting, her attorney suggested that she submit to hypnosis in order to refresh her memory. Petitioner was hypnotized twice by Doctor Bettye Back, a licensed neuropsychologist with training in the field of hypnosis. Doctor Back interviewed petitioner for an hour prior to the first hypnosis session, taking notes on petitioner's general history and her recollections of the shooting.[25] [2] Both hypnosis sessions were recorded on tape. Petitioner did not relate any new information during either of the sessions, but, after the hypnosis, she was able to remember that at the time of the incident she had her thumb on the hammer of the gun, but had not held her finger on the trigger. She also recalled that the gun had discharged when her husband grabbed her arm during the

---

[25] [n.2] Doctor Back's handwritten notes regarding petitioner's memory of the day of the shooting read as follows:

"Pt states she & husb. were discussing moving out to a trailer she had prev. owned. He was 'set on' moving out to the trailer — felt they should discuss. She bec[ame] upset & went to another room to lay down. Bro. came & left. She came out to eat some of the pizza, he wouldn't allow her to have any. She said she would go out and get [something] to eat he wouldn't allow her — He pushed her against a wall an end table in the corner [with] a gun on it. They were the night watchmen for business that sets behind them. She picked gun up stated she didn't want him hitting her anymore. He wouldn't let her out door, slammed door & 'gun went off & he fell & he died' [pt looked misty eyed here — near tears]" (additions by Doctor Back)."

scuffle. As a result of the details that petitioner was able to remember about the shooting, her counsel arranged for a gun expert to examine the handgun, a single-action Hawes.22 Deputy Marshal. That inspection revealed that the gun was defective and prone to fire, when hit or dropped, without the trigger's being pulled.

When the prosecutor learned of the hypnosis sessions, he filed a motion to exclude petitioner's testimony. The trial judge held a pretrial hearing on the motion and concluded that no hypnotically refreshed testimony would be admitted. The court issued an order limiting petitioner's testimony to "matters remembered and stated to the examiner prior to being placed under hypnosis." At trial, petitioner introduced testimony by the gun expert, but the court limited petitioner's own description of the events on the day of the shooting to a reiteration of the sketchy information in Doctor Back's notes.[26] [4] The jury convicted petitioner on the manslaughter charge and she was sentenced to 10 years' imprisonment and a $10,000 fine.

On appeal, the Supreme Court of Arkansas rejected petitioner's claim that the limitations on her testimony violated her right to present her defense. The court concluded that "the dangers of admitting this kind of testimony outweigh whatever probative value it may have," and decided to follow the approach of states that have held hypnotically refreshed testimony of witnesses inadmissible *per se*. Although the court acknowledged that "a defendant's right to testify is fundamental," it ruled that the exclusion of petitioner's testimony did not violate her constitutional rights. Any "prejudice or deprivation" she suffered "was minimal and resulted from her own actions and not by any erroneous ruling of the court." We granted certiorari, to consider the constitutionality of Arkansas' *per se* rule excluding a criminal defendant's hypnotically refreshed testimony.

II.

Petitioner's claim that her testimony was impermissibly excluded is bottomed on her constitutional right to testify in her own defense. At this point in the development of our adversary system, it cannot be doubted that a defendant in a criminal case has the right to take the witness stand and to testify in his or her own defense. . . .

. . . .

The right to testify on one's own behalf at a criminal trial has sources in several provisions of the Constitution. It is one of the rights that "are essential to due process of law in a fair adversary process." *Faretta v. California*, 422 U.S. 806, 819 n.15 (1975). The necessary ingredients of the Fourteenth Amendment's guarantee that no one shall be deprived of liberty without due process of law include a right to be heard and to offer testimony:

---

[26] [n.4] When petitioner began to testify, she was repeatedly interrupted by the prosecutor, who objected that her statements fell outside the scope of the pretrial order. Each time she attempted to describe an event on the day of the shooting, she was unable to proceed for more than a few words before her testimony was ruled inadmissible. For example, she was unable to testify without objection about her husband's activities on the morning of the shooting, about their discussion and disagreement concerning the move to her trailer, about her husband's and his brother's replacing the shock absorbers on a van, and about her brother-in-law's return to eat pizza. She then made a proffer, outside the hearing of the jury, of testimony about the fight in an attempt to show that she could adhere to the court's order. The prosecution objected to every detail not expressly described in Doctor Back's notes or in the testimony the doctor gave at the pretrial hearing. The court agreed with the prosecutor's statement that "ninety-nine percent of everything [petitioner] testified to in the proffer" was inadmissible.

"A person's right to reasonable notice of a charge against him, *and an opportunity to be heard in his defense* — a right to his day in court — are basic in our system of jurisprudence; and these rights include, as a minimum, a right to examine the witnesses against him, to offer testimony, and to be represented by counsel." (Emphasis added.) *In re Oliver*, 333 U.S. 257, 273 (1948).

The right to testify is also found in the Compulsory Process Clause of the Sixth Amendment, which grants a defendant the right to call "witnesses in his favor," a right that is guaranteed in the criminal courts of the States by the Fourteenth Amendment. Logically included in the accused's right to call witnesses whose testimony is "material and favorable to his defense," *United States v. Valenzuela-Bernal*, 458 U.S. 858, 867 (1982), is a right to testify himself, should he decide it is in his favor to do so. In fact, the most important witness for the defense in many criminal cases is the defendant himself. There is no justification today for a rule that denies an accused the opportunity to offer his own testimony. Like the truthfulness of other witnesses, the defendant's veracity . . . can be tested adequately by cross-examination.

. . . .

The opportunity to testify is also a necessary corollary to the Fifth Amendment's guarantee against compelled testimony. In *Harris v. New York*, 401 U.S. 222, 230 (1971), the Court stated: "Every criminal defendant is privileged to testify in his own defense, or to refuse to do so." *Id.*, at 225. . . .

III.

The question now before the Court is whether a criminal defendant's right to testify may be restricted by a state rule that excludes her posthypnosis testimony. This is not the first time this Court has faced a constitutional challenge to a state rule, designed to ensure trustworthy evidence, that interfered with the ability of a defendant to offer testimony.

. . . .

Just as a State may not apply an arbitrary rule of competence to exclude a material defense witness from taking the stand, it also may not apply a rule of evidence that permits a witness to take the stand, but arbitrarily excludes material portions of his testimony. In *Chambers v. Mississippi*, 410 U.S. 284 (1973), the Court invalidated a State's hearsay rule on the ground that it abridged the defendant's right to "present witnesses in his own defense." *Id.*, at 302. Chambers was tried for a murder to which another person repeatedly had confessed in the presence of acquaintances. The State's hearsay rule, coupled with a "voucher" rule that did not allow the defendant to cross-examine the confessed murderer directly, prevented Chambers from introducing testimony concerning these confessions, which were critical to his defense. This Court reversed the judgment of conviction, holding that when a state rule of evidence conflicts with the right to present witnesses, the rule may "not be applied mechanistically to defeat the ends of justice," but must meet the fundamental standards of due process. *Ibid.* In the Court's view, the State in *Chambers* did not demonstrate that the hearsay testimony in that case, which bore "assurances of trustworthiness" including corroboration by other evidence, would be unreliable, and thus the defendant should have been able to introduce the exculpatory testimony. *Ibid.*

Of course, the right to present relevant testimony is not without limitation. The right "may, in appropriate cases, bow to accommodate other legitimate interests in the criminal trial process." *Id.*, at 295.[27] [11] But restrictions of a defendant's right to testify may not be arbitrary or disproportionate to the purposes they are designed to serve. In applying its evidentiary rules a State must evaluate whether the interests served by a rule justify the limitation imposed on the defendant's constitutional right to testify.

IV.

The Arkansas rule enunciated by the state courts does not allow a trial court to consider whether posthypnosis testimony may be admissible in a particular case; it is a *per se* rule prohibiting the admission at trial of any defendant's hypnotically refreshed testimony on the ground that such testimony is always unreliable. Thus, in Arkansas, an accused's testimony is limited to matters that he or she can prove were remembered before hypnosis. This rule operates to the detriment of any defendant who undergoes hypnosis, without regard to the reasons for it, the circumstances under which it took place, or any independent verification of the information it produced.

In this case, the application of that rule had a significant adverse effect on petitioner's ability to testify. It virtually prevented her from describing any of the events that occurred on the day of the shooting, despite corroboration of many of those events by other witnesses. Even more importantly, under the court's rule petitioner was not permitted to describe the actual shooting except in the words contained in Doctor Back's notes. The expert's description of the gun's tendency to misfire would have taken on greater significance if the jury had heard petitioner testify that she did not have her finger on the trigger and that the gun went off when her husband hit her arm.

In establishing its *per se* rule, the Arkansas Supreme Court simply followed the approach taken by a number of States that have decided that hypnotically enhanced testimony should be excluded at trial on the ground that it tends to be unreliable. Other States that have adopted an exclusionary rule, however, have done so for the testimony of *witnesses*, not for the testimony of a *defendant*. The Arkansas Supreme Court failed to perform the constitutional analysis that is necessary when a defendant's right to testify is at stake.[28] [15]

Although the Arkansas court concluded that any testimony that cannot be proved to be the product of prehypnosis memory is unreliable, many courts have eschewed a *per se* rule and permit the admission of hypnotically refreshed testimony. Hypnosis by

---

[27] [n.11] Numerous state procedural and evidentiary rules control the presentation of evidence and do not offend the defendant's right to testify. *See, e.g., Chambers v. Mississippi*, 410 U.S., at 284, 302 ("In the exercise of this right, the accused, as is required of the State, must comply with established rules of procedure and evidence designed to assure both fairness and reliability in the ascertainment of guilt and innocence"); *Washington v. Texas*, 388 U.S. 14, 23 n.21 (1967) (opinion should not be construed as disapproving testimonial privileges or nonarbitrary rules that disqualify those incapable of observing events due to mental infirmity or infancy from being witnesses).

[28] [n.15] The Arkansas court relied on a California case, *People v. Shirley*, 723 P.2d 1354, *cert. denied*, 459 U.S. 860 (1982), for much of its reasoning as to the unreliability of hypnosis. But while the California court adopted a far stricter general rule - barring entirely testimony by any witness who has been hypnotized - it explicitly excepted testimony by an accused:

"[W]hen it is the defendant himself — not merely a defense witness — who submits to pretrial hypnosis, the experience will not render his testimony inadmissible if he elects to take the stand. In that case, the rule we adopt herein is subject to a necessary exception to avoid impairing the fundamental right of an accused to testify in his own behalf." 723 P.2d, at 1384.

This case does not involve the admissibility of testimony of previously hypnotized witnesses other than criminal defendants and we express no opinion on that issue.

trained physicians or psychologists has been recognized as a valid therapeutic technique since 1958, although there is no generally accepted theory to explain the phenomenon, or even a consensus on a single definition of hypnosis. The use of hypnosis in criminal investigations, however, is controversial, and the current medical and legal view of its appropriate role is unsettled.

. . . .

We are not now prepared to endorse without qualifications the use of hypnosis as an investigative tool; scientific understanding of the phenomenon and of the means to control the effects of hypnosis is still in its infancy. Arkansas, however, has not justified the exclusion of *all* of a defendant's testimony that the defendant is unable to prove to be the product of prehypnosis memory. A State's legitimate interest in barring unreliable evidence does not extend to *per se* exclusions that may be reliable in an individual case. Wholesale inadmissibility of a defendant's testimony is an arbitrary restriction on the right to testify in the absence of clear evidence by the State repudiating the validity of all posthypnosis recollections. The State would be well within its powers if it established guidelines to aid trial courts in the evaluation of posthypnosis testimony and it may be able to show that testimony in a particular case is so unreliable that exclusion is justified. But it has not shown that hypnotically enhanced testimony is always so untrustworthy and so immune to the traditional means of evaluating credibility that it should disable a defendant from presenting her version of the events for which she is on trial.

In this case, the defective condition of the gun corroborated the details petitioner remembered about the shooting. The tape recordings provided some means to evaluate the hypnosis and the trial judge concluded that Doctor Back did not suggest responses with leading questions. Those circumstances present an argument for admissibility of petitioner's testimony in this particular case, an argument that must be considered by the trial court. Arkansas' *per se* rule excluding all posthypnosis testimony infringes impermissibly on the right of a defendant to testify on his own behalf.

The judgment of the Supreme Court of Arkansas is vacated, and the case is remanded to that court for further proceedings not inconsistent with this opinion.

It is so ordered.

NOTE

Note that the Supreme Court in *Rock* did not say that the defendant's testimony was admissible, but only that the trial court may not exclude the defendant from testifying without "performing the constitutional analysis that is necessary." *Rock, supra,* 483 U.S. at 58. Some states have adopted guidelines to help a trial court assess the reliability of such testimony. *See State v. Butterworth,* 792 P.2d 1049, 1057 (Kan. 1990) (adopting the *Hurd* guidelines); *State v. Holden,* 554 So. 2d 121, 126 (La. Ct. App. 1989) (defendant must demonstrate strict compliance with *Hurd* guidelines by clear and convincing evidence).

PROBLEMS

Problem 4-6. Assume that a person witnesses a violent murder and is so traumatized by the event that he has no present memory of what happened. If the witness is hypnotized, and after hypnosis remembers what happened and can identify the murderer, is his testimony admissible in a state that follows a *per se* rule of excluding such testimony? Does it make any difference if the witness is called by the defense and is prepared to say that the defendant did *not* commit the crime? *See Contreras v. State,* 718 P.2d 129, 139 (Alaska 1986); *Bundy v. State,* 471 So. 2d 9, 17–18 (Fla. 1985); *Burral v. State,* 724 A.2d 65, 81 (Md. 1999).

Problem 4-7. On July 26, 1995, firefighters put out a fire at the home of Katherine Heath. When the fire had cooled Heath's body was found. An investigation revealed that Heath had been shot in the head, and that the fire had been deliberately started after she died in what investigator's concluded was an apparent attempt to hide the murder.

Police arrested two suspects, George and Wesley. Both were seen at Heath's home the night of the murder and fire. George agrees to help police in return for immunity from prosecution, but claims to have an incomplete memory of what happened. Police hypnotize George and his memory is refreshed. He is now prepared to testify that he and Wesley killed Heath and then set fire to her house.

When confronted with George's statement Wesley confesses, but later claims that his confession was false. Wesley then undergoes hypnosis. While under hypnosis he states that George killed Heath and that he, Wesley, tried to stop him.

Wesley is charged with murder and George is not charged based on his receiving immunity.

(A) Is George's hypnotically refreshed testimony admissible?

(B) If you were investigating this case *before* George was hypnotized, what, if anything, could you do to make his subsequent testimony as admissible as possible?

At trial Wesley takes the witness stand and denies he murdered Heath and set fire to her house. He is then impeached with the inconsistent statement in his confession.

(C) Is the prior consistent statement he made while hypnotized admissible for the purpose of rehabilitation?

See United States v. Solomon, 753 F.2d 1522, 1524–26 (9th Cir. 1985).

[b]   Narcoanalysis ("Truth Serums")

Narcoanalysis involves the interrogation of an individual who has been given a drug that depresses the central nervous system. Drugs such as sodium pentothal, sodium amytal, brevital sodium, and scopolamine are used in narcoanalysis, and are commonly referred to as "truth serums." Proponents of narcoanalysis assert that a person with less control over his or her central nervous system will be more relaxed, more talkative, and have less emotional control. The result of this decreased control, it is claimed, is twofold: (1) a decrease in inhibitions and, arguably, an inability to lie; and (2) a stimulation of repressed information.

Narcoanalysis, as a method of compelling a person to tell the truth, has been viewed with a considerable degree of skepticism. The criticisms are similar to those made against receiving testimony from a person who has been hypnotized. For example, opponents claim that only those people who are inclined to confess anyway will confess, and that even if effective in some cases, "truth serums" have no effect on certain individuals. Further, critics argue that narcoanalysis is not reliable because individuals under the influence of a "truth serum" become suggestible and inclined to assert fancy as well as fact.

Narcoanalysis has been uniformly rejected by the courts when offered to prove the truth of the matter asserted while under the influence of a "truth serum." The *Cox* case that follows is typical of cases rejecting the admissibility of statements made by a person under the influence of a "truth serum" drug.

PEOPLE v. COX
271 N.W.2d 216 (Mich. App. 1978)

RILEY, PRESIDING JUDGE.

This case involves a matter of first impression in Michigan, namely the admissibility of expert testimony concerning the results of and conclusions drawn from an interview with the defendant conducted while defendant was under the influence of brevital sodium, a so-called "truth serum" drug.

Defendant Michael Cox was tried on a charge of second-degree murder, and convicted of the lesser offense of careless discharge of a firearm resulting in death. He was sentenced to one year of detention in the Detroit House of Correction and a $1,000 fine.

The incident in question began when both defendant and decedent, and several friends of both, stopped to aid a disabled motorist. An altercation ensued between defendant and decedent, with defendant eventually being pushed by decedent into the on-coming traffic lane, and culminating in the shooting which caused decedent's fatal injury.

Defendant testified that after decedent pushed him into the road, he saw decedent approaching him armed with a baseball bat. Defendant asserted that he fired the fatal shots in self-defense. There was conflicting testimony from other witnesses as to whether decedent, or anyone present, was armed with a bat. However, at the scene of the shooting, the police found a bat in the car of decedent's friend.

At trial the defense sought to introduce the testimony of a psychiatrist who had interviewed defendant after administering a dose of brevital sodium. On a special record the tape recording of that interview was played. The psychiatrist testified that in his opinion the defendant truthfully believed that he had seen decedent armed with a baseball bat. The psychiatrist testified also that his opinion was based solely upon this interview. The trial court ruled that the tape and the testimony concerning the results of the interview and the psychiatrist's opinion were inadmissible. The psychiatrist was allowed to testify generally on certain psychiatric conditions and occurrences, but without reference to defendant or the particular case.

As stated previously, no Michigan case has as yet dealt specifically with the admissibility of the results of a truth serum test. Therefore, we must look for the standards for admissibility by analogy to similar forms of scientific testing evidence. The most appropriate analogy is to polygraph evidence.

The standard for admissibility of polygraph results is the so-called *Davis/Frye* test, which was recently reaffirmed by the [Michigan] Supreme Court. . . .

Tests similar to the *Davis/Frye* standard, which require a showing of a general scientific reliability of truth serum tests prior to admission of the evidence, have been employed by other states which have ruled on evidence obtained by the use of such drugs. The large majority of states which have applied this type of standard to truth serum evidence has found it lacking in scientific recognition and accordingly excluded it from admission.

Applying this test to the case at bar, we find that the trial judge correctly ruled that the results of the brevital sodium test, and the witness's opinions relating to those results, were inadmissible. The psychiatrist himself admitted upon inquiry from the court that there was no medical evidence or studies on the reliability of this drug as a truth serum. Absent such evidence, the court was obligated to rule that the testimony was too uncertain to be allowed before a jury, where it would have had a potentially significant impact.

Affirmed.

NOTES

1. *Offered on Issue of Mental Condition.* Note that offering an opinion about a person's mental condition based upon an examination of that individual that included the use of a "truth serum" presents a different evidentiary issue from that presented when a psychiatrist gives an opinion that an individual the psychiatrist examined while under the influence of a "truth serum" was telling the truth. For example, in *Harper v. State*, 292 S.E.2d 389 (Ga. 1982), a psychiatrist was allowed to testify that "based on [his] own interviews . . . and other reports the defendant suffered from a defect in memory," but was not allowed to testify that, based on the sodium amytal interview, the defendant was telling the truth. *Id.* at 394–95.

Where relevant, expert opinion on an individual's mental condition may be admissible, and *statements made by an individual during an interview with a psychiatrist while under the influence of a "truth serum" may be admissible* as part of the basis for the expert opinion on mental condition. Those same statements (made while under the influence of a "truth serum"), however, if offered for their truth would be inadmissible.

2. *Confession.* Using "truth serum" to induce a confession presents constitutional problems with the confession's voluntariness. *See Townsend v. Sain*, 372 U.S. 293, 307–08 (1963) ("It is difficult to imagine a situation in which a confession would be less the product of a free intellect, less voluntary, than when brought by a drug having the effect of a "truth serum.").

C. DEOXYRIBONUCLEIC ACID (DNA)

[1]   Introduction

The validity of the basic theory underlying DNA analysis, and of established techniques used to create a DNA profile, is universally acknowledged. In fact, courts often take judicial notice of the reliability of DNA theory and established methods for performing DNA testing, and several state legislatures have passed statutes recognizing DNA evidence as reliable and admissible.

Simply put, the theory is that all individuals have DNA, that an individual's DNA is unique to that individual (except in the case of identical twins), and that it is possible, *if testing techniques are properly applied*, to identify an individual by his or her DNA.

Nonetheless, the forensic use of DNA in criminal cases has not been without controversy, and courts have excluded DNA evidence in certain circumstances. Generally speaking, admissibility problems have involved two issues.

First, critics argued that because DNA testing is a complex process, errors are a realistic possibility if reliable testing protocols[29] are not strictly applied. Accordingly, it was argued that even if DNA theory and testing techniques are valid, additional evidentiary hurdles — in the form of affirmative proof that testing procedures were properly applied — ought to be imposed upon DNA testing.

Second, criticism has been directed at probability estimates that typically accompany evidence that the DNA profile in two samples "match." Probability estimates state the likelihood that another person might have the same DNA profile as that found in the two samples (typically a crime scene sample and a sample taken from a suspect). It is not unusual to find such probability estimates in the one-in-several billion range. Critics have argued that these probabilities are misunderstood and misleading. Additionally, it has been argued that if the database used to calculate these probabilities is not accurate, the astounding and damning probabilities are also unreliable, misleading, and highly prejudicial.

An examination of how courts have dealt with these two principal attacks to the admissibility of DNA evidence is the focus of this section. The first issue examined is that of whether using proper test procedures is an issue of weight for the jury or admissibility for the court.

[2]   The Use of Proper Procedures to Create A Dna Profile and Declare A "Match" — an Admissibility Requirement or A Weight Issue for The Jury?

The first area of controversy that arose with the use of DNA evidence in criminal cases concerned the complicated nature of performing a DNA test. The Arizona Supreme Court described DNA testing as a three-step process. First, a DNA "print" or "profile" must be made of the crime scene sample and of the sample to which the crime scene sample is being compared. The second step is determining whether the two profiles "match." If the samples match, the third step requires computing the probability that the match is random or coincidental. *See State v. Bible*, 858 P.2d 1152, 1180 (Ariz. 1993).

The present focus is upon the first step — the creation of a DNA profile from crime scene and other biological samples. As a general proposition, two methods have been used to create a DNA profile for forensic purposes: restriction fragment length polymorphism (RFLP testing) and polymerase chain reaction (PCR-based testing[30]). RFLP testing was the first widely used method for creating a DNA profile, and it dominated the reported cases until the mid 1990s, when DNA testing using PCR technology became the dominant forensic method.

---

[29] Protocols are the steps a technician follows when performing DNA testing from receipt of a specimen through the final result. *See* Taylor v. State, 889 P.2d 319, 323 n.6 (Okla. Crim. App. 1995).

[30] PCR is not itself a method of DNA typing, but a technique used to process and replicate DNA. Later methods of DNA profiling that are based on PCR technology are sometimes collectively referred to as PCR testing. *See* United States v. Ewell, 252 F. Supp. 2d 104, 107 (D.N.J. 2003) (discussing PCR technology). PCR technology is examined in some detail in section 4, *infra*.

RFLP technology was used in the late 1980s when courts were first presented with evidence based upon DNA profiling, and were deciding whether any additional admissibility hurdles ought to be employed with DNA evidence. Accordingly, the complex nature of RFLP DNA testing is an important factor to keep in mind when reading cases from that period. RFLP testing involved a six-step process that could take weeks to complete. This complexity (and its attendant possibility of error) persuaded some courts to require the proponent of DNA evidence to affirmatively show that correct test procedures were applied in the particular case being litigated, as a condition for admissibility.

The examination of the weight versus admissibility issue begins in England, in 1984, with the first forensic use of DNA. The passage that follows, excerpted from *DNA in the Courtroom: A Trial Watcher's Guide*, explains that the way DNA was introduced to the legal system fueled the controversy over whether evidence of correct test procedures should be viewed as an admissibility hurdle. Following the excerpt from *DNA in the Courtroom*, a rather simplified explanation of DNA biology and the RFLP technique is presented.

[a]   The Beginning

HOWARD COLEMAN & ERIC SWENSON, DNA IN THE COURTROOM: A TRIAL WATCHER'S GUIDE, 2–7 (1994)[31]

In the Beginning

The forensic use of DNA started with the work of Alec Jeffreys, a geneticist at the University of Leicester in Britain's Midlands. In 1984, Jeffreys invented the techniques that took human identification from the laboratory to the courtroom. With his co-workers, he . . . demonstrated that forensic samples, dried stains several years old, contained sufficient DNA to yield conclusive results. Jeffreys proved that even small fragments of DNA molecules were virtually unique to individuals. With appropriate dramatic flair, he called the process he invented "DNA fingerprinting," a term most forensic scientists dislike because it is confusing and can be misleading.

The "fingerprint" produced by the test bears a superficial resemblance to a supermarket bar code with the differences between individuals revealed by the spacing between the 15 or 20 lines called bands. The differences between specimens are measured by a process called Restriction Fragment Length Polymorphism (RFLP) analysis.

Jeffreys' new form of genetic typing and the law were linked from the beginning. He sought high-profile forensic tests for his brainchild. First, he applied it to an immigration case. A boy from Ghana sought to emigrate to Britain, claiming that his mother was already a resident. Conventional blood tests were not conclusive beyond confirming that the two could be related. DNA analysis showed beyond reasonable doubt that the relationship was as claimed, and the Home Office put its stamp of approval on the new technology.

Finding the Pitchfork in the Haystack

A detective in the East Midlands read of the [immigration] case and sought Jeffreys' help in solving the vicious murder and rape of two British schoolgirls. The police held a

---

prime suspect in the case, a kitchen porter at an insane asylum who had confessed to one of the murders. They brought Jeffreys semen samples from the murder scenes and a blood sample from the suspect. Jeffreys confirmed that the same person committed both crimes but it was not the suspect the police held. On November 21, 1986, the kitchen porter became the first person in the world to have his innocence proven by DNA testing.

Both the police and villagers in the area felt strongly that the killer was someone in their midst. Police were prompted to try something entirely new. All male residents between the ages of 17 and 34 were asked to voluntarily submit a blood sample. Within a month, a thousand men had been "blooded." By May 1987 the number had risen to more that 3,600. Summer turned to Fall, [and] it seemed that this experiment was destined to be as unproductive as the previous, more conventional efforts.

Then the police received an unexpected tip. A bakery manager chatting in a pub with some of her employees learned that one of their colleagues, Colin Pitchfork, had convinced another baker to be blooded in his stead. After four long years and the disappointment of the porter's false confession, the detectives felt this was the break they were looking for. They went to Pitchfork's home and moments after arresting him, he confessed. He became the 4,583rd and last man to be tested in the hunt for the Midlands killer. His sample provided a perfect match to the sperm taken from his two young victims. It was September of 1987 and forensic DNA was on its way.

Commercial Development in the United States

It also was in 1987 that the British firm of Cellmark Diagnostics opened a branch in Germantown, Maryland and introduced Jeffreys' methods in the United States. The firm is part of Imperial Chemical Industries, a giant British company, which previously established a DNA laboratory in Abingdon, England. When Cellmark set up its operation in this country, it had only one other competitor, Lifecodes Corporation of Valhalla, New York. Founded in 1982, Lifecodes began forensic DNA testing in 1987 and took the lion's share of the market early.

Lifecodes performed the tests in the first case in the United States in which a criminal was identified by DNA. The trial of accused rapist Tommy Lee Andrews began in Orlando, Florida on November 3, 1987. A scientist from Lifecodes and a M.I.T. biologist testified that semen from the victim matched Andrews' DNA, and that Andrews' print would be found in only 1 in 10 billion individuals. On November 6, 1987, the jury returned a guilty verdict and Andrews was subsequently sentenced to 22 years in prison.

This case was heavily reported by the press, creating a media blitz favorable to the new technology. Defense attorneys were caught off guard by the technology and largely accepted it without question. Other cases quickly followed with the same result. Judges and juries were clearly impressed with this new technology.

The introduction of DNA methods to the courtroom by private companies was unique in the history of forensic science. The sharp competition, the proprietary approach of the industry and their desire to keep their products and processes under wraps did not create a favorable environment in which to launch a new technology with such vast potential for changing the criminal justice system. Patent challenges, litigation, and technology-licensing questions became the norm and continue to impede the introduction of technological improvements.

The usual methods of testing new scientific methods are publication and peer review. The requirements for standardization and replication in multiple labs and evaluation of test performance under exacting environmental conditions are of paramount importance in the validation of a forensic test. These did not occur as the commercial laboratories maintained secrecy while rushing to get a return on their substantial investment and start-up costs.

In essence, the major private companies were racing with each other to the courtroom. They hoped to license their procedures and sell their proprietary materials and reagents to as many crime laboratories as they could. They used different tools that produced incompatible results which precluded comparison. As DNA testing became established, some labs were overwhelmed with casework. Systems were not yet in place to ensure quality control, nor had the labs performed sufficient validation studies. They were run like research labs, having been started by academic scientists, not forensic scientists. While the juggernaut of DNA seemed unstoppable, the very speed with which it was moving boded ill.

Rush to Judgment

Case after case involving DNA evidence was won by the prosecution on the basis of testing and testimony provided by Lifecodes and Cellmark. The two companies, while competing for the same business, often joined forces to promote the new technology to the bench, bar, and law enforcement. Their job was made easier by an adulatory press that wrote numerous stories about the miracle technology that fingered criminals with unerring accuracy.

Judges accepted the assertions of industry witnesses at face value and juries were wowed by the big numbers they were offered. In the words of a Massachusetts Supreme Court justice, DNA had acquired an "aura of infallibility." One juror in Queens put it succinctly when he said, "You can't argue with science." Judge Joseph Harris of Albany, N.Y., after sentencing a defendant on a murder and rape charge that hinged on DNA evidence, called it the "single greatest advance in the search for truth since the advent of cross-examination."

The reaction within the defense bar ranged from bemusement to shell shock. One Florida prosecutor commiserated with attorneys representing guilty clients. "If they print your guy with this stuff, you're dead. You can't combat it. There is no defense to it." Defense attorney Robert Brower's assessment was equally unequivocal. He felt that DNA evidence threatened the constitutional right to a fair trial. "In rape cases, when the semen has been matched with the defendant's and the chance that it came from another person is 33 billion to 1, you don't need a jury."

Across the board, the new technology was changing the criminal justice system, and defense attorneys didn't like this development. Of course, they could hope that at least some of the DNA convictions would be reversed on appeal. In the meantime, they were clearly on the defensive as they never had been before.

New York v. Castro: The Chink in the Armor

When police arrived at the Bronx apartment of Jeffrey Otero in February 1987, they discovered a scene of terrible carnage. Vilma Ponce, Otero's seven months pregnant common-law wife, lay on the living room floor, nude from the waist down. She was perforated by more than sixty knife wounds. In the bathroom, police found the body of her two-year-old daughter, Natasha, also repeatedly stabbed.

Police interviewed Jose' Castro, the janitor of a neighboring building who fit Otero's description of the suspect. The detective noticed what he thought might be a dried bloodstain on Castro's watch and asked if he could retain it for examination. Shortly thereafter, Castro was arrested and charged with the double murder. The dried blood on Jose' Castro's watch and how it was handled led to the first notable courtroom challenge to DNA typing.

Police turned the watch, along with blood samples from Castro and the two victims, over to the Lifecodes Corporation. Scientists analyzed the dried blood and during the 15 week long pre-trial evidentiary hearing, testified that the DNA from the stain matched that of Vilma Ponce, and that the frequency of her patterns in the Hispanic population were 1:189,200,000.

The defense undertook a thorough examination of the genetic analyses and mounted the first extended (and eventually successful) effort to have DNA evidence excluded. What also occurred in the Castro case that contributed to this turn of events was an unprecedented out-of-court meeting between two defense and two prosecution scientific witnesses after they had testified. These scientists all agreed that Lifecodes had failed to use generally accepted scientific techniques in reaching their results matching the blood found on Castro's watch with that of Vilma Ponce. The quality of the data they produced was poor and they did not even follow their own procedures for interpreting the data.

As a result. . . , the judge ruled that the inclusionary tests suggesting that Ponce was the source of the blood stain were inadmissible, while allowing the exclusionary evidence that the blood did not come from Castro. After almost one hundred cases where DNA evidence met little or no resistance and never was ruled inadmissible, the defense obtained their first victory. Later that year, in what was to be the anti-climax to the case, Castro confessed to the murders, admitting that the blood on his watch came from Vilma Ponce, and pled guilty.

The FBI and Mounties Ride to the Rescue

Fortunately, the Federal Bureau of Investigation and the Royal Canadian Mounted Police entered the picture at about this time, with a salutary effect. The FBI saw the potential for the forensic use of DNA testing at about the same time that Alec Jeffreys was conducting his breakthrough experiments. Along with the National Institutes of Health, the FBI began collaborative research and in 1987, set up its own research unit to establish DNA identification techniques for the Bureau. After one year of testing, ending in late 1988, the FBI set up their own DNA laboratory at their Pennsylvania Avenue headquarters. The RCMP soon followed with their own DNA laboratory.

The Bureau benefitted from the experience of DNA lab pioneers here and in Europe, and was not locked into a single technology or product. When the FBI lab went on-line, it used a combination of four different DNA probes, including those developed by GeneLex, Dr. Raymond White of the Howard Hughes Medical Center, Lifecodes, and Cellmark. DNA probes and primers are the key patented biochemicals used to identify individual genetic differences.

The main result of the FBI and RCMP beginning their own DNA testing was standardization of a chaotic industry. The Federal agency established detailed laboratory protocols, performed appropriate validation studies, and cut through the competing systems, methods, and tools to establish a standardized system that is used in almost all North American laboratories today. The raising of standards became easier once standardization was achieved.

[b]   DNA Science and the RFLP Technique

A basic understanding of the science and testing procedures applicable to DNA testing is helpful in appreciating both the significance of DNA as a tool to identify people, and in understanding the legal issues that have been generated by the forensic use of DNA testing. The excerpt that follows is from *Commonwealth v. Blasioli*, a case decided by the Pennsylvania Supreme Court in 1998. In the excerpt the Pennsylvania Supreme Court discusses both the scientific principles that apply to DNA testing. The excerpt is provided, at this point, only for its explanation of the scientific principles underlying DNA testing.

COMMONWEALTH v. BLASIOLI
713 A.2d 1117 (Pa. 1998)

SAYLOR, JUSTICE.

. . . .

In addressing the merits of the parties' arguments, a brief description of the scientific principles and procedures applied in DNA analysis is necessary. DNA is genetic material found in most types of cells of the human body, including white blood cells and cells contained in semen and hair follicles.[32] [4] DNA constitutes the primary element of an organism's total genetic information, known as its genome. In the process of cellular division, DNA functions essentially as a template, providing a blueprint for resulting cells. . . . DNA also . . . determines an organism's unique physical composition.

A DNA molecule consists of strands in the shape of a ladder, twisted into a characteristic shape resembling a spiral staircase, which is described as a double helix. Each side of the ladder is composed of repeated sequences of phosphate and sugar olecules, with a nitrogen-containing chemical called a base extending toward the opposite side to join a complimentary base, together forming a rung of the ladder.[33] [5] Each unit of a strand, containing one sugar molecule, one phosphate molecule and one base, is called a nucleotide.

Each pair of nucleotide bases joined to form the rungs of the DNA ladder is called a base pair, of which there are over three billion in any single DNA molecule. It is the unique, repeating sequences of the base pairs along the double strands of DNA that provides the instructions for individual human characteristics. A gene, the fundamental unit of heredity, is a functional unit of DNA containing the base pair sequence responsible for a particular characteristic. The human genome is estimated to comprise

---

[32] [n.4] In every nucleated cell in the human body, long strands of DNA are compressed and entwined into bodies called chromosomes, of which there are twenty-three pairs, one-half of each pair in an individual being donated by one's father and the other by the mother.

[33] [n.5] There are four kinds of nucleotide bases in DNA: adenine (A), guanine (G), cytosine (C) and thymine (T). Due to their chemical composition, these can fit together only as follows: adenine will pair only with thymine, and cytosine will pair only with guanine. This strict pairing requires that the order of bases on one side of a DNA ladder will determine the order on the other side, establishing the basis for accurate cell reproduction upon splitting of a DNA molecule.

at least 100,000 genes. Alternative forms of genes are known as alleles,[34] [6] and the position of a gene or allele on a chromosome is known as its locus.

Large segments of human DNA are the same from person to person, accounting for human characteristics that are generally shared. Indeed, from the sequence of the 3 billion base pairs, only about 3 million differ from one individual to another (except in the case of identical twins, who have identical DNA). It is the existence of such differences in the sequencing of base pairs, known as "polymorphisms," that provides the basis for DNA identification.[35] [7]

NOTES AND QUESTIONS

1. *Another Explanation of DNA Biology.* In *People v. Brown*, 110 Cal. Rptr. 2d 750 (Cal. Ct. App. 2001), the court presented a "simplified" explanation of DNA biology. The description is consistent with that given by the court in *Blasioli, supra* ; however, it presents the topic in terms more familiar to the non-scientist.

1. Genetic Profiling. We begin with some simplified biology. The genetics of a human cell can be compared to a library, the *genome*, composed of 46 books, each a single *chromosome.* The text contained in the books is written in *DNA,* the chemical language of genetics. The library is compiled by the owner's parents, each of whom contributes 23 books, which are then matched up and arranged together in 23 paired sets inside the sacrosanct edifice of the *nucleus.* During embryonic development, the original library is copied millions of times so that each cell in the human body contains a copy of the entire library.

Twenty-two of the twenty-three paired sets of books are entitled "Chromosome 1" through "Chromosome 22"; externally, the two paired books of each set appear to be identical in size and shape. However, the twenty-third set, which contains information on gender, consists of one book entitled "Chromosome X" (given by the mother) and one book entitled either "Chromosome X" or "Chromosome Y" (given by the father and determining the sex of the library's owner). The 22 sets comprising "Chromosome 1" through "Chromosome 22" address an enormous variety of topics describing the composition, appearance, and function of the owner's body. In addition, they include a considerable amount of what appears to be nonsense. The two paired books of each set, one book from each parent, address identical topics, but may contain slightly different information on those topics. Thus, two paired books opened to the same page contain corresponding paragraphs, but the text within those corresponding paragraphs may vary between the two books. For example, within the paragraph addressing eye color, one book may describe blue eyes while the other book of the set may describe brown eyes.

The two corresponding, but potentially variant, paragraphs in the two paired books are called *alleles.* If, for a particular topic (i.e., at a particular region or *locus* on the DNA), the allele from the mother is A and the corresponding allele

---

[34] [n.6] For example, the gene for the production of eyes may take the form of a blue-eyed allele or a green-eyed allele. The difference between the alleles results from the sequence of the base pairs along the DNA strands. Each parent contributes one copy of each gene, so every individual has two copies or alleles of each gene.

[35] [n.7] Such identification is also referred to as DNA identity testing, profiling, fingerprinting, typing or genotyping.

from the father is B, the *genotype* at that locus is designated AB. The text of two corresponding alleles at any locus may be identical (a *homozygous* genotype, e.g., AA) or different (a *heterozygous* genotype, e.g., AB). Regardless, one person's genetic text is, in general, extremely similar to another person's; indeed, viewed in its vast entirety, the genetic text of one human library is 99.9 percent identical to all others. As a result, the text of most corresponding paragraphs varies only slightly among members of the population.

Certain alleles, however, have been found to contain highly variable text. For example, alleles are composed of highly variable text when they describe structures requiring enormous variability. Also, some alleles appear to contain gibberish that varies greatly, or repeated strings of text that vary not in text but in repeat number. These variants (*polymorphisms*) found at certain *loci* render each person's library unique [Identical twins, however, share essentially identical DNA] and provide forensic scientists a method of differentiating between libraries (people) through the use of forensic techniques that rely on the large number of variant alleles possible at each variable locus. For example, the combined libraries of the human population may contain two variant alleles at a particular locus, three at another, nine at another, and so on. Since each person receives two alleles for each locus, the number of possible combinations is further increased.

When a sample of DNA — usually in the form of hair, blood, saliva, or semen — is left at the crime scene by a perpetrator, a forensic genetic analysis is conducted. First, DNA analysts create a genetic "profile" or "type" of the perpetrator's DNA by determining which variants or alleles exist at several variable loci. Second, the defendant's DNA is analyzed in exactly the same manner to create a profile for comparison with the perpetrator's profile. If the defendant's DNA produces a different profile than the perpetrator's, even by only one allele, the defendant could not have been the source of the crime scene DNA, and he or she is absolutely exonerated. If, on the other hand, the defendant's DNA produces exactly the same genetic profile, the defendant could have been the source of the perpetrator's DNA — but so could any other person with the same genetic profile. Third, when the perpetrator's and defendant's profiles are found to match, the statistical significance of the match must be explained in terms of the rarity or commonness of that profile within a particular population that is, the number of people within a population expec ted to possess that particular genetic profile, or, put another way, the probability that a randomly chosen person in that population possesses that particular genetic profile. Only then can the jury weigh the value of the profile match."

People v. Brown, 110 Cal. Rptr. 2d 750, 753–55 (Cal. Ct. App. 2001).

2. *Alleles.* One point should be stressed. The excerpt from *Blasioli, supra* , correctly notes that an "allele" is one of two or more alternative forms of a gene on a chromosome at a particular site. Much of current DNA testing examines sites along the DNA molecule that differ among people, but which do not contain any genes. Such sites are sometimes referred to as "junk DNA" because these sites have no known function and appear to simply be "spacers" between the genes. In DNA testing the term "allele" is expanded, and is used to refer to any DNA region that is used for analysis whether that region contains a gene or is simply a "spacer." Such non-gene alleles are sometimes referred to as "Variable Number Tandem Repeats" (VNTRs) because the same sequence of base pairs are repeated successively, but for numbers of times that differ from person to person. *See People v. Venegas*, 954 P.2d 525, 532 n. 10, n. 11 (Cal. 1998).

3. *The Six-Step RFLP Method of DNA Testing.* In *State v. Davis*, 814 S.W.2d 593 (Mo. 1991), the Missouri Supreme Court considered the admissibility of DNA evidence. In that case the court discussed the six-step RFLP process.

The DNA fingerprinting process . . . involves six steps:

1) *Extraction.* The DNA is chemically extracted from the blood sample and purified to obtain a high molecular DNA.

2) *Fragmentation.* The DNA molecule, too large to deal with as a single unit, is then cut into fragments by a restricting enzyme which, depending upon the enzyme selected, cuts the DNA fragment precisely at a designated point.

3) *Electrophoresis.* The DNA fragments are then placed in an agarose gel between two electrically charged poles which assist in separating the fragments by size, the smaller fragments moving more readily through the gel than the large. The end result is an orderly pattern of the fragments in parallel lines.

4) *Southern Blotting.* Named for Dr. Ed Southern who pioneered the process in the mid-1970's, the DNA band pattern in the agarose gel is then transferred to a nylon membrane which resembles a sheet of heavy blotting paper. During this process, the DNA strands are "unzipped" from one another at their base pairings.

5) *Hybridization.* Radioactive tagged probes, which are small DNA fragments developed in the laboratory, are then introduced onto the nylon membrane. The probes locate and attach themselves to recognized complementary base sequences, in essence "zipping" back parts of the DNA fragments.

6) *Autoradiograph.* The excess probes are washed away and the nylon membrane is then placed next to a sheet of x-ray film and exposed for several days. The end product is a series of dark parallel bands resembling the Universal Bar Codes on labels commonly found in retail stores to identify stacks of merchandise. The result is known as an autoradiograph or commonly an autorad. This then is the DNA fingerprint.

State v. Davis, 814 S.W.2d 593, 598–99 (Mo. 1991).

4. To better understand the legal issues that accompany the admissibility of DNA evidence it is essential to have some basic knowledge of DNA biology, methodology, and terminology. Refer back to *Blasioli, supra* , and Notes 1, 2, and 3 in answering these questions.

(A) Which cells in the human body contain DNA?

(B) What are "base pairs" (or nucleotides)?

(C) How many base pairs, or "rungs of the DNA ladder" are contained in a single DNA molecule? How many base pairs differ from person to person?

(D) DNA is apportioned into 46 discrete sections. What are these sections called?

(E) What is a gene?

(F) What are different types, or alternate forms, of genes called?

(G) What is a "polymorphic site"?

(H) How many steps are there in the RFLP method for creating a DNA profile?

[c]   The Judicial Response

Two points made in the excerpt from *DNA in the Courtroom: A Trial Watcher's Guide, supra,* bear repeating. First, DNA was initially introduced into the courtroom by *private companies* who were trying to make a return on their initial investment and start-up costs, and who were in competition with other companies. Sharp competition and the desire to keep one's products and processes under wraps precluded the peer review and empirical testing that usually occurred when a new scientific technique was initially brought to the courtroom.

Second, in the first major challenge to DNA evidence in 1989, *People v. Castro,* 545 N.Y.S.2d 985 (N.Y. Sup. Ct. 1989), defense and prosecution witnesses agreed that the laboratory that performed the DNA testing, Lifecodes Corporation, had failed to follow generally accepted scientific techniques in reaching their results. In fact, Lifecodes had not even followed their own procedures for interpreting the data their testing had produced.

Accordingly, while courts had no reason to doubt the validity of DNA theory and the RFLP technique, the way DNA technology was introduced to the legal system, and the sloppiness exhibited by Lifecodes in the *Castro* case, suggested that there were reasons to be wary of the way a DNA test was performed in a particular case. The *Perry* case and the Notes that follow *Perry* discuss the judicial response to these issues.

EX PARTE PERRY v. STATE
586 So. 2d 242 (Ala. 1991)

KENNEDY, JUSTICE.

Waylon Dwight Perry was convicted of capital murder, and the trial court, accepting the jury's recommendation, sentenced Perry to life imprisonment without parole. . . . We granted certiorari review to address one issue: Whether DNA evidence, which was used to identify Perry as the perpetrator of the crime, is admissible in Alabama. . . .

In July 1988 Bryce Wallace was strangled to death in his house. When law enforcement officers investigated, they found bloodstains on Wallace's clothing and on the front doorknob of Wallace's house. Those bloodstains were later analyzed with a procedure called "DNA print analysis" [using the RFLP method for creating a DNA profile] by Lifecodes Corporation ("Lifecodes"), a New York corporation that performs DNA tests in relation to criminal and paternity lawsuits.

. . . .

At trial the State called as its first two witnesses Joanne Squeglia and Dr. Kevin McElfresh. Squeglia testified at some length concerning how she performed the DNA testing procedures comparing the DNA of the individual whose blood was on Wallace and on Wallace's front doorknob to Perry's DNA. Dr. McElfresh, the assistant manager of Lifecodes' forensics laboratory, testified that he interpreted the results of the tests Squeglia performed. Dr. McElfresh explained the procedures that Lifecodes normally performs in DNA analysis; when the State asked Dr. McElfresh to state the conclusions that he drew from that analysis, Perry's attorney objected, with this statement:

> "For the record, we object to Dr. McElfresh's opinion — his rendering an opinion as to the identity on the blood type in relationship to Waylon Perry because the Lifecodes test has not been proven trustworthy in Alabama. We maintain that it is not trustworthy. There are several things that can cause variations in this type testing; and that his testimony with regard to a conclusion of identity should be excluded."

Dr. McElfresh testified that Perry's DNA "matched" the DNA of the blood found on Wallace and on Wallace's front doorknob. We refer to this testimony as testimony concerning DNA "matching" evidence. Dr. McElfresh also testified that . . . the probability of finding similar DNA was 1 in 209,100,000. We refer to this testimony as evidence of "DNA population frequency statistics."

Perry argues that the trial court erred by submitting the DNA evidence to the jury without first holding a hearing outside the presence of the jury as to its admissibility. Such a hearing is necessary, Perry argues, because, the trial court otherwise is presuming that the evidence is admissible, although DNA evidence is novel scientific evidence that this Court has never held to be admissible. Such a holding, Perry contends, turns the only contention about the DNA evidence to an argument over its proper weight without ever addressing the threshold issue of admissibility.

. . . Perry . . . challenges the admissibility of the DNA evidence because such evidence has not previously been held admissible by this Court and because there is the possibility that DNA testing can produce flawed results. . . .

    . . . .

The Frye Test and Admitting Novel Scientific Evidence

In Alabama, whether novel scientific evidence is admissible is determined normally by using the test established in *Frye v. United States*, 293 F. 1013 (D.C. Cir. 1923). . . .

Other courts have discussed what *Frye* requires to permit the introduction of DNA evidence and whether the *Frye* requirements should be modified somewhat in relation to the admission of DNA evidence. Cf. . . . *[People v.] Castro*, [545 N.Y.S.2d 985 (Sup. Ct. 1989)]; United States v. Two Bulls, 918 F.2d 56 (8th Cir. 1990); For example, in *Castro*, the court, addressing the admissibility of DNA evidence, wrote:

> "The court has advanced the following three prong analysis to aid in the evaluation and resolution of the issues presented:

>> "Prong I. Is there a theory, which is generally accepted in the scientific community, which supports the conclusion that DNA forensic testing can produce reliable results?

>> "Prong II. Are there techniques or experiments that currently exist that are capable of producing reliable results in DNA identification and which are generally accepted in the scientific community?

>> "Prong III. Did the testing laboratory perform the accepted scientific techniques in analyzing the forensic samples in this particular case?

"In dealing with DNA identification tests, some courts have considered all three questions as part of the inquiry under *Frye*.

"Others, in guarding the province of the trier of the facts, have indicated that the third question goes to the weight of the evidence, not the admissibility under *Frye*.

. . . .

"[T]his court [concludes] that a different approach is required in this complex area of DNA identification. The focus of this controversy must be shifted. It must be centered around the resolution of the third prong.

"It is the view of this court that given the complexity of the DNA multi-system identification tests and the powerful impact that they may have on a jury, passing muster under *Frye* alone is insufficient to place this type of evidence before a jury without a preliminary, critical examination of the actual testing procedures performed in a particular case.

"Accordingly, the first two prongs of the analysis deal strictly and exclusively with the *Frye* issue. The third prong is the subject of a pre-trial hearing on the question of the admissibility of the particular evidence presented in this case."

545 N.Y.S.2d at 987–88.

In *Two Bulls*, a case of first impression in the federal circuit courts, the Eighth Circuit Court of Appeals adopted a standard similar to *Castro's*. After holding that *Frye* and Rule 702 of the Federal Rules of Evidence would require the establishment of similar foundations to allow the admission of DNA evidence, the court wrote:

"We hold that it was error for the trial court to determine the admissibility of the DNA evidence without determining whether the testing procedures used by the FBI lab in this case were conducted properly. In weighing the overall admissibility of such evidence, the court should hear testimony from experts on both sides as to the scientific acceptability and reliability of any novel scientific tests. The trial judge should rule as a matter of law (1) whether the DNA evidence is scientifically acceptable, (2) whether there are certain standard procedures that should be followed in conducting these tests, and (3) whether these standards were followed in this case. If the trial court is preliminarily satisfied that these requirements have been met the evidence should be admitted and the jury should be allowed to determine the weight that should be allocated to it.

918 F.2d at 61.

. . . .

Each of the cases from which we have quoted, as well each case that we have reviewed concerning the admissibility of DNA evidence, including cases from jurisdictions that do not follow *Frye*, note one similar concern with the admission of the evidence: however accepted and proper the scientific theory underlying DNA evidence analysis is, and however acceptable the techniques for DNA testing based on that theory, there remains the possibility for error in the . . . performance of the tests. . . . As regards the concern for the problems in the use of a particular technique, the sole source of disagreement seems to be whether *Frye* or some other source of law requires that for

DNA evidence to be admissible, it must be shown that there was no error in the . . . performance of the tests.

. . . Like every other court that has addressed the admissibility of DNA evidence, we recognize the possibility of error in the . . . performance of the tests as a legitimate concern. . . . Accordingly, considering both this concern and the *Frye* test, we hold that the following three-pronged test, substantially similar to that announced in *Castro*, is the test by which to determine the admissibility of the contested evidence:

I. Is there a theory, generally accepted in the scientific community, that supports the conclusion that DNA forensic testing can produce reliable results?

II. Are there current techniques that are capable of producing reliable results in DNA identification and that are generally accepted in the scientific community?

III. In this particular case, did the testing laboratory perform generally accepted scientific techniques without error in the performance . . . of the tests?

We believe that our statement of the third prong says in substance what the court in *Castro* meant.

Admissibility Analysis Under the
Three-Pronged Test

Prong I: The Theory.

Considering both the record in this case and the holdings of other courts that have addressed this issue, we hold that as to the DNA "matching" evidence there is a theory, generally accepted in the scientific community, that supports the conclusion that DNA forensic testing can produce reliable results. . . .

Prong II: Techniques.

Considering the holdings of other courts that have addressed this issue, we hold that there are current techniques that are capable of producing reliable results in DNA "matching" and that are generally accepted in the scientific community. . . .

Prong III: Performance and Interpretation of Accepted Techniques.

The third prong asks: In this particular case, did the testing laboratory perform generally accepted scientific techniques without error in the performance . . . of the tests?

In order to answer this question, we must make two inquiries. First, were the techniques used by the testing laboratory generally accepted in the scientific community? Second, was there error in the performance . . . of the tests?

Regarding the first inquiry, we recognize and are almost persuaded by the holdings in other cases that have involved the question whether Lifecodes' techniques are generally accepted in the scientific community. In each instance, Lifecodes' techniques were held to be generally accepted in the scientific community. The record before us does not support such a holding, however. . . . Squeglia and Dr. McElfresh testified in a limited, conclusory manner that the techniques they used were generally accepted in the scientific community. Considering the import of this issue, we will not hold that that testimony of Squeglia and Dr. McElfresh, who both have an obvious interest in validating Lifecodes' techniques, was sufficient to support a holding that those techniques are generally accepted in the scientific community.

We note that if in the future it is proved to this Court that certain techniques are generally accepted in the scientific community and then those same techniques are *exclusively* used in other cases, it may be possible to hold as a matter of law that the techniques are generally accepted in the scientific community.

The evidence in the record before us is not sufficient for us to determine whether there was error in the performance . . . of the tests.[36] Perry cross-examined Dr. McElfresh on this issue, but Perry did not provide his own evidence to establish that there was error in the performance . . . of the tests. The cases that we have discussed in relation to other issues of admissibility strongly suggest that DNA evidence can meet every other requirement of admissibility but nevertheless fail on this requirement.

. . . .

Finally, in regard to whether there was error in the performance . . . of the tests, we note that this challenge to admissibility will be available even if the challenge under the first portion of the third prong is determined as a matter of law.

To summarize our discussion of the third prong of the admissibility test, we hold that the evidence in the record before us is insufficient for us to determine whether there was error under either of the two inquiries that must be addressed in the third prong of the analysis. . . .

. . . .

Procedures for Challenging DNA Evidence

Earlier, we stated that Perry contends that the trial court erred by submitting the DNA evidence to the jury without first holding a hearing concerning its admissibility. As we explain presently, we do not hold that the trial court has necessarily erred.

We do hold, however, that if the admissibility of DNA evidence is challenged, the trial court should conduct a hearing outside the presence of the jury to address the considerations raised in this opinion. That hearing can be conducted either as a preliminary hearing or when the court chooses, but it should be held outside the presence of the jury, because the admissibility of the evidence is what is challenged. . . .

DNA evidence is discoverable at least by the defendant. The defendant's fair trial and due process rights . . . clearly require that the prosecution allow the defendant access to the DNA evidence.

. . . .

---

[36] [n.1] We are aware of the testimony of Squeglia and Dr. McElfresh that a DNA test cannot indicate a match when there is no match, because the test will simply fail to provide any results if it is improperly performed. Similar claims were made by scientists in [other cases]. From these statements, the State contends that a match, if made, cannot be flawed. We strongly reject both this contention and the testimony supporting it as hyperbole. Our discussion particularly of *Castro* . . . indicates that there can be errors in both the performance of the tests and their interpretation, both of which can lead to an improper "match."

Judgment

. . . Because of the novelty of the issues presented in this case, because only with this opinion have we established methods for admitting DNA evidence in Alabama, because the record does not sufficiently indicate whether the evidence was admissible, and considering the potentially devastating impact on Perry's defense caused by the DNA evidence presented at trial, we remand this cause to the Court of Criminal Appeals with instructions for it to remand for the trial court to conduct an evidentiary hearing to determine the admissibility of both the DNA "matching" evidence and the DNA population frequency statistical evidence. If the trial court determines that either the "matching" evidence or the population frequency statistical evidence is inadmissible, then the admission of the testimony was improper and the trial court should enter an order granting Perry a new trial. . . .

Remanded with Instructions.

NOTES

1. *DNA Theory and Technique; Judicial Notice and Legislative Admissibility.* In *Perry* the Alabama Supreme Court found that DNA theory and the RFLP technique were generally accepted. Many courts (including Alabama) have taken judicial notice of the reliability of DNA science, theory, and of specific techniques used in creating a DNA profile. *See e.g., United States v. Beasley*, 102 F.3d 1440, 1448 (8th Cir. 1996) (PCR method); *United States v. Martinez*, 3 F.3d 1191, 1197–98 (8th Cir. 1993) (RFLP method; *State v. Traylor*, 656 N.W.2d 885, 893 (Minn. 2003) (PCR-STR technology); *State v. Butterfield*, 27 P.3d 1133, 1143 (Utah 2001) (PCR-STR method); *Turner v. State*, 746 So. 2d 355, 362 (Ala. 1998) (RFLP technique); *Taylor v. State*, 889 P.2d 319, 338–39 (Okla. Crim. App. 1995) (RFLP method). DNA evidence has been so well received that several states have passed legislation regarding the admissibility of DNA evidence. For example, Connecticut's statute provides:

> In any criminal proceeding, DNA (deoxyribonucleic acid) testing shall be deemed to be a reliable scientific technique and the evidence of a DNA profile comparison may be admitted to prove or disprove the identity of any person. . . .

CONN. GEN. STAT. ANN. § 54-86k (2001). *See Armstead v. State*, 673 A.2d 221, 230 n.12 (Md. 1996) (listing 12 states that legislatively admit DNA evidence). *See also* HOWARD COLEMAN & ERIC SWENSON, DNA IN THE COURTROOM: A TRIAL WATCHER'S GUIDE 113–20 (1994) (same); Michael J, Short, Comment, *Forensic DNA Analysis: An Examination of Common Objections Raised to the Admission of DNA Fingerprinting as Illustrated by* State v. Pierce, 19 U. DAYTON L. REV. 133, 143 n.101 (1993) [hereinafter *Forensic DNA Analysis*].

It is important to remember, however, that there is more than one technique or method for preparing a DNA profile. That is, just because a court has judicially noticed the RFLP testing or PCR technology as reliable does not mean that a new technique for creating a DNA profile will be able to avoid scrutiny under *Daubert* or *Frye*. *See State v. Traylor*, 656 N.W.2d 885, 890 (Minn. 2003) ("We have already concluded that 'DNA typing is generally acceptable.' [W]e explicitly emphasized, however, that our holding . . . of general acceptance was limited to the principles underlying RFLP testing. As such, this new testing methodology [PCR-STR] presents a question of first impression for us."); *Turner v. State*, 746 So. 2d 355, 362 (Ala. 1998) ("We recognize that the state of scientific theories and the techniques for producing DNA evidence is not static, and that the scientific community undoubtedly will produce new theories and techniques regarding DNA. Each new theory and technique will be subject to the test set out above [*Daubert*] until its reliability warrants judicial notice.").

2. DNA Test Performance — The Majority View; Errors in Test Performance Is a Weight (Not an Admissibility) Issue. As a general proposition, courts accept the science and theory underlying DNA testing, as well current methods used for producing a DNA profile. Accordingly, a significant issue concerns whether the proponent of DNA evidence must present affirmative evidence to establish that an accepted technique or method of DNA testing was actually performed correctly in the particular case before the court.

While there is authority for each view, the trend favors treating procedural deficiencies as a matter of weight for the jury. *See* 2 SCIENTIFIC EVIDENCE § 18.05[b], at 104 (4th ed. 2007) (noting the trend); Edward J. Imwinkelried, *The Debate in the DNA Cases Over the Foundation for the Admission of Scientific Evidence: The Importance of Human Error as a Cause for Forensic Misanalysis*, 69 WASH. U.L.Q. 19, 21 (1991) ("[C]ourts have tended to rule that any deficiencies in the specific manner in which the analyst conducts the DNA typing test affect the weight but not the admissibility of the evidence."). Indeed, six years after the Alabama Supreme Court issued its opinion in *Perry, supra*, the Court held that pursuant to a state statute, Alabama courts must use the *Daubert* test when determining the admissibility of DNA evidence, and that procedural deficiencies in DNA testing are a weight consideration for the jury — not an admissibility requirement for the proponent of DNA evidence.

> Whether otherwise reliable testing procedures were performed without error in a particular case goes to the weight of the evidence, not its admissibility. Only if a party challenges the performance of a reliable and relevant technique and shows that the performance was so particularly and critically deficient that it undermined the reliability of the technique, will evidence that is otherwise reliable and relevant be deemed inadmissible.

Turner v. State, 746 So. 2d 355, 361 (Ala. 1998).

Courts that fall into the majority (or weight camp) include both *Frye* and *Daubert* jurisdictions. *See Taylor v. State*, 889 P.2d 319, 330 n.46 (Okla. Crim. App. 1995) (*Daubert* jurisdiction; "allegations of error in the testing process affect the weight of scientific . . . evidence but not its admissibility"); *State v. Davis*, 814 S.W.2d 593, 603 (Mo. 1991) (Court uses *Frye* test and concludes that "manner in which the [DNA] tests were conducted goes more to the credibility of the witness and the weight of the evidence. . . ."). In *United States v. Shea*, 957 F. Supp. 331 (D.N.H. 1997) the court explained the weight approach.

> Shea . . . challenges the reliability of the DNA evidence by pointing to several alleged deficiencies in the FBI's evidence handling and quality control procedures. Shea contends that the FBI laboratory mishandled the evidence by packaging the dried blood samples in individual paper coin envelopes and storing them together. [Shea's expert,] Dr. Riley theorizes that this practice is fatally flawed because DNA from one sample could migrate through a paper coin envelope and contaminate other similarly packaged samples. . . .

> I need not address the merits of Shea's arguments. Instead, I join the many courts that have addressed similar issues by concluding that because such

arguments concern the way in which a method is applied in a particular case rather than the validity of the method, they affect the weight that should be given to the evidence rather than its admissibility.

Id. at 340–41.

3. *Amended Rule 702.* Several Federal Circuits have held that mistakes in arriving at test results are a matter of weight for the jury to decide. *United States v. Jakobetz*, 955 F.2d 786, 800 (2d Cir. 1992) (pre-*Daubert* DNA case using a reliability test; performing correct test protocols goes to weight); *United States v. Bonds*, 12 F.3d 540, 563 (6th Cir. 1993) (criticisms concerning laboratory mistakes are for the jury); *United States v. Chischilly*, 30 F.3d 1144, 1154 (9th Cir. 1994) (impact of imperfectly conducted lab procedures is an issue going to weight, not admissibility of DNA evidence). One factor that bears watching is how (if at all) amended Rule 702 will impact this issue. On December 31, 2000, an amendment to Rule 702 went into effect that provided, among other things, that scientific evidence would be admissible, "if . . . the [expert] witness has applied the principles and methods reliably to the facts of the case." Fed. R. Evid. 702. *See* 2 SCIENTIFIC EVIDENCE § 18.05[b], at 104 (4th ed. 2007) (the 2000 amendment to Rule 702 "seems to reinstate the requirement that the proponent make a foundational showing that the expert utilized correct test procedures").

4. *DNA Test Performance — The Minority View; Evidence of Proper Test Performance Is an Admissibility Requirement.* States that require the proponent of DNA evidence to establish that an accepted testing technique was correctly applied are concerned with whether a DNA analyst complied with correct test protocol in conducting the test in question. *See e.g., United States v. Coronado-Cervantes*, 912 F. Supp. 497, 500 (D.N.M. 1996) ("compliance with standard protocol in applying the RFLP technique is essential and goes to admissibility, rather than to merely the weight of DNA evidence"). *See also,* 2 SCIENTIFIC EVIDENCE § 18.05[b], at 100-03 (4th ed. 2007).

In *Ex Parte Hutcherson*, 677 So. 2d 1205, 1209 (Ala. 1996) (a case decided prior to Alabama overruling *Perry; see* Note 2 above), the Alabama Supreme Court held that complying with the third prong of *Perry* required *affirmative testimony* — not generalities — from the proponent's expert, and that the presentation should include what quality controls were used. "[The expert] failed to sufficiently meet the third prong [of *Perry*] because he explained only one type of quality control procedure used and did not testify as to other quality controls procedures used except to state generally that quality controls were used." *Id. See also, Commonwealth v. Vao Sok*, 683 N.E.2d 671, 682–83 (Mass. 1997) (PCR testing; court finds PCR technology reliable, but since PCR test kits had no "User's Guides," admissibility depends upon proponent of evidence demonstrating that laboratory "in fact properly utilized the kits to achieve reliable results").

People v. Miles, 577 N.E.2d 477 (Ill. Ct. App. 1991), is an Illinois case finding that the proponent had demonstrated proper test procedures.

> When a case arrives at Cellmark [the testing laboratory], it is assigned to one person, who is responsible for performing tests and following testing procedures. Cellmark requires its scientists to follow a written protocol in performing tests. Expiration dates ensure chemicals used in the process are fresh. . . . [I]nstruments and equipment are kept in working order. A second Cellmark employee witnesses all steps in the chain of custody as well as many test procedures. Once the autorads are developed, the molecular biologist presents them to a Ph.D. scientist for review. The Ph.D. scientist reviews the

entire case file in interpreting the autorad. Two Ph.D. scientists separately review each case and each writes a report of findings. The reports are combined in the final document sent to the client. A laboratory supervisor reviews the report before it is released to the client.

Id. at 483–84.

5. *A Third View: Applying an Accepted Technique Distinguished from "Careless Testing."* Some jurisdictions appear to take a middle approach. For example, California draws a distinction between *failure to use correct scientifically accepted procedures* (that precludes admissibility), and *"careless testing"* (that affects the weight of the evidence but not its admissibility). Recall that this differs from the two-part approach taken by the Alabama Supreme Court in *Perry*.

> The third prong asks: In this particular case, did the testing laboratory perform generally accepted scientific techniques without error in the performance . . . of the tests?
>
> In order to answer this question, we must make two inquiries. First, were the techniques used by the testing laboratory generally accepted in the scientific community? Second, was there error in the performance . . . of the tests?
>
> . . . .
>
> . . . [I]n regard to whether there was error in the performance . . . of the tests, we note that this challenge to admissibility will be available even if the challenge under the first portion of the third prong is determined as a matter of law.

Perry, supra, 586 So. 2d at 250, 253.

Contrast the two-part admissibility test just described with the California approach. In *People v. Venegas,* 954 P.2d 525 (Cal. 1998), the California Supreme Court explained what showing must be made to satisfy the third prong of its *Frye* test (called the *Kelly* test in California). *Id.* at 546.

> The *Kelly* test's third prong does not apply the *Frye* requirement of general scientific acceptance — it assumes the methodology and technique in question has already met that requirement. Instead, it inquires into the matter of whether *the procedures actually utilized in the case* were in compliance with that methodology and technique, as generally accepted by the scientific community. The third-prong inquiry is thus case specific; "it cannot be satisfied by relying on a published appellate decision
>
> . . . .
>
> The *Kelly* test's third prong does not, of course, cover all derelictions in following the prescribed scientific procedures. Shortcomings such as mislabeling, mixing the wrong ingredients, or failing to follow routine precautions against contamination may well be amenable to evaluation by jurors without the assistance of expert testimony. Such readily apparent missteps involve "the degree of professionalism" with which otherwise scientifically accepted methodologies are applied in a given case, and so amount only to "[c]areless testing affect[ing] the weight of the evidence and not its admissibility."
>
> The *Kelly* third-prong inquiry involves further scrutiny of a methodology or technique that has already passed muster under the . . . first prong of the *Kelly* test in that the general acceptance of its validity by the relevant scientific

community has already been established. The issue of the inquiry is whether the procedures utilized in the case at hand complied with that technique.

Venegas, supra, 954 P.2d at 545, 547. In *People v. Brown,* 110 Cal. Rptr. 2d 750, 769–70 (Cal. Ct. App. 2001), the California Court of Appeals added; "[t]he third-prong hearing will not approach the complexity of a full- blown *Kelly* hearing. All that is necessary in the limited third-prong hearing is a foundational showing that correct scientific procedures were used. Where the prosecution shows that the correct procedures were followed, criticisms of the techniques go to the weight of the evidence, not its admissibility."

In the 1993 case of *United States v. Martinez,* 3 F.3d 1191 (8th Cir. 1993), the Eighth Circuit set up a process for ensuring correct test performance that is similar to the California approach in that not all test application errors result in the exclusion of DNA evidence.

> [T]he reliability inquiry set forth in *Daubert* mandates that there be a preliminary showing that the expert properly performed a reliable methodology in arriving at his methodology. . . . [T]he inquiry extends beyond simply the reliability of the principles or methodologies in the abstract. In order to determine whether scientific *testimony* is reliable the court must conclude that the testimony was derived from the application of a reliable methodology or principle in the particular case.

> . . . .

> [W]e conclude that the court should make an initial inquiry into the particular expert's application of the scientific principle or methodology in question. The court should require the testifying expert to provide affidavits attesting that he properly performed the protocols involved in DNA profiling. If the opponent of the evidence challenges the application of the protocols in a particular case, the district court must determine whether the expert erred in applying the protocols, and if so, whether such error so infected the procedure as to make the results unreliable.

> [T]his inquiry is of necessity a flexible one. Not every error in the application of a particular methodology should warrant exclusion. An alleged error in the application of a reliable methodology should provide the basis for exclusion of the opinion only if that error negates the basis for the reliability of the principle itself. We agree with the Third Circuit that an allegation of failure to properly apply a scientific principle should provide the basis for exclusion of an expert opinion only if "a reliable methodology was so altered [by a particular expert] as to skew the methodology itself. . . ."

Id. at 1197–98 (emphasis in original). *See also, People v. Morganti,* 50 Cal. Rptr. 2d 837, 852 (Cal. Ct. App. 1996) (testimony that PCR testing "kit" contained a "User's Guide"and testimony that the "User's Guide" contained correct scientific procedures for conducting PCR testing; evidence that "User's Guide" procedures were followed sufficient for admissibility).

QUESTIONS

1. In *Perry*, the Alabama Supreme Court divides its "third prong," or test application inquiry into two questions: "were the techniques used . . . generally accepted in the scientific community," and "was there error in the performance of the tests." What is the difference between these two inquiries? *See United States v. Shea*, 957 F. Supp. 331, 340 (D.N.H. 1997) ("Testing errors can occur either because a test has inherent limitations or because the people involved in collecting, handling or testing samples are not sufficiently skilled.").

The *Perry* court states that its two-part test application inquiry is "in substance what the court in *Castro* meant." Is dividing the third prong into these two inquiries consistent with *Castro*, or is the approach of the California Supreme Court in *Venegas, supra* , (see Note 4(B) above) more consistent with *Castro*?

2. Why is it that the courts in *Castro* and *Ex parte Perry* feel that a third prong must be added to *Frye*, and why does the Eighth Circuit in *Martinez* (*see* Note 5 above) feel that *Daubert* requires a demonstration of proper application in the case of DNA testing even though the Eighth Circuit (and many other courts) takes judicial notice of the reliability of the DNA theory and technique?

3. Why should the foundation for the admissibility of DNA evidence be laid *outside* the hearing of the jury?

4. How confident are you that a jury could properly assess the weight to accord a scientist's failure to properly perform one of the steps involved in DNA testing?

PROBLEMS

Problem 4-8. Defendant is accused of murdering his wife. DNA testing revealed that defendant's blood was found on clothing his wife was wearing when she was killed. At his trial the prosecution seeks to offer the DNA evidence. The only DNA expert called by the prosecution is Dr. Daniel Garner, the director of laboratories at Cellmark, Inc., the private corporation that performed the DNA testing. Dr. Garner is prepared to testify to the RFLP process employed by Cellmark and his review of the DNA testing data, and to give a conclusion — that blood stains found on the deceased's clothing were those of the defendant.

The defendant objects because Dr. Garner did not perform the DNA test himself and because he did not personally observe or oversee the testing. While defendant admits that DNA theory and the RFLP process, in general, are reliable, he argues that the results of this particular test may be unreliable. Because the prosecution offered no testimony about what procedures were followed and what precautions were taken to avoid contamination, band shifting, and human error, the defendant objects to the admission of the DNA evidence. Furthermore, since Dr. Garner was not present at the testing he cannot respond to such questions on cross-examination.

Should the DNA test results be admitted? *See State v. Davis*, 814 S.W.2d 593, 602–03 (Mo. 1991); *Taylor v. State*, 889 P.2d 319, 330 n.46 (Okla. Crim. App. 1995).

Problem 4-9. Assume that in a murder investigation Criminalist Matt Martin takes a blood sample from a suspect at the police station. Assume that proper department regulations require the blood sample to be kept in the possession of the criminalist and delivered to the state crime laboratory for testing. Instead of going directly to the crime laboratory Criminalist Martin goes to the scene of the murder to collect additional evidence. At the murder scene he encounters Detective Mo Fitzgerald, who is also gathering evidence. Criminalist Martin gives the suspect's blood sample to Detective Fitzgerald at the murder scene and asks him to take it to the crime laboratory while he (Criminalist Martin) continues to gather evidence at the murder scene (including the collection of blood samples). Detective Fitzgerald agrees and places the suspect's blood sample in his pocket. Eventually, Detective Fitzgerald leaves the murder scene and takes the blood sample to the crime laboratory for testing. The suspect is charged with murder based in part on DNA testing that concluded that his DNA profile was found in blood collected at the crime scene.

If both Criminalist Matt Martin and Detective Mo Fitzgerald testify that they did nothing wrong, does the violation of department regulations in the handling of the suspect's blood sample make the subsequent DNA test results inadmissible? *See United States v. Martinez*, 3 F.3d 1191, 1198 (8th Cir. 1993); *People v. Venegas*, 954 P.2d 525, 547 (Cal. 1998).

Problem 4-10. Defendant Smith is accused of a brutal rape and murder in a state that follows an admissibility rule similar to that of Alabama (*Ex parte Perry, supra*). His fingerprints were in the house of the victim, blood consistent with his blood type and not the victim's was found in the victim's home, and an eyewitness saw Smith leave the victim's home just before the body was discovered.

In addition to obtaining the above evidence, the state had DNA testing performed on semen samples found on the victim's clothing. The result of RFLP testing indicated a "match," and the state's DNA expert is prepared to testify that the chances of a random match are one in 6 million. At trial the state's DNA testimony is given before the jury (i.e., there is no *pretrial hearing* on admissibility of the DNA evidence). The prosecution's DNA testimony is summarized as follows:

> The State presented the testimony of Sarah Elaine Scott, a forensic scientist, who testified that she identifies and characterizes bodily fluids. Scott has a master's degree and has had special training in serological research by the FBI, the American Academy of Forensic Scientists, and several private corporations that do serological work. She testified that she collected fluid stains from the victim and her home.

> Scott stated that she tested blood [and semen] taken from the victim at the autopsy, along with blood stains found at the crime and blood samples taken from the defendant. . . .

> Scott testified that DNA matching and testing were generally accepted in the scientific community. . . . She further testified that the techniques used in her lab were generally accepted in the scientific community. . . .

Defense counsel objects to the admissibility of DNA testimony because there was no testimony regarding what quality controls Scott used in her laboratory in general, and what quality controls were used in this case. Defense counsel's objections are overruled, and Smith is convicted and sentenced to death.

(A) If in a state that follows *Ex parte Perry's* approach of making two inquiries when considering whether there was correct test application in this case, what result? *See Ex parte Hutcherson*, 677 So. 2d 1205, 1208–09 (Ala. 1996).

(B) If in a state that follows the weight approach, what result? *See State v. Pierce*, 597 N.E.2d 107, 113–14 (Ohio 1992).

[3]   The Debate Over the Significance of A Match[37]

[a]   Overview

DNA testing produces two distinct but interrelated items of information. First, whether the DNA profile found in two samples (e.g., a crime scene sample and a sample taken from the defendant) matches, and second, if a match exists, the statistical likelihood that another individual, chosen at random, might also possess the DNA profile found in both samples. This statistical assessment — performed after a match is declared — is called "population frequency analysis." In explaining the importance of calculating the statistical significance of a match, the Arizona Supreme Court stated:

> Absent laboratory error, a declared match means that only one of the following is true: (1) the samples came from the same individual; (2) the samples came from identical twins; or (3) the samples came from different individuals but, by pure chance, *the DNA segments examined* match (although comparison of the entire DNA sequence from each individual would not match). It is the probability favoring a random match (the third of these three alternatives) that provide the telling and crucial bottom line of DNA evidence.

State v. Bible, 858 P.2d 1152, 1185 (Ariz. 1993) (emphasis added). The California Supreme Court described the significance of population frequency analysis this way:

> A determination that the DNA profile of a evidentiary sample matches the profile of a suspect establishes that the two profiles are consistent, but the determination would be of little significance if the evidentiary profile also matched that of many or most other human beings. The evidentiary weight of the match with the suspect is therefore inversely dependent upon the statistical probability of a similar match with the profile of a person drawn at random from the relevant population.

People v. Venegas, 954 P.2d 525, 547–48 (Cal. 1998).

The calculation of the probability that someone other than the accused would possess a DNA profile matching that contained in a crime scene sample has generated much controversy, and has led to the rejection of DNA evidence in some cases. The concerns that led some courts to reject DNA evidence have been, for the most part, addressed. Nonetheless, weight attacks on population frequency statistics can still be made. To comprehend the legal issues involved in this controversy, three things need to be understood.

The selective nature of DNA profiling. First, because of the "selective" nature of DNA profiling, statistics are critical to add meaning to the declaration of a match. In DNA testing an individual's entire DNA sequence is not examined. Recall that there are roughly 3 billion base pairs (or "rungs") in a DNA molecule. Approximately 99.9% of these base pairs are identical in every human being. This identity of DNA is what makes humans human. What distinguishes humans *from each other* is the fact that certain *sections* of DNA differ (less than 1%).[38] These unique sections, or sites, where DNA

---

[37] *See generally* Committee on DNA Technology in Forensic Science, National Research Council, *DNA Technology in Forensic Science* 74–95 (1992).

[38] *See* 2 SCIENTIFIC EVIDENCE § 18.02, at 13 (4th ed. 2007) ("approximately 99.9% of the base pairs found in all human beings are the same"). *See also* Brim v. State, 779 So. 2d 427, 444 n.38 (Fla. Dist. Ct. App. 2000) (stating that by "rough analogy" looking at five loci [the number of sites tested in the *Brim* case] "is

base pairs may be arranged differently among individuals, are called polymorphic sites. Different or alternative versions of DNA at polymorphic sites that are examined for forensic purposes are called "alleles." Some alleles are genes, and are responsible for coding for a trait in an individual (e.g., hair or eye color). Other alleles are referred to as "Variable Number Tandem Repeats" (VNTRs) or "Short Tandem Repeats"(STRs), and have no known effect on a person's traits.

Because each person's DNA is unique (except for identical twins), if scientists looked at all alleles at all polymorphic sites, they could, with absolute certainty, identify an individual. Because this is currently not possible, scientists look at only a few alleles at specific sites (loci) in a crime scene sample and in the sample taken from a suspect, victim, or other person. The FBI, as of this writing, examines 13 sites containing 26 alleles. If the alleles at the sites examined are the same in both samples, scientists declare a "match" and then calculate the *probability* of another human being having the same alleles at the 13 sites examined. In sum, statistical analysis is necessary because current DNA typing examines only several of the numerous sites of genetic variation.

Calculating the probability of a "random match." The second thing that must be understood is how population frequency statistics are calculated. To begin with, scientists calculate how frequently each allele found at each site (locus) appears in a relevant population. To do this scientists need a database of DNA profiles from several population groups. This database can be compiled from a variety of sources such as blood banks, hospitals, clinics, genetics laboratories, law enforcement personnel, etc. The populations that serve as the database are usually grouped by race. For example, laboratories conducting DNA testing may have a database of allele frequencies for Caucasians, Hispanics, and African-Americans.

By looking at DNA profiles in the relevant database, scientists conclude how often a particular allele appears at a particular site in that database. For example, if 300 Hispanic individuals have DNA profiles developed, and one allele appears on 30 of those profiles, scientists conclude that allele appears at that DNA location on one out of every 10 Hispanic people. In essence, this is a calculation of how often a particular allele appears in that population.

Once a scientist knows the frequency for individual alleles at specific sites, he or she looks at the pair of alleles that are actually found at a particular site (locus), and calculates the frequency for that pair of alleles at that site. For example, if one allele at a site appears 10% of the time (one in 10), and the other allele at that site appears 20% of the time (one in five), then the frequency for that specific *pair* of alleles at that specific site is 0.04% (2 x.10 x.20 =.04). Then, the allele frequencies at each of the sites examined are multiplied together to get the frequency for the entire profile. For example, if only five sites (loci) are examined in a particular case (remember the FBI currently examines 13 loci), and it has been determined that the frequency for each pair of alleles at those five sites was.10 (one in 10), scientists use the product rule (multiplying one out of 10, by one out of 10, by one out of 10, by one out of 10, by one out of 10) and conclude that the frequency for that five-loci profile is one in 100,000 (.00001). Continuing with this example, if, in a specific case, the defendant's DNA profile matches that in a crime scene sample at those five loci, then scientists would estimate that the probability of a randomly selected person from the database population genetically matching the defendant's profile and the crime scene sample would be one in 100,000.

---

comparable to identifying a 4000-mile highway by examining only 5 pieces of road totaling less that 1½ feet in length").

Dispute over the use of the product rule. Obviously, the accuracy of such calculations depends upon the reliability of the database used to determine individual allele frequencies, and the appropriateness of using the product rule with DNA testing. The product rule, of course, posits that the probability of several events occurring together is the product of their individual probabilities. For example, according to the product rule, the probability of "heads" coming up on three successive coin tosses is the probability of heads coming up on the first toss (one in two), multiplied by the probability of heads on the second toss (one in two), multiplied by the probability of heads on the third toss (one in two), resulting in an overall probability of one in eight.

The validity of using the product rule in any context depends upon two factors: the *validity* of the individual probabilities, and the *independence* of each event occurring individually. In the context of DNA analysis, both of these factors have been challenged by the assertion that "population substructures" exist that affect both the frequency and independence of alleles within certain "sub-populations." The materials that follow examine the judicial response to the scientific debate over population substructures and the product rule in DNA analysis.

PROBLEM

Problem 4-11. In an article that appeared in the August 1994 issue of *Trial*, William C. Thompson used a hypothetical to illustrate the problem of population substructures. This problem is loosely based on that illustration.

Suppose a population survey of 500 Europeans showed that 10% (one in 10) have blond hair, 10% have blue eyes, and 10% have fair skin. Using this database of 500 Europeans and the product rule, one could conclude that one out of every 1,000 Europeans have all three traits: blond hair, blue eyes, and fair skin.

Now assume that a murder is committed in Norway and the murder is recorded on a surveillance camera. The picture captured by the surveillance camera shows that the murderer was a blond-haired, blue-eyed man with fair skin, but the picture quality is not good enough to make out any features of the man's face. If the police arrest a blond-haired, blue-eyed Norwegian man with fair skin, are the odds one in 1,000 that another person randomly selected in Norway would have all three traits? *See* William C. Thompson, *DNA Evidence in Criminal Law: New Developments*, TRIAL, Aug. 1994, at 36.

[b] The Judicial Response to the Scientific Debate Over Population Substructures

In the early 1990s a few courts rejected DNA evidence because of a dispute within the scientific community. A few well-respected scientists felt that broad racial categories (e.g., Caucasian, African-American, Hispanic) may contain genetically distinct sub-populations. For example, within the Caucasian racial group there could be genetically distinct sub-populations such as Italian, Polish, Irish, etc. Within the Hispanic racial group there could be genetically distinct sub-populations such as Cuban, Mexican, etc. These scientists argued that for these sub-populations (that may mate within their own ethnic group) the frequency of alleles observed in the broader racial category might be inaccurate. Accordingly, allele frequencies calculated upon the frequency alleles were observed in the broad racial groups would not be accurate for the sub-populations — and using the product rule to multiply these inaccurate frequencies would only exaggerate the inaccuracies.

Other scientists (perhaps the majority) acknowledged the existence of such sub-populations, or "population substructures," but contended that existing methods of population frequency analysis was conservative enough to compensate for these variations. In 1992 the highly respected National Academy of Science's National Research Council (NRC) issued a report acknowledging the dispute and the existence of population substructures, and — rather than resolving the dispute — proposed circumvention of any alleged population substructure problem through application of what it called the "modified ceiling method." The modified ceiling method of calculating probabilities retained the product rule but modified the allele frequency data to which it was applied. The "modified ceiling method" would result in admittedly inaccurate probabilities (as a result of modifying — or manipulating — the allele frequency data), but these probabilities would be biased in favor of the defendant.

The two cases that follow illustrate the issues involved in the dispute, the judicial response to the NRC's modified ceiling method, and how the debate subsided as scientific research increased. First, in *State v. Johnson* the Arizona Supreme Court explains why it initially found the use of the product rule with DNA analysis to be suspect, and then explains the effect of the NRC's "modified ceiling method" upon admissibility.

STATE v. JOHNSON
922 P.2d 294 (Ariz. 1996)

FELDMAN, CHIEF JUSTICE.

We granted review in this case to re-examine questions involving the admissibility of DNA profile probability statistics. The questions addressed are those left open by *State v. Bible*, 858 P.2d 1152 (1993), our previous opinion on this subject.

FACTS AND PROCEDURAL BACKGROUND

On the morning of July 9, 1991, in Sierra Vista, Arizona, a storekeeper was surprised by an intruder as she opened her business. The intruder overpowered the woman and raped her. The woman was taken to the emergency room where Sierra Vista police interviewed her and gathered her clothing. . . .

Terry Hogan, a criminalist at the Arizona Department of Public Safety (DPS) crime laboratory, found that DNA extracted from blood and semen stains on the clothes . . . matched the DNA of a suspect, Robert Wayne Johnson. At Johnson's jury trial on sexual assault charges, the state presented evidence of the DNA match, and Hogan testified, over objection, that the probability of such a match occurring randomly was one in 312 million. [Hogan used an approach called the "modified ceiling method" and the product rule to calculate the probability of a random match.] The jury evidently believed that odds of one to 312 million established guilt beyond a reasonable doubt and found Johnson guilty of one count of sexual assault. . . . The court of appeals affirmed. . . .

Johnson then petitioned this court for review, claiming that the trial judge erred in admitting Hogan's testimony about the odds of a random match between Johnson's DNA and DNA extracted from the semen stains. In light of the importance of the issue and the uncertainty of the law on the point, we granted review of Johnson's claim regarding admission of the DNA evidence.

DISCUSSION

A. DNA analysis

DNA analysis involves three basic steps: (1) creating the DNA profiles of evidence samples; (2) determining whether profiles of different samples match; and (3) if samples match, articulating the significance of the match, preferably by computing the probability of a random match.

Hogan used restricted fragment length polymorphism (RFLP) to create the DNA profiles and determine that they matched. The scientific principles underlying RFLP, its validity, and the process for declaring a match are well-documented and unchallenged here. . . .

RFLP produces a picture or DNA profile of the suspect's blood, semen, or other specimen, which is compared to the DNA profile produced from the evidence sample. . . .

If the two DNA profiles do not match then the suspect is positively excluded. If they do match, the evidence sample came either from the suspect or an identical twin, or the match was a complete coincidence. If there is no identical twin, as in the present case, the significance of a match can be expressed in terms of the probability that the suspect's DNA profile would occur randomly. The probability can be expressed either qualitatively — "probable," "highly probable" — or mathematically, as Hogan did in this case: one in 312 million. The issue under review concerns only this third step of DNA analysis: are DNA probability statistics produced by the modified ceiling method and expressed mathematically admissible under the standard for new scientific evidence? We held in *Bible* that admission of such evidence calculated by the product rule was error. *Bible*, 858 P.2d at 1180.

B. The standard for admitting new scientific evidence

. . . .

[T]he *Frye* rule, which has been followed without causing significant problems since it was first adopted in 1962, remains the rule in Arizona.

C. Admissibility of probability evidence

1. State v. Bible

In *Bible*, we reviewed the admissibility of DNA probability evidence calculated with the product rule[39] [3] and held that the DNA probability calculations based on Cellmark

---

[39] [n.3] The product rule is described as follows:

Suppose, for example, that a pair of DNA [profiles] match on two bands, and that one band reflects an allele found in ten percent of the population and the other an allele found in fifty percent of the population. Applying the product rule, an analyst would conclude that the probability of a coincidental match on both alleles is $0.10 \times 0.50 = .05$, or a five percent probability.

Laboratory's application of the product rule were inadmissible because,

> [f]or purposes of *Frye*, these probability calculations are flawed in three ways: (1) they are impermissibly based on the disputed assumption of linkage equilibrium; (2) the database relied on is of disputed statistical validity; and (3) the database relied on is [concededly] not in Hardy-Weinberg equilibrium.

The modified ceiling method, which was used to calculate the probabilities introduced at Johnson's trial, is inextricably linked to the product rule. Therefore, as a threshold requirement, the modified ceiling method must produce results untainted by the shortcomings articulated for the product rule in *Bible*.

2. Assumption of linkage equilibrium

Cellmark's application of the product rule was rejected in *Bible*, in part because of "the disputed assumption of linkage equilibrium." Linkage equilibrium refers to the principle of independent assortment, which states that the frequency of occurrence of alleles expressing different genetic traits will be determined independently of the frequency of the occurrence of other alleles in the sample. The National Research Council (NRC), in its 1992 report, *DNA Technology in Forensic Science* (NRC report),[40] [4] illustrates the principle thusly:

> From a statistical standpoint, the situation is analogous to estimating the proportion of blond, blue-eyed, fair-skinned people in Europe by separately counting the frequencies of people with blond hair, people with blue eyes, and people with fair skin and calculating their proportions [by application of the product rule].

NRC report at 76.

Thus, by way of illustration only, linkage equilibrium assumes that whether a person inherits the allele for blue eyes is unrelated to whether that person inherits the allele for blond hair or fair skin. Of course, as the NRC report points out, these three traits tend to co-occur in Nordics. Therefore the actual frequency of these three traits occurring together (assuming each trait occurs one time in ten) is not simply a straight calculation under the product rule of .10 x .10 x .10 equals 1 in 1000. Instead, because of the co-occurrence of such observable, physical traits in certain sub-populations, the actual frequency in the *total* population of all three traits appearing in any one individual is probably considerably higher than 1 in 1000. *Id.*

This does not, however, necessarily invalidate the assumption of linkage equilibrium because the alleles chosen to create the DNA profile with the RFLP protocol are non-coding, that is, they are not responsible for producing any observable characteristic. *See* NRC report at 77. Furthermore, these alleles are known to be extremely variable from person to person, and scientific studies have not shown any statistical correlation between them. Thus, as the NRC report makes clear, the assumption of linkage

---

William C. Thompson & Simon Ford, *DNA Typing*, 75 VA. L. REV. 45, 81–82 (1989).

40 [n.4] The National Research Council's members are drawn from the councils of the National Academy of Sciences, the National Academy of Engineering, and the Institute of Medicine. The members who prepared this report were chosen for their special competencies. The report was reviewed by a group other than the authors who prepared it, according to procedures approved by a Report Review Committee, consisting of members of the National Academy of Sciences, the National Academy of Engineering, and the Institute of Medicine.

equilibrium inherent in protocols such as RFLP is well-grounded and has been proved accurate for purposes of DNA profiles. NRC report at 77. Accordingly, the assumption of linkage equilibrium for purposes of RFLP analysis and use in applying the product rule has been demonstrated to be generally accepted in the relevant scientific community. NRC report at 77.

3. Hardy-Weinberg equilibrium

The statistical validity of the product rule also assumes that mates are chosen randomly within any population, resulting in an equally random occurrence of any particular allele. Populations that are in random-mating proportions are said to be in Hardy-Weinberg equilibrium. See THE EVALUATION OF FORENSIC DNA EVIDENCE 4-2 (National Academy Press 1996) (prepublication copy) (1996 NRC report).

Of course people who live in close geographic proximity to each other are more likely to choose each other as mates, and people often select mates on the basis of certain physical, racial, cultural, and behavioral characteristics. However, the alleles used in DNA profiling do not represent physical, racial, cultural, and behavioral characteristics and are therefore not the basis for the choice of mates. Accordingly, the alleles used for profiling remain in Hardy-Weinberg equilibrium. Id.

Our concern with Hardy-Weinberg equilibrium in Bible was not with the general acceptance of the scientific principle but instead was limited to Cellmark's admittedly defective database. Hogan testified to testing for and finding the DPS database in Hardy-Weinberg equilibrium. Nothing in the record refutes this testimony.

4. Statistical validity of the database - size, randomness and representativeness

To estimate the probability that a defendant's DNA is the same as that taken from a crime scene, the expert relies on a previously constructed database. This database allows the expert to calculate the frequency of the alleles with which such a match could be expected in the general population.

. . . Johnson also challenges the statistical validity of the DPS database used in this case. Thus, we must determine whether the DPS database, which is comprised of samples from blood banks, is generally accepted in the relevant scientific community.

With respect to size, "the scientific community now generally agrees that a database consisting of as few as 150 individuals will suffice, so long as the individuals are unrelated." . . . The DPS database consisted of approximately 200 samples for each of four racial groups.

As for randomness, the NRC report concludes that to be sufficiently random, the database need only consist of samples drawn at random from designated populations. NRC report at 77, 83. Randomness is satisfied when there is linkage equilibrium and Hardy-Weinberg equilibrium. See NRC report at 83. Finally, to ensure the database is sufficiently representative, the modified ceiling method calls for samples drawn from at least three racial populations. NRC report at 91. The DPS database was drawn from four different racial populations. Three of these populations were used by Hogan in his calculations, and the samples were identified only by race.

Hogan tested for and found the database to be in Hardy-Weinberg equilibrium. We have already determined that the assumption of linkage equilibrium has been sufficiently proven. Thus, we believe the size, randomness, and representativeness of the

DPS database were such that the database was generally accepted in the relevant scientific community.

5. *The modified ceiling method*

The modified ceiling method is an application of the product rule. This method, however, has the added dimension of addressing any effect subpopulations might have on product rule calculations. Subpopulations refer to stratifications within distinct racial groups. The modified ceiling method addresses the possible effects of subpopulations by making product rule calculations more conservative. It does this by utilizing databases containing frequency information on at least three principal racial populations. The occurrence frequency of alleles represented in the [DNA profile] are calculated for each racial population. If any allele's frequency in any of the populations is less than ten percent, that allele is assigned the frequency of ten percent. In other words, no allele will be assumed to occur less frequently than ten percent of the time in any of the several populations, regardless of how infrequently it might actually have occurred. If an allele's frequency is greater than ten percent in any population, then the highest observed frequency is used [in] comput[ing] the . . . [frequency] for that [allele]. This results in moving the highest observed frequency, if it was over ten percent, higher still. Employing these occurrence frequencies for the individual alleles, the product rule is then applied to determine the probability of a suspect's DNA profile occurring randomly. This probability is both race-neutral and conservative, thereby accounting for any effect of subpopulations. NRC report at 13, 91–92. Any error in the probability would be in the direction of increased probability of a random match, so that the final calculation favors defendants. *Id.*

6. *Admissibility of the modified ceiling method under Frye*

. . . .

At the *Frye* hearing, Hogan testified that the modified ceiling method is recommended by the NRC. Other courts have recognized that

> the [NRC] is a distinguished cross section of the scientific communi- ty. . . . Thus, that committee's conclusion regarding the reliability of forensic DNA typing, specifically RFLP analysis, and the proffer of a conservative method for calculating probability estimates can easily be equated with general acceptance of those methodologies in the relevant scientific community.

United States v. Porter, 618 A.2d 629, 643 n. 26 (D.C.App.1992). We, too, believe that endorsement by the NRC of the modified ceiling method is strong evidence of general acceptance within the relevant scientific community. But we need not rely solely on the NRC's endorsement. Several other courts have addressed this issue and found the modified ceiling method to be generally accepted. *See Commonwealth v. Lanigan*, 641 N.E.2d 1342 (1994); *State v. Bloom*, 516 N.W.2d 159, 167 (Minn.1994); *State v. Anderson*, 881 P.2d 29, 47 (1994).

These judicial views are supported by the weight of scientific opinion. Eric S. Lander and Bruce Budowle were two of the principal antagonists involved in the initial debate over forensic DNA typing. *See DNA Fingerprinting Dispute Laid to Rest*, 371 Nature 735 (Oct.1994). Both Lander and Budowle have concluded that following the NRC's report "there is no scientific reason to doubt the accuracy of forensic DNA typing results," such as the modified ceiling method. *Id.*

Most telling, perhaps, is that those forensic experts who take issue with the modified ceiling method do so because they believe it produces excessively conservative results that unduly favor the defendant.

. . . We fail to see any prejudice to a defendant in results produced by a method that, if biased, is biased in the defendant's favor.

Based on our review of the NRC reports, legal commentary, scientific literature, and consideration and acceptance of the modified ceiling method by other jurisdictions, we conclude that the method is generally accepted in the relevant scientific community and that DNA probability calculations computed with that method are admissible under *Frye*. Our holding extends only to the issue presented in this case - the modified ceiling method. . . . [W]e do not at this time address the admissibility of probability statistics calculated with the "pure" product rule.

. . . .

CONCLUSION

. . . DNA probability evidence calculated by use of the RFLP protocol and with the modified ceiling method is generally accepted in the relevant scientific community and is therefore admissible under the *Frye* test, subject to proper foundational showing. Upon such a showing, the significance of a DNA profile match may be explained with probability estimates based on the method's calculations. Accordingly, we approve the court of appeals' opinion finding that the trial judge did not err in permitting testimony on the mathematical probability of Johnson's DNA profile occurring randomly and affirm Johnson's conviction and sentence.

QUESTIONS

1. There could be three explanations for a "match" between two DNA profiles. What are the three possible explanations?

2. Why had the Arizona Supreme Court previously (in the *Bible* case) found probability calculations based upon the product rule to be inadmissible?

3. What is the "assumption of linkage equilibrium"? Why does the *Johnson* court feel that the "assumption of linkage equilibrium" is valid for DNA profiles even though in certain sub-populations some traits appear more frequently than in the total population?

4. How does the "modified ceiling method" work in favor of the defendant in a criminal case?

5. What one probability calculation issue does the *Johnson* court leave unaddressed?

In *Commonwealth v. Blasioli*, the Pennsylvania Supreme Court was presented with a challenge to the admissibility of probability statistics as applied to forensic DNA testing. *Blasioli* discusses the NRC's updated 1996 report, and addresses the issue left undecided by the *Johnson* case — whether the product rule in its "pure" form (without using the "modified ceiling method") may be used to calculate probabilities in DNA testing.

COMMONWEALTH v. BLASIOLI
713 A.2d 1117 (Pa. 1998)

SAYLOR, JUSTICE.

We allowed appeal to determine whether evidence of statistical probabilities calculated using the product rule is admissible at trial in a criminal case to assist the trier of fact in assessing the probative significance of a deoxyribonucleic acid ("DNA") match. We agree with the trial court and the Superior Court that the product rule, as applied in DNA forensic analysis, is generally accepted in the relevant scientific communities and that such evidence therefore meets the standard for admissibility.

In May, 1993, J.D. was assaulted and raped. The crimes occurred late at night . . . while she was walking home . . . along a poorly-lit road. During the attack, the assailant held his hand over J.D.'s eyes, and J.D. closed her eyes throughout the encounter for fear that her assailant would take her life if she saw his face. . . .

. . . .

In September, 1993 . . . Appellant Donald J. Blasioli ("Blasioli") [became a suspect in the rape of J.D.]

[P]olice obtained a warrant authorizing them to obtain samples of Blasioli's hair and blood. DNA testing performed at the Pennsylvania State Police laboratory [using the RFLP method] resulted in a determination of a match between Blasioli's blood sample and the semen sample obtained from J.D. immediately after the crimes. Based upon this evidence, Blasioli was arrested and charged with rape, indecent assault, simple assault and unlawful restraint.

Prior to trial, the Commonwealth disclosed its intent to present testimony concerning both the results of the DNA testing and certain probabilities derived from those tests using statistical methods known as the product rule and the ceiling principle. Specifically, the Commonwealth sought to introduce expert testimony that: the probability of a random occurrence in the general population of a DNA profile matching both Blasioli's and the crime sample, calculated using the product rule, was one in 10 billion; and the probability calculated using the ceiling principle was one in 30 million. After a pre-trial hearing pursuant to *Frye v. United States*, 293 F. 1013 (D.C.Cir.1923), the trial court ruled that the evidence met the standard of admissibility for novel scientific evidence.

At trial, J.D. testified to the circumstances of the crimes, but was unable to identify Blasioli as the perpetrator. The Commonwealth presented its scientific evidence through the testimony of expert witnesses, and Blasioli presented an expert to refute the Commonwealth's evidence. The jury found Blasioli guilty of all charges. . . . On direct appeal, the Superior Court affirmed, and this appeal followed.

In determining whether novel scientific evidence is admissible in criminal trials, Pennsylvania courts apply the test set forth in *Frye*, 293 F. at 1013. Pursuant to *Frye*, to be admissible, such evidence must have gained general acceptance in the relevant scientific community. . . .

In addressing the merits of the parties' arguments, a brief description of the scientific principles and procedures applied in DNA analysis is necessary. . . .

. . . .

After DNA profiles are created for both the crime scene and suspect samples, the [profiles] are measured and compared according to their length. If the similarities are such that they fall within a narrow margin, known as a match window, the samples are declared a match.

. . . .

The statistical assessment performed after a match has been declared is called population frequency analysis. The object is to determine the overall likelihood that someone other than the suspect would possess DNA matching that in the sample obtained from the crime scene.[41] [12] The first step is to determine, for each matching allele, the likelihood that such an allele would appear in a randomly selected individual. . . .

. . . .

Once the probability of random occurrence is calculated for each individual allele, the individual probabilities may be combined to determine an overall probability of random matching across the genetic profile. In order to make this calculation, scientists have employed the product rule. . . .

. . . .

Valid use of the product rule in any context depends upon the statistical independence of each component factor of the equation. Independence exists where the outcome of the first event does not impact upon the outcome of the second event. Validity of the rule in DNA forensic analysis depends upon whether individual alleles are actually statistically independent, requiring that the probability of finding one allele is not significantly affected by having found any other allele.[42] [18]

In this case, Blasioli maintains that use of the product rule is not generally accepted in relevant scientific communities, in particular because of an asserted lack of statistical independence of allele frequency. For many years, some scientists argued that the product rule can validly be applied only where members of racial and ethnic groups represented by a database intermix randomly, without regard to religion, ethnicity or geography. The view was premised upon the theory that population substructures affect the frequency of alleles and undermine the independence of such genetic factors and, hence, valid application of the product rule.[43] [19] Among these critics were two prominent population geneticists, Professors Daniel Hartl and Richard Lewontin. Furthermore, in its 1992 report, the NRC noted the existing dispute and proposed that

---

[41] [n.12] The analysis does not yield the probability that a particular defendant is the source of the crime sample or committed the crime at issue; instead, it provides only an estimate of the probability that a randomly selected person from the general population would genetically match the crime sample as well as the suspect.

[42] [n.18] The NRC illustrated this independence principle by referring to the example of individuals in the Nordic population with alleles for blonde hair, blue eyes and fair skin. If each trait carried a one-in-ten probability of occurrence, application of the product rule would result in a one-in-one-thousand probability that an individual would have all three traits. The combination, however, occurs commonly in the Nordic population, raising concerns about the validity of the application of the product rule to allele frequency calculations.

[43] [n.19] Population substructures occur when a certain subsection of the population, for example, a racial or ethnic group, selectively mates within that same subsection, resulting in the interrelation of certain genetic traits. Several theories developed which suggested that truly random mating across racial and ethnic lines was necessary to independence in the distribution of individual alleles in a population. The terms "linkage equilibrium," "gametic phase balance," and "Hardy-Weinberg equilibrium" identify versions of such theories. For example, Hardy-Weinberg equilibrium referred to a state in which one allele at a locus is not predictive of the other allele at that locus (one allele is inherited from the mother, the other from the father).

a conservative modification of the product rule, known as the ceiling principle, be used in calculating the probability of a genetic match.

Importantly, the NRC's 1992 report did not constitute an outright rejection of the product rule. Instead, the NRC merely recommended that, until data could be assembled from which to assess the impact of any significant population substructuring, the ceiling principle could be applied to impose an appropriate degree of conservatism.

The suggestion in the 1992 NRC Report, however, that substructuring could impact upon the validity of the product rule in DNA forensic analysis persuaded a number of courts that general agreement in the scientific community was lacking. While substantial debate ensued, it is noteworthy that no empirical data existed to support theories postulating a substantial impact of substructuring upon DNA forensic analysis.

Several events subsequently occurred, indicating that the controversy over the use of the product rule has dissipated. In 1993, the FBI conducted an extensive, international study of VNTR frequency data. *See* LABORATORY DIVISION, FEDERAL BUREAU OF INVESTIGATION, UNITED STATES DEPARTMENT OF JUSTICE, 1-A VNTR POPULATION DATA: A WORLDWIDE STUDY 2 (Feb. 1993). The study concluded that population frequency calculation using the product rule was reliable, valid and meaningful, without forensically significant consequences resulting from population substructure as had been postulated by some scientists.[44] [21]

Additionally, in 1994, Dr. Eric Lander, a former leading opponent of the use of the product rule, coauthored an article in which he declared that the "DNA fingerprinting wars are over." E. Lander & B. Budowle, *DNA Fingerprinting Dispute Laid to Rest*, 371 NATURE 735, 735 (Oct. 27, 1994). In the article, the authors stated that the 1992 NRC Report "failed to state clearly enough that the ceiling principle was intended as an ultra-conservative calculation, which did not bar experts from providing their own 'best estimates' based on the product rule." They noted that the FBI's laboratory maintained a "remarkable" database, and that, reassuringly, "observed variation is modest for the loci used in forensic analysis and random matches are quite rare, supporting the notion that the FBI's implementation of the product rule is a reasonable best estimate."

. . . .

Additionally, in 1996, the NRC reexamined the methodology issue and also concluded that the use of the ceiling principle for forensic purposes is unnecessary, not only because the principle overstates the effect of population substructuring, but also because of the current abundance of data regarding different ethnic groups within the major races. . . .

A majority of jurisdictions have acknowledged these developments - including the FBI study, the article by Lander and Budowle, and the 1996 NRC report - and have concluded that the controversy over the use of the product rule has been sufficiently resolved.[45] [23]

At the *Frye* hearing in this case, the Commonwealth presented evidence of general acceptance of the product rule in the relevant scientific disciplines. Such evidence

---

[44] [n.21] It is important to note that the relevant question is not whether some such substructuring exists, but whether the deviations it induces have an appreciable effect upon the relative frequency of the particular, highly-variable alleles selected for DNA profiling.

[45] [n.23] We recognize that several of these jurisdictions employ the federal standard enunciated in *Daubert*, which has been characterized as more lenient than the *Frye* test.

included citation to numerous scientific texts and journals and the testimony of professors of human genetics and statistics from prominent universities. At trial, Blasioli was permitted to contest the Commonwealth's DNA forensic evidence, including the statistical expressions based upon the product rule and the ceiling principle. Blasioli did so through the testimony of an expert who emphasized the theoretical impact of population substructuring along the lines advanced by Lewontin and Hartl. The expert also offered an alternative analysis known as the counting method, whereby he determined that the chances of another genetic match in this case were 1 in 2,220.[46] [25]

While we are cognizant of the fact that unanimity among scientists does not exist, unanimity is not required for general acceptance. . . . At present . . . it is clear from the scientific commentary, the clear weight of judicial authority, and the evidence in this case that the product rule has gained general acceptance across the disciplines of population genetics, human genetics and population demographics. As such, any remaining dispute as to the validity of the product rule should not result in the exclusion of evidence based upon this statistical method in criminal trials in Pennsylvania.

In sum, we hold that statistical evidence based upon the product rule was properly admitted at the trial in this case. Accordingly, the judgment of sentence is affirmed.

NOTES

1. *The Dispute Over the Admissibility of Probability Statistics Dissipates.* While several courts (primarily in the early 1990s) initially excluded probability statistics because of the dispute over population substructures, the dispute appears over. In *People v. Soto*, the California Supreme Court declared,

> [i]t is clear from the evidence in the record, the clear weight of judicial authority, and the published scientific commentary, that the unmodified product rule, as used in the DNA forensic analysis in this case, has gained general acceptance in the relevant scientific community and therefore meets the [*Frye*] standard for admissibility.

People v. Soto, 981 P.2d 958, 977 (Cal. 1999). Virtually every court that has commented on this issue since the publication of the NRC's updated 1996 Report has held that the probability estimates calculated with the product rule (without using the modified ceiling method) are admissible.

2. *Population Substructures and Weight Attacks.* It is important to remember that the existence of population substructures with the potential to impact probability estimates has not been refuted. In this regard consider the following excerpts from two opinions by the California Supreme Court. First, in *People v. Venegas* the Court discussed why there is not a single, interracial database for the United States.

> Major laboratories that do RFLP analysis, including the FBI and Cellmark, have developed their own separate population databases for each of several broad racial or ethnic categories such as Caucasian, Black, and Hispanic, the assumption being that mating among members of any one of those categories of

---

[46] [n.25] This method is simply an enumeration of how many times an event occurred in a given set of observations.

the United States population is sufficiently random to justify using them in conjunction with the product rule to calculate the frequency of a DNA profile.

In a footnote the Court added,

Conversely, the laboratories do not use a single interracial United States database, presumably because the incidence of random mating between members of the different racial categories is deemed low enough to preclude use of the product rule to calculate an overall frequency statistic for the United States population as a whole.

People v. Venegas, 954 P.2d 525, 537, 537 n. 22.

Second, in *People v. Soto* the Court added that,

[i]t is important to note that the relevant question . . . is not whether some population substructuring exists, but whether the deviations it induces have an appreciable effect upon the relative frequency of the particular, highly variable alleles selected for DNA profiling. None of the experts, so far as we are aware, believe that population substructuring has absolutely no effect on frequencies obtained under the unmodified product rule. They conclude instead that when, as in the present case, the probabilities of a random match are very rare - one in the multimillions or billions - substantial variations in such frequencies have no practical significance. We have no occasion in this case to consider whether substructuring could be a cause of material variation in much higher frequencies, *e.g.* one in several hundred.

People v. Soto, supra, 981 P.2d at 977.

Accordingly, the California Supreme Court appears to have left the door open to an admissibility challenge based upon population substructuring. Admissibility attacks aside, all courts should allow evidence of population substructure as a weight attack when population frequency statistics are computed with the "pure" product rule.

3. Admitting Testimony of a Match Without Testimony of the Probability of a Random Match. Most courts agree with the view taken by the Massachusetts Supreme Court in *Commonwealth v. Lanigan*, 641 N.E.2d 1342, 1346 (Mass. 1994), and hold that testimony of a "match" between a sample of DNA found at a crime scene and the defendant's DNA is meaningless and inadmissible without testimony of the probability of a random match. *See, e.g., People v. Coy*, 620 N.E.2d 888, 895 (Mich. Ct. App. 2000) (evidence of a potential match inadmissible "absent some accompanying interpretive evidence regarding the likelihood of the potential match."); *State v. Cauthron*, 846 P.2d 502, 516 (Wash. 1993); *but see State v. Bible*, 858 P.2d 1152, 1190 (Ariz. 1993) (testimony of a match admissible without accompanying statistical probability testimony). *See also State v. Carter*, 524 N.W.2d 763, 783 (Neb. 1994) (discusses cases on both sides of issue before following the majority approach of not admitting evidence of a match without accompanying probability estimate). Accordingly, if a court should conclude that probability statistics are inadmissible, it may very well also hold that testimony about a match may not be admissible.

QUESTIONS

1. In *Blasioli* why does the Pennsylvania Supreme Court declare that "the controversy over the use of the product rule has dissipated"?

2. Even though the *Blasioli* court admits the probability evidence, does the court acknowledge that there may be valid concerns over the impact of population substructures and the use of the product rule? If so, why are probability estimates calculated with the "pure" product rule deemed reliable enough to be admissible?

PROBLEM

Problem 4-12. Assume that a man is murdered in Miami, Florida. An autopsy indicates that he was beaten to death with a baseball bat after a violent struggle. Blood from the victim and from another person is found at the crime scene. Police arrest a Cuban immigrant and charge him with the murder. At his trial the state offers DNA evidence indicating a match between the defendant's DNA profile and the DNA profile found in blood at the crime scene. The state's DNA expert states, that based upon a database of 500 Hispanics in Houston, Texas, and San Diego, California, and using the "pure" product rule, the chances of a random match with another Hispanic person would be one in 97 million.

(A) Assume you represent the defendant. What arguments would you make that the probability estimate is flawed?

(B) Assume that you represent the prosecution. What arguments would you make that the probability estimate is accurate and admissible?

[c]   What Does the Probability of a Random Match Really Mean?

Is it possible that a jury could be so overwhelmed by the magnitude of probability statistics their admission evidence would constitute error? (That is, that the jury would mistakenly equate the probability of a random match with the probability that the defendant is innocent.) Beyond this, even if a jury could appreciate and weigh such probabilities, should the way the probabilities are expressed be modified to include laboratory error rate? Both of those issues were presented to the trial court in our next case, *United States v. Shea.*

UNITED STATES v. SHEA
957 F. Supp. 331 (D.N.H. 1997)

MEMORANDUM OPINION

BARBDORO, DISTRICT JUDGE.

Two men wearing masks and gloves broke into the Londonderry, branch of the First New Hampshire Bank about an hour after closing on August 4, 1995. One of the robbers apparently cut himself when he entered the building, as bloodstains were discovered inside the bank and in a stolen minivan believed to have been used as a getaway vehicle.

The government later charged Anthony Shea with the robbery and proposed to base its case in part on expert testimony comparing Shea's DNA with DNA extracted from several of the bloodstains. The government's expert, a forensic scientist employed by the FBI, used a method of DNA analysis known as Polymerase Chain Reaction ("PCR"), in determining that Shea has the same DNA profile as the person who left several of the blood stains at the crime scene and in the getaway vehicle. The expert also concluded that the probability of finding a similar profile match if a DNA sample were drawn randomly from the Caucasian population is 1 in 200,000.

Shea moved to exclude the DNA evidence prior to trial. Although he conceded that the scientific principles underlying PCR are generally accepted in the fields of molecular biology and forensic science, he argued that . . . evidence of a random match probability is barred by Fed. R. Evid. 403 because the risk that the jury would be misled by the evidence substantially outweighs its probative value.

After holding an evidentiary hearing and carefully considering Shea's arguments, I denied his motion to exclude. Shea subsequently was convicted of attempted bank robbery and several related charges. In this opinion, I explain why I admitted the DNA evidence.

. . . .

II.

. . . .

B. Rule 403

Rule 403 requires the exclusion of otherwise admissible expert testimony if the probative value of the evidence is substantially outweighed by "the danger of unfair prejudice, confusion of the issues, or misleading the jury, or by considerations of undue delay, waste of time, or needless presentation of cumulative evidence." Fed. R. Evid. 403. Expert testimony must be closely scrutinized for compliance with Rule 403 because, as the court in *Daubert* [*v. Merrell Dow Pharmaceuticals, Inc.*] recognized, "[e]xpert evidence can be both powerful and quite misleading. . . ." *Daubert*, 509 U.S. at 595. Nevertheless, relevant and reliable expert testimony ordinarily should be admitted notwithstanding Rule 403 unless the potential that it will be used improperly substantially outweighs any legitimate persuasive value that the evidence may have. *See* [*In re Paoli R.R. Yard PCB Litig.*, 35 F.3d 717, 747 (3d Cir. 1994)] (expert testimony should not be excluded simply because it is complex unless there is something about the particular technique at issue that overwhelms the jury's ability to independently assess the evidence).

III.

Shea [asserts] that the government should be barred from informing the jury of the probability of a random match because it will mislead the jury. . . .

C. Juror Confusion

Evidence that a defendant's DNA profile matches DNA extracted from an evidence sample suggests that the defendant cannot be excluded as a potential contributor, but it is of little value, standing alone, in proving the defendant's guilt. Giving the jury a random match probability estimate for the profile is one way of helping it assess the potential significance of a DNA profile match. However, because such evidence also has the potential to mislead, Rule 403 requires that the probative value of the evidence must be carefully balanced against the danger of unfair prejudice.

Shea argues that a jury would be so overwhelmed by evidence of a random match probability that it could not properly assess the possibility that a profile match is false unless a laboratory or industry error rate is calculated and combined with the random match probability estimate. Shea bases this argument on the following reasoning: (1) a random match probability estimate is meaningless if the declared DNA profile match is false; (2) the best evidence of whether a match is false in a particular case is the laboratory's false match error rate; (3) if the laboratory's false match error rate cannot be determined, the next best evidence is the industry's false match error rate; (4) jurors cannot understand the significance of a laboratory's error rate unless it is combined with the random match probability estimate. Because the FBI laboratory does not calculate a PCR false match error rate and the government refuses to combine what Shea suggests is the industry's PCR error rate with the random match probability estimate, Shea argues that the estimate is inherently misleading.

I reject Shea's argument because it is built on several flawed premises. First, I cannot accept Shea's contention that a laboratory or industry error rate is the best evidence of whether a test was properly performed in a particular case. Juries must decide whether a particular test was performed correctly based on all of the relevant evidence. This determination can never be precisely quantified because it will often depend in part on subjective factors such as the credibility of the person who performed the test. At best, evidence of a laboratory's past proficiency should be considered as one of several factors in making this important judgment.[47] [42] Shea's method for dealing with the probability of a false match is thus seriously flawed because it would deprive the jury of the opportunity to determine the probability of a false match based on all of the pertinent evidence.

Second, I am unconvinced by Shea's claim that a jury cannot properly assess the potential of a false match unless a false match error rate is calculated and combined with the random match probability estimate. Shea relies on testimony and research conducted by Dr. Jay Koehler to support this contention. Although Dr. Koehler's research suggests that jurors could become confused if evidence of a false match error rate and a random match probability estimate are presented with little or no explanation, it does not support Shea's broader contention that jurors cannot be made to understand such evidence even if it is properly explained. In a real trial setting, the parties are given an opportunity to explain the significance of statistical evidence through expert testimony. Further, if a trial judge concludes that jurors could be confused by statistical evidence, the judge can deliver carefully crafted instructions to insure that the evidence is properly understood. Notwithstanding Dr. Koehler's research, I am confident that the concerns Shea raises can be properly addressed through expert testimony and, if necessary, clarifying jury instructions.

Shea next argues that a random match probability estimate is inherently misleading because the jury inevitably will confuse the probability of a random match with the potentially very different probability that the defendant is not the source of the matching samples. This type of incorrect reasoning is often referred to as the fallacy of the transposed conditional, or the prosecutor's fallacy. The probability of a random

---

[47] [n.42] The parties assume that error rate information is admissible at trial. This assumption may well be incorrect. Even though a laboratory or industry error rate may be logically relevant, a strong argument can be made that such evidence is barred by Fed. R. Evid. 404 because it is inadmissible propensity evidence. I need not determine whether error rate information is ever admissible, however, because the point is not essential to my analysis, and the government did not object to Shea's effort to introduce error rate information at trial.

match is the conditional probability of a random match given that someone other than the defendant contributed the evidence sample. The potentially different probability that someone other than the defendant contributed the sample given the existence of a match can only be determined by considering all of the evidence in the case.[48] [44] Shea argues, based on research conducted by Dr. Koehler, that the jury will inevitably confuse these two probabilities.

Although I acknowledge that a jury could become confused concerning the meaning and potential significance of a random match probability estimate, I am confident that the risk of confusion is acceptably small if the concept is properly explained. Moreover, because such an estimate can be extremely valuable in helping the jury appreciate the potential significance of a DNA profile match, it should not be excluded merely because the concept requires explanation. Accordingly, I decline to exclude the government's random match probability estimate pursuant to Rule 403.

IV.

After carefully considering Shea's motion to exclude the DNA evidence, I reached the following conclusion[ ]:

. . . .

(4) When the significance of a random match probability estimate is properly explained, the probative value of the evidence is not substantially outweighed by the limited potential that jurors could be misled.

Accordingly, I denied the defendant's motion to exclude.

NOTE

Another Rationale for Not Modifying Statistical Probability Estimates to Take into Account Laboratory Error Rates. In *People v. Reeves*, 109 Cal. Rptr. 2d 728 (Cal. Ct. App. 2001), Reeves's expert contended that "laboratory error rates should be the dominant statistic for evaluating the weight of a match." *Id.* at 750. The expert argued that a laboratory could make a mistake in sampling or testing that could result in a "false positive" match. According to the expert, the chances of a laboratory making such a mistake ranged from "one in hundreds to one in thousands." *Id.* If true, this suggests that laboratory error rate is much greater than the probability of an erroneous identification due to a coincidental match of the DNA profiles. The court illustrated the expert's contentions in a footnote.

> Mueller [Reeves' expert] supported this opinion with an example of a hypothetical missile that, when fired, has only a 1 in 1 billion chance of missing its target. However, in 1 out of 5 tries the missile does not fire at all. The probability that the missile will not function correctly is therefore 1 in 5, or 20 percent.

Id. at 750 n. 15.

---

[48] [n.44] To illustrate how these two probabilities can be very different, consider a hypothetical case where: (1) the defendant's DNA profile is correctly found to match DNA left by the perpetrator at the crime scene during the commission of the crime; (2) the random match probability estimate for the observed DNA profile is 1 in 1,000,000; and (3) undisputed evidence establishes that the defendant did not commit the crime. In this hypothetical case, the random match probability estimate is 1 in 1,000,000 even though the probability that someone other than the defendant contributed the evidence sample is 1.

In rejecting Reeves's contention the court noted that the NRC had addressed the issue and decided that laboratory error rates should not be included in such calculations.

In a section titled "Should an Error Rate Be Included in Calculations?" (1996 NRC Rep., *supra*, at pp. 85–87), the 1996 NRC Report listed four reasons why laboratory error should not be combined with random match probability calculations. First, the relevant statistic is not a general error rate for the testing laboratory, or laboratories in general, but whether the laboratory has committed an error in this particular case. But the risk of error in a particular case depends on many variables, and no simple equation exists to translate them into a probability statistic. (*Id.* at pp. 85–86.) Second, a testing laboratory would have to undergo an unrealistically large number of proficiency tests to allow the estimation of a statistically valid probability of error. (*Id.* at p. 86.) Third, although it might be possible to generate a probability statistic by pooling data from the proficiency tests of several laboratories, producing an " 'industry-wide' " error rate, this statistic would unfairly penalize better laboratories. Fourth, an error rate estimated by a laboratory's historical performance on proficiency tests will almost certainly be too high, since errors will be investigated and corrected after they are discovered, and thus errors committed in the past are not likely to recur. The committee concluded: "[W]e believe that a calculation that combines error rates with match probabilities is inappropriate. The risk of error is properly considered case by case, taking into account the record of the laboratory performing the tests, the extent of redundancy, and the overall quality of the results." Moreover, a suspect's "best insurance" against the possibility of a false match due to laboratory error is the opportunity to have testing repeated at another facility. The committee therefore advised investigative agencies to retain samples for retesting whenever feasible.

Reeves, supra, 109 Cal. Rptr. 2d at 751–52.

ANDRE A. MOENSSENS, A MISTAKEN DNA IDENTIFICATION? *WHAT DOES IT MEAN?* (Updated October 2000), http://www.forensic-evidence.com/site/EVID/EL_DNAerror.html[49]

Various press reports released in early February make mention of a British case wherein a local police department confessed to having identified an innocent person as a criminal by a DNA test that was said to be in error. A U.K. police agency that had secured near 100 convictions on the basis of DNA testing, admitted that, as far back as April of 1999, they had matched a sample taken from the scene of a burglary to six loci on the DNA molecule of one of 700,000 persons whose DNA was collected in the national database. The suspect was a man with advanced Parkinson's disease, who could not drive and could barely dress himself. He lived 200 miles from the site of the burglary. His blood sample had been taken when he was arrested, and then released, after hitting his daughter in a family dispute. He was arrested despite his protestations of innocence and alibi evidence that he was babysitting a sick daughter at home. Police dismissed these protestations stating that "it had to be him" since the DNA matched. The odds of the arrestee's DNA being wrongly matched against that of the crime scene were said to be **one in 37 million.**

---

[49] Copyright 2008 by Andre A. Moenssens. Reprinted with permission.

It is only when the suspect's solicitor demanded a retest using additional markers, after the suspect had been in jail for months, that further testing was done. This testing, using a total of 10 loci, showed an exclusion at the additional four loci. The interpretation of the original test's results, given by law enforcement officials, were proven to be inaccurate. The suspect was then released from custody. The new British ten-loci test, it is said, only "offers a one in one billion chance of a mismatch" according to Scotland's *Evening News* of February 9, 2000!

Was the result reported after an examination of six loci an "erroneous" or "false" identification? No. There was indeed a "match" at six loci. What confuses lawyers, judges, lay persons, and indeed the police who make use of the results, is that they do not understand the true meaning of the statistics used by the experts. All but the initiated believe that when a DNA "match" is reported with odds of one in 37 million, we will encounter a like match in the DNA pattern only once in 37 million people. To test whether this is a common misunderstanding, the author [Prof. Moenssens], when lecturing to some 100+ trial judges, asked them what they understood the meaning of the testimony to be. All those who responded viewed the report as having said *that this defendant's particular DNA pattern would occur only once in 37 million individuals.*

According to DNA scientist Keith Inman, co-author with Norah Rudin of the recently published treatises, AN INTRODUCTION TO FORENSIC DNA ANALYSIS (CRC Press, 1997), and PRINCIPLES AND PRACTICE OF CRIMINALISTICS (CRC Press, 2000), it should be understood that the calculated frequency is an estimate, and can be off by an order of magnitude in either direction. Further, Inman said that "studies show that when databases grow, more loci (more discriminating loci) are required to support a strong inference of a common source." In other words, despite the statistical calculation of 1 in 37 million on six loci, *that does NOT mean that the six loci cannot match more than one person in 37 million.* According to population geneticists, it is indeed possible to have the six loci match in perhaps many dozens of individuals whose DNA is contained in a databank of 700,000.

Knowing that the non-expert judges, lawyers, and lay jurors will take the one in 37 million testimony to mean what it appears to say, is it ethical for a forensic expert to testify to the staggering statistical probabilities without explaining what the true meaning of the testimony is? And what obligation does the DNA analyst have to tell the jury that they must integrate the DNA evidence with other evidence when deciding whether the suspect is the perpetrator?

Keith Inman regards a "hit" (or "match") as nothing more than probable cause to look at the individual whose DNA has been matched to a sample stored in the database more closely, not the definitive and final disposition of his future in the criminal justice system. He states that "detectives and attorneys (perhaps even a few forensic scientists) need to be much better educated about the inferential nature of physical evidence. With well informed investigative people, the potential for arresting innocent people, as perhaps occurred in the U.K. case, will be minimized, **while with ill-informed or biased agents, mistakes will happen with 13 loci, too.**" [Emphasis supplied by editor.]

The police in Great Britain maintain a DNA database which has grown from 470,000 potential suspects in 1998 to over 700,000 during 1999. The U.K. database is managed by the Forensic Science Service. It is now reported that ten loci will henceforth be used routinely when comparing known samples against unknown DNA fragments. The FBI is reported to test 13 different loci, which minimizes the chance of matching an innocent suspect by chance. State and local laboratories, however, do not always test as many loci as are used by our top national law enforcement agency.

Will this result in wholesale appeals by the thousands of persons convicted through DNA testing? Stephen Niezgoda of the FBI is reported to have characterized the possibilities as "mind-blowing" in a story that appeared in USA Today on February 8. The story also suggests that U.S. officials recognize similar mismatches may occur here as DNA testing occurs more routinely. The American database of DNA specimen is reported to be about half of the one existing in the U.K. The larger the database, the greater the possibility for adventitious hits, which is how Mr. Inman characterized the British case.

Perhaps a disturbing sidelight is that this misinterpretation of the statistical results in light of the case circumstances was revealed by British authorities only in January of 2000 when a law enforcement conference of DNA specialists worldwide met in Washington D.C. The mistake was not publicly acknowledged for almost a year after it occurred. When British authorities were questioned about the failure to reveal the error, a Home Affairs spokesperson said, "No system is 100 percent foolproof." It must also be noted that the retest was done at the insistence of the defendant's attorney. The unlikelihood of this suspect being able to commit the crime of which he was accused did not spark the retest. Forensic Science Service officials were said to have refused comment on the case to the press.

The U.K.'s *Daily News* of February 11, 2000, reported that when the mistake was discovered some six months later, the arrestee was released without an apology and given a brief letter stating that charges against him were being dropped because "there was not enough evidence to provide a realistic chance of conviction." No admission of error to the innocent person who had been arrested was to be forthcoming. The cavalier way in which law enforcement agencies deny making mistakes, and admit them only when the evidence is so overwhelming that errors can no longer be denied, does more to undermine the public confidence in law enforcement than the mere fact of the discovery of an error itself would do.

Yet, DNA reliability has been lauded nationally as the most reliable evidence known, and persons criticizing the meaning of the proffered statistical calculations have been treated as lunatics and "Neanderthals." It is clear that many people do not understand statistics, and law enforcement officers, prosecutors, defense attorneys, judges and jurors should also understand that DNA matches based on six DNA loci — or whatever number of loci tested — are not the end of the inquiry, but only the beginning of more investigative hard work.

QUESTIONS

1. There was no allegation of laboratory error in the case described by Professor Moenssens. That is, the accused's DNA did match the crime scene DNA at the six loci initially examined, and there was no error in calculating a one-in-37 million probability of a random match. Recall that in the conclusion of the *Shea* opinion, Judge Barbadoro wrote that "[w]hen significance of a random match probability estimate is *properly explained*, the probative value of the evidence is not substantially outweighed by the limited potential that jurors could be misled." (emphasis added).

Bearing all this in mind, just how should the significance of a random match probability estimate be "explained" to a jury so that they will not be misled?

2. Should every person who has been convicted based upon a match at six loci (or fewer) have their conviction reviewed?

[d]   Can DNA Evidence *Alone* Be Sufficient to Convict?

The article by Professor Moenssens, above, leads to a different, but related, issue. Should DNA evidence *by itself* be legally sufficient to convict?

The next case involves a prosecution for robbery and rape. At trial the victim identified a spectator in the courtroom — not the defendant — as her assailant. [The victim had identified the defendant in a pretrial lineup; however, evidence of the pretrial lineup was excluded at defendant's trial. Accordingly, *the misidentification of the spectator was the only eyewitness evidence in the case*]. Despite not being identified as the assailant, the defendant was convicted. The conviction was based upon DNA evidence that the probability of another individual's DNA randomly matching the DNA profile found in a semen sample recovered from the victim was one in 500 million. After conviction the defendant moved the trial court for an order of dismissal.

PEOPLE v. RUSH
630 N.Y.S.2d 631 (Sup. Ct. Kings Co. N.Y. 1995)

ALAN D. MARRUS, JUSTICE.

This case presents an issue of apparent first impression in New York. In a criminal prosecution, can DNA evidence alone establish a legally sufficient case of a defendant's guilt? While there appears to be general acceptance of the notion that DNA evidence alone can exculpate a defendant accused or even convicted of a crime,[50] [1] no reported decision in New York has determined that DNA evidence alone can inculpate a defendant sufficiently to support a guilty verdict.

Here the People commenced trial with a complainant who had been robbed and raped at knifepoint by a stranger. Several weeks after the crime, the complainant selected the defendant's photograph from a photographic array as the person who perpetrated the crime. About two weeks later, she identified the defendant in a corporeal lineup. When the complainant testified at trial, however, she identified a spectator in the courtroom as her assailant. As a result, evidence of the previous lineup identification of the defendant had to be precluded.

The only other evidence of identification offered by the prosecution came from an F.B.I. special agent who is an expert in forensic DNA analysis. He performed a DNA profiling test using anal and vaginal swabs taken from the complainant at a hospital shortly after the rape and two dried blood samples, one taken from the complainant and one from the defendant. . . . The expert's conclusion was "that the probability of selecting another individual at random from the population that would have the same set of DNA profiles was less than 1 in 500 million for the black, the white, and the Hispanic populations." The only other evidence offered at trial which in any way related

---

[50] [n.1] According to information supplied by the Innocence Project at Cardozo Law School, seven defendants convicted and imprisoned for criminal activity were exonerated and freed from custody based on DNA evidence developed after their convictions. Marion Coakley (Suffolk Co., NY); Kerry Kotler (Suffolk Co., NY); Brian Piczcek (Ohio); Terry Chalmers (Westchester Co., NY); Kurt Bloodsworth (Maryland); Charles Dabbs (Westchester Co., NY); and Glendall Woodall (West Virginia). Two other defendants were granted clemency based on DNA evidence. Edward Honaker (Virginia) and Tony Snyder (Virginia).

to identification was the testimony of an acquaintance of the defendant who saw him in the vicinity of the crime three days before the crime took place.

At the close of the People's case, the defendant moved to dismiss the case on the ground that the evidence was legally insufficient to make out a prima facie case for the jury. The court reserved decision until after the jury deliberated and reached a verdict. The jury subsequently convicted the defendant of rape in the first degree and robbery in the first degree.

The standard for a trial order of dismissal is whether the evidence offered by the prosecution is legally sufficient. Legally sufficient evidence means "competent evidence which, if accepted as true, would establish every element of an offense charged and the defendant's commission thereof." "Legally sufficient evidence" and "prima facie case" are often used interchangeably, but neither standard is as rigorous as "proof beyond a reasonable doubt."

The evidence of defendant's guilt was entirely circumstantial:

(1) the complainant was robbed and raped;

(2) swabs taken from her vagina and anus shortly after the rape contained semen;

(3) the semen samples matched the DNA profile of the defendant sufficiently to estimate that the odds were 1 in 500 million that another person was the source of that DNA;

(4) the complainant testified that before the rape she had not engaged in sexual intercourse for at least four or five years; and

(5) the defendant was seen in the area where the rape took place three days before the crime.

Circumstantial evidence is legally sufficient when "the hypotheses of guilt . . . flow[s] naturally from the facts proved, and [is] consistent with them and . . . exclude[s] 'to a moral certainty' every reasonable hypothesis of innocence."

To determine whether the evidence here meets that standard, this court has reviewed cases where fingerprint evidence was deemed sufficient to establish the identity of the perpetrator. But a fingerprint expert will testify that the fingerprints left at the scene "match" those of the defendant. The DNA expert here was clear, however, to distinguish his finding from a fingerprint match:

Q.   Agent, recently in the news there's been a lot of the use of the term DNA fingerprinting suggesting the possibility of absolute identification. Can the DNA comparisons you described result in such an absolute identification?

A.   No, they cannot. The DNA tests that I do and I've described to you do not result in an absolute identification, as a fingerprint comparison results in an absolute identification."

. . . .

DNA profiling evidence . . . is a relative newcomer to New York trials. Indeed, it was only a little more than a year ago that our highest State court determined that DNA evidence is admissible. *People v. Wesley*, 83 N.Y.2d 417, 633 N.E.2d 451 (1994). But in declaring that DNA evidence should be admissible, the New York Court of Appeals observed that "[s]uch evidence, consisting of unique genetic characteristics belonging to an individual, can provide *strong evidence* of a person's presence at and participation in a criminal act." *People v. Wesley* at 421, 633 N.E.2d 451 (emphasis added). Yet it appears that neither that Court, the Appellate Division, nor any of the State trial courts have issued a reported decision sustaining a criminal conviction on DNA evidence alone.

For guidance on this issue, therefore, decisions from other jurisdictions have been consulted. There appear to be two reported decisions in the United States, both of which have upheld criminal convictions where the sole evidence linking the defendant to the crime is DNA evidence. In *Springfield v. State*, 860 P.2d 435 (1993), the Wyoming Supreme Court upheld a rape conviction based entirely on DNA evidence developed, as here, by the F.B.I. laboratory. The victim, while able to give a general description of her assailant, was unable to make an identification, although she did testify that the defendant "resembles him." The DNA expert found a match between the defendant's blood sample and samples recovered from a stain on the victim's panties and from her anus. The probability that another Indian person would have the same DNA was estimated to be at 1 in 250,000. The Wyoming Supreme Court concluded that "the evidence was sufficient for 'reasonable and rational individuals' to conclude that the [defendant] was the perpetrator." 860 P.2d at 449.

In California, the Court of Appeals, in *People v. Soto*, 35 Cal.Rptr.2d 846 (1994) has also upheld a defendant's conviction for rape where the identifying evidence of the defendant came solely from DNA. There, the victim was unable to identify her assailant because he wore a mask during the attack. But a DNA match between a seminal stain on the victim's bedspread and the defendant's blood resulted in the statistical probability of 1 in 189 million that another Hispanic could have provided that sample. The court determined that "corroboration of identifying evidence was not required for DNA comparison." 35 Cal.Rptr.2d at 860.

. . . .

Identification evidence from an eyewitness inculpating a defendant, which can be unreliable and the product of suggestiveness, would not be relied upon by a court in the face of contradictory DNA evidence (*see* footnote 1). Why then should not the opposite be true — that DNA evidence should be relied upon, even in the face of contradictory eyewitness identification evidence exculpating a defendant? Indeed, that is exactly what the jury has done here in finding the defendant guilty.

The DNA evidence at the trial was the product of careful evaluation by a recognized expert in a prominent laboratory using a scientific technique to determine a statistical probability. The eyewitness identification evidence came from an injured and traumatized rape victim using impaired vision while in the unfamiliar capacity of a witness in a strange courtroom setting.

DNA evidence is not completely infallible — no evidence is. . . . . [T]his court is well aware that there may be "a significant margin of error in scientific analysis." Critics of forensic science are able to cite examples of sloppy laboratory performance to support their claim that there is room for "drastic improvement.

There can be little doubt, however, that the perils of eyewitness identification testimony far exceed those presented by DNA expert testimony. Acquittals in criminal prosecutions based entirely on eyewitness identification evidence are legion, as are reversals and vacaturs of convictions premised entirely on such evidence. New York State courts have even given serious consideration to admitting expert testimony to discredit eyewitness identification evidence. Where the prosecution is confronted with an irreconcilable conflict between eyewitness identification evidence and DNA identification evidence, it is likely to rely on the DNA evidence.

This court is, therefore, satisfied that the testimony of even one DNA expert that there is a genetic match between the semen recovered from the victim of a rape and the blood of the defendant, a total stranger, and the statistical probability that anyone else was the source of that semen are 1 in 500 million is legally sufficient to support a guilty verdict. The defendant's motion for a trial order of dismissal is, therefore, denied.

NOTES

1. ***The Rush Appeal.*** Rush's conviction was upheld on appeal. *People v. Rush*, 672 N.Y.S.2d 362 (1982). The appeals court stated that,

> It is well settled that a jury verdict must be sustained if, ' "after viewing the evidence in the light most favorable to the prosecution, any rational trier of fact could have found the essential elements of the crime beyond a reasonable doubt" ' (*People v. Contes*, 60 N.Y.S.2d 620, 621, quoting *Jackson v. Virginia*, 443 U.S. 307, 319). It is also settled that a defendant's guilt may be established through the introduction of circumstantial evidence. . . . [T]he evidence introduced here was sufficient to establish the defendant's guilt beyond a reasonable doubt.
>
> The defendant first claims that DNA evidence cannot serve as the sole evidence supporting his conviction because it is circumstantial in nature and is not absolute or infallible. This claim is not persuasive. Virtually no evidence is absolutely conclusive in its probative import, and the defendant cites no authority which imposes such a standard of absolute certitude. Legal sufficiency "does not mean that absolute or metaphysical certainty is required" Further, it is well settled that "[c]ircumstantial evidence is not a disfavored form of proof and, in fact, may be stronger than direct evidence." It has been observed that "[c]ircumstantial evidence is frequently more reliable and stronger than direct proof by eyewitness testimony.
>
> The scientific evidence adduced was not insufficient to establish the defendant's guilt beyong a reasonable doubt. . . .
>
> . . . The unrebutted scientific testimony introduced by the People established that the DNA recovered from the crime scene matched the defendant's DNA. According to the People's expert, the chance that another person's profile would produce such a match was virtually nonexistent, i.e., 500 million to one. The foregoing evidence constituted highly probative evidence that the jury could properly credit as establishing the defendant's guilt beyond a reasonable doubt. Moreover, although the victim misidentified the defendant at trial, any conflicting inferences to be drawn from her testimony were for the jury to resolve, and we cannot conclude on the record before us that its verdict was against the weight of the evidence."

Rush, supra, 672 N.Y.S.2d at 363–64.

Other cases have held that DNA evidence alone is legally and factually sufficient to convict. *See State v. Toomes*, 191 S.W.3d 122, 129–30 (Tenn. Ct. App. 2005) ("Agent James, we note, testified that probabilities of finding the defendant's profile within the

African-American population was 1 in 5 billion, 128 million; within the Caucasian population it was 1 in 22 billion, 870 million; within the Southeastern Hispanic population it was 1 in 90 billion, 910 million, and within the Southwestern Hispanic population it was 1 in 185 billion, 700 million. The confluence of these factors persuades us that the evidence was sufficient to support the defendant's conviction for aggravated rape."); *Roberson v. State*, 16 S.W.3d 156, 159 & 162 (Tex. App. 2000) (probability of a random match one in 5.5 billion legally and factually sufficient to convict in the absence of any eyewitness or other circumstantial evidence of identity).

2. *Court in the U.K. Finds DNA Statistics Insufficient to Convict Without Corroboration.* In the case of *R. v. Watters*, Court of Appeal (Criminal Division) October 19, 2000, the court held that without corroborating evidence DNA evidence was insufficient to convict. *See DNA Statistics Found Insufficient to Convict without Corroboration*, http://www.forensic-evidence.com/site/EVID/DNA_Watters.html (last visited, March 20, 2009).

3. *CODIS.* In 1994 Congress enacted the "DNA Identification Act." 42 U.S.C. §§ 14131-34 (1994). This Act authorized the FBI to establish a national database of DNA profiles from persons convicted of crimes, crime scene samples, and unidentified human remains. The national DNA database is known as the "Combined DNA Index System" (CODIS). All 50 states have enacted statutes creating a statewide database of DNA profiles and use the CODIS software developed by the FBI. Whose DNA profile is included in a particular state's database varies from state to state. At a minimum, however, all states collect DNA profiles from felony sexual offenders.

The FBI selected 13 STR loci to serve as the standard for the CODIS system. The national database consists of the 50 state databases, all of which use common procedures to create a DNA profile. The national database is continually growing. As of January of 2009 there were 6,652,752 offender profiles in the database.

The national database makes it possible to compare an unknown crime scene sample with every individual's DNA profile in the national database. Professors Donnelley and Friedman refer to this sort of search as a "trawl search." *See* Peter Donnelley and Richard D. Friedman, *DNA as Evidence*, THE UNIVERSITY OF MICHIGAN LAW QUADRANGLE NOTES 87, 89 (Fall/Winter 2000). A trawl search makes it possible for an individual to be connected to a crime even though the individual was never a suspect, and even though there may not be any evidence to corroborate the DNA match. It was a trawl search of the national database in England and Wales that was the subject of the "mistaken" DNA identification discussed in the article by Professor Mansions in subsection [c] *supra*, of this chapter.

The expanding national database will inevitably lead to cases where an individual is connected to a crime *solely* on the basis of a DNA match. Inevitably, more courts will have to grapple with the issue of whether DNA match evidence alone is sufficient to convict.

[4]   Polymerase Chain Reaction (PCR)

Most of the DNA cases presented above discuss the admissibility of DNA evidence generated by the RFLP technique. RFLP testing was, at one time, the dominant method for creating a DNA profile in criminal cases. That distinction now belongs to the testing based on the polymerase chain reaction (PCR) technique. The PCR technique was introduced in the late 1980s, and by the mid- to late 1990s had replaced the RFLP technique as the dominant method for developing a DNA profile in criminal cases.

PCR-based testing has significant advantages over RFLP testing. PCR-based test results can be available much quicker, and can be used on samples too small for RFLP testing. For example, PCR technology makes it possible to analyze DNA extracted from items such as saliva on a postage stamp or a cigarette butt.

> One major drawback of RFLP analysis is that it requires a relatively large, nondegraded DNA sample. Unfortunately, many crime scenes . . . yield only a minute amount of genetic information about the perpetrator. PCR . . . testing, is designed to overcome this obstacle. PCR is like a "genetic photocopy machine." It is a laboratory technique that can increase the amount of testable DNA in a crime sample.

State v. Moeller, 548 N.M.2d 465, 480 (S.D. 1996).

PCR is not itself a method of DNA typing, but a technique of sample preparation that replicates, or "amplifies" specific polymorphic sections of DNA. Once DNA is amplified by PCR it still must be typed to identify the alleles that are present. First-generation PCR technology amplified and typed, or identified, alleles of only one gene at one site — the DQ alpha gene. Accordingly, early PCR testing was not nearly as discriminating as RFLP technology that looked at alleles at several polymorphic sites. Over time, however, PCR technology improved and was able to amplify and examine alleles at additional sites, and thereby become much more discriminating. The *Vao SOK* case that follows describes the second generation of PCR testing that identifies alleles at multiple sites, or loci. The Notes following the *Vao SOK* case discuss the third generation of PCR-based DNA typing, known as PCR-STR testing, which examines alleles at 13 sites.

COMMONWEALTH v. Vao SOK
683 N.E.2d 671 (Mass. 1997)

GREANEY, JUSTICE.

This interlocutory appeal, in which the Commonwealth is the appellant, arises from . . . murder proceedings in the Superior Court: the defendant Vao Sok is charged with . . . kidnapping, rape, and murder. . . . The Commonwealth sought to introduce in evidence . . . deoxyribonucleic acid (DNA) test results derived from the polymerase chain reaction (PCR) method. Citing *Daubert v. Merrell Dow Pharmaceuticals, Inc.*, 509 U.S. 579, the defendant . . . filed a "motion in limine to exclude evidence of DNA testing or in the alternative to conduct a *Daubert* hearing[.]" [A] judge in the Superior Court conducted an evidentiary hearing on the defendant's . . . claims. The judge subsequently entered a memorandum and order in which he ruled that the results of the DQa PCR-based DNA testing could be admitted in evidence against . . . defendant, but that the results of the Polymarker (PM) PCR-based DNA testing and the D1S80 PCR-based DNA testing should be excluded. . . . The Commonwealth [petitioned] for relief . . . challenging the judge's decision with respect to the PM and D1S80 test results. . . . We conclude that the PCR-based tests at issue in this case meet the test of scientific reliability. . . .

1. *Background.* (a)[51] [4]. . . . There are different methods used in DNA forensic testing including Restriction Fragment Length Polymorphism (RFLP) and PCR amplification and allele identification. RFLP analysis requires a larger segment of DNA than does PCR analysis and involves a time-consuming testing process. RFLP targets loci on DNA molecules that are known to have different lengths because of variations in the number of times that a sequence of base pairs is repeated. These loci are referred to as variable number tandem repeats (VNTRs). . . . The RFLP process was not used in the cases before us.

PCR-based testing is an alternative method of analyzing forensic DNA samples that compares polymorphic DNA sequences through "allele-specific probe analysis," a very different process from RFLP, which looks at the length of the DNA sequence. The goal of a PCR-based approach is to determine whether certain alleles are actually present or absent in a sample. Two DNA samples taken from the same individual will contain the same alleles. Samples from different individuals are apt to contain different alleles. Thus, finding the same alleles in two different samples supports the conclusion that the samples have a common source. As with RFLP, if a match is identified, calculations are performed to determine how often such a match is likely to occur in the population. Where an individual's sample matches a provided sample of DNA, the individual cannot definitely be excluded as the possible source of the provided sample of DNA, but where key alleles do not match, the individual is excluded as the source.

PCR-based analysis involves the making of millions of copies of particular short segments of DNA in an amplification process, similar to the mechanism by which DNA normally replicates itself.[52] [5] After the segments are replicated, different genetic marker typing tests are performed, depending on the particular polymorphic locus being probed. . . . Different typing kits were used to amplify and detect the genetic markers. After the genetic markers have been identified, the DNA profile is compared to another profile from a known source. If an appropriate correlation appears, a statistical analysis is performed, based on population databases, and the probability of a random match for a particular sequence is estimated from the frequency with which that sequence appears in the relevant databases.

PCR-based testing is extremely valuable for forensic science. It permits DNA profiling of samples containing much smaller quantities of DNA-such as saliva on a cigarette butt-than can be tested by the RFLP method, and test results are available promptly, often within twenty-four hours. . . .

---

[51] [4] Some additional definitions of terms used in this opinion are provided to assist in the understanding of the technology involved. The position that a gene or other DNA fragment occupies on the DNA molecule is called a locus. Each person has two genes, each with possibly a multiple of alleles, at each locus. An individual's genotype is his or her gene makeup. The genotype for a group of loci that have been analyzed is the individual's DNA profile. A genetic marker is "an easily detected gene or chromosome region used for identification."

[52] [n.5] This amplification process consists of three steps as follows:

"First, each double-stranded segment is separated into two strands by heating. Second, these single-stranded segments are hybridized with primers, short DNA segments (20–30 nucleotides in length) that complement and define the target sequence to be amplified. Third, in the presence of the enzyme DNA polymerase, and the four nucleotide building blocks (A, C, G, and T), each primer serves as the starting point for the replication of the target sequence. A copy of the complement of each of the separated strands is made, so that there are two double-stranded DNA segments. This three-step cycle is repeated, usually 20–35 times. The two strands produce four copies; the four, eight copies; and so on until the number of copies of the original DNA is enormous."

(b) All the DNA testing in [this] case . . . was done at CBR Laboratories in Boston (CBR) in 1994 and 1995. . . . PCR amplification and typing were performed . . . by means of three available scientific DNA genetic marker kits: the Amplitype HLA DQa Amplification and Typing Kit;[53] [9] the AmpliType PM PCR Amplification and Typing Kit; and the AmpliFLP D1S80 PCR Amplification Kit. These kits are marketed by Perkin-Elmer Corporation, Inc., under licenses from Roche Molecular Systems, which holds the patents on the kits. In his memorandum, the judge described in considerable detail the steps taken in the use of the kits, and explicitly set forth the testing process in each case [and] the results of the tests. . . .

. . . It is important to point out here that the evidentiary value of PCR-based tests lies in their combination with one another. The likelihood of a coincidental match between different samples of DNA is relatively high if only DQA1 testing is done. When that testing is combined with PM testing, however, the joint power of discrimination of the two tests is over 99.9%; that is, over 99.9% of the time, two randomly-chosen individuals will have a different combination of DQa and PM types. When D1S80 testing is used in conjunction with DQA1 and PM testing, the power of discrimination increases to 99.99%. Thus, testing at multiple genetic loci increases the likelihood of detecting sampling errors or contamination, and the PM and D1S80 tests provide an important tool in cross-validation of DQA1 testing to ensure accuracy in the exclusion of an individual based on a comparison of different DNA samples.

2. *The [trial] judge's decision.* . . . The judge saw the problem before him as calling, at the outset, for a determination of the "reliability of [the PCR-based] methodology and [the DQA1, PM, and D1S80 test kits] in general, and specifically their reliability when employed in a forensic setting." The judge recognized that . . . the overarching issue [was] the scientific "reliability of the process underlying the expert testimony."

We summarize the judge's conclusions (expressing his reasoning with respect to the merits and his rulings of law) as follows:

(1) The PCR method is a scientifically valid and reliable method of amplifying samples of DNA, and . . . [is a] scientifically valid method[ ] of comparing DNA samples if . . . prescribed procedures are followed.

(2) The three kits used by CBR are "undoubtedly . . . designed and intended to produce reliable results." The kits will provide such results only if they are used in accordance with the protocols established by their manufacturer and are processed by knowledgeable and well-trained analysts with an adequate background in forensic DNA analysis.

. . . .

(6) The DQA1 technique and the Amplitype HLA DQa Amplification and Typing Kit are reliable, and the DQa results obtained in each of the cases may be admitted in evidence. The judge based this ruling on scientific articles he had examined, the testimony at the hearing, and the "rather overwhelming support that has been given to the [DQa] technique by the appellate courts of other jurisdictions."

(7) The Commonwealth did not sustain its burden of proof with regard to the reliability of the PM and D1S80 test kits, and the results of tests utilizing those kits are therefore excluded.

---

[53] [n.9] DQa is the product of the DQA gene, found at the DQA1 locus.

3. *Standards of review.* . . . In considering the issue of scientific validity, our review is *de novo* because a trial judge's conclusion will have applicability beyond the facts of the case before him. The question of the validity of a particular scientific methodology is thus entitled to the same standard of review as a conclusion of law.

. . . .

4. *Application of the standards of review.* The conclusions in the judge's decision set forth above are directed . . . to the issue of the scientific validity of PCR-based testing. In examining these conclusions de novo, we keep in mind that forensic DNA typing "is a rapidly developing field, and new understanding may be expected as more studies and tests are conducted." Thus, consideration of the scientific validity of the DNA tests in issue is not frozen at the date almost two years ago when the hearing was held. Rather, our determination must be made in light of current scientific knowledge.

DNA profiling evidence from RFLP analysis has been shown to be a scientifically valid methodology. Similarly, DNA profiling evidence by PCR-based analysis, both in general and specifically at the DQA1 locus, has been demonstrated to be a valid technique, as noted both in scientific research and in a large number of appellate cases. [T]he judge's conclusions validating . . . the PCR-based metholog[y] [is] clearly correct.

We next confront the issue of the validity of PCR-based testing at the PM and D1S80 loci. . . . [T]he judge concluded that the PCR-based tests at all three loci are designed to be reliable, so long as they are used in accordance with established protocols.

The judge's ruling with respect to the PM and D1S80 test kits was based . . . on his determination that the underlying methodology for these tests had not yet reached a stage of acceptance sufficient to support a ruling of scientific validity. In so deciding, the judge considered the following:

> (a) two Commonwealth expert witnesses were naturally, and perhaps understandably, biased in favor of the admissibility of the PCR-based tests;

> (b) other Commonwealth experts were not nearly as enthusiastic in their endorsement of the PM and D1S80 techniques as they were of the DQa technique;

> (c) the PM technique has a weakness not present in the DQa technique because the PM test must use a compromise temperature to test the multiple genetic markers; and

> (d) at the time of the evidentiary hearing, the PM technique had not been reviewed by any appellate court, and the D1S80 technique had received only cursory review by the Court of Appeals of Georgia in *Redding v. State*, 464 S.E.2d 824 (1995).

We conclude, based on events occurring since the judge concluded the hearing, that testing at the PM and D1S80 loci has been scientifically validated. An authoritative work in this field by the National Research Council, The Evaluation of Forensic DNA Evidence (1996) (1996 NRC Report), has found that PM testing is "beginning to be widely used" and has been validated with tests for "robustness" (reliability) by various studies. *Id.* at 72. The Report goes on to find that the "value [of the D1S80 technique] for forensic analysis has been validated in a number of tests." *Id.* at 72, 117. The Report concludes that the "technology [for DNA profiling] and the methods for estimating frequencies and related statistics have progressed to the point where the admissibility of properly collected and analyzed DNA data should not be in doubt." *Id.* at 73. . . .

In addition to the 1996 NRC Report, other validation studies have been issued that demonstrate the reliability of PM and D1S80 testing. . . .

We have not been referred to any published scientific study or article that questions the reliability of PCR-based DNA analysis or its general acceptance in the relevant community of forensic scientists. . . .

Further, the courts that have considered PM and D1S80 testing to date have found both to be scientifically reliable when properly done. Such cases probably represent the first wave of what undoubtedly will be many more decisions accepting PM and D1S80 testing for consideration by triers of fact.[54] [20]

Thus we are satisfied that PCR-based testing at the PM and D1S80 loci is a scientifically valid means of comparing DNA profiles and that such testing is admissible as evidence when the tests are properly conducted.

. . . .

6. *Disposition.* The case is remanded to the county court for the entry of a judgment consistent with this opinion.

So ordered.

NOTES

1. *Court Acceptance of DNA Evidence Derived from PCR Technology.* As mentioned in *Vao SOK*, PCR technology as a means for amplifying discrete sections of DNA is widely accepted. *See United States v. Beasley*, 102 F.3d 1440, 1447–48 n.4 (8th Cir. 1996) (validating DQA1 and PM testing, and listing 16 states that have sustained the admissibility of DNA evidence derived from PCR technology); *United States v. Shea*, 957 F. Supp. 331, 338 (D.N.H. 1997) (validating DQA1, PM, and D1S80 testing); *United States v. Lowe*, 954 F. Supp. 401, 418 (D. Mass. 1997) (DQA1, PM, and D1S80); *State v. Gore*, 21 P.2d 262, 272- 273 & 273 n.8 (Wash. 2001) (DQ-alpha, PM, and D1S80 testing generally accepted; collecting cases finding PM and D1S80 testing to be admissible); *Brodine v. State*, 936 P.2d 545 (Alaska. Ct. App. 1997) (validating PM, DQA1, and D1S80 testing); *State v. Pooler*, 696 So. 2d 22, 52–53 (La. Ct. App. 1997) (no error in allowing jury to view DQA1, PM, and D1S80 test results, on charts, in jury room); *Keen v. Commonwealth*, 485 S.E.2d 659 (Va. 1997) (testimony on DQA1 and PM tests admissible); *People v. Pope*, 672 N.E.2d 1321 (Ill. 1996) (validating DQA1 and PM testing); *People v. Morales*, 643 N.Y.S.2d 217 (N.Y. 1996) (validating DQA1 and PM testing); *Redding v. State*, 464 S.E.2d 824 (Ga. 1995) (validating DQA1 and D1S80 testing).

Concern over correct testing procedures as essential to ensuring reliable PCR test results is, of course, the same issue that courts have dealt with in regard to RFLP analysis. *See* section C. [2], *supra*, of this chapter. As with RFLP testing, courts are

---

[54] [n.20] In *Commonwealth v. Rosier*, 685 N.E. 2d 739 (1997), we have approved yet another type of PCR-based testing involving short tandem repeats of a few nucleotide units (STRs). This process permits testing at a large number of sites, and "[a]s more STRs are developed and validated, this system is coming into wide use." 1996 NRC Report, supra at 71. This is yet another indication of the rapid pace at which PCR-based technology is developing and the scientific recognition that new systems are receiving as they are validated for forensic use.

split on whether proper test procedure is a weight or admissibility issue. *Compare State v. Russell*, 882 P.2d 747, 761 (Wash. 1994) (*Frye* does not require acceptance of the laboratory testing procedures; concerns over errors can be argued to the jury) *with State v. Carter*, 524 N.W.2d 763, 779 (Neb. 1994) (trial court decides preliminarily "whether the test conducted properly followed [accepted methodology]").

2. Short Tandem Repeat (PCR-STR) Testing. At footnote 20 of *Vao SOK, supra* , the Massachusetts Supreme Court mentions that it has approved "yet another type of PCR-based testing involving short tandem repeats of a few nucleotide units (STRs)." *Vao SOK, supra*, 683 N.E.2d at 691 n.20.

PCR-STR testing has become widely used and is a powerful identification tool. PCR-STR testing at 13 loci is the standard used by the FBI for compiling the national DNA database (CODIS).

In *People v. Shreck*, 22 P.3d 68 (Colo. 2001), the Colorado Supreme Court joined a growing list of courts to find PCR-STR analysis to be reliable and admissible. *Shreck* involved a rape where PCR-STR analysis of rape kit samples determined that the probability that the contributor was not the defendant (but a random third person) was one in 5.3 quadrillion (5.3 quadrillion = 5,300,000,000,000,000 = 5.3 × 1015). *Shreck, supra*, 22 P.3d at 72. The Colorado Supreme Court described STR analysis.

> Polymerase chain reaction ("PCR") is a process by which DNA fragments too small to be suitable for RFLP analysis can be analyzed. Under the PCR process, these DNA fragments are duplicated many times, thus allowing very small samples to be accurately tested. PCR also permits testing in a relatively short time in comparison to prior methods that required the decay of radioactive materials. Finally, unlike RFLP testing, which destroys the sample, PCR processing allows a technician to reproduce and verify test results by creating a larger sample for testing.

> . . . .

> [One] form of PCR testing involves the use of locations on the DNA strand containing short tandem repeats ("STR") of baseline patterns. STR testing reveals length differences between chromosomes on different people with the same base pair sequences. There are thirteen locations at which the number of STRs are known to vary from person to person. Thus, if all thirteen locations of the known and questioned sample are identical, a match is considered to have been made.

> When STR loci are amplified through the PCR process separately and run on a separate gel, the system is called "monoplex." Multiplex systems add more than one set of PCR primers to a reaction so as to be able to amplify several loci together and run them simultaneously. Monoplex systems and multiplex systems that amplify and run three loci simultaneously, ("triplex"), have been in use for many years.

> The commercial kits used to perform the STR testing at issue in this case were manufactured by Perkins Elmer Biosystems ("PE"). These kits, called AmpFLSTR Profiler Plus ("Profiler Plus") and AmpFLSTR Cofiler ("Cofiler"), employ a combination sixplex and nineplex system that is able to read all thirteen locations at the same time. In January 1999, when they were used in this case, the kits were relatively new to the market.

Shreck, supra, 22 P.2d at 68. Other cases finding PCR-STR technology to be reliable and admissible include, *State v. Traylor,* 656 N.W.2d 885, 900 (Minn. 2003) (generally accepted under Minnesota's version of the *Frye* test); *State v. Butterfield,* 27 P.3d 1133, 1143–44 (Utah 2001) (PCR-STR reliability can be judicially noticed); *State v. Rokita,* 736 N.E.2d 205, 211 (Ill. Ct. App. 2000) (noting that STR-based testing is now generally accepted in the relevant scientific community); *People v. Allen,* 85 Cal. Rptr. 2d 655, 659–60 (Cal. App.1999) (STR testing is generally accepted under *Frye*); *Commonwealth v. Rosier,* 685 N.E.2d 739, 743 (Mass.1997) (PCR-based tests, including STR, are scientifically valid); *State v. Jackson,* 582 N.W.2d 317, 325 (Neb. 1998) (holding that the trial court correctly determined that PCR-based STR DNA testing used was generally accepted).

   3. *PCR-Based Testing and the Statistics Issue.* Recall that the many courts take the position that without testimony about the frequency of a random match, testimony that a crime scene sample "matched" the suspect's is meaningless and, therefore, testimony about the match itself is inadmissible. *See United States v. Yee,* 134 F.R.D. 161, 181 (N.D. Ohio) ("Without the probability assessment, the jury does not know whether the patterns are as common as two eyes, or as unique as the Mona Lisa."). Accordingly, at one point in time, several courts considering the admissibility of DNA evidence *generated by the RFLP method* found such evidence inadmissible because the calculation of statistics (not the evidence of a match) was unreliable. *See* Section C. [3], *supra* this chapter; *State v. Carter,* 524 N.W.2d 763, 783 (Neb. 1994) (court collects cases).

   Probability estimates calculated with the product rule are routinely admissible with DNA profiles generated by PCR testing. In fact, PCR testing avoided much of the controversy that plagued probability estimates associated with the product rule and RFLP testing, described in section C. [3], *supra,* of this chapter. There are two reasons for this.

   (A) The First Generation of PCR Testing. To begin with, the probability statistics that were initially offered with PCR evidence were of a different magnitude than the statistics that were being offered with RFLP testing. This is because the first generation of PCR testing looked at only one gene, the DQ alpha gene, and there were only six variations (alleles) of this gene. Because alleles are inherited in pairs, one from each parent, there were only 21 possible combinations of pairs of this gene. *See People v. Morganti,* 50 Cal. Rptr. 2d 837, 849 (Cal. App. 1996); HOWARD COLEMAN & ERIC SWENSON, DNA IN THE COURTROOM: A TRIAL WATCHER'S GUIDE 55–56 (1994).

   RFLP testing, by contrast, looks at several alleles and, by using the product rule, generates statistics that can run into the billion-to-one range. Initially, therefore, PCR testing was less discriminating than RFLP testing, and the population frequency testimony was much less dramatic. In *Morganti, supra* , the court described it this way:

> . . . [A]pplying statistics to PCR test results presents a fundamentally different issue from the controversy involving RFLP testing. . . .

> . . . [U]nder the PCR method, for a 1.2, 4 allele, the percentage frequency is 10.4 percent. In the rarest situation, that of a 1.3, 1.3 allele, the frequency is 1.2 percent of Caucasians. . . . Here the data base . . . [is] from samples observed and a percentage only is given. Eliminated . . . [with] the PCR method is . . . an unusual amount of speculation or conjecture when you attempt to project in the millions of people of certain classes as in RFLP method. That simply isn't present under the PCR method. . . .

Id. at 854.

As a result, most cases dealing with the admissibility of PCR and the DQ alpha gene did not even discuss the reliability of the estimate of a random match. *See, e.g., State v. Russell*, 882 P.2d 747, 761 (Wash. 1994) (estimate that 90 to 95% of the population but not defendant could be excluded); *State v. Moeller*, 548 N.W.2d 465, 478 (S.D. 1996) (one out of 13 estimate); *State v. Lyons*, 863 P.2d 1303, 1306 (Or. App. 1993) (estimate that 2% to 3% of the Caucasian population could share the gene type); *State v. Hill*, 895 P.2d 1238, 1246 (Kan. 1995) (7% of the population and the defendant could not be excluded); *Clarke v. State*, 813 S.W.2d 654 (Tex. App. 1991) (no discussion at all); *People v. Lee*, 537 N.W.2d 233, 250 (Mich. App. 1995) (allele type appears in 4.3% of the Caucasian population and 8% of the black population). *But see State v. Carter*, 524 N.W.2d 763, 776 & 783 (Neb. 1994) (estimate that DQ alpha type appears in 8.9% of black and 6.8% of white population inadmissible because of disagreement in scientific community over population substructure).

(B) Debate Over the Product Rule Dissipates as PCR Testing Becomes More Discriminating. Second, by the time PCR testing began to look at multiple loci and use the product rule to generate probability estimates into the millions and billions, the debate over the appropriateness of using the product rule had subsided. The Washington Supreme Court summarized the issues and their resolution in *State v. Gore*, 21 P.3d 262 (Wash. 2001).

> We have not previously addressed the issue whether the product rule is admissible for determining statistical probabilities where PCR testing is involved. The issue here is whether the rule may be used to multiply results of the three PCR testing results (DQ-alpha, polymarker, and D1S80) together to determine statistical probabilities.

> The chief questions raised by Gore are whether linkage equilibrium and Hardy-Weinberg equilibrium have been established for the alleles at loci involved in the PCR testing in this case. . . .

> . . . [A] number of published articles have appeared in roughly the last five years which support use of product rule calculations using the PCR techniques at issue here. . . .

> Moreover, the 1996 NRC report also states that the product rule may be used with PCR testing. Committee on DNA Forensic Science: *An Update, The Evaluation of Forensic DNA Evidence* 119 (National Academy Press 1996). The report specifically states, as to the newest of the typing methods used here, D1S80, that it has been evaluated for agreement with Hardy-Weinberg. *Id.* at 117.

> Other courts have found use of the product rule admissible based on PCR results. . . .

> We conclude that use of the product rule for calculating probabilities of a random match of a genetic profile in the human population is generally accepted in the scientific community and is admissible to calculate frequencies where the PCR-based systems at issue in this case are involved.

Gore, supra, 21 P.3d at 274–75. Other courts reach similar results. *See United States v. Lowe*, 954 F. Supp. 401 (D. Mass.1996) (*Daubert* test; polymarker and D1S80); *People v. Wright*, 72 Cal. Rptr. 2d 246 (Cal. Ct. App. 1998) (*Kelly-Frye* standard); *State v. Carter,*

586 N.W.2d 818 (Neb. 1998) (*Frye-Houser* test; polymarker and DQ-alpha); *Common-wealth v. Rosier*, 685 N.E.2d 739 (Mass. 1997) (modified *Daubert;* polymarker test); *State v. Harvey*, 699 A.2d 596 (N.J. 1997) (reliability standard; polymarker test); *People v. Pope*, 672 N.E.2d 1321 (Ill. 1996) (*Frye* test; polymarker and DQ-alpha typing).

4. *Mitochondrial DNA (mtDNA) Analysis.* The techniques for creating a DNA profile already discussed (RFLP and PCR) involve the analysis of *nuclear* DNA. That is, the DNA material examined with these techniques is contained in the nucleus of the cell. There is, however, a second type of DNA material contained in a cell called *mitochondrial DNA* (mtDNA). Unlike nuclear DNA, mtDNA is not stored in the cell's nucleus. Mitochondrial DNA is contained within the cell's mitochondria. Mitochondria are circular structures that surround the nucleus of the cell. Also, unlike nuclear DNA that contains genetic material inherited from both the mother and father, mtDNA contains only genetic material inherited from the mother.

From a forensic point of view there are advantages and disadvantages with mtDNA analysis. A primary advantage is that mtDNA can be extracted from material where nuclear DNA is unavailable — like the shaft of a hair (nuclear DNA can only be found in the living cells of the hair's root). A general overview of mtDNA analysis was provided by the Tennessee Supreme Court in *State v. Scott*, 33 S.W.3d 746 (Tenn. 2000).

> . . . Generally speaking, every cell contains two types of DNA material: nuclear DNA and mitochondrial DNA. Nuclear DNA material is found in the nucleus of the cell, and the analysis of nuclear DNA is the traditional form of DNA analysis with which most people are now commonly familiar. With analysis of an individual's nuclear DNA profile, the possibility exists that each individual, with the exception of identical twins, has a unique profile with respect to anyone else in the world.

> By way of contrast, mtDNA comes from mitochondria in cells, and analysis of mtDNA provides significantly less ability to discriminate among possible donors. For example, because mtDNA is only inherited from the mother, all maternal relatives will share the same mtDNA profile. The final result in mtDNA typing analysis is that the defendant is either excluded as a possible contributor of the genetic material or he or she is included within the class of possible contributors. Because it is not possible to achieve the extremely high level of exclusion provided by nuclear DNA, mtDNA typing has been said to be a test more of exclusion than one of identification.

> Nevertheless, mtDNA typing has several advantages over traditional nuclear DNA typing. First, while any given cell contains only one nucleus, that same cell may contain hundreds or thousands of mitochondria from which to conduct analysis. MtDNA, therefore, can be obtained from some sources that nuclear DNA cannot, such as from bone, teeth, or hair shafts. Moreover, mtDNA can be obtained from small amounts of material, from degraded material, or even from dead cells.

> MtDNA analysis does have some shortcomings, however. The most important of these is the extreme sensitivity of the material, which renders it particularly susceptible to contamination. The State's expert admitted that all who handle mtDNA must be cognizant of the greater potential for contamina tion and that in any mtDNA laboratory, the contamination controls must be heightened. The potential for contamination seems to be greatest when the mtDNA is exposed to other organic materials or fluids. Moreover, the available

database of mtDNA sequences, to which mtDNA profiles are compared to identify whether a particular profile commonly occurs within the population, is relatively small when compared to the database compiled for nuclear DNA profiles. Although the smaller size of the database is due to the relative infancy of forensic mtDNA analysis, the ability to identify common types of mtDNA profiles in the general population is certainly more restricted than that of traditional nuclear DNA analysis.

Scott, supra, 33 S.W.3d at 756–57.

MtDNA analysis is based upon PCR amplification. *See State v. Underwood,* 518 S.E.2d 231, 237 (N.C. App. 1999) (court provides succinct explanation of mtDNA method of analysis), MtDNA testing has been found reliable and admissible in both *Daubert* and *Frye* jurisdictions. *See Wagner v. State,* 864 A.2d 1037, 1049 (Md. 2005) (*Frye* jurisdiction); *State v. Pappas,* 776 A.2d 1091, 1107 n.6 (Conn. 2001) (collects cases).

QUESTIONS

1. What are the advantages of PCR testing as compared to RFLP testing?

2. How many steps are there in PCR amplification?

3. What are the total number of polymorphic sites examined with PCR-STR testing for the national database (CODIS)?

4. How does mtDNA differ from traditional, or nuclear, DNA?

5. What are advantages and disadvantages of mtDNA testing?

[5]   Summary

The Acceptance of DNA "Match" and "Probability" Evidence. The forensic use of DNA evidence is, obviously, here to stay. While the forensic use of DNA did have a very "uneven" first 10 years, there were reasons for this. As explained in *DNA in the Courtroom: A Trial Watchers Guide:*

There is plenty of blame to allocate for causing confusion about DNA. To summarize:

- Forensic DNA testing was developed rapidly and by short-sighted commercial interests, the first time a major forensic technology had been introduced by the private sector. One result was that standards were not developed as quickly as they should have been;

- Prosecution witnesses oversold DNA evidence, claiming that the probability of a random match was as low as 1:738,000,000,000,000, creating false expectations about the technology and stacking the odds against the defendant;

- Overeager and hardnosed prosecutors urged these exaggerated figures and denied or delayed legitimate defense requests, exacerbating the inherently adversarial American legal system;

- Expert witnesses, often deriving the bulk of their income from witness fees, have a vested interest in making sure the controversy continues so that they can keep testifying;

- Inaccurate media that thrives on the sensational and the controversial has spread misinformation and disinformation about DNA;

- The judiciary is not always judicious, and is sometimes indifferent to the choices it could exercise to more speedily and certainly strive for justice.

HOWARD COLEMAN & ERIC SWENSON, DNA IN THE COURTROOM: A TRIAL WATCHER'S GUIDE 18 (1994).[55]

The above notwithstanding, there never was an indication that DNA was not, ultimately, going to be accepted by the courts in criminal cases. As problems surfaced that threatened the admissibility of DNA evidence (e.g., questionable test procedures or questions about the database used in making statistical probability estimates), one of three things happened to facilitate admissibility: scientists modified and standardized testing procedures, courts decided the problems were more of weight than admissibility, or state legislatures stepped in and legislated admissibility for DNA evidence.

There is no reason to doubt that the future will see new techniques for performing DNA analysis. Also, there is little reason to doubt that evolving DNA technology will — after an initial period of scrutiny — be judicially noticed as reliable. Evidentiary issues of the future will likely focus more on how DNA technology and evidence fits within the values embodied in our criminal justice system rather than whether DNA "match" and "probability" evidence is, or is not, admissible.

The Future; DNA and "Fairness" Issues. With admissibility challenges based upon reliability diminishing, courts have been forced to confront how such powerful and complex evidence fits within the framework of our criminal justice system and the values it represents. For example, if the prosecution plans to use DNA evidence against an indigent defendant, must the state provide the defendant with a DNA expert? Some states have said "yes." *See State v. Scott*, 33 S.W.3d 746, 755 (Tenn. 2000); *Dubose v. State*, 662 So. 2d 1189 (Ala. 1995); *Cade v. State*, 658 So. 2d 550 (Fla. Dist. Ct. App. 1995). Consider also whether the erroneous admission of DNA evidence can ever be "harmless error." *See Hutcherson v. State*, 677 So. 2d 1205, 1209 (Ala. 1996) ("admission of DNA evidence without [admissibility hearing] can never be harmless error"); *State v. Carter*, 524 N.W.2d 763, 786 (Neb. 1994) (erroneous admission of DNA not harmless given prejudicial nature of DNA evidence and the "unusual circumstances" of the case); *but see Nelson v. State*, 628 A.2d 69, 77 (Del. 1993) (erroneous admission of DNA evidence harmless error). Finally, as the CODIS database continues to grow, more courts will be faced with the issue of whether evidence of a DNA match and the accompanying probability of a random match is sufficient to convict even if there is no other evidence of guilt to corroborate the DNA evidence. *See People v. Rush*, section C. [3][d], *supra.*

In sum, while each new technique for creating a DNA profile has been found admissible, there remain unresolved "fairness" and policy issues for courts and legislatures to address. Beyond this, inevitable advances in DNA technology will likely spawn new legal challenges.

---

[55] Copyright © 1994 by the GeneLex Corporation. Reprinted with permission.

Chapter 5

EVIDENCE BASED ON RESEARCH IN SOCIAL AND BEHAVIORAL SCIENCE

A. INTRODUCTION: "SOFT SCIENCE"

[1]   Characteristics of "Soft Science"

Scientific evidence is commonly thought of as including evidence based upon research and study in one of the natural or physical sciences such as chemistry, physics, medicine, or biology. Typically, such research and study leads to the development of a technique, machine, or process that can be used to "scientifically" analyze physical evidence associated with a crime and produce a result that serves as the base for an expert opinion. Examples of such techniques include toxicology tests used to identify drugs, and DNA tests used to create an individual's DNA profile.

Not all evidence referred to as "scientific" is based on research in natural or physical science. This chapter examines the admissibility of evidence that is based upon research and study in social and behavioral sciences such as sociology and psychology. For lack of a more descriptive term, the expert opinion testimony examined in this chapter is sometimes referred to as "soft science" to distinguish it from expert opinion testimony based upon principles or techniques rooted in one of the natural or physical sciences, which is often referred to as "hard science."

A distinguishing characteristic of expert testimony based upon research in behavioral and social science is the unique (and somewhat vague) terminology employed by experts in this area. Frequently (but not always), such experts testify about "syndromes" and "profiles." Just what qualifies for the designation "syndrome" or "profile" is unclear. One commentator has suggested that "syndrome" usually refers to a condition that an important party to the case (victim or defendant) is suffering from, while "profile" references a set of characteristics likely possessed by the perpetrator of a crime.[1] Examples of syndromes that have been used in criminal cases include rape trauma syndrome, battered woman syndrome, and child sexual abuse accommodation syndrome. Examples of profiles that have been used in criminal cases include the battering parent profile, the child sexual abuser profile, and the drug courier profile.

Regardless of whether one refers to such evidence as soft science, syndrome and profile evidence, or "nontraditional" psychological and social science evidence, certain characteristics distinguish this type of evidence from all others. We begin our

---

[1] David McCord, *Syndromes, Profiles and Other Mental Exotica: A New Approach to the Admissibility of Nontraditional Psychological Evidence in Criminal Cases*, 66 Or. L. Rev. 19, 24 n.14 (1987) ("The imprecision of the designations can be seen by the fact that the battering parent phenomenon has been interchangeably referred to as a 'syndrome' or a 'profile.' ").

examination with an excerpt from an article by Professor David McCord that identifies nine characteristics of such evidence.

DAVID McCORD, SYNDROMES, PROFILES AND OTHER MENTAL EXOTICA: A NEW APPROACH TO THE ADMISSIBILITY OF NONTRADITIONAL PSYCHOLOGICAL EVIDENCE IN CRIMINAL CASES, 66 Or. L. Rev. 19, 27–35 (1987)[2]

The Characteristics of Nontraditional Psychological Evidence

There are nine characteristics that distinguish nontraditional psychological evidence from all other types of evidence. These characteristics will be examined individually along with the evidentiary concerns that they normally elicit from courts.

A. *Comparison of Individual's Behavior With That of Others in Similar Circumstances*

Psychological researchers engage in detailed observation of the behavior of individuals who for one reason or another have become the object of researchers' scrutiny. The researcher ascertains what behavior an individual exhibits and the circumstances which gave rise to that behavior. Over time, researchers recognize correlations between certain behaviors and certain causal circumstances. If a strong enough correlation becomes apparent, then researchers can predict that an individual subjected to certain circumstances will likely exhibit certain behaviors thereafter. The analysis can also work retrospectively. If an individual exhibits certain behavior, the researcher may infer that the behavior may have been caused by the individual being subjected to certain circumstances. For example, researchers studying rape victims began to notice that a large percentage of those individuals exhibited common reactions and that those reactions did not result from any other set of circumstances. Accordingly, over time the concept of "rape trauma syndrome" developed to designate behavior common to rape victims. All nontraditional psychological evidence follows this pattern of a comparison of an individual's behavior with a database consisting of the behavior of others in similar circumstances who have been studied in the past.

B. *Not Offered on Issue of Defendant's Sanity*

The one and only traditional usage of psychological evidence in criminal cases is on the issue of insanity. A short history of courts' dealings with psychological evidence offered on the issue of insanity is illuminating, since courts have treated nontraditional psychological evidence so differently.

Until a few decades into the nineteenth century, expert testimony was relatively rare at insanity trials. Rather, the observations of laypersons and arguments of counsel were the grist of the defense. This was true because "before the early nineteenth century the medical profession was not particularly interested in mental disorders, and knew little about them," and the legal profession saw "little need for expert advice on the issue of

---

[2] Reprinted by permission of Professor McCord and the University of Oregon. Copyright © 1987 by University of Oregon.

insanity."[3] [21] In the late nineteenth century, however, under the dominating influence of Sigmund Freud, doctors and other researchers became enamored with the workings of the human mind. As the nineteenth century progressed:

> The monolithic term "insanity" acquired shape and substance. Mental disorders came in different degrees and distinct varieties, and changed over time. The sane mind was not a pure intellect whose ability to "know," "think," and "understand" might be placed higher or lower along a linear scale of cognitive development, but rather a conglomerate of reason and emotion, a complex structure in which disturbances of one part might wreak subtly pervasive alterations in the rest.[4] [23]

As psychological researchers learned more, they became more confident in their competence to diagnose mental illness. Consequently, they became more frequent participants in cases involving insanity defenses until they became the standard fixtures that they are today.

While the history of the use of psychological testimony on the insanity defense is easily understood, it is not so easy to understand why this kind of testimony insinuated itself into the fabric of insanity defense trials without so much as a token objection to its admissibility. The fact that this type of testimony met with few substantive objections has been noted but not explained. Various hypotheses may explain the phenomenon. For example, perhaps no fundamental difference was perceived between traditionally accepted medical testimony and expert psychological medical testimony. Or perhaps since the past mental state of the defendant is a notoriously difficult issue, courts were happy for any assistance that could be rendered on the issue. Or perhaps psychological testimony was simply "in vogue" when it first sought entry into the legal arena, and it did not occur to anyone to challenge its validity. Whatever the explanation, psychological testimony on the issue of insanity became entrenched in the law without having to overcome any substantive objections to its admissibility.

The distinguishing characteristic of nontraditional psychological evidence is simply that it is not offered in connection with an insanity defense. Accordingly, it has not received the benefit of the law's unexamined acceptance of psychological diagnoses relating to insanity.

C. *Scientific, But Not "Hard" Scientific*

Psychological research is obviously "scientific." However, many people perceive degrees of science with some disciplines being more "scientific" than others. The most obvious division is between the social sciences and the physical sciences. The former, often characterized as "soft" sciences, may be perceived as less "scientific" than the "hard" physical sciences. Psychological research is somewhat of a hybrid. It looks like a social science, yet it is closely related to medicine, a discipline with many characteristics of "hard" science. While most people would admit that psychological research is more "scientific" than other social sciences such as history or sociology, most would also contend that it is nowhere near as "scientific" as the physical sciences such as biology, chemistry, and physics.

---

[3] [n.21] [T. MAEDER, CRIME AND MADNESS] 37 (1985).

[4] [n.23] T. MAEDER, *supra* note [21], at 37.

Categorizing psychological research as "scientific" from an evidentiary perspective is important because some types of "scientific" evidence have traditionally been required to meet more stringent standards of admissibility than nonscientific expert testimony. The most famous special test for scientific evidence is described in *Frye v. United States*. The *Frye* test requires that the scientific evidence be generally accepted in the scientific community from which it arose before it is admissible. Thus, when confronted with nontraditional psychological evidence, courts must decide whether to apply a *Frye*-type test to the evidence, which is admittedly "scientific," but not nearly so "scientific" as the physical science evidence to which the test has traditionally been applied.

D. *Not Far Removed From Common Understanding*

Expert psychological testimony concerning a defendant's sanity is often esoterically expressed in psychological jargon that is far removed from the common experience of the ordinary juror. By contrast, most types of nontraditional scientific evidence are much closer to the common understanding of the ordinary juror, yet, may fall beyond the common experience of jurors. Nontraditional psychological evidence often deals with circumstances that jurors probably suspect involve peculiar psychological consequences not associated with everyday existence. Yet jurors are without sufficient information to have any great insight into what those peculiar consequences might be. For example, most jurors would probably suspect there was something "funny" happening psychologically with a woman who is repeatedly battered by a man, yet continues to voluntarily live with him, until she eventually kills him to avoid further beatings. Yet most jurors are probably unable to do any more than speculate about what those "funny" psychological factors are. Battered woman syndrome testimony is introduced for the purpose of explaining those factors. Since most types of nontraditional psychological evidence are not too far removed from the common experience of the jury, testimony concerning them is unlikely to be esoteric and can be easily conveyed to and understood by the jury. From an evidentiary perspective, though, this raises the question whether such testimony tells the jurors anything they do not already know.

E. *Injection of Expert Testimony Where Historically It Has Not Been Used*

For decades, and in some cases for centuries, juries have decided questions upon which nontraditional psychological evidence is now being offered without the benefit of expert testimony. For example, juries have decided rape cases and eyewitness identification cases without the benefit of expert testimony regarding rape trauma syndrome and the fallibility of eyewitness identifications. More important, the legal system assumes that juries are competent to decide and, for the most part, have correctly decided those cases without the benefit of such expert testimony.

The current attitude of the legal system toward expert testimony is somewhat schizophrenic. On the one hand, the last three decades or so have seen a veritable explosion in the use of expert testimony at trial. Liberal standards for the admissibility of expert testimony have been codified. For example, Federal Rule of Evidence 702 allows such testimony whenever it "will assist" the trier of fact. Barriers to expert opinion, such as the ultimate issue rule, have been abolished. On the other hand, courts often exhibit concern about the role of the jury being preempted by expert testimony. A continuing concern of the courts is the so-called "battle of the experts" which is viewed as a waste of time, unnecessary, and confusing. Many courts seem to hold either an implicit trust of lay jurors to hear the "facts" and decide the case correctly or an implicit distrust of experts to assist juries in correctly deciding the cases. Although no court has ever explicitly stated, "We have never needed this before, so why should we need it now?" [N]ontraditional psychological evidence often has to hurdle this unstated objection.

F. *Reflects Directly on Witness Credibility*

Most nontraditional psychological evidence, while not explicitly directed at witness credibility, does reflect on the credibility of at least one key witness in the case. For example, in a rape case where the defendant admits intercourse but contends that it was consensual, testimony that the complainant is suffering from rape trauma syndrome (a syndrome which does not ensue from consensual intercourse) directly reflects on the credibility of both the complainant and the defendant. Some types of testimony reflect directly on the credibility of only the defendant. For example, battered woman syndrome testimony and pathological gamblers' syndrome testimony directly reflect on the credibility of the defendant's explanation of his behavior. Testimony regarding the fallibility of eyewitness identification reflects directly on the credibility of the key eyewitnesses in a case.

Of course all testimony in a case has some bearing on the credibility of all other testimony in the case. Thus, it is difficult to draw bright lines among degrees of "direct" reflection of some testimony on the credibility of other testimony. Nonetheless, most nontraditional psychological evidence is not in a gray area - it directly reflects upon the credibility of the testimony of some key witness or witnesses in a case. From an evidentiary perspective, this is important since traditionally determining the credibility of witnesses is within the sole province of the jury. This legal bromide has led many courts to hold that such testimony is therefore an improper comment on witness credibility.

G. *Impact on the Jury Unknown But Suspect*

One of the greatest ironies surrounding the law of evidence is that, while its major goal is to allow the jury the best possible opportunity to decide a case correctly, very little is actually known about how juries decide cases. Rules of evidence and trial practice are formulated largely on the basis of lawyers' hunches, intuitions, and informed speculation concerning the impact that certain evidence will have on the jury. Numerous provisions of the rules of evidence incorporate lawyers' value judgments concerning evidence that is more harmful than helpful to a jury's deciding a case in the best possible manner. For example, the hearsay rule is premised upon the intuition that jurors may overvalue hearsay, and for that reason it should be excluded from evidence. Another example is the rule excluding evidence that the defendant is insured against the liability being asserted against him.

Nontraditional psychological evidence immediately conjures up for many lawyers and judges two basic intuitions concerning the impact of such evidence on juries. First, expert testimony may tend to overawe a jury to the extent that the jury simply acquiesces to the expert's opinion rather than reaching its own decision. Second, expert testimony, characterized as "scientific," may have a particular tendency to cause such acquiescence by jurors. These two intuitions surface either in the form of an "unfair prejudice" objection or an objection that the jurisdiction's special test for scientific evidence has not been met.

H. *Research Findings in Nonlegal Sources*

Research findings regarding most nontraditional psychological evidence can be found in nonlegal sources such as medical texts, medical journals, and social science periodicals. These materials are not typically found in a law library, and most lawyers have no training in researching these materials even when they are easily available. Thus, it is not surprising that most judicial opinions dealing with nontraditional psychological evidence exhibit either no research into the nonlegal literature or a very cursory search. At key points in opinions where one would expect to find an in depth analysis of the nonlegal literature, one is more likely to find the court resorting to a bare conclusion, pithily formulated in a legal catchphrase such as "not beyond the ken of the jury," "invades the province of the jury," "unfairly prejudicial," or "will (or will not) assist the jury."

I. *Cutoff Point Not Easily Established*

A sentiment rarely expressed by courts, but one which the devoted reader of judicial opinions in this area can detect, is: "If we allow this evidence, where will it all end? Is everything becoming an expert issue?" For example, if a court allows the psychologist to testify in one case that another witness is or is not telling the truth, then why not allow such testimony with respect to every witness in every case? Or, if a court allows a psychologist to testify in one case regarding the factors that make eyewitness identification fallible, then why not allow such testimony in every case where there is the slightest question of identity? Similarly, if a court allows a psychologist to testify in one case that the defendant's psychological profile is incompatible with commission of the crime charged, how can any subsequent case be distinguished? Although the "opening the floodgates" argument is rarely articulated, it is easily discernible.

Courts are also concerned with the admission of nontraditional psychological evidence to exculpate defendants whom the courts think are deserving of punishment. The three prime examples of this concern are battered woman syndrome, pathological gamblers' syndrome, and XYY chromosome syndrome. Some courts do not believe that a woman who could have left but instead chose violence, a pathological gambler, and a person with an unusual genetic makeup should be excused from criminal liability. If persons suffering from these syndromes are excused, cannot other defendants find "syndromes" of which they are victims to the extent that the criminal law becomes riddled with suspect excuses?

The nine characteristics set forth above distinguish nontraditional psychological evidence from traditional psychological evidence and from all other kinds of evidence. Although not all of these nine characteristics are found *only* in nontraditional psychological evidence, the combination of them is unique to nontraditional psychological evidence.

[2]   Admissibility Issues: Evidence Rules 702 and 403

As suggested in the preceding excerpt from the article by Professor McCord, "soft" science presents several distinct, but related, admissibility problems. Unfortunately, as you will see, courts often blur the distinctions between these admissibility concerns. It may help to organize the admissibility concerns into three categories.

First, an initial evidentiary hurdle requires a determination that the proffered expert testimony is needed. The question here — stated in relation to a Rule 702 admissibility requirement — is whether the testimony will "assist the trier of fact."? Put another way, is there anything here that a typical juror does not already know? For example, do we really need an expert to tell the jury that an eyewitness' recall of an observed event diminishes over time? Do we really need an expert to explain to a jury that a woman who has been raped may have a fear of being alone? Courts express this concern in different ways. For example, a court may ask whether: (a) the evidence is beyond the ken of the jury, (b) the evidence invades the province of the jury, (c) the evidence constitutes an improper comment on witness credibility, or (d) the evidence is so general as to be irrelevant. Regardless of the terminology, courts that disallow such testimony on one of the above grounds (or some similar ground) are concerned that the proffered testimony is, at a minimum, not needed. That is, it will not assist the jury in determining any factual issue because it is not so "scientific," "technical," or "specialized" as to be beyond the common understanding of the jury. Courts often state that cross-examination and/or detailed jury instructions are adequate substitutes for expert testimony that is within the jury's understanding.

Second, if the proposed testimony survives the first admissibility hurdle and is considered specialized or "expert enough" to be of assistance to the trier of fact, the court must then grapple with whether the jurisdiction's admissibility test for "hard" science — *Daubert* or *Frye* — should be applied, and, if so, whether it is satisfied.[5] All federal courts use an admissibility test known as the "*Daubert* test," which requires the trial court to determine whether expert testimony is both reliable and relevant. A majority of state courts use the *Daubert* test or a similar "reliability" test. All federal courts (and most state courts) apply *Daubert* to determine the admissibility of expert testimony based upon research in social and behavioral science. On the other hand, a minority of state courts use the *Frye* general acceptance test to determine the admissibility of scientific evidence. The *Frye* test asks whether the research underlying the expert's opinion is generally accepted by scientists in the pertinent field. State courts using the *Frye* standard differ on whether such expert testimony is "scientific" and, therefore, subject to the general acceptance test.

Third, even if the expert testimony survives the first two hurdles, courts sometimes express concern over the possibility that such evidence will mislead, confuse, and/or prejudice the jury. These are the concerns embodied in Rule 403 of the Federal Rules of Evidence, and in Rule 403's state counterparts. Sometimes this concern leads courts to exclude the testimony altogether; in other cases courts may restrict what the expert can say. For example, assume that in a prosecution for rape the defense asserts that the alleged victim consented to sexual intercourse. Assume further that an expert has examined the victim and has concluded that she is suffering from "rape trauma syndrome," and that she had been raped. Should the expert be permitted to tell the jury that the victim "had been raped" or has "rape trauma syndrome"?

As you read through the cases that follow, ask yourself if the court is concerned (1) that the proffered testimony may not be appropriate for expert opinion because it will not assist the trier of fact, (2) that, even if helpful, the testimony does not satisfy the jurisdiction's evidentiary test for admissibility (*Frye* or *Daubert*), or (3) that the expert testimony may be more prejudicial and misleading than probative.

---

[5] The *Daubert* and *Frye* standards are examined in Chapter 2, *supra*.

B. EYEWITNESS IDENTIFICATIONS

[1]   The Accuracy of Eyewitness Identifications

The first area of "soft" science to be examined concerns the admissibility of expert testimony on the accuracy and reliability of eyewitness identifications. For years researchers have asserted that faulty eyewitness identifications were a major cause of wrongful convictions. *See e.g.*, Elizabeth A. Loftus, *Ten Years in the Life of an Expert Witness*, 10 LAW & HUM. BEHAV. 241, 243 (1986) (citing a 1983 Ohio State University Doctoral Study concluding that more than one-half of all wrongful convictions were the result of faulty eyewitness identifications). Initial concerns were based primarily upon controlled experiments (staged crimes) where eyewitnesses to the staged event were found to be inaccurate in their identifications. More recently, the forensic use of DNA technology has borne out these claims.

The forensic use of DNA did not begin until the late 1980s. Scores of individuals who were tried and convicted of crimes prior to the late 1980s have been exonerated when DNA technology was used to analyze evidence from their cases. When the trials of the DNA- exonerated individuals were studied, it was revealed that false identification evidence accounted for more false convictions than all other causes combined. *See* Brandon L. Garrett, *Judging Innocence*, 108 COLUM. L. REV. 55, 78 (2008) (158 of 200 cases (79%) involved eyewitness identifications); Gary Wells, Mark Small, Steven Penrod, Roy S. Malpass, Solomon M. Fulero & C.A.E. Brimacombe, *Eyewitness Identification Procedures: Recommendations for Lineups and Photospreads*, 22 LAW & HUM. BEHAV. 603, 605 (1998) (40 DNA exonerated cases studied; 36 cases [90%] included one or more false eyewitness identifications); Barry Scheck, Peter Neufeld & Jim Dwyer, *Freeing the Innocent*, THE CHAMPION 18, 20–21 (March 2000) (mistaken identification a factor in 53 of first 60 cases of wrongful convictions).

Of course, not all criminal cases with eyewitness identifications involve biological evidence that can be subjected to DNA analysis. Two questions are raised. First, what is it that makes eyewitness identifications suspect, and second, what should a jury be told in a particular case about the reliability of seemingly "certain" eyewitness identifications? As to the latter question, one possibility is to permit an expert to explain to the jury why an eyewitness in a particular case may be confident in an identification and yet may be wrong. The materials that follow in this section examine both questions: factors that contribute to inaccurate eyewitness identifications, and how the courts have reacted to expert testimony on this subject.

PAUL C. GIANNELLI & EDWARD J. IMWINKELRIED, 1 SCIENTIFIC EVIDENCE § 9.02, at 494–97 (4th ed. 2007)[6]

§ 9.02 Eyewitness Identifications.

Both courts and commentators have noted the problems of eyewitness identifications. For example, in *United States v. Wade*, the U.S. Supreme Court wrote: "The vagaries of eyewitness identification are well-known; the annals of criminal law

---

are rife with instances of mistaken identification."[7] [5] In *Actual Innocence*, Barry Scheck and his colleagues examined 62 of the first DNA exonerations secured through Cardozo Law School's Innocence Project to ascertain what factors contributed to these miscarriages of justice. Eighty-four percent involved eyewitness misidentifications.[8] [6]

Although psychological research on eyewitness identification dates back a hundred years,[9] [7] most of the research has been reported in the last few decades. This research emphasizes the complex nature of human perception and memory. Human memory does not function like a videotape recorder, accurately recording all images which can subsequently be fully retrieved. Rather, it is a constructive process, in which many factors play a part.

The perception and memory process can be divided into three stages. The first is the acquisition stage, during which the event is perceived and entered in the memory. The second is the retention stage — the time between the event and its recollection. The third stage is the retrieval stage during which the information relating to the event is recalled. Inaccuracies can be introduced at all three stages.

In the acquisition stage, the literature indicates that witnesses are more accurate when:

(1) exposure time is longer rather than shorter,

(2) events are less rather than more violent,

(3) witnesses are not subject to extreme stress,

(4) witnesses are free from biased expectations,

(5) witnesses are young adults rather than children, and

(6) witnesses are asked to report on salient aspects of an event rather than peripheral aspects.

Retention of information in memory (second stage) can be influenced by numerous factors. Two principal points emerge from the research. First, the longer the interval between the event and the recollection of the event, the greater the lapse in memory. Moreover, the lapse in memory does not decrease at a uniform rate; it decreases sharply immediately after the event and then more slowly over a period of time. This phenomenon is known as the "curve of forgetting." Second, new information enters the memory between the event and its recollection: "External information provided from the outside can intrude into the witness' memory, as can his own thoughts, and both can cause dramatic changes in his recollection."

Finally, the way in which information is retrieved (third stage) can influence memory. For example, the method of questioning, the type of identification procedure employed, the status of the questioner, and nonverbal communication clues all may distort memory.

---

[7] [n. 5] United States v. Wade, 388 U.S. 218, 228 [(1967)].

[8] [n.6] Barry Scheck et al., Actual Innocence: Five Days to Execution and Other Dispatches from the Wrongly Convicted 246 (2000).

[9] [n.7] Wells & Loftus, *Eyewitness Research: Then and Now*, in Eyewitness Testimony: Psychological Perspectives 1, 3 (G. Wells & E. Loftus eds. 1984) ("over 85% of the entire published literature has surfaced since 1978").

Factors

Research has identified a number of factors that may affect eyewitness identifications.

First, cross-racial identifications present special problems. Dr. Elizabeth Loftus, a prominent researcher in this field, notes that people "have greater difficulty in recognizing faces of another race than faces of their own race. This cross-racial identification problem is not due to the fact that people have greater prejudices or less experience with members of the other race."[10] [14]

Second, "weapon focus" frequently interferes with a person's ability to identify faces; that is, when a weapon is used in a crime, the witness' attention will focus on the weapon rather than the facial features of the person holding the weapon.

Third, "unconscious transference" may lead to misidentifications. A witness who has seen an innocent suspect at an earlier time may misidentify that suspect because he "looks familiar." For example, a witness may view a photographic display that includes a picture of the innocent suspect. No identification is made. Later, the witness picks the innocent suspect out of a lineup, unconsciously remembering the face from the photo display.

Fourth, research indicates that the relationship between the accuracy of an identification and a witness' confidence in the identification is not strong. Indeed, two researchers have concluded that "the eyewitness accuracy-confidence relationship is weak under good laboratory conditions and functionally useless in forensically representative settings."[11] [18]

Jury Impact

The research also reveals that the impact of eyewitness identifications on juries is substantial. In commenting on the research, Dr. Loftus has written that eyewitness testimony "is likely to be believed by jurors, especially when it is offered with a high level of confidence, even though the accuracy of an eyewitness and the confidence of that witness may not be related to one another at all."[12] [20]

---

[10] [n. 14] E. Loftus, Eyewitness Testimony [(1979)], at 139.

[11] [n.18] Wells & Murray, *Eyewitness Confidence*, in Eyewitness Testimony: Psychological Perspectives 155, 165 (G. Wells & E. Loftus eds. 1984).

[12] [n. 20] E. Loftus, Eyewitness Testimony [(1979)], at 19.

[2]   The Admissibility of Expert Testimony

[a]   Trial Court Exclusion and the Abuse of Discretion Standard

UNITED STATES v. RINCON
28 F.3d 921 (9th Cir. 1994)

T.G. NELSON, CIRCUIT JUDGE:

I. OVERVIEW

Hugo Rincon (Rincon) was convicted on two counts of unarmed bank robbery. [The indictment charged Rincon with the robbery of two different banks on different days in April, 1988. The demand note in each robbery was the same: "This is a robbery. Don't make it a murder. Give me all the money now." The robber wore sunglasses during the first robbery and, in the second, the robber spoke Spanish and wore a baseball cap.

[The teller at the first bank to be robbed was unable to make an in-court identification, but picked Rincon out of a photo spread three to four months after the robbery. There were four eyewitnesses to the second bank robbery who identified Rincon at one time or another. One witness made an in-court identification and picked Rincon out of a photo spread three months after the robbery. Two other witnesses were unable to make in-court identifications but had picked Rincon out of a photo spread about a year after the robbery. The fourth witness to the second bank robbery made an in-court identification of Rincon but did not make a photo spread identification.

[Rincon did not testify at the trial. His defense consisted of presenting himself to the jury in order to contrast his appearance with that of a surveillance photograph of the robber which the government had introduced as a trial exhibit.] On Rincon's first appeal to this court, he contended that the district court erred in refusing to admit expert testimony regarding the reliability of eyewitness identification. We affirmed the district court's exclusion of that expert testimony in *United States v. Rincon (Rincon I)*, 984 F.2d 1003 (9th Cir. 1993). After the Supreme Court's recent decision in *Daubert v. Merrell Dow Pharmaceuticals, Inc.*, regarding the admissibility of expert testimony, the Court remanded this case and asked us to reexamine that issue in light of *Daubert*. We remanded to the district court for reconsideration. The district court upheld its earlier decision to exclude the expert testimony. We affirm.

II. BACKGROUND

. . . .

On remand to the district court, Rincon again proffered the testimony of an experimental psychologist and full professor at the Claremont Graduate School of Psychology, Kathy Pezdek, Ph.D. If permitted to testify, Dr. Pezdek would explain to the jury, among other things, the three phases of eyewitness identification, including perceiving and encoding, storage and retention, and retrieval of information. Dr. Pezdek would also testify as to the effect of various psychological factors on each phase, including stress, the observer's state of mind, suddenness, suggestibility, and cross-ethnic identifications. In addition, she would testify that empirical research contradicts numerous lay notions of eyewitness identifications. Dr. Pezdek, however, would offer no definitive opinion concerning the reliability or certainty of the witnesses' identifications in this case. After reconsidering the issue, the district court affirmed its earlier order denying Rincon's motion *in limine* and excluding the expert testimony. Rincon challenges the district court's exclusion of the expert testimony.

III. EXPERT TESTIMONY

We review for abuse of discretion the district court's decision regarding the admissibility of expert testimony on the reliability of eyewitness identifications.

In *Daubert*, the Supreme Court held that Fed. R. Evid. 702 supersedes the general acceptance standard established in *Frye*. It noted, however, that notwithstanding its holding, the Federal Rules of Evidence still place limits on the admissibility of scientific evidence. . . . The Court established a two-part test for determining whether to admit expert testimony: "[T]he trial judge must determine at the outset, pursuant to Rule 104(a), whether the expert is proposing to testify to (1) scientific knowledge that (2) will assist the trier of fact to understand or determine a fact in issue." These preliminary questions must be established by a preponderance of proof. Finally, the Court stated that evidence otherwise admissible may be excluded under Rule 403 if its probative value is substantially outweighed by the danger of unfair prejudice, confusion of the issues, or misleading the jury.

On remand, the district court excluded the expert testimony on eyewitness identification, ruling that:

1.   The proposed testimony invades the province of the jury (i.e., it does not assist the trier of fact);

2.   No showing has been made that the testimony relates to an area that is recognized as a science; and

3.   The testimony is likely to confuse the jury.

Moreover, the district court stated that "the proposed expert eyewitness identification testimony is being offered by the defense more in the role of an advocate and not as a scientifically valid opinion." We conclude that the district court did not abuse its discretion in excluding Dr. Pezdek's testimony because Rincon's proffer failed to satisfy the admissibility standard established in *Daubert*.

A. *Scientific Knowledge*

"[I]n order to qualify as 'scientific knowledge,' an inference or assertion must be derived by the scientific method. Proposed testimony must be supported by appropriate validation — i.e., 'good grounds,' based on what is known." The scientific knowledge requirement establishes a standard of evidentiary reliability. The district court must make a preliminary assessment as to whether the reasoning or methodology underlying the testimony is scientifically valid. *Daubert* set forth several factors which the district court may consider in determining whether a theory or technique constitutes "scientific knowledge," including: (1) whether the theory or technique can be or has been tested; (2) whether the theory or technique has been subjected to peer review and publication; (3) the known or potential rate of error; and (4) the particular degree of acceptance within the scientific community. This list is not exhaustive. Nor did the Court "presume to set out a definitive checklist or test."

The first inquiry, then, under *Daubert* is whether the proposed testimony of Dr. Pezdek was on a "scientific" subject. On remand, the district court denied Rincon's motion on three grounds, one of which was that "no showing has been made that the testimony relates to an area that is recognized as a science."

In the initial motion, Rincon asserted that Dr. Pezdek held a Ph.D. in psychology from the University of Massachusetts at Amherst, and was a full professor at the Claremont Graduate School of Psychology. She would testify that there are three phases of eyewitness identification: perception and encoding; storage and retention (memory); and retrieval. In turn, the perception and encoding phase [is] affected by the factors of stress, duration of exposure, cross-racial identification, and availability of facial features (whether or not the face is partially obscured). The storage and retrieval stages are affected by time delay and suggestibility.

Dr. Pezdek would also discuss certain lay notions of eyewitness identification that are contradicted by research, such as: the certainty of the identification is a measure of the reliability of the identification; accuracy of memory is improved by stress; and memory of a face does not diminish over time.

The declaration of Rincon's counsel which accompanied the motion expanded on each of these matters, with statements such as: "There is a wealth of research supporting this point. . . ."; "The research is clear. . . ."; "The research suggests. . . ." However, none of the research was submitted or described so that the district court could determine if the studies were indeed scientific on the basis the Court explained in *Daubert*: "whether the reasoning or methodology underlying the testimony is scientifically valid. . . ."

On remand, Rincon supplemented the record with a copy of an article entitled *The "General Acceptance" of Psychological Research on Eyewitness Testimony*.[13] [4] The article described a survey of sixty-three experts on eyewitness testimony relating to their views of the scientific acceptance of research on a number of topics, including those that Dr. Pezdek would testify to. As the article said:

> The results are discussed in relation to the "general acceptance" provision of the *Frye* test and the limitations of this test for determining the admissibility of expert testimony.

Id. at 1089.

However, while the article identified the research on some of the topics, it did not discuss the research in sufficient detail that the district court could determine if the research was scientifically valid. In the argument before the district court, counsel for Rincon told the court that Dr. Pezdek could testify about the studies that had been done on the various topics. However, he again did not offer or describe the studies themselves. The district court's determination that Rincon had not shown the proposed testimony related to a scientific subject is supported by the record.

B. *Assist Trier of Fact*

Even when a theory or methodology satisfies the "scientific knowledge" requirement, in order to be admissible, expert testimony must also "assist the trier of fact to

---

[13] [n.4] Kassin, Ellsworth & Smith, *The "General Acceptance" of Psychological Research on Eyewitness Testimony*, Am. Psychologist, Aug. 1989, at 1089–98.

understand or to determine a fact in issue." This second requirement relates primarily to relevance. It requires the district court to make a preliminary determination as to whether the scientific knowledge can be applied to facts of the case at hand.

The expert testimony Rincon offered was no doubt relevant to his defense. A determination that evidence is relevant does not end the inquiry. Rather, *Daubert* reiterates that the district court may nonetheless exclude relevant expert evidence pursuant to Rule 403 "if its probative value is substantially outweighed by the danger of unfair prejudice, confusion of the issues, or misleading the jury." "Expert evidence can be both powerful and quite misleading because of the difficulty in evaluating it. Because of that risk, the judge in weighing possible prejudice against probative force under Rule 403 of the present rules exercises more control over experts than over lay witnesses." Thus, *Daubert* in no way altered the discretion that resides with the district court judge to determine whether such evidence is properly admitted.

In this case, the district court found that Dr. Pezdek's testimony would not assist the trier of fact and that it would likely confuse or mislead the jury. Rincon argues that the district court erred in excluding the evidence because Dr. Pezdek's testimony was relevant evidence which would have helped the jury arrive at an informed decision. Her testimony would have addressed factors that [affect] eyewitness identifications, such as passage of time, stress, identification from the lower half of the face, the relationship between certainty and accuracy, and cross-ethnic identifications. We decline to disturb the district court's ruling.

Even though the factors about which Dr. Pezdek was to testify may have been informative, the district court conveyed that same information by providing a comprehensive jury instruction to guide the jury's deliberations. As Rincon's own article on such expert eyewitness testimony suggests, alternative solutions exist.

> [O]ur results should not be taken to imply that using psychological experts is the best possible solution for the problems arising from eyewitness testimony-
> . . . . *[B]ecause expert testimony is costly, an alternative would be to educate jurors through cautionary instructions.*[14] [5]

The district court gave the jury in this case a comprehensive instruction on eyewitness identifications. The instruction addressed many of the factors about which Dr. Pezdek would have testified. The district court instructed the jury to consider whether: (1) the eyewitness had the capacity and adequate opportunity to observe the offender based upon the length of time for observation as well as the conditions of observation; (2) the identification was the product of the eyewitness's own recollection or was the result of subsequent influence or suggestiveness; (3) the eyewitness has made inconsistent identifications; and (4) the eyewitness was credible. The instruction also pointed out the danger of a showup versus the reliability of a lineup with similar individuals from which the eyewitness must choose. Finally, it permitted the jury to consider, as a factor bearing upon the reliability of the eyewitness testimony, the length of time which may have elapsed between the occurrence of the crime and the eyewitness's identification.[15] [6]

. . . Given the powerful nature of expert testimony, coupled with its potential to mislead the jury, we cannot say that the district court erred in concluding that the

---

[14] [n.5] Kassin, *supra* note 4, at 1097–98 (emphasis added) (internal citation omitted).

[15] [n.6] We also note, as we did in *Rincon I*, that the eyewitnesses were subject to cross-examination which gave Rincon the opportunity to reveal any deficiencies in their identifications.

proffered evidence would not assist the trier of fact and that it was likely to mislead the jury.

Notwithstanding our conclusion, we emphasize that the result we reach in this case is based upon an individualized inquiry, rather than strict application of the past rule concerning expert testimony on the reliability of eyewitness identification. Our conclusion does not preclude the admission of such testimony when the proffering party satisfies the standard established in *Daubert* by showing that the expert opinion is based upon "scientific knowledge" which is both reliable and helpful to the jury in any given case. District courts must strike the appropriate balance between admitting reliable, helpful expert testimony and excluding misleading or confusing testimony to achieve the flexible approach outlined in *Daubert*. The district court struck such a balance in this case.

. . . .

V. CONCLUSION

Rincon has failed to produce sufficient evidence either that the testimony proffered here is based upon "scientific knowledge" or that it would have assisted the trier of fact in this particular case. Accordingly, we conclude that the district court did not abuse its discretion in excluding Dr. Pezdek's testimony. . . .

Affirmed.

NOTES

1. ***Majority Rule: Trial Court Discretion.*** As a general proposition, court's excluding expert testimony on eyewitness reliability have found that the testimony would not be helpful. Most appellate court decisions are consistent with *Rincon, supra*, and find that a trial court is well within its discretion in finding that expert testimony would provide the jury with little, if any, information that could not be provided by jury instructions and a thorough cross-examination of the eyewitness. *See e.g. United States v. Crotteau*, 218 F.3d 826, 833 (7th Cir. 2000) ("[T]he trial court did not abuse its discretion in excluding the expert testimony of the psychologist. Such testimony was not necessary because the defense extensively cross-examined the eyewitness regarding the reliability of her identification, the experienced trial judge provided the jury with clear, concise, and unambiguous cautionary instructions on the reliability of her identifications, and the [witnesses] identification of [the defendant] as the robber was substantially corroborated by other testimony . . ."); *Jones v. State*, 862 S.W.2d 242, 244 (Ark. 1993) ("the trial court has wide discretion in such matters and [it is not an] abuse of discretion [to] refuse[ ] such testimony on the ground that it was a matter of common knowledge and would not assist the trier of fact.").

See also CHARLES T. MCCORMICK, 1 MCCORMICK ON EVIDENCE § 206, at 881 (Kenneth S. Broun ed., 6th ed. 2006) ("these decisions seem almost invariably to be upheld").

More recent cases have, however, appeared more receptive. Federal courts have held that it would be an abuse of discretion to reject such testimony out-of-hand without holding a *Daubert* hearing. *United States v. Smithers*, 212 F.3d 306, 314 (6th Cir. 2000) (listing post-*Daubert* cases finding that it was not an abuse of discretion to exclude expert testimony on eyewitness identifications, but commenting that "the cases indicate that courts must consider whether the testimony would be helpful or confusing to the jury"); *United States v. Amador-Galvan*, 9 F.3d 1414, 1417–18 (9th Cir. 1994) (expert testimony on reliability of eyewitness identification must be evaluated under *Daubert*, and remanding case for *Daubert* inquiry). *See* 1 SCIENTIFIC EVIDENCE § 9.02[d], at 504 (4th ed. 2007) ("*Daubert* decision caused some courts to reevaluate their positions on this issue.").

2. Cross-Examination and Jury Instructions as Alternatives for Expert Testimony. The court in *Rincon* noted that unreliable eyewitness identifications can be addressed by "comprehensive jury instructions" and cross-examination. As mentioned in Note 1 above, other courts that have upheld the exclusion of expert testimony on eyewitness identifications have felt that any such problem could be eliminated with special cautionary instructions to the jury. On the other hand, some jurisdictions hold that generic instructions on witness credibility and burden of proof are sufficient. *See Brodes v. State*, 614 S.E.2d 766, 769 n.6 (Ga. 2005) (listing states that find jury instructions on eyewitness identification either "superfluous" or "an impermissible judicial comment on the evidence").

Both remedial devices (jury instructions and cross-examination) assume that the jury is capable, without help from an expert, of understanding the problems and weaknesses of eyewitness identifications if they are asked to focus on those problems. The leading case on cautionary jury instructions is *United States v. Telfaire*, 469 F.2d 552 (D.C. Cir. 1972). *Telfaire* provided the following model set of jury instructions. The sentences in brackets ([]) were to be used only if appropriate to the facts of the case.

Appendix: Model Special Instructions on Identification

One of the most important issues in this case is the identification of the defendant as the perpetrator of the crime. The Government has the burden of providing identity, beyond a reasonable doubt. It is not essential that the witness himself be free from doubt as to the correctness of his statement. However, you, the jury, must be satisfied beyond a reasonable doubt of the accuracy of the identification of the defendant before you may convict him. If you are not convinced beyond a reasonable doubt that the defendant was the person who committed the crime, you must find the defendant not guilty.

Identification testimony is an expression of belief or impression by the witness. Its value depends on the opportunity the witness had to observe the offender at the time of the offense and to make a reliable identification later.

In appraising the identification testimony of a witness, you should consider the following:

(1) Are you convinced that the witness had the capacity and an adequate opportunity to observe the offender?

Whether the witness had an adequate opportunity to observe the offender at the time of the offense will be affected by such matters as how long or short a time was available, how far or close the witness was, how good were lighting conditions, whether the witness had had occasion to see or know the person in the past.

[In general, a witness bases any identification he makes on his perception through the use of his senses. Usually the witness identifies an offender by the sense of sight-but this is not necessarily so, and he may use other senses.]

(2) Are you satisfied that the identification made by the witness subsequent to the offense was the product of his own recollection? You may take into account both the strength of the identification, and the circumstances under which the identification was made.

If the identification by the witness may have been influenced by the circumstances under which the defendant was presented to him for identification, you should scrutinize the identification with great care. You may also consider the length of time that lapsed between the occurrence of the crime and the next opportunity of the witness to see defendant, as a factor bearing on the reliability of the identification.

[You may also take into account that an identification made by picking the defendant out of a group of similar individuals is generally more reliable than one which results from the presentation of the defendant alone to the witness.]

[(3) You make take into account any occasions in which the witness failed to make an identification of defendant, or made an identification that was inconsistent with his identification at trial.]

(4) Finally, you must consider the credibility of each identification witness in the same way as any other witness, consider whether he is truthful, and consider whether he had the capacity and opportunity to make a reliable observation on the matter covered in his testimony.

I again emphasize that the burden of proof on the prosecutor extends to every element of the crime charged, and this specifically includes the burden of proving beyond a reasonable doubt the identity of the defendant as the perpetrator of the crime with which he stands charged. If after examining the testimony, you have a reasonable doubt as to the accuracy of the identification, you must find the defendant not guilty.

Telfaire, supra., 469 F.2d at 558–59. Not all courts that require cautionary jury instructions require the instructions to be as comprehensive as the model instructions found in *Telfaire. See e.g. Brodes v. State,* 614 S.E.2d 766, 767 n.1 (Ga. 2005) (one-paragraph pattern jury instruction); *Nelson v. State,* 362 So. 2d 1017, 1022 (Fla. Dist. Ct. App. 1978) (finding jury instructions adequate although not as "elaborate" as the model instructions contained in *United States v. Telfaire, supra*).

QUESTIONS

1. What is the rationale for the court's opinion in *Rincon* regarding the proffered expert testimony and the scientific knowledge requirement of *Daubert*? Is expert testimony on the fallibility of eyewitness identifications not scientific knowledge, or is it merely that the plaintiff failed to offer enough evidence in this case for the trial court to find that such testimony was scientific knowledge?

2. If, as the court states, "[t]he expert testimony Rincon offered was no doubt relevant to his defense," why is it that it would not assist the trier of fact?

3. What alternatives to expert testimony exist to inform the jury on the shortcomings of eyewitness identifications?

4. Compare the model jury instructions on eyewitness identifications from the *Telfaire* case in Note 2 above with the proposed testimony from Dr. Pezdek summarized in the *Rincon* case. Are you persuaded that cautionary jury instructions are an adequate alternative to expert testimony?

[b]   Limited Admissibility: Defining When Exclusion of Expert Testimony Constitutes an Abuse of Discretion

A number of courts have found trial court exclusion of expert testimony on the subject of eyewitness identifications to be an abuse of discretion in certain circumstances. *People v. McDonald* is one such case. As you read *McDonald*, note the factors that the court found pertinent to its finding that the trial court had abused its discretion.

PEOPLE v. McDONALD
690 P.2d 709 (Cal. 1984)

Mosk, Justice.

We address here a contention that is increasingly heard in the courts of California and our sister jurisdictions, i.e., that it may be an abuse of discretion to exclude the testimony of a psychologist who is a qualified expert witness on psychological factors shown by the evidence that may affect the accuracy of an eyewitness identification of the defendant. As will appear, we hold that on a proper showing such testimony is admissible, and that it should have been admitted in the case at bar.

Defendant was charged . . . with the murder of Jose Esparza. . . . He pleaded not guilty. . . . The jury convicted him of the murder and . . . fixed the penalty at death. . . .

At trial it was established without dispute that August 20, 1979, was payday for Esparza, a restaurant worker. At 4 p.m. he took a break from his job to cash his paycheck. Shortly after 5 p.m. he was shot and killed by a black man at the intersection of Pine and Seventh Streets in downtown Long Beach. The principal issue was the identity of the perpetrator. The prosecution presented seven eyewitnesses who identified defendant as that person with varying degrees of certainty, and one eyewitness who categorically testified that defendant was *not* the gunman. . . . Four prosecution witnesses positively identified defendant in the courtroom as the perpetrator; in the testimony of each, however, there were factors that could have raised reasonable doubts in the minds of jurors as to the accuracy of the identification. [Three of the four witnesses who positively identified McDonald at trial either failed to pick McDonald's picture out of a pretrial photo spread or picked McDonald's picture at the pretrial photo spread but admitted, at that time, to being unsure if McDonald was the person they saw. There was no evidence that the fourth witness who positively identified McDonald at trial had ever identified McDonald before trial, and, as to this eyewitness, serious discrepancies existed between the version of events he gave police the day of the crime and his testimony at trial]. . . .

. . . .

None of the other prosecution witnesses were positive in their courtroom identifications of defendant. . . .

. . . .

The prosecution witnesses were in general agreement in their description of the clothing worn by the gunman, but two [prosecution witnesses] claimed the man had a large, round, gold earring in his left ear, about the size of a quarter, while none of the other witnesses testified that he wore any such distinctive jewelry. In addition, two [prosecution] witnesses . . . described the man as having "pockmarks" or "acne-like" scars on the lower part of his face, while none of the other witnesses so testified.

Finally, one of the prosecution's own witnesses unequivocally testified that the black man at the scene was *not* defendant. . . .

. . . .

The prosecution offered no other evidence to connect defendant with the crime in this case. The defense, however, called six witnesses to establish that on the date of the shooting (Aug. 20, 1979) defendant was visiting his grandfather in Saraland, Alabama, near Mobile. . . .

. . . .

I. *Expert Testimony on Eyewitness Identification*

Defendant contends the court abused its discretion in excluding the testimony of an expert witness on the psychological factors that may affect the accuracy of eyewitness identification. Prior to trial the defense moved for an order admitting the testimony of Dr. Robert Shomer. Dr. Shomer is a practicing psychologist and professor of psychology of almost 20 years' experience. . . . The People do not question the witness' qualifications.

At the hearing on the motion Dr. Shomer explained that he proposed to inform the jury of various psychological factors that may affect the reliability of eyewitness identification, and to "help to counter some common misconceptions" about the process. He noted first that all eyewitness identification begins with the observer's initial perception of the event. The physical circumstances affecting that observation are generally known to laymen, such as lighting, distance, and duration. But psychological factors may also influence the accuracy of the perception: Dr. Shomer intended to review for the jury the results of certain experimental studies showing that perception may be affected by such factors as the observer's state of mind, his expectations, his focus of attention at the time, the suddenness of the incident, the stressfulness of the situation, and differences in the race and/or age of the observer and the observed. On the latter point he would have testified, for example, that there are substantial decreases in accuracy when the two persons are of different races or ages.

The next phase of the process is memory. Dr. Shomer intended to discuss with the jury the evidence showing that memory is not merely a passive recording event, producing an imperishable reproduction of the scene perceived; rather, it is both a selective and a constructive process, in which old elements fade and are lost while new elements — subsequent information or suggestions — are unconsciously interwoven into the overall recollection until the subject cannot distinguish one from the other.

The last step is retrieval. Dr. Shomer proposed to review the studies establishing that recall may be affected by such factors as the subject's expectations, his suggestibility[,] the phrasing of the questions asked of him, and even the size and type of the photographs he is shown. For example, Dr. Shomer would have explained to the jury that witnesses who are asked to identify criminals in lineups or photo displays tend to find the experience psychologically unpleasant and wish to terminate it. Because of this self-induced pressure, such witnesses may subconsciously take a simple request to point out the offender if he is in the lineup and convert it into a demand that they find the face in the lineup that is the "most similar" to the offender; that alternative appears more legitimate to them than admitting they cannot identify anyone at all.

Turning to the case at bar, Dr. Shomer made it clear that he did not propose to offer an opinion that any particular witness at this trial was or was not mistaken in his or her identification of defendant. But he did intend to point out various psychological factors that could have affected that identification in the present case. Thus he emphasized that from the viewpoint of the witnesses the shooting of Esparza on a busy street corner was a sudden and unexpected event, occurring some distance away, and that because of parked and passing cars their observations were largely discontinuous. He also referred to the youth of certain of the witnesses, the words used in making the pretrial photographic identifications of defendant, and the ambiguity of those identifications. Dr. Shomer particularly noted the effect of the "cross-racial factor" in this case, emphasizing that the one witness who was certain that defendant, a black, was not the black man at the scene was herself a black; by contrast, two of the witnesses who positively identified defendant at trial as the assailant were of the same ethnic origin (Hispanic) as the victim.

Finally, Dr. Shomer intended to explain to the jury that empirical research has undermined a number of widespread lay beliefs about the psychology of eyewitness identification, e.g., that the accuracy of a witness's recollection increases with his certainty, that accuracy is also improved by stress, that cross-racial factors are not significant, and that the reliability of an identification is unaffected by the presence of a weapon or violence at the scene.

On this showing, defendant offered the testimony of Dr. Shomer as an aid to the jurors in weighing the eyewitness identifications in this case. The People objected on the sole ground that to admit the testimony would "usurp the jury's function," citing *People v. Johnson* (1974) 112 Cal. Rptr. 834, and similar decisions. The trial court . . . ruled the testimony inadmissible. The court declared that it "fully agreed" with the reasoning of *Johnson*. . . . [T]he court concluded that to allow Dr. Shomer to testify "would be invading the province of the jury." Defendant protested that Dr. Shomer would not give an opinion on the credibility of any particular witness, but would simply provide the jurors with information to help them determine the accuracy of the various identifications put before them. The court stood by its ruling, adding the further grounds that it intended to give a standard instruction on discrepancies in testimony, that expert testimony on eyewitness identification "maybe would have a tendency" to "maybe cause confusion in the jurors' minds," and that such testimony "is really not what I consider scientific enough at this point in time" to be admissible.

. . . .

B.

A traditional way of bringing scientific information to the attention of the judicial system, of course, is by the testimony of expert witnesses. But when that testimony relates to psychological factors affecting the accuracy of eyewitness identification, the courts have shown reluctance to admit it: appellate decisions almost unanimously hold that rulings excluding such evidence do not constitute an abuse of discretion. We inquire whether that reluctance remains justified.[16] [10]

This court has not previously addressed the admissibility of expert testimony on eyewitness identification. The leading case in this state — followed by the trial court in the case at bar — is *People v. Johnson.* There the sole evidence connecting the defendants with a robbery-murder at a liquor store was the eyewitness identification of the surviving robbery victims. The defense sought to discredit that identification on various grounds, including the offer of expert testimony by a psychologist as to the ability of eyewitnesses to accurately perceive, remember and relate, and the distorting effects of excitement and fear on those functions. The trial court excluded the testimony, and the Court of Appeal upheld the ruling on [several] grounds. None, however, is immune from criticism.

First, the opinion reasons that although [the California] Evidence Code section 780, subdivision (c), permits a witness to be impeached by discrediting his capacity to perceive, recollect or communicate, "it does" not follow that a party has a right to impeach a witness by calling another witness to testify as to the former's capacity." The argument misses the point. The expert witness in *Johnson* — just as Dr. Shomer here — would not have testified that any particular prosecution witness lacked the *capacity* to perceive, remember and relate; rather, he would simply have informed the jury of certain psychological factors that may impair the accuracy of a typical eyewitness identification, including the emotions of excitement or fear, with supporting references to experimental studies of such phenomena. Such evidence . . . bear[s] on the credibility of a witness.

Second, the *Johnson* opinion states that [California] Evidence Code section 801, subdivision (a), "limits expert testimony to subjects beyond the range of common experience." This paraphrase of the statutory scheme, however, is both incomplete and misleading. To begin with, by its terms section 801 applies only to expert testimony "in the form of an opinion." If an expert testifies not as to his opinion but as to *facts* within his special knowledge, section 801 is inapplicable. Factual testimony by an expert is admissible if it complies with the general statutory requirements that the witness be "qualified" by his special knowledge and that his evidence be relevant to the issues.[17] [11] Much of the proposed testimony of the psychologist in *Johnson* and of Dr. Shomer here would have related primarily to matters of fact: the *contents* of eyewitness identification studies reported in the professional literature — their methodology, their data, and their findings — are facts, verifiable by anyone who can read and understand the studies in question.

In any event, to the extent these cases may involve opinion testimony by the psychologist witness, the *Johnson* paraphrasing of section 801, subdivision (a), errs by omission. The statute does not flatly limit expert opinion testimony to subjects "beyond common experience"; rather, it limits such testimony to such subjects *"sufficiently* beyond common experience *that the opinion of an expert would assist the trier of fact"*

---

[16] [n.10] Of course, the virtual unanimity of appellate decisions on the topic may well be misleading. Expert testimony on eyewitness identification is usually offered by the defendant. In cases in which the testimony is *admitted*, the issue will not arise on appeal: if the defendant is convicted, he cannot complain of the admission of his own evidence; and if he is acquitted, no appeal is possible in any event. It follows that appellate courts ordinarily confront the issue only when the testimony has been *excluded*; and in all such cases appellate courts tend to affirm, because of the deference traditionally accorded to discretionary rulings of trial courts. . . .

[17] [n.11] The testimony also remains subject to the court's general discretionary power to exclude evidence that is unduly time-consuming or confusing, and to its special discretionary power to limit the number of expert witnesses called by any party.

(italics added). The emphasized words, omitted by the *Johnson* court, make it clear that the admissibility of expert opinion is a question of degree. The jury need not be wholly ignorant of the subject matter of the opinion in order to justify its admission; if that were the test, little expert opinion testimony would ever be heard. Instead, the statute declares that even if the jury has some knowledge of the matter, expert opinion may be admitted whenever it would "assist" the jury. It will be excluded only when it would add nothing at all to the jury's common fund of information, i.e., when "the subject of inquiry is one of such common knowledge that men of ordinary education could reach a conclusion as intelligently as the witness." (*People v. Cole* (1956) 301 P.2d 854.)

We apply this test to expert testimony on eyewitness identification. It is doubtless true that from personal experience and intuition all jurors know that an eyewitness identification can be mistaken, and also know the more obvious factors that can affect its accuracy, such as lighting, distance, and duration. It appears from the professional literature, however, that other factors bearing on eyewitness identification may be known only to some jurors, or may be imperfectly understood by many, or may be contrary to the intuitive beliefs of most. For example, in the case at bar Dr. Shomer would have testified to the results of studies of relevant factors that appear to be either not widely known to laypersons or not fully appreciated by them, such as the effects on perception of an eyewitness's personal or cultural expectations or beliefs, the effects on memory of the witness's exposure to subsequent information or suggestions, and the effects on recall of bias or cues in identification procedures or methods of questioning.

. . . .

We conclude that although jurors may not be totally unaware of the foregoing psychological factors bearing on eyewitness identification, the body of information now available on these matters is "sufficiently beyond common experience" that in appropriate cases expert opinion thereon could at least "assist the trier of fact."[18] [15]

[Lastly], the *Johnson* opinion also upholds the trial court's ruling on the ground that to admit expert psychological evidence on eyewitness identification would "invade the province" or "usurp the function" of the jury, because such evidence "embraces the ultimate issue." As Dean Wigmore has said, however, such language "is so misleading, as well as so unsound, that it should be entirely repudiated. . . ." Specifically referring to expert psychological evidence on eyewitness identification, the author of a leading treatise on the topic asserts that "the objection based upon the 'province of the jury' is no more than a shibboleth which, if accepted, would deprive the jury of important information useful and perhaps necessary for a proper decision on a difficult issue." (Wall, Eye-Witness Identification in Criminal Cases (1965) p. 213.)

---

[18] [n.15] We realize there is a minority view on this question: two psychologists are on record as opposing the use of expert testimony on the factors affecting eyewitness identification. They argue that for most of these factors, the claimed effect on witness accuracy either is not proved or is probably obvious to jurors. (Egeth & McCloskey, *Expert Testimony About Eyewitness Behavior: Is It Safe and Effective?*, in Expert Testimony: Psychological Perspectives, p. 283; see also Egeth & McCloskey, *Eyewitness Identification: What Can a Psychologist Tell a Jury?* (1983), 38 Am. Psychologist 550.) Their reasoning, however, has been vigorously disputed by their peers. And on close examination it appears the principal complaint of Egeth and McCloskey is not so much that expert testimony on eyewitness identification should never be admissible, as that it is too soon to admit it: additional research is needed. But this is a frequent conclusion of academic authors. As the present case makes plain, appellate judges do not have the luxury of waiting until their colleagues in the sciences unanimously agree that on a particular issue no more research is necessary. Given the nature of the scientific endeavor, that day may never come.

The reasons for these criticisms are several. The expert testimony in question does not seek to take over the jury's task of judging credibility: as explained above, it does not tell the jury that any particular witness is or is not truthful or accurate in his identification of the defendant. Rather, it informs the jury of certain factors that may affect such an identification in a typical case; and to the extent that it may refer to the particular circumstances of the identification before the jury, such testimony is limited to explaining the potential effects of those circumstances on the powers of observation and recollection of a typical eyewitness. The jurors retain both the power and the duty to judge the credibility and weight of all testimony in the case, as they are told by a standard instruction.

Nor could such testimony in fact usurp the jury's function. As is true of all expert testimony, the jury remains free to reject it entirely after considering the expert's opinion, reasons, qualifications, and credibility. . . .

Finally, California has abandoned the "ultimate issue" rule in any event: "in this state we have followed the modern tendency and have refused to hold that expert opinion is inadmissible merely because it coincides with an ultimate issue of fact." (*People v. Cole* (1956) *supra*, 301 P.2d 854, and cases cited.). . . .

C.

For the reasons stated, the challenged ruling excluding the expert testimony of Dr. Shomer is not supported by the trial court's professed "agreement" with the reasoning of *Johnson*, . . . or by its flat assertion that such expert testimony would "invade the province" of the jury.

Nor is the ruling supported by the court's announced intent to give the standard instruction on discrepancies in testimony. The instruction contains only a few general remarks on the topic;[19] [19] it does not even begin to convey to the jury the specific data on the eyewitness identification process that Dr. Shomer's testimony would have provided[.] Nor, again, is the ruling supported by the court's speculation that this testimony might tend to confuse the jurors. Evidence that is relevant to the prime theory of the defense cannot be excluded in wholesale fashion merely because the trial would be simpler without it. Rather, it should be accompanied by instructions clearly explaining to the jury the purpose for which it is introduced. . . .

Lastly, the ruling is not supported by the court's opinion that expert testimony on eyewitness identification is not yet "scientific enough" to be admissible. . . . [T]he court was implicitly invoking the *Kelly-Frye* rule, i.e., the rule that evidence based on a new scientific method of proof is admissible only on a showing that the procedure has been generally accepted as reliable in the scientific community in which it developed. (*People v. Kelly* (1976) 549 P.2d 1240; *Frye v. United States* (D.C. Cir. 1923), 293 Fed. 1013.

We are not persuaded . . . that the *Kelly-Frye* rule applies to expert testimony on eyewitness identification. It is important to distinguish in this regard between expert testimony and scientific evidence. When a witness gives his personal opinion on the stand — even if he qualifies as an expert — the jurors may temper their acceptance of

---

[19] [n.19] E.g., "Failure of recollection is a common experience; and innocent misrecollection is not uncommon. It is a fact, also, that two persons witnessing an incident or a transaction often will see or hear it differently."

his testimony with a healthy skepticism born of their knowledge that all human beings are fallible. But the opposite may be true when the evidence is produced by a machine: like many laypersons, jurors tend to ascribe an inordinately high degree of certainty to proof derived from an apparently "scientific" mechanism, instrument, or procedure. Yet the aura of infallibility that often surrounds such evidence may well conceal the fact that it remains experimental and tentative. For this reason, courts have invoked the *Kelly-Frye* rule primarily in cases involving novel devices or processes such as lie detectors, "truth serum," Nalline testing, experimental systems of blood typing, "voiceprints," identification by human bite marks, microscopic analysis of gunshot residue, and hypnosis. . . . In some instances the evidence passed the *Kelly-Frye* test, in others it failed; but in all such cases "the rule serves its salutary purpose of preventing the jury from being misled by unproven and ultimately unsound scientific methods."

Here, by contrast, no such methods are in issue. We have never applied the *Kelly-Frye* rule to expert medical testimony, even when the witness is a psychiatrist and the subject matter is as esoteric as the reconstitution of a past state of mind or the prediction of future dangerousness. . . . We see no reason to require a greater foundation when the witness is a qualified psychologist who will simply explain to the jury how certain aspects of everyday experience shown by the record can affect human perception and memory, and through them, the accuracy of eyewitness identification testimony. Indeed, it would be ironic to exclude such testimony on *Kelly-Frye* grounds on the theory that jurors tend to be unduly impressed by it, when jurors are far more likely to be unduly impressed by the eyewitness testimony itself.

D.

It remains true, of course, that "[w]here expert opinion evidence is offered, much must be left to the discretion of the trial court." Yet that discretion is not absolute: in various contexts it has been held that trial courts committed reversible error in excluding expert testimony. . . .

. . . Here . . . the expert witness was undoubtedly qualified to testify on the particular matters he proposed to address. . . . [W]e decline to assume that the subject matter of Dr. Shomer's testimony would have been fully known to the jurors; rather, the professional literature persuades us to the contrary. [Further] the record establishes that Dr. Shomer's testimony would have been of significant assistance to the jury. Because no other evidence connected defendant with the crime, the crucial factor in the case was the accuracy of the eyewitness identifications. Yet on that issue the evidence was far from clear. As we noted at the outset, in the testimony of each of the witnesses who identified defendant in the courtroom there were elements that could have raised reasonable doubts as to the accuracy of the identification. . . . Further doubts could have arisen from the dramatic declaration in open court by a prosecution witness that the defendant was *not* the perpetrator, and from the testimony of six witnesses that defendant was not in the state on the day the crime was committed.

In these circumstances the exclusion of Dr. Shomer's testimony undercut the evidentiary basis of defendant's main line of defense — his attack on the accuracy of the eyewitness identifications — and deprived the jurors of information that could have assisted them in resolving that crucial issue. The ruling excluding such testimony was therefore unsupported by the record. We have previously shown (Part I C, *ante*) that it was unsupported by the law. It follows that the ruling constituted an abuse of discretion.

An error in excluding expert testimony may be found harmless. In the case at bar, however, the record compels us to conclude that the error was prejudicial. As we have seen, the issue affected by the ruling was crucial, given the absence of any other evidence connecting defendant with the crime; and the evidence on that issue was close, given the potential weaknesses in the prosecution's testimony and the presence of both eyewitness and alibi testimony favorable to the defense. An error that impairs the jury's determination of an issue that is both critical and closely balanced will rarely be harmless. Rather, after an examination of the whole record we find it reasonably probable that a result more favorable to defendant would have been reached in the absence of this error. There has therefore been a miscarriage of justice, and the judgment must be reversed.

We reiterate that the decision to admit or exclude expert testimony on psychological factors affecting eyewitness identification remains primarily a matter within the trial court's discretion. . . . We expect that such evidence will not often be needed, and in the usual case the appellate court will continue to defer to the trial court's discretion in this matter.[20] [24] Yet deference is not abdication. When an eyewitness identification of the defendant is a key element of the prosecution's case but is not substantially corroborated by evidence giving it independent reliability, and the defendant offers qualified expert testimony on specific psychological factors shown by the record that could have affected the accuracy of the identification but are not likely to be fully known to or understood by the jury, it will ordinarily be error to exclude that testimony.

. . . .

The judgment is reversed.

NOTES

1. ***Abuse of Discretion in Limited Circumstances.*** Initially, expert testimony on eyewitness fallibility met with uniform disapproval from the appellate courts. *See, e.g., Caldwell v. State*, 594 S.W.2d 24, 28–29 (Ark. Ct. App. 1980) (science of human perception testimony is new and invades the province of the trier of fact). In the last half of the 1980s, beginning with *State v. Chapple*, 660 P.2d 1208 (Ariz. 1983), appellate courts began looking more favorably upon such testimony. *See Williams v. State*, 594 So. 2d 1225, 1227 (Ala. 1992) ("It is clear . . . that there is presently a trend in the law to allow expert testimony on the subject of human memory. . . . We further hold, however, that the admissibility of such evidence is . . . subject to the discretion of the trial court."). *See also United States v. Downing*, 753 F.2d 1224, 1232 (3d Cir. 1985).

Other jurisdictions have found a trial court's exclusion of expert testimony on the reliability of eyewitness identification testimony to be an abuse of discretion in limited situations such as those described in *McDonald, supra*. *See People v. LeGrand*, 867 N.E.2d 374, 379–80 (N.Y. 2007) (case turns solely on uncorroborated eyewitness testimony); *State v. DuBray*, 77 P.3d 247, 255 (Mont. 2004) ("[W]e agree with the California Supreme Court's reasoning [in *People v. McDonald*] and now adopt the

---

[20] [n.24] Even when the trial court correctly excludes such testimony, the defendant may be entitled to a special instruction specifically directing the jury's attention to other evidence in the record . . . that supports his defense of mistaken identification and could give rise to a reasonable doubt of his guilt. . . .

limited admissibility rule in Montana. It shall be an abuse of discretion for a district court to disallow expert testimony on eyewitness testimony when no substantial corroborating evidence exists."); *Johnson v. State*, 526 S.E.2d 549, 552–53 (Ga. 2000) (case turns solely on uncorroborated eyewitness testimony).

2. *The Applicability of Frye.* The *Frye* test was formulated to place an extra hurdle in the path of admissibility for "hard" scientific evidence. Jurisdictions that use the *Frye* test do not always apply it to "soft science." *See e.g., Campbell v. People*, 814 P.2d 1, 7–8 (Colo. 1991) (*Frye* does not apply to expert testimony on eyewitness identifications); *People v. Hampton*, 746 P.2d 947, 951 (Colo. 1987) (*Frye* applies to cases involving the manipulation of physical evidence). Sometimes courts either apply — or do not apply — the *Frye* test, without addressing the issue. *See State v. MacLennan*, 702 N.W.2d 219, 231 (Minn. 2005) (surveying *Frye* states in cases involving expert testimony on the battered child syndrome).

QUESTIONS

1. California is a *Frye* state. Did the *McDonald* court rule that expert testimony on eyewitness identifications was generally accepted? If so, why was such evidence admissible?

2. The *Rincon* case upheld the trial court's exclusion of expert testimony; *McDonald* found the exclusion to be an abuse of discretion. Just where is it that *Rincon* and *McDonald* disagree, or does the testimony offered in *McDonald* meet the *Rincon* standard?

PROBLEMS

Problem 5-1. Assume that an *unmasked* man with a shotgun walks into a fast food restaurant just before closing. There are two customers and eight employees in the restaurant. The gunman asks for money, and after getting all the money in the cash register orders all the employees and the two customers to stand next to each other. The gunman says "You are going to get hurt," fires into the group, and then flees. Three people are killed, and the rest are injured.

Defendant, Bill Smith, is arrested and charged with capital murder in the case. Evidence produced against him at trial includes testimony of the seven surviving victims of the robbery. Five of the eyewitnesses state that they are "certain" that Smith was the man who robbed the restaurant, and two of the eyewitnesses state that they are "pretty certain" Smith was the robber. Smith is an African-American, and four of the eyewitnesses are African-American; the other three eyewitnesses are white. Other evidence connecting Smith to the crime includes testimony from a friend of Smith who states that Smith asked him to help in the robbery. Further, the police found a shotgun and live shotgun shells in Smith's apartment that were consistent with the shotgun and shells used in the robbery-murder. Finally, $880 in small bills (no bill larger than a $20) was found at Smith's apartment when he was arrested the day after the crime — $1,100 in small bills had been taken in the robbery.

Smith presents no alibi witnesses and does not take the stand at his trial. Smith seeks to offer an expert witness on eyewitness testimony. If allowed to testify, the expert will describe the psychological factors that affect the reliability of eyewitness testimony. The trial court rules that the expert cannot testify because her testimony does not relate to a matter sufficiently beyond common experience to assist the trier of fact: because such evidence does not satisfy the *Frye* test or the *Daubert* test, and because the time that would be consumed if it were admitted substantially outweighs what little probative value it has.

Smith is convicted and sentenced to death. On appeal he claims that it was reversible error to exclude his expert's testimony. How should the appellate court rule in a jurisdiction that follows *McDonald? See People v. Sanders*, 905 P.2d 420, 434–36 (Cal. 1996).

Problem 5-2. A woman was driving home from work late at night when a man fell over in front of her car. She stopped, and the man got up and opened her door and said, "I have a gun. This is a robbery." The man ordered her to drive to a secluded spot just off the highway where he raped her. He then got out of the car and ran.

The victim worked with a police artist in drawing a sketch of her attacker. She stated that her attacker's face was "ingrained in her memory." A suspect matching the sketch was arrested and photographed. The victim identified the man in the photograph as the man who attacked her.

At trial the victim testifies and identifies the defendant as her attacker. She states that the attack took place for nearly one hour and that she was able to see her attacker's face clearly several times when the car's interior was illuminated by the headlights of passing cars. She states she was face to face with her attacker throughout most of the attack. The state offers no physical evidence to connect defendant with the crime.

The defendant seeks to admit expert testimony on eyewitness identifications. If allowed to testify, the defendant's expert will say that stress diminishes a witness' ability to accurately make an identification, that a witness may unconsciously try to complete an incomplete recollection, and that a witness' beliefs about the accuracy of his or her observations may be unconsciously influenced by outside factors (such as nonverbal cues from others). The trial court excludes the testimony, stating that the jury can understand the psychological factors that affect eyewitness identification and that cross-examination can bring out any deficiencies that are present.

Defendant is convicted and appeals. How should the appellate court rule on appeal? *See State v. Percy*, 595 A.2d 248, 252–53 (Vt. 1991).

C. SYNDROMES

[1]   Rape Trauma Syndrome

PAUL C. GIANNELLI & EDWARD J. IMWINKELRIED, 1 SCIENTIFIC EVIDENCE § 9.04 & § 9.04[a], at 524–28 (4th ed. 2007)[21]

§ 9.04 Rape Trauma Syndrome.

Burgess and Holmstrom coined the phrase "rape trauma syndrome" (RTS) to describe the behavioral, somatic, and psychological reactions of rape and attempted rape victims.[22] [176] Based on interviews with 146 women, they found that victims usually progress through a two-phase process — an acute phase and a long-term reorganization phase. Impact reactions in the acute phase involve either an "expressed style," in which fear, anger, and anxiety are manifested, or a "controlled style," in which these feelings are masked by a composed or subdued behavior. Somatic reactions include physical trauma, skeletal muscle tension, gastrointestinal irritability, and genitourinary disturbance. In addition, a wide gamut of emotional reactions, ranging from fear, humiliation, and embarrassment to anger, revenge, and self-blame, are exhibited.

The second phase, the reorganization phase, typically began two to six weeks after the attack and was a period in which the victim attempted to reestablish her life. This period was characterized by activity, such as changing residences, changing telephone numbers, or visiting family members. Nightmares and dreams were common. Rape-related phobias, such as fear of being alone or fear of having people behind their back, and difficulties in sexual relationships also were prominent.

Other studies elaborated on the initial research, sometimes confirming the earlier studies and sometimes providing additional insights. "Subsequent research, which is much more rigorous, conceptualizes rape trauma in terms of specific symptoms rather than more general stages or recovery."[23] [178]

RTS is now recognized as a type of post-traumatic stress disorder (PTSD), and such disorders are included in the most recent edition of the American Psychiatric Association's Diagnostic and Statistical Manual of Mental Disorders. This approach to RTS, however, does not focus on the two-stage model of recovery posited by Burgess and Holmstrom, but rather on specific symptoms.

Critics have questioned the scientific basis for RTS evidence. After surveying the literature (1984), one commentator concluded that "definitional problems, biased research samples, and the inherent complexity of the phenomenon vitiate all attempts to establish empirically the causal relationship implicit in the concept of a rape trauma

---

[21] Copyright © 2007 by Matthew Bender & Co., a member of the LEXISNEXIS Group. Reprinted with permission. All rights reserved.

[22] [n.176] Burgess & Holmstrom, *Rape Trauma Syndrome*, 131 Am. J. Psychiatry 981 (1974). *See also* Burgess, *Rape Trauma Syndrome*, 1 Behav. Sci. & Law 97 (Summer 1983).

[23] [n.178] Frazier & Borgida, *Rape Trauma Syndrome: A Review of Case Law and Psychological Research*, 16 Law & Hum. Behav. 293, 299 (1992).

syndrome."[24] [181] Some of the research problems included: (1) unrepresentative samples, (2) failure to distinguish between victims of rapes, attempted rapes, and molestation, and (3) failure to account for individual idiosyncratic and incident-specific reactions. In 1989 a psychologist concluded that "research on the rape trauma syndrome is not probative on prior consent, prior trauma, nor the cause of the complainant's current behavior."

A 1992 review of the literature by Frazier and Borgida included a number of findings: Although victims experience a range of symptoms, only a few symptoms have been studied consistently — fear and anxiety, depression, social maladjustment, and sexual dysfunction. Later studies also documented symptoms identified for PTSD — recurrent nightmares, irritability, and hypervigilance.[25] [184] They concluded:

> In our opinion, although early studies were plagued by numerous methodological problems. . . , several studies have since been conducted that are much more sophisticated methodologically . . . These studies have assessed victim recovery at several points after the assault using standardized assessment measures and have employed carefully matched control groups. This research has established that rape victims experience more depression, anxiety, fear, and social adjustment and sexual problems than women who have not been victimized. Research on PTSD among rape victims is more recent but consistently suggests that many victims experience PTSD symptoms following an assault. Initially high symptom levels generally abate by 3 to 4 months postassault, although significant levels of distress continue for many victims.[26] [185]

The focus of much of the research was to understand the victim's reactions in order to provide assistance to the victim. The focus was not to evaluate a victim's reactions in order to establish the fact that a rape had occurred, which is how RTS evidence is sometimes used at trial. There is an accepted body of research concerning the aftereffects of rape. The critical issue, however, is how the research is used in court.

Frazier and Borgida also reviewed expert testimony in the reported cases. In several instances they found testimony that was unsupported by research. For example, in *Lessard v. State*,[27] [186] the expert testified that it is "very common" for a victim to ask an assailant not to tell anyone about the assault. Frazier and Borgida concluded that "this particular behavior has not been documented in the research literature."[28] [187] Their conclusions concerning court testimony are noteworthy:

> In sum, experts in recent cases have described a broad range of symptoms and behaviors as consistent with RTS, some of which do not appear to be based on research. Testimony that is not research based often seems to be prompted by a defendant's claims that a complainant's behavior was inconsistent with having

---

[24] [n.181] Note, *Checking the Allure of Increased Conviction Rates: The Admissibility of Expert Testimony on Rape Trauma Syndrome in Criminal Proceedings*, 70 Va. L. Rev. 1657, 1678 (1984).

[25] [n.184] Frazier & Borgida, *Rape Trauma Syndrome: A Review of the Case Law and Psychological Research*, 16 Law & Hum. Behav. 293, 300 (1992).

[26] [n.185] *Id.* at 301.

[27] [n.186] 719 P.2d 227, 233 (Wyo. 1986).

[28] [n.187] Frazier & Borgida, *Rape Trauma Syndrome: A Review of the Case Law and Psychological Research*, 16 Law & Hum. Behav. 293, 304 (1992).

been raped. If virtually any victim behavior is described as consistent with RTS, the term soon will have little meaning. Indeed, some critics have argued that this already is the case. . . .[29] [188]

Jury Studies

Social scientists have also attempted to determine whether the typical jury is generally knowledgeable about the aftereffects of rape, and what the impact of expert testimony on this subject will have on a jury. In 1988 Frazier and Borgida administered an 18-item questionnaire on sexual assault to two groups of experts: rape experts and PTSD experts. The responses of the experts were then compared to those of two nonexpert groups (students and nonacademic university staff). The nonexpert groups scored markedly lower on the questionnaire than did the experts — near chance levels (57% and 58% correct). Significantly, the nonexperts were unaware of the behavioral changes a victim often experiences following a rape. This study suggests that jurors often need to be informed about this subject in order to understand the evidence.

. . . .

The studies also indicated that jurors did not automatically accept the expert's testimony, and that expert testimony was important in acquaintance rape and lack of physical resistance situations.

[a] Admissibility: Lack of Consent

The prosecution may offer RTS evidence at trial for two different purposes: (1) to prove lack of consent by the alleged victim, and (2) to explain post-incident conduct by a victim that a jury might perceive as inconsistent with the claim of rape. The courts divide over the first use but generally accept the second use.

---

[a]   Rape Trauma Syndrome: Offered by Prosecution to Prove Lack of Consent

Prosecuting attorneys have experienced some difficulty in obtaining convictions for rape in situations where the victim has no obvious physical injuries that suggest force was used, and where the accused admits having sexual intercourse with the complaining witness but claims such intercourse was consensual. In cases that are essentially "swearing matches" between the accused and the victim, expert testimony that the victim suffered from symptoms that are associated with forcible rape (rape trauma syndrome) strengthens the case for lack of consent. The prosecuting attorney asks the jury to accept expert testimony that rape victims display certain characteristics or symptoms (rape trauma syndrome). The prosecutor then offers evidence that the complainant has these same characteristics or symptoms. The jury is then asked to infer, or the expert offers an opinion that, the complainant must have been raped, since she has symptoms of rape trauma syndrome.

Courts are fairly evenly split on the admissibility of expert testimony concerning rape trauma syndrome when offered to prove lack of consent to an admitted occurrence of sexual intercourse. In July of 1982 the case of *State v. Marks* became the first

---

[29] [n.188] *Id.* at 304–05.

reported case upholding the admission of expert testimony on rape trauma syndrome to prove lack of consent. It was followed six weeks later by the Minnesota case of *State v. Saldana*, which reached the opposite conclusion.

STATE v. MARKS
647 P.2d 1292 (Kan. 1982)

HERD, JUSTICE:

This is an appeal from a jury conviction of rape and aggravated sodomy.

At approximately 10:00 p.m., July 4, 1980, the victim, a twenty-one-year-old student at Emporia State University, went to an Emporia private club called "The Attic." The club opened late because of a fireworks display that night. The victim was the club's first customer that evening. She testified she went to the club because she was upset over a recent breakup with her boyfriend.

Shortly after the victim arrived at the club, Elmore Marks, Jr. entered. He made his way to her booth and sat down. A conversation ensued with the victim talking about school and work. Marks fabricated a grandiose story about his being a Ph.D and an M.D. and how he was in the process of writing an analytical book about people. He indicated the background for the book consisted of a series of interviews with people of varied experiences. The victim naively swallowed Marks' line and agreed to be interviewed for the book.

After two drinks and an hour and a half discussion the victim agreed to go with Marks to the house of one of his friends in order that he might arrange a trip to Nassau to pay her for assisting with the book. They drove to the house, which actually belonged to Marks, and there he pretended to make reservations for the trip. Later Marks told his victim she looked nervous and gave her a small white pill as a remedy. She took the pill and became dizzy and light-headed. Marks then produced another pill virtually forcing it down her. Her dizziness grew worse. Marks led her to the bedroom where she laid down. Marks then pulled up a chair, took pad and pencil in hand and began interrogating the victim about her sex life. When she refused to answer, Marks became angry and started taking off her clothing. He also choked her briefly and attempted smothering her with a pillow. The victim fought back but her dizziness prevented her from escaping. Marks threatened if she did not stop fighting he would kill her. After a long struggle he succeeded in removing the victim's clothing and forced her to have sexual intercourse and oral sodomy with him. After giving his victim a shower and massage, Marks drove her to her car.

Upon returning to her apartment, the victim tearfully related the episode to her roommate who called the police and drove her to the hospital. The examining physician found a lacerated area near the opening of the victim's vagina but no other bruises or marks.

Several days later the victim rode with the police and guided them to Marks' residence. A search warrant was obtained and the house was searched. Marks was arrested and charged with rape and aggravated sodomy. After conviction this appeal followed.

. . . .

Appellant . . . attacks the admission of the expert testimony of Dr. Herbert Modlin, a board certified psychiatrist and neurologist who practices psychiatry and teaches at the Menninger Foundation. He is also one of a small number of doctors to be certified in the field of forensic psychiatry.

During his testimony Dr. Modlin discussed the diagnosis and treatment of "post traumatic stress disorders." The condition is caused when a person experiences a "very frightening, stressful event" and manifests itself in a kind of "psychological hangover." According to Dr. Modlin a type of post traumatic stress disorder labeled "rape trauma syndrome" is the result of a sexual assault. Symptoms of rape trauma syndrome include fear of offender retaliation, fear of being raped again, fear of being home alone, fear of men in general, fear of being out alone, sleep disturbance, change in eating habits and sense of shame.

Dr. Modlin examined the victim two weeks after the rape. Based upon his psychiatric evaluation Dr. Modlin testified he was of the opinion she had been the victim of "a frightening assault, an attack" and that she was suffering from the post-traumatic stress disorder known as rape trauma syndrome.

. . . .

Appellant does not contend Dr. Modlin lacks the requisite "special knowledge, skill, experience or training," to testify as an expert in this area. He argues that expert testimony regarding rape trauma syndrome should be per se inadmissible in a case where consent is the defense because it invades the province of the jury.

The identification of rape trauma syndrome is a relatively new psychiatric development. Even so, if the presence of rape trauma syndrome is detectable and reliable as evidence that a forcible assault did take place, it is relevant when a defendant argues the victim consented to sexual intercourse. As such an expert's opinion does not invade the province of the jury. It is merely offered as any other evidence, with the expert subject to cross-examination and the jury left to determine its weight.

In *State v. Washington*, 622 P.2d 986 (1981), we stated "before a scientific opinion may be received in evidence at trial, the basis of that opinion must be shown to be generally accepted as reliable within the expert's particular scientific field." See also *Frye v. United States*, 293 F. 1013 (D.C. Cir. 1923). Although *Washington* involved physical scientific evidence, the same test is applicable to the admission of testimony regarding a psychiatric diagnosis.

An examination of the literature clearly demonstrates that the so-called "rape trauma syndrome" is generally accepted to be a common reaction to sexual assault. As such, qualified expert psychiatric testimony regarding the existence of rape trauma syndrome is relevant and admissible in a case such as this where the defense is consent.

. . . .

Admissibility of expert testimony . . . lies within the sound discretion of the trial court, and the court's decision will not be reversed on appeal unless it is shown that discretion was abused. Here the judge considered the qualifications of Dr. Modlin, the basis and relevancy of his testimony and allowed him to testify. There is no showing of abuse of discretion.

. . . .

The judgment is affirmed.

STATE v. SALDANA
324 N.W.2d 227 (Minn. 1982)

SCOTT, JUSTICE.

Camilo Saldana appeals from his conviction of criminal sexual conduct in the first degree. At trial appellant admitted that sexual intercourse had occurred but claimed it was consensual. To rebut appellant's claim, the state presented an expert witness who described the typical post-rape symptoms and behavior of rape victims, and gave her opinion that the complainant was a victim of rape and had not fabricated her allegations. We find that the admission of such testimony requires the reversal of appellant's conviction, and we remand for a new trial.

Our concern is directed toward the testimony of Lynn Dreyer, a counselor for sexual assault victims, who testified for the state. Dreyer, the director of the Victim Assistance Program in Mankato, holds a bachelor's degree in psychology and social work. Dreyer testified that she met Martha Fuller, the complainant, 10 days after the alleged rape and that she counseled Fuller for approximately a 10-week period. In her testimony, Dreyer explained the stages that a rape victim typically goes through and discussed typical behavior of victims after a rape. She then described Fuller's reactions as she had observed them. In response to a question, Dreyer testified that it was not unusual that Fuller did not report the incident until the following day and that many rape victims never report a rape. Dreyer stated that Fuller was the victim of "acquaintance rape," that she definitely believed Fuller was a victim of sexual assault and rape, and that she did not think Fuller fantasized or "made it up."

The issue is whether admission of testimony concerning typical post-rape symptoms and behavior of rape victims, opinions that Fuller was a victim of rape, and an opinion that Fuller did not fantasize the rape was reversible error.

To be admissible, expert testimony must be helpful to the jury in reaching its decision:

> The basic requirement of Rule 702 is the helpfulness requirement. If the subject of the testimony is within the knowledge and experience of a lay jury and the testimony of the expert will not add precision or depth to the jury's ability to reach conclusions about that subject which is within their experience, then the testimony does not meet the helpfulness test.

State v. Helterbridle, 301 N.W.2d 545, 547 (Minn. 1980). If the jury is in as good a position to reach a decision as the expert, expert testimony would be of little assistance to the jury and should not be admitted. Expert testimony may also be excluded if its probative value is substantially outweighed by the danger of unfair prejudice, confusion, or misleading the jury. Under this test of admissibility, we must examine each segment of Dreyer's testimony.

Dreyer's discussion of the stages a rape victim typically goes through was essentially an explanation of "rape trauma syndrome," although she did not so label it. On the facts of the case before us, such testimony is of no help to the jury and produces an extreme danger of unfair prejudice. The factual question to be decided by the jury is whether the alleged criminal conduct occurred. It is not necessary that Fuller react in a typical manner to the incident. Fuller need not display the typical post-rape symptoms and behavior of rape victims to convince the jury that her view of the facts is the truth.

Rape trauma syndrome is not the type of scientific test that accurately and reliably determines whether a rape has occurred. The characteristic symptoms may follow *any* psychologically traumatic event. American Psychiatric Association, *Diagnostic and Statistical Manual of Mental Disorders* 236 (3d ed. 1980). At best, the syndrome describes only symptoms that occur with some frequency, but makes no pretense of describing every single case. The jury must not decide this case on the basis of how most people react to rape or on whether Fuller's reactions were the typical reactions of a person who has been a victim of rape. Rather, the jury must decide what happened in *this* case, and whether the elements of the alleged crime have been proved beyond a reasonable doubt.

The scientific evaluation of rape trauma syndrome has not reached a level of reliability that surpasses the quality of common sense evaluation present in jury deliberations. As we stated in refusing to permit introduction of "battering parent" syndrome, the evidence may not be introduced "until further evidence of the scientific accuracy and reliability of syndrome or profile diagnoses can be established." *State v. Loebach*, 310 N.W.2d 58, 64 (Minn. 1981). Permitting a person in the role of an expert to suggest that because the complainant exhibits some of the symptoms of rape trauma syndrome, the complainant was therefore raped, unfairly prejudices the appellant by creating an aura of special reliability and trustworthiness. Since jurors of ordinary abilities are competent to consider the evidence and determine whether the alleged crime occurred, the danger of unfair prejudice outweighs any probative value. To allow such testimony would inevitably lead to a battle of experts that would invade the jury's province of fact-finding and add confusion rather than clarity.

Rape trauma syndrome is not a fact-finding tool, but a therapeutic tool useful in counseling. Because the jury need be concerned only with determining the facts and applying the law, and because evidence of reactions of other people does not assist the jury in its fact-finding function, we find the admission of expert testimony on rape trauma syndrome to be error.

The second segment of Dreyer's testimony of questionable admissibility is her opinion that Fuller was raped.[30] [4] The issue is whether the state may introduce expert testimony in a rape prosecution that, in the expert's opinion, a rape in fact occurred.

The primary criterion for admissibility is the helpfulness requirement as discussed above. An expert witness may testify in the form of an opinion, Minn. R. Evid. 702, and opinion testimony is not objectionable merely because it embraces an ultimate issue to be decided by the jury, Minn. R. Evid. 704. However, according to the Advisory Committee Comment to Rule 704, opinions involving a legal analysis or mixed questions

---

[30] [n.4] The prosecutor elicited the following testimony from Dreyer:

Q: Can you explain to the jury the stages that Martha Fuller went through since the date of this incident? [Objection overruled.]

A: . . . She has went through a lot because her rape is what we call acquaintance rape, where it involves someone that they know, and she's gone through a lot of feelings of guilt and internalizing the pain, because it is a friend and a personal friend of her husband [sic].

. . . .

Q: From your professional involvement with Martha Fuller, do you have an opinion Miss Dreyer, as to whether or not this incident actually took place?

A: I definitely believe that Martha was a victim of assault.

Q: Of a sexual assault?

A: Sexual assault and rape.

of law and fact are deemed to be of no use to the jury.

A majority of the courts that have considered the issue have held that admission of a doctor's opinion that rape or sexual assault had occurred is error.[31] [5] A few courts in other jurisdictions have permitted a doctor who has physically examined the complaining witness shortly after the alleged rape to give an opinion that sexual intercourse was not voluntary.

The admission of Dreyer's testimony constitutes error under the majority rule. Furthermore, because Dreyer is not a physician, never physically examined Martha Fuller and did not meet Fuller until 10 days after the alleged rape, the admission of Dreyer's testimony constitutes error even under the minority rule.

We conclude that the admission of Dreyer's testimony was error. Because the jurors were equally capable of considering the evidence and determining whether a rape occurred, Dreyer's opinion was not helpful. Her testimony was a legal conclusion which was of no use to the jury. Furthermore, the danger of unfair prejudice outweighed any probative value. . . .

The final segment of Dreyer's testimony was her opinion that Fuller had not fantasized the rape.[32] [7] Once a witness is deemed competent, expert opinions concerning the witness's reliability in distinguishing truth from fantasy are generally inadmissible because such opinions invade the jury's province to make credibility determinations. Expert testimony concerning the credibility of a witness should be received only in "unusual cases." An example of such an unusual case is a sexual assault case where the alleged victim is a child or mentally retarded.

The admission of Dreyer's testimony that Martha Fuller did not fantasize or fabricate her story was erroneous. First, there are no unusual circumstances in this case which warrant the admission of expert testimony concerning the credibility of Fuller, who is an adult with at least average intelligence. Second, Dreyer, who had no medical education or training, was unqualified to determine whether a person could differentiate between reality and fantasy or to detect whether a person was telling the truth or fabricating a story. Finally, the question and answer did not concern Fuller's general tendency to fantasize or fabricate but whether she fantasized or fabricated the particular facts at issue. Dreyer was simply stating her opinion that Fuller was telling the truth. Because credibility is the sole province of the jury, admission of the testimony was erroneous.

The final question for our determination is whether the erroneous admission of Dreyer's testimony mandates reversal of appellant's conviction and a new trial. Appellant admitted that sexual intercourse occurred. The sole issue in dispute was whether the sexual intercourse was voluntary. The evidence produced at trial could be interpreted to support the claim of either the complainant or appellant. The jury's determination depended largely upon which party it believed. Under these circum

---

[31] [n.5] The examining physician may of course testify to observations of physical and emotional conditions, examinations and tests performed, and medical conclusions reached.

[32] [n.7] The prosecutor asked the question as follows:

Q: Is there any way that this could have been consensual and that she fantasiased [sic]? [Objection overruled.]

A: I first of all believe that because rape is a crime of violence and a person is very humiliated and physically abused in a rape, that leads me to believe that not many women would fantasias [sic] or make something like this up when you know the degree of humiliation she will have to live with and speaking personally; Martha I do not think she fantasiased [sic] or made it up.

stances, Dreyer's testimony, presented as the unbiased opinion of an expert, may well have tipped the balance.

We hold that in this prosecution for criminal sexual conduct where the defendant claimed consent it was reversible error for an expert to testify concerning typical post-rape symptoms and behavior of rape victims and give opinions that the complainant was a victim of rape and had not fantasized the rape. Our holding is necessary to ensure accuracy in the truth-seeking process and to guarantee fairness to the accused. We reverse appellant's conviction and remand for a new trial.

Reversed and remanded.

NOTES

1. ***Traditional Methods for Proving Absence of Consent.*** Offering evidence concerning the alleged victim's condition after a rape on the issue of consent is neither new nor controversial. Physical evidence (such as bruises, swelling, and abrasions) and evidence of the victim's emotional state (such as crying and nervousness) are, and have been, admissible as indicating that intercourse was forcible rather than consensual. *See Smelcher v. State*, 385 So. 2d 653 (Ala. Crim. App. 1980) (physical conditions); *People v. Weaver*, 290 N.E.2d 691 (Ill. Ct. App. Ct. 1972) (physical conditions); *Simmons v. State*, 504 N.E.2d 575 (Ind. 1987) (testimony of victim's father and sister concerning their observations about victim's "behavior and fears" held relevant and admissible on issue of fact of rape); *Collins v. State*, 365 So. 2d 113 (Ala. Crim. App. 1978) (emotional state); Nicole Rosenberg Economou, *Defense Expert Testimony on Rape Trauma Syndrome: Implications for the Stoic Victim*, 42 HASTINGS L.J. 1143, 1159 (1991). What distinguishes this type of evidence from rape trauma syndrome evidence is that it is *not* in the form of expert opinion: firsthand observations are admitted — without an accompanying opinion — for the jury's consideration.

Expert opinion that intercourse was not consensual has, however, been admitted by many courts where the opinion was that of the examining physician, and the opinion was based *purely* on physical evidence such as bruising or bleeding. *See, e.g., State v. Miller*, 117 N.W.2d 447 (Iowa 1962); *State v. Ring*, 339 P.2d 461 (Wash. 1959). A minority of courts have allowed treating physicians to offer an opinion as to whether intercourse was forcible based both upon their physical examination and upon their observation of the victim's emotional state. *See People v. LaPorte*, 303 N.W.2d 222 (Mich. 1981) (no error in admitting attending physician's expert opinion, based upon the victim's physical and emotional conditions shortly after the incident, that there had been penetration against the will of the complainant).

2. ***Rape Trauma Syndrome on Issue of Credibility.*** It should be remembered that the general rule, reflected in Fed. R. Evid. 608, is that opinion evidence is not admissible to bolster or support the credibility of a witness who has testified *until the witness' character for truthfulness has been attacked.* Whether testimony that contradicts a victim's testimony constitutes an "attack" on the victim's character for truthfulness is unclear. The Advisory Committee Note to Fed. R. Evid. 608 states that "whether evidence in the form of contradiction is an attack upon the character of a witness must depend on the circumstances."

Even if contradictory testimony is considered an "attack" on the victim's character, Fed. R. Evid. 608 reflects the common law rule in limiting the type of evidence that can be offered to support credibility to reputation and opinions that pertain to the witness' *character* for truthfulness. Accordingly, an expert offering an opinion that a woman was "telling the truth" or "was not fantasizing" when she said sex was without consent would face problems of admissibility if the theory of admissibility is that the testimony supports or rehabilitates the credibility of the complaining witness.

3. Courts Accepting Evidence of Rape Trauma Syndrome on Consent. Several courts in addition to Kansas, *Marks, supra,* have admitted expert testimony concerning RTS on the issue of consent. *See State v. Huey,* 699 P.2d 1290 (Ariz. 1985); *Simmons v. State,* 504 N.E.2d 575 (Ind. 1987); *State v. Gettier,* 438 N.W.2d 1 (Iowa 1989); *State v. Allewalt,* 517 A.2d 741 (Md. 1986); *State v. Liddell,* 685 P.2d 918 (Mont. 1984); *State v. McCoy,* 366 S.E.2d 731 (W. Va. 1988); *People v. Douglas,* 538 N.E.2d 1335 (Ill. App. Ct. 1989); *State v. Whitman,* 475 N.E.2d 486 (Ohio Ct. App. 1984). Although the cases are not in complete agreement, most *Frye* jurisdictions that have addressed the issue have conditioned admissibility of rape trauma syndrome evidence upon satisfaction of the *Frye* test. *See State v. Baby,* 946 A.2d 463, 492 n.26 (Md. 2008) (listing cases; noting jurisdictions that have refused admissibility for failure satisfy *Frye's* general acceptance test).

4. Courts Rejecting Evidence of Rape Trauma Syndrome on Consent. The *Saldana* case is instructive in that it addresses many of the arguments commonly employed against syndrome evidence. The *Saldana* court found rape trauma syndrome to be inadmissible for several reasons:

> (1) Irrelevancy — "The jury must not decide this case on the basis of how most people react to rape or on whether [the victim's] reactions were typical reactions of a person who has been the victim of a rape. Rather the jury must decide what happened in *this case.*" *Saldana, supra,* 324 N.W.2d at 230.

> (2) Reliability — "Rape trauma syndrome is not the type of scientific test that accurately and reliably determines whether a rape has occurred." *Saldana, supra,* 324 N.W.2d at 229.

> (3) Not helpful to jury — "[J]urors of ordinary abilities are competent to consider the evidence and determine whether the alleged crime occurred." *Id.* at 230.

> (4) Unfair prejudice — "Permitting a person in the role of an expert to suggest that because the complainant exhibits some of the symptoms of rape trauma syndrome, the complainant was therefore raped, unfairly prejudices the appellant by creating an aura of special reliability and trustworthiness. . . . . [T]he danger of unfair prejudice outweighs any probative value." *Id.* at 230.

In addition to Minnesota, courts in Wyoming, *Chapman v. State,* 18 P.3d 1164 (Wyo. 2001); North Carolina, *State v. Hall,* 412 S.E.2d 883 (N.C. 1992); New York, *People v. Taylor,* 552 N.Y.S.2d 883 (N.Y. 1990); California, *People v. Coleman,* 768 P.2d 32 (Cal. 1989), and Washington, *State v. Black,* 745 P.2d 12 (Wash. 1987), have refused to admit evidence of rape trauma syndrome when offered to prove lack of consent in a rape prosecution.

5. Limited Admissibility: Certain Forms of Expert Testimony Permitted. Note that some jurisdictions that do not allow an expert to testify that a rape occurred (i.e., in most cases, that the victim did not consent to sexual intercourse) based upon a finding of rape trauma syndrome will often allow an expert to speak in general terms about the victim's symptoms, about the characteristics of rape trauma syndrome, and to opine that the victim's symptoms are "consistent with" rape trauma syndrome. In this manner the jury is able to hear expert testimony about rape trauma syndrome, but are left to draw their own conclusions on the ultimate issue of whether the alleged victim was or was not raped. This, obviously, is a rather fine distinction to draw, and transforms the prohibition against rape trauma syndrome evidence on the issue of consent into prohibition of certain *forms* of expert testimony. *See* DAVID L. FAIGMAN, MICHAEL J. SAKS, JOSEPH SANDERS & EDWARD K. CHENG, 2 MODERN SCIENTIFIC EVIDENCE: THE LAW AND SCIENCE OF EXPERT TESTIMONY § 15:3, at 426–27 (2008–2009) ("Most courts stress in unequivocal terms that RTS cannot be used to prove that a rape occurred. Courts divide this restriction into *two testimonial prohibitions.* First, experts are usually prohibited from offering an opinion about the 'ultimate issue' that a rape occurred. . . . The second . . . prohibition . . . precludes experts from commenting on the credibility of the alleged victim or the veracity of similarly situated people.") (emphasis added).

There are four "forms," or levels of specificity, of expert opinion discussed in the cases. The first (and most general) level is testimony from an expert that describes the general characteristics of the syndrome but offers no testimony about the victim. The second level is testimony describing the general characteristics of the syndrome *and* testimony that the complainant's symptoms match or are *consistent with* the syndrome. The third level describes general characteristics of the syndrome, adds that the complainant's symptoms are consistent with the syndrome, *and further adds an opinion that the complainant was raped or, alternatively, is suffering from rape trauma syndrome.* The fourth level is testimony in which the expert adds an opinion bolstering the credibility of the complainant by stating an opinion that the complainant did not fantasize the attack. *See generally* David McCord, *The Admissibility of Expert Testimony Regarding Rape Trauma Syndrome in Rape Prosecutions,* 26 B.C. L. REV. 1143, 1179–80 (1985).

A general description of the syndrome coupled with testimony from the complainant or other lay witness as to the complainant's symptoms and behaviors, with the jury left to determine if the complainant's behavior matches the syndrome, is not controversial. The second level, allowing the expert to say that the complainant's behaviors were *consistent with* rape trauma syndrome or a traumatic experience, also appears to be admissible. *See, e.g., Hall v. State,* 670 A.2d 962, 967 (Md. 1996) (prosecutor's question concerning whether the victim's disorders "were consistent"with disorders in children who had been sexually abused proper); *State v. McCoy,* 366 S.E.2d 731, 736–37 (W.Va. 1988) (expert testimony regarding the existence of symptoms "consistent with rape trauma syndrome is relevant and admissible."); *State v. Galindo,* 973 S.W.2d. 574, 576 (Mo. App. 1998) ("[M]ost the doctor could have testified to was that the victim's symptoms were consistent with a traumatic experience, even a stressful sexual experience, but [expert] could not say that [the victim] was raped. . . .")

The third level of expert specificity — expert opinion including a conclusion that the alleged victim was raped or was suffering from rape trauma syndrome — presents admissibility problems. *See Hutton v. State,* 663 A.2d 1289, 1301 (Md. 1995) ("Testimony by an expert that the alleged victim suffered from post traumatic stress disorder as a result of sexual abuse goes beyond the limits of proper expert expression."); *People v. Coleman,* 768 P.2d 32, 49 (Cal. 1989) (expert testimony that "complaining witness is suffering from rape trauma syndrome . . . is likely to mislead the jury into inferring that such a classification reflects a scientific judgment that the witness was, in fact raped.").

Finally, courts generally prohibit expert testimony that can be construed as a direct comment on the credibility of the alleged victim. *State v. Brodniak*, 718 P.2d 322, 327–29 (Mont. 1982). Testimony that the victim was raped or did not fantasize the incident falls into this category. *See State v. Taylor*, 663 S.W.2d 235, 239 (Mo.1984) (expert opines that victim did not fantasize the incident; inadmissible as a direct comment on credibility); *State v. McCoy*, 366 S.E.2d 731, 737 (W.Va. 1988) (expert opinion based upon rape trauma syndrome that victim "was indeed raped" inadmissible for impermissibly bolstering the credibility of the victim).

6. *Syndromes Developed as Therapeutic Tools.* Does the purpose for which the syndrome was originally developed have any bearing on its admissibility? Consider the following passage from *People v. Bledsoe*, 681 P.2d 291 (Cal. 1984), in which the California Supreme Court rejected the use of rape trauma syndrome testimony on the issue of consent:

> [I]n this case, the prosecution introduced the rape trauma syndrome testimony, not to rebut misconceptions about the presumed behavior of rape victims, but rather as a means of proving — from the alleged victim's post-incident trauma — that a rape in the legal sense had, in fact, occurred. . . .
>
> Unlike fingerprints, blood tests, lie detector tests, voiceprints or the battered child syndrome, rape trauma syndrome was not devised to determine the "truth" or "accuracy" of a particular past event — i.e., whether, in fact, a rape in the legal sense occurred — but rather was developed by professional rape counselors as a therapeutic tool, to help identify, predict and treat emotional problems experienced by the counselors' clients or patients. As the professional literature makes clear — and as the expert testimony in this case also reveals — because in the past women who have brought charges of rape have traditionally had their credibility or motives questioned by the police and others, rape counselors are taught to make a conscious effort to avoid judging the credibility of their clients. . . .
>
> Thus, as a rule, rape counselors do not probe inconsistencies in their clients' descriptions of the facts of the incident, nor do they conduct independent investigations to determine whether other evidence corroborates or contradicts their clients' renditions. Because their function is to help their clients deal with the trauma they are experiencing, the historical accuracy of the clients' descriptions of the details of the traumatizing events is not vital in their task. To our knowledge, all of the studies that have been conducted in this field to date have analyzed data that have been gathered through this counseling process and, as far as we are aware, none of the studies has attempted independently to verify the "truth" of the clients' recollections or to determine the legal implication of the clients' factual accounts.
>
> . . . .
>
> Given the history, purpose and nature of the rape trauma syndrome concept, we conclude that expert testimony that a complaining witness suffers from rape trauma syndrome is not admissible to prove that the witness was raped. We emphasize that our conclusion in this regard is not intended to suggest that rape trauma syndrome is not generally recognized or used in the general scientific community from which it arose, but only that it is not relied on in that community for the purpose for which the prosecution sought to use it in this case, namely, to prove that a rape in fact occurred. Because the literature does

not even purport to claim that the syndrome is a scientifically reliable means of proving that a rape occurred, we conclude that it may not properly be used for that purpose in a criminal trial.

People v. Bledsoe, 681 P.2d 291, 299–301 (Cal. 1984).

PROBLEMS

Problem 5-3. Consider the situation sometimes referred to as "date rape." The defendant asserts mistake of fact as a defense; i.e., he admits that sexual intercourse took place and he does not contest the complaining witness' assertions that she did not consent. Rather, the defendant contends that he had an honest and reasonable (but mistaken) belief that the complainant consented to sexual intercourse. Should expert testimony of rape trauma syndrome be admitted in such a case? On what issue? If it is admissible, what would you allow the expert to say in addition to describing the syndrome? *See People v. Bledsoe*, 681 P.2d 291, 300 n.12 (Cal. 1984).

If the defendant asserted an alibi defense, would testimony of rape trauma syndrome be admissible?

If the case is a civil case where the victim is seeking damages, would the expert testimony be relevant? On what issue?

Problem 5-4. Consider the situation where the complaining witness claims to have been raped at knife point, but the defense is that no sexual activity took place at all. Is testimony from an expert about rape trauma syndrome admissible? On what issue? The problem below is based upon such a case.

A police officer on a routine patrol came upon the defendant emerging from a wooded area with his pants down. A partially dressed woman was standing nearby. When the woman saw the police officer, she ran toward him and stated that she had been raped at knife point.

The woman claimed that the defendant, an acquaintance, was giving her a ride home when he pulled off the road, threatened her with a switchblade knife, and forced her to have intercourse. When she (falsely) told him she had gonorrhea, he stopped raping her and forced her to perform oral sex. She states that she ran toward the lights of the police car as it went by.

Defendant claims that he stopped the car to go urinate and the complainant followed him into the woods. She began unbuttoning her shirt and asked for sex. He declined because he was feeling sick from having had too much to drink, and the complainant, furious, left the woods. He emerged from the woods and saw the patrol car there. When the defendant was arrested, the police found a switchblade knife in his pocket. All of the state's tests on hair and saliva samples, and a physical examination of the victim, fail to confirm that sex took place.

A doctor at the hospital where the complaining witness was taken had undergone training in rape trauma syndrome and, in fact, was a trained rape counselor. The doctor testified that the complaining witness was emotional and tearful but able to describe the incident. Further, the doctor testified that the complainant's emotional state was consistent with rape trauma syndrome, and that she believed that the complainant had been raped.

The defendant is convicted and appeals, asserting that no sexual activity took place and that the expert testimony on rape trauma syndrome should not have been admitted. Assume that the trial took place in a state that follows *State v. Marks.* How should the appellate court rule? *See State v. Bressman*, 689 P.2d 901, 907–08 (Kan. 1984); *State v. Hall*, 412 S.E.2d 883, 889 (N.C. 1992).

Problem 5-5. If the defendant in *Marks* had evidence that the victim had prior unpleasant sexual experiences, would he be allowed to question the victim on the witness stand about these experiences? Why would such testimony be relevant? If admissible, does that mean that admitting evidence of rape trauma syndrome erodes the protections afforded by rape shield statutes like Fed. R. Evid. 412? *See* Susan Stefan, *The Protection Racket: Rape Trauma Syndrome, Psychiatric Labeling and Law*, 88 NW. U. L. REV. 1271, 1324–27 (1994); David McCord, *The Admissibility of Expert Testimony Regarding Rape Trauma Syndrome in Rape Prosecutions*, 26 B.C. L. REV. 1143, 1209 (1985).

[b]   Rape Trauma Syndrome: Offered by the Prosecution to Explain the Victim's Behavior

Sometimes a defendant in a rape case will offer evidence of the alleged victim's post-incident conduct and assert that such conduct is inconsistent with the victim's claim of rape. Those jurisdictions that do not accept testimony of rape trauma syndrome to establish lack of consent tend to be more open to receiving such evidence when offered to rebut evidence offered by the defendant. In the next case, *People v. Taylor*, the New York Court of Appeals finds that rape trauma syndrome is not admissible to prove that a rape occurred, and then deals with whether such testimony is admissible for the apparently more limited purpose of explaining conduct of the complainant that would seem to be inconsistent with a rape.

PEOPLE v. TAYLOR
PEOPLE v. BANKS
552 N.Y.S.2d 883 (N.Y. 1990)

WACHTLER, CHIEF JUDGE.

In these two cases, we consider whether expert testimony that a complaining witness has exhibited behavior consistent with "rape trauma syndrome" is admissible at the criminal trial of the person accused of the rape. Both trial courts admitted the testimony and the Appellate Division affirmed in both cases. . . . While we recognize that the unchecked admission of expert testimony in this area has peculiar dangers, we believe that under certain circumstances and subject to certain limitations evidence of rape trauma syndrome is both relevant and admissible. We believe, however, that the trial court in *Banks* erred in allowing the expert to testify under the facts present in that case.

I. *People v. Taylor*

On July 29, 1984, the complainant, a 19-year-old Long Island resident, reported to the town police that she had been raped and sodomized at gunpoint on a deserted beach near her home. The complainant testified that at about nine that evening she had received a phone call from a friend, telling her that he was in trouble and asking her to meet him at a nearby market in half an hour. Twenty minutes later, the same person called back and changed the meeting place. The complainant arrived at the agreed-upon place, shut off the car engine and waited. She saw a man approach her car and she unlocked the door to let him in. Only then did she realize that the person who had approached and entered the car was not the friend she had come to meet. According to the complainant, he pointed a gun at her, directed her to nearby Clarke's Beach, and once they were there, raped and sodomized her.

The complainant arrived home around 11:00 P.M., woke her mother and told her about the attack. Her mother then called the police. Sometime between 11:30 P.M. and midnight, the police arrived at the complainant's house. At that time, the complainant told the police she did not know who her attacker was. She was taken to the police station where she described the events leading up to the attack and again repeated that she did not know who her attacker was. At the conclusion of the interview, the complainant was asked to step into a private room to remove the clothes that she had been wearing at the time of the attack so that they could be examined for forensic evidence. While she was alone with her mother, the complainant told her that the defendant John Taylor, had been her attacker. The time was approximately 1:15 A.M. The complainant had known the defendant for years, and she later testified that she happened to see him the night before the attack at a local convenience store.

Her mother summoned one of the detectives and the complainant repeated that the defendant had been the person who attacked her. The complainant said that she was sure that it had been the defendant because she had had ample opportunity to see his face during the incident. . . . He was arrested on July 31, 1984, and was indicted by the Grand Jury on one count of rape in the first degree, two counts of sodomy in the first degree and one count of sexual abuse in the first degree.

The defendant's first trial ended without the jury being able to reach a verdict. At his second trial, the Judge permitted Eileen Treacy, an instructor at the City University of New York, Herbert Lehman College, with experience in counseling sexual assault victims, to testify about rape trauma syndrome. The prosecutor introduced this testimony for two separate purposes. First, Treacy's testimony on the specifics of rape trauma syndrome explained why the complainant might have been unwilling during the first few hours after the attack to name the defendant as her attacker where she had known the defendant prior to the incident. Second, Treacy's testimony that it was common for a rape victim to appear quiet and controlled following an attack, responded to evidence that the complainant had appeared calm after the attack and tended to rebut the inference that because she was not excited and upset after the attack, it had not been a rape. At the close of the second trial, the defendant was convicted. . . .

II. *People v. Banks*

On July 7, 1986, the defendant Ronnie Banks approached the 11-year-old complainant, who was playing with her friends in the City of Rochester. The complainant testified that the defendant told her to come to him and when she did not, he grabbed her by the arm and pulled her down the street. According to the complainant, the defendant took her into a neighborhood garage where he sexually assaulted her. The complainant returned to her grandmother's house, where she was living at the time. The next morning, she told her grandmother about the incident and the police were contacted. The defendant was arrested and charged with three counts involving forcible compulsion —rape in the first degree, sodomy in the first degree and sexual abuse in the first degree — and four counts that were based solely on the age of the victim — rape in the second degree, sodomy in the second degree, sexual abuse in the second degree and endangering the welfare of a child.

At trial, the complainant testified that the defendant had raped and sodomized her. In addition, she and her grandmother both testified about the complainant's behavior following the attack. Their testimony revealed that the complainant had been suffering from nightmares, had been waking up in the middle of the night in a cold sweat, had been afraid to return to school in the fall, had become generally more fearful and had been running and staying away from home. Following the introduction of this evidence, the prosecution sought to introduce expert testimony about the symptoms associated with rape trauma syndrome.

Clearly, the prosecution, in an effort to establish that forcible sexual contact had in fact occurred, wanted to introduce this evidence to show that the complainant was demonstrating behavior that was consistent with patterns of response exhibited by rape victims. The prosecutor does not appear to have introduced this evidence to counter the inference that the complainant consented to the incident, since the 11-year-old complainant is legally incapable of consent. Unlike *Taylor*, the evidence was not offered to explain behavior exhibited by the victim that the jury might not understand; instead, it was offered to show that the behavior that the complainant had exhibited after the incident was consistent with a set of symptoms commonly associated with women who had been forcibly attacked. The clear implication of such testimony would be that because the complainant exhibited these symptoms, it was more likely than not that she had been forcibly raped.

The Judge permitted David Gandell, an obstetrician-gynecologist on the faculty of the University of Rochester, Strong Memorial Hospital, with special training in treating victims of sexual assault, to testify as to the symptoms commonly associated with rape trauma syndrome. After Gandell had described rape trauma syndrome he testified hypothetically that the kind of symptoms demonstrated by the complainant were consistent with a diagnosis of rape trauma syndrome. At the close of the trial, the defendant was acquitted of all forcible counts and was convicted on the four statutory counts. He was sentenced to indeterminate terms of 3½ to 7 years on the rape and sodomy convictions and to definite one-year terms on the convictions of sexual abuse in the second degree and endangering the welfare of a child.

III. *Rape Trauma Syndrome*

In a 1974 study rape trauma syndrome was described as "the acute phase and long-term reorganization process that occurs as a result of forcible rape or attempted forcible rape. This syndrome of behavioral, somatic, and psychological reactions is an acute stress reaction to a life-threatening situation" (Burgess & Holmstrom, *Rape Trauma Syndrome*, 131 Am. J. Psychiatry 981, 982 [1974]). Although others had studied the reactions of rape victims prior to this publication, the Burgess and Holmstrom identification of two separate phases in a rape victim's recovery has proven enormously influential.

. . . .

. . . The question before us today . . . is whether [rape trauma] syndrome, which has been the subject of study and discussion for the past 16 years, can be introduced before a lay jury as relevant evidence in these two rape trials.

We realize that rape trauma syndrome encompasses a broad range of symptoms and varied patterns of recovery. Some women are better able to cope with the aftermath of sexual assault than other women. It is also apparent that there is no single typical profile of a rape victim and that different victims express themselves and come to terms with the experience of rape in different ways. We are satisfied, however, that the relevant scientific community has generally accepted that rape is a highly traumatic event that will in many women trigger the onset of certain identifiable symptoms (*see Frye v. United States*, 293 F. 1013 (D.C. Cir.); *People v. Hughes*, 453 N.E.2d 484).

We note that the American Psychiatric Association has listed rape as one of the stressors that can lead to posttraumatic stress disorder (American Psychiatric Association, Diagnostic & Statistical Manual of Mental Disorders 247, 248 [3d ed. rev. 1987] [DSM III-R]). According to DSM III-R, there is an identifiable pattern of responses that can follow an intensely stressful event. The victim who suffers from posttraumatic stress disorder will persistently reexperience the traumatic event in a number of ways, as through dreams, flashbacks, hallucinations, or intense distress at exposure to events that resemble or symbolize the traumatic event. The victim will also avoid stimuli that he or she associates with the trauma. Finally, the victim will experience "persistent symptoms of increased arousal," which could include difficulty in falling or staying asleep, sudden outbursts of anger, or difficulty concentrating. While the diagnostic criteria for posttraumatic stress disorder that are contained in DSM III-R have convinced us that the scientific community has accepted that rape as a stressor can have marked, identifiable effects on a victim's behavior, we would further note that although rape trauma syndrome can be conceptualized as a posttraumatic stress disorder, victims of rape will often exhibit peculiar symptoms — like a fear of men — that are not commonly exhibited by victims of other sorts of trauma.

We are aware that rape trauma syndrome is a therapeutic and not a legal concept. Physicians and rape counselors who treat victims of sexual assault are not charged with the responsibility of ascertaining whether the victim is telling the truth when she says that a rape occurred. That is part of the truth-finding process implicated in a criminal trial. We do not believe, however, that the therapeutic origin of the syndrome renders it unreliable for trial purposes. Thus, although we acknowledge that evidence of rape trauma syndrome does not by itself prove that the complainant was raped, we believe that this should not preclude its admissibility into evidence at trial when relevance to a particular disputed issue has been demonstrated.

IV. *The Law*

Having concluded that evidence of rape trauma syndrome is generally accepted within the relevant scientific community, we must now decide whether expert testimony in this area would aid a lay jury in reaching a verdict. . . .

. . . [R]ape is a crime that is permeated by misconceptions. Society and law are finally realizing that it is an act of violence and not a sexual act. . . . Studies have shown that one of the most popular misconceptions about rape is that the victim by behaving in a certain way brought it on herself. For that reason, studies have demonstrated that jurors will under certain circumstances blame the victim for the attack and will refuse to convict the man accused. Studies have also shown that jurors will infer consent where the victim has engaged in certain types of behavior prior to the incident.

. . . .

Because cultural myths still affect common understanding of rape and rape victims and because experts have been studying the effects of rape upon its victims only since the 1970's, we believe that patterns of response among rape victims are not within the ordinary understanding of the lay juror. For that reason, we conclude that introduction of expert testimony describing rape trauma syndrome may under certain circumstances assist a lay jury in deciding issues in a rape trial.

In reaching our conclusions in this area, we note that an extensive body of case law has developed concerning the admissibility of this type of evidence. There is no uniform approach to the admission of evidence of rape trauma syndrome among the States that have considered the question. . . .

. . . .

Among those States that have allowed such testimony to be admitted, the purpose for which the testimony was offered has proven crucial. A number of States have allowed testimony of rape trauma syndrome to be admitted where the defendant concedes that sexual intercourse occurred, but contends that it was consensual. . . .

Other States have permitted the admission of this testimony where it was offered to explain behavior exhibited by the complainant that might be viewed as inconsistent with a claim of rape. . . .

Having concluded that evidence of rape trauma syndrome can assist jurors in reaching a verdict by dispelling common misperceptions about rape, and having reviewed the different approaches taken by the other jurisdictions that have considered the question, we, too, agree that the reason why the testimony is offered will determine its helpfulness, its relevance and its potential for prejudice. In the two cases now before us, testimony regarding rape trauma syndrome was offered for entirely different purposes. We conclude that its admission at the trial of John Taylor was proper, but that its admission at the trial of Ronnie Banks was not.

As noted above, the complaining witness in *Taylor* had initially told the police that she could not identify her assailant. Approximately two hours after she first told her mother that she had been raped and sodomized, she told her mother that she knew the defendant had done it. The complainant had known the defendant for years and had seen him the night before the assault. We hold that under the circumstances present in this case, expert testimony explaining that a rape victim who knows her assailant is more fearful of disclosing his name to the police and is in fact less likely to report the rape at all was relevant to explain why the complainant may have been initially unwilling to report that the defendant had been the man who attacked her. Behavior of this type is not within the ordinary understanding of the jury and testimony explaining this behavior assists the jury in determining what effect to give to the complainant's initial failure to identify the defendant. This evidence provides a possible explanation for the complainant's behavior that is consistent with her claim that she was raped. As such, it is relevant.

Rape trauma syndrome evidence was also introduced in *Taylor* in response to evidence that revealed the complainant had not seemed upset following the attack. We note again in this context that the reaction of a rape victim in the hours following her attack is not something within the common understanding of the average lay juror. Indeed, the defense would clearly want the jury to infer that because the victim was not upset following the attack, she must not have been raped. This inference runs contrary to the studies cited earlier, which suggest that half of all women who have been forcibly raped are controlled and subdued following the attack. Thus, we conclude that evidence of this type is relevant to dispel misconceptions that jurors might possess regarding the ordinary responses of rape victims in the first hours after their attack. We do not believe that evidence of rape trauma syndrome, when admitted for that express purpose, is unduly prejudicial.

The admission of expert testimony describing rape trauma syndrome in *Banks*, however, was clearly error. As we noted earlier, this evidence was not offered to explain behavior that might appear unusual to a lay juror not ordinarily familiar with the patterns of response exhibited by rape victims. We conclude that evidence of rape trauma syndrome is inadmissible when it inescapably bears solely on proving that a rape occurred, as was the case here.

Although we have accepted that rape produces identifiable symptoms in rape victims, we do not believe that evidence of the presence, or indeed of the absence, of those symptoms necessarily indicates that the incident did or did not occur. Because introduction of rape trauma syndrome evidence by an expert might create such an inference in the minds of lay jurors, we find that the defendant would be unacceptably prejudiced by the introduction of rape trauma syndrome evidence for that purpose alone. We emphasize again that the therapeutic nature of the syndrome does not preclude its admission into evidence under all circumstances. We believe, however, that its usefulness as a fact-finding device is limited and that where it is introduced to prove the crime took place, its helpfulness is outweighed by the possibility of undue prejudice. Therefore, the trial court erred in permitting the admission of expert testimony regarding rape trauma syndrome under the facts present in *Banks*.

On this record, we cannot conclude that the introduction of the evidence of rape trauma syndrome evidence in *People v. Banks* was harmless error. Accordingly, in *People v. Banks*, the order of the Appellate Division should be reversed and a new trial ordered.

In *People v. Taylor*: Order affirmed.

In *People v. Banks*: Order reversed and a new trial ordered.

NOTE

Rape Trauma Syndrome Used to Explain Victim Behavior: Examples. Most (if not all) courts, even those that reject rape trauma syndrome testimony on the issue of consent, have permitted such testimony if offered to explain victim behavior. *See, e.g., People v. Bledsoe*, 681 P.2d 291, 298 (Cal. 1984). In addition to the situation described in *Taylor*, courts have permitted expert testimony about rape trauma syndrome to explain lack of resistance during an attack, *Perez v. State*, 653 S.W.2d 878, 882 (Tex. Crim. App. 1983), delay in reporting attack, *State v. Roles*, 832 P.2d 311, 318 (Idaho Ct. App. 1992), and why the victim may return for further contact with her attacker if the victim was in a previous trust relationship with her attacker, *Commonwealth v. Mamay*, 553 N.E.2d 945, 951 (Mass. 1990). *See also Pulinario v. Goord*, 291 F. Supp. 2d 154, 159–60, 181 (E.D.N.Y. 2003) (granting habeas corpus petition; holding woman charged with murder had a constitutional right to present evidence that she was suffering from RTS at the time she shot and killed the man who, she claimed, had previously raped her).

QUESTION

If a complainant exhibits behavior that may appear to the jury to be inconsistent with having been raped (e.g., not resisting, delay in reporting attack, calm demeanor after attack, etc.), may the prosecutor offer rape trauma testimony *in the prosecution's case in chief*, or must the state wait until the accused uses the "unusual" behavior of the victim as probative of either consent or that no sex occurred at all? Does offering such evidence in the prosecution's case in chief constitute rehabilitating a witness who has not had her credibility attacked? *See State v. Roles*, 832 P.2d 311, 318 (Idaho Ct. App. 1992) (proper for state to offer rape trauma syndrome testimony in its case in chief since defendant's counsel brought complainant's behavior before the jury in his opening statement); *People v. Hampton*, 746 P.2d 947, 948–49 (Colo. 1987) (admissible after defense cross-examines victim); *Cf. Commonwealth v. Mamay*, 553 N.E.2d. 945, 951 (Mass. 1990) (no defense objection noted to offering expert testimony to explain behavior in case in chief).

PROBLEMS

Problem 5-6. Four years ago a man dressed as a police officer gained entry into a woman's home on the pretense of being on police business. He thereafter raped the woman at gunpoint and beat her. The victim immediately called the police and reported the crime. There is no dispute that a violent, forcible rape took place.

Two weeks after the attack the police called the victim to the police station to look at photos that included the defendant, a man named Gallagher. She could not identify Gallagher as her attacker. She then (the same day) went to the police station and was asked to look at Gallagher but could not identify him as her attacker.

Four years later the victim again looked at photographs at the police station. This time she picked Gallagher out as her attacker. Gallagher was charged with rape.

At trial, in front of the jury, the victim identified Gallagher as her attacker. On cross-examination of the victim, Gallagher's attorney attacked the identification as unreliable because she (the victim) could not identify the defendant two weeks after the crime. On rebuttal the prosecution called an expert on rape trauma syndrome. She testified that the victim has rape trauma syndrome and that two weeks after the rape, when she was asked to identify her attacker, she was in an acute phase and was not able to perform normal day-to-day functions, so it is understandable that she would have difficulty in identifying her attacker at that time. Furthermore, the expert testifies, an identification four years later is "particularly credible" because it occurred after the acute phase and resulted from a flashback, in which traumatic events that have been "actively stored in the mind" come flooding back into consciousness.

The expert testimony is admitted and the defendant is convicted. Was the expert testimony properly admitted? *See Commonwealth v. Gallagher*, 547 A.2d 355, 357–58 (Pa. 1988).

Problem 5-7. A State Police officer is charged with rape. His defense is that he stopped the victim's car for erratic driving but that nothing happened after that. The victim's story is that she was driving to a wedding when she was pulled over by the defendant, a uniformed police officer, operating a State Police vehicle. Defendant approached her car and asked for her license and registration. Defendant told her that she had failed to signal when she was changing lanes and had been driving erratically. He instructed her to get out of her car and walk a straight line toward his car. She complied, and he told her to get into his car. Defendant then told her she could be in serious trouble and referred to possible charges of driving while intoxicated that could be brought against her.

The victim stated that she drank one or two beers two hours earlier. The defendant instructed her to blow in his face. After she did so he put his mouth on hers, drew her toward him, and put his hand down her blouse. When she asked what he was doing, the defendant put his mouth on hers again. The victim, who had observed that defendant had a gun, stated that she froze in fear. Defendant then told her he was going to "make it" with her and that he had to go to the State Police barracks to get a condom. Apparently thinking she might be able to get away, the victim suggested that she drive her car. Defendant agreed but he kept her license and registration and directed her to follow him. Fearing he would follow her if she escaped, she complied. Upon arriving at the barracks, defendant took the victim by the hand and placed her in his car. He then went into the barracks. The victim said she was still frozen with fear because she did not know if the defendant had friends in the barracks who knew what he was doing. Defendant returned to his car and drove to a deserted area. Defendant then raped, sodomized, and sexually assaulted her. Afterward, defendant drove the victim back to her car, and she left.

The victim went to the wedding as planned and did not tell anyone about the assault. After being unable to eat or sleep for one week, the victim called a rape crisis hotline and eventually gave them permission to make a report to the State Police. There is no physical evidence to support that a rape took place.

Defendant was indicted, tried, and found guilty of rape. Defendant testifies that no attack took place and questions the credibility of the victim's story because the victim did not try to escape before the rape and she did not report the rape for one week. The victim's testimony at trial was as described above.

In addition to presenting the victim's testimony, the prosecution called an expert witness on rebuttal to testify regarding rape trauma syndrome. She was asked to assume certain facts about a hypothetical woman. The hypothetical involved the victim's version of the facts from the stop of her vehicle until defendant's first advances. The expert was asked how the hypothetical woman would react. The expert said that the victim would react by doing exactly as she was told because of various factors such as the authority figure, the gun, the order, and her view of this as something she must do. The expert stated that this hypothetical woman would not try to escape because of fear and stress about what else the officer might do.

The expert was then asked about what happened *after* the attack. The expert stated that the woman would probably not report the incident because of "fear of who this person [her attacker] was."

The defendant claims that the trial court erred in admitting the expert testimony concerning rape trauma syndrome to explain the victim's behavior.

(A) Was testimony about the victim's behavior *before* the attack admissible?

(B) Was testimony about the victim's behavior *afterwards* (the delay in reporting the attack) admissible? *See New York v. Bennett*, 593 N.E.2d 279, 283–85 (N.Y. 1992).

[c]   Rape Trauma Syndrome: Offered by the Defense

What if a *defendant* calls an expert to testify that the alleged victim did not exhibit any of the symptoms of rape trauma syndrome? May expert testimony be used as a shield as well as a sword? The *Henson* case below examines this issue.

HENSON v. STATE
535 N.E.2d 1189 (Ind. 1989)

DEBRULER, JUSTICE.

Defendant Rickey J. Henson was convicted in a jury trial of Rape, . . . Criminal Deviate Conduct, . . . Criminal Confinement, and Battery. . . . He was sentenced to fifteen years for Rape, forty-five years for Criminal Deviate Conduct, both of which were to be served concurrently, fifteen years for Criminal Confinement and five years for Battery, both of which were to be served consecutive to each other as well as to the first two sentences.

On appeal, Henson argues that . . . the trial court erred by not allowing the testimony of an expert witness that the victim's conduct after the alleged rape was inconsistent with that of a person who had suffered a traumatic forcible rape. . . .

The facts which tend to support the conviction are as follows: Henson was at a crowded bar in Kokomo and asked J.O., who was sitting alone, if he could join her. She consented and the two exchanged names, but otherwise did not speak. Two other men joined them at the table and J.O. danced with them during the course of the evening but not with Henson. J.O. stayed at the bar until it closed and then left to have more drinks at the home of one of the bar's waitresses. After she got in her car, but before she could shut the door, Henson approached her with a knife, pushed her over to the passenger's seat, got in the car and drove to a secluded place. He then forced her to have sexual intercourse with him as well as oral sex. He also attempted to cut her blouse off with the knife and J.O. received superficial lacerations as a result. The next evening, J.O. returned to the same bar where she stayed for two hours and drank.

At trial, one witness testified that J.O. was drinking as well as dancing on the evening after the rape allegedly occurred. Defendant then called a psychologist, Dr. David Gover, and established that the witness was an expert in the study and treatment of post-traumatic stress syndrome. Defendant's counsel then asked the following question:

Q.   Doctor, in your professional opinion, a person who has allegedly suffered
            a traumatic, forcible rape, would it be consistent in your experience that
            a person who had gone through a situation such as that would go back to
            the same place the act allegedly occurred and socialize, drink, dance, on
            the same day of the alleged act?

After establishing that Dr. Gover had never consulted with J.O. personally and that he had no firsthand knowledge of the incident in question, the prosecution objected to the question. The objection was sustained on the grounds that the testimony was not relevant and that a proper foundation had not been laid. There followed a lengthy offer to prove, out of the jury's presence, in which the objection was again sustained on the grounds that the testimony was too speculative.

The testimony of Dr. Gover would clearly have been relevant to the issues at trial. Evidence is relevant if it is material and has probative value. Evidence is material if it is offered to prove a matter in issue. Evidence has probative value if it has any tendency to make the existence of any fact that is of consequence to the determination of the action . . . more or less probable than it would be without the evidence. Here, Dr. Gover's testimony would have tended to prove that J.O.'s behavior after the incident was inconsistent with that of a victim who had suffered a traumatic rape such as that which J.O. recounted. The evidence therefore would have a tendency to make it less probable that a rape in fact occurred, clearly a matter in issue at trial, and was therefore relevant.

Still, where an expert is to give opinion testimony in the form of an answer to a hypothetical question, more than mere relevance is required to make the evidence admissible. A proper foundation must be laid which is two-fold. First, the expert's ability to give such an opinion must be established through testimony showing he has the requisite knowledge, skill, education or experience on which to base the opinion. However, firsthand knowledge of the facts are not required. It is well established in our state that an expert may give opinion testimony even though he does not have personal knowledge of the facts on which his opinion is based. Second, there must be a proper evidentiary foundation supporting the facts that are included in the hypothetical question. That is to say, a hypothetical question is proper if it embraces facts that have been placed into evidence. . . . Additionally, an expert may not testify as to matters which are within the common knowledge and experience of the jurors. This would include testimony directly expressing an opinion as to the credibility of other witnesses, an area well within a juror's common knowledge and experience.

Here both foundations were met. The record indicates that, once counsel for the defendant had fully explored Dr. Gover's credentials, the trial court was fully satisfied with the psychologist's ability to testify. The evidence shows Dr. Gover had worked extensively with patients who had suffered from post-traumatic stress syndrome and these included patients with rape in their backgrounds. Moreover, there was ample evidence to support the facts embraced by the hypothetical question posed to Dr. Gover by defendant's counsel. One witness for the prosecution had testified that J.O. had returned to the bar on the evening after the alleged rape and was drinking and dancing; and J.O. herself admitted she was drinking at the same bar that evening. . . .

   . . . .

The State argues here that the trial court did not abuse its discretion in refusing to allow Dr. Gover to testify because his testimony would have amounted to an opinion as to J.O.'s credibility. We cannot agree. The record shows that Dr. Gover would have testified merely that some of J.O.'s behavior was inconsistent with that of a person who had suffered a traumatic rape. While this would have tended to show that J.O.'s testimony was not credible, it was not direct testimony as to her credibility. All testimony which contradicts one party's version of a set of events raises questions about that party's credibility; however, that does not make the testimony inadmissible. If that were the case, a defendant would be hard pressed to ever present any sort of defense in his own behalf since the core of any defense usually involves a denial that the alleged criminal conduct occurred. Because Dr. Gover would not have expressed a direct opinion as to J.O.'s credibility, his testimony was not inadmissible on this ground.

The State also argues that the testimony was too speculative. . . . [T]he record clearly reflects Dr. Gover's competence to give an opinion as to behavior of the victim without having interviewed her. On cross-examination, he stated that it would not have been particularly helpful to talk with the victim since he was merely making a general observation that certain behavior, of which there was evidence from previous testimony, was inconsistent with post-traumatic stress syndrome. To argue that evidence is too speculative is to say merely that it is lacking in probative value. There is little doubt that an alleged rape victim's conduct after the fact is probative of whether a rape in fact occurred. The prosecution in this case was clearly aware of this as they introduced testimony regarding J.O.'s behavior after the rape was reported: she was upset, had difficulty sleeping and was shaking when she identified the defendant in a photo lineup. It cannot be said, therefore, that the testimony of Dr. Gover was lacking in probative value. That the expert did not personally interview the victim bears on the weight of the evidence not on its admissibility; and such facts may be brought out by opposing counsel on cross-examination just as any perceived deficiencies in the facts underlying the hypothetical question are brought out.

. . . .

Moreover, this Court has already recognized the admissibility of rape trauma syndrome evidence in [*State v.*] *Simmons.* It would be fundamentally unfair to allow the use of such testimony by the State, as was the case in *Simmons*, and then deny its use by a defendant here. In so holding, we are not unmindful of the considerable body of literature in this area and recent case law in other jurisdictions. The commentators and case law address, for the most part, whether evidence of post-traumatic stress syndrome in the form of rape trauma syndrome should be admissible at all. . . . Since we have already crossed that hurdle our decision here is focused more on the issue above: whether, having allowed a trial court to admit such testimony when offered by the State to prove a rape was committed, we can say it is not an abuse of discretion to exclude it when offered by a defendant to prove that one was not. We conclude, in light of our decision in *Simmons*, that to bar the defendant from presenting such evidence exceeds the discretion of the trial court; and, in this case, the trial court's ruling impinged upon the substantial rights of appellant to present a defense and was reversible error.

. . . .

The judgment of the trial court is accordingly vacated and this case is remanded for a new trial.

PROBLEMS

Problem 5-8. Assume that you are in a state that allows evidence of rape trauma syndrome on the issue of consent. The state, in a rape prosecution, does *not* plan to offer any evidence on rape trauma syndrome. The defendant, however, wishes to offer evidence that the victim is not suffering from rape trauma syndrome to support the defense theory that sexual intercourse was consensual. The defense makes a motion to compel the victim to see a psychiatrist so that the psychiatrist can testify that the victim does not have rape trauma syndrome.

(A) Should the defense be able to compel the victim to be examined by a psychiatrist? Does your answer depend upon whether the state seeks to offer such evidence? See *Clark v. Commonwealth*, 551 S.E.2d 642, 644 (Va. 2001); *Gilpin v. McCormick*, 921 F.2d 928, 931 (9th Cir. 1990); *State v. Liddell*, 685 P.2d 918 (Mont. 1984); *State v. McQuillen*, 689 P.2d 822, 827, 830 (Kan. 1984); *Lickey v. State*, 827 P.2d 824, 826 (Nev. 1992); *People v. Wheeler*, 602 N.E.2d 826, 832–33 (Ill. 1992).

(B) Assume that the trial court does not allow the defense expert to examine the victim before trial. Can the defense attorney ask the victim on cross-examination if she has had sex since the attack? If so, can the defense attorney ask how many times the victim has had sex since the attack? If so, why is the victim's post-attack sex life relevant? *See State v. Jones*, 615 N.E.2d 713, 718–19 (Ohio Ct. App. 1992).

As a matter of policy, should the defendant be allowed to "invade the victim's privacy" in such a way? *See* Jennifer J. Hackman, Comment, Henson v. State: *Rape Trauma Syndrome Used by the Defendant as Well as the Victim*, 19 AM. J. TRIAL ADVOC. 453, 464 (1995); Nicole Rosenberg Economou, Note, *Defense Expert Testimony on Rape Trauma Syndrome: Implications for the Stoic Victim*, 42 HASTINGS L. J. 1143, 1169–70 (April 1991); Susan Stefan, *The Protection Racket: Rape Trauma Syndrome, Psychiatric Labeling and Law*, 88 NW. U. L. REV. 1271, 1328–29 (1994). *Compare* Fed. R. Evid. 412.

Problem 5-9. Defendant, a male, is charged with grand larceny and extortion. The state claims that the defendant had consensual homosexual relations with the victim and thereafter threatened to expose the victim as a homosexual if the victim did not pay him $5,000. Defendant claims that he was the victim of homosexual rape and that he (the defendant) demanded $5,000 from the complaining witness in the form of compensation for the "wrong" the complaining witness did to him.

To support his claim that he was raped and to explain why he did not report the alleged rape to the police, the defendant is prepared to call an expert witness to testify that he (the defendant) is suffering from rape trauma syndrome, or "male sexual victimization syndrome." Should the evidence be allowed? If so, what foundation must be presented? *See People v. Yates*, 637 N.Y.S.2d 625 (N.Y. Sup. Ct. 1995); *State v. Borchardt*, 478 N.W.2d 757 (Minn. 1991).

[2]   Child Sexual Abuse Syndrome

The evidentiary issues that accompany expert testimony based upon the child sexual abuse syndrome are similar to the evidentiary issues just encountered with rape trauma syndrome. This is because expert testimony based upon either syndrome is most helpful in the same type of case — where it is difficult to prove that any unlawful sexual contact ever occurred. In adult rape cases this type of case occurs when there are no signs of physical injury, and the defendant admits sexual intercourse occurred but claims that the victim consented. One commentator described how proving unlawful sexual contact occurred can be a problem in cases of child sexual abuse:

> The sexual offender is often a relative or a trusted adult with whom the child spends time alone. Eyewitnesses to the molestation are therefore rare. In addition, sexual abuse is typically a nonviolent crime. Children who are abused by a trusted adult usually are manipulated psychologically and do not resist their abusers. Physical injury can provide valuable medical evidence of the sexual abuse, but this evidence is often lacking because the abuse is committed without force. Furthermore, the sexual abuse may involve an act other than penetration of the vagina or anus. Crimes such as petting, fondling, or oral copulation usually do not involve forceful physical contact and do not leave physical scars. A lapse of time between the sexual abuse and disclosure may also contribute to the lack of medical evidence.[33] [2]

---

[33] Kathy L. Hensley, Note, *The Admissibility of "Child Sexual Abuse Accommodation Syndrome" in*

As one might expect, rape trauma syndrome and child sexual abuse syndrome expert testimony are typically offered for similar reasons: (1) to prove that nonconsensual sex occurred — in the case of a child, to prove that a sex act occurred (whether consensual or not); (2) to explain conduct of the victim that a jury may perceive as inconsistent with having been sexually attacked or abused; and (3) to support the credibility of the victim. This latter point is particularly important when the victim is a young child and has difficulty expressing what happened.

Courts that admit expert testimony on child sexual abuse syndrome vary on what they will allow the expert to say. As with rape trauma syndrome, there are four levels of expert testimony regarding child sexual abuse syndrome: (1) narrative testimony concerning the characteristics of the syndrome; (2) narrative testimony on the general characteristics of the syndrome coupled with an opinion that the child displayed characteristics *consistent with* the syndrome; (3) an opinion that the child is, in fact, the victim of child sexual abuse or is suffering from child sexual abuse syndrome; and (4) an opinion that bolsters the victim's credibility by asserting that the child is "telling the truth."[34]

There are, however, noteworthy differences between the two syndromes that play a significant role in determining admissibility. First, expert testimony on child sexual abuse syndrome is not offered on the issue of consent. It is offered as proof that the alleged sexual abuse *actually occurred*. Unlike adult rape cases, in child sexual abuse cases, consent to sexual contact is not a defense because a child is legally incapable of giving consent for such conduct.

Second, and perhaps most significantly, there is disagreement over just what characteristics constitute child sexual abuse syndrome. The Utah Supreme Court noted this problem in a 1989 case that concluded that it was reversible error to admit expert testimony of child sexual abuse syndrome:

> [T]he child abuse profile consists of a long list of vague and sometimes conflicting psychological characteristics that are relied upon to establish the fact of injury in a specific case as well as the cause. And neither the record nor our independent research demonstrates that there is general acceptance of child abuse profile evidence as a determinant of abuse either by the legal community . . . or by the scientific community.
>
> . . . .
>
> [S]uffice it to say, then, that the literature in the area is disparate and contradictory and that child abuse experts have been unable to agree on a universal symptomology of sexual abuse, especially a precise symptomology that is sufficiently reliable to be used confidently in a forensic setting as a determinant of abuse.

State v. Rimmasch, 775 P.2d 388, 401 (Utah 1989). Compounding this problem is the fact that, even though most children do react in some way to sexual abuse, approximately 20% of abused children display no observable reactions.[35] Nonetheless, many courts

---

California Criminal Courts, 17 PAC. L.J. 1361, 1368–69 (1986). Copyright © 1986 by the University of the Pacific, McGeorge School of Law. Reprinted by permission.

[34] *See generally* 1 SCIENTIFIC EVIDENCE § 9.05[a], at 536 (4th ed. 2007); David McCord, *The Admissibility of Expert Testimony Regarding Rape Trauma Syndrome in Rape Prosecutions*, 26 B.C. L. REV. 1143, 1179–80 (1985).

[35] John E.B. Myers, Jan Bays, Judith Becker, Lucy Berliner, David L. Corwin & Karen J. Saywitz, *Expert*

admit testimony from experts on child sexual abuse syndrome as probative of the fact that the child was sexually abused. Often these courts do not address the reliability or general acceptance of such syndrome testimony. The *Dunkle* case that follows takes the opposite view and is typical of cases that find such evidence unreliable and inadmissible to prove that child sexual abuse occurred.

COMMONWEALTH v. DUNKLE
602 A.2d 830 (Pa. 1992)

CAPPY, JUSTICE.

We are called upon to decide whether the trial court erred in permitting expert testimony about the behaviors exhibited by children who have been sexually abused . . . in a case in which the appellee was charged with sexual abuse of a minor. Additionally, we must decide whether the expert testimony was properly admitted to explain why sexually abused children may not recall certain details of the assault, to explain why they may not give complete details, and to explain why they may delay reporting the incident. . . .

We hold that expert testimony concerning typical behavior patterns exhibited by sexually abused children should not have been admissible in the case before us. We also hold that it was error to permit an expert to explain why sexually abused children may not recall certain details of the assault, why they may not give complete details, and why they may delay reporting the incident. . . .

FACTUAL AND PROCEDURAL HISTORY

The appellee, Neil Dunkle, was charged with rape, indecent assault, corruption of minors, simple assault and criminal attempt to commit involuntary deviate sexual intercourse. Following a jury trial, he was found guilty of all charges except rape. . . . The acts for which he was convicted concerned a sexual assault upon his teenage stepdaughter.

These charges arose out of a complaint made by the appellee's stepdaughter that in April of 1983, the appellee entered her bathroom while she was showering and, after forcing her to the floor, sexually assaulted her, forced her to engage in oral intercourse, and raped her.

During the trial, the Commonwealth called Susan Slade to testify as an expert witness. [O]ver the objection of the defense, the trial court permitted her to testify. Ms. Slade (who is not a psychiatrist or a psychologist) testified about behavior patterns that occurred in children who had been sexually abused. Additionally, she testified about why a victim would delay reporting an offense, why a victim might be unable to recall exact dates and times of an alleged offense, and why victims of sexual abuse omitted details of the incident when they first told their story. At no time during her testimony did the expert witness relate any of her testimony to the child in question.

According to the complaining witness, the appellee had assaulted her in April, 1983. The victim did not report the offenses to anyone in authority until April, 1986. Additionally, there was testimony that the victim omitted details of the assault when she first reported the incident and was unable to recall specific dates and times.

Testimony in Child Sexual Abuse Litigation, 68 NEB. L. REV. 1, 67 (1989).

In addition to the expert testimony, there was testimony by those who knew the victim concerning changes in her behavior after the alleged assault occurred. . . .

Following the conviction, the appellee appealed and the Superior Court reversed, holding that the expert's testimony was used to buttress the credibility of the victim in violation of *Commonwealth v. Seese*, 517 A.2d 920 (1986). We granted the Commonwealth's petition for allowance of appeal to address the issue of whether the expert witness should have been permitted to testify. . . .

DISCUSSION

In order for us to adequately explain our reasoning, we divide this opinion into [two] sections; the first dealing with the testimony concerning the behavior patterns of sexually abused children — the so-called "Child Sexual Abuse Syndrome." The second section of the opinion addresses the testimony about why children delay reporting incidents of child abuse. . . .

Testimony About the "Child Sexual Abuse Syndrome"

Testimony concerning typical behavior patterns exhibited by sexually abused children is also referred to as the "Sexually Abused Child Syndrome," "the Child Abuse Syndrome," and the "Child Sexual Abuse Accommodation Syndrome."

This Court has long recognized that in order for an expert to testify about a matter, the subject about which the expert will testify must have been "sufficiently established to have gained general acceptance in the particular field in which it belongs." (the so-called "*Frye* standard"). In its brief, the Commonwealth refers to the "Child Abuse Syndrome." This syndrome is an attempt to construct a diagnostic or behavioral profile about sexually abused children. The existence of such a syndrome as either a generally accepted diagnostic tool or as relevant evidence is not supportable. Several commentators note that the so-called "sexual abuse syndrome" is not specific enough to sexually abused children to be accurate.

> The principal flaw with the notion of a specific syndrome is that no evidence indicates that it can discriminate between sexually abused children and those who have experienced other trauma. Because the task of a court is to make such discriminations, this flaw is fatal. In order for a syndrome to have discriminant ability, not only must it appear regularly in a group of children with a certain experience, but it also must not appear in other groups of children who have not had that experience.[36] [2]

According to the literature on the subject, there is no one classical or typical personality profile for abused children. The difficulty with identifying a set of behaviors exhibited by abused children is that abused children react in a myriad of ways that may not only be dissimilar from other sexually abused children, but may be the very same behaviors as children exhibit who are not abused. . . . As another commentator aptly notes:

> [O]ne cannot reliably say that a child exhibiting a certain combination of behaviors has been sexually abused rather than, for instance, physically abused,

---

[36] [n.2] Haugaard & Reppucci, The Sexual Abuse of Children, A Comprehensive Guide to Current Knowledge and Intervention Strategies 177–178 (1988).

neglected, or brought up by psychotic or antisocial parents. Although future research may support identification of victims by their behaviors, such identification is currently not possible.[37] [5]

In the case *sub judice*, the expert testified that the "victim usually experiences initially a lot of fear of the offender, a lot of anger towards the alleged offender." The "victim is usually very confused," "the children initially feel very, very guilty." The expert also testified that the "child is usually very confused over the relationship." The child "frequently expresses many of the positive things that weren't in the relationship." "Child victims of sexual abuse usually have a very low self esteem." Additionally, "children frequently withdraw after the disclosure of sexual abuse, they will isolate themselves [and] not want contact with other people." "[T]hey are not performing as well as they did at school, they are disassociating themselves with common practices or common friends at the school, they're [sic] grades frequently will fall, they have [an] inability to concentrate on their school work."

While all of these behavior patterns may well be typical of sexually abused children, even a layperson would recognize that these behavior patterns are not necessarily unique to sexually abused children. They are common to children whose parents divorce and to psychologically abused children.[38] [7]

. . . .

In [one] study of sexually abused children, the authors remark that *all* maltreated children may react similarly — whether the victims of sexual abuse or another type.

> The degree to which sexually abused children differ from other maltreated children or children from chaotic and violent households may be small. In the best study to date, 267 children were followed prospectively, and 60 to 86 were identified as maltreated at different ages through age 6 years, including 11 sexually abused children. [The study concluded]: *There are more similarities than differences among the groups of maltreated children. . . .* All have difficulty meeting task demands at school, all seem to have an abiding anger, all are unpopular with their peers, and all have difficulty functioning independently in school and laboratory situations. *The problems are not abuse-specific*; [the authors go on to state] [t]he common problems . . . all can be tied to the lack of nurturance. . . . [A]ll [parents] failed to provide sensitive, supportive care for their child.[39] [13]

Based on the foregoing, it is clear that the testimony about the uniformity of behaviors exhibited by sexually abused children is not "sufficiently established to have gained general acceptance in the particular field in which it belongs" and should have been excluded.

---

[37] [n. 5] Haugaard & Reppucci, *supra* note 2, p. 178.

[38] [n.7] In a study on psychologically maltreated children, the authors note the following behaviors that may be exhibited:

> *Children:* feel unloved, inferior, low self-esteem, negative view of the world; anxiety and aggressiveness turned [inward] or outward; inadequate social behavior. *Adolescents:* feeling similar to children's but response may be more severe; may become truants, runaways, destructive, depressed, suicidal. Gabarino, Guttmann & Seeley, *The Psychologically Battered Child* Table 2, Components Involved in Identification of Psychological Maltreatment, 69 (1986).

[39] [n.13] Freidrich, *Psychotherapy of Sexually Abused Children and Their Families*, 25 (1990) (emphasis supplied).

Intertwined with the notion of "general acceptance in the particular field" is the understanding of what constitutes relevant and therefore admissible evidence. We have long held that "[a]ny analysis of the admissibility of a particular type of evidence must start with a threshold inquiry as to its relevance and probative value." . . .

The expert testimony about the behavior patterns exhibited by sexually abused children does not meet this threshold determination. While it may "bear upon a matter in issue," it does not render the desired inference more probable than not. It simply does not render any inference at all. Rather, it merely attempts — in contravention of the rules of evidence — to suggest that the victim was, in fact, exhibiting symptoms of sexual abuse. This is unacceptable.

The expert witness also testified that sexually abused children exhibit the following behaviors: Runaway behavior, anger, rebellion, acting out, becoming promiscuous, getting involved with drugs, alcohol, not doing school work, regression to earlier behavior, suicide attempts or thoughts of suicide, depression, eating disorders, nightmares, and bed wetting. It is virtually impossible to clinically describe the elements of the "child abuse syndrome" with any realistic degree of specificity.[40] [15]

We do not believe that the testimony in question was probative. Clearly, drug and alcohol abuse, eating disorders, low self-esteem and not doing school work are common phenomena not solely related to child abuse. To permit the jury to speculate that they might be, however, violates every notion of what constitutes probative and relevant evidence. It is neither scientifically supportable nor legally supportable. Such a laundry list of possible behaviors does no more than invite speculation and will not be condoned.[41]

---

[40] [15] Richard A. Gardner, M.D., a practicing child psychiatrist, in a recent book entitled *Sex Abuse Hysteria, Salem Witch Trials Revisited* (1991), contends that many normal behaviors are often taken as "evidence" of child abuse, namely bedwetting in young children, nightmares, temper tantrums, and masturbation. *Id.* at 60–65. Furthermore, many of the so-called abnormal behaviors attributed to victims of sexual abuse in fact have "nothing to do with sex abuse." These include "depression, phobias, tics, obsessive compulsive rituals, conduct disorders, antisocial behavior, hyperactivity, attention deficit disorder, headaches, gastrointestinal complaints (nausea, cramps, diarrhea), musculoskeletal complaints, etc." *Id.* at 65.

[41] In her book, *Handbook on Sexual Abuse of Children, Assessment and Treatment Issues,* 77 (1988), Lenore Walker includes a compilation of a study showing what percentage of sexually abused children exhibited what behaviors. This study was funded by the National Institute of Mental Health and was meant to describe the effects of sexual abuse on a sample of 369 sexually abused children.

Table 5.1 Proportion of Abused Sample Exhibiting Checklist Symptoms

Symptom	%Present	Symptom	%Present
Panic/anxiety attacks	5.7	Fearful of abuse stimuli	30.1
Behavioral regression	3.8	Suicidal thoughts or actions	5.7
Runs away/takes off	2.7	Psychosomatic complaints	10.0
Excessive autonomic arousal	4.6	Ritualistic behavior	1.1
Depression	18.7	Indiscriminate affection-giving or receiving	6.5
Withdrawal from usual activity or relations	15.2	Low self-esteem	32.8
Sexually victimizes others	3.0	Places self in dangerous situations	4.9
Generalized fear	11.7	Violent fantasies	2.4
Suicidal attempts	1.9	Emotional upset	22.8
Body image problems	7.9	Prostitution	0.8
Repressed anger/hostility	19.2	Obsessional, repetitive/recurrent thoughts	5.4

. . . .

The damage created by this testimony was also compounded by the testimony about those who knew the child in question. There was testimony admitted about the behaviors exhibited by the child after the alleged incident. As such, the prosecution's introduction of the testimony by those who observed the child served to confirm certain behavior patterns that the expert suggested were exhibited by abused children. Permitting an expert to testify about an unsupportable behavioral profile and then introducing testimony to show that the witness acted in conformance with such a profile is an erroneous method of obtaining a conviction. For this reason, we hold that the expert should not have been permitted to testify about behavior patterns generally exhibited by abused children and that the error requires reversal.

Testimony Concerning Delays in Reporting and Omissions in Reporting

The remainder of the expert witness's testimony concerned explanations for (1) why a sexually abused child would delay reporting the incident to family members; (2) why abused children omit details of the incident; and (3) why a sexually abused child may have an inability to recall dates or times of the incident.

In addition to expert testimony meeting the tests of relevancy and the *Frye* standard of admissibility, expert testimony is admitted only when the subject matter is beyond the knowledge or experience of the average layman. When the issue is one of common knowledge, expert testimony is inadmissible.

It is understood why sexually abused children do not always come forward immediately after the abuse: They are afraid or embarrassed; they are convinced by the abuser not to tell anyone; they attempt to tell someone who does not want to listen; or they do not even know enough to tell someone what has happened. In the case *sub judice*, the expert testified that a "[m]ajor reason would be any threats that were made to the child." Also, she stated that "[t]hey also could not disclose for fear of embarrassment, for fear they are damaged in some way, they are not a perfect person." "[T]hey do not disclose

Symptom	%Present	Symptom	%Present
Daydreaming	13.8		
Major problems with police	0.3	Shoplifting/stealing	2.2
Eating disorders	0.8	Nonacademic school behavior problems	9.2
Psychotic episode	-		
Overly compliant/too anxious to please 20.1	13.8	Nightmares/sleep disorders	
Drug/alcohol abuse	2.2	Inability to form/maintain relationships	8.7
Age-inappropriate sexual behavior	7.9	Academic problems	15.4
		Aggressive behavior	14.4
Hurts self physically	1.4	Inappropriate/destructive peer relationships	7.0
Minor problems with police	3.3	peer relationships	7.0

As this chart graphically demonstrates, sexually abused children (1) cannot be fit into any specific behavior patterns; (2) for every symptom that was exhibited by any percentage, an even larger number do not exhibit that symptom; and (3) not one, single symptom was exhibited by a majority of sexually abused children. Clearly, these types of percentages cannot constitute probative evidence.

out of fear of loss that they may have to leave the home, that someone within the home may have to leave them. . . ." All of these reasons are easily understood by lay people and do not require expert analysis.

. . . .

In the final analysis, the reason for the delay must be ascertained by the jury and is based on the credibility of the child and the attendant circumstance of each case. We believe that the evidence presented through the fact witnesses, coupled with an instruction to the jury that they should consider the reasons why the child did not come forward, including the age and circumstances of the child in the case, are sufficient to provide the jury with enough guidance to make a determination of the importance of prompt complaint in each case.[42] [19] Not only is there no *need* for testimony about the reasons children may not come forward, but permitting it would infringe upon the jury's right to determine credibility.

We are also convinced that sexually abused children may sometimes omit the horrid details of the incident for the same reasons that they do not always promptly report the abuse: fear, embarrassment and coercion by the abusing adult. Additionally, it is often clear that children do not always comprehend what has occurred and the need for complete description of the events. Children often omit details in describing many events, and it is no wonder that they often do not fully describe the details of an especially upsetting event.

However, we do not believe that there is any clear need for an expert to explain this to a jury. This understanding is well within the common knowledge of jurors. Additionally, the prosecutor is able to elicit such information from the child during testimony. As such, the need for expert testimony in this area is not apparent.

As with the issue of prompt complaint, however, there may be other reasons why children omit details; namely, the story they are relating is fabricated or imagined. In either event, the credibility of the child may well be measured by the reasons they relate for omitting details. As such, we believe that to permit expert testimony to buttress the testimony of the child would be to impermissibly interfere with the jury's function to judge credibility. . . . We are confident that jurors are well equipped to judge the credibility of children without need of expert advice.

The final issue we address is whether expert testimony is appropriate to explain why a child may have an inability to recall dates or times of the incident. It is universally understood that children, especially young children, may not be able to recall with specificity when things occurred to them. So too, when disclosure is delayed, the child may not be able to remember specific dates or times due simply to the passage of time. Again, however, an expert simply is not necessary to explain this to a jury.

. . . We find that it was error for the trial court to admit an expert's testimony on the subject of delay of reporting, omission of details, and the inability to recall dates and times.

---

[42] [n.19] Although the standard jury instructions concerning credibility do not contain an instruction about considering the child's age, we have approved of such a charge in *Commonwealth v. Snoke*, 580 A.2d 295 (1990). In that case, we found that the trial judge's instructions concerning credibility were proper where he stated, *inter alia*, "you should consider whether the witness' testimony was [a]ffected by reason of youth." 580 A.2d at 299, n.2.

We are all aware that child abuse is a plague in our society and one of the saddest aspects of growing up in today's America. Nevertheless, we do not think it befits this Court to simply disregard long-standing principles concerning the presumption of innocence and the proper admission of evidence in order to gain a greater number of convictions. A conviction must be obtained through the proper and lawful admission of evidence in order to maintain the integrity and fairness that is the bedrock of our jurisprudence. No shortcuts are permissible that erode this concept, no matter how noble the purpose. For these reasons, we affirm so much of the decision of the Superior Court which held that the testimony of the Commonwealth's expert should have been excluded.

. . . .

McDermott, Justice, concurring and dissenting.

. . . .

Regarding the majority's second issue, I believe the majority is ascribing to the average juror incredible sophistication regarding the effect of sexual abuse on the workings of a young mind. Moreover, to say, as the majority does, that "[a]ll of these reasons (i.e., reasons for delaying the report of such abuse) are easily understood by lay people and do not require expert analysis," "[t]his understanding (i.e. referring to why victims sometimes omit details) is well within the common knowledge of jurors," and "[i]t is universally understood that children, especially young children, may not be able to recall with specificity when things occurred to them," basically trivializes an entire field of child psychology by implying that everybody already knows these facts as surely as they know that apples fall down.

Finally, it greatly concerns me that the majority would continue to permit, as no doubt they must, defense counsel to attack the credibility of the child-victim on all of these grounds, yet afford the Commonwealth no means to parry these defense tactics; this despite the fact that on this point there is sufficient expert unanimity to conclude that such evidence is reliable.[43] [4]

Therefore, as to the majority's holding on the second issue, I dissent and would allow expert testimony that did not specifically refer to the victim in the trial at hand.

NOTES

1. *To Prove Abuse Occurred.* Courts are split on the issue of whether child sexual abuse syndrome is reliable enough to be a proper subject for expert opinion testimony when offered to prove that abuse occurred.

(A) Courts Finding Testimony Inadmissible. In addition to the *Dunkle* case, courts finding such evidence inadmissible include *Irving v. State*, 705 So. 2d 1021, 1023 (Fla. Dist Ct. App. 1998) (child sexual abuse accommodation syndrome (CSAAS) not proven to be generally accepted; error to admit expert testimony that victim exhibited symptoms consistent with CSAAS); *State v. York*, 564 A.2d 389, 391 (Me. 1989) (testimony of clinical features of child sexual abuse inadmissible absent empirical evidence establishing scientific reliability); *State v. Rimmasch*, 775 P.2d 388, 401 (Utah

---

[43] [n.4] Indeed, if one takes the majority at its word, there is such unanimity that it has become accepted common knowledge.

1989) (there is a lack of consensus about the child abuse profile's ability to determine abuse). *See generally People v. Peterson*, 537 N.W.2d 857, 866–67 (Mich. 1995) (discussing cases).

In *State v. Foret*, the Louisiana Supreme Court considered whether expert testimony on the issue of whether abuse occurred was admissible under the *Daubert* test:

> [T]he court finds that this type of evidence is of highly questionable scientific validity, and fails to unequivocally pass the *Daubert* threshold test of scientific reliability. In any capacity, it is highly unlikely that it will be useful to a jury on the issue of a witness' credibility, especially as a tool for determining whether or not abuse actually occurred.

State v. Foret, 628 So. 2d 1116, 1127 (La. 1993).

(B) Courts Finding Testimony Admissible. Courts that admit such testimony do not focus on whether there is general agreement in the field (the *Frye* test) or to any significant degree on whether the syndrome testimony is reliable; rather the focus appears to be on the fact that such testimony is *needed* to assist the jury in assessing credibility of the victim. Reliability under such an analysis is pertinent only to balancing probativeness with prejudice as set forth in Fed. R. Evid. 403.

The Minnesota case of *State v. Myers*, 359 N.W.2d 604 (Minn. 1984), is typical of cases that admit expert testimony on child sexual abuse syndrome. In *Myers* the defendant denied that sexual abuse occurred, but the victim, an eight-year-old girl, testified that it did occur. The prosecution called an expert, Dr. Bell, who first testified about the characteristics displayed by children who are the victims of child sexual abuse, and then testified about those same characteristics that she had observed in the complainant. The Minnesota Supreme Court, which two years earlier had held that evidence of rape trauma syndrome in a case involving an adult was inadmissible (*State v. Saldana*, 324 N.W.2d 227 (Minn. 1982)), stated:

> [T]he issue to be resolved is whether or not the emotional and psychological characteristics observed in sexually abused children [are] a proper subject of expert testimony.
>
> The basic consideration in admitting expert testimony under Minn. R. Evid. 702 is whether it will assist the jury in resolving the factual questions presented. As we explained in *State v. Helterbridle*, 301 N.W.2d 545, 547 (Minn. 1980):
>
> > If the subject of the testimony is within the knowledge and experience of a lay jury and the testimony of the expert will not add precision or depth to the jury's ability to reach conclusions about that subject which is within that experience, then the testimony does not meet the helpfulness test.
>
> In making this determination, the trial court may also consider the concerns expressed in Minn. R. Evid. 403. Even helpful, relevant evidence may be excluded if the trial court concludes that its probative value is substantially outweighed by the danger of unfair prejudice or of misleading the jury. In applying these considerations to Dr. Bell's testimony, we conclude that the admission of that segment of her testimony in which she described the traits and characteristics typically found in sexually abused children and those she had observed in the complainant was not erroneous."

State v. Myers, supra, 359 N.W.2d at 609. The court in *Myers* concluded with this observation about the reliability of the expert's opinion:

> The reliability of expert opinion testimony with regard to the existence or cause of the condition goes not to the admissibility of the testimony but to its relative weight. As in other cases, the defendant is free to test the value of the expert's testimony through cross-examination and, when appropriate, presentation of his own expert witnesses.

Id. at 611. *See also State v. Charles,* 398 S.E.2d 123, 141 (W.Va. 1990) (expert can give opinion that child has been sexually abused based upon child sexual abuse syndrome since probative value of testimony outweighs its potential for prejudice); *Sexton v. State,* 529 So. 2d 1041, 1049–50 (Ala. Crim. App. 1988) (admitting expert opinion testimony on child sexual abuse syndrome stating, "Though it may not have possessed a high degree of *reliability* (in the sense that "[t]he behavioral scientific literature conclusively demonstrates that there is no general acceptance of the ability of experts in the field to diagnose a child as having been sexually abused"), it did have a high degree of *understandability* . . . [and] most significantly, . . . its *necessity* was extremely great.).

Who has the better view? Do you agree with the *Myers* court's view that the inability of researchers to know what caused the child's symptoms (i.e., divorce, psychological abuse, sexual abuse, etc.) "goes not to the admissibility of the testimony but to its relative weight"? Are you persuaded by the *Dunkle* court's view that the inability to know what caused the symptoms creates enough unreliability to make testimony unreliable and inadmissible?

2. *Explaining Behavior — Majority Admit.* The *Dunkle* case is in the distinct minority in refusing to allow expert testimony to explain behavior of a child that appears inconsistent with having been sexually abused. Most courts, even those that do not allow evidence of child sexual abuse syndrome to prove that a sexual assault occurred, follow the view presented by Justice McDermott in his dissent in *Dunkle* and admit such testimony to explain inconsistent behavior. *See, e.g., People v. Peterson,* 537 N.W.2d 857, 866–67 (Mich. 1995); *State v. Matthews,* 864 P.2d 644, 649 (Idaho 1993); *State v. Lindsey,* 720 P.2d 73, 74–75 (Ariz. 1986).

The case for admissibility on this issue is strengthened because evidence of child sexual abuse syndrome is usually offered in rebuttal to a defense claim that the particular behavior in question is inconsistent with allegations of sexual abuse. The opinion of the Delaware Supreme Court in *Wheat v. State,* 527 A.2d 269 (Del. 1987), is representative of such cases. In *Wheat,* the victim recanted her allegations of sexual abuse while the defendant was in jail awaiting trial. *Id.* at 270. The defense argued at trial that the victim recanted because she was "tired of lying." *Id.* at 271. The prosecution offered testimony from an expert. The expert was not allowed to opine whether the victim was truthful, but was permitted to explain that "between thirty percent and forty percent of children [who are sexually abused] recant, alter or otherwise minimize their original allegations of sexual abuse. . . ." *Id.* The Delaware Supreme Court upheld the admission of the expert testimony stating:

> We emphasize that limited use of expert testimony in child sexual abuse prosecutions is appropriate to assist the finder of fact, whether judge or jury, in evaluating the psychological dynamics and resulting behavior patterns of alleged victims of child abuse, where the child's behavior is not within the common experience of the average juror. To the extent such expert testimony is given in general terms and directed to behavior factors in evidence, it is

admissible. To the extent it attempts to quantify the veracity of a particular witness or provide a statistical test for truth telling in the courtroom, it is clearly unacceptable.

Wheat, supra, 527 A.2d at 275. *See also State v. Matthews,* 864 P.2d 644, 649 (Idaho 1993) (role of experts is to provide testimony on subjects beyond the common sense, experience, and education of the average juror; behavior patterns of young victims of incest or molestation fall into that category).

3. *Credibility.* Perhaps the most noteworthy difference between evidence of rape trauma syndrome and child sexual abuse syndrome is the receptiveness of some courts to admitting child sexual abuse syndrome evidence to enhance the credibility of the abused child. The Louisiana Supreme Court, for example, in *State v. Foret,* found that expert testimony on child sexual abuse accommodation syndrome did not satisfy the reliability test contained in *Daubert* to justify the admission of such evidence to prove abuse occurred. The *Foret* court did, however, allow such evidence for the limited purpose of rebutting attacks on the victim's credibility based upon inconsistent statements, limited disclosures, delays in reporting, or recantations. *State v. Foret,* 628 So. 2d 1116, 1129–30 (La. 1993).

The Minnesota Supreme Court in *State v. Myers,* 359 N.W.2d 604 (Minn. 1984), explained the difference in attitude:

> There can be no doubt that an indirect effect of that portion of Dr. Bell's testimony [on child sexual abuse syndrome] was to bolster the complainant's credibility. . . . The test is not whether opinion testimony embraces an ultimate issue to be decided by the jury but whether or not the expert's testimony, if believed, will help the jury to understand the evidence or to determine a fact in issue. With respect to most crimes the credibility of a witness is peculiarly within the competence of the jury, whose common experience affords sufficient basis for the assessment of credibility. . . . The nature, however, of the sexual abuse of children places lay jurors at a disadvantage. Incest is prohibited in all or almost all cultures, and the common experience of the jury may represent a less than adequate foundation for assessing the credibility of a young child who complains of sexual abuse. If the victim of a burglary failed to report the crime promptly, a jury would have good reason to doubt that person's credibility. A young child subjected to sexual abuse, however, may for some time be either unaware or uncertain of the criminality of the abuser's conduct. As Dr. Bell testified, uncertainty becomes confusion when an abuser who fulfills a caring-parenting role in the child's life tells the child that what seems wrong to the child is, in fact, all right. Because of the child's confusion, shame, guilt, and fear, disclosure of the abuse is often long delayed. When the child does complain of sexual abuse, the mother's reaction frequently is disbelief, and she fails to report the allegations to the authorities. By explaining the emotional antecedents of the victim's conduct and the peculiar impact of the crime on other members of the family, an expert can assist the jury in evaluating the credibility of the complainant.

> In *State v. Saldana,* 324 N.W.2d 227 (Minn. 1982), we ruled inadmissible expert testimony regarding rape trauma syndrome because evidence of the typical reactions of a woman who has been raped does not assist the jury in determining whether or not the sexual act was consensual in a particular case and because the testimony furnishes no assistance to jurors, who are as capable

as the expert in assessing the credibility of the alleged adult rape victim. In *Saldana*, however, we recognized that when the alleged victim of a sexual assault is a child or mentally retarded person there is presented one of those "unusual cases" in which expert testimony concerning credibility of a witness should be received. In the case of a sexually abused child consent is irrelevant and jurors are often faced with determining the veracity of a young child who tells of a course of conduct carried on over an ill-defined time frame and who appears an uncertain or ambivalent accuser and who may even recant. Background data providing a relevant insight into the puzzling aspects of the child's conduct and demeanor which the jury could not otherwise bring to its evaluation of her credibility is helpful and appropriate in cases of sexual abuse of children, and particularly of children as young as this complainant.

State v. Myers, 359 N.W.2d 604, 609–10 (Minn. 1984). *See also Sexton v. State*, 529 So. 2d 1041, 1048–49 (Ala. Crim. App. 1988).

Most courts that permit expert testimony on the credibility issue do not, however, permit the expert to comment *directly* on the child's credibility. *United States v. Hadley*, 918 F.2d 848, 852 (9th Cir. 1990) (improper to testify that children "*could be believed*"; general testimony, however, that bolsters credibility is permissible); *State v. Charles*, 398 S.E.2d 123, 141 (W.Va. 1990) (expert may not give opinion on whether or not he personally believes the child); *State v. Moran*, 728 P.2d 248, 252 (Ariz. 1986) (expert may not tell the jury who is correct or incorrect); *But see State v. Geyman*, 729 P.2d 475, 479 (Mont. 1986) (expert is permitted to assess credibility of complainant).

4. *Anatomically Correct Dolls*. Experts often use anatomically correct dolls in therapy sessions with children who allegedly are the victims of sexual abuse. Children sometimes will act out behaviors with dolls that they cannot or will not verbalize. *See, e.g., State v. Hester*, 760 P.2d 27, 37–38 (Idaho 1988).

Often, based upon observing children interact with dolls, an expert is able to form an opinion relative to whether the child was sexually abused. One issue presented with such testimony concerns how the expert utilizes observations about how the child interacted with dolls. If the child's interactions with anatomically correct dolls are used by the expert to form an expert opinion about child abuse, then the *Frye* or *Daubert* tests may have to be satisfied. The Ninth Circuit (in a pre-*Daubert* case) held that expert opinion testimony based on play therapy with anatomically correct dolls must qualify under the *Frye* test and was inadmissible. *United States v. Gillespie*, 852 F.2d 475, 480–81 (9th Cir. 1988).

On the other hand, if the way the child interacted with the anatomically correct dolls is used by the expert merely to illustrate and explain the expert's opinion (and not as a "scientific technique"), the testimony may be admitted. Courts in Texas and Colorado have held that such dolls are not used as "scientific techniques" and, accordingly, do not have to satisfy *Frye* or any other test designed to ensure scientific reliability of an expert's opinion. *Reyna v. State*, 797 S.W.2d 189, 193 (Tex. Crim. App. 1990) (dolls are not scientific method of proof; rather, they are a tool to aid the jury in understanding the witness' testimony); *Stevens v. People*, 796 P.2d 946, 955 (Colo. 1990) (dolls are corroboration for child's hearsay statements).

5. *Expert Testimony on "Suggestive" and Leading Interview Techniques*. Many (if not most) researchers feel that young children are particularly susceptible to suggestion, and that improper questioning and/or suggestive interviewing can result in false accusations of child abuse. Stephen J. Ceci & Richard D. Friedman, *The*

Suggestibility of Children: Scientific Research and Legal Implications, 86 CORNELL L. REV. 33, 71 (Nov. 2000). Many, but not all, courts have allowed expert testimony on the suggestibility of children, improper questioning techniques, and the possibility that a false memory of child abuse had been implanted. *State v. Sargent*, 738 A.2d 351, 353–54 (N.H. 1999) (once defendant makes a "particularized showing" that improper interviewing techniques were used, expert testimony is admissible); *State v. Gersin*, 668 N.E.2d 486, 488 (Ohio 1996) ("[A] defendant in a child sexual abuse case may present testimony as to the proper protocol for interviewing child victims regarding their abuse."). *Contra State v. Ellis*, 669 A.2d 752, 753–54 (Me. 1996).

Note that the admissibility of such testimony may result in a "battle of the experts." For example, the prosecution may present an expert to testify about child sexual abuse syndrome and explain that the syndrome is characterized by behaviors exhibited by sexually abused children that include recantations, inconsistent disclosures, or delayed disclosure. On the other hand, the defense might then call an expert to testify that these same characteristics might be caused by improper interview techniques that result in the implantation of false memories. *Sargent, supra*, 738 A.2d at 352.

PROBLEMS

Problem 5-10. Assume that a defendant is charged with sexual abuse of a minor — a boy seven years old. Defendant maintains that he did nothing to the child and asks the court to compel the child to undergo a psychiatric examination to enable his expert to testify whether the child has child sexual abuse syndrome.

(A) Should the child be compelled to undergo such an examination? If so, how is this different (if it is) from compelling an adult rape victim to undergo a psychiatric exam to determine if she has the symptoms of rape trauma syndrome?

(B) Does it matter whether the state plans to use expert testimony of child sexual abuse syndrome in its case in chief?

(C) What if the child and/or the child's parents refuse to let the child be examined by a psychiatrist?

See State v. Maday, 507 N.W.2d 365, 372 (Wis. App. 1993).

Problem 5-11. Defendant was charged with sexual abuse of his daughter. The alleged incidents began when defendant's daughter was seven and ended when she was 13. The daughter went to authorities with her accusations when she turned 17. Defendant denies all allegations and asserts that his daughter "made up" the allegations because of conflict between the defendant and his wife (his daughter's mother). The only evidence against defendant is his daughter's testimony and testimony from an expert on child sexual abuse accommodation syndrome.

Based upon interviews with the daughter, the expert stated that "the daughter had, in fact, been abused." When asked by the prosecutor to explain the basis for her opinions that the daughter had been sexually abused, the expert responded: "Well, specifically, in my opinion, one does not give this kind of information with the amount of details and the amount of clarity unless one has experienced it." Later, on redirect examination, the prosecutor asked the expert to explain what the daughter had to gain by accusing her father of sexual abuse. The expert stated:

> One of the things that we do when we are doing a clinical interview and looking at the reality of the statements is to consider the alternative hypothesis,

which is that the individual is not telling the truth; and based on the richness of the detail and the uniqueness of some of the incidents that she described, I can't see that — well, then, if you would consider the alternative that [the daughter] is not telling the truth, then you would have to look at the consequences of the lie and what — why she would lie. And in talking with [the daughter] and reviewing her test data, I think she has only to lose. . . . [S]o I don't know what she would have to gain.

Based largely on the expert testimony, the defendant is convicted. On appeal the defendant argues that admitting the expert opinion violates Fed. R. Evid. 608(a). Rule 608(a) provides:

(a) *Opinion and reputation evidence of character*

The credibility of a witness may be attacked or supported by evidence in the form of opinion or reputation, but subject to these limitations: (1) the evidence may refer only to character for truthfulness or untruthfulness, and (2) evidence of truthful character is admissible only after the character of the witness for truthfulness has been attacked by opinion or reputation evidence or otherwise.

Defendant concedes that he attacked his daughter's credibility at trial but maintains that admitting expert opinion that she is telling the truth, is still improper under Rule 608(a). Was the expert opinion proper? Why? *See State v. Rimmasch*, 775 P.2d 388, 391–93 (Utah 1989).

[3]   Battered Woman Syndrome

PAUL C. GIANNELLI & EDWARD J. IMWINKELRIED, 1 SCIENTIFIC EVIDENCE § 9.03, at 508–17 (4th ed. 2007)[44]

§ 9.03 Battered Woman Syndrome.

The battered woman syndrome (BWS) describes a pattern of violence inflicted on a woman by her mate. In 1979 Dr. Lenore Walker, one of the principal researchers in this field, published her seminal text, *The Battered Woman*. She described a battered woman as follows:

A battered woman is a woman who is repeatedly subjected to any forceful physical or psychological behavior by a man in order to coerce her to do something he wants her to do without any concern for her rights. Battered women include wives or women in any form of intimate relationships with men. Furthermore, in order to be classified as a battered woman, the couple must go through the battering cycle at least twice. Any woman may find herself in an abusive relationship with a man once. If it occurs a second time, and she remains in the situation, she is defined as a battered woman.[45] [92]

Dr. Walker's initial findings were based on a nonrandom sample of 110 battered women who were mostly white and middle-class. A later study (1984) involved a more

---

[44] Copyright © 2007 by Matthew Bender & Co., a member of the LEXISNEXIS Group. Reprinted with permission. All rights reserved.

[45] [n.92] L. Walker, The Battered Woman xv (1979).

representative sample of 435 women. In her second book, *The Battered Woman Syndrome*, Walker defined the syndrome by incidents of violence: "A battered woman is a woman . . . who is or has been in an intimate relationship with a man who repeatedly subjects or subjected her to forceful physical and/or psychological abuse."[46] [93] Two acute battering incidents qualified as "repeated" incidents.

Cycle of Violence

According to Dr. Walker, the violence associated with this type of relationship is neither constant nor random. Instead, it follows a pattern. Dr. Walker identified a three-stage cycle of violence. The first stage is the "tension building" phase, during which small abusive episodes occur. These episodes gradually escalate over a period of time. The tension continues to build until the second stage — the acute battering phase — erupts. During this phase, in which most injuries occur, the battering is out of control. Psychological abuse in the form of threats of future harm is also prevalent. The third phase is a calm, loving period during which the batterer is contrite, seeks forgiveness, and promises to refrain from future violence. This phase provides a positive reinforcement for the woman to continue the relationship in the hope that the violent behavior will not recur. The cycle then repeats itself.

In addition, the batterer is often extremely jealous of the spouse's time and attention, a factor that further isolates her from friends and outside support. Moreover, numerous obstacles, both psychological and economic, often prevent the battered spouse from leaving her mate. Walker used Martin Seligman's theory of "learned helplessness" to explain the woman's condition.

In sum, the battered woman feels "trapped in a deadly situation." Caught in this cycle, she sometimes strikes back and kills.

Criticism

The BWS is not without its critics. In 1984 Professor Faigman questioned the validity of the underlying research:

> The prevailing theories of battered woman syndrome have little evidentiary value in self-defense cases. The work of Lenore Walker, the leading researcher on battered woman syndrome, is unsound and largely irrelevant to the central issues in such cases. The Walker cycle theory suffers from significant methodological and interpretative flaws that render it incapable of explaining why an abused woman strikes out at her mate when she does. Similarly, Walker's application of learned helplessness to the situation of battered women does not account for the actual behavior of many women who remain in battering relationships.[47] [98]

A decade later, he and a colleague would write: "The syndrome, first proposed in the 1970's and based on the clinical observations of a single researcher, has yet to be corroborated by serious and rigorous empirical work. . . . Given the lack of a scientific basis and its failure to achieve specific political and policy goals, the battered woman

---

[46] [n.93] L. Walker, The Battered Woman Syndrome 203 (1984). *See also* L. Walker, Terrifying Love: Why Battered Women Kill and How Society Responds (1989).

[47] [n.98] Faigman, *The Battered Woman Syndrome and Self-Defense: A Legal and Empirical Dissent,* 72 Va. L. Rev. 619, 647 (1986).

syndrome can be expected to soon pass from the legal scene."[48] [99] Another critic wrote: "Reduced to its essence, battered-woman syndrome is not a physicians' diagnosis but an advocate's invention. It means: Blame the deceased."[49] [100]

A 1992 review of the research literature indicated that BWS had attained, to a large extent, scientific acceptance. Citing a survey involving experts in the field, Schuller and Vidmar concluded:

> The degree of expert consensus shown in the Dodge and Greene survey tends to suggest that the scientific literature bearing on a battered woman's circumstances and situation is sound. There are, however, some aspects of the testimony — the cycle pattern of violence and the development of learned helplessness — that are not universal across battering relationships.[50] [102]

The widespread legal acceptance of BWS is a product of the work of feminist scholars, who have attacked the traditional law of self-defense as based upon a male-oriented perspective. Such scholarship, however, also recognizes that BWS may perpetuate stereotypes: "Dueling stereotypes are likely to become the focus of the trial process. While the prosecution attempts to discredit the defendant for not living up to the standard of a 'good wom[a]n,' the defense counters with an equally distorted portrayal of the defendant as ultra-feminine: passive, helpless victim."[51] [103] Another author suggested that most proposals for law reform concerning this subject are based on two assumptions, both of which are wrong. The first assumption is that a majority of cases involve nonconfrontational situations (e.g., spouse asleep or hired killer); however, a survey of the cases reveals that approximately 75% of the cases involve confrontations.[52] [104] The second assumption is that traditional self-defense law excluded a female perspective. The author argues that while it is true that self-defense law developed in cases with male defendants, it is not true that the law ignored "the context of a woman defendant's actions."[53] [105]

Several studies on the impact of BWS evidence on juries have been reported.

[a]   Admissibility: Self-defense

The admissibility of expert testimony on BWS has produced much commentary and initially divided the courts. It was first introduced in the 1979 case of *Ibn-Tamas v. United States.*[54] [108] Several different evidentiary issues are raised.

---

[48] [n.99] Faigman & Wright, *Battered Woman Syndrome in the Age of Science,* 39 Ariz. L. Rev. 67, 114 (1997).

[49] [n.100] Caplan, *Battered Wives, Battered Justice,* Nat'l Rev. 49, 40 (Feb. 1991).

[50] [n.102] Schuller & Vidmar, *Battered Woman Syndrome Evidence in the Courtroom: A Review of the Literature,* 16 Law & Hum. Behav. 273, 281 (1992).

[51] [n.103] Jenkins & Davidson, *Battered Women in the Criminal Justice System: An Analysis of Gender Stereotypes,* 8 Behav. Sci. & Law 161, 169 (1990).

[52] [n.104] Maguigan, *Battered Women and Self-Defense: Myths and Misconceptions in Current Reform Proposals,* 140 U. Pa. L. Rev. 379, 397 (1991) (surveying appellate decisions).

[53] [n.105] *Id.* at 405.

[54] [n. 108] Ibn-Tamas v. United States, 407 A.2d 626, 634–35 (D.C. 1979), *appeal after remand,* 455 A.2d 893 (D.C. 1983).

Relevancy

The first issue concerns the relevancy of BWS evidence. Typically, the evidence is offered in support of a self-defense claim in a homicide prosecution. A few courts have declared that BWS evidence is simply irrelevant to a self-defense claim. This seems wrong. While being a battered woman by itself is no defense to homicide, the syndrome may explain two elements of a self-defense claim: (1) the defendant's subjective fear of serious injury or death and (2) the reasonableness of that belief. Similarly, this evidence also would be admissible on the subjective fear element in a jurisdiction that recognized "imperfect self-defense," which reduces murder to voluntary manslaughter.

Numerous courts have recognized the relevancy of BWS evidence for this purpose. For example, the evidence explains why a battered woman has not left her mate. According to the New Jersey Supreme Court, "[o]nly by understanding these unique pressures that force battered women to remain with their mates, despite their long-standing and reasonable fear of severe bodily harm and the isolation that being a battered woman creates, can a battered woman's state of mind be accurately and fairly understood.[55] [113] Another court admitted BWS evidence to help explain a battered woman's conduct after killing her mate.[56] [114] The Georgia Supreme Court summed up the majority view as follows:

> [T]he battered person syndrome is not a separate defense, but . . . evidence of battered person syndrome is relevant in a proper case as a component of justifiable homicide by self-defense. . . . [E]vidence that a defendant suffered from battered person syndrome is only another circumstance which, if believed by the jury, would authorize a finding that a reasonable person, who had experienced prior physical abuse such as was endured by the defendant, would reasonably believe that the use of force against the victim was necessary, even though that belief may have been, in fact, erroneous.[57] [115]

. . . .

Beyond Jurors' Knowledge

A second issue is whether BWS evidence is a proper subject for expert testimony- . . . . Most courts . . . find[] that "a battering relationship embodies psychological and societal features that are not well understood by lay observers."[58] [117] The research appears to support this conclusion; it "suggests that jurors are misinformed on some aspects of wife abuse and that some jurors are likely to be more misinformed than others. Nevertheless, the surveys have not found overwhelming endorsement of the 'myths' about abuse."

Scientific Basis

A final issue relates to the scientific basis for BWS evidence. Some courts excluded expert testimony on this subject because its scientific validity had not been sufficiently established. Rejecting this argument, other courts have concluded that a "sufficient

---

[55] [n. 113] State v. Kelly, 97 N.J. 178, 196, 478 A.2d 364, 372 (1984). *See also* Fielder v. State, 756 S.W.2d 309, 319 (Tex. Crim. App. 1988).

[56] [n. 114]People v. Minnis, 118 Ill. App. 3d 345, 356–57, 455 N.E.2d 209, 218 (1983) (BWS "might extend to [explain] dismemberment" of husband after killing, a point which the prosecution legitimately exploited).

[57] [n. 104] State v. Smith, 486 S.E.2d 819, 822 (1997).

[58] [n. 117] State v. Kelly, 97 N.J. 178, 209, 478 A.2d 364, 379 (1984). . . .

scientific basis" has been established. According to a federal district court, "[t]he general acceptance of expert testimony on the battered woman syndrome has been acknowledged by legal authorities as well as the scientific community."

Trend Toward Acceptance

After initial setbacks, the trend favored admissibility of BWS evidence. . . . Several states . . . enacted statutes admitting BWS evidence. Nevertheless, refusal to admit BWS evidence is probably not unconstitutional.

In *Nguyen v. State*, the Georgia Supreme Court held that psychological abuse alone justified the presentation of expert testimony on the battered woman syndrome: "verbal and/or emotional abuse can warrant the introduction of expert evidence and the giving of a requested charge on battered person syndrome." The lower court had ruled that physical abuse was required. The Supreme Court however, limited the circumstances under which such evidence may be used. "[T]he psychological abuse inflicted on the accused must have been of such an extreme nature that it engendered in the accused a 'reasonable belief in the imminence of the victim's use of unlawful force.' Psychological abuse which humiliates, embarrasses or abases an individual is deplorable, but such abuse, when unaccompanied by other acts or verbal statements giving rise to a reasonable fear of imminent physical harm, cannot alone justify the admission of expert evidence on the battered person syndrome." The court then ruled that the defendant had made a sufficient showing.

Several limitations on admissibility should be noted. First, some courts permit experts to explain the syndrome only in general terms, describing the salient characteristics of BWS. Accordingly, the expert "should not be allowed to testify as to the ultimate fact that the particular defendant actually suffers from battered woman syndrome."

Second, the substantive law of self-defense may limit admissibility. Traditionally self-defense law required "imminent" danger of death or serious bodily injury. Typically, a killing in the absence of a confrontation falls outside this rule. Accordingly, several courts have held that a battered woman who kills a sleeping spouse cannot claim the defense. Similarly, some courts refuse to recognize the use of BWS evidence in the "murder-for-hire" cases. The opposing view is that the battered woman may justifiably believe she is in "imminent" danger, even though she is not being beaten or threatened at the time of the killing. To solve these problems, one commentator argued that the legal definition of self-defense was too restrictive and should be modified to recognize "psychological self-defense."[59] [133]

As indicated in the preceding excerpt from SCIENTIFIC EVIDENCE, there is a clear trend to admit evidence of the battered woman syndrome. Typically, such evidence is considered reliable and is generally accepted and relevant when a woman who has killed her batterer asserts that the killing was in self-defense. Problems with the battered woman syndrome occur when it is used as a defense in situations that do not involve a violent attack by the alleged batterer; as when the battered woman kills during a lull in the violence while her batterer is sleeping. In the next case, *People v. Yaklich*, a woman hired two "hit men" to kill her husband and at her murder trial offered evidence that she

---

[59] [n.133] Ewing, *Psychological Self-Defense: A Proposed Justification for Battered Woman Who Kill*, 14 LAW & HUM. BEHAV. 579 (1990).

suffered from the battered woman syndrome to support either that the killing was in self-defense or that it was committed under duress.

PEOPLE v. YAKLICH
833 P.2d 758 (Colo. App. 1991)

Opinion by JUDGE ROTHENBERG.

In this appeal, the People challenge the propriety of several rulings made by the trial court during the jury trial of defendant, Donna Yaklich, for the murder of her husband. We disapprove two of the trial court's rulings and, in view of this, we find the People's other arguments moot.

On December 12, 1985, Charles and Eddie Greenwell shot and killed Yaklich's husband in the driveway of his home as he stepped out of his truck. Yaklich was inside the house asleep.

After her husband's death, Yaklich received payment under his three life insurance policies, and she admitted that she paid the Greenwells $4,200 in several installments for murdering her husband. Consequently, she was brought to trial on a charge of first degree murder and conspiracy to murder under a theory that she had been motivated to arrange her husband's death in order to obtain the insurance money.

The defense, however, maintained that Yaklich suffered from the "battered woman syndrome" and that her actions were justifiable acts of self-defense and were committed under duress resulting from years of physical and psychological battering by her husband.

According to the defense, Yaklich lived in a constant state of fear of her husband, and, at the time of his death, she believed she was in imminent danger of being killed by him or receiving great bodily injury from him. The defense also contended that Yaklich believed and had reasonable grounds to believe that there was a real or apparent necessity to act to avoid the imminent danger of death or great bodily injury.

The defense presented expert and other testimony in support of its battered woman theory. In contrast, the People's expert witness gave her opinion that Donna Yaklich did not fit the profile of a battered woman.

At the close of the evidence, over the People's objections, the trial court instructed the jury on Yaklich's affirmative defenses of self-defense and duress. It also gave the jury definitions of "imminent danger," "apparent necessity," and "reasonable belief." The jury acquitted Yaklich of murder in the first degree. However, it convicted her of conspiracy to commit murder in the first degree, and the court sentenced her to forty years in prison.

The central issue on appeal is whether a woman who has hired a third party to kill her abuser but who presents evidence that she suffered from the battered woman syndrome is entitled to a self-defense instruction. We hold that a self-defense instruction is not available in a contract-for-hire situation, even though the accused presents credible evidence that she is a victim of the battered woman syndrome. Accordingly, we disapprove the trial court's ruling on that issue.

I.

The General Assembly has codified the law of self-defense at § 18-1-704, C.R.S. (1986 Repl. Vol. 8B). That statute permits an individual to use deadly physical force against another if the individual using deadly force reasonably believes that the other individual has used or imminently will use unlawful life-threatening force.

"Imminent" has not been expressly defined by statute or by Colorado case law in the context of self-defense. . . .

Yaklich contends that in the context of a battered woman situation in which the woman kills her abuser, "imminent" should be defined as: "likely to happen without delay, threatening, menacing, or impending, not immediate." Thus, according to Yaklich, a woman who kills her abuser or, as here, who hires another to kill her abuser is nevertheless entitled to a self-defense instruction even though she was not threatened with harm contemporaneously with the killing.

This is a case of first impression in Colorado, and in order to analyze and evaluate Yaklich's contention properly, it is necessary to examine briefly the battered woman syndrome as it relates to the issue of self-defense in Colorado.

II.

The "battered woman syndrome" constitutes a series of common characteristics that appear in women who are physically and psychologically abused over an extended period of time by the dominant male figure in their lives. (Although in rare circumstances, the victim of "battered woman syndrome" may be a male, the literature suggests that the vast majority of victims are women.)

Numerous cases across the country have held that the battered woman syndrome is "a recognized phenomenon in the psychiatric profession and is defined as a technical term of art in professional diagnostic textbooks."

Studies in this area have revealed that in a battering relationship, violence does not occur all the time. Rather, there is a "cycle of violence" which has three phases: (1) a tension building phase; (2) an acute battering phase; and (3) a tranquil and loving phase. The cycle of violence is continually repeated until the victim becomes unable to predict her own safety or the effect that her behavior will have on the abuser. As a result, the woman is reduced to a state of learned helplessness.

According to the testimony, one very important and often misunderstood aspect of the battered woman syndrome is the fact that many battered women cannot safely leave their abusive mates. In fact, abuse often escalates at the time of separation, and it is then that battered women face the greatest danger of being murdered. Many abusers have been known to pursue the women who leave them and subject them to brutal attacks.

Additionally, battered women may not psychologically or emotionally have the alternative of leaving the abuser because of their low self-esteem, their emotional and economic dependency, the absence of another place to go, and the woman's legitimate fear of the abuser's response to her leaving. Thus, according to the expert testimony, battered women become trapped in their own fear and often feel that their only recourse is to kill the batterer or be killed.

The battered woman syndrome is not in itself a defense to the charge of assault or murder, that is, the existence of the syndrome does not of itself establish the legal right of a woman to kill her abuser. Rather, evidence of the battered woman syndrome may, in certain circumstances, be considered in the context of self-defense. In Crocker, *The Meaning of Equality for Battered Women Who Kill Men in Self Defense*, 8 Harv. Women's L.J. 121, 132–33 (1985), the author explains:

> Lay witnesses may establish the history of threats and physical abuse experienced by the defendant. In situations where the uninformed juror would not see any threat or impending danger, expert witnesses help elucidate how a battering relationship generates different perspectives of danger, imminence, and necessary force.

> Expert testimony also attacks unstated stereotypic assumptions by explaining why the defendant stayed in the relationship, why she never sought help from police or friends, or why she feared increased violence. . . . [J]urors on their own or encouraged by the prosecution, may assume that the defendant stayed in the abusive relationship because the abuse was not serious or because she enjoyed it. Expert testimony demonstrates that women stay most often because they cannot or are afraid to leave.

III.

In the reported cases where battered women have killed their abusers and have contended that they acted in self-defense, one of three scenarios is generally present: (1) the battered woman has killed her abuser at the time he was attacking her; (2) the battered woman has killed her abuser during a lull in the violence (such as while the abuser was sleeping); and (3) the battered woman has hired a third party to kill her abuser.

A.

In situations in which the battered woman has killed her abuser at the moment of attack, virtually all jurisdictions have held that the woman is entitled to a self-defense instruction.

B.

In situations in which the woman has killed her abuser during a lull in the violence, there is a split of authority on whether she is entitled to a self-defense instruction. A key factor in the resolution of the issue has been the manner in which the particular jurisdiction defines "imminent danger."

Jurisdictions which define imminent danger as *immediate* danger have generally refused to allow a self-defense instruction to a defendant in this battered woman situation. *See People v. Aris*, 264 Cal. Rptr. 167 (1989) (self-defense instruction not justified because battered wife was not facing immediate peril when she shot and killed sleeping husband); *State v. Norman*, [378 S.E.2d 8 (N.C. 1989)] (self-defense instruction refused where wife shot and killed sleeping husband because, at the time of the killing, wife was not confronted with an instantaneous choice between killing husband and being killed); *State v. Stewart*, 763 P.2d 572 (Kan. 1988) (self-defense instruction refused where wife shot sleeping husband because there was no lethal threat to wife contemporaneous with the killing).

Other jurisdictions have defined "imminent danger" to mean something other than immediate danger and have held that a battered woman who kills her abuser during a lull in the violence is entitled to a self-defense instruction. *See State v. Gallegos*, 719 P.2d 1268 (N.M. 1986) (woman who shot and stabbed husband while he was lying in bed was entitled to self-defense instruction); *State v. Allery*, [682 P.2d 312] (self-defense instruction proper where battered wife shot husband while he was lying on couch, despite absence of any violent act immediately preceding shooting); *State v. Leidholm*, 334 N.W.2d 811 (N.D. 1983) (self-defense instruction justified where battered woman stabbed husband while he slept).

No Colorado case has yet decided this issue.

C.

We are aware of only three reported cases that discuss the issue of whether to give a self-defense instruction under circumstances in which the battered women have hired third parties to kill their abusers. Two arose in the state of Missouri and one arose in the state of Tennessee.

In *State v. Anderson*, 785 S.W.2d 596 (Mo. App. 1990), a wife hired several men to kill her abusive husband. At her trial for murder, the court refused to allow her expert to testify that she suffered from the battered woman syndrome. On appeal, she contended that the trial court erred in refusing to allow her to present expert testimony supporting her self-defense claim and in refusing to instruct the jury on self-defense.

The Missouri Court of Appeals rejected her arguments and stated:

> [T]he facts of the killing here do not support a self-defense claim or use of the battered spouse syndrome. [Defendant] hired or lured the killers into the crime. There was no evidence of self-defense of assaults of the husband *when he was shot*. [Defendant] had been talking for over three months prior to the murder about how to have her husband killed, with payment to the assailants out of his insurance proceeds. (Emphasis added.)

The Missouri court concluded that the woman did not prove she was in immediate danger at the time her husband was killed and, thus, failed to make a *prima facie* showing of self-defense. *See also State v. Martin*, 666 S.W.2d 895 (Mo. App. 1984) (no error in excluding evidence of battered spouse syndrome where wife hired hit man to kill her abusive husband but failed to show she was in immediate danger at the time he was killed); *State v. Leaphart*, 673 S.W.2d 870 (Tenn. Crim. App. 1983) (no error in trial court's failure to give a self-defense instruction where wife was not in immediate danger at time husband was killed by hired killers).

IV.

In summary, Yaklich contends that when a murder defendant presents evidence that she meets the criteria of being a battered woman and raises self-defense as her theory of the case, she is then entitled to a self-defense instruction. She further contends that "imminent" danger is not limited to immediate danger but should be defined more broadly as: "likely to happen without delay, impending, [but] not immediate." Thus, according to Yaklich, the trial court properly instructed the jury.

However, even if we were to adopt Yaklich's definition of imminent, we still would not agree that a self-defense instruction is available in a contract-for-hire case for three reasons. First, to our knowledge, no jurisdiction in the country has held that a battered woman is entitled to a self-defense instruction in a murder-for-hire case, no matter how the jurisdiction has defined imminent.

Secondly, a self-defense instruction in a murder-for-hire situation would undermine ancient notions of self-defense which originated in the common law and were later codified in Colorado law. As the North Carolina Supreme Court has stated: "The killing of another human being is the most extreme recourse to our inherent right of self-preservation and can be justified in law only by the utmost real or apparent necessity brought about by the decedent. . . ." *State v. Norman, supra.*

Finally, we cannot overlook the fact that Yaklich's participation in the death of her husband was not merely peripheral. Had it not been for Yaklich, the Greenwells would not have been involved in this murder. Thus, in our view, we would be establishing poor public policy if Yaklich were to escape punishment by virtue of an unprecedented application of self-defense while the Greenwells were convicted of murder.

We recognize that the alternatives available to battered women have proven "tragically inadequate" in many cases, and in reaching this conclusion, we do not minimize the dangers that battered women face. Nevertheless, we conclude that the result reached reasonably balances an individual's inherent and time honored right of self-preservation with the great value our society places on human life.

Here, the uncontroverted evidence was that Yaklich approached several people about having her husband killed and that she met with Eddie Greenwell several times over an eight-month period. She paid the Greenwells after they killed her husband, and, at the time the contract killing was performed by the Greenwells, she was in her house sleeping.

We therefore hold that under either the People's or Yaklich's definition of "imminent," Yaklich's evidence, even if taken as true, was insufficient as a matter of law to support her theory that she was in imminent danger at the time her husband was killed. Therefore, the trial court erred in giving a self-defense instruction to the jury. *See People v. Banks*, 804 P.2d 203 (Colo. App. 1990) (a defendant is entitled to an instruction embodying her theory of the case only if there is some evidence to support it).

. . . .

V.

The People next contend that the trial court erred in submitting an instruction to the jury on the affirmative defense of duress because Yaklich did not act "at the direction of another person" when she hired the Greenwells to kill her husband. Again we agree.

At the time Yaklich's husband was killed, the duress statute did not require a person to act "at the direction of another person" in order to establish the defense of duress. See § 18-1-708, C.R.S. (1986 Repl. Vol. 8B). Nevertheless, the case law required such a condition to exist.

Here, since there was no testimony that Yaklich acted "at the direction of another person," we disapprove the trial court's ruling giving a duress instruction.

. . . .

The trial court's rulings allowing a self-defense instruction and a duress instruction are disapproved.

NOTES

1. *Donna Yaklich.* Donna Yaklich's story was made into a TV movie, *Cries Unheard: The Donna Yaklich Story*, which initially aired in January of 1994. Donna Yaklich's request to have her sentence reduced was denied in March of 1994. She was granted parole in October of 2005. Eddie Greenwell (who fired the gun that killed Donna Yaklich's husband) was sentenced to 30 years in prison, and his brother, Charles, received a 20-year sentence.

2. *Scientific Reliability and "Helpfulness."* Note that the court in *Yaklich* gave very brief treatment to the issue of whether the battered woman syndrome is reliable or generally accepted. Instead the court simply states, "[n]umerous cases across the country have held that the battered woman syndrome is 'a recognized phenomenon in the psychiatric profession and is defined as a technical term of art in professional diagnostic textbooks.'" *People v. Yaklich, supra*, 833 P.2d at 760. This appears consistent with the modern trend of cases. *See, e.g., State v. Hennum*, 441 N.W.2d 793, 798–99 (Minn. 1989) (court reviews cases that admitted expert testimony on battered woman syndrome and concludes that the "theory underlying the battered woman syndrome . . . has gained . . . scientific acceptance"); *State v. Allery*, 682 P.2d 312, 313–16 (Wash. 1984). The evidentiary issue presented by battered woman syndrome evidence appears not to involve its reliability, but rather how, when, and to what issues it applies in a criminal case.

A related issue concerns whether expert testimony on the battered woman syndrome is a proper subject for expert testimony. That is, whether such expert testimony is helpful in the sense that it provides information not within the jurors' common understanding. Note again that the appellate court in *Yaklich* deals with this issue in very brief fashion by citing from an article that appeared in the Harvard Women's Law Journal. *People v. Yaklich, supra*, 833 P.2d at 761. Once again, this appears consistent with the modern trend of cases that find expert testimony on the battered woman necessary to dispel "common sense" misperceptions such as that the woman in a battering relationship is free to leave at any time, or that the woman must "enjoy" the beatings or else she would leave. *See e.g., People v. Christel*, 537 N.W.2d 194, 201–02 (Mich. 1995) (admissible to explain behavior where victim's responses are "incomprehensible" to average people); *State v. Ciskie*, 751 P.2d 1165, 1172 (Wash. 1988) (admissible to explain failure to report abuse and why victim did not leave relationship). Some states have legislatively recognized the admissibility of battered woman syndrome testimony. *See, e.g.,* Mo. Ann. Stat. § 563.033 (Vernon 1992); Ohio Rev. Code Ann. § 2901.06 (Anderson 1991).

There are a few reported cases that reject the use of expert testimony on the battered woman syndrome for lack of relevance, *People v. White*, 414 N.E.2d 196, 200 (Ill. App. 1980), for being within the common understanding of the jury, *State v. Thomas*, 423 N.E.2d 137, 140 (Ohio 1981), and for not having a sufficient scientific basis, *Buhrle v. State*, 627 P.2d 1374, 1378 (Wyo. 1981). These cases, however, appear to be contrary to the modern trend. *See* 1 Scientific Evidence § 9.03[a], at 515 (4th ed. 2007); *State v. Koss*, 551 N.E.2d 970, 974 (Ohio 1990) (overrules earlier case, *State v. Thomas*, finding battered woman syndrome inadmissible).

3. *Imperfect Self-Defense.* In addition to being admissible to prove self-defense, many courts admit evidence of the battered woman syndrome to prove an imperfect self-defense. Where recognized, imperfect self-defense reduces an intentional killing from murder to manslaughter. Imperfect self-defense requires only a *subjective* fear of imminent danger; there is no requirement that this subjective fear be "reasonable" as is the case with "perfect" self-defense. Those states that recognize imperfect self-defense hold that expert testimony on the battered woman syndrome is relevant on the subjective honesty of the woman's belief that she was in danger.

In *People v. Aris*, 264 Cal. Rptr. 167 (Cal. App. 1989), a woman killed her husband by shooting him five times while he slept. After first holding that perfect self-defense was not available in a case where a woman with battered woman syndrome kills her batterer while he sleeps, *Id.* at 172–76 & 179, the court addressed the applicability of imperfect self-defense and the battered woman syndrome:

> Although Dr. Walker's opinion that defendant reasonably perceived herself to be in danger was irrelevant to the reasonableness of her self-defense because it was based on an evaluation of her subjective mental state, for that very reason Dr. Walker's opinion slightly reframed is highly relevant to the first element of self-defense — defendant's actual, subjective perception that she was in danger and that she had to kill her husband to avoid that danger. Not only is the opinion relevant to the excuse of imperfect self-defense which requires only an actual perception, but also the justification of complete self-defense because it requires both actual as well as reasonable perception.

> The relevance to the defendant's actual perception lies in the opinion's explanation of how such a perception would reasonably follow from the defendant's experience as a battered woman. This relates to the prosecution's argument that such a perception of imminent danger makes no sense when the victim is asleep and a way of escape open and, therefore, she did not actually have that perception.

> . . . .

> Although [battered woman syndrome] testimony is admissible, both in general and as it applies to the particular defendant, trial courts should recognize the possibility that the jury in a particular case may misuse such evidence to establish the reasonableness requirement for perfect self-defense, for which purpose it is irrelevant as previously discussed. Therefore, upon request whenever the jury is instructed on perfect self-defense, trial courts should instruct that such testimony is relevant only to prove the honest belief requirement for both perfect and imperfect self-defense, not to prove the reasonableness requirement for perfect self-defense."

Id. at 181.

4. *Battered Woman Syndrome Evidence Offered by the Prosecution.* Expert testimony of the battered woman syndrome is usually offered by the defense. There are, however, situations where the prosecution has offered such evidence. The most common example of prosecution use of battered woman evidence involves the prosecution of a batterer. Battered woman syndrome evidence is used to explain the victim's behavior; i.e., why the victim recanted, did not leave, or delayed in reporting the battering incident. *State v. Grecinger*, 569 N.W.2d 189, 197 (Minn. 1997) (expert testimony on battered woman syndrome admissible in prosecution's case-in-chief where it is intro duced after victim's credibility has been attacked to help jury understand inconsistent statements or delay in seeking prosecution of the batterer). *See generally*, 1 SCIENTIFIC EVIDENCE § 9.03[d], at 520–21 (4th ed. 2007).

QUESTIONS

1. Would evidence of the battered woman syndrome have been admissible in *Yaklich* if the defendant had killed her husband herself, in the couple's driveway, instead of hiring the Greenwells to do it for her? If so, why?

2. Would evidence of the battered woman syndrome have been admissible in *Yaklich* if, on the day following a particular severe beating, she had hired the Greenwells to kill her husband and they had killed him that day? If so, why?

3. What does "imminent" mean in the context of Colorado's self-defense statute?

4. If a woman kills her spouse and claims self-defense, what issues, *in all cases*, would testimony of the battered woman syndrome be relevant to prove?

PROBLEMS

Problem 5-12. Assume that a woman on trial for murder wishes to offer evidence of the battered woman syndrome to support her claim of self-defense. Assume further that the prosecution doubts the validity of her claim that she is a battered spouse, and asks the court to order her to submit to examination by a prosecution psychologist. What result? How is this different from the situation encountered where the defendant sought to have the victim of a rape examined by a defense expert to determine if the victim had rape trauma syndrome? *See State v. Hennum*, 441 N.W.2d 793, 800 (Minn. 1989); *Hickson v. State*, 630 So. 2d 172, 173, 175–76 (Fla. 1993); Mo. ANN. STAT. § 563.033 (Vernon 1992).

Problem 5-13. Assume that a woman is charged with selling marijuana. Her defense is that she sold drugs under duress at the direction of her battering husband. She seeks to offer evidence that she is a battered spouse to prove the coercion she was under. She admits that there were periods of relative calm in her relationship with her husband.

Assume that in this jurisdiction the defense of duress requires (1) that the defendant be under an unlawful and present, imminent, and impending threat such as would induce a well-grounded apprehension of death or serious bodily injury; (2) that the defendant had not placed herself recklessly or negligently in a situation where she would be forced to choose criminal conduct; (3) that the defendant had no reasonable legal alternative to violating the law; and (4) that there was a direct causal relationship between the avoidance of the threatened harm and the criminal conduct taken by the defendant.

Should the defendant be able to offer evidence of the battered woman syndrome to support her defense of duress? *See United States v. Willis*, 38 F.3d 170, 174–77 (5th Cir. 1994).

Problem 5-14. Defendant is charged with raping, beating, and kidnapping his wife. The charges stem from an incident that occurred one year ago. Defendant and his estranged wife had an argument outside a tavern over an alleged affair involving defendant's wife and another man. Defendant is alleged to have taken his wife by force to the apartment where he was staying, and where he kept her against her will overnight. During the night he is alleged to have beaten and raped his wife. The next day defendant left his apartment, and his wife went to the police and reported the kidnapping, rape, and beating. Charges were brought against her husband. Two months later, before trial, defendant's wife wrote the prosecutor asserting that her accusations were untrue and that all contact with her husband on the night in question was consensual. Charges were then dropped.

The following spring defendant's wife returned to the prosecutor's office and asked that the dismissed charges be refiled, which they were. At defendant's trial the prosecution seeks to offer evidence that the victim, defendant's wife, was a battered woman, to explain why she recanted her original accusations.

May the prosecution offer such evidence to explain the victim's behavior? *See State v. Schaller*, 544 N.W.2d 247, 250–53 (Wis. Ct. App. 1995); *People v. Christel*, 537 N.W.2d 194, 201–04 (Mich. 1995).

[4]   Syndromes: Where to Draw the Line

At the beginning of this chapter, nine characteristics of nontraditional psychological evidence were identified.[60] One of those characteristics was that the cut-off point for admissibility of similar types of expert testimony is not easily determined. Nowhere in the area of soft science is this characteristic more controversial than when "new" syndromes are offered as a defense in a criminal trial, or when an existing syndrome is wrenched from the context in which it had been accepted by the courts, and offered as a defense in a different situation. This difficulty in "drawing the line" is illustrated in the cases that follow.

[a]   Extending the Coverage of Accepted Syndromes: The Battered Child Syndrome

STATE v. JANES
822 P.2d 1238 (Wash. Ct. App. 1992)

AGID, JUDGE.

Andrew G. Janes appeals his conviction for the second degree murder of his stepfather, Walter Jaloveckas, and for two counts of second degree assault. He assigns error to the trial court's failure to allow an instruction on self-defense and to various evidentiary rulings excluding expert testimony regarding the battered child syndrome that he contends would have been relevant to establishing that defense. . . . We agree that he should have been permitted to present evidence of the battered child syndrome and reverse.

On August 30, 1988, the appellant, Andrew Janes (Andy), shot and killed his stepfather, Walter Jaloveckas, as Jaloveckas walked through the front door of their home. Andy then triggered the alarm system in the home to summon the police and fire department. When police arrived, Andy fired at them, as well as at some empty cars and at the telephone in his house. Mountlake Terrace Police Officer James Blackburn and a bystander, Eve Flores, were slightly injured in the shooting.

---

[60] *See* David McCord, *Syndromes, Profiles and Other Mental Exotica: A New Approach to the Admissibility of Nontraditional Psychological Evidence in Criminal Cases*, 66 OR. L. REV. 19, 27–35 (1987).

Andy was charged by information with one count of murder in the first degree (premeditated), and two counts of assault in the second degree.[61] [1] He was found guilty of the lesser included offense of murder in the second degree and of both assault charges. The trial court found that Andy had suffered a pattern of ongoing abuse at the hands of the decedent and imposed an exceptional sentence of 10 years on the murder conviction.[62] [2]

An understanding of the nature of the relationship between Andy and his stepfather is important to an understanding of our decision. Jaloveckas moved in with the Janes family in November 1978 when Andy was 7 years old, after Andy's biological father abandoned the family earlier that year. After the family moved into a home of their own in 1980, Jaloveckas became increasingly abusive and subject to unpredictable and sometimes physically violent outbursts of anger. There is extensive testimony in the record with respect to the details of the abuse, which included incidents where Jaloveckas beat or hit Andy, his brother and Gale Janes, their mother, smashed a stereo and bicycles with a sledgehammer, and threatened to torture, kill, or send the boys away for such transgressions as being tardy in completing chores or taking some of his marijuana.[63] [3] While Jaloveckas' actions were reported to Child Protective Services (CPS) on three occasions, CPS did not follow up on those reports. On at least two of the three occasions Ms. Janes or Andy requested that CPS not follow up out of fear of reprisal by Jaloveckas.

On the evening of August 29, an incident occurred that the appellant contends triggered the events of the next day. After a loud argument during which Jaloveckas yelled angrily at Ms. Janes for about 45 minutes, Jaloveckas stopped by Andy's room and spoke to him in a low tone. Ms. Janes testified that when Jaloveckas used a low tone, it usually meant that he was making a threat. She did not hear what he actually said, and Andy could not remember what was said. The next morning Ms. Janes woke Andy after Jaloveckas left for work and told him that he should be sure to get all his work done because Jaloveckas was still angry.

One of Andy's school friends testified that he stopped by Andy's home on the way to school. Andy brought out a shotgun and loaded it, showed it to his friend and told him he was going to kill Jaloveckas. Andy left the shotgun under some clothes in his room, went to school and left after two classes. After returning home, Andy broke a padlock off the door to the bedroom shared by Ms. Janes and Jaloveckas in which Jaloveckas kept his supply of alcohol and marijuana. Andy drank whiskey, smoked marijuana, and retrieved a shotgun and loaded 9-mm. handgun that belonged to Jaloveckas. When Jaloveckas returned at 4:30 p.m., Andy shot him as he entered the home. Jaloveckas died from two gunshot wounds to the head.

There is no dispute that Andy killed his stepfather. Instead, defense counsel sought to base Andy's defense on a theory of justifiable homicide. The defense argued that Andy acted in self-defense because he perceived himself to be in imminent danger of serious bodily harm as a consequence of a condition analogous to "battered woman

---

[61] [n.1] Count 2 charged Andy with assault on the police officers on whom he fired; count 3 charged him with assault on Eve Flores.

[62] [n.2] The standard range was 13–18 years. The court imposed standard range sentences of 20 months on each assault, to run concurrently with each other and with the 10-year sentence on the murder conviction. The State has not appealed the exceptional sentence.

[63] [n.3] Jaloveckas sold and used both marijuana and cocaine during the years that he lived with the Janes family.

syndrome," stemming from the 10 years of abuse he had suffered at the hands of his stepfather. The trial court ruled, however, that in the absence of evidence showing that Andy was in fact in imminent danger at the time of the shooting, there was an insufficient factual basis to support giving an instruction regarding self-defense.

Although the court did not permit testimony supporting the defense of justifiable homicide, it did permit the defense experts, Dr. Christopher Varley and Dr. Bruce Olson, to testify on the defense of diminished capacity. Both testified that Andy suffered from post traumatic stress disorder, primarily as a result of abuse at the hands of Jaloveckas, and that as a result of this disorder, Andy's capacity for premeditation was "impaired." The court instructed the jury that it could consider a mental illness or disorder where the existence of a particular mental state was a necessary element of a particular crime.

I. *Battered Child Syndrome*

A defendant is entitled to have his theory of the case submitted to the jury under appropriate instructions when the theory is supported by sufficient evidence in the record. The issue of self-defense is properly raised if the defendant produces "any evidence" tending to show self-defense. *State v. Adams*, 641 P.2d 1207 (Wash. App. 1982) ("[O]nly where no plausible evidence appears in the record upon which a claim of self-defense might be based is an instruction on [self-defense] not necessary."). The question of whether there is sufficient evidence to raise a claim of self-defense is a question of law for the trial court, which must apply a subjective standard, viewing the evidence from the perspective of the defendant at the time of the act. Here, the trial court held, following an offer of proof, that evidence of the battered child syndrome could not, as a matter of law, support a finding of self-defense because, it concluded, there was no "imminent threat" to Andy at the time of the shooting. It therefore excluded the testimony and refused the proffered instruction. For the reasons stated below, we hold that it was error to exclude testimony concerning the battered child syndrome and to refuse to submit the issue of the reasonableness of Andy's perceptions, in light of expert testimony on the battered child syndrome, to the jury.[64] [5]

Self-defense requires a showing of (1) reasonable apprehension of a design to commit a felony or to do some great personal injury, and (2) imminent danger of that design being accomplished. While the "imminent danger" prong requires the jury to find that the victim honestly and reasonably believed that the aggressor intended to inflict serious bodily injury in the near future, there need be no evidence of an actual physical assault to demonstrate the immediacy of the danger. Fear alone does not entitle a defendant to a self-defense instruction. *State v. Kidd*, 786 P.2d 847 (Wash. App. 1990) (criminal culpability is not lessened when one acts in self-defense due to an honest but *unreasonable* belief in the need for force). Some evidence of aggressive or threatening behavior, gestures, or communication by the victim is typically required to show that the defendant's belief that he or she was in imminent danger of great bodily harm was reasonable.

. . . Washington uses a subjective standard to evaluate the imminence of the danger a defendant faced at the time of the act. This requires the court and the jury to evaluate

---

[64] [n.5] The latter holding assumes, of course, that the testimony is sufficient to support giving the instruction.

the reasonableness of the defendant's perception of the imminence of that danger in light of all the facts and circumstances known to the defendant at the time he acted, including the facts and circumstances as he perceived them before the crime. Because battering itself can alter the defendant's perceptions, Washington courts have held that expert testimony with respect to the battered woman syndrome is admissible to explain a woman's perception that she had no alternative but to act in the manner that she did.[65] [6] As the *Walker* court explained:

> The function of evidence of the battered woman syndrome, offered through expert testimony, is merely to assist the trier of fact in evaluating the reasonableness of both the use of force and the degree of force used in a case involving the recognized circumstances of self-defense. That the defendant is a victim of a battering relationship is not alone sufficient evidence to submit the issue of self-defense to a jury. It is the *perceived imminence* of danger, based on the appearance of some threatening behavior or communication, which supplies the justification to use deadly force under a claim of self-defense.

(Emphasis added.) *State v. Walker*, 700 P.2d 1168 (Wash. 1985).

In analyzing the question of whether the jury should have been permitted to hear expert testimony concerning the battered child syndrome in the context of the defendant's claim of self-defense here, we consider: (1) whether scientific understanding of the battered child syndrome is sufficiently developed so as to be generally admissible, and (2) whether the expert testimony offered would have been helpful to the trier of fact in the context of this case.

While no Washington case has yet recognized the "battered child syndrome" in this context,[66] [8] the pertinent literature indicates that there is a sufficient scientific basis to justify extending the battered woman syndrome to analogous situations affecting children. *See, e.g.*, Comment, *Killing Daddy: Developing a Self-Defense Strategy for the Abused Child*, 137 U. Pa. L. Rev. 1281 (1989); Van Sambeek, *Parricide as Self-Defense*, 7 Law & Inequality 87 (1988–89); P. Mones, When a Child Kills: Abused Children Who Kill Their Parents (1991).

Neither law nor logic suggests any reason to limit to women recognition of the impact a battering relationship may have on the victim's actions or perceptions. We have noted in other contexts that children are both objectively and subjectively more vulnerable to the effects of violence than are adults. For that reason, the rationale underlying the admissibility of testimony regarding the battered woman syndrome is at least as compelling, if not more so, when applied to children. Children do not reach the age of majority until they are 18 years of age. Until then, they have virtually no independent ability to support themselves, thus preventing them from escaping the abusive atmosphere. Further, unlike an adult who may come into a battering relationship with at least some basis on which to make comparisons between current and past experiences, a child has no such equivalent life experience on which to draw to put the

---

[65] [n.6] The scientific basis and relevancy of testimony regarding battered woman syndrome is now well established. *State v. Hanson*, 793 P.2d 1001, *review denied*, 803 P.2d 325 (1990), *citing State v. Allery*, 682 P.2d 312 (1984) (testimony concerning battered woman syndrome admissible to explain defendant's perception of the threat and the reasonableness of the force employed in self-defense against the threat).

[66] [n.8] Washington courts have recognized "battered child syndrome" in the context of admitting evidence to show that the injuries of the child victim of a batterer are not accidental, but are instead the result of physical abuse by a person of mature strength. *E.g.*, *State v. Toennis*, 758 P.2d 539, *review denied*, 111 Wash. 2d 1026 (1988); *State v. Mulder*, 629 P.2d 462 (1981).

battering into perspective. There is therefore every reason to believe that a child's entire world view and sense of self may be conditioned by reaction to that abuse. Van Sambeek, *supra* at 98.

For these reasons, we recognize that the battered child syndrome is the functional and legal equivalent of the battered woman syndrome, and hold that scientific understanding of the battered child syndrome is sufficiently developed to make testimony concerning that syndrome admissible in appropriate cases.

After reviewing the offer of proof and arguments in the record, we also conclude that the information the appellant's experts offered concerning the battered child syndrome and its application in this case would have been helpful to the trier of fact. Without it, the jury could not adequately evaluate the reasonableness of Andy's perception that he was in imminent danger of death or serious bodily harm at the time he killed his stepfather.

The testimony offered by the appellant's experts and a review of the materials cited by the appellant illustrate just how counter-intuitive and difficult to understand the dynamics of the relationship between a batterer and his victim can be. For example, it is unlikely that the average juror would be able to understand, without Dr. Olson's testimony on hypervigilance in the battered child, the significance of Andy's claim that he acted in self-defense.[67] [10] Battered children live in an environment wholly different from the safe and nurturing home depicted by traditional values and social expectations. The impact of long-term abuse on a child's emotional and psychological responses is a matter that is thus beyond the average juror's understanding. Without expert testimony to put the child's perceptions into context, a jury cannot fairly evaluate the reasonableness of the child's perception of the imminence of the danger to which he or she reacted. The jury in this case should, on remand, be permitted to hear the testimony and evaluate the reasonableness of Andy's perceptions and actions in light of the battered child syndrome evidence.

II. *Diminished Capacity*

. . . The State argues that the trial court erred by allowing the diminished capacity instruction. . . .

. . . .

The trial court . . . did not err in allowing an instruction on diminished capacity. A diminished capacity instruction is to be given "whenever there is substantial evidence of such a condition and such evidence logically and reasonably connects the defendant's alleged mental condition with the inability to possess the required level of culpability to commit the crime charged." Here, there is substantial evidence in the record to support the diminished capacity instruction. Defendant's experts testified that Andy suffered from posttraumatic stress disorder and that Andy's ability to premeditate was "im

---

[67] [n.10] Hypervigilance is a heightened ability to discern preaggressive behavior in others, a condition which occurs with long-term abuse. In this context, the defense experts could have explained to the jury that a child may notice a change in the usual pattern of abuse which would be almost imperceptible to one who has not been abused. This, in turn, may suggest to the victim of abuse a level of imminent and acute danger very different from that perceived by one not continuously exposed to an abusive environment. Other psychological effects that may contribute to a child's sense that he or she has no alternatives include learned helplessness, depression, isolation, low self-esteem, fear of reprisal, a belief in the omnipotence of the batterer, and a belief in the futility of either resistance or flight. *See* P. Mones, When a Child Kills: Abused Children Who Kill Their Parents (1991).

paired" as a result. The foundation requirements . . . were met, and the jury was properly instructed on that basis.

    . . . .

Reversed and remanded.

NOTES

1. *The* **Janes** *Appeal.* In an opinion issued April 8, 1993, the Washington Supreme Court reviewed the appellate court decision in the *Janes* case. *State v. Janes*, 850 P.2d 495 (Wash. 1993). The Washington Supreme Court upheld the appellate court's ruling that expert testimony on the battered child syndrome was admissible to prove self-defense, and it remanded the case to the trial court to determine if the history of abuse suffered by Andrew Janes, and the circumstances surrounding the murder of Walter Jaloveckas, provided sufficient evidence to warrant a trial court instruction on self-defense. *Id.* at 496.

Specifically, as to the battered child syndrome, the Washington Supreme Court agreed with the appellate court and held that it was the "functional and legal equivalent of the battered woman syndrome." *Id.* at 503. Because the court had previously held that the battered woman syndrome satisfied the *Frye* test and was admissible on the issue of self-defense, it had no difficulty holding that the battered child syndrome also satisfied *Frye* and was admissible, where relevant, to prove self-defense. *Id.*

As to admissibility of expert testimony on the battered child syndrome on the *specific facts* of the *Janes* case, the Washington Supreme Court was less clear. The Washington Supreme Court remanded the case to the trial court stating that

> the trial court should reconsider its ruling denying the self-defense instruction in light of principles discussed in this opinion. If the trial court determines that some evidence existed to justify a self-defense instruction, then it should order a new trial. Otherwise, Andrew's conviction stands. . . .

Id. at 506. In June of 1993 the trial court ordered a new trial for Andrew Janes. At the second trial the jury heard expert testimony on the battered child syndrome and self-defense. The second trial ended in a hung jury, and Janes then pleaded guilty to manslaughter. He was sentenced to time served (61 months) on the manslaughter charge and an additional nine months for an unrelated incident. *See* Karen Alexander, *Judge Sentences Janes; He'll Spend Two More Months in Jail*, SEATTLE TIMES, 1st Ed., Mar. 15, 1995, Section: Snohomish, at B1.

2. *The Two Battered Child Syndromes.* As indicated in the court's opinion, the phrase "battered child syndrome" is used in two different contexts. (*See* footnote 8 of the court's opinion.) First, the battered child syndrome that is admissible without controversy involves *medical* testimony about the type of injuries a child received. This sort of testimony is typically received when an adult is accused of battering a child and the adult asserts that the child's injuries were accidental or self-inflicted. Testimony on this type of battered child syndrome was received in the case of *State v. Loebach*, 310 N.W.2d 58 (Minn. 1981):

> Dr. Robert ten Bensel, an expert on child abuse, testified concerning the so-called "battered child syndrome." He concluded that it fit this case almost perfectly. The baby had not thrived and there were no organic reasons for this disclosed by the autopsy. The baby was in the 95th percentile by weight when

born, but in only the 10th percentile at death; it was in the 95th percentile by height when born, but in only the 50th at death. At death, the baby had multiple bruises and injuries of different parts of the body, including the head. These injuries were both old and new. Dr. ten Bensel testified that he had never before seen rib fractures like those revealed by the autopsy. He testified that the fractures were so close to the spine that it would require almost total compression of the ribs and total squeezing of the body to cause these injuries. He also testified that throwing the baby in the air and catching it could not have caused such fractures. As for the hemorrhaging, some were 1 to 3 weeks old and some had occurred within 24 hours of death. The fresh bleeding was the result of multiple blows. The multiple injuries were clearly not caused by accidents of the kind the defendant stated and were not self-inflicted. Dr. ten Bensel was firmly convinced that the baby's death was the final result of nonaccidental physical abuse of the baby over a period of time.

State v. Loebach, 310 N.W.2d at 61–62. *See State v. Heath*, 957 P.2d 449, 464–65 (Kan. 1998) ("battered child syndrome is an accepted medical diagnosis" and other state courts have approved its use);1 SCIENTIFIC EVIDENCE § 9.03[e], at 522–23 (4th ed. 2007); Annot., *Admissibility of Expert Medical Testimony on Battered Child Syndrome*, 98 A.L.R.3d 306 (1980).

The second, and more controversial, type of evidence also designated as the battered child syndrome is *psychologically* based and is the type of evidence that was the focal point of the *Janes* case; using evidence of a child being battered as a defense or partial defense to a murder charge. *State v. Smullen*, 844 A.2d 429 n.13 (Md. 2004) (distinguishing the medical diagnosis "battered child syndrome" and listing cases that accept the medical diagnosis syndrome).

In sum, the first battered child syndrome looks at physical injuries to the child and is typically offered by the prosecution. The second battered child syndrome looks at psychological damage caused to the child by being battered and is typically offered by the child as a defense when the child attacks his or her batterer.

3. *Acceptance of the Battered Child Syndrome.* *Janes* was the first reported appellate case in the United States to admit expert testimony concerning the battered child syndrome on the issue of self-defense. Other jurisdictions have appeared receptive to battered child syndrome testimony. *See State v. MacLennan*, 702 N.W.2d 219, 234 (Minn. 2005) ("Like expert testimony on battered woman syndrome, we conclude that expert testimony on battered child syndrome may help to explain a phenomenon not within the understanding of an ordinary lay person."); *State v. Smullen*, 844 A.2d 429, 449–50 (Md. 2004) (recognizing battered child syndrome as an extension of state's statutorily recognized battered spouse syndrome); *State v. Nemeth*, 694 N.E.2d 1332, 1336 (Ohio 1998) (expert testimony on battered child syndrome admissible); *State v. Hines*, 696 A.2d 780, 787 (N.J. 1997) (citing *Janes, supra*, and holding evidence of defendant's post-traumatic stress disorder arising from child abuse admissible in support of her self-defense claim).

The few jurisdictions that do not accept the battered woman syndrome on the issue of self-defense will likely have difficulty accepting expert testimony on battered child syndrome when offered to prove self-defense. *See, e.g., Jahnke v. State*, 682 P.2d 991, 1008 (Wyo. 1984) (battered son testimony rejected because defendant not under attack at time he killed).

4. *Diminished Capacity.* The significance of the diminished capacity defense should not be overlooked. In those jurisdictions that do not permit syndrome testimony to establish perfect self-defense, evidence of the syndrome may still be admitted to negate a mental element required for conviction of the most serious homicides. The argument made is similar to that accepted by the trial court in the *Janes* case; because of abuse inflicted over a long period of time, the defendant's perception was altered so that he or she did not form (or could not form) the mental state necessary for the most serious homicide charged. *See* Section E, *infra* of this chapter.

QUESTIONS

1. What authority does the Washington Court of Appeals rely on in determining that "there is a sufficient scientific basis to justify extending the battered woman syndrome to analogous situations affecting children"?

2. Consider the article that follows:

Associated Press, *Abuse Syndrome Develops Comfortable Home in Courts*, SEATTLE TIMES, March 31, 1994, Final Edition, Section: Local News, at B4.[68]

In the hours after he was shot to death in a Seattle middle-school hallway, teacher Neal Summers was recalled by stunned colleagues and students as a dedicated teacher, an exemplary human being.

When his killer confessed a few days later, Summers had some new labels: sexual abuser, pedophile.

Darrell Allen Cloud, 24, of White Center said he killed the Whitman Middle School teacher to end a decade of abuse that began when he was 14. Cloud, divorced, engaged to be married and living miles from Summers' North Seattle home, was an adult long past the age of consent.

But his attorney contends he suffered battered person's syndrome as a result of his long relationship with Summers.

"Self-defense is the defense of the '90s," one prosecutor said in a recent interview with *The News Tribune* of Tacoma. "It's definitely a trend."

And the definition is expanding.

King County Prosecutor Norm Maleng, whose office will take Cloud to trial in June, argues the legal definition requires immediate or imminent fear of bodily harm or death. "We condemn an adult sexually abusing a child," Maleng said. "But we cannot excuse murder as the appropriate response."

But that has changed, beginning in the mid-1980s, when juries began accepting psychologists' arguments that battered wives, like prisoners of war, may lose touch with reality as they struggle alone in a world of terror and violence — and self-defense may come in response to less obvious signals.

Some people respond to their sense of overwhelming, hopeless pain by killing themselves. Others turn on their tormenters.

The domestic-abuse syndrome has been expanded to cover male victims of long-term physical or sexual abuse — notably Andrew Janes, who was 17 when

---

[68] Copyright © 1994 by The Associated Press. Reprinted with permission.

he ambushed and shotgunned his abusive stepfather in suburban Mountlake Terrace.

Janes was convicted of second-degree murder in 1988, when a judge refused to allow evidence of self-defense, but the state Supreme Court last year granted him a new trial at which he will be permitted to argue he thought it was only a matter of time before his stepfather killed him.

. . . .

"We're coming close to making revenge killing legal," said Seth Aaron Fine, a deputy prosecutor in Snohomish County.

It's a tough concept for prosecutors to swallow.

"I'm not denying that abuse victims suffer long-lasting trauma in every aspect of their lives, but it shouldn't be a defense for everything," said Barbara Corey-Boulet, a deputy prosecutor in Pierce County. "It allows some people to escape responsibility for clear criminal conduct."

Jeff Sullivan, prosecutor for Yakima County, said he plans to ask the Legislature to narrow the definition. He complained that gang members who shoot in response to a rival gang's hand signal have tried to use it.

"My concern is, where do we cut it off?" Sullivan asked. "Do we say to every abused person, 'You don't have to take it, just kill him'?"

. . . .

Cloud's case is murk[y].

An expert witness called in by [the defense] considers Cloud psychotic. Prosecutors likely will call in their own experts to assess the defendant, in custody in lieu of $250,000 bail.

A gifted athlete, Cloud's reputation for a hot temper predates his relationship with Summers.

"What the teacher did was not OK — he was an offender. But there were many problems in this kid's life before he ever met teacher X," said Karil Klingbeil, director of social work at Harborview Medical Center and an associate professor at the University of Washington.

But Klingbeil . . . said she has no trouble understanding why Cloud kept returning to Summers. Victims rarely evolve out of their role with the abuser, she said: once a victim, always a victim. The abuse can cause normal development to stall. "Just because a child reaches the age of majority doesn't mean they think like adults," Klingbeil said.The trial likely will focus on Summers' impact on Cloud, Corey-Boulet said. "You end up trying not the defendant, but the victim," she said.

Members of the public, hearing excerpts from such a trial — like the Menendez brothers' trials for killing their parents, which both ended in hung juries — may dismiss the allegations.

People don't like hearing ill of the dead, and there is a risk of backlash against the defense, said Janes' appeal attorney, Lenell Nussbaum.

But the evidence is graphic and compelling for jurors, said Robert Aronson, a UW law professor. "If you sat there and hear the kind of abuse somebody took in detail, you can see how some jurors would say they can't find this person guilty beyond a reasonable doubt."

If someone can be abused by a parent (battered child syndrome) or a spouse (battered woman syndrome) and become afflicted with the battered child or battered woman syndrome, why can't a defendant who has killed an abusive friend assert that years of physical and emotional battering by the friend resulted in the "battered friend syndrome"?

Put another way, can a person in a relationship other than that of parent-child or husband-wife become afflicted with a syndrome that is the equivalent of the battered child or battered woman syndrome? Why shouldn't there be a syndrome called the "battered *person* syndrome"? *See, e.g., State v. Williams*, 787 S.W.2d 308, 312 (Mo. Ct. App. 1990) ("battered syndrome" applies whether woman is married or not); *People v. Yates*, 637 N.Y.S.2d 625 (N.Y. Sup. Ct. 1995) (male rape trauma syndrome); *State v. Borchardt*, 478 N.W.2d 757 (Minn. 1991) (male rape trauma syndrome); David S. Dupps (Student Note), *Battered Lesbians: Are They Entitled to a Battered Woman Defense?*, 29 J. Fam. L. 879, 898–99 (1990–91).

If an expert will so testify, what principled ground would a court have for excluding such evidence if there is precedent in the jurisdiction for admitting evidence of the battered child and/or battered woman syndrome?

3. Prior to killing his stepfather, Andrew Janes made a tape recording explaining his actions. After reading the text of Andrew Janes's recording (presented below), does your view of the battered child syndrome change? If not, does your view of the appropriateness of the battered child syndrome in the specific facts of the *Janes* case change? Finally, if the battered child syndrome is truly beyond the ken of the average juror and is the proper subject of expert testimony, is it possible that the comments below cannot be appreciated without the aid of an expert?

> I declare war on Walt and whoever else. I feel that what I am doing is right. He — Walter has made mine and my mom's life and my brother's life miserable. My mom is never happy. She doesn't smile anymore, and I can't handle this shit. My mom was trying to get him to stop doing drugs, dealing drugs. She's tried everything and he won't stop. There's nothing she can do. From his drug dealing I have become addicted. I've tried to quit, but I can't. And I don't want this in my life anymore. So I shall take care of the problem myself. Mom, if you find this, I hope you will forgive me. I'm doing this in your best wishes. I hope you will be happier without Walter. I think I'm going crazy, Mom. This shit has just been too much. If the police should find this before you, I'm not responsible for my actions. I do not know what I'm doing.

State v. Janes, 850 P.2d 495, 497 (Wash. 1993).

4. If you are uncomfortable with syndromes like the battered child syndrome or the battered woman syndrome being used as a complete defense for a homicide charge, is the problem one that can be addressed in an evidentiary ruling, or is the problem inherent in the definition of self-defense?

5. Finally, consider the way the trial judge handled the *Janes* case. The trial judge did not allow evidence of the battered child syndrome to establish self-defense but did allow it on the diminished capacity defense and (apparently) considered it in arriving at what sentence to impose. *See State v. Janes, supra,* 822 P.2d at 1240 n.2. Is this the better way to deal with defendants who claim to be suffering from a syndrome? *See* Travis H.D. Lewin, *Psychiatric Evidence in Criminal Cases for Purposes Other Than the Defense of Insanity,* 26 Syracuse L. Rev. 1051 (Fall 1975).

[b]   "New" Syndromes

The *Janes* case presented the "slippery slope" problem of a syndrome defense gradually being expanded into analogous fact patterns. The *Werner* case that follows takes a further step — expanding a syndrome defense into entirely new fields.

WERNER v. STATE
711 S.W.2d 639 (Tex. Crim. App. 1986) (en banc)

Onion, Presiding Judge.

A jury found appellant guilty of murder and assessed punishment at 10 years' confinement in the Department of Corrections.

The evidence showed that appellant shot and killed Tarbell Griffin Travis, after Travis allegedly damaged an automobile owned by appellant's friend, Kenneth Netterville.

On appeal the appellant raised four grounds of error, the second of which contended the trial court erred in refusing to allow him to introduce certain evidence on the condition of his mind "at the time of the offense" by virtue of the testimony of a psychiatrist. The Court of Appeals found the excluded evidence was not relevant to any issue. . . . We granted appellant's petition to determine whether the Court of Appeals was correct in overruling the second ground of error relating to the Holocaust syndrome.

The facts form the necessary backdrop for a discussion of appellant's contention. The 21-year-old appellant left work about 10:45 p.m. on April 1, 1982. He bought a six pack of beer and about 11 p.m. went to the Netterville residence on Stillbrooke in Houston to see Kenneth Netterville. Approximately 45 minutes later while he was on the porch with Kenneth's sister, Carole, appellant saw a car driven by the deceased, Tarbell Travis, speeding onto Stillbrooke from Greenwillow. The car swerved to miss a parked car and collided with Netterville's vehicle on the opposite side of the street. The car backed into Greenwillow and took off at a high rate of speed. Kenneth Netterville came out of the house and gave appellant a pistol stating "Let's go get him" and instructing appellant to go "that way."

Appellant found the vehicle on Spellman Street where the deceased Travis and his passenger, John Christensen, had gotten out to inspect the damage to the vehicle in which they were riding. Appellant parked his car parallel to the other vehicle and got out carrying a flashlight in one hand and the pistol in the other hand. Christensen testified appellant said, "What the hell do you think you're doing? You hit my friend's car. I ought to shoot you." Christensen recalled the deceased responded, "Well, then, why don't you?" At this time appellant shot the deceased in the chest from which wound he expired.

Appellant testified that he pursued the deceased's vehicle "to hold whoever hit my friend's car for the police." After he found the vehicle he stated he "yelled at him to get up against the car," and the deceased replied, "You're just going to have to shoot me, you son of a bitch." Appellant testified the deceased made a "shrugging" motion with his shoulders and took a step towards him. With the flashlight he saw the deceased's face and the deceased "looked crazy." He couldn't see the deceased's hands and didn't know whether the deceased was armed. Appellant stated he was in fear of his life, and to protect himself he shot the deceased in the chest.

Appellant did not know the deceased and apparently had not seen the deceased before the occasion in question. At no time during his testimony was he asked or did he state that he was a son or grandson of survivors of the Holocaust, or that stories about the Holocaust had any influence upon his state of mind at the time of the offense.

The excluded testimony was preserved for review by informal bills of exception. . . .

. . . .

Appellant . . . proffered the testimony of Dr. Rudolph Roden, a board-certified psychiatrist, who received a degree in Russian Literature from Charles University in Prague, Czechoslovakia in 1948, a medical degree from Queen's University in Kingston, Ontario in 1955, and a Ph.D. from the University of Montreal in 1965. It was stated Dr. Roden had come to this country three years before from Canada; was board-certified in psychiatry; that Dr. Roden's particular interest was research into the area of survivors and children of survivors of Nazi concentration camps; that the doctor himself was incarcerated in concentration camps from 1940 to 1945. It was also offered that Dr. Roden had lectured and written articles in the field of his specialty. He had conducted seminars in pre-Freudian and Freud, Freud's general psychological theory, male chauvinism, survivor syndrome, and survival.

It was proffered that Dr. Roden would testify that beginning in August, 1982, four months after the alleged offense, he began to see the appellant as a patient, and saw him some 18 or 19 times. Dr. Roden learned that the appellant's paternal grandmother was Jewish, his paternal grandfather was Protestant, and after the grandfather's death in 1941 or 1942 appellant's grandmother and his half-Jewish father and other members of the family were placed in concentration camps, that the father and grandmother survived, the other members of the family did not. Dr. Roden also learned the appellant grew up with stories of concentration camps told to him by his father and grandmother, who related seeing people beaten to death who did not fight back. Dr. Roden determined appellant showed "some" of the characteristics of an individual who has the syndrome associated with children of survivors of Nazi concentration camps.

It was also stated Dr. Roden would testify that the appellant told him of the events that occurred on the night in question. Dr. Roden related that appellant told him the moment he (appellant) pulled the trigger that he wasn't thinking about anything except protecting himself. Dr. Roden would testify, however, "that one does not need to be thinking of an event for another event in one's life to have an effect, a subconscious effect on him;" that the appellant disliked injustice, and one of the greatest injustices was the Holocaust, and that his knowledge thereof shaped his view of self-defense, that the act of the deceased in "running into a car and leaving the scene" was an unjust act in the appellant's view, and he sought to right the wrong by detaining the deceased for the police. Dr. Roden would testify that appellant's background caused him to make the decision to protect himself if his life was threatened, and though at the moment the alleged offense occurred he was not thinking of the Holocaust, it "was his state of mind to defend himself because he comes from a family that did not."

The State objected to the proffered testimony of Dr. Roden on the ground of relevancy, that if self-defense is urged the "test to be made by the jury in applying the standard of an ordinary and prudent person [is] the Defendant's position at the time of the offense."

The appellant disclaimed there was any issue of insanity at the time of the commission of the offense. . . .

The court overruled the proffer of Dr. Roden's testimony stating:

> " THE COURT: In light of the Defendant's testimony, the fact that there is no legal authority at all for such testimony coming before the jury, and because there are no two people alike, everybody is different, everybody comes from a different background, different things happen in the past, because there is no special breed of people that should be treated differently, all must come within the standard of law that we have in the state of Texas, and although the Holocaust is an example of man's inhumane acts towards their fellow man, the Court is going to sustain the objection at this time."

. . . .

There is no claim that the testimony of the appellant in his own behalf was limited or restricted in any way. He simply did not testify that he was suffering from a Holocaust syndrome, or that it had any effect on his actions that night. It was not mentioned at all. What appellant does assert is that it was error to exclude . . . the opinion testimony of a psychiatrist. . . . Dr. Roden stated appellant told him he was not thinking of the Holocaust at the time of the event in question, that appellant showed "some" of the characteristics of a child of a survivor of the Holocaust, that in his opinion [it] could have had a subconscious effect on him.

It is well established that evidence must be relevant to a contested fact or issue to be admissible. It has been said that in order to determine whether any evidence is admissible, the trial judge should compare its probative value, if any, with the prejudicial and inflammatory aspects of the testimony. The determination of this admissibility is within the sound discretion of the trial judge. That determination will not be reversed on appeal unless a "clear abuse" of discretion by the trial judge is shown.

It is also settled that evidence of collateral facts which does not in some logical way tend to prove or disprove the matters in issue is not admissible. And this rule of exclusion is particularly true when the irrelevant evidence tends to create sympathy for the deceased or his family, or to prejudice the defendant before the jury.

. . . .

Appellant argues the excluded evidence was material to his claim of self-defense, that his use of deadly force arose from a perception, reasonable to him, that he needed to resort to the use of deadly force for self protection, and that a reasonable person, with his background and experience, would not have retreated.

The trial court did not find that the excluded evidence was relevant and therefore admissible, and for there to be reversible error the trial court must have clearly abused its discretion.

The State argues that appellant was not entitled to the defense of self-defense, and certainly not deadly force self-defense, under the facts of the case. . . . Thus the proffered evidence was not material to any contested issue in the case, and was properly excluded; that if self-defense was raised, evidence of the asserted "Holocaust Syndrome" was properly excluded as an impermissible attempt to broaden the right of self-defense beyond [the] parameters established by V.T.C.A., Penal Code, §§ 9.31, 9.32 and 1.07(31).

Appellant used deadly force in shooting the deceased in the chest with a pistol. Section 9.32 (Deadly Force in Defense of Person) provides the use of deadly force is justified in self-defense only when three conditions are all present: (1) the defendant would have been justified in using force under § 9.31; (2) a reasonable person in the defendant's situation would not have retreated; and (3) the use of deadly force was reasonably believed to be immediately necessary to protect the defendant against another's use or attempted use of unlawful deadly force, or to prevent the imminent commission of specified violent crimes.

Appellant testified he did not see any weapon in the possession of the deceased or his companion, Christensen. He did not, and plainly could not have testified that he reasonably believed it necessary to shoot the deceased in order to defend himself against the deceased's use or attempted use of deadly force. In absence of evidence of use or attempted use of deadly force by the deceased, the statutory defense permitted by § 9.32 is not available, and a defendant is not entitled to a jury instruction. Further, there is nothing in the record to indicate a reasonable person in appellant's circumstance would not have retreated, hence the statutory defense was not raised and need not have been submitted to the jury. Thus the excluded evidence was not relevant to any real contested issue in the case, and the court in ruling the same inadmissible did not err.

Be that as it may, even if the self-defense issue was validly before the jury the proffered testimony was still immaterial. . . . Dr. Roden's testimony was that, although appellant continued to disclaim [sic] he was not thinking of the Holocaust at the time of the offense, he showed "some" characteristics of the syndrome associated with children of the survivors of the Holocaust, and the same might have had a subconscious effect on him. All that can be inferred from this evidence is that appellant may have been more susceptible to actions in self-defense. It did not establish that appellant did in fact act under the influence of the Holocaust on the night of the offense. The self-defense statutes permit the use of force only when and to the degree a person "reasonably believes" it immediately necessary. As stated in V.T.C.A., Penal Code, § 1.07(31), a "reasonable belief" is one that would be held by an "ordinary and prudent man in the same circumstances as the actor." Although the test assumes that a defendant may act on appearances as viewed from his standpoint, the test also assumes the "ordinary prudent man test of tort law." Practice Commentary to V.T.C.A., Penal Code, § 9.31 (Searcy and Patterson).

The evidence excluded only tended to show that possibly appellant was not an ordinary and prudent man with respect to self-defense. This did not entitle appellant to an enlargement of the statutory defense on account of his psychological peculiarities. A similar point was recently made in *Gonzales v. State*, 689 S.W.2d 900, 903 (Tex. Cr. App. 1985), with regard to V.T.C.A., Penal Code, § 19.04(c) (Voluntary manslaughter), which also utilizes the "reasonable man."

> "Appellant seems to contend that because he is an Hispanic farm worker who was living with a Caucasian woman on a low income he should be granted more latitude in the degree of insult, etc., sufficient to enrage him. Yet appellant fails to recognize that the standard of the reasonable man, the person of ordinary temper, is employed precisely to avoid different applications of the law of

manslaughter to defendants of different races, creed, color, sex, or social status."

. . . .

We conclude that the Court of Appeals reached the right result in overruling appellant's ground of error #2. . . .

The judgment of the Court of Appeals is affirmed.

TEAGUE, JUDGE, dissenting.

. . . .

The subject "The Holocaust Syndrome" appears to be a new type of syndrome in psychiatric circles. Excluding a reference to one book entitled *Adolescent Psychiatry: Developmental and Clinical Studies*, at p. 66 (1982), all other references that counsel for the appellant directs us to are articles found in three newspapers. My independent research has yet to find a single reported court case which has discussed this syndrome.

Although there appears to be a paucity of case law regarding "The Holocaust Syndrome," this in itself should not have been reason for the trial judge to have excluded Dr. Roden's testimony; to the contrary, this is probably the best reason why such testimony should have been admitted in this case. Dr. Roden's testimony was highly relevant on the issue of the condition of the appellant's state of mind at the time he fired the fatal shot, and would have aided the jury, all of whom were probably totally unfamiliar with this type syndrome, in better deciding what the appellant's state or condition of his mind was when he shot the deceased, and how his suffering from "The Holocaust Syndrome" affected the condition of his mind at that time.

. . . .

In this instance, there is no challenge by the State to Dr. Roden's qualifications to testify on the subject "The Holocaust Syndrome." From his impressive list of credentials, as well as his study of the subject, Dr. Roden appears to possess special knowledge upon the specific matter about which his expertise was sought.

If scientific, technical, or other specialized knowledge will assist the trier of fact to better understand the evidence or determine a fact in issue, a witness is qualified as an expert by knowledge, skill, experience, training, or education, and he should be able to testify in the form of opinion evidence.

In this instance, I find that the subject "The Holocaust Syndrome" was beyond the ken of the average lay person. The jury was entitled to know that when the appellant fired the fatal shot he believed that because of his past experiences, if his life was ever threatened, he would act to protect himself, and that is why he acted in the manner in which he did, i.e., that his state of mind at the time was affected, not only by that which he visually saw on the night in question, but also because of his belief that it was necessary for him to defend himself because he comes from a family who did not defend themselves, thus causing them to perish in the Holocaust. Dr. Roden's proffered testimony as to what effect being a descendant of a survivor of "The Holocaust" had upon the appellant, as to his reasonable belief of danger, was not only relevant and material as to his state of mind, but it was also relevant and material on his defense of self-defense, on which the jury was instructed.

. . . .

Although there are obvious differences between the syndrome now known as "The Battered Wife Syndrome" and the syndrome now known as "The Holocaust Syndrome," in principle they have much in common. Today, it is not unusual for our more enlightened trial courts to admit testimony of expert witnesses on "The Battered Wife Syndrome," as relevant to explain the legitimacy of a wife's reactions to threats of danger from her spouse, and to counteract prosecutorial claims that the wife's continued presence in the home means that the homicide was not necessary. It should be obvious to almost anyone that without such testimony it would be difficult, if not impossible, for persons unfamiliar with how "The Battered Wife Syndrome" manifests itself to understand what effect the actions of the former spouse had on the state or condition of the wife's mind when she shot and killed her former spouse. In any event, it simply cannot be logically argued that such testimony would not be of assistance to the trier of fact in determining what the condition of the defendant's mind might have been when the offense was committed.

All courts are not in agreement that expert testimony in "The Battered Woman Syndrome" type case is always admissible. Some courts have held that such testimony is relevant to the issue of self-defense and therefore admissible, other courts have held that such testimony is admissible for reasons other than self-defense, while other courts hold that such testimony is absolutely inadmissible.

. . . .

. . . [T]he lack of uniformity is not surprising; attempts to expand testimony into new fields have often resulted in judicial confusion and inconsistency. . . .

. . . .

For the above and foregoing reasons, I respectfully dissent.

NOTES

1. *Syndromes Used by the Prosecution.* When applied to a defendant and used by the prosecution to help secure a conviction, expert testimony on the defendant having a syndrome can come very close to being evidence of a character or propensity to commit a crime. In *People v. Phillips*, 175 Cal. Rptr. 703 (Cal. Ct. App. 1981), the defendant was accused of murdering one of her two adopted daughters by deliberately administering a sodium compound into her daughter's food. To suggest a motive for the mother's conduct the state presented expert testimony on "Munchausen's syndrome by proxy." The state's expert explained that Munchausen's syndrome by proxy is "one in which an individual either directly or through the vehicle of a child feigns, simulates, or actually fabricates a physical illness." *Id.* at 709. The state's expert continued and explained that the mother with Munchausen's syndrome by proxy is transferring her "own unmet parental needs onto pediatricians, nurses, [and] spouses and [gets] from these people through [her] child's illness the attention and sympathy [she] never got from [her] own parents." *Id.* The court found evidence of the syndrome admissible to show motive even though the defendant had not placed her mental condition in issue. *Id.* at 712.

A similar character evidence problem is presented when the prosecution offers evidence of a criminal "profile" and applies the profile to a defendant to suggest that the defendant committed a crime. The use of profiles as character evidence is discussed in the next section.

2. *Expanding Syndromes.* The admissibility of a variety of syndromes and mental conditions has been considered by the courts. Sometimes such evidence is offered by the accused as a complete or partial defense, and sometimes it is offered by the prosecution to show motive or explain why a crime victim might have acted as he or she did. For example, in addition to the syndromes already examined, courts have been presented with "narcissistic personality disorder," *United States v. Cohen*, 510 F.3d 1114, 1123 (9th Cir. 2007) (defendant's "will was in the service of irrational beliefs as a result of narcissistic personality disorder"; offered as mens rea defense to tax evasion charge); "flight/flee syndrome," *State v. Nazario*, 726 So.2d 349, 349–50 (Fla. Dist. Ct. App. 1999) (precludes defendant from forming an intent to kill, but rather, caused him to kill out of an involuntary survival instinct"); "neonaticide syndrome," *People v. Wernick*, 674 N.E.2d 322, 323 (N.Y. 1996) (killing of newborn within 24 hours of birth due to feelings of isolation and denial; offered to support insanity defense); "parental alienation syndrome," *People v. Fortin*, 706 N.Y.S.2d 611, 612–13 (Cty. Ct. 2000) (the programming of a child by one parent into a campaign of denigration directed against the other; offered to show why niece may have falsely accused uncle of rape); "Vietnam post-traumatic stress syndrome," *State v. Felde*, 422 So. 2d 370, 376 (La. 1982) (individual behaves as though they are reexperiencing combat; offered to support insanity defense); "Munchausen syndrome by proxy," *People v. Phillips*, 175 Cal. Rptr. 703, 707 (Cal. App. 1981) (patient beguiles a physician into performing unnecessary medical procedures; offered by prosecution to show motive for harming child); "detail phobia," *United States v. Barta*, 888 F.2d 1220 (8th Cir. 1989) (proffered in prosecution for filing false tax returns to show lack of intent); "Hispanic farm worker syndrome," *Gonzales v. State*, 689 S.W.2d 900 (Tex. Crim. App. 1985) (Hispanic living with a Caucasian woman more readily enraged at insults; offered to support adequate provocation element of voluntary manslaughter); "intermittent explosive disorder," *Kramer v. United States*, 579 F. Supp. 314, 316 (D. Md. 1984) (disorder causes discrete episodes of loss of control that result in violent outbursts); "pathological" or "compulsive" gambling syndrome, *United States v. Lewellyn*, 723 F.2d 615 (8th Cir. 1983), and "pseudologia fantastica," *United States v. Shay*, 57 F.3d 126, 129–30 (1st Cir. 1995) (condition causing person to "spin webs of lies"). *See also* Wally Owens, Student Note, *State v. Osby, The Urban Survival Defense*, 22 Am. J. Crim. L. 809 (1995).

QUESTIONS

1. What, precisely, is Werner's defense? How is testimony of the Holocaust syndrome relevant to this defense?

2. Why does the prosecution contend that evidence of the Holocaust syndrome is inadmissible?

3. Would it have made any difference to the appellate court in *Werner* if Werner himself had been in a concentration camp rather than having just heard about it from his father and grandmother?

4. On the reasoning of the court in *Werner*, would a woman be entitled to offer evidence of the battered woman syndrome in similar circumstances? On what issue? *See Pierini v. State*, 804 S.W.2d 258, 259 (Tex. App. 1991) (defendant offered battered woman syndrome testimony to explain why she stayed with and "loved" man who battered her and whom she killed).

D. PROFILES

[1]   Profiles Offered by the Prosecution to Suggest the Defendant Committed a Crime

Assume that an expert who has studied the background and lifestyles of hundreds of parents who battered their children develops a "profile" of characteristics possessed by the typical child batterer. If the accused in a criminal case fits the profile (and the profile is deemed to be either "reliable" or, alternatively, not subject to the jurisdiction's test for scientific evidence), will the prosecution be allowed to offer evidence of the "battering parent profile" *and* evidence tending to show that the defendant fit the profile? If so, for what purpose? In *State v. Loebach* the Supreme Court of Minnesota was presented with those questions.

STATE v. LOEBACH
310 N.W.2d 58 (Minn. 1981)

YETKA, JUSTICE.

On July 31, 1978, appellant was charged with third-degree murder and first-degree manslaughter in connection with the June 1, 1978, death of his three-month-old son Michael. [Appellant was tried before a jury, found] guilty of third-degree murder[,] . . . [and] sentenced to a maximum term of 15 years. This appeal followed. We affirm.

The issues raised on appeal [include]:

1. Whether the trial court erred in admitting testimony as to appellant's background and personality traits used to prove he fit the diagnosis of a "battering parent"[.]

. . . .

The victim, Michael Loebach, was born February 13, 1978. His mother, Anna, who had been serving in the U.S. Army in Georgia, was pregnant with Michael when she met appellant, who was also serving in the U.S. Army. She and appellant were married a month before the baby was born. Anna was discharged in December because of her pregnancy. Appellant received a general discharge in early March. In late March of 1978, they began living in an apartment building in Millville, Minnesota, where Anna's half-sister lived.

Both appellant and Anna looked for jobs, but only Anna was successful. She began work as a waitress in Rochester in mid-April. Because appellant remained unemployed, he acted as the babysitter whenever Anna worked. With one exception, the baby was in the custody and presence of either or both Anna and appellant during his entire short life. The one exception was in April, when appellant and Anna took a weekend trip and left the baby with Anna's half-sister. It was undisputed that the baby was not injured in any way on that occasion. The evidence was clear that the baby had no "accidents" and showed no bruises before Anna began leaving him in appellant's care while she worked.

. . . .

There was . . . testimony that the baby had numerous facial scratches, head bumps and black eyes during this period, but the explanation by both Anna and appellant was that the baby scratched himself a lot, bumped his head on the crib, and poked his eye until it was black and blue. Anna also admitted that she saw appellant "spank" the baby once.

. . . .

The baby died sometime on the evening of June 1, 1978, when Anna was at work and appellant was in charge. The testimony of a number of appellant's neighbors who visited with appellant in the hall that evening was that appellant was drinking and was unusually sociable. One of these neighbors, Mrs. Lori Stock, went in to look at the baby around 8:00 or 8:30 p.m. that evening while appellant and Mr. Stock were talking. She testified that she put her hand on the baby, who was lying on his abdomen with his head facing the wall, but did not notice anything unusual. Mrs. Stock testified that she did not touch the baby for more than a moment because appellant came in and asked her to leave because he didn't want her to wake the baby. Sometime around 11:00 p.m., Anna arrived home but could not get into the apartment. Her loud pounding on the door failed to wake appellant. With the help of neighbors, Anna was able to get into the apartment through a window. Anna testified that when she got in, she found appellant asleep on the bathroom floor. She apparently checked the baby when she first arrived but did not notice anything wrong. When she checked the baby again at midnight, she noticed how cold he was and immediately knew that he was dead. She then ran out to the neighbors for help. The baby was in the same position it had been in when Mrs. Stock saw it at 8:00 or 8:30 that evening. There is strong medical evidence that the baby was dead by 9:00 p.m., possibly even when Mrs. Stock touched him sometime before that hour.

. . . .

A sheriff's deputy testified that appellant, who was obviously intoxicated, told him when he arrived that the baby had not been acting right, had not taken milk, and had died of crib death. Concerning bruises on the baby, appellant said he must have squeezed Michael too hard and that when he was giving the baby a bath, the baby must have slipped out.

The coroner, a licensed physician, testified that he immediately noticed an unusual bruise high on the baby's cheek near the temple and some 2- or 3-day-old bruises on the baby's back. Further, he testified that as he examined the baby, appellant interjected, in explanation of the bruises, that he had tossed the baby in the air playfully and that when he caught it, his fingernails had caused the back bruises. Both appellant and Anna objected when the doctor stated that he was ordering an autopsy. One witness testified that appellant was enraged by this.

The autopsy revealed back bruises, several bruises above one ear, one bruise on the jaw, and one between the nipples. The internal examination revealed 2- or 3-week-old rib fractures close to the spine. It also revealed that although there was no skull fracture, there was extensive brain hemorrhaging, some of which was caused by injuries occurring within the previous 24 hours and some by injuries 3 or more weeks old. It was determined that the hemorrhaging caused the death and that the injuries which caused the hemorrhaging were caused by some blunt force.

Appellant, in an interview by an investigator, repeated his version of the cause of the back bruises, claiming this incident occurred 2 to 3 days before the baby's death. Appellant also claimed that the baby often picked at his eye and even hit himself on the head. He admitted shouting at the baby if it cried, admitted spanking the baby, and admitted slapping it once in Georgia. The investigator testified that Anna said she occasionally noticed spots on the baby's head and that appellant's explanation was that the baby poked himself. The investigator also testified that Anna admitted asking appellant on two or three occasions if he had abused the baby and that Anna said his reply, which she believed, was that he had not.

. . . .

Dr. Robert ten Bensel, an expert on child abuse, testified concerning the so-called "battered child syndrome." He concluded that it fit this case almost perfectly. . . . Dr. ten Bensel was firmly convinced that the baby's death was the final result of nonaccidental physical abuse of the baby over a period of time.

Dr. ten Bensel also was permitted to testify, over a general objection by defense counsel, that battering parents tend to have similar personality traits and personal histories.

Defense counsel objected generally to the state's calling of two witnesses from appellant's past in an attempt to prove appellant fit the pattern of a "battering parent." Judith Carpenter is a former case worker who was assigned to appellant when he was a juvenile in Illinois. She testified that appellant's mother, who raised appellant alone, had abused him until he was old enough to fight back, that his mother expected too much of him, and that appellant was not good at controlling his anger. Charles Nelson, an employee of a school for disturbed adolescent boys which appellant attended for 3 years until he reached age 18, testified that appellant often withdrew from others, had a low frustration level, and was adolescent in behavior. Testimony from other witnesses also aided in showing that appellant fit the "battering parent" profile. There was testimony that appellant and Anna were isolated and did not have contact with many people and that in April 1978, appellant had slapped her and broken her nose. Defense counsel did not object to the testimony concerning the broken nose.

The defense strategy for countering this testimony was partly to show that the "battering parent" profile also fit Anna and that it did not necessarily fit appellant. In cross-examining Anna's sister, defense counsel elicited testimony that appellant was proud, confident and not lacking in self-esteem, whereas Anna was hypertense, unable to cope, unable to handle liquor, and was herself a victim of child abuse. Appellant's direct testimony, however, tended to corroborate the state's evidence that he fit the profile. He testified that his mother called him the man of the family and that he developed a bad temper.

Appellant denied abusing the baby. He testified that he did not see anyone else abuse the baby and that he had no explanation for the injuries the doctor found in the autopsy, although he thought he might have broken the baby's ribs when he accidently dropped the baby one day. He also testified that for a period of time, until warned by Mrs. Hermanson, [defendant's sister-in-law], that it was dangerous, he had playfully thrown the baby high in the air and caught it. He testified that he stopped doing this 1 to 2 months before the baby died. He also testified that while he admitted slapping the baby once, the slap was more like a love pat.

1. Appellant contends that the state's use of evidence of his character constitutes prejudicial error and warrants reversal. The specific testimony objected to concerns that given by the state's expert, Dr. ten Bensel, and the two prosecution witnesses who knew appellant as an adolescent.

On direct examination, Dr. ten Bensel was asked to state the characteristics of a "battering parent." According to Dr. ten Bensel, the "battering parent" syndrome is an "inner (sic) generational phenomena" in that adults who abuse their children were often abused themselves. The doctor testified that abusing parents frequently experience role reversal and often expect their children to care for them. He also stated that battering parents often exhibit similar characteristics such as low empathy, a short fuse, low [sic] temper, short temper, low boiling point, high blood pressure, strict authoritarianism, uncommunicativeness, low self-esteem, isolation and lack of trust. Dr. ten Bensel did not testify that appellant possessed any of these characteristics, but the state's witnesses, Judith Carpenter and Charles Nelson, suggested that he did.

The obvious purpose for the introduction of the Carpenter and Nelson testimony and other character evidence was to demonstrate that appellant fit within the "battering parent" profile. The general rule as to the admission of such character evidence is contained in Minn. R. Evid. 404(a) which provides in relevant part as follows:

> (a) *Character evidence generally.* Evidence of a person's character or a trait of his character is not admissible for the purpose of proving that he acted in conformity therewith on a particular occasion, except:
>
>> (1) *Character of accused.* Evidence of a pertinent trait of his character offered by an accused, or by the prosecution to rebut the same;

Appellant did not put his character in evidence in this case so the cited exception to the rule's general prohibition does not apply.

Even prior to the adoption of the Minnesota Rules of Evidence by this court, the general prohibition against the use of character evidence was well established in Minnesota. In *City of St. Paul v. Harris*, 184 N.W. 840 (1921), the long history of the rule was recognized by the court when it noted, "No rule of criminal law is more thoroughly established than the rule that the character of the defendant cannot be attacked until he himself puts it in issue by offering evidence of his good character." 184 N.W. at 840.

There are three basic reasons for the exclusion of character evidence used to prove a criminal defendant acted in conformity with such character. First, there is the possibility that the jury will convict a defendant in order to penalize him for his past misdeeds or simply because he is an undesirable person. Second, there is the danger that a jury will overvalue the character evidence in assessing the guilt for the crime charged. Finally, it is unfair to require an accused to be prepared not only to defend against immediate charges, but also to disprove or explain his personality or prior actions. . . .

The state argues that the potential for prejudice to defendants that justifies the rule excluding character evidence is outweighed by the public interest in assuring conviction of persons who batter children. The state's position is that the difficulties involved in prosecuting those who abuse children warrant an exception to the general rule. The victim, as the state's expert testified, is usually an infant and therefore particularly defenseless. Children who are abused are also almost wholly dependent on those who inflict the abuse. The victims' age and dependence act to prevent them from testifying against abusing caretakers. Finally, abuse almost always occurs when the child is in the exclusive care of a battering caretaker. These features of abuse cases make it very difficult to establish a defendant's guilt by means of direct evidence. The state contends, therefore, that an exception to the general rule is necessary to offset these obstacles to the prosecution of battering individuals.

. . . .

We . . . hold that in future cases the prosecution will not be permitted to introduce evidence of "battering parent" syndrome or to establish the character of the defendant as a "battering parent" unless the defendant first raises that issue. We feel this finding is required until further evidence of the scientific accuracy and reliability of syndrome or profile diagnoses can be established.

Our determination that the "battering parent" evidence should not have been admitted does not affect the result of this case in the court below. A defendant claiming error in the trial court's reception of evidence has the burden of showing both the error and the prejudice resulting from the error. A reversal is warranted only when the error substantially influences the jury to convict.

The record in this case indicates that the "battering parent" testimony consisted of only a small percentage of the evidence. The record also reveals that there was overwhelming evidence of appellant's guilt even without the "battering parent" testimony.

. . . .

In light of this substantial evidence to support appellant's conviction, the error in admitting "battering parent" testimony was not prejudicial.

. . . .

The conviction is affirmed.

NOTES

1. *The Battering Parent Profile: Inadmissible as General Character Evidence.* The *Loebach* case is in the majority in both its refusal to allow the prosecution to use evidence of the battering parent profile in its *case in chief*, and in basing its decision upon the rule that precludes the prosecution from offering evidence of the accused's character unless the accused first puts his or her character in issue. *See Sanders v. State*, 303 S.E.2d 13, 18 (Ga. 1983); Annot., *Admissibility at Criminal Prosecution of Expert Testimony on Battering Parent Syndrome*, 43 A.L.R.4th 1203 (1986).

2. *The Sex Offender Profile.* A somewhat analogous situation involves sex offenses, particularly child sexual abuse. Prosecutors have, on occasion, attempted to offer evidence of the profile of a child sexual abuser accompanied by evidence tending to show that the defendant fits the profile. Courts have rejected such evidence primarily because it violates the ban on the prosecution putting the defendant's character in evidence. The reasoning is the same as in cases that exclude expert opinion of the battering parent profile for violating the character evidence rule. For example, in *United States v. Gillespie*, 852 F.2d 475 (9th Cir. 1988), the trial court admitted testimony from a government expert that

> the characteristics of a molester include an early disruption in the family environment, often with one parent missing: a relationship with the parent of the opposite sex who is dominant; unsuccessful relationships with women; a poor self-concept; and general instability in the background.

Id. at 480. On appeal the Ninth Circuit held that it was error to admit such testimony because the defendant had not put his character in issue or testified that he had any character traits that would make him incapable of molesting children.

Courts that have admitted similar testimony when offered by the prosecution have done so in cases that involve sexual offenses and have characterized the evidentiary issue in such a way that the character evidence issue is ignored or not implicated. Two cases illustrate this approach.

First, in *State v. Hickman*, 337 N.W.2d 512 (Iowa 1983), the defendant was accused of raping and then murdering a co-worker by stabbing her 39 times. Defendant took the witness stand and (as to the rape charge) claimed that there was consensual intercourse, not rape. In rebuttal, the prosecution called a psychiatrist who had made a study of the psychology of rapists and who had examined defendant and defendant's medical history. The psychiatrist testified about various types of rapists and characterized defendant as "of the class of aggressive, antisocial or sociopathic, hatred rapists." *Id.* at 516. The Iowa Supreme Court, without mentioning the obvious character evidence issue, held such testimony was admissible to *rebut* defendant's claim of consensual intercourse. *Id.*

Second, in *Slayton v. State*, 633 S.W.2d 934 (Tex. Crim. App. 1982), defendant was charged with indecency with a child. In its case in chief the state called a psychiatrist who testified that the accused was the type of person who might expose himself to a child. *Id.* at 936. Even though such testimony appears to violate the rule against the prosecution putting the defendant's character in evidence, the court, without addressing the character issue, held, "It is not error for a psychiatrist to express his opinion that an accused is capable of forming an *intent* to perform the act with which he is charged." *Id.* (Emphasis added.)

3. *The Reliability of Profile Evidence.* Also militating against admissibility of profile evidence is the fact that there appears to be some question as to the scientific reliability of such evidence. Of course, the reliability issue rarely arises when it is the prosecution, in its case in chief, offering profile testimony because the character evidence rule makes such testimony inadmissible without considering its reliability. When, however, the *defendant* offers profile evidence, which is not prohibited by the ban on character evidence, courts are forced to consider reliability issues. Profile reliability issues in this context are discussed in the *St. Pierre* case *infra* this chapter, and the notes that follow.

To illustrate, consider the situation where a defendant is permitted to offer character evidence in the form of opinion testimony stating that the defendant did not have the character of a child batterer. The character evidence ban presented by Fed. R. Evid. 404(a) and its state counterparts would, presumably, be overcome, and the state could offer opinion character evidence in rebuttal to the defendant's character evidence pursuant to Fed. R. Evid. 404(a)(1). The question that then arises is whether expert opinion based upon the battering parent profile (or whatever profile is pertinent in the case) is scientifically valid enough so that it may be used for rebuttal evidence consistent with Rule 404(a)(1) and its state counterparts.

The question of scientific reliability of profile evidence has not been directly addressed by the courts in the context of the battering parent profile. At least one commentator, however, has expressed concern over the reliability of such evidence. *See* John E.B. Myers, Jan Bays, Judith Becker, Lucy Berliner, David L. Corwin & Karen J. Saywitz, *Expert Testimony in Child Sexual Abuse Litigation*, 68 NEB. L. REV. 1, 142 (1989) ("Regardless of which party offers battering parent syndrome evidence, serious questions persist about the syndrome's reliability."). *Cf. Flanagan v. State*, 625 So. 2d 827, 828 (Fla. 1993) (sex offender profile cannot satisfy the *Frye* test).

4. *The Prejudicial Effect of Criminal Profile Evidence.* In addition to evidentiary problems associated with character evidence and scientific reliability, when the pros ecution offers evidence of a criminal profile to suggest that the accused fits the profile, troubling problems of unfair prejudice appear. In *United States v. Gillespie*, 852 F.2d 475 (9th Cir. 1988), the Ninth Circuit, in dicta, commented that testimony concerning criminal profiles is "highly undesirable" as substantive evidence because of its low probative value and its inherent prejudicial effect. *Id.* at 852. *See also United States v. White*, 890 F.2d 1012, 1014 (8th Cir. 1989) (predictive profiles are "inherently prejudicial because of the potential they have for including innocent citizens"); *United States v. Hernandez-Cuartas*, 717 F.2d 552, 554–55 (11th Cir. 1983) (testimony of profile of a drug courier ordinarily inadmissible as substantive evidence of guilt); *Hall v. State*, 692 S.W.2d 769, 773 (Ark. App. 1985) (expert profile testimony distractive and prejudicial).

5. *Modus Operandi Evidence.* In two situations experts (usually prosecution experts) are allowed to testify to what is termed "modus operandi" evidence. Sometimes expert testimony about the habits or methods of certain types of criminals, or criminal enterprises, is offered as *background information* to help the jury understand the significance of certain conduct that otherwise may appear to be innocent conduct. For example, if a defendant who was arrested for drug trafficking possessed a small amount of drugs rolled inside a dollar bill in his shirt pocket, an expert may testify that that is more consistent with a dealer's sample than possession of drugs for personal use. *See Commonwealth v. Munera*, 578 N.E.2d 418, 422 (Mass. App. 1991). Such evidence, called modus operandi evidence, is often admitted by courts.

In the second situation, a defendant will sometimes present evidence that his conduct is innocent, making modus operandi rebuttal evidence admissible. In the *Munera* case the defendant was charged with trafficking in cocaine. Munera's attorney, in his opening statement, asked the jury to consider that the defendant's simple lifestyle was inconsistent with the money typically made by cocaine dealers. In rebuttal the prosecution offered expert testimony that modest stash pads and a low profile was the modus operandi of drug dealers. *Commonwealth v. Munera, supra*, 578 N.E.2d at 422.

The problem with such evidence, from the standpoint of the defense, is that it closely resembles profile evidence, and a jury may assume that the defendant is guilty because his or her conduct fits what an expert testifies to as the modus operandi of other typical criminals. Courts are quite emphatic in holding that if the evidence is offered as substantive evidence of guilt, it is inadmissible. *United States v. Hernandez-Cuartas*, 717 F.2d 552, 555 (11th Cir. 1983) (drug courier profile evidence denounced when offered as substantive evidence of guilt; admissible when offered as background information to help the jury appreciate the significance of unfamiliar conduct). However, if modus operandi evidence is offered as background or rebuttal evidence, it may be admissible. *See United States v. White*, 890 F.2d 1012, 1014 (8th Cir. 1989).

QUESTION

In the *Loebach* case, the Minnesota Supreme Court held that the prosecution would not be permitted to introduce evidence of the battering parent profile to establish the character of the defendant as a battering parent "unless the defendant first raises the issue." *State v. Loebach, supra*, 310 N.W.2d at 64. The court, however, seemed to qualify its ruling by concluding, "[w]e feel this finding is required *until* further evidence of the scientific accuracy and reliability of syndrome or profile diagnoses can be established." *Id.* (Emphasis added.)

If it were shown that profiles of the battering parent (or the child molester) had achieved "scientific accuracy and reliability," would that justify an exception to the ban on the prosecution placing the defendant's character in evidence? If scientific accuracy were achieved, what arguments would support admissibility of such evidence? What arguments would support keeping such evidence inadmissible even though it had been shown to be scientifically reliable? *See* Thomas N. Bulleit, Jr., Student Note, *The Battering Parent Syndrome: Inexpert Testimony as Character Evidence*, 17 U. MICH. J.L. REF. 653, 668–69 (1984); *United States v. White*, 890 F.2d 1012, 1014 (8th Cir. 1989).

PROBLEMS

Problem 5-15. Defendants are charged with conspiracy to persuade a minor to engage in sexually explicit conduct for the purpose of producing visual or print media in violation of federal statutes. Defendants claim that the non-sexual but nude photos of children found in their possession (and which they published in magazines) were "innocent nude studies" and not child pornography, and, further, that they were planning to cast a "legitimate film" for which they needed some nude photos to assist in casting. A critical issue at trial, therefore, is whether the photos were obtained with the intent of using them to produce and distribute child pornography or for legitimate purposes.

At trial the district court permits testimony by an FBI agent who is qualified as an expert on "the characteristic behaviors of pedophiles." The FBI expert testifies that pedophiles "characteristically derive sexual satisfaction from and collect even such ostensibly non-sexual nude photos of children [as those in this case]," and that such photos "rather than more graphic ones, are frequently published in magazines distributed to pedophiles in an attempt to circumvent laws against obscenity and child pornography." Further, the FBI expert testifies that pedophiles often use the term "nude studies" as a "code word" to refer to such non-obscene photographs.

Defendants are convicted and appeal. Defendants challenge such testimony as unfairly prejudicial and cite *United States v. Gillespie*, 852 F.2d 475, 479–80 (9th Cir. 1988) (profile offered by the prosecution violates the character evidence rule unless defendant first places his or her character in issue, and "testimony of criminal profiles is highly undesirable as substantive evidence").

Is there an argument for admitting such testimony that does not conflict with Fed. R. Evid. 404(a)'s ban on character evidence? *See United States v. Cross*, 928 F.2d 1030, 1050 (11th Cir. 1991); *United States v. White*, 890 F.2d 1012, 1014 (8th Cir. 1989).

Problem 5-16. Defendant is convicted of child molestation. At trial the defendant offered testimony from a priest that defendant was not the type of person who would molest children. In rebuttal the state offered evidence from a clinical psychologist as to the common characteristics of child molesters. The expert stated that child molesters (1) have an early disruption in their family environment, (2) often have one parent missing, (3) have one parent of the opposite sex who is dominant, (4) have unsuccessful relationships with women, (5) have a poor self-concept, and (6) generally are unstable. The profile fits defendant based upon evidence offered by other witnesses at trial.

On appeal defendant challenges the admissibility of the profile evidence. Was the profile evidence properly admitted? *See United States v. Gillespie*, 852 F.2d 475, 479–80 (9th Cir. 1988).

[2]   Profiles Offered by the Defense to show that Defendant's Character is Incompatible with the Crime Charged

Assume that the prosecution does not offer evidence of a profile in its case in chief. The defendant, however, calls an expert witness who testifies as to the characteristics, or profile, of a person who would commit the crime, and then testifies that, based upon an examination of the defendant, it is his or her expert opinion that the defendant does not possess the characteristics that fit the profile.

Recall that Fed. R. Evid. 404(a) states:

> (a) *Character evidence generally.* Evidence of a person's character or a trait of character is not admissible for the purpose of proving action in conformity therewith on a particular occasion, *except*:
>
>> (1) *Character of accused.* In a criminal case, evidence of a pertinent trait of character *offered by an accused*, or by the prosecution to rebut the same. . . .

Fed. R. Evid. 404(a) (emphasis added). Fed. R. Evid. 405(a) governs the methods of proof that can be utilized to prove character (when character evidence is permitted by Fed. R. Evid. 404), and it lists "testimony in the form of an opinion" as a permitted form of proof. Further, the Advisory Committee Note to Rule 405(a) provides:

> In recognizing opinion as a means of proving character, the rule departs from usual contemporary practice in favor of that of an earlier day. . . . If character is defined as the kind of person one is, then account must be taken of varying ways of arriving at the estimate. These may [include] the opinion of the psychiatrist based upon examination and testing.

Is expert opinion evidence that the defendant does not fit the profile of a person who would commit the crime charged, *if offered initially by the defendant*, admissible as within Rule 404(a)(1)'s exception? What other evidence hurdles must be overcome by the accused who proffers such evidence?

UNITED STATES v. ST. PIERRE
812 F.2d 417 (8th Cir. 1987)

HENRY WOODS, DISTRICT JUDGE.

The appellant, Ronald Kaye St. Pierre, was convicted of two counts of carnal abuse and sentenced to imprisonment for a concurrent term of eleven years on each count. The victim was his twelve-year-old stepdaughter, Tarace. . . . Appellant does not attack the sufficiency of the evidence but contends that the court erred in several evidentiary rulings. . . . We affirm.

No useful purpose would be served by a detailed recounting of the sordid facts in this case. When Tarace was an infant, appellant married her mother. He began a pattern of sexual abuse in July, 1984 when his stepdaughter was barely eleven years of age. It continued until October, 1985 and consisted of over fifty episodes of sexual intercourse. The two incidents for which St. Pierre was indicted and convicted occurred in July, 1985. Tarace related them in specific detail to the jury. The relationship ended in October, 1985 when appellant assaulted his wife after an argument over his girlfriend. When the family found refuge in a church-sponsored shelter, Tarace confided to her mother that appellant had been sexually abusing her. A physical examination corroborated her story.

. . . .

III.

The appellant . . . contends that the trial court erred in permitting Dr. [Mary] Curran, [a] clinical psychologist [who examined Tarace], to testify as to certain traits and characteristics of sexually abused children as compared with those exhibited by Tarace. The testimony of Dr. Curran that the scientific community recognizes certain emotional and psychological characteristics in sexually abused children stands uncontradicted in the record. After detailing these traits, the expert was permitted to describe those exhibited by the victim herein. She did not testify as to whether she thought Tarace was telling the truth.

A fundamental test for the admission of expert testimony is whether it will assist the jury in resolving the factual issues before it. These cases present difficult problems for the jury. The testimony of the accused and the victim is generally in direct conflict. The crime is secretive with extreme pressures against revelation, especially when committed in a family setting.

The Supreme Court of Minnesota addressed this precise evidentiary problem in *State v. Myers*, 359 N.W.2d 604 (Minn. 1984). That court recognized that the type of testimony presented by Dr. Curran could be very helpful because jurors are at a disadvantage when dealing with sexual abuse of children. "Incest is prohibited in all or almost all cultures, and the common experience of the jury may represent a less than adequate foundation for assessing the credibility of a young child who complains of sexual abuse." *Id.* at 610. This court has commented that the "special concerns arising in the prosecution of child abuse cases have not been fully met by the development of new methods of practice." *United States v. Cree*, 778 F.2d 474, 478 n.7 (8th Cir. 1985). There was no error in admitting this testimony.

IV.

Appellant moved to have an expert examine him to determine whether he fits the profile of a sexual offender. The motion was denied. The burden rested upon him to satisfy the court that relevant expert testimony was necessary to present an adequate defense. The decision to appoint an expert is entrusted to the sound discretion of the trial judge in light of the particular facts. Appellant has cited no decision or scientific treatise that recognizes the acceptability of such testimony. One of the standards for admissibility is that it must have gained the acceptance of the particular field or scientific community to which it belongs. The Supreme Court of New Jersey recently applied this standard to expert testimony offered by a psychiatrist that the accused did not have the psychological profile of a rapist. The testimony was rejected. There was no showing that the scientific community recognized the existence of identifiable traits common to rapists. *State v. Cavallo*, 443 A.2d 1020, 1026 (N.J. 1982). "A review of the cases in other jurisdictions does not persuade us that it is generally accepted in the medical or legal communities that psychiatrists possess such knowledge or capabilities." *Id.* at 1027. The trial judge did not abuse his discretion in denying appellant's motion.

. . . .

VI.

No errors appear in the various rulings and orders of the district judge, and he is in all respects affirmed.

NOTE

Majority View. The *St. Pierre* case expresses the majority view of refusing to admit expert testimony that the defendant did not fit a pertinent offender profile. As indicated in *St. Pierre*, the courts that refuse to admit such testimony focus (primarily) on the lack of scientific validity for such profiles. In *State v. Parkinson*, 909 P.2d 647 (Idaho App. 1996), the Idaho Court of Appeals commented that "the introduction of expert testimony regarding whether the defendant fits an alleged "sexual offender" profile has been almost universally rejected." *Id.* at 651. The court continued:

> Various reasons have been given for rejection of this type of evidence, including that it has not gained general acceptance in the scientific community, that it invades the province of the jury and unfairly prejudices the prosecution, and that it does not assist the trier of fact to understand the evidence or determine a fact in issue.

Id. See also State v. Hulbert, 481 N.W.2d 329, 332–33 (Iowa 1992) (profile of a child molester); *State v. Cavaliere*, 663 A.2d 96, 100 (N.H. 1995) (sex offender profile); *State v. Cavallo*, 443 A.2d 1020, 1026–29 (N.J. 1982) (psychological traits of a rapist); *People v. John W.*, 229 Cal. Rptr. 783, 785 (Cal. App. 1986) (sexual deviant profile); *State v. Holcomb*, 643 S.W.2d 336, 341 (Tenn. Crim. App. 1982) (no psychological pathology indicating rape); *State v. Parkinson*, 909 P.2d 647, 651 (Idaho App. 1996) (sex offender profile; court lists cases excluding such evidence).

The California Supreme Court has taken a contrary view. In *People v. Stoll*, 783 P.2d 698 (Cal. 1989), the defendant was charged with several counts of lewd and lascivious conduct with children. The defense sought to introduce opinion testimony by a psychologist that, based upon interviews and personality tests conducted by the psychologist, the defendant displayed no signs of deviance or abnormality. The trial court refused to allow such testimony because it did not satisfy the *Frye* test for new or novel scientific techniques. The California Supreme Court reversed, holding that the *Frye* test did not apply to such testimony, and that the expert's opinion was authorized by rules allowing the defendant to introduce testimony concerning his or her character to show nondisposition to commit the crime charged. *Id.* at 699, 707–08.

QUESTION

In *St. Pierre* the Eighth Circuit accepted expert opinion testimony on child sexual abuse syndrome to prove that a sexual attack occurred but rejected expert opinion testimony on the sexual offender profile to prove that the sexual attack did not occur. From the court's point of view, what factors distinguish the child sexual abuse syndrome from the sexual abuser profile as far as admissibility is concerned?

PROBLEMS

Problem 5-17. The *St. Pierre* case was decided before the United States Supreme Court announced its decision in *Daubert v. Merrell Dow Pharmaceuticals, Inc.*, 509 U.S. 579 (1993). Recall that in *Daubert* Justice Blackmun wrote that *Daubert's* criteria for the admissibility of scientific evidence applied to *all* scientific evidence, not just novel or recently developed scientific techniques. *Id.* at 592 n.11. Assuming that *Daubert* applies, would profile evidence like that offered in *St. Pierre* satisfy the *Daubert* test? What argument could you make that *Daubert's* criteria does not apply to expert opinion of profiles? *See State v. Parkinson*, 909 P.2d 647, 652–53 (Idaho App. 1996).

Problem 5-18. Defendant is accused of sexual abuse of his 11-year-old stepdaughter. The defendant's stepdaughter testified that she, her mother, and her stepfather (the defendant) were watching television when she (the victim) noticed that her stepfather was naked. She testified that when her mother got up to go to the bathroom her stepfather removed her pajama bottoms and engaged in sexual intercourse with her.

The defendant denies that any sexual activity took place and offers the testimony of a psychologist. The psychologist is prepared to testify to two things. First, that he examined the defendant and "found no scientific objective data of deviant sexual interest and could not, therefore, recommend any particular form of therapy for his (the defendant's) sexuality." This first opinion is offered for the purpose of showing that the defendant did not exhibit behavior characteristics consistent with persons who are likely to commit sexual crimes against children.

Second, the psychologist is prepared to testify that instances of sexual misconduct do not take place in the manner described by the victim.

(A) Is the psychologist's opinion that the defendant did not display behavior characteristics consistent with persons likely to commit sex crimes admissible? Are there any other foundation requirements that need to be met? *See People v. John W.*, 229 Cal. Rptr. 783–88 (Cal. App. 1986).

(B) Is the psychologist's opinion that sexual misconduct does not occur in the manner described by the victim admissible? *See People v. John W.*, 229 Cal. Rptr. 783, 784 n.2 (Cal. App. 1986); *United States v. Cross*, 928 F.2d 1030, 1050 n.66 (11th Cir. 1991).

E. DIMINISHED CAPACITY

An identifying characteristic of nontraditional psychological and social science evidence is that it is not offered on the issue of the defendant's sanity.[69] As Professor McCord points out, there is nothing "nontraditional" about such evidence; courts have for many years accepted psychiatric testimony when it is offered to prove that the defendant was (or was not) legally "insane."[70]

Consider the situation where a defendant in a criminal case suffers from an abnormal mental condition that does not meet the legal definition of insanity. Nonetheless, because of this mental abnormality, the defendant was incapable of forming requisite mens rea necessary to be convicted of the charged crime. Stated differently, the defendant knew

---

[69] David McCord, *Syndromes, Profiles and Other Mental Exotica: A New Approach to the Admissibility of Nontraditional Psychological Evidence in Criminal Cases*, 66 OR. L. REV. 19, 28 (1987).

[70] *Id.* at 28–29.

that the acts he or she performed were "wrong," but because of a mental condition short of what the law considers "insanity," the defendant did not or could not appreciate just "how wrong" they were. Is expert testimony about such a condition admissible to show that the defendant had a diminished or partial understanding of the significance of the acts he or she performed? Since most criminal statutes require a particular state of mind to exist at the time a criminal act occurs, expert testimony on the defendant's emotional or mental condition *not amounting to insanity* would, arguably, be relevant to show that a defendant did not have the state of mind necessary to commit the offense charged. If such evidence were admitted to negate a mental state, this would be a nontraditional use of such psychological evidence.

The use of psychological evidence to negate a mental state is usually referred to as the "diminished (or partial) capacity" or "diminished responsibility" defense." With the diminished capacity defense the defendant's expert psychological testimony is aimed at negating the mental state required to commit the offense. If successful, this defense usually results not in complete exculpation but in conviction of a lower-grade offense. For example, if a defendant charged with first-degree murder was permitted to offer evidence tending to show that, because of diminished mental capacity, he or she did not or could not premeditate, the defendant could still be found guilty of a lower grade of homicide not requiring premeditation.

The threshold admissibility question is one of relevance. Some jurisdictions take the view that mental or emotional conditions that do not constitute insanity do not diminish responsibility for an offense. In such jurisdictions a person is either sane or insane; there is no "partial insanity." *See, e.g., Bethea v. United States*, 365 A.2d 64, 86 (D.C. 1976) (court objects to abandonment of "traditional legal theory"; mental deficiency is an "all-or-nothing defense"). Accordingly, in such jurisdictions testimony of diminished capacity is irrelevant to any issue of guilt or innocence and is inadmissible.

On the other hand, many jurisdictions see the testimony as going directly to the existence of a mental state that is an element of the crime charged. In these jurisdictions testimony that the accused could not or did not form a particular mental state because of diminished capacity is relevant and admissible.

In jurisdictions that deem such testimony relevant to show the absence of a required mental state, admissibility issues similar to those already examined in other areas of nontraditional evidence must be addressed. For example, courts examine whether the expert is qualified, whether there is a scientific basis for the particular type of diminished capacity, and whether there is anything in the proffered expert opinion that is beyond the jury's understanding.

COMMONWEALTH v. WALZACK
360 A.2d 914 (Pa. 1976)

Nix, Justice.

Today we must decide whether psychiatric evidence is admissible to be evaluated by the jury when an accused offers it to negate the element of specific intent required for a conviction of murder of the first degree thereby reducing the crime to murder of the second degree. We are persuaded by the vast weight of authority that psychiatric evidence should be admissible for this purpose and, therefore, we hold that the learned court below erred in excluding the proffered testimony from the jury's consideration.

Prior to analyzing the specific facts of this case, it is necessary to clarify what we do not decide in today's opinion. First, appellant has not raised the defense of insanity and today's decision in no way affects the vitality of the M'Naughten test as the sole standard in this Commonwealth for determining criminal responsibility where the actor alleges mental illness or defect. Second, for reasons that will be discussed hereinafter, we do not view the position adopted today as inferentially accepting the irresistible impulse test which we have previously expressly rejected. Third, we do not here reach the question of the applicability of the principles announced herein to crimes requiring a specific intent other than murder of the first degree.

Appellant, Michael Walzack, was tried before a jury and convicted of murder of the first degree in the shooting death of one Ole Toasen. Following a penalty hearing, appellant was sentenced to life imprisonment . . . [T]his direct appeal followed.

During the trial, the defense admitted the killing and attempted to establish its position through the testimony of appellant and a Dr. Willis. When called to the stand, the defense made an offer of proof indicating that the witness [Dr. Willis] did not intend to contest appellant's sanity at the time of the incident, under the M'Naghten standard. The defense conceded that appellant was sane, that he could tell the difference between right and wrong and that he knew the nature and quality of his act. The single stated purpose in offering the witness was to demonstrate that as a result of a surgical procedure, a lobotomy, which appellant had undergone, he did not possess sufficient mental capacity to form the specific intent required for a conviction of murder of the first degree.[71] [6]

In rejecting the psychiatric evidence, the trial court relied on a number of our earlier closely divided decisions. . . .

Appellant was charged with and convicted of murder of the first degree. The Legislature defined the elements of this crime as:

> "All murder which shall be perpetrated by means of poison, or by lying in wait, or by any other kind of *willful, deliberate and premeditated killing*, or which shall be committed in the perpetration of, or attempting to perpetrate any

---

[71] [n.6] While the offer was not as precise as it might have been, the reference to "diminishing the degree of responsibility of the Defendant for this crime" was sufficient to alert the trial judge of the intended purpose of the testimony. In this area, nomenclature has been a source of obfuscation. The concept has been referred to as partial responsibility, diminished responsibility and partial insanity. Criminal Law, LaFave & Scott, p. 326. Probably, the most accurate label would be "diminished capacity" since the thrust of the doctrine relates to the accused's ability to perform a specified cognitive process. See *Commonwealth v. Tomlinson*, 284 A.2d 687, 695 n.3 (1971) (Dissenting opinion, Roberts, J., in which Mr. Chief Justice Jones and Mr. Justice Pomeroy joined):

> "Although the terms 'partial' and 'diminished' responsibility are the common vehicles used by writers and courts to describe the theory we discuss today, they are highly misleading. They connote that the defendant is somehow not fully responsible for his actions. In actuality the defendant is fully responsible, but only for a crime which does not require the elements of premeditation and deliberation."

In *State of New Mexico v. Padilla*, the Supreme Court of New Mexico advised:

> "The doctrine contended for by the defendant is sometimes referred to as that of 'diminished' or 'partial responsibility.' This is actually a misnomer, and the theory may not be given an exact name. However, it means the allowing of proof of mental derangement short of insanity as evidence of lack of deliberate or premeditated design. In other words, it contemplates full responsibility, not partial, but only for the crime actually committed." *State of New Mexico v. Padilla*, 347 P.2d 312, 314 (1959)."

arson, rape, robbery, burglary, or kidnapping, shall be murder in the first degree." (Emphasis added.) Penal Code, Act of June 24, 1939, P.L. 872, § 701."

Under this section the term "willful, deliberate and premeditated" describes the mental state that must accompany the act before a nonfelony murder can be murder of the first degree.

It is axiomatic that the Commonwealth must prove each element of a crime beyond a reasonable doubt. It is equally as clear that the requisite intent of an offense is one of the elements of the crime. Consequently, in the instant trial, it was incumbent upon the Commonwealth to prove beyond a reasonable doubt that appellant had the specific intent to kill to support the finding of murder of the first degree.

. . . .

In the instant case, appellant attempted to introduce expert testimony concerning his mental capacity to form the type of specific intent a conviction for murder of the first degree requires. This testimony obviously would have "significantly advanced the inquiry" as to the presence or absence of an essential element of the crime. Thus, the exclusion of the proffered testimony cannot be based upon a lack of relevancy. Also, there is no basis for finding the tendered testimony incompetent for other reasons. Although early decisions in this jurisdiction can be found that express doubt as to the reliability of psychiatric testimony, our more recent decisions make clear that psychiatry has a legitimate scientific basis. While recognizing that psychiatry might well be less exact than some of the other medical disciplines we are nevertheless cognizant of the "tremendous advancements made in the field." *Commonwealth v. McCusker*, 292 A.2d 286, 287 (1972). In *Commonwealth v. McCusker, supra*, after noting many of the areas in criminal law where we have accepted a psychiatrist's opinion, we observed:

> ". . . (t)he reliance we have consistently placed upon the competence of psychiatric evidence belies any concern that it is not a sufficiently recognized and accepted medical science capable of offering quality expert guidance." *Id*. at 291."

We have long accepted psychiatric evidence on the issue of whether an accused is competent to stand trial. Similarly, we have long permitted psychiatric evidence under the M'Naghten test to determine whether an accused was insane at the time of the crime. More recently we have allowed psychiatric evidence for the purpose of determining whether an accused acted in the heat of passion when committing a homicide; whether an accused subjectively believed he was in imminent danger of death or serious bodily injury under his claim of self-defense; whether an accused was capable of making a detailed written confession; and, we have long accepted psychiatric evidence at the penalty stage of trial.

Having determined that psychiatric evidence possesses sufficient reliability for its admission for the purposes announced herein we must ascertain whether there are any policy reasons that might justify ruling it incompetent. Early opinions of this Court have suggested that acceptance of the doctrine of diminished capacity is tantamount to acceptance of the irresistible impulse test for insanity. We do not agree. The doctrines of diminished capacity and irresistible impulse involve entirely distinct considerations. Irresistible impulse is a test for insanity which is broader than the M'Naghten test. Under the irresistible impulse test a person may avoid criminal responsibility even though he is capable of distinguishing between right and wrong, and is fully aware of the nature and quality of his act provided he establishes that he was unable to refrain from acting. An accused offering evidence under the theory of diminished capacity *concedes general criminal liability*. The thrust of this doctrine is to challenge the capacity of the actor to possess a particular state of mind required by the legislature for the commission of a certain degree of the crime charged.

In adopting the position we announce today, we are buttressed by the fact that many jurisdictions in the country accept this view. Of these jurisdictions, a number of them embrace the M'Naghten rule as we do.

. . . In a more expansive explanation of the rationale supporting this view, the Iowa Supreme Court stated:

> "We believe that failure to recognize there can be an unsoundness of mind of such a character as to negative a specific intent to commit a particular crime, is to ignore the great advancements which have been made in the field of psychiatry. The results which have been achieved confirm its growing reliability. We do not consider this position contradictory to our adherence to the right and wrong test of insanity. We do not pretend there are no mental disorders except those which qualify under this test, but rather limit the defense of insanity to the types of mental illness in which the defendant cannot comprehend the nature or consequences of his act. Weihofen in his text *Mental Disorder as a Criminal Defense* states that if we recognize the basic principle that a person should not be punished for a crime if he did not entertain the requisite state of mind, "there is no logical escape from the proposition that a person cannot be held guilty of a deliberate and premeditated killing when he did not deliberate and premeditate, and indeed was incapable of deliberating and premeditating. If, however, he was able to understand the nature of the act he was committing and if he intended to do that act, he should be held guilty of murder in the second degree or manslaughter. There is no logic in the 'all or nothing' assumption underlying so many court opinions on the subject - that a person is either 'sane' and wholly responsible for all his acts, or 'insane' and wholly irresponsible."[72] [19] *State v. Gramenz*, 126 N.W.2d 285 (1964).

Once it is determined that the proffered evidence was both relevant and competent, due process requires its admission. Article I, Section 9 of the Pennsylvania Constitution sets forth the rights of an accused in criminal prosecutions. "

> "Even the most myopic interpretation of this clause would necessarily concede the right to offer relevant evidence to challenge a material issue of fact." *Commonwealth v. Graves*, 334 A.2d 661, 665, n.7 (1975)."

It is inconsistent with fundamental principles of American jurisprudence to preclude an accused from offering relevant and competent evidence to dispute the charge against him. This, of course, includes any of the elements that comprise that charge.

Judgment of sentence reversed and a new trial awarded.

---

[72] [n.19] Legal textwriters and authorities are virtually unanimous in their approval of the position we adopt today. The foremost is, perhaps, the American Law Institute's Model Penal Code. In Section 4.02 of the proposed official draft the institute provides:

> "Evidence that the defendant suffered from a mental disease or defect is admissible whenever it is relevant to prove that the defendant did or did not have a state of mind which is an element of the offense."

Others are too numerous to single out.

EAGEN, J. (dissenting).

In *Commonwealth v. McCusker*, 292 A.2d 286 (1972), a majority of this Court overruled a multitude of prior decisions and held that psychiatric testimony is admissible at trial to aid the fact finder in determining if one who kills another did so in the heat of passion. Today a majority of the Court takes a further leap into the unknown and attributes to the science of psychiatry the ability to say with a reasonable degree of certainty that the instant killer, *who admittedly was sane and acted with malice and had the mental capacity to know what he was doing and to know what he was doing was wrong*, lacked the mental capacity to form a specific intent to kill. I dissented in *McCusker*, and I dissent here again.

The science of psychiatry has advanced materially in recent years and undoubtedly is now able to present reliable information as to human behavior in certain situations; however, the psychiatric testimony, here involved, is so patently devoid of reliability it should not receive judicial sanction.

Some psychiatrists will continue to dig up excuses for criminal behavior . . . even though some such 'excuses' may border on the ridiculous and be totally lacking in scientific reliability. Unfortunately, some members of the judiciary will join them in accepting these excuses.

. . . I submit that my position represents the long and well established view that such testimony is not admissible for the purposes which the majority now holds it admissible. Moreover, nothing in the record before this Court shows this testimony is anymore reliable today than yesterday. Because the trial court had no power to overturn our prior rulings, it did not hear evidence to establish the reliability of this testimony. Yet the majority reverses our prior rulings based not on a showing of reliability in the record but on *their personal* knowledge and beliefs about psychiatry. If the majority is concerned with facts, they would at least remand the case for a hearing on reliability. Thus, while I defer to the well established rule, the majority not only expresses their personal beliefs, they subject the entire Commonwealth to those beliefs and they do so in the face of division as to the reliability of such testimony even within the psychiatric field.

. . . .

O'BRIEN, J., joins in this dissent.

NOTES

1. *Three Views of Diminished Capacity Defense.*

(A) Limited Admissibility. A few states permit the use of the diminished capacity defense but limit its availability. The limitation takes one of two forms. First, some states, similar to the holding in *Walzack*, allow such evidence only in murder prosecutions to negate the intent or premeditation elements in first-degree murder cases. *See Commonwealth v. Garcia*, 479 A.2d 473, 476 (Pa. 1984). Second, some states take a slightly more expansive approach and admit such evidence to negate the "specific intent" element (but not a general intent element) of any crime. *See State v. Jacobs*, 607 N.W.2d 679, 684 (Iowa 2000). *See also* JOSHUA DRESSLER, UNDERSTANDING CRIMINAL LAW § 26.02[B][3], at 396–97 (4th ed. 2006). In reality this version of diminished capacity defense generally serves only as a partial defense because there is almost always a lesser-intent crime facing the person with a diminished capacity. *Id.*

(B) Inadmissibility. A significant minority of states exclude evidence of diminished responsibility altogether. *See* PAUL H. ROBINSON, 1 CRIMINAL LAW DEFENSES § 64(a), at 275 n.6 (1984) (collection of cases). In these states evidence of mental disease or defect is admissible to prove insanity or nothing — mental abnormality short of the legal definition of insanity is not considered on the issue of guilt or innocence for the crime charged. *See, e.g., Chestnut v. State*, 538 So. 2d 820, 823 (Fla. 1989) (rejecting diminished capacity defense and noting that the state is not constitutionally required to recognize the defense). Some courts reason that it belongs to the legislature, not the judiciary, to recognize a new defense. *See, e.g., Johnson v. State*, 439 A.2d 542, 554 (Md. 1982). Other courts in this category have reasoned that expert testimony on the defendant's mental state invades the province of the jury on the ultimate issue of fact. *See, e.g., State v. Hobson*, 671 P.2d 1365, 1386–87 (Kan. 1983).

(C) Complete Admissibility. While the positions of some states are not entirely clear, approximately 12 to 15 states, by statute or court decision, permit evidence of a mental disease or defect — short of legally defined insanity — to be admitted to negate any culpable state of mind that is an element of an offense. *See Hendershott v. People*, 653 P.2d 385, 393–94 (Colo. 1982). *See also* PAUL H. ROBINSON, 1 CRIMINAL LAW DEFENSES § 64(a), at 273 n.3 (1984) (citations to cases and statutes). This view is consistent with the "relevancy" view of the Model Penal Code:

> Evidence that the defendant suffered from a disease or defect is admissible whenever it is relevant to prove that the defendant did or did not have a state of mind which is an element of the offense.

MODEL PENAL CODE § 4.02(1).

2. *Syndromes That Result in Diminished Capacity.* Bear in mind that there may be some overlap between a defense based upon a syndrome and the diminished responsibility defense. A syndrome, rather than retardation, physical injury, or some other form of mental illness, may be asserted as the *cause* of diminished capacity. For example, in a homicide case a defendant may assert that because of the battered woman syndrome or the battered child syndrome (or some other syndrome) they could not form the specific intent necessary to premeditate or deliberate before an intentional killing. Alternatively, the defendant could argue that because of such a syndrome he or she honestly (but incorrectly) perceived a threat to safety and acted in self-defense rather than with premeditation or malice and, accordingly, should not be convicted of first-degree murder. Recall that this occurred in the case of *State v. Janes*, 822 P.2d 1238, 1244 (Wash. Ct. App. 1992), where child abuse syndrome was asserted as the cause of Janes's diminished capacity.

In *United States v. Cohen*, 510 F.3d 1114 (9th Cir. 2007) the defendant, Cohen, was an income tax protester who had been charged and convicted of aiding and abetting in the filing of false federal income tax returns. Cohen argued on appeal that his conviction should be overturned because the trial court excluded expert testimony from a psychiatrist that Cohen suffered from "narcissistic personality disorder" and, as a result, he did not intend to violate the law. The psychiatrist's report described Cohen's "narcissistic personality disorder" as follows:

> In the report, [the psychiatrist] Dr. Roitman diagnoses Cohen as suffering from a narcissistic personality disorder, and concludes that Cohen "did not intend to violate the law, as would be the case with a criminal who acted out of a desire for personal gain" but rather [h]is behavior is driven by a mental disorder as opposed to criminal motivation. . . . Although it is true Mr. Cohen was not

delusional or psychotic and was in possession of basic mental faculties, his will was in the service of irrational beliefs as a result of narcissistic personality disorder.

Cohen, supra, 510 F.3d at 1123. The Ninth Circuit reversed. Although the Court did not mention diminished capacity, it found that,

> Dr. Roitman's testimony would have been highly probative on the issue of whether Cohen could have formed the requisite *mens rea*, and was unlikely to cause significant confusion with the jury if properly constrained by compliance with the rules of evidence.

Id. at 1127. *Cf. State v. Nazario,* 726 So.2d 349, 350 (Fla. Dist. Ct. App. 1999) (holding expert testimony on the "flight/flee syndrome and how the effects of this syndrome precluded [defendant] from forming an intent to kill, but rather, caused him to kill out of an involuntary survival instinct" was inadmissible because of Florida's longstanding refusal to allow diminished capacity defenses).

QUESTIONS

1. The majority in *Walzack* states that "psychiatric evidence possesses sufficient reliability for its admission for the purposes announced herein." *Commonwealth v. Walzack, supra,* 360 A.2d at 919. What, exactly, are those "purposes"?

2. What policy considerations would restrict the admission of admittedly relevant evidence on the mental state element of a criminal charge to cases that involve first-degree murder, or to cases that involve specific-intent but not general-intent crimes? *See* JOSHUA DRESSLER, UNDERSTANDING CRIMINAL LAW § 26.02 [B][3] & [4], at 396–98 (4th ed. 2006). Can it be constitutional for a state to restrict a defendant from offering admittedly relevant evidence? *Compare State v. Mott,* 931 P.2d 1046, 1051–52 (Ariz. 1997) (constitutional), *with State v. White,* 109 P.3d 1199, 1209 (Kan. 2005) (not constitutional). *See* PAUL H. ROBINSON, CRIMINAL LAW DEFENSES § 64(a), at 277 (1984).

PROBLEMS

Problem 5-19. Defendant is charged with theft of a ring from a jewelry store. The theft took place in a state that recognizes the diminished responsibility defense. At trial defendant is prepared to offer testimony from two experts about defendant's mental aberrations at the time of the theft. If allowed to testify, the experts would say that defendant knew it was wrong to steal, but because of his mental aberrations he did not have the intent necessary to commit the crime. The prosecution argues that allowing the partial or diminished responsibility defense in this situation is improper because it will result in a complete acquittal, there being no lesser included offense to theft if the mental state element is negated. The expert testimony is excluded by the trial judge.

Should evidence on the diminished responsibility defense be admitted in theft cases where it will result in a complete defense? *See State v. Booth,* 588 P.2d 614, 615–16 (Or. 1978).

Problem 5-20. If a jurisdiction accepts the diminished responsibility defense, does it matter what *caused* the diminished responsibility? If you think that the cause of the diminished responsibility affects admissibility, what is your objection? Consider the following two scenarios:

(A) On March 10, 1993, Dr. David Gunn, a doctor who performed abortions, was shot and killed. Michael Griffin, an anti-abortion protester, was charged in the killing. Attorneys representing Griffin hoped to present evidence that Griffin had diminished capacity brought on by intense exposure to anti-abortion propaganda. *See generally* Stephanie Salter, *Insane by Reason of Anti-Abortion Propaganda*, S.F. EXAMINER, Feb. 22, 1994, at A13. Should Griffin be allowed to offer expert testimony that he suffered from diminished capacity?

(B) On March 9, 1996, a man named Jonathan Schmitz shot and killed an acquaintance named Scott Amedure. A few days before the shooting both men had appeared on "The Jenny Jones Show" (a nationally syndicated afternoon "talk" show), where Scott Amedure revealed that he had a crush on Schmitz. Attorneys for Schmitz planned to present evidence that Schmitz was suffering from diminished capacity at the time of the shooting brought on by depression, alcoholism, and Graves disease (a thyroid condition). *See generally* S.F. EXAMINER, July 9, 1996, Nation Datelines, A5; S.F. EXAMINER, Oct. 15, 1996, Nation Datelines, A9. Should Schmitz be allowed to offer expert testimony that he suffered from diminished capacity?

Chapter 6

CHARACTER EVIDENCE

A. INTRODUCTION

The admissibility of character evidence is principally governed under the Federal Rules of Evidence by Rules 404 and 405. Federal Rule of Evidence 404(a) carefully limits the circumstances under which character evidence may be admitted. Generally, character evidence is inadmissible for the purpose of proving that a person acted in conformity with that character.[1] This rule is necessary because of the high degree of prejudice that inheres in character evidence. In *Michelson v. United States*,[2] the Supreme Court opined: "The overriding policy of excluding such evidence, despite its probative value, is the practical experience that its disallowance tends to prevent confusion of issues, unfair surprise, and undue prejudice."[3] At the same time, the ban against the admissibility of character evidence is not absolute. Rule 404(a) recognizes three exceptions to the use of character evidence to prove action in conformity with that character. First, a criminal defendant may offer evidence of a pertinent trait of his own character.[4] For example, "[a] defendant puts his character at issue when he offers testimony as to honesty or his good reputation,"[5] or his peaceful disposition when charged with a crime of violence. The Advisory Committee's Note states that this exception is "so deeply imbedded in our jurisprudence as to assume almost constitutional proportions and to override doubts of the basic relevancy of the evidence."[6] After

---

[1] Fed. R. Evid. 404(a) provides:

(a) Character evidence generally. Evidence of a person's character or a trait of character is not admissible for the purpose of proving action in conformity therewith on a particular occasion, except:

  (1) Character of accused. Evidence of a pertinent trait of character offered by an accused, or by the prosecution to rebut the same, or if evidence of a trait of character of the alleged victim of the crime is offered by the accused and admitted under 404 (a) (2), evidence of the same trait of character of the accused offered by the prosecution;

  (2) Character of victim. Evidence of a pertinent trait of character of the alleged victim of the crime offered by an accused, or by the prosecution to rebut the same, or evidence of a character trait of peacefulness of the victim offered by the prosecution in a homicide case to rebut evidence that the victim was the first aggressor;

  (3) Character of witness. Evidence of the character of a witness, as provided in rules 607, 608, and 609.

Evidence of a rape victim's character is discussed *infra* this chapter at Section C.2.

[2] 335 U.S. 469, 476 (1948).

[3] *See also* Advisory Committee's Notes to Fed. R. Evid. 404.

[4] Fed. R. Evid. 404(a)(1).

[5] *United States v. Keiser*, 57 F.3d 847, 853 (9th Cir. 1995); *see also* Fed. R. Evid. 404 Advisory Committee's Notes ("Illustrations are: evidence of a violent disposition to prove that the person was the aggressor in an affray. . . .").

[6] Fed. R. Evid. 404(a)(1). One commentator has offered the following explanation on why a criminal defendant is entitled to introduce evidence of his own character:

  About the best one can do with this puzzle is to guess that somewhere, somehow the rule was relaxed to allow the criminal defendant with so much at stake and so little available in the way of

a defendant takes this initial step, the prosecution may rebut by offering contrary character evidence. Furthermore, character evidence offered pursuant to Fed. R. Evid. 404(a)(1) must be in the form of reputation or opinion evidence rather than specific instances of conduct.[7]

As a second exception to the general rule against the use of character evidence to prove propensity, Rule 404(a)(2) permits an accused to offer evidence of a pertinent trait of an alleged victim's character.[8] For example, in an assault prosecution, Rule 404(a)(2) would permit evidence of an alleged victim's violent character to support a claim that the defendant was acting in self-defense. "The advisory committee's note to this rule indicates that a victim's 'violent disposition' is exactly the sort of evidence this rule was intended to encompass."[9] Again, 404(a)(2) permits the prosecution to introduce character evidence in rebuttal, and the prosecution may offer evidence of the same character trait of the accused (pursuant to 404(a)(1)), as well as the alleged victim. While the rule would appear to allow evidence of a rape victim's character on the issue of consent, Fed. R. Evid. 412 narrowly restricts evidence of the complainant's past sexual behavior.[10]

Third, evidence of a witness's character is authorized as provided in Rules 607, 608, and 609.[11] Such evidence may be received to impeach or rehabilitate the credibility of a witness and applies to all party and nonparty witnesses in both civil and criminal cases.

Assuming that character evidence is properly admissible under Rule 404(a), Rule 405(b) determines what form that evidence may take.[12] Rule 405(a) provides that in all cases in which evidence of character is admissible, proof may be made by testimony as to reputation or by testimony in the form of an opinion. Thus, if properly admissible, character evidence may always be received in the form of reputation or opinion testimony. In contrast, the rule restricts the admissibility of specific instances of conduct. Rule 405 states in straightforward manner that evidence of specific acts is admissible only when a person's character is an "essential element of a charge, claim, or defense."[13] Although specific instances of conduct are the most convincing of the three methods of proving character provided by the rule, the Advisory Committee's Notes explain that "it possesses the greatest capacity to arouse prejudice, to confuse, to surprise and to consume time."[14] Thus, the use of specific instances of conduct is confined to cases in which character is, in the strict sense, in issue.

---

conventional proof to have special dispensation to tell the factfinder just what sort of person he really is.

Uviller, *Evidence of Character to Prove Conduct: Illusion, Illogic, and Injustice in the Courtroom*, 130 U. PA. L. REV. 845, 855 (1982).

[7] *See* Fed. R. Evid. 405(a). *See also Michelson v. United States*, 335 U.S. 469, 477 (1948) ("The witness may not testify about defendant's specific acts or courses of conduct. . . ."); *State v. Elmer*, 21 F.3d 331, 335 (9th Cir. 1994).

[8] Fed. R. Evid. 404(a)(2).

[9] *United States v. Keiser*, 57 F.3d 847, 853 (9th Cir. 1995); *see also* Fed. R. Evid. 404 Advisory Committee's Notes ("Illustrations are: evidence of a violent disposition to prove that the person was the aggressor in an affray. . . .").

[10] *See* Fed. R. Evid. 412, *infra.*

[11] Fed. R. Evid. 404(a)(3).

[12] *See United States v. Keiser*, 57 F.3d 847, 855 (9th Cir. 1995); *United States v. Talamante*, 981 F.2d 1153, 1156 (10th Cir. 1992).

[13] Fed. R. Evid. 405(b).

[14] Fed. R. Evid. 405 Advisory Committee's Notes.

Finally, Rule 404(b) prohibits evidence of other crimes, wrongs or acts to prove the character of a person in order to show action in conformity therewith. "The rule is designed to avoid a danger that the jury will punish the defendant for offenses other than those charged, or at least that it will convict when unsure of guilt, because it is convinced that the defendant is a bad man deserving of punishment."[15] The evidence may, however, be admitted if offered for other purposes, such as proof of motive, opportunity, intent, preparation, plan, knowledge, identity, or absence of mistake or accident.[16]

B. PROPER USE OF THE DEFENDANT'S CHARACTER

[1]   Evidence of a Pertinent Trait of Accused's Character Offered by the Accused — Fed. R. Evid. 404(a)(1)

[a]   Invoking the Exception

As previously discussed, Rule 404(a)(1) creates an exception to the use of character evidence to prove propensity. Under the rule, a defendant may offer evidence of a pertinent trait of his own character. An accused clearly invokes this exception by calling a character witness to give reputation or opinion testimony on a pertinent trait of his character. In *Michelson v. United States*,[17] the defendant put his general character at issue when he called five witnesses who testified that he enjoyed a good reputation for honesty and truthfulness. In contrast, an accused does not raise the issue of his character by merely taking the witness stand and providing general background information.[18] In *United States v. Gillespie*,[19] the court reversed the defendant's conviction for causing the transportation of a three-year-old child victim in interstate and foreign commerce for illegal sexual purposes on the grounds that the district court erred in admitting the testimony of a clinical psychologist on characteristics common to child molesters. The Ninth Circuit reasoned that the defendant's testimony as to his childhood was general background information, which did not put his character at issue.[20]

Additionally, a prosecutor cannot "open his own door" to such character evidence by asking defendant or a defense witness about defendant's character and then offering rebuttal evidence. In *United States v. Gilliland*,[21] the prosecution asked a defense

---

[15] *United States v. Hill*, 953 F.2d 452, 457 (9th Cir. 1991) (quoting *United States v. Brown*, 880 F.2d 1012, 1014 (9th Cir. 1989)).

[16] Fed. R. Evid. 404(b) provides:

> Other crimes, wrongs, or acts. Evidence of other crimes, wrongs, or acts is not admissible to prove the character of a person in order to show action in conformity therewith. It may, however, be admissible for other purposes, such as proof of motive, opportunity, intent, preparation, plan, knowledge, identity, or absence of mistake or accident, provided that upon request by the accused, the prosecution in a criminal case shall provide reasonable notice in advance of trial, or during trial if the court excuses pretrial notice on good cause shown, of the general nature of any evidence it intends to introduce at trial.

[17] 335 U.S. 469 (1948).

[18] Of course, when the defendant takes the stand his veracity may be attacked, like any other witness, by character evidence offered under Fed. R. Evid. 608 or 609.

[19] 852 F.2d 475, 480 (9th Cir. 1988).

[20] *Id.*

[21] 586 F.2d 1384 (1978).

witness on cross-examination whether the defendant was the kind of person who would commit the crime of transporting a stolen automobile across state lines in violation of the Dyer Act, 18 U.S.C. § 2312. When the witness testified that the defendant would not commit such a crime, the prosecution cross-examined him about defendant's prior criminal record. In reversing defendant's conviction, the Tenth Circuit held that the government may not turn a defense witness into a character witness "by asking him what kind of man defendant was, and then use those questions to bootstrap into the case evidence of defendant's prior convictions which it was prohibited from using in its case-in-chief."[22]

Furthermore, the trait of character admitted into evidence by the defendant must be "pertinent" to the crime charged. For example, evidence of the defendant's "reputation for truth and veracity" is properly excluded in a prosecution for a crime of violence[23] and a narcotics prosecution.[24] The defendant's reputation for honesty is not relevant to whether he committed a violent felony or drug trafficking offense. However, evidence that the defendant has a "law-abiding" character is properly admissible in any criminal prosecution.[25]

[b]   Defensive Use of Character Evidence by the Prosecution

UNITED STATES v. BRIGHT
588 F.2d 504 (5th Cir. 1979)

Ainsworth, Circuit Judge.

Edgar Lee Whitten and Louin Ray Bright appeal their convictions for mail fraud under 18 U.S.C. §§ 2 and 1341.

* * *

. . . Appellant Whitten asserts that the trial court abused its discretion in allowing the Government to cross-examine one of his character witnesses regarding Whitten's alleged reprimand by a judge and bar association for unprofessional conduct. The witness, an attorney, testified under direct examination that Whitten had a good general reputation in his community for veracity and integrity and declared that he would believe Whitten under oath. On cross-examination, the Government asked this witness whether he had "heard that Mr. Whitten was reprimanded by Judge Dick Thomas in November of last year for unprofessional conduct?," and the witness replied, "No, sir, I had not." During recross-examination, the Government queried, "But you had not heard that Mr. Whitten had been reprimanded by the Bar Association through Judge Thomas in DeSoto County?" Whitten's character witness responded, "I was not aware of either one of them." The Government then asked, "Well, the State Bar then, the Mississippi

---

[22] *Id.* at 1389.

[23] *Darland v. United States*, 626 F.2d 1235, 1237 (5th Cir.1980).

[24] *United States v. Jackson*, 588 F.2d 1046, 1055 (5th Cir. 1979). *Cf. United States v. Moore*, 27 F.3d 969, 974 (4th Cir.1994) (in prosecution for various fraudulent activities defendant called a number of character witnesses to testify about his general reputation and honesty in the community).

[25] *See United States v. Diaz*, 961 F.2d 1417, 1419 (9th Cir. 1992); *United States v. Daily*, 921 F.2d 994, 1014 (10th Cir. 1991); *United States v. Barry*, 814 F.2d 1400, 1402 (9th Cir. 1987); *United States v. Salvidar*, 710 F.2d 699, 705–07 (11th Cir. 1983); *United States v. Angelini*, 678 F.2d 380, 381 (1st Cir. 1982); *United States v. Hewitt*, 634 F.2d 277, 278–80 (5th Cir. 1981).

State Bar?," and the witness answered, "I was not aware of that, no sir." Whitten's counsel objected to each of these questions and, at the close of trial, moved for a mistrial; the lower court overruled the objections and denied the motion.

Arguing that he was "substantially prejudiced by this type of cross-examination," Whitten contends that the district judge should have invoked his discretionary power under Fed. R. Evid. 403 to stop this line of questioning, since "its probative value (was) substantially outweighed by the danger of unfair prejudice." Fed. R. Evid. 403. We disagree. When a witness has testified in support of the defendant's good character, the trial court may in its discretion allow the Government to attempt to undermine the credibility of that witness on cross-examination "by asking him whether he has heard of prior misconduct of the defendant which is inconsistent with the witness' direct testimony." *United States v. Wells*, 5 Cir., 1976, 525 F.2d 974, 976. However, there are "two important limitations upon judicial discretion in admitting inquiries concerning such prior misconduct: first, a requirement that the prosecution have some good-faith factual basis for the incidents inquired about, and second, a requirement that the incidents inquired about are relevant to the character traits involved at trial." *Id.* at 977. Those requirements are both satisfied here. During a conference in chambers after the defendants rested their case, Whitten's lawyer moved for a mistrial, arguing that "the government offered no evidence whatsoever of this highly prejudicial statement" "about a censure from the DeSoto County Bar, the Mississippi State Bar Association for unethical conduct." The Government replied that it was "prepared to show the basis on which we asked the question, that it is a fact, and that our questions were based on that fact." It said that if Whitten's attorney "will stipulate to the letter of reprimand we will introduce that in the record" and volunteered to "move to reopen and call Mr. Whitten for further cross-examination on the matter" if his counsel "thinks it necessary that we prove it." In our view, the Government's proffer of a letter of reprimand for stipulation and its willingness to reopen the case and attempt to prove the fact of Whitten's reprimand demonstrated the necessary "good-faith factual basis for the incidents inquired about." Those incidents were also "relevant to the character traits involved at trial." The character witness, an attorney, testified to Whitten's good reputation for honesty and integrity and the alleged reprimand for unprofessional conduct was relevant to Whitten's community reputation regarding those traits.

Affirmed.

NOTE

The prosecution may challenge the admission of the defendant's character evidence on two fronts. First, when a witness has testified in support of the defendant's good character, the prosecution may "attempt to undermine the credibility of that witness on cross-examination 'by asking him whether he has heard of prior misconduct of the defendant which is inconsistent with the witness' direct testimony.' " *Bright*, 588 F.2d at 511–12 (5th Cir. 1979) (citation omitted). Second, the government may call rebuttal character witnesses to testify regarding the defendant's poor character. *See United States v. Moore*, 27 F.3d 969, 974 (4th Cir. 1994) ("Once Moore introduced evidence of his trustworthiness and dependability in business matters, his claim to possession of those traits was open to rebuttal by the government under Rule 404(a)(1), either by direct testimony of reputation, or, as here, by inquiry on cross-examination into relevant instances of conduct."); *United States v. Murphy*, 768 F.2d 1518, 1535 (7th Cir. 1985) (holding that it was proper for the government to call witnesses to testify in rebuttal that defendant had a "reputation for dishonesty"). While the rebuttal character witness may testify in the form of reputation or opinion, evidence on specific instances of conduct is prohibited. *See* Fed. R. Evid. 405(a).

[2] Evidence of Prior Bad Acts Offered for Purposes Other than to Prove the Defendant Acted in Conformity — Fed. R. Evid. 404(b)

Federal Rule of Evidence 404(b) prohibits evidence of "[o]ther crimes, wrongs or acts" to show the defendant's bad character and propensity to violate the law. On the other hand, evidence of other bad acts is admissible for certain purposes unrelated to a defendant's propensity to commit crime. Rule 404(b) enumerates nine purposes for which specific acts evidence may be admitted. These include: "proof of motive, opportunity, intent, preparation, plan, knowledge, identity, or absence of mistake or accident." The federal courts generally have construed this list as illustrative rather than exclusive. Stated another way, "Rule 404(b) is a rule of inclusion," and evidence is admissible under this rule if "relevant to an issue in the case other than [the] defendant's criminal propensity."[26] Evidence admissible under Rule 404(b) may nevertheless be excluded under Rule 403 "where its probative value is substantially outweighed by its prejudicial effect."[27]

Although evidence of the accused's prior conduct may be relevant to the determination of his guilt, "this evidence is excluded as a policy matter, in order to guard against the extreme danger that its introduction might lead a jury to convict an innocent defendant on the theory that he is a 'bad person' deserving of punishment."[28] As Wigmore explained, evidence of the accused's past crimes is excluded "not because it has no appreciable probative value but because it has too much."[29]

Despite the general ban on evidence of other crimes or wrongs to prove a propensity to commit similar crimes, an exception was created by Congress in 1994 for cases involving sexual offenses. In 1994 Congress added Rules 413, 414, and 415 to the Federal Rules of Evidence. Rule 413 permits the admission of evidence of prior sexual assaults committed by the accused, and Rule 414 permits the admission of evidence of prior child molestation offenses committed by the accused in criminal cases that involve accusations of sexual assault or child molestation "for its bearing on any matter to which it is relevant." Rule 415 is the civil case equivalent of Rules 413 and 414. The judicial reaction to Rules 413 and 414 is discussed below at section B[2][g].

---

[26] *United States v. Meling*, 47 F.3d 1546, 1557 (9th Cir. 1995) (citations omitted).

[27] *United States v. Hayden*, 85 F.3d 153, 159 (4th Cir. 1996); *see also Meling*, 47 F.3d at 1557; *United States v. Tracy*, 12 F.3d 1186, 1194 (2d Cir. 1993) ("Rule 403 gives the trial judge discretion to exclude relevant evidence on the ground that its potential for unfair prejudice substantially outweighs its probative value.").

[28] Joan L. Larsen, *Of Propensity, Prejudice, and Plain Meaning: The Accused's Use of Exculpatory Specific Acts Evidence and the Need to Amend Rule 404(b)*, 87 Nw. U. L. Rev. 651, 658 (1993).

[29] J. Wigmore, Evidence in Trials at Common Law § 58.2 (Peter Tillers ed., 1983).

[a]   Standard of Proof

UNITED STATES v. HUDDLESTON
485 U.S. 681 (1988)

Chief Justice Rehnquist delivered the opinion of the Court.

*   *   *

. . . This case presents the question whether the district court must itself make a preliminary finding that the Government has proved the "other act" by a preponderance of the evidence before it submits the evidence to the jury. We hold that it need not do so.

Petitioner, Guy Rufus Huddleston, was charged with one count of selling stolen goods in interstate commerce, 18 U.S.C. § 2315, and one count of possessing stolen property in interstate commerce, 18 U.S.C. § 659. The two counts related to two portions of a shipment of stolen Memorex videocassette tapes that petitioner was alleged to have possessed and sold, knowing that they were stolen.

The evidence at trial showed that a trailer containing over 32,000 blank Memorex videocassette tapes with a manufacturing cost of $4.53 per tape was stolen from the Overnight Express yard in South Holland, Illinois, sometime between April 11 and 15, 1985. On April 17, 1985, petitioner contacted Karen Curry, the manager of the Magic Rent-to-Own in Ypsilanti, Michigan, seeking her assistance in selling a large number of blank Memorex videocassette tapes. After assuring Curry that the tapes were not stolen, he told her he wished to sell them in lots of at least 500 at $2.75 to $3 per tape. Curry subsequently arranged for the sale of a total of 5,000 tapes, which petitioner delivered to the various purchasers — who apparently believed the sales were legitimate.

There was no dispute that the tapes which petitioner sold were stolen; the only material issue at trial was whether petitioner knew they were stolen. The District Court allowed the Government to introduce evidence of "similar acts" under Rule 404(b), concluding that such evidence had "clear relevance as to [petitioner's knowledge]." App. 11. The first piece of similar act evidence offered by the Government was the testimony of Paul Toney, a record store owner. He testified that in February 1985, petitioner offered to sell new 12" black and white televisions for $28 apiece. According to Toney, petitioner indicated that he could obtain several thousand of these televisions. Petitioner and Toney eventually traveled to the Magic Rent-to-Own, where Toney purchased 20 of the televisions. Several days later, Toney purchased 18 more televisions.

The second piece of similar act evidence was the testimony of Robert Nelson, an undercover FBI agent posing as a buyer for an appliance store. Nelson testified that in May 1985, petitioner offered to sell him a large quantity of Amana appliances — 28 refrigerators, 2 ranges, and 40 icemakers. Nelson agreed to pay $8,000 for the appliances. Petitioner was arrested shortly after he arrived at the parking lot where he and Nelson had agreed to transfer the appliances. A truck containing the appliances was stopped a short distance from the parking lot, and Leroy Wesby, who was driving the truck, was also arrested. It was determined that the appliances had a value of approximately $20,000 and were part of a shipment that had been stolen.

Petitioner testified that the Memorex tapes, the televisions, and the appliances had all been provided by Leroy Wesby, who had represented that all of the merchandise was obtained legitimately. Petitioner stated that he had sold 6,500 Memorex tapes for Wesby on a commission basis. Petitioner maintained that all of the sales for Wesby had been on a commission basis and that he had no knowledge that any of the goods were stolen.

In closing, the prosecution explained that petitioner was not on trial for his dealings with the appliances or the televisions. The District Court instructed the jury that the similar acts evidence was to be used only to establish petitioner's knowledge, and not to prove his character. The jury convicted petitioner on the possession count only.

* * *

We granted certiorari, to resolve a conflict among the Courts of Appeals as to whether the trial court must make a preliminary finding before "similar act" and other Rule 404(b) evidence is submitted to the jury. We conclude that such evidence should be admitted if there is sufficient evidence to support a finding by the jury that the defendant committed the similar act.

Federal Rule of Evidence 404(b) — which applies in both civil and criminal cases — generally prohibits the introduction of evidence of extrinsic acts that might adversely reflect on the actor's character, unless that evidence bears upon a relevant issue in the case such as motive, opportunity, or knowledge. Extrinsic acts evidence may be critical to the establishment of the truth as to a disputed issue, especially when that issue involves the actor's state of mind and the only means of ascertaining that mental state is by drawing inferences from conduct. The actor in the instant case was a criminal defendant, and the act in question was "similar" to the one with which he was charged. Our use of these terms is not meant to suggest that our analysis is limited to such circumstances.

Before this Court, petitioner argues that the District Court erred in admitting Toney's testimony as to petitioner's sale of the televisions. The threshold inquiry a court must make before admitting similar acts evidence under Rule 404(b) is whether that evidence is probative of a material issue other than character. The Government's theory of relevance was that the televisions were stolen, and proof that petitioner had engaged in a series of sales of stolen merchandise from the same suspicious source would be strong evidence that he was aware that each of these items, including the Memorex tapes, was stolen. As such, the sale of the televisions was a "similar act" only if the televisions were stolen. Petitioner acknowledges that this evidence was admitted for the proper purpose of showing his knowledge that the Memorex tapes were stolen. He asserts, however, that the evidence should not have been admitted because the Government failed to prove to the District Court that the televisions were in fact stolen.

Petitioner argues from the premise that evidence of similar acts has a grave potential for causing improper prejudice. For instance, the jury may choose to punish the defendant for the similar rather than the charged act, or the jury may infer that the defendant is an evil person inclined to violate the law. Because of this danger, petitioner maintains, the jury ought not to be exposed to similar act evidence until the trial court has heard the evidence and made a determination under Federal Rule of Evidence 104(a) that the defendant committed the similar act. Rule 104(a) provides that "[p]reliminary questions concerning the qualification of a person to be a witness, the existence of a privilege, or the admissibility of evidence shall be determined by the court, subject to the provisions of subdivision (b)." According to petitioner, the trial court must make this preliminary finding by at least a preponderance of the evidence.

We reject petitioner's position, for it is inconsistent with the structure of the Rules of Evidence and with the plain language of Rule 404(b). Article IV of the Rules of Evidence deals with the relevancy of evidence. Rules 401 and 402 establish the broad principle that relevant evidence — evidence that makes the existence of any fact at issue more or less probable — is admissible unless the Rules provide otherwise. Rule 403 allows the trial judge to exclude relevant evidence if, among other things, "its probative value is substantially outweighed by the danger of unfair prejudice." Rules 404 through 412 address specific types of evidence that have generated problems. Generally, these latter Rules do not flatly prohibit the introduction of such evidence but instead limit the purpose for which it may be introduced. Rule 404(b), for example, protects against the introduction of extrinsic act evidence when that evidence is offered solely to prove character. The text contains no intimation, however, that any preliminary showing is necessary before such evidence may be introduced for a proper purpose. If offered for such a proper purpose, the evidence is subject only to general strictures limiting admissibility such as Rules 402 and 403.

Petitioner's reading of Rule 404(b) as mandating a preliminary finding by the trial court that the act in question occurred not only superimposes a level of judicial oversight that is nowhere apparent from the language of that provision, but it is simply inconsistent with the legislative history behind Rule 404(b). The Advisory Committee specifically declined to offer any "mechanical solution" to the admission of evidence under 404(b). Advisory Committee's Notes on Fed. Rule Evid. 404(b), 28 U.S.C. App., p. 691. Rather, the Committee indicated that the trial court should assess such evidence under the usual rules for admissibility: "The determination must be made whether the danger of undue prejudice outweighs the probative value of the evidence in view of the availability of other means of proof and other factors appropriate for making decisions of this kind under Rule 403." *Ibid.*; see also S. Rep. No. 93-1277, p. 25 (1974) ("[I]t is anticipated that with respect to permissible uses for such evidence, the trial judge may exclude it only on the basis of those considerations set forth in Rule 403, i.e., prejudice, confusion or waste of time.").

Petitioner's suggestion that a preliminary finding is necessary to protect the defendant from the potential for unfair prejudice is also belied by the Reports of the House of Representatives and the Senate. The House made clear that the version of Rule 404(b) which became law was intended to "plac[e] greater emphasis on admissibility than did the final Court version." H.R. Rep. No. 93-650, p. 7 (1973). The Senate echoed this theme: "[T]he use of the discretionary word 'may' with respect to the admissibility of evidence of crimes, wrongs, or other acts is not intended to confer any arbitrary discretion on the trial judge." S. Rep. No. 93-1277, *supra*, at 24. Thus, Congress was not nearly so concerned with the potential prejudicial effect of Rule 404(b) evidence as it was with ensuring that restrictions would not be placed on the admission of such evidence.

We conclude that a preliminary finding by the court that the Government has proved the act by a preponderance of the evidence is not called for under Rule 104(a). This is not to say, however, that the Government may parade past the jury a litany of potentially prejudicial similar acts that have been established or connected to the defendant only by unsubstantiated innuendo. Evidence is admissible under Rule 404(b) only if it is relevant. "Relevancy is not an inherent characteristic of any item of evidence but exists only as a relation between an item of evidence and a matter properly provable in the case." Advisory Committee's Notes on Fed. Rule Evid. 401, 28 U.S.C. App., p. 688. In the Rule 404(b) context, similar act evidence is relevant only if the jury can reasonably conclude that the act occurred and that the defendant was the actor. *See United States v. Beechum,* 582 F.2d 898, 912–913 (CA5 1978) (*en banc*). In the instant case, the evidence that petitioner was selling the televisions was relevant under the Government's theory only if the jury could reasonably find that the televisions were stolen.

Such questions of relevance conditioned on a fact are dealt with under Federal Rule of Evidence 104(b). *Beechum, supra,* at 912–913; *see also* E. Imwinkelried, Uncharged Misconduct Evidence § 2.06 (1984). Rule 104(b) provides:

> When the relevancy of evidence depends upon the fulfillment of a condition of fact, the court shall admit it upon, or subject to, the introduction of evidence sufficient to support a finding of the fulfillment of the condition.

In determining whether the Government has introduced sufficient evidence to meet Rule 104(b), the trial court neither weighs credibility nor makes a finding that the Government has proved the conditional fact by a preponderance of the evidence. The court simply examines all the evidence in the case and decides whether the jury could reasonably find the conditional fact — here, that the televisions were stolen — by a preponderance of the evidence. See 21 C. Wright & K. Graham, Federal Practice and Procedure § 5054, p. 269 (1977). The trial court has traditionally exercised the broadest sort of discretion in controlling the order of proof at trial, and we see nothing in the Rules of Evidence that would change this practice. Often the trial court may decide to allow the proponent to introduce evidence concerning a similar act, and at a later point in the trial assess whether sufficient evidence has been offered to permit the jury to make the requisite finding.[7] If the proponent has failed to meet this minimal standard of proof, the trial court must instruct the jury to disregard the evidence.

We emphasize that in assessing the sufficiency of the evidence under Rule 104(b), the trial court must consider all evidence presented to the jury. "[I]ndividual pieces of evidence, insufficient in themselves to prove a point, may in cumulation prove it. The sum of an evidentiary presentation may well be greater than its constituent parts." *Bourjaily v. United States,* 483 U.S. 171, 179–180 (1987). In assessing whether the evidence was sufficient to support a finding that the televisions were stolen, the court here was required to consider not only the direct evidence on that point — the low price of the televisions, the large quantity offered for sale, and petitioner's inability to produce a bill of sale — but also the evidence concerning petitioner's involvement in the sales of other stolen merchandise obtained from Wesby, such as the Memorex tapes and the Amana appliances. Given this evidence, the jury reasonably could have concluded that the televisions were stolen, and the trial court therefore properly allowed the evidence to go to the jury.

We share petitioner's concern that unduly prejudicial evidence might be introduced under Rule 404(b). See *Michelson v. United States,* 335 U.S. 469, 475–476 (1948). We think, however, that the protection against such unfair prejudice emanates not from a requirement of a preliminary finding by the trial court, but rather from four other

---

[7] "When an item of evidence is conditionally relevant, it is often not possible for the offeror to prove the fact upon which relevance is conditioned at the time the evidence is offered. In such cases it is customary to permit him to introduce the evidence and 'connect it up' later. Rule 104(b) continues this practice, specifically authorizing the judge to admit the evidence 'subject to' proof of the preliminary fact. It is, of course, not the responsibility of the judge sua sponte to insure that the foundation evidence is offered; the objector must move to strike the evidence if at the close of the trial the offeror has failed to satisfy the condition." 21 C. Wright & K. Graham, Federal Practice And Procedure § 5054, pp. 269–270 (1977) (footnotes omitted).

sources: first, from the requirement of Rule 404(b) that the evidence be offered for a proper purpose; second, from the relevancy requirement of Rule 402 — as enforced through Rule 104(b); third, from the assessment the trial court must make under Rule 403 to determine whether the probative value of the similar acts evidence is substantially outweighed by its potential for unfair prejudice, *see* Advisory Committee's Notes on Fed. Rule Evid. 404(b), 28 U.S.C. App., p. 691; S. Rep. No. 93-1277, at 25; and fourth, from Federal Rule of Evidence 105, which provides that the trial court shall, upon request, instruct the jury that the similar acts evidence is to be considered only for the proper purpose for which it was admitted. *See United States v. Ingraham*, 832 F.2d 229, 235 (1st Cir. 1987).

QUESTION

In *Huddleston*, while sharing petitioner's concern with the potential prejudicial effect of Rule 404(b) evidence, the Supreme Court nonetheless held that the district court need not make a preliminary finding that the government has proved the "other act" by a preponderance of the evidence before it submits the "similar acts" evidence to the jury. Do you agree with the Supreme Court's ruling? If the government is not required to prove by a preponderance of the evidence that the defendant committed the "similar acts," what protections are otherwise afforded the defendant against unduly prejudicial evidence being introduced under Rule 404(b)? *See United States v. Esparsen*, 930 F.2d 1461, 1476 (10th Cir. 1991), where the court stated:

> In *Huddleston*, the Supreme Court explained that protection from unfair prejudice of 404(b) evidence comes from (1) Rule 404(b)'s requirement that the evidence be offered for a proper purpose, (2) Rule 402's relevancy requirement, (3) Rule 403's requirement that the evidence be more probative than prejudicial, and (4) Rule 105's requirement that the trial court, upon request, instruct the jury that the evidence should only be considered for the purpose for which it was admitted (citations omitted).

Are these protections adequate to prevent unfair prejudice from the introduction of Rule 404(b) evidence?

[b]   Motive

UNITED STATES v. LLOYD
71 F.3d 1256 (7th Cir. 1995)

COFFEY, CIRCUIT JUDGE.

A federal grand jury indicted Willie E. Lloyd of being a felon in possession of a firearm, a 9mm Ruger semi-automatic pistol, in violation of 18 U.S.C. § 922(g)(1). Lloyd filed a pre-trial motion to quash the warrant authorizing the search of his person and apartment; the motion was denied. Lloyd was convicted before a jury and sentenced to a term of ninety-six months imprisonment, to be followed by a three year term of supervised release, and ordered to pay a special assessment of $50. Lloyd appeals his conviction as well as the denial of his motion to quash the warrant. We AFFIRM.

On March 6, 1994, Detective Anthony Wojcik of the Chicago Police Department ("CPD") received information from a confidential informant ("CI") that Willie E. Lloyd was in possession of two handguns. Lloyd and the CI were members of the Vice Lords, a Chicago street gang, and Lloyd was the leader of the faction known as the Unknown Vice Lords. The CI, who belonged to the Conservative Vice Lords, informed Wojcik that late in the evening of March 5, he met Lloyd in an apartment on West Jackson Street in Chicago, Illinois. He described the building as a "brown brick, six-flat unit on the southeast corner of Jackson and Keeler," and informed him that the apartment was on the first floor, on the west side of the building. The CI also told Wojcik that the door to the apartment was bordered in white stone.

While the CI was in the flat with Lloyd, the defendant displayed two black handguns to the CI: a 9mm Ruger semi-automatic pistol which was loaded as well as a 9mm Glock semi-automatic pistol, also loaded. When Lloyd exhibited these firearms, he stated that he kept them in the apartment for "security purposes." After showing the CI his firearms, Lloyd placed them on a shelf in the closet of the rear bedroom, located directly off the kitchen.

*   *   *

Based upon this information, the officer prepared an affidavit in support of a search warrant and appeared with the CI before a Cook County Circuit Judge who found that there was probable cause to believe that Lloyd was a felon in possession of a firearm and issued the warrant for the search of Lloyd's person and the first floor west apartment in the building.

*   *   *

Lt. Farrell and Sgt. Mingey testified that after the forcible entry into the apartment, they observed Lloyd standing in the rear of the flat, with a "dark colored" firearm in his right hand. As Farrell hollered "He's got a gun," Lloyd ran into the bedroom off the kitchen, and closed and dead-bolted the door. Lt. Farrell broke down the door and upon entry witnessed Lloyd, standing near a window on the west wall of the bedroom, throw a gun out through a broken window with his right hand. He immediately placed Lloyd under arrest.

While Farrell, Mingey, and a few other officers were gaining access to the apartment, CPD officers Lawrence Knysch and Victor Rodriguez stood on the west side of the apartment building. At trial, Knysch and Rodriguez asserted that the area around the apartment building was well illuminated with street lights as well as from light coming through a window in the west apartment on the first floor. The officers also testified that they heard their companion officers enter the apartment, followed by a lot of noise and commotion. Knysch stated that while he was on the outside detail some twenty five feet away from the window, he witnessed the defendant Lloyd pull back a shade, bang on the window above them with a gun in his right hand, break the glass, and throw out the gun. Rodriguez testified that he was approximately fifteen feet from the window, and that he was positive that he saw Lloyd throw the firearm from the window.

Knysch and Rodriguez retrieved the loaded 9mm Ruger semi-automatic handgun, and Rodriguez immediately yelled up to the officers inside the apartment that he and Knysch had recovered the Ruger. Farrell stated that he then conducted a pat-down search of Lloyd, as the defendant stated: "You got me. You got me. My brothers should have been out there."

While Lt. Farrell was arresting Lloyd, Sgt. Mingey found Shean Fisher (also known as Shean Woods) and Che Williams laying on the floor in the middle bedroom of the apartment. When Officer Rodriguez searched the closet of this bedroom, he discovered a third weapon, a loaded.25 caliber Lorcin handgun under some clothes. At the time of the search, the following individuals were also present in the apartment: Renee Fitzgerald and Keith Melton, Kim Taylor, Ms. Taylor's six children, and Mookie Lloyd, the defendant's three year old son.

The government called Fisher, who was seventeen years of age at the time of his arrest, to testify at trial. He stated that Lloyd was the chief of his street gang, the Unknown Vice Lords, and that he and Williams, then sixteen years old, were Lloyd's security guards on the night of his arrest. According to Fisher, their duties included watching the apartment "to make sure nothing or no one don't come through there," protecting Lloyd from rival gang members, and to warn him if the police were approaching. As security guards, Fisher and Williams were positioned near the front door of the apartment, and Fisher stated that they were usually armed. At the time of Lloyd's arrest, Fisher was carrying the.25 caliber Lorcin, but Williams, who according to Fisher ordinarily carried the Ruger while on guard duty, was unarmed.

*   *   *

The prosecution also called Officer Michael Cronin to testify. Cronin had been employed by the CPD for 23 years, and spent the last thirteen years of his tour of duty in the Gang Investigations Section. He had been assigned to the west side area in the city of Chicago for the last ten years, and stated that he was familiar with both Lloyd and the Vice Lords, including the defendant's faction, the Unknown Vice Lords. During the time Cronin was investigating the Vice Lords, he testified that he had occasion to speak with Lloyd, who informed the officer that he was the leader of the Unknown Vice Lords. Cronin further stated that he had previously observed Lloyd accompanied by fellow gang members acting as "security guards," and that within the year before the defendant's arrest, there were two separate attempts on Lloyd's life from members of rival street gangs.[4]

Lloyd called Renee Fitzgerald, his girlfriend and the mother of his son, to testify on his behalf. She asserted that on the evening of March 6, she and Lloyd were in the rear bedroom of the apartment, changing their son's diaper, when she heard someone in the apartment shouting "Five-O!" She further stated that at this time, Williams knocked on the rear bedroom door, and that when she opened it, Williams handed her the Ruger and asked her to get rid of it. According to Fitzgerald, upon receiving the gun, she closed and locked the door, broke the rear bedroom window with her fist, and threw the gun to the ground. When queried during cross-examination if she injured her hand as she broke the window, she stated no and that she had only sustained a scratch. She contended that she had not seen Lloyd in possession of a gun at any time during that day. On cross examination, she admitted that Fisher and Williams were security guards for Lloyd, and that Williams carried the Ruger as part of his guard duties. She also contradicted Fisher's testimony by stating that Lloyd was no longer the leader of the Unknown Vice Lords at the time of his arrest, although he had once been the faction's chief.

*   *   *

The jury returned a verdict of guilty, and the trial judge entered a judgment in accordance with the verdict, finding that Lloyd was guilty of being a felon in possession

---

[4] Prior to trial, the government filed a motion in limine, seeking to admit Cronin's testimony in order to establish; (1) the context of the defendant's statement "My brothers should have been out there"; (2) the relationship between Lloyd, Williams and Fisher; and (3) the defendant's motive to possess the Ruger as protection in case there were any more assassination attempts. Over Lloyd's objection, the trial court admitted the evidence.

of a firearm, in violation of 18 U.S.C. § 922(g)(1).

* * *

III. DISCUSSION

* * *

B. Evidence of Prior Bad Acts

Lloyd maintains that the trial court abused its discretion when it allowed Officer Cronin to testify that the defendant was the leader of the Unknown Vice Lords, employed security guards from the ranks of his gang, and that he had been the target of two assassination attempts within the previous year. He posits that the evidence received was not sufficiently similar to the crime with which he was charged (possession of a firearm by a felon), and that because of the strong societal bias against members of street gangs, the admission of that testimony was unduly prejudicial. The trial judge admitted the evidence for the limited purposes of establishing "one, the context of the defendant's post-arrest statement, two the relationship between the defendant and other persons in the apartment at the time of the search, and three the defendant's motive to possess a handgun," as well as why Lloyd felt the necessity to employ armed security guards.

"Under Federal Rule of Evidence 404(b), evidence of other misconduct is not admissible to show that the defendant acted in conformity therewith, but may be admissible for other purposes, *such as proof of motive*, opportunity, intent, preparation, plan, knowledge, or identity." *United States v. Wilson*, 31 F.3d 510, 514 (7th Cir. 1994) (citations omitted, emphasis added). . . .

> In determining the admissibility of Rule 404(b) evidence, the court must determine whether (1) the evidence is directed toward establishing a matter in issue other than the defendant's propensity to commit the crime charged; (2) the evidence shows that the other act is similar enough and close in time to be relevant to the matter in issue; (3) the evidence is sufficient to support a jury finding that the defendant committed the similar act; and (4) the probative value of the evidence is not substantially outweighed by the danger of unfair prejudice.

Wilson, 31 F.3d at 514–15 (citations omitted).

Under the requirements of *Wilson*, the trial judge determined that Officer Cronin's testimony was (1) directed at establishing a matter other than Lloyd's propensity to commit the crime charged, and was (2) "relevant to the matter in issue," Lloyd's possession of the gun. *Id.* at 514. Information concerning Lloyd's employment of security guards was admitted in evidence not to demonstrate that he had a propensity to possess a gun, but rather, to establish that considering the totality of the circumstances surrounding Williams' and Fisher's relationship to the defendant, vis-a'-vis the weapons and their employment status, Lloyd retained constructive possession of the guns they carried while on guard duty. . . .

Furthermore, Rule 404(b) specifically states that evidence of prior acts is admissible to establish motive. The assassination attempts on Lloyd provided a possible motive for his possession of the firearms and use of armed guards — protecting his own life, as well as the lives of his girlfriend and child, both of whom were present during the last attempt on his life. Although the defendant argues that motive was not one of the elements the government was required to prove in order to gain a conviction, motive to possess a firearm was "relevant to the matter in issue," *Wilson*, 31 F.3d at 514, because it makes possession "more probable . . . than it would be without the evidence." Fed. R. Evid. 403.

The second element of *Wilson* also requires that the acts occur close enough in time to the crime charged to be relevant to the matter in issue. . . . The substance of Officer Cronin's testimony concerned the year prior to Lloyd's arrest for the instant offense and this circuit has found that far greater time periods were close enough in proximity to be relevant for purposes of Rule 404(b) analysis. *See, e.g., United States v. Kreiser*, 15 F.3d 635, 640–41 (7th Cir. 1994) (seven years before the current charges for conspiring to possess with intent to distribute cocaine, the defendant was involved in a similar cocaine transaction); and *United States v. Goodapple*, 958 F.2d 1402, 1407 (7th Cir. 1992) (a defendant charged with possession with intent to distribute valium, obtained and distributed drugs from a hospital in which he worked five years earlier).

The third element of our analysis is also directed at establishing the relevancy of the 404(b) evidence. . . . We have also made it clear that this prong of our Rule 404(b) analysis need not be unduly rigid: we have stated that "when evidence is offered to prove intent, the degree of similarity is relevant only insofar as the acts are sufficiently alike to support an inference of criminal intent. . . . *The prior acts need not be duplicates of the one for which the defendant is now being tried.*" *United States v. York*, 933 F.2d 1343, 1351 (7th Cir.), *cert. denied*, 502 U.S. 916 (1991) (quotations and citations omitted); *see also United States v. Elizondo*, 920 F.2d 1308, 1320 (7th Cir. 1990) ("[t]here is no requirement that acts used to show the existence *of a common scheme or plan be identical, just that the charged and uncharged prior events have sufficient points in common.*").

Thus, while the assassination attempts and use of security guards, as recounted by Officer Cronin, were not identical to the crime with which Lloyd was charged, they were nonetheless relevant because they support an inference that Lloyd, aware that his life might be in danger, possessed firearms and made use of armed security guards to protect himself. Furthermore, Cronin's testimony "complete[d] what would otherwise be a . . . conceptual void in the story of the crime," *United States v. Spaeni*, 60 F.3d 313, 316 (7th Cir.), *petition for cert. filed*, No. 95-6386 (Oct. 12, 1995), because Lloyd's statement that his "brothers should have been out there," only becomes clear when it is understood as a reference to his teenaged security guards, Williams and Fisher.

Finally, we turn our attention to balancing the prejudicial and probative value of Officer Cronin's testimony. This court has stated that "[b]ecause evidence of membership in a street gang is likely to be damaging to [a defendant] in the eyes of the jury, district courts must consider carefully the admissibility of such evidence." *United States v. Rodriguez*, 925 F.2d 1049, 1053 (7th Cir. 1991) (quotation omitted). The requirement that the probative value of Rule 404(b) evidence must not be substantially outweighed by its prejudicial value "overlaps with Rule 403, which states that 'evidence may be excluded if its probative value is substantially outweighed by the danger of unfair prejudice.' " [*United States v. Torres*, 977 F.2d 321, 328 (7th Cir. 1992)] (quoting Fed. R. Evid. 403). "Relevant evidence is inherently prejudicial. . . . Rule 403 was never intended to exclude relevant evidence simply because it is detrimental to one party's case; rather, the relevant inquiry is whether any *unfair prejudice* from the evidence substantially outweighs its probative value." *Cook v. Hoppin*, 783 F.2d 684, 689 (7th Cir. 1986) (quotations and citations omitted).

"When balancing the prejudice and probative value, the courts of the various circuits have found the scale tipped in favor of admitting evidence of prior bad acts in cases where the acts involved, or explained, the circumstances of the crime charged, where the acts provided the background for, or development of, the crime charged, and where the acts completed the story of the crime on trial." *United States v. Jordan*, 722 F.2d 353, 356 (7th Cir. 1983). "[T]his court has long recognized that gang membership has probative value under appropriate circumstances," *Rodriguez*, 925 F.2d at 1053 (quotation omitted), and has held that "evidence of gang members' lifestyle is admissible when it is intricately related to the facts of [a] case." *Id.* at 1054 (quotation omitted).

Thus, even though the testimony of Officer Cronin aided the prosecution in establishing Lloyd's guilt, our inquiry, as mandated by Fed. R. Evid. 403, is whether the evidence's probative value was outweighed by the risk of *unfair* prejudice. The use of the guards was probative of Lloyd's intent to illegally possess a firearm, as well as assuring that he would have sufficient forewarning if police were approaching. Thus, Officer Cronin's testimony helped to establish Lloyd's actual and constructive possession of the loaded Ruger . . . and the highly probative nature of his testimony outweighs the risk of unfair prejudice to Lloyd. *See Torres*, 977 F.2d at 328.

* * *

Affirmed.

NOTES AND QUESTIONS

1. Generally, motive is not an element of a crime but may be relevant to prove intent or the identity of the defendant as the perpetrator of the crime. *See United States v. Sebolt*, 460 F.3d 910, 917 (7th Cir. 2006) ("Prior instances of sexual misconduct with a child victim may establish a defendant's sexual interest in children and thereby serve as evidence of the defendant's motive to commit a charged offense involving sexual exploitation of children."); *United States v. Deciccio.* 370 F.3d 206, 214 (1st Cir. 2004) (evidence of defendant's tax liabilities admissible to prove motive to commit arson and other crimes charged in indictment). *United States v. Bradshaw*, 690 F.2d 704, 708 (9th Cir. 1982) (even though motive need not be proven as an element of the offense, it is "far from irrelevant").

2. *The Test for Admission of Rule 404(b) Evidence.* In determining whether prior bad act evidence is properly admissible under Rule 404(b), several federal circuits require that the evidence satisfy two requirements: (1) it must have some special relevance to a material issue other than propensity; and (2) the probative value of the evidence must not be substantially outweighed by the danger of unfair prejudice. *See United States v. Lopez*, 340 F.3d 169 (3d Cir. 2003); *United States v. Trenkler*, 61 F.3d 45 (1st Cir. 1995); *United States v. Mitchell*, 49 F.3d 769 (D.C. Cir. 1994); and *United States v. Cordell*, 912 F.2d 769 (5th Cir. 1990). At least two circuits additionally require that the "other crimes" evidence be similar to the charged crime and committed reasonably close in time. *See United States v. Abumayyaleh*, 530 F.3d 641 (8th Cir. 2008); *United States v. Curry*, 79 F.3d 1489 (7th Cir. 1996). The Fourth Circuit applies a unique four-part test in determining the admissibility of prior bad act evidence: (1) the evidence must be relevant, i.e., sufficiently related to the charged offense; (2) it must be necessary, i.e., an essential part of the crime on trial or necessary to proved the context of the crime; (3) it must be reliable; and (4) its probative value must not be substantially outweighed by the danger of unfair prejudice. *See United States v. Hill* 322 F.3d 301 (4th Cir. 2003). *See also United States v. Vizcarra-Martinez*, 66 F.3d 1006

(9th Cir. 1995 (applying a different four-part test, other crimes evidence admissible if: (1) it tends to prove a material point; (2) the prior act is not too remote in time; (3) the evidence is sufficient to support a finding that the defendant committed the other act; and (4) (in cases where knowledge and intent are at issue) the act is similar to the offense charged"). Where prior crimes are offered to prove motive, they need not be similar in nature to be admissible. *See United States v. Shriver*, 842 F.2d 968, 974 (7th Cir. 1988). Finally, several circuits also require that the trial court give a limiting instruction. *See United States v. Merriweather*, 78 F.3d 1070 (6th Cir. 1996); *United States v. Edwards*, 69 F.3d 419 (10th Cir. 1994); and *United States v. Pitre*, 960 F.2d 1112 (2d Cir. 1992).

3. Should the "motive" exception to Rule 404(b) be narrowly or liberally construed? Should evidence of a defendant's drug addiction be admitted to prove motive for commission of a burglary? Robbery? For cases admitting drug use to prove motive for robbery, *see United States v. Madden*, 38 F.3d 747, 751–52 (4th Cir. 1994) (evidence of defendant's prior drug use admissible if the financial needs of defendant's drug habit are sufficient to establish motive for the robbery); *United States v. Miranda*, 986 F.2d 1283, 1285 (9th Cir. 1993) (drug use admissible to demonstrate motive in robbery case). *But see United States v. Sutton*, 41 F.3d 1257, 1259 (8th Cir. 1994) (in bank robbery prosecution, court found prior drug use to be of slight probative value, which did not outweigh the risk of unfair prejudice).

[c]   Intent

UNITED STATES v. TORRES
977 F.2d 321 (7th Cir. 1992)

COFFEY, CIRCUIT JUDGE.

Dennis Torres was charged with intentionally threatening a federal witness in violation of 18 U.S.C. § 1513. At trial the government introduced evidence of prior acts of violence by Torres under Federal Rule of Evidence 404(b), alleging that this evidence, though unrelated to the charged crime, was introduced solely to establish Torres's intent when making the threats. A jury found him guilty, and the court, departing upward from the Sentencing Guidelines, sentenced him to 85 months in prison. Torres now challenges the admission of the prior acts evidence introduced to prove intent, and the upward departure, and we affirm.

In August of 1990 a grand jury indicted eleven members of a cocaine distribution ring in Milwaukee, Wisconsin. One of these eleven was Diane Blas, who agreed to cooperate with the government and provide information about the ring. During her interviews Blas told the government that she and her husband had sold half-ounce packages of cocaine to Dennis Torres. She also revealed that Torres had been involved in the "Georgia Stop," during which he and Blas's husband, along with their travelling companions, were stopped by a Georgia state trooper who discovered two ounces of cocaine in one of the caravan vehicles. Torres had not been named in the conspiracy indictment, but he told police that he knew Blas was cooperating with the authorities and had informed them of his drug-related conduct.

On the morning of March 5, 1991, Juan Glarza, Diane Blas's father, was working at his wife's grocery store. Also present was Torrey Bodie, a salesman who was taking Glarza's grocery order. Around 8:15 a.m. Dennis Torres entered the store and asked for

Diane Blas. Juan Glarza told him that Diane was not there. Torres became visibly agitated, and, in extremely vulgar and menacing language, threatened to severely harm Blas, Glarza, and Glarza's store. He told Glarza to tell Blas that he (Torres) was going to kill her for naming him to authorities, and then said that he also planned to destroy Glarza and the grocery store.

After making the threats Torres backed towards the door and reached into his coat pocket. Fearful that he might be reaching for a gun, Glarza pulled his gun from behind the grocery counter and fired a shot into the floor near Torres. Part of the floor or the bullet ricocheted into Torres's leg. At this time Torres grabbed Bodie and used him as a shield as he exited the store and jumped into a waiting getaway car.

*   *   *

The government's theory at trial was that Torres intentionally threatened the property and persons of Juan Glarza and Diane Blas in retaliation for Blas's informing the federal prosecutors about his drug activity. To buttress this theory the government, in addition to presenting Glarza's and Bodie's versions of the grocery store incident, also introduced evidence of two prior acts committed by Torres in order to prove his intent to retaliate against Blas. Torres objected to the admission of evidence regarding these acts, arguing that it was being introduced for an improper purpose; namely, revealing his propensity toward criminal behavior. *See* Fed. R. Evid. 404(b). The court overruled the objection, finding that the evidence was properly introduced for the purpose of demonstrating his retaliatory intent at the time of the threats, and was not being used merely to show a penchant for crime.

The first prior act was described by the mother of Torres's child, Lisetta Miranda. Miranda testified that in April of 1989, when she was living with the defendant, someone stole a television and VCR from their apartment. She heard on the street that Jose Santiago had done it, and so advised Torres. The two of them then drove to a car wash where they observed Santiago. Torres got out of his vehicle, argued with Santiago, and thereafter drew a gun and opened fire. Miranda could not remember where Torres was pointing the gun as he fired, but officer William Sincere later found bullet holes in the overhead door and wall of the car wash. No charges were filed in connection with this incident.

The second prior act introduced to prove Torres's retaliatory intent occurred on September 21, 1989, after reports of a street fight in Torres's neighborhood. Milwaukee police officer Cindy Rosenthal went to investigate the scene of the fight and discovered a partially loaded .22 automatic pistol clip. Approximately half an hour later, while still on the scene, Rosenthal heard shots close by. Witnesses advised her that a large white auto and a damaged silver Nissan automobile were involved in the shooting. Shortly thereafter Officer Rosenthal saw the silver Nissan on a nearby street and ordered the driver to pull over. Two of the car's occupants were arrested after officers saw a gun inside. Thirty-five minutes later, while waiting for a truck to tow the Nissan from the scene, Rosenthal observed the other vehicle (a large white auto) involved in the shooting, pass through an alley right in front of her. She pursued the vehicle until it stopped at a nearby house. Torres got out of the car and Rosenthal ordered him to freeze, after which backup officers instituted a search of his person and vehicle. Torres had about $2,000 cash and two live .22 bullets on his person. He also had two guns, one a .22 caliber revolver, hidden under the armrest cushion in his car. The .22 clip recovered from the fight scene fit the .22 revolver Torres had tucked under the armrest. Torres was charged with two misdemeanor counts of carrying concealed weapons, which charges were pending at the time of the conduct charged herein.

*   *   *

III. DISCUSSION

A. Evidence of Prior Bad Acts

*   *   *

. . . The principle behind [Rule 404(b)] is that evidence of crimes or acts other than those charged should not be admissible merely to show that the defendant, having committed other bad acts, has a propensity toward crime or a bad character. *See United States v. Harvey*, 959 F.2d 1371, 1373–74 (7th Cir. 1992). Such evidence may be admissible, however, to prove some other fact at issue, such as motive, opportunity, intent, or the other elements outlined by the Rule. *Id.* Here the government presented the other acts evidence as proof of Torres's retaliatory intent. He now appeals the court's decision to admit the evidence over his objection, arguing that the evidence failed to demonstrate his intent and was merely used to attack his character before the jury.

*   *   *

This Circuit applies a four-part test when examining Rule 404(b) evidence, which may be admitted where:

> (1) the evidence is directed toward establishing a matter in issue other than the defendant's propensity to commit the crime charged, (2) the evidence shows that the other act is similar enough and close enough in time to be relevant to the matter in issue, (3) the evidence is sufficient to support a jury finding that the defendant committed the similar act, and (4) the probative value of the evidence is not substantially outweighed by the danger of unfair prejudice.

United States v. Lennartz, 948 F.2d 363, 366 (7th Cir. 1991); *United States v. Robinson*, 956 F.2d 1388, 1395 (7th Cir. 1992), *petition for cert. filed*, 61 U.S.L.W. 3200 (July 23, 1992). Torres maintains that the evidence of the car wash shooting and the concealed weapons incident did not meet the first, second, and fourth parts of this test, and thus should have been excluded. We examine each part in turn.

1. Matter at Issue Other Than Propensity

The first requirement is that the evidence must be relevant to some matter at issue in the case (i.e., intent), rather than merely establishing the defendant's propensity to commit crimes. In *United States v. Shackleford*, 738 F.2d 776 (7th Cir. 1984), we held that other acts evidence of intent always relates to a matter at issue other than propensity when the defendant is charged with a specific intent crime.

> When the crime charged requires proof of specific intent, we have held that, because it is a material element to be proved by the government, it is necessarily in issue and the government may submit evidence of other acts in an attempt to establish the matter in its case-in-chief, assuming the other requirements of Rules 404(b) and 403 are satisfied.

Id. at 781. Torres was charged under 18 U.S.C. § 1513, which is titled "Retaliating against a witness, victim, or an informant." To establish a violation, the government must demonstrate that the defendant "knowingly engage[d]" in conduct threatening the person or property of another "with intent to retaliate" against a witness, victim, or informant for providing information to a law enforcement officer concerning a federal offense. 18 U.S.C. § 1513. Since the government was required to establish that Torres acted not only knowingly, but also with an intent to retaliate, this is a specific intent crime. *See* 1 W. LaFave & A. Scott, Substantive Criminal Law, § 3.5, at 315 (1986) (specific intent "designate[s] a special mental element which is required above and beyond any mental state required with respect to the *actus reus* of the crime.") The Rule 404(b) evidence thus went to a matter at issue, and therefore meets the first part of the admissibility test.

2. Similarity and Temporal Proximity

The second section of the Rule 404(b) test requires that the other acts be sufficiently similar and close enough in time to the charged act to be relevant to the matter they are offered to prove — in this case Torres's intent. As to the temporal proximity requirement, we have recognized that the analysis must be flexible, observing that "Questions about 'how long is too long' do not have uniform answers; the answers depend on the theory that makes the evidence admissible." *United States v. Beasley,* 809 F.2d 1273, 1277 (7th Cir. 1987). By the same token, questions about "how similar is similar enough" also do not have uniform answers; these answers too depend on the theory that makes the evidence admissible, and must be reached on a case-by-case basis. Thus, similarity means more than sharing some common characteristics; the common characteristics must relate to the purpose for which the evidence is offered. As the Fifth Circuit stated: "Where the issue addressed is the defendant's intent to commit the offense charged, the relevancy of the extrinsic offense derives from the defendant's indulging himself in the same state of mind in the perpetration of both the extrinsic and charged offenses." *United States v. Beechum,* 582 F.2d 898, 911 (5th Cir. 1978) (*en banc*). We thus examine each of the extrinsic criminal acts in this case to determine whether Torres committed them with the same type of retaliatory intent that he allegedly harbored when he threatened Blas and Glarza for the former's cooperation with federal authorities, and whether the prior acts occurred within a time period proximate enough to be relevant to the charged offense.

The first extrinsic act is Torres's shooting into the car wash at the man who allegedly stole his television and VCR. This act, which took place just less than two years before the incident at the grocery store, was clearly a violent act of retaliation by which Torres hoped to intimidate someone he believed had wronged him. It is thus similar to the charged offense of threatening to retaliate against a government witness who may have incriminated him. Evidence of the car wash shooting showed that Torres intended to frighten and intimidate Jose Santiago by firing bullets in his direction; this evidence was relevant to the issue of whether he had a similar intent when threatening Glarza and Blas. Further, the close similarity of the mental states during each act erases any difficulty as to their probity that might arise by their occurring nearly two years apart; two years is plainly recent enough when the acts are so alike. *Cf. United States v. Harrod,* 856 F.2d 996, 1002 (7th Cir. 1988) (five-year-old convictions admissible under Rule 404(b) because of their close similarity to the charged offense); *United States v. Chaimson,* 760 F.2d 798, 807 (7th Cir. 1985) (similar acts committed five years ago admissible under Rule 404(b)). The evidence of the car wash shooting is thus sufficiently similar and also close enough in time to satisfy the second element of the Rule 404(b) test.

The second extrinsic act occurred on September 21, 1989, some twenty months before the threats in the grocery store. On that date Torres was arrested with concealed weapons in his car and live bullets in his pocket. Moreover, a spent .22 clip found at the scene of the nearby street fight matched the unloaded .22 pistol recovered from the defendant's vehicle, another piece of evidence leading to the conclusion that Torres had in fact fired shots during the fight. The district judge stated that the relevancy of this incident may have been tenuous as to Torres's intent, but admitted it nonetheless, inferring from the nature of Torres's conduct after the street fight that he must have been engaged in retaliatory activity.

> [T]he court is, frankly, not fully apprized as to precisely what was at issue with regard to the shooting incident that occurred on September 21st in the 2600 block of North Holton with regard to shots being fired.

> However, the court simply cannot overlook the reality that when shots are fired, [and] a vehicle leaves the scene as opposed to awaiting law enforcement authorities or contacting law enforcement authorities, one is left with the inescapable conclusion that there was untoward conduct which could clearly be described and determined by a fact-finder that was retaliatory in nature.

Trial Transcript, at 91. Though this reasoning — that leaving a scene where shots have been fired somehow proves retaliatory intent — is suspect, we nevertheless affirm the court's decision to admit this evidence because, as explained below, we believe it to be sufficiently similar and recent in time to satisfy the second element of the Rule 404(b) test. In other words, while the fact that Torres left the scene of the shooting has questionable relevance, the evidence, when considered in its totality, adequately demonstrates that he acted with retaliatory intent in the past, making it admissible under Rule 404(b) and eliminating the reservations and problems we might have about the trial court's unusual reasoning. . . .

The most salient aspect of this incident is that Torres was found with concealed weapons in his vehicle, and strong circumstantial evidence demonstrated that he had fired this gun during a street fight a few hours before (the clip found at the fight scene fit the gun found hidden in his car shortly after the fight; witnesses said his car had been involved in a second shooting incident thirty minutes after the fight; he was carrying bullets for that gun in his pockets when stopped). Such evidence is probative of Torres's intent at the grocery store because it demonstrates that when he is crossed or under attack he retaliates with a weapon in a violent fashion. Street fights arouse strong emotions, and Torres acted on his emotion by firing a .22 pistol. Similarly, the evidence at trial established that Blas's cooperation with law enforcement officials had angered Torres, and that Glarza believed Torres was carrying a gun in his coat. Thus, the concealed weapons incident was relevant to prove Torres's intent when threatening Glarza — the intent to violently retaliate against perceived enemies. Further, the street fight took place only twenty months before the threats here, making it recent enough to be relevant. . . . Accordingly, it was not error to admit this evidence.

* * *

3. Probative Value Versus Prejudice

Torres's third challenge to the admission of the other acts evidence is that its probative value was outweighed by its danger of unfair prejudice. This aspect of the Rule 404(b) analysis overlaps with Rule 403, which states that "evidence may be excluded if its probative value is substantially outweighed by the danger of unfair prejudice." Fed. R. Evid. 403. . . . In other words, the more probative the evidence, the more the court will tolerate some risk of prejudice, while less probative evidence will be received only if the risk of prejudice is more remote. *See Beechum*, 582 F.2d at 914 ("It is the incremental probity of the evidence that is to be balanced against its potential for undue prejudice.").

The district judge found no danger of unfair prejudice because the evidence would be limited to the issue of intent, without exposing unnecessary details simply to make the defendant look bad. This determination is treated with great deference because of the trial judge's first-hand exposure to the witnesses and evidence as a whole, and because of his familiarity with the case and ability to gauge the likely impact of the evidence in the context of the entire proceeding. . . .

As to the car wash shooting, we agree with the district court's decision that its probative value outweighed the risk of prejudice. The incident was similar to the crime charged and no evidence beyond the essential facts of the incident was adduced. Additionally, any reflection on Torres's character was merely incidental to the proof of his intent to intimidate and retaliate against Blas, and the likelihood of misusing the evidence was reduced by the court's limiting instruction to the jury. . . . Finally, even though the government might have been able to prove Torres's intent with Glarza's and Bodie's testimony alone, the evidence had significant probative value to the government, and admitting it was not an abuse of discretion.

A similar analysis applies to the evidence of the concealed weapons incident. Like the car wash shooting, this incident was probative of the defendant's intent due to its relatively recent occurrence and similarity to the charged conduct. It was also subject to the court's limiting instruction and, though there may have been some danger of prejudice to Torres, we agree with the trial court that this danger did not substantially outweigh the event's probative value.

*   *   *

IV. CONCLUSION

We affirm Torres's conviction and hold that the evidence of the car wash shooting and the concealed weapons incident was properly admitted under Rule 404(b). . . .

Affirmed.

NOTES AND QUESTIONS

1. When offered to prove intent, the prior acts must generally involve similar conduct. *See United States v. Brand*, 467 F.3d 179, 197 (2d Cir. 2006) (possession of child pornography was relevant to proving whether defendant traveled across state lines to engage in sexual activity with a minor or for a more benign reason); *United States v. Sebolt*, 460 F.3d 910, 917 (7th Cir. 2006) ("Prior instances of sexual misconduct with a child victim may establish a defendant's sexual interest in children and thereby serve as evidence of the defendant's motive to commit a charged offense involving sexual exploitation of children."); *United States v. Hinton*, 31 F.3d 817, 822 (9th Cir. 1994) (the victim, the assailant, the manner of the assault and the nature of the harm involved in the present and prior acts were sufficiently similar and thus admissible to prove intent to kill); *United States v. Jackson*, 84 F.3d 1154 (9th Cir. 1996) (evidence of similar drug transactions admissible to prove intent to participate in conspiracy). It is unclear from the *Torres* facts what was at issue with regard to the shooting incident that occurred on September 21st (the second prior act). The shooting could have been a retaliatory shooting connected to gang activity. At the same time, it could just as easily have been a shooting in self-defense or attempted robbery. How is an unexplained prior shooting relevant to the charged act of threatening a witness? The court states that the fact that Torres left the scene "when considered in its totality, adequately demonstrates that he acted with retaliatory intent in the past, making it admissible under Rule 404(b)." *Torres*, 977 F.2d at 327. Do you agree?

2. Is it certain whether Torres even possessed a weapon when he threatened Glarza? If not, how are the prior bad acts, each of which involved possession and use of a firearm, sufficiently similar to be relevant on the issue of intent?

3. *The Materiality of Intent.* Intent must be a genuine issue in the case before prior act evidence may be proved. Is intent always a "material issue" within the meaning of Rule 404(b) when a defendant is charged with a specific intent crime? A majority of circuits hold that when a defendant is charged with a specific intent crime, "intent is always at issue regardless of whether [a] defendant has made it an issue." *United States v. Johnson*, 27 F.3d 1186, 1191 (6th Cir. 1994). In these circuits, if the government must prove intent as an element of the crime, a defendant through a general denial of guilt cannot preclude the government from introducing prior bad acts to establish intent. *See, e.g., United States v. Edouard*, 485 F.3d 1324 (11th Cir. 2007) ("A defendant who enters a not guilty plea makes a material issue which imposes a substantial burden on the government to prove intent, which it may prove by qualifying Rule 404(b) evidence absent affirmative steps by the defendant to remove intent as an issue."); *United States v. Johnson*, 439 F.3d 947, 952 (8th Cir. 2006) (defendant's complete denial of participation in drug conspiracy does not remove the issue of intent as a matter of dispute in the case); *United States v. Misher*, 99 F.3d 664, 670 (5th Cir. 1996) ("A defendant places his intent in issue when he has pled not guilty in a drug conspiracy case and, therefore, evidence of past drug transactions can be used to establish criminal intent."); *accord Johnson*, 27 F.3d at 1192; *United States v. Mazzanti*, 888 F.2d 1165, 1171 (7th Cir. 1989); *United States v. Harrison*, 942 F.2d 751, 760 (10th Cir. 1991); *United States v. Diaz-Lizaraza*, 981 F.2d 1216, 1224 (11th Cir. 1993).

What if the defendant makes an unequivocal offer to concede both the intent and knowledge elements of a charged criminal offense? Is either intent or knowledge still a "material issue" in the case? The issue has generated divergent views. In *United States v. Crowder*, 87 F.3d 1405 (D.C. Cir. 1996) (*en banc*), the District of Colombia Court of Appeals, sitting en banc, answered the question in the negative, holding that when the defendant offers to concede knowledge and intent, evidence of prior drug sales is inadmissible to prove either knowledge or intent. *Id.* at 1410. The Supreme Court, however, vacated the D.C. Circuit Court's opinion in *Crowder* (*Crowder I*) and remanded the case for further consideration in light of the Court's decision in *Old Chief v. United States*, 519 U.S. 172 (1997). *See United States v. Crowder*, 519 U.S. 1087 (1997). On remand, the D.C. Circuit reversed itself, holding that "despite a defendant's unequivocal offer to stipulate to an element of an offense, Rule 404(b) does not preclude the government from introducing evidence of other bad acts." *United States v. Crowder*, 141 F.3d 1202, 1203 (D.C. Cir. 1998) (*Crowder II*). The D.C. Circuit reasoned as follows:

Our original en banc decision rested on the following theory: "a defendant's offer to concede knowledge and intent combined with an explicit jury instruction that the Government no longer needs to prove either element" results in the other crimes evidence having, as "its only purpose," proof of the defendant's propensity, which Rule 404(b) forbids. The idea was that the proposed stipulation (and instruction) "completely removed" knowledge and intent from the trial; that evidence of the defendant's other crimes therefore could no longer be considered relevant to those elements; and that if the evidence had no other nonpropensity purpose, its only function would be to prove what Rule 404(b) barred.

Tested against the Supreme Court's *Old Chief* decision, the theory of *Crowder I* fails. *Old Chief's* holding ultimately rested on Federal Rule of Evidence 403, which authorizes trial courts to exclude evidence if its "probative value is substantially outweighed by the danger of unfair prejudice. . . ." But before getting to Rule 403, the Court had to dispose of a preliminary question, a question that bears directly on the *Crowder I* theory. The defendant in *Old Chief* claimed, as *Crowder I* held, that a defense stipulation to an element of a crime completely removes the element from trial, thereby rendering other evidence of the element irrelevant and thus inadmissible. The Supreme Court rejected this argument. A defendant's offer to stipulate or concede an element of an offense, the Court concluded, does not deprive the government's evidence of relevance. *See Old Chief*, 519 U.S. at [178]. There does not have to be an "actual issue" about the facts sought to be proven. As the Court put it, "evidentiary relevance under Rule 401 [is not] affected by the availability of alternative proofs of the element," such as a defendant's concession or offer to stipulate. *Id.* In support, the Court quoted the statement in the advisory committee notes to Rule 401 that the "fact to which the evidence is directed need not be in dispute." *Id.* The Court then summed up: "If, the, relevant evidence is inadmissible in the presence of other evidence related to it, its exclusion must rest not on the ground that the other evidence has rendered it 'irrelevant,' but on its character as unfairly prejudicial, cumulative or the like, its relevance notwithstanding." *Id.* at [179].

Other courts have adopted the position taken in *Crowder II*. *See United States v. Hill*, 249 F.3d 707, 712 (8th Cir. 2001) ("[A] criminal defendant may not stipulate or admit his way out of the full evidentiary force of the case as the Government chooses to present it."); *United States v. Johnson*, 439 F.3d 947 (8th Cir. 2006) (same).

4. Prior bad act evidence may be admissible to challenge a defense claim of entrapment. In *United States v. Horn*, 277 F.3d 48, 57 (1st Cir. 2002), the court posited that "where a defendant employs entrapment as a defense to criminal liability, prior bad acts relevant to a defendant's predisposition to commit a crime are highly probative and can overcome the Rule 404(b) bar." *Accord United States v. Brand*, 467 F.3d 179, 189 (2d Cir. 2006); *United States v. Johnson*, 439 F.3d 884 (8th Cir. 2006); *United States v. Hardwell*, 80 F.3d 1471 (10th Cir. 1996); *United States v. Williams*, 31 F.3d 522, 527 (7th Cir. 1995); *United States v. Simtob*, 901 F.2d 799, 807 (9th Cir. 1990).

PROBLEM

Problem 6-1. *Evidence of Sexual Assault to Show Motive to Kidnap.* The defendant, Nopporn Sriyuth, is a naturalized citizen of the United States, having immigrated to this country from Thailand. The defendant went to Detroit and met Chindavone "Von" Phongsavath, a Laotian national, and her family. Von's mother and sister approached Sriyuth about the possibility of a pre-arranged wedding between Von and himself. Von objected to the marriage as she was currently seeing someone else. Her family encouraged the defendant to take Von away for awhile so that she would forget about her boyfriend. Consequently, the defendant bought a 9-mm Taurus handgun and kidnapped Von. He took her to Scranton, Pennsylvania where they stayed with his friends. While there, the defendant raped Von. The day after the rape, Von was able to call the police from a neighbor's home. The defendant was arrested and charged with kidnapping and the use of a firearm in relation to the kidnapping. Prior to trial, the defendant filed a motion in limine to preclude the government from introducing any evidence about the sexual assault as it was not relevant to proving the kidnapping. And even if relevant, the defendant argued, the evidence should be excluded under Fed. R. Evid. 403 as the danger of unfair prejudice substantially outweighed its probative value. The government argued that the sexual assault evidence was admissible under Fed. R. Evid. 404(b) to prove the defendant's motive or purpose to kidnap Von. Furthermore, the evidence of the sexual assault tended to establish that Von did not consent to the kidnapping and was thus admissible to show the defendant's intent to kidnap. How should the court rule? Is the evidence admissible under Rule 404(b)? If so, under the theories advanced by the government? If the evidence is admissible, should it nevertheless be excluded under Rule 403? *See United States v. Sriyuth*, 98 F.3d 739 (3d Cir. 1996).

[d]   Plan or Scheme

UNITED STATES v. DECICCO
370 F.3d 206 (1st Cir. 2004)

The government appeals from a pair of orders excluding evidence in the prosecution of Gary P. DeCicco ("DeCicco"). The government indicted DeCicco for four counts of violating 18 U.S.C. § 1341 and two counts of violating 18 U.S.C. §§ 844(h)(1) and (2). The district court excluded evidence related to prior bad acts by DeCicco. After careful review, we reverse.

I. FACTUAL BACKGROUND

DeCicco purchased a two story brick warehouse located at 17 Rear Heard Street, in Chelsea, Massachusetts, on August 8, 1989 ("the Heard Street warehouse"). Before securing the mortgage on the Heard Street warehouse, DeCicco applied to the City of Chelsea for an occupancy permit to use the building as a warehouse for his moving companies. The city denied the application, noting that the Heard Street warehouse was surrounded by residential properties and had a narrow driveway to provide access to and from the street. DeCicco used the building as a warehouse, notwithstanding the City of Chelsea's opposition. In the ensuing dispute, the City of Chelsea prevented DeCicco from using the property as a warehouse.

After the permit was denied, DeCicco paid $65,000 for the Heard Street warehouse. The purchase was financed with a $104,000 loan from Somerset Bank, which was secured by a mortgage on the property. As proof of insurance on the property, DeCicco submitted an insurance binder from the John M. Biggio Insurance Agency, signed by Andrew Biggio, and covering the property for the first month that DeCicco owned it.

DeCicco was in arrears on his mortgage to Somerset Bank by September 1991. Somerset Bank obtained a foreclosure order on the Heard Street warehouse. DeCicco had other outstanding obligations to Somerset Bank: a $400,000 loan used to build a new warehouse in Revere, Massachusetts ("the Revere warehouse") and a short term $80,000 commercial loan. Liens were imposed on both the Heard Street warehouse and the Revere warehouse, as well as on other properties owned by DeCicco's businesses.

In October 1991, two years after purchase, DeCicco obtained insurance on the Heard Street warehouse. Two applications were completed by the broker: a standard form application and an "arson" application. An insurance binder was issued by Lincoln Insurance Company and an expert was retained to examine the property. The inspector never managed to speak with DeCicco, but he visited the property and determined that, contrary to DeCicco's representations that the property was occupied, the Heard Street warehouse was in fact empty. On March 3, 1992, Lincoln Insurance Company cancelled the policy on the Heard Street warehouse due to DeCicco's alleged misrepresentations. A notice advised DeCicco that the policy would be cancelled effective at 12:01 a.m. on March 13, 1992.

In the meantime, Somerset Bank informed DeCicco that he was behind on his payments and that foreclosure proceedings would follow unless the bank received the amount owed by March 2, 1992.

On March 11, 1992, a fire broke out at the Heard Street warehouse. Investigators of the Chelsea Fire Department determined that the fire was started intentionally; the arsonist used a liquid accelerator on the support pillars, in order to bring down the building as quickly as possible. Due to the Fire Department's quick response, little damage was done to the warehouse. DeCicco did not file a claim related to this fire and a period of three years and two months transpired during which the Heard Street warehouse went uninsured.

In the meantime, DeCicco hired Richard Stewart ("Stewart"), an accountant. Stewart was allegedly retained because DeCicco had significant tax liabilities and wanted to institute sound bookkeeping practices for his businesses. Regardless, it is undisputed that DeCicco owed more than one million dollars to the Internal Revenue Service ("IRS") and other monies to the Massachusetts Department of Revenue ("DOR"). DeCicco also owed over $10,000 in real estate taxes to the City of Chelsea and an undisclosed amount to the City of Revere.

On May 7, 1995, Scottsdale Insurance Company ("Scottsdale") issued an insurance policy for the Heard Street warehouse, listing DeCicco as the beneficiary. DeCicco told the Scottsdale agent that the building was a new purchase, even though DeCicco had owned it for nearly six years. He also told the Scottsdale agent that there was no mortgage on the property. The policy was for a one year term and provided coverage of up to $125,000.

On July 9, 1995, the Heard Street warehouse was intentionally set on fire by means of four separate fires started on the second floor. The Fire Department again responded quickly and the property was spared. DeCicco hired an insurance adjustor to assist him in filing an insurance claim, but that claim was never filed.

During the early morning hours of July 21, 1995, a third fire broke out in the Heard Street warehouse. Investigators determined that the fire was set with an accelerant poured at the base of the support columns. The third time proved to be the last. This time, a much larger fire injured several firefighters as well as some surrounding residential property. Per the City of Chelsea's order, the Heard Street warehouse was demolished because the damage was too extensive.

DeCicco obtained payments for the third fire from Scottsdale, for a total aggregate amount of $116,964.

The government alleges that, in violation of 18 U.S.C. § 1341, DeCicco transmitted false and fraudulent insurance claims for building loss insurance proceeds to Scottsdale. Four distinct acts of mail fraud are alleged. In addition, DeCicco was charged with two counts of knowingly using fire to commit a felony, in violation of 18 U.S.C. §§ 844(h)(1) and 2.

DeCicco filed a motion in limine seeking the exclusion of the following evidence at trial: any testimony of Richard Stewart, the accountant; and any evidence related to any fires at the Heard Street warehouse or any other property which pre dated July 9, 1995. The district court orally granted the motion on the first day of trial. The government appeals from this ruling.

*   *   *

III. ANALYSIS

A. Exclusion of Evidence Related to 1992 Fire

DeCicco sought to exclude evidence of the March 1992 fire from the government's case in chief. DeCicco argued, *inter alia*, that the fire was evidence of other crimes which should be excluded under Fed. R. Evid. 404(b), and that there was insufficient evidence that he committed the prior bad act.

Federal Rule of Evidence 404(b) provides that:

> Evidence of other crimes, wrongs or acts is not admissible to prove the character of a person in order to show action in conformity therewith. It may, however, be admissible for other purposes, such as proof of motive, opportunity, intent, preparation, plan, knowledge, identity or absence of mistake.

Therefore, mere propensity evidence is never admissible solely to show a character inclined towards unlawful behavior. The same evidence may be admissible, however, even if it may be construed as propensity evidence, if it is used to show any of the other elements set out in the rule. *See United States v. Taylor*, 284 F.3d 95, 101 (1st Cir.2002) (stating that Rule 404(a) codified the general prohibition against bad acts evidence, but Rule 404(b) allows for the admission of evidence of prior bad acts to prove elements other than propensity). We review the admissibility of this type of evidence under a two pronged test: first, a court must determine whether the evidence in question has any special relevance exclusive of defendant's character or propensity; and second, notwithstanding its special relevance, whether the evidence meets the standard set forth in Fed. R. Evid. 403.

The government argues that evidence of the March 1992 fire is probative of a common plan or scheme to burn the Heard Street warehouse for the insurance proceeds, or, in the alternative, that it is probative of identity. Before delving into these arguments, we consider the threshold question whether the government has proffered enough evidence to show, by a preponderance of the evidence, that DeCicco committed the March 1992 fire.

1. Sufficiency of the Evidence Argument

Under *Huddleston v. United States*, 485 U.S. 681, 689 (1988), "similar act evidence is relevant only if the jury can reasonably conclude that the act occurred and that the defendant was the actor." (citing *United States v. Beechum*, 582 F.2d 898, 912 13 (5th Cir.1978) (en banc)). In the instant case, DeCicco does not question the occurrence of the March 1992 fire but vigorously defends his innocence as to the arson.

The government proffered the following circumstantial evidence that DeCicco committed the 1992 arson:

> that 29 hours before he [knew] that the insurance on the building [was] going to be cancelled and at a time when he [was] under financial pressure both from the City of Chelsea, which [had] filed a tax title proceeding based on nonpayment of city taxes, and he's being chased by his bank for payment on the loan, there is a fire.

DeCicco's counsel stated that "[t]here was no evidence [as to the 1992 fire]. There's a lot of circumstantial stuff, but there's no evidence that ties the defendant to this fire, either that he did it, [or] that he hired anybody to do it. There's no physical evidence." The government attempted to develop its "common scheme or plan" theory by stating that

> the fact that three years goes by is actually significant because . . . the standard insurance form requires you to tell an insurance company if you've had an insurance cancelled within the previous three years. Now a false answer on that will when it's discovered, which it almost surely will be is a basis for voiding the policy.
>
> So after the fire in 1992 failed to work, three years goes by, and then the defendant insures the building again. Maybe six or seven weeks after he gets the insurance there's a second fire intentionally set in the building. That's one of the charged fires. That doesn't work.
>
> Twelve days later there's a huge fire that finally takes the building down. So if you look at the time table. . . .

At this point in the discussion, the district court decided to exclude the evidence from the government's case in chief.

We find that circumstantial evidence was presented from which a jury could find by a preponderance of evidence that the 1992 arson occurred and that DeCicco was responsible. *See Huddleston*, 485 U.S. at 690 (stating that there must be enough evidence for a jury to reasonably conclude by a preponderance of the evidence that the prior bad act was committed). The jury can weigh the totality of the evidence to determine whether a preponderance of the evidence shows that DeCicco committed the first arson. *See Huddleston*, 485 U.S. at 690 (citing 21 C. Wright & K. Graham, *Federal Practice and Procedure* § 5054, p. 269 (1977)). The evidence adduced as to the timing of the 1992 fire and the fact that DeCicco was the sole beneficiary on the policy, as well as other evidence, such as the similar accelerant and method used, are probative as to the

1992 fire. Therefore, we agree with the government that there is enough evidence for a jury to find that DeCicco started the 1992 fire.

2. Special Relevance as to Common Scheme or Plan

The district court abused its discretion when it refused to consider the government's argument as to the common scheme or plan in this case. As to the special relevance under Rule 404(b), the government argued to the district court, *inter alia*, that there was a common scheme or plan to burn the Heard Street warehouse for the insurance proceeds. "We have focused on two factors to determine the probative value of prior bad act evidence: 'the remoteness in time of the other act and the degree of resemblance to the crime charged.'" *United States v. Varoudakis*, 233 F.3d 113, 119 (1st Cir. 2000) (quoting *Frankhauser*, 80 F.3d at 648).

In this case, the first fire occurred three years prior to the two fires charged in the Indictment. In *United States v. González Sánchez*, 825 F.2d 572, 581–83 (1st Cir.1987), we affirmed the admissibility of other fires for the purpose of showing a common scheme to defraud using arson of property. In *González Sánchez*, the fires occurred two months and six months before the final fire that destroyed the property. *Id.* at 577. Nevertheless, the distinction here (that three years elapsed) can be explained when viewed in the context of the cancellation of the Lincoln Insurance policy. DeCicco had to wait three years to obtain insurance because any other policy provider would have reviewed prior cancellations, i.e., Scottsdale would have found out about the Lincoln Insurance policy cancellation and Scottsdale's insurance policy never would have issued. In addition, three years is not so remote a time as to reduce the probative value of this evidence. *See Frankhauser*, 80 F.3d at 649 (time span of seven years is not too remote); *see also United States v. Hadfield*, 918 F.2d 987, 994 (1st Cir.1990) (five years between prior bad act and charged act is acceptable).

The degree of resemblance of the crimes also favors inclusion of the evidence. Both the 1992 fire and the final fire were set in the same manner: an accelerant was poured on the base of the support pillars on the first floor of the Heard Street warehouse. They are the same type of crime, and, more importantly, the object of all fires was the same property. These factors tend to show that the previous offense leads in progression to the two charged fires, or, put more simply, that DeCicco had one common scheme to burn the Heard Street warehouse, which had previously proven financially unsuccessful. *Cf. United States v. Lynn*, 856 F.2d 430, 435 (1st Cir.1988) (reversing the admission of prior bad act evidence under the common scheme or plan theory, because the prior bad act did not lead in progression to the second act). Therefore, the district court erred in not considering whether the 1992 fire was relevant to a common scheme or plan to burn the Heard Street warehouse for the insurance proceeds. The evidence is probative of a common scheme or plan and should be introduced to that effect.

3. Rule 403 Analysis

The second bar to the admission of prior bad acts evidence is Rule 403. *See Varoudakis*, 233 F.3d at 121 (stating that a district court must exclude 404(b) evidence where its probative value is outweighed by the danger of unfair prejudice, confusion of issues, misleading the jury or other considerations). The district court did not make a finding in this respect. We find that, while this evidence is prejudicial, it does not violate Rule 403. "[T]here is always some danger that the jury will use [Rule 404(b) other act] evidence not on the narrow point for which it is offered but rather to infer that a defendant has a propensity towards criminal behavior." *United States v. Trenkler*, 61 F.3d 45, 56 (1st Cir.1995). The risk here is not too great as to surpass the probative value of evidence, which, if found credible by a properly instructed jury, would show that the defendant had a common plan to burn the Heard Street Warehouse. *Cf. Gilbert*, 229 F.3d at 25 (affirming the exclusion of evidence under Rule 403, in a murder case, that defendant attempted to murder her husband because it was particularly inflammatory and highly susceptible of being misused by the jury). Therefore, we find that the district court abused its discretion and reverse the exclusion of the evidence regarding the 1992 fire.

B. Exclusion of Accountant's Testimony

*   *   *

DeCicco argued to the district court that the testimony of Stewart was not admissible to show motive or intent under Fed. R. Evid. 404(b), and was otherwise unduly prejudicial under Fed. R. Evid. 403. The government argues that this evidence was limited to Stewart's testimony regarding the calculation of individual taxes DeCicco owed as of the time of the July 1995 fires (including penalties and interest), the tax years for which those determinations were made, and other information regarding DeCicco's tax liabilities at the time of the July 1995 Heard Street warehouse fires, and that this testimony was relevant to the issue of motive to commit arson and the other crimes charged in the Indictment.

> [Editor's note: The court found that the district court further abused its discretion when it excluded evidence of defendant's tax liabilities. The court held that such evidence was admissible to prove motive to commit arson and other crimes charged in indictment. Therefore, the district judge's exclusion of Stewart's testimony was reversed.]

IV. CONCLUSION

For the reasons stated above, we reverse and remand for further proceedings consistent with this opinion.

NOTES AND QUESTIONS

1. *Sufficiency of the Evidence.* In *DeCicco*, the court stated that there was sufficient circumstantial evidence for a jury to find by a preponderance of the evidence that the 1992 arson occurred and DeCicco was responsible. *See Huddleston v. United States*, 485 U.S. 681, 689 (1998) ("similar act evidence is relevant only if the jury can reasonably conclude that the act occurred and the defendant was the actor"). What evidence was introduced to prove the defendant started the 1992 fire. Do you agree with the court that the evidence satisfied the standard for admission of Rule 404(b) evidence under *Huddleston*?

2. *Special Relevance as to Common Scheme or Plan.* The *DeCicco* court focused on two factors in determining the probative value of prior bad act evidence (the 1992 arson): " 'the remoteness in time of the other act and the degree of resemblance to the crime charged.' " *DeCicco*, 370 F.3d at 212 (internal citations omitted). The first fire occurred three years prior to the two fires charged in the indictment. Doesn't the remoteness in time between the prior bad act and the charged offenses weigh against a finding that the defendant was involved in a common scheme or plan to burn the warehouse for the purpose of collecting the insurance proceeds? The court also found that the degree of similarity between the crimes favored inclusion of the prior bad act evidence. Specifically, the court found that the fires were set in the same manner and involved the same property. *Id.* The court further posited that "[t]hese factors tend to show that the previous offense leads in progression to the two charged offenses. . . ." *Id.* at 212–13. In order for prior bad act evidence to be admissible to prove common plan or scheme must the evidence lead in progression to the charged offense? In other words, are there three requirements for admission of prior bad acts to prove common plan or scheme? Must the prior bad acts be (1) proximate in time, (2) closely resemble, and (3) lead in progression to the charged crime? Must all three requirements be satisfied or can the absence of evidence with respect to one factor be offset by a strong showing in another?

In analyzing what constitutes a "plan" for purposes of Rule 404(b), one court posited "[t]hat a sequence of acts resembles a design when examined in retrospect is not enough; the prior conduct must be intertwined with what follows, such that the prior conduct and the charged act are 'mutually dependent.' " *State v. Melcher*, 678 A.2d 146 (N.H. 1996). Do you agree with the court's "mutual dependency" requirement for admission of evidence under the "plan" exception to Rule 404(b)? In other words, for prior bad act evidence to be admissible for the purpose of establishing a common plan or scheme, must the success of the charged offense be dependent upon the uncharged crimes? For a more liberal application of the "plan" exception, see *United States v. Gipson*, 446 F.3d 828 (8th Cir. 2006) (evidence of defendant's prior arrests for selling drugs admissible to prove common scheme or plan to sell cocaine base from same apartment complex); *United States v. Conway*, 73 F.3d 975 (10th Cir. 1995) (evidence of prior drug arrests for selling crack cocaine from motel on same street as motel from which defendant charged in instant case with selling cocaine, admissible to show common plan or scheme); and *United States v. Murphy*, 768 F.2d 1518, 1535 (7th Cir. 1985) (in bribery prosecution, evidence that judge "had been receiving envelops full of cash month after month for eight years was admissible to establish a common plan or scheme").

3. *Rule 403 Analysis.* Rule 403 imposes an additional hurdle to the admission of prior bad acts evidence. The district court must exclude Rule 404(b) evidence offered to prove common scheme or plan where its probative value is outweighed by the danger of unfair prejudice, confusion of issues, misleading the jury, or by considerations of undue delay or waste of time. Doesn't the fact that the arson involved the same property create an unreasonable danger that the jury will consider the prior arson evidence for propensity purposes? In other words, the jury could conclude that if the defendant committed the 1992 arson, he must have committed the two fires charged in the indictment. Doesn't Rule 404(b) prohibit prior bad act evidence from being used for proving propensity?

4. *Prior Bad Acts Evidence to Prove "Context."* Some courts admit evidence of prior bad acts to provide the context in which the crime occurred. *See United States v. Smith*, 441 F.3d 254 (4th Cir. 2006) (testimony that defendant's son used to deliver drugs for his father was admissible prior bad acts evidence, in drug conspiracy prosecution; son's testimony provided part of the context of the crime and revealed basis for son's knowledge of father's drug operation); *United States v. Fleck*, 413 F.3d 883 (8th Cir. 2005) ("One of the exceptions to the general rule that evidence of other crimes committed by a defendant is inadmissible is when the proof provides the context in which the crime occurred — 'the res gestae.' "); *United States v. Moore*, 735 F.2d 289, 292 (8th Cir. 1984) ("[A jury] cannot be expected to make its decision in a void-without knowledge of the time, place, and circumstances of the acts which form the basis of the charge.").

PROBLEM

Problem 6-2. *Prior Familial Sexual Abuse to Show Common Plan or Scheme.* The defendant was charged with several counts of taking indecent liberties with a child and rape as a result of his molestation of his two step-granddaughters. At the trial, the government sought to elicit testimony from three other female family members whom the defendant allegedly molested when they were teenagers. The first witness was the mother of the two victims and the daughter of the defendant's wife. She alleged that the defendant began molesting her at the age of sixteen and continued to have sexual relations with her after she married and gave birth to the victims. The second witness was also the daughter of the defendant's wife. She claimed that defendant molested her and raped her when she was twelve years old. The third witness married the defendant's son when she was fourteen as she was pregnant with his child. After she gave birth, the defendant began stopping by daily to have sexual intercourse with her. With all witnesses and the victims, the abuse began at puberty with the defendant showering them with gifts during the time he was molesting them and threatening them if they told anyone. None of the witnesses ever brought charges against the defendant. All of them agreed to testify against the defendant at trial. The government argued that their testimony was admissible under Fed. R. Evid. 404(b) in order to show a common plan or scheme. The defendant objected to the introduction of their testimony, claiming that their allegations occurred anywhere from seven to twenty-seven years ago and that they were too remote to establish a common plan. Furthermore, the victims in this case were not even alive when some of the alleged prior abuse happened and thus defendant could not have devised a plan to abuse them. Should the district court admit the testimony regarding the prior incidents of sexual abuse under Rule 404(b) as evidence of a common plan or scheme? *See State v. Frazier*, 476 S.E.2d 297 (N.C. 1996).

[e]   Knowledge

UNITED STATES v. VIZCARRA-MARTINEZ
66 F.3d 1006 (9th Cir. 1995)

REINHARDT, CIRCUIT JUDGE.

This appeal presents various factual and legal questions regarding the sentence and conviction of the defendant, Fernando Vizcarra-Martinez. Although we decline the defendant's invitation to reverse his conviction based upon the insufficiency of the evidence and find no merit in his claim that the evidence seized during the search of his car was improperly admitted, we conclude that the district court committed reversible error by admitting evidence of his drug use to prove that he conspired to possess and possessed hydriodic acid with knowledge that it would be used to manufacture methamphetamine. Because we reverse on this ground, we do not consider Vizcarra-Martinez's remaining contentions regarding the district court's evidentiary rulings and its sentencing decision.

Vizcarra-Martinez was indicted with six other defendants. He was charged in Count I with conspiracy to wrongfully possess a listed chemical knowing and having reasonable cause to believe that it would be used to manufacture methamphetamine; he was also charged in Count II with wrongful possession of a listed chemical knowing and having reasonable cause to believe that it would be used to manufacture methamphetamine. . . . Vizcarra-Martinez moved to exclude evidence of his possession of a personal-use amount of methamphetamine and certain post-arrest statements. The motions were denied. After a trial, the jury returned a verdict of guilty on both counts. Vizcarra-Martinez was sentenced to concurrent sentences of 70 months, to be followed by a three-year term of supervised release.

*   *   *

IV.

*   *   *

A. "Other Act" Evidence

The government initially maintains that we need not evaluate the district court's decision to admit the evidence in question under Rule 404. It asserts that the evidence was not "other act" evidence, and was exempted from the requirements of Rule 404, because it was "inextricably intertwined" with the underlying offense. We disagree.

There are generally two categories of cases in which we have concluded that "other act" evidence is inextricably intertwined with the crime with which the defendant is charged and therefore need not meet the requirements of Rule 404(b). First, we have sometimes allowed evidence to be admitted because it constitutes a part of the transaction that serves as the basis for the criminal charge. For example, in *United States v. Williams*, 989 F.2d 1061, 1070 (9th Cir. 1993), we concluded that contemporaneous sales of cocaine and crank by the defendant were inextricably intertwined with the crime with which the defendant was charged: the sale of cocaine. As we noted in *Williams*, "[t]he policies underlying rule 404(b) are inapplicable when offenses committed as part of a 'single criminal episode' become other acts simply because the defendant 'is indicted for less than all of his actions.' " *Williams*, 989 F.2d at 1070 (quoting *United States v. Soliman*, 813 F.2d 277, 278 (9th Cir. 1987)). Thus, when it is clear that particular acts of the defendant are part of, and thus inextricably intertwined with, a single criminal transaction, we have generally held that the admission of evidence regarding those acts does not violate Rule 404(b).

Second, we have allowed "other act" evidence to be admitted when it was necessary to do so in order to permit the prosecutor to offer a coherent and comprehensible story regarding the commission of the crime; it is obviously necessary in certain cases for the government to explain either the circumstances under which particular evidence was obtained or the events surrounding the commission of the crime. This exception to Rule 404(b) is most often invoked in cases in which the defendant is charged with being a felon in possession of a firearm. For example, in *United States v. Daly*, 974 F.2d 1215, 1216 (9th Cir. 1992), evidence regarding a shoot-out was considered to be "inextricably intertwined" with the charge that the defendant was a felon in possession of a firearm. We based our holding upon the fact that "evidence regarding the shoot-out was necessary to put [the defendant's] illegal conduct into context and to rebut his claims of self defense." *Id.* Recognizing the difficulty that the prosecution would encounter in proving that the defendant possessed a gun and in rebutting his proffered defense without relating the facts surrounding the commission of the crime, we observed that "the prosecution is not restricted to proving in a vacuum the offense of possession of a firearm by a felon. . . .'[The jury] cannot be expected to make its decision in a void — without knowledge of the time, place, and circumstances of the acts which form the basis of the charge.'" *Id.* (quoting *United States v. Moore*, 735 F.2d 289, 292 (8th Cir. 1984)).

It is clear that the evidence in this case does not fall within either of these exceptions. Coincidence in time is insufficient. The mere fact that a defendant is in possession of a small amount of a prohibited narcotic substance at the time he commits a crime is not enough to support the introduction of the evidence of drug usage. There must be a sufficient contextual or substantive connection between the proffered evidence and the alleged crime to justify exempting the evidence from the strictures of Rule 404(b). Here, there was no such relationship. First, the defendant's personal use of methamphetamine was, unquestionably, not a part of the transaction with which he was charged — possession of hydriodic acid with knowledge that it would be used to manufacture methamphetamine. The prosecution presented absolutely no evidence that the methamphetamine in question was obtained from a member of the conspiracy or that Vizcarra-Martinez had been involved in its manufacture or distribution. Second, it is clear that the prosecution would encounter little difficulty in presenting the evidence relevant to its case against the defendant — his possession of hydriodic acid and the circumstances surrounding the commission of that crime — without offering into evidence the personal-use amount of methamphetamine the police discovered in the defendant's pocket upon arrest. The methamphetamine found in the defendant's pocket had nothing to do with the incidents leading to the search, nor did it have any bearing upon the commission of the crime. Thus, we reject the government's contention that the contested evidence was so inextricably intertwined with the crime as to fall outside the scope of Rule 404(b).

B. Rule 404(b) Test

Because we conclude that the evidence in question represents "other act" evidence, we must apply our court's four-part test to determine whether it should have been excluded. Under Rule 404(b):

> Evidence of prior criminal conduct may be admitted if (1) the evidence tends to prove a material point; (2) the prior act is not too remote in time; (3) the evidence is sufficient to support a finding that the defendant committed the other act; and (4) (in cases where knowledge and intent are at issue) the act is similar to the offense charged.

United States v. Mayans, 17 F.3d 1174, 1181 (9th Cir. 1994). In applying this test, we have repeatedly emphasized that:

> "Extrinsic act evidence is not looked upon with favor." We have stated that "[o]ur reluctance to sanction the use of evidence of other crimes stems from the underlying premise of our criminal system, that the defendant must be tried for what he did, not for who he is." Thus, "guilt or innocence of the accused must be established by evidence relevant to the particular offense being tried, not by showing that the defendant has engaged in other acts of wrongdoing."

United States v. Bradley, 5 F.3d 1317, 1320 (9th Cir. 1993) (quoting *United States v. Hodges*, 770 F.2d 1475, 1480 (9th Cir. 1985)).

Vizcarra-Martinez does not argue that the prior act in this case is too remote in time or that the evidence is insufficient to support a finding that he had in his possession a personal-use amount of methamphetamine. Instead, he rests his case upon the contention that the evidence does not tend to prove a material point and that his alleged possession of an amount of methamphetamine suitable for personal use is not sufficiently similar to the offense charged to justify its admission. In essence, Vizcarra-Martinez argues that the fact that he used methamphetamine does not tend to prove that he was aware that the chemicals he was delivering would be used to manufacture methamphetamine or that he intended to participate in a conspiracy to do so.

The defendant's arguments regarding relevancy and similarity[5] are closely related, *see United States v. Hernandez-Miranda*, 601 F.2d 1104, 1109 (9th Cir. 1979) ("The greater is the dissimilarity of the two offenses, the more tenuous is the relevance."), and we address them both together. We conclude that the evidence regarding Vizcarra-Martinez's drug use was not sufficiently relevant to the charged offense and that it does not tend to prove the requisite knowledge.

In order to admit evidence concerning other "bad acts," the government must prove "a logical connection between the knowledge gained as a result of the commission of the [other] act and the knowledge at issue in the charged act." *Mayans*, 17 F.3d at 1181–82. Here, there exists no logical connection between the knowledge that the defendant might have gained by using methamphetamine and the knowledge that the government must prove that he possessed at the time of his arrest — that is, knowledge of the use to which the hydriodic acid in his possession would be put as well as knowledge of the scope and purpose of the conspiracy.[6]

We conclude that evidence of possession of a small quantity of drugs does not tend to prove that a defendant is aware of the use to which a particular chemical in his possession will be put — more specifically, that possession of a small amount of methamphetamine for personal use does not tend to prove that Vizcarra-Martinez was aware that hydriodic acid could be transformed into methamphetamine through a complicated manufacturing process. Viewing the case from "common human experience," *Hernandez-Miranda*, 601 F.2d at 1108, it is clear that most people who use drugs — indeed, most people who use legal chemical substances, such as cleaning fluid or paint or medicine — do so without having the faintest idea as to how the substance is produced or what ingredients are required to manufacture it. We simply cannot assume, as the government requests us to, that Vizcarra-Martinez's use of methamphetamine tended to

---

[5] We recognize that "in cases involving the use of prior crimes to show 'opportunity, knowledge, preparation or motive,' similarity may or may not be necessary depending upon the circumstances." *United States v. Miller*, 874 F.2d 1255, 1269 (9th Cir. 1989); *see also United States v. Bailleaux*, 685 F.2d 1105, 1110 n.1 (9th Cir. 1982). We do not consider whether our courts' four-part test regarding admission of evidence under Rule 404(b) requires that the "bad act" in question be precisely similar to the charged offense. Instead, we simply use the similarity inquiry as a means to assess the relevance and probative value of the evidence. *See United States v. Hernandez-Miranda*, 601 F.2d 1104, 1109 (noting the relationship between the similarity and relevance inquiries); *see also United States v. Bibo-Rodriguez*, 922 F.2d 1398, 1402 (9th Cir.) ("Similarity, to the extent that it bears on the relevance of the subsequent act, is necessary to indicate knowledge and intent."), *cert. denied*, 501 U.S. 1234 (1991).

[6] While this court has suggested there may be a logical connection between knowledge of the *use* of cocaine and knowledge of the *use* of heroin, we have not suggested such a connection between knowledge of the use of a drug and knowledge of that drug's manufacturing process. *See, e.g., United States v. Marshall*, 526 F.2d 1349, 1360–61 (9th Cir. 1975), *cert. denied*, 426 U.S. 923 (1976) (admitting evidence of possession of cocaine at the time of offense when defendant charged with the conspiracy to possess and distribute heroin); *United States v. Perez*, 491 F.2d 167, 171–72 (9th Cir.), *cert. denied*, 419 U.S. 858 (1974) (same).

prove that he knew that the chemical in his possession would be used in the methamphetamine manufacturing process. There may have been other reasons that the defendant was aware of the purpose of the hydriodic acid delivery, but his personal drug use was not one of them. Indeed, we would be especially reluctant to sanction the use of such evidence where, as here, the government has not presented any evidence indicating that the methamphetamine in question was produced by the members of the conspiracy.

Similarly, we hold that evidence that the defendant used methamphetamine, or possessed a small amount of the drug, does not tend to prove that he participated in a conspiracy to manufacture it. We believe that this is precisely the type of abuse that Rule 404 was designed to prevent: bad act evidence cannot be used to prove a defendant's propensity to commit a crime. . . . Indeed, in *United States v. Mehrmanesh*, 689 F.2d 822, 832 (9th Cir. 1982), we explicitly rejected the government's argument that "the jury could infer that since [the defendant] used drugs he was likely to participate in their importation." The rationale for our holding in *Mehrmanesh* is equally persuasive in this case.

Irrespective of any inference that may be drawn from evidence of an individual's *possession or use* of a drug in assessing their knowledge, intent, or motive to *possess or distribute* another drug, . . . there is an important distinction to be drawn between an individual's private use of a small quantity of a drug and his knowledge of the drug's manufacturing process or his participation in a large-scale conspiracy to possess precursor chemicals in order to manufacture that drug. In *United States v. Blackstone*, 56 F.3d 1143, 1145 (9th Cir. 1995), we distinguished between an individual's possession of marijuana for personal use and drug trafficking.[7] An assumed connection between drug trafficking and guns may be explained by the theory that "drug traffickers typically possess weapons to guard their drugs and money." *Id.* "[B]ut nothing suggests that those who possess small quantities of marijuana for personal use feel equally compelled to carry weapons." *Id.* Likewise, nothing suggests an individual who possesses a small quantity of methamphetamine for personal use feels compelled to participate in a conspiracy to manufacture that drug.

As we noted in *United States v. Bibo-Rodriguez*, 922 F.2d 1398 (9th Cir.), *cert. denied*, 501 U.S. 1234 (1991), " '[t]he relevant factor is the type of activity undertaken, *not the identity of the drugs.*' " *Id.* at 1402 (emphasis added) (quoting *United States v. Moschiano*, 695 F.2d 236, 245 (7th Cir. 1982), *cert. denied*, 464 U.S. 831 (1983)); *see also United States v. McLister*, 608 F.2d 785, 789 (9th Cir. 1979) (concluding that a conviction for possessing marijuana should not be used to convict the defendant for distribution of cocaine because it has "little probative value . . . to prove *any* of the purposes listed in Rule 404(b)" (emphasis added)). . . . The government has, in effect, invited us to draw conclusions regarding the knowledge and criminal propensities of drug users without providing any legal or factual support for doing so. Rule 404(b), and common sense, prevent us from concluding that this evidence was properly admitted.

A second, independent justification prevents us from upholding the admission of the disputed evidence. Even if we found the government's arguments to be persuasive — and we do not — we would nevertheless be compelled to conclude that the district court

---

[7] In *Blackstone* we found: "The evidence that [the defendant] had marijuana for his personal use was simply not relevant to his knowing possession of [a] gun. . . . The reasons the courts have been willing to assume that drug-trafficking is relevant to the question whether the defendant possessed a firearm do not support drawing a connection between the possession of marijuana for personal use and the possession of a firearm." *Id.*

erred in light of our decision in *United States v. Hill*, 953 F.2d 452 (9th Cir. 1991). In *Hill*, we held that evidence that a defendant had used cocaine could not be admitted as evidence to convict him of conspiracy and attempt to possess with intent to distribute cocaine. Despite the fact that the defendant had used the same drug that he was convicted of possessing with intent to distribute, we held that the evidence was inadmissible because "the testimony at issue had no direct bearing on the elements of conspiracy in this case." *Hill*, 953 F.2d at 457.[8]

We are at a loss as to how we could hold that the evidence in this case was properly admitted since the relationship between the charged offense and the "other act" evidence in this case is even more attenuated than was the relationship in *Hill*. Given that *Hill* prevents the prosecution from using evidence that the defendant used a drug to convict him for possessing precisely the same drug with intent to distribute, we cannot conclude that evidence of Vizcarra-Martinez's use of methamphetamine was properly admitted to prove that he possessed an entirely different substance — a precursor chemical which can only be transformed into that drug through a complex manufacturing process — with the requisite knowledge and intent necessary to support a conviction.[9]

*   *   *

CONCLUSION

For the reasons set forth above, we reverse and remand for further proceedings not inconsistent with this opinion.

---

[8] Similarly, we have held in numerous other cases that evidence of drug use or mere possession cannot be used to prove that the defendant possessed a different type of drug with intent to distribute. *See, e.g., United States v. Mehrmanesh*, 689 F.2d 822, 831 (9th Cir. 1982) (concluding that admission of evidence concerning the defendant's use of cocaine cannot be admitted as evidence when the underlying offense is the import and attempted distribution of heroin); *United States v. Bramble*, 641 F.2d 681, 683 (9th Cir. 1981) ("[t]he appellant's conviction of possession of marijuana is not probative of his predisposition to sell cocaine"); *Enriquez v. United States*, 314 F.2d 703, 713 (9th Cir. 1963) (holding that a conviction for possessing marijuana is not sufficiently similar to the offense of selling heroin that it could be considered to be admissible).

[9] We note that there is considerable confusion in our cases regarding the appropriate treatment of Rule 404(b) challenges, in large part due to the highly fact-specific nature of the inquiry involved. Indeed, at first glance some of our opinions appear to be in considerable tension. *Compare, e.g., United States v. Ramirez-Jiminez*, 967 F.2d 1321, 1326 (9th Cir. 1992) (holding that "[w]hen offered to prove knowledge, however, the prior act may not be similar to the charged act as long as the prior act was one which would tend to make the existence of the defendant's knowledge more probable than it would be without the evidence") *with Mayans*, 17 F.3d at 1181 ("In cases where knowledge and intent are at issue . . . the act [must be] similar to the offense charged."). However, our court has made every effort to explain and reconcile these cases. *See, e.g., United States v. Miller*, 874 F.2d 1255, 1269 (9th Cir. 1989) (explaining that whether similarity is required to prove knowledge or intent depends heavily upon the facts of the case and the probative use to which the evidence will be put); *see also United States v. Bailleaux*, 685 F.2d 1105, 1110 n.1 (9th Cir. 1982) (same). There is some possibility that our treatment of cases in which evidence of a defendant's previous possession of drugs has been admitted to prove possession of a narcotic with intent to distribute may be inconsistent in some respects. *Compare United States v. Bramble*, 641 F.2d 681, 683 (9th Cir. 1981) and *Enriquez v. United States*, 314 F.2d 703, 713 (9th Cir. 1963) *with United States v. Arambula-Ruiz*, 987 F.2d 599 (9th Cir. 1993); *United States v. Marshall*, 526 F.2d 1349 (9th Cir. 1975), *cert. denied*, 426 U.S. 923 (1976); *United States v. Perez*, 491 F.2d 167 (9th Cir.), *cert. denied sub nom. Lombera v. United States*, 419 U.S. 858 (1974). However, these inconsistencies, if they do exist, have no bearing upon the question before us in this case since, as we note above, the connection between the admitted evidence and the charged offense is far more attenuated than in any of the cases in which the admission of evidence of drug possession has been approved.

FERNANDEZ, CIRCUIT JUDGE, DISSENTING:

I agree that the evidence was sufficient to sustain the verdict and that there was probable cause to search Vizcarra-Martinez's car. However, I do not agree that it was prejudicial error to admit the small amount of methamphetamine that Vizcarra-Martinez had on his person when he was arrested.

Often we have even said that possession or use of a drug on a prior occasion is relevant to show the knowing possession of drugs on a second occasion. *See United States v. Santa-Cruz*, 48 F.3d 1118 (9th Cir. 1995); *United States v. Hegwood*, 977 F.2d 492 (9th Cir. 1992), *cert. denied*, 113 S. Ct. 2348 (1993); *United States v. Milner*, 962 F.2d 908 (9th Cir.), *cert. denied*, 113 S. Ct. 614 (1992); *United States v. Marshall*, 526 F.2d 1349 (9th Cir. 1975), *cert. denied*, 426 U.S. 923 (1976); *United States v. Perez*, 491 F.2d 167 (9th Cir.), *cert. denied*, 419 U.S. 858 (1974). It is true that those cases involved prior and current possession of drugs, whereas this case involves possession of a drug and of a precursor chemical. It is also true that a person could possess a drug and not know what chemicals went to make it up. Still, it is also true that a person *could* possess a little cocaine and still not know what heroin was. *But see Marshall*, 526 F.2d at 1360–61 (possession of cocaine could lead to inference of knowledge of heroin); *Perez*, 491 F.2d at 171–72 (same). And a person *could* have used drugs and still not know that a package had drugs in it. *But see Hegwood*, 977 F.2d at 497 (prior use of cocaine is relevant to knowledge, intent, absence of mistake). And a person *could* have used drugs and still not have conspired to distribute them. *But see Santa Cruz*, 48 F.3d at 1120 (prior possession of cocaine relevant to knowing participation in drug deal 12 weeks later); *Milner*, 962 F.2d at 912–13 (evidence of drug use relevant to show person conspiring to distribute drug). Coulds are interesting, but they do not make evidence irrelevant or inadmissible. So it is here.

Another concept militates against a determination that the admission of the methamphetamine was unfairly prejudicial. We have not been overly prissy about making sure that a defendant knew exactly what drugs he was transporting. We have considered one combination of chemicals to be as good as another. So if a person thought he had marijuana, but had cocaine or heroin, he could be prosecuted for cocaine or heroin possession. *See United States v. Ramirez-Ramirez*, 875 F.2d 772, 774 (9th Cir. 1989); *United States v. Lopez-Martinez*, 725 F.2d 471, 475 (9th Cir.), *cert. denied*, 469 U.S. 837 (1984). Cf. *United States v. Davis*, 501 F.2d 1344, 1345–46 (9th Cir. 1974) (psilocybin mushrooms versus LSD). It is easy to infer that Vizcarra-Martinez knew he was illicitly transporting a chemical substance of some kind. His clandestine activity, his driving to the pickup place with one of the major co-conspirators in tow, his lies, his threats, and his pay all tended to show that he was not just some poor unknowing wretch who was transporting water or gasoline for all he knew. We cannot get inside his head to determine whether he thought he was transporting methamphetamine itself or something to make methamphetamine with. But we can discount his claim that he had no idea at all about what it might be.

Vizcarra-Martinez's possession of methamphetamine was relevant to undercut his total ignorance argument and it did add a piece to the puzzle, even though what the picture was going to be was pretty clear already.

Therefore, I respectfully dissent.

NOTES AND QUESTIONS

1. In *Vizcarra-Martinez*, the court held that there existed no logical connection between the knowledge that the defendant might have gained by using methamphetamine and the knowledge of the use to which the hydriodic acid in his possession would be put, i.e., to manufacture methamphetamine. Viewing the case from "common human experience," the court opined that "it is clear that most people who use drugs — indeed, most people who use legal chemical substances, such as cleaning fluid or paint or medicine — do so without having the faintest idea as to how the substance is produced or what ingredients are required to manufacture it." *Id.* at 1014–15. Do you agree with the court's view that drug abusers are totally ignorant as to how illegal drugs are produced or what ingredients are required to manufacture them?

Despite Judge Reinhardt's remarks to the contrary, the process of manufacturing methamphetamine is not particularly complicated and requires little more than a basic understanding of chemistry.[30] In fact, one of the things that makes trafficking in methamphetamine attractive is that the drug can be easily manufactured in crude laboratories. The chemicals and equipment necessary to manufacture methamphetamine are readily available and inexpensive.[31] Additionally, hydriodic acid is an essential precursor chemical for manufacturing methamphetamine.[32] When viewed from the "common human experience" of a regular methamphetamine user, this is likely a well-known fact.

2. In *Vizcarra-Martinez*, the court offered as a second, independent justification for excluding the disputed evidence, its earlier decision in *United States v. Hill*, 953 F.2d 452 (9th Cir. 1991), which it stated compelled the conclusion that the district court erred in admitting the methamphetamine evidence. The facts in *Hill*, however, appear easily distinguishable from those in *Vizcarra-Martinez*. In *Hill*, the government sought to introduce evidence that the defendant had used small amounts of cocaine five years earlier to prove his participation in a drug conspiracy. There, the Ninth Circuit correctly held that drug use five years earlier was not relevant to prove any of the essential elements of conspiracy which are: (1) an agreement to accomplish an illegal objective, (2) coupled with one or more overt acts in furtherance of the illegal purpose, and (3) intent to commit the underlying substantive offense. The logical connection (between drug usage and defendant's intent to distribute drugs or enter into a conspiratorial agreement to do so some five years later) is tenuous at best. Obviously, the critical factor in *Hill* was that the prior incidents of drug usage were extremely remote in time, a fact which the *Vizcarra-Martinez* court omitted from its discussion.

3. The court in *Vizcarra-Martinez* correctly observed that there is "considerable confusion" among the courts regarding the appropriate treatment of incidents of prior drug possession or usage under Rule 404(b). There is an apparent split in authority

---

[30] *See* James R. Sevick, Precursor and Essential Chemicals in Illicit Drug Production: Approaches to Enforcement, at 5.31 (1993) (hereinafter " Precursor and Essential Chemicals") ("The knowledge of chemistry needed to set up and operate a lab is about equivalent to that learned in a high school.").

[31] *See* Drugs, Crime, and the Justice System, a National Report from the Bureau of Justice Statistics, at 41 (1992):

> The expertise required to run such a laboratory is fairly minimal, and the equipment and chemicals required to make the drugs are readily available and inexpensive, especially in relation to the profits realized. . . . The production of methamphetamine is fairly easy and cheap. Setting up a lab to produce a substantial amount of the drug may cost less than $2,000 and be enormously profitable — one day's production may be worth $70,000.

[32] *See* Precursor and Essential Chemicals, at 10.

regarding whether evidence of drug use or mere possession may be used to prove that a defendant knowingly possessed a different type of drug with intent to distribute. For cases excluding such evidence, *see United States v. Vo*, 413 F.3d 1010 (9th Cir. 2005); *United States v. Bramble*, 641 F.2d 681, 683 (9th Cir. 1981) (defendant's conviction of possession of marijuana is not probative of his intent to sell cocaine). For cases taking the opposite view and admitting the evidence, see *United States v. Perkins*, 548 F.510 (7th Cir. 2008); *United States v. Marshall*, 526 F.2d 1349, 1360–61 (9th Cir. 1976) (possession of cocaine could lead to inference of knowledge of heroin); *United States v. Perez*, 491 F.2d 167, 171–72 (9th Cir. 1974) (same). Which is the better view? Why?

4. In light of the court's holding in *Vizcarra-Martinez*, would evidence that the defendant possessed a small quantity of cocaine on a prior occasion be admissible in a criminal prosecution for possession of cocaine base knowing and having reasonable cause to believe it would be used to manufacture cocaine?

5. Evidence of narcotics trafficking may be properly admitted to show knowing possession of a weapon. *See United States v. Till*, 434 F.3d 880 (6th Cir. 2006) (containing a recent string-cite of cases). *See also United States v. Carrasco*, 257 F.3d 1045 (9th Cir. 2001). At the same time, at least one circuit has held that evidence that the defendant possessed a small quantity of marijuana for his personal use was not relevant to his knowing possession of a firearm. *See United States v. Blackstone*, 56 F.3d 1143, 1145 (9th Cir. 1995).

6. Where the crimes are "inextricably intertwined," some courts hold that Fed. R. Evid. 404(b) does not apply, reasoning that the uncharged crime is not an extrinsic offense or "other" crime, but instead is simply part of the proof of the charged offense. *See* MUELLER & KIRKPATRICK, EVIDENCE, § 4.20, at 261 (1995). In *Vizcarra-Martinez*, the Ninth Circuit recognized generally two categories of cases where the "other act" evidence is inextricably intertwined with the crime charged. First, "other" crime evidence is admissible if "it constitutes a part of the transaction that serves as the basis for the criminal charge." 66 F.3d at 1012. *See also United States v. Chin*, 83 F.3d 83 (4th Cir. 1996) (evidence of prior contract murder inextricably intertwined with criminal enterprise, including defendant's heroin business, and therefore not extrinsic evidence in prosecution for selling heroin and conducting a continuing criminal enterprise); *United States v. Nicholson*, 17 F.3d 1294 (10th Cir. 1994) (evidence of marijuana and heroin possession by defendant at the time of his arrest for cocaine possession inextricably intertwined and thus admissible in cocaine prosecution); *United States v. Freeman*, 434 F.3d 369 (5th Cir. 2005) ("uncharged offense arose out of the same series of transactions, because the funds were co-mingled and used to make lulling payments to investors from both schemes"); *United States v. Montgomery*, 384 F.3d 1050 (9th Cir. 2004). Second, "other act" evidence is admitted when "it [is] necessary in order to permit the prosecutor to offer a coherent and comprehensible story regarding the commission of the crime; . . . to explain either the circumstances under which particular evidence was obtained or the events surrounding the commission of the crime." *Vizcarra-Martinez*, 66 F.3d at 1011–12; *see also United States v. Daly*, 974 F.2d 1215, 1216 (9th Cir. 1992) (evidence of shoot-out considered to be inextricably intertwined with charge that defendant was a felon in possession of a firearm).

7. In *Vizcarra-Martinez*, what if the defendant was charged with conspiracy to manufacture methamphetamine and the small quantity possessed at the time of his arrest was represented to be a sample of the methamphetamine being manufactured? Would the methamphetamine possessed by the defendant be admissible under the "inextricably intertwined" theory? If so, under which of the two categories articulated by the Ninth Circuit?

8. In determining whether "other act" evidence should be admitted under Rule 404(b), the court in *Vizcarra-Martinez* applied a four-part test. Evidence of prior criminal conduct may be admitted if "(1) it tends to prove a material point; (2) the prior act is not too remote in time; (3) the evidence is sufficient to support a finding that the defendant committed the other act; and (4) (in cases where knowledge and intent are at issue) the act is similar to the offense charged." *Vizcarra-Martinez, supra,* 66 F.3d at 1013.

[f]   Identity

UNITED STATES v. TRENKLER
61 F.3d 45 (1st Cir. 1995)

STAHL, CIRCUIT JUDGE.

Following a lengthy criminal trial, a jury convicted defendant Alfred Trenkler of various charges stemming from a bomb explosion in Roslindale, Massachusetts ("the Roslindale bomb"). On appeal, Trenkler challenges the admission of evidence relating to his participation in a prior bombing that occurred five years earlier in Quincy, Massachusetts ("the Quincy bomb"). . . . After careful review, we affirm.

On October 28, 1991, a bomb exploded at the Roslindale home of Thomas L. Shay ("Shay Sr."), killing one Boston police officer and severely injuring another. The two officers, members of the Boston Police Department Bomb Squad, had been dispatched to Shay Sr.'s home to investigate a suspicious object located in Shay Sr.'s driveway. Shay Sr. had earlier reported that, while backing his 1986 Buick Century into the street the day before, he had heard a loud noise emanating from beneath the floorboard of his automobile. Shay Sr. added that, subsequently, he found the suspicious object resting near the crest of his driveway.

Following the explosion, a massive investigation ensued involving a variety of federal, state and local law-enforcement agencies. On June 24, 1993, this investigation culminated with the return of a three-count indictment charging Trenkler and Thomas A. Shay ("Shay Jr."), Shay Sr.'s son, with responsibility for the Roslindale bombing. Trenkler filed a successful severance motion, and the government tried the two defendants separately. Shay Jr. was tried first, and a jury convicted him on counts of conspiracy and malicious destruction of property by means of explosives.

At Trenkler's trial, the thrust of the government's case was that Trenkler had built the Roslindale bomb for Shay Jr. to use against his father. To establish Trenkler's identity as the builder of the bomb, the government offered, *inter alia,* evidence that Trenkler had previously constructed a remote-control device, the Quincy bomb, which exploded in Quincy, Massachusetts, in 1986. The government contended that unique similarities in design, choice of components, and overall *modus operandi* between the two bombs compelled the conclusion that Trenkler had designed and built both devices. Prior to trial, the government filed a motion *in limine* seeking to admit the "similarity" evidence. Following a day-long evidentiary hearing, the district court ruled the evidence admissible, finding that it was relevant on the issues of identity, skill, knowledge, and intent. Although Trenkler did not testify at trial, his counsel stipulated at the evidentiary hearing that Trenkler had built the Quincy bomb.[3]

1986 Quincy Bomb

Trenkler constructed the Quincy bomb in 1986 for a friend, Donna Shea. At the time, Shea was involved in a dispute with the owners of the Capeway Fish Market and she wanted the bomb to use as a means to intimidate them. At her request, Trenkler assembled a remote-control, radio-activated explosive device. The device was later attached to the undercarriage of a truck belonging to the Capeway Fish Market and detonated in the middle of the night. The resulting bomb blast caused no injuries and little property damage.

In building the Quincy bomb, Trenkler used as the explosive material a military flash simulator typically utilized to mimic gunfire in combat exercises. To provide remote-control capabilities, Trenkler employed a radio-receiver he had removed from a small toy car. Trenkler wrapped the bomb in duct tape and attached a large donut-shaped speaker magnet to enable the bomb to adhere to the undercarriage of the truck. Other components Trenkler used included a "double throw" toggle switch, four AA batteries, two six-volt batteries, an electric relay, solder, various wires, and a slide switch.

Testimony at trial established that Trenkler purchased some of the electrical components for the Quincy bomb from a Radio Shack store. On one occasion, Trenkler sought to obtain needed components by sending Shea's eleven-year-old nephew into a Radio Shack store with a list of items to purchase while Trenkler remained waiting outside. Shea's nephew, however, was unable to find all of the items, and Trenkler eventually came into the store to assist him.

1991 Roslindale Bomb

* * *

Testimony from government investigators and Shay Sr. established that the Roslindale bomb was a remote-control, radio-activated device with an explosive force supplied by two or three sticks of dynamite connected to two electrical blasting caps. A black wooden box weighing two or three pounds and measuring approximately eight- to ten-inches long, five- to six-inches wide and one- to two-inches deep housed the bomb. A large donut-shaped magnet and several smaller round magnets attached to the box were used to secure the device to the underside of Shay Sr.'s automobile. Other components used in the construction of the bomb included duct tape, a "single throw" toggle switch, four AA batteries, five nine-volt batteries, a Futaba radio receiver, solder, various wires, and a slide switch.

* * *

Both the government and Trenkler elicited testimony from their respective explosives experts explaining the similarities and differences between the two bombs. Both experts testified at length concerning the electronic designs, the choice of components and the method of construction. The government's expert opined that the two incidents shared many similar traits and characteristics, evincing the "signature" of a single bomb

---

[3] During the original 1986 investigation of the Quincy bombing, Trenkler admitted building the bomb. In 1987, the Commonwealth of Massachusetts brought charges against Trenkler for his involvement in the Quincy bombing, but the charges were dismissed.

maker. He further stated that he had no doubt "whatsoever" that the same person built both bombs. Trenkler's expert, on the other hand, stated that too many dissimilarities existed to conclude that the same person built both bombs. Moreover, Trenkler's expert testified that the similarities that existed lacked sufficient distinguishing qualities to identify the two bombs as the handiwork of a specific individual.

*   *   *

II. DISCUSSION

*   *   *

A. Quincy Bombing Evidence

We begin with Trenkler's contention that the district court erred in admitting the evidence of the Quincy bombing.

1. Fed. R. Evid. 404(b): Other Act Evidence

In general, Rule 404(b) proscribes the use of other bad-act evidence solely to establish that the defendant has a propensity towards criminal behavior. Rule 404(b)'s proscription, however, is not absolute: the rule permits the use of such evidence if it bears on a material issue such as motive, knowledge or identity. In this Circuit, we have adopted a two-part test for determining the admissibility of Rule 404(b) evidence. *E.g., United States v. Williams*, 985 F.2d 634, 637 (1st Cir. 1993). First, the district court must determine whether the evidence has some "special relevance" independent of its tendency simply to show criminal propensity. . . . Second, if the evidence has "special relevance" on a material issue, the court must then carefully conduct a Rule 403 analysis to determine if the probative value of the evidence is not substantially outweighed by the danger of unfair prejudice. *Williams*, 985 F.2d at 637. As with most evidentiary rulings, the district court has considerable leeway in determining whether to admit or exclude Rule 404(b) evidence. Accordingly, we review its decision only under the lens of abuse of discretion. . . .

2. Identity

*   *   *

a. Rule 404(b) Evidence: Special Relevance

When, as in this case, Rule 404(b) evidence is offered because it has "special relevance" on the issue of identity, we have required, as a prerequisite to admission, a showing that there exists a high degree of similarity between the other act and the charged crime. *See United States v. Ingraham*, 832 F.2d 229, 231–33 (1987), *cert. denied*, 486 U.S. 1009 (1988). Indeed, the proponent must demonstrate that the two acts exhibit a commonality of distinguishing features sufficient to earmark them as the handiwork of the same individual. *Id.* at 231. This preliminary showing is necessary because

> [a] defendant cannot be identified as the perpetrator of the charged act simply because he has at other times committed the same commonplace variety of criminal act except by reference to the forbidden inference of propensity. The

question for the court[,therefore, must be] whether the characteristics relied upon are *sufficiently idiosyncratic* to permit an inference of pattern for purposes of proof.

United States v. Pisari, 636 F.2d 855, 858–59 (1st Cir. 1981) (internal quotations and citations omitted) (emphasis added).

* * *

Trenkler contends that the array of similarities between the two incidents amounts to no more than a collection of "prosaic commonalit[ies that] cannot give rise to an inference that the same person was involved in both acts without reference to propensity." *United States v. Garcia-Rosa*, 876 F.2d 209, 225 (1st Cir. 1989), *cert. denied*, 493 U.S. 1030, *cert. granted and vacated on other grounds sub nom. Rivera-Feliciano v. United States*, 498 U.S. 954 (1990). However, in resolving whether the evidence supports an inference that the two incidents are "sufficiently idiosyncratic," we have cautioned that "an exact match is not necessary." *Ingraham*, 832 F.2d at 232. The test must focus on the "totality of the comparison," demanding not a "facsimile or exact replica" but rather the "'conjunction of several identifying characteristics *or* the presence of some highly distinctive quality.'" *Id.* at 232–33 (quoting *Pisari*, 636 F.2d at 859) (emphasis added); *see also United States v. Myers*, 550 F.2d 1036, 1045 (5th Cir. 1977) ("[A] number of common features of lesser uniqueness, although insufficient to generate a strong inference of identity if considered separately, may be of significant probative value when considered together."). In this case, we think the balance of the evidence tilts sufficiently towards admission to satisfy the first step of the Rule 404(b) analysis. Accordingly, we believe that the district court did not abuse its discretion in determining that the numerous similarities in components, design, and technique of assembly, combined with the similar *modus operandi* and the closeness of geographic proximity between the two events, sufficiently support the inference that the same person built both bombs.

We begin by noting that the government's explosives expert, Thomas Waskom, testified that his analysis of the similarities shared by the two incidents left him with no doubt "whatsoever" that the same individual built both bombs. Our own review of the record reveals that the two bombs did indeed share a number of similar components and characteristics. Both bombs were remote-controlled, radio-activated, electronic explosive devices. Both were homemade mechanisms, comprising, in general, electronic components easily purchased at a hobby store. Both had similar, though not identical, firing and fusing circuits with separate battery power supplies for each. Both had switches in their fusing circuits to disconnect the radio receivers. To energize their respective radio receivers, both devices utilized similar power supplies, consisting of four AA batteries. Both employed many similar components such as batteries, duct tape, toggle switches, radio receivers, antennas, solder, electrical tape, and large round speaker magnets. Moreover, both used a distinctive method (i.e., twisting, soldering, and taping) to connect some, though not all, of the wires used. Though we hardly find any of these factors by themselves to be "highly distinctive," the coalescence of them is fairly persuasive.[15] Indeed, even Trenkler's expert witness, Denny Kline, testified at the pretrial hearing that, in light of these similarities, "there is a possibility, a *probability*, that maybe *there is a connection* between the maker of these two bombs." (Emphasis added.)

---

[15] On the other hand, Trenkler argues that the differences between the two bombs are more significant. Some of the differences that Trenkler cites include:

*   *   *

Accordingly, we believe some significance is properly attributed to the simple fact that both incidents are bombings. A bombing, in and of itself, is, arguably, a fairly distinctive method for intimidating or killing an individual. . . . In addition, both incidents involved not simply bombs, but remote-control bombs that were placed underneath automotive vehicles.

*   *   *

In *United States v. Pisari*, 636 F.2d 855 (1st Cir. 1981), we reversed the district court's decision to admit evidence of a prior robbery solely on the issue of identity, where the only similarity between it and the charged offense was that a knife was used. Similarly, in *Garcia-Rosa*, 876 F.2d at 224–25, we refused to sanction the admission of a prior drug transaction where the only characteristic linking it to the charged drug deal was the characteristic exchange of a sample of drugs prior to the sale. In *Garcia-Rosa*, we held that a single "prosaic commonality" was insufficient "to give rise to an inference that the same person was involved in both acts without reference to propensity." *Id.* at 225. *See also United States v. Benedetto*, 571 F.2d 1246, 1249 (2d Cir. 1978) (no signature where shared characteristic is merely "a similar technique for receiving the cash: the passing of folded bills by way of a handshake").

In the present case, however, the government presented more than a single "prosaic commonality." Indeed, the government propounded a laundry list of similarities in design, component selection, construction and overall *modus operandi*. On the other hand, Trenkler offered a fairly impressive list of differences between the two incidents. In the absence of one or more highly distinctive factors that in themselves point to idiosyncracy, we must examine the combination of all the factors. Had Trenkler been unable to point to any significant differences, we suspect he would have had little chance in establishing an abuse of discretion in allowing the evidence. Similarly, had the government found but three or four common characteristics to establish sufficient similarity, we doubt that the admission of the evidence would have been granted or sustained. Here, in the middle, with substantial evidence on either side and conflicting expert opinions, could a reasonable jury have found it more likely than not that the same person was responsible for both bombs? We think the answer is yes. *See Ingraham*, 832 F.2d at 233 (admitting evidence) ("[G]iven the host of important comparables, the discrepancies — though themselves not unimportant — go to the weight of the

---

Roslindale Bomb	Quincy Bomb
Two or three sticks of dynamite unwrapped in a magazine page and electrical blasting caps which killed one officer and severely injured another	Military flash simulator used which produced only minor damage
Futuba remote control system which used a small electrical servo motor	Radio receiver taken from toy car
"Single throw" toggle switch used to send power to dynamite	Relay allowed power to be sent to explosives; "double throw" toggle switch used as safety
Five nine-volt batteries provided power to firing system	Two six-volt batteries supplied power to firing system
Device was housed in a black wooden box	Device was wrapped in silver duct tape

challenged evidence, not to its admissibility.").

b. Rule 404(b) Evidence: Probative Value and Unfair Prejudice

Resolving that the district court did not abuse its discretion in determining that a rational jury could infer that it was more likely than not that the same person built both bombs, however, does not end the analysis. We must also review the trial court's determination that the probative value of the evidence was not substantially outweighed by the risk of unfair prejudice. Several factors weigh heavily in this balancing, such as the government's need for the evidence, . . . the strength of evidence establishing the similarity of the two acts, . . . the inflammatory nature of the evidence, and the degree to which it would promote an inference based solely on the defendant's criminal propensity, *see United States v. Rubio-Estrada*, 857 F.2d 845, 851–52 (1st Cir. 1988) (Torruella, J., dissenting) (explaining inherent unfair prejudice in evidence of prior bad acts). . . .

We believe the district court acted well within its broad discretion in admitting the evidence. First, the evidence was important to the government's case. The evidence that Trenkler had built the Quincy bomb corroborated David Lindholm's testimony, identifying Trenkler as the builder of the Roslindale bomb. Second, although the evidence of similarity could have been more compelling, it was nonetheless substantial: Indeed, the government's explosives expert testified that he had no doubt "whatsoever" that the same person designed and constructed both bombs.

On the other hand, we disagree with the district court that the evidence did not pose any risk of unfair prejudice. As with all "bad act" evidence, there is always some danger that the jury will use the evidence not on the narrow point for which it is offered but rather to infer that the defendant has a propensity towards criminal behavior. Nonetheless, outside the context of propensity, the evidence was not unduly inflammatory. The Quincy bomb did not kill or injure any individual and caused little property damage. Moreover, the district court minimized any risk of unfair prejudice by carefully instructing the jury not to use the evidence of the Quincy bombing to infer Trenkler's guilt simply because he was a bad person or because the fact he had a built a bomb in the past made it more likely he had built the bomb in this case. In sum, we believe that the district court did not abuse its discretion in determining that the probative value of the Quincy bomb evidence was not substantially outweighed by the risk of unfair prejudice.

*   *   *

III. CONCLUSION

. . . [W]e affirm Trenkler's conviction.

UNITED STATES v. LUNA
21 F.3d 874 (9th Cir. 1994)

FLETCHER, CIRCUIT JUDGE.

Defendants Richard Pin˜a and Robert Todd Torres were convicted of robbing the Western Financial Savings Bank in Fresno, California; Pin˜a, Torres, and David Luna were convicted of robbing the Bank of America, also in Fresno. Evidence of two subsequent Oregon bank robberies for which Luna and Pin˜a were alleged to have been responsible was admitted, under Fed. R. Evid. 404(b), to prove the identity of the Fresno bank robbers.

Luna and Pin˜a contend that the district court erred in admitting the evidence of the two Oregon bank robberies. We agree, and reverse Luna's and Pin˜a's convictions on that basis. . . .

A. The First Charged Robbery: Western Financial Savings Bank

On March 12, 1992, the Western Financial Savings Bank, in Fresno, was robbed by two gunmen. The robbery was performed "takeover style": after a loud entry, the robbers ordered all of the bank employees and customers, at gunpoint, to get on the floor. One of the robbers then jumped over the counter, made the tellers open their drawers, and began emptying money into a pillowcase-like bag. The other robber stood guard on top of the counter. Two of the tellers were grabbed or pulled by the hair. The robbers were also verbally abusive to the tellers.

The robbers were dressed in dark sweatpants and sweatshirts, with nylon stocking masks over their heads. At least one robber wore gloves, which according to one witness were not surgical gloves. One or both of the robbers wore baseball hats.

After three or four minutes, the robbers left the bank, yelling, as they went out, "this is Crips 107." The robbers were observed by a gardener, who was standing outside the bank raking flower beds; he watched them run by with their guns and their bag of money, one robber shedding his stocking mask as he ran. Baseball hats were later found in the hallway in front of the bank. The robbers jumped into a car which was then driven off, probably by a third person.

After the robbery, one victim was able to make a positive identification of Torres from a police photo spread, and again identified Torres in court. Probation officers identified both Torres and Pin˜a from bank surveillance photographs.

B. The Second Charged Robbery: Bank of America

On March 23, 1992, between 10:30 and 11:00 a.m., three men, at least two of them armed, robbed the Bank of America in Fresno. This robbery also was committed takeover style; when the men burst into the bank, they shouted out, according to different witnesses, "Everybody down," or "This is a robbery," or "This is a holdup. Don't move." All three robbers jumped over the counters; they pulled the cash cans out of the tellers' drawers and threw them onto the floor. They loaded the money into bags described variously as white bank bags, canvas bags, beige bags, and pillowcases. The robbers used foul language with the tellers, but did not physically abuse anybody until, on the way out, one of them struck the bank manager in the face.

The robbers were dressed in dark sweatpants and sweatshirts. Two wore ski masks; one wore a nylon stocking mask. At least one robber wore surgical gloves. One of the bank tellers saw a tattoo on the left side of the neck of one of the robbers. The teller testified that the tattoo was consistent with a tattoo that Torres had on the left side of his neck at the time of trial.

After the robbery, at 11:45 a.m., Deputy Elerick of the Fresno County Sheriff's Department recognized a car he had stopped on March 11, 1992. Elerick also recognized the occupants from the previous stop: the driver was Luna and one of the passengers was Pin˜a. Elerick followed the car; after it ran three stop signs, he attempted to make a vehicle stop. Rather than pulling over, however, the car stopped in the middle of the street. Elerick approached the car, but after seeing Luna reach down toward the floorboard, ran back toward his own vehicle. The car started to move again; Elerick chased it for a short distance; the car stopped, and three persons jumped out and fled. The car, which was still running, rolled over the curb and then stopped beneath a tree. The third person who jumped from the car, according to Elerick, was an Hispanic male in his late teens or early twenties, between 5'5" and 5'9", and weighing between 130 and 150 lbs.

Inside the car, officers found a revolver later discovered to have one of Torres' fingerprints on it. The customer service manager at the Bank of America testified that this revolver was similar to the gun one of the robbers had brandished. Also in the car, the officers found a semiautomatic handgun (in the area where Luna had been reaching), a bag of surgical gloves, and several torn-out yellow pages from a phone book, listing financial institutions. Outside the car, police discovered an L.A. Kings baseball hat; "Crips 107" was written under the bill. Police also found a maroon sweatshirt near a house that the suspects had run past; witnesses from the bank identified it as similar to a sweatshirt one of the robbers had been wearing. Upon investigation, the police found that the car belonged to Pin˜a's girlfriend.

C. The First Uncharged Robbery: Security Pacific Bank

On April 20, 1992, at approximately 11:00 a.m., two men burst through the doors of the Security Pacific Bank, in Beaverton, Oregon, and ordered everyone inside to get down on the floor. One man remained in the lobby area with his gun drawn; the other jumped over the tellers' counter and forced the tellers to open their cash drawers and give him money. This robber had a bag which one witness said might have been a pillowcase and which other witnesses described as light, whitish, or beige. The robbers yelled profanities at the bank employees, and the robber behind the counter grabbed one teller by the arm and attempted to pick up another teller by his hair.

The robbers wore nylon stocking masks and were dressed in sweatshirts and sweatpants; the pants of one robber may have been blue, and his shirt may have been a lighter color. The robber who remained in the lobby wore a hat; the counter-jumper did not. The robbers wore gloves which may have been either cotton or surgical gloves.

Also on the morning of April 20, a witness in the vicinity saw a car speeding away from the bank; reddish-colored smoke that could have been from a dye packet was coming out of the car. The witness saw three persons in the car. One person was holding onto the roof of the car with a surgical-gloved hand, while throwing items out of the car with the other hand. Two of these items turned out to be a baseball hat and a woman's nylon stocking.

On that same day, half a mile from the bank, an FBI agent inspected an abandoned car which looked as if it had been stolen, and which had reddish dye stains in the interior. Money was scattered through the car. A semiautomatic handgun was also inside. The car had been left with its engine running.

Parole officers looking at bank surveillance photographs later identified the robbers as Pin˜a and Luna. On April 24, a police officer stopped a car driven by a man named Jimmy Ray Vaughn. The two other people in the car gave the names of Paul Lopez and Ralph Rey, but were later identified as Pin˜a and Luna. Luna was wearing a baseball hat and blue sweats.

D. The Second Uncharged Robbery: Far West Savings Bank

At approximately 10:50 a.m. on April 28, 1992, two men wearing nylon stockings on their heads made a very loud entrance into the Far West Savings Bank in Hillsboro, Oregon. One of them brandished a gun. First one and then the other robber came over the tellers' counter. They forced a teller to open his drawer, and when he didn't give them enough money, pushed him and tossed him back and forth between them. They also took money from the purse of one of the women in the bank. They were verbally abusive. The robbers wore blue and red sweatsuits, and baseball hats. One robber wore gloves which a witness described as being "more like white cotton work gloves"; the other wore white gloves made of a material the witness did not recall.

Just before 11:00 a.m. that same day, Officer Sarrett of the Washington County Sheriff's Office learned that a bank robbery had taken place, and drove toward Hillsboro to try to find the robbers. On his way to town, he noticed that the driver of a car coming toward him was staring straight ahead without looking from side to side. His suspicions alerted, Sarrett turned around and followed. He turned on his overhead lights, and the car sped away from him. He lost it briefly and soon thereafter found it abandoned in the middle of the road, with the ignition on. A bystander (holding a pillowcase) told him that three men had fled from the car. Sarrett gave chase, but did not find the escapees.

Inside the abandoned car, officers later found a blue sweat shirt, a woman's purse, and a tall yellow bank bag from the Far West bank. Inside the bag was $3000. Three traffic citations in the glove compartment bore the name of Jimmy Ray Vaughn. Inside the bank, officers found an L.A. Kings baseball hat.

Also on April 28, 1992, three men, out of breath, dirty, and wet, appeared at the house of Lydia Caballero, in Cornelius, Oregon. One of the men, whom Caballero knew to be David Luna, had no shirt on. The other men were Pin̄a and Vaughn; they asked for Candy, who shared the house with Caballero, and who was Luna's cousin. Caballero suspected the men had robbed a bank, and confronted them with this. Luna admitted that this was indeed what had happened, and told Caballero to keep quiet. Instead, Caballero notified her aunt, who worked for the sheriff's department. The three men were eventually arrested at Caballero's house. Caballero later identified Pin̄a and Luna in surveillance photographs from the Security Pacific robbery.

* * *

DISCUSSION

A. Use of Other Crimes Evidence

* * *

Recently, this court restated a 4-part test for the application of Rule 404(b): Evidence of prior or subsequent criminal conduct may be admitted if (1) the evidence tends to prove a material point; (2) the other act is not too remote in time; (3) the evidence is sufficient to support a finding that defendant committed the other act; and (4) (in certain cases) the act is similar to the offense charged.[1]*Garcia-Orozco*, 997 F.2d at 1304 (*citing United States v. Bibo-Rodriguez*, 922 F.2d 1398, 1400 (9th Cir.), *cert. denied*, 111 S. Ct. 2861 (1991)). If the evidence in question satisfies these requirements, the trial court must then apply Fed. R. Evid. 403. . . .

When the other acts evidence is introduced to prove identity, as it was here, "the characteristics of the other crime or act [must] be 'sufficiently distinctive to warrant an inference that the person who committed the act also committed the offense at issue.' " *United States v. Perkins*, 937 F.2d 1397, 1400 (9th Cir. 1991) (quoting *United States v. Andrini*, 685 F.2d 1094, 1097 (9th Cir. 1982)). Conversely, " 'if the characteristics of both the prior offense and the charged offense are not in any way distinctive, but are similar to numerous other crimes committed by persons other than the defendant, no inference of identity can arise.' " *Id.* (quoting *United States v. Powell*, 587 F.2d 443, 448 (9th Cir. 1978)). In this case, Luna, joined by Pin˜a, argues that those elements which were common to the charged and the uncharged acts were not sufficiently distinctive to permit the requisite inference to be drawn.

In its offer of proof, the government provided the following "summary of the common factors running through all four robberies":

> (1) they are all "take-over robberies"; (2) at least one or more robbers wore white surgical gloves, which is very unusual; (3) a white pillow case was used to take the money; (4) one robber stayed in the lobby area and was armed with a handgun; (5) the second robber was the counter jumper who removed money from multiple drawers; (6) the counter jumper grabbed the hair of the tellers in order to force them to the ground and to move them about; (7) the robbers wore long sleeve sweatshirts and sweatpants; (8) one or more of the robbers wore dark women's nylon stockings over their face; (9) the robbers wore baseball caps; (10) the robbers spoke with a Hispanic accent; (11) the robbers appeared to be between 20–30 years old; (12) a car was usually found abandoned with its engine running near the scene of the robbery; (13) the robbers used an excessive amount of profanity to intimidate and take control of the employees and customers; and (14) the robberies all occurred between 10:30 a.m. and 11:30 a.m. Govt's Amended Notice of Intention to Offer Defendant's Subsequent Acts at Trial at 6–7.

As noted, the district court ruled that the evidence would be admitted, but after hearing the testimony of the witnesses to the two charged robberies, expressed its concern that those crimes did not fit the pattern promised by the government. In particular, the court noted that in neither robbery did it appear that one robber had stood guard in the lobby area while the other had vaulted the counter; nor was it true that in both robberies the tellers had been grabbed by the hair. Indeed, the trial judge was so concerned with the discrepancies between the offer of proof and the proof that had come in that he stated "[m]aybe we better get an order out to the U.S. Attorney's Office, any representations that are made are made under oath, or any affidavits are under oath because I am not hearing the same case you told me I was going to hear." Tr. at 325.

---

[1] *Garcia-Orozco* pointed out that similarity is a prerequisite when the other crimes evidence is introduced to prove intent. As set forth below, similarity is also a prerequisite when the other crimes evidence is used to prove identity. Indeed, "[a] much greater degree of similarity between the charged crime and the uncharged crime is required when the evidence of the other crime is introduced to prove identity than when it is introduced to prove a state of mind." *United States v. Myers*, 550 F.2d 1036, 1045 (5th Cir. 1977); John W. Strong, McCormick on Evidence, § 190, p. 805 (4th ed. 1992).

*   *   *

A more accurate summary of the points of similarity is as follows. All the robberies were conducted takeover style, i.e., rather than robbing individual tellers and attempting to hide that fact from the rest of the bank, the robbers announced their presence to one and all and took control of the bank. The robberies all occurred between 10:30 and 11:30 a.m., and the robbers entered the banks noisily. In each case, the robbers wore sweatpants, sweatshirts, some kind of mask, and gloves. The robbers were armed. At least one robber jumped over the counter. The robbers swore at the tellers and pushed, tossed, or struck one or more bank employees. They took money out of one or more of the tellers' drawers and put it into bags. They used a getaway car in all of the robberies, and in both of the uncharged crimes and one of the charged crimes, they abandoned the car with its motor running.

On the other hand, there were also differences. Three of the robberies were perpetrated by two persons, while the fourth was carried out by three. In two cases, the robbers commanded everybody in the bank to get down; in one case, according to one witness the robbers did not tell everyone in the bank to get down, while according to another witness they did; in the fourth case, there is no mention of the robbers telling anyone to get down. In two of the robberies, all of the robbers went over the counter; in one robbery, one went over the counter while another stood guard in the lobby; in another robbery, one went over the counter while one stood guard on top of it. The robbers wore surgical gloves in some cases and cotton gloves (or possibly combinations of cotton and surgical gloves) in others. They wore nylon masks in three cases, and a combination of ski masks and nylon masks in the fourth. Baseball hats were identified in some but not all cases; in one case one robber wore a hat and the other did not. It does not appear that the robbers used their own bags to carry out the money in all cases: in one of the uncharged acts, a yellow bag bearing the name of the robbed bank (and containing money) was found in the robbers' car. It is also not clear that the same kind of bag was used in those cases where the robbers apparently did bring their own: the bags were described variously as white and as beige, and as pillowcases and as canvas-type bags. In one case, the robbers used physical violence in an especially gratuitous manner, striking an employee on their way out; in other cases, they used violence in an apparent attempt to get the tellers to open their drawers and give them money. They used violence of different kinds, sometimes pulling the hair of the tellers, sometimes bruising their arms, and sometimes both. In some cases, the robbers identified themselves as members of the Crips gang; in others, they did not. The robbers' getaway car appeared to be a stolen vehicle in some, but not in all cases.

We must determine whether the common characteristics of the four robberies are "sufficiently distinctive to warrant an inference that the person who committed the [uncharged] act[s] also committed the offense[s] at issue," or whether those common features are so generic that such an inference cannot be drawn.

We conclude that the common features in this case were largely generic. This case very much fits the pattern of *United States v. Myers*, 550 F.2d 1036 (5th Cir. 1977), in which the Fifth Circuit, in holding that other crimes evidence had been admitted erroneously, specifically discussed which elements of an armed bank robbery might be considered distinctive, and which are merely generic. The *Myers* court held that it was reversible error to admit other acts evidence to prove identity under Rule 404(b) where the charged and the uncharged acts had the following in common:

> (1) both crimes were bank robberies, (2) perpetrated . . . between two and three o'clock in the afternoon. In both robberies the victimized bank was [3]

located on the outskirts of a town, [4] adjacent to a major highway. In both robberies the participants [5] used a revolver, [6] furnished their own bag for carrying off the proceeds, and wore [7] gloves and [8] masks crudely fashioned from nylon stockings.

Id. at 1046. Each of these eight factors, the Fifth Circuit held, "is a common component of armed bank robbery," and hence the fact that those elements were present in both the charged and the uncharged robberies meant virtually nothing. *Id.*

In the present case, the government relies on many of the same "common components": guns, masks, gloves, bags.[5] Other common elements also collapse into generic features of a takeover robbery, in which it is almost by definition necessary to intimidate people: the loud entry; the profanity; the abuse of bank employees.

This case also shares another important feature with *Myers*. Here, as there, different numbers of perpetrators are alleged to have been responsible for the different robberies (sometimes two perpetrators, sometimes three). This difference takes on particular significance when it is recalled that the government promised that the evidence would reveal that all of the robberies were characterized by a neat, two-man division of labor (counter jumper and guard), but the evidence never did reveal this. A fixed number of persons did not play fixed roles, but rather a varying number of persons divided up the work of robbing a bank differently in almost every case.

Moreover, according to the government's own theory of the case, not only different numbers of persons but also different combinations of persons were responsible for the different robberies: Pin˜a and Torres for Western Financial; Pin˜a, Luna, and Torres for the Bank of America; Pin˜a and Luna (and possibly Vaughn) for the two Oregon robberies. Without necessarily adopting Luna's argument that the lack of identity of alleged perpetrators is in itself fatal to a Rule 404(b) identity theory, we do agree that the differences in personnel, like the other differences detailed above, significantly lessen the purportedly distinctive quality of the charged and uncharged crimes. The more combinations of people who are in the business of carrying out the same supposedly distinctive brand of crime, the less distinctive that "brand" becomes.

Given the various differences among the four crimes, given the generic quality of the elements the crimes did share in common, and given the differences which existed even within the concededly common elements of the four crimes, . . . we conclude that the trial court erred in admitting the other crimes evidence for the purpose of showing identity.[7]

---

[5] Perhaps if the robbers had used identical kinds of masks, gloves, and bags in every crime, the government would have come closer to proving a distinctive quality running through all four robberies. But as indicated above, there were important differences as to the kinds of masks, gloves, and bags which were used; similarly, although the robbers wore sweats in all cases, they did not wear the same color sweats. Given these differences, the common elements take on an even more generic quality: disguises for hands, face, and body; something to carry away the money in. These are elements that are common to most bank robberies; they are hardly distinctive.

[7] In those cases where other crimes evidence has been admitted to establish a bank robber's identity, the common features were generally more distinctive than are the common features here. *See, e.g., United States v. Perry*, 438 F.3d 642, 648 (6th Cir. 2006) (evidence of uncharged bank robbery was properly admitted to prove identity in separate bank robbery prosecution where defendant entered both banks carrying a gun in a bookbag and siught to purchase money orders after requesting change for a $50 bill); *United States v. Mack*, 258 F.3d 548, 553–54 (6th Cir. 2001) (uncharged bank robbery evidence admissible to prove identity in prosecution for six other bank robberies, where defendant's use of ski mask, leaping over the teller counter upon entering and leaving bank in unindicted robbery were sufficiently similar to methods used in charged

* * *

Affirmed in part; reversed in part; and remanded.

NOTES AND QUESTIONS

1. In *Trenkler*, the court posited that a "high degree of similarity" is required where the "other act" evidence is offered to prove identity. *Trenkler, supra*, 61 F.3d at 52. The test for admissibility advanced by the court is whether the shared characteristics of the other act and the charged offense are "sufficiently idiosyncratic" that a reasonable jury could find more likely than not that the same person committed them both. *Id.* at 53. At the same time, the court commented that "an exact match is not necessary." *Id.* at 54 (citation omitted). Instead, "[t]he test must focus on the 'totality of the comparison,' demanding not a 'facsimile or exact replica' but rather the 'conjunction of several identifying characteristics or the presence of some highly distinctive quality.'" *Id.* (citation omitted). Thus, the other act evidence is admissible in either of two cases: (1) the prior act shares several similarities with the charged offense, and (2) where the similarities, while fewer in number, are of a highly distinctive quality. The *Trenkler* court ultimately found none of the factors by themselves to be "highly distinctive," but based upon a combination or "coalescence" of similarities ruled that the evidence of the prior bombing was properly admissible to prove identity. *Id.* at 54–55.

In contrast, the *Luna* court based admissibility exclusively on whether the characteristics of the other crime or act are "'sufficiently distinctive to warrant an inference that the person who committed the act also committed the offense at issue,'" not on a totality of the comparison and number of similarities between the charged bank robberies and other acts. *Luna*, 21 F.3d at 878–79 (citation omitted). If the *Luna* case had been decided by the *Trenkler* court, would the First Circuit have reached a different result? Conversely, in the absence of any "highly distinctive" characteristics between the two bombings in *Trenkler*, coupled with a number of dissimilar features recognized by the court, do you think the *Luna* court would have excluded evidence of the Quincy bombing? Are the rulings in *Trenkler* and *Luna* consistent?

2. After resolving whether the evidence of the Quincy bombing was properly admissible under Fed. R. Evid. 404(b) to prove identity, the *Trenkler* court proceeded to consider the Fed. R. Evid. 403 issue. What factors did the court consider in balancing whether the risk of unfair prejudice substantially outweighed the probative value of the evidence? Can you think of any other factors that should have been considered by the court?

3. Do you agree with the court's statement in *Trenkler* that the district court minimized any risk of unfair prejudice by instructing the jury not to use the evidence of

---

robberies, and court noted other similarities between the charged and uncharged bank robberies); *United States v. Johnson*, 820 F.2d 1065, 1069–70 (9th Cir. 1987) (in both the two charged acts and the one uncharged act, a lone man robbed a bank, and before asking the teller to hand over all of the money in the drawer, asked for change — the same amount of change in the uncharged act as in one of the charged acts (quarters for a $5 bill)); *United States v. Powers*, 978 F.2d 354, 361 (7th Cir. 1992) (in all robberies, robber wore hat, suit, glasses, and moustache; robber carried a briefcase and handed the teller typewritten notes of similar size, content, and style), *cert. denied*, 113 S. Ct. 1323 (1993); *United States v. Morgan*, 936 F.2d 1561, 1572 (10th Cir. 1991) (in both robberies, robber used stolen car to drive to banks, wore mask made out of sweat pants, and used a weapon), *cert. denied*, 112 S. Ct. 1190 (1992); *United States v. Hudson*, 884 F.2d 1016, 1021 (7th Cir. 1989) (in all robberies, two men came into credit union; the taller man asked for change, and both men jumped over or ran behind the counter when the teller opened the drawer to get the change; they then grabbed the cash, and fled), *cert. denied*, 496 U.S. 939 (1990).

the Quincy bombing to infer Trenkler's guilt or to surmise that because he had built a bomb in the past he was more likely to have built the bomb in this case? Is it unrealistic to believe that the jury will follow the district court's limiting instruction? Do you think the jury will be able to consider the other act evidence on the issue of identity, but refrain from considering this same evidence and drawing the inference that because the defendant constructed a bomb on one occasion he likely constructed the bomb at issue?

4. For cases admitting prior act evidence to show identity by establishing a distinctive *modus operandi*, see *United States v. Gonzales*, 533 F.3d 1057 (9th Cir. 2008); *United States v. Carlton*, 534 F.3d 97 (2d Cir. 2008); *United States v. Patterson*, 20 F.3d 809 (10th Cir.1994); *United States v. Sappe*, 898 F.2d 878 (2d Cir. 1990); *United States v. Connelly*, 874 F.2d 412, 417–18 (7th Cir. 1989); *United States v. Woods*, 613 F.2d 629, 635 (6th Cir. 1980).

For cases excluding the other act evidence, *see United States v. Carroll*, 207 F.3d 465 (8th Cir. 2000); *Government of Virgin Islands v. Pinney*, 967 F.2d 912, 916 (3d Cir. 1992) (although two rapes involved minors of same age, occurred in the same apartment, involved similar behavior and concluded with similar warnings to enforce the victims' silence, court held that evidence was "neither sufficiently detailed nor significantly unusual" to establish identity); *United States v. Benedetto*, 571 F.2d 1246, 1249 (2d Cir. 1978) (rejecting evidence of prior bribe made by technique of passing cash by way of handshake, stating "that method of bribery is about as unique as using glassine envelopes to package heroin").

PROBLEM

Problem 6-3. *Identity of the Defendant in Multiple Murders.* The defendant was charged with capital murder relating to the kidnapping, sexual assault, and murder of eight-year-old Bertha M. After his arrest, the defendant confessed to a similar kidnapping, sexual assault and murder of nine-year-old Nancy S., ten years earlier. Prior to trial, the defendant also confessed to kidnapping, sexual assault and murder of Bertha M., but, at trial, the defendant recanted his confession to the Bertha M. murder. The government then offered the defendant's confession to the Nancy S. murder, arguing that the "Nancy" confession was admissible under Rule 404(b) to establish the defendant's identity as the Bertha M. murderer and to rebut his claim that the "Bertha" confessions were inaccurate and involuntary. Below is the government's chart outlining the similarities between the two murders:

BERTHA MARTINEZ CASE	NANCY SHOEMAKER CASE
VICTIM PROFILE	VICTIM PROFILE
— One (1) Victim	— One (1) Victim
— Female Victim	— Female Victim
— Child Victim	— Child Victim
— Same Approx. Age (8 yrs. old)	— Same Approx. Age (9 yrs. old)
— Victim Was "Unknown Stranger"	— Victim Was "Unknown Stranger"
KIDNAPPING	KIDNAPPING
— Victim Was Abducted	— Victim Was Abducted
— Victim Was Abducted/Public Area	— Victim Was Abducted/Public Area
— Victim Was Abducted Near Victim's Home	— Victim Was Abducted Near Victim's Home

BERTHA MARTINEZ CASE	NANCY SHOEMAKER CASE
— Victim Was Physically Relocated (. . . City Park/Comanche St. Residence)	— Victim Was Physically Relocated (. . . Bell/Plaine, Kansas)
DEFENDANT HAD "NEXUS" TO LOCATION OF ABDUCTION	**DEFENDANT HAD "NEXUS" TO LOCATION OF ABDUCTION**
— Defendant Was Resident of Nearby Brown School Area	— Defendant Delivered "Penny Power" Circulars in This Area
<u>VICTIM WAS PHYSICALLY ASSAULTED</u>	<u>VICTIM WAS PHYSICALLY ASSAULTED</u>
<u>VICTIM WAS SEXUALLY ASSAULTED</u>	<u>VICTIM WAS SEXUALLY ASSAULTED</u>
<u>VICTIM WAS MURDERED</u>	<u>VICTIM WAS MURDERED</u>
— Defendant "Strangled" Victim	— Defendant "Strangled" Victim
<u>VICTIM'S BODY WAS "DUMPED"</u>	<u>VICTIM'S BODY WAS "DUMPED"</u>
DEFENDANT COMMITTED OFFENSE WITH CO-ACTOR	**DEFENDANT COMMITTED OFFENSE WITH CO-ACTOR**
— Woody and Murlene Brought	— Donny Wacker
DEFENDANT INVOLVED WITH "SEARCH"	**DEFENDANT INVOLVED WITH "SEARCH"**
<u>DEFENDANT CLAIMED "TROPHY" FROM CRIME</u>	<u>DEFENDANT CLAIMED "TROPHY" FROM CRIME</u>
— Wore Bertha Martinez's Under-wear	— Took Nancy Shoemaker's Under-wear

The defendant argued that the "Nancy" confession was irrelevant to any non-character-conformity purpose under Rule 404(b). Furthermore, the defendant contended that admission of the "Nancy" confession was unfairly prejudicial and, thus, inadmissible under Fed. R. Evid. 403. Is the "Nancy" confession admissible under Rule 404(b) to show the defendant's identity as the "Bertha" murderer and to rebut the defendant's claim that the "Bertha" confessions were involuntary? Should the "Nancy" confession be excluded under Rule 403? *See Lane v. State*, 933 S.W.2d 504 (Tex. Crim. App. 1996).

[g]   Evidence of Prior Sexual Assault or Child Molestation *to Prove Propensity* — Rules 413 and 414

Federal Rules of Evidence 413 and 414 were enacted by Congress on September 13, 1994, to be effective one hundred fifty days thereafter. The key parts of these Rules provide as follows:

Rule 413. Evidence of Similar Crimes in Sexual Assault Cases

(a) In a criminal case in which the defendant is accused of an offense of sexual assault, evidence of the defendant's commission of another offense or offenses of sexual assault is admissible, and may be considered for its bearing on any matter to which it is relevant.

* * *

Rule 414. Evidence of Similar Crimes in Child Molestation Cases

(a) In a criminal case in which the defendant is accused of an offense of child molestation, evidence of the defendant's commission of another offense of child molestation is admissible, and may be considered for its bearing on any matter to which it is relevant.

*   *   *

In subsequent subsections both rules require the government to provide notice and disclosure to the defendant fifteen days prior to trial, of any evidence it intends to offer regarding the defendant's prior sexual assault or child molestation offenses.

These Rules were controversial. Congress adopted Rules 413 and 414 (and their civil case counterpart, Rule 415) despite the recommendations of the Advisory Committee of Evidence Rules, the Advisory Committee on Criminal and Civil Rights (with the exception of the Department of Justice), the Standing Committee (with the exception of the Department of Justice), and the Judicial Conference that they were undesirable and that Rule 404(b) sufficiently addressed the admission of evidence relating to the defendant's prior bad acts.

As mentioned, Rules 413 and 414 provide that prior acts of sexual misconduct may be admitted and considered "for its bearing on any matter to which it is relevant." Obviously, the inference a jury is likely to draw is the propensity inference; that is, since the accused committed this type of crime before he or she probably did it again this time. Accordingly, these Rules stand in contrast to the traditional ban on propensity evidence represented by Rules 404(a) and 404(b).

UNITED STATES v. CASTILLO
140 F.3d 874 (10th Cir.1998)

Tacha, Circuit Judge.

A jury convicted Serefino Castillo of four counts of sexual abuse in violation of 18 U.S.C. § 2242(1) and four counts of sexual abuse of a minor in violation of 18 U.S.C. § 2243(a). At trial, the district court admitted certain evidence against the defendant pursuant to Federal Rule of Evidence 414. The defendant now appeals the admission of that evidence, contending . . . (2) that Rule 414 violated his constitutional rights to due process and equal protection under the Fifth Amendment, as well as the right to be free of cruel and unusual punishment under the Eighth Amendment, and (3) that the Rule 414 evidence should have been excluded because of its great prejudicial value. We hold that Rule 414 . . . does not violate the Constitution. We remand this case to the district court, however, for an adequate explanation of its Rule 403 determination.

*   *   *

Serefino Castillo lives on the Navajo Reservation in Crownpoint, New Mexico. He and his wife have five children. The indictment charged the defendant with four acts of sexual abuse — three acts towards his daughter N.C. and one towards his daughter C.C. Each of these alleged acts gave rise to one count of sexual abuse under 18 U.S.C. § 2242 and one count of sexual abuse of a minor under 18 U.S.C. § 2244. At trial, the district court allowed N.C. to testify not only to the three acts of abuse against her with which the defendant was charged, but also to a fourth act of sexual abuse against her that was not charged in the indictment. Similarly, C.C. testified to two acts of sexual abuse committed against her by the defendant in addition to the one charged in the indictment. The district court admitted the evidence pursuant to Rule 414.

DISCUSSION

I. Federal Rule of Evidence 414

. . . .

A. Constitutional Challenges to Rule 414

Federal Rule of Evidence 414 reads, in pertinent part:

> In a criminal case in which the defendant is accused of an offense of child molestation, evidence of the defendant's commission of another offense or offenses of child molestation is admissible, and may be considered for its bearing on any matter to which it is relevant.

Fed. R. Evid. 414(a). This rule allows the prosecution to use evidence of a defendant's prior acts for the purpose of demonstrating to the jury that the defendant had a disposition of character, or propensity, to commit child molestation. In the cases to which this rule applies, it replaces the restrictive Rule 404(b), which prevents parties from proving their cases through "character" or "propensity" evidence. Here, the trial court admitted evidence of the defendant's prior acts of child molestation under Rule 414 for the purpose of demonstrating his character. Mr. Castillo now challenges the admission of that evidence on constitutional grounds. We review de novo the district court's conclusion that Rule 414 is constitutional.

1. Due Process

We first consider whether Federal Rule of Evidence 414 violates the due process rights of a criminal defendant under the Fifth Amendment. . . . The defendant here . . . challenges the rule in the abstract, thus presenting us with a facial challenge rather than an as-applied challenge.

a. Prior Cases

In *United States v. Enjady*, this court recently held that Federal Rule of Evidence 413, which allows character evidence in sexual assault cases, does not on its face violate the due process rights of a defendant. 134 F.3d 1427, 1433–34 (10th Cir.1998). We now hold that Rule 414 does not on its face violate the Due Process Clause.

*   *   *

b. Analysis

The Due Process Clause has limited operation beyond the specific guarantees enumerated in the Bill of Rights. The Due Process Clause will invalidate an evidentiary rule only if the rule "violates those fundamental conceptions of justice which lie at the base of our civil and political institutions and which define the community's sense of fair play and decency." *United States v. Lovasco*, 431 U.S. 783, 790 (1977). The Supreme Court has "defined the category of infractions that violate 'fundamental fairness' very narrowly." *Dowling v. United States*, 493 U.S. 342, 352–53 (1990). For three reasons, we conclude that Rule 414 falls outside that narrow category.

First, "[o]ur primary guide in determining whether the principle in question is fundamental is, of course, historical practice." *Montana v. Egelhoff*, 518 U.S. 37, 41–44 (1996). The ban on propensity evidence dates back to English cases of the seventeenth century. In addition, courts in the United States have enforced the ban throughout our nation's history, and we assume for purposes of this case, without deciding the matter, that because of the ban's lineage and significance in our jurisprudence, it is a protection that the Due Process Clause guarantees.

Nonetheless, the historical record regarding evidence of one's sexual character is much more ambiguous. More than a century ago, courts regularly admitted a defendant's prior acts as proof of the crime of incest. For example, the Michigan Supreme Court said:

> The general rule in criminal cases is well settled, that the commission of other, though similar offenses by the defendant, can not be proved for the purpose of showing that he was more likely to have committed the offense for which he is on trial. . . . But the courts in several of the States have shown a disposition to relax the rule in cases where the offense consists of illicit intercourse between the sexes.

People v. Jenness, 5 Mich. 305, 319–20 (Mich.1858). In the nineteenth and early twentieth centuries, some states developed a "lustful disposition" rule, allowing evidence of sexual acts other than the one charged in order to prove the defendant's disposition to commit a sex crime. Many of the cases in this area of the law concern sexual offenses against children. By the early 1920's, twenty-three states had a "lustful disposition" exception applicable to cases of statutory rape. Today, an even greater number of states retain the "lustful disposition" rule in cases involving sex offenses, including cases of child molestation.

Thus, the history of evidentiary rules regarding a criminal defendant's sexual propensities is ambiguous at best, particularly with regard to sexual abuse of children. The existence of this ambiguity does not leave us uncertain of the constitutional result, however; rather, it favors the government. As the Supreme Court stated in *Egelhoff*, "It is not the [government] which bears the burden of demonstrating that its rule is 'deeply rooted,' but rather [the defendant] who must show that the principle of procedure *violated* by the rule (and allegedly required by due process) is 'so rooted in the traditions and conscience of our people as to be ranked as fundamental.' " *Egelhoff*, 518 U.S. at 47.

In addition to the historical record, it is significant that other rules of evidence have been found constitutional even though they allow evidence presenting a risk of prejudice similar to that presented by Rule 414 evidence. When a court admits evidence of a defendant's propensities, such as evidence of the defendant's prior criminal acts, it creates " 'the risk that a jury will convict for crimes other than those charged — or that, uncertain of guilt, it will convict anyway because a bad person deserves punishment.' " *Old Chief v. United States*, 519 U.S. 172, ___, 117 S.Ct. 644, 650 (1997) Those risks of prejudice are present not only when the evidence is offered to show propensity, but whenever a defendant's prior bad acts are admitted. Whenever such evidence is before the jury, the jury may be tempted to convict for the prior bad act, or what it says about the defendant's character, rather than what it says about the likelihood that the defendant committed the charged crime. Therefore, the Supreme Court has described the risk of prejudice associated with evidence admitted under Rule 404(b) — which allows evidence of prior bad acts — in almost precisely the same terms as that associated with propensity evidence. The Court has said that Rule 404(b) evidence presents the risk that "the jury may choose to punish the defendant for the similar rather than the charged act, or [that] the jury may infer that the defendant is an evil person inclined to violate the law." *Huddleston v. United States*, 485 U.S. 681, 686 (1988). Nevertheless, since the Court upheld the common law equivalent of Rule 404(b) there has been no doubt that it is a constitutional rule. Similarly, a state does not violate due process when it allows evidence of a defendant's prior conviction, relevant only to his sentencing, at the guilt-determination stage.

The third and most significant factor favoring Rule 414's constitutionality is the existence of procedural protections in Rule 402 and, in particular, Rule 403. In *Huddleston*, the Supreme Court addressed the argument that because evidence of prior acts is so prejudicial, a district court should not admit 404(b) evidence unless the proponent of the evidence has proved the existence of the prior act by a preponderance of the evidence. Although *Huddleston* was not a constitutional decision, it is important to our inquiry because the defendant here — like those in *Huddleston* — argues that "prior acts" evidence creates an unacceptable risk of prejudice. The *Huddleston* Court ruled that even when evidence has a potentially great prejudicial effect, as Rule 404(b) evidence does, Rules 402 and 403 adequately control the prejudicial effect.

Rule 402 requires that all evidence be logically relevant to a material issue in the case. Rule 402 applies to Rule 414 evidence. More importantly, however, the Rule 403 balancing test applies to evidence admitted under Rule 414. Rule 403 excludes evidence, even if it is logically relevant, if its prejudicial effect substantially outweighs its probative value. Because of the presence of these protections, only a very narrow question remains — whether admission of Rule 414 evidence that is both relevant under 402 and not overly prejudicial under 403 may still be said to violate the defendant's due process right to a fundamentally fair trial. To ask the question is to answer it.

The due process violation that the defendant alleges here is that Rule 414 evidence is so prejudicial that it violates the defendant's fundamental right to a fair trial. Application of Rule 403, however, should always result in the exclusion of evidence that has such a prejudicial effect. *See* Fed. R. Evid. 403 (excluding evidence if its probative value is *substantially outweighed by danger of unfair prejudice*). Thus, application of Rule 403 to Rule 414 evidence eliminates the due process concerns posed by Rule 414.

For the above reasons, we hold that Rule 414 on its face does not violate the constitutional guarantee of due process. Thus, when reviewing a trial court's decision to admit Rule 414 evidence for constitutional error, the appellate court must engage in a case-specific inquiry only, asking whether the evidence in the case was "so prejudicial in the context of the proceedings as a whole that [the defendant] was deprived of the fundamental fairness essential to the concept of due process." *Scrivner v. Tansy*, 68 F.3d 1234, 1239–40 (10th Cir.1995).

2. Equal Protection

Rule 414 also does not violate the Constitution's promise of equal protection under the law. Although there is no Equal Protection Clause in the Fifth Amendment, the equal protection standards of the Fourteenth Amendment are incorporated into the Fifth Amendment's promise of due process. Under those standards, if a law "neither burdens a fundamental right nor targets a suspect class, we will uphold the legislative classification so long as it bears a rational relation to some legitimate end." *Romer v. Evans*, 517 U.S. 620, 631 (1996). In the previous portions of this opinion, we determined that the admission of character evidence allowed by Rule 414 does not burden the defendant's fundamental due process rights. Furthermore, the defendant does not belong to a suspect class. While the rule does treat those accused of child molestation differently than other criminal defendants, such a classification is not subject to a heightened standard of review. Therefore, we ask only whether Rule 414 has a rational basis.

Under the rational basis test, if there is a "plausible reason [] for Congress' action, our inquiry is at an end." *United States R.R. Retirement Bd. v. Fritz*, 449 U.S. 166, 179 (1980). We need not find that the legislature ever articulated this reason, nor that it actually underlay the legislative decision, nor even that it was wise. There are plausible reasons for the enactment of Rule 414. "Congress' objective of enhancing effective prosecution of sexual assaults is a legitimate interest." The government has a particular need for corroborating evidence in cases of sexual abuse of a child because of the highly secretive nature of these sex crimes and because often the only available proof is the child's testimony. Rule 414 does not violate the Equal Protection Clause.

3. Eighth Amendment

Mr. Castillo also argues that Rule 414 violates the Eighth Amendment's prohibition against cruel and unusual punishment. In *Robinson v. California*, 370 U.S. 660, 666–68 (1962), the Supreme Court held that the government infringes on an individual's Eighth Amendment rights when it imposes criminal punishment based on one's status, e.g., as a drug addict, rather than one's actions, e.g., purchasing drugs. According to Mr. Castillo, Rule 414 punishes him for his status as a person with a sexual interest in minors.

Rule 414 does not violate the Eighth Amendment. The rule does not impose criminal punishment at all; it is merely an evidentiary rule. In response, the defendant argues that because the evidence has such a strong prejudicial effect on juries, Rule 414 works as a *de facto* punishment for one's status as a sex offender. For the defendant to be correct, juries would have to ignore courts' instructions to them that they consider only *the crime charged* in deciding whether to convict. A central assumption of our jurisprudence is that juries follow the instructions they receive. Furthermore, as the Court did in *Huddleston*, we conclude above that the protections of Rules 402 and 403 adequately control any risk of prejudice. Thus, we find the defendant's Eighth Amendment argument unavailing.

B. The 403 Balancing Test

Having determined that Rule 414 is constitutional, and because Rule 403 applies to Rule 414 evidence, we ask whether the trial court nonetheless should have excluded the Rule 414 evidence under Rule 403 because of its prejudicial effect. We review a district court's decision on Rule 403 for abuse of discretion. Rule 403 allows a court to exclude evidence "if its probative value is substantially outweighed by the danger of unfair prejudice, confusion of the issues, or misleading the jury, or by considerations of undue delay, waste of time, or needless presentation of cumulative evidence." Fed. R. Evid. 403. Because of the unique nature of character evidence, it is important that the trial court "make a reasoned, recorded" statement of its 403 decision when it admits evidence under Rules 413–415. The district court need not make detailed factual findings in support of its Rule 403 determination. However, "[b]ecause of the sensitive nature of the balancing test in these cases, it will be particularly important for a district court to fully evaluate the proffered Rule 413 [or 414] evidence and make a clear record of the reasoning behind its findings."

In the present case, the district court responded as follows to a request that it make a finding under Rule 403:

> I'm not at all certain that under 413 I have to make a decision on 403. It seems to me that 413 is self-executing. . . . And if I have to make a finding under 403, then I find it's relevant and the probative value is not substantially outweighed by any prejudice.

This statement falls short of our minimum requirements. As we said in a similar case:

> [T]he district court's summary disposition of this issue renders it impossible for us to review the propriety of its decision. . . . Without any reasoned elaboration by the district court we have no way of understanding the basis of its decision. . . . As an appellate court, we are in no position to speculate about the possible considerations which might have informed the district court's judgment. Instead, we require an on the record decision by the court explaining its reasoning in detail.

United States v. Roberts, 88 F.3d 872, 882 (10th Cir.1996) We therefore remand this case to the district court for an explanation of its ruling under Rule 403.

* * *

CONCLUSION

We REMAND this case for the limited purpose of requiring the district court to clarify the reasoning underlying its evidentiary ruling under Rule 403. . . .

NOTES AND QUESTIONS

1. Note the critical role played by Rule 403 in preventing Rule 414 (and Rule 413) from violating the due process clause. A potential due process violation exists because Rule 414 (and Rule 413) evidence carries so much prejudice that it may jeopardize the accused's fundamental right to fair trial guaranteed by the due process clause. Rule 403 scrutiny saves Rule 414 evidence from a due process violation, however, because Rule 403's purpose is to exclude evidence that is overly prejudicial. As the court mentioned in *Castillo*, "[a]pplication of Rule 403 . . . should always result in the exclusion of evidence that has such a prejudicial effect" [and] "eliminates the due process concerns posed by Rule 414." *Castillo, supra*, 140 F.3d at 883. *See also, United States v. Guardia*, 135 F.3d 1326, 1330 (10th Cir. 1998) (Rule 403 balancing test applies to Rule 413 evidence.)

In a previous case, *United States v. Enjady*, 134 F.3d 1427 (10th Cir. 1998), the Tenth Circuit discussed the application of 403 balancing in the context of Rule 413.

> Rule 403 requires that if the trial court concludes the probative value of the similar crimes evidence is outweighed by the risk of unfair prejudice it must exclude the evidence. But the exclusion of relevant evidence under Rule 403 should be used infrequently, reflecting Congress' legislative judgment that the evidence "normally" should be admitted. *See* 140 Cong. Rec. H8992 (S.Molinari,

Aug. 21, 1994). Rule 403 balancing in the sexual assault context requires the court to consider: 1) how clearly the prior act has been proved; 2) how probative the evidence is of the material fact it is admitted to prove; 3) how seriously disputed the material fact is; and 4) whether the government can avail itself of any less prejudicial evidence. When analyzing the probative dangers, a court considers: 1) how likely is it such evidence will contribute to an improperly-based jury verdict; 2) the extent to which such evidence will distract the jury from the central issues of the trial; and 3) how time consuming it will be to prove the prior conduct.

Enjady, supra, 143 F.3d at 1433.

2. Should the application of Rule 403 be more "restrained" when evidence is offered pursuant to Rules 413 and 414? In *United States v. LeCompte*, 131 F.3d 767 (8th Cir. 1997), the Eighth Circuit seemed to think so.

Rule 414 and its companion rules — Rule 414 and Rule 415 — are "general rules of admissibility in sexual assault and child molestation cases for evidence that the defendant has committed offenses of the same type on other occasions. . . . The new rules will supersede in sex offense cases the restrictive aspects of Federal Rule of Evidence 404(b)" 140 Cong. Rec. H8992 (daily ed. Aug. 21, 1994) (statement of Rep. Molinari).

Evidence offered under Rule 414 is still subject to the requirements of Rule 403. This Court has recognized that evidence otherwise admissible under Rule 414 may be excluded under Rule 403's balancing test. However, Rule 403 must be applied to allow Rule 414 its intended effect.

. . . In light of the strong legislative judgment that evidence of prior sexual offenses should ordinarily be admissible, we think the District Court erred in its assessment that the probative value of T.T.'s testimony [concerning a prior uncharged sex offense committed by the defendant, Lecompte] was substantially outweighed by the danger of unfair prejudice. . . .

[T]he danger of unfair prejudice noted by the District Court was that presented by the "unique stigma" of child sexual abuse, on account of which LeCompte might be convicted not for the charged offense, but for his sexual abuse of T.T. This danger is one that all propensity evidence in such trials presents. It is for this reason that the evidence was previously excluded, and it is precisely such holdings that Congress intended to overrule.

LeCompte, supra, 131 F.3d at 769–70.

The Tenth Circuit disagrees. In *United States v. Guardia*, 135 F.3d 1326, (10th Cir. 1998, it characterized the view expressed by the Eighth Circuit in *LeCompte* a "misapplication" of Rule 403's balancing test.

[A] court could perform a restrained 403 analysis because of the belief that Rule 413 embodies a legislative judgment that propensity evidence regarding sexual assaults is never too prejudicial or confusing and generally should be admitted. *See United States v. LeCompte*, 131 F.3d 767, 769–70 (8th Cir. 1977).

We find [this] interpretation illogical. . . .

*   *   *

With regard to [this] potential misapplication of Rule 413, the government urges us to approve a lenient 403 balancing test. We agree that Rule 413, like all other Rules of admissibility, favors the introduction of evidence. Rule 413, however, contains no language that supports an especially lenient application of Rule 403. Furthermore, courts apply Rule 403 in undiluted form to Rules 404(a)(1)–(3), the other exceptions to the ban on propensity evidence. Those rules allow a criminal defendant to use character evidence of himself, his victim, or in limited circumstances, of other witnesses, in order to "prov[e] action in conformity therewith." Fed. R. Evid. 404(a) (1–3). Like Rule 413, these rules carve out exceptions to Rule 404(a) and reflect a legislative judgment that certain types of propensity evidence should be admitted. Courts have never found, however, that because the drafters made exceptions to the general rule of 404(a), they tempered Rule 403 as well.

*   *   *

When balancing Rule 413 evidence under 403, then, the district court should not alter its normal process of weighing the probative value of the evidence against the danger of unfair prejudice. In Rule 413 cases, the risk of prejudice will be present to varying degrees. Propensity evidence, however, has indisputable probative value. That value in a given case will depend on innumerable considerations including the similarity of the prior acts to the acts charged, the closeness in time of the prior acts to the charged acts, the frequency of the prior acts, the presence or lack of intervening events, and the need for evidence beyond the testimony of the defendant and the alleged victim. Because of the sensitive nature of the balancing test in theses cases, it will be particularly important for a district court to fully evaluate the proffered Rule 413 evidence and make a clear record of the reasoning behind its findings.

Guardia, supra, 143 F.3d at 1330–31.

Which view do you find more persuasive; the Eight Circuit's or the Tenth Circuit's? If Rule 403 balancing is a constitutional requirement to ensure the accused a fair trial (as the Tenth Circuit discussed in *Castillo*) would a lenient or restrained application of Rule 403 be constitutional?

UNITED STATES v. HORN
523 F.3d 882 (8th Cir. 2008)

Following a jury trial, Maurice Hollow Horn was convicted of two counts of abusive sexual contact, in violation of 18 U.S.C. §§ 1153, 2244(a)(1), 2241(c), and 2246(3). The district court denied Hollow Horn's motion for new trial and sentenced him to concurrent terms of 34 months' imprisonment. Hollow Horn appeals. We affirm.

I. BACKGROUND

During a 2004–2005 FBI investigation of Hollow Horn for suspected sexual misconduct against a young girl, two other girls R.R.A. and H.C. informed law enforcement officers that Hollow Horn had inappropriately touched them at a birthday party in 1999. At the time of the alleged inappropriate touching, both R.R.A. and H.C. were under twelve years of age.

*   *   *

At trial, the evidence established that in July 1999, several girls attended the 10th birthday party for Hollow Horn's daughter, Maurisa. The girls included R.R.A., who is Maurisa's first cousin (and Hollow Horn's niece) and H.C., who is Maurisa's second cousin (and the daughter of Hollow Horn's first cousin, Laudine). The party began at Hollow Horn's home. The adults also set up a tent outside of Maurisa's grandmother's home a few hundred yards away, so that the girls could have a sleep over. Five girls from the party started out in the tent that night, including Maurisa, R.R.A., and H.C. However, R.R.A. who was 7 years old at the time became scared, left the tent, and went into her grandmother's house to sleep on the couch. The other four girls spent the night in the tent.

R.R.A. testified that as she began to doze off on the couch, Hollow Horn (her uncle) entered the room wearing only his underwear and sat down on the couch near her feet. R.R.A. testified that Hollow Horn removed her covers and touched her vagina, rubbing it in an "up and down" motion with his hand over her panties but underneath the long shirt that she was wearing. Hollow Horn continued this rubbing for a couple of seconds before R.R.A. kicked him in the side, causing him to stop. Hollow Horn then placed the covers back on R.R.A., told her to be quiet and go back to sleep, and walked out of the room. Although her grandmother was in the house, R.R.A. did not yell out or otherwise call for help because she was scared of Hollow Horn. R.R.A. testified that her fear also prevented her from reporting the incident to her family or the police.

H.C., who was 10 years old at the time of the party, testified that she was asleep inside the tent with the three other girls, when she was awakened by someone rubbing her breasts in a circular motion. H.C. testified that she opened her eyes when she felt someone lift up her nightgown, exposing her stomach, and she saw Hollow Horn trying to remove her panties. At that point, but before her panties were removed, H.C. told Hollow Horn to stop, and he complied. Hollow Horn then left the tent without speaking. Although there were three other girls in the tent, H.C. testified that she did not call out for help or otherwise wake up the other girls because she was scared. As with R.R.A, H.C.'s fear prevented her from reporting this incident at that time.

After an offer of proof by the government, the district court, over Hollow Horn's objection, allowed H.C.'s mother, Laudine, to testify pursuant to Federal Rule of Evidence 413. Laudine testified that Hollow Horn raped her at a New Year's Eve party on the night of December 31, 1987 or early morning of January 1, 1988, when Laudine was 20 years old. Laudine testified that she became intoxicated at the party and passed out. When she came to, she found her pants at her ankles, her shirt pulled up, and Hollow Horn her first cousin having sex with her. Laudine testified that she told Hollow Horn to get off of her, and he moved back, pulled up his pants, and watched as she got dressed. . . . After Laudine's police report was filed, a tribal prosecution was commenced, but Laudine subsequently withdrew the complaint due to pressure from her mother. In withdrawing the complaint, Laudine did not recant her allegation. Nevertheless, after the complaint was withdrawn, Hollow Horn was not prosecuted for the alleged rape. Laudine further testified that she would not have consented to sex with Hollow Horn.

After the government rested, the defense called 12 witnesses, most of whom had been at the 1999 birthday party, including the other young girls at the party. The defense witnesses generally testified that they were unaware of any sexual contact between Hollow Horn and R.R.A. or H.C. Hollow Horn also took the stand. He testified that he had not had any sexual contact with either R.R.A. or H.C. and denied that he had gone to the tent site or Maurisa's grandmother's house on the night of the birthday party.

Hollow Horn's testimony confirmed that he had been at the same New Year's party as Laudine on December 31, 1987 and January 1, 1988, but he denied that he had sex or any sexual contact with Laudine.

The jury subsequently found Hollow Horn guilty on both counts of abusive sexual contact one count each relating to his contact with R.R.A. and H.C. On January 4, 2007, more than three months after Hollow Horn's conviction, but prior to his sentencing, Delores Curley, who had testified at the trial, sent a letter to defense counsel stating that she believed that R.R.A.'s parents had coached the girl's testimony, based on statements Curley claimed that she heard the girl's parents make to R.R.A. while they were all in the witness room prior to and after R.R.A.'s testimony. The district court postponed Hollow Horn's sentencing to allow the defense to investigate Curley's claim. Thereafter, Curley signed an affidavit in which she averred that before R.R.A.'s testimony, Curley overheard R.R.A.'s father ask the girl: "Remember what you're supposed to say?"; and that when R.R.A. returned from testifying, R.R.A.'s mother asked: "Did you say what we told you to say?"

Hollow Horn moved for a new trial based on the newly discovered evidence, and the district court conducted an evidentiary hearing. Curley testified at the hearing that she wrote the letter because she did not want Hollow Horn to be imprisoned based upon manufactured testimony. Curley admitted that although R.R.A. was the government's first witness and that Curley was the last witness, she did not inform counsel for either side or the court of the alleged coaching until over three months after Hollow Horn's conviction. Curley also acknowledged that her letter to defense counsel had been written at the behest of Hollow Horn's mother and that the letter was faxed to defense counsel by Hollow Horn's sister.

R.R.A.'s parents also testified at the evidentiary hearing. Her father denied making the alleged statements or any similar comments. He testified that he simply told R.R.A. to not be scared, but that he did not tell R.R.A. what to say and did not tell her to accuse Hollow Horn. The father also testified that he had not heard R.R.A.'s mother tell or suggest to R.R.A. what to say. R.R.A.'s mother also testified, and she likewise denied making the alleged statements or anything similar. The mother confirmed that the government had informed her and her husband that they could not talk to each other about the trial when they were in the witness room, and she denied that she did anything to interfere with Hollow Horn's right to a fair trial or that her dislike for Hollow Horn would cause her to do so.

The district court denied Hollow Horn's motion for a new trial. Subsequently, the district court sentenced Hollow Horn to 34 months' imprisonment on each count, with the sentences to run concurrently.

II. DISCUSSION

* * *

A. Admission of Rule 413 Evidence

As stated above, the district court, over Hollow Horn's objection, allowed H.C.'s mother, Laudine, to testify pursuant to Federal Rule of Evidence 413, that Hollow Horn had raped her in 1988. On appeal, Hollow Horn argues that the district court erred in admitting Laudine's testimony regarding his alleged rape of her. The district court admitted the evidence under Rules 413 and 403 and gave a limiting instruction to the jury. We review these evidentiary rulings by the district court for abuse of discretion.

"Evidence of prior bad acts is generally not admissible to prove a defendant's character or propensity to commit crime." *Gabe*, 237 F.3d at 959 (citing Fed. R. Evid. 404(b)). Congress, however, modified this rule in sex offense cases when it adopted Rules 413 and 414 of the Federal Rules of Evidence. *Id.* In sexual assault and child molestation cases, "evidence that the defendant committed a prior similar offense 'may be considered for its bearing on any matter to which it is relevant,' including the defendant's propensity to commit such offenses." *Id.* (citing Fed. R. Evid. 413(a), 414(a)). . . . If the evidence of the defendant's prior sexual offense is relevant, "the evidence is admissible unless its probative value is 'substantially outweighed' by one or more of the factors enumerated in Rule 403, including 'the danger of unfair prejudice.' " *Gabe*, 237 F.3d at 959 (citing *United States v. LeCompte*, 131 F.3d 767, 769 (8th Cir.1997)).

Federal Rule of Evidence 413(a) states: "In a criminal case in which the defendant is accused of an offense of sexual assault, evidence of the defendant's commission of another offense or offenses of sexual assault is admissible, and may be considered for its bearing on any matter to which it is relevant." The definition of an "offense of sexual assault" for purposes of Rule 413, includes, among other things: "contact, without consent, between any part of the defendant's body . . . and the genitals or anus of another person," as well as "an attempt . . . to engage in [such] conduct. . . ." Fed. R. Evid. 413(d). Laudine's testimony qualifies as Rule 413 evidence because it is evidence that Hollow Horn committed another offense of sexual assault. Hollow Horn was charged with abusive sexual contact, which undeniably meets the definition of an offense of sexual assault. But, as discussed above, to be admissible, the Rule 413 evidence must also be relevant and its probative value must not be substantially outweighed by the danger of unfair prejudice. *Gabe*, 237 F.3d at 959 ("If relevant, [Rule 413] evidence is admissible unless its probative value is 'substantially outweighed' by one or more of the factors enumerated in Rule 403, including 'the danger of unfair prejudice.' ").

The district court found that Hollow Horn's alleged rape of Laudine was relevant, and that its probative value outweighed the danger of unfair prejudice. Hollow Horn's alleged rape of Laudine occurred approximately 11 and a half years prior to the date of Hollow Horn's alleged abusive sexual contact with R.R.A. and H.C., and the alleged rape was of a 20 year old, not a child. Nonetheless, we agree with the district court that the evidence was relevant and probative. Both offenses involved sexual assaults of defenseless victims. The instant charges involve Hollow Horn's alleged sexual assault of sleeping minor victims, and the earlier alleged rape also involved an unconscious victim. Furthermore, Hollow Horn was related to all three alleged victims. Additionally, in all three instances, the accusers testified that once they realized what Hollow Horn was doing, they took action, either verbally or physically, to make him stop, and he did so. Thus, the district court did not abuse its discretion in ruling that the Rule 413 evidence was relevant.

We must next decide whether the probative value of Laudine's testimony was "substantially outweighed by its potential for unfair prejudice." *United States v. Withorn*, 204 F.3d 790, 794 (8th Cir. 2000). Laudine's testimony was undoubtedly prejudicial to Hollow Horn as evidence admitted under Rule 413 is very likely to be. Rule 403, however, "is concerned only with 'unfair prejudice, that is, an undue tendency to suggest decision on an improper basis.' " *Gabe*, 237 F.3d at 960 (quoting *United States v. Yellow*, 18 F.3d 1438, 1442 (8th Cir.1994)). Laudine's testimony is prejudicial to Hollow Horn for the same reason it is probative it tends to prove his propensity to commit sexual assaults on vulnerable female members of his family when presented with an opportunity to do so undetected. *See Gabe,* 237 F.3d at 960 (finding witness's testimony that defendant sexually molested her 20 years earlier admissible under Rule 414, stating that the "testimony is prejudicial . . . for the same reason it is probative it tends to prove his propensity to molest young children in his family when presented with an opportunity to do so undetected"). Because this specific type of propensity evidence is admissible under Rule 413, Hollow Horn has not shown that its prejudice was *unfair. See id.* (ruling that because Rule 414 evidence is admissible to prove propensity, the resulting prejudice from the admission of the Rule 414 evidence was not "*unfair* prejudice").

Although the prior sexual assault alleged against Hollow Horn was over 11 years prior to the alleged sexual offenses at issue here, "Congress expressly rejected imposing any time limit on prior sex offense evidence," when it enacted Rule 413. *Id.* (citing 140 CONG. REC. H8968 01, H8992 (daily ed. Aug. 21, 1994) (statement by Rep. Molinari) ("No time limit is imposed on the uncharged offenses for which evidence may be admitted; as a practical matter, evidence of other sex offenses by the defendant is often probative and properly admitted, notwithstanding very substantial lapses of time in relation to the charged offense or offenses.")). Further, we have previously held that a district court did not abuse its discretion in admitting Rule 414 evidence despite a 20 year lapse in time between the prior act and the current one. *See Gabe,* 237 F.3d at 960 (finding no abuse of discretion in district court's allowance under Rule 414 of witness's testimony that defendant, who was on trial for child molestation offenses, had molested her 20 years earlier). Additionally, despite the passage of time in this case, the district court also found Laudine's testimony to be credible.

"There is a strong legislative judgment that evidence of prior sexual offenses should ordinarily be admissible." *Crawford,* 413 F.3d at 876 (quoting *LeCompte,* 131 at 769). Moreover, the district court gave a limiting instruction thereby decreasing the danger that Hollow Horn was *unfairly* prejudiced by Laudine's testimony.[9] *See id.* ("Limiting instructions decrease the danger of unfair prejudice"). For all of these reasons, we hold that the district court did not abuse its discretion in allowing Laudine's testimony.

*   *   *

III. CONCLUSION

Accordingly, we affirm the judgment of the district court.

---

[9] After Laudine's direct examination at trial, but prior to her cross examination, the district court instructed the jury, stating:

> Ladies and gentlemen of the jury, . . . this is evidence that is received for a limited purpose only. Congress passed a rule that said that in cases of alleged sexual assaults that evidence of other alleged sexual assaults may be admissible in evidence.

> It's it doesn't mean that the Defendant is guilty of the crimes for which he's on charge here. But the jury can give this evidence plus the cross examination, of course, as much weight as you want to give it. And so that's the purpose of this evidence.

> Normally, as I said before, the fact that you were speeding five years ago doesn't mean that you were speeding yesterday or something of that nature, okay?

Trial Transcript 138:24 139:11.

NOTES AND QUESTIONS

(1) **Probative value.** In *Horn*, the victims of sexual molestation were under twelve years of age at the time of the charged sexual assaults. However, the Rule 413 evidence involved an alleged rape against a 20-year-old adult victim, not a child. Despite the disparity in age between the child victims and the adult rape victim, the court found that the prior sexual assault evidence was relevant and probative. Do you agree with the court's reasoning? *See United States v. Horn*, 523 F.3d at 888. Should the court require proof of substantial similarity between the uncharged prior sexual conduct and the charged sexual assault before admitting such evidence under Rule 413? In *United States v. Tail*, 459 F.3d 854 (8th Cir. 2006), the court held that defendant's prior conviction for second degree rape was properly admitted under Rule 413(d)(2) "because it involved the same victim and an act that occurred close in time and under circumstances similar to the crime charged." *Id.* at 858. *See also United States v. Seymour*, 468 F.3d 378, 385 (6th Cir. 2006) (finding a similarity between the uncharged and charged sexual assaults where all four alleged victims were part of defendant's extended family, and all four were allegedly assaulted on a bed after defendant arrived in an intoxicated state).

(2) **Unfair prejudice.** Evidence admitted under either Rule 413 or Rule 414 must be subjected to the balancing test in Rule 403. *See, e.g., United States v. Seymour*, 468 F.3d 378, 383–84 (6th Cir. 2006); *United States v. Benais*, 460 F.3d 1059, 1063 (8th Cir. 2006); *Seeley v. Chase*, 443 F.3d 1290, 1294–95 (10th Cir. 2006); *United States v. Crawford*, 413 F.3d 873, 875 (8th Cir. 2005); *United States v. LeMay*, 260 F.3d 1018, 1027 (9th Cir. 2001). Pursuant to Rule 403, evidence is admissible only where the probative value is not substantially outweighed by the potential for "unfair prejudice." Fed. R. Evid. 403. However, both Rules 413 and 414 permit evidence of prior uncharged sexual assaults to prove propensity. Thus, because this specific type of propensity evidence is admissible under Rules 413 and 414, prejudice resulting from the admission of such evidence, does note constitute *unfair* prejudice. *See United States v. Horn*, 523 F.3d 882, 888 (8th Cir. 2008); *United States v. Tail*, 459 F.3d 854, 858 (8th Cir. 2006); *United States v. Gabe*, 237 F.3d 954, 960 (8th Cir. 2001). One federal circuit holds that "[t]o require the exclusion of [Rule 413] evidence based on the asserted 'inflammatory nature' of sexual offenses would be at odds with the 'strong legislative judgment' in favor of admitting such evidence that Congress expressed in adopting Rule 413." *United States v. Tail*, 459 F.3d 854, 858 (8th Cir. 2006); *United States v. Medicine Horn*, 447 F.3d 620, 623 (9th Cir. 2006) (same); *United States v. LeCompte*, 131 F.3d 767, 770 (8th Cir. 1997) (same).

If evidence tending to prove the defendant's propensity to commit sexual assaults does not constitute unfair prejudice under Rule 403, what other factors would weigh in favor of exclusion of prior-sexual assault-evidence? Should evidence of uncharged sexual assaults be excluded if such evidence would tend to confuse the jury relating to the offenses charged in the case? What if the admission of such evidence would have triggered mini-trials concerning allegations of sexual abuse unrelated to the case? Finally, if the defendant would be forced to devote a significant amount of time and effort during trial refuting allegations of uncharged sex crimes, should evidence of prior sexual assaults be excluded?

(3) **Proximity in time.** In *Horn*, the alleged prior sexual assault occurred over 11 years prior to the child sexual molestation offenses charged in the case. In *United States v. Gabe*, 237 F.3d 954 (8th Cir. 2001), the Rule 414 evidence admitted at trial occurred 20 years prior to the offense of child sexual molestation alleged in the

indictment. In both cases, despite the passage of time, the Eighth Circuit found that the district court had not abused its discretion in admitting the evidence. Should a time limit be imposed on the admission of prior sex offense evidence?

(4) *Limiting instruction.* The court stated that the limiting instruction given to the jury decreased the danger that Horn would be unfairly prejudiced by Laudine's testimony. *United States v. Horn,* 523 F.3d at 889. *See also United States v. Tail,* 459 F.3d 854, 858 (8th Cir. 2006) ("Such cautionary instructions decrease any danger of unfair prejudice."); *United States v. Crawford,* 413 F.3d 873, 876 (9th Cir. 2005) (same). Do you agree? Is a limiting instruction likely to neutralize the risk of unfair prejudice resulting from testimony of prior uncharged sexual assaults, especially in a child-molestation case?

(6) When a defendant is on trial for child sexual molestation is Rule 414 the exclusive rule governing the admissibility of prior sexual assault evidence, and not the more general Rule 413? In other words, in cases involving child sexual molestation, does Rule 414 limit the admission of evidence of prior sexual offenses to those against *children,* and not adult victims, or should evidence of prior sexual assaults admissible under Fed. R. Evid. 413 also be admissible in child molestation cases? In *Horn,* the court rejected defendant's argument that Rule 414 is the exclusive rule governing the admissibility of prior sexual assault evidence in child molestation cases. Because Rule 414(c) expressly states that "[t]his rule shall not be construed to limit the admission or consideration of evidence under any other rule," the court found no incompatibility between the two rules. *Horn,* 523 F.3d at 888. *See also United States v. Seymour,* 468 F.3d 378, 385 (6th Cir. 2006) (same).

[3]   Reverse 404(b) — Evidence of Prior Bad Acts Offered by the Defendant to Prove Another Person Committed the Offense Charged

As previously discussed, the prohibition on the use of specific acts evidence codified in Rule 404(b) was intended to protect the accused from the unduly prejudicial effects of specific acts evidence offered by the prosecution. However, when the accused — rather than the prosecution — seeks to introduce evidence of the prior bad acts of a third person to prove that he committed the crime, should the same standard for barring admissibility of propensity evidence apply? Since the concerns of prejudice are not present when the accused seeks to introduce prior bad acts evidence of a third party to raise a reasonable doubt as to his culpability for the crime charged, should the courts apply a more relaxed standard for admissibility of "reverse Rule 404(b)" evidence? Rule 404(b) makes no distinction between prosecutorial and defensive use of specific acts evidence.[33]

---

[33] *See* Joan L. Larsen, *Of Propensity, Prejudice, and Plain Meaning: The Accused's Use of Exculpatory Specific Acts Evidence and the Need to Amend Rule 404(b),* 87 Nw. U. L. Rev. 651 (1993) (making the case for application of a more liberal standard for admissibility of Rule 404(b) evidence when offered by the defendant).

UNITED STATES v. STEVENS
935 F.2d 1380 (3d Cir. 1991)

BECKER CIRCUIT JUDGE.

. . . [H]aving been convicted of aggravated sexual assault and robbery both within the special territorial jurisdiction of the United States in violation of 18 U.S.C. §§ 2241 and 2111, [defendant] respectively mounts a multi-pronged challenge to his conviction. . . .

Stevens advances several evidentiary challenges. . . . He [] remonstrates about the district court's refusal to admit the testimony of one Tyrone Mitchell under Fed. R. Evid. 404(b), or more accurately, under a seldomly used subspecies of Rule 404(b) known as "reverse 404(b)." Stevens proffered Mitchell's testimony that he (Mitchell) was the victim of a crime which was so similar to the instant crime that the investigating officers believed that the same individual had committed both. Mitchell also would have testified that he, unlike the victims here, did not identify Stevens as his assailant. According to Stevens, Mitchell's testimony would have tended to show that some unknown third person had perpetrated both crimes, and that the victims had misidentified him as their attacker.

. . . We also think that Stevens should have been allowed to call Tyrone Mitchell as a witness and to introduce other evidence concerning the parallels between the Mitchell crime and the crime *sub judice.* When a defendant proffers "other crimes" evidence under Rule 404(b) there is no possibility of prejudice to the defendant; therefore the other crime need not be a "signature" crime. Instead, it only need be sufficiently similar to the crime at bar so that it is relevant under Fed. R. Evid. 401 and 402, and that its probative value is not substantially outweighed by Fed. R. Evid. 403 considerations. Applying this standard to the instant case, we are satisfied that the Mitchell crime clears the relatively low relevancy hurdle. . . .

At about 9:30 p.m. on April 15,1989, a damp and chilly Saturday evening, two white Air Force police officers, Jane Smith and Tony McCormack, were strolling back to their dormitories at Fort Dix, New Jersey, after having seen a movie at a nearby shopping mall. Because a light rain was falling, the officers decided to sit and chat under a glass-enclosed bus shelter.

A few minutes later, a black male, wearing a wool cap and a tan nylon jogging suit, entered the shelter, paused for a moment about ten feet away from the officers, and then asked them who they were. Both officers stood, but neither responded to the inquiry. The man approached the officers and, standing just a few feet away, reached his right hand into the small of his back and drew a small, silver handgun from his pants. Pointing the gun at McCormack's chest, the man demanded McCormack's wallet. McCormack handed over his wallet, which contained an unsigned $100 money order. To assure himself that McCormack was not withholding any cash, the man quickly frisked him; once satisfied he told McCormack to sit down.

. . . [The attacker forced Smith to perform fellatio on him.]

* * *

At the station, Smith and McCormack met Christine Amos, a military police investigator. . . . Before leaving to arrange for transportation to the hospital, Amos invited Smith and McCormack to take a look at the wanted board on the wall and to see if anyone resembled their assailant. This wanted board consisted of eight posters containing mostly composite sketches but also some photographs. McCormack rose, approached the wanted board, and almost immediately focused upon a photograph of the defendant, Richard Stevens. McCormack said: "[T]his is him. This is the man." Smith agreed that the photograph resembled their attacker, but thought that it made him appear a bit heavier. When Amos returned, Smith and McCormack informed her that they had identified a photograph of their assailant. Amos removed the poster of Stevens from the wall and then accompanied Smith to Walson Army Community Hospital.

. . . Smith was met by Agent Timothy Jackson of the United States Army Criminal Investigation Division ("CID"). Smith and Agent Jackson returned to the Fort Dix military police station where Smith recounted to Agent Jackson that evening's traumatic events. Agent Jackson also showed Smith an array of six photographs from which she identified Stevens as her attacker. While Smith was at the hospital, another CID agent interviewed McCormack and showed him the same photographic spread. Like Smith, he identified Stevens as the assailant.

. . . Based on the victims' identifications a federal grand jury sitting in the District of New Jersey returned a two-count indictment charging Stevens with aggravated sexual assault and robbery in the first degree, both within the special territorial jurisdiction of the United States. . . .

*   *   *

In January of 1990, Stevens was tried before a jury, which ultimately became deadlocked, so a mistrial was declared. Stevens was retried in March of 1990 on the same charges. Following a four-day trial, this jury convicted Stevens on both counts. Stevens thereafter filed a motion for judgment of acquittal, Fed. R. Crim. P. 29(c), which was denied by the district court. The court then sentenced Stevens to concurrent terms of 168 months of incarceration, together with concurrent terms of three years supervised release and special assessments totalling $100. This appeal followed, over which we have jurisdiction pursuant to 28 U.S.C. § 1291.

*   *   *

VI. THE REVERSE 404(b) ISSUE

To shore up his theory that Smith and McCormack misidentified him as the perpetrator, Stevens sought to introduce under Fed. R. Evid. 404(b) the testimony of Tyrone Mitchell, the victim of a similar crime at Fort Dix. Three days after Smith and McCormack were assaulted, Mitchell, a black man, was robbed at gunpoint by another black man who, according to Mitchell's description, resembled Smith's and McCormack's attacker. Unlike Smith and McCormack, however, Mitchell stated that Stevens was not his assailant. Stevens reasons that Mitchell's failure to identify him tends to establish that he did not assault Smith and McCormack. The syllogism goes as follows. In view of the many parallels between the two crimes, one person very likely committed both; and because Stevens was exonerated by Mitchell, a black man whose identification (or lack thereof) is arguably more reliable than that of the two white victims, Stevens was not that person. The critical question is, of course, one of degree of similarity.

The similarities between the Mitchell robbery and the Smith and McCormack robbery/sexual assault are significant. Both crimes: (1) took place within a few hundred yards of one another; (2) were armed robberies; (3) involved a handgun; (4) occurred between 9:30 p.m. and 10:30 p.m.; (5) were perpetrated on military personnel; and (6) involved a black assailant who was described similarly by his victims. Indeed, based on these similarities, the United States Army Criminal Investigation Division came to believe, initially, that the same person had committed both crimes. Agent Jackson, the CID officer assigned to investigate the instant crime, reported that:

> [T]his office is currently investigating a second Armed Robbery that occurred on the night of 18 Apr 89, at the NCO Academy. The suspect in the second armed robbery matches the physical description in the Armed Robbery/Forced Sodomy.

He further remarked:

> [The Mitchell] Robbery has a lot of similarities with . . . ([the Smith] and McCormack Robbery/Sodomy) excluding the sexual aspects. The subject, in both files, had a gun, stole wallets and rummaged through the victims pockets and were in the same areas on post.

Stevens, as a result, quickly became the CID's leading suspect in the Mitchell robbery, as well as the Smith and McCormack robbery/sexual assault. CID Agent Bronisz stated: "Dix CID is certain that STEVENS robbed MITCHELL of his ID." The FBI, cognizant of this fact, thus had Mitchell view Stevens in the same lineup and on the same day that Smith and McCormack viewed him. Mitchell, however, did not identify Stevens as his assailant.

An additional, and even more striking, parallel subsequently developed which made the similarities between the two crimes more difficult to dismiss as mere coincidence. Mitchell was robbed of various items, including his military identification card. This card later was used to cash two stolen checks at the Fort Meade exchange in Maryland. Significantly, McCormack's stolen money order, like Mitchell's identification, also ended up near Fort Meade: it was cashed by someone other than Stevens at the Odenton Pharmacy located across the street from Fort Meade. That the fruits of the Mitchell and McCormack robberies, which occurred within days of one another at Fort Dix, New Jersey, both surfaced near Fort Meade, Maryland, is undoubtedly probative that the same individual committed both offenses.

The analytical basis for Stevens's proffer of Mitchell's testimony was a rarely-used variant of Rule 404(b), known as "reverse 404(b)." In contrast to ordinary other crimes evidence, which is used to incriminate criminal defendants, "reverse 404(b)" evidence is utilized to exonerate defendants. As Wigmore's treatise points out:

> It should be noted that ["other crimes"] evidence may be also available to *negative the accused's guilt.* E.g., if A is charged with forgery and denies it, and if B can be shown to have done a series of similar forgeries connected by a plan, this plan of B is some evidence that B and not A committed the forgery charged. This mode of reasoning may become the most important when A alleges that he is a victim of *mistaken identification.*

2 Wigmore, Wigmore on Evidence § 304, at 252 (J. Chadbourn rev. ed. 1979) (emphases in original). Despite its rarity, several cases discuss "reverse 404(b)" evidence at length. We will discuss these cases *in extenso* in order to illuminate how "reverse 404(b)" evidence has been used in the past.

In *Commonwealth v. Murphy*, 282 Mass. 593, 185 N.E. 486 (1933), there was no evidence connecting the defendant to the offenses except for the victims' identifications. To offset these identifications, the defendant offered evidence of three similar crimes, one of which occurred while he was in custody. He also sought to introduce evidence that two of the victims of the other crimes had stated that he looked somewhat like (but was not) the assailant, and that the third victim had admitted to misidentifying him as the assailant. On appeal, the Supreme Judicial Court of Massachusetts reversed the trial court's exclusion of this evidence, emphasizing that the jury was entitled to consider it in evaluating the victims' identifications: "No one we think will deny that if the evidence offered is the truth it well might shake confidence in the identifications upon which alone this conviction rests." *Id.* at 596–597.

In *State v. Bock*, 229 Minn. 449, 39 N.W.2d 887 (1949), the defendant, who was convicted of uttering a forged check, appealed from the trial court's refusal to admit evidence that checks identical to that which he allegedly passed were negotiated on the same day and in a like manner by someone else. The Supreme Court of Minnesota reversed, holding that:

> [The defendant] should . . . have the right to show that crimes of a similar nature have been committed by some other person when the acts of such other person are so closely connected in point of time and method of operation as to cast doubt upon the identification of the defendant as the person who committed the crime charged against him. *Id.* at 458.

Likewise, the defendant in *Holt v. United States*, 342 F.2d 163 (5th Cir. 1965), proffered "reverse 404(b)" evidence to bolster his defense of misidentification. More specifically, he attempted to introduce evidence that he had been misidentified twice before as the perpetrator of virtually identical offenses. *Id.* at 164–65. The district court excluded this evidence on relevancy grounds, but the Fifth Circuit reversed, noting that the proffered evidence tended to support defendant's assertions that another man who resembled him had committed the identical crime, and that he had been misidentified. *Id.* at 166. In these circumstances, the court stated, the evidence was relevant and of substantial probative value. The jury should have been allowed to consider it on the question of identity. . . . *Id.*

Two New Jersey cases are also helpful. In *State v. Garfole*, 76 N.J. 445, 388 A.2d 587 (1978), the defendant, who was charged with sexually molesting two children, sought to introduce evidence that he had been indicted on charges arising out of five similar episodes; that the charges arising out of four of those episodes had been dismissed; and that he had an alibi for all but two of the episodes. . . . The trial court rejected this proffer, stating that it was irrelevant to the specific charge at issue.

The New Jersey Supreme Court disagreed, noting that the evidence clearly had some relevance to the case. . . . The Court then turned to the question whether the other crimes were sufficiently relevant (i.e., similar) to outweigh countervailing considerations such as undue consumption of time and confusion of the issues. The Court observed, in this regard, that the trial court had imposed on the defendant the same standard of similarity that would have applied if the State had offered the evidence, in essence requiring that the other crimes be so distinctive as to constitute "signature" crimes. This, the Court held, was error:

> We are of the view . . . that a lower standard of degree of similarity of offenses may justly be required of a defendant using other-crime evidence defensively than is exacted from the State when such evidence is used incriminatorily. . . . [O]ther-crimes evidence submitted by the prosecution has the distinct capacity of prejudicing the accused. . . . Therefore a fairly rigid standard of similarity may be required of the State if its effort is to establish the

existence of a common offender by the mere similarity of the offenses. But *when the defendant is offering that kind of proof exculpatorily, prejudice to the defendant is no longer a factor, and simple relevance to guilt or innocence should suffice as the standard of admissibility*, since ordinarily, and subject to rules of competency, an accused is entitled to advance in his defense any evidence which may rationally tend to refute his guilt or buttress his innocence of the charge made.

Id. at 452–53 (emphasis added) (footnote and citation omitted). The Court thus instructed the trial court to rebalance the probative value of the evidence against the countervailing considerations, keeping in mind that prejudice to the defendant is not a factor when the defendant offers the other crimes evidence.

The Superior Court of New Jersey explored this same issue in *State v. Williams*, 214 N.J. Super. 12, 518 A.2d 234 (1986), wherein the defendant appealed his conviction for attempted murder on the ground that the trial court improperly had excluded his "reverse 404(b)" proffer. The victim, who ultimately identified the defendant (her ex-boyfriend) as the perpetrator, was grabbed from behind, told not to scream, and (after a brief struggle) stabbed nine times. She also stated that her attacker had "pull[ed] on her clothes" prompting the investigating officer to report the attack as a possible rape attempt. . . . At trial, the defendant sought to adduce evidence of two similar crimes committed at the same time of day and at the same location by an individual who lived nearby. In both of the other crimes, the perpetrator grabbed his victim from behind, threatened her with a knife, and raped her; one of the victims was stabbed eight times following the rape.

In refusing to admit this evidence, the trial court stated that it would unduly confuse the jury, and that the other crimes were not sufficiently similar to outweigh the potential confusion. On appeal, the Superior Court reversed, concluding that the parallels between the three crimes satisfied the diminished standard of similarity articulated in *Garfole*:

All three incidents occurred within a block of [the perpetrator's] home in the early hours of the morning. [The perpetrator] committed one offense before the [instant] attack and went on to commit one after it. All three victims were grabbed suddenly and threatened. All incidents involved the use of a knife. In one case the victim was stabbed eight times, in this case nine times. In two cases the victim was actually raped and in this case there was evidence from which a sexual element could be inferred.

Id. at 21. Had the trial court admitted this evidence, the Superior Court noted, it would have shown that someone else had committed similar crimes in the same area and at about the same time, which, in turn, would have undercut the persuasiveness of the victim's identification.

The precise rationale for the district court's exclusion of Stevens's "reverse 404(b)" evidence is difficult to glean from the record. It appears that the court barred the evidence on relevancy grounds, holding that the Mitchell robbery was a "separate offense . . . not directly related or tied . . . to this defendant."

The government defends the district court's exclusion by asserting that a defendant may avail himself of Rule 404(b) in only three "constrained" circumstances, none of which apply to the instant case. First, the government submits, the defense may introduce evidence that the government induced others to commit crimes in order to show that the defendant was induced to commit the charged offense. *See United States v. Rodriguez*, 917 F.2d 1286, 1289–91 (11th Cir. 1990). This usage obviously has no bearing on Stevens's case. Second, the government argues, Rule 404(b) permits a defendant to introduce evidence that another person committed a similar crime, and that he (the defendant) was misidentified as the perpetrator of that similar crime. *Holt* and *Murphy*, the government contends, are of examples of this line of cases, which, the government asserts, is unavailable to Stevens because Mitchell never misidentified him as the assailant. Finally, the government states, defendants may invoke Rule 404(b) to admit evidence of other crimes "where those other crimes were sufficiently numerous and similar in their execution as to form a clear pattern." Appellee's Br. at 28. This is the so-called "signature" crime exception. The government maintains that this use, which supposedly is typified by *Bock* and *Garfole*, is also unavailable to Stevens, because Stevens has proffered evidence of only one other crime, and because that crime was dissimilar in that there was no sexual assault.

Based on our survey of the case law, we believe that the district court imposed too stringent a standard of similarity on Stevens, and that the government has unnecessarily compartmentalized the permissible uses of "reverse 404(b)" evidence. "It is well established that a defendant may use similar 'other crimes' evidence defensively if in reason it tends alone or with other evidence to negate his guilt of the crime charged against him." *Williams*, 214 N.J. Super. at 20. In our view, the most persuasive treatment of "reverse 404(b)" evidence is found in *Garfole, see supra* at 1402–03, wherein the New Jersey Supreme Court observed that a lower standard of similarity should govern "reverse 404(b)" evidence because prejudice to the defendant is not a factor. We agree with the reasoning of *Garfole* and with its holding that the admissibility of "reverse 404(b)" evidence depends on a straightforward balancing of the evidence's probative value against considerations such as undue waste of time and confusion of the issues. Recasting this standard in terms of the Federal Rules of Evidence, we therefore conclude that a defendant may introduce "reverse 404(b)" evidence so long as its probative value under Rule 401 is not substantially outweighed by Rule 403 considerations.

Given the flexible contours of the above equation, we reject the government's attempt to impose hard and fast preconditions on the admission of "reverse 404(b)" evidence. More specifically, the defendant, in order to introduce other crimes evidence, need not show that there has been more than one similar crime, that he has been misidentified as the assailant in a similar crime, or that the other crime was sufficiently similar to be called a "signature" crime. These criteria, although relevant to measuring the probative value of the defendant's proffer, should not be erected as absolute barriers to its admission. Rather, a defendant must demonstrate that the "reverse 404(b)" evidence has a tendency to negate his guilt, and that it passes the Rule 403 balancing test.

* * *

The similarities between the Mitchell robbery and the Smith and McCormack robbery/sexual assault are demonstrated amply, in our view, by the facts that the CID was convinced that the same person had committed both crimes, and that the fruits of both robberies (i.e., McCormack's money order and Mitchell's military identification) ended up in Fort Meade. That the Mitchell robbery lacked a sexual element, we think, is not fatal to Stevens's proffer, because Mitchell, unlike McCormack, did not have a female companion. While we readily concede that the two attacks are by no means "signature" crimes, this is simply not the test. All that is necessary is that the evidence satisfy the relevancy standard of Rule 401. Having determined that Stevens's "reverse

404(b)" proffer was relevant under Rule 401 (i.e., it had a tendency to make Stevens's guilt less probable), we turn now to the countervailing Rule 403 considerations.

Under the circumstances of this case, the potential for waste of time or for misleading the jury, if the "reverse 404(b)" evidence were admitted, was minimal. Although the government objected to Mitchell's testimony, it agreed to stipulate to all of the essential facts regarding the Mitchell robbery in the event that his testimony were admitted. Stevens maintains that, as a result of this stipulation, Mitchell would have been a "fifteen-minute" witness, who simply would have testified regarding the details of the robbery and his viewing of the lineup. In addition, Stevens probably would have asked CID Agent Jackson and FBI Agent Maxwell some questions on cross-examination about the similarities between the Mitchell robbery and the Smith and McCormack robbery/ sexual assault and about the government's initial suspicion that Stevens had robbed Mitchell.

Thus, even if Stevens's estimate of "fifteen-minutes" was overly optimistic, there was no appreciable risk that Stevens's presentation of "reverse 404(b)" evidence would have degenerated into a mini-trial about whether or not Stevens had robbed Mitchell. Nor was there any real danger that Stevens's portrayal of the parallels between the two crimes would have obstructed the orderly progress of the trial or would have distracted the jurors' attention from the real issues in this case. The government, in fact, does not dispute seriously these points. The thrust of its challenge to Stevens's reverse 404(b) evidence was that it did not pass muster under Rule 401, not Rule 403. We thus conclude that the probative value of the Mitchell robbery was not substantially outweighed by the prospect of undue delay or confusion of the issues.

*   *   *

VIII. CONCLUSION

We conclude that the district court erred . . . by excluding evidence about the similarities between the Mitchell robbery and the Smith and McCormack robbery/ sexual assault. Because these errors were not harmless, the judgment of sentence will be reversed and the case remanded for a new trial.

NOTES AND QUESTIONS

1. What is the test for the admissibility of "reverse 404(b)" evidence? What factors should be considered in determining admissibility of such evidence?

2. For a general discussion of "reverse 404(b)" and the need to amend Fed. R. Evid. 404(b) to allow greater use as a "shield" by the defendant, see Joan L. Larsen, *Of Propensity, Prejudice, and Plain Meaning: The Accused's Use of Exculpatory Specific Acts Evidence and the Need to Amend Rule 404(b)*, 87 Nw. U. L. Rev. 651 (1993).

PROBLEM

Problem 6-4. *Nondistinctive Crimes Under Reverse 404(b).* The police pulled over a vehicle for operating without functioning headlights. The defendant was the passenger in the vehicle driven by Jim Miller's girlfriend. Upon investigation, the police learned that the defendant had a previous felony conviction and that the license plates were not registered to the stopped vehicle. They asked the driver and the defendant to exit the vehicle. The police patted the defendant down and saw that he was wearing an empty shoulder holster. He denied having a weapon, explaining that he was not permitted to carry one because of his prior felony conviction. A search of the vehicle turned up a fully loaded.44 caliber Sturm Ruger revolver under the passenger seat where the defendant had been seated.

The vehicle the defendant had been riding in belonged to Jim Miller. The police determined that this vehicle was stolen and an arrest warrant was issued against Jim Miller. At the time of Miller's arrest, he was driving another stolen vehicle. In searching the second vehicle, the police found a handgun under the driver's side seat.

In the defendant's trial for felon in possession of a firearm, the defendant sought to introduce the evidence of Miller's arrest and evidence of the gun being found in the second vehicle under Fed. R. Evid. 404(b). The defendant argued that this evidence established that the identity of the person who hid the gun under the defendant's seat was Miller, who had possession of and access to both vehicles. The government countered that hiding a weapon under a car seat was not a distinctive crime and, therefore, could not be used to establish identity. Should the court admit the Miller arrest evidence under the identity exception to Rule 404(b)? *See United States v. Spencer*, 1 F.3d 742 (9th Cir. 1992).

C. PROPER USE OF THE VICTIM'S CHARACTER

[1] Evidence of a Pertinent Trait of Victim's Character Offered by the Accused — Fed. R. Evid. 404(a)(2)

UNITED STATES v. KEISER
57 F.3d 847 (9th Cir. 1995)

CYNTHIA HOLCOMB HALL, CIRCUIT JUDGE.

Ronald Keiser shot Victor Romero, paralyzing him from the waist down. The shooting occurred inside the boundaries of Fort Peck Indian Reservation in Montana. Keiser was indicted and convicted of violating 18 U.S.C. § 113(f) (assault resulting in serious bodily injury). He is currently serving a prison term of 71 months. He raises on appeal two claims regarding his conviction: (1) that the district court's instruction on self-defense and defense of another was not appropriate under the facts of this case; and (2) that the district court improperly excluded testimony regarding an incident outside the courtroom at trial that would have revealed the victim's violent character. He does not challenge his sentence. . . . We affirm.

The regrettable events giving rise to this prosecution occurred early in the morning of December 19, 1992, in Wolf Point, Montana. A group of people gathered at a home across the street from the home of the defendant, Ronald Keiser. The gathering was raucous. Members of the group had been drinking at various bars and the drinking apparently was continuing at the after-hours party.

Keiser went across the street to complain about the party. Testimony regarding the details of what happened next is conflicting, but it appears that several arguments ensued. Keiser may have slapped a woman; a scuffle began; a guest tried to throw Keiser out of the house; Keiser pulled a chunk of hair out of the head of one of the guests.

Keiser then returned home and was quite upset. His girlfriend was unable to calm him down, so she called the defendant's brother, Randy Keiser, to come over. Randy came and was successful in calming the defendant down. Randy then left the defendant's house and returned to his pickup truck, which was parked on the street between the two houses.

At around the same time as Randy was leaving, however, Victor Romero, the brother of the girl whom the defendant allegedly slapped, arrived at the house across the street. Angered that someone had slapped his sister, Romero set off across the street with two companions. En route, they encountered Randy, the brother of the defendant, sitting in his pickup truck as it warmed up. Romero saw Randy in the truck and, thinking it was Randy who had slapped his sister, began hitting and shoving Randy, who was still sitting in the driver's seat of his truck.

The defendant watched these events from inside his house. He testified that he saw one of the two men who were with Romero remove a gun from the back of a parked Ford Escort station wagon, place it in the back of his pants, and head in Randy's direction. He therefore feared the three men were about to kill his brother. Ronald retrieved a rifle from his bedroom. When he saw what he thought was a gun being used in the assault on his brother, he shot at the people by the truck, hitting Romero.

The bullet passed through Romero's kidney, colon, and small intestine, and lodged in his spine. Romero is now paralyzed from the waist down, and uses a wheelchair and a colostomy bag.

Keiser was arrested four days later and indicted on the charge of violating 18 U.S.C. § 113(f). His theory at trial was that he had acted in defense of his brother, who he reasonably believed was in danger because of the assault by three armed and angry men.

During the second day of trial, the defense called the defendant's brother, Randy Keiser. Defense counsel began to ask Randy about an incident that had occurred the day prior in the lobby outside the courtroom. The prosecutor objected to the line of questioning as irrelevant and the court sustained the objection.

Counsel then approached the bench and defense counsel made an offer of proof:

> My purpose in this was not — yesterday afternoon Victor Romero [the victim] was with his family and friends in the presence of court security. He looked at this witness and he said words to the effect, there he is, that's the f_____'s brother. And I want you to remember his face, remember his face. . . . And he had to be taken out of there, he was screaming. I think that's indicative of he wanted to get revenge, it is indicative of his actions on the night in question. This is not the sympathetic individual that comes in here and says he was very calm and collected. And I think it is indicative of his state of mind now and his state of mind at the time. I think it is relevant.

Tr. of May 11, 1993, at 271–72. The court again sustained the objection. Keiser was convicted on May 11, 1993 and is incarcerated for a term of 71 months.

* * *

III.

Keiser's only defense in this case was that he was justified in shooting into the muster because he was acting in defense of his brother, whom Romero was assaulting at the time of the shooting. Keiser sought to introduce testimony about this incident outside the courtroom in order to bolster his self-defense claim. He argues on appeal that the incident "tend[s] to show the character of Mr. Romero for anger and violence." Admission of Randy Keiser's testimony regarding the incident would have "show[n] the jury the true nature of the 'victim.' " The government responds that the testimony "would have added absolutely nothing material to the trial," because "the appellant did not personally know the victim, nor did he therefore have personal knowledge of the victim[']s character." We think that neither party has properly addressed the legal questions this proffered testimony raises.

The question whether defendants may introduce specific violent or aggressive acts of the victim in order to bolster a claim of self-defense has begotten a host of written opinions, both in the federal courts and in state courts interpreting analogies to the Federal Rules of Evidence. The analytic approaches, as well as the answers these approaches have yielded, are myriad. Some courts have reasoned that a victim's violent nature is an essential element of a claim of self-defense and that defendants should therefore be allowed to introduce evidence of specific acts in order to prove that character.[7] Some have concluded that the victim's violent nature is not essential to the claim of self-defense, and therefore limit the defendant to the use of reputation or opinion evidence to show the victim's character for violence.[8] Others, on the other hand, have refused to admit specific acts on the rationale that their use would be circumstantial rather than direct.[9] Others still admit specific acts under the theory that the acts themselves bear on the defendant's state of mind and the reasonableness of his use of force in self-defense.[10] At least one court admits specific acts under the theory that the victim's character is an essential element of self-defense, but limits the acts to those of which the defendant had personal knowledge at the time of the crime,[11] and another admits specific acts as character evidence because the acts are essential to determining the defendant's state of mind.[12] This Court has not yet addressed this question.

Our task, therefore, is not simple. It is made significantly easier, however, by clarification of what this case is not about. Keiser makes no claim on appeal that the

---

[7] *E.g., Gottschalk v. State*, 881 P.2d 1139, 1143 (Alaska Ct. App. 1994); *Thompson v. State*, 306 Ark. 193, 813 S.W.2d 249, 251 (1991); *State v. Dunson*, 433 N.W.2d 676, 681 (Iowa 1988); *Gonzales v. State*, 838 S.W.2d 848, 859 (Tex. Ct. App. 1992); *State v. Koon*, 190 W. Va. 632, 440 S.E.2d 442, 450 (1993).

[8] *E.g., State v. Smith*, 222 Conn. 1, 608 A.2d 63, 72 (1992) (applying state common law); *State v. Alexander*, 52 Wash. App. 897, 765 P.2d 321, 324 (1988); *cf. United States v. Piche*, 981 F.2d 706, 713 (4th Cir. 1992) (excluding evidence of specific acts of racial violence because the victim's tendency to engage in racial violence is not an essential element of any defense).

[9] *E.g., United States v. Talamante*, 981 F.2d 1153, 1156 (10th Cir. 1992) ("use of evidence of a victim's violent character to prove that the victim was the aggressor is circumstantial use of character evidence"); *Bingham v. Baker*, 28 Fed. R. Evid. Serv. (Callaghan) 267, 272, 1989 WL 87863 (8th Cir. 1989) (per curiam) ("[The victim's] violent temper was only relevant as circumstantial evidence of his conduct, that is, as evidence that [the victim] acted in conformity therewith."); *Perrin v. Anderson*, 784 F.2d 1040, 1045 (10th Cir. 1986).

[10] *E.g., State v. Cano*, 154 Ariz. 447, 449, 743 P.2d 956, 958 (Ariz. App. 1987); *State v. Bland*, 337 N.W.2d 378, 383 (Minn. 1983); *State v. Duncan*, 111 N.M. 354, 356, 805 P.2d 621, 623 (1991); *State v. Latham*, 519 N.W.2d 68, 71 (S.D. 1994).

[11] *People v. Boles*, 127 Mich. App. 759, 339 N.W.2d 249, 252 (1983).

[12] *Green v. State*, 614 So. 2d 926, 934 (Miss. 1992).

incident outside the courtroom — which obviously occurred after the shooting — was relevant to his state of mind at the time of the shooting or the reasonableness of his belief that force in self-defense was necessary. Thus, we need not, and do not, reach the question whether specific acts are admissible to bolster the assertion that the defendant's belief in the need for force was reasonable. Instead, we need only decide whether testimony regarding this incident should have been admitted *as character evidence*, i.e., as evidence from which the jury could infer that the victim, at the time of the shooting, was likely to be behaving in accordance with his violent character.

Put another way, introduction of specific acts as victim character evidence would support the proposition that the victim was in fact using unlawful force, whereas introduction of specific acts to prove the defendant's state of mind would support the proposition that the defendant's belief that force was necessary was reasonable. These two propositions are separate elements of the defense of self-defense or defense of another. . . .

A. Relevance of the Excluded Testimony

The Federal Rules of Evidence provide an exception to the general rule against character evidence as propensity evidence in the case of "[e]vidence of a pertinent trait of character of the victim of the crime offered by an accused." Fed. R. Evid. 404(a)(2). The advisory committee's note to this rule indicates that a victim's "violent disposition" is exactly the sort of evidence this rule was intended to encompass. *See* Fed. R. Evid. 404 advisory committee's note ("Illustrations are: evidence of a violent disposition to prove that the person was the aggressor in an affray. . . .").

Thus, whether Romero is a violent and angry person is certainly relevant to the defendant's claim that he was acting in defense of his brother. Romero's violent character makes it more likely that his behavior on the night of the shooting was violent — which supports the defendant's defense that he was shooting to protect his brother — than it would be if Romero were peaceable.

The government, however, argues that because the incident occurred after the shooting, it has no bearing on whether the defendant acted reasonably at the time of the shooting. It reasons that, at the time of the shooting, the defendant did not "have personal knowledge of the victim[']s character."

This argument misapprehends the purpose of presenting testimony regarding the victim's character. Rule 404(a)(2) provides one of the few instances in which character evidence is admissible to allow the jury to infer that a person acted on a specific occasion in conformity with his character. The rule does not contemplate that the character evidence will somehow reveal the defendant's state of mind at the time he acted in self-defense.

The structure of the rule supports this conclusion. Section 404(a) establishes the general prohibition: "Evidence of a person's character or a trait of his character is not admissible *for the purpose of proving that he acted in conformity therewith on a particular occasion*. . . ." Fed. R. Evid. 404(a) (emphasis added). The rule then provides three exceptions to the prohibition, one of which is the exception for character of the victim provided in section 404(a)(2). The fact that section 404(a)(2) is an exception to the rule against introducing character evidence to imply that a person acted in conformity with that character on a particular occasion suggests that the very purpose of victim character evidence is to suggest to the jury that the victim did indeed act in conformity with his violent character at the time of the alleged crime against him. The purpose is not to provide insight into the reasonableness of the thought processes of the defendant. Thus, whether the defendant knew of the victim's character at the time of the crime has no bearing on whether victim character evidence should come in under section 404(a)(2). . . .

Furthermore, a smattering of federal cases indirectly supports the contention that the relevance of victim character in an assault case stems from its making it more likely that the victim was in fact using unlawful force — a proposition that, if true, would give rise to the defendant's justified use of force — rather than its bearing on the defendant's state of mind. These cases show that whether the defendant knew of the victim's character does not affect the relevance of the evidence. For instance, the Court of Appeals for the Tenth Circuit, in *Perrin v. Anderson*, 784 F.2d 1040 (10th Cir. 1986), reasoned that testimony of nondefendants regarding the violent nature of the victim was relevant to the claim of self-defense. *Id.* at 1045. Such testimony would only be relevant to allow the jury to infer that the victim was also acting violently on the occasion in question; it would be entirely irrelevant to whether the defendants actually knew of the victim's violent nature.[15]

These cases suggest a common understanding in the federal courts that "personal knowledge" of the victim's propensity for violence is simply not a prerequisite for admission of victim character evidence under Rule 404(a)(2). We therefore hold that Romero's violent nature is relevant to Keiser's theory of defense of his brother.

B. Form of the Excluded Testimony

Despite its relevance, the testimony regarding the altercation outside the courtroom was properly excluded. Under the Federal Rules of Evidence, only reputation or opinion evidence is proper to show that the victim of an assault had a propensity toward violence. The excluded testimony, on the other hand, would have constituted paradigmatic "specific act" evidence.

After a court determines that character evidence is admissible under Rule 404, it must next turn to Rule 405 to determine what form that evidence may take. *See United States v. Talamante*, 981 F.2d 1153, 1156 (10th Cir. 1992) (" Federal Rule of Evidence 405 establishes the permissible methods of proving character under Rule 404(a)(2).") (footnote omitted), *cert. denied*, 113 S. Ct. 1876 (1993). Rule 405 provides:

Methods of Proving Character

(a) Reputation or opinion

In all cases in which evidence of character or a trait of character of a person is admissible, proof may be made by testimony as to reputation or by testimony in the form of an opinion. . . .

(b) Specific instances of conduct

---

[15] *But see Boles*, 339 N.W.2d at 252 ("[U]nless the defendant could show that he knew of that incident or that it was directly connected with the homicide, the evidence should be excluded."); *Latham*, 519 N.W.2d at 71 ("[O]nly specific instances of conduct known to [the defendant] at the time of the incident in question were relevant."); *State v. Woodson*, 181 W. Va. 325, 382 S.E.2d 519, 524 n.5 (1989) ("We expressly overrule any suggestion . . . that Rule 405(b) . . . permits the defendant to introduce specific acts of violence by the victim against third parties even though he has no knowledge of them at the time he claimed to have acted in self-defense.").

In cases in which character or a trait of character of a person is an essential element of a charge, claim, or defense, proof may also be made of specific instances of that person's conduct.

Fed. R. Evid. 405.

No published opinion of this Court has addressed whether Rule 405(b) authorizes a defendant claiming self-defense to introduce specific acts demonstrating his victim's propensity for violence. We conclude, however, that the language of the rule, the teaching of out-of-Circuit authority, and the theory supporting admission of victim character evidence all lead to the conclusion that victim character evidence introduced to support a claim of self-defense or defense of another should be limited to reputation or opinion evidence.

The language of the rule states in straightforward manner that evidence of specific instances of conduct may only be made when a person's character is "an essential element of a . . . defense." Some courts have analyzed particular efforts to introduce specific act evidence to determine whether character is, as the rule states, an "essential element." *E.g.,* [*United States v. Piche*, 981 F.2d 706, 713 (4th Cir. 1992)] ("Because the evidence of character that [the defendant] attempts to admit is not an essential element of a charge, claim, or defense, however, proof of character is limited to reputation or opinion evidence in accord with Rule 405(a)."). Not all courts have conducted their analyses in strict conformity with this language, however. Other courts, for instance, have analyzed the question using different terminology, concluding that whether proof of specific instances of conduct is admissible depends upon whether the use of character evidence is "circumstantial" or "direct." *E.g., Talamante*, 981 F.2d at 1156 ("When character is used circumstantially to create an inference that a person acted in conformity with his or her character, Rule 405 allows proof of character only by reputation and opinion.").

This lack of uniformity in methodology appears to stem from some courts' reliance on language in the advisory committee's note to Rule 404, which rule governs when character evidence is admissible in the first instance. The note provides an overview of the situations in which character evidence may have relevance, and observes that character may arise in two fundamentally different ways. Character may be "in issue," as when a statute specifies the victim's chastity as an element of the crime of seduction, or when the defense to a defamation action is the truth of the allegedly defamatory statement. On the other hand, character may have relevance only circumstantially, in order to suggest an inference that a person acted in conformity with his character on a specific occasion. Fed. R. Evid. 404 Advisory Committee's Notes.

In contrast to these other courts, we find that reliance on the advisory committee's note to Rule 404 — which merely establishes a nomenclature for discussing the ways in which "character" might have relevance — in order to determine what form evidence may take under Rule 405 is misguided. The note to Rule 404 begins with the assertion that "[t]his subdivision [section 404(a)] deals with the basic question whether character evidence should be admitted." The note to Rule 405, on the other hand, begins by clarifying that Rule 405 "deals only with allowable methods of proving character, not with the admissibility of character evidence, which is covered in Rule 404." These notes deal with separate questions, as do the evidence rules they explain.

Thus, the distinction that the Rule 404 note establishes between character "in issue" and character evidence as "circumstantial" does not guide our inquiry here. Instead, we conduct our Rule 405 inquiry according to the terms of the Rule itself, which requires courts to determine whether the character a party seeks to prove constitutes "an essential element of a charge, claim, or defense." Fed. R. Evid. 405(b). The relevant question should be: would proof, or failure of proof, of the character trait by itself actually satisfy an element of the charge, claim, or defense? If not, then character is not essential and evidence should be limited to opinion or reputation. . . .

Our object in this case, therefore, is to determine whether Romero's violent character is an "essential element" of Keiser's defense. We conclude, by reference to the model instruction we expressly approved in Part II, that Romero's violent character does not constitute an essential element of Keiser's claim that the shooting was justified because he was acting in defense of his brother. Even had Keiser proven that Romero is a violent person, the jury would still have been free to decide that Romero was not using or about to use unlawful force, or that the force Romero was using was not likely to cause death or great bodily harm, or that Keiser did not reasonably believe force was necessary, or that he used more force than appeared reasonably necessary. On the other hand, a successful defense in no way depended on Keiser's being able to show that the Romero has a propensity toward violence. A defendant could, for example, successfully assert a claim of self-defense against an avowed pacifist, so long as the jury agrees that the defendant reasonably believed unlawful force was about to be used against him. Thus, even though relevant, Romero's character is not an essential element of Keiser's defense. *Cf.* [*State v. Alexander,* 765 P.2d 321, 324 (Wash. App. 1988)] (holding that character is not an essential element of self-defense because "[t]he self-defense issue could be resolved without any evidence of, or reliance upon, a character trait of [the victim] or the defendant").[21]

Thus, exclusion of the proffered testimony regarding the verbal altercation outside the courtroom was proper because the victim's violent nature is not essential to a successful claim of self-defense. Keiser's claim of self-defense neither rises nor falls on his success in proving that Romero has a penchant for violent outbursts. Thus, Keiser had no right to introduce evidence of the incident outside the courtroom to buttress his defense. We therefore affirm the district court's exclusion of the testimony. . . . Keiser's conviction is

Affirmed.

NOTES AND QUESTIONS

1. In *Keiser,* the court observed that the question of whether a defendant may introduce specific violent acts of the victim in order to bolster a claim of self-defense has divided the courts. The court remarked: "The analytic approaches, as well as the answers these approaches have yielded, are myriad." *Keiser,* 57 F.3d at 854. The *Keiser* court then proceeded to outline the various approaches taken:

> Some courts have reasoned that a victim's violent nature is an essential element of a claim of self-defense and that defendants should therefore be allowed to introduce evidence of specific acts in order to prove that character. Some have concluded that the victim's violent nature is not essential to the claim of self-defense, and therefore limit the defendant to the use of reputation or

---

[21] *But see Thompson,* 813 S.W.2d at 251 ("as an essential element of her defense, appellant clearly had the right to introduce specific instances of [the victim's] violent character"); *Boles,* 339 N.W.2d at 252 (same); *Gonzales,* 838 S.W.2d at 859 ("A victim's aggressive character is an essential element of the defense of self-defense.").

opinion evidence to show the victim's character for violence. Others, on the other hand, have refused to admit specific acts on the rationale that their use would be circumstantial rather than direct. Others still admit specific acts under the theory that the acts themselves bear on the defendant's state of mind and the reasonableness of his use of force in self-defense. At least one court admits specific acts under the theory that the victim's character is an essential element of self-defense, but limits the acts to those of which the defendant had personal knowledge at the time of the crime, and another admits specific acts as character evidence because the acts are essential to determining the defendant's state of mind.

Id. at 852–53. The admissibility of specific instances of conduct by the victim to prove "violent disposition" raises two important issues. First, in the absence of personal knowledge of the victim's violent propensity, is the evidence relevant? The answer to this question implicates Rules 402, 403, and 404. Second, if deemed relevant, what is the method of proof? In other words, is proof limited to testimony in the form of reputation or opinion, or may the defendant introduce evidence of specific instances of conduct? This question is determined by Rule 405, and the answer turns on whether the character or trait of character of a person is an "essential element of a charge, claim, or defense." Fed. R. Evid. 405. The courts are divided on this issue as well. *See Keiser*, 57 F.3d at 855.

2. On the question of whether "personal knowledge" of the victim's propensity for violence is a prerequisite for admission of victim character evidence under Rule 404(a)(2), the *Keiser* court responded in the negative. The court posited:

[W]hether Romero (victim) is a violent and angry person is certainly relevant to the defendant's claim that he was acting in defense of his brother. Romero's violent character makes it more likely that this behavior on the night of the shooting was violent — which supports the defendant's defense that he was shooting to protect his brother — than it would be if Romero were peaceable.

Id. at 853. This view, however, is not uniformly embraced. *See, e.g., People v. Boles*, 339 N.W.2d 249, 252 (Mich. App. 1983) ("[U]nless the defendant could show that he knew of that incident or that it was directly connected with the homicide, the evidence should be excluded.") *rev'd on other grounds*, 358 N.W.2d 894 (1994); *State v. Latham*, 519 N.W.2d 68, 71 (S.D. 1994) ("[O]nly specific instances of conduct known to [the defendant] at the time of the incident in question were relevant."). Which is the better view? Why?

3. The *Keiser* court held that the victim's violent character was not an "essential element" of the claim of self-defense. The court stated: "The relevant question should be: would proof, or failure of proof, of the character trait by itself actually satisfy an element of the charge, claim, or defense? If not, then character is not essential and evidence should be limited to opinion or reputation." *Id.* at 856. Other courts have adopted the opposite view, reasoning that a victim's violent nature is an essential element of a claim of self-defense and, therefore, the defendant should be allowed to introduce evidence of specific acts to prove the victim's character. *E.g., Gottschalk v. State*, 881 P.2d 1139, 1143 (Alaska App. 1994); *Thompson v. State*, 813 S.W.2d 249, 251 (Ark. 1991); *Gonzales v. State*, 838 S.W.2d 848, 859 (Tex. App. 1992). Do you agree with the position adopted in *Keiser* or the opposing view?

4. Is the evidence of the victim's violent conduct always relevant when the defendant raises a claim of self-defense? How would the court in *Keiser* answer this question?

5. Should admissibility depend on the purpose for which the character evidence is being offered? For example, when offered to prove the defendant's state of mind and whether the use of force was necessary and reasonable, should knowledge of the victim's violent propensity be a precondition to admissibility? Moreover, it could be convincingly argued that since the evidence is being offered to prove state of mind rather than propensity, Rule 404(a)(2) is not applicable. What if the defendant claims that the victim was the first aggressor? In this situation, is character evidence relevant to show merely that the victim is a violent person? Should knowledge of the victim's violent character be a prerequisite to admissibility?

6. *Keiser* involved a claim of defense of another. The court stated that admission of evidence of the violent outburst outside the courthouse was not being sought to prove the defendant's state of mind at the time of the shooting, nor was it intended to show that the victim was the first aggressor. For what purpose was evidence of the victim's violent character being offered?

[2]   Evidence of Rape Victim's Character for Chastity — Fed. R. Evid. 412 (Rape Shield Statute)

[a]   Introduction

At common law, a rape defendant was permitted virtually unlimited cross-examination of a complaining witness's sexual past. The complainant's character for chastity was considered relevant on two issues. First, it was maintained that prior consensual sexual activity with the defendant made it more likely that the alleged rape victim consented to the sexual encounter that was the subject of the criminal prosecution. "[T]he underlying thought here is that it is more probable that an unchaste woman would assent . . . than a virtuous one."[34] In *People v. Abbot*, 19 Wend. 192 (N.Y. 1838), a case decided over 150 years ago, the New York appellate court memorialized this sexist view. The court distinguished between a woman "who has already submitted herself to the lewd embraces of another, and the coy and modest female severely chaste and instinctively shuddering at the thought of impurity. . . ." *Id.* at 196. The *Abbot* court further opined: "And will you not more readily infer assent in the practiced Messalina, in loose attire, than in the reserved and virtuous Lucretia?"[35] *Id.* at 195. Thus, evidence of prior sexual behavior was admitted to attack the victim's moral character. Second, evidence of prior sexual relations outside of marriage was deemed probative on the issue of a complainant's credibility on the theory that "promiscuity imports dishonesty."[36] Thus, evidence of unchastity was admitted to challenge a complainant's veracity.

---

[34] Berger, *Man's Trial, Woman's Tribulation: Rape Cases in the Courtroom*, 77 Colum. L. Rev. 1, 15 (1977).

[35] Messalina was the wife of Claudius I. She had a reputation for greed and lust that was supposedly unknown to her husband until she publicly married her lover. *See Messalina*, The Columbia Electronic Encyclopedia, (6th ed. 2000) www.encyclopedia.com/articles /08365.html. Lucretia, or Lucrece, is a woman of Roman legend renowned for her virtue. According to legend, she was raped and, after asking her husband to avenge her, she stabbed herself to death. *See Lucrece*, The Columbia Electronic Encyclopedia, www. encyclopedia.com/articles/08365.html.

[36] Berger, *supra* note 34, at 16; *see also* Harriet R. Galvin, *Shielding Rape Victims in the State and Federal Courts: A Proposal for the Second Decade*, 70 Minn. L. Rev. 763, 766 (1986) (hereinafter *Rape Shield Laws*); Frank Tuerkheimer, *A Reassessment and Redefinition of Rape Shield Laws*, 50 Ohio St. L.J. 1245, 1254 (1989).

The traditional rationale that a woman's unchastity has probative value on the question of whether or not she was raped is emphatically rejected by rape shield legislation. During the 1970s, a rape-law reform movement, supported by a coalition of women's rights organizations and the law enforcement establishment, persuaded legislators from across the nation to enact rape shield laws significantly restricting evidence of a victim's past sexual behavior. The advocates of rape shield legislation advanced four fundamental arguments for excluding evidence of prior sexual conduct. First, admission of evidence of prior sexual behavior "twice traumatizes" the complainant — first by the rape and then a second time by the criminal justice system.[37] Rape shield laws aim to safeguard the alleged victim against the invasion of privacy, harassment, and "potential embarrassment associated with public disclosure of intimate sexual details and infusion of sexual innuendo into the factfinding process."[38] Second, rape-shield proponents claim that the changing moral climate in this country simply invalidated the underpinnings of the common law doctrine, rendering unchastity evidence irrelevant for its stated purposes. As one commentator noted: "Because the decision to engage in consensual nonmarital sexual activity is no longer a decision to defy conventional norms, the behavior is 'character-neutral' and does not support the inference 'if she strayed once, she'll stray again.' "[39] The mere fact that the complainant has engaged in prior consensual sexual activity simply lacks probative value as a predictor of future behavior. Moreover, a criminal defendant has no constitutional right to present irrelevant, prejudicial evidence in his behalf.[40] Next, admission of prior sexual activity creates jury confusion by shifting the focus of the criminal trial away from the issue of the defendant's innocence or guilt to an inquisition of the victim's morality.[41] Finally, restricting evidence of prior sexual conduct furthers effective law enforcement. Permitting evidence of unchastity deters rape victims from reporting sex crimes to the authorities for fear of being publicly humiliated by disclosure of the most intimate details of the complainant's personal life. Thus, by severely restricting evidence of the complainant's unchastity, the drafters of rape shield laws sought to remove a major impediment to reporting sex crimes.[42]

While existing rape shield statutes vary widely in scope, their single common characteristic is a rejection of the previous automatic admissibility of proof of the

---

[37] *See* Galvin, *Rape Shield Laws, supra* note 35, at 795.

[38] Fed. R. Evid. 412, Notes of Advisory Committee, 1994 Amendment.

[39] Galvin, *Rape Shield Laws, supra* note 35, at 799 (quoting Ordover, *Admissibility of Patterns of Similar Sexual Conduct: The Unlamented Death of Character for Chastity*, 63 CORNELL L. REV. 90, 97 (1977)).

[40] *See* Galvin, *Rape Shield Laws, supra* note 35, at 806; Tanford & Bocchino, *Rape Victim Shield Laws and the Sixth Amendment*, 128 U. PA. L. REV. 544, 558, 560 (1980).

[41] *See State v. Budis*, 580 A.2d 283, 288 (N.J. App. Div. 1990) ("Among the remedial aims of rape shield laws is the protection of victims from harassment and invasion of privacy; encouragement of sex crime reporting; and avoidance of juror confusion."); Tuerkheimer, *supra* note 35, at 1250.

[42] *See* Galvin, *Rape Shield Laws, supra* note 35, at 797 ("[T]he legal systems's treatment of rape victims should be changed to encourage reporting of rape, which will lead to apprehension and conviction of rapists, which, in turn, will deter future rapists."); Tuerkheimer, *supra* note 35, at 1250–51.

Congressman Holtzman, the chief sponsor of H.R. 4727, which enacted Fed. R. Evid. 412, stated:

> Too often in this country victims of rape are humiliated and harassed when they report and prosecute the rape. Bullied and cross-examined about their prior sexual experiences, many find the trial almost as degrading as the rape itself. Since rape trials become inquisitions into the victim's morality, not trials of the defendant's innocence or guilt, it is not surprising that it is the least reported crime. It is estimated that as few as one in ten rapes is ever reported.

124 Cong. Rec. H. 11944 (daily ed. Oct. 10, 1978).

complainant's prior sexual behavior.[43] There are four distinct conceptual approaches to rape-shield legislation.[44] The most restrictive approach is represented by the Michigan statute.[45] The statutes modeled on the Michigan rape shield law prohibit the introduction of any evidence of prior sexual conduct by the complaining witness subject to certain enumerated exceptions. The statutory exceptions are highly specific, reflecting a legislative determination of those circumstances in which sexual conduct evidence will be critical to the defendant's theory of the case.[46] Evidence of past sexual conduct is inadmissible unless it falls within one or more of these statutory exceptions. Prior sexual relations with the defendant are usually excepted,[47] as are sexual relations with third parties to explain physical evidence of sexual activity such as pregnancy, semen, or venereal disease.[48]

The Michigan-type statutes have been criticized as being underinclusive. It is argued that the statutorily enumerated exceptions are unduly restrictive and exclude evidence of unchastity highly relevant to a legitimate defense theory. In a small number of cases, courts have held the Michigan-style statutes unconstitutional *as applied* in particular factual settings.[49]

A substantially less restrictive approach is taken by Arkansas and eight other states that have adopted a similar statutory scheme.[50] In these jurisdictions, the rape shield statutes create no substantive evidentiary exclusions but rather require an *in camera* determination on the issue of whether the probative value of evidence outweighs its

---

[43] Rape shield laws have been enacted in 48 of the 50 states. In addition, the Federal Rules of Evidence, Fed. R. Evid. 412, and the Code of Military Justice, Mil. R. Evid. 412, also embody the principle, as does the common law of the two states that have not enacted a rape shield statute. *See State ex rel. Pope v. Superior Court*, 545 P.2d 946 (Ariz. 1976); *State v. Johns*, 615 P.2d 1260 (Utah 1980).

[44] *See* Galvin, *Rape Shield Laws, supra* note 35, for a comprehensive and scholarly examination of the nation's rape shield laws.

[45] *See* MICH. COMP. LAWS ANN. § 750.520j (West Supp. 1985). Twenty-five states have modeled rape shield statutes on the Michigan law. *See* Galvin, *Rape Shield Laws, supra* note 35, at 773 (appendix Table 1). Those statutes include: ALA. CODE § 12-21-203 (Supp. 1985); FLA. STAT. ANN. § 794.022(2)–(3) (West 1985); GA. CODE ANN. § 24-2-3 (1985); ILL. ANN. STAT. ch 38, § 115-7 (Smith-Hurd Supp. 1985); IND. CODE ANN. § 35-37-4-4 (Burns 1985); KY. REV. STAT. § 510.145 (1985); LA. REV. STAT. ANN. § 15:498 (West 1981); ME. R. EVID. 412; MD. ANN. CODE art. 27, § 461A (1982); MASS. ANN. LAWS ch. 233, § 21B (Law. Co-op. 1985); MINN. R. EVID. 404(c); MO. ANN. STAT. § 491.015 (Vernon Supp. 1986); MONT. CODE ANN. § 45-5-511(4) (1985); NEB. REV. STAT. § 28-321 (Supp. 1984); N.H. REV. STAT. ANN. § 632-A:6 (Supp. 1983); N.J. STAT. ANN. 2C:14-7; N.C. R. EVID. 412; OHIO REV. CODE ANN. § 2907.02(D) (Page Supp. 1984); PA. CONS. STAT. ANN. tit. 18, § 3104 (Purdon 1983); S.C. CODE ANN. § 16-3659.1 (Law. Co-op. 1985); TENN. CODE ANN. § 40-17119 (1982); VT. STAT. ANN. tit. 13, § 3255 (Supp. 1985); VA. CODE § 18.2-67.7 (1982); W. VA. CODE § 61-8B-11 (1984); and WIS. STAT. ANN. §§ 972.11(2), 972.31(11) (West 1985).

[46] *See* Galvin, *Rape Shield Laws, supra* note 35, at 773, 812. This formulation has been described as the "inflexible legislative rule" approach. *See* Berger, *Man's Trial, Woman's Tribulation: Rape Cases in the Courtroom*, 77 COLUM. L. REV. 1, 32 (1977).

[47] All twenty-five statutes adopting the Michigan approach permit the introduction of evidence of prior sexual conduct between the defendant and the complaining witness. Professor Galvin posits that "[t]his evidence is probative of the complainant's state of mind toward the particular defendant, permitting an inference that the state of mind continued to the occasion in question." Galvin, *Rape Shield Laws, supra* note 35, at 815.

[48] *See Johnson v. State*, 632 A.2d 152, 155 (Md. App. 1993); *State v. Budis*, 580 A.2d 283, 287 (N.J. App. Div. 1990).

[49] *See Budis*, 580 A.2d at 292; *State v. Pulizzano*, 456 N.W.2d 325 (Wis. 1990).

[50] ARK. STAT. ANN. § 411810.2(b) (1977); ALASKA STAT. § 12.45.045 (Supp. 1985); COLO. REV. STAT. § 18-3-407 (1978); IDAHO CODE § 18-6105 (1979); KAN. STAT. ANN. § 21-3525 (Supp. 1984); N.M.R. EVID. 413; R.I. GEN. LAWS § 11-37-13 (1981); S.D. CODIF. LAWS ANN. § 23A-22-15 (1979); and WYO. STAT. ANN. § 6-2-312 (1983).

prejudicial effects. In contrast to the Michigan statute, which has been assailed for stripping the trial courts of their discretion to determine the relevancy of sexual conduct evidence, the Arkansas approach has been criticized for vesting trial judges with nearly unfettered discretion to admit sexual conduct evidence. "Because the statutes lack any substantive restrictions on the admissibility of sexual conduct evidence . . . judges are free to permit its introduction as they were prior to the enactment of the legislation."[51] Thus, while the Michigan approach suffers from being underinclusive, the Arkansas-type statute is criticized for being overinclusive and permitting prior sexual conduct evidence to prove that the complainant acted in conformity.

A third group of statutes modeled on the federal rape shield provision, Fed. R. Evid. 412, combines features of both the restrictive and the discretionary approaches. In the six jurisdictions following the federal approach, sexual conduct evidence is generally prohibited, subject to certain enumerated exceptions.[52] The key feature of this statutory scheme, however, is a "constitutional catch-all" provision that permits introduction of unexcepted sexual conduct evidence "the exclusion of which would violate the constitutional rights of the defendant"[53] or when required in the "interests of justice."[54] The obvious problem with this approach is that the statute offers the defendant no guidance in determining whether admission of the evidence is constitutionally mandated.

As a procedural matter, Fed. R. Evid. 412(c) requires notice and a hearing prior to admitting the evidence.[55] The hearing must be conducted *in camera*, affording the victim and the parties the right to be present and an opportunity to be heard. The purpose of the *in camera* hearing is to protect the privacy of the rape victim in the event the court finds the evidence of specific instances of prior sexual conduct inadmissible.

Finally, under the California approach, evidence of the complaining witness's conduct is divided into two broad categories depending on the purpose for which it is offered: (1) evidence relating to consent and (2) evidence relating to credibility. The California statute prohibits evidence of the former (relating to consent), while admitting evidence of the latter (relating to credibility). The critical flaw in this legislation is that sexual conduct evidence does not neatly break down into "consent" or "credibility" uses. Quite often evidence that establishes consent by the complainant will simultaneously impeach her credibility, and vice versa. Thus, the statute "invites the danger of resurrecting the concept that 'promiscuity imports dishonesty,'" a concept that has been uniformly rejected by courts and legislators.[56] As noted by one commentator: "[I]n cases where the issues of consent and credibility merge, the statute may result in the admission of the kind of evidence rape shield laws are designed to avoid — prior

---

[51] Galvin, *Rape Shield Laws, supra* note 35, at 774.

[52] Conn. Gen. Stat. Ann. § 54-86F (West 1985); Haw. R. Evid. 412; Iowa R. Evid. 412; N.Y. Crim. Proc. Law § 60.42 (McKinney 1981); Or. Rev. Stat. Ann. § 40.210 (1988); Tex. R. Crim. Evid. 412.

[53] Fed. R. Evid. 412(b)(1)(C).

[54] N.Y. Crim. Proc. Law § 60.42(5) (McKinney 1981).

[55] Fed. R. Evid. 412(c)(1).

[56] Tuerkheimer, *supra* note 36, at 1250; *see also State v. Budis*, 580 A.2d 283, 288 (N.J. App. Div. 1990) ("By enacting this rape shield law, our Legislature has adopted a view nearly universally accepted by courts, legislators and legal writers: that in a rape case evidence of a complainant's prior sexual conduct is generally irrelevant or if not entirely irrelevant, has a probative value which is substantially outweighed by countervailing facts such as prejudice.").

sexual acts offered to prove consent in the instant case."[57] Inexplicably, the Washington and Nevada rape shield statutes, based on California's law, recognize the consent/credibility dichotomy but adopt the opposite view on admissibility. These jurisdictions admit the past sexual conduct evidence for purposes of proving consent but not lack of credibility.[58]

[b]   The Confrontation Clause Dilemma

A tension exists between the legitimate state interest in "protect[ing] rape victims from the degrading and embarrassing disclosure of intimate details about their private lives"[59] and preserving the defendant's Sixth Amendment right of confrontation. While the state's interest on behalf of rape victims is compelling, the Sixth Amendment guarantees the defendant's right to effective cross-examination. *See Olden v. Kentucky*, 488 U.S. 227, 231 (1988), and *Davis v. Alaska*, 415 U.S. 308 (1974). As between these competing interests, Fed. R. Evid. 412 recognizes that the right of confrontation is paramount to Rule 412's policy of shielding a rape victim from potential embarrassment. Rule 412(b)(1)(C) explicitly provides that evidence of the complainant's prior sexual behavior is inadmissible unless exclusion would violate the constitutional rights of the defendant. Determining at what point the complainant's rights protected under rape shield legislation infringe upon the defendant's rights afforded under the Sixth Amendment Confrontation Clause has confounded the courts. The following cases are illustrative of circumstances where the rape complainant's rights were held to give way to the defendant's right to a fair trial.

UNITED STATES v. BEGAY
937 F.2d 515 (10th Cir. 1991)

HOLLOWAY, CHIEF JUDGE.

Defendant Begay, an Indian, appeals his conviction and sentence on one count of aggravated sexual abuse of an Indian child in Indian country in violation of 18 U.S.C. §§ 1153 (offenses committed within Indian Country), 2241(c) (sexual acts with persons under twelve years of age), and 2245(2) (sexual act). Begay was sentenced to imprisonment for 108 months and a supervised release term of five years.

Begay contends that the district court erroneously restricted his right to cross-examination in violation of the Confrontation Clause of the Sixth Amendment by excluding evidence of relevant incidents of the alleged victim's prior sexual activity under Federal Rules of Evidence 412(b)(2)(A) and 403. . . . We reverse and remand for a new trial. . . .

There was evidence tending to show the following:

At the time of the alleged assault in early December 1987, Begay lived in a three-room residence on an Indian reservation in New Mexico with his sister, Betty, his girlfriend, Anna R., and her eight year old daughter, D.R. (D.). Begay, Anna and D. regularly slept together in the same bed, with Anna between Begay and D. On or about the evening of December 1, 1987, Begay was intoxicated and went to bed. Only D. was

---

[57] *Id.*

[58] WASH. REV. CODE ANN. § 9A.44.020 (1988); NEV. REV. STAT. §§ 48.069, 50.090 (1986).

[59] 124 Cong. Rec. H. 11944 (daily ed. Oct. 10, 1978) (statement of Rep. Mann).

in Begay's bed as Anna had decided to sleep in a different bed in the same room because of her period.

After noticing some movement, Anna became concerned that Begay might be molesting her daughter. Anna turned on the light, "threw the covers off of them," and saw Begay in his shorts and D.'s pants zipped down, with Begay "hugging [D.]." II R. at 73–74. Begay got dressed, "said he was going to kill himself and just took off" from the house. *Id.* at 76. Anna's and D.'s accounts of the incident are similar, although D. specifically testified at trial that Begay undressed her, laid on her, and put his penis in her, and went up and down.

On December 28, 1987, D.'s relatives reported the incident to Irene Poyer, a social worker with the Navajo Tribe. Shortly thereafter during an interview at the Begay residence, D. informed Poyer that Begay had sexual intercourse with her.

Following this early December 1987 incident, D. was examined for the first time on March 30, 1988, by Doctor Robert Wagner. The examination revealed an "unusually" large hymenal opening and a "streaky area that . . . [Dr. Wagner] considered to be an abrasion of some sort." *Id.* at 83. During cross-examination by Begay's counsel, Dr. Wagner further testified that it was impossible to determine strictly on the basis of D.'s physical examination whether her symptoms reflected one violent sexual penetration or repeated penetrations over a period of time. Moreover, after cross-examination, during an offer of proof by Begay (which was excluded), out of the hearing of the jury, Dr. Wagner also testified that it was impossible to determine from the physical examination alone whether D.'s symptoms were caused by Begay or during earlier incidents with John Jim. In connection with this offer of proof D.'s brother, Aaron R., would have testified that he saw Jim assault D. on three separate occasions in the summer immediately preceding the Begay incident. This offer was also excluded. Jim has pled guilty to aggravated sexual assault upon D.

On April 18, 1988, Begay and Esther Keeswood, a juvenile presenting officer with the Navajo Tribe, both appeared before the Navajo children's court in a dependency case to review a petition to place D. in a different living environment. Keeswood testified that when she questioned Begay during the hearing, Begay admitted having sexual intercourse with D.

On May 24, 1988, criminal investigator Semans of the Bureau of Indian Affairs questioned Begay at the Shiprock Police Station about D.'s allegations that he had sexually abused her. Although Begay was not in custody when he arrived at the station with Anna R., nevertheless Semans informed Begay in English of his Miranda rights. Furthermore, Officer Cowboy was present at the meeting and he likewise advised Begay in Navajo of "his rights." Begay indicated that he understood his rights and was more comfortable communicating in English.

When confronted by the officers with allegations and medical findings of sexual abuse, Begay responded, "if D. said it was true, then that's what happened." [II R. at 100.] Later, he reiterated this response to the officers but said that he was too drunk on the evening of the incident to recall exactly what happened. After a brief period, Begay admitted in greater detail that he initially thought that D. was Anna until he touched her. Begay nevertheless, "inserted his penis inside of her vagina." *Id.* at 101. Begay subsequently signed a written statement reflecting his third admission after Semans reviewed it orally with him.

On February 7, 1989, a federal grand jury returned a one-count indictment against Begay, charging him with "engag[ing] in a sexual act with . . . an Indian female who had not yet attained the age of twelve (12) years." I R. at 1. Begay filed a motion to suppress the May 24, 1988 confession that he made to Officers Semans and Cowboy at the Shiprock Police Station. Begay claimed that his confession was involuntary because "he was scared" and because "he didn't know that [Jim] was being investigated for a prior act of penetration." Brief for Appellant at 5. The district court denied Begay's motion at a suppression hearing before trial.

Jerry Harris, an investigator for the Public Defender's Office, interviewed D. on March 24, 1989. He asked her if Begay "had put himself inside her or something to that effect, and she replied to me no." II R. 164. This was related in testimony before the jury at trial. In an offer of proof, rejected by the trial judge, Harris said he questioned D. about the Jim incident and contrasted it with the Begay incident. Harris said basically his question to D. was "did Carl Begay do the same thing to her that John Jim did, as far as — you know, getting inside her and that type thing, and she replied to me no." *Id.* at 183. This offer was rejected at trial.

Before trial Begay filed a motion to offer evidence, pursuant to Rule 412, seeking to introduce proof which involved references to D.'s past sexual activity with Jim. The court denied the motion after a hearing. After a two-day trial, the jury found Begay guilty as charged by the indictment, the judgment of conviction and the sentence were entered, and this appeal followed.

II.

Begay's primary claim of error is that the district court violated the Confrontation Clause of the Sixth Amendment by improperly excluding evidence under Rules 403 and 412, Fed. R. Evid. He says that admission of the evidence was "constitutionally required" and should have been allowed under Rule 412(b)(1). Begay argues that the trial judge's rulings erroneously denied him the opportunity to explain the physical evidence of D.'s condition, relied on heavily by the prosecution, by showing earlier sexual acts that could have caused the conditions; and that he was wrongly denied the right to cross-examine D. in a manner necessary to show the weakness of her testimony against Begay as to whether he was actually guilty of the sexual act with penetration as charged, all in violation of the Confrontation Clause.

* * *

The Sixth Amendment's Confrontation Clause states: "In all criminal prosecutions, the accused shall enjoy the right . . . to be confronted with the witnesses against him." The Clause provides two types of protections for defendants, the right physically to face those who testify against him and the right of cross-examination — "a primary interest of the [Clause]." *Kentucky v. Stincer*, 482 U.S. 730, 736 (1987) (citing *Douglas v. Alabama*, 380 U.S. 415, 418 (1965)). *See Olden v. Kentucky*, 488 U.S. 227, 231 (1988); *Pennsylvania v. Ritchie*, 480 U.S. 39, 51 (1987). *See also Coy v. Iowa*, 487 U.S. 1012, 1021 (1988) (defendant's right to confrontation violated where screen prevented complaining witnesses from viewing him, allegedly justified by legislatively imposed presumption of trauma).

The Supreme Court has long held that the rights to confront and cross-examine witnesses and to call witnesses in one's behalf are essential to due process. *See Chambers v. Mississippi*, 410 U.S. 284, 294 (1973). Indeed, the Court has emphasized that cross-examination "is critical for ensuring the integrity of the factfinding process" and "is the principal means by which the believability of a witness and the truth of his testimony are tested." *Stincer*, 482 U.S. at 736; *Davis v. Alaska*, 415 U.S. 308, 316 (1974). Accordingly, we recently held that a "defendant's right to confrontation may be violated if the trial court precludes an entire relevant area of cross-examination." *United States v. Lonedog*, 929 F.2d 568, 570 (10th Cir. 1991) (citing *United States v. Atwell*, 766 F.2d 416 (10th Cir.), *cert. denied*, 474 U.S. 921 (1985)).

The trial judge said the case presented a "close question" on permitting the cross-examination that Begay sought. Nevertheless the court ruled at the pretrial hearing held pursuant to Rule 412 that evidence of the Jim incidents was inadmissible under Rule 403 because it "would be totally unfair to . . . [D. to] subject [her] to the examination of any other rape . . . and [it would] prejudice the jury against the young child." II R. at 11. Furthermore, he said it would create "confusion of the critical issue of the case because the defense would be attempting to retry or try a case of rape on the part of another defendant who pled guilty to the offense." *Id.* at 12. This reasoning is pertinent both under Rule 403 and under the similar probativeness versus prejudice test provided in Rule 412(c)(3).

Relevant evidence is any evidence having a tendency to make the existence of a material fact more or less probable than it would be without the evidence. *See United States v. Shomo*, 786 F.2d 981, 985 (10th Cir. 1986); Fed. R. Evid. 401. Materiality is defined by substantive law. Here the aggravated sexual abuse statute, 18 U.S.C. § 2241, requires proof, for a charge of abuse of a child under 12, of a "sexual act." 18 U.S.C. § 2241(c). And a "sexual act" includes contact between the penis and vulva occurring "upon penetration, however slight." *Id.* at § 2245(2)(A).

Here the significance of the excluded evidence is magnified when the lesser offense of abusive sexual contact is considered. The trial judge instructed that the indictment "necessarily include[d] the lesser offense of abusive sexual contact of a child," found at 18 U.S.C. § 2244. . . . Consequently, any evidence proving or disproving a "sexual act," as charged in the indictment for aggravated sexual abuse with penetration, or the lesser offense of "sexual contact," as explained in the trial judge's lesser-included-offense instruction, is relevant and admissible unless specifically excluded by another rule of evidence. *United States v. Esch*, 832 F.2d 531, 535 (10th Cir. 1987), *cert. denied*, 485 U.S. 991 (1988); *Shomo*, 786 F.2d at 985. *See United States v. Neal*, 718 F.2d 1505, 1509–10 (10th Cir. 1983), *cert. denied*, 469 U.S. 818 (1984).

Contrary to the trial court's ruling, we conclude that cross-examination about the Jim incidents was relevant and probative on the central issue whether D.'s memory was clear and accurate on critical details about the Begay incident as contrasted with the Jim incidents. Further, cross-examination of Dr. Wagner was likewise relevant and of critical importance. The rejected offers of proof included his statement that his physical findings about D.'s condition would be consistent with proof that Jim had full sexual intercourse with D. on at least two occasions several months before the Begay incident, although the doctor could not differentiate as to time lengths when the conditions were caused.

Having determined that the Jim incidents were relevant, we should also consider the trial court's additional ruling that even if the incidents were relevant, "any relevancy would be totally outweighed by [their] prejudicial effect. . . ." II R. at 12, referring to the traumatic effect on D. Begay argues that the district court erred in finding that the probative value of cross-examination of D., Dr. Wagner, Officer Semans and Harris concerning the Jim incident was outweighed by its prejudicial effect.

*   *   *

We are unable to agree with the rulings of the trial judge rejecting Begay's efforts to cross-examine and to proffer evidence on critical facts about the Jim incidents. As we have noted, the prosecution relied heavily on the testimony concerning the enlarged hymen and the abrasion, conditions the doctor testified about for the prosecution. In closing argument the prosecutor came back to this point to argue that "[t]he evidence that was presented by Dr. Wagner was consistent with someone who had been sexually penetrated. That speaks for itself." II R. at 270. The prosecuting attorney also argued to the jury that "[s]he was examined, ladies and gentlemen, by a physician, and the examination was consistent with that sexual assault." *Id.* at 266. And in his rebuttal, the prosecutor bore down on the medical evidence again: "Medical evidence. Does that medical evidence that you heard from Doctor Wagner, does that suggest that nothing happened, that this is all just a big bruja about nothing?," *id.* at 292, "you've got the medical evidence. . . ." *Id.* at 293. Leaving the state of the evidence and such argument unanswered by proof of the Jim incidents was crippling to the defense of Begay.

In these circumstances, we are convinced that it was error to restrict the cross-examination of D. and to reject the offers of proof by cross-examination of Dr. Wagner and other witnesses respecting the Jim incidents in order to counter the damaging evidence of the child's physical condition, which the prosecution was obviously relying on to point to the defendant's guilt. We feel there was an abuse of discretion in holding that such evidence was more prejudicial than probative for purposes of Rule 403 and 412. Furthermore, we are convinced that under Rule 412(b)(1), the evidence should have been admitted as constitutionally required to protect Begay's rights under the Confrontation Clause. *See United States v. Nez*, 661 F.2d 1203, 1205 (10th Cir. 1981). We are persuaded by the reasoning in *United States v. Saunders*, 736 F. Supp. 698, 703 (E.D. Va. 1990):

> Although the Rule provides no guidance as to the meaning of the phrase "constitutionally required," it seems clear that the Constitution requires that a criminal defendant be given the opportunity to present evidence that is relevant, material and favorable to his defense. *See United States v. Valenzuela-Bernal*, 458 U.S. 858, 867 (1982) (To establish 6th Amendment violation, defendant must show that he was precluded from offering evidence "material and favorable to his defense.") (footnote omitted); *Washington v. Texas*, 388 U.S. 14, 16 (1967) (6th Amendment violation occurs when defendant is arbitrarily deprived of "testimony . . . relevant and material, . . . and vital to the defense"). . . .

In sum, we hold that the trial judge's rulings under Rule 412 and Rule 403, rejecting critical proof and cross-examination, were in error. . . . The judgment is reversed and the cause is remanded for a new trial and further proceedings consistent with this opinion.

NOTES AND QUESTIONS

1. Does the court in *Begay* set forth a clear standard for determining when excluding evidence of past sexual conduct violates the defendant's rights under the Confrontation Clause? The court opined that the phrase "constitutionally required" means "that a criminal defendant be given the opportunity to present evidence that is *relevant,* *material and favorable to his defense." Begay*, 937 F.2d at 523 (emphasis added). In so doing, does the court merely restate Fed. R. Evid. 402, which authorizes the admissibility of relevant evidence, rather than articulate a constitutional standard? Is the Sixth Amendment violated whenever a defendant is denied the opportunity to cross-examine a witness on evidence that is relevant, or does proof of a breach of the Confrontation Clause require a higher showing? Must the evidence be necessary to prove a central issue in the case?

2. The *Begay* court found that the Confrontation Clause was violated because "cross examination about the Jim incidents was relevant and probative on the central issue whether D.'s memory was clear and accurate on the critical details about the Begay incident as contrasted with the Jim incidents." *Id.* at 521. It can be argued that in every case where the rape victim is a child, the complainant's memory is a "central" issue. Thus, does excluding evidence of the prior sexual behavior of a child rape victim always violate the Confrontation Clause?

3. Is the evidence concerning the prior sexual conduct with Jim admissible under the alternative source of injury exception provided by Rule 412(b)(1)(B) (as amended 1994)? The exception protects the defendant's right to show that past contact with persons other than the accused was the source of semen or "injury" rather than conduct with the defendant. This evidence is not relevant when the issue is consent, but only when the defendant denies the sexual incident and claims another person is the source of semen or injury. This exception to the general rule excluding evidence of prior sexual behavior represents a legislative determination that an alternative source of semen or injury evidence is highly relevant and material to the presentation of a defense and its admission is, therefore, constitutionally required. *See State v. Budis*, 580 A.2d 283, 289 (N.J. App. Div. 1990); Galvin, *Shielding Rape Victims in the State and Federal Courts: A Proposal for the Second Decade*, 70 Minn. L. Rev. 763, 812 (1986).

4. One issue raised by the facts in *Begay* is whether evidence of prior sexual acts with someone other than the defendant may be admitted to prove an alternative source of an enlarged hymen. In other words, does an enlarged hymen constitute an "injury" for purposes of the rule? The federal circuits are split on this issue. In *United States v. Shaw*, 824 F.2d 601 (8th Cir. 1987), *cert. denied*, 484 U.S. 1068 (1988), the Eighth Circuit held that the term "injury" does not include an enlarged hymen. In contrast, the Tenth Circuit in *Begay* rejected the reasoning in *Shaw* and concluded that the evidence is admissible where the prosecution has made this particular injury — the condition of the hymen — directly relevant on the question of the defendant's guilt or innocence. *Begay*, 937 F.2d at 523 n.10; *see also Tague v. Richards*, 3 F.3d 1133 (7th Cir. 1993) (holding that exclusion of evidence of prior molestation by the victim's father to show an alternative source of hymen injury violated the defendant's confrontation rights; however, error was harmless). The injury exception to Rule 412 was amended in 1994 to include evidence of injury "or other physical evidence." Thus, evidence otherwise inadmissible under the rule is admissible if offered to prove that a person other than the accused was the "source of semen, injury or other physical evidence." Consequently, for those courts that hold that the "injury" exception does not extend to evidence of an enlarged hymen, the insertion of the language "or other physical evidence," which broadens the scope of coverage of the exception, would appear to have resolved the issue in favor of inclusion. Do you agree?

5. Does the injury exception to Rule 412 encompass emotional injury or behavior? Is evidence of prior sexual conduct admissible to provide an alternative explanation for why the victim exhibited the behavioral symptoms of a sexually abused child? In *United*

States v. Shaw, 824 F.2d 601, 603 n.2 (8th Cir. 1987), the court held that "Rule 412's injury requirement exception does not apply to emotional injuries unaccompanied by cognizable physical consequence." *But see United States v. Bear Stops*, 997 F.2d 451, 455 (8th Cir. 1993), where the court held that evidence that the victim was sexually assaulted by three older boys was constitutionally required to be admitted to provide an alternative explanation for the victim's behavioral manifestations identified as frequently observed in sexually abused children. Which position is the better view? Why?

[c]   Introduction of Evidence of Prior Sexual Behavior to Prove Knowledge by Victim of Minor Years

As previously noted, in support of finding a Confrontation Clause violation, the *Begay* court stressed the fact that the prosecution relied heavily on the medical testimony concerning the victim's enlarged hymen and abrasions to corroborate the victim's testimony. The court posited that "[l]eaving the state of the evidence and such argument unanswered by proof of the Jim incidents was crippling to the defense of Begay." *Begay*, 937 F.2d at 523. What if the defendant sought to introduce evidence of prior sexual incidents involving the child victim and a third party not to prove an alternative source of injuries to the victim, but instead, to establish an alternate source of sexual knowledge? In other words, should evidence of prior sexual conduct with a third party be admitted to rebut an inference that a child rape victim could not have known of such intimate sexual acts unless they occurred with the defendant? Would excluding evidence of an alternative source of sexual knowledge violate the defendant's Sixth Amendment right of confrontation?

STATE v. BUDIS
580 A.2d 283 (N.J. App. Div. 1990)

Long, Judge.

After a jury trial, defendant James G. Budis was convicted of two counts of sexual penetration on T.D., a child of less than thirteen years of age, contrary to N.J.S.A. 2C:14-2(a)(1). He was sentenced to concurrent custodial terms of fifteen years on each conviction. An appropriate Violent Crimes Compensation Board penalty was also imposed. . . .

* * *

We have carefully reviewed this record in light of the claims advanced by defendant and conclude that defendant was denied a fair trial because of an interpretation of N.J.S.A. 2C:14-7 which precluded admission of crucial defense evidence. Accordingly, we reverse and remand for a new trial. This ruling renders moot the remaining issues raised in defendant's brief.

In May 1988, T.D., who was then 10 years old, was playing a Nintendo game with a relative. The game featured two characters boxing. While playing the game, T.D. commented that it looked like one of the characters "was sucking the other guy off." This comment was reported to her father, who confronted T.D. in order to discover where she had heard of such a thing. In response, T.D. mentioned the names of her former stepfather, H.D., and the defendant. The father, in turn, made a report to the Division of Youth and Family Services, which contacted the Somerset County Prosecutor.

An investigation was conducted by a detective from the Somerset County Prosecutor's Office, who met with T.D. and taped two statements. In the first statement, T.D. said that defendant, who is her father's cousin, was visiting on an evening in July 1987, when the family went swimming in the apartment complex pool at night. According to T.D., defendant took her back into the apartment to get changed, and once inside he placed his erect penis in her mouth and her vagina, but that nothing came out of his penis. She said that a few days later the family went to Dorney Park for her brother's birthday. Defendant went with them and slept over. During the night, he came into her bedroom and once again placed his erect penis in her mouth and her vagina.

The second statement referred to T.D.'s former stepfather, H.D. In her statement, T.D. said that on five or six occasions during the fall of 1986 while they were living in the same household, H.D. took her into his bedroom at night and placed his erect penis in her mouth and her vagina. She said that he did this for about an hour at a time, but that nothing came out of his penis. Upon questioning, H.D. admitted to three sexual encounters with T.D. He was indicted and subsequently pled guilty to one count of sexual assault and one count of aggravated sexual assault. He has since been sentenced.

On May 25, 1988, the detective sought to question the defendant about T.D.'s allegations. Defendant acknowledged that two sexual encounters with T.D. occurred during the previous summer but differed with T.D.'s description of the events. Defendant said that on the occasion of T.D.'s brother's birthday, he slept on the couch. Shortly after he went to sleep, he awoke to find that T.D. had taken his penis "out through the side of my shorts and was jerking me off and then started licking and kissing" it; he pushed her away after "maybe five minutes at the most." Defendant said that on the other occasion, when he visited the apartment complex to go swimming, he went into the apartment by himself to get changed. When he had "stripped down," defendant noticed T.D. was behind him; she grabbed his penis and testicles and began to stroke and kiss them for about a minute. Defendant said that "[a]t that point, it felt good." On both occasions, defendant had an erection but did not ejaculate. Defendant said that he warned T.D. not to do anything like this again or he would have to tell her father. Defendant subsequently was arrested and indicted on two counts of sexual penetration in violation of N.J.S.A. 2C:14-2a(1).

At trial, the testimony of T.D. was essentially the same as her prior statements to the police. When defendant was confronted on cross-examination with his prior inculpatory answers, he gave these explanations. He said that his statement that what T.D. did to him after they went swimming "felt good" meant that "it didn't hurt." He also said that his description of what T.D. did when he woke up on the couch as lasting "maybe five minutes" was a figure of speech; it actually was only a few seconds before he pushed her away.

During discussions outside the presence of the jury, defense counsel indicated that he needed to elicit testimony as to the prior sexual abuse to which T.D. had been subjected by her stepfather in order to show sexual knowledge for the purpose of preventing the jury from dismissing outright defendant's testimony that a child would be inclined to initiate sexual contact. The trial judge ruled that the rape shield statute (N.J.S.A. 2C:14-7) precluded the admission of the evidence:

> First of all I — I do not agree with the contention of defense counsel that you can show as to a child that which you couldn't show as to an adult woman. That to me is absolutely beyond belief. If an adult engaged in each of these alleged acts with an adult male, you could not show it in a charge of aggravated sexual

assault involving another and distinct different, different person. You would not be permitted. And it's urged to me that you should be permitted to do it with a child.

First of all, I will not permit any examination of this child with respect to any sexual activity other than the sexual activity charged in this indictment. Either by direct examination or cross-examination.

I will permit the examination of the detective within the limited area, to wit, did he investigate allegations of sexual abuse by her stepfather. And I will not permit the details of those — that alleged sexual abuse to be brought before this jury. . . .

Although the testimonial portion of the trial only lasted two days, the jury deliberated for one full day and for a portion of a second day before reaching a verdict.

The Sixth Amendment to the United States Constitution guarantees the right of the accused in a criminal prosecution "to be confronted with the witnesses against him." This right has been extended by the Fourteenth Amendment to protect the accused in state proceedings. *Pointer v. Texas*, 380 U.S. 400 (1965); *State v. Williams*, 182 N.J. Super. 427, 434, 442 A.2d 620 (App. Div. 1982). Art. 1, par. 10 of the New Jersey Constitution (1947) concomitantly provides that "in all criminal prosecutions the accused shall have the right . . . to be confronted with the witnesses against him. . . ." Confrontation means more than merely being allowed to address a witness physically. A primary interest secured by confrontation is the right to meaningful cross-examination. *Davis v. Alaska*, 415 U.S. 308, 315 (1974) (citing *Douglas v. Alabama*, 380 U.S. 415, 418 (1965)). "Cross examination is the principal means by which the believability of a witness and the truth of his testimony are tested." *Id.* at 316. The right to confront and cross examine witnesses is crucial to due process. *In re Oliver*, 333 U.S. 257 (1948). It is not, however, without limitation and may, "in appropriate cases, bow to accommodate other legitimate interests in the criminal trial process." *Chambers v. Mississippi*, 410 U.S. 284, 295 (1973) (citing *Mancusi v. Shibbs*, 408 U.S. 204 (1972)). *See State v. Crandall*, 120 N.J. 649, 577 A.2d 483 (1990). Whenever the right to confrontation is denied or diminished, the integrity of the factfinding process is called into question. *Berger v. California*, 393 U.S. 314 (1969). Thus, the competing state interest must be closely examined and, even if legitimate, must give way where the defendant's confrontation rights are directly implicated. *Davis v. Alaska, supra.*

In this case, defendant's request to inquire into the victim's prior sexual abuse was denied based upon N.J.S.A. 2C:14-7, New Jersey's so-called rape shield law. . . .

Rape shield laws have been enacted in 48 of the 50 states, including New Jersey; the Federal Rules of Evidence and the Code of Military Justice also embody the principle, as does the common law of the two states which have not enacted a rape shield statute. In general, these laws operate to protect rape victims from the humiliation of unwarranted public disclosure of the details of their prior sexual activity. Tanford and Bocchino, *Rape Shield Laws and the Sixth Amendment*, 128 U. Pa. L. Rev. 544 (1980). By their enactment, a victim's moral character is eliminated as an issue in a rape case and evidence of unchastity is precluded as a way of impeaching a victim's credibility. "In enacting rape-shield legislation, reformers sought to remove sexist assumptions from the fact-finding process, putting to rest the common-law notions that unchaste women are more likely to consent and to lie under oath than their virtuous sisters." Galvin, *Shielding Rape Victims in the State and Federal Courts: A Proposal for the Second Decade*, 70 Minn. L. Rev. 763 (1986).

Among the remedial aims of rape shield laws is the protection of victims from harassment and invasion of privacy; encouragement of sex crime reporting; and avoidance of juror confusion. All of these salutary aims are advanced by N.J.S.A. 2C:14-7. By enacting this rape shield law, our Legislature has adopted a view nearly universally accepted by courts, legislators and legal writers: that in a rape case evidence of a complainant's prior sexual conduct is generally irrelevant or if not entirely irrelevant, has a probative value which is substantially outweighed by countervailing factors such as prejudice. Thus, it can be said that this statute incorporates an important issue of public policy.

*   *   *

N.J.S.A. 2C:14-7 is much different from its predecessor, which did nothing more than require the trial judge to make an evaluation of the proffered prior sexual conduct evidence and allow its admission only if it met traditional relevancy standards and if its probative value was not outweighed by countervailing factors. On the contrary, although N.J.S.A. 2C:14-7 incorporates the provisions of N.J.S.A. 2A:84A-32.1 requiring the judge to make a relevancy determination and to evaluate the probative value of the proffered evidence, it precludes the judge from admitting evidence of prior sexual conduct unless it is material to "negating the element of force or coercion or to proving that the source of semen, pregnancy or disease is a person other than the defendant." By this formulation, New Jersey has joined 25 other states which generally proscribe the admission of prior sexual conduct evidence subject to very specific exceptions and allow no judicial discretion to admit unexcepted evidence.[3] This formulation has been described as the "inflexible legislative rule" approach [Berger, *Man's Trial, Woman's Tribulation: Rape Cases in the Courtroom*, 77 Colum. L. Rev. 1, 32 (1977)] and has been characterized as a legislative effort to pre-determine

> precisely those circumstances in which sexual conduct evidence is highly relevant and material to the presentation of a defense and, therefore, constitutionally required. [Galvin, *supra*, at 812].

Indeed, our statute denominates its exceptions as relevancy judgments thus barring all but the excepted evidential classes as irrelevant per se. What makes the scheme problematic is the fact that relevance is not an inherent characteristic of any particular piece of evidence. It is rather the logical relationship between the proffered evidence and the material fact sought to be proved. Evid. R. 1(2). For this reason, a matter of relevance ordinarily "must be considered in the full factual setting. . . ." *Lowenstein v. Newark Bd. of Education*, 35 N.J. 94, 105, 171 A.2d 265 (1961).

This is not to suggest that every general rule regarding the relevancy of evidence is invalid on its face. Where the same kind of evidence is frequently offered to prove the same material proposition, a standardized rule may be appropriate. Thus, for example, to the extent that our statute declares evidence of prior sexual conduct with third parties irrelevant to those issues on which it was traditionally admitted at common law, i.e., consent and lack of good moral character, it is not objectionable. The problem arises out of the Legislature's undertaking to anticipate, predict and prescribe every single factual context in which sexual conduct evidence might be relevant to a legitimate theory of defense. Without a fail-safe mechanism allowing the trial judge discretion to admit

---

[3] Alabama, Florida, Georgia, Illinois, Indiana, Kentucky, Louisiana, Maine, Maryland, Massachusetts, Michigan, Minnesota, Missouri, Montana, Nebraska, New Hampshire, North Carolina, Ohio, Pennsylvania, South Carolina, Tennessee, Vermont, Virginia, West Virginia and Wisconsin. . . .

critical defense evidence which is not the subject of an exception, statutes like ours have the potential, as applied, to conflict with a defendant's right to a fair trial. *See* [Cannel, Criminal Code Annotated, Comments 2, 4, N.J.S.A. 2C:14-7 (1991)].

Whether this is the case depends upon resolution of the issue of whether and to what extent unexcepted prior sexual conduct evidence is relevant and necessary to the defense. This requires an assessment of the proffer in light of the record, leaving aside for the moment any consideration of the statute. Here, the jury was presented with what was essentially a two-witness case. Although other witnesses testified, the outcome depended on whether the jury believed the victim or the defendant. Clearly, if the jury believed the victim there was ample evidence to support the verdict. However, there was also evidence elicited during trial which, if believed by the jury, could have warranted defendant's acquittal on one or both of the counts against him. This consisted of defendant's version of the two sexual encounters as having been entirely initiated by T.D. and his testimony that he immediately rejected her advances.

The problem with defendant's version of the events is the probable jury skepticism over the suggestion that a nine-year-old would know enough about sex to initiate such encounters. The reason why defendant proffered the evidence of the victim's prior sexual initiation through sexual abuse by her step-father was to dispel the devastating implication that this child of tender years could not have known of such intimate sexual acts unless they occurred at defendant's initiation. Contrary to the State's argument that this was irrelevant, we think an exquisitely important piece of evidence was excluded from the jurors' consideration.

We are not alone in this view. In *State v. Howard*, 121 N.H. 53, 426 A.2d 457 (1982), the Supreme Court of New Hampshire analyzed a similar issue this way:

> We believe that the average juror would perceive the average twelve-year-old-girl as a sexual innocent. Therefore, it is probable that jurors would believe that the sexual experience she describes must have occurred in connection with the incident being prosecuted; otherwise, she could not have described it. However, if statutory rape victims have had other sexual experiences, it would be possible for them to provide detailed, realistic testimony concerning an incident that may never have happened. To preclude a defendant from presenting such evidence to the jury, if it is otherwise admissible, would be obvious error. [*Howard*, 426 A.2d at 462.]

. . . .

Like results were reached in *Summitt v. State*, 101 Nev. 159, 697 P.2d 1374 (1985) and *People v. Ruiz*, 71 A.D.2d 569, 418 N.Y.S.2d 402 (App. Div. 1979). *See also State v. Jacques*, where the Maine Supreme Court opined that:

> Where the victim is a child, as in this case, the lack of sexual experience is automatically in the case without specific action by the prosecutor. A defendant therefore must be permitted to rebut the inference a jury might otherwise draw that the victim was so naive sexually that she could not have fabricated the charge. A number of jurisdictions with similar rules permit the admission of evidence of prior sexual activity for the limited purposes of rebutting the jury's natural assumption concerning a child's sexual innocence and of protecting the defendant's rights. *Commonwealth v. Ruffen*, 399 Mass. 811, 507 N.E.2d 684 (1987); *State v. Peterson*, 35 Wash. App. 481, 667 P.2d 645 (1983); *State v.*

Carver, 37 Wash. App. 122, 678 P.2d 842 (1984); *State v. Baker*, 127 N.H. 801, 508 A.2d 1059 (1986). [*Jacques*, 558 A.2d 706, 708 (Me. 1989).]

The most recent decision on point is *State v. Pulizzano*, 456 N.W.2d 325, decided by the Wisconsin Supreme Court on June 12, 1990. There the trial judge, relying on Wisconsin's rape shield law, prohibited the admission of evidence that the child victim had previously been sexually assaulted. The evidence was proffered for the purpose of explaining that the victim had an alternate source of sexual knowledge. The Wisconsin Supreme Court held that although the statute barred the admission of the evidence, it was not unconstitutional on its face. However, according to the court, the statute, as applied, impermissibly infringed on defendant's rights to confrontation and compulsory process, which prevailed over the state's interest in promoting effective law enforcement. The court concluded that

> to establish a constitutional right to present otherwise excluded evidence of a child complainant's prior sexual conduct for the limited purpose of proving an alternative source of sexual knowledge, prior to trial the defendant must make an offer of proof showing: (1) that the prior acts clearly occurred; (2) that the acts closely resembled those of the present case; (3) that the prior act is clearly relevant to a material issue; (4) that the evidence is necessary to the defendant's case; and (5) that the probative value of the evidence outweighs its prejudicial effect. [*Pulizzano, supra*, 456 N.W.2d at 335.]

But see State v. Clarke, 343 N.W.2d 158 (Iowa 1984); *People v. Arenda*, 416 Mich. 1, 330 N.W.2d 814 (1982).

Here, the State concedes that the prior acts did occur and that they closely resembled those in the present case. In fact, T.D. used nearly identical language to describe the events. However, the State disagrees as to the relevance and necessity of the evidence to the defense. The State's main argument is that the point of the proffer was to prove the victim's actual conduct on a given occasion based upon prior specific acts contrary to Evid. R. 47. This is not correct. The point of the evidence was not the victim's activity but her capacity to have acted as defendant says she did. Thus, it was offered not to invoke an inference as to how the victim behaved on the date of the crime but to establish a source of knowledge or familiarity with sexual matters under circumstances in which lack of knowledge and a concomitant lack of capacity to act was the likely inference which would be drawn by the factfinder.

* * *

The State finally urges that the admission of this evidence would "gut the core protection of the statute, and defeat all of the legitimate interests protected by it." We disagree. In our view, its admission would not violate any of the overall remedial goals of the rape shield law. The evidence was not offered to establish any of the classic inferences the law was meant to interdict. Inclination to consent was not an issue in the case because of the victim's age. Further, the proffered testimony as to T.D.'s prior victimization did not implicate her own "conduct" and could not place her moral character in issue in any way. *See State v. Carver, supra.* It was unlikely to prejudice her in the jury's eyes. Indeed, the contrary is true. Sympathy for her plight was the more likely response. Nor would it have confused the jury. Rather, it would have tended to explain what might otherwise appear unexplainable — how a nine-year-old child could have learned of the details of sexual intimacies other than from the defendant. The admission of the evidence would not have inhibited the reporting of abuse cases because children generally are not aware of the legal consequences of reporting. Likewise, because of the limited purpose for which evidence was offered, embarrassment or harassment of the victim was unlikely. Indeed, this evidence could have been elicited from another witness testifying as to T.D.'s statements, from the official documents involving T.D.'s step-father's convictions, or by stipulation, in any event with an appropriate limiting instruction. In sum, not only would the "core protection" of the statute not be gutted, but none of the policy considerations informing the statute would be diminished by the admission of this evidence.

We conclude that, as applied to bar the admission of what we view as crucial defense evidence, N.J.S.A. 2C:14-7 violated defendant's Sixth Amendment rights. While we recognize the virtue of the rape shield law and the state's important interest in the protection of rape victims and especially of children and perceive no facial defect in the statute, where evidence of a victim's prior sexual conduct is highly relevant and probative of a fact other than moral character or inclination to consent, a defendant's right to present it is constitutionally protected. Thus, consistent with *Chambers* and *Davis*, this defendant's confrontation rights required that evidence of T.D.'s prior victimization be admitted notwithstanding that the evidence would otherwise have been excluded by the rape shield law.

We emphasize that our holding here is not meant to detract from the importance of the general principles embodied in N.J.S.A. 2C:14-7. In so doing, we affirm that evidence of a victim's prior sexual conduct with a person other than defendant is irrelevant either to prove a lack of moral character bearing on her credibility or on the issue of whether she consented to defendant's advances. We also affirm the need for the trial judge to assiduously evaluate proffered defense evidence in terms of relevance and in terms of the traditional requirement that its probative value not be outweighed by countervailing factors. Even where a determination of admissibility is made, we underscore the need for the trial judge to swiftly and unequivocally circumscribe cross-examination of a victim which is unnecessarily repetitive and harassing. We hold only that N.J.S.A. 2C:14-7 cannot be read in such a way as to deny a defendant a right to a fair trial. Here, that means that evidence of this child victim's prior sexual abuse should have been admitted to rebut the inference that she could not have known of the sexual experiences she described unless they occurred in connection with the incident being prosecuted.

* * *

We reverse and remand this case for a new trial consistent with this opinion.

NOTES AND QUESTIONS

1. In *Budis*, the court rejected the prosecution's claim that the admission of the evidence would "gut the core protection of the statute, and defeat all of the legitimate interests protected by it." *Budis, supra,* 580 A.2d at 291–92. In response, the court stated:

> The admission of the evidence would not have inhibited the reporting of abuse cases because children generally are not aware of the legal consequences of reporting. Likewise, because of the limited purpose for which evidence was offered, embarrassment or harassment of the victim was unlikely.

Id. Do you agree with the court's statement? Are the parents likely to permit a child abuse victim to testify at trial if the defendant is allowed to cross-examine her on prior instances of sexual conduct? At the same time, if the child abuse victim refuses to testify, the defendant in all likelihood goes free.

2. The court's conclusion that it is unlikely that a child abuse victim would be embarrassed or harassed by the admission of the evidence of prior sexual abuse is based on the assumption that the evidence would be admitted through some other witness. *Budis*, 580 A.2d at 291–92. Would a different result in *Budis* be justified if the child victim had to be cross-examined in order for the evidence to be admitted?

3. The New Jersey rape shield statute provides that "[e]vidence of previous sexual conduct shall not be considered relevant unless it is material to negating the element of force or coercion or to proving that the source of semen, pregnancy or disease is a person other than the defendant." N.J.S.A. 2C:14-7. This type of rape shield statute has been characterized as the "inflexible legislative rule" approach. Berger, *Man's Trial, Woman's Tribulations: Rape Cases in the Courtroom*, 77 COLUM. L. REV. 1, 32 (1977). The statute represents a legislative effort to pre-determine precisely those circumstances in which sexual conduct evidence is highly relevant and material to the presentation of a defense theory, and thus, constitutionally required. At the same time, it reflects a legislative judgment that in all but the excepted evidential classes enumerated in the statute, the evidence is irrelevant *per se*. This type of statutory scheme has been criticized as being fundamentally flawed. The criticism is directed at the legislature's inability to pre-determine in a factual vacuum those circumstances when evidence of a victim's prior sexual conduct is highly relevant and necessary to a legitimate defense theory. *See* Galvin, *Shielding Rape Victims in the State and Federal Courts: A Proposal for the Second Decade*, 70 MINN. L. REV. 763 (1986). Would a preferable approach be to explicitly provide in the rape shield statute that if evidence of the victim's past sexual behavior is offered to prove either consent, lack of good moral character, or to impeach the complainant's credibility, the evidence is inadmissible *per se*, but if offered for other purposes admissibility is to be governed by traditional relevancy rules? If the evidence is offered for purposes other than those prohibited by statute, the trial judge would be accorded wide discretion in determining whether the evidence is relevant and whether the probative value is outweighed by the prejudicial effects. In determining whether the probative value is outweighed by countervailing factors, the court should evaluate, among other considerations, the probability that admission of the evidence will create undue prejudice, confusion of the issues, or unwarranted invasion of the privacy of the complaining witness. Which statutory approach is preferable?

4. It should be noted that a number of jurisdictions with rape shield statutes like N.J.S.A. 2C:14-7 have declared admissible prior sexual conduct evidence not the subject of a statutory exception when such evidence was necessary to protect defendant's constitutional rights of confrontation and due process. *See State v. Budis*, 580 A.2d 283, 292 n.5 (N.J. Super. 1990); *Raines v. State*, 382 S.E.2d 738 (Ga. 1989); *State v. Jacques*, 558 A.2d 706 (Me. 1989); *Thomas v. State*, 483 A.2d 6, 18 (Md. 1983) ("Of course, rape shield laws may not be used to exclude probative evidence in violation of a defendant's constitutional rights of confrontation and due process."); *Commonwealth v. Ruffen*, 507 N.E.2d 684, 688 (Mass. 1987) ("[D]espite the general statutory policy prohibiting inquiry into a victim's prior sexual experiences, the Constitution requires that a defendant be permitted to introduce evidence which may materially affect the credibility of the victim's testimony."); *People v. Hackett*, 365 N.W.2d 120, 124 (Mich. 1984) (reaffirming that evidence otherwise excluded by the rape shield statute may be admissible where constitutionally required); *State v. Kroshus*, 447 N.W.2d 203 (Minn. App. 1989) (same); *State v. Howard*, 426 A.2d 457 (N.H. 1981); *Commonwealth v. Black*, 487 A.2d 396 (Pa. 1985) (holding that it was constitutionally impermissible to exclude, under a rape shield law, evidence of prior sexual conduct with third persons offered to reveal a specific bias against the accused and therefore a motive to make a false accusation); *State v. Green*, 260 S.E.2d 257, 264 (W. Va. 1979); *State v. Pulizzano*, 456 N.W.2d 325 (Wis. 1990).

[d]   Admission of Prior Sexual Behavior to Prove Bias or Motive to Fabricate Charges

The Supreme Court has consistently held that restricting the defendant's cross-examination of a key prosecution witness on the issue of bias and motive violates the Confrontation Clause. In *Olden v. Kentucky*, 488 U.S. 227 (1988), the Supreme Court reversed a rape conviction, holding that the defendant had a right to inquire into the rape complainant's cohabitation with another man to show bias. In *Davis v. Alaska*, 415 U.S. 308 (1974), the Supreme Court held that failure to admit evidence of a prior juvenile adjudication, otherwise barred by state policy, to show "possible biases, prejudices, or ulterior motives of the witness" violated defendant's right of confrontation. *Id.* at 316.

Should evidence of past sexual relations be admitted to prove a motive or bias to falsify the rape charge that is the subject of prosecution? Does failure to admit bias or motive evidence infringe upon the defendant's right of confrontation? In *Commonwealth v. Black*, 487 A.2d 396 (Pa. 1985), the defendant argued that his daughter's rape complaint was designed to remove him from the house so that she could continue an ongoing sexual relationship with her brother. The trial court excluded the evidence since it did not fit any of the exceptions of the Pennsylvania rape shield law. The Pennsylvania appeals court reversed on the authority of *Davis v. Alaska*, in which the Supreme Court held that excluding proof relating to motive to lie offends the defendant's rights under the Confrontation Clause.

In *Johnson v. State*, 632 A.2d 152 (Md. App. 1993), the victim, who was addicted to crack cocaine, accused the defendant and his co-defendant of rape. According to the defendant, the sexual relations with the victim occurred while the victim was "freaking" for drugs, i.e., exchanging sex for drugs. The defendant testified that one William Jackson, promised the victim crack cocaine if she would engage in sexual relations, an offer which extended to sexual relations with both defendant and the co-defendant, as well as Jackson. When Jackson did not "pay" the victim, she accused the defendant of rape. Thus, the defendant maintained that the complainant's rape allegation was a vindictive response to not receiving drugs for the sexual relations she engaged in with the defendant. The evidence is substantially probative and material to establishing that the victim had an ulterior motive in falsely accusing him of rape. In corroboration of his defense, the defendant proffered that the victim had "freaked" for drugs in the recent past, and he sought to cross-examine her on this subject.

At an *in camera* hearing held to determine the admissibility of alleged prior incidents of "sex in exchange for drugs," the complainant testified that she had been "freaking" for crack for approximately six months. She further admitted to "freaking" for crack cocaine one week prior to being raped. The victim explained that when she wanted to get high, she would engage in sex for crack cocaine at any time of the day or night. She specifically denied "freaking" for cocaine on the occasion at issue in the case or having previously engaged in sexual relations with either the defendant or the co-defendant.

The Maryland rape shield statute expressly recognized an ulterior motive exception to the general prohibition against admitting evidence of specific instances of prior sexual activity. Nevertheless, the trial court ruled that the probative value of the proffered evidence was outweighed by the prejudicial effects. In reversing the rape conviction, the Maryland Court of Appeals reasoned:

> First, there is a close connection between the sexual conduct evidence and the petitioner's defense; in order to establish that he was falsely accused because the victim did not get the cocaine she was promised, it was necessary for the petitioner to establish the basis for the bargain. Moreover, viewed in light of the victim's activities during the hours preceding the alleged rape, and her addiction and its effect on her (causing her to have sex for cocaine at any time of the day or night when she wanted to get high), the evidence that she freaked for cocaine within a week of the alleged rape is highly probative. *Furthermore, there is little danger that the evidence will be misused by the jury, that its attention will be diverted from the real issue in the case.* As we have seen, rather than offer extrinsic evidence of the fact to be proved, the petitioner elicited the admission from the victim herself; at the in-camera hearing the court held on the subject, the victim made the admission the petitioner sought. Thus, this is not a case in which the jury is required to credit testimony from an extrinsic source, in the face of denial by the victim. Finally, the evidence is necessary to the petitioner's defense. The central focus of this case is the very issue upon which the contested evidence relates: whether the victim, in fact, engaged in sex for drugs rather than being raped. Inasmuch as the petitioner's defense was clear, uncomplicated, and not inherently unbelievable, the probative value of the evidence to prove it outweighed, substantially, its potential for unfair prejudice.

Johnson, 632 A.2d at 161 (emphasis added). While it was not necessary to reach the confrontation issue, the Maryland Court of Appeals cited with approval other cases that reached the same result on confrontation grounds.[60]

NOTES AND QUESTIONS

1. Does the ruling in *Johnson* suggest that motive and bias is always at issue when the complainant is a prostitute? If so, does this mean that in every case where the complainant has engaged in prostitution, evidence of prior sexual acts is admissible? Is a prostitute-complainant less worthy of belief than a virtuous woman? In effect, doesn't the court's ruling implicate sexist presumptions rejected by rape shield statutes? Should evidence of the victim's history of prostitution be admitted to prove bias and motive? Consent? *See State ex rel. Pope v. Mohave Superior Court*, 545 P.2d 946, 953 (1926) (evidence of victim's reputation as prostitute and prior acts of prostitution admissible to support defense of consent to act of prostitution); *Demers v. State*, 547 A.2d 28, 36–37 (1988) (the Constitution requires admission of evidence of past prostitution because it is probative of defense's theory of consent to prostitution);

---

[60] The following cases were cited by the Maryland Court of Appeals: *People v. Varona*, 143 Cal. App. 3d 566 (1983); *Commonwealth v. Joyce*, 415 N.E.2d 181, 186–87 (Mass. 1981) (despite the fact that the Massachusetts rape shield statute does not contain an ulterior motive exception, evidence of prior instances of prostitution offered to prove victim's bias or motive to lie held admissible. "Where . . . facts are relevant to a showing of bias or motive to lie, the general evidentiary rule of exclusion must give way to the constitutionally based right of effective cross-examination."); *People v. Slovinski*, 420 N.W.2d 145, 153–56 (Mich. 1988) (prior acts of the prostitution admissible on issue of consent); *State v. Howard*, 426 A.2d 457 (N.H. 1981) (right of confrontation may require admission of specific acts of sexual conduct of statutory rape victim when defense is denial of contact); *State v. Jalo*, 557 P.2d 1359 (Or. 1976) (rape shield statute which did not permit evidence of victim's ulterior motive infringed upon the defendant's right of confrontation); *State v. Herndon*, 426 N.W.2d 347 (Wis. 1988) (same); *Commonwealth v. Black*, 487 A.2d 396 (Pa. 1985) (same).

Commonwealth v. Joyce, 415 N.E.2d 181, 187 (1981) (victim's history of prostitution admissible to show bias or motive to fabricate, but not to demonstrate consent to prostitution); *People v. Slovinski*, 420 N.W.2d 145, 153–56 (1988) (prior acts of victim's prostitution admissible on issue of consent to vindicate the defendant's due process and confrontation rights, but not to impeach victim's veracity or credibility); *Drake v. State*, 836 P.2d 52, 55 (1992) (rape shield laws restricting admissibility of victim's prior sexual conduct do not apply to acts of illegal prostitution); *State v. Williams*, 487 N.E.2d 560, 563 (1986) (where complainant testified that she did not consent to sex with men because she was a lesbian, it was constitutional error to exclude evidence of her reputation in the community as a prostitute); and *State v. Green*, 260 S.E.2d 257, 264 (1979) (it would be unconstitutional to exclude evidence that complainant was a prostitute where "the defendant alleges the prosecutrix actually consented to an act of prostitution"). *But see Jeffries v. Nix*, 912 F.2d 982, 987 (8th Cir. 1990) (evidence of prostitution inadmissible because "even if [victim] did exchange sex for money on previous occasions, there is no evidence that she offered to do so in this situation); *Hagins v. United States*, 639 A.2d 612, 614–16 (D.C. 1994) (doubting relevance of victim's history of prostitution to defendant's theory of consent to prostitution); *People v. Tennin*, 515 N.E.2d 1056, 1059 (1987) (same); *State v. Philbrick*, 551 A.2d 847, 851 (Me. 1988) (evidence that rape victim was a prostitute inadmissible where offered only to impeach her character); *Holloway v. State*, 695 S.W.2d 112, 117 (Tex. Crim. App. 1985) (evidence of recent prostitution material to defendant's theory of consent to prostitution, but more prejudicial than probative), *aff'd*, 751 S.W.2d 866, 870–71 (Tex. Crim. App. 1988) (affirming because evidence of recent prostitution was not even material to the defendant's theory).

2. Do you agree with the court's statement in *Johnson* that "there is little danger that the evidence will be misused by the jury, that its attention will be diverted from the real issue in the case"? Isn't the jury in *Johnson* likely to find the complainant, who admittedly exchanged sex for drugs, morally less deserving of protection under the rape shield law? If evidence of prior incidents of "freaking" is admitted, do you think this will cause the jury's attention to shift from the issue of innocence or guilt of the defendant to the moral character of the complainant?

[e]   Evidence of Complainant's Prior False Allegations of Rape

UNITED STATES v. STAMPER
766 F. Supp. 1396 (W.D.N.C. 1991)

Seymour, Circuit Judge.

*   *   *

A. Procedural History

On December 3, 1990, the captioned criminal case was called for trial, and jury selection began. On that day Defendant filed a brief supporting his position on the proffered evidence.

On December 4, 1990, after voir dire had resulted in the selection of eight jurors, the Government notified the Court of the complainant's desire to have independent counsel appointed for the protection of her privacy interests, pursuant to the policies enunciated in *Doe v. United States*, 666 F.2d 43, 46 (4th Cir. 1981), *In re McDaniel*, 861 F.2d 714 (4th Cir. 1988) (unpublished opinion), and *United States v. Saunders*, 736 F. Supp. 698, 700 (E.D. Va. 1990). After consulting with the complainant, the Court appointed attorney Steven Lindsay to represent her interests. The Court then conducted an *in camera* hearing to determine the admissibility of Defendant's proffered evidence. The Court heard testimony from, and all three parties were permitted to examine, the following witnesses: complainant; complainant's mother, Maxine Beck; complainant's father, Jack Beck; and two of the three men previously accused by the complainant of sexual abuse, Robert Francis "Bobby" Stamper (complainant's uncle) and Reuben Teesataskie (the live-in boyfriend of complainant's mother). Upon the Court's own motion, the case was continued so as to provide Mr. Lindsay adequate time for preparation and to allow the Court to consider Defendant's evidentiary motion. . . . The Court therefore excused the eight jurors already selected.

The Government, counsel for the Defendant, and counsel for the complainant have since filed briefs on the question of Rule 412 evidence. . . .

B. The In Camera Hearing

At the *in camera* hearing described above, the evidence showed:

1. Complainant is the daughter of Maxine and Jack Beck, who were divorced prior to the events herein contemplated. Jack Beck remarried and lives in the Bird Town section of the Cherokee Indian Reservation. Maxine Beck lives with her boyfriend Teesataskie in the Big Cove section of the same reservation.

2. In early 1989, approximately one year before the allegations in the instant case, complainant made allegations of sexual fondling against three persons known by both complainant and her natural parents: Teesataskie, complainant's uncle by marriage Bobby Stamper, and her first cousin Maney.

3. The prior allegations were made when complainant was living with her mother and Teesataskie, and at a time when pronounced "difficulties" existed among complainant, her mother, and Teesataskie.

4. As a result of the prior allegations (and immediately after they were made), complainant moved from her mother's house to her father's house. The move was made for the purpose of getting complainant away from Teesataskie.

5. Complainant subsequently wrote a letter, the pertinent part of which reads: "Well, I told my dad that my step dad [sic] sexually abused me. Then my dad made me talk to a councilor. The councilor's name is John. John went and told my step dad what I said (*which is not true*)." Defendant's Exhibit 3 (handwritten letter, dated March 20, 1989, from complainant to recipient identified only as Kathy) (emphasis added). Complainant therein identified Teesataskie as her "step dad," but he and complainant's mother were unmarried live-ins. There was no mention in the letter of Bobby Stamper or Maney, or of the allegations once leveled against them.

6. Upon discovery of the letter, it was submitted to the Cherokee Police Department. Subsequently, the investigations pending against Teesataskie, Maney, and Bobby Stamper were halted, and no charges were ever brought against any of the three men.

7. Complainant admitted that she had lied about the three prior alleged occurrences of sexual abuse.

8. Complainant has since disaffirmed this letter and other recantings, saying that the prior allegations are true. Complainant claims that the phrase "(which is not true)" refers to the next sentence in the letter: "Reuben went and stood over my little sister Candi, and started crying because *he is afraid* some people will *take her away* for what he did!" Defendant's Exhibit 3 (emphasis in original). In other words, complainant contends, contrary to the way it reads literally, that the letter merely refutes the notion that someone would deprive Teesataskie of his custody of Candi because of the sexual molestation allegations, and does not disaffirm her allegations of sexual abuse against Teesataskie.

9. The allegations giving rise to the present case were made when complainant was living with her father, and when "difficulties" arose between complainant and her father. More specifically, complainant was caught sneaking back into her father's house after spending an entire evening out with one Allen Littlejohn. On at least one other occasion, and without her father's knowledge, complainant had snuck out of her father's house late at night to see Littlejohn and subsequently returned undetected. Upon discovering his daughter's late-night activities, Jack Beck threatened to send complainant to "detention." Defendant, against whom the present allegations were made, is an acquaintance of complainant and a co-employee, acquaintance/friend, and fishing buddy of her father.

* * *

11. As a result of the present allegations (and immediately after they were made), complainant moved from her father's house back into her mother's house, still inhabited also by Teesataskie.

C. Issues Presented

Title 18, United States Code, §§ 2243(a) and 1153 make it a crime for an Indian person knowingly to engage in a sexual act in Indian country with another person at least 12 years old but not yet 16 and at least four years younger than the accused. Defendant is charged in two counts with commission of this offense on July 5, 1990, and again on July 16, 1990. On those dates, the complainant was a twelve year-old schoolgirl, and the Defendant was a twenty year-old dispatcher with the Cherokee Police Department. He was married, his wife of one year was expecting their first child in some five months, and he was attending community college in pursuit of law enforcement certification.

The issue before the Court might be stated as follows: in a prosecution for statutory rape, where the Government's sole incriminating evidence is the complainant's testimony and where the complainant has admitted in writing to falsely accusing her mother's boyfriend of sexual molestation on a prior occasion and has made accusations against two others under circumstances tending to show ulterior motives on her part, should the Court find to be admissible (a) cross examination of the complainant concerning such accusations, and (b) testimony by all three prior accusees that the accusations against them were false. Such evidence, according to the Defendant, is necessary to demonstrate that complainant's allegations against him are not true, but rather are part of a continuing scheme on her part to manipulate others for her own selfish purposes.

II. DISCUSSION

* * *

B. The Confrontation Clause and Davis v. Alaska

The question remaining is whether the proffered evidence is constitutionally required to be admitted. "In all criminal prosecutions, the accused shall enjoy the right . . . to be confronted with the witnesses against him." U.S. Const. amend. VI. "[A] primary interest secured by [the confrontation clause of the sixth amendment] is the right of cross-examination." *Douglas v. Alabama*, 380 U.S. 415, 418 (1965).

The case of *Davis v. Alaska*, 415 U.S. 308 (1974), with its confrontation clause analysis, requires the admission of the evidence Defendant seeks. In that case, the United States Supreme Court allowed evidence of a prior juvenile adjudication, otherwise barred by state policy, to show "possible biases, prejudices, or ulterior motives of the witness as they might relate directly to the issues or personalities in the case at hand." *Id.* at 316. According to the *Davis* Court, the State's policy interest in preserving the anonymity of a juvenile offender "cannot require [the] yielding of so vital a constitutional right as the effective cross-examination for bias of an adverse witness-. . . . [T]he State cannot, consistent with the right of confrontation, require the [Defendant] to bear the full burden of vindicating the State's interest in the secrecy of juvenile criminal records." *Id.* at 320. "[T]he exposure of a witness' motivation in testifying is a proper and important function of the constitutionally protected right of cross-examination." *Id.* at 316–17 (citing *Greene v. McElroy*, 360 U.S. 474, 496 (1959)).

In the instant case, Defendant offers evidence of complainant's prior allegations to show that, because she previously made false allegations of sexual abuse and fondling, the complainant is now making "false accusations of a similar nature, with the same intent, motivation and plan to move her residence from one parent to another and to divert attention from herself and place it on an alleged perpetrator to show her motivation, intent and plan in this case." Defendant's Brief on Proffered Evidence, at 7. Such language has its roots in the *Davis* "possible biases, prejudices, or ulterior motives" language. *Davis*, 415 U.S. at 316. *See also Hoover v. Maryland*, 714 F.2d 301, 305 (4th Cir. 1983); *Chavis v. North Carolina*, 637 F.2d 213, 225–26 (4th Cir. 1980). The lack of physical evidence of rape in the instant case makes complainant the "crucial" witness, in that the "accuracy and truthfulness of [her] testimony [are the] key elements in the [Government's] case." *Davis*, 415 U.S. at 317. Therefore, the jury is "entitled to have the benefit of the defense theory before them so that they [may] make an informed judgment as to the weight to place on [complainant's] testimony which provide[s] 'a crucial link in the proof . . . of [Defendant's] act.' " *Id.* (quoting *Douglas*, 380 U.S. at 419). *See also* [1 S. Saltzburg & M. Martin, Federal Rules of Evidence Manual, at 396–97]. In order to confront the complainant effectively, to elucidate the facts and legal issues here in question fully, and to present a defense in a constitutionally viable trial, Defendant must be allowed to set before the jury the proffered evidence of ulterior motives of the complainant. The sixth amendment and *Davis* mandate that the proffered evidence be admitted.

The Government argues that the prior allegations of sexual abuse and fondling lodged by complainant are rendered inadmissible as evidence of "past sexual behavior" under Fed. R. Evid. 412. . . . The Government has cited case law from other circuits which concluded that the exclusion of prior allegations of rape under Rule 412 was not reversible error. *United States v. Bartlett*, 856 F.2d 1071 (8th Cir. 1988); *United States v. Azure*, 845 F.2d 1503 (8th Cir. 1988); *United States v. Cardinal*, 782 F.2d 34 (6th Cir.), *cert. denied*, 476 U.S. 1161 (1986). However, on the present facts and for the reasons discussed herein, the Court finds that Defendant's right of confrontation is paramount to Rule 412's policy of shielding a rape victim from potential embarrassment. *See Davis*, 415 U.S. at 319.

*   *   *

Defendant is charged with a serious crime, one for which, upon conviction, he would likely serve time in prison. Testifying against him is a complainant whose interest in avoiding the embarrassing disclosure of intimate details of her private life has been recognized and, with limited exceptions, shielded by Rule 412. In assessing the balance to be struck between these competing interests, it cannot be ignored that her charges are largely unsubstantiated outside of her own testimony. No physical evidence of rape, sexual abuse, or fondling by Defendant has been presented. In the end, the jury will believe her or the Defendant. Defendant, a law enforcement dispatcher before these charges were brought, seeks to offer exculpatory evidence that the complainant's charges against him were motivated by the bias and ulterior motive of a willful adolescent from a broken home bent on manipulating those who had custody of her and control of her activities.

C. General Credibility Versus Scheme of Fabrication

It is not merely a general credibility attack that is at stake here. The question on these facts, rather, is whether Defendant must face prison deprived of the effective ability to develop in evidence the plan or scheme purportedly motivating his accuser, whose state of mind is an essential element of his defense of fabrication. The sixth amendment necessitates this development of Defendant's theory of defense, for only in this way can the Defendant fully and effectively confront the complainant. *See* 1 S. Saltzburg & M. Martin, at 397 ("A Judge may not bar relevant evidence that itself establishes a defense recognized in law."). Defendant's proffered evidence goes beyond the general provisions of Rule 404(b), for the Defendant does not wish to show that the prior false allegations of sexual abuse, under similar circumstances, establish a mere propensity to fabricate. Rather, Defendant seeks to put forth these allegations as proof of a contrived ulterior motive and plan. In that sense the Court should give, at least if requested by the Government, an instruction that the prior falsehoods by the alleged victim, if so found by the jury, would not in themselves prove falsity in the instant case, but could be considered on the question of motive or plan, if any, behind the accusations in the case at hand. Fed. R. Evid. 105.

Defendant's theory of defense seeks evidentiary support for the proposition that we have here an adolescent girl given (arguably) to lying for the purposes of manipulating her custodians, avoiding therapy, keeping her younger sister Candi at home, and the like. This line of attack on her credibility and motivation is constitutionally required, for not to admit it would be to block out an area of possible truth constituting the very context in which the charges arose. Defendant is entitled to offer the evidence necessary to prove his theory of the case by showing that complainant's charges against him did not evince a single isolated instance of manipulative behavior, but rather were part of an ongoing scheme or, at least, a scheme revealed by the like motives and *modus operandi* of schemes past. While it is true that the complainant now contends that she did not mean what she said in her letter, and withdrew her allegations of sexual abuse solely to keep Candi in her home, what her actual behavior and motivations might have been are for the jury to determine.

There are several facts in the instant case indicative of a contrived scheme of fabrication on the part of the complainant. Both the prior (Teesataskie, Bobby Stamper, and Maney) and the present (Defendant) allegations were made at times of pronounced difficulties between the complainant and the natural parent with whom she was living at the time, and both allowed complainant to move from one parent's home to another. The fact that the prior and the present allegations were separated by just one year significantly increases the probative value of the prior allegations. 124 Cong. Rec. H11,945, daily ed. Oct. 10, 1978 (statement of Rep. Mann, pertaining to Rule 412) ("In determining the admissibility of such evidence, the court will consider . . . the amount of time that lapsed between the alleged prior acts and the rape charged in the prosecution. The greater the lapse of time, of course, the less likely it is that such evidence will be admitted."). All of the allegations were made against older men who either dwelt in or frequented the custodial parent's home. The letter pertaining to the Teesataskie allegations and complainant's *in camera* testimony pertaining to all three prior allegations create reasonable doubt as to the veracity of these prior allegations. Finally, the Court notes that complainant moved back in with her mother and Teesataskie of her own volition after the present allegations were lodged, despite the fact that she had moved out of that home one year earlier for the presumed purpose of getting away from Teesataskie. This event tends to show her earlier allegations against Teesataskie were untrue. These remarkable similarities lend substantial credence to the defense theory of an ongoing scheme of fabrication by the complainant.

It is precisely the extensive similarities between the present and the prior allegations that removes the instant case from the general credibility attacks prohibited by the *Bartlett, Azure,* and *Cardinal* line of cases cited by the Government. *Azure* is irrelevant in this context because it dealt only with evidence presented for general witness impeachment and to show the source of injury to the prosecuting witness. *Azure,* 845 F.2d at 1506. The court did not discuss the confrontation clause exception to Rule 412 exclusion of evidence. *Id.* at 1505. The offer of proof in that case does not approach the complexity, and ample substantiation, of the *Davis*-type defense theory of complainant's motive or scheme of fabricated sexual abuse allegations in the instant case.

* * *

The instant case more closely approaches the facts in the Supreme Court decision *Olden v. Kentucky,* 488 U.S. 227 (1988). In *Olden,* the defense theory was that the defendant and the complainant had engaged in consensual sexual relations, and that the complainant had fabricated the charges of rape against the defendant in order to protect her ongoing relationship with her live-in boyfriend. *Olden,* 488 U.S. at 230. The Supreme Court began by reiterating the central principle of *Davis,* that " 'the exposure of a witness' motivation in testifying is a proper and important function of the constitution-ally protected right of cross-examination.' " *Id.* at 231 (quoting *Davis,* 415 U.S. at 316–17). It followed, according to the *Olden* Court, that " '[a] reasonable jury might have received a significantly different impression of [the witness'] credibility had [defense counsel] been permitted to pursue his proposed line of cross-examination.' " *Olden,* 488 U.S. at 232 (quoting *Delaware v. Van Arsdall,* 475 U.S. 673, 680 (1986)). The Court thus found reversible error in the trial court's exclusion of evidence pertaining to the complainant's relationship with her live-in boyfriend. *Olden,* 488 U.S. at 233.

In the instant case, Defendant has vigorously asserted a motive or scheme of fabrication by the complainant and has produced substantial supporting evidence. The absence of Defendant's proffered evidence pertaining to the three prior allegations would deprive the jury members of substantial information relevant to their duty of witness credibility assessment. Any ambiguity potentially posed by this evidence is to be resolved by the jury. *See Saunders,* 736 F. Supp. at 701.

The Court is of the view that Defendant's substantial interest in presenting an adequate defense, predicated on the concept of complainant's motive or scheme, against the very real possibility of an extended loss of liberty, Defendant's sixth amendment right to confront witnesses against him, and the general constitutional importance of effective cross-examination outweighs the possibility of embarrassment complainant might suffer upon the revelation of her prior allegations of sexual abuse against the three. *See Davis*, 415 U.S. at 319; *Lawson v. Murray*, 837 F.2d 653, 656 (4th Cir.), *cert. denied*, 488 U.S. 831 (1988); *United States v. Bodden*, 736 F.2d 142, 145 (4th Cir. 1984); Galvin, *Shielding Rape Victims in the State and Federal Courts: A Proposal for the Second Decade*, 70 Minn. L. Rev. 763, 839 (1986).

*   *   *

Finally, Rule 412 does not bar admission of evidence of the complainant's past sexual behavior where such evidence is offered to demonstrate the accused's state of mind. *See Doe*, 666 F.2d at 48; *Saunders*, 736 F. Supp. at 702. However, "admissibility still hinges on whether the evidence passes muster under Rule 403, Fed. R. Evid." and whether it is relevant to the issues in question. *Saunders*, 736 F. Supp. at 702, 704 (citing *Doe*). The Court agrees with the *Saunders* court that "the Fourth Circuit doubtless intends careful application of the state of mind exception to ensure that it is not used to avoid the Rule [412]." *Saunders*, 736 F. Supp. at 704, n.8. Conversely, particularly in light of the *Davis* decision, the Court believes Rule 412 cannot be manipulated by the Government or the complainant so as to envelop the complainant's motivation or state of mind in a shroud of statutory inadmissibility, thereby depriving Defendant of "a proper and important function of the constitutionally protected right of cross-examination." *Davis*, 415 U.S. at 316–17.

III. ORDER

IT IS, THEREFORE ORDERED that Defendant's motion for the admission of evidence pertaining to the complainant's prior allegations of sexual abuse and fondling against Reuben Teesataskie, Robert Francis "Bobby" Stamper, and Kenneth Junior "Buffy" Maney is hereby ALLOWED.

NOTES AND QUESTIONS

1. The *Stamper* court recognized an exception to Rule 412 to prove the accused's "state of mind." The court stated:

> Rule 412 does not bar admission of evidence of the complainant's past sexual behavior where such evidence is offered to demonstrate the accused's state of mind. . . . [P]articularly in light of the *Davis* decision, the Court believes Rule 412 cannot be manipulated by the Government or the complainant so as to envelop the complainant's motivation or state of mind in a shroud of statutory inadmissibility, thereby depriving Defendant of a "proper and important function of the constitutionally protected right of cross-examination." (citation omitted).

Stamper, 766 F. Supp. at 1406. What is the justification for this exception? Did the court merely fashion its own exception to the rule's explicit ban on past sexual behavior when relevant to the accused's state of mind? What are the appropriate limits of the court's enunciated "state of mind" exception? Doesn't consent go to the victim's state of mind?

Does this exception risk opening the door to the admission of past sexual conduct to prove that the complainant consented?

2. One other federal circuit has recognized an exception to Fed. R. Evid. 412 for the purpose of proving the *defendant's* state of mind. In *Doe v. United States*, 666 F.2d 43 (4th Cir. 1981), when confronted with the question of whether "evidence of the defendant's 'state of mind as a result of what he knew of [the victim's] reputation'" was admissible under Fed. R. Evid. 412(a), the court stated: "There is no indication . . . that this evidence was intended to be excluded when offered solely to show the accused's state of mind." 666 F.2d at 47, 48; *see also United States v. Saunders*, 736 F. Supp. 698, 705 (E.D. Va. 1990) (suggesting that evidence that the defendant had knowledge that the complainant had shown a preference for combative sex in her prior sexual relations with others may be relevant to prove the defendant's state of mind where the defendant claims that he reasonably interpreted the victim's protestations and struggles as invitations, rather than denials, of consent). For a critical analysis of *Doe, see* Spector & Foster, *Rule 412 and the Doe Case: The Fourth Circuit Turns Back the Clock*, 35 OKLA. L. REV. 87 (1982). Should an exception to Fed. R. Evid. 412 be recognized for the defendant's state of mind?

3. Rule 412(a)(1) prohibits evidence offered to prove that any alleged victim engaged in "other sexual behavior." A threshold question is whether demonstrably false past allegations of rape or sexual abuse lodged by the alleged victim constitute evidence of "other sexual behavior." If the answer is indeed "no," then Rule 412 is inapplicable. Several courts have excluded such evidence from coverage under their individual versions of rape shield statutes. *See, e.g., United States v. Tail*, 459 F.3d 854, 861 (8th Cir. 2006) (excluding evidence of allegations of prior false accusations, reasoning that admission of such evidence would have triggered "mini-trials" and "increased the danger of jury confusion and speculation"); *Covington v. State*, 703 P.2d 436, 442 (Alaska App.), *different results reached on other grounds*, 711 P.2d 1183 (1985); *West v. State*, 719 S.W.2d 684 (Ark. 1985); *People v. Burrell-Hart*, 237 Cal. Rptr. 654, 656 (1987); *State v. Barber*, 766 P.2d 1288 (Kan. 1989); *Cox v. State*, 443 A.2d 607, 613–14 (Md. App. 1982); *People v. Hackett*, 365 N.W.2d 120, 125 (Mich. 1984) (*dicta*); *People v. Garvie*, 384 N.W.2d 796, 798 (1986); *People v. Mandel*, 403 N.Y.S.2d 63, 68 (1978), *rev'd on other grounds*, 48 N.Y.2d 952, 401 N.E.2d 185 (1979); *State v. Baron*, 292 S.E.2d 741, 743 (N.C. App. 1982); *State v. Le Clair*, 730 P.2d 609 (Or. App. 1986); *In re Pittsburgh Action Against Rape*, 428 A.2d 126 (Pa. 1981). *See also* C. Wright & K. Graham, FEDERAL PRACTICE AND PROCEDURE § 5384, at 546; § 5387, at 579–80 (1980); Galvin, *Shielding Rape Victims in the State and Federal Courts: A Proposal for the Second Decade*, 70 MINN. L. REV. 763, 859, 863 n.476 (1986).

PROBLEM

Problem 6-5. *Pattern of Sexual Conduct.* Does the defendant have a right to introduce evidence of a pattern between "other" sexual acts and the one alleged? Professor Berger poses a hypothetical case where a woman over a brief period goes to singles bars on Saturday nights, picks up strangers, takes them home with her, and then has consensual sexual relations with them. After doing so on more than twenty occasions, she meets the defendant at the same bar, takes him home with her, and then, according to her, she is sexually assaulted; according to him, their sexual relations were consensual. Should the defendant be permitted to prove the prior consensual sexual acts between the complaining witness and other men to bolster his defense of consent? Would exclusion of evidence of a pattern of sexual conduct violate the defendant's rights under the Confrontation Clause? Is a "pattern of conduct" exception consistent with the policies underlying rape shield legislation or merely a thinly veiled attempt to resurrect common law sexist assumptions? *See* Berger, *Man's Trial, Woman's Tribulation: Rape Cases in the Courtroom*, 77 COLUM. L. REV. 1, 59 (1977); *see also* Galvin, *Rape-Shield Laws*, at 831. Note that three states provide an exception for evidence that exhibits a pattern of consensual sexual conduct on the part of the complainant when the circumstances so closely resemble the facts of the alleged rape as to raise the inference that she consented on the occasion in question. *See* Fla. Stat. Ann. § 794.022(2) (West Supp. 1985); Minn. R. Evid. 404(c)(A)(i); N.C.R. Evid. 412.

Chapter 7

HEARSAY — ADMISSIONS

A. THE ACCUSED'S CONDUCT — CONSCIOUSNESS OF GUILT

Defendant's flight or escape from custody is generally viewed by the courts as an "admission by conduct" and admissible as evidence probative of the defendant's "consciousness of guilt."[1] The admission of such evidence is based on an inference that only the guilty flee. An often-quoted statement from Wigmore's treatise on evidence states that "the wicked flee, even when no man pursueth, but the righteous are as bold as a lion."[2] At the same time, admission by conduct on the issue of consciousness of guilt is not limited to evidence of flight or escape from custody. An accused's " 'resistance to arrest, concealment, assumption of a false name, and related conduct, are admissible as evidence of consciousness of guilt, and thus of guilt itself.' "[3] Additionally, efforts to alter one's identity may be admitted to show consciousness of guilt.[4]

Evidence of physical threats to a witness may be admissible to prove consciousness of guilt if related to the offense charged.[5] Admission of evidence to show consciousness of guilt may implicate Fed. R. Evid. 404(b), which prohibits evidence of "[o]ther crimes, wrongs, or acts" to prove that the defendant acted in conformity therewith. The defendant against whom the evidence is admissible may request a limiting instruction to the jury, cautioning it not to consider the threat as proof of the defendant's violent character, but only as proof of consciousness of guilt.[6]

If a defendant fails to act by refusing to comply with a court order to provide fingerprints, voice exemplars, or handwriting specimens, such failure may be probative of consciousness of guilt and admissible on that basis. The courts are in accord that the

---

[1] *See United States v. Barnes*, 140 F.3d 737, 738 (8th Cir. 1998); *United States v. Felix-Gutierrez*, 940 F.2d 1200, 1207 (9th Cir. 1991); *United States v. Dillon*, 870 F.2d 1125, 1126 (6th Cir. 1989); *United States v. Kord*, 836 F.2d 368, 372 (7th Cir. 1988); *United States v. Martinez*, 681 F.2d 1248, 1256 (10th Cir. 1982); *United States v. Myers*, 550 F.2d 1036, 1049 (5th Cir. 1977).

[2] 2 J. WIGMORE, EVIDENCE § 276 (Chadbourn rev. 1979).

[3] *United States v. Clark*, 45 F.3d 1247, 1250 (8th Cir. 1995) (quoting 2 J. WIGMORE, EVIDENCE § 276, at 122 (Chadbourn rev. 1979); *see also United States v. Felix-Gutierrez*, 940 F.2d 1200, 1207–08 (9th Cir. 1991) (court did not abuse its discretion in admitting evidence of defendant using assumed names).

[4] *See Felix-Gutierrez*, 940 F.2d at 1208 (defendant's behavior in having a distinctive tattoo removed and submitting to cosmetic facial surgery admissible as evidence of consciousness of guilt).

[5] *See United States v. Hayden*, 85 F.3d 153, 159 (4th Cir. 1996) ("Evidence of witness intimidation is admissible to prove consciousness of guilt and criminal intent under Rule 404(b), if the evidence (1) is related to the offense charged and (2) is reliable."); *United States v. Mickens*, 926 F.2d 1323, 1328 (2d Cir. 1991) (evidence that defendant made a hand gesture in the shape of a gun as his former attorney entered the courtroom to testify was properly admitted to prove consciousness of guilt); *United States v. Smith*, 629 F.2d 650, 651–52 (10th Cir. 1980) ("Evidence of threats to prosecution witness is admissible as showing consciousness of guilt if a direct connection is established between the defendant and the threat.").

[6] *See United States v. Tracy*, 12 F.3d 1186, 1195 (2d Cir. 1993).

defendant's failure to act under these circumstances is admissible to show consciousness of guilt.[7]

What is the test for the admissibility of flight evidence as circumstantial evidence of consciousness of guilt? In other words, how do courts determine the probative value of flight evidence? The federal circuits generally apply a four-step inquiry. The probative value of flight as evidence of a defendant's consciousness of guilt depends on the degree of the confidence with which four inferences can be drawn: (1) infer flight from behavior; (2) infer consciousness of guilt from flight; (3) infer consciousness of guilt concerning the crime charged from consciousness of guilt; and (4)infer actual guilt of the crime charged from consciousness of guilt concerning the crime charged.[8] Application of the four-part test is discussed in *United States v. Dillon*.

UNITED STATES v. DILLON
870 F.2d 1125 (6th Cir. 1989)

MERRITT, CIRCUIT JUDGE.

Appellant Thomas J. Dillon was indicted for, and convicted of, various drug offenses: 21 U.S.C. § 841(a)(1) (distribution of cocaine); 21 U.S.C. § 846 (conspiracy to possess cocaine with intent to distribute it); 21 U.S.C. § 843(b) (use of telephone to facilitate the crimes of conspiracy and distribution). He appeals on [the ground] that the District Court erred by admitting evidence of his flight and by giving the jury an instruction on flight. . . . Because we see no reason to find error . . . we affirm Dillon's conviction.

Flight evidence comes in as an admission of guilt by conduct. Cleary, McCormick on Evidence § 271, at 803 (3d ed. 1984). The Supreme Court has expressed skepticism as to its value:

> [W]e have consistently doubted the probative value in criminal trials of evidence that the accused fled the scene of an actual or supposed crime. In *Alberty v. United States*, 162 U.S. 499, 511 [. . . (1896)], this Court said: ". . . it is not universally true that a man, who is conscious that he has done a wrong, 'will pursue a certain course not in harmony with the conduct of a man who is conscious of having done an act which is innocent, right and proper,' since it is a matter of common knowledge that men who are entirely innocent do sometimes fly from the scene of a crime through fear of being apprehended as the guilty parties, or from an unwillingness to appear as witnesses. Nor is it true as an accepted axiom of criminal law that 'the wicked flee when no man pursueth, but the righteous are as bold as a lion.'"

Wong Sun v. United States, 371 U.S. 471, 483 n. 10 (1963). Where evidence of flight has genuine probative value, however, it is "generally admissible as evidence of guilt, and

---

[7] *See, e.g.*, *United States v. Jackson*, 886 F.2d 838, 846 (7th Cir. 1989) ("We believe the evidence of the defendant's refusal to furnish writing exemplars, like evidence of flight and concealment, is probative of consciousness of guilt, or in other words guilty knowledge."); *United States v. Terry*, 702 F.2d 299, 314 (2d Cir. 1983) (defendant's refusal to furnish palm print was admissible as consciousness of guilt); *United States v. Franks*, 511 F.2d 25, 35–36 (6th Cir. 1975) (upheld jury instruction that jury could infer defendant's consciousness of guilt from his refusal to provide court-ordered voice exemplar).

[8] *See United States v. Levine*, 5 F.3d 1100, 1107 (7th Cir. 1993); *United States v. Felix-Gutierrez*, 940 F.2d 1200, 1207–08 (9th Cir. 1991); *United States v. Hankins*, 931 F.2d 1256, 1261 (8th Cir. 1991); *United States v. Dillon*, 870 F.2d 1125, 1126–27 (6th Cir. 1989); *United States v. Myers*, 550 F.2d 1036, 1049 (5th Cir. 1977).

. . . juries are given the power to determine 'how much weight should be given to such evidence.' " *United States v. Touchstone*, 726 F.2d 1116, 1119 (6th Cir. 1984) (citations omitted). The task for a District Court in determining whether to admit evidence of flight, thus, is to determine whether the proffered evidence in fact tends to prove guilt and not merely the terror that may befall an innocent person confronted by the criminal justice system, and whether the evidence, even if probative of guilt, is so prejudicial that its admission offends Fed. R. Evid. 403. Our task is to review those determinations for an abuse of discretion. *United States v. Hernandez-Bermudez*, 857 F.2d 50, 53 (1st Cir. 1988); *United States v. Lepanto*, 817 F.2d 1463, 1467 (10th Cir. 1987).

The Fifth Circuit has devised a four-step analysis of flight evidence that, as many courts have recognized, allows an orderly inquiry into the inferences proposed by evidence of flight. . . . According to this formulation, the probative value of flight evidence

> depends upon the degree of confidence with which four inferences can be drawn: (1) from the defendant's behavior to flight; (2) from flight to consciousness of guilt; (3) from consciousness of guilt to consciousness of guilt concerning the crime charged; and (4) from consciousness of guilt concerning the crime charged to actual guilt of the crime charged.

United States v. Myers, 550 F.2d 1036, 1049 (5th Cir. 1977), *cert. denied*, 439 U.S. 847 (1978). All four inferences must be "reasonabl[y] support[ed]" by the evidence. *Myers*, 550 F.2d at 1050.

In the present case, Dillon was charged with, and convicted of, supplying Edward Knezevich with cocaine between December 1982 and March 26, 1983. Knezevich obtained a pound of cocaine from Dillon on the latter date and sold it, through a pre-arranged deal, to Sheila Bezotsky. Bezotsky was cooperating with the FBI, and Knezevich was arrested when he delivered the cocaine to her. All those events took place in Columbus, where Dillon then lived.

Knezevich was eventually convicted for his role in this deal. After his conviction he was subpoenaed to testify before a Grand Jury. On December 19, 1984, Knezevich told Dillon that he would testify the next day before a Grand Jury, and that he intended to tell the truth about Dillon's role in the cocaine deal. Knezevich also testified that, as part of his agreement with the government, he would attempt to contact Dillon, wearing a hidden tape recorder, on December 20; that he had tried to find Dillon; and that he had failed to find him.

Dillon's ex-wife testified that Dillon did not keep his engagement to take custody of their children, on Christmas day. She also testified that, ever since that day and for the next two years, Dillon contacted her only by phone, and that she had no way of knowing whether he was in Columbus or not.

Dillon was arrested in Florida in June 1987. The FBI agent who arrested him testified that he was living there under an assumed name. There is no evidence that he denied to the FBI agent arresting him that he was Thomas Dillon. He was indicted on the present charges on July 30, 1987.

At trial, the government attempted to prove that Dillon had fled Columbus after learning about Knezevich's planned Grand Jury testimony, and that such a flight proved Dillon's awareness of his guilt of the crimes charged. Dillon preserved his appeal from the admission of evidence of flight by timely objections at trial. He seeks to persuade this Court that his departure from Columbus came at least two years after the alleged offense and well before the indictment was filed, so that he had "nothing to flee from." To accept this argument we would have to ignore the crucial fact that the government adduced evidence suggesting that Dillon fled Columbus within days after hearing from a co-conspirator that the co-conspirator was about to implicate Dillon in a big cocaine deal in Grand Jury testimony. The real question before us is whether the evidence, *including* Dillon's December 19 conversation with Knezevich, his unexplained failure to keep his Christmas plans with his children, and his subsequent phone rather than personal contacts with his ex-wife, are sufficiently probative of a guilty conscience to overcome the prejudice it entails. We conclude that the four *Myers* inferences are all adequately supported by the evidence introduced at Dillon's trial.

The first question is whether the evidence supports the inference that there has been a "flight" in the first place. The *Myers* court found that no such inference was allowable where the jury could infer flight only by resort to "conjecture and speculation." *Myers*, 550 F.2d at 1050. We believe that the evidence before Dillon's jury allowed a sound inference, not merely a speculative one, that he had fled. Dillon's ex-wife testified that, only six days after hearing from Knezevich about the latter's planned Grand Jury testimony, he broke an important family commitment and from then on contacted her by phone from an undisclosed location. He was arrested in Florida, where he was living under an assumed name. We do not believe it would be unreasonable for a jury to infer from these undisputed facts that Dillon fled Columbus soon after his conversation with Knezevich.

In this case, the second and third inferences — (2) that the defendant is afflicted with a guilty consciousness (3) of the crime charged — involve examination of two interrelated factors: immediacy and the defendant's knowledge that he is in trouble with the law. For flight evidence to be admissible, the timing of flight must itself indicate the sudden onset or the sudden increase of fear in the defendant's mind that he or she will face apprehension for, accusation of, or conviction of the crime charged. Flight immediately after the crime charged, of course, will tend to prove guilt of that crime. *See Myers*, 550 F.2d at 1051. But the mental crisis that precipitates flight may fail to occur immediately after the crime, only to erupt much later, when the defendant learns that he or she is charged with the crime and sought for it. *United States v. Hernandez-Miranda*, 601 F.2d 1104, 1106–07 (9th Cir. 1979) (flight immediately after crime is important only where defendant does not know, or might not know, of charges against him); *United States v. Jackson*, 572 F.2d at 640–41 (immediacy may become irrelevant where defendant knows she is charged and sought).

We reject Dillon's argument that these cases allow introduction of evidence of a postponed flight only when that flight occurs after the defendant learns of the charges against him or her. Rather, these cases recognize that flight may be proven where it occurs after any event which would tend to spark a sharp impulse of fear of prosecution or conviction in a guilty mind. This might occur long after the defendant learns of the charges, as it did in *Touchstone*, where defendants did not flee until the heat of trial became unbearable. *Touchstone*, 726 F.2d at 1120. And it can occur long before the defendant learns of the charges: for instance, when flight occurs after the defendant is served, himself, with a subpoena to appear before a Grand Jury. *United States v. Grandmont*, 680 F.2d 867, 869–70 (1st Cir. 1982). Indeed, the "commencement of an investigation" may substitute for accusation as the precipitating event. *United States v. Beahm*, 664 F.2d at 420 (dictum).

Dillon argues that he departed Columbus a year and nine months after the crime at the earliest, that the indictment was issued after his arrest, and that nothing in the interim constitutes notice of the sort that courts have recognized as a substitute for immediacy-after-the-crime. This reasoning ignores the December 19 conversation with Knezevich and urges a wooden and literalistic reading of the case law. Common sense on this question is loud and clear: a guilty defendant is almost as unequivocally put on notice of his peril by a convicted co-conspirator who is on the verge of testifying before a Grand Jury about their common crime, as he would be by hearing from someone that he is charged and sought. We see no flaws in an inference from such notice to the defendant's guilty consciousness of the crime charged.

Dillon raises no argument that the fourth *Myers* inference — from guilty consciousness to actual guilt — is unsupported by record evidence. We, therefore, hold that the District Court did not abuse its discretion in admitting evidence of flight at Dillon's trial. . . .

NOTES AND QUESTIONS

1. As stated by the court in *Dillon*, the first question in the four-part inquiry is whether the evidence supports the inference that there has been a "flight." *Dillon*, 870 F.2d at 1128. The court added that no such inference is allowable where the jury could infer flight only by resort to " 'conjecture and speculation.' " *Id.* (*quoting United States v. Myers*, 550 F.2d 1036, 1050 (5th Cir. 1977). After examining the evidence, the court concluded that the evidence allowed a sound inference, not merely a speculative one, that the defendant had fled. What facts did the court rely on in reaching this conclusion? *See United States v. Samples*, 456 F.3d 875 (8th Cir. 2006) (in robbery prosecution where defendant claimed temporary insanity, prosecutor's rebuttal argument that defendant's post-arrest flight demonstrated consciousness of guilt was not improper); *United States v. Oliver*, 397 F.3d 369 (6th Cir. 2005) (evidence of defendant's flight from a residential halfway house was admissible as evidence of guilt); *United States v. Felix-Gutierrez*, 940 F.2d 1200, 1207–08 (9th Cir. 1991) ("Felix's behavior in fleeing from Costa Rica, hiding in Los Angeles, having his distinctive tattoo removed in Reno, submitting to cosmetic facial surgery, and using assumed names strongly supports the inference that his conduct constituted flight.").

2. The *Dillon* court posited that the second and third inferences — (2) that the defendant is afflicted with a guilty consciousness (3) of the crime charged — involve examination of two interrelated factors: "immediacy and the defendant's knowledge that he is in trouble with the law." *Dillon*, 870 F.2d at 1128. To support an inference of consciousness of guilt, must the flight occur immediately after the commission of the crime charged? While immediacy of flight is a highly relevant factor, it is not dispositive. The court in *Dillon* stated: "[F]light may be proven where it occurs after any event which would tend to spark a sharp impulse of fear of prosecution or conviction in a guilty mind." *Id.*; *see also United States v. Levine*, 5 F.3d 1100, 1108 (7th Cir. 1993) (evidence of flight properly admitted even though defendant did not flee for more than a year after the murders; evidence at trial indicated that defendant closely monitored the on-going investigation and left his home when he realized he would be indicted).

3. *Inferring Consciousness of Guilt.* Is it improper to infer consciousness of guilt when other possible reasons existed for flight? Some courts have questioned the conventional wisdom that only the guilty flee, one of which asserted that " 'men who are entirely innocent do sometimes fly from the scene of a crime' for a multitude of reasons, including, for example, hesitation to confront even false accusations, fear that they will be unable to prove their innocence, or protection of a guilty party." *United States v. Hernandez-Bermudez*, 857 F.2d 50, 54 (1st Cir. 1988) (citations omitted). In *United States v. Clark*, 45 F.3d 1247, 1251 (8th Cir. 1995), the defendant argued that it was improper to infer consciousness of guilt of carjacking when he had so many other reasons to flee — there were guns in the car, he had possession of someone else's checkbook, his driver's license was invalid, and he suspected the car was stolen. The court rejected the defendant's argument, stating: "The existence of other possible reasons for flight does not render the inference impermissible or irrational." *Kattar*, 840 F.2d at 131. Do you agree? At the very least, is the inference of consciousness of guilt pertaining to the crime charged substantially weakened by the existence of other reasons for flight?

4. *Consciousness of Guilt and Character Evidence.* Should admission of evidence offered to demonstrate consciousness of guilt be evaluated under Fed. R. Evid. 404(b), which governs evidence of "[o]ther crimes, wrongs, or acts"? Rule 404(b) prohibits using evidence of other acts "to prove the character of a person in order to show action in conformity therewith." It may, however, be admissible for other purposes, such as proof of "motive, opportunity, intent, preparation, plan, knowledge, identity, or absence of mistake or accident." Fed. R. Evid. 404(b). Is the defendant against whom the "other act" evidence is admissible entitled to a limiting instruction to the jury, cautioning it not to consider the evidence as proof of the defendant's violent character, but only as proof of consciousness of guilt? *See United States v. Benedetti*, 433 F.3d 111 (1st Cir. 2005) (probative value of evidence of defendant's four-year flight following his indictment was not outweighed by the danger or unfair prejudice); *United States v. Tracy*, 12 F.3d 1186, 1195 (2d Cir. 1993) (where the court determines that probative value of death threat outweighs its potential for unfair prejudice, the defendant may request a limiting instruction cautioning jury not to consider threat as proof of the defendant's violent character, but only as proof of consciousness of guilt); *United States v. Esparsen*, 930 F.2d 1461, 1475 (10th Cir. 1991) (holding that jury should have been instructed to consider evidence of the defendant's threats to government witness only as proof of knowledge, not as evidence of violent character); *United States v. Mickens*, 926 F.2d 1323, 1328 (2d Cir. 1991) (admissibility of evidence that the defendant made hand gesture in the shape of a gun as his former attorney entered courtroom to testify against the defendant evaluated under Fed. R. Evid. 404(b)).

5. Is admission of flight evidence or other evidence offered to show consciousness of guilt ultimately limited by Fed. R. Evid. 403? Under Rule 403, the trial court should exclude relevant evidence if the potential for unfair prejudice substantially outweighs its probative value. *See United States v. Benedetti*, 433 F.3d 111 (1st Cir. 2005) (probative value of evidence of defendant's four-year flight following his indictment was not outweighed by the danger or unfair prejudice); *United States v. Tracy*, 12 F.3d 1186, 1195 (2d Cir. 1993) ("Evidence of threats of death is subjected to the same Rule 403 balancing test as other relevant evidence."); *United States v. Hayden*, 85 F.3d 153, 158–59 (4th Cir. 1996) (same). Thus, even if the defendant's conduct evidences consciousness of guilt, should the court exclude the evidence if its probative value is substantially outweighed by the possibility of unfair prejudice?

PROBLEM

Problem 7-1. *False Exculpatory Statements as Evidence of Consciousness of Guilt.* The defendant, Ernest Perkins, entered a Southern California Bank, placed a pouch on the counter, and handed the teller a note that read: "This is a robbery. I have a gun and want all of your large money." While the teller was placing the money in the pouch, the defendant repeated that he had a gun and only wanted large bills. The defendant walked out of the bank and a witness saw him drive away in a blue Datsun. Later, police investigators questioned the defendant while he was reporting to his probation officer. The defendant was given his Miranda warnings and signed a written waiver. Officer Dezihan asked the defendant if he was involved in any bank robberies. The defendant denied any involvement. Dezihan then inquired how the defendant got to the probation office. The defendant claimed a friend had dropped him off as he did not own a vehicle. The defendant was arrested and the police found keys in his pocket that belonged to a blue Datsun registered to the defendant. The Datsun was parked within a couple of blocks of the probation office. The government sought to introduce the defendant's false exculpatory statement to Officer Dezihan denying ownership of any vehicle as evidence of consciousness of guilt. The defendant objected to the admission of the evidence, arguing that his statement was only admissible for impeachment purposes if he chose to testify. Should the district court limit the introduction of the defendant's statement only to impeachment or should it be admitted as evidence of consciousness of guilt? *See United States v. Perkins*, 937 F.2d 1397 (9th Cir. 1991).

B.   VICARIOUS ADMISSIONS OF THE ACCUSED — STATEMENTS OF A CO-CONSPIRATOR

Federal Rule of Evidence 801(d)(2)(E) provides: "A statement is not hearsay if . . . [t]he statement is offered against a party and is . . . a statement by a co-conspirator of a party during the course and in furtherance of the conspiracy." The Supreme Court has emphasized the importance of co-conspirator statements as a means of proof. In *United States v. Inadi*, the Court indicated that such statements "are usually irreplaceable as substantive evidence" in part because they "provide evidence of the conspiracy's context that cannot be replicated."[9] The admissibility of co-conspirator statements against the defendant is based on an agency theory of conspiracy. The defendant (who must himself be a conspirator) is held to be responsible for acts of another done during the course and in furtherance of the conspiracy. "Under the agency theory, 'each member of a conspiracy is the agent of each of the other conspirators whenever he is acting — including speaking — to promote the conspiracy (hence the requirement that the statement be in furtherance of the conspiracy).' "[10]

There are three foundational prerequisites which must be established to admit a co-conspirator's statements under Rule 801(d)(2)(E): (1) the existence of a conspiracy and that both the defendant and the declarant were members of the conspiracy; (2) the declarant's statements were made "during the course of"; and (3) "in furtherance of" the conspiracy.[11] In *Bourjaily v. United States*, the Supreme Court addressed three questions regarding the admission of statements under Rule 801(d)(2)(E): (1) whether the court must determine by independent evidence that the conspiracy existed and that the defendant and the declarant were members of the conspiracy; (2) the quantum of

---

[9] *United States v. Inadi*, 475 U.S. 387, 395–96 (1986). *See United States v. Pallais*, 921 F.2d 684, 687 (7th Cir. 1990) ("[C]oconspirator's statements 'are reliable in the same sense that contracts or negotiations among legitimate business partners usually portray accurately the affairs of those involved.' ") (Citations omitted.)

[10] *United States v. Perez*, 989 F.2d 1574, 1577 (10th Cir. 1993) (quoting *Pallais*, 921 F.2d at 687); *see also* Fed. R. Evid. 801(d)(2)(E) advisory committee's note; 4 J. WEINSTEIN & M. BERGER, WEINSTEIN'S EVIDENCE ¶ 801(d)(2)(E) at 801-308 to -311 (1992).

[11] *See Bourjaily v. United States*, 483 U.S. 171, 175 (1987); *United States v. Tellier*, 83 F.3d 578, 580 (2d Cir. 1996); *United States v. Williamson*, 53 F.3d 1500, 1517–18 (10th Cir. 1995).

proof on which such determinations must be based; and (3) whether a court must examine the circumstances of the proffered statement to determine its reliability.

[1]   Standard of Proof

BOURJAILY v. UNITED STATES
483 U.S. 171 (1987)

CHIEF JUSTICE REHNQUIST delivered the opinion of the Court.

Federal Rule of Evidence 801(d)(2)(E) provides: "A statement is not hearsay if . . . [t]he statement is offered against a party and is . . . a statement by a coconspirator of a party during the course and in furtherance of the conspiracy." We granted certiorari to answer three questions regarding the admission of statements under Rule 801(d)(2)(E): (1) whether the court must determine by independent evidence that the conspiracy existed and that the defendant and the declarant were members of this conspiracy; (2) the quantum of proof on which such determinations must be based; and (3) whether a court must in each case examine the circumstances of such a statement to determine its reliability. . . .

In May 1984, Clarence Greathouse, an informant working for the Federal Bureau of Investigation (FBI), arranged to sell a kilogram of cocaine to Angelo Lonardo. Lonardo agreed that he would find individuals to distribute the drug. When the sale became imminent, Lonardo stated in a tape-recorded telephone conversation that he had a "gentleman friend" who had some questions to ask about the cocaine. In a subsequent telephone call, Greathouse spoke to the "friend" about the quality of the drug and the price. Greathouse then spoke again with Lonardo, and the two arranged the details of the purchase. They agreed that the sale would take place in a designated hotel parking lot, and Lonardo would transfer the drug from Greathouse's car to the "friend," who would be waiting in the parking lot in his own car. Greathouse proceeded with the transaction as planned, and FBI agents arrested Lonardo and petitioner immediately after Lonardo placed a kilogram of cocaine into petitioner's car in the hotel parking lot. In petitioner's car, the agents found over $20,000 in cash.

Petitioner was charged with conspiring to distribute cocaine, in violation of 21 U.S.C. § 846, and possession of cocaine with intent to distribute, a violation of 21 U.S.C. § 841(a)(1). The Government introduced, over petitioner's objection, Angelo Lonardo's telephone statements regarding the participation of the "friend" in the transaction. The District Court found that, considering the events in the parking lot and Lonardo's statements over the telephone, the Government had established by a preponderance of the evidence that a conspiracy involving Lonardo and petitioner existed, and that Lonardo's statements over the telephone had been made in the course of and in furtherance of the conspiracy. Accordingly, the trial court held that Lonardo's out-of-court statements satisfied Rule 801(d)(2)(E) and were not hearsay. Petitioner was convicted on both counts and sentenced to 15 years. The United States Court of Appeals for the Sixth Circuit affirmed. . . . We affirm.

Before admitting a co-conspirator's statement over an objection that it does not qualify under Rule 801(d)(2)(E), a court must be satisfied that the statement actually falls within the definition of the Rule. There must be evidence that there was a conspiracy involving the declarant and the nonoffering party, and that the statement was made "during the course and in furtherance of the conspiracy." Federal Rule of

Evidence 104(a) provides: "Preliminary questions concerning . . . the admissibility of evidence shall be determined by the court." Petitioner and the Government agree that the existence of a conspiracy and petitioner's involvement in it are preliminary questions of fact that, under Rule 104, must be resolved by the court. The Federal Rules, however, nowhere define the standard of proof the court must observe in resolving these questions.

We are therefore guided by our prior decisions regarding admissibility determinations that hinge on preliminary factual questions. We have traditionally required that these matters be established by a preponderance of proof. Evidence is placed before the jury when it satisfies the technical requirements of the evidentiary Rules, which embody certain legal and policy determinations. The inquiry made by a court concerned with these matters is not whether the proponent of the evidence wins or loses his case on the merits, but whether the evidentiary Rules have been satisfied. Thus, the evidentiary standard is unrelated to the burden of proof on the substantive issues, be it a criminal case or a civil case. The preponderance standard ensures that before admitting evidence, the court will have found it more likely than not that the technical issues and policy concerns addressed by the Federal Rules of Evidence have been afforded due consideration. . . . We think that our previous decisions in this area resolve the matter. *See, e.g., Colorado v. Connelly,* [497 U.S. 157, 167–69 (1986)] (preliminary fact that custodial confessant waived rights must be proved by preponderance of the evidence); *Nix v. Williams,* 467 U.S. 431, 444, n.5 (1984) (inevitable discovery of illegally seized evidence must be shown to have been more likely than not); *United States v. Matlock,* 415 U.S. 164 (1974) (voluntariness of consent to search must be shown by preponderance of the evidence); *Lego v. Twomey,* 404 U.S. 477 (1971) (voluntariness of confession must be demonstrated by a preponderance of the evidence). Therefore, we hold that when the preliminary facts relevant to Rule 801(d)(2)(E) are disputed, the offering party must prove them by a preponderance of the evidence.

Even though petitioner agrees that the courts below applied the proper standard of proof with regard to the preliminary facts relevant to Rule 801(d)(2)(E), he nevertheless challenges the admission of Lonardo's statements. Petitioner argues that in determining whether a conspiracy exists and whether the defendant was a member of it, the court must look only to independent evidence — that is, evidence other than the statements sought to be admitted. Petitioner relies on *Glasser v. United States,* 315 U.S. 60 (1942), in which this Court first mentioned the so-called "bootstrapping rule." The relevant issue in *Glasser* was whether Glasser's counsel, who also represented another defendant, faced such a conflict of interest that Glasser received ineffective assistance. Glasser contended that conflicting loyalties led his lawyer not to object to statements made by one of Glasser's co-conspirators. The Government argued that any objection would have been fruitless because the statements were admissible. The Court rejected this proposition:

> "[S]uch declarations are admissible over the objection of an alleged co-conspirator, who was not present when they were made, only if there is proof *aliunde* that he is connected with the conspiracy. . . . Otherwise, hearsay would lift itself by its own bootstraps to the level of competent evidence." *Id.,* at 74–75.

The Court revisited the bootstrapping rule in *United States v. Nixon,* 418 U.S. 683 (1974), where again, in passing, the Court stated: "Declarations by one defendant may also be admissible against other defendants upon a sufficient showing, by *independent evidence*, of a conspiracy among one or more other defendants and the declarant and if the declarations at issue were in furtherance of that conspiracy." *Id.*, at 701, and n.14 (emphasis added) (footnote omitted). Read in the light most favorable to petitioner, *Glasser* could mean that a court should not consider hearsay statements at all in determining preliminary facts under Rule 801(d)(2)(E). Petitioner, of course, adopts this view of the bootstrapping rule. *Glasser*, however, could also mean that a court must have some proof *aliunde*, but may look at the hearsay statements themselves in light of this independent evidence to determine whether a conspiracy has been shown by a preponderance of the evidence. The Courts of Appeals have widely adopted the former view and held that in determining the preliminary facts relevant to co-conspirators' out-of-court statements, a court may not look at the hearsay statements themselves for their evidentiary value.

Both *Glasser* and *Nixon*, however, were decided before Congress enacted the Federal Rules of Evidence in 1975. These Rules now govern the treatment of evidentiary questions in federal courts. Rule 104(a) provides: "Preliminary questions concerning . . . the admissibility of evidence shall be determined by the court. . . . In making its determination it is not bound by the rules of evidence except those with respect to privileges." Similarly, Rule 1101(d)(1) states that the Rules of Evidence (other than with respect to privileges) shall not apply to "[t]he determination of questions of fact preliminary to admissibility of evidence when the issue is to be determined by the court under rule 104." The question thus presented is whether any aspect of *Glasser*'s bootstrapping rule remains viable after the enactment of the Federal Rules of Evidence.

Petitioner concedes that Rule 104, on its face, appears to allow the court to make the preliminary factual determinations relevant to Rule 801(d)(2)(E) by considering any evidence it wishes, unhindered by considerations of admissibility. That would seem to many to be the end of the matter. Congress has decided that courts may consider hearsay in making these factual determinations. Out-of-court statements made by anyone, including putative co-conspirators, are often hearsay. Even if they are, they may be considered, *Glasser* and the bootstrapping rule notwithstanding. But petitioner nevertheless argues that the bootstrapping rule, as most Courts of Appeals have construed it, survived this apparently unequivocal change in the law unscathed and that Rule 104, as applied to the admission of co-conspirator's statements, does not mean what it says. We disagree.

Petitioner claims that Congress evidenced no intent to disturb the bootstrapping rule, which was embedded in the previous approach, and we should not find that Congress altered the rule without affirmative evidence so indicating. It would be extraordinary to require legislative history to *confirm* the plain meaning of Rule 104. The Rule on its face allows the trial judge to consider any evidence whatsoever, bound only by the rules of privilege. We think that the Rule is sufficiently clear that to the extent that it is inconsistent with petitioner's interpretation of *Glasser* and *Nixon*, the Rule prevails.

Nor do we agree with petitioner that this construction of Rule 104(a) will allow courts to admit hearsay statements without any credible proof of the conspiracy, thus fundamentally changing the nature of the co-conspirator exception. Petitioner starts with the proposition that co-conspirators' out-of-court statements are deemed unreliable and are inadmissible, at least until a conspiracy is shown. Since these statements are unreliable, petitioner contends that they should not form any part of the basis for establishing a conspiracy, the very antecedent that renders them admissible.

Petitioner's theory ignores two simple facts of evidentiary life. First, out-of-court statements are only *presumed* unreliable. The presumption may be rebutted by appropriate proof. Second, individual pieces of evidence, insufficient in themselves to prove a point, may in cumulation prove it. The sum of an evidentiary presentation may well be greater than its constituent parts. Taken together, these two propositions demonstrate that a piece of evidence, unreliable in isolation, may become quite probative when corroborated by other evidence. A per se rule barring consideration of these hearsay statements during preliminary factfinding is not therefore required. Even if out-of-court declarations by co-conspirators are presumptively unreliable, trial courts must be permitted to evaluate these statements for their evidentiary worth as revealed by the particular circumstances of the case. Courts often act as factfinders, and there is no reason to believe that courts are any less able to properly recognize the probative value of evidence in this particular area. The party opposing admission has an adequate incentive to point out the shortcomings in such evidence before the trial court finds the preliminary facts. If the opposing party is unsuccessful in keeping the evidence from the factfinder, he still has the opportunity to attack the probative value of the evidence as it relates to the substantive issue in the case. . . .

We think that there is little doubt that a co-conspirator's statements could themselves be probative of the existence of a conspiracy and the participation of both the defendant and the declarant in the conspiracy. Petitioner's case presents a paradigm. The out-of-court statements of Lonardo indicated that Lonardo was involved in a conspiracy with a "friend." The statements indicated that the friend had agreed with Lonardo to buy a kilogram of cocaine and to distribute it. The statements also revealed that the friend would be at the hotel parking lot, in his car, and would accept the cocaine from Greathouse's car after Greathouse gave Lonardo the keys. Each one of Lonardo's statements may itself be unreliable, but taken as a whole, the entire conversation between Lonardo and Greathouse was corroborated by independent evidence. The friend, who turned out to be petitioner, showed up at the prearranged spot at the prearranged time. He picked up the cocaine, and a significant sum of money was found in his car. On these facts, the trial court concluded, in our view correctly, that the Government had established the existence of a conspiracy and petitioner's participation in it.

We need not decide in this case whether the courts below could have relied solely upon Lonardo's hearsay statements to determine that a conspiracy had been established by a preponderance of the evidence. To the extent that *Glasser* meant that courts could not look to the hearsay statements themselves for any purpose, it has clearly been superseded by Rule 104(a). It is sufficient for today to hold that a court, in making a preliminary factual determination under Rule 801(d)(2)(E), may examine the hearsay statements sought to be admitted. As we have held in other cases concerning admissibility determinations, "the judge should receive the evidence and give it such weight as his judgment and experience counsel." *United States v. Matlock*, 415 U.S. 164, 175 (1974). We have no reason to believe that the District Court's factfinding of this point was clearly erroneous. We hold that Lonardo's out-of-court statements were properly admitted against petitioner.

We also reject any suggestion that admission of these statements against petitioner violated his rights under the Confrontation Clause of the Sixth Amendment. That Clause provides: "In all criminal prosecutions, the accused shall enjoy the right . . . to be confronted with the witnesses against him."

[Editors' note — The Supreme Court proceeded to analyze whether the admission of Lonardo's out-of-court statements violated the Sixth Amendment Confrontation Clause applying the test enunciated in *Ohio v. Roberts*, 448 U.S. 56 (1980). In *Crawford v. Washington*, 541 U.S. 36 (2004), the Court overturned *Roberts*. The Court adopted a new test, holding that the Confrontation Clause bars the admission of "testimonial" statements. *Id.* at 68. *See* discussion of *Crawford infra*, at Chapter 8. In *Crawford*, the Court further suggested that co-conspirator statements fall within an exception to the right of confrontation. The Court opined: "Most of the hearsay exceptions covered statements that by their nature were not testimonial — for example, business records or statements in furtherance of a conspiracy." *Id.* at 56.]

The judgment of the Court of appeals is

Affirmed.

* * *

NOTES AND QUESTIONS

1. The Supreme Court in *Bourjaily* ruled that the offering party must prove the foundational facts pertinent to Rule 801(d)(2)(E) by a preponderance of the evidence. Thus, the proponent of the statement must prove each of three essential facts by a preponderance of the evidence: (1) the existence of a conspiracy and that both the defendant and the declarant were members of the conspiracy, (2) the statement was made "during the course," and (3) "in furtherance" of the conspiracy. *Bourjaily*, 483 U.S. at 175–76.

2. *The Need for Corroborating Evidence.* In *Bourjaily*, the Supreme Court rejected petitioner's argument that in determining whether a conspiracy existed and whether the defendant and the declarant were members of this conspiracy, the court must only look to independent evidence. The Court held that the proffered co-conspirator statement itself may be considered along with other evidence to prove the existence of a conspiracy and the participation of both the defendant and the declarant in the conspiracy. The Court, however, left open the question whether "the courts below could have relied solely upon . . . [the] hearsay statements to determine that a conspiracy had been established by a preponderance of the evidence." *Id.* at 181.

This question was answered in the negative by the court in *United States v. Tellier*, 83 F.3d 578 (2d Cir. 1996). In *Tellier*, the court opined that in the absence of some independent corroborating evidence, of the defendant's knowledge of and participation in the conspiracy, the out-of-court statements are inadmissible. *Id.* at 580. It should be emphasized that the government's burden on the conspiracy issue involves a two-part inquiry. First, the government must prove the existence of a conspiracy, and second, that both the defendant and the declarant were members of this conspiracy. While the government in *Tellier* introduced independent evidence of a marijuana conspiracy and the declarant's participation in the conspiracy, there was no independent, corroborating evidence to implicate the defendant in the marijuana scheme. The only evidence offered by the government to link appellant to the conspiracy was Robin Tellier's extra-judicial statement. Thus, the second prong of the two-part inquiry was not satisfied. *See also United States v. Al-Moayad*, 545 F.3d 129 (2d Cir. 2008) (requiring independent, corroborating evidence of defendant's knowledge and participation in the conspiracy); *United States v. Conrad*, 507 F.3d 424 (6th Cir. 2007) (same).

3. *The Procedure for Meeting the Burden of Proof.* In many cases, co-conspirator statements are admitted provisionally, subject to later proof of the predicate facts. In the event that the government fails to establish the prerequisites for admissibility set forth in *Bourjaily*, the jury is instructed to disregard the statements. In *United States v. James*, 590 F.2d 575 (5th Cir. 1979), the Fifth Circuit suggested a "preferred order of proof" in which the court holds a pretrial hearing outside the jury's presence to decide whether to admit the statement, "reasoning that coconspirator statements have great impact and that provisionally admitting them runs the risk of mistrial or an instruction of dubious effect striking what the jury has already heard if the necessary foundation (or connecting) evidence is not offered or proves unpersuasive." MUELLER & KIRKPATRICK, EVIDENCE § 8.33, at 913 (1995). *But see United States v. Baltas*, 236 F.3d 27 (1st Cir. 2001) (declining to require a *James* hearing, admitting the hearsay evidence provisionally, "subject to [a] final *Petrozziello* determination, which should be made 'at the close of all the evidence' and 'out of the hearing of the jury' "); *United States v. Darden*, 70 F.3d 1507 (8th Cir. 1995) (same). What problems do you perceive in using the pretrial hearing approach? What problems do you perceive in using the provisional admittance method?

4. What if the defendant is acquitted on the conspiracy count? Does this render inadmissible the declarations of the co-conspirators on the substantive charge? Despite an acquittal on the conspiracy count, since different standards of proof govern the two determinations, the courts have uniformly upheld the admissibility of the co-conspirator statements on the substantive counts. *See United States v. Hernandez-Miranda*, 78 F.3d 512, 513 (11th Cir. 1996) ("[O]nce the court has determined that the government has made the requisite showing of a conspiracy, 'the admission of testimony under the co-conspirator exception to the hearsay rule is not rendered retroactively improper by subsequent acquittal of the alleged co-conspirator.' ") (citations omitted); *United States v. Peralta*, 941 F.2d 1003, 1006 (9th Cir. 1991); *United States v. Carroll*, 860 F.2d 500, 506 (1st Cir. 1988); *United States v. Clark*, 613 F.2d 391, 402–04 (2d Cir. 1979); *United States v. Cravero*, 545 F.2d 406, 419 (5th Cir. 1976) ("[e]arlier acquittal signifies that the government failed to prove the declarant a participant in the conspiracy beyond a reasonable doubt; this circumstance in no way forecloses the government, in a subsequent case, from establishing by slight or even preponderant evidence, the declarant's participation"); *United States v. Blackshire*, 538 F.2d 569, 571 (4th Cir. 1976) (same).

[2]   The First Requirement — Proof of a Conspiracy Between the Declarant and the Defendant

UNITED STATES v. BREITKREUTZ
977 F.2d 214 (6th Cir. 1992)

RYAN, CIRCUIT JUDGE.

Defendant Frank B. Breitkreutz was convicted of conspiring to distribute methamphetamine in violation of 21 U.S.C. § 846. On appeal, he assigns error to [an] . . . evidentiary ruling [] . . . admitting a purported drug ledger as the statement of a coconspirator. . . . Finding no error in [the ruling] of the district court, we shall affirm the judgment of conviction.

In March 1988, agents of the Drug Enforcement Administration (DEA) and the Tennessee Bureau of Investigation (TBI) searched the residence of Ray and Lisa Loudermilk in Cleveland, Tennessee and discovered a small quantity of methamphetamine. The Loudermilks agreed to cooperate with the government, and helped set up their supplier, Craig Van Riper, in a controlled buy in Pigeon Forge, Tennessee. Van Riper, in turn, led authorities to his supplier, Frank Santiago, who operated out of Athens, Georgia. Santiago then identified Mark Ruff as his source. Ruff, who lived in northern California, told government agents that he had two main sources for methamphetamine: his stepfather, Ferrell Clements, and defendant, Frank Breitkreutz.

As the DEA and TBI began their probe in Tennessee, local authorities in California were already involved in investigating defendant, Clements, and others suspected of involvement in methamphetamine distribution in the San Francisco Bay area. As part of their investigation, in January 1988, the San Pablo, California Police Department searched the residence of the defendant and his wife, Janet Breitkreutz. In this search, they located cash, firearms, large quantities of chemicals used to manufacture methamphetamine, a book detailing the manufacture of methamphetamine, receipts for glassware often used to produce methamphetamine, and several sheets of paper containing names, phone numbers, dollar amounts, lists of chemicals, and various calculations and other notations. Authorities also searched another house used by the Breitkreutzes and confiscated more chemicals and glassware used in methamphetamine production and a large number of "baggies," which are often used in drug distribution.

In November 1988, a federal grand jury sitting in Tennessee returned an indictment charging the defendant with participation in a "chain" conspiracy to distribute and possess with intent to distribute methamphetamine. Also named as coconspirators in the indictment were Clements, Ruff, Castle, Santiago, Van Riper, and "other persons known and unknown to the Grand Jury." In a superseding indictment issued in April 1989, Janet Breitkreutz was named as a conspirator as well. Clements, Ruff, and Castle entered into plea agreements, and each later testified before the grand jury as to their involvement in the conspiracy. Defendant, in the meantime, jumped a $100,000 bond issued by a magistrate judge in California in November 1988 and remained a fugitive until his arrest in December 1990.

At defendant's trial, the government called Ruff and Castle as witnesses, and also introduced evidence seized in the January 1988 searches at the Breitkreutzes' residence. According to Ruff's testimony, he and defendant began trafficking in narcotics in the summer of 1987, after Ruff's discharge from the military. Ruff had been receiving relatively small quantities of methamphetamine from his stepfather, and supplying Santiago, an acquaintance from the army, with the drugs via Federal Express shipments to Georgia. As Santiago expanded his distribution network and the quantities needed by Santiago became larger, Ruff turned to defendant as his primary source for methamphetamine. Ruff said that the switch was necessary because his stepfather was an unreliable source. Ruff testified to having supplied Santiago with approximately 60 pounds of methamphetamine over a period of months. He estimated that about two-thirds of this amount he received from defendant, the rest from his stepfather and from another supplier, Donnie Phillips.

Castle, a childhood friend of Ruff, testified that on a few occasions he acted as a courier of drugs and money. Following the January 1988 search of the Breitkreutz residence in California, the conspirators became more circumspect in their affairs and employed Castle, who had no prior links to the drug trade, to make several trips to

Santiago's home in Georgia, once carrying about 20 pounds of methamphetamine and returning to California with $200,000 cash. Castle also testified that on one occasion, at Ruff's direction, he accompanied defendant and Janet Breitkreutz to a hotel at the Stockton, California airport, where he was given a duffel bag, containing about ten pounds of methamphetamine, to deliver to Ruff.

Several documents purported to be drug ledgers, as well as other evidence of methamphetamine trafficking seized in the January 1988 searches of the Breitkreutzes' residences, were admitted into evidence at defendant's trial through the testimony of Detective Doug Hearn of the San Pablo Police Department. With respect to the documents seized, Hearn testified that, based on his experience in narcotics investigations, he interpreted them to be records and notes used to keep track of sales, receipts, and other calculations related to the sale of methamphetamine. He also testified to the seizure of cash, assorted weapons, and equipment and chemicals used to manufacture methamphetamine.

Defendant was convicted following a jury trial and now appeals.

* * *

B.

Defendant also challenges the district court's admission into evidence of certain documents the parties have described as drug ledgers. At oral argument, defendant addressed only the admission of Exhibit M-21, and we shall limit our discussion to this exhibit. Exhibit M-21 was seized from Janet Breitkreutz's purse and listed several chemicals, including methylamine, methyl alcohol, acetic anhydrides, sodium acetate, and sodium hydroxide, and certain items of equipment, including vacuum pump, ice vapor trap, and boiling beads, often used to produce methamphetamine. It also contained a list of names and notations as follows:

Jeanne	21
Cousin	22
Corena (2)	5, 6
Doug (4)	4, 2, 3, 1
Dino (2)	15, 16
Debbie (2)	13, 14
Dave (2)	8, 9
Joan (2)	7, 12
James (2)	10, 11
Larry (2)	X4, X5
Bill (1)	17
Mark (2)	*X2, X1, X7*
My friend (2)	X3, X8, 25
My friend Rick (1)	24
Korena	19, X6

The government offered the ledger as evidence that defendant was involved in a methamphetamine distribution conspiracy. The district court admitted the various documents, explaining that it was satisfied by a preponderance of the evidence that there was a conspiracy to manufacture and distribute methamphetamine in existence, and that these documents were made by the Defendant himself, which, of course, make them admissible as an admission, [or] if they were not made by him, they were made by somebody who was . . . obviously involved in this conspiracy, because they involve on their face statements regarding business transactions surrounding the methamphetamine deals that we're concerned with here.

Since the parties have concentrated most of their attention on the so-called coconspirator's exclusion to the rule against hearsay, Fed. R. Evid. 801(d)(2)(E), we shall focus on this rule as well. Rule 801(d)(2)(E) states that "a statement by a coconspirator of a party during the course and in furtherance of the conspiracy" is not hearsay when introduced against the nonoffering party. There are three foundational prerequisites which must be established to admit a coconspirator's statements under Rule 801(d)(2)(E): that a conspiracy existed; that defendant was a member of the conspiracy; and that the declarant's statement was made during the course and in furtherance of the conspiracy. . . . These preliminary matters are findings of fact to be made by the district court pursuant to Fed. R. Evid. 104(a). They must be established by a preponderance of the evidence, *Bourjaily*, 483 U.S. at 176 . . . and are reviewed only for clear error. *Id.* at 181.

Defendant contends that the government's failure to identify the author of the ledger renders it inadmissible, relying on *United States v. Mouzin*, 785 F.2d 682 (9th Cir.), *cert. denied*, 479 U.S. 985 (1986). In *Mouzin*, the Ninth Circuit examined the admission of an alleged cocaine distribution ledger found in the home of the defendant. The ledger lacked explicit references to cocaine, contained names which the government could not identify at trial, and which could not be linked to defendant by means other than fingerprints. *Id.* at 691–92. The court held that the ledger was not admissible as the statement of a coconspirator under Rule 801(d)(2)(E), declaring that "[k]nowledge of the identity of the declarant is essential to a determination that the declarant is a conspirator whose statements are integral to the activities of the alleged conspiracy." *Id.* at 691–92.

We do not think that the precise identity of a declarant is necessarily required for admission under Rule 801(d)(2)(E) and conclude that, with respect to the admission of Exhibit M-21 in this case, there existed ample circumstantial evidence "that there was a conspiracy involving the declarant and the nonoffering party, and that the statement was made 'during the course of and in furtherance of the conspiracy.'" *Bourjaily*, 483 U.S. at 175.

First, we find overwhelming, indeed uncontroverted, evidence that a conspiracy to distribute methamphetamine existed and that defendant was part of it. Defendant has admitted as much repeatedly. Moreover, Exhibit M-21 was found in the purse of defendant's wife during a successful search of the Breitkreutzes' shared residence for evidence of narcotics trafficking, along with vast quantities of chemicals and equipment used to manufacture methamphetamine. Under these circumstances, the district court was not clearly erroneous in finding that these facts were sufficient to support a conclusion, by a preponderance of the evidence, that Janet Breitkreutz, or some other member of a methamphetamine conspiracy, made the statements contained in Exhibit M-21, and that defendant and the declarant were linked to the same drug conspiracy.

Next, the statements contained in Exhibit M-21 themselves, along with the circumstances of their seizure, also allowed the district court to reasonably conclude that the statements were made during the course and in furtherance of the drug conspiracy. The contents of Exhibit M-21 demonstrate a running account of methamphetamine production and distribution, necessary to track various sales and keep the conspirators' drug trade profitable. The document was seized along with other evidence indicating a large-scale methamphetamine trafficking operation by the Breitkreutzes. We hold that the district court, under these circumstances, could properly determine, by a preponderance of the evidence, that the statements contained in Exhibit M-21 were made during the course and in furtherance of a drug conspiracy.

Because the government established all the necessary foundational requirements by a preponderance of the evidence, and the district court's findings on these matters were not clearly erroneous, we find no abuse of the district court's discretion in admitting the drug ledger under Rule 801(d)(2)(E). To repeat, the identity of the actual author was not necessary in this case, given the overwhelming circumstantial evidence, essentially undisputed by defendant, that a methamphetamine distribution conspiracy existed, that he was a part of such a conspiracy, and that the statements in Exhibit M-21 were made during the course and in furtherance of a conspiracy to distribute methamphetamine.

* * *

We find no merit in the defendant's various assignments of error and therefore AFFIRM the judgment of the district court.

NOTES AND QUESTIONS

1. There is a split in the federal circuits on whether the author of the entries in a drug ledger must be identified as a prerequisite to admission of the evidence under Rule 801(d)(2)(E). In *United States v. Mouzin*, 785 F.2d 682 (9th Cir. 1986), a drug ledger written in Spanish was seized from the home of a co-conspirator whose fingerprints were also found on it. However, "[t]he ledger did not mention the name of anyone that the government was able to identify at trial," nor was there any reference to cocaine, which was the basis of the drug conspiracy. *Id.* at 691. The court held that the drug ledger was inadmissible as a statement of a co-conspirator under Rule 801(d)(2)(E), declaring that "[k]nowledge of the identity of the declarant is essential to a determination that the declarant is a conspirator whose statements are integral to the activities of the alleged conspiracy" *Id.* at 692–93. Did the Ninth Circuit *sua sponte* establish an additional foundational requirement for admission of a co-conspirator statement? Should the government be required to establish the actual identity of the declarant as a condition for admissibility of a co-conspirator statement under Rule 801(d)(2)(E)? In other words, if it is clear from the surrounding circumstances that the ledger entries were made by a member of the conspiracy, and in furtherance of the conspiracy, should it matter whether the author of the entries can be identified?

2. Following *Mouzin*, the Ninth Circuit has maintained that some evidence as to the identity of the author of drug ledgers is "a necessary corollary" to establishing the three foundational requirements under Rule 801(d)(2)(E). *See United States v. Smith*, 893 F.2d 1573, 1578 (9th Cir. 1990). However, direct proof of the identity of the author of the ledgers is not required. *United States v. Gil*, 58 F.3d 1414, 1420 (9th Cir. 1995) (drug ledgers found in the defendants' residence with references to a nickname used by one defendant, coupled with the fact that some entries in the ledger corresponded to surveilled activities, adequately identified the defendants as authors of the ledger); *Smith*, 893 F.2d at 1578 (co-conspirator testimony that the defendant kept drug ledgers as a record of transactions was sufficient to establish with reasonable certainty that defendant authored the ledger); *United States v. Schmit*, 881 F.2d 608, 613–14 (9th Cir. 1989) (use of distinctive code words, plus reference to "Dad" in drug ledgers, sufficient to establish that defendant's son was the author). Do these cases signal a retreat by the Ninth Circuit from its earlier ruling in *Mouzin* that knowledge of the declarant's identity is essential to the admissibility of drug ledgers as co-conspirator statements? Are these cases factually distinguishable from *Mouzin*?

3. In contrast to the Ninth Circuit in *Mouzin*, the Sixth Circuit in *Breitkreutz* admitted the out-of-court statement in the absence of evidence establishing the identity of the declarant. Further, the Third Circuit in *United States v. Cruz*, 910 F.2d 1072 (3rd Cir. 1990), held that "[u]nidentifiability may be important in some situations, but when the statement itself and the surrounding circumstances provide sufficient evidence of reliability, unidentifiability will not be particularly important." Id. at 1081 n.10. The Eighth Circuit also posited that "[w]hat is essential is that the government show that the unknown declarant was more likely than not a [co]conspirator." *United States v. Helmel*, 769 F.2d 1306, 1313 (8th Cir. 1985). The Seventh Circuit has followed the reasoning of the Third, Sixth, and Eighth Circuits. *See United States v. DeGudino*, 722 F.2d 1351, 1356 (7th Cir. 1983). Should extra-judicial statements be admitted into evidence if the government establishes by a preponderance that the unidentified declarant was a coconspirator? *See also United States v. Mahasin*, 362 F.3d 1071 (8th Cir. 2004) ("It was not necessary for the declarant to have been formally charged as a coconspirator or even be identified, so long as the statement in question was itself sufficiently reliable in demonstrating the applicability of Rule 801(d)(2)(E)."); *United States v. Squillacote*, 221 F.3d 542, 563-64 (4th Cir. 2000) (foreign documents were admissible as coconspirator statements notwithstanding government's inability to identify the declarants). Do you find the reasoning in *Breitkreutz* or in *Mouzin* more persuasive? Why? Was there sufficient evidence to establish that the author of the drug ledgers in *Mouzin* was a co-conspirator under the preponderance of the evidence test?

4. The circuits hold that "'[p]roof of the existence of a buyer-seller relationship, without more, is inadequate to tie the buyer to a larger conspiracy.'" *United States v. Williamson*, 53 F.3d 1500, 1518 (10th Cir. 1995); *see also United States v. Hawkins*, 547 F.3d 66 (2d Cir. 2008) (same); *United States v. Gee*, 226 F.3d 885, 893 (7th Cir. 2000) (same). In *Williamson*, the court remarked: "In the absence of some evidence demonstrating that the [defendant] knowingly and voluntarily joined the conspiracy and accepted the conspiratorial objectives, he cannot be transformed into a coconspirator merely because he bought drugs from a known member of a drug conspiracy." 53 F.3d at 1518. Thus, it would be clear error to admit the out-of-court statement made by the drug seller against the drug buyer. At the same time, the government is not required to prove that there was a formal agreement, and circumstantial evidence indicating the defendant's membership in the conspiracy may properly be considered. *See United States v. Stephenson*, 53 F.3d 836, 843 (7th Cir. 1995). In *Stephenson*, the court stated that the government must show that the defendant "(1) knew of the conspiracy, and (2) intended to associate himself with the criminal scheme." *Id.* (citations omitted).

5. Does the fact that one party to a conversation is a government informant preclude the admission of the conspirator's statements under Rule 801(d)(2)(E)? The courts have consistently held that "the appropriate focus is on whether the statements were 'made by' a member of the conspiracy, and not on whether the statements were 'made to' a member of the conspiracy." *United States v. Williamson*, 53 F.3d 1500, 1519 (10th Cir. 1995); *see also United States v. Colon-Diaz*, 521 F.3d 29 (1st Cir. 2008) (statements made by a coconspirator are admissible under Rule 801(d)(2)(E), provided that they meet the Rule's foundational requirements, " 'regardless of whether the third party is a tipster, an informant, and undercover officer, or a mere acquaintance' ") (quoting *United States v. Piper*, 298 F.3d 47 (1st Cir. 2007)); *United States v. Frazier*, 280 F.3d 835 (8th Cir. 2002) (same); *United States v. Mealy*, 851 F.2d 890, 901 (7th Cir. 1988).

[3]   The Second Requirement — Statements Made During the Pendency of the Conspiracy

UNITED STATES v. HADDAD
976 F.2d 1088 (7th Cir. 1992)

HARLINGTON WOOD, JR., SENIOR CIRCUIT JUDGE.

Defendant Fadi B. Haddad appeals his conviction on a single-count indictment charging him with knowingly and intentionally attempting to possess with intent to distribute approximately one kilogram of cocaine in violation of 21 U.S.C. §§ 841(a)(1) and 846. We affirm.

On April 23, 1991, a grand jury returned a single-count indictment charging Haddad with knowingly and intentionally attempting to possess with intent to distribute approximately one kilogram of cocaine in violation of 21 U.S.C. §§ 841(a)(1) and 846 and 18 U.S.C. § 2. . . . The jury returned a verdict of guilty.

Prior to the events testified to at trial Fadi Haddad was a 24-year-old bartender at a tavern called Colombo's in Milwaukee, Wisconsin. One of his co-workers was James Jackson, a government informant. On February 27, 1991, James Jackson introduced Haddad to Charles Unger, who was working undercover as a member of a Drug Enforcement Administration task force. Arrangements were made for Haddad to meet Unger and Jackson at a tavern in West Allis, Wisconsin, and supply Unger with one kilogram of cocaine for $25,000. Haddad did not appear. After Haddad did not show up, Unger sent Jackson to Colombo's. Jackson talked with Haddad and informed Unger that Haddad wanted to see cash before he would set up any transaction. Unger then went to see Haddad at Colombo's to display cash to Haddad.

Jackson contacted Haddad the following day, February 28, 1991. Haddad, Jackson and Unger then met at Denny's Restaurant. Unger believed the transaction was to take place at Denny's; however, Haddad advised him that his contacts who were supposed to supply the cocaine would not come to the restaurant. Unger explained that he did not want to meet Haddad's people and that he wanted to stay at Denny's. Haddad then told Unger about a friend who had "bugged him about something like this for a long time." (Presumably Haddad meant a cocaine transaction.) Finally, Haddad told Unger, "We did the connection, the first time is always hard, the hardest thing." Haddad also told Unger he had been burned before. The parties arranged another rendezvous location.

The parties went to a gas station on 55th and North where Unger testified that Haddad's source supply was to meet him, but when they arrived Haddad pulled up along side Unger's car and told Unger and Jackson they had to go to North and Lisbon. They travelled seven blocks to that location and waited. Eventually Unger testified he got tired of waiting for the deal to go through. He contacted Haddad the next day to find out what the problem was. Haddad told Unger he never got in contact with his source. After Haddad revealed he was having trouble getting in contact with his source,

Unger attempted to make an arrangement for a one kilogram exchange to occur at what Unger purported to be his residence at 102nd and Lincoln. Haddad did not appear to make the exchange.

Then on March 15, 1991, Unger received a page on his electronic pager from Haddad. Unger testified that Haddad offered to sell him two ounces of "the finest" cocaine. Unger replied that he had no interest in such a small amount. Unger told Haddad he would possibly get together with him later, but the two never met. Subsequently, Unger went to Colombo's with another undercover agent to pay Haddad a social visit and have some cocktails. The two men did not talk specifically about drug transactions.

On April 1, 1991, Haddad contacted Unger at approximately 11:30 in the morning. At Haddad's request, Unger went to meet him at Auto Stereo where Haddad was employed. Haddad told Unger he had been in contact with a supplier of cocaine in Chicago. Haddad said that he could get a kilogram of cocaine if Unger gave him the money up front. Unger replied that if he was going to put up $25,000 he needed some collateral. Since Haddad had mentioned he owned ten cars, Unger asked for keys and titles to five of Haddad's vehicles. Haddad agreed.

Haddad next contacted Unger on April 12, 1991. Unger and Haddad met at Denny's Restaurant. Haddad informed Unger that he was ready to go through with the deal at any time. Haddad also informed Unger that the price for a kilogram of cocaine would be $28,000. Unger did not want to make the exchange that day because he needed time to set up surveillance. The following day after Haddad tried to reach Unger several times by pager, Unger and Haddad arranged a meeting for 6:30 p.m. at Denny's Restaurant. Haddad and a friend, Ali Charri, met Unger in the parking lot of Denny's. They were driving a rented car. Haddad supplied Unger with titles to three automobiles, a BMW, a Cadillac and a Volkswagen GTI. After receiving the titles, Unger stepped to the rear of his automobile and took out a box which Haddad was led to believe contained $25,000 in cash. Unger gave this box to Haddad. Unger then took out a roll of money from his pocket which Haddad was led to believe was approximately $3,000 in cash. He gave the roll of money to Haddad. Haddad took the money and went to his car. Haddad and Charri were then arrested.

After his arrest, Charri agreed to place a police-monitored call to John Leydon, Haddad's supplier of cocaine in Chicago. Leydon had been repeatedly paging Haddad, after Haddad was arrested. Charri called Leydon and told him that he and Haddad would not be able to make it to Chicago. Leydon replied that the suppliers in Chicago were angry with the delay and the deal would have to be canceled. While Charri was making the phone call, Haddad was being questioned. Haddad told DEA officers that his source of cocaine was a man named Tony in Milwaukee. He agreed to set up an immediate meeting with Tony for the agents to record. However, when Tony arrived he did not have a kilogram of cocaine for sale. Instead Tony said he thought Haddad was going to supply the cocaine.

At trial Haddad testified he became involved in the transaction with Unger only because the government informant, Jackson, kept badgering him. He also testified he had no additional experience in drug trafficking prior to being contacted by Jackson. Haddad then testified that the only reason he knew what to do in his February 28th meeting with Unger was by following the instructions of a restaurant customer named Phil, who appeared to Haddad to be a person "on drugs," and Phil's friend, Ray. Haddad also testified that he gave the name "Tony" to the agents questioning him because he was nervous and because he wanted to avoid trouble for his friend Leydon. Haddad said he had no conversations with Tony concerning cocaine deals prior to the April 13th meeting Haddad set up with government agents.

On cross-examination the government confronted Haddad with his own recorded statements concerning his experience in negotiating prior drug transactions. The government also demonstrated that Haddad's contacts with Phil (Burns) and Ray (Rivera) went back to December of 1990, well before Haddad's negotiations with Unger which began in February of 1991. The government additionally showed Haddad had a number of unexplained cash deposits in his checking account during the time he was attempting to sell cocaine. And finally, the government introduced a tape-recorded, post-arrest conversation between Haddad and Tony during which Haddad referred to prior drug transactions between the two men.

ANALYSIS

The first issue Haddad raises on appeal is whether the trial court correctly admitted statements made over the telephone by John Leydon to Ali Charri, after Charri and Haddad were arrested. Haddad argues the trial court erred in admitting the statements because the government did not establish the existence of the conspiracy and because the government did not establish that the conversation was in furtherance of any conspiracy.

Federal Rule of Evidence 104(a) requires a district judge to determine whether co-conspirator statements are relevant before they will be admitted. *United States v. Martinez de Ortiz*, 907 F.2d 629, 632 (7th Cir.) (*en banc*), *cert. denied*, 111 S. Ct. 684 (1991). Additionally, Federal Rule of Evidence 801(d)(2)(E) provides for the admissibility of co-conspirator statements at trial if the government establishes by a preponderance of evidence that: (1) a conspiracy existed; (2) the defendant and the declarant were members of the conspiracy when the statements were made; and (3) the statements were made in furtherance of the conspiracy. *See United States v. D'Antoni*, 874 F.2d 1214, 1217 (7th Cir. 1989). We will not disturb the trial court's decision to admit co-conspirator statements under these three factors unless we find the court's decision to be clearly erroneous. *United States v. Van Daal Wyk*, 840 F.2d 494, 496 (7th Cir. 1988).

In a detailed analysis the trial court set out the reasons which it believed supported a finding that a conspiracy existed between Haddad, Charri and Leydon. The trial court relied on Charri's testimony that Leydon was awaiting Charri's and Haddad's arrival with $25,000 when Charri and Haddad were arrested; that Leydon was not aware of their arrest and repeatedly attempted to page Haddad on his beeper; and that when Charri contacted Leydon after Charri's arrest, the planned cocaine transaction was to take place so far as Leydon knew. The court also considered the content of the statements themselves. Finally, the court pointed to other evidence of joint membership in a "criminal misadventure" such as Agent Unger's testimony that Haddad identified Chicago as the location of his cocaine supplier. Based on all this evidence the trial court found it more likely than not that Haddad, Charri and Leydon were co-conspirators in a joint venture to purchase cocaine in Chicago and deliver it to Agent Unger in Milwaukee.

Moreover, we believe there is ample evidence in the record to support the conclusion that the relationship between Haddad and Leydon was more than a buyer-seller relationship. Evidence of a buyer-seller relationship standing alone is insufficient to support a conspiracy conviction. *United States v. Townsend*, 924 F.2d 1385, 1394 (7th Cir. 1991). The details presented by the government at trial indicated that the relationship between Haddad and Leydon was ongoing and that the parties intended to make cocaine transactions in the future. For example, there was evidence of two months of negotiations between Haddad and Agent Unger with Haddad referring to his cocaine supplier from Chicago (Leydon). And in one transcript of a recorded conversation between Haddad and Agent Unger, Haddad stated to Agent Unger that if Agent Unger wanted cocaine sold in the future all Agent Unger had to do was to contact Haddad because Haddad had people in place who would "dump" the cocaine in a day or two. The government speculated at oral argument to this court that perhaps the relationship between the co-conspirators and the unidentified person from whom the co-conspirators obtained a kilogram of cocaine in Chicago (via Leydon) was buyer-seller. But as between Haddad and Leydon, there was ample discussion and activity produced at trial that supported the existence of a conspiracy. Based on our review of the record we are satisfied with the trial court's analysis of the existence of the conspiracy for purposes of the admission of Leydon's statements made to Charri after Charri was arrested.

Similarly, we agree with the trial court's discussion of whether the co-conspirator statements were made in furtherance of the conspiracy. Haddad advances an argument that co-conspirator statements are not admissible if the conspiracy ends in failure. Haddad cites an advisory committee note to Rule 801(d)(2)(E) in support of his position. The note provides in relevant part:

> The limitation upon the admissibility of statements of co-conspirators to those made "during the course and in furtherance of the conspiracy" . . . is consistent with the position of the Supreme Court in denying admissibility to statements made after the objectives of the conspiracy have either failed or been achieved. (citations omitted).

Haddad says the conspiracy in this case ended when Haddad and Charri were both arrested. Haddad reasons that since Leydon was the only remaining unarrested participant in the conspiracy, he was incapable of carrying out the goals of the conspiracy. Haddad also contends that the conspiracy could not be carried out by Charri, who was acting as a government informant, because a person cannot conspire with a government informant who secretly intends to frustrate the conspiracy. Haddad cites *United States v. Lively*, 803 F.2d 1124, 1126 (11th Cir. 1986), to support his latter argument.

The conspiracy between Haddad, Charri and Leydon was not automatically terminated by Haddad's and Charri's arrest. *See United States v. Mealy*, 851 F.2d 890, 901 (7th Cir. 1988). In *Mealy* we said, "a co-conspirator's arrest does not automatically terminate a conspiracy; the remaining conspirators may continue to carry out the goals of the conspiracy notwithstanding the arrest of one of the partners." *Id.* The trial court found that as long as Leydon remained at large, the conspiracy was alive. The court found further that it did not matter whether Charri was an informant because his statements were not being offered as out-of-court statements; rather, the government sought to introduce Leydon's statements, and Leydon had no idea that Charri and Haddad were in custody when Leydon spoke to Charri.

We think the trial court correctly analyzed the issue of whether Leydon's statements were made in furtherance of the conspiracy. Leydon spoke to Charri about the status of the transaction and when Charri and Haddad were going to arrive in Chicago to pick up a kilogram of cocaine. Moreover, while Leydon was talking with Charri about the cocaine transaction, Haddad was attempting to mislead government agents by fingering a person in Milwaukee, Tony, as his supplier of cocaine in an attempt to protect his friend, Leydon. At the time of Charri's phone call to Leydon, Haddad and Leydon were still acting on behalf of the conspiracy, and Leydon's statements to Charri were properly admitted as co-conspirator statements made in furtherance of an existing conspiracy.

*   *   *

CONCLUSION

Fadi B. Haddad's conviction for attempting to possess cocaine with the intent to distribute in violation of 21 U.S.C. §§ 841(a) and 846 and the sentence imposed by the district court are Affirmed.

NOTES AND QUESTIONS

1. *Withdrawing from the Conspiracy.* As the court stated in *Haddad*, the arrest of one co-conspirator does not automatically terminate the conspiracy. *Haddad*, 976 F.2d at 1093. "[T]he remaining conspirators may continue to carry out the goals of the conspiracy notwithstanding the arrest of one of the partners." *United States v. Mealy*, 851 F.2d 890, 901 (7th Cir. 1988); *see also United States v. Williams*, 87 F.3d 249, 253 (8th Cir. 1996). *But see United States v. Melton*, 131 F.3d 1400 (10th Cir. 1997) ("Although a conspirator's arrest or incarceration by itself is insufficient to constitute his withdrawal from the conspiracy . . . an arrest may under certain circumstances amount to a withdrawal."). As a general rule, a conspiracy is presumed to continue until one takes affirmative steps to withdraw from the conspiracy, which usually involves notifying others in the venture, or confessing to law enforcement authorities. *See* Model Penal Code §§ 5.03(6) (recognizing an affirmative defense where defendant thwarted success of venture under circumstances manifesting complete and voluntary renunciation) and 5.03(7)(c) (conspiracy is terminated where defendant abandons agreement by "advis[ing] those with whom he conspired" or informs law enforcement authorities) (1974); *see also United States v. United States Gypsum Co.*, 438 U.S. 422, 464–65 (1978); *Williams*, 87 F.3d at 253 ("[A] conspiracy is presumed to exist until there has been an affirmative showing that it has been terminated so long as there is 'a continuity of purpose and a continued performance of acts.'") (citations omitted); *United States v. Walker*, 796 F.2d 43, 49 (4th Cir. 1986) ("The defendant must show affirmative acts inconsistent with the object of the conspiracy and communicated in a manner reasonably calculated to reach his co-conspirators.").

2. Are statements made during the concealment phase of the conspiracy admissible under Rule 801(d)(2)(E)? Resolution of the issue turns on whether the main objective of the conspiracy has been achieved. If the "main aim" of the conspiracy has been attained, the out-of-court statements are inadmissible. In *Krulewitch v. United States*, 336 U.S. 440 (1949), the Supreme Court held that statements made after the central criminal purposes of a conspiracy had been achieved were inadmissible if made to conceal the crime. In *Grunewald v. United States*, 353 U.S. 391, 401–02 (1957), the Court subsequently explained and reaffirmed its holding in *Krulewitch*:

> The crucial teaching of *Krulewitch* . . . is that after the central criminal purposes of a conspiracy have been attained, a subsidiary conspiracy to conceal may not be implied from circumstantial evidence showing merely that the

conspiracy was kept a secret and that the conspirators took care to cover up their crime in order to escape detection and punishment. As was there stated, allowing such a conspiracy to conceal to be inferred or implied from mere overt acts of concealment would result in a great widening of the scope of conspiracy prosecutions, since it would extend the life of a conspiracy indefinitely. Acts of covering up, even though done in the context of a mutually understood need for secrecy, cannot themselves constitute proof that concealment of the crime after its commission was part of the initial agreement among the conspirators- . . . . Sanctioning the Government's theory would for all practical purposes wipe out the statute of limitations in conspiracy cases, as well as extend indefinitely the time within which hearsay declarations will bind coconspirators.

3. If the conspiracy is ongoing, post-arrest conspirator statements are admissible under Rule 801(d)(2)(E) if intended to allow the conspiracy to continue by misleading law enforcement officers. *See United States v. Williams,* 87 F.3d 249, 254 (8th Cir. 1996); *United States v. Alonzo,* 991 F.2d 1422, 1426 (8th Cir. 1993); *United States v. Garcia,* 893 F.2d 188, 190 (8th Cir. 1990); *United States v. Fahey,* 769 F.2d 829, 839 (1st Cir. 1985).

PROBLEM

Problem 7-2. *Post-Arrest Co-conspirator Statements.* Defendant Louis Williams was a member of a conspiracy to steal blank United States Treasury checks from a St. Louis postal center. Williams recruited a Mexican citizen to cash the checks in Mexico in exchange for a portion of the proceeds. The remaining funds were channeled back into a Texas bank account maintained by one of the co-conspirators. On behalf of Williams, Tommie Penson made a series of wire transfers into bank accounts maintained by Williams.

The St. Louis postal center received a copy of one check for $10,000,000. Postal inspectors immediately began an investigation. Penson was subsequently arrested in connection with the fraudulent scheme. Following his arrest, Penson told investigators that he funded wire transfers with money borrowed from an unidentified source, denied knowing about the stolen Treasury checks, and maintained he was not in Mexico when one of the stolen checks had been presented. The unidentified source was believed to be Williams. Penson's last statement was subsequently proven false.

After his arrest, Penson remained in contact with Williams. Penson and Williams continued to disburse funds from one of the stolen United States Treasury checks. Williams was eventually arrested and charged with conspiracy, money laundering, forgery and receiving stolen United States Treasury checks. Penson did not testify at Williams' trial, and the government sought to introduce Penson's post-arrest statements under Fed. R. Evid. 801(d)(2)(E). Williams objected to their admission, arguing that Penson's statements were not in furtherance of the conspiracy since he had already been arrested. Should the district court admit Penson's post-arrest statements as co-conspirator's statements under Rule 801(d)(2)(E)? If admitted, might any error constitute harmless error? *See United States v. Williams,* 87 F.3d 249 (8th Cir. 1996) (modifying the statement of the facts).

[4]   The Third Requirement — Statements that "Further" the Conspiracy

STATE v. CORNELL
842 P.2d 394 (Or. 1992)

Unis, Justice.

Defendant appeals from convictions on two counts of felony murder for the homicide of John Ruffner, allegedly committed during the course of robbing him and burglarizing his residence. Defendant was originally indicted with Mark Allen Pinnell in October 1985 for one count of aggravated murder and two counts of felony murder. In January 1988, defendant and Pinnell were indicted on five counts of aggravated murder. Defendant's motion for a separate trial was allowed in March 1988. In that trial, defendant was acquitted of aggravated murder and convicted on both counts of felony murder, which were merged for purposes of sentencing. The Court of Appeals affirmed the judgment of the trial court. *State v. Cornell*, 820 P.2d 11 (Or. App. 1991). We allowed review to consider defendant's challenge of the introduction of evidence of statements of a coconspirator under OEC 801(4)(b)(E).

We take the following statement of facts from the Court of Appeals' opinion:

"Defendant and Pinnell got the victim's name and phone number from the Swing N Sway magazine, where people advertise for sexual contacts. They drove to the victim's residence in a car borrowed from Dixie Timmons, Pinnell's ex-wife. They were accompanied by a woman named Velma Varzali. She stayed in the car when defendant and Pinnell went into the victim's residence. Several hours later the two men returned to the car and loaded it with personal property taken from the residence. Later that same day, defendant wrote checks on the victim's account and used his credit cards.

"The next day, the victim's body was discovered on the bathroom floor of his apartment. His feet and hands were tied behind his back with an electric appliance cord and there was a cord around his neck. Evidence at trial described this type of restraint as 'hog-tying.' The victim died of asphyxiation, because of the cord around his neck and the wad of toilet paper stuffed in his mouth. [The victim had been struck on the right side of his head, which caused a tear of his ear.] The apartment had been ransacked and several items of property taken, including the victim's wallet and checkbook.

"When defendant and Pinnell were arrested a few days later at Timmons' house, defendant had the victim's checkbook and credit cards and was wearing two rings taken from the victim. The police also seized several items of the victim's property that were at Timmons' house.

"During trial, the state introduced evidence that defendant and Pinnell had assaulted and robbed Randy Brown about 10 days before they killed Ruffner. The state's theory for admission of the evidence was that the facts of the Brown assault were so similar to the Ruffner homicide that it was relevant to identify the two men as the perpetrators of that killing." *Id.* at 13.

The trial court, over defendant's objection, allowed the state to introduce, through the testimony of other witnesses, eleven statements made by Pinnell.[3] The Court of

---

[3] Setting out the full text of Pinnell's statements would serve no useful purpose. The one statement that

Appeals held that the trial court did not err in admitting the statements as statements of a coconspirator under OEC 801(4)(b)(E). The Court of Appeals also held that the admission of the coconspirator statements did not violate defendant's confrontation rights under either Article I, section 11, of the Oregon Constitution or the Sixth Amendment to the United States Constitution. We affirm.

When "offered against a party," OEC 801(4)(b)(E) treats as "not hearsay" "[a] statement by a coconspirator of a party during and in furtherance of the conspiracy." OEC 801(4)(b)(E) requires that the party seeking to introduce a statement by a coconspirator must establish, as foundational requirements: (1) that there was a conspiracy in which both the accused and the declarant were members; (2) that the declarant made his or her statement "during the course" of the conspiracy; and (3) that the statement was made "in furtherance of the conspiracy." Whether the foundational requirements are met is a preliminary question of fact to be determined by the trial court under OEC 104(1), and each requirement is to be established by a preponderance of the evidence. . . . [8]

In the present case, the statements at issue — Pinnell's statements — were offered by the state against a party (defendant). Thus, in order to admit Pinnell's statements under OEC 801(4)(b)(E), the trial court was required to find by a preponderance of the evidence (1) that there was a conspiracy with respect to the Ruffner and Brown crimes and that both defendant and the declarant (Pinnell) were members of that conspiracy, (2) that Pinnell's statements were made "during the course" of the conspiracy, and (3) that Pinnell's statements were made "in furtherance of the conspiracy." The trial court found that the foundational requirements were met and admitted Pinnell's statements under OEC 801(4)(b)(E).

On review, we determine whether there was sufficient evidence to support the trial court's finding, by a preponderance of the evidence, that the preliminary foundational requirements were met. [*State v. Carlson*, 214, 808 P.2d 1002, 1010 (Or. 1991)]. In making this determination, "[w]e view the record consistent with the trial court's ruling, . . . accepting reasonable inferences and reasonable credibility choices that the trial judge could have made." *Id.*

The substantive law defines a conspiracy. ORS 161.450(1) states that a criminal conspiracy exists if, "with the intent that conduct constituting a crime punishable as a felony or a Class A misdemeanor be performed, [a] person agrees with one or more [other] persons to engage in or cause the performance of such conduct." Although the substantive law defines a criminal conspiracy, the Oregon Evidence Code states the evidentiary principles concerning the admissibility of coconspirator statements. A person need not be charged with or found guilty of criminal conspiracy or of the underlying crime in order to be a coconspirator under OEC 801(4)(b)(E). *See State v. Gardner*, 358 P.2d 557 (Or. 1961) (prior to adoption of evidence code, admissibility of statements of coconspirators did not depend on including conspiracy in indictment); 2 McCormick on Evidence § 259, at 168 (4th ed. 1992) (citing federal cases) ("[t]he existence of a conspiracy in fact is sufficient to support admissibility, and a conspiracy count in the indictment is not required and the declarant need not be charged"). Because there usually is no formal agreement to begin a conspiracy, the very existence of a conspiracy usually must be inferred from the facts surrounding the statements. 4

---

raises the closest question as to its admissibility is discussed *infra*, 314 Or. at 680, 842 P.2d at 398.

[8] OEC 801(4)(b) includes in its definition of statements of a party-opponent, "(E) [a] statement by a coconspirator of a party during the course and in furtherance of the conspiracy."

Weinstein & Berger, Weinstein's Evidence ¶ 801(d)(2)(E)[01], at 801-335 (1992). . . .

Based on the facts in the record, summarized above, and accepting reasonable inferences and reasonable credibility choices that the trial judge could have made, we conclude that there was sufficient evidence to support the trial judge's finding, by a preponderance of the evidence, that a conspiracy existed with respect to the Ruffner and Brown crimes and that defendant and Pinnell were members of that conspiracy.

"During the Course" of the Conspiracy Requirement

For the purpose of applying the coconspirator exemption in OEC 801(4)(b)(E), the duration of a conspiracy is not limited by the commission of the elements of the underlying crime. Conduct before or after the commission of the elements of the underlying crime [is] part of a conspiracy, if the conduct is either in planning, preparing for, or committing the crime, or in eluding detection for, disposing of, or protecting the fruits of the crime. Here, the alleged conspiracy included robbing the victims. At a minimum, a conspiracy to rob continues until the articles stolen are removed from the scene of the crime and are disposed of in some manner. *See State v. Gardner, supra,* 358 P.2d at 561 (so stating under former conspiracy statute).

In this case, the challenged statements by Pinnell were made before or shortly after one of the robberies and before the stolen articles had been disposed of. There was sufficient evidence to support the trial judge's finding, by a preponderance of the evidence, that Pinnell's statements were made "during the course" of the conspiracy.

"In Furtherance of the Conspiracy" Requirement

Pinnell's statements must also have been made "in furtherance of the conspiracy." This requirement goes beyond the temporal requirement that the statement be made "during the course" of the conspiracy and focuses on whether the statement was intended in some way to advance the objectives of the conspiracy. A statement in furtherance of a conspiracy must have been meant to advance the objectives of the conspiracy in some way, i.e., it must be made in furtherance of planning, preparing, or committing the crime, or in furtherance of eluding detection for, disposing of, or protecting the fruits of the crime. Whether this prerequisite is met is determined in the context in which the particular statement is made. Weinstein & Berger, *supra,* ¶ 801(d)(2)(E)[01], at 801-318 to -323. When a statement is made in the presence of a coconspirator, a statement that would not otherwise be in furtherance of the conspiracy may be in furtherance of the conspiracy if the statement demonstrates a desire to encourage a coconspirator to carry out the conspiracy or to develop camaraderie in order to ensure the success of the continuing conspiracy.

In this case, defendant challenges the introduction of a coconspirator's statement, related by Varzali, that "I went for the ear, but ol' [defendant] had got there first." If this statement had been made to the police or out of the presence of defendant, it might be difficult to see how it could be in furtherance of the conspiracy. Here, however, the statement was made in defendant's presence, and the record reflects that defendant was "really quiet" and "very upset." Although the alleged crime had been completed just prior to the statement, defendant and the coconspirator were fleeing from the scene with the stolen articles; the conspiracy was continuing. In these circumstances, a trier of fact would be entitled to infer that the coconspirator's statements were made to encourage defendant, a coconspirator, to carry out the conspiracy or to develop camaraderie with defendant in order to ensure the success of the continuing conspiracy. There was, therefore, sufficient evidence to support the trial judge's finding, by a preponderance of the evidence, that the statement was made in furtherance of the conspiracy.

We have examined the other statements made by Pinnell and, accepting reasonable inferences and reasonable credibility choices that the trial judge could have made, we find that there was sufficient evidence to support the trial judge's finding, by a preponderance of the evidence, that each statement was made during the course of and in furtherance of the conspiracy.

We conclude that the eleven statements made by Pinnell were admissible as statements of a coconspirator under OEC 801(4)(b)(E).

* * *

The decision of the Court of Appeals and the judgment of the circuit court are affirmed.

NOTES AND QUESTIONS

1. Do you agree with the court in *Cornell* that Pinnell's statement to Varzali, that "I went for the ear, but ol' [defendant] had got there first," *Cornell*, 842 P.2d at 399, was in furtherance of the conspiracy to rob and murder Ruffner, or to dispose of the fruits of the crime? Do you find the court's reasoning convincing that Pinnell's statement was in furtherance of the conspiracy because it was made to "develop camaraderie with the defendant in order to ensure the success of the continuing conspiracy"? *Id.* What danger do you perceive in applying the court's "camaraderie" standard for determining whether the out-of-court statement was "in furtherance" of the conspiracy?

2. The requirement that the statements be in furtherance of the conspiracy "is designed both to assure their reliability and to be consistent with the presumption that the coconspirator would have authorized them." *United States v. Lieberman*, 637 F.2d 95, 103 (2d Cir. 1980). The courts' liberal construction of Rule 801(d)(2)(E)'s "in furtherance" requirement, however, places in doubt whether this requirement provides a meaningful limitation on admissibility. Examples of statements which may be found to satisfy the "in furtherance" requirement include

> statements made to induce enlistment or further participation in the group's activities; statements made to prompt further action on the part of conspirators; statements made to reassure members of a conspiracy's continued existence; statements made to allay a co-conspirator's fears; and statements made to keep co-conspirators abreast of an ongoing conspiracy's activities.

United States v. Perez, 989 F.2d 1574, 1578 (10th Cir. 1993) (*quoting United States v. Nazemian*, 948 F.2d 522, 529 (9th Cir. 1991). Additionally, in *United States v. Pallais*, 921 F.2d 684, 688 (7th Cir. 1990), the court posited: "Even commenting on a failed operation is in furtherance of the conspiracy, because people learn from their mistakes. Even identification of a coconspirator by an informative nickname such as "Big Guy" is in furtherance of the conspiracy, because it helps to establish, communicate, and thus confirm the lines of command in the organization." Finally, "[s]tatements made to keep co-conspirators informed about the progress of the conspiracy, to recruit others, or to control damage to the conspiracy are made in furtherance of the conspiracy." *United States v. Stephenson*, 53 F.3d 836, 845 (7th Cir. 1995); *see also United States v.*

Williamson, 53 F.3d 1500, 1520 (10th Cir. 1995)*(statements describing the particular roles of other co-conspirators are in furtherance of the conspiracy).*

3. The courts uniformly hold that "idle chatter" is not "in furtherance" of the conspiracy and thus is inadmissible hearsay. *See United States v. Stephenson*, 53 F.3d 836, 845 (7th Cir. 1995); *United States v. Johnson*, 927 F.2d 999, 1002 (7th Cir. 1991); *United States v. Pallais*, 921 F.2d 684, 688 (7th Cir. 1990) ("Mere chitchat, casual admissions of culpability, and other noise and static in the information stream are not admissible."); *United States v. Lieberman*, 637 F.2d 95, 103 (2d Cir. 1980). Statements are not in furtherance of the conspiracy if they are "mere narratives," that is, " 'statements relating to past events, even those connected with the operation of the conspiracy where the statement serves no immediate or future conspiratorial purpose.' " *United States v. Perez*, 989 F.2d 1574, 1578 (10th Cir. 1993) (citations omitted). Is Pinnell's out-of-court statement in *Cornell* merely "idle chatter"?

4. When inquiring whether a statement was made "in furtherance" of a conspiracy, must the government prove that the statement actually advanced the goals of the conspiracy? The federal courts have consistently ruled that it is enough if the declarant intended to promote the conspiratorial objectives. Actual facilitation of the objectives of the conspiracy is not required. *See United States v. Perez*, 989 F.2d 1574, 1578 (10th Cir. 1993); *United States v. Hamilton*, 689 F.2d 1262, 1270 (6th Cir. 1982) (government is not required to prove that statements "must actually further conspiracy" so long as they were "intended to").

5. Does the successful completion of the underlying offense which is the objective of the conspiracy necessarily terminate the conspiracy? Does this then preclude the admission of any statement made after the commission of the underlying offense from being a statement made in furtherance of the conspiracy? The courts have generally answered this question in the negative. *See Wallace v. State*, 426 N.E.2d 34, 42–43 (Ind. 1981) (holding that statements regarding payment from insurance proceeds, made by co-conspirators after the murder had taken place, were admissible because the statements were in furtherance of the objective of the conspiracy); *Willoughby v. State*, 660 N.E.2d 570, 581 (Ind. 1996) (same); *Cf. Grunewald v. United States*, 353 U.S. 391, 401–02 (1957) (if "main aim" of the conspiracy has been attained, the out-of-court statements are not admissible as co-conspirator statements).

6. Post-arrest statements amounting to confessions to known law enforcement agents are not in furtherance of the conspiracy. *See United States v. Rodriguez Alvarado*, 985 F.2d 15, 18–19 (1st Cir. 1993); *United States v. Alonzo*, 991 F.2d 1422, 1425–26 (8th Cir. 1993); *United States v. Gomez*, 927 F.2d 1530, 1535 (11th Cir. 1991); *United States v. Meachum*, 626 F.2d 503, 510–11 n.8 (5th Cir. 1980).

PROBLEM

Problem 7-3. *Co-conspirator Statements to Impress.* Defendant Carl Fielding, Robert ("Bobby") Flores, Rafael Flores, and others were charged with importation of marijuana and conspiracy among the same persons to import with the intent to distribute marijuana from Mexico. Bobby and Rafael Flores were the sources of marijuana. Fielding allegedly handled the stateside operations.

At trial, the district court admitted testimony from David Wagner, a government informant, and Dixon McClary, a DEA Special Agent. Their testimony consisted almost entirely of out-of-court statements made to them by co-conspirators Bobby and Rafael

Flores. At a meeting in Los Angeles with the Floreses, Wagner introduced himself as a big dealer and told them that he was interested "in doing a scam just like the one Carl (the defendant) was engaged in." At this meeting, Wagner attempted to initiate a new drug transaction, but was told that there was trouble with the defendant because he had not paid Bobby some $68,000 from an earlier trip which had been undertaken during the course of the conspiracy. Wagner offered his assistance, which was accepted, in collecting the debt.

The Floreses and Wagner went to Seattle to settle the financial dispute with defendant Fielding. At the airport, the Floreses and Wagner met Agent McClary, who was acting in an undercover capacity. Bobby made statements to Wagner and McClary connecting defendant Fielding to the conspiracy. Bobby stated that "he didn't like the way Carl dealt, he didn't like having to be on the dole and coming up to Seattle [to collect money from Carl] a few thousand dollars at a time." The Floreses further stated that they were planning to use physical force against the defendant. McClary and Wagner refused to provide them with a machete and talked them out of the use of force.

Eventually, Fielding, Bobby and Rafael were arrested. However, Bobby and Rafael Flores, who were Mexican nationals, were deported to Mexico before Fielding's trial. Thus, they were not available as trial witnesses and did not testify at the defendant's trial.

Are Bobby and Rafael's out-of-court statements made to Wagner and McClary properly admissible under Fed. R. Evid. 801(d)(2)(E) as co-conspirator statements against the defendant Fielding? Were these statements made in furtherance of the conspiracy to import marijuana with the intent to distribute? *See United States v. Fielding*, 645 F.2d 719 (9th Cir. 1981).

C.   VICARIOUS ADMISSIONS OF THIRD PARTIES OFFERED AGAINST THE GOVERNMENT — FED. R. EVID. 801(d)(2)(B)

Evidence otherwise inadmissible as hearsay — an out-of-court statement "offered in evidence to prove the truth of the matter asserted,"[12] may nonetheless be admitted as a non-hearsay statement if offered against the government when "the [Government] has manifested an adoption or belief in its truth."[13] An admission by a party opponent is not hearsay under this rule if the statement is either "(A) the party's own statement, in either an individual or a representative capacity or (B) a statement of which the party has manifested an adoption or belief in its truth. . . ."[14] For example, witness statements contained in a police report, otherwise inadmissible hearsay, may be admissible against the government if it is established that the government has "manifested an adoption or belief in [the] truth" of those statements.[15]

Admissibility of out-of-court statements under Rule 801(d)(2) involves a two-part inquiry. First, we must determine whether the government is a "party-opponent" for purposes of Rule 801(d)(2) in a criminal case. In *United States v. Kattar*,[16] the court

---

[12]   FED. R. EVID. 801(c).

[13]   FED. R. EVID. 801(d)(2)(B).

[14]   FED. R. EVID. 801(d)(2).

[15]   *See United States v. Warren*, 42 F.3d 647, 655 (D.C. Cir. 1994).

[16]   840 F.2d 118, 130 (1st Cir. 1988).

answered that question in the affirmative. The court stated:

> We agree with Judge Bazelon that "the Federal Rules clearly contemplate that the federal government is a party-opponent of the defendant in criminal cases." *United States v. Morgan*, 581 F.2d 933, 937 n.10 (D.C. Cir. 1978). We can find no authority to the contrary or reasons to think otherwise. Whether or not the entire federal government in all its capacities should be deemed a party-opponent in criminal cases, the Justice Department certainly should be considered such. (Citations omitted.)

The second inquiry is whether the government has manifested an adoption or belief in the truth of the proffered out-of-court statements. In *United States v. Warren*, 42 F.3d 647, 655 (D.C. Cir. 1994), the D.C. Circuit found that the government had expressed its belief in the out-of-court statements:

> The District Court excluded . . . Officer Holman's statement that Smith leased the apartment, contained in a statement of facts attached to the criminal complaint against Warren, App. 4. . . .

> This statement plainly was relevant, and therefore admissible under the Federal Rules of Evidence. Evidence is relevant if it has a tendency to make the existence of a material fact "more probable or less probable than it would be without the evidence." Fed. R. Evid. 401. Here, the evidence that Smith leased the apartment made it less likely that Warren owned the drugs found there, albeit marginally so. However, the District Court excluded this statement as hearsay — an out-of-court statement "offered in evidence to prove the truth of the matter asserted." Fed. R. Evid. 801(c). This was error. Officer Holman's statement . . . was contained in a sworn statement of facts submitted to a federal magistrate. Where, as here, "the government has indicated in a sworn affidavit to a judicial officer that it believes particular statements are trustworthy, it may not sustain an objection to the subsequent introduction of those statements on grounds that they are hearsay." *United States v. Morgan*, 581 F.2d 933, 938 (D.C. Cir. 1978). Instead, Officer Holman's statement was admissible under Federal Rules of Evidence 801(d)(2)(B) as a non-hearsay statement offered against the Government "of which the [Government] has manifested an adoption or belief in its truth." Fed. R. Evid. 801(d)(2)(B); see *Morgan*, 581 F.2d at 937–38; *United States v. Kattar*, 840 F.2d 118, 131 (1st Cir. 1988) (finding statements admissible under Rule 801(d)(2)(B) where Justice Department manifested belief in their truthfulness by submitting them to federal courts).

NOTES AND QUESTIONS

1. Should "the entire federal government in all its capacities . . . be deemed a party-opponent in criminal cases"? *United States v. Kattar*, 840 F.2d 118, 130 (1st Cir. 1988). Should the term "party-opponent," for purposes of Fed. R. Evid. 801(d)(2)(B), be construed to encompass any federal governmental agency? Only the United States Department of Justice? What if a state agency is assisting in a federal prosecution? Is the state agency a "party-opponent"?

2. Should the government be deemed to have "manifested an adoption or belief in [the] truth" of statements contained in any affidavits or briefs filed with the court? This appears to be the position adopted by the court in *United States v. Kattar*, 840 F.2d

118, 131 (1st Cir. 1988). *See also United States v. Warren*, 42 F.3d 647, 655 (D.C. Cir. 1994) (finding that the government "manifested an adoption or belief in the truth" of statements contained in a sworn statement of facts attached to a criminal complaint submitted to a federal magistrate). In support of its finding that statements in government briefs were admissible under Rule 801(d)(2)(B) as statements of which the party-opponent "has manifested an adoption or belief in its truth," the *Kattar* court stated that "[t]he government cannot indicate to one federal court that certain statements are trustworthy and accurate, and then argue to a jury in another federal court that those same assertions are hearsay." *Kattar*, 840 F.2d at 131. Do you agree? Should there then be a *per se* rule that the government has manifested a belief in the truth of every statement in all documents or briefs filed with the court? Does the *Kattar* court adopt an overly simplistic view of whether the government has manifested an adoption or belief in the truth of a particular statement for purposes of Rule 801(d)(2)(B)? Doesn't it depend on the particular facts of the case?

Chapter 8

HEARSAY — EXCEPTIONS WHERE THE AVAILABILITY OF THE DECLARANT IS IMMATERIAL

A. INTRODUCTION

The exceptions to the hearsay rule recognized in Fed. R. Evid. 803 "proceed upon the theory that under appropriate circumstances a hearsay statement may possess circumstantial guarantees of trustworthiness sufficient to justify nonproduction of the declarant in person at the trial even though he may be available."[1] All the hearsay exceptions rest on the belief that the declarations possess particular assurances of credibility which justify admission. In addition to the trustworthiness rationale, admission is based on necessity. Furthermore, because surrounding circumstances often enhance their reliability, some out-of-court declarations are considered to be of greater probative value than the present testimony of the declarant.[2]

Application of the Rule 803 hearsay exceptions within the criminal context raises unique problems. For example, the Confrontation Clause of the Sixth Amendment guarantees that "[i]n all criminal prosecutions, the accused shall enjoy the right . . . to be confronted with the witnesses against him." Thus, even though the hearsay statement may satisfy the statutory requirements imposed by Rule 803, admitting the statement may nevertheless violate the defendant's confrontation rights. Accordingly, every hearsay declaration proffered under Rule 803 must be measured for admission by the constitutional standard as well as the statutory requirements.

Traditionally, the courts have interpreted the Sixth Amendment Confrontation Clause as affording criminal defendants two types of protection: the right to physically face the witnesses who testify against the defendant, and the right to cross-examine them. *Pennsylvania v. Ritchie*, 480 U.S. 39, 51 (1987). The Confrontation Clause is designed "to ensure the reliability of the evidence against a criminal defendant by subjecting it to rigorous testing in the context of an adversary proceeding before the trier of fact." *Maryland v. Craig*, 497 U.S. 836, 845 (1990). For decades, Sixth Amendment challenges to hearsay declarations have been considered under the test established by the United States Supreme Court in *Ohio v. Roberts*, 448 U.S. 56 (1980). In *Roberts*, the Supreme Court held that when there is a showing of unavailability, a hearsay statement "is admissible only if it bears adequate 'indicia of reliability.' " *Id.* at 66. Under *Roberts*, reliability can be inferred where the out-of-court statement (1) falls within a firmly rooted exception to the hearsay rule or (2) contains such particularized guarantees of trustworthiness that adversarial testing of the statement would add little to the assessment of whether the evidence is reliable. *Id.*

---

[1] Advisory Committee Notes to Rule 803.

[2] CHARLES T. McCORMICK, 2 McCORMICK ON EVIDENCE § 273at 215 (John W. Strong, ed., 5th ed. 1999) ("Being spontaneous, the hearsay statements [concerning the declarant's present bodily condition and symptoms] are considered of greater probative value than the present testimony of the declarant.").

In *Crawford v. Washington*, 541 U.S. 36 (2004), the Supreme Court overruled *Roberts*, establishing a new standard for the admissibility of hearsay statements under the Confrontation Clause. The Court explicitly rejected the *Roberts* "indicia of reliability" test, holding that the Sixth Amendment Confrontation Clause bars prosecutors from proving guilt with hearsay that is "testimonial" in nature unless the declarant testifies, or the declarant is unavailable and there was "a prior opportunity for cross-examination." *Id.* at 68. Thus, after *Crawford*, the critical issue in determining whether admission of a hearsay statement violates the Confrontation Clause is whether the statement is "testimonial." If the statement is not testimonial, the courts are free to apply the relevant hearsay rules to determine the statement's admissibility. However, the Court left "for another day any effort to spell out a comprehensive definition of 'testimonial.'" *Id.* In the absence of such a definition, the courts have struggled in determining whether a challenged statement is "testimonial" or "nontestimonial" for purposes of the Confrontation Clause.

This chapter addresses the Rule 803 hearsay exceptions that are the frequent subject of dispute in criminal litigation, including an examination of whether admission of the hearsay evidence withstands scrutiny under the Sixth Amendment Confrontation Clause.

B. THE SIXTH AMENDMENT CONFRONTATION CLAUSE — LIMITATIONS ON THE ADMISSIBILITY OF "TESTIMONIAL" STATEMENTS

CRAWFORD v. WASHINGTON
541 U.S. 36 (2004)

SCALIA, J., delivered the opinion of the Court.

Petitioner Michael Crawford stabbed a man who allegedly tried to rape his wife, Sylvia. At his trial, the State played for the jury Sylvia's tape-recorded statement to the police describing the stabbing, even though he had no opportunity for cross-examination. The Washington Supreme Court upheld petitioner's conviction after determining that Sylvia's statement was reliable. The question presented is whether this procedure complied with the Sixth Amendment's guarantee that, "[i]n all criminal prosecutions, the accused shall enjoy the right . . . to be confronted with the witnesses against him."

I.

On August 5, 1999, Kenneth Lee was stabbed at his apartment. Police arrested petitioner later that night. After giving petitioner and his wife *Miranda* warnings, detectives interrogated each of them twice. Petitioner eventually confessed that he and Sylvia had gone in search of Lee because he was upset over an earlier incident in which Lee had tried to rape her. The two had found Lee at his apartment, and a fight ensued in which Lee was stabbed in the torso and petitioner's hand was cut.

Petitioner gave the following account of the fight:

"Q. Okay. Did you ever see anything in [Lee's] hands?

"A. I think so, but I'm not positive.

"Q. Okay, when you think so, what do you mean by that?

"A. I could a swore I seen him goin' for somethin' before, right before everything happened. He was like reachin', fiddlin' around down here and stuff . . . and I just . . . I don't know, I think, this is just a possibility, but I think, I think that he pulled somethin' out and I grabbed for it and that's how I got cut . . . but I'm not positive. I, I, my mind goes blank when things like this happen. I mean, I just, I remember things wrong, I remember things that just doesn't, don't make sense to me later."

Sylvia generally corroborated petitioner's story about the events leading up to the fight, but her account of the fight itself was arguably different-particularly with respect to whether Lee had drawn a weapon before petitioner assaulted him:

"Q. Did Kenny do anything to fight back from this assault?

"A. (pausing) I know he reached into his pocket . . . or somethin' . . . I don't know what.

"Q. After he was stabbed?

"A. He saw Michael coming up. He lifted his hand . . . his chest open, he might [have] went to go strike his hand out or something and then (inaudible).

"Q. Okay, you, you gotta speak up.

"A. Okay, he lifted his hand over his head maybe to strike Michael's hand down or something and then he put his hands in his . . . put his right hand in his right pocket . . . took a step back . . . Michael proceeded to stab him . . . then his hands were like . . . how do you explain this . . . open arms . . . with his hands open and he fell down . . . and we ran (describing subject holding hands open, palms toward assailant).

"Q. Okay, when he's standing there with his open hands, you're talking about Kenny, correct?

"A. Yeah, after, after the fact, yes.

"Q. Did you see anything in his hands at that point?

"A. (pausing) um um (no)."

The State charged petitioner with assault and attempted murder. At trial, he claimed self-defense. Sylvia did not testify because of the state marital privilege, which generally bars a spouse from testifying without the other spouse's consent. In Washington, this privilege does not extend to a spouse's out-of-court statements admissible under a hearsay exception, so the State sought to introduce Sylvia's tape-recorded statements to the police as evidence that the stabbing was not in self-defense. Noting that Sylvia had admitted she led petitioner to Lee's apartment and thus had facilitated the assault, the State invoked the hearsay exception for statements against penal interest, Wash. Rule Evid. 804(b)(3) (2003).

Petitioner countered that, state law notwithstanding, admitting the evidence would violate his federal constitutional right to be "confronted with the witnesses against him." Amdt. 6. According to our description of that right in *Ohio v. Roberts*, 448 U.S. 56 (1980), it does not bar admission of an unavailable witness's statement against a criminal defendant if the statement bears "adequate 'indicia of reliability.' " *Id.*, at 66. To meet that test, evidence must either fall within a "firmly rooted hearsay exception" or bear "particularized guarantees of trustworthiness." *Ibid.* The trial court here admitted the statement on the latter ground, offering several reasons why it was trustworthy: Sylvia was not shifting blame but rather corroborating her husband's story that he acted in self-defense or "justified reprisal"; she had direct knowledge as an eyewitness; she was describing recent events; and she was being questioned by a "neutral" law enforcement officer. The prosecution played the tape for the jury and relied on it in closing, arguing that it was "damning evidence" that "completely refutes [petitioner's] claim of self-defense." The jury convicted petitioner of assault.

The Washington Court of Appeals reversed. It applied a nine-factor test to determine whether Sylvia's statement bore particularized guarantees of trustworthiness, and noted several reasons why it did not: The statement contradicted one she had previously given; it was made in response to specific questions; and at one point she admitted she had shut her eyes during the stabbing. The court considered and rejected the State's argument that Sylvia's statement was reliable because it coincided with petitioner's to such a degree that the two "interlocked." The court determined that, although the two statements agreed about the events leading up to the stabbing, they differed on the issue crucial to petitioner's self-defense claim: "[Petitioner's] version asserts that Lee may have had something in his hand when he stabbed him; but Sylvia's version has Lee grabbing for something only after he has been stabbed."

The Washington Supreme Court reinstated the conviction, unanimously concluding that, although Sylvia's statement did not fall under a firmly rooted hearsay exception, it bore guarantees of trustworthiness. . . .

We granted certiorari to determine whether the State's use of Sylvia's statement violated the Confrontation Clause.

II.

The Sixth Amendment's Confrontation Clause provides that, "[i]n all criminal prosecutions, the accused shall enjoy the right . . . to be confronted with the witnesses against him." We have held that this bedrock procedural guarantee applies to both federal and state prosecutions. *Pointer v. Texas*, 380 U.S. 400, 406 (1965). As noted above, *Roberts* says that an unavailable witness's out-of-court statement may be admitted so long as it has adequate indicia of reliability-*i.e.*, falls within a "firmly rooted hearsay exception" or bears "particularized guarantees of trustworthiness." 448 U.S., at 66. Petitioner argues that this test strays from the original meaning of the Confrontation Clause and urges us to reconsider it.

A.

* * *

The right to confront one's accusers is a concept that dates back to Roman times. The founding generation's immediate source of the concept, however, was the common law. English common law has long differed from continental civil law in regard to the manner in which witnesses give testimony in criminal trials. The common-law tradition is one of live testimony in court subject to adversarial testing, while the civil law condones examination in private by judicial officers.

Nonetheless, England at times adopted elements of the civil-law practice. Justices of the peace or other officials examined suspects and witnesses before trial. These examinations were sometimes read in court in lieu of live testimony, a practice that "occasioned frequent demands by the prisoner to have his 'accusers,' *i.e.* the witnesses against him, brought before him face to face." 1 J. Stephen, History of the Criminal Law of England 326 (1883).

Pretrial examinations became routine under two statutes passed during the reign of Queen Mary in the 16th century. These Marian bail and committal statutes required justices of the peace to examine suspects and witnesses in felony cases and to certify the results to the court. It is doubtful that the original purpose of the examinations was to produce evidence admissible at trial. Whatever the original purpose, however, they came to be used as evidence in some cases, resulting in an adoption of continental procedure.

The most notorious instances of civil-law examination occurred in the great political trials of the 16th and 17th centuries. One such was the 1603 trial of Sir Walter Raleigh for treason. Lord Cobham, Raleigh's alleged accomplice, had implicated him in an examination before the Privy Council and in a letter. At Raleigh's trial, these were read to the jury. Raleigh argued that Cobham had lied to save himself: "Cobham is absolutely in the King's mercy; to excuse me cannot avail him; by accusing me he may hope for favour." Suspecting that Cobham would recant, Raleigh demanded that the judges call him to appear, arguing that "[t]he Proof of the Common Law is by witness and jury: let Cobham be here, let him speak it. Call my accuser before my face. . . ." The judges refused, and, despite Raleigh's protestations that he was being tried "by the Spanish Inquisition," the jury convicted, and Raleigh was sentenced to death.

One of Raleigh's trial judges later lamented that " 'the justice of England has never been so degraded and injured as by the condemnation of Sir Walter Raleigh.' " Through a series of statutory and judicial reforms, English law developed a right of confrontation that limited these abuses. For example, treason statutes required witnesses to confront the accused "face to face" at his arraignment. Courts, meanwhile, developed relatively strict rules of unavailability, admitting examinations only if the witness was demonstrably unable to testify in person. Several authorities also stated that a suspect's confession could be admitted only against himself, and not against others he implicated.

One recurring question was whether the admissibility of an unavailable witness's pretrial examination depended on whether the defendant had had an opportunity to cross-examine him. In 1696, the Court of King's Bench answered this question in the affirmative, in the widely reported misdemeanor libel case of *King v. Paine*, 5 Mod. 163, 87 Eng. Rep. 584. The court ruled that, even though a witness was dead, his examination was not admissible where "the defendant not being present when [it was] taken before the mayor . . . had lost the benefit of a cross-examination."

*   *   *

B.

Controversial examination practices were also used in the Colonies. Early in the 18th century, for example, the Virginia Council protested against the Governor for having "privately issued several commissions to examine witnesses against particular men *ex parte*," complaining that "the person accused is not admitted to be confronted with, or defend himself against his defamers." A decade before the Revolution, England gave jurisdiction over Stamp Act offenses to the admiralty courts, which followed civil-law rather than common-law procedures and thus routinely took testimony by deposition or private judicial examination. Colonial representatives protested that the Act subverted their rights "by extending the jurisdiction of the courts of admiralty beyond its ancient limits." John Adams, defending a merchant in a high-profile admiralty case, argued: "Examinations of witnesses upon Interrogatories, are only by the Civil Law. Interrogatories are unknown at common Law, and Englishmen and common Lawyers have an aversion to them if not an Abhorrence of them." Draft of Argument in *Sewall v. Hancock* (Oct. 1768 - Mar. 1769), in 2 Legal Papers of John Adams 194, 207 (L. Wroth & H. Zobel eds.1965).

Many declarations of rights adopted around the time of the Revolution guaranteed a right of confrontation. See Virginia Declaration of Rights § 8 (1776); Pennsylvania Declaration of Rights § IX (1776); Delaware Declaration of Rights § 14 (1776); Maryland Declaration of Rights § XIX (1776); North Carolina Declaration of Rights § VII (1776); Vermont Declaration of Rights Ch. I, § X (1777); Massachusetts Declaration of Rights § XII (1780); New Hampshire Bill of Rights § XV (1783), all reprinted in 1 B. Schwartz, The Bill of Rights: A Documentary History 235, 265, 278, 282, 287, 323, 342, 377 (1971). The proposed Federal Constitution, however, did not. At the Massachusetts ratifying convention, Abraham Holmes objected to this omission on the ground that it would lead to civil-law practices: "The mode of trial is altogether indetermined; . . . whether [the defendant] is to be allowed to confront the witnesses, and have the advantage of cross-examination, we are not yet told. . . . [W]e shall find Congress possessed of powers enabling them to institute judicatories little less inauspicious than a certain tribunal in Spain, . . . the *Inquisition.*" 2 Debates on the Federal Constitution 110–111 (J. Elliot 2d ed. 1863). . . . The First Congress responded by including the Confrontation Clause in the proposal that became the Sixth Amendment.

*   *   *

III.

This history supports two inferences about the meaning of the Sixth Amendment.

A.

First, the principal evil at which the Confrontation Clause was directed was the civil-law mode of criminal procedure, and particularly its use of *ex parte* examinations as evidence against the accused. It was these practices that the Crown deployed in notorious treason cases like Raleigh's; that the Marian statutes invited; that English law's assertion of a right to confrontation was meant to prohibit; and that the founding-era rhetoric decried. The Sixth Amendment must be interpreted with this focus in mind.

*   *   *

This focus also suggests that not all hearsay implicates the Sixth Amendment's core concerns. An off-hand, overheard remark might be unreliable evidence and thus a good candidate for exclusion under hearsay rules, but it bears little resemblance to the civil-law abuses the Confrontation Clause targeted. On the other hand, *ex parte* examinations might sometimes be admissible under modern hearsay rules, but the Framers certainly would not have condoned them.

The text of the Confrontation Clause reflects this focus. It applies to "witnesses" against the accused-in other words, those who "bear testimony." 2 N. Webster, An American Dictionary of the English Language (1828). "Testimony," in turn, is typically "[a] solemn declaration or affirmation made for the purpose of establishing or proving some fact." *Ibid.* An accuser who makes a formal statement to government officers bears testimony in a sense that a person who makes a casual remark to an acquaintance does not. The constitutional text, like the history underlying the common-law right of confrontation, thus reflects an especially acute concern with a specific type of out-of-court statement.

Various formulations of this core class of "testimonial" statements exist: "*ex parte* in-court testimony or its functional equivalent-that is, material such as affidavits, custodial examinations, prior testimony that the defendant was unable to cross-examine, or similar pretrial statements that declarants would reasonably expect to be used prosecutorially;" "extrajudicial statements . . . contained in formalized testimonial materials, such as affidavits, depositions, prior testimony, or confessions," *White v. Illinois*, 502 U.S. 346, 365 (1992) (THOMAS, J., joined by SCALIA, J., concurring in part and concurring in judgment); "statements that were made under circumstances which would lead an objective witness reasonably to believe that the statement would be available for use at a later trial," Brief for National Association of Criminal Defense Lawyers et al. Regardless of the precise articulation, some statements qualify under any definition-for example, *ex parte* testimony at a preliminary hearing.

Statements taken by police officers in the course of interrogations are also testimonial under even a narrow standard. Police interrogations bear a striking resemblance to examinations by justices of the peace in England. The statements are not *sworn* testimony, but the absence of oath was not dispositive. Cobham's examination was unsworn, yet Raleigh's trial has long been thought a paradigmatic confrontation violation. . . . [footnote omitted].

In sum, even if the Sixth Amendment is not solely concerned with testimonial hearsay, that is its primary object, and interrogations by law enforcement officers fall squarely within that class. [footnote omitted].

B.

The historical record also supports a second proposition: that the Framers would not have allowed admission of testimonial statements of a witness who did not appear at trial unless he was unavailable to testify, and the defendant had had a prior opportunity for cross-examination. The text of the Sixth Amendment does not suggest any open-ended exceptions from the confrontation requirement to be developed by the courts. Rather, the "right . . . to be confronted with the witnesses against him," Amdt. 6, is most naturally read as a reference to the right of confrontation at common law, admitting only those exceptions established at the time of the founding. As the English authorities above reveal, the common law in 1791 conditioned admissibility of an absent witness's examination on unavailability and a prior opportunity to cross-examine. The Sixth Amendment therefore incorporates those limitations. . . . [footnote omitted].

We do not read the historical sources to say that a prior opportunity to cross-examine was merely a sufficient, rather than a necessary, condition for admissibility of testimonial statements. They suggest that this requirement was dispositive, and not merely one of several ways to establish reliability. This is not to deny, as THE CHIEF JUSTICE notes, that "[t]here were always exceptions to the general rule of exclusion" of hearsay evidence. Several had become well established by 1791. But there is scant evidence that exceptions were invoked to admit *testimonial* statements against the accused in a *criminal* case. [footnote omitted]. Most of the hearsay exceptions covered statements that by their nature were not testimonial-for example, business records or statements in furtherance of a conspiracy. . . . [footnote omitted].

IV.

Our case law has been largely consistent with these two principles. Our leading early decision, for example, involved a deceased witness's prior trial testimony. *Mattox v. United States*, 156 U.S. 237 (1895). In allowing the statement to be admitted, we relied on the fact that the defendant had had, at the first trial, an adequate opportunity to confront the witness: "The substance of the constitutional protection is preserved to the prisoner in the advantage he has once had of seeing the witness face to face, and of subjecting him to the ordeal of a cross-examination. This, the law says, he shall under no circumstances be deprived of. . . ." *Id.*, at 244.

Our later cases conform to *Mattox's* holding that prior trial or preliminary hearing testimony is admissible only if the defendant had an adequate opportunity to cross-examine. [citations omitted]. Even where the defendant had such an opportunity, we excluded the testimony where the government had not established unavailability of the witness. [citation omitted]. We similarly excluded accomplice confessions where the defendant had no opportunity to cross-examine. [citations omitted]. In contrast, we considered reliability factors beyond prior opportunity for cross-examination when the hearsay statement at issue was not testimonial.

Even our recent cases, in their outcomes, hew closely to the traditional line. *Ohio v. Roberts*, 448 U.S., at 67–70, admitted testimony from a preliminary hearing at which the defendant had examined the witness. *Lilly v. Virginia*, excluded testimonial statements that the defendant had had no opportunity to test by cross-examination. And *Bourjaily v. United States*, 483 U.S. 171, 181–184 (1987), admitted statements made unwittingly to a Federal Bureau of Investigation informant after applying a more general test that did *not* make prior cross-examination an indispensable requirement. [footnote omitted].

* * *

Our cases have thus remained faithful to the Framers' understanding: Testimonial statements of witnesses absent from trial have been admitted only where the declarant is unavailable, and only where the defendant has had a prior opportunity to cross-examine. [footnote omitted].

V.

Although the results of our decisions have generally been faithful to the original meaning of the Confrontation Clause, the same cannot be said of our rationales. *Roberts* conditions the admissibility of all hearsay evidence on whether it falls under a "firmly rooted hearsay exception" or bears "particularized guarantees of trustworthiness." 448 U.S., at 66. This test departs from the historical principles identified above in two respects. First, it is too broad: It applies the same mode of analysis whether or not the hearsay consists of *ex parte* testimony. This often results in close constitutional scrutiny in cases that are far removed from the core concerns of the Clause. At the same time, however, the test is too narrow: It admits statements that *do* consist of *ex parte* testimony upon a mere finding of reliability. This malleable standard often fails to protect against paradigmatic confrontation violations.

* * *

A.

Where testimonial statements are involved, we do not think the Framers meant to leave the Sixth Amendment's protection to the vagaries of the rules of evidence, much less to amorphous notions of "reliability". . . . Admitting statements deemed reliable by a judge is fundamentally at odds with the right of confrontation. To be sure, the Clause's ultimate goal is to ensure reliability of evidence, but it is a procedural rather than a substantive guarantee. It commands, not that evidence be reliable, but that reliability be assessed in a particular manner: by testing in the crucible of cross-examination. The Clause thus reflects a judgment, not only about the desirability of reliable evidence (a point on which there could be little dissent), but about how reliability can best be determined.

The *Roberts* test allows a jury to hear evidence, untested by the adversary process, based on a mere judicial determination of reliability. It thus replaces the constitutionally prescribed method of assessing reliability with a wholly foreign one. In this respect, it is very different from exceptions to the Confrontation Clause that make no claim to be a surrogate means of assessing reliability. For example, the rule of forfeiture by wrongdoing (which we accept) extinguishes confrontation claims on essentially equitable grounds; it does not purport to be an alternative means of determining reliability.

*   *   *

Dispensing with confrontation because testimony is obviously reliable is akin to dispensing with jury trial because a defendant is obviously guilty. This is not what the Sixth Amendment prescribes.

B.

The legacy of *Roberts* in other courts vindicates the Framers' wisdom in rejecting a general reliability exception. The framework is so unpredictable that it fails to provide meaningful protection from even core confrontation violations.

Reliability is an amorphous, if not entirely subjective, concept. There are countless factors bearing on whether a statement is reliable; the nine-factor balancing test applied by the Court of Appeals below is representative. Whether a statement is deemed reliable depends heavily on which factors the judge considers and how much weight he accords each of them. Some courts wind up attaching the same significance to opposite facts. . . . The Virginia Court of Appeals found a statement more reliable because the witness was in custody and charged with a crime (thus making the statement more obviously against her penal interest), see *Nowlin v. Commonwealth*, 40 Va.App. 327, 335–338 (2003), while the Wisconsin Court of Appeals found a statement more reliable because the witness was *not* in custody and *not* a suspect, see *State v. Bintz*, 2002 WI App. 204, ¶ 13. Finally, the Colorado Supreme Court in one case found a statement more reliable because it was given "immediately after" the events at issue, *Farrell, supra,* at 407, while that same court, in another case, found a statement more reliable because two years had elapsed, *Stevens v. People*, 29 P.3d 305, 316 (Colo.2001).

The unpardonable vice of the *Roberts* test, however, is not its unpredictability, but its demonstrated capacity to admit core testimonial statements that the Confrontation Clause plainly meant to exclude. Despite the plurality's speculation in *Lilly*, 527 U.S., at 137, that it was "highly unlikely" that accomplice confessions implicating the accused could survive *Roberts*, courts continue routinely to admit them. [citations omitted]. One recent study found that, after *Lilly*, appellate courts admitted accomplice statements to the authorities in 25 out of 70 cases-more than one-third of the time. Kirst, Appellate Court Answers to the Confrontation Questions in *Lilly v. Virginia*, 53 Syracuse L.Rev. 87, 105 (2003). Courts have invoked *Roberts* to admit other sorts of plainly testimonial statements despite the absence of any opportunity to cross-examine. [citations omitted].

C.

Roberts' failings were on full display in the proceedings below. Sylvia Crawford made her statement while in police custody, herself a potential suspect in the case. Indeed, she had been told that whether she would be released "depend[ed] on how the investigation continues." In response to often leading questions from police detectives, she implicated her husband in Lee's stabbing and at least arguably undermined his self-defense claim. Despite all this, the trial court admitted her statement, listing several reasons why it was reliable. In its opinion reversing, the Court of Appeals listed several *other* reasons why the statement was *not* reliable. Finally, the State Supreme Court relied exclusively on the interlocking character of the statement and disregarded every other factor the lower courts had considered. The case is thus a self-contained demonstration of *Roberts'* unpredictable and inconsistent application.

* * *

Where nontestimonial hearsay is at issue, it is wholly consistent with the Framers' design to afford the States flexibility in their development of hearsay law-as does *Roberts*, and as would an approach that exempted such statements from Confrontation Clause scrutiny altogether. Where testimonial evidence is at issue, however, the Sixth Amendment demands what the common law required: unavailability and a prior opportunity for cross-examination. We leave for another day any effort to spell out a comprehensive definition of "testimonial." [footnote omitted]. Whatever else the term covers, it applies at a minimum to prior testimony at a preliminary hearing, before a grand jury, or at a former trial; and to police interrogations. These are the modern practices with closest kinship to the abuses at which the Confrontation Clause was directed.

* * *

The judgment of the Washington Supreme Court is reversed, and the case is remanded for further proceedings not inconsistent with this opinion.

NOTES AND QUESTIONS

1. What is the "principal evil" that the Sixth Amendment Confrontation Clause was designed to address? *Crawford v. Washington*, 541 U.S. 36, 50 (2004). Do all hearsay statements implicate this core concern?

2. *Testimonial statements.* In *Crawford v. Washington*, the Supreme Court stated: "We leave for another day any effort to spell out a comprehensive definition of 'testimonial.'" *Id.* at 68. However, the Court noted that there is a "core class" of testimonial statements barred by the Confrontation Clause. *Id.* at 51. What out-of-court declarations fall within this "core class" of testimonial statements? The Court posited that "[s]tatements taken by police officers in the course of interrogations are . . . testimonial" *Id.* at 52. What other types of hearsay statements are "testimonial" and therefore inadmissible under the Confrontation Clause? Are statements that "declarants would reasonably expect to be used prosecutorially" testimonial in nature?

Id. at 51. Any such statements or only those made in response to police questioning that a declarant would reasonably expect to be used at a later trial?

3. Does Confrontation Clause protection extend to situations where governmental or law enforcement involvement does not exist? Stated another way, are statements made to non-governmental officials "nontestimonial"? In *People v. Stechly*, 870 N.E.2d 333 (Ill. 2007), the Illinois Supreme Court held that statements to non-governmental officials may be testimonial, but not always. *But see Clarke v. United States*, 943 A.2d 555, 557 (D.C. App. 2008) (holding that victim-declarant's statement to mother was nontestimonial, but noting that "the fact alone that a statement was made to" a non-state actor does not make it per se nontestimonial); *State v. Kemp*, 212 S.W.3d 135, 150 (Mo. 2007) (holding victim's statement to neighbors asking for help and describing how she was harmed and by whom, was nontestimonial because "an accuser who makes a formal statement to government officers bears testimony in a sense that a person who makes a casual remark to an acquaintance does not."); *United States. v. Peneaux*, 432 F.3d 882, 896 (8th Cir. 2005) (child victim's statements to his foster mother were not testimonial). *See also* Michael H. Graham, *Crawford/Davis "Testimonial" Interpreted, Removing the Clutter; Application Summary*, 62 U. MIAMI L. REV. 811, 827 (2007–2008) (statements made to a non-governmental official are clearly non-testimonial "falling outside the core meaning of the Confrontation Clause — the principal evil of civil-law-type ex parte examinations admitted against the accused"). Do you agree with Professor Graham?

4. *Relevant factors.* What factors are relevant in determining whether out-of-court statements are "testimonial" for purposes of the Sixth Amendment Confrontation Clause? Justice Scalia states that the text of the Confrontation Clause applies to " 'witnesses' against the accused . . . those who 'bear testimony.' " *Crawford*, 541 U.S. at 51. He further asserts that " '[t]estimony' . . . is typically '[a] solemn declaration or affirmation made for the purpose of establishing or proving some fact.' An accuser who makes a formal statement to government officers bears testimony in a sense that a person who makes a casual remark to an acquaintance does not." *Id.* Thus, in determining whether a hearsay statement is testimonial does it matter whether the statement was the product of "interrogation," formal or informal, or made under circumstances indicating "solemnity"? *See* Michael H. Graham, *Crawford/Davis "Testimonial" Interpreted, Removing the Clutter; Application Summary*, 62 U. MIAMI L. REV. 811, 821 (2007–2008). Are testimonial statements limited to statements "accusatory in nature," meaning statements that assist law enforcement in the apprehension or prosecution of a criminal defendant? Are statements that "declarants would reasonably expect to be used prosecutorily," or that "were made under circumstances which would lead an objective witness reasonably to believe that the statement would be available for use at a later trial" testimonial? *Crawford*, 541 U.S. at 51–52. *See also United States v. Summers*, 414 F.3d 1287, 1302 (10th Cir. 2005) ("a statement is testimonial if a reasonable person in the position of the declarant would objectively foresee that his statement might be used in the investigation or prosecution of a crime").

5. In *Crawford*, Justice Scalia stated:

> Involvement of government officers in the production of testimony with an eye toward trial presents unique potential for prosecutorial abuse-a fact borne out time and again throughout a history with which the Framers were keenly familiar. *Id.* at 56 n.7.

Thus, are reports prepared with an "eye toward trial," such as a drug chemist report certifying that an unknown substance is a controlled substance or a breath-analyzer report indicating the driver's blood-alcohol level was above the legal limit, testimonial statements even if they fall within the business or public records exception to the hearsay rule? Aren't such reports always prepared with an "eye toward trial"? *See State v. Caulfield*, 722 N.W.2d 304 (Minn. 2006).

6. *Multi-part inquiry.* After *Crawford*, courts must undertake a two-step inquiry before admitting hearsay statements. "First, it must be determined whether the hearsay evidence is admissible under the applicable rules of evidence. Second, if the evidence is admissible under the rules, it must be determined whether the hearsay statement is testimonial or nontestimonial." *United States v. Arnold*, 486 F.3d 177, 199 (6th Cir. 2007) (*en banc*). *See also United States v. Mendez*, 514 F.3d 1035, 1043 (10th Cir. 2008) (applying a three-part test: "(1) whether the challenged evidence is hearsay; (2) whether it is testimonial; and (3) if the evidence is testimonial, whether its introduction was harmless error").

7. Post-*Crawford*, while the Confrontation Clause plainly restricts the admission of testimonial statements, does it place any restrictions on the admission of nontestimonial statements? *Crawford* left the question open. *See Crawford*, 541 U.S. at 61. For example, does the Confrontation Clause require the proponent of a nontestimonial statement to prove that it bears sufficient indicia of reliability? In *Whorton v. Bockting* 549 U.S. 406 (2007), the Supreme Court stated that "the Confrontation Clause has no application to 'out-of-court nontestimonial statement[s].' "

8. Note that the Confrontation Clause does not restrict the use of prior testimonial statements where the declarant appears for cross-examination at trial. In *Crawford*, the Court stated that "when the declarant appears for cross-examination at trial, the Confrontation Clause places no constraints at all on the use of his prior testimonial statements." *Crawford*, 541 U.S. at 59 n.9. In such a case, the admissibility of the out-of-court statement is determined by whether the statement falls within a hearsay exception, including the residual exception. *See* Fed. R. Evid. 807.

9. *Exceptions to Crawford.* In *Crawford*, Justice Scalia asserted: "Most of the hearsay exceptions covered statements that by their nature were not testimonial — for example, business records or statements in furtherance of a conspiracy." *Id.* at 56. Are statements in business records or made in furtherance of a conspiracy nontestimonial or do such statements constitute an exception to the ruling in *Crawford*? Are there other exceptions to the rule in *Crawford*?

(a) *Dying declarations.* In *Crawford*, the Supreme Court recognized one possible exception to the common law prohibition of testimonial statements against the accused in a criminal case. The Court stated:

> The one deviation we have found involves dying declarations. The existence of that exception as a general rule of criminal hearsay law cannot be disputed. [citations omitted]. Although many dying declarations may not be testimonial, there is authority for admitting even those that clearly are. [citations omitted]. We need not decide in this case whether the Sixth Amendment incorporates an exception for testimonial dying declarations. If this exception must be accepted on historical grounds, it is *sui generis. Id.* at 56, note 6.

In *State v. Lewis*, 235 S.W.3d 136 (Tenn. 2007), the Tennessee Supreme Court recognized an exception to the rule in *Crawford* for dying declarations. *See* discussion *infra*, at Chapter 9. The court declared: "Because the admissibility of the dying declaration is . . . deeply entrenched in the legal history of this state, it is also our view that this single hearsay exception survives the mandate of *Crawford* regardless of its testimonial nature." *Id.* at 148. However, the courts remain divided on the issue. *See, e.g., Harkins v. State*, 143 P.3d 706 (Nev. 2006) (dying declaration admissible despite its testimonial nature); but see *United States v. Jordan* (D. Colo. 2005) (admitting dying declaration goes against "sweeping prohibitions" of *Crawford*).

(b) *Business and public records.* In *Crawford*, the Supreme Court stated that "[m]ost of the hearsay exceptions covered statements that by their nature were not testimonial — for example, business records or statements in furtherance of a conspiracy." *Crawford*, 541 U.S., at 56. Some courts have taken the position that out-of-court statements that fall into either the business or public records exception to the hearsay rule are nontestimonial. *See, e.g., United States v. Mendez*, 514 F.3d 1035 (10th Cir. 2008) (drug ledgers and ICE database are not testimonial); *United States v. Torres-Villalobos*, 487 F.3d 607, 613 (8th Cir. 2007) (warrants of deportation are public records and not testimonial); *United States v. Weiland*, 420 F.3d 1062, 1076–77 (9th Cir. 2005) (records of conviction and routine certifications of public records are not testimonial); *United States v. Lopez-Moreno*, 420 F.3d 420, 437 (5th Cir. 2005) (ICE computer records are public records and not testimonial); *State v. Forte*, 619 S.E.2d 853 (N.C. 2006) (lab reports of DNA analysis are not testimonial). *But see State v. Johnson*, 982 So.2d 672 (Fla. 2008) (holding that state drug laboratory report was testimonial); *State v. Caulfield*, 722 N.W.2d 304 (Minn. 2006) (same).

(c) *Co-conspirator statements.* Does *Crawford* affect the admissibility of co-conspirator statements? *See Bourjaily v. United States*, 483 U.S. 171 (1987). The courts have consistently held that co-conspirator statements are neither hearsay nor "testimonial" in nature. *See e.g., United States v. Hargrove*, 508 F.3d 445 (7th Cir. 2007); *United States Bridgeforth*, 441 F.3d 864, 869 n.1 (9th Cir. 2006); *United States v. Martinez*, 430 F.3d 317, 329 (6th Cir. 2005); *United States v. Delgado*, 401 F.3d 290, 299 (5th Cir. 2005); *United States v. Hendricks*, 395 F.3d 173, 183–84 (3d Cir. 2005); *United States v. Saget*, 377 F.3d 223, 224–25 (2d Cir. 2004).

10. *Harmless error.* A Confrontation Clause violation under *Crawford* is subject to the constitutional harmless error analysis. In his concurrence in *Crawford*, Chief Justice Rehnquist stated that "the mistaken application of [the majority's] new rule by courts which guess wrong as to the scope of the rule is subject to harmless error analysis." *Crawford*, 541 U.S. at 76 (Rehnquist, C.J., concurring). *See also United States v. Arnold*, 486 F.3d 177, 201 (6th Cir. 2007) (en banc) (applying a harmless error analysis); *United States v. Mendez*, 514 F.3d at 1043 (10th Cir. 2008) (same); *United States v. Robinson*, 389 F.3d 582, 593 (6th Cir. 2004) (same) (citing *Delaware v. Van Arsdall*, 475 U.S. 673, 684 (1986)). Under the harmless error rule, a constitutional error does not mandate reversal and a new trial if the error was harmless beyond a reasonable doubt. What factors are relevant in determining whether the admission of a testimonial statement constituted harmless or prejudicial error? In *Delaware v. Van Arsdall*, the Supreme Court declared:

> Whether such an error is harmless in a particular case depends on a host of factors, all readily accessible to reviewing courts. These factors include the importance of the witness' testimony in the prosecution's case, whether the testimony was cumulative, the presence or absence of evidence corroborating or contradicting the testimony of the witness on material points, the extent of

cross-examination otherwise permitted, and, of course, the overall strength of the prosecution's case.

Van Arsdall, 475 U.S. at 684.

In *State v. Caulfield*, 722 N.W.2d 304, 314 (Minn. 2006), the court considered the following factors in determining whether the admission of a state drug lab report, which the court concluded was "testimonial" under *Crawford*, constituted harmless error:

> When determining whether a jury verdict was surely attributable to an erroneous admission of evidence, the reviewing court considers the manner in which the evidence was presented, whether it was highly persuasive, whether it was used in closing argument, and whether it was effectively countered by the defendant. "[O]verwhelming evidence of guilt is a factor, often a very important one, in determining whether, beyond a reasonable doubt, the error has no impact on the verdict."

Id. (citations omitted). Applying these factors, the *Caulfield* court concluded that the erroneous admission of the drug lab report was not harmless beyond a reasonable doubt. *Id.* at 317.

11. *Police interrogations.* The Supreme Court in *Crawford* stated that the term "testimonial" covers police interrogations. Why are statements made during police interrogations "testimonial" in nature? Are statements made in response to police questioning always "testimonial"? Does it matter whether the statements were voluntered by the declarant or the product of police interrogation? Does it depend on whether the *primary purpose* of the police interrogation was to confront an emergency or explain past events? In *Davis v. Washington*, 547 U.S. 813 (2006), the Supreme Court retreated from its position in *Crawford* that statements made during a police interrogation are testimonial for purposes of the Confrontation Clause. Apparently, while some statements elicited during interrogations by law enforcement officers fall squarely within the core class of testimonial hearsay, other such statements do not. What is the determinative factor?

[1]   The "Primary Purpose" Test

DAVIS v. WASHINGTON
547 U.S. 813 (2006)

SCALIA, J., delivered the opinion of the Court.

These cases require us to determine when statements made to law enforcement personnel during a 911 call or at a crime scene are "testimonial" and thus subject to the requirements of the Sixth Amendment's Confrontation Clause.

I.

A.

The relevant statements in *Davis v. Washington*, No. 05-5224, were made to a 911 emergency operator. . . . When the operator answered the initial call, the connection terminated before anyone spoke. She reversed the call, and Michelle McCottry answered. In the ensuing conversation, the operator ascertained that McCottry was involved in a domestic disturbance with her former boyfriend Adrian Davis, the petitioner in this case:

> "911 Operator: Hello.
>
> "Complainant: Hello.
>
> "911 Operator: What's going on?
>
> "Complainant: He's here jumpin' on me again.
>
> "911 Operator: Okay. Listen to me carefully. Are you in a house or an apartment?
>
> "Complainant: I'm in a house.
>
> "911 Operator: Are there any weapons?
>
> "Complainant: No. He's usin' his fists.
>
> "911 Operator: Okay. Has he been drinking?
>
> "Complainant: No.
>
> "911 Operator: Okay, sweetie. I've got help started. Stay on the line with me, okay?
>
> "Complainant: I'm on the line.
>
> "911 Operator: Listen to me carefully. Do you know his last name?
>
> "Complainant: It's Davis.
>
> "911 Operator: Davis? Okay, what's his first name?
>
> "Complainant: Adrian
>
> "911 Operator: What is it?
>
> "Complainant: Adrian.
>
> "911 Operator: Adrian?
>
> "Complainant: Yeah.
>
> "911 Operator: Okay. What's his middle initial?
>
> "Complainant: Martell. He's runnin' now."

As the conversation continued, the operator learned that Davis had "just r[un] out the door" after hitting McCottry, and that he was leaving in a car with someone else. McCottry started talking, but the operator cut her off, saying, "Stop talking and answer my questions." She then gathered more information about Davis (including his birthday), and learned that Davis had told McCottry that his purpose in coming to the house was "to get his stuff," since McCottry was moving. McCottry described the context of the assault, after which the operator told her that the police were on their way. "They're gonna check the area for him first," the operator said, "and then they're gonna come talk to you."

The police arrived within four minutes of the 911 call and observed McCottry's shaken state, the "fresh injuries on her forearm and her face," and her "frantic efforts to gather her belongings and her children so that they could leave the residence."

The State charged Davis with felony violation of a domestic no contact order. "The State's only witnesses were the two police officers who responded to the 911 call. Both officers testified that McCottry exhibited injuries that appeared to be recent, but neither officer could testify as to the cause of the injuries." McCottry presumably could have testified as to whether Davis was her assailant, but she did not appear. Over Davis's objection, based on the Confrontation Clause of the Sixth Amendment, the trial court admitted the recording of her exchange with the 911 operator, and the jury convicted him. The Washington Court of Appeals affirmed. The Supreme Court of Washington, with one dissenting justice, also affirmed, concluding that the portion of the 911 conversation in which McCottry identified Davis was not testimonial, and that if other portions of the conversation were testimonial, admitting them was harmless beyond a reasonable doubt. We granted certiorari.

B.

In *Hammon v. Indiana*, No. 05-5705, police responded . . . to a "reported domestic disturbance" at the home of Hershel and Amy Hammon. They found Amy alone on the front porch, appearing " 'somewhat frightened,' " but she told them that " 'nothing was the matter.' " She gave them permission to enter the house, where an officer saw "a gas heating unit in the corner of the living room" that had "flames coming out of the . . . partial glass front. There were pieces of glass on the ground in front of it and there was flame emitting from the front of the heating unit."

Hershel, meanwhile, was in the kitchen. He told the police "that he and his wife had 'been in an argument' but 'everything was fine now' and the argument 'never became physical.' " By this point Amy had come back inside. One of the officers remained with Hershel; the other went to the living room to talk with Amy, and "again asked [her] what had occurred." Hershel made several attempts to participate in Amy's conversation with the police, but was rebuffed. The officer later testified that Hershel "became angry when I insisted that [he] stay separated from Mrs. Hammon so that we can investigate what had happened." After hearing Amy's account, the officer "had her fill out and sign a battery affidavit." Amy handwrote the following: "Broke our Furnace & shoved me down on the floor into the broken glass. Hit me in the chest and threw me down. Broke our lamps & phone. Tore up my van where I couldn't leave the house. Attacked my daughter."

The State charged Hershel with domestic battery and with violating his probation. Amy was subpoenaed, but she did not appear at his subsequent bench trial. The State called the officer who had questioned Amy, and asked him to recount what Amy told him and to authenticate the affidavit. Hershel's counsel repeatedly objected to the admission of this evidence. At one point, after hearing the prosecutor defend the affidavit because it was made "under oath," defense counsel said, "That doesn't give us the opportunity to cross examine [the] person who allegedly drafted it. Makes me mad." Nonetheless, the trial court admitted the affidavit as a "present sense impression," and Amy's statements as "excited utterances" that "are expressly permitted in these kinds of cases even if the declarant is not available to testify." The officer thus testified that Amy "informed me that she and Hershel had been in an argument. That he became irrate [sic] over the fact of their daughter going to a boyfriend's house. The argument became . . . physical after being verbal and she informed me that Mr. Hammon, during the verbal part of the argument was breaking things in the living room and I believe she stated he broke the phone, broke the lamp, broke the front of the heater. When it became physical he threw her down into the glass of the heater.

"She informed me Mr. Hammon had pushed her onto the ground, had shoved her head into the broken glass of the heater and that he had punched her in the chest twice I believe."

The trial judge found Hershel guilty on both charges, and the Indiana Court of Appeals affirmed in relevant part. The Indiana Supreme Court also affirmed, concluding that Amy's statement was admissible for state law purposes as an excited utterance; that "a 'testimonial' statement is one given or taken in significant part for purposes of preserving it for potential future use in legal proceedings," where "the motivations of the questioner and declarant are the central concerns;" and that Amy's oral statement was not "testimonial" under these standards. . . . We granted certiorari.

II.

The Confrontation Clause of the Sixth Amendment provides: "In all criminal prosecutions, the accused shall enjoy the right . . . to be confronted with the witnesses against him." In *Crawford v. Washington*, 541 U.S. 36, 53–54 (2004), we held that this provision bars "admission of testimonial statements of a witness who did not appear at trial unless he was unavailable to testify, and the defendant had had a prior opportunity for cross examination." A critical portion of this holding, and the portion central to resolution of the two cases now before us, is the phrase "testimonial statements." Only statements of this sort cause the declarant to be a "witness" within the meaning of the Confrontation Clause. It is the testimonial character of the statement that separates it from other hearsay that, while subject to traditional limitations upon hearsay evidence, is not subject to the Confrontation Clause.

Our opinion in *Crawford* set forth "[v]arious formulations" of the core class of " 'testimonial' " statements, *ibid.*, but found it unnecessary to endorse any of them, because "some statements qualify under any definition," *id.*, at 52. Among those, we said, were "[s]tatements taken by police officers in the course of interrogations." *Id.*, at 53. The questioning that generated the deponent's statement in *Crawford* which was made and recorded while she was in police custody, after having been given *Miranda* warnings as a possible suspect herself "qualifies under any conceivable definition" of an " 'interrogation,' " 541 U.S., at 53, n.4. We therefore did not define that term, except to say that "[w]e use [it] . . . in its colloquial, rather than any technical legal, sense," and that "one can imagine various definitions. . . , and we need not select among them in this case." *Ibid.* The character of the statements in the present cases is not as clear, and these cases require us to determine more precisely which police interrogations produce testimony.

Without attempting to produce an exhaustive classification of all conceivable statements or even all conceivable statements in response to police interrogation as either testimonial or nontestimonial, it suffices to decide the present cases to hold as follows: Statements are nontestimonial when made in the course of police interrogation under circumstances objectively indicating that the primary purpose of the interrogation is to enable police assistance to meet an ongoing emergency. They are testimonial when the circumstances objectively indicate that there is no such ongoing emergency, and that the primary purpose of the interrogation is to establish or prove past events potentially relevant to later criminal prosecution. [footnote omitted].

III.

A.

In *Crawford*, it sufficed for resolution of the case before us to determine that "even if the Sixth Amendment is not solely concerned with testimonial hearsay, that is its primary object, and interrogations by law enforcement officers fall squarely within that class." *Id.*, at 53. Moreover, as we have just described, the facts of that case spared us the need to define what we meant by "interrogations." The *Davis* case today does not permit us this luxury of indecision. The inquiries of a police operator in the course of a 911 call [footnote omitted] are an interrogation in one sense, but not in a sense that "qualifies under any conceivable definition." We must decide, therefore, whether the Confrontation Clause applies only to testimonial hearsay; and, if so, whether the recording of a 911 call qualifies.

The answer to the first question was suggested in *Crawford*, even if not explicitly held:

> "The text of the Confrontation Clause reflects this focus [on testimonial hearsay]. It applies to 'witnesses' against the accused in other words, those who 'bear testimony.' 1 N. Webster, An American Dictionary of the English Language (1828). 'Testimony,' in turn, is typically 'a solemn declaration or affirmation made for the purpose of establishing or proving some fact.' Ibid. An accuser who makes a formal statement to government officers bears testimony in a sense that a person who makes a casual remark to an acquaintance does not." 541 U.S., at 51.

A limitation so clearly reflected in the text of the constitutional provision must fairly be said to mark out not merely its "core," but its perimeter.

*   *   *

The question before us in *Davis*, then, is whether, objectively considered, the interrogation that took place in the course of the 911 call produced testimonial statements. When we said in *Crawford* that "interrogations by law enforcement officers fall squarely within [the] class" of testimonial hearsay, we had immediately in mind (for that was the case before us) interrogations solely directed at establishing the facts of a past crime, in order to identify (or provide evidence to convict) the perpetrator. The product of such interrogation, whether reduced to a writing signed by the declarant or embedded in the memory (and perhaps notes) of the interrogating officer, is testimonial. It is, in the terms of the 1828 American dictionary quoted in *Crawford*, " '[a] solemn declaration or affirmation made for the purpose of establishing or proving some fact.' " 541 U.S., at 51. . . . A 911 call, on the other hand, and at least the initial interrogation conducted in connection with a 911 call, is ordinarily not designed primarily to "establis[h] or prov[e]" some past fact, but to describe current circumstances requiring police assistance.

The difference between the interrogation in *Davis* and the one in *Crawford* is apparent on the face of things. In *Davis*, McCottry was speaking about events as they were actually happening, rather than "describ[ing] past events," *Lilly v. Virginia*, 527 U.S. 116, 137 (1999) (plurality opinion). Sylvia Crawford's interrogation, on the other hand, took place hours after the events she described had occurred. Moreover, any reasonable listener would recognize that McCottry (unlike Sylvia Crawford) was facing an ongoing emergency. Although one might call 911 to provide a narrative report of a crime absent any imminent danger, McCottry's call was plainly a call for help against bona fide physical threat. Third, the nature of what was asked and answered in Davis, again viewed objectively, was such that the elicited statements were necessary to be able to resolve the present emergency, rather than simply to learn (as in *Crawford*) what had happened in the past. That is true even of the operator's effort to establish the identity of the assailant, so that the dispatched officers might know whether they would be encountering a violent felon. And finally, the difference in the level of formality between the two interviews is striking. Crawford was responding calmly, at the station house, to a series of questions, with the officer interrogator taping and making notes of her answers; McCottry's frantic answers were provided over the phone, in an environment that was not tranquil, or even (as far as any reasonable 911 operator could make out) safe.

We conclude from all this that the circumstances of McCottry's interrogation objectively indicate its primary purpose was to enable police assistance to meet an ongoing emergency. She simply was not acting as a witness; she was not testifying. What she said was not "a weaker substitute for live testimony" at trial. . . . No "witness" goes into court to proclaim an emergency and seek help.

*   *   *

This is not to say that a conversation which begins as an interrogation to determine the need for emergency assistance cannot, as the Indiana Supreme Court put it, "evolve into testimonial statements," 829 N.E.2d, at 457, once that purpose has been achieved. In this case, for example, after the operator gained the information needed to address the exigency of the moment, the emergency appears to have ended (when Davis drove away from the premises). The operator then told McCottry to be quiet, and proceeded to pose a battery of questions. It could readily be maintained that from that point on, McCottry's statements were testimonial, not unlike the "structured police questioning" that occurred in *Crawford*. This presents no great problem. Just as, for Fifth Amendment purposes, "police officers can and will distinguish almost instinctively between questions necessary to secure their own safety or the safety of the public and questions designed solely to elicit testimonial evidence from a suspect," *New York v. Quarles*, 467 U.S. 649, 658–659 (1984), trial courts will recognize the point at which, for Sixth Amendment purposes, statements in response to interrogations become testimonial. Through in limine procedure, they should redact or exclude the portions of any statement that have become testimonial, as they do, for example, with unduly prejudicial portions of otherwise admissible evidence. . . .

B.

Determining the testimonial or nontestimonial character of the statements that were the product of the interrogation in *Hammon* is a much easier task, since they were not much different from the statements we found to be testimonial in *Crawford*. It is entirely clear from the circumstances that the interrogation was part of an investigation into possibly criminal past conduct as, indeed, the testifying officer expressly acknowledged. There was no emergency in progress; the interrogating officer testified that he had heard no arguments or crashing and saw no one throw or break anything. When the officers first arrived, Amy told them that things were fine and there was no immediate threat to her person. When the officer questioned Amy for the second time, and elicited the challenged statements, he was not seeking to determine (as in *Davis*) "what is happening," but rather "what happened." Objectively viewed, the primary, if not indeed the sole, purpose of the interrogation was to investigate a possible crime which is, of course, precisely what the officer should have done.

It is true that the *Crawford* interrogation was more formal. It followed a *Miranda* warning, was tape recorded, and took place at the station house. While these features certainly strengthened the statements' testimonial aspect made it more objectively apparent, that is, that the purpose of the exercise was to nail down the truth about past criminal events none was essential to the point. It was formal enough that Amy's interrogation was conducted in a separate room, away from her husband (who tried to intervene), with the officer receiving her replies for use in his "investigat[ion]." What we called the "striking resemblance" of the *Crawford* statement to civil law ex parte examinations, 541 U.S., at 52, is shared by Amy's statement here. Both declarants were actively separated from the defendant officers forcibly prevented Hershel from participating in the interrogation. Both statements deliberately recounted, in response to police questioning, how potentially criminal past events began and progressed. And both took place some time after the events described were over. Such statements under official interrogation are an obvious substitute for live testimony, because they do precisely what a witness does on direct examination; they are inherently testimonial. [footnote omitted].

* * *

Both Indiana and the United States as amicus curiae argue that this case should be resolved much like *Davis.* For the reasons we find the comparison to *Crawford* compelling, we find the comparison to *Davis* unpersuasive. The statements in *Davis* were taken when McCottry was alone, not only unprotected by police (as Amy Hammon was protected), but apparently in immediate danger from Davis. She was seeking aid, not telling a story about the past. McCottry's present tense statements showed immediacy; Amy's narrative of past events was delivered at some remove in time from the danger she described. And after Amy answered the officer's questions, he had her execute an affidavit, in order, he testified, "[t]o establish events that have occurred previously."

* * *

We affirm the judgment of the Supreme Court of Washington in No. 05-5224. We reverse the judgment of the Supreme Court of Indiana in No. 05-5705, and remand the case to that Court for proceedings not inconsistent with this opinion.

JUSTICE THOMAS, concurring in the judgment in part and dissenting in part.

A.

* * *

The Confrontation Clause provides that "[i]n all criminal prosecutions, the accused shall enjoy the right . . . to be confronted with the witnesses against him. . . ." U.S. Const., Amdt. 6. We have recognized that the operative phrase in the Clause, "witnesses against him," could be interpreted narrowly, to reach only those witnesses who actually testify at trial, or more broadly, to reach many or all of those whose out of court statements are offered at trial. Because the narrowest interpretation of the Clause would conflict with both the history giving rise to the adoption of the Clause and this Court's precedent, we have rejected such a reading.

Rejection of the narrowest view of the Clause does not, however, require the broadest application of the Clause to exclude otherwise admissible hearsay evidence. The history surrounding the right to confrontation supports the conclusion that it was developed to target particular practices that occurred under the English bail and committal statutes passed during the reign of Queen Mary, namely, the "civil law mode of criminal procedure, and particularly its use of ex parte examinations as evidence against the accused." *Crawford*, supra, at 43, 50. . . .

In *Crawford*, we recognized that this history could be squared with the language of the Clause, giving rise to a workable, and more accurate, interpretation of the Clause. " '[W]itnesses,' " we said, are those who " 'bear testimony.' " 541 U.S., at 51 (quoting 1 N. Webster, An American Dictionary of the English Language (1828)). And " '[t]esti-mony' " is " '[a] solemn declaration or affirmation made for the purpose of establishing or proving some fact.' " *Ibid.* (quoting Webster, supra). Admittedly, we did not set forth a detailed framework for addressing whether a statement is "testimonial" and thus subject to the Confrontation Clause. But the plain terms of the "testimony" definition we endorsed necessarily require some degree of solemnity before a statement can be deemed "testimonial."

This requirement of solemnity supports my view that the statements regulated by the Confrontation Clause must include "extrajudicial statements . . . contained in formal-ized testimonial materials, such as affidavits, depositions, prior testimony, or confes-sions." *White*, supra, at 365. Affidavits, depositions, and prior testimony are, by their very nature, taken through a formalized process. Likewise, confessions, when extracted by police in a formal manner, carry sufficient indicia of solemnity to constitute formalized statements and, accordingly, bear a "striking resemblance" to the examina-tions of the accused and accusers under the Marian statutes. [footnote omitted].

*   *   *

The Court all but concedes that no case can be cited for its conclusion that the Confrontation Clause also applies to informal police questioning under certain circum-stances. Instead, the sole basis for the Court's conclusion is its apprehension that the Confrontation Clause will "readily be evaded" if it is only applicable to formalized testimonial materials. *Ante*, at 2276. But the Court's proposed solution to the risk of evasion is needlessly overinclusive. Because the Confrontation Clause sought to regulate prosecutorial abuse occurring through use of ex parte statements as evidence against the accused, it also reaches the use of technically informal statements when used to evade the formalized process. That is, even if the interrogation itself is not formal, the production of evidence by the prosecution at trial would resemble the abuses targeted by the Confrontation Clause if the prosecution attempted to use out of court statements as a means of circumventing the literal right of confrontation. In such a case, the Confrontation Clause could fairly be applied to exclude the hearsay statements offered by the prosecution, preventing evasion without simultaneously excluding evidence offered by the prosecution in good faith.

The Court's standard is not only disconnected from history and unnecessary to prevent abuse; it also yields no predictable results to police officers and prosecutors attempting to comply with the law. In many, if not most, cases where police respond to a report of a crime, whether pursuant to a 911 call from the victim or otherwise, the purposes of an interrogation, viewed from the perspective of the police, are both to respond to the emergency situation and to gather evidence. Assigning one of these two "largely unverifiable motives" primacy requires constructing a hierarchy of purpose that will rarely be present and is not reliably discernible. It will inevitably be, quite simply, an exercise in fiction.

*   *   *

B.

Neither the 911 call at issue in *Davis* nor the police questioning at issue in *Hammon* is testimonial under the appropriate framework. Neither the call nor the questioning is itself a formalized dialogue. [footnote omitted]. Nor do any circumstances surrounding the taking of the statements render those statements sufficiently formal to resemble the Marian examinations; the statements were neither Mirandized nor custodial, nor accompanied by any similar indicia of formality. Finally, there is no suggestion that the prosecution attempted to offer the women's hearsay evidence at trial in order to evade confrontation. Accordingly, the statements at issue in both cases are nontestimonial and admissible under the Confrontation Clause.

The Court's determination that the evidence against Hammon must be excluded extends the Confrontation Clause far beyond the abuses it was intended to prevent. When combined with the Court's holding that the evidence against Davis is perfectly admissible, however, the Court's *Hammon* holding also reveals the difficulty of applying the Court's requirement that courts investigate the "primary purpose[s]" of the investigation. The Court draws a line between the two cases based on its explanation that *Hammon* involves "no emergency in progress," but instead, mere questioning as "part of an investigation into possibly criminal past conduct," *ante*, at 2269–2270, and its explanation that *Davis* involves questioning for the "primary purpose" of "enabl[ing] police assistance to meet an ongoing emergency," *ante*, at 2277. But the fact that the officer in *Hammon* was investigating Mr. Hammon's past conduct does not foreclose the possibility that the primary purpose of his inquiry was to assess whether Mr. Hammon constituted a continuing danger to his wife, requiring further police presence or action. It is hardly remarkable that Hammon did not act abusively towards his wife in the presence of the officers, and his good judgment to refrain from criminal behavior in the presence of police sheds little, if any, light on whether his violence would have resumed had the police left without further questioning, transforming what the Court dismisses as "past conduct" back into an "ongoing emergency." [footnote omitted]. Nor does the mere fact that McCottry needed emergency aid shed light on whether the "primary purpose" of gathering, for example, the name of her assailant was to protect the police, to protect the victim, or to gather information for prosecution. In both of the cases before the Court, like many similar cases, pronouncement of the "primary" motive behind the interrogation calls for nothing more than a guess by courts.

II.

Because the standard adopted by the Court today is neither workable nor a targeted attempt to reach the abuses forbidden by the Clause, I concur only in the judgment in *Davis v. Washington*, and respectfully dissent from the Court's resolution of *Hammon v. Indiana.*

NOTES AND QUESTIONS

1. *Davis* appears to have narrowed the ruling in *Crawford* in two important respects. First, in *Crawford v. Washington*, the majority stated that at a minimum the definition of "testimonial" includes statements made during "police interrogations." *Crawford*, 541 U.S. at 68. After *Davis*, "[s]tatements are nontestimonial when made in the course of police interrogation under circumstances objectively indicating that the primary purpose of the interrogation is to enable police assistance to meet an ongoing emergency." *Davis*, 547 U.S. at 822. Second, in *Crawford*, the Supreme Court stated that one possible definition of "testimonial" includes whether statements made by the nontestifying out-of-court declarant were statements "that declarants would reasonably expect to be used prosecutorily," or "were made under circumstances which would lead an objective witness reasonably to believe that the statements would be available for use at a later trial." *Crawford*, 541 U.S. at 51–52. In *Davis*, were McCottry's 911 statements that Davis was beating on her and her later statement that Davis had just run out the door after hitting her, statements an objective witness would reasonably expect or believe would be used against the defendant at a later trial? *See* Michael H. Graham, *Crawford/Davis "Testimonial" Interpreted, Removing the Clutter, Application Summary*, 62 U. Miami L. Rev. 811, 817 (2007–2008) ("If a statement to law enforcement reporting a current crime and a subsequent statement reporting a past crime do not meet the . . . concept of 'reasonable expect or belief,' it is hard to imagine a statement that would."). After *Davis*, is the declarant's reasonable belief or expectation that the hearsay statements could be used against the defendant at trial no longer a relevant consideration for determining whether the statement is testimonial? Has the focus shifted away from the declarant's reasonable expectation or belief to the law enforcement officer's primary purpose for eliciting the statement or primary purpose on receipt?

2. *Primary purpose test*. In *Davis v. Washington*, the U.S. Supreme Court held that "[s]tatements are not testimonial when made in the course of police interrogation under circumstances objectively indicating that the primary purpose of the interrogation is to enable police assistance to meet an ongoing emergency." *Id*. at 822. In *Davis*, the "emergency" involved the curtailment of an ongoing crime involving domestic violence. However, the Court did not define what it meant by "emergency." What other types of emergencies might be implicated by the *Davis* Court's primary purpose test? Are statements made by a child victim to a nurse conducting a forensic examination to determine whether the child was sexually abused for the purpose of meeting an ongoing emergency? *See State v. Kransky*, 736 N.W.2d 636 (Minn. 2007) (holding that the primary purpose of the child victim's statements to a nurse was to assess and protect the child's health and welfare, and thus the statements were not testimonial). Are statements made to the police *after* the emergency has ceased "testimonial"? What factors are relevant in determining whether the emergency has subsided?

3. What is the scope of the holding in *Davis*? Is *Davis* limited to statements obtained pursuant to police questioning, e.g., statements made to a police officer during a 911 call, or elicited at a crime scene? Does *Davis* stand for the proposition that statements obtained pursuant to police questioning in response to an emergency are always nontestimonial, while statements made to a police officer in the absence of such an emergency are always testimonial? Stated another way, are statements obtained pursuant to police questioning, but not in response to an emergency, always testimonial?

One commentator maintains that "while *Davis* expressly states that it is not presenting a comprehensive definition of 'testimonial,' *Davis* may nevertheless . . . have done so, or come very close to having done so, and thus be the 'another day' referred to in *Crawford*." Michael H. Graham, *Crawford/Davis "Testimonial" Interpreted, Removing the Clutter; Application Summary*, 62 U. MIAMI L. REV. 811, 817 (2007–2008). "[U]nder *Crawford* and *Davis* a hearsay statement is 'testimonial' when, and only when, the statement of a nongovernmental official (1) was made to or elicited by a police officer, other law enforcement personnel, or a judicial officer ('government official'), and (2) was made to or elicited by a government official under circumstances objectively indicating at the time that the primary purpose to which the statement will be used by the government is to establish or prove past events potentially relevant to later criminal prosecution." *Id.* at 819–20. Conversely, a hearsay statement is "nontestimonial" if the primary purpose for making or eliciting the statement was for some other purpose. *Id.* at 820. Do you agree with the commentator's interpretation of *Davis*? Did *Davis* articulate a comprehensive test for determining whether hearsay statements are testimonial, despite the Court's declaration to the contrary?

4. *Child victim's statements.* In *State v. Buda*, 949 A.2d 761 (N.J. 2008), the New Jersey Supreme Court held that a child's statements to a member of the Division of Youth and Family Services' (DYFS) Office of Child Abuse Control at a hospital, where the child was taken with severe injuries were not testimonial. The court posited that the DYFS worker "was responding to a life-threatening emergency no different in kind than the function being performed by the 911 operator in *Davis*; she was seeking information from a victim to determine how best to remove the very real threat of continued bodily harm and even death from this three-year-old child." *Id.* at 778. The court further reasoned that the primary obligation of a DYFS worker is not to collect evidence of past events for purposes of future prosecution, but to protect the child. *Id.* at 779. The DYFS worker had not become an extension of law enforcement, the court explained. Do you agree? Are the statements of the child victim to a social worker the functional equivalent of the 911 statements in *Davis*?

5. Justice Thomas, concurring in *Davis* and dissenting in *Hammon*, maintains that the statements in both cases are nontestimonial. Why does he disagree with the majority's interpretation of what constitutes a "testimonial" statement? Under Justice Thomas' definition, what kinds of statements would be deemed "testimonial?" How narrowly would he define the term "testimonial" for purposes of the Confrontation Clause? Should the Sixth Amendment Confrontation Clause be construed to cover only statements obtained during a formal custodial interrogation after warnings given pursuant to *Miranda v. Arizona*, 384 U.S. 436 (1966)?

6. Justice Thomas is critical of the majority's standard stating that it "yields no predictable results to police officers and prosecutors attempting to comply with the law." *Davis*, 547 U.S. at 838. Justice Thomas further posits that "[i]n many, if not most, cases where police respond to a report of a crime, whether pursuant to a 911 call from the victim or otherwise, the purposes of an interrogation, viewed from the perspective of the police, are *both* to respond to the emergency situation *and* to gather evidence." *Id.* at 839 (emphasis in original). Do you agree with Justice Thomas that determining the "primary" motive behind the police interrogation is nothing more than guess work by the courts? *Id.* at 841–42 (Thomas, J., concurring in part and dissenting in part). If so, do you agree with Justice Thomas' assessment that the majority's "primary purpose" test is unpredictable and unworkable?

7. Hearsay statements may begin as an interrogation by police to determine the need for emergency assistance (nontestimonial) and evolve into questioning intended to prove past events (testimonial). The Court in *Davis* stated that through *in limine* procedures, trial courts should redact or exclude the portions of any statement that have become testimonial. *Davis*, 547 U.S. at 828–29. How difficult will it be to parse out statements obtained in response to an emergency and statements that merely implicate the defendant in criminal activity?

8. *Forfeiture by Wrongdoing.* In *Davis*, the Court recognized the doctrine of forfeiture by wrongdoing, stating that "one who obtains the absence of a witness by wrongdoing forfeits the constitutional right to confrontation." *Davis*, 547 U.S., at 833. *See also Crawford v. Washington*, 541 U.S. 36, 62 (2004) ("the rule of forfeiture by wrongdoing (which we accept) extinguishes confrontation claims on essentially equitable grounds"); Fed. R. Evid. 804(f)(6). If a defendant engages in wrongful conduct that prevents the witness from testifying at trial, does she forfeit her Sixth Amendment right to object to the witness's testimony on confrontation grounds? If so, does forfeiture by wrongdoing constitute an exception to the Sixth Amendment prohibition on the admissibility of testimonial statements? In *Giles v. California*, 128 S. Ct. 2678 (2008), the Supreme Court narrowly construed forfeiture by wrongdoing to require proof that the defendant intended to prevent the witness from testifying. *See* discussion *infra*, at Chapter 9.

C. EXCITED UTTERANCE

Rule 803(2) of the Federal Rules of Evidence provides an exception to the hearsay rule for any "statement relating to a startling event or condition made while the declarant was under the stress of the excitement caused by the event or condition." The rationale for the excited utterance exception is that "such statements are given under circumstances that eliminate the possibility of fabrication, coaching, or confabulation. . . ."[3] Statements made under the influence of a startling event are considered trustworthy for two reasons:

> The stimulus leaves the speaker momentarily incapable of fabrication, and his memory is fresh because the impression has not yet passed from his mind. In short, risks of insincerity and memory lapse are removed.[4]

For a hearsay statement to be admitted under this exception, three conditions must be met: "(1) a startling event must have occurred; (2) the declarant must have made the statement while under the stress or excitement caused by the event; and (3) the statement must relate to the startling event."[5]

In the criminal law context, the exciting event often involves a declarant who is a percipient witness to or victim of a crime. The exception imposes a subjective standard. What is important is that the declarant was actually excited, and the fact that another

---

[3] *Idaho v. Wright*, 497 U.S. 805, 820 (1990); *see also Dutton v. Evans*, 400 U.S. 74, 89, 91 (1970) (declarant did not misrepresent defendant's involvement in the crime, since the statement was spontaneous); *United States v. Sowa*, 34 F.3d 447, 453 (7th Cir. 1994) (the relevant inquiry is whether the statements " 'were made under such circumstances and so recently after the occurrence of the transaction as to preclude the idea of reflection or deliberation' ") (citations omitted).

[4] MUELLER & KIRKPATRICK, EVIDENCE § 8.35, at 916–17 (1995).

[5] *United States v. Sowa*, 34 F.3d 447, 453 (7th Cir. 1994); *see also Territory of Guam v. Cepeda*, 69 F.3d 369, 372 (9th Cir. 1995).

person might not have been does not matter. There are several factors probative on the ultimate question of whether the statement was the product of stress and excitement or reflective thought: the nature of the event,[6] the age of the declarant,[7] the appearance, behavior or condition of the speaker,[8] and timing.[9] No one factor is dispositive. At the same time, the exception only exempts hearsay statements "relating" to the exciting event or condition. While the subject matter of an excited utterance usually involves a description of the startling event, the statement need only "relate" to the startling event.[10] In this respect, Rule 803(2) is broader in application than Rule 803(1), the present sense impression exception, which permits hearsay statements "describ[ing] or explain[ing] an event or condition made while the declarant was perceiving the event or condition, or immediately after."

[1]   The Confrontation Clause — The Requirement of Unavailability

UNITED STATES v. ARNOLD
486 F.3d 177 (6th Cir. 2007) (en banc)

Joseph Arnold challenges his felon in possession of a firearm conviction, contending that the evidence does not support the verdict, that the district court violated his Confrontation Clause rights by admitting testimonial hearsay and that the district court made several erroneous evidentiary rulings during the course of the trial. We affirm.

I.

At 7:43 a.m. on September 19, 2002, Tamica Gordon called 911 and told the emergency operator: "I need police. . . . Me and my mama's boyfriend got into it, he went in the house and got a pistol, and pulled it out on me. I guess he's fixing to shoot me, so I got in my car and [inaudible] left. I'm right around the corner from the house." Gordon identified her mother's boyfriend as Joseph Arnold, a convicted murderer whom the State had recently released from prison.

About five minutes after the dispatcher told three police officers about Gordon's call, the officers arrived at 1012 Oak View, the residential address that Gordon had provided to the 911 operator. Gordon exited her car and approached the officers, "crying," "hysterical," "visibly shaken and upset," and exclaimed that Arnold had pulled a gun on her and was trying to kill her. JA 112 14. She described the gun as a "black handgun." JA 127.

Soon after the officers arrived, Arnold returned to the scene in a car driven and owned by Gordon's mother. Gordon became visibly anxious again, exclaiming, "that's him, that's the guy that pulled the gun on me, Joseph Arnold, that's him." JA 115. She

---

[6] *See Territory of Guam v. Cepeda*, 69 F.3d 369, 372 (9th Cir. 1995).

[7] *Id.*

[8] *Id.* at 372 (robbery victims appeared "quite panic[ked]" when making statements); *United States v. Rivera*, 43 F.3d 1291, 1296 (9th Cir. 1995) (fifteen-year-old rape victim was crying and in a semi-hysterical state at the time she made statements); *Morgan v. Foretich*, 846 F.2d 941, 946 (4th Cir. 1988) (child nearly hysterical).

[9] *Id.* at 372; *United States v. Sowa*, 34 F.3d 447, 453 (7th Cir. 1994).

[10] *See Bemis v. Edwards*, 45 F.3d 1369, 1372 n.1 (9th Cir. 1995).

also told the officers that "he's got a gun on him." JA 116. Arnold exited the car, and the police patted him down to determine if he was carrying a weapon. When the pat down did not produce a weapon, the officers asked Gordon's mother for permission to search the car. She consented, and the officers found a black handgun inside a clear, plastic bag directly under the passenger seat where Arnold had been sitting.

A grand jury charged Arnold with being a felon in possession of a firearm. *See* 18 U.S.C. § 922(g)(1). When Gordon did not appear to testify at Arnold's trial in response to a government subpoena, the district court ruled (1) that the government could admit a redacted recording of the 911 call (without the reference to Arnold as a convicted murderer) and Gordon's two statements at the scene under the "excited utterance" exception to the hearsay rule and (2) that the applicability of this well established hearsay exception authorized the introduction of this evidence under the Confrontation Clause. . . . The jury found Arnold guilty of the single charge.

III.

Arnold . . . challenges the admissibility of three out of court statements the 911 call, Gordon's initial statements to police officers upon their arrival at the crime scene and Gordon's statement to officers upon Arnold's return to the scene under the excited utterance exception to the hearsay rule. Under Rule 803(2) of the Federal Rules of Evidence, a court may admit out of court statements for the truth of the matter asserted when they "relat[e] to a startling event or condition made while the declarant was under the stress of excitement caused by the event or condition." To satisfy the exception, a party must show three things. "First, there must be an event startling enough to cause nervous excitement. Second, the statement must be made before there is time to contrive or misrepresent. And, third, the statement must be made while the person is under the stress of the excitement caused by the event." *Haggins v. Warden, Fort Pillow State Farm*, 715 F.2d 1050, 1057 (6th Cir.1983). All three inquiries bear on "the ultimate question": "[W]hether the statement was the result of reflective thought or whether it was a spontaneous reaction to the exciting event." *Id.* at 1058 (internal quotation marks omitted). We apply abuse of discretion review to a district court's application of the rule. *See United States v. Beverly*, 369 F.3d 516, 540 (6th Cir.2004).

The 911 Call. Gordon's statements to the 911 operator readily satisfy the first and third prongs of the test. As to the first requirement, being threatened by a convicted murderer wielding a semi automatic handgun amounts to a startling event that would prompt at least nervous excitement in the average individual, if not outright trauma. As to the third requirement, Gordon plainly remained in this state of anxiety during the 911 call. Throughout the call, the operator had to tell her to "calm down" and "quit yelling" and often had difficulty understanding her frantic pleas for help.

The record also supports the district court's finding that the call took place soon after Arnold threatened Gordon "slightly more than immediately" after the threat, in the district court's words which satisfies the second factor. The district court listened to the tape of the 911 call five times, noted that Gordon said "*he's* fixing to shoot me," not that he "*was* fixing to shoot me," JA 52 (emphasis added), and ultimately concluded that there was an immediacy to her statements. Arnold does not challenge the district court's factual conclusions regarding the meaning of the tape.

Case law supports the view that Gordon made the statement "before there [was] time to contrive or misrepresent." *Haggins*, 715 F.2d at 1057. *Haggins*, for example, upheld the admission of statements by a four year old child made more than an hour after the incident but while the child was still suffering the trauma from it. Other cases have upheld the admission of statements that also were made after the startling event but well within the traumatic range of it. *See, e.g., United States v. Baggett*, 251 F.3d 1087, 1090 & n.1 (6th Cir. 2001) (applying the excited utterance exception to statements made several hours after the last of several spousal beatings over a three day period); *see also United States v. McCullough*, 150 Fed.Appx. 507, 510 (6th Cir.2005) (applying exception to statements made "not . . . longer than two and a half hours" after witnessing companion's arrest); *United States v. Green*, 125 Fed.Appx. 659, 662 (6th Cir.2005) (applying exception to statements made three hours after the startling event); *see also United States v. Alexander*, 331 F.3d 116, 123 (D.C.Cir.2003) (applying exception to statements made 15 to 20 minutes after the startling event); *United States v. Cruz*, 156 F.3d 22, 30 (1st Cir.1998) (applying exception to statements made four hours after the startling event); *United States v. Tocco*, 135 F.3d 116, 128 (2d Cir.1998) (applying exception to statements made within three hours of the startling event).

Contrary to Arnold's suggestion, our cases do not demand a precise showing of the lapse of time between the startling event and the out of court statement. The exception may be based solely on "[t]estimony that the declarant still appeared nervous or distraught and that there was a reasonable basis for continuing [to be] emotional[ly] upset," *Haggins*, 715 F.2d at 1058 (internal quotation marks omitted); a conclusion that eliminates an unyielding requirement of a time line showing precisely when the threatening event occurred or precisely how much time there was for contrivance. The district court made this exact finding, a finding supported by evidence that, in the words of *Haggins*, "will often suffice." 715 F.2d at 1058 (internal quotation marks omitted). . . .

Gordon's statement to officers upon their arrival at the scene. When the officers arrived at the scene soon after learning of the 911 call, Gordon exited her car and approached the officers, "crying," "hysterical," "visibly shaken and upset," and exclaimed that Arnold had threatened her with a gun. JA 112 14. For many of the same reasons the district court had authority to admit the 911 call, it had authority to admit this statement. It remained the case that a startling event had occurred. The time that had passed between the end of the 911 call and the officers' arrival on the scene 5 to 21 minutes, based on the officers' testimony that the dispatch contacted them "about 8:00" or "a little bit before 8:00," JA 71, 112, 139, (meaning the dispatch could have occurred any time between the end of the 911 call at 7:45 and 8:00) and that they arrived five to six minutes later did not give Gordon sufficient time to misrepresent what had happened. . . . And as shown by Gordon's frantic statements to the officers upon their arrival, she remained visibly agitated by Arnold's threat. The court did not abuse its discretion in admitting the statement.

Gordon's statement to officers when Arnold pulled up next to the police car. Soon after the officers' arrival, which is to say from 30 seconds to 5 minutes after they reached the scene, a car with Arnold in it pulled up next to the police car, at which point Gordon made the last of her statements admitted as an excited utterance. "[T]hat's him," she said, "that's the guy who pulled a gun on me, Joseph Arnold, that's him." JA 115. The district court permissibly admitted this statement as part of the same emotional trauma that captured Gordon's earlier statement to the officers. On top of that, the unexpected appearance of the victim's assailant independently suffices to establish a startling event followed by an understandably excited verbal response. [citations omitted]. The district court did not abuse its discretion in admitting the statement.

*   *   *

IV.

A.

At trial, Arnold also challenged the admissibility of these three statements under the Confrontation Clause of the Sixth Amendment. . . . Under *Crawford v. Washington*, 541 U.S. 36 (2004), when the prosecution seeks to introduce "testimonial" statements against a criminal defendant, when in the words of the Sixth Amendment the "accused" is being subjected to "witnesses against him," U.S. Const. amend. VI, the defendant generally has a right to confront those witnesses without regard to what the modern day Federal (or State) Rules of Evidence have to say about the matter. The Confrontation Clause, *Crawford* thus establishes, bars the "admission of *testimonial statements* of a witness who did not appear at trial unless he was unavailable to testify, and the defendant had had a prior opportunity for cross examination." 541 U.S. at 53–54 (emphasis added).

In announcing this rule, *Crawford* chose not to provide a "comprehensive" definition of "testimonial" hearsay, *id.* at 68, but it did offer initial guidance on the meaning of the term. The Court explained that "testimony" involves " '[a] solemn declaration or affirmation made for the purpose of establishing or proving some fact.' " *Id.* at 51, (quoting 2 N. Webster, *An American Dictionary of the English Language* (1828)). And it explained that testimonial hearsay at a minimum includes "a formal statement to government officers" by "[a]n accuser" in the form of an affidavit, a deposition, prior testimony or the like. *Id.* at 51– 52. While these initial explanations sufficed to resolve *Crawford*, which involved statements made during a station house interrogation, the Court reviewed two consolidated cases last Term that required it to give further definition to the line between testimonial and nontestimonial hearsay. *See Davis v. Washington*, 126 S.Ct. 2266 (2006).

"Statements are nontestimonial," *Davis* explained, "when made in the course of police interrogation under circumstances objectively indicating that the primary purpose of the interrogation is to enable police assistance to meet an ongoing emergency. They are testimonial when the circumstances objectively indicate that there is no such ongoing emergency, and that the primary purpose of the interrogation is to establish or prove past events potentially relevant to later criminal prosecution." *Id.* at 2273–74. *Davis* applied this definition to two recurring types of witness statements: statements to 911 operators and statements to the police at the scene of the crime.

"A 911 call . . . and at least the initial interrogation conducted in connection with a 911 call," the Court held, "is ordinarily not designed primarily to 'establis[h] or prov[e]' some past fact, but to describe current circumstances requiring police assistance." *Id.* at 2276. In reaching this conclusion, the Court noted four distinctions between the 911 call before it and the interrogation at issue in *Crawford*. The accuser, Michelle McCottry, "was speaking about events *as they were actually happening*," not describing events "hours" after they occurred. *Id.* "[A]ny reasonable listener would recognize that McCottry (unlike Sylvia Crawford) was facing an ongoing emergency," prompting her to make "a call for help against bona fide physical threat." *Id.* "[T]he nature of what was asked and answered in *Davis*" demonstrated that "the elicited statements were necessary to be able to *resolve* the present emergency, rather than simply to learn (as in *Crawford*) what had happened in the past." *Id.* And there was a "striking" "difference in the level of formality" of the two statements, with Crawford "responding calmly" at the police station to the officer's questions and the officer taking notes about the answers while "McCottry's frantic answers were provided over the phone, in an environment that was not tranquil, or even . . . safe." *Id.* at 2276–77.

"[T]he circumstances of McCottry's interrogation," the Court concluded, "objectively indicate its primary purpose was to enable police assistance to meet an ongoing emergency." *Id.* at 2277. She thus "was not acting as a *witness;* she was not *testifying."* *Id.* The Court acknowledged that an interrogation that begins as a plea for help may turn into testimony once the emergency purposes of the 911 call have been satisfied.

The Court reached a different conclusion in the second case, which also stemmed from a domestic dispute and which concerned Amy Hammon's statements to investigating police officers at her home after the police responded to a "reported domestic disturbance." *Id.* at 2272 (internal quotation marks omitted). The characterization of these statements was "much easier" to resolve, the Court held, because they "were not much different" from the statements in *Crawford. Id.* at 2278. The interrogation arose from "an investigation into possibly criminal past conduct"; "[t]here was no emergency in progress"; Hammon told the officers when they arrived that "things were fine"; when an officer eventually questioned Hammon a second time and elicited the challenged statements, "he was not seeking to determine . . .'what is happening,' but rather 'what happened' "; the police separated Hammon from her husband during the interview and prohibited him from intervening; and the interview "took place some time after the events described were over." *Id.* Under these circumstances, the Court held, Hammon's answers to the officers' questions amounted to testimonial statements.

In reaching this conclusion, the Court rejected the theory "that virtually any 'initial inquiries' at the crime scene" will be nontestimonial. *Id.* at 2279. At the same time, it cautioned, it was not "hold[ing] the opposite that *no* questions at the scene will yield nontestimonial answers. We have already observed of domestic disputes that officers called to investigate . . . need to know whom they are dealing with in order to assess the situation, the threat to their own safety, and possible danger to the potential victim." *Id.* "Such exigencies," the Court added, "may *often* mean that 'initial inquiries' produce nontestimonial statements. But in cases like this one, where [Hammon's] statements were neither a cry for help nor the provision of information enabling officers immediately to end a threatening situation, the fact that they were given at an alleged crime scene and were 'initial inquiries' is immaterial." *Id.*

As *Davis's* assessment of the 911 call and the on the scene statements indicates, the line between testimonial and nontestimonial statements will not always be clear. Even if bona fide 911 calls frequently will contain at least some nontestimonial statements (assuming the emergency is real and the threat ongoing) and even if a victim's statements to police at the scene of the crime frequently will contain testimonial statements (assuming the emergency has dissipated), that will not always be the case, and difficult boundary disputes will continue to emerge. Each victim statement thus must be assessed on its own terms and in its own context to determine on which side of the line it falls.

1. The 911 Call

Gordon's statements to the 911 emergency operator offer a close analogy to McCottry's statements in *Davis.* As in *Davis,* we assume for the sake of argument that the inquiries of the 911 operator amount to "acts of the police." 126 S.Ct. at 2274 n.2. And as in *Davis*, we do not doubt that Gordon sought protection from an ongoing emergency. When Gordon fled from her gun wielding assailant, the defendant remained at large and remained (in the present tense) "fixing to shoot" her. *See id.* at 2276 ("McCottry was speaking about events *as they were actually happening*, rather than describing past events."). The tape of the 911 call itself makes clear that Gordon had made "a call for help against [a] bona fide physical threat." *Id.* The 911 operator's handling of the call shows that she was trying to "elicit[ ] statements . . . necessary to be able to resolve the present emergency," *id.* (emphasis omitted), by attempting to compose Gordon and by seeking to understand the gravity of the peril she faced. Gordon's frantic responses "were provided over the phone, in an environment that was not tranquil, or even . . . safe" because she had just left the house and had no reason to know whether Arnold was following her or not. *Id.* at 2277. The fear that the district court noted in Gordon's voice communicated that she was scarcely concerned with testifying to anything but simply was seeking protection from a man with a gun who had killed before and who had threatened to kill again. The primary purpose and effect of the 911 operator's questioning was to resolve the crisis, with the questions and answers coming in spite of, not because of, the possibility of a later criminal trial.

Nor had the "exigency of the moment . . . ended," *id.* at 2277, before Gordon made the 911 call. While Gordon left the house and entered her car around the corner before making the 911 call rather than trying to make the call in Arnold's presence, that did not make the emergency less real or less pressing. It is one thing for the *assailant* to start "runnin[g]" after his victim calls 911, to leave in a car and to give the victim an opportunity to lock the door, all of which happened in *Davis* and all of which suggested that the responses to the 911 operator may have evolved into testimonial hearsay. *Id.* at 2271, 2277. It is another thing for the *victim* to flee the house and for the assailant still to be "fixing to shoot" her. In *Davis*, the assailant left the scene in a car because he knew the police were on their way, and there thus was no reason to think that he would be back factors that markedly diminished the peril the victim faced. Gordon by contrast left the residence, went around the corner and called the police. At the time she made the call, she had no reason to know whether Arnold had stayed in the residence or was following her. What she did know is that he had a gun; he had just threatened her; he was still in the vicinity; there was still "somebody runnin' around with a gun" nearby, *United States v. Thomas*, 453 F.3d 838, 844 (7th Cir.2006); there was in short an "emergency in progress," *Davis*, 126 S.Ct. at 2278. . . .

2. Gordon's statement to officers upon their arrival at the crime scene

While it may often be the case that on the scene statements in response to officers' questions will be testimonial because the presence of the officers will alleviate the emergency, this is not one of those cases. Neither the brief interval of time after the 911 call nor the arrival of the officers ended the emergency. Arnold remained at large; he did not know that Gordon had called 911; and for all Gordon (or the officers) knew Arnold remained armed and in the residence immediately in front of them or at least in the nearby vicinity.

The exchange between Gordon and the officers also suggests that the officers primarily were focused on meeting the emergency at hand, not on preparing a case for trial. As soon as the police arrived and before they had a chance to ask her a question, Gordon exited her car, "walked towards [them], . . . crying and . . . screaming, [and] said Joseph Arnold pulled a gun on her, [and] said he was going to kill her." JA 114. The officers tried to "tell [] her to gather herself and [to] slow down." JA 115.

While the fact that Gordon's initial statement was unprompted and thus not in response to police interrogation does not by itself answer the inquiry, *Davis*, 126 S.Ct. at 2274 n.1, this reality at least suggests that the statement was nontestimonial. So, too, does the distress that the officers described in her voice, the present tense of the emergency, the officers' efforts to calm her and the targeted questioning of the officers as to the nature of the threat, all of which suggested that the engagement had not reached the stage of a retrospective inquiry into an emergency gone by. No reasonable officer could arrive at a scene while the victim was still "screaming" and "crying" about a recent threat to her life by an individual who had a gun and who was likely still in the vicinity without perceiving that an emergency still existed. . . .

During the few moments the officers spoke to Gordon, moreover, the primary purpose, measured objectively, of the question they asked her for "a description of the gun," JA 133 was to avert the crisis at hand, not to develop a backward looking record of the crime. Contrary to the contention of the partial dissent, this question did not transform the encounter into a testimonial interrogation. Asking the victim to describe the gun represented one way of exploring the authenticity of her claim, one way in other words of determining whether the emergency was real. And having learned who the suspect was and having learned that he was armed, they surely were permitted to determine what kind of weapon he was carrying and whether it was loaded information that has more to do with preempting the commission of future crimes than with worrying about the prosecution of completed ones. What officers would not want this information either to measure the threat to the public or to measure the threat to themselves? *Cf. Davis*, 126 S.Ct. at 2276 (911 operator's questions regarding assailant's identity objectively aimed at addressing emergency because "the dispatched officers might" then "know whether they would be encountering a violent felon"). And what officer under these circumstances would have yielded to the prosecutor's concern of building a case for trial rather than to law enforcement's first and most pressing impulse of protecting the individual from danger?

Nor does the fact that Gordon made her statement to investigating police officers on the scene by itself establish that it was testimonial. *Davis* disclaimed creating any such rule. 126 S.Ct. at 2279. Officers investigating domestic disputes, it observed, "need to know whom they are dealing with in order to assess the situation, the threat to their own safety, and possible danger to the potential victim. . . . Such exigencies may often mean that initial inquiries produce nontestimonial statements." *Id.* Gordon's statements also stand in marked contrast to Amy Hammon's on the spot testimonial statements in *Davis*. Here, by all accounts, the officers sought only to bring initial calm to the situation (by reassuring the victim) and to understand the threat to the public and their own safety (by learning that Arnold had a loaded semiautomatic handgun). To the extent they made inquiries at all, they never strayed from asking questions clarifying the extent of the emergency and obtaining information necessary to resolve it. Hammon in comparison told the arriving officers that "things were fine . . . and there was no immediate threat to her person"; she spoke with officers while "actively separated from the defendant" who had been detained and was with other officers in a different room; she "deliberately recounted, in response to police questioning, how potentially criminal past events began and progressed"; and then she summarized all of this in an affidavit for the officers. *Id.* at 2278. The ongoing emergency questioning in the former offers a poor analogy to the structured, distress free questioning in the latter.

3. Gordon's statement to officers when Arnold suddenly returned to the scene

Gordon's statement to the officers when Arnold returned to the scene bears even less resemblance to testimony than her initial statement to the officers. Her exclamation "that's him, that's the guy that pulled the gun on me" was prompted not by *ex parte* questioning by the officers but by Arnold's sudden reappearance. When she not only described Arnold as her assailant but also added that "he's got a gun on him," JA 116, no one can doubt that Gordon *and* the officers faced a risky situation or that Gordon sought to obtain their protection. This was not a statement prepared for court. "No 'witness,' " after all, "goes into court to proclaim an emergency and seek help." *Davis*, 126 S.Ct. at 2277. The statement thus "was not 'a weaker substitute for live testimony' at trial," *id.* (quoting *United States v. Inadi*, 475 U.S. 387, 394 (1986)), but had independent evidentiary value separate and apart from any "courtroom analogue[ ]," *id.* It was nontestimonial. . . .

Noting that Gordon used "past tense" verbs at several points during the 911 call, the dissent contends that there was no longer an ongoing emergency when Gordon made the 911 call and when the officers arrived on the scene. But the entire 911 conversation begins with, and takes place in the context of, a present tense plea for help: "I need police." Gordon's "past tense" statements described discrete facts contributing to what, from an objective perspective, constituted an ongoing emergency requiring police protection. . . .

Nor, once the officers arrived, is it the case that Gordon did nothing "consistent with an ongoing emergency." Dissent at 215. That she rushed up to the officers and was so upset that she initially "couldn't speak," JA 73, surely bespeaks the conduct of one who feels threatened and who could blame her under the circumstances? And by remaining near the house, she hardly showed otherwise. She called 911 after she got out of the house, and the 911 operator told her that the officers "would be over there as soon as they can" and to "be watching for them." Staying near the house thus offered the quickest route to making contact with the officers. And staying near her car at the same time gave her an immediate departure option if Arnold found her before the officers did. . . . For these reasons, we affirm.

NOTES AND QUESTIONS

1. *Multi-Part Test.* What are the requirements for the admission of out-of-court statements under the excited-utterance exception to the hearsay rule? In *Arnold*, were those requirements satisfied for the three statements admitted into evidence under the hearsay exception? The 911 call? Gordon's statements to police officers upon their arrival to the scene? Gordon's statement to officers when Arnold pulled up next to the police car?

2. *Lack of Time to Contrive.* The lapse of time between the startling event and the out-of-court statement is highly relevant in determining spontaneity and therefore admissibility. The majority concluded that Gordon lacked the time, between Arnold threatening her with a gun and her 911 call, to contrive or fabricate her statements. Did the time that elapsed between the end of the 911 call and the officers' arrival at the scene give Gordon sufficient time to misrepresent what had happened? In dissent, Judge Moore argued that the government failed to satisfy its burden that Gordon's statements were made before she had time to contrive or misrepresent. *See Arnold.* 486 F.3d at 211 (Moore, J., dissenting). As a general matter, what lapse of time between the startling event and making the statements is acceptable? *See Arnold*, 486 F.3d at 185

(citing cases where the statements were made three to four hours after the startling event).

3. *Independent Corroboration.* In her dissent, Judge Moore maintains that the government failed to introduce any evidence of the alleged "startling event" outside of the hearsay statements themselves. *See Arnold*, 486 F.3d at 207 (Moore, J., dissenting). In her view, a hearsay statement cannot serve as the sole evidence of the alleged startling event that spurred the statement. *Id.* Judge Moore reasons that "excited utterances are admissible because the startling event and corresponding state of alarms renders it 'unlikely that the statement is contrived or the product of reflection.' " *Id.* at 208 (internal citations omitted). Moreover, "without some corroborating evidence of such an exciting event, the district court lacks the capacity to make such a determination, or to determine even that there was such an event" according to Judge Moore. *Id.* The majority, on the other hand, maintains that there was considerable non-hearsay evidence to corroborate the startling event, detailing the following evidence:

> (1) Gordon's act of calling 911; (2) the fear and excitement exhibited by the tenor and tone of Gordon's voice during the 911 call; (3) Gordon's distraught demeanor personally observed by Officers Brandon and Newberry upon their arrival at the scene; (4) Gordon's renewed excitement upon seeing Arnold return; and (5) the gun matching Gordon's description found underneath the passenger seat in which Arnold was sitting.

Arnold, 486 F.3d at 185. Do you agree with Judge Moore or the majority?

4. *Application of the Primary Purpose Test.* In *Arnold*, the majority held that Gordon's hearsay statements were elicited in response to an emergency and thus were nontestimonial under *Davis*. Do you agree? What factors demonstrate that the primary purpose in eliciting Gordon's statements was to confront an ongoing emergency? Do Gordon's hearsay statements offer a close analogy to McCottry's or Hammon's statements in *Davis*?

5. *Nontestimonial Statements Evolving into Testimonial Statements.* In Judge Griffin's opinion concurring in part and dissenting in part, he agrees with the majority that Gordon's 911 telephone call and her initial 30- second narrative on-the-scene statement, and her later spontaneous statement, "that's him, that's the guy that pulled the gun on me, Joseph Arnold, that's him," were nontestimonial statements. *Arnold*, 486 F.3d at 196 (Griffin, J., concurring in part and dissenting in part). However, Judge Griffin dissented from the majority's analysis pertaining to the complainant's hearsay statements made in response to police interrogation, reasoning that "[o]nce Gordon was safely in the protective custody of the three police officers, the perceived emergency had ceased." *Id.* at 200. After that point, her responses to questions asked by the police describing the weapon were testimonial and therefore subject to defendant's right to confrontation. Do you agree with Judge Griffin's position? Are these statements similar to Amy Hammon's narrative of past events set forth in her battery affidavit in *Davis v. Washington*, 547 U.S. 813, 820 (2006)? Did the statements in *Arnold* "evolve" from an initial response to an emergency into testimonial statements?

6. *An Exception to Crawford?* Should statements related to a startling event made while the declarant was under the stress of the excitement be recognized as an exception to the rule in *Crawford*? In *State v. Buda*, 949 A.2d 761 (N.J. 2008), the court stated that "[s]uch statements are admissible under the rationale that excitement suspends the declarant's powers of reflection and fabrication." *Id.* at 770. Because such statements are not the product of reflective thought, how can they be construed as testimonial? Do

statements made while the declarant was under the stress or excitement caused by the event fall within the abuses targeted by the Confrontation Clause? *See United States v. Lucian*, 414 F.3d 174, 175 (1st Cir. 2005) (holding that excited utterances are not testimonial).

D. STATE OF MIND

Federal Rule of Evidence 803(3) excepts from the hearsay rule "[a] statement of the declarant's then existing state of mind, emotion, sensation, or physical condition (such as intent, plan, motive, design, mental feeling, pain and bodily health), but not including a statement of memory or belief to prove the fact remembered or believed."[11] In the criminal context, the state of mind hearsay exception operates to admit hearsay statements in three different situations: (1) statements as to then-existing mental or emotional condition; (2) statements as to then-existing physical condition; and (3) certain statements probative of the declarant's subsequent conduct.[12] The underlying rationale for the state of mind exception is based on the contemporaneity of the statement and the unlikelihood that the declarant would deliberately or consciously misrepresent his state of mind or physical condition. Additionally, being spontaneous, the hearsay statements are considered of greater probative value than the present testimony of the declarant.[13]

The state of mind exception explicitly excludes "statements of memory or belief [proffered] to prove the fact remembered or believed." This provision "is necessary to prevent the exception from swallowing the hearsay rule."[14] The Advisory Committee Note to Rule 803(3) provides that exclusion of such statements is "necessary to avoid the virtual destruction of the hearsay rule which would otherwise result from allowing state of mind, provable by a hearsay statement, to serve as the basis for an inference of the happening of the event which produced the state of mind." Thus, while admitting statements of condition, Rule 803(3) excludes statements of belief. In other words, statements as to why the declarant held the particular state of mind are inadmissible under the rule. For example, the state of mind exception would permit a witness to testify to declarant's condition — "I'm scared" — but exclude statements of belief — "I'm scared because [someone] threatened me."[15] Similarly, self-diagnostic statements of the declarant's then-existing physical condition are excluded under the hearsay exception. While Rule 803(3) would permit such statements as "I am in pain," the

---

[11] Fed. R. Evid. 803(3).

[12] Rule 803(3) also authorizes hearsay statements of belief and intent concerning the declarant's will. This provision has no application in criminal prosecutions and thus will not be analyzed.

[13] McCormick adds:

> Special reliability is provided by the spontaneous quality of the declarations, assured by the requirement that the declaration purport to describe a condition presently existing at the time of the statement. This assurance of reliability is always effective in that some statements describing present symptoms are almost certainly calculated misstatements. Nevertheless, a sufficiently large percentage are probably spontaneous to justify the exception.

> Being spontaneous, the hearsay statements are considered of greater probative value than the present testimony of the declarant.

Charles T. McCormick, 2 McCormick on Evidence § 273 at 214–15 (John W. Strong, ed., 5th ed. 1999).

[14] *United States v. Cardascia*, 951 F.2d 474, 487 (2d Cir. 1991).

[15] *See United States v. Fontenot*, 14 F.3d 1364, 1371 (9th Cir. 1994). This exclusion from the state of mind exception grew out of Justice Cardozo's opinion in *Shepard v. United States*, 290 U.S. 96 (1933), where the Supreme Court refused to admit the statement by the defendant's wife that "Dr. Shepard has poisoned me." The Court posited: "The testimony now questioned faced backward and not forward. . . . What is even more important, it spoke to a past act, and even more than that, to an act by some one not the speaker." *Id.* at 104.

declarant's statements identifying the person responsible for inflicting the pain would be inadmissible.

Rule 803(3) is limited to statements of the declarant's state of mind. An out-of-court statement relating a third party's state of mind falls outside the scope of the hearsay exception. Additionally, Rule 803(3) requires that the declaration be directed at a present condition. This means that the statement must be made contemporaneously with the physical or mental condition being described. Statements concerning a past condition are considered less trustworthy because of potential defects in memory, perception, and time for reflection.[16] Where the statement does not concern a "then existing" condition, but is a narrative of a past event formulated after time for reflection, it is inadmissible.

Rule 803(3) further permits a declarant's statement to prove the occurrence of subsequent relevant conduct.[17] Out-of-court statements of a declarant's plan, design or intention are admissible to prove that he acted in accord with that plan, design or intention. At the same time, the House Judiciary Committee made clear that the rule is restricted to proving a declarant's future conduct, not the future conduct of another person.[18] The federal courts have consistently excluded statements of intent offered to prove subsequent conduct of someone other than the declarant.

State of mind is often highly relevant in a criminal case. The victim's hearsay statement may be admissible to rebut the defendant's claim of self-defense or lack of criminal intent, or to prove that the victim in an extortion case feared the defendant. At the same time, the defendant's out-of-court declaration may be relevant to show that he lacked the requisite state of mind for conviction. However, when proffered by the defendant, the self-serving nature of the statement raises serious questions of trustworthiness, and thus whether the statements are properly admissible under the state of mind exception. The cases and notes that follow examine the application of Rule 803(3) within the criminal context.

---

[16] *See United States v. Harvey,* 959 F.2d 1371, 1375 (7th Cir. 1992) ("To be admissible under Rule 803(3) . . . a statement must be made under circumstances showing that the declarant had no time to reflect and perhaps misrepresent his thoughts."); *United States v. Jackson,* 780 F.2d 1305, 1315 (7th Cir. 1986) (to be admissible under Rule 803(3), three requirements must be satisfied: "(1) 'the statements must be contemporaneous with the . . . event sought to be proven'; (2) 'it must be shown that the declarant had no chance to reflect — that is, no time to fabricate or to misrepresent his thoughts'; and (3) 'the statements must be shown to be relevant to an issue in the case.' " (Citations omitted.)

[17] *See Mutual Life Ins. Co. v. Hillmon,* 145 U.S. 285 (1892) (endorsing the use of statements of plan or intent to show that the planned or intended act was undertaken).

[18] The House Judiciary Committee stated:

> [T]he Committee intends that the Rule be construed to limit the doctrine of [*Hillmon*], so as to render statements of intent by a declarant admissible only to prove his future conduct, not the future conduct of another person.

H.R. Rep. No. 93-650, 93d Cong., 1st Sess. 13–14 (1973).

[1]   Statements Showing the Victim's State of Mind Used to Rebut the Accused's Defense

UNITED STATES v. DONLEY
878 F.2d 735 (3rd Cir. 1989)

HIGGINBOTHAM, JR., CIRCUIT JUDGE.

This is an appeal of a sentence of life imprisonment for a conviction of first degree murder imposed under the new guidelines ("Sentencing Guidelines") promulgated by the United States Sentencing Commission, pursuant to the Sentencing Reform Act of 1984, as amended, 18 U.S.C. § 3551 et seq. (Supp. V 1987), and 28 U.S.C. §§ 991–998 (Supp. V 1987). . . .

Except as noted, the following facts are essentially undisputed. Linda K. Donley was serving as a Sergeant in the United States Air Force at the time of her murder. She lived with her husband, Malcolm C. Donley ("Donley"), and their daughter in family housing at McGuire Air Force Base, where she was stationed. The Donleys had been having domestic difficulties for some months, and the McGuire Housing Office was considering terminating Mrs. Donley's entitlement to base housing because of domestic disturbances at her residence. Mrs. Donley wanted to separate from her husband. She had devised a plan to convince him that they were being evicted and that she was going to move in with her parents. She hoped that he would move out of their home first, and she would then stay on in the base housing. The day before her death, Linda Donley had begun to pack, and her mother, who was visiting her, heard her mention to her husband the impending move and the separation. The following night, her husband Malcolm Donley killed her by repeatedly striking her in the head with a hatchet and a meat cleaver. He also cut her neck with a knife.

Mr. Donley never denied killing his wife, but claimed that he had done so in the heat of passion shortly after finding her in their bedroom with another man. The prosecution introduced evidence to show that Mrs. Donley had gone to bed and was asleep when her husband attacked and killed her. The jury returned a conviction of murder in the first degree. The Presentence Report recommended no departure from the Sentencing Guidelines and the district court imposed a sentence of life imprisonment, which it considered to be mandatory under federal law for first degree murder.

II.

The appellant challenges a number of evidentiary and other rulings by the district court, only one of which we will discuss here. He claims that the District Court erred in allowing the government to introduce testimony by the victim's mother, Mrs. Brown, as to hearsay statements by the victim to show her plan and state of mind. Donley claims, first, that the statements were inadmissible hearsay used to prove his own future conduct, and second, that they were extremely prejudicial to him. . . .

With regard to the first question, whether the statements of the victim's mother qualify as an exception to the rule barring hearsay evidence under Rule 803(3) of the Federal Rules of Evidence, our review is plenary. Federal Rule of Evidence 803(3) provides for an exception to the hearsay rule if the statement is introduced to show the declarant's then existing state of mind, such as his intent, plan or design.[2] The evidence may also be used to prove or explain acts or conduct of the declarant. The question for us on review is whether the statements indeed go to show what the government claims they show. That is a question of relevancy and our standard of review for relevancy rulings is plenary. . . .

The government used Mrs. Brown's testimony to show that the deceased had a plan to convince her husband that they were being evicted, and that she acted shortly before her death to further her plan. Linda Donley had started packing up the apartment and her mother testified that she heard her daughter make several statements to the appellant regarding the packing, the separation agreement and the division of property. Donley claims that the testimony was used to show not just the plan and state of mind of the deceased, but also his future conduct. We do not agree. The testimony went not to show that the defendant was soon to kill the declarant, but, rather, to show the existence of the deceased's plan to move out of the base apartment and separate from her husband. The government properly sought to persuade the jury to infer from her statements that she had such a plan and, in turn, to infer from that plan and the defendant's awareness of it that he had a motive for murder other than the one he claimed. The motive for murder was contested. The appellant claimed that he killed his wife because he had found her with another man. The government claimed, however, that the defendant killed her because of the imminent marital separation. The government was entitled to introduce testimony from which the jury might reasonably infer the existence of the motive the government proposed, provided the testimony was not inadmissible on other grounds.

Under *Mutual Life Insurance Co. v. Hillmon*, 145 U.S. 285, (1892), out-of-court statements showing the declarant's intention were admitted because his intention "was a material fact bearing upon the question in controversy." *Id.* at 299–300. Donley contends that the testimony by Mrs. Brown was unnecessary because the victim's plan was not disputed, and the hearsay testimony should therefore have been excluded. It is true that the uncontested testimony of another witness, Captain Swanson, showed the existence of the plan. However, the mother's testimony was needed to show that the victim was putting into effect her plan to separate from the appellant and to force him out of the base housing shortly before she was killed. It was not just the existence of the plan, the government claims, but its imminent realization, that provided the motive for murder.

Donley further argues that the hearsay statements of the victim cannot go to show his motive because Mrs. Brown could testify only that her daughter had said them, not that he had heard or responded to them. He concludes that they therefore should not have been admitted. The fact that the mother could not be certain that the appellant heard what the victim had said does not make the testimony inadmissible, nor does it mean that it cannot be useful in establishing motive. The testimony offers evidence from which the jury might have inferred that the appellant heard the statements, but even if he did not hear them, the evidence was still admissible. Statements admitted under Fed. R. Evid. 803(3) to show the declarant's intent or plan may be used to show that the declarant acted in accord with that plan. *See Mutual Life Insurance Co. v. Hillmon*, 145 U.S. 285 (1892).

---

[2] The Federal Rules of Evidence provide that the following are not excluded by the hearsay rule: A statement of the declarant's then existing state of mind, emotion, sensation, or physical condition (such as intent, plan, motive, design, mental feeling, pain and bodily health). . . . Fed. R. Evid. 803(3).

Lastly, the appellant claims that the testimony of the victim's mother, even if relevant, was extremely prejudicial to him. Prejudice does not in itself, however, make the testimony inadmissible. The question that the trial court had to decide was whether the probative value of the testimony was outweighed by the danger of unfair prejudice. Fed. R. Evid. 403. Mrs. Brown's testimony was relevant, as discussed above, and nothing in the record suggests that it was overly emotional. The district court concluded that the danger of unfair prejudice did not outweigh the probative value of the testimony, and we conclude that the district court did not abuse its discretion in making that determination. We therefore hold that the district court acted properly in admitting the hearsay evidence by the victim's mother to show the victim's state of mind and plan.

* * *

IV.

For the foregoing reasons, we will affirm the decision of the district court.

NOTES AND QUESTIONS

1. Rule 803(3) permits hearsay evidence to prove the declarant's state of mind. For purposes of the hearsay exception, "state of mind" includes the declarant's "intent, plan, motive, design, mental feeling, pain and bodily health." Fed. R. Evid. 803(3). What was the government's theory for admitting Mrs. Brown's testimony, which included hearsay declarations by Linda Donley, the murder victim? What was the appellant's defense? Were the out-of-court declarations relevant to rebutting that defense?

2. Appellant Donley maintained that the hearsay statements were admitted to prove his motive and intent. Is Donley correct? Is the hearsay evidence being offered to prove both Linda Donley's plan and intent to leave appellant, as well as to prove appellant's motive and intent to kill? Does Rule 803(3) permit out-of-court declarations to prove the state of mind of someone other than the declarant? *See Shepard v. United States*, 290 U.S. 96, 98 (1933) (excluding declarant's hearsay statements offered to prove an act committed by someone else — that declarant was dying from poison given by her husband); *United States v. Joe*, 8 F.3d 1488, 1493 n.4 (10th Cir. 1993) ("An out-of-court statement relating a third party's state of mind falls outside the scope of the hearsay exception because such a statement necessarily is one of memory or belief.").

Associated Press

Judge: Call to Abuse Line Can't Be Used Against Simpson

SANTA MONICA, Calif. — The judge in the O.J. Simpson civil trial told jurors Thursday that testimony about a call to a battered-women's hot line from someone who identified herself as "Nicole" cannot be taken as evidence that Simpson threatened or stalked his former wife. . . .

[Judge] Fujisaki told jurors that the testimony given Wednesday by women's shelter worker Nancy Ney could be considered only to determine what Nicole Simpson may have been feeling at the time, not what Simpson was doing.

Ney, of Sojourn House, testified that a woman named Nicole with the same personal history as Nicole Simpson called five days before the 1994 murders of

Nicole Brown Simpson and her friend Ronald Goldman. The woman named Nicole reported being stalked and receiving a death threat from a famous ex-husband, Ney testified.

"The testimony is received only to show her [Nicole Simpson's] state of mind and to explain her conduct," Fujisaki told jurors. "The jury must not consider the substance of [the caller's] statements to Nancy Ney as evidence of any event or whether such events occurred."

The defense had objected to allowing Ney's testimony, arguing that it was hearsay and that the caller's identity wasn't certain because she did not give her last name. The evidence was not allowed in Simpson's criminal trial. . . .

The judge's instruction means that jurors can only interpret the testimony as what Nicole Simpson was thinking in her own mind.

The judge said her state of mind was relevant in this case because it helped explain what she may have said or done at a dance recital just hours before her murder. Simpson was also at that recital. . . . Chicago Tribune, Dec. 8, 1996, Sec. 1, at 5.

Was the testimony of Nancy Ney properly admitted into evidence under the state of mind exception? What is the relevance of Nicole Brown Simpson's state of mind five days before the 1994 murders? Is Judge Fujisaki's limiting instruction to the jury not to use Ney's testimony as substantive evidence of whether O.J. Simpson stalked or threatened his former wife, sufficient to prevent the jury from misusing the testimony? Is the hearsay evidence sufficiently trustworthy to withstand scrutiny under the Confrontation Clause?

3. In a prosecution under the Hobbs Act, 18 U.S.C. § 1951, the victim's state of mind is an essential element of the government's case. For purposes of the statute, the term "extortion" "means the obtaining of property from another, with his consent, induced by wrongful use of actual or threatened force, violence, or fear, or under color of official right." 18 U.S.C. § 1951. The government must prove not only the defendant's intent but the victim's fearful state of mind at the time of the extortion. It is well-settled that statements by the victim indicating fear of the defendant are admissible in a prosecution for extortion. *See United States v. Collins*, 78 F.3d 1021, 1036 (6th Cir. 1996) ("In a prosecution based upon extortion through fear of economic loss, the state of mind of the victim of extortion is highly relevant."); *United States v. Goodoak*, 836 F.2d 708, 713–14 (1st Cir. 1988) (hearsay statements properly admitted to prove victim's state of mind and whether defendant had threatened him); *United States v. Grassi*, 783 F.2d 1572, 1577–78 (11th Cir. 1986) (same); *United States v. Tuchow*, 768 F.2d 855, 866 (7th Cir. 1988) (same); *United States v. Kelly*, 722 F.2d 873, 878 (1st Cir. 1983) (same).

4. In a homicide case where the defendant claims self-defense, Rule 803(3) permits statements by the victim that he feared the defendant to rebut the claim that the victim was the aggressor. *See United States v. Day*, 591 F.2d 861, 881–86 (D.C. Cir. 1978); *United States v. Brown*, 490 F.2d 758, 767–69 (D.C. Cir. 1973).

5. While Rule 803(3) permits hearsay to prove the declarant's subsequent conduct, hearsay is also admissible to establish the declarant's state of mind that is inconsistent with the declarant voluntarily taking certain action. In *United States v. Hartmann*, 958 F.2d 774 (7th Cir. 1992), the murder victim's wife, her lover, and an accomplice were convicted on various fraud counts in connection with a scheme to defraud insurance companies of the proceeds of life and mortgage insurance policies on the victim's life. At trial, the district court admitted several of the murder victim's "beyond-the-grave statements" concerning his failed marriage (including the adulterous acts of his wife), his desire to change beneficiaries on his insurance policies, and his fear of being murdered by his wife and her lover. On appeal, the court affirmed the convictions and upheld the admissibility of the murder victim's hearsay statements, reasoning that hearsay is admissible under Rule 803(3) to establish a deceased declarant's state of mind that is inconsistent with the declarant voluntarily taking certain action. The court posited:

> Werner's [the murder victim's] statements that he feared Debra and Korabik [the defendants] would murder him were also properly admitted. The district court admitted these statements under Fed. R. Evid. 803(3) to prove Werner's attitude toward his insurance policies; that is, if Werner feared that his wife and her lover were planning to kill him, it would be extremely unlikely that Werner deliberately would make his murder even more attractive by naming his wife as beneficiary to lucrative policies that insured his life.

Id. at 783. Do you agree with the court's ruling? Should the murder victim's statements have been excluded under Fed. R. Evid. 403?

PROBLEM

Problem 8-1. *Statements Looking Backward and Forward.* The defendant represented the International Union of Operating Engineers ("IUOE"). Some members of the IUOE were working for the Terry Contracting Company, which had received the bid to build the Connecticut turnpike. Defendant contacted the owner of Terry Contracting, Harry Terker, and threatened that Harry would need to give him money in order to ensure that no labor disputes arose during the construction of the turnpike. Later that day, Harry had lunch with his son, Richard. Harry told Richard about defendant's threat and the money he demanded. Richard asked his father what he was going to do and Harry replied that he was going to send the extortion money to the defendant. Shortly after this luncheon, Harry died of a stroke and Richard took over the business.

Defendant was indicted for one count of extortion. During his trial, the government sought to introduce Richard's testimony describing his conversation with his father about the defendant's extortion threat. The government argued that this testimony was admissible under Fed. R. Evid. 803(3) as it demonstrated the declarant's state of mind. The government maintained that Harry's intent to pay the defendant inferred that he sent the money to the defendant. The defendant objected to the introduction of this testimony, contending that it included backward-looking statements about defendant's conduct which prompted Harry's statement. In other words, the hearsay declaration was being offered to prove a past event, i.e., that the defendant extorted money from Harry. Such statements are prohibited under Rule 803(3) (". . . but not including a statement of memory or belief to prove the fact remembered or believed.") Are Richard's statements properly admissible under Rule 803(3)? *See United States v. Annunziato,* 293 F.2d 373 (2d Cir. 1961) (modifying the facts).

**[2]   Statements of the Accused Offered by the Defense — The
Self-Serving Problem**

UNITED STATES v. DiMARIA
727 F.2d 265 (2d Cir. 1984)

FRIENDLY, CIRCUIT JUDGE:

Appellant Leonard DiMaria was convicted in the District Court for the Eastern
District of New York, after trial before Judge Bramwell and a jury, on three counts of
an indictment charging, respectively, possession of cigarettes stolen while moving in
interstate commerce in violation of 18 U.S.C. § 659 (Count III), possession of
contraband cigarettes in violation of 18 U.S.C. § 2342 (Count IV) and conspiracy to
commit both substantive offenses in violation of 18 U.S.C. § 371 (Count I). He was
sentenced to ten years' imprisonment on Count III and to five years' imprisonment on
Counts I and IV, the sentences to run concurrently.

The Government's proof established the following: On February 9, 1981, John Bott
drove a tractor-trailer containing 950 cases of Philip Morris cigarettes worth over
$200,000, from Richmond, Virginia, toward its ultimate destination in Jersey City, New
Jersey. One night during the course of the trip Bott pulled into a rest area on the New
Jersey Turnpike and went to sleep in the cab of his truck. He was awakened by a man
who placed a gun to his head and ordered him to surrender his rig. Bott was removed
from the cab of the tractor and placed in the rear of a van. When, several hours later,
he was released from the van, his tractor-trailer and its load of cigarettes were gone.

Shortly thereafter Robert Russell, a long-time associate of one of DiMaria's co-
defendants, Anthony Billeci, received a telephone call from another co-defendant asking
him to go to the Tunnel Diner in Jersey City. Russell there met Irving Birnbaum,
Anthony Billeci and John Gouker, all co-defendants, and a fourth unidentified man.
They discussed using a storage yard at the Walsh Trucking Company in Jersey City to
store a stolen trailer that Billeci and Birnbaum had obtained until they could find a
buyer for the load. Gouker made arrangements with John DiRoma, the yard manager,
also a co-defendant, to use the yard of the Walsh Trucking Company in Jersey City.

On February 14 the FBI began a surveillance of the yard and two refrigerated
trucks therein, which bore the logo IRL on the side, and the New York City Police
Department began surveillances on Billeci and Birnbaum in response to information
that a truckload of cigarettes had been hijacked. At approximately 8:50 p.m. on
February 17, the City detectives observed Billeci and Birnbaum arrive at a social club
on Glenwood Road in Brooklyn that DiMaria frequented. After an hour Billeci and
Birnbaum walked outside the club with DiMaria and an unidentified male. After a brief
conversation Billeci and Birnbaum left in Birnbaum's Cadillac while DiMaria and the
unidentified man left in another car.

Late the following evening, February 18, Billeci and Birnbaum again drove to the
social club. Over the next two hours, until about 2:00 a.m., Billeci, Birnbaum and
DiMaria repeatedly left the club, talked while walking up and down the sidewalk, and
then reentered the club.

On the afternoon of the next day, February 19, co-defendant Anthony Apice rented
a Hertz tractor. Two men drove the tractor to the Walsh Trucking yard and when
unable to open the gate, drove three blocks away where Billeci and Birnbaum, in the

latter's Cadillac, pulled alongside. The men returned to the Walsh yard, unlocked the gate, and unsuccessfully attempted to connect the tractor to one of the IRL trailers. Billeci and Birnbaum arrived in time to see this debacle. The second trailer was then attached to the Hertz tractor and was pulled from the yard. Billeci locked the gate, and he and Birnbaum left.

The Hertz tractor and the IRL trailer were then driven to the Best Deli in Brooklyn, where the drivers were replaced by another pair who drove the rig to the Brooklyn Terminal Market. The rig was followed by an Oldsmobile which had been seen near DiMaria's social club on the two evenings when he met with Billeci and Birnbaum. In the storage yard at the Brooklyn Terminal Market, the tractor was unhitched from the IRL trailer and was driven back to the Best Deli where the new crew left. Billeci's and Birnbaum's men replaced them, and the tractor, Billeci and Birnbaum left the area. The trailer remained at the yard, being guarded through the night by the Oldsmobile and its unidentified occupant.

On the next day, Friday, February 20, the second IRL trailer arrived at the Terminal Market and was positioned near the first. An "S & R" van leased by Richard Lustparten entered the yard and approached the trailers. Cases of cigarettes were loaded from the trailers into the van. Early in the evening co-defendants Sal Miciotta and Joseph Monteleone arrived at the market and maintained guard over the two trailers throughout the night. The denouement came about 4:00 p.m. on Saturday, February 21. A white Cadillac led a Barn rental van into the market. Each vehicle carried two passengers. DiMaria got out of the Cadillac and directed the van as it backed up into the space between the two IRL trailers. The four men loaded the van with cigarettes from the trailers; one case was cut open on the loading dock. DiMaria and Miciotta started to drive away in the Cadillac and the two other men prepared to depart in the Barn van. The FBI agents stopped both vehicles. They found in the Cadillac a half-case in the trunk. A search of Miciotta revealed a number of keys which fit the locks of the doors of the two IRL trailers and three tally sheets . . . and a part of the bill of lading taken from John Bott containing a computer print-out listing of the contents of the original trailer as it had left Philip Morris in Richmond. Execution of search warrants recovered 670 cases of assorted Philip Morris cigarettes from the trailer, and 45 cases of various brands from the Barn rental van.

* * *

We thus come to the serious point raised by DiMaria. The defense sought to elicit from FBI Special Agent MacDonald that as the agents approached him, DiMaria said:

> I thought you guys were just investigating white collar crime; what are you doing here? I only came here to get some cigarettes real cheap.

The defense contended that cheap or even "real cheap" cigarettes meant bootleg cigarettes, i.e., cigarettes brought from a low-tax state for sale in a high-tax state, rather than stolen cigarettes, and that the statement thus tended to disprove the state of mind required for conviction under 18 U.S.C. § 659 (Count III), and also under the conspiracy count which charged a conspiracy to violate both 18 U.S.C. § 659 and 18 U.S.C. § 2342, since the jury was charged that it could convict if it found DiMaria guilty of conspiring to commit either crime. The defense did not explain with particularity why the statement was not inculpatory rather than exculpatory with regard to Count IV which charged possession of contraband cigarettes in violation of 18 U.S.C. § 2342; the theory must be that the reference to getting "some cigarettes real cheap" could be considered by the jury as negating an intention to possess a quantity in excess of 60,000 which § 2341(2) requires for a conviction. Admissibility was predicated on Fed. R. Evid. 803(3) which excepts from the hearsay rule, even though the declarant is available as a witness:

> A statement of the declarant's then existing state of mind, emotion, sensation, or physical condition (such as intent, plan, motive, design, mental feeling, pain, and bodily health), but not including a statement of memory or belief to prove the fact remembered or believed unless it relates to the execution, revocation, identification or terms of declarant's will.

After hearing argument, the judge excluded the statement.

Our decision in *United States v. Marin*, 669 F.2d 73, 84 (1982), which the Government cited to the judge as dispositive in its favor, is totally irrelevant. We there upheld the exclusion of a portion of a post-arrest statement by the defendant Romero that a co-defendant, Marin, had placed a bag of narcotics in Romero's car. This was not a statement of Romero's existing state of mind; it fell squarely within the exception to the Rule 803(3) exception banning "a statement of memory or belief to prove the fact remembered or believed."

The Government's claim that, apart from the authority of *Marin*, DiMaria's statement falls within the exception to the exception is baseless. The Advisory Committee's Notes explain that the exception to the exception was "necessary to avoid the virtual destruction of the hearsay rule which could otherwise result from allowing state of mind, provable by a hearsay statement, to serve as the basis for an inference of the happening of the event which produced the state of mind." The comment, as the Notes indicate, derived from Justice Cardozo's opinion in *Shepard v. United States*, 290 U.S. 96, 98 (1933), where the Government had attempted to use the state of mind exception to justify the admission of a declaration by the defendant's wife that "Dr. Shepard has poisoned me." In repelling this the Court said:

> It [the Government] did not use the declarations by Mrs. Shepard to prove her present thoughts and feelings, or even her thoughts and feelings in times past. It used the declarations as proof of an act committed by some one else, as evidence that she was dying of poison given by her husband.

*   *   *

> The testimony now questioned faced backward and not forward. . . . What is even more important, it spoke to a past act, and more than that, to an act by some one not the speaker. *Id.* at 104, 106.

DiMaria's statement had none of these characteristics. It stated, or so the jury could find, that his existing state of mind was to possess bootleg cigarettes, not stolen cigarettes. It was not offered to prove that the cigarettes were not stolen cigarettes but only to show that DiMaria did not think they were. It would defy reality to predicate any contrary conclusion on the use of the words "I came" rather than "I am." DiMaria's remark was not a statement, like Mrs. Shepard's, of what he or someone else had done in the past. It was a statement of what he was thinking in the present. . . . The trial judge initially recognized this, before being distracted by the Government's erroneous reliance on *Marin*, when he said "this statement goes directly to the 659 count, and his state of mind."

The Assistant United States Attorney also stated in objection that DiMaria's remark was "an absolutely classic false exculpatory statement." False it may well have been but if it fell within Rule 803(3), as it clearly did if the words of that Rule are read to mean what they say, its truth or falsity was for the jury to determine. Dean Wigmore strongly endorsed the admissibility of such a statement at common law, 6 Wigmore, Evidence § 1732, at 159–62 (Chadbourn rev. 1976). Dealing with the argument that declarations of a mental state by an accused could readily be trumped up, he protested "the singular fallacy . . . of taking the possible trickery of guilty persons as a ground for excluding evidence in favor of a person not yet proved guilty," *id.* at 160, and contended that to sustain the argument would be inconsistent with the presumption of innocence.

It is true that Dean Wigmore would permit the exclusion of a statement of existing state of mind if "the circumstances indicate plainly a motive to deceive," *id.* (footnote omitted). McCormick, Evidence § 294, at 695 n.56 (Cleary 2d ed. 1972), cit[ing] . . . *Smith v. Smith*, 364 Pa. 1, 70 A.2d 630 (1950), which held that the self-serving nature of such a declaration went only to its weight. The Federal Rules of Evidence have opted for the latter view. The Advisers' Introductory Note: The Hearsay Problem, endorses Professor Chadbourn's criticism of § 63(4)(c) of the Commissioner's proposed Uniform Rules of Evidence, saying, "For a judge to exclude evidence because he does not believe it has been described as 'altogether atypical, extraordinary,'" citing Chadbourn, *Bentham and the Hearsay Rule — A Benthamic View of Rule 63(4)(c) of the Uniform Rules of Evidence*, 75 Harv. L. Rev. 932, 947 (1962).[5]

It is doubtless true that all the hearsay exceptions in Rules 803 and 804 rest on a belief that declarations of the sort there described have "some particular assurance of credibility." See Introductory Note, *supra*. But the scheme of the Rules is to determine that issue by categories; if a declaration comes within a category defined as an exception, the declaration is admissible without any preliminary finding of probable credibility by the judge, save for the "catch-all" exceptions of Rules 803(24) and 804(b)(5) and the business records exception of Rule 803(6) ("unless the source of information or the method or circumstance of preparation indicate lack of trustworthiness"). As Judge Weinstein has stated, "the scheme adopted for the hearsay article in the federal rules is that of a system of class exceptions coupled with an open-ended provision in Rules 803(24) and 804(b)(5), and with the exemption of certain prior statements from the definition of hearsay." 4 Weinstein's Evidence ¶ 800[02], at 800–13 (1981), even though this excludes certain hearsay statements with a high degree of trustworthiness and admits certain statements with a low one. This evil was doubtless thought preferable to requiring preliminary determinations of the judge with respect to trustworthiness, with attendant possibilities of delay, prejudgment and encroachment on the province of the jury. There is a peculiarly strong case for admitting statements like DiMaria's, however suspect, when the Government is relying on the presumption of guilty knowledge arising from a defendant's possession of the fruits of a crime recently after its commission.

The Government argues that if exclusion of the statement was erroneous, the error was harmless because of the strength of the evidence against DiMaria, the ambiguous nature of the statement, the doubt that the jury would credit it, and the fact that counsel was allowed to argue that DiMaria was only trying to buy some cigarettes cheap and did not know they were stolen. The evidence with respect to guilty knowledge, while entirely sufficient, was not overpowering. As indicated above, the interpretation and the credibility of DiMaria's statement were for the jury. Counsel's argument was no substitute for the argument that could have been made if DiMaria's statement had been

---

[5] Professor Chadbourn added:

   In terms of the time honored formula, credibility is a matter of fact for the jury, not a matter of law for the judge.

admitted. As we have often remarked, we cannot but wonder why, if the statement was so insignificant as the Government now claims, the prosecutor was at such pains to have it excluded.

The judgment of conviction is reversed and the cause is remanded for a new trial consistent with this opinion. . . .

NOTES AND QUESTIONS

1. What was the defense theory for admitting the defendant's hearsay statements: "I thought you guys were just investigating white collar crime; what are you doing here? I only came here to get some cigarettes real cheap"? *DiMaria*, 727 F.2d 270. What was the government's theory for excluding them?

2. It is fundamental to criminal law that every crime requires proof of the union of an *actus reus* and *mens rea*. In order to convict for commission of a crime, the government must prove that the defendant possessed the *mens rea* or state of mind prescribed by statute. Thus, the defendant's state of mind is always at issue in a criminal case. Does *DiMaria* require admission under Rule 803(3) of every post-arrest statement made by a defendant denying knowledge or the intent to commit the crime charged, regardless of how self-serving? Would the court have reached a different result in *DiMaria* had the defendant made the statement some time after his arrest and the seizure of the contraband?

3. Are a defendant's self-serving statements sufficiently trustworthy? The court in *DiMaria* observed that Dean Wigmore would permit the exclusion of a statement of existing state of mind if "the circumstances indicate plainly a motive to deceive." *DiMaria*, 727 F.2d at 271 (citations omitted). Does the court require a preliminary finding of probable credibility as a precondition to admitting the defendant's hearsay statements? If not, why not? *See United States v. Cardascia*, 951 F.2d 474, 487 (2d Cir. 1991) ("the self-serving nature of a statement is considered when the jury weighs the evidence at the conclusion of the trial"); *United States v. Peak*, 856 F.2d 825, 834 (7th Cir. 1988) (the court does not have discretion to exclude testimony because the judge does not believe the witness). How does the court in *DiMaria* propose dealing with the self-serving problem?

4. Near the end of the Second Circuit's opinion in *DiMaria* the court refers to the so-called " 'catch all exceptions' " of "Rules 803(24) and 804(b)(5)." The contents of these two Rules were combined into one new Rule — Rule 807 — in a 1997 amendment to the Federal Rules of Evidence. The substance meaning of the Rules 803(24) and 804(b)(5) were not changed by this amendment.

In discussing the "catch-all" exceptions (now catch all *exception*; *i.e.* Rule 807) and the business records exception of Rule 803(6), the *DiMaria* court noted that these Rules require preliminary determinations by the judge with respect to trustworthiness. Should a similar trustworthiness determination be required where the circumstances indicate a motive to deceive? The *DiMaria* court rejected such a preliminary determination. Why?

E.   MEDICAL DIAGNOSIS OR TREATMENT

Rule 803(4) permits hearsay testimony regarding, "[s]tatements made for purposes of medical diagnosis or treatment and describing medical history, or past or present symptoms, pain or sensations or the inception or general character of the cause or external source thereof insofar as reasonably pertinent to diagnosis or treatment." The basis for this exception emanates from the patient's own selfish motive "that the effectiveness of the treatment depends on the accuracy of the information provided to the doctor."[19] Since the declarant is seeking effective medical treatment, it is assumed that the information provided to a physician for that purpose is sufficiently trustworthy. The Supreme Court has further affirmed this rationale, commenting that "statements made in the course of receiving medical care . . . are made in contexts that provide substantial guarantees of trustworthiness."[20]

The medical treatment exception, however, does not permit admission of any statement made to a physician. To fit the exception, it is essential that the statement be "reasonably pertinent to treatment or diagnosis." There are several questions that arise in determining whether a hearsay statement is "reasonably pertinent" to treatment or diagnosis. For example, are statements by an alleged victim of child abuse identifying the sexual abuser "reasonably pertinent" to treatment or diagnosis? Is the identity of the perpetrator necessary to promote effective treatment? If so, under what theory of treatment? While the guarantee of trustworthiness extends to statements about the injury, since the patient will want to be diagnosed correctly and treated appropriately, does this same presumption of reliability extend to statements of culpability? What if the victim of sexual abuse is an adult? Should statements made by a patient identifying her attacker be treated differently depending on whether they were made by a child or adult victim?

While the typical statement offered under the exception is made by the patient directly to the doctor, the exception is not limited to patient-doctor declarations. It extends to statements made by family members, as well as Good Samaritans[21] who bring the patient in for medical services. Thus, for example, statements made by a parent or guardian to a doctor for medical purposes qualify under the exception.[22] The statements are deemed sufficiently trustworthy because of the parent or guardian's interest in ensuring that the child is properly diagnosed and treated.

The exception is also not limited to statements made to the treating or diagnosing physician. Statements made to clerical intake personnel, administrative assistants, nurses, and emergency medical responders should qualify under the exception. Whether statements made to a psychiatrist for purposes of obtaining medical treatment and diagnosis fit within the exception is less certain. The underlying rationale for the medical diagnosis exception may not extend with equal validity to a patient seeking psychiatric treatment for the obvious reason that statements considered "reasonably pertinent" for purposes of psychiatric diagnosis or treatment could lead to an expansive application of the exception. As one commentator accurately noted: "Given the uncertainties and tenta

---

[19] CHARLES T. MCCORMICK, 2 MCCORMICK ON EVIDENCE § 277, at 233 (John W. Strong ed., 5th ed. 1999); *see also* FED. R. EVID. 803(4), Advisory Committee's Note; 6 J. WIGMORE, EVIDENCE IN TRIALS AT COMMON LAW § 1719 (Chadbourn rev. ed. 1976).

[20] *White v. Illinois*, 502 U.S. 346, 355 (1992).

[21] *See Navarro de Cosme v. Hospital Pavia*, 922 F.2d 926, 931–32 (1st Cir. 1991).

[22] *See United States v. Lovejoy*, 92 F.3d 628, 632 (8th Cir. 1996); *United States v. Yazzie*, 59 F.3d 807, 813–14 (9th Cir. 1994).

tiveness of psychiatric diagnoses, virtually any statement would be considered 'reasonably pertinent,' so the exception would cover almost anything."[23]

The medical examination exception must also satisfy the requirements of the Sixth Amendment Confrontation Clause. The critical question is whether statements made for the purpose of receiving medical diagnosis or treatment are "testimonial" statements or as articulated by the Supreme Court in *Crawford v. Washington*, 541 U.S. 36 (2004) and its progeny. For example, are statements made by a child victim of sexual abuse to a social worker the functional equivalent of police interrogation? The cases and notes that follow will examine the statutory requirements for admission of hearsay statements under Rule 803(4), as well as whether such statements may be barred by the Confrontation Clause.

UNITED STATES v. PENEAUX
432 F.3d 882 (8th Cir. 2005)

A jury convicted Sherman Peneaux on four counts of aggravated sexual abuse of a child, T.P., and on two counts of assault, and the district court imposed concurrent sentences of 180 months for the sexual abuse offenses and 60 months for the assault convictions. Peneaux appeals, arguing that there was insufficient evidence to sustain his convictions, that hearsay statements were improperly admitted, and that his constitutional right to confrontation was violated. We affirm.

I.

In March 2002 the South Dakota Department of Social Services (DSS) removed T.P. and her siblings, N.P. and Fianna, from the custody of their parents, Sherman Peneaux and Juanita Swalley, based on allegations that Peneaux had abused Fianna. At that time T.P. was three years old, and N.P. was two. The children were placed in the Spotted Tail Crisis Center, and T.P. subsequently reported that Peneaux had sexually abused her and extinguished a cigarette on her body. T.P. made the statements to tribal police investigator Grace Her Many Horses, forensic investigator Lora Hawkins, child care case worker Zane McClarnnan, pediatrician Dr. Lori Strong, and two different foster parents, Edith Connot and Penny Norris. . . .

The case went to trial in September 2004, and the government called tribal investigator Grace Her Many Horses after other witnesses had provided background information. She testified without objection about statements T.P. made during an interview with her. She reported that T.P. told her that she had been sexually and physically abused. Then the government called T.P. to the stand; her testimony was inconsistent. On direct examination T.P. denied that Peneaux had abused her, but acknowledged that she had previously told people that she had been sexually abused. The prosecutor presented her with drawings of a naked man and woman and asked her to mark the part of Peneaux's body which had touched her and the part of her body which Peneaux had touched. T.P. circled the genital region and anus on both the male and female diagrams. When she was asked to identify the areas she had marked, she called them the "pee pee" and "butt." Without objection the diagrams were received into evidence as exhibits. T.P. was also asked how she received the burn mark on her stomach. She responded that Peneaux had inflicted it with a lit cigarette, but she denied he had ever burned her when questioned by defense counsel.

---

[23] MUELLER & KIRKPATRICK, EVIDENCE § 8.41, at 955 (1995).

The government called other individuals with whom T.P. had spoken prior to trial. Zane McClarnnan, an employee of the Spotted Tail Crisis Center, testified that T.P. told him that "my dad likes to undress me" and would "lay on top of me." T.P.'s stepmother, Juanita Swalley, was asked about statements she had made to the FBI and whether she had disclosed that T.P. told her "daddy was doing loving to me" and other similar comments. Swalley answered that she could not remember precisely what she had told the agents, but she acknowledged that she had signed the statement she gave to the FBI. The defense did not object to the testimony of either of these witnesses.

Foster parent Edith Connot testified to an incident she had observed at her home. She saw T.P. under her kitchen table touching the genitals of her four year old son. When Connot explained that such behavior was inappropriate, T.P. replied that her father touched her in that way. Again there was no objection by the defense. T.P.'s other foster parent, Penny Norris, testified that she saw many little white marks on T.P.'s body. T.P. told her that Peneaux had burned her with his cigarettes when Norris asked if she had been bitten by bugs. Norris also testified to statements made by N.P., T.P.'s brother, that Peneaux had also burned him with a cigarette. No objection was raised to any of this testimony. The defense did object to testimony Norris gave about a conversation she had with Dr. Allison during a wellness check of T.P. which she had arranged after learning that Peneaux might have physically and sexually abused the child. Norris reported that Dr. Allison had remarked that the circular marks on T.P. could be cigarette burns.

The government next called forensic investigator Lora Hawkins, who testified to statements T.P. had made during two separate interviews. Hawkins testified that during the first interview T.P. told her that "my daddy gets on top of me," that "my daddy touches my pee pee," and that he wanted her to touch "by his pee pee." Hawkins also testified that when asked where Peneaux had touched her, T.P. grabbed her crotch. Hawkins further testified that during their second interview, T.P. "consistently presented the same information" and told her that Peneaux had touched her genitals both with his fingers and his penis and that he had tried to penetrate her anus with his penis. Not only did the defense not object to Hawkins' testimony, it offered to introduce the video recordings of these interviews into evidence if the government did not. Peneaux's counsel also had written transcripts of the videos made and entered them into evidence.

Dr. Lora Strong, a pediatrician who examined both T.P. and her brother, was another government witness. She testified about T.P.'s statements indicating that Peneaux had abused her sexually and physically and about her own physical findings. When Dr. Strong asked T.P. whether anyone had touched her where "she goes pee from," T.P. responded yes. When asked who had done it, she stated "Sherman." When asked where Peneaux hurt her, T.P. pointed to her genital area. When asked about her circular scar, T.P. replied "Sherman hurt me." When asked how, she answered "burn with cigarette."

Although the defense did not object to Dr. Strong's testimony about T.P., it did object to her testimony about T.P.'s brother, N.P. No grounds were given for the objection, and it was overruled. Dr. Strong then testified that N.P. had a circular scar on his right knee which was similar to the one found on T.P. She also testified that when she asked N.P. how he got hurt, he responded "burn." When asked what that meant, he answered "Sherman" and "Sherman hurt."

* * *

The defense called witnesses who testified that they never saw Peneaux sexually or physically abuse T.P. or his other children. The assistant to T.P.'s health care provider testified that T.P. had been examined numerous times before she was removed from her parents' custody and nothing in her records indicated she had been burned. No physical evidence indicating sexual abuse had been reported, and Dr. Strong had noted that her genitals were normal for her age. Although the mark on her stomach was consistent "with the possibility" of a cigarette burn, Dr. Strong admitted something else could have caused it. Betty Kallinger, a physician's assistant at the Horizon Health Care Mission where T.P. was often treated, testified that T.P.'s medical records did not indicate that she had been burned and that the scar could have resulted from an infected sore.

* * *

III.

Peneaux complains that the district court improperly admitted T.P.'s prior inconsistent statements as substantive evidence. He devotes much of his brief to arguing that unsworn prior inconsistent statements cannot be admitted as substantive evidence under Rule 801(d)(1)(A). The government does not refute this argument, but instead contends that these statements were properly admitted in this case as substantive evidence under Rule 807, the residual exception to the hearsay rule, and Rule 803(4), the exception for statements related to medical diagnosis or treatment. Peneaux cites no authority for the proposition that a jury cannot consider residual hearsay as substantive evidence, and we have repeatedly allowed the admission of residual hearsay testimony for that purpose. If the testimony was properly admitted, it may be considered as substantive evidence, and the district court was not obligated to tell the jury it could not consider inconsistent statements as substantive evidence.

* * *

Peneaux contends that Dr. Strong's testimony about what T.P. told her was inadmissible under Rule 803(4), which requires that hearsay statements be reasonably pertinent to medical diagnosis or treatment. Because Peneaux did not preserve this alleged error, we review for plain error. *Olano*, 507 U.S. at 732–36. Under this rule the proponent of the evidence must show that the statement is of the type reasonably relied on by a physician in treatment or diagnosis and that the declarant's motive in making the statement was consistent with promoting treatment. *United States v. Iron Shell*, 633 F.2d 77, 84 (8th Cir.1980). While a declarant's statements identifying the party allegedly responsible for her injuries may normally not be reasonably pertinent to treatment or diagnosis, *Iron Shell*, 633 F.2d at 84, we have consistently found that "a statement by a child abuse victim that the abuser is a member of the victim's immediate household presents a sufficiently different case from that envisaged by the drafters of Rule 803(4) that it should not fall under the general rule" and that such statements "are reasonably pertinent" to treatment or diagnosis. *Renville*, 779 F.2d at 436–37; *see also United States v. Gabe*, 237 F.3d 954, 958 (8th Cir.2001); *Balfany*, 965 F.2d at 581; *U.S. v. Provost*, 875 F.2d 172, 177 (8th Cir.1989).

T.P.'s statements identifying Peneaux as the abuser are of the type reasonably relied upon by a physician for treatment or diagnosis. *See Renville*, 779 F.2d at 436–37; *Shaw*, 824 F.2d at 608. Due to the nature of child sexual abuse, a doctor must be able to identify and treat not only physical injury, but also the emotional and psychological problems that typically accompany sexual abuse by a family member. Moreover, such a statement may be relevant to prevent future occurrences of abuse and to the medical safety of the child. Dr. Strong explained that identification of the abuser is a matter of great concern because if the person who brought the child to the clinic is the abuser, the child should not leave with that individual. She also testified about her need to report problem relationships to the state as mandated by a South Dakota law requiring physicians to prevent an abused child from being returned to an environment where the child cannot be adequately protected from recurrent abuse. S.D. Codified Laws § 26–8A–3 (2005).

The more difficult Rule 803(4) question relates to T.P.'s motive. The motive requirement means that the victim must have had a "selfish subjective motive of receiving proper medical treatment" or the state of mind of someone seeking medical treatment. *United States v. Turning Bear*, 357 F.3d 730, 739 (8th Cir. 2004); *Gabe*, 237 F.3d at 958. To satisfy this rule, a proponent must show that a child understands "the medical significance of being truthful." *United States v. Sumner*, 204 F.3d 1182, 1186 (8th Cir. 2000). This requirement is especially important in sexual abuse cases since "not even an adult necessarily understands the connection between a sex abuser's identity and her medical treatment." *Gabe*, 237 F.3d at 958.

Dr. Strong testified that she told T.P. what they were going to "visit about" and showed T.P. her medical equipment. She also explained to T.P. that as her doctor she needed to treat her for any types of germs that might be on her private parts and that it was important for her to be honest in answering questions because germs could make her sick. According to Dr. Strong's testimony T.P. appeared to understand what the doctor had explained to her, and that evidence was relevant on the issue of the little girl's understanding of the need to tell the truth. Even if Dr. Strong's testimony were erroneously admitted, however, it would not have been plain error since Peneaux's substantial rights were not affected in light of the significant amount of other evidence identifying Peneaux as T.P.'s abuser. Dr. Strong was one of many witnesses who testified that T.P. had identified Peneaux before trial as her abuser. Many of T.P.'s prior statements were admissible under Rule 807, and others were not objected to at trial or on this appeal.

* * *

An error in admitting hearsay testimony in a child sexual abuse case is harmless if the evidence was cumulative to other hearsay testimony to which the defendant did not object. *Gabe*, 237 F.3d at 958–59. Norris testified that Allison had stated that the circular scar on N.P. "could be burns," but Norris later testified without objection that N.P. said Peneaux had burned him. Moreover, T.P.'s testimony that she had seen Peneaux burn N.P. with a cigarette had already been admitted without objection, and Peneaux has not challenged that evidence on appeal. Although Peneaux objected to Dr. Strong's testimony about her physical examination of N.P., he did not object to admission of the videotape of the physical examinations she conducted of both children. T.P. had already testified that Peneaux had burned her and that had been confirmed by Dr. Strong. The jury was able to view and compare the scars from T.P. and N.P. and make its own findings from all this evidence. We conclude that permitting Penny Norris to testify to Dr. Allison's comments was at most harmless error.

Peneaux contends that the district court violated his right to confrontation by allowing Dr. Strong and Penny Norris to testify about N.P.'s statements because they were testimonial in nature, citing *Crawford v. Washington*, 541 U.S. 36 (2004). Peneaux argues that Dr. Strong was acting on behalf of the Child Advocacy Center when she talked to N.P. and he made the statements, and that the Center is a collaborative effort between the medical system, law enforcement, social services, and the judiciary. N.P.'s statements to Penny Norris were "elicited through the foster parent's interrogation" he claims. Since foster parents are answerable to DSS, he contends that such questioning could result in a report to the agency and a referral to law enforcement.

In *Crawford*, the Supreme Court held that the confrontation clause bars the admission of testimonial statements unless the accused has had a prior opportunity to cross examine an unavailable declarant. *Crawford*, 541 U.S. at 53–54. The Court gave some examples of a "core class of testimonial statements," including affidavits, depositions, and prior testimony not subject to cross examination. *Id.* at 52. The closest the Court came to defining the term "testimonial statement" was in its catchall example of "statements that were made under circumstances which would lead an objective witness reasonably to believe that the statement would be available for use at a later trial." *Id.* After this general discussion the Court decided that "[s]tatements taken by police officers in the course of interrogations are also testimonial" even when unsworn. *Id.* The Court also indicated that it was speaking of interrogation in a colloquial sense rather than a technical one. *Id.* at 53 n.4.

We applied *Crawford* in *United States v. Bordeaux*, 400 F.3d 548 (8th Cir.2005), a case involving a child sex abuse victim who was only available by closed circuit television for much of her testimony and for all of her cross examination. The district court in *Bordeaux* had admitted a videotaped statement of the child victim made in an interview with someone the government referred to as a "forensic interviewer." Two videotapes had been made, and one was specifically prepared for law enforcement purposes. *Id.* at 555. We held that the admission of the child's statement had violated the defendant's confrontation rights because (1) the purpose of her interview had been "to collect information for law enforcement" so her statement was testimonial, and (2) the child had not been available in the courtroom for cross examination. *Id.* We review a confrontation clause challenge de novo and the "underlying factual determinations for clear error." *Id.* at 552.

The case before the court differs from *Bordeaux* in important ways. N.P. was taken to Dr. Strong by his foster parents for a medical examination after they noticed "some marks on his body". Dr. Strong is a pediatrician, and no forensic interview preceded her meeting with N.P. Dr. Strong's interview with N.P. was for the purpose of ensuring his health and protection, and there is no evidence that the interview resulted in any referral to law enforcement. The interview lacked the "formality of . . . questioning," the substantial "government involvement," and "the law enforcement purpose" present in *Bordeaux*. 400 F.3d at 555–56. Dr. Strong testified at trial and was available for cross examination about her physical findings and about her interview with N.P. Although N.P. did not testify, his statements to Dr. Strong about his burn were merely cumulative to the testimony other witnesses had given without objection about what N.P. had said about his scar. N.P. was also not the victim of the charged offense, unlike the child whose interview at issue in *Bordeaux*. Where statements are made to a physician seeking to give medical aid in the form of diagnosis or treatment, they are presumptively nontestimonial. *See State v. Vaught* 682 N.W.2d 284, 291 (Neb.2004); *compare State v. Snowden*, 867 A.2d 314, 329–30 (Md. 2005) (declining to extend the reasoning of *Vaught* to testimony of social workers). N.P.'s statements to Dr. Strong fall into the this treatment category and were nontestimonial in nature.

Appellant also complains that the statements of N.P. to Penny Norris are testimonial under *Crawford* because Norris was an agent of the state when she elicited statements from N.P. The premise of this argument is that foster parents are agents of the state, yet Peneaux cites no case treating foster parents as such. A contrary body of case law indicates that foster parents are generally not considered agents of the state. *See White v. Chambliss*, 112 F.3d 731, 739 (4th Cir.1997) (state has no affirmative duty for children placed in foster care); *Weller v. Dep't of Social Servs. for Baltimore*, 901 F.2d 387, 392 (4th Cir.1990) ("the harm suffered by a child at the hands of his foster parents is not harm inflicted by state agents"); *K.H. Through Murphy v. Morgan*, 914 F.2d 846, 852 (7th Cir.1990) ("We may assume, without having to decide . . . that the foster parents, even if paid by the state, are not state agents for constitutional purposes"); *Lintz v. Skipski*, 807 F. Supp. 1299, 1306–07 (W.D.Mich.1992) ("This Court is unaware of any case which has held that foster parents are [S]tate actors."). We conclude that Penny Norris was not an agent of the state and that N.P.'s statements to her were not testimonial within the meaning of *Crawford*.

IV.

In sum, we conclude that there was sufficient evidence for a reasonable jury to find Peneaux guilty of sexual abuse and assault, that the admission of Dr. Allison's statements about N.P. was at most harmless error, and that the able trial judge did not otherwise err or abuse his discretion in admitting disputed evidence. We therefore affirm the judgment of the district court.

NOTES AND QUESTIONS

1. *Multi-Part Test.* For a hearsay statement to be admissible under Rule 803(4), the statement must be reasonably pertinent to medical diagnosis or treatment. The *Peneaux* court set forth two requirements for admission under the hearsay exception: (1) the proponent of the statement must show that the statement is of the type "reasonably relied on by a physician in treatment or diagnosis" and (2) "the declarant's motive in making the statement was consistent with promoting treatment." *Peneaux*, 432 F.3d at 893. *See also Lovejoy v. United States*, 92 F.3d 628, 632 (8th Cir. 1996) (applying the two-part test for determining a statement's admissibility under Rule 803(4)); *Morgan v. Foretich*, 846 F.2d 941, 949 (4th Cir. 1988) (same). At the same time, the Tenth Circuit has expressly rejected this two-part test as "not contemplated by the rule and not necessary to ensure that the rule's purpose is carried out." *United States v. Joe*, 8 F.3d 1488, 1494 (10th Cir. 1993). The Tenth Circuit asserts that "the plain language of Rule 803(4) should guide [the court] in determining the admissibility of statements made for purposes of medical diagnosis or treatment." *Id.* at 1494 n.5. Which is the better view? Does the text of Rule 803(4) provide support for the two-part test?

2. *Statements Identifying the Perpetrator of Child Sexual Abuse.* Ordinarily, statements identifying the sexual abuser do not fall within the medical examination exception. FED. R. EVID. 803(4), ADVISORY COMMITTEE'S NOTE. However, in *Peneaux*, the court permitted the statement by the child victims identifying the defendant. Other courts have held that statements made by a child to a physician which identify the sexual abuser are "reasonably pertinent to diagnosis or treatment." *See United States v. Lovejoy*, 92 F.3d 628, 632 (8th Cir. 1996); *United States v. Joe*, 8 F.3d 1488, 1493 (10th Cir. 1993); *United States v. Balfany*, 965 F.2d 575, 579 (8th Cir. 1992); *Morgan v. Foretich*, 846 F.2d 941, 949 (4th Cir. 1988). Are statements by a child victim identifying the abuser of the type reasonably relied upon by a physician for treatment or diagnosis? Does it matter whether the abuser is a member of the victim's immediate household? What if the abuser was a next door neighbor or close family friend, not a member of the victim's immediate household? What is the medical purpose of questioning the child victim about the identity of the abuser? What dangers do you perceive in interpreting the medical diagnosis exception to include statements of culpability?

3. Statements Identifying the Perpetrator of Adult Sexual Abuse. Should the medical examination exception be interpreted to include statements made by an adult victim of sexual abuse identifying her estranged husband as the abuser? Is the identity of the abuser reasonably pertinent to treatment in virtually every sexual assault case, even those *not* involving children? *See United States v. Joe*, 8 F.3d 1488 (10th Cir. 1993), and Problem 8-2.

4. Statements Made to a Social Worker or Foster Parent. In *Peneaux*, the court admitted out-of-court statements made by T.P. to a tribal investigator, social worker, pediatrician, and T.P.'s foster parents. The court also admitted hearsay statements by N.P., T.P.'s brother, to Penny Norris, a foster parent, and Dr. Lora Strong. *Peneaux*, 432 F.3d at 888–89. Are T.P.'s and N.P.'s statements admissible under Rule 803(4)? Some, but not others? What were T.P.'s and N.P.'s motives in making each of these hearsay statements? In each case, were the children's motives "consistent with promoting [medical] treatment"? *Peneaux*, 432 F.3d at 893.

5. Statements Made by the Parent or Child Guardian. Are hearsay statements made under Rule 803(4) identifying the sexual abuser limited to those made by the child-patient? What if the hearsay statements to a doctor identifying the assailant in a child molestation case are made by a parent or guardian? In *United States v. Yazzie*, 59 F.3d 807 (9th Cir. 1994), the court cautioned against admitting such statements:

> A parent's statement to a doctor identifying the assailant in a child molestation case must be treated as suspect. Indeed, one of the most bitter ironies of these cases is that the perpetrators are usually parents or relatives who are supposed to act in the child's best interest. In the drama that unfolds during the medical examination of a child molestation victim, a parent's or guardian's motive for casting blame may or may not be in the child's best interest or for the purpose of medical diagnosis. For example, a parent might misidentify the assailant in an effort to protect the other spouse, to avoid reprisal from the other spouse, to avoid having suspicion cast upon him or her, or to incriminate the other spouse for personal motives.

Id. at 813 (citations omitted).

Despite this strong admonition to the contrary, the court in *Yazzie* ultimately ruled that the parent's statements were properly admitted under the medical treatment exception. *Yazzie*, 59 F.3d at 813. *See also Lovejoy v. United States*, 92 F.3d 628, 632 (8th Cir. 1996) (statements made by the child victim's mother to a nurse implicating the defendant as the sexual abuser properly admitted under the medical diagnosis exception). In light of all of the dangers that weigh against trustworthiness, why do you think the court in *Yazzie* admitted the parent's statements?

6. Admission of Out-of-Court Statements Where the Child Victim Testifies. While T.P. testified at trial, N.P. did not. Is the Sixth Amendment Confrontation Clause implicated in both cases? In *Crawford v. Washington*, 541 U.S. 36 (2004), the majority stated: "The Clause does not bar admission of a statement so long as the declarant is present at trial to defend or explain it." *Id.* at 58 n.9.

STATE v. KRASKY
736 N.W.2d 636 (Minn. 2007)

Appellant State of Minnesota appealed from a pretrial order barring admission of statements made to a nurse by a child victim, T.K., who was incompetent to testify at trial by reason of her young age. The court of appeals reversed, holding that admission of the statements would not violate the Confrontation Clause rights of respondent Edward Richard Krasky, and Krasky appealed. We vacated and remanded for reconsideration in light of our decisions in *State v. Bobadilla*, 709 N.W.2d 243 (Minn.), *cert. denied* 549 U.S. 953 (2006), and *State v. Scacchetti*, 711 N.W.2d 508 (Minn. 2006), both of which dealt with application of the Confrontation Clause to statements by child victims to medical professionals. On remand, the court of appeals affirmed the district court order barring admission of T.K.'s statements. The state now brings this appeal, arguing that T.K.'s statements to a nurse are not testimonial and therefore admission of those statements poses no Confrontation Clause problem. We reverse.

On April 22, 2004, T.K.'s foster mother discovered six year old T.K. engaging in sexual behavior with M.K., her younger sister. When T.K.'s foster mother discussed this behavior with T.K., T.K. said that Krasky, her biological father, had engaged in various sexual behaviors with T.K. and M.K. Over the next several days, T.K. continued to engage in inappropriate behavior with her sister and again mentioned to her foster mother certain sexual behavior with Krasky.[1]

On May 12, 2004, the Willmar Police Department received a child protection report concerning T.K. (presumably made by the foster mother). Thereafter, Timothy Manuel, a detective with the Willmar Police Department, and Charlotte Hand, a social worker with Kandiyohi County Family Services who conducts child protection investigations, discussed the situation and decided to have Midwest Children's Resource Center (MCRC) interview and examine T.K. [footnote omitted]. On May 20, 2004, T.K.'s foster mother gave T.K. a ride to MCRC where they were met by Hand and Tina Mages, the girls' adoption social worker.

MCRC nurse Margaret Carney first spoke to the foster mother, who described T.K.'s inappropriate behavior and the comments T.K. made regarding the sexual abuse. The foster mother also relayed some limited medical history. While Hand and Mages watched from an observation room, Carney interviewed T.K. and performed a physical examination of her. The interview and the examination were videotaped, although the physical exam was conducted out of view of the camera. Carney told T.K. that T.K. was being assessed in order to evaluate T.K.'s health and it was important for T.K. to tell the truth. During the assessment, T.K. repeatedly stated that Krasky touched her genitals, penetrated her, and made her touch his genitals. Following the assessment, Carney tested T.K. for sexually transmitted diseases and made a recommendation for psychotherapy by a therapist who specializes in children who have been sexually abused.

Krasky was charged with multiple counts of both first and second degree criminal sexual conduct in violation of Minn.Stat. §§ 609.342, 609.343 (2006). The state gave notice to Krasky that it intended to admit at trial T.K.'s statements to Carney or the videotape of the interview, and Krasky made a timely motion to suppress T.K.'s out of

---

[1] As of April 2004, Krasky had not had any contact with T.K. in approximately 18 months, having been incarcerated for much of that period in connection with various assault convictions stemming from physical abuse of T.K. and his other children.

court statements claiming that admission of them would violate his right of confrontation. At a hearing on October 12, 2004, the prosecutor argued that Krasky had forfeited his confrontation rights by creating a violent atmosphere in the home. The state stipulated that T.K. and M.K. were not competent witnesses and were therefore unavailable to testify. The district court determined that T.K., then six years old, was incompetent to testify and therefore unavailable because T.K. "lacks the capacity to truthfully and accurately relate the facts about the defendant's alleged abuse," apparently due to her young age and developmental delays. The court concluded that T.K.'s statements during the MCRC interview and examination were testimonial and that the statements were therefore inadmissible. . . .

The state appealed from the pretrial order, and the court of appeals reversed the court's order suppressing T.K.'s statements. [footnote omitted]. The court held that the statements were not testimonial because they were made at least in part for medical purposes and, as a result, the court concluded that admission of the statements would not violate Krasky's rights under the Confrontation Clause. Krasky appealed, and we granted review, stayed Krasky's appeal, and ultimately remanded to the court of appeals for reconsideration in light of our decisions in *Bobadilla*, 709 N.W.2d at 243, and *Scacchetti*, 711 N.W.2d at 508.

On remand, the court of appeals considered not only the *Bobadilla* and *Scacchetti* decisions, but also *Davis v. Washington*, 547 U.S. 813 (2006), which had been recently decided. The court of appeals interpreted *Davis* as establishing that statements are testimonial when made in a nonemergency situation in response to government questions about past events that are potentially relevant to later criminal prosecution. The court determined that T.K.'s statements were made to Carney in a nonemergency situation because T.K. had been removed from Krasky's home and his parental rights had been terminated. Further, the court concluded, without explanation, that there was "no identified medical reason for the interview." The court of appeals concluded that T.K.'s statements were testimonial and could not be admitted at trial. . . . This appeal followed.

The sole issue in this case is whether statements made by a child victim to a nurse at MCRC are testimonial, and therefore inadmissible under the Confrontation Clause. [footnote omitted]. When appealing from a pretrial order suppressing evidence, the state must establish that the order was erroneous. We employ a de novo standard of review when determining whether admission of evidence will violate a criminal defendant's rights under the Confrontation Clause. *State v. Caulfield*, 722 N.W.2d 304, 308 (Minn. 2006).

The Sixth Amendment states that "[i]n all criminal prosecutions the accused shall enjoy the right * * * to be confronted with the witnesses against him." U.S. Const. amend. VI; *see also* Minn. Const. art. 1, § 6 ("The accused shall enjoy the right * * * to be confronted with the witnesses against him * * *"). This clause requires that all prior testimonial statements be excluded in criminal trials unless the declarant is unavailable to testify at trial and the defendant has had a prior opportunity to cross examine the declarant regarding the statement. *See Crawford v. Washington*, 541 U.S. 36, 68 (2004). The state bears the burden of proving a declarant's statements are not testimonial.

*   *   *

In this case, the assessment of T.K. was conducted at a children's hospital rather than at a law enforcement center, and no law enforcement officer was present. The referral to MCRC was a joint decision made by social services and law enforcement, but there is no indication that the MCRC nurse who conducted the assessment of T.K. in this case was acting as a proxy for law enforcement. Accordingly, T.K.'s statements to Carney are clearly less the product of a police interrogation than the statements at issue in *Bobadilla.* As in *Scacchetti*, we conclude that a nurse practitioner employed by MCRC is not a government actor. 711 N.W.2d at 514–15.

We conclude that the primary purpose of T.K.'s statements to Carney was to assess and protect T.K.'s health and welfare. Carney conducted a physical examination of T.K., questioned the foster mother about T.K.'s medical history, tested T.K. for sexually transmitted diseases, recommended that T.K. receive psychotherapy, and repeatedly told T.K. that an examination was necessary in order to ensure that T.K. was healthy. That Krasky had been incarcerated and no longer possessed parental rights at the time of Carney's assessment does not mean that T.K.'s future health and welfare were not in question. The harms of child abuse are not limited to the abused child's physical well being. Although future acts of abuse were unlikely given that Krasky's parental rights had been terminated and he was incarcerated at the time T.K. reported the abuse, Carney's recommendation that T.K. receive psychotherapy indicates that her mental health was still at risk. Further, unlike in *Bobadilla* and *Scacchetti*, there is no indication in the record that T.K. was examined after she first reported the abuse and before meeting with Carney. Therefore, it could be said that T.K.'s current physical health remained in doubt. In addition, seeking an assessment from Carney was a natural response to T.K.'s inappropriate behavior towards other children and, following the assessment, T.K. was eventually removed from foster care and the company of the other children living there. Consequently, we conclude that T.K.'s statements to Carney were nontestimonial and that admission of those statements will not violate Krasky's rights under the Confrontation Clause. [footnote omitted].

* * *

Krasky argues that the Supreme Court's holding in *Davis v. Washington* calls into question the validity of our holdings in *Bobadilla* and *Scacchetti* (both decided before *Davis*). Krasky's reliance on *Davis* is misplaced. The *Davis* case involved two separate domestic violence cases. 126 S.Ct. at 2270–73. In the first case, a 911 operator gathered information about an assailant and details of the assault. *Id.* at 2270–72. The victim never testified and the district court admitted the victim's out of court statements to the 911 operator. *Id.* at 2271. In the second case, police arrived at the victim's home in response to a report of domestic abuse. *Id.* at 2272. The victim told the police that the assailant (her husband) had assaulted her and she signed an affidavit describing the assault. The *Davis* Court concluded that the 911 call in the first case did not produce a testimonial statement because the circumstances indicated that "its *primary purpose* was to enable police assistance to meet an ongoing emergency." *Id.* at 2277 (emphasis added). With respect to the on scene statements in the second case, the court held that there was no emergency in progress and that the "*primary*, if not indeed the sole, *purpose* of the interrogation was to investigate a possible crime." *Id.* at 2278 (emphasis added).

Krasky argues that Carney was not assessing or responding to an immediate danger and, therefore, she was merely seeking to preserve evidence for trial. We do not read the *Davis* opinion to hold that only those statements made in response to an immediate danger are nontestimonial. The facts of *Davis* required the court "to determine more precisely which police interrogations produce testimony" and the precise question was whether emergency calls to police are treated differently than statements made in the regular course of a police investigation. *Id.* at 2273–74. The court specifically noted that its holding was limited to its facts. *Id.* at 2278 n.5 ("[O]ur holding is not an exhaustive classification of all conceivable statements or even all conceivable statements in response to police interrogation, but rather a resolution of the cases before us and those like them."(internal quotation marks and citations omitted)). We conclude that the *Davis* decision leaves undisturbed our conclusions in *Bobadilla* and *Scacchetti* that statements elicited by a medical professional for the primary purpose of protecting a child sexual assault victim's health and welfare are nontestimonial.

We conclude that T.K.'s statements to Carney are nontestimonial and admission of those statements will not violate Krasky's right of confrontation under the Sixth Amendment. [footnote omitted]. The decision of the court of appeals is reversed.

DISSENT

PAGE, Justice (dissenting).

I respectfully dissent, for two reasons. First, on the facts presented here, the child's statements at Midwest Children's Resource Center (MCRC) are testimonial under the Supreme Court's decision in *Davis v. Washington*, 547 U.S. 813 (2006). Second, even if the child's statements at MCRC are not testimonial, they are not admissible as hearsay because they formed the basis for the district court's finding that the child was incompetent to testify. I therefore conclude that the district court properly excluded the statements.

* * *

We first applied what guidance there was in *Crawford* to statements made to a 911 operator and to police officers during a field investigation. *State v. Wright*, 701 N.W.2d 802 (Minn.2005), *vacated and remanded*, 548 U.S. 923 (2006). In *Wright*, in the absence of a more definitive explanation from the Supreme Court, we listed eight considerations we thought relevant to whether a statement is testimonial. Those considerations included such things as "whether the declarant was a victim or an observer" and "whether it was the police or the declarant who initiated the conversation." *Id.* at 812.[1]

We then applied our eight part test to statements by child sexual abuse victims in *State v. Bobadilla*, 709 N.W.2d 243 (Minn. 2006), and *State v. Scacchetti*, 711 N.W.2d 508 (Minn. 2006). In *Bobadilla*, the court concluded that statements by a child sexual abuse victim to a child protection worker were not testimonial by reference to what it concluded was the "main purpose" of the interview: "assessing and responding to imminent risks to [the child's] health and welfare." 709 N.W.2d at 255. I dissented in *Bobadilla* because the interview of the child was part of a police interrogation, in the presence of a police officer, conducted by "a government official who was taking the statement as a surrogate interviewer for the police." *Id.* at 257 (Page, J., dissenting). In *Scacchetti*, we concluded that the child's statements were not testimonial because they were made to a pediatric nurse practitioner whose "purpose in interviewing and examining [the child] was to assess her medical condition," 711 N.W.2d at 515; "no government actor initiated, participated, or was involved in any way," *id.* at 514.

* * *

---

[1] The eight considerations we listed were: (1) whether the declarant was a victim or an observer; (2) the declarant's purpose in speaking with the officer; (3) whether it was the police or the declarant who initiated the conversation; (4) the location where the statements were made; (5) the declarant's emotional state; (6) the level of formality and structure of the conversation; (7) the officer's purpose in speaking with the declarant; and (8) if and how the statements were recorded. *Wright*, 701 N.W.2d at 812–13.

From the Supreme Court's reasoning in *Davis*, it appears to me that some of the eight factors we recounted in *Wright* such as whether the declarant was a victim or an observer may no longer be germane to the analysis. Instead, the Court's distinction between testimonial and nontestimonial statements appears to depend on four factors: (1) when the statement was made (for example, whether the statement was made contemporaneous with or after the incident); (2) what the statement describes (for example, whether the statement describes a current emergency or past events); (3) if describing a current emergency, whether the declarant's statement is necessary to resolve the current emergency; and (4) the circumstances giving rise to the statement (such as by whom the statement was initiated and the level of its formality).

From what this record discloses about T.K.'s statements to MCRC, they are testimonial. The questioning took place approximately 18 months after Krasky's last contact with T.K. There was no current emergency; as the court acknowledges, by the time T.K. was interviewed at MCRC, Krasky had already been incarcerated and his parental rights had been terminated. T.K.'s statements to MCRC recounted, in response to questions, how past criminal events began and progressed. That is to say, the nurse elicited from T.K. a narrative of her alleged abuse at the hands of Krasky. The questioning was intended as a substitute for, and indeed produced, "precisely what a witness does on direct examination." *Davis*, 126 S.Ct. at 2278. Indeed, the nurse began her questioning of T.K. by asking T.K. to do what the court asks witnesses to do: promise to tell the truth. Finally, the interview at MCRC was at the behest of government actors, having been arranged by the police, in conjunction with a county social worker. On this record, T.K.'s statements at MCRC were testimonial and therefore inadmissible in the absence of T.K.'s testimony or a previous opportunity for Krasky to cross examine her.

The court in this case rests its decision on what it characterizes as "the primary purpose of T.K.'s statements to Carney," that is, "to assess and protect T.K.'s health and welfare." Doing so is misguided. First, to say the "primary purpose" of the statement was to assess T.K.'s health begs the question because that "primary purpose" does not alter the fact that another purpose for taking the statement was to assist in the prosecution of Krasky. Second, Carney's purpose in questioning T.K. may have been to assess T.K.'s health, but it cannot be said on this record that T.K. had any understanding of why she was at MCRC and therefore I cannot assume that in answering Carney's questions T.K. thought she was protecting her health and welfare. Finally, even if T.K. understood the purpose of the MCRC examination, it seems to me that the court's reliance on "the primary purpose of T.K.'s statements to Carney" is simply a fallback to the historical underpinnings of the hearsay exception under Minn. R. Evid. 803(4) for "[s]tatements made for purposes of medical diagnosis and treatment," namely, that statements made for purposes of medical treatment provide " 'special assurance of reliability' " because of " 'the patient's belief that accuracy is essential to effective treatment.' " *State v. Robinson*, 718 N.W.2d 400, 404 (Minn. 2006) (quoting 2 John W. Strong, et al., *McCormick on Evidence* § 277, at 247 (4th ed.1992)). If anything is clear in the Supreme Court's definition of "testimony," it is that statements are not to be categorized as "nontestimonial" (and therefore admissible) simply because a court believes them to be inherently reliable. *See Crawford*, 541 U.S. at 61 ("Admitting statements deemed reliable by a judge is fundamentally at odds with the right of confrontation."). I therefore conclude that T.K.'s statements at MCRC are testimonial under *Davis*.

* * *

Finally, I note that only T.K.'s statements to Carney during the MCRC are at issue here. *Crawford* distinguished between "[a]n accuser who makes a formal statement to government officers" and "a person who makes a casual remark to an acquaintance." 541 U.S. at 51. This case began after T.K.'s foster mother reprimanded her for inappropriately touching T.K.'s sister, and T.K. defended herself on grounds that Krasky did the same to her. I do not believe that the Supreme Court's concern with testimonial statements in *Crawford* and *Davis* is meant to reach T.K.'s spontaneous statements to her foster mother that alerted the foster mother to the possibility of abuse in the first place. Nor does T.K.'s age inappropriate behavior, such as pretending to masturbate, constitute testimony. Similarly, although I find T.K.'s statements to Carney inadmissible, the results of Carney's physical examination of T.K. would still be admissible. Thus, without expressing any opinion as to the viability of the state's case on remand, I do not believe that excluding T.K.'s statements to Carney necessarily bars prosecution of Krasky. . . . I respectfully dissent.

NOTES AND QUESTIONS

1. *Primary Purpose Test.* In *Krasky*, the majority and dissent sharply disagreed over whether an emergency existed at the time of the questioning of the child. The dissent argued there was no medical emergency, observing that the questioning took place approximately 18 months after the defendant's last contact with the T.K. *Krasky*, 736 N.W.2d at 647 (Paige, J., dissenting). The dissent characterized the majority's application of the "primary purpose" test as "simply a fallback to the historical underpinnings of the hearsay exception." *Id.* at 648. The dissent maintained that the majority conflated the "primary purpose" test with the requirements for admissibility under the medical treatment and diagnosis exception to the hearsay rule. According to the majority, the primary purpose of T.K.'s statements to nurse Carney was to assess and protect T.K.'s health and welfare. The majority further argued that the ruling in *Davis v. Washington*, 547 U.S. 813 (2006) is not limited to statements made in response to an "immediate danger." *Id.* at 643. Do you agree with the majority or dissent?

2. *Statement Made for Multiple Purposes.* What if the questioning has multiple purposes, e.g., for medical diagnosis and treatment, and to collect evidence to be used in a criminal prosecution? Are the statements elicited during such questioning testimonial under *Davis*?

3. *Relevant Factors for Determining the "Primary Purpose" of the Questioning.* In Judge Paige's dissenting opinion, he maintains that the distinction between testimonial and nontestimonial statements under *Davis'* "primary purpose" test may depend on four factors:

> (1) when the statement was made (for example, whether the statement was made contemporaneous with or after the incident); (2) what the statement describes (for example, whether the statement describes a current emergency or past events); (3) if describing a current emergency, whether the declarant's statement is necessary to resolve the current emergency; and (4) the circumstances giving rise to the statement (such as by whom the statement was initiated and the level of its formality).

Id. at 647 (Paige, J., dissenting). Do you agree? Are these relevant factors for determining whether the primary purpose of the questioning was to respond to a medical emergency?

4. *Functional Equivalent of Police Interrogation.* In *Crawford*, the Supreme Court noted that statements made during the course of interrogations are testimonial because police interrogations bear the "closest kinship to the abuses at which the Confrontation Clause was directed." *Crawford*, 541 U.S. at 68. Does questioning by a doctor, nurse, or social worker as part of a sexual assault examination, at the behest of the police, constitute the "functional equivalent" of a police interrogation? *See Crawford*, at 51 (stating that a "core class" of testimonial' statements exist, which include *ex parte* in-court testimony or its "functional equivalent"). In such a case, is the person conducting the forensic examination acting as an agent of the police? The courts that have considered the issue are divided. *See State v. Hooper*, 176 P.3d 911 (Idaho 2007) (because there was a clear connection between the police and nurse who conducted the forensic interview, the interview was the functional equivalent of a police interrogation and the statements were testimonial); *State v. Mark*, 101 P.3d 349 (Or. 2004) (same); *State v. Snowden*, 867 A.2d 314 (Md. 2005) (same). *But see People v. Vigil*, 127 P.3d 916 (Colo. 2006) (statements to a doctor conducting a sexual assault exam were nontestimonial where the police officer was not involved in the medical exam and not present in the examination room); *State v. T.T.* 815 N.E.2d 789 (Ill. 2004) (holding that statements by a child to a physician describing the cause of symptoms and pain and the general character of the assault were nontestimonial); *People v. Geno*, 683 N.W.2d 687 (Mich. App. 2004) (child's response to an interviewer who was not a government employee was not testimonial); *State v. Vaught*, 682 N.W.2d 284 (Neb. 2004) (statement by a child victim to a physician, admitted under the medical diagnosis or treatment exception, was not testimonial). Further, in *People v. Vigil*, 127 P.3d 916 (Colo. 2006), the Colorado Supreme Court stated: "The fact that the doctor was a member of the child protection team does not, in and of itself, make him a government official absent a more direct and controlling police presence." *Id.* at 923–24. Do you agree? Does the issue ultimately turn on the whether the doctor is being directed and controlled by the police? Whether the police officer was present during the questioning? Whether the police officer and social worker, who conducted the questioning were working together?

In *Krasky*, Nurse Carney conducted the assessment of T.K. at a children's hospital. There were no law enforcement officers present at the time and, according to the majority, there was no indication that Carney was acting as a proxy for law enforcement when she conducted the assessment of T.K. *Id.* at 641. Does the primary purpose test articulated by the Supreme Court in *Davis* apply in the absence of custodial interrogation or its functional equivalent?

5. *Focusing on the Objective Witness or Surrounding Circumstances?* Are statements to a doctor testimonial if the circumstances would have led an objective witness reasonably to believe that the statements would be available for use at a later trial? *See Crawford*, 541 U.S. at 52. Does the term "objective witness" refer to an objectively reasonable person in the declarant's position? In *People v. Vigil*, 127 P.3d 916 (Colo.2006), the court applied an objective test "focusing on the reasonable expectations of a person in the declarant's position." *Id.* at 924. *See also United States v. Cromer*, 389 F.3d 662, 675 (6th Cir. 2004) (same). Applying the objective witness standard, would a child believe that his statements to a doctor describing the source of his pain and his symptoms would be used in a later trial? *See Vigil*, at 926 ("We hold that no objective witness in the position of the child would believe that his statements to the doctor would be used at trial."). However, one court has adopted a different approach focusing instead on whether the circumstances surrounding the questioning indicate that the statements will be available for trial. *See State v. Snowden*, 867 A.2d 314, 329 (Md. 2005). Which is the better approach, a declarant-centered approach (an objectively reasonable person in

the declarant's position) or focusing on the circumstances of the questioning, for determining whether a statement is testimonial?

PROBLEM

Problem 8-2. *Statements of Adult Victim of Sexual Abuse Identifying the Abuser.* The defendant, Melvin Joe, and his wife, Julia, were in the process of obtaining a divorce. They had one child together, Jessica. Defendant, upset over the impending divorce, went on a drunken binge. He drove his mother's Chevy Blazer over to Julia's home. He knocked on the door and when there was no answer, he kicked opened the door and entered the home brandishing an unloaded.22 caliber rifle. Defendant and Julia fought and he became physically abusive. Julia's neighbor, Matilda Washburn, came over to help Julia convince the defendant to leave. While the defendant agreed to leave the home, he persisted in circling Julia's house. Afraid of what the defendant might do, Julia and Matilda attempted to flee to Matilda's home with Jessica. While Jessica fled safely to Matilda's home, the defendant struck Julia with the Blazer. As he was turning around to take another run at Julia, Matilda was able to help Julia climb onto an abandoned pick-up truck bed that was sitting on four wooden stumps in a field next to Matilda's home.

Not deterred by the new obstacle, defendant proceeded to ram the bed from the end opposite where the two women stood huddled. Upon impact, defendant continued to accelerate, knocking the truck bed off the wooden stumps and pushing it over onto Julia and Matilda Washburn. Eventually, defendant accelerated enough to drive the bed so far forward that he ran over the two women. Both women died of massive internal and external injuries. Defendant then placed Julia's body in the Blazer and drove a few miles away. The police found the abandoned Blazer with the keys in the ignition along with Julia's body.

Defendant was charged with two counts of first degree murder. His defense was that at the time of the killings he was so intoxicated and enraged over the pending divorce that he did not have the requisite specific intent necessary to sustain a conviction for first degree murder. To rebut the defense theory, the government sought to introduce the testimony of Dr. Smoker. Dr. Smoker had treated Julia for rape, eight days before her murder. During the medical examination, Julia told Dr. Smoker that the defendant raped her and that she was afraid because he threatened to kill her if he found her with another man. The government argued that these statements to Dr. Smoker were admissible under Fed. R. Evid. 803(4) as statements for purpose of medical diagnosis. The defendant objected, contending that Julia's statements were not relevant to Dr. Smoker's medical treatment and therefore were not admissible under Rule 803(4). The government countered that in treating victim's of domestic violence and abuse, the identity of the perpetrator is relevant. Dr. Smoker needed to know the identity of Julia's rapist in order to counsel her about the rape. Are Julia's statements to Dr. Smoker admissible under Rule 803(4)? While Rule 803(4) permits the introduction into evidence of statements by a child abuse victim to a physician identifying the abuser, should this exception be expanded to admit statements by adult victims to doctors which identify the abuser? *See United States v. Joe*, 8 F.3d 1488 (10th Cir. 1993).

F. BUSINESS AND PUBLIC RECORDS

The admissibility of laboratory, scientific, or other law enforcement reports in criminal cases raises a unique set of problems under the Federal Rules of Evidence. The business records exception, Fed. R. Evid. 803(6), would appear to permit their admission into evidence, assuming that the statutory requirements are satisfied.[25] Rule 803(6) requires that the transaction in question (1) be recorded "at or near the time" of its occurrence (2) "by, or from information transmitted by, a person with knowledge," (3) kept in the course of a "regularly conducted business activity," and (4) that it was the regular practice of that business to make the document. Records prepared and kept in the ordinary course of business are presumed reliable for two reasons. "First, businesses depend on such records to conduct their own affairs; accordingly, the employees who generate them have a strong motive to be accurate and none to be deceitful. Second, routine and habitual patterns of creation lend reliability to business records."[26] The Advisory Committee's Note to Rule 803(6) further provides:

> The element of unusual reliability of business records is said variously to be supplied by systematic checking, by regularity and continuity which produce habits of precision, by actual experience of business in relying upon them, or by a duty to make an accurate record as part of a continuing job or occupation." (Citations omitted.)

Additionally, the justification for excepting business records is grounded on necessity. Since business records often contain information derived from a variety of sources, Rule 803(6) averts the need for calling all persons involved in the transaction. Furthermore, the rule recognizes that if all the participants in the business transaction were called to testify, they often would be unable to recall matters beyond those contained in the report due to their involvement in a large number of such transactions.[27] Thus, for example, when made on a routine basis, a laboratory report containing the analysis of a suspected controlled substance would be admissible as a business record under Fed. R. Evid. 803(6). Moreover, nothing in the language of the business record exception would restrict its admission in a criminal case.

Under the "public records" exception, Fed. R. Evid. 803(8), this same laboratory report, if prepared pursuant to a criminal investigation, would be excluded when offered against the accused in a criminal proceeding (see discussion of Rule 803(8)(B) and (C) below). The justification for the public records exception is likewise based on necessity and a presumption of reliability. The Advisory Committee's Note to Rule 803(8) states: "Justification for the exception is the assumption that a public official will perform his duty properly and the unlikelihood that he will remember details independently of the

---

[25] Rule 803(6), the business records exception, exempts from the hearsay rule:

A memorandum, report, record, or data compilation, in any form, of acts, events, conditions, opinions, or diagnoses, made at or near the time by, or from information transmitted by, a person with knowledge, if kept in the course of a regularly conducted business activity, and if it was the regular practice of that business activity to make the memorandum, report, record, or data compilation, all as shown by the testimony of the custodian or other qualified witness, unless the source of information or the method or circumstances of preparation indicate lack of trustworthiness. The term "business" as used in this paragraph includes business, institution, association, profession, occupation, and calling of every kind, whether or not conducted for profit.

[26] *United States v. Blackburn*, 992 F.2d 666, 670 (7th Cir. 1993); *see also* MICHAEL H. GRAHAM, HANDBOOK OF FEDERAL EVIDENCE § 803.6, at 867 (3d ed. 1991); GLENN WEISSENBERGER, FEDERAL RULES OF EVIDENCE § 803.29, at 409 (1987) (hereinafter WEISSENBERGER).

[27] WEISSENBERGER § 803.29, at 410.

record."[28] The trustworthiness of the statement is "premised on the assumption that public officials perform their duties properly without motive or interest other than to submit accurate and fair reports."[29] Necessity arises from the lack of independent memory. It is highly unlikely that a public official would have an independent memory of a particular agency action or entry where the duties require constant repetition of routine tasks. This would lead to calling numerous witnesses to testify to prove the activities reported in the public records, which would be both inconvenient and costly.

Both Rule 803(8)(B) and (C) provide restrictions on the admission of public records in criminal cases. Rule 803(8)(B) permits the admission of "records, reports, statements, or data compilations in any form, of public offices or agencies," setting forth matters observed pursuant to a legal duty to report, excluding, however, in criminal cases matters observed by police officers and other law enforcement personnel."[30] Rule 803(8)(C) allows evidence of factual findings resulting from investigations made pursuant to authority granted by law "in civil actions and proceedings and against the government in criminal cases." Thus, public reports containing factual findings resulting from an investigation are only admissible when offered against the government and are inadmissible when offered against a defendant in criminal cases.

The law enforcement exception in Rule 803(8)(B) is based on the presumed unreliability of observations made by law enforcement officials at the scene of the crime "because of the adversarial nature of the confrontation between the police and the defendant in criminal cases."[31] Congress was concerned about prosecutors attempting to prove their cases in chief simply by putting into evidence police officers' reports of their contemporaneous observations of crime."[32] At the same, the Rule 803(8)(C) requirement that evidence of factual findings contained in investigative reports may only be offered against the government is based upon the apparent concern of the drafters of the rule that use of records in criminal cases would cause "almost certain collision with confrontation rights."[33]

The problem with the formal structure of the Rule 803 exceptions is that only Rule 803(8) contains restrictions on the use of hearsay documents in criminal cases. None of the other hearsay exceptions, including the business records exception, limit the use of hearsay documents in criminal prosecutions. If hearsay statements prohibited under Rule 803(8)(B) or (C) can be admitted into evidence under Rule 803(6), the limiting aspects of Rule 803(8) are easily circumvented. In order to resolve this internal inconsistency in the hearsay rules, should the limitations imposed by Rule 803(8)(B) and (C) be read into the other hearsay exceptions, including Rule 803(6)? Stated another

---

[28] FED. R. EVID. 803(8), Advisory Committee Note.

[29] *United States v. Versaint*, 849 F.2d 827, 832 (3d Cir. 1988).

[30] Rule 803(8) provides: Public records and reports.

Records, reports, statements, or data compilations, in any form, of public offices or agencies, setting forth (A) the activities of the office or agency, or (B) matters observed pursuant to duty imposed by law as to which matters there was a duty to report, excluding, however, in criminal cases matters observed by police officers and other law enforcement personnel, or (C) in civil actions and proceedings and against the government in criminal cases, factual findings resulting from an investigation made pursuant to authority granted by law, unless the sources of information or other circumstances indicate lack of trustworthiness.

[31] S. Rep. No. 1277, 93d Cong., 2d Sess. (1974), *reprinted in* U.S.C.C.A.N. 7051, 7064; *see also United States v. Orozco*, 590 F.2d 789, 793 (9th Cir. 1979).

[32] *Orozco*, 590 F.2d at 794 (quoting *United States v. Grady*, 544 F.2d 598, 604 (2d Cir. 1976)).

[33] FED. R. EVID. 803(8) Advisory Committee Note.

way, if public records are inadmissible under the public records exception, does Rule 803(8) prohibit their admission under any other hearsay exception?

The leading case is *United States v. Oates*.[34] In *Oates*, the government sought to introduce against a criminal defendant the official report and handwritten worksheet of the Customs Service chemist whose analysis had revealed that a substance seized from the defendant's companion was heroin. The chemist did not testify at trial. The court held that the term "other law enforcement personnel" in Rule 803(8)(B) should be read "to include, at the least, any officer or employee of a governmental agency which has law enforcement responsibilities."[35] The court concluded that chemists of the United States Customs Service clearly fall within this definition. Thus, the chemist's report and worksheet prepared in connection with the analysis of the alleged controlled substance were inadmissible under the Rule 803(8)(B) restriction. The court went on to conclude that the same prohibitions should be read into Rule 803(6), and might preclude admission under other hearsay exceptions as well.

The ruling in *Oates*, however, is controversial. Some federal courts have rejected the logic of *Oates* altogether, while others have substantially narrowed its application. The admissibility of law enforcement reports under Fed. R. Evid. 803(8) and 803(6) will be analyzed in the cases and notes that follow.

[1]   Sixth Amendment Confrontation Clause — Reports Prepared in Anticipation of Litigation

MELENDEZ-DIAZ v. MASSACHUSETTS
129 S. Ct. 2527 (2009)

JUSTICE SCALIA delivered the opinion of the Court.

The Massachusetts courts in this case admitted into evidence affidavits reporting the results of forensic analysis which showed that material seized by the police and connected to the defendant was cocaine. The question presented is whether those affidavits are "testimonial," rendering the affiants "witnesses" subject to the defendant's right of confrontation under the Sixth Amendment.

I.

*   *   *

Melendez-Diaz was charged with distributing cocaine and with trafficking in cocaine in an amount between 14 and 28 grams. At trial, the prosecution placed into evidence [the substances seized by police]. It also submitted three "certificates of analysis" showing the results of the forensic analysis performed on the seized substances. The certificates reported the weight of the seized bags and stated that the bags "[h]a[ve] been examined with the following results: The substance was found to contain: Cocaine." The certificates were sworn to before a notary public by analysts at the State Laboratory Institute of the Massachusetts Department of Public Health, as required under Massachusetts law.

---

[34] 560 F.2d 45 (2d Cir. 1977).

[35] *Id.* at 68.

Petitioner objected to the admission of the certificates, asserting that our Confrontation Clause decision in *Crawford v. Washington*, 541 U.S. 36 (2004), required the analysts to testify in person. The objection was overruled, and the certificates were admitted pursuant to state law as "prima facie evidence of the composition, quality, and the net weight of the narcotic . . . analyzed." (citation omitted).

The jury found Melendez-Diaz guilty. He appealed, contending, among other things, that admission of the certificates violated his Sixth Amendment right to be confronted with the witnesses against him. The Appeals Court of Massachusetts rejected the claim, relying on the Massachusetts Supreme Judicial Court's decision in *Commonwealth v. Verde*, 827 N.E.2d 701, 7057–706 (2005), which held that the authors of certificates of forensic analysis are not subject to confrontation under the Sixth Amendment. The Supreme Judicial Court denied review. We granted certiorari.

II.

The Sixth Amendment to the United States Constitution, made applicable to the States via the Fourteenth Amendment, provides that "[i]n all criminal prosecutions, the accused shall enjoy the right . . . to be confronted with the witnesses against him." In *Crawford*, after reviewing the Clause's historical underpinnings, we held that it guarantees a defendant's right to confront those "who 'bear testimony'" against him. 541 U.S., at 51. A witness's testimony against a defendant is thus inadmissible unless the witness appears at trial or, if the witness is unavailable, the defendant had a prior opportunity for cross-examination. *Id.*, at 54.

Our opinion described the class of testimonial statements covered by the Confrontation Clause as follows:

> "Various formulations of this core class of testimonial statements exist: *ex parte* in-court testimony or its functional equivalent — that is, material such as affidavits, custodial examinations, prior testimony that the defendant was unable to cross-examine, or similar pretrial statements that declarants would reasonably expect to be used prosecutorially; extrajudicial statements . . . contained in formalized testimonial materials, such as affidavits, depositions, prior testimony, or confessions; statements that were made under circumstances which would lead an objective witness reasonably to believe that the statement would be available for use at a later trial." *Id.*, at 51–52 (internal quotation marks and citations omitted).

There is little doubt that the documents at issue in this case fall within the "core class of testimonial statements" thus described. Our description of that category mentions affidavits twice. The documents at issue here, while denominated by Massachusetts law "certificates," are quite plainly affidavits: "declaration[s] of facts written down and sworn to by the declarant before an officer authorized to administer oaths." Black's Law Dictionary 62 (8th ed.2004). They are incontrovertibly a "'solemn declaration or affirmation made for the purpose of establishing or proving some fact.'" *Crawford, supra*, at 51 (quoting 2 N. Webster, An American Dictionary of the English Language (1828)). The fact in question is that the substance found in the possession of Melendez-Diaz and his codefendants was, as the prosecution claimed, cocaine — the precise testimony the analysts would be expected to provide if called at trial. The "certificates" are functionally identical to live, in-court testimony, doing "precisely what a witness does on direct examination." *Davis v. Washington*, 547 U.S. 813, 830 (2006) (emphasis deleted).

Here, moreover, not only were the affidavits " 'made under circumstances which would lead an objective witness reasonably to believe that the statement would be available for use at a later trial,' " *Crawford, supra*, at 52, but under Massachusetts law the *sole purpose* of the affidavits was to provide "prima facie evidence of the composition, quality, and the net weight" of the analyzed substance, Mass. Gen. Laws, ch. 111, § 13. We can safely assume that the analysts were aware of the affidavits' evidentiary purpose, since that purpose — as stated in the relevant state-law provision — was reprinted on the affidavits themselves.

In short, under our decision in *Crawford* the analysts' affidavits were testimonial statements, and the analysts were "witnesses" for purposes of the Sixth Amendment. Absent a showing that the analysts were unavailable to testify at trial *and* that petitioner had a prior opportunity to cross-examine them, petitioner was entitled to " 'be confronted with' " the analysts at trial. *Crawford, supra*, at 54.[1]

*   *   *

III.

Respondent and the dissent advance a potpourri of analytic arguments in an effort to avoid this rather straightforward application of our holding in *Crawford*. Before addressing them, however, we must assure the reader of the falsity of the dissent's opening alarum that we are "sweep[ing] away an accepted rule governing the admission of scientific evidence" that has been "established for at least 90 years" and "extends across at least 35 States and six Federal Courts of Appeals."

The vast majority of the state-court cases the dissent cites in support of this claim come not from the last 90 years, but from the last 30, and not surprisingly nearly all of them rely on our decision in *Ohio v. Roberts*, 448 U.S. 56 (1980), or its since-rejected theory that unconfronted testimony was admissible as long as it bore indicia of reliability, *id.*, at 66. As for the six Federal Courts of Appeals cases cited by the dissent, five of them postdated and expressly relied on *Roberts*. The sixth predated *Roberts* but relied entirely on the same erroneous theory. See *Kay v. United States*, 255 F.2d 476, 480–481 (C.A.4 1958) (rejecting confrontation clause challenge "where there is reasonable necessity for [the evidence] and where . . . the evidence has those qualities of reliability and trustworthiness").

A review of cases that predate the *Roberts* era yields a mixed picture. As the dissent notes, three state supreme court decisions from the early 20th century denied confrontation with respect to certificates of analysis regarding a substance's alcohol content. But other state courts in the same era reached the opposite conclusion. At least this much is entirely clear: In faithfully applying *Crawford* to the facts of this case, we are not overruling 90 years of settled jurisprudence. It is the dissent that seeks to

---

[1] Contrary to the dissent's suggestion, we do not hold, and it is not the case, that anyone whose testimony may be relevant in establishing the chain of custody, authenticity of the sample, or accuracy of the testing device, must appear in person as part of the prosecution's case. While the dissent is correct that "[i]t is the obligation of the prosecution to establish the chain of custody," this does not mean that everyone who laid hands on the evidence must be called. As stated in the dissent's own quotation, from *United States v. Lott*, 854 F.2d 244, 250 (C.A.7 1988), "gaps in the chain [of custody] normally go to the weight of the evidence rather than its admissibility." It is up to the prosecution to decide what steps in the chain of custody are so crucial as to require evidence; but what testimony *is* introduced must (if the defendant objects) be introduced live. Additionally, documents prepared in the regular course of equipment maintenance may well qualify as nontestimonial records. See *infra*, at [section D].

overturn precedent by resurrecting *Roberts* a mere five years after it was rejected in *Crawford*.

We turn now to the various legal arguments raised by respondent and the dissent.

A.

Respondent first argues that the analysts are not subject to confrontation because they are not "accusatory" witnesses, in that they do not directly accuse petitioner of wrongdoing; rather, their testimony is inculpatory only when taken together with other evidence linking petitioner to the contraband. This finds no support in the text of the Sixth Amendment or in our case law.

The Sixth Amendment guarantees a defendant the right "to be confronted with the witnesses *against him*." (Emphasis added.) To the extent the analysts were witnesses (a question resolved above), they certainly provided testimony *against* petitioner, proving one fact necessary for his conviction — that the substance he possessed was cocaine. The contrast between the text of the Confrontation Clause and the text of the adjacent Compulsory Process Clause confirms this analysis. While the Confrontation Clause guarantees a defendant the right to be confronted with the witnesses "against him," the Compulsory Process Clause guarantees a defendant the right to call witnesses "in his favor." U.S. Const., Amdt. 6. The text of the Amendment contemplates two classes of witnesses — those against the defendant and those in his favor. The prosecution *must* produce the former; the defendant *may* call the latter. Contrary to respondent's assertion, there is not a third category of witnesses, helpful to the prosecution, but somehow immune from confrontation.

* * *

B.

Respondent and the dissent argue that the analysts should not be subject to confrontation because they are not "conventional" (or "typical" or "ordinary") witnesses of the sort whose *ex parte* testimony was most notoriously used at the trial of Sir Walter Raleigh. It is true, as the Court recognized in *Crawford*, that *ex parte* examinations of the sort used at Raleigh's trial have "long been thought a paradigmatic confrontation violation." 541 U.S., at 52. But the paradigmatic case identifies the core of the right to confrontation, not its limits. The right to confrontation was not invented in response to the use of the *ex parte* examinations in *Raleigh's Case*, 2 How. St. Tr. 1 (1603). That use provoked such an outcry precisely because it flouted the deeply rooted common-law tradition "of live testimony in court subject to adversarial testing." *Crawford, supra*, at 43–47

In any case, the purported distinctions respondent and the dissent identify between this case and Sir Walter Raleigh's "conventional" accusers do not survive scrutiny. The dissent first contends that a "conventional witness recalls events observed in the past, while an analyst's report contains near-contemporaneous observations of the test." It is doubtful that the analyst's reports in this case could be characterized as reporting "near-contemporaneous observations"; the affidavits were completed almost a week after the tests were performed. But regardless, the dissent misunderstands the role that "near-contemporaneity" has played in our case law. The dissent notes that that factor was given "substantial weight" in *Davis*, but in fact that decision *disproves* the dissent's position. There the Court considered the admissibility of statements made to police officers responding to a report of a domestic disturbance. By the time officers arrived the assault had ended, but the victim's statements — written and oral — were sufficiently close in time to the alleged assault that the trial court admitted her affidavit as a "present sense impression." *Davis*, 547 U.S., at 820 (internal quotation marks omitted). Though the witness's statements in *Davis* were "near-contemporaneous" to the events she reported, we nevertheless held that they could *not* be admitted absent an opportunity to confront the witness. *Id.*, at 830.

A second reason the dissent contends that the analysts are not "conventional witnesses" (and thus not subject to confrontation) is that they "observe[d] neither the crime nor any human action related to it." The dissent provides no authority for this particular limitation of the type of witnesses subject to confrontation. Nor is it conceivable that all witnesses who fit this description would be outside the scope of the Confrontation Clause. For example, is a police officer's investigative report describing the crime scene admissible absent an opportunity to examine the officer? The dissent's novel exception from coverage of the Confrontation Clause would exempt all expert witnesses — a hardly "unconventional" class of witnesses.

A third respect in which the dissent asserts that the analysts are not "conventional" witnesses and thus not subject to confrontation is that their statements were not provided in response to interrogation. As we have explained, "[t]he Framers were no more willing to exempt from cross-examination volunteered testimony or answers to open-ended questions than they were to exempt answers to detailed interrogation." *Davis, supra*, at 822–823, n.1. Respondent and the dissent cite no authority, and we are aware of none, holding that a person who volunteers his testimony is any less a " 'witness against' the defendant," than one who is responding to interrogation. In any event, the analysts' affidavits in this case *were* presented in response to a police request. If an affidavit submitted in response to a police officer's request to "write down what happened" suffices to trigger the Sixth Amendment's protection (as it apparently does, see *Davis*, 547 U.S., at 819–820), then the analysts' testimony should be subject to confrontation as well.

C.

Respondent claims that there is a difference, for Confrontation Clause purposes, between testimony recounting historical events, which is "prone to distortion or manipulation," and the testimony at issue here, which is the "resul[t] of neutral, scientific testing." Relatedly, respondent and the dissent argue that confrontation of forensic analysts would be of little value because "one would not reasonably expect a laboratory professional . . . to feel quite differently about the results of his scientific test by having to look at the defendant."

This argument is little more than an invitation to return to our overruled decision in *Roberts*, 448 U.S. 56, which held that evidence with "particularized guarantees of trustworthiness" was admissible notwithstanding the Confrontation Clause. *Id.*, at 66. What we said in *Crawford* in response to that argument remains true:

> "To be sure, the Clause's ultimate goal is to ensure reliability of evidence, but it is a procedural rather than a substantive guarantee. It commands, not that evidence be reliable, but that reliability be assessed in a particular manner: by testing in the crucible of cross-examination. . . . Dispensing with confrontation because testimony is obviously reliable is akin to dispensing with jury trial

because a defendant is obviously guilty. This is not what the Sixth Amendment prescribes." 541 U.S., at 61–62.

Respondent and the dissent may be right that there are other ways — and in some cases better ways — to challenge or verify the results of a forensic test. But the Constitution guarantees one way: confrontation. We do not have license to suspend the Confrontation Clause when a preferable trial strategy is available.

Nor is it evident that what respondent calls "neutral scientific testing" is as neutral or as reliable as respondent suggests. Forensic evidence is not uniquely immune from the risk of manipulation. According to a recent study conducted under the auspices of the National Academy of Sciences, "[t]he majority of [laboratories producing forensic evidence] are administered by law enforcement agencies, such as police departments, where the laboratory administrator reports to the head of the agency." National Research Council of the National Academies, Strengthening Forensic Science in the United States: A Path Forward 6-1 (Prepublication Copy Feb. 2009) (hereinafter National Academy Report). And "[b]ecause forensic scientists often are driven in their work by a need to answer a particular question related to the issues of a particular case, they sometimes face pressure to sacrifice appropriate methodology for the sake of expediency." Id., at S-17. A forensic analyst responding to a request from a law enforcement official may feel pressure — or have an incentive — to alter the evidence in a manner favorable to the prosecution.

Confrontation is one means of assuring accurate forensic analysis. While it is true, as the dissent notes, that an honest analyst will not alter his testimony when forced to confront the defendant, the same cannot be said of the fraudulent analyst. Like the eyewitness who has fabricated his account to the police, the analyst who provides false results may, under oath in open court, reconsider his false testimony. And, of course, the prospect of confrontation will deter fraudulent analysis in the first place.

Confrontation is designed to weed out not only the fraudulent analyst, but the incompetent one as well. Serious deficiencies have been found in the forensic evidence used in criminal trials. One commentator asserts that "[t]he legal community now concedes, with varying degrees of urgency, that our system produces erroneous convictions based on discredited forensics." Metzger, Cheating the Constitution, 59 Vand. L.Rev. 475, 491 (2006). One study of cases in which exonerating evidence resulted in the overturning of criminal convictions concluded that invalid forensic testimony contributed to the convictions in 60% of the cases. Garrett & Neufeld, Invalid Forensic Science Testimony and Wrongful Convictions, 95 Va. L.Rev. 1, 14 (2009).

* * *

Like expert witnesses generally, an analyst's lack of proper training or deficiency in judgment may be disclosed in cross-examination.

This case is illustrative. The affidavits submitted by the analysts contained only the bare-bones statement that "[t]he substance was found to contain: Cocaine." At the time of trial, petitioner did not know what tests the analysts performed, whether those tests were routine, and whether interpreting their results required the exercise of judgment or the use of skills that the analysts may not have possessed. While we still do not know the precise tests used by the analysts, we are told that the laboratories use "methodology recommended by the Scientific Working Group for the Analysis of Seized Drugs." At least some of that methodology requires the exercise of judgment and presents a risk of error that might be explored on cross-examination. See 2 P. Giannelli & E.

Imwinkelried, Scientific Evidence § 23.03[c], pp. 532–533, ch. 23A, p. 607 (4th ed.2007) (identifying four "critical errors" that analysts may commit in interpreting the results of the commonly used gas chromatography/mass spectrometry analysis); Shellow, The Application of *Daubert* to the Identification of Drugs, 2 Shepard's Expert & Scientific Evidence Quarterly 593, 600 (1995) (noting that while spectrometers may be equipped with computerized matching systems, "forensic analysts in crime laboratories typically do not utilize this feature of the instrument, but rely exclusively on their subjective judgment").

The same is true of many of the other types of forensic evidence commonly used in criminal prosecutions. "[T]here is wide variability across forensic science disciplines with regard to techniques, methodologies, reliability, types and numbers of potential errors, research, general acceptability, and published material." National Academy Report S-5. See also *id.*, at 5-9, 5-12, 5-17, 5-21 (discussing problems of subjectivity, bias, and unreliability of common forensic tests such as latent fingerprint analysis, pattern/impression analysis, and toolmark and firearms analysis). Contrary to respondent's and the dissent's suggestion, there is little reason to believe that confrontation will be useless in testing analysts' honesty, proficiency, and methodology — the features that are commonly the focus in the cross-examination of experts.

D.

Respondent argues that the analysts' affidavits are admissible without confrontation because they are "akin to the types of official and business records admissible at common law." But the affidavits do not qualify as traditional official or business records, and even if they did, their authors would be subject to confrontation nonetheless.

Documents kept in the regular course of business may ordinarily be admitted at trial despite their hearsay status. See Fed. Rule Evid. 803(6). But that is not the case if the regularly conducted business activity is the production of evidence for use at trial. Our decision in *Palmer v. Hoffman*, 318 U.S. 109 (1943), made that distinction clear. There we held that an accident report provided by an employee of a railroad company did not qualify as a business record because, although kept in the regular course of the railroad's operations, it was "calculated for use essentially in the court, not in the business." *Id.*, at 114. The analysts' certificates — like police reports generated by law enforcement officials — do not qualify as business or public records for precisely the same reason. See Rule 803(8) (defining public records as "excluding, however, in criminal cases matters observed by police officers and other law enforcement personnel").

*   *   *

The dissent identifies a single class of evidence which, though prepared for use at trial, was traditionally admissible: a clerk's certificate authenticating an official record — or a copy thereof — for use as evidence. But a clerk's authority in that regard was narrowly circumscribed. He was permitted "to certify to the correctness of a copy of a record kept in his office," but had "no authority to furnish, as evidence for the trial of a lawsuit, his interpretation of what the record contains or shows, or to certify to its substance or effect." *State v. Wilson*, 75 So. 95, 97 (1917). The dissent suggests that the fact that this exception was " 'narrowly circumscribed' " makes no difference. To the contrary, it makes all the difference in the world. It shows that even the line of cases establishing the one narrow exception the dissent has been able to identify simultaneously vindicates the general rule applicable to the present case. A clerk could by affidavit *authenticate* or provide a copy of an otherwise admissible record, but could not do what the analysts did here: *create* a record for the sole purpose of providing evidence against a defendant.

Far more probative here are those cases in which the prosecution sought to admit into evidence a clerk's certificate attesting to the fact that the clerk had searched for a particular relevant record and failed to find it. Like the testimony of the analysts in this case, the clerk's statement would serve as substantive evidence against the defendant whose guilt depended on the nonexistence of the record for which the clerk searched. Although the clerk's certificate would qualify as an official record under respondent's definition — it was prepared by a public officer in the regular course of his official duties — and although the clerk was certainly not a "conventional witness" under the dissent's approach, the clerk was nonetheless subject to confrontation.

Respondent also misunderstands the relationship between the business-and-official-records hearsay exceptions and the Confrontation Clause. As we stated in *Crawford:* "Most of the hearsay exceptions covered statements that by their nature were not testimonial — for example, business records or statements in furtherance of a conspiracy." 541 U.S., at 56. Business and public records are generally admissible absent confrontation not because they qualify under an exception to the hearsay rules, but because — having been created for the administration of an entity's affairs and not for the purpose of establishing or proving some fact at trial — they are not testimonial. Whether or not they qualify as business or official records, the analysts' statements here — prepared specifically for use at petitioner's trial — were testimony against petitioner, and the analysts were subject to confrontation under the Sixth Amendment.

E.

Respondent asserts that we should find no Confrontation Clause violation in this case because petitioner had the ability to subpoena the analysts. But that power — whether pursuant to state law or the Compulsory Process Clause — is no substitute for the right of confrontation. Unlike the Confrontation Clause, those provisions are of no use to the defendant when the witness is unavailable or simply refuses to appear. Converting the prosecution's duty under the Confrontation Clause into the defendant's privilege under state law or the Compulsory Process Clause shifts the consequences of adverse-witness no-shows from the State to the accused. More fundamentally, the Confrontation Clause imposes a burden on the prosecution to present its witnesses, not on the defendant to bring those adverse witnesses into court. Its value to the defendant is not replaced by a system in which the prosecution presents its evidence via *ex parte* affidavits and waits for the defendant to subpoena the affiants if he chooses.

F.

Finally, respondent asks us to relax the requirements of the Confrontation Clause to accommodate the " 'necessities of trial and the adversary process.' " It is not clear whence we would derive the authority to do so. The Confrontation Clause may make the prosecution of criminals more burdensome, but that is equally true of the right to trial by jury and the privilege against self-incrimination. The Confrontation Clause — like those other constitutional provisions — is binding, and we may not disregard it at our convenience.

We also doubt the accuracy of respondent's and the dissent's dire predictions. The dissent, respondent, and its *amici* highlight the substantial total number of controlled-substance analyses performed by state and federal laboratories in recent years. But only some of those tests are implicated in prosecutions, and only a small fraction of those cases actually proceed to trial. See Brief for Law Professors as *Amici Curiae* 7–8 (nearly 95% of convictions in state and federal courts are obtained via guilty plea).

Perhaps the best indication that the sky will not fall after today's decision is that it has not done so already. Many States have already adopted the constitutional rule we announce today, while many others permit the defendant to assert (or forfeit by silence) his Confrontation Clause right after receiving notice of the prosecution's intent to use a forensic analyst's report. Despite these widespread practices, there is no evidence that the criminal justice system has ground to a halt in the States that, one way or another, empower a defendant to insist upon the analyst's appearance at trial. Indeed, in Massachusetts itself, a defendant may subpoena the analyst to appear at trial, and yet there is no indication that obstructionist defendants are abusing the privilege.

*   *   *

Defense attorneys and their clients will often stipulate to the nature of the substance in the ordinary drug case. It is unlikely that defense counsel will insist on live testimony whose effect will be merely to highlight rather than cast doubt upon the forensic analysis. Nor will defense attorneys want to antagonize the judge or jury by wasting their time with the appearance of a witness whose testimony defense counsel does not intend to rebut in any fashion. The *amicus* brief filed by District Attorneys in Support of the Commonwealth in the Massachusetts Supreme Court case upon which the Appeals Court here relied said that "it is almost always the case that [analysts' certificates] are admitted without objection. Generally, defendants do not object to the admission of drug certificates most likely because there is no benefit to a defendant from such testimony." Given these strategic considerations, and in light of the experience in those States that already provide the same or similar protections to defendants, there is little reason to believe that our decision today will commence the parade of horribles respondent and the dissent predict.

*   *   *

This case involves little more than the application of our holding in *Crawford v. Washington*, 541 U.S. 36. The Sixth Amendment does not permit the prosecution to prove its case via *ex parte* out-of-court affidavits, and the admission of such evidence against Melendez-Diaz was error.[2] [14] We therefore reverse the judgment of the Appeals Court of Massachusetts and remand the case for further proceedings not inconsistent with this opinion.

---

[2] We of course express no view as to whether the error was harmless. The Massachusetts Court of Appeals did not reach that question and we decline to address it in the first instance. In connection with that determination, however, we disagree with the dissent's contention, that "only an analyst's testimony suffices to prove [the] fact" that "the substance is cocaine." Today's opinion, while insisting upon retention of the confrontation requirement, in no way alters the type of evidence (including circumstantial evidence) sufficient to sustain a conviction.

JUSTICE KENNEDY, with whom THE CHIEF JUSTICE, JUSTICE BREYER, and JUSTICE ALITO join, dissenting.

The Court sweeps away an accepted rule governing the admission of scientific evidence. Until today, scientific analysis could be introduced into evidence without testimony from the "analyst" who produced it. This rule has been established for at least 90 years. It extends across at least 35 States and six Federal Courts of Appeals. Yet the Court undoes it based on two recent opinions that say nothing about forensic analysts: *Crawford v. Washington*, 541 U.S. 36 (2004), and *Davis v. Washington*, 547 U.S. 813 (2006).

*   *   *

Crawford and *Davis* dealt with ordinary witnesses — women who had seen, and in two cases been the victim of, the crime in question. Those cases stand for the proposition that formal statements made by a conventional witness — one who has personal knowledge of some aspect of the defendant's guilt — may not be admitted without the witness appearing at trial to meet the accused face to face. But *Crawford* and *Davis* do not say — indeed, could not have said, because the facts were not before the Court — that anyone who makes a testimonial statement is a witness for purposes of the Confrontation Clause, even when that person has, in fact, witnessed nothing to give them personal knowledge of the defendant's guilt.

Because *Crawford* and *Davis* concerned typical witnesses, the Court should have done the sensible thing and limited its holding to witnesses as so defined.

*   *   *

The Court's opinion suggests this will be a body of formalistic and wooden rules, divorced from precedent, common sense, and the underlying purpose of the Clause. Its ruling has vast potential to disrupt criminal procedures that already give ample protections against the misuse of scientific evidence. For these reasons, as more fully explained below, the Court's opinion elicits my respectful dissent.

I.

A.

1.

The Court says that, before the results of a scientific test may be introduced into evidence, the defendant has the right to confront the "analyst." One must assume that this term, though it appears nowhere in the Confrontation Clause, nevertheless has some constitutional substance that now must be elaborated in future cases. There is no accepted definition of analyst, and there is no established precedent to define that term.

Consider how many people play a role in a routine test for the presence of illegal drugs. One person prepares a sample of the drug, places it in a testing machine, and retrieves the machine's printout — often, a graph showing the frequencies of radiation absorbed by the sample or the masses of the sample's molecular fragments. A second person interprets the graph the machine prints out — perhaps by comparing that printout with published, standardized graphs of known drugs. Meanwhile, a third person — perhaps an independent contractor — has calibrated the machine and, having done so, has certified that the machine is in good working order. Finally, a fourth person — perhaps the laboratory's director — certifies that his subordinates followed established procedures.

*　　*　　*

It is possible to read the Court's opinion, however, to say that all four must testify. Each one has contributed to the test's result and has, at least in some respects, made a representation about the test. Person One represents that a pure sample, properly drawn, entered the machine and produced a particular printout. Person Two represents that the printout corresponds to a known drug. Person Three represents that the machine was properly calibrated at the time. Person Four represents that all the others performed their jobs in accord with established procedures.

And each of the four has power to introduce error. A laboratory technician might adulterate the sample. The independent contractor might botch the machine's calibration. And so forth. The reasons for these errors may range from animus against the particular suspect or all criminal suspects to unintentional oversight; from gross negligence to good-faith mistake. It is no surprise that a plausible case can be made for deeming each person in the testing process an analyst under the Court's opinion.

Consider the independent contractor who has calibrated the testing machine. At least in a routine case, where the machine's result appears unmistakable, that result's accuracy depends entirely on the machine's calibration. The calibration, in turn, can be proved only by the contractor's certification that he or she did the job properly. That certification appears to be a testimonial statement under the Court's definition: It is a formal, out-of-court statement, offered for the truth of the matter asserted, and made for the purpose of later prosecution. It is not clear, under the Court's ruling, why the independent contractor is not also an analyst.

Consider the person who interprets the machine's printout. His or her interpretation may call for the exercise of professional judgment in close cases. If we assume no person deliberately introduces error, this interpretive step is the one most likely to permit human error to affect the test's result. This exercise of judgment might make this participant an analyst. The Court implies as much.

And we must yet consider the laboratory director who certifies the ultimate results. The director is arguably the most effective person to confront for revealing any ambiguity in findings, variations in procedures, or problems in the office, as he or she is most familiar with the standard procedures, the office's variations, and problems in prior cases or with particular analysts. The prosecution may seek to introduce his or her certification into evidence. The Court implies that only those statements that are actually entered into evidence require confrontation. This could mean that the director is also an analyst, even if his or her certification relies upon or restates work performed by subordinates.

The Court offers no principles or historical precedent to determine which of these persons is the analyst. All contribute to the test result. And each is equally remote from the scene, has no personal stake in the outcome, does not even know the accused, and is concerned only with the performance of his or her role in conducting the test.

*　　*　　*

Today's decision demonstrates that even in the narrow category of scientific tests that identify a drug, the Court cannot define with any clarity who the analyst is. Outside this narrow category, the range of other scientific tests that may be affected by the Court's new confrontation right is staggering. *See, e.g., Comment, Toward a Definition of "Testimonial": How Autopsy Reports Do Not Embody the Qualities of a Testimonial Statement*, 96 Cal. L.Rev. 1093, 1094, 1115 (2008) (noting that every court post-*Crawford* has held that autopsy reports are not testimonial, and warning that a contrary rule would "effectively functio[n] as a statute of limitations for murder").

2.

It is difficult to confine at this point the damage the Court's holding will do in other contexts. Consider just two — establishing the chain of custody and authenticating a copy of a document.

It is the obligation of the prosecution to establish the chain of custody for evidence sent to testing laboratories — that is, to establish "the identity and integrity of physical evidence by tracing its continuous whereabouts." 23 C.J. S., Criminal Law § 1142, p. 66 (2008). Meeting this obligation requires representations — that one officer retrieved the evidence from the crime scene, that a second officer checked it into an evidence locker, that a third officer verified the locker's seal was intact, and so forth. The iron logic of which the Court is so enamored would seem to require in-court testimony from each human link in the chain of custody. That, of course, has never been the law.

*   *   *

Because the Court is driven by nothing more than a wooden application of the *Crawford* and *Davis* definition of "testimonial," divorced from any guidance from history, precedent, or common sense, there is no way to predict the future applications of today's holding. Surely part of the justification for the Court's formalism must lie in its predictability. There is nothing predictable here, however, other than the uncertainty and disruption that now must ensue.

B.

With no precedent to guide us, let us assume that the Court's analyst is the person who interprets the machine's printout. This result makes no sense. The Confrontation Clause is not designed, and does not serve, to detect errors in scientific tests. That should instead be done by conducting a new test. Or, if a new test is impossible, the defendant may call his own expert to explain to the jury the test's flaws and the dangers of relying on it. And if, in an extraordinary case, the particular analyst's testimony is necessary to the defense, then, of course, the defendant may subpoena the analyst. The Court frets that the defendant may be unable to do so "when the [analyst] is unavailable or simply refuses to appear." But laboratory analysts are not difficult to locate or to compel. As discussed below, analysts already devote considerable time to appearing in court when subpoenaed to do so. Neither the Court, petitioner, nor *amici* offer any reason to believe that defendants have trouble subpoenaing analysts in cases where the analysts' in-court testimony is necessary.

The facts of this case illustrate the formalistic and pointless nature of the Court's reading of the Clause. Petitioner knew, well in advance of trial, that the Commonwealth would introduce the tests against him. The bags of cocaine were in court, available for him to test, and entered into evidence. Yet petitioner made no effort, before or during trial, to mount a defense against the analysts' results. Petitioner could have challenged the tests' reliability by seeking discovery concerning the testing methods used or the qualifications of the laboratory analysts. He did not do so. Petitioner could have sought to conduct his own test. Again, he did not seek a test; indeed, he did not argue that the drug was not cocaine. Rather than dispute the authenticity of the samples tested or the accuracy of the tests performed, petitioner argued to the jury that the prosecution had not shown that he had possessed or dealt in the drugs.

Despite not having prepared a defense to the analysts' results, petitioner's counsel made what can only be described as a *pro forma* objection to admitting the results without in-court testimony, presumably from one particular analyst. Today the Court, by deciding that this objection should have been sustained, transforms the Confrontation Clause from a sensible procedural protection into a distortion of the criminal justice system.

It is difficult to perceive how the Court's holding will advance the purposes of the Confrontation Clause. One purpose of confrontation is to impress upon witnesses the gravity of their conduct. A witness, when brought to face the person his or her words condemn, might refine, reformulate, reconsider, or even recant earlier statements. A further purpose is to alleviate the danger of one-sided interrogations by adversarial government officials who might distort a witness's testimony. The Clause guards against this danger by bringing the interrogation into the more neutral and public forum of the courtroom.

But neither purpose is served by the rule the Court announces today. It is not plausible that a laboratory analyst will retract his or her prior conclusion upon catching sight of the defendant the result condemns. After all, the analyst is far removed from the particular defendant and, indeed, claims no personal knowledge of the defendant's guilt. And an analyst performs hundreds if not thousands of tests each year and will not remember a particular test or the link it had to the defendant.

This is not to say that analysts are infallible. They are not. It may well be that if the State does not introduce the machine printout or the raw results of a laboratory analysis; if it does not call an expert to interpret a test, particularly if that test is complex or little known; if it does not establish the chain of custody and the reliability of the laboratory; then the State will have failed to meet its burden of proof. That result follows because the State must prove its case beyond a reasonable doubt, without relying on presumptions, unreliable hearsay, and the like. The State must permit the defendant to challenge the analyst's result. The rules of evidence, including those governing reliability under hearsay principles and the latitude to be given expert witnesses; the rules against irrebuttable presumptions; and the overriding principle that the prosecution must make its case beyond a reasonable doubt — all these are part of the protections for the accused. The States, however, have some latitude in determining how these rules should be defined.

The Confrontation Clause addresses who must testify. It simply does not follow, however, that this clause, in lieu of the other rules set forth above, controls who the prosecution must call on every issue. Suppose, for instance, that the defense challenges the procedures for a secure chain of custody for evidence sent to a lab and then returned to the police. The defense has the right to call its own witnesses to show that the chain of custody is not secure. But that does not mean it can demand that, in the prosecution's case in chief, each person who is in the chain of custody — and who had an undoubted opportunity to taint or tamper with the evidence — must be called by the prosecution under the Confrontation Clause. And the same is true with lab technicians.

The Confrontation Clause is simply not needed for these matters. Where, as here, the defendant does not even dispute the accuracy of the analyst's work, confrontation adds nothing.

C.

For the sake of these negligible benefits, the Court threatens to disrupt forensic investigations across the country and to put prosecutions nationwide at risk of dismissal based on erratic, all-too-frequent instances when a particular laboratory technician, now invested by the Court's new constitutional designation as the analyst, simply does not or cannot appear.

Consider first the costs today's decision imposes on criminal trials. Our own Court enjoys weeks, often months, of notice before cases are argued. We receive briefs well in advance. The argument itself is ordered. A busy trial court, by contrast, must consider not only attorneys' schedules but also those of witnesses and juries. Trial courts have huge caseloads to be processed within strict time limits. Some cases may unexpectedly plead out at the last minute; others, just as unexpectedly, may not. Some juries stay out longer than predicted; others must be reconstituted. An analyst cannot hope to be the trial court's top priority in scheduling. The analyst must instead face the prospect of waiting for days in a hallway outside the courtroom before being called to offer testimony that will consist of little more than a rote recital of the written report.

As matters stood before today's opinion, analysts already spent considerable time appearing as witnesses in those few cases where the defendant, unlike petitioner in this case, contested the analyst's result and subpoenaed the analyst. By requiring analysts also to appear in the far greater number of cases where defendants do not dispute the analyst's result, the Court imposes enormous costs on the administration of justice.

Setting aside, for a moment, all the other crimes for which scientific evidence is required, consider the costs the Court's ruling will impose on state drug prosecutions alone. In 2004, the most recent year for which data are available, drug possession and trafficking resulted in 362,850 felony convictions in state courts across the country. *See* Dept. of Justice, Bureau of Justice Statistics, M. Durose & P. Langan, Felony Sentences in State Courts 2004, p. 2 (July 2007). Roughly 95% of those convictions were products of plea bargains, which means that state courts saw more than 18,000 drug trials in a single year.

*   *   *

The Federal Government may face even graver difficulties than the States because its operations are so widespread. For example, the FBI laboratory at Quantico, Virginia, supports federal, state, and local investigations across the country. Its 500 employees conduct over one million scientific tests each year. The Court's decision means that before any of those million tests reaches a jury, at least one of the laboratory's analysts must board a plane, find his or her way to an unfamiliar courthouse, and sit there waiting to read aloud notes made months ago.

The Court purchases its meddling with the Confrontation Clause at a dear price, a price not measured in taxpayer dollars alone. Guilty defendants will go free, on the most technical grounds, as a direct result of today's decision, adding nothing to the truth-finding process. The analyst will not always make it to the courthouse in time. He or she may be ill; may be out of the country; may be unable to travel because of inclement weather; or may at that very moment be waiting outside some other courtroom for another defendant to exercise the right the Court invents today. If for any reason the analyst cannot make it to the courthouse in time, then, the Court holds, the jury cannot learn of the analyst's findings (unless, by some unlikely turn of events, the defendant previously cross-examined the analyst). The result, in many cases, will be that the prosecution cannot meet its burden of proof, and the guilty defendant goes free on a technicality that, because it results in an acquittal, cannot be reviewed on appeal.

The Court's holding is a windfall to defendants, one that is unjustified by any demonstrated deficiency in trials, any well-understood historical requirement, or any established constitutional precedent.

II.

All of the problems with today's decision — the imprecise definition of "analyst," the lack of any perceptible benefit, the heavy societal costs — would be of no moment if the Constitution did, in fact, require the Court to rule as it does today. But the Constitution does not.

The Court's fundamental mistake is to read the Confrontation Clause as referring to a kind of out-of-court statement — namely, a testimonial statement — that must be excluded from evidence. The Clause does not refer to kinds of statements. Nor does the Clause contain the word "testimonial." The text, instead, refers to kinds of persons, namely, to "witnesses against" the defendant. Laboratory analysts are not "witnesses against" the defendant as those words would have been understood at the framing. There is simply no authority for this proposition.

Instead, the Clause refers to a conventional "witness" — meaning one who witnesses (that is, perceives) an event that gives him or her personal knowledge of some aspect of the defendant's guilt. Both *Crawford* and *Davis* concerned just this kind of ordinary witness — and nothing in the Confrontation Clause's text, history, or precedent justifies the Court's decision to expand those cases.

A.

The Clause states: "In all criminal prosecutions, the accused shall enjoy the right . . . to be confronted with the witnesses against him." U.S. Const., Amdt. 6. Though there is "virtually no evidence of what the drafters of the Confrontation Clause intended it to mean," *White v. Illinois*, 502 U.S. 346 (1992) (THOMAS, J., concurring in part and concurring in judgment), it is certain the Framers did not contemplate that an analyst who conducts a scientific test far removed from the crime would be considered a "witnes[s] against" the defendant.

The Framers were concerned with a typical witness — one who perceived an event that gave rise to a personal belief in some aspect of the defendant's guilt. There is no evidence that the Framers understood the Clause to extend to unconventional witnesses. As discussed below, there is significant evidence to the contrary. . . . The Court goes dangerously wrong when it bases its constitutional interpretation upon historical guesswork.

The infamous treason trial of Sir Walter Raleigh provides excellent examples of the kinds of witnesses to whom the Confrontation Clause refers. *Raleigh's Case*, 2 How. St. Tr. 1 (1603). Raleigh's accusers claimed to have heard Raleigh speak treason, so they were witnesses in the conventional sense. We should limit the Confrontation Clause to witnesses like those in Raleigh's trial.

The Court today expands the Clause to include laboratory analysts, but analysts differ from ordinary witnesses in at least three significant ways. First, a conventional witness recalls events observed in the past, while an analyst's report contains near-contemporaneous observations of the test. An observation recorded at the time it is made is unlike the usual act of testifying. A typical witness must recall a previous event that he or she perceived just once, and thus may have misperceived or misremembered. But an analyst making a contemporaneous observation need not rely on memory; he or she instead reports the observations at the time they are made. . . . The Court cites no authority for its holding that an observation recorded at the time it is made is an act of "witness[ing]" for purposes of the Confrontation Clause.

Second, an analyst observes neither the crime nor any human action related to it. Often, the analyst does not know the defendant's identity, much less have personal knowledge of an aspect of the defendant's guilt. The analyst's distance from the crime and the defendant, in both space and time, suggests the analyst is not a witness against the defendant in the conventional sense.

Third, a conventional witness responds to questions under interrogation. But laboratory tests are conducted according to scientific protocols; they are not dependent upon or controlled by interrogation of any sort. Put differently, out-of-court statements should only "require confrontation if they are produced by, or with the involvement of, adversarial government officials responsible for investigating and prosecuting crime." 96 Cal. L.Rev., at 1118. There is no indication that the analysts here — who work for the State Laboratory Institute, a division of the Massachusetts Department of Public Health — were adversarial to petitioner. Nor is there any evidence that adversarial officials played a role in formulating the analysts' certificates.

Rather than acknowledge that it expands the Confrontation Clause beyond conventional witnesses, the Court relies on our recent opinions in *Crawford* and *Davis*. The Court assumes, with little analysis, that *Crawford* and *Davis* extended the Clause to any person who makes a "testimonial" statement. But the Court's confident tone cannot disguise the thinness of these two reeds. Neither *Crawford* nor *Davis* considered whether the Clause extends to persons far removed from the crime who have no connection to the defendant. Instead, those cases concerned conventional witnesses.

*   *   *

C.

In addition to lacking support in historical practice or in this Court's precedent, the Court's decision is also contrary to authority extending over at least 90 years, 35 States, and six Federal Courts of Appeals.

Almost 100 years ago three state supreme courts held that their state constitutions did not require analysts to testify in court. . . . Just two state courts appear to have read a state constitution to require a contrary result. *State v. Clark*, 290 Mont. 479, 484–489 (1998) (laboratory drug report requires confrontation under Montana's Constitution, which is "[u]nlike its federal counterpart"); *State v. Birchfield*, 342 Or. 624 (2007).

As for the Federal Constitution, before *Crawford* the authority was stronger still: The Sixth Amendment does not require analysts to testify in court. All Federal Courts of Appeals to consider the issue agreed. . . . Some 24 state courts, and the Court of

Appeals for the Armed Forces, were in accord. Eleven more state courts upheld burden-shifting statutes that reduce, if not eliminate, the right to confrontation by requiring the defendant to take affirmative steps prior to trial to summon the analyst. Because these burden-shifting statutes may be invalidated by the Court's reasoning, these 11 decisions, too, appear contrary to today's opinion. . . .

On a practical level, today's ruling would cause less disruption if the States' hearsay rules had already required analysts to testify. But few States require this. At least sixteen state courts have held that their evidentiary rules permit scientific test results, calibration certificates, and the observations of medical personnel to enter evidence without in-court testimony. The Federal Courts of Appeals have reached the same conclusion in applying the federal hearsay rule.

* * *

The Court rejects the well-established understanding — extending across at least 90 years, 35 States and six Federal Courts of Appeals — that the Constitution does not require analysts to testify in court before their analysis may be introduced into evidence. The only authority on which the Court can rely is its own speculation on the meaning of the word "testimonial," made in two recent opinions that said nothing about scientific analysis or scientific analysts.

III.

In an attempt to show that the "sky will not fall after today's decision," the Court makes three arguments, none of which withstands scrutiny.

A.

In an unconvincing effort to play down the threat that today's new rule will disrupt or even end criminal prosecutions, the Court professes a hope that defense counsel will decline to raise what will soon be known as the *Melendez-Diaz* objection. The Court bases this expectation on its understanding that defense attorneys surrender constitutional rights because the attorneys do not "want to antagonize the judge or jury by wasting their time."

The Court's reasoning is troubling on at least two levels. First, the Court's speculation rests on the apparent belief that our Nation's trial judges and jurors are unwilling to accept zealous advocacy and that, once "antagonize[d]" by it, will punish such advocates with adverse rulings. The Court offers no support for this stunning slur on the integrity of the Nation's courts. It is commonplace for the defense to request, at the conclusion of the prosecution's opening case, a directed verdict of acquittal. If the prosecution has failed to prove an element of the crime — even an element that is technical and rather obvious, such as movement of a car in interstate commerce — then the case must be dismissed. Until today one would not have thought that judges should be angered at the defense for making such motions, nor that counsel has some sort of obligation to avoid being troublesome when the prosecution has not done all the law requires to prove its case.

Second, even if the Court were right to expect trial judges to feel "antagonize[d]" by *Melendez-Diaz* objections and to then vent their anger by punishing the lawyer in some way, there is no authority to support the Court's suggestion that a lawyer may shirk his or her professional duties just to avoid judicial displeasure. There is good reason why the

Court cites no authority for this suggestion — it is contrary to what some of us, at least, have long understood to be defense counsel's duty to be a zealous advocate for every client.

*　*　*

The Court surmises that "[i]t is unlikely that defense counsel will insist on live testimony whose effect will be merely to highlight rather than cast doubt upon the forensic analysis." This optimistic prediction misunderstands how criminal trials work. If the defense does not plan to challenge the test result, "highlight[ing]" that result through testimony does not harm the defense as the Court supposes. If the analyst cannot reach the courtroom in time to testify, however, a *Melendez-Diaz* objection grants the defense a great windfall: The analyst's work cannot come into evidence. Given the prospect of such a windfall (which may, in and of itself, secure an acquittal) few zealous advocates will pledge, prior to trial, not to raise a *Melendez-Diaz* objection. Defense counsel will accept the risk that the jury may hear the analyst's live testimony, in exchange for the chance that the analyst fails to appear and the government's case collapses. And if, as here, the defense is not that the substance was harmless, but instead that the accused did not possess it, the testimony of the technician is a formalism that does not detract from the defense case.

*　*　*

C.

In a further effort to support its assessment that today's decision will not cause disruption, the Court cites 10 decisions from States that, the Court asserts, "have already adopted the constitutional rule we announce today." The Court assures us that "there is no evidence that the criminal justice system has ground to a halt in the[se] States."

On inspection, the citations prove far less reassuring than promised. Seven were decided by courts that considered themselves bound by *Crawford*. . . .

Moreover, because these seven courts only "adopted" the Court's position in the wake of *Crawford*, their decisions are all quite recent. These States have not yet been subject to the widespread, adverse results of the formalism the Court mandates today.

*　*　*

Laboratory analysts who conduct routine scientific tests are not the kind of conventional witnesses to whom the Confrontation Clause refers. The judgment of the Appeals Court of Massachusetts should be affirmed.

NOTES AND QUESTIONS

(1) *"Analysts."* In *Melendez-Diaz*, the Court held that before the results of a scientific test may be introduced into evidence, the Sixth Amendment Confrontation Clause guarantees the defendant the right to confront the "analyst." In a drug case, who is the "analyst"? In his dissenting opinion, Justice Kennedy maintains that there are many people who play a role in a routine test for the presence of illegal drugs. He observed:

One person prepares a sample of the drug, places it in a testing machine, and retrieves the machine's printout — often, a graph showing the frequencies of radiation absorbed by the sample or the masses of the sample's molecular fragments. A second person interprets the graph the machine prints out — perhaps by comparing that printout with published, standardized graphs of known drugs. Meanwhile, a third person — perhaps an independent contractor — has calibrated the machine and, having done so, has certified that the machine is in good working order. Finally, a fourth person — perhaps the laboratory's director — certifies that his subordinates followed established procedures.

Id. at 2544.

After *Melendez-Diaz*, must the prosecution call all four individuals to testify before the drug laboratory results may be admitted into evidence? Are all four of these individuals witnesses against the accused?

(2) ***Ordinary witnesses.*** In his dissenting opinion, Justice Kennedy argues that *Crawford* and *Davis* dealt with "ordinary witnesses," meaning those witnesses who had personal knowledge of some aspect of the defendant's guilt. *Id.* at 2550–52. Writing for the majority, Justice Scalia maintains that anyone who makes a testimonial statement is a witness for purposes of the Confrontation Clause. Do you agree with Justice Kennedy or Justice Scalia? Should the Sixth Amendment Confrontation Clause be interpreted to guarantee the right to confront only "ordinary" or "typical" witnesses? Is a lab analyst a so-called "ordinary" or accusatory witness?

(3) ***Purposes of the Confrontation Clause.*** Justice Kennedy argues that the purposes of the Confrontation Clause are not advanced by the Court's holding. He states:

It is not plausible that a laboratory analyst will retract his or her prior conclusion upon catching sight of the defendant the result condemns. After all, the analyst is far removed from the particular defendant and, indeed, claims no personal knowledge of the defendant's guilt. And an analyst performs hundreds if not thousands of tests each year and will not remember a particular test or the link it had to the defendant.

Id. at 2548. Do you agree? What are the benefits of being able to cross-examine the drug analyst? In short, does the Court's holding advance the purposes of the Confrontation Clause? Do the benefits of cross-examination outweigh the costs imposed on the administration of justice?

(4) ***Potential for Abuse.*** In dissent, Justice Kennedy maintains that the Court's decision is a "windfall" to defendants and will impose enormous costs on the administration of justice. *Id.* at 2549–50. Scalia downplays these concerns, stating that the "sky will not fall after today's decision." *Id.* at 2540. Scalia further opines:

Defense attorneys and their clients will often stipulate to the nature of the substance in the ordinary drug case. It is unlikely that defense counsel will insist on live testimony whose effect will be merely to highlight rather than cast doubt upon the forensic analysis.

Id. at 2542. Do you agree with Justice Scalia or Justice Kennedy?

(5) ***Business Record Exception.*** Justice Scalia rejected respondent's argument that the certificates of analysis sworn by analysts at the state laboratory were admissible

without confrontation because they constituted documents kept in the regular course of business under the business or public records exception to the hearsay rule. *Id.* at 2538. What is Justice Scalia's reasoning? Why do the drug analysts' affidavits not qualify as official or business records?

(6) ***Autopsy Reports and Other Scientific Tests.*** The holding in *Melendez-Diaz* has application to autopsy reports and other routine scientific tests. After *Melendez-Diaz*, must the medical examiner testify before the autopsy report describing the victim's injuries may be admitted into evidence? With respect to other scientific tests, does the Court's holding require confrontation of certificates stating that instruments were in good working order at the time of a test? For example, must the analyst testify prior to the admission of a certificate that a breathalyzer machine was operating properly?

(7) ***Harmless Error.*** The majority expressed no view as to whether admitting the analyst's affidavit was harmless error. *Id.* at 2542 n. 14. When would introducing drug test results without calling the analyst to testify constitute harmless error? It is conceivable that if the identity of the suspected cocaine was proven by other types of evidence (including circumstantial evidence), the failure to confront the analyst could constitute harmless error.

(8) ***Justice Thomas' Concurrence.*** Note that *Melendez-Diaz* was a 5-4 decision, but Justice Thomas, who voted with the majority, wrote a concurring opinion restating his view that the Confrontation Clause is only implicated by extrajudicial statements, "insofar as they are in formalized testimonial materials, such as affidavits, depositions, prior testimony or confessions." *Id.* at *13. Justice Thomas then added the following:

> I join in the Court's opinion in this case because the documents at issue in this case "are quite plainly affidavits." As such, they fall within the "core class of testimonial statements" governed by the Confrontation Clause."

Id. Does Justice Thomas' concurrence limit the impact of *Melendez-Diaz*? For example, is it fair to say that a majority of the Court endorse the proposition put forth by Justice Scalia that,

> [b]usiness and public records are generally admissible absent confrontation not because they qualify under an exception to the hearsay rules, but because — *having been created for the administration of an entity's affairs and not for the purpose of establishing or proving some fact at trial* — they are not testimonial.

Id. at *11 (emphasis added).

(9) In ***Melendez-Diaz***, the Supreme Court held that admitting into evidence " "affidavits" " reporting the results of forensic analysis violated the Sixth Amendment Confrontation Clause absent a showing that the analyst was unavailable to testify at trial *and* the petitioner had a prior opportunity to cross-examine him. Is the Court's holding limited to "affidavits" reporting the results of forensic tests or does it extend to medical examiner's reports as well? The question would seem to depend on Justice Thomas' view of whether a medical examiner's report falls within the core category of "testimonial" statements.

UNITED STATES v. FELIZ
467 F.3d 227 (2d Cir. 2006)

Defendant appellant Jose Erbo appeals his conviction in the United States District Court for the Southern District of New York, following a jury trial, for racketeering activities, 18 U.S.C. § 1962(c), conspiring to violate racketeering laws, in violation of 18 U.S.C. § 1962(d), conspiring to commit and committing murder in aid of racketeering, in violation of 18 U.S.C. § 1959(a), using and carrying firearms in connection with the murders and conspiracies to commit murder, in violation of 18 U.S.C. § 924(c), and conspiring to distribute and possess with the intent to distribute powder cocaine and crack, in violation of 21 U.S.C. §§ 812, 841(a)(1), 841(b)(1)(A), and 846.

Erbo raises numerous challenges to his conviction and sentence, all but one of which we address in a summary order affirming the District Court. In this opinion we address Erbo's contention that the admission of autopsy reports against a defendant who has had no opportunity to cross examine the author of the reports violates the defendant's rights under the Confrontation Clause as articulated by the Supreme Court in *Crawford v. Washington*, 541 U.S. 36 (2004). Because we conclude that autopsy reports are not testimonial within the meaning of *Crawford* and, thus, do not come within the ambit of the Confrontation Clause, we find no constitutional error in the admission of the autopsy reports.

BACKGROUND

From at least 1991 until 1997, Erbo led a violent cocaine distribution organization in New York City known as "Tito's Crew." Erbo and other members of Tito's Crew distributed large amounts of crack and cocaine and committed multiple murders. On February 4, 1999, the Government charged Erbo and others in a seventeen count indictment, which included charges of racketeering as well as murder, and conspiracy to commit murder, in aid of racketeering. In September 1999, he was convicted on weapons charges in the Dominican Republic and sentenced to two years' imprisonment. Upon his completion of that sentence in April 2001, the Dominican Republic surrendered Erbo to the United States pursuant to an extradition request. He subsequently pled not guilty, and trial commenced on May 9, 2002.

In order to establish the manner and cause of death for each of Erbo's victims in the charged homicides, the Government offered nine autopsy reports through the testimony of Dr. James Gill, an employee of the Office of the Chief Medical Examiner of New York ("Medical Examiner's Office"). Dr. Gill had not conducted any of the autopsies detailed in the reports. Erbo, therefore, objected to the admission of the reports on the grounds that they were inadmissible hearsay and violated his right to confrontation under the Sixth Amendment. The District Court admitted the autopsy reports over that objection, concluding that the Government had established a proper foundation for their admission as business records. Using the recorded observations in the autopsy reports, Dr. Gill testified before the jury as to the causes of death of the nine victims.

* * *

DISCUSSION

I. The Confrontation Clause Analysis, Before and After *Crawford*

The Confrontation Clause states that "[i]n all criminal prosecutions, the accused shall enjoy the right . . . to be confronted with the witnesses against him." U.S. CONST. amend. VI. Prior to *Crawford*, standards of reliability demarcated the boundaries of the Confrontation Clause's protections. . . . *Crawford*, however, "substantially alter[ed] the . . . existing Confrontation Clause jurisprudence," *Saget*, 377 F.3d at 226, announcing a per se bar on the admission of a class of out of court statements the Supreme Court labeled "testimonial" unless the declarant is unavailable and the defendant has had a prior opportunity to cross examine the declarant regarding the statement. *Crawford*, 541 U.S. at 59, 68; *United States v. Stewart*, 433 F.3d 273, 290 (2d Cir.2006); *United States v. Logan*, 419 F.3d 172, 177 (2d Cir.2005). *Crawford's* per se bar applies "regardless of whether [the testimonial] statement falls within a firmly rooted hearsay exception or has particularized guarantees of trustworthiness." *Saget*, 377 F.3d at 226 (citing *Crawford*, 541 U.S. at 68 69). . . . Rather, "[w]here testimonial statements are at issue, the only indicium of reliability sufficient to satisfy constitutional demands is the one the Constitution actually prescribes: confrontation." *Id.* at 68–69.

*   *   *

II. Crawford and the Scope of "Testimonial" Evidence

The *Crawford* Court declined to "spell out a comprehensive definition of 'testimonial.'" *Crawford*, 541 U.S. at 68, but it did offer a number of observations that suggest the contours of that definition. First, the Court noted that both the historical background and text of the Confrontation Clause indicate that "the principal evil at which [it] was directed was the civil law mode of criminal procedure, and particularly its use of ex parte examinations as evidence against the accused." *Id.* at 50. According to the Court, "the Sixth Amendment" and, presumably the term testimonial as well, "must be interpreted with this focus in mind." *Id.* at 50. Consistent with that approach, the Court suggested that an "off hand, overheard remark" would not be testimonial under the Sixth Amendment because "it bears little resemblance to the civil law abuses the Confrontation Clause targeted." *Id.* at 51. Along the same lines, the Court indicated that a statement produced through the "[i]nvolvement of government officers" and with an "eye towards trial" is testimonial because it "presents [a] unique potential for prosecutorial abuse a fact borne out time and again through a history with which the Framers were keenly familiar." *Id.* at 56 n.7.

Second, the Court stated that "[v]arious formulations of th[e] core class of 'testimonial' statements exist": (1) "'ex parte in court testimony or its functional equivalent that is, material such as affidavits, custodial examinations, prior testimony that the defendant was unable to cross-examine, or similar pretrial statements that declarants would reasonably expect to be used prosecutorially,'" *id.* at 51; (2) "'extrajudicial statements . . . contained in formalized testimonial materials, such as affidavits, depositions, prior testimony, or confessions,'" *id.* at 51 52 (quoting *White v. Illinois*, 502 U.S. 346, 365 (1992) (Thomas, J., concurring)); and (3) "'statements that were made under circumstances which would lead an objective witness reasonably to believe that the statement would be available for use at a later trial,'" *Id.* at 52. Importantly, while noting that these three formulations "all share a common nucleus and then define the Clause's coverage at various levels of abstraction around it," *id.*, the Court "found it unnecessary to endorse any of them, because 'some statements qualify under any definition,' " *Davis*, 126 S.Ct. at 2273 (quoting *Crawford*, 541 U.S. at 52).

Third, the Court provided several concrete examples of testimonial and nontestimonial statements. "Whatever else the term [testimonial] covers, it applies at a minimum to prior testimony at a preliminary hearing, before a grand jury, or at a former trial; and to police interrogations." *Crawford*, 541 U.S. at 68. The Court reasoned that "[t]hese are the modern practices with closest kinship to the abuses at which the Confrontation Clause was directed." *Id.* In contrast, the Court stated that "[m]ost of the hearsay exceptions covered statements that by their nature were not testimonial for example, business records or statements in furtherance of a conspiracy." *Id.* at 56.

Relying on this final example, the Government argues that *Crawford* specifically excludes business records from the definition of testimonial. While this argument has superficial appeal, the Supreme Court's several examples of what constitute testimonial statements and this Court's subsequent discussion of that same issue requires us to probe why it is that a business record, such as the autopsy reports at issue here, is not also testimonial and subject to the Confrontation Clause. At the outset, we acknowledge that several courts have rejected arguments similar to the Government's, characterizing *Crawford's* reference to business records as *dicta* and requiring a case by case determination of whether the statements in the business records are testimonial. *See, e.g., State v. Crager*, 844 N.E.2d 390, 398–99 (2005) (refusing to adopt a per se exclusion of all business records from scrutiny under *Crawford*); *People v. Mitchell*, 32 Cal.Rptr.3d 613, 621 (2005) (stating that the *Crawford* Court did not intend that "all documentary evidence which could broadly qualify in some context as a business record . . . automatically be considered non testimonial").

III. The Autopsy Reports Are Admissible as Business Records

We disagree with these courts, however, holding instead that testimonial statements within the meaning of *Crawford* and *Davis* would not qualify as business records under FED. R. EVID. 803(6). Stated differently, we hold that a statement properly admitted under FED. R. EVID. 803(6) cannot be testimonial because a business record is fundamentally inconsistent with what the Supreme Court has suggested comprise the defining characteristics of testimonial evidence.[4]

We look first to the definition of a business record. Rule 803(6) of the Federal Rules of Evidence defines a business record as:

> [a] memorandum, report, record, or data compilation, in any form, of acts, events, conditions, opinions, or diagnoses, made at or near the time by, or from information transmitted by, a person with knowledge, if kept in the course of a regularly conducted business activity, and if it was the regular practice of that business activity to make the memorandum, report, record or data compilation.

FED. R. EVID. 803(6). We know that because Rule 803(6) requires business records to be kept in the regular course of a business activity, records created in anticipation of litigation do not fall within its definition. *See Certain Underwriters at Lloyd's, London v. Sinkovich*, 232 F.3d 200, 205 n.4 (4th Cir.2000) (noting that it "is well established that

---

[4] It should be noted that Chief Justice Rehnquist appears to have read *Crawford* to exclude business records from the definition of "testimonial" simply by virtue of their status as business records. *See Crawford*, 541 U.S. at 76 (Rehnquist C.J., concurring) ("To its credit, the Court's analysis of 'testimony' excludes at least some hearsay exceptions, such as business records and official records.").

documents made in anticipation of litigation are inadmissible under the business records exception"). This Court has further construed Rule 803(6) to exclude records in criminal cases containing observations made by police officers or other law enforcement personnel. *See Rosa*, 11 F.3d at 331–32 (citing *United States v. Oates*, 560 F.2d 45, 70 (2d Cir.1977)).

Because business records cannot be made in anticipation of litigation or include observations made by law enforcement personnel, they "bear[ ] little resemblance to the civil law abuses the Confrontation Clause targeted." *Crawford*, 541 U.S. at 51; *see also id.* at 50 (stating that "the principal evil at which the Confrontation Clause was directed was the civil law mode of criminal procedure, and particularly its use of ex parte examinations as evidence against the accused"). *Crawford* itself suggests that the very same characteristics that preclude a statement's classification as a business record are likely to render the statement testimonial. *See id.* at 56 n.7 (describing as testimonial, statements produced through the "[i]nvolvement of government officers" and made "with an eye towards trial"). Indeed, "[t]he essence of the business record exception contemplated in *Crawford* is that such records or statements are not testimonial in nature because they are prepared in the ordinary course of regularly conducted business and are 'by their nature' not prepared for litigation." *People v. Durio*, 794 N.Y.S.2d 863, 867 (N.Y.Sup.Ct. 2005) (quoting *Crawford*, 541 U.S. at 56); *see also United States v. Cervantes– Flores*, 421 F.3d 825, 834–35 (9th Cir. 2005) (holding that a document analogous to a business record was not testimonial, in part, because it did not "resemble the examples of testimonial evidence given by the Court" in *Crawford*).

Erbo argues, based in large part on our decision in *Saget*, that regardless of their classification as business records, autopsy reports must be testimonial because a medical examiner preparing such a report must have a reasonable expectation the reports may be available for use in a subsequent trial. In *Saget*, we stated that *"Crawford* at least suggests that the determinative factor in determining whether a declarant bears testimony is the declarant's awareness or expectation that his or her statements may later be used at a trial." *Saget*, 377 F.3d at 228. If this statement in *Saget* were controlling, autopsy reports would be testimonial and subject to the Confrontation Clause requirements that the witness be unavailable and the accused have had a prior opportunity to cross examine him or her. That is, although autopsy reports are not prepared for use at trial, *see Rosa*, 11 F.3d at 332 (stating, "a medical examiner . . . bears more similarity to a treating physician than he does to one who is merely rendering an opinion for use in the trial of a case" (internal quotation marks omitted)); *Durio*, 794 N.Y.S.2d at 869 ("That [an autopsy report] may be presented as evidence in a homicide trial does not mean that it was composed for that accusatory purpose or that its use by a prosecutor is the inevitable consequence of its composition."); *see also People v. Washington*, 654 N.E.2d 967 (1995) ("The mandate of [the Medical Examiner's Office] is clear, to provide an impartial determination of the cause of death."), any medical examiner preparing such a report must expect that it *may* later be available for use at trial.

We do not believe, however, that this statement in *Saget* should be read to have adopted such an expansive definition of testimonial. Though helpful in framing the discussion of the issues under consideration in *Saget*, those statements concerning the scope of "testimonial" did not determine the outcome in that case. *See Saget*, 377 F.3d at 229 ("We need not attempt to articulate a complete definition of testimonial statements in order to hold that [the declarant's] statements did not constitute testimony."). Furthermore, this Court's subsequent decision in *Mungo*, in which we considered *Crawford's* observation that "'statements taken by police officers in the course of interrogations are also testimonial,'" suggests some further strictures on the scope of that term. *See Mungo*, 393 F.3d at 336 n.9 (quoting *Crawford*, 541 U.S. at 52). While acknowledging that interrogation might include "any asking of questions," *id.*, we speculated the Supreme Court intended the word to include only questioning characterized by "'formality, command, and thoroughness for full information and circumstantial detail,'" *id.* (quoting *Webster's Third New International Dictionary* 1182 (1976) (definition for "interrogate")). That "more limited meaning," we reasoned, "is more consistent with the other types of testimonial statements," such as trial testimony and depositions, mentioned by the Court. *Id.* This discussion in *Mungo*, like that in *Saget*, is also *dicta.* Nonetheless, because a declarant responding to any type of questioning, as in *Mungo*, could still reasonably anticipate a responsive statement would be available for use at trial, *Mungo's* dicta undermine any suggestion that the reasonable expectation of the declarant should be what distinguishes testimonial from nontestimonial statements. Certainly, practical norms may lead a medical examiner reasonably to expect autopsy reports may be available for use at trial, but this practical expectation alone cannot be dispositive on the issue of whether those reports are testimonial.

Finally, we return to the decision in *Crawford* and note that the Supreme Court expressly declined to adopt a specific formulation of when a statement is "testimonial." 541 U.S. at 68. Given that the Supreme Court did not opt for an expansive definition that depended on a declarant's expectations, we are hesitant to do so here. In addition, we point out that the characterization of business records as nontestimonial only accords with the need to preserve the efficiency and integrity of the truth seeking process. Chief Justice Rehnquist praised what he considered to be *Crawford's* per se exclusion of business records from the definition of testimonial. He wrote, "the Court's analysis of 'testimony' excludes at least some hearsay exceptions, such as business records and official records. To hold otherwise would require numerous additional witnesses without any apparent gain in the truth seeking process." *Crawford*, 541 U.S. at 76 (Rehnquist, C.J., concurring). Another court recognized the practical difficulties we avoid in considering autopsy reports nontestimonial:

> Years may pass between the performance of the autopsy and the apprehension of the perpetrator. This passage of time can easily lead to the unavailability of the examiner who prepared the report. Moreover, medical examiners who regularly perform hundreds of autopsies are unlikely to have any independent recollection of the autopsy at issue in a particular case and in testifying invariably rely entirely on the autopsy report. Unlike other forensic tests, an autopsy cannot be replicated by another pathologist. Certainly it would be against society's interests to permit the unavailability of the medical examiner who prepared the report to preclude the prosecution of a homicide case.

Durio, 794 N.Y.S.2d at 869 (holding that autopsy reports are not testimonial by virtue of their status as business records). In sum, therefore, we hold that where a statement is properly determined to be a business record as defined by FED. R. EVID. 803(6), it is not testimonial within the meaning of *Crawford*, even where the declarant is aware that it may be available for later use at trial.

In this case, the autopsy reports qualified as business records under Rule 803(6). Autopsy reports are "reports kept in the course of a regularly conducted business activity"; the Office of the Chief Medical Examiner of New York conducts thousands of routine autopsies every year, without regard to the likelihood of their use at trial. Nor do the Chief Medical Examiner's reports constitute the observations of a police officer;

§ 557 of the New York City Charter describes the office as an "independent office" within the Department of Health and Mental Hygiene. *See also Rosa*, 11 F.3d at 332 (holding that the employees of the Medical Examiner's Office are "physicians and pathologists," not "attorneys" and that autopsy reports are business records); *Washington*, 86 N.Y.2d at 192 (holding that under New York law, the Medical Examiner is "not subject to the control of the prosecutor"); *Durio*, 794 N.Y.S.2d at 867 (holding that "[u]nder New York law an autopsy report can be considered a business record. . . ."). Because the autopsy reports are business records as defined in FED. R. EVID. 803(6), they are nontestimonial.

IV. The Autopsy Reports Are Admissible as Public Records

We hold that the autopsy reports are equally admissible as public records. For reasons substantially analogous to those outlined above, we find that public records are, indeed, nontestimonial under *Crawford*, 541 U.S. at 36. The Federal Rules of Evidence define public records as "Records, reports, statements . . . in any form, of public offices or agencies, setting forth (A) the activities of the office or agency, or (B) matters observed pursuant to duty imposed by law as to which matters there was a duty to report. . . ." FED. R. EVID. 803(8) (A B). But this Rule is not unlimited. As with Rule 803(6), governing the admissibility of business records, Rule 803(8) excludes reports of "matters observed by police officers and law enforcement personnel. . . ." FED. R. EVID. 803(8)(B). In addition, Rule 803(8) excludes documents prepared for the ultimate purpose of litigation, just as does Rule 803(6). *United States v. Bohrer*, 807 F.2d 159, 162 (10th Cir.1986). In his interpretation of the *Crawford* opinion, Chief Justice Rehnquist considered public records alongside business records to fall outside the "testimonial" ambit of the Confrontation Clause. *Id.* at 76. (Rehnquist, C.J., concurring). These factors suggest that public records, like business records, "bear [] little resemblance to the civil law abuses the Confrontation Clause targeted." *Crawford*, 541 U.S. at 51, 124 S.Ct. 1354. We thus hold that public records are nontestimonial, and not subject to the strictures of the Confrontation Clause.

In this case, the autopsy reports qualified as public records. They are "record[s] . . . setting forth . . . activities of the office . . . or . . . matters observed pursuant to duty imposed by law as to which matters there was a duty to report. . . ." FED. R. EVID. 803(8) (A-B). According to § 557(f) of the New York City Charter, the Chief Medical Examiner has the duty to conduct autopsies in various situations, including when presented with "persons dying from criminal violence, by casualty, by suicide, suddenly . . . when unattended by a physician, in a correctional facility or in any suspicious or unusual manner or where an application is made pursuant to law for a permit to cremate the body of a person." As noted above, these reports are routine, and do not constitute the "observations of police officers." *See also Washington*, 86 N.Y.2d at 192 (holding that the Medical Examiner is "not subject to the control of the prosecutor"); *Rosa*, 11 F.3d at 332 (holding that autopsy reports are public records); *Durio*, 794 N.Y.S.2d at 868 (holding that autopsies qualify as public records under New York law). Because autopsy reports are public records under FED. R. EVID. 803(8), they are nontestimonial.

CONCLUSION

For the foregoing reasons, even though Erbo had no opportunity to cross examiné the medical examiners who prepared the autopsy reports, their admission into evidence did not violate the Confrontation Clause. . . . [T]he judgment of conviction is AF-FIRMED.

NOTES AND QUESTIONS

1. *Per se Exclusion of Business Records.* In *Feliz*, the court held that "a statement properly admitted under Fed. R. Evid. 803(6) cannot be testimonial because a business record is fundamentally inconsistent with what the Supreme Court has suggested comprise the defining characteristics of testimonial evidence." *Id.* at 234. Thus, the court adopted a per se exclusion of all business records from scrutiny under *Crawford*? Do you agree with the court's decision? Should the determination of whether statements in business records are testimonial be made on a case-by-case basis?

2. *Prepared with an "eye towards trial."* In *Crawford v. Washington*, 541 U.S. 36 (2004), the Supreme Court indicated that a statement produced through the "[i]nvolvement of government officers" and with an "eye towards trial" is testimonial because it "presents [a] unique potential for prosecutorial abuse — a fact borne out time and again through a history with which the Framers were keenly familiar." *Id.* at 56 n.7. Are autopsy reports prepared with an "eye towards trial"? Are such reports made in anticipation of litigation, at least where the medical examiner concludes that the cause of death was homicide? Do such reports present a potential for prosecutorial abuse?

3. *The "Objective Witness" Test.* The *Feliz* court downplayed the importance of the fact that an autopsy report was prepared in anticipation of being used in a homicide trial. The court stated that "practical norms may lead a medical examiner reasonably to expect autopsy reports may be available for use at trial, but this practical expectation alone may cannot be dispositive on the issue of whether those reports are testimonial." *Feliz*, 467 F.3d at 235. In *Crawford*, the Supreme Court referred to a "core class" of testimonial statements, which included, for example, " 'statements that were made under circumstances which would lead an objective witness reasonably to believe that the statement would be available for use at a later trial.' " *Id.* at 53 (internal citations omitted). *See also State v. Caulfield*, 722 N.W.2d 304 (Minn. 2006) ("We have said the critical determinative factor in assessing whether a statement is testimonial is whether it was prepared for litigation."). Is *Feliz* inconsistent with the ruling in *Crawford*?

4. *Reliability and Necessity.* In *Crawford*, Chief Justice Rehnquist wrote, "the Court's analysis of 'testimony' excludes at least some hearsay exceptions, such as business records and official records. To hold otherwise would require numerous additional witnesses without any apparent gain in the truth-seeking process." *Crawford*, 541 U.S. at 76 (Rehnquist, C.J., concurring). The government in *Feliz* cited to Chief Justice Rehnquist's statement to support its argument that *Crawford* specifically excludes business records from the definition of testimonial. However, isn't Chief Justice Rehnquist's statement merely *dicta*? Do you agree with Chief Justice Rehnquist's statement that to hold that business records are testimonial "would require numerous additional witnesses without any apparent gain to the truth-seeking process"? Would requiring the medical examiner to testify advance the "truth-seeking process"? What kinds of questions might be asked by defense counsel on cross examination? Finally, the *Feliz* court argued that the passage of time may lead to the unavailability of the medical examiner who prepared the report and "it would be against society's interest to permit the unavailability of the medical examiner who prepared the report to preclude the prosecution of a homicide case." *Feliz*, 467 3d. At 236 (quoting

People v. Durio, 794 N.Y.2d 863, 869 (N.Y. Sup. Ct. 2005)). Do you find the court's necessity argument compelling?

5. *Split of Authority.* The courts remain divided on whether autopsy reports are "testimonial" in nature. In addition to the Second Circuit in *Feliz*, at least one other court has held that autopsy reports are nontestimonial and admissible under the business and public records exception. *See State v. Craig*, 853 N.E.2d 621 (Ohio 2006). However, in *State v. Johnson*, Minn. Ct. App., No. A07-1189 (Oct. 14, 2008), the Minnesota appellate court reached the opposite result. The court held that a forensic laboratory report prepared for use in a criminal prosecution was a "testimonial" statement subject to the requirements of the Confrontation Clause. *See also State v. Crager*, 164 Ohio App.3d 816, 844 N.E.2d 390, 389–99 (2005) (refusing to adopt a per se exclusion of all business records from scrutiny under *Crawford*); *People v. Mitchell*, 131 Cal. App. 4th 1210, 32 Cal.Rptr.3d 613, 621 (2005) (stating that *Crawford* did not intend that "all documentary evidence which could broadly qualify in some context as a business record . . . automatically be considered non-testimonial"). Other courts have distinguished between statements of fact and statements of opinion in autopsy reports, holding that the latter are testimonial but the former are not. *See Rollins v. State*, 897 A.2d 821 (Md. 2006).

[2]   Reports of Non-Adversarial Matters

UNITED STATES v. ENTERLINE
894 F.2d 287 (8th Cir. 1990)

Beam, Circuit Judge.

Nick Cloyd Enterline appeals from his conviction by a jury on two counts of transporting in interstate commerce a motor vehicle, knowing that it was stolen, in violation of 18 U.S.C. §§ 2312 and 2(b) (1988), and on two counts of possessing with the intent to sell a motor vehicle, knowing that its identification number had been removed or otherwise altered, in violation of 18 U.S.C. § 2321 (1988). Enterline was acquitted of count five of receiving or selling a motor vehicle, knowing that it was stolen, in violation of 18 U.S.C. § 2313 (1988). The district court sentenced Enterline to fifteen years in prison. We affirm.

Enterline was indicted by a grand jury on the five counts on November 16, 1988. From 1981 until his indictment, Enterline operated a vehicle salvage business from a lot in Fayetteville, Arkansas. A building on the lot also served as his residence. The auto salvage business provided Enterline with the cover for the changeover scheme in which the government implicated him. Enterline would purchase a wrecked or salvaged vehicle, and would have stolen for him an automobile of the same year, make and model. He would then attach the vehicle identification number from the salvaged car to the stolen vehicle, thus providing a new identity for the machine. The automobile would then be registered. Specifically, the indictment charged the following: counts one and two charged the transportation and possession, with the intent to sell, of a 1984 Cadillac Seville; count three charged the transportation of a 1987 Chevrolet Astro van; count four charged the possession, with the intent to sell, of a 1986 Chevrolet Camaro IROC; and count five charged the possession of a 1985 Chevrolet Suburban.

The trial involved complicated and lengthy testimony from more than twenty-five government witnesses. Each related, piecemeal, facts involving Enterline's dealings with each vehicle charged in the changeover scheme. The government's case made use of the testimony of four convicted car thieves who testified that they stole the particular vehicles charged in the indictment at the specific request of Enterline. Enterline denied that he ordered any of the vehicles stolen, and argued that all were legitimately purchased and sold as part of his salvage business.

II. DISCUSSION

A. *Hearsay Objection to Testimony*

On appeal, Enterline challenges the testimony of Edward Satterfield, a Special Agent of the FBI, based in Little Rock, Arkansas. Satterfield participated in the investigation of the scheme, and was present at Enterline's residence in Fayetteville on August 8, 1987, when law enforcement officers executed a search warrant. As part of that search, officers from the auto theft unit of the Tulsa Police Department seized several vehicle identification number plates, as well as shipping manifests, from vehicles on Enterline's property. Satterfield then ran a computer check on the identification numbers, and found that several of the vehicles had been reported stolen. Satterfield testified that the computer report indicated that three vehicles not charged in the indictment, but present on Enterline's property, had been reported stolen, and that two vehicles not charged had been renumbered. While this portion of Satterfield's testimony did not concern vehicles charged in the indictment, Enterline argues on appeal not that the testimony was inadmissible under Federal Rule of Evidence 404(b), but that the testimony was hearsay and not admissible through any exception in the rules. We disagree, since Satterfield's testimony from the computer report, while hearsay, was admissible under the public records exception, Federal Rule of Evidence 803(8)(B).

Satterfield derived his conclusion that several cars on Enterline's property were reported stolen from a computer report comparing the identification numbers given to Satterfield with vehicle identification numbers from all cars reported stolen. The computer report is clearly hearsay, since it is an out of court statement offered to prove the truth of the matter asserted — that the cars on Enterline's property were reported stolen. The report nevertheless qualifies as a public record within Rule 803(8)(B). The hearsay exception for public records is based on both the necessity for admitting such records and their inherent trustworthiness. Indeed, were the computer record not admissible as a public record to prove that the cars were reported stolen, the difficulty of proving that simple fact would be enormous. Thus, this circuit has admitted, for example, under Rule 803(8), certified documents from the Missouri Department of Revenue to prove ownership of an automobile. *See United States v. King*, 590 F.2d 253, 255 (8th Cir. 1978), *cert. denied*, 440 U.S. 973 (1979). Our concern is thus not whether the public records exception applies in this case, but whether the computer report falls within the exclusion found in Rule 803(8)(B) for matters observed by law enforcement officers in a criminal case. We hold that it does not.

It is clear that the exclusion concerns matters observed by the police at the scene of the crime. Such observations are potentially unreliable since they are made in an adversary setting, and are often subjective evaluations of whether a crime was committed. The exclusion seeks to avoid admitting an officer's report of his observations in lieu of his personal testimony of what he observed. "In adopting this exception, Congress was concerned about prosecutors attempting to prove their cases in chief simply by putting into evidence police officers' reports of their contemporaneous observations of crime." *United States v. Orozco*, 590 F.2d 789, 794 (9th Cir.) (quoting *United States v. Grady*, 544 F.2d 598, 604 (2d Cir. 1976)), *cert. denied*, 442 U.S. 920 (1979). Similarly, this circuit explained, in dictum, that Rule 803(8)(B) contains an exclusion for criminal cases because police reports are not "reliable evidence of whether the allegations of criminal conduct they contain are true." *United States v. Bell*, 785 F.2d 640, 644 (8th Cir. 1986).

Thus, the subject matter of the public record or report determines its admissibility; the exclusion applies only to "matters observed by police officers and other law enforcement personnel." Other circuits have found that reports not containing matters observed by officers in an adversarial setting do not fall within the exclusion to Rule 803(8)(B). In *Orozco*, the Ninth Circuit considered a computer report that the car in which defendants were arrested had crossed the Mexican border on the night of the arrest. The computer report was made by United States Customs officials at the border, who, as standard procedure, enter vehicle license numbers into a computer to determine whether the same vehicle has crossed the border within a seventy-two hour period. The Ninth Circuit held the computer report admissible, finding it significant that "the simple recordation of license numbers of all vehicles which pass [the] station is not of the adversarial confrontation nature which might cloud [an official's] perception." *Orozco*, 590 F.2d at 793. Thus, the situation provided little opportunity for an inaccurate report. *Id.*

Similarly, in [*United States v. Quezada*, 754 F.2d 1190 (5th Cir. 1985)], the Fifth Circuit admitted a warrant of deportation in a proceeding in which defendant was charged with illegal re-entry into the United States following his deportation. The warrant contained a record made by the agent that the defendant had departed the country. The Fifth Circuit found that the information in the warrant required no more of the law enforcement officer than to "mechanically register an unambiguous factual matter." *Quezada*, 754 F.2d at 1194. Thus, "[i]n the case of documents recording routine, objective observations, made as part of the everyday function of the preparing official or agency, the factors likely to cloud the perception of an official engaged in the more traditional law enforcement functions of observation and investigation of crime are simply not present." *Id. Cf. United States v. Hernandez-Rojas*, 617 F.2d 533, 534–35 (9th Cir.), *cert. denied*, 449 U.S. 864 (1980) (notation of departure on warrant "has none of the features of the subjective report made by a law enforcement official in an on-the-scene investigation, which investigative reports lack sufficient guarantees of trustworthiness because they are made in an adversary setting"); *United States v. Puente*, 826 F.2d 1415, 1417–18 (5th Cir. 1987) (admitting computer report made at Mexican border on same rationale as *Orozco* and *Quezada*).

Similarly, the facts of this case are not within the purpose of the exclusion. The computer report does not contain contemporaneous observations by police officers at the scene of a crime, and thus presents none of the dangers of unreliability that such a report presents. Rather, the report merely contains, and is based on, facts: that cars with certain vehicle identification numbers were reported to have been stolen. Neither the notation of the vehicle identification numbers themselves nor their entry into a computer presents an adversarial setting or an opportunity for subjective observations by law enforcement officers. The officers were not recording their observations of crime, but were recording facts presented to them. Thus, the computer compilation, while hearsay, is simply not a report susceptible to the dangers which the exclusion set forth in Rule 803(8)(B) was designed to avoid. *Cf. United States v. Johnson*, 722 F.2d 407, 409–10 (8th Cir. 1983) (admission of certified document containing a serial number report from the manufacturer of a gun on grounds that report was not a matter observed by law enforcement personnel). Accordingly, we find no error in the district court's admission of Satterfield's testimony.

*   *   *

III. CONCLUSION

We have considered Enterline's other arguments on appeal and find them to be without merit. Accordingly, for the reasons stated, we affirm the judgment of the district court.

NOTES AND QUESTIONS

1. In *Enterline*, the Eighth Circuit held that the computer report comparing the identification numbers found during the execution of the search warrant on the defendant's property with vehicle identification numbers from cars reported stolen does not fall within the exclusion found in Rule 803(8)(B) for matters observed by law enforcement personnel in a criminal case. What is the reasoning of the court?

2. In *Enterline*, the court stated that the hearsay exception for public records is based both on necessity and the inherent reliability of such evidence. The court, however, limited its discussion to the trustworthiness of records prepared by a public official as part of a routine procedure in a non-adversarial setting. In *United States v. Quezada*, 754 F.2d 1190 (5th Cir. 1985), the court addressed the necessity justification for the hearsay exception. *Quezada* involved the admissibility of INS Form I-205, a warrant of deportation, which contained virtually all of the information needed for proving defendant's prior arrest and deportation in a prosecution for illegally reentering the country. The court observed:

> [I]n a case like the one at bar, the absolute necessity of proving the government's case through the use of public records is unquestionable. In the years 1977–81, the INS processed for departure from the country, on average, more than 1,000,000 aliens annually. In 1981, more than 260,000 aliens were processed in the State of Texas alone, with over 6,000 of those having been officially deported. Given these numbers, it is unlikely that testimony by an INS officer as to the deportation of a particular individual could be based on anything other than recorded observations with such testimony being merely cumulative to the more reliable written record of deportation.

Id. at 1194–95.

Thus, the case for necessity is based on two grounds. First, the expense and inconvenience of having to call to testify every public official involved in the public transaction or event is prohibitive. Second, since INS officials are involved in processing hundreds of thousands of aliens for departure annually, the public official is likely to have little, if any, independent memory of a particular entry in an INS document. The recorded document of deportation therefore constitutes the more reliable evidence.

3. What is the justification for excluding matters observed by law enforcement officers in criminal cases as required by Rule 803(8)(B)? In support of its decision admitting the computer report, the court in *Enterline* stated: "The computer report does not contain contemporaneous observations by police officers at the scene of the crime, and thus presents none of the dangers of unreliability that such a report presents." *Enterline, supra*, 894 F.2d at 290. Does the court's ruling limit the Rule 803(8)(B) prohibition to matters observed at the scene of the crime? Should Rule 803(8)(B) be construed to read: ". . . excluding, however, in criminal cases matters observed by police officers and other law enforcement personnel [*at the scene of the crime*]"? (Emphasis added.)

4. *Enterline* could be read as simply recognizing an exception to the exclusion created by Rule 803(8)(B). If so, what are the requirements for admitting into evidence under the public records exception matters otherwise observed by police officers and other law enforcement personnel?

5. Are police reports of matters observed by law enforcement officers beyond the scene of the crime sufficiently reliable? *See United States v. Puente*, 826 F.2d 1415, 1418 (5th Cir. 1987) (admitting computer report listing the license plate number of every vehicle coming into the United States from Mexico, finding that the "information was recorded by a public official as part of a routine procedure in a non-adversarial setting"); *United States v. Quezada*, 754 F.2d 1190 (5th Cir. 1985) (admitting a warrant of deportation in a proceeding in which defendant was charged with illegal re-entry into the United States following his deportation, reasoning that the warrant required no more of the law enforcement officer than to "mechanically register an unambiguous factual matter"); *United States v. Orozco*, 590 F.2d 789, 793 (9th Cir. 1979) (admitting a computer report that the car in which defendants were arrested had crossed the Mexican border on the night of the arrest, reasoning that "the simple recordation of license numbers of all vehicles which pass [the] station is not of the adversarial confrontation nature which might cloud [an official's] perception").

[2]   "Law Enforcement Personnel"

PROBLEM

Problem 8-3. *Reports Prepared by a Private Company at the Request of the Government.* Defendant robbed a bank wearing a handkerchief and brandishing a long-barreled revolver. During his getaway he forced a bank customer to escort him out of the bank. He directed the customer to take him to his (the customer's) car, where he ordered the customer into the passenger seat. Defendant then drove the car a short distance before letting the customer out. The defendant later abandoned the car. The car was discovered by police and returned to the customer.

The customer found a pair of unfamiliar eyeglasses in the car and turned them over to the FBI. Special Agent Roth sent the glasses to Edward H. Schmidt and Sons, a company that manufactured eyeglasses. Schmidt and Sons used a lensometer machine to determine the prescription of each lens. They also determined that the eyeglasses had designer frames by "Geoffrey Beene" which were anywhere from eight to twelve months old. Agent Roth then contacted companies who had sold "Geoffrey Beene" frames in the last year. Seventeen sales of "Geoffrey Beene" frames had been made and only one of these sales matched the prescription in the eyeglasses found in the customer's vehicle. This sale was to the defendant. Furthermore, defendant attempted to purchase an identical pair of replacement eyeglasses a few days after the robbery.

Defendant was charged with bank robbery. At his trial, the government sought to introduce the computer printouts of the lensometer readings for each lens of the eyeglasses found in the customer's vehicle. Defendant objected, arguing that Fed. R.

Evid. 803(8)(B) and (C) precluded the introduction into evidence of the computer printouts of the lensometer readings. He claimed that Schmidt and Sons was an agent of the government who had prepared the printouts in preparation for prosecution. The government responded that the business records exception in 803(6), rather than the public records exception, determined the admissibility of the lensometer computer printouts. As Schmidt and Sons made the printouts in the regular course of business, the government argued that the printouts were admissible under Rule 803(6). Does Rule 803(8) apply to private business records compiled at the request of the government in anticipation of prosecution? Are the lensometer printouts admissible under the business records exception? If admissible under the business records exception, should the printouts still be excluded under the public records exception because of the restrictions in Rule 803(8)(B) and (C)? *See United States v. Blackburn*, 992 F.2d 666 (7th Cir. 1993) (facts modified).

G. RESIDUAL HEARSAY RULE

The residual exception contained in Fed. R. Evid. 807,[36] authorizes admission of hearsay statements that are inadmissible under any of the enumerated exceptions to the hearsay rule, but that have "equivalent circumstantial guarantees of trustworthiness." Rule 807 is a 1997 amendment to the Federal Rules of Evidence that combined and replaced residual exceptions contained in Rules 803(24) and 804(b)(5). The Advisory Committee's Note to Rule 807 states,

> The contents of Rule 803(24) and Rule 804(b)(5) have been combined and transferred to a new Rule 807. This was done to facilitate additions to Rules 803 and 804. No change in meaning is intended.

Accordingly, case law construing former Rules 803(24) and 804(b)(5) should be considered applicable to Rule 807. When cases in this chapter refer to and examine these former Rules (*i.e.* 803(24) and 804(b)(5)), one should consider the discussion as applicable to the residual exception's new residence — Rule 807.

Originally, Congress enacted the residual exception to provide flexibility in rare instances when sufficiently trustworthy and necessary hearsay could not satisfy the requirements of a specified categorical exception. In examining the legislative history, it is clear that Congress envisioned that the "residual exceptions will be used very rarely, and only in exceptional circumstances."[37] This legislative intent is further buttressed by the Senate Judiciary Report on the Federal Rules of Evidence: "The committee does not intend to establish a broad license for trial judges to admit hearsay statements that do not fall within one of the other exceptions. . . . The residual exceptions are not meant

---

[36] Fed. R. Evid. 807 provides:

A statement not specifically covered by Rule 803 or 804 but having equivalent circumstantial guarantees of trustworthiness, is not excluded by the hearsay rule, if the court determines that (A) the statement is offered as evidence of a material fact; (B) the statement is more probative on the point for which it is offered than any other evidence which the proponent can procure through reasonable efforts; and (C) the general purposes of these rules and the interests of justice will best be served by admission of the statement into evidence. However, a statement may not be admitted under this exception unless the proponent of it makes known to the adverse party sufficiently in advance of the trial or hearing to provide the adverse party with a fair opportunity to prepare to meet it, the proponent's intention to offer the statement and the particulars of it, including the name and address of the declarant.

[37] S. Rep. No. 1277, 93d Cong., 2d Sess. 11 (1974), reprinted in 1974 U.S.C.C.A.N. 7051, 7066.

to authorize major judicial revisions of the hearsay rule, including its present exceptions."[38]

To admit hearsay evidence under the residual exception, the district court must find that (1) the statement bears circumstantial guarantees of trustworthiness equivalent to those that warrant the admission of hearsay under the other exceptions enumerated in Rule 803 (or, when applicable, Rule 804); (2) the statement relates to a material fact; (3) the statement is more probative on the point for which it is offered than any other reasonably obtainable evidence; (4) the general purposes of the rules of evidence and the interests of justice are served by the statement's admission; and (5) the offering party has provided the opposing party reasonable notice before trial of his intention to use the statement.

[1]   The Confrontation Clause — Demonstrating "Particularized Guarantees of Trustworthiness"

UNITED STATES v. PENEAUX
432 F.3d 882 (8th Cir. 2005)

A jury convicted Sherman Peneaux on four counts of aggravated sexual abuse of a child, T.P., and on two counts of assault, and the district court imposed concurrent sentences of 180 months for the sexual abuse offenses and 60 months for the assault convictions. Peneaux appeals, arguing that there was insufficient evidence to sustain his convictions, that hearsay statements were improperly admitted, and that his constitutional right to confrontation was violated. We affirm.

I.

In March 2002 the South Dakota Department of Social Services (DSS) removed T.P. and her siblings, N.P. and Fianna, from the custody of their parents, Sherman Peneaux and Juanita Swalley, based on allegations that Peneaux had abused Fianna. At that time T.P. was three years old, and N.P. was two. The children were placed in the Spotted Tail Crisis Center, and T.P. subsequently reported that Peneaux had sexually abused her and extinguished a cigarette on her body. T.P. made the statements to tribal police investigator Grace Her Many Horses, forensic investigator Lora Hawkins, child care case worker Zane McClarnnan, pediatrician Dr. Lori Strong, and two different foster parents, Edith Connot and Penny Norris. . . .

The case went to trial in September 2004, and the government called tribal investigator Grace Her Many Horses after other witnesses had provided background information. She testified without objection about statements T.P. made during an interview with her. She reported that T.P. told her that she had been sexually and physically abused. Then the government called T.P. to the stand; her testimony was inconsistent. On direct examination T.P. denied that Peneaux had abused her, but acknowledged that she had previously told people that she had been sexually abused. The prosecutor presented her with drawings of a naked man and woman and asked her to mark the part of Peneaux's body which had touched her and the part of her body which Peneaux had touched. T.P. circled the genital region and anus on both the male

---

[38] *Id.* at 20, reprinted in U.S.C.C.A.N. at 7066. For an excellent and thoughtful examination of the legislative history and application of the residual exceptions, *see* David A. Soneshein, *The Residual Exceptions to the Federal Hearsay Rule: Two Exceptions in Search of a Rule*, 57 N.Y.U. L. Rev. 867 (1982).

and female diagrams. When she was asked to identify the areas she had marked, she called them the "pee pee" and "butt." Without objection the diagrams were received into evidence as exhibits. T.P. was also asked how she received the burn mark on her stomach. She responded that Peneaux had inflicted it with a lit cigarette, but she denied he had ever burned her when questioned by defense counsel.

The government called other individuals with whom T.P. had spoken prior to trial. Zane McClarnnan, an employee of the Spotted Tail Crisis Center, testified that T.P. told him that "my dad likes to undress me" and would "lay on top of me." T.P.'s stepmother, Juanita Swalley, was asked about statements she had made to the FBI and whether she had disclosed that T.P. told her "daddy was doing loving to me" and other similar comments. Swalley answered that she could not remember precisely what she had told the agents, but she acknowledged that she had signed the statement she gave to the FBI. The defense did not object to the testimony of either of these witnesses.

Foster parent Edith Connot testified to an incident she had observed at her home. She saw T.P. under her kitchen table touching the genitals of her four year old son. When Connot explained that such behavior was inappropriate, T.P. replied that her father touched her in that way. Again there was no objection by the defense. T.P.'s other foster parent, Penny Norris, testified that she saw many little white marks on T.P.'s body. T.P. told her that Peneaux had burned her with his cigarettes when Norris asked if she had been bitten by bugs. Norris also testified to statements made by N.P., T.P.'s brother, that Peneaux had also burned him with a cigarette. No objection was raised to any of this testimony. The defense did object to testimony Norris gave about a conversation she had with Dr. Allison during a wellness check of T.P. which she had arranged after learning that Peneaux might have physically and sexually abused the child. Norris reported that Dr. Allison had remarked that the circular marks on T.P. could be cigarette burns.

The government next called forensic investigator Lora Hawkins, who testified to statements T.P. had made during two separate interviews. Hawkins testified that during the first interview T.P. told her that "my daddy gets on top of me," that "my daddy touches my pee pee," and that he wanted her to touch "by his pee pee." Hawkins also testified that when asked where Peneaux had touched her, T.P. grabbed her crotch. Hawkins further testified that during their second interview, T.P. "consistently presented the same information" and told her that Peneaux had touched her genitals both with his fingers and his penis and that he had tried to penetrate her anus with his penis. Not only did the defense not object to Hawkins' testimony, it offered to introduce the video recordings of these interviews into evidence if the government did not. Peneaux's counsel also had written transcripts of the videos made and entered them into evidence.

Dr. Lora Strong, a pediatrician who examined both T.P. and her brother, was another government witness. She testified about T.P.'s statements indicating that Peneaux had abused her sexually and physically and about her own physical findings. When Dr. Strong asked T.P. whether anyone had touched her where "she goes pee from," T.P. responded yes. When asked who had done it, she stated "Sherman." When asked where Peneaux hurt her, T.P. pointed to her genital area. When asked about her circular scar, T.P. replied "Sherman hurt me." When asked how, she answered "burn with cigarette."

Although the defense did not object to Dr. Strong's testimony about T.P., it did object to her testimony about T.P.'s brother, N.P. No grounds were given for the objection, and it was overruled. Dr. Strong then testified that N.P. had a circular scar on his right knee which was similar to the one found on T.P. She also testified that when she asked N.P. how he got hurt, he responded "burn." When asked what that meant, he answered "Sherman" and "Sherman hurt."

*   *   *

The defense called witnesses who testified that they never saw Peneaux sexually or physically abuse T.P. or his other children. The assistant to T.P.'s health care provider testified that T.P. had been examined numerous times before she was removed from her parents' custody and nothing in her records indicated she had been burned. No physical evidence indicating sexual abuse had been reported, and Dr. Strong had noted that her genitals were normal for her age. Although the mark on her stomach was consistent "with the possibility" of a cigarette burn, Dr. Strong admitted something else could have caused it. Betty Kallinger, a physician's assistant at the Horizon Health Care Mission where T.P. was often treated, testified that T.P.'s medical records did not indicate that she had been burned and that the scar could have resulted from an infected sore.

At the conclusion of the government's case the defense moved for a judgment of acquittal which was denied. The defense again moved for judgment of acquittal at the conclusion of all the evidence; the court reserved ruling on the motion and submitted the case to the jury. The jury returned guilty verdicts on all counts, and the defense moved for judgment notwithstanding the verdict and alternatively for a new trial. Both motions were denied. Peneaux appeals, arguing that there was insufficient evidence to sustain his convictions and that the district court abused its discretion by admitting statements which were hearsay and which violated his constitutional right to confrontation.

*   *   *

III.

Peneaux complains that the district court improperly admitted T.P.'s prior inconsistent statements as substantive evidence. He devotes much of his brief to arguing that unsworn prior inconsistent statements cannot be admitted as substantive evidence under Rule 801(d)(1)(A). The government does not refute this argument, but instead contends that these statements were properly admitted in this case as substantive evidence under Rule 807, the residual exception to the hearsay rule, and Rule 803(4), the exception for statements related to medical diagnosis or treatment. Peneaux cites no authority for the proposition that a jury cannot consider residual hearsay as substantive evidence, and we have repeatedly allowed the admission of residual hearsay testimony for that purpose. *United States v. Dorian*, 803 F.2d 1439, 1443–46 (8th Cir.1986); *United States v. Renville*, 779 F.2d 430, 439 (8th Cir.1985). If the testimony was properly admitted, it may be considered as substantive evidence, and the district court was not obligated to tell the jury it could not consider inconsistent statements as substantive evidence.

In order for testimony to be admissible under Rule 807 there must be a showing that (1) the statement has equivalent circumstantial guarantees of trustworthiness to the other hearsay exceptions; (2) the statement is offered as evidence of a material fact; (3) the statement is more probative on the point for which it is offered than any other evidence which the proponent can procure through reasonable efforts; (4) the general purposes of the rules and the interests of justice will best be served by its admission; and (5) adequate notice must be given to the opposing party. *See* Fed. R. Evid. 807; *United*

States v. Balfany, 965 F.2d 575, 581–82 (8th Cir.1992). We review the district court's determination of admissibility of residual hearsay testimony for abuse of discretion. Where the defendant has failed to preserve the error for appeal, however, we review the admission of evidence only for plain error.

Peneaux complains that T.P.'s out of court statements to Zane McClarnnan, Penny Norris, Juanita Swalley, and Lora Hawkins should not have been admitted under Rule 807. He argues that prior inconsistent unsworn statements are not evidence of a material fact and cannot be more probative than the victim's own testimony. According to him, admission of such statements is contrary to the congressional intent limiting the use of statements admitted under Rule 801. Because Peneaux did not object to this testimony during trial we review its admission only for plain error. In order to establish plain error, a party must demonstrate (1) an error, (2) that is plain, and (3) which affects substantial rights. If those elements are met, we will not reverse unless the "error seriously affect[s] the fairness, integrity or public reputation of judicial proceedings." *United States v. Olano*, 507 U.S. 725, 732–36 (1993).

In this case there is no issue about adequate notice under Rule 807. Well before trial the government complied with the rule by filing notice of its intent to introduce T.P.'s prior out of court statements through the testimony of Zane McClarnnan, Penny Norris, Lora Hawkins, and Juanita Swalley. The notice also provided information about the nature of the statements or where they could be located, along with the names, addresses, and phone numbers of the witnesses. The defense made no response or objection to the notice, and it did not object at trial to the admission of T.P.'s out of court statements through the testimony of these witnesses.

Although Peneaux has not argued that these statements are untrustworthy, we nevertheless consider the issue, for "as the trustworthiness of a statement increases, the justification for excluding it decreases." *United States v. Shaw*, 824 F.2d 601, 609 n.9 (8th Cir.1987), *rev'd on other grounds* 24 F.3d 1040 (8th Cir.1994). We consider many factors in determining whether particular statements are trustworthy, including whether the questions were open ended, whether the child used age appropriate language in describing the abuse, and whether the child repeated the same facts consistently to adults.

Here, T.P. consistently alleged both sexual and physical abuse prior to trial, she used language appropriate for a young child in talking about the abuse, she circled the parts of her body that Peneaux had touched on an anatomically correct diagram, and there was no allegation of coercion or coaching. Her out of court statements were either made in response to open ended questions from Lora Hawkins and Penny Norris or were simply volunteered to Zane McClarnnan. At trial she admitted that she had made these prior statements although she challenged their veracity. The fact that T.P. testified at trial and was subject to cross examination "vitiates the main concern of the hearsay rule." *Renville*, 779 F.2d at 440. The jury was able to weigh her statements and accord them whatever weight they deemed appropriate. We conclude that T.P.'s prior out of court statements admitted under Rule 807 possessed equivalent circumstantial guarantees of trustworthiness to the other hearsay exceptions.

The materiality requirement in Rule 807 is merely a "restatement of the general requirement that evidence must be relevant." *McCormick on Evidence* § 324 (5th ed.2003); *see Huff v. White Motor Corp.*, 609 F.2d 286, 294 (7th Cir.1979) (materiality question is similar to Rule 401 relevance inquiry). Evidence is relevant if it has "any tendency to make the existence of any fact that is of consequence to the determination of the action more probable or less probable than it would be without the evidence." Fed. R. Evid. 401. The out of court statements of T.P. to Zane McClarnnan, Penny Norris, Juanita Swalley and Lora Hawkins are relevant to the issues here, for they identified both the type of abuse inflicted upon T.P. and her abuser.

We have previously upheld the admission of residual hearsay statements where the child victim testified at trial, *Grooms*, 978 F.2d 425, and recanted earlier accusations. *Renville*, 779 F.2d at 439–40. As we explained in *Shaw*, "a deferential standard of review" is appropriate where the district judge "was able to watch and listen to the witnesses as they testified," as is the case here. *Shaw*, 824 F.2d at 609. Where testifying adults are able to provide information that the victim is unwilling or unable to give, this testimony may come in under Rule 807.

Congress added Rule 803(24), the predecessor to Rule 807, because it could not foresee every possible evidentiary scenario. And while Congress intended the residual hearsay exception to "be used very rarely, and only in exceptional circumstances," S.Rep. No. 1277, 93d Cong., 2d Sess., at 20 (1974), exceptional circumstances generally exist when a child sexual abuse victim relates the details of the abusive events to an adult. *Shaw*, 824 F.2d at 609; *Dorian*, 803 F.2d at 1443–46; *United States v. Cree*, 778 F.2d 474, 476–78 (8th Cir.1985); *Renville*, 779 F.2d at 439–41. Here, the trial testimony of T.P. was inconsistent and at times unclear. The testimony of McClarnnan, Norris, Swalley, and Hawkins aided the jury in its fact finding task to determine whether T.P.'s allegations were true. The admission of this hearsay testimony was thus in the interest of justice and consistent with the requirements of Rule 807.

We conclude that the admission of T.P.'s prior out of court statements complied with Rule 807. The government provided the requisite notice and the statements were trustworthy, material, and more probative than T.P.'s hesitant trial testimony. Admission of the evidence was also consistent with the structure and purpose of the Federal Rules of Evidence. Finding no error in its admission, we need not discuss the remaining *Olano* factors.

*   *   *

IV.

In sum, we conclude that there was sufficient evidence for a reasonable jury to find Peneaux guilty of sexual abuse and assault, that the admission of Dr. Allison's statements about N.P. was at most harmless error, and that the able trial judge did not otherwise err or abuse his discretion in admitting disputed evidence. We therefore affirm the judgment of the district court.

NOTES AND QUESTIONS

1. *Circumstantial Guarantees of Trustworthiness.* In order to be admissible under Rule 807, hearsay statements must possess "circumstantial guarantees of trustworthiness" equivalent to those covered by Rule 803 and 804. At trial, T.P. denied being sexually abused. Why are T.P.'s prior inconsistent statements sufficiently trustworthy? What factors properly relate to whether the out-of-court statements made by the child victim are trustworthy? What importance should be placed on whether the statements were made in response to open ended or leading questions? Whether the statements were volunteered? In *Idaho v. Wright*, 497 U.S. 805 (1990), the Supreme Court stated that evidence corroborating the truth of a hearsay statement should not

be considered in finding that the statement bears "particularized guarantees of trustworthiness."

2. *Materiality*. The proponent of the hearsay statement must prove that it relates to a material fact. Is the materiality requirement in Rule 807 merely a restatement of the general rule that evidence must be relevant? *See* Fed. R. Evid. 401.

3. *Probativeness*. This requirement for admissibility under the residual exception really involves two elements. First, the proponent of the statement must prove that no other admissible evidence presently before the court is as probative as the hearsay. Second, it must be demonstrated that the proponent could not procure evidence with a greater, or equivalent, probative worth by reasonable efforts. Probative evidence is evidence which logically tends to make the existence of a particular fact more likely than it would be without such evidence. Thus, this first criterion for admission under the residual exception requires that the hearsay be excluded when there exists other equally probative evidence which corroborates the out-of-court declarations. For example, where there are other competent eyewitnesses to the crime available to testify, hearsay should not be admitted. Stated another way, hearsay evidence that is merely cumulative is not more probative than other available evidence, and as such, should be excluded under the rule. In contrast, the easiest case for admission occurs when the proffered hearsay is the only evidence of the material fact at issue. *See United States v. Zannino*, 895 F.2d 1, 7 (1st Cir. 1990) (declarant's former testimony was highly probative because unavailable declarant was only person with personal knowledge on point for which evidence was offered); *Huff v. White Motor Corp.*, 609 F.2d 286 (7th Cir. 1979) (because the hearsay evidence was the only direct evidence of the material fact for which it was offered, the court ruled it met the probativeness requirement of the residual exception); *see also* David A. Soneshein, *The Residual Exceptions to the Federal Hearsay Rule: Two Exceptions in Search of a Rule*, 57 N.Y.U. L. Rev. 867 (1982).

A number of courts have liberally interpreted the probativeness requirement. In *United States v. Grooms*, 978 F.2d 425, 427 (8th Cir. 1992), despite the fact that three young girls testified, giving their accounts of abusive sexual conduct that occurred between the defendant and themselves, the court permitted an FBI agent to recount in his testimony statements made to him by the three victims during an interview at the girls' school. While the children's earlier hearsay statements to the FBI agent appeared merely to corroborate the testimony at trial, the court admitted the hearsay, reasoning that the agent's testimony was more detailed because it contained specific descriptions of the incidents including the dates and places of the abuse. Thus, the court concluded that the agent's testimony had the probative value required for admission under the residual hearsay exception. *See also United States v. NB*, 59 F.3d 771, 776 n.6 (8th Cir. 1995) (citing *Grooms* with approval and reaching the same result on the admission of prior statements by child witness); *accord United States v. Shaw*, 824 F.2d 601, 610 (8th Cir. 1987) ("[T]he social worker's testimony was more probative than the child's because it contained specific details of the abuse that the victim could not provide."); *United States v. Toney*, 599 F.2d 787 (6th Cir. 1979) (out-of-court statement admitted under the residual exception despite the fact that it was cumulative of defendant's own testimony).

4. *Reasonable Efforts To Procure Other Admissible Evidence*. The probativeness requirement also requires that hearsay evidence be more probative "than any other evidence which the proponent can procure through reasonable efforts." Fed. R. Evid. 807. Under this element, hearsay that may be highly probative may nonetheless be

excluded where the proponent has failed to carry the burden of showing the unavailability of other evidence on the relevant point. *See deMars v. Equitable Life Assur. Soc'y*, 610 F.2d 55 (1st Cir. 1979) (the district court erred in permitting the plaintiff's attorney to read to the jury a letter by an unavailable physician which contained the physician's opinion of the cause of death because the plaintiff had failed to show that more probative evidence was unavailable). Additionally, what constitutes "reasonable efforts" is determined on a case-by-case analysis. At the very least, the proponent must establish the likely nonexistence of other probative evidence or, if such evidence likely exists, that it would be unreasonably difficult to obtain.

5. *The General Purposes Of The Rules And The Interests Of Justice.* In most cases, this criterion for admission of evidence under the residual exception is found to be satisfied with only minimal analysis by the courts. *See, e.g., United States v. Munoz*, 16 F.3d 1116, 1122 (11th Cir. 1994) ("This requirement is essentially a restatement of Rule 102 (citations omitted). The district court's admission of this evidence was consistent with the general requirement in that rule to provide a speedy, inexpensive and fair trial designed to reach the truth."); *United States v. Zannino*, 895 F.2d 1, 8 (1st Cir. 1990) ("[A]llowing the jury to hear Smoot's former testimony was consonant with both the interests of justice and the Federal Rules' general purposes."). This requirement is generally viewed to be satisfied so long as the other requirements of the residual exceptions are met and admission of the evidence does not offend other provisions of the Federal Rules of Evidence. *See United States v. Friedman*, 593 F.2d 109 (9th Cir. 1979) (finding that the interests of justice were met when the other requirements of the residual exception were satisfied). One court has reasoned that the "interests of justice" would not be served "by the admission of proffered grand-jury testimony if its trustworthiness and reliability were open to troubling doubt." *United States v. Fernandez*, 892 F.2d 976, 982 (11th Cir. 1989). In contrast, the Eighth Circuit posited that the "interests of justice" would be furthered by the admission of hearsay statements, given under oath before a grand jury, where the witness refused to testify because he had been intimidated by the defendant. The court ruled that "[t]o deprive the jury of the substance of this testimony merely because Carlson caused Tindall not to testify at the trial would be antithetical to the truthseeking function of our judicial system and would not serve the interests of justice." *United States v. Carlson*, 547 F.2d 1346, 1355 (8th Cir. 1976). Finally, one commentator has cogently explained the requirement in the following manner:

> A reasonable interpretation of clause (C) requires that the admission of hearsay not be inconsistent with the interests of justice. While this standard should be viewed flexibly, the additional requirement that the proffer not undermine the spirit or letter of the other Federal Rules of Evidence should be viewed more stringently. Thus, if the admission of the hearsay under the residual exception runs afoul of some other Federal Rule, the other rule should control to exclude the hearsay. Where Congress has specifically addressed an issue in another rule, the more general language of the residual exceptions must give way. Otherwise, litigants will be able to circumvent the particularized requirements envisioned by Congress.

David A. Soneshein, *The Residual Exceptions to the Federal Hearsay Rule: Two Exceptions in Search of a Rule*, 57 N.Y.U. L. Rev. 867, 900 (1982).

6. *Notice.* The residual exception requires the proponent of the out-of-court declaration to provide the opponent with notice of his intention to offer it "sufficiently in advance of the trial or hearing to provide the adverse party with a fair opportunity to

prepare to meet it." While the language of the rule appears quite clear, the federal circuits remain divided on whether the notice must be given before trial. The flexible rule adopted by a majority of the courts that have considered the matter permit the admission of hearsay under the residual exception despite the absence of pretrial notice to the adverse party when the proponent only became aware of the need to offer the evidence after the commencement of trial. In this case, any prejudice is cured by affording the opponent a continuance in order to provide "a fair opportunity to contest the use of the statement." *United States v. Bailey*, 581 F.2d 341, 348 (3d Cir. 1978) (citations omitted); *see also United States v. Carlson*, 547 F.2d 1346 (8th Cir. 1976); *United States v. Leslie*, 542 F.2d 285 (5th Cir. 1976). In *Furtado v. Bishop*, 604 F.2d 80 (1st Cir. 1979), the court adopted the view that failure to give pretrial notice can be excused where the proponent of the hearsay statement is blameless and could not have anticipated the need for the evidence and where the opponent was given sufficient opportunity to prepare and contest it.

The Second Circuit has adopted a strict approach to the notice requirement. In *United States v. Ruffin*, 575 F.2d 346, 348 (2d Cir. 1978), the court held that "Rule 803(24) . . . can be utilized only if notice of an intention to rely upon it is given in advance of trial. 'There is absolutely no doubt that Congress intended that the requirement of advance notice be rigidly enforced.'" (citations omitted). The fact that the party proffering the hearsay discovered the need for the evidence only after the start of trial was deemed irrelevant. Which is the better view? Why?

7. Should the residual hearsay exception be rarely used and only in exceptional cases? Why or why not?

8. *Adequate Opportunity for Cross-Examination.* In *Crawford v. Washington*, 541 U.S. 36 (2004), the Supreme Court "reiterate[d] that, when the declarant appears for cross-examination at trial, the Confrontation Clause places no constraints on the use of his prior testimonial statements. *Id.* at 59 n.9 (citing *California v. Greenwood*, 399 U.S. 149, 162 (1970)). Should the Court's language be strictly construed, or should a court consider whether the declarant's testifying provided the defendant with an adequate opportunity for cross-examination? *See State v. Holliday*, 745 N.W.2d 556 (Minn. 2008) (holding the admission of declarant's hearsay statements to a police officer did not violate the Confrontation Clause where the declarant testified at trial, despite the declarant's inability to remember the substance of his statement due to regular drug use).

Problem 8-4. *The Business Records and the Residual Hearsay Exceptions: The Problem of Double Hearsay.* The defendants were indicted for conspiring to commit wire fraud, money laundering and use of unauthorized access devices. The charges stemmed from their fraudulent use of 270 stolen credit cards to obtain over $500,000 in cash. Defendants posed as legitimate business owners and obtained the equipment necessary to process the false charges on the stolen credit cards. Defendants were caught after credit card holders reported the unauthorized charges to the banks issuing the credit cards. Bank representatives took down information from the card holders and then transferred these statements onto the bank's computers. Printouts of these unauthorized use reports were provided to the government.

The government sought to introduce the computer printouts, containing the victims' statements under the business records exception. Defendants objected, arguing that these printouts contained double hearsay and were inadmissible under Fed. R. Evid. 803(6). The government countered that the computer printouts were admissible under

Rule 803(6), while the victims' statements were admissible under the residual hearsay exception in Fed. R. Evid. 807. Do they contain double hearsay? Are these printouts admissible under the business records exception? Are the victims' statements admissible under the residual hearsay exception? *See United States v. Ismoila*, 100 F.3d 380 (5th Cir. 1996).

Chapter 9

HEARSAY — EXCEPTIONS REQUIRING
THAT THE DECLARANT BE UNAVAILABLE

A. UNAVAILABILITY — AN OVERVIEW

Federal Rule of Evidence 804(b) recognizes five exceptions to the hearsay rule.[1] Statements covered by these exceptions are considered trustworthy, but less so than those exempted from the hearsay rule by Rule 803. Under Rule 804(b), the admissibility of statements is conditioned on the "unavailability" of the declarant as defined by Rule 804(a). "Unavailability represents a kind of necessity, which is one of two traditional bases for hearsay exceptions (the other being trustworthiness)."[2] Thus, in the "usual case (including cases where prior cross-examination has occurred), the prosecution must either produce, or demonstrate the unavailability of, the declarant whose statement it wishes to use against the defendant."[3] Furthermore, in discussing "unavailability," the Supreme Court has stated that a "witness is not 'unavailable' for purposes of . . . the exception to the confrontation requirement unless the prosecutorial authorities have made a *good-faith effort* to obtain his presence at trial."[4]

A declarant is "unavailable as a witness" under Rule 804(a) where: (1) the declarant is exempt from testifying due to privilege; (2) the declarant refuses to testify; (3) the declarant testifies to a lack of memory; (4) the declarant is unable to testify due to death, illness or infirmity; and (5) the declarant is absent and the proponent of the declarant's statement has been unable to obtain the testimony by process or other reasonable means.[5]

---

[1] Federal Rule of Evidence 804(b) provides that the following are not excluded by the hearsay rule if the declarant is unavailable as a witness: (1) former testimony; (2) statement under belief of impending death; (3) statement against interest; (4) statement of personal or family history; and (5) the catch-all exception based upon "circumstantial guarantees of trustworthiness." The first three exceptions, former testimony, statement under belief of impending death, and statement against interest, frequently arise in the criminal context, and thus will be examined in this chapter. The Rule 804(b)(5) residual hearsay exception is virtually identical to Rule 803(24)'s catch-all exception, except that Rule 804(b)(5) requires that the declarant be unavailable. The Rule 803(24) catch-all exception was covered in Chapter 8. Thus, its Rule 804(b)(5) counterpart will not be covered again in this chapter.

[2] MUELLER & KIRKPATRICK, EVIDENCE, § 8.53, at 1000 (1995); *see also Burns v. Clusen*, 798 F.2d 931, 936–37 (7th Cir. 1986) ("[I]n conformance with the Framers' preference for face-to-face accusation, the Sixth Amendment establishes a rule of necessity.").

[3] *Ohio v. Roberts*, 448 U.S. 56, 65 (1980), overturned on other grounds, *Crawford v. Washington*, 541 U.S. 36 (2004);

[4] *Id.* at 74 (supplying the emphasis) (quoting *Barber v. Page*, 390 U.S. 719, 724–25 (1968)).

[5] FED. R. EVID. 804(a).

[1]   Privilege

Rule 804(a)(1) provides that a witness is unavailable if he "is exempted by ruling of the court on the ground of privilege from testifying concerning the subject matter of his statement." Under this provision, unavailability is established if the declarant properly invokes a common law privilege[6] or asserts his Fifth Amendment privilege against self-incrimination.[7] In either case, the declarant's bare assertion of the privilege is insufficient to make the witness unavailable. Rule 804(a)(1) requires that the declarant be "exempted by ruling of the court" from testifying based on the witness's assertion of privilege. Thus, prior to admitting the prior statement the court must rule upon the validity of the witness's assertion of the privilege.

Unavailability under this provision arises most frequently when the declarant asserts his Fifth Amendment privilege against self-incrimination[8] or claims the spousal privilege.[9]

[2]   Refusal to Testify

A declarant is unavailable under Fed. R. Evid. 804(a)(2) if he "persists in refusing to testify concerning the subject matter of his statement despite an order of the court to do so." Unavailability under this subsection often arises in a criminal setting when the declarant is granted use immunity by the government, thus removing his constitutional privilege against self-incrimination, but nevertheless refuses to testify despite a court order to do so.[10] Although Rule 804(a)(2) normally requires the court to order a witness to testify before a finding of unavailability is made, such an order is not always necessary. For example, failure to order the witness to testify was not inappropriate when, during an *in camera* hearing, the witness stated that he would not obey a court order requiring him to testify.[11]

---

[6] The Federal Rules of Evidence acknowledge the authority of the federal courts to continue the evolutionary development of testimonial privileges in federal criminal trials "governed by the principles of the common law as they may be interpreted . . . in the light of reason and experience." FED. R. EVID. 501. *See also Trammel v. United States*, 445 U.S. 40 (1980) (discussing the spousal privilege).

[7] *See United States v. Kimball*, 15 F.3d 54, 55 n.3 (5th Cir. 1994) ("it is clear that a witness who is unavailable because he has invoked the Fifth Amendment privilege against self-incrimination is unavailable under the terms of 804(a)(1)") (citations omitted); *United States v. Vernor*, 902 F.2d 1182, 1186 (5th Cir. 1990) (same).

[8] *See United States v. Lowe*, 65 F.3d 1137, 1145 (4th Cir. 1995) (having asserted his Fifth Amendment privilege against self-incrimination, declarant was unavailable under Fed. R. Evid. 804(a)(1)); *United States v. Thomas*, 62 F.3d 1332, 1337 (11th Cir. 1995) (same); *United States v. Nagib*, 56 F.3d 798, 804 (7th Cir. 1995) (same); *United States v. Matthews*, 20 F.3d 538, 545 (2d Cir. 1994) (same); *United States v. Fischl*, 16 F.3d 927, 928 (8th Cir. 1994) (same); *United States v. Innamorati*, 996 F.2d 456, 474 (1st Cir. 1993) (same); *United States v. Triplett*, 922 F.2d 1174, 1182 (5th Cir. 1991) (same); *United States v. Arthur*, 949 F.2d 211, 216 (6th Cir. 1991).

[9] *See United States v. Trammel*, 445 U.S. 40, 52–53 (1980) (holding that only the witness spouse holds a testimonial privilege, and defendant spouse cannot prevent witness spouse from testifying); *United States v. Donlon*, 909 F.2d 650, 653 (1st Cir. 1990) (finding witness that claimed spousal privilege was unavailable and thus her grand jury testimony was admissible under 804(b)(5)); *United States v. Chapman*, 866 F.2d 1326 (11th Cir. 1989) (witness claiming marital privilege is unavailable).

[10] *See Williamson v. United States*, 512 U.S. 594, 597–98 (1994); *United States v. Gomez-Lemos*, 939 F.2d 326, 328 (6th Cir. 1991).

[11] *See Jennings v. Maynard*, 946 F.2d 1502, 1505 (10th Cir. 1991).

[3]   Lack of Memory

Pursuant to Rule 804(a)(3), a witness is unavailable if he "testifies to a lack of memory of the subject matter of the declarant's statement."[12] The Notes of the Advisory Committee provide that the lack of memory must be established by the testimony of the witness himself, which contemplates the witness taking the stand and being subject to cross-examination.

It is unclear whether unavailability under this subsection requires proof that the witness has no memory of the events to which his hearsay statements relate, or whether unavailability is established where the witness's memory has merely faded with time. At least one court has held that where the witness did remember the general subject matter of the out-of-court statement, his lack of memory as to the details was not sufficient to make the testimony admissible.[13]

[4]   Death or Infirmity

Rule 804(a)(4) establishes that a declarant is unavailable if he "is unable to be present or to testify at the hearing because of death or then existing physical or mental illness or infirmity."[14] When the declarant is suffering from some mental or physical illness and is unavailable on that basis, the issue is whether the court properly exercised discretion in not continuing the trial for a reasonable period to afford the witness enough time to recover from the infirmity and thus be available to testify. The determination of the admissibility of prior testimony based on unavailability due to illness or infirmity is a matter left to the discretion of the trial judge.[15]

Generally, the courts require a balancing test. "A judge must weigh the desirability of a speedy trial against the possibility that a further delay may find the declarant competent [or physically able to testify]."[16] The trial court's finding of unavailability because of "then existing physical or mental illness or infirmity" has been upheld where the declarant had delivered a child a week prior to trial and had been hospitalized with chest pains the day before she was to testify;[17] where the key witness was unavailable for five months after triple-bypass open-heart surgery;[18] and where elderly witnesses

---

[12] *See People v. Ramey*, 604 N.W.2d 275 (Ill. 1992); *State v. Jenkins*, 483 N.E.2d 262, 271 n. 11 (Wis. App.); *State v. Gonzales*, 817 P.2d 1186 (N.M. 1991).

[13] *See North Mississippi Communications, Inc. v. Jones*, 792 F.2d 1330, 1336 (5th Cir. 1986).

[14] *See United States v. Shaw*, 69 F.3d 1249, 1251 (4th Cir. 1995) (death of witness prior to trial renders the witness unavailable); *United States v. Hilliard*, 11 F.3d 618, 619 (6th Cir. 1993) (same); *United States v. Williams*, 989 F.2d 1061, 1068 (9th Cir. 1993) (same); *Virgin Islands v. Joseph*, 964 F.2d 1380, 1386 n.6 (3d Cir. 1992) (same); *United States v. Gabay*, 923 F.2d 1536, 1540 (11th Cir. 1991) (same); *United States v. DeVillio*, 983 F.2d 1185, 1189 (2d Cir. 1993) (co-defendant murdered prior to trial was unavailable); *United States v. Mokol*, 939 F.2d 436, 437 (7th Cir. 1991) (police officer murdered prior to trial was unavailable); *United States v. Panzardi-Lespier*, 918 F.2d 313, 316 (1st Cir. 1990) (informant murdered prior to trial was unavailable).

[15] *See United States v. Donaldson*, 978 F.2d 381, 392 (7th Cir. 1992) (upholding trial court's ruling on unavailability where witness had delivered a child shortly before trial and was seriously ill at the time of trial); *United States v. Campbell*, 845 F.2d 1374, 1378 (6th Cir. 1988) (elderly witnesses suffering from severe health problems that prevented them from traveling declared to be unavailable); *United States v. Faison*, 679 F.2d 292, 295–96 (3d Cir. 1982) (witness, who was in the hospital suffering from a heart attack, was unavailable).

[16] *Burns v. Clusen*, 798 F.2d 931, 937–38 (7th Cir. 1986).

[17] *United States v. Donaldson*, 978 F.2d 381, 393–94 (7th Cir. 1992).

[18] *United States v. Koller*, 956 F.2d 1408, 1415 (7th Cir. 1992); *see also United States v. Lang*, 904 F.2d 618, 621 (11th Cir. 1990) (witness recovering from heart attack is unavailable).

were permanently unavailable.[19] In the case of a mental rather than a physical disability, the trial court's determination is often more difficult because of greater uncertainty as to prognosis.[20]

[5]   Absence

According to Rule 804(a)(5), a witness is "unavailable" if he "is absent from the hearing and the proponent of a statement has been unable to procure the declarant's attendance (or in the case of a hearsay exception under subdivision (b)(2), (3), or (4), the declarant's attendance or testimony) by process or other reasonable means." Before the witness is found unavailable and his hearsay statements are admitted under Rule 804(b)(2), (3), or (4), the Rule requires that not only must the declarant be unavailable, but his "testimony," which includes a deposition, must be unavailable. Thus, at least for purposes of Rules 804(b)(2), (3), and (4), "reasonable means" must be employed to take the witness's deposition when the witness cannot appear at trial. Otherwise, the "reasonableness" requirement is satisfied if the proponent of the statement attempts in good faith to locate and subpoena the witness.[21]

In federal trials, the government must not only subpoena the witness but must also make reasonable efforts to secure his or her attendance and to enforce the subpoena. What constitutes "reasonable efforts" by the government, however, is unclear.[22] The Supreme Court has stated that the "ultimate question is whether the witness is unavailable despite good-faith efforts undertaken prior to trial."[23] What if the witness is living abroad? Does the reasonableness standard require the government to obtain the witness's return by extradition?[24]

---

[19] *United States v. Campbell*, 845 F.2d 1374, 1378 (6th Cir. 1988); *see also United States v. Calkins*, 906 F.2d 1240, 1243 (8th Cir. 1990) (permanent disability resulting from a stroke suffered by elderly witness made her unavailable).

[20] *See Burns v. Clusen*, 798 F.2d 931, 943 (7th Cir. 1986) (court erred in finding sexual assault victim unavailable where finding of unavailability was made on confused and "stale" record).

[21] *See United States v. Flenoid*, 949 F.2d 970, 972 (8th Cir. 1991) (district court erred in excluding hearsay statement where defendant attempted in good faith to locate and subpoena witness). *Compare United States v. Martinez-Perez*, 916 F.2d 1020, 1023 (5th Cir. 1990) (government failed to satisfy its burden of demonstrating good faith efforts to locate witness where government merely assumed witness was outside United States and beyond reach of the trial court). Additionally, in *Barber v. Page*, 390 U.S. 719 (1968), the Supreme Court held that admission of hearsay statements upon a simple showing that a prosecution witness was absent from the state may be insufficient to satisfy the defendant's right of confrontation.

[22] *Christian v. Rhode*, 41 F.3d 461, 467 (9th Cir. 1994) ("While no court has articulated a standard for the diligence required of the prosecution in attempting to secure the defendant's presence at a deposition to be used at trial, it is clear that herculean efforts are not required."); *State v. Lee*, 925 P.2d 1091, 1100 (Haw. 1996) ("[P]rosecution's reasonable efforts to secure the presence of the declarant 'require a search equally as vigorous as that which the government would undertake to find a critical witness if it had no prior testimony to rely upon in the event of unavailability.' ").

[23] *Ohio v. Roberts*, 448 U.S. 56, 74 (1980), overturned on other grounds, Crawford v. Washington, 541 U.S. 36 (2004); *see also United States v. Quinn*, 901 F.2d 522, 528 (6th Cir. 1990) (finding that government failed to satisfy its burden of demonstrating that a witness was unavailable as required to admit her suppression hearing testimony).

[24] *See United States v. Curbello*, 940 F.2d 1503, 1506 (11th Cir. 1991) (Court erred in admitting hearsay statement where government failed to "represent that it had made any request of Bahamian government to make [the witness] available through extradition or any other means to attend trial."). *Compare United States v. Casamento*, 887 F.2d 1141, 1169 (2d Cir. 1989) (unavailability of witness established by government affidavit that Italian government had refused request to extradite the witness to the United States).

[6]   Procurement of Unavailability of Declarant

Unavailability as defined in Rule 804(a)(1) to (5) is further subject to the condition that the proponent of the statement may not create the condition of unavailability and then benefit therefrom. Rule 804(a) provides that a declarant is not unavailable under the rule "if his exemption, refusal, claim of lack of memory, inability, or absence is due to the procurement or wrongdoing of the proponent of his statement for the purpose of preventing the witness from attending or testifying."[25] The rule was "designed to ensure one access to testimony where, by the actions of the opponent, or at least through no fault of the testimony's proponent, a desired witness becomes unavailable."[26] The rule was not intended to permit the proponent of the statement to create his own necessity or unavailability. "[C]learly the clause means a party cannot claim someone is unavailable if he intimidates him into refusing to testify, or kills him to silence him, or kidnaps or hides him to block process."[27]

Where a prosecutor is negligent in releasing a witness on her own recognizance so that she disappears and cannot be located, a close question arises whether the government's actions were so egregious as to preclude a finding of unavailability.[28] At the same time, the government's failure to immunize a witness who asserts his privilege against self-incrimination does not constitute "procurement or wrongdoing" under Rule 804(a).[29]

B.   THE SIXTH AMENDMENT CONFRONTATION CLAUSE

See supra, Chapter 8 discussing *Crawford v. Washington*, 541 U.S. 26 (2004) (holding absent a showing that the declarant is unavailable and the defendant had a prior opportunity for cross-examination, the Confrontation Clause prohibits the admission of out-of-court statements that are "testimonial" in nature).

C.   "UNAVAILABILITY" AND THE VICTIM OF CHILD ABUSE — THE PROBLEM OF TRAUMA AND BEING "PSYCHOLOGICALLY UNAVAILABLE"

MARYLAND v. CRAIG
497 U.S. 836 (1990)

JUSTICE O'CONNOR delivered the opinion of the Court.

This case requires us to decide whether the Confrontation Clause of the Sixth Amendment categorically prohibits a child witness in a child abuse case from testifying

---

[25] FED. R. EVID. 804(a). *See United States v. Kimball*, 15 F.3d 54, 56 (5th Cir. 1994) (holding that defendant who created his own unavailability by invoking his Fifth Amendment privilege against self-incrimination was not unavailable for purposes of Rule 804(a)).

[26] *United States v. Kimball*, 15 F.3d 54, 56 (5th Cir.1994).

[27] MUELLER & KIRKPATRICK, EVIDENCE § 8.56, at 1012 (1995).

[28] *See United States v. Hazelett*, 32 F.3d 1313, 1317 (8th Cir. 1994) (raising the concern, but ultimately not deciding question because the declarant's statements were not sufficiently against her penal interest to be admitted under Rule 804(b)(3)).

[29] *See United States v. Lang*, 589 F.2d 92, 95–96 (2d Cir. 1978) (the power of the Executive Branch to grant immunity to a witness is discretionary and no obligation exists to seek such immunity).

against a defendant at trial, outside the defendant's physical presence, by one-way closed circuit television.

In October 1986, a Howard County grand jury charged respondent, Sandra Ann Craig, with child abuse, first and second degree sexual offenses, perverted sexual practice, assault, and battery. The named victim in each count was a 6-year-old girl who, from August 1984 to June 1986, had attended a kindergarten and prekindergarten center owned and operated by Craig.

In March 1987, before the case went to trial, the State sought to invoke a Maryland statutory procedure that permits a judge to receive, by one-way closed circuit television, the testimony of a child witness who is alleged to be a victim of child abuse. To invoke the procedure, the trial judge must first "determin[e] that testimony by the child victim in the courtroom will result in the child suffering serious emotional distress such that the child cannot reasonably communicate." Md. Cts. & Jud. Proc. Code Ann. § 9-102(a)(1)(ii) (1989). Once the procedure is invoked, the child witness, prosecutor, and defense counsel withdraw to a separate room; the judge, jury, and defendant remain in the courtroom. The child witness is then examined and cross-examined in the separate room, while a video monitor records and displays the witness' testimony to those in the courtroom. During this time the witness cannot see the defendant. The defendant remains in electronic communication with defense counsel, and objections may be made and ruled on as if the witness were testifying in the courtroom.

In support of its motion invoking the one-way closed circuit television procedure, the State presented expert testimony that the named victim as well as a number of other children who were alleged to have been sexually abused by Craig, would suffer "serious emotional distress such that [they could not] reasonably communicate," § 9-102(a)(1)(ii), if required to testify in the courtroom. The Maryland Court of Appeals characterized the evidence as follows:

> "The expert testimony in each case suggested that each child would have some or considerable difficulty in testifying in Craig's presence. For example, as to one child, the expert said that what 'would cause him the most anxiety would be to testify in front of Mrs. Craig. . . . ' The child 'wouldn't be able to communicate effectively.' As to another, an expert said she 'would probably stop talking and she would withdraw and curl up.' With respect to two others, the testimony was that one would 'become highly agitated, that he may refuse to talk or if he did talk, that he would choose his subject regardless of the questions' while the other would 'become extremely timid and unwilling to talk.'" 316 Md. 551, 568–569 (1989).

Craig objected to the use of the procedure on Confrontation Clause grounds, but the trial court rejected that contention, concluding that although the statute "take[s] away the right of the defendant to be face to face with his or her accuser," the defendant retains the "essence of the right of confrontation," including the right to observe, cross-examine, and have the jury view the demeanor of the witness. App. 65–66. The trial court further found that, "based upon the evidence presented . . . the testimony of each of these children in a courtroom will result in each child suffering serious emotional distress . . . such that each of these children cannot reasonably communicate." *Id.*, at 66. The trial court then found the named victim and three other children competent to testify and accordingly permitted them to testify against Craig via the one-way closed circuit television procedure. The jury convicted Craig on all counts, and the Maryland Court of Special Appeals affirmed the convictions.

The Court of Appeals of Maryland reversed and remanded for a new trial. The Court of Appeals rejected Craig's argument that the Confrontation Clause requires in all cases a face-to-face courtroom encounter between the accused and his accusers, but concluded:

> "[U]nder § 9-102(a)(1)(ii), the operative 'serious emotional distress' which renders a child victim unable to 'reasonably communicate' must be determined to arise, at least primarily, from face-to-face confrontation with the defendant. Thus, we construe the phrase 'in the courtroom' as meaning, for sixth amendment and [state constitution] confrontation purposes, 'in the courtroom in the presence of the defendant.' Unless prevention of 'eyeball-to-eyeball' confrontation is necessary to obtain the trial testimony of the child, the defendant cannot be denied that right." *Id.*, at 566.

Reviewing the trial court's finding and the evidence presented in support of the § 9-102 procedure, the Court of Appeals held that, "as [it] read *Coy [v. Iowa*, 487 U.S. 1012 (1988)], the showing made by the State was insufficient to reach the high threshold required by that case before § 9-102 may be invoked." *Id.* 316 Md., at 554–555.

We granted certiorari to resolve the important Confrontation Clause issues raised by this case.

II.

The Confrontation Clause of the Sixth Amendment, made applicable to the States through the Fourteenth Amendment, provides: "In all criminal prosecutions, the accused shall enjoy the right . . . to be confronted with the witnesses against him."

We observed in *Coy v. Iowa* that "the Confrontation Clause guarantees the defendant a face-to-face meeting with witnesses appearing before the trier of fact." 487 U.S., at 1016. . . . This interpretation derives not only from the literal text of the Clause, but also from our understanding of its historical roots. . . .

We have never held, however, that the Confrontation Clause guarantees criminal defendants the *absolute* right to a face-to-face meeting with witnesses against them at trial. Indeed, in *Coy v. Iowa*, we expressly "le[ft] for another day . . . the question whether any exceptions exist" to the "irreducible literal meaning of the Clause: 'a right to *meet face to face* all those who appear and give evidence *at trial.*' " 487 U.S., at 1021 (quoting [*California v. Green*, 399 U.S. 149, 175 (1970)] (Harlan, J., concurring)). The procedure challenged in *Coy* involved the placement of a screen that prevented two child witnesses in a child abuse case from seeing the defendant as they testified against him at trial. . . . In holding that the use of this procedure violated the defendant's right to confront witnesses against him, we suggested that any exception to the right "would surely be allowed only when necessary to further an important public policy" — *i.e.*, only upon a showing of something more than the generalized, "legislatively imposed presumption of trauma" underlying the statute at issue in that case. *Id.*, at 1021, *see also id.*, at 1025 (O'Connor, J., concurring). We concluded that "[s]ince there ha[d] been no individualized findings that these particular witnesses needed special protection, the judgment [in the case before us] could not be sustained by any conceivable exception." *Id.*, at 1021. Because the trial court in this case made individualized findings that each of the child witnesses needed special protection, this case requires us to decide the question reserved in *Coy.*

The central concern of the Confrontation Clause is to ensure the reliability of the evidence against a criminal defendant by subjecting it to rigorous testing in the context of an adversary proceeding before the trier of fact. The word "confront," after all, also means a clashing of forces or ideas, thus carrying with it the notion of adversariness. As we noted in our earliest case interpreting the Clause:

> "The primary object of the constitutional provision in question was to prevent depositions or *ex parte* affidavits, such as were sometimes admitted in civil cases, being used against the prisoner in lieu of a personal examination and cross-examination of the witness in which the accused has an opportunity, not only of testing the recollection and sifting the conscience of the witness, but of compelling him to stand face to face with the jury in order that they may look at him, and judge by his demeanor upon the stand and the manner in which he gives his testimony whether he is worthy of belief." [*Mattox v. United States*, 156 U.S. 237, 242–43 (1895)].

As this description indicates, the right guaranteed by the Confrontation Clause includes not only a "personal examination," 156 U.S., at 242, but also "(1) insures that the witness will give his statements under oath — thus impressing him with the seriousness of the matter and guarding against the lie by the possibility of a penalty for perjury; (2) forces the witness to submit to cross-examination, the 'greatest legal engine ever invented for the discovery of truth'; [and] (3) permits the jury that is to decide the defendant's fate to observe the demeanor of the witness in making his statement, thus aiding the jury in assessing his credibility." *Green, supra*, 399 U.S., at 158.

The combined effect of these elements of confrontation — physical presence, oath, cross-examination, and observation of demeanor by the trier of fact — serves the purposes of the Confrontation Clause by ensuring that evidence admitted against an accused is reliable and subject to the rigorous adversarial testing that is the norm of Anglo-American criminal proceedings.

We have recognized, for example, that face-to-face confrontation enhances the accuracy of fact finding by reducing the risk that a witness will wrongfully implicate an innocent person. *See Coy, supra*, 487 U.S., at 1019–1020 ("It is always more difficult to tell a lie about a person 'to his face' than 'behind his back.' . . . That face-to-face presence may, unfortunately, upset the truthful rape victim or abused child; but by the same token it may confound and undo the false accuser, or reveal the child coached by a malevolent adult"). . . . We have also noted the strong symbolic purpose served by requiring adverse witnesses at trial to testify in the accused's presence. *See Coy*, 487 U.S., at 1017 ("[T]here is something deep in human nature that regards face-to-face confrontation between accused and accuser as 'essential to a fair trial in a criminal prosecution' ") (quoting *Pointer v. Texas*, 380 U.S. 400, 404 (1965)).

Although face-to-face confrontation forms "the core of the values furthered by the Confrontation Clause," *Green*, 399 U.S., at 157, we have nevertheless recognized that it is not the *sine qua non* of the confrontation right.

For this reason, we have never insisted on an actual face-to-face encounter at trial in every instance in which testimony is admitted against a defendant. Instead, we have repeatedly held that the Clause permits, where necessary, the admission of certain hearsay statements against a defendant despite the defendant's inability to confront the declarant at trial. *See, e.g., Mattox*, 156 U.S., at 243 ("[T]here could be nothing more directly contrary to the letter of the provision in question than the admission of dying declarations."); *Pointer, supra*, 380 U.S., at 407 (noting exceptions to the confrontation right for dying declarations and "other analogous situations"). In *Mattox*, for example, we held that the testimony of a Government witness at a former trial against the defendant, where the witness was fully cross-examined but had died after the first trial, was admissible in evidence against the defendant at his second trial. We explained:

> "There is doubtless reason for saying that . . . if notes of [the witness'] testimony are permitted to be read, [the defendant] is deprived of the advantage of that personal presence of the witness before the jury which the law has designed for his protection. But general rules of law of this kind, however beneficent in their operation and valuable to the accused, must occasionally give way to considerations of public policy and the necessities of the case. To say that a criminal, after having once been convicted by the testimony of a certain witness, should go scot free simply because death has closed the mouth of that witness, would be carrying his constitutional protection to an unwarrantable extent. The law in its wisdom declares that the rights of the public shall not be wholly sacrificed in order that an incidental benefit may be preserved to the accused." *Id.*, at 243.

We have accordingly stated that a literal reading of the Confrontation Clause would "abrogate virtually every hearsay exception, a result long rejected as unintended and too extreme." [*Ohio v. Roberts*, 448 U.S. 56, 63 (1980)]. Thus, in certain narrow circumstances, "competing interests, if 'closely examined,' may warrant dispensing with confrontation at trial." *Id.*, at 64. We have recently held, for example, that hearsay statements of nontestifying co-conspirators may be admitted against a defendant despite the lack of any face-to-face encounter with the accused. *See Bourjaily v. United States*, 483 U.S. 171 (1987); *United States v. Inadi*, 475 U.S. 387 (1986). Given our hearsay cases, the word "confronted," as used in the Confrontation Clause, cannot simply mean face-to-face confrontation, for the Clause would then, contrary to our cases, prohibit the admission of any accusatory hearsay statement made by an absent declarant — a declarant who is undoubtedly as much a "witness against" a defendant as one who actually testifies at trial.

In sum, our precedents establish that "the Confrontation Clause reflects a preference for face-to-face confrontation at trial," *Roberts, supra*, 448 U.S., at 63, a preference that "must occasionally give way to considerations of public policy and the necessities of the case." *Mattox, supra*, 156 U.S., at 243. "[W]e have attempted to harmonize the goal of the Clause — placing limits on the kind of evidence that may be received against a defendant — with a societal interest in accurate fact finding, which may require consideration of out-of-court statements." *Bourjaily, supra*, 483 U.S., at 182. We have accordingly interpreted the Confrontation Clause in a manner sensitive to its purposes and sensitive to the necessities of trial and the adversary process. . . . Thus, though we reaffirm the importance of face-to-face confrontation with witnesses appearing at trial, we cannot say that such confrontation is an indispensable element of the Sixth Amendment's guarantee of the right to confront one's accusers. . . .

. . . .

That the face-to-face confrontation requirement is not absolute does not, of course, mean that it may easily be dispensed with. As we suggested in *Coy*, our precedents confirm that a defendant's right to confront accusatory witnesses may be satisfied absent a physical, face-to-face confrontation at trial only where denial of such confrontation is necessary to further an important public policy and only where the reliability of the testimony is otherwise assured. *See* 487 U.S., at 1021. . . .

III.

Maryland's statutory procedure, when invoked, prevents a child witness from seeing the defendant as he or she testifies against the defendant at trial. We find it significant, however, that Maryland's procedure preserves all of the other elements of the confrontation right: The child witness must be competent to testify and must testify under oath; the defendant retains full opportunity for contemporaneous cross-examination; and the judge, jury, and defendant are able to view (albeit by video monitor) the demeanor (and body) of the witness as he or she testifies. Although we are mindful of the many subtle effects face-to-face confrontation may have on an adversary criminal proceeding, the presence of these other elements of confrontation — oath, cross-examination, and observation of the witness' demeanor — adequately ensures that the testimony is both reliable and subject to rigorous adversarial testing in a manner functionally equivalent to that accorded live, in-person testimony. These safeguards of reliability and adversariness render the use of such a procedure a far cry from the undisputed prohibition of the Confrontation Clause: trial by *ex parte* affidavit or inquisition. . . . Rather, we think these elements of effective confrontation not only permit a defendant to "confound and undo the false accuser, or reveal the child coached by a malevolent adult," *Coy, supra*, 487 U.S., at 1020, but may well aid a defendant in eliciting favorable testimony from the child witness. Indeed, to the extent the child witness' testimony may be said to be technically given out of court (though we do not so hold), these assurances of reliability and adversariness are far greater than those required for admission of hearsay testimony under the Confrontation Clause. . . . We are therefore confident that use of the one-way closed circuit television procedure, where necessary to further an important state interest, does not impinge upon the truth-seeking or symbolic purposes of the Confrontation Clause.

The critical inquiry in this case, therefore, is whether use of the procedure is necessary to further an important state interest. The State contends that it has a substantial interest in protecting children who are allegedly victims of child abuse from the trauma of testifying against the alleged perpetrator and that its statutory procedure for receiving testimony from such witnesses is necessary to further that interest.

We have of course recognized that a State's interest in "the protection of minor victims of sex crimes from further trauma and embarrassment" is a "compelling" one. *Globe Newspaper Co. v. Superior Court of Norfolk County*, 457 U.S. 596, 607 (1982). . . . In *Globe Newspaper*, . . . we held that a State's interest in the physical and psychological well-being of a minor victim was sufficiently weighty to justify depriving the press and public of their constitutional right to attend criminal trials, where the trial court makes a case-specific finding that closure of the trial is necessary to protect the welfare of the minor. . . . This Term, in *Osborne v. Ohio*, 495 U.S. 103 (1990), we upheld a state statute that proscribed the possession and viewing of child pornography, reaffirming that " '[i]t is evident beyond the need for elaboration that a State's interest in "safeguarding the physical and psychological well-being of a minor" is "compel-ling." ' " *Id.*, at 109 (quoting [*New York v. Ferber*, 458 U.S. 747, 756–57 (1982)]).

We likewise conclude today that a State's interest in the physical and psychological well-being of child abuse victims may be sufficiently important to outweigh, at least in some cases, a defendant's right to face his or her accusers in court. That a significant majority of States have enacted statutes to protect child witnesses from the trauma of giving testimony in child abuse cases attests to the widespread belief in the importance of such a public policy. . . . Thirty-seven States, for example, permit the use of videotaped testimony of sexually abused children; 24 States have authorized the use of one-way closed circuit television testimony in child abuse cases; and 8 States authorize the use of a two-way system in which the child witness is permitted to see the courtroom and the defendant on a video monitor and in which the jury and judge are permitted to view the child during the testimony.

The statute at issue in this case, for example, was specifically intended "to safeguard the physical and psychological well-being of child victims by avoiding, or at least minimizing, the emotional trauma produced by testifying." *Wildermuth v. State*, 310 Md. 496, 518 (1987). . . .

Given the State's traditional and " 'transcendent interest in protecting the welfare of children,' " [*Ginsberg v. New York*, 390 U.S. 629, 640 (1968)], and buttressed by the growing body of academic literature documenting the psychological trauma suffered by child abuse victims who must testify in court, . . . we will not second-guess the considered judgment of the Maryland Legislature regarding the importance of its interest in protecting child abuse victims from the emotional trauma of testifying. Accordingly, we hold that, if the State makes an adequate showing of necessity, the state interest in protecting child witnesses from the trauma of testifying in a child abuse case is sufficiently important to justify the use of a special procedure that permits a child witness in such cases to testify at trial against a defendant in the absence of face-to-face confrontation with the defendant.

The requisite finding of necessity must of course be a case-specific one: The trial court must hear evidence and determine whether use of the one-way closed circuit television procedure is necessary to protect the welfare of the particular child witness who seeks to testify. . . . The trial court must also find that the child witness would be traumatized, not by the courtroom generally, but by the presence of the defendant. . . . Denial of face-to-face confrontation is not needed to further the state interest in protecting the child witness from trauma unless it is the presence of the defendant that causes the trauma. In other words, if the state interest were merely the interest in protecting child witnesses from courtroom trauma generally, denial of face-to-face confrontation would be unnecessary because the child could be permitted to testify in less intimidating surroundings, albeit with the defendant present. Finally, the trial court must find that the emotional distress suffered by the child witness in the presence of the defendant is more than *de minimis*, i.e., more than "mere nervousness or excitement or some reluctance to testify," *Wildermuth, supra*, 310 Md., at 524. We need not decide the minimum showing of emotional trauma required for use of the special procedure, however, because the Maryland statute, which requires a determination that the child witness will suffer "serious emotional distress such that the child cannot reasonably communicate," § 9-102(a)(1)(ii), clearly suffices to meet constitutional standards.

. . . .

In sum, we conclude that where necessary to protect a child witness from trauma that would be caused by testifying in the physical presence of the defendant, at least where such trauma would impair the child's ability to communicate, the Confrontation Clause does not prohibit use of a procedure that, despite the absence of face-to-face confrontation, ensures the reliability of the evidence by subjecting it to rigorous adversarial testing and thereby preserves the essence of effective confrontation. Because there is no dispute that the child witnesses in this case testified under oath, were subject to full cross-examination, and were able to be observed by the judge, jury, and defendant as they testified, we conclude that, to the extent that a proper finding of necessity has been made, the admission of such testimony would be consonant with the Confrontation Clause.

. . . .

. . . We therefore vacate the judgment . . . and remand the case for further proceedings not inconsistent with this opinion.

NOTES AND QUESTIONS

1. The Supreme Court in *Craig* upheld the constitutionality of closed circuit trial testimony by witnesses alleged to be the victims of child abuse, but only upon a case-by-case "adequate showing of necessity." *Craig*, 497 U.S. at 855. The Court identified several prerequisites to allowing a child to testify on videotape. What findings must the trial court make as a precondition to admitting videotaped testimony from a child witness? *See id.*; *United States v. Boyles*, 57 F.3d 535, 546 (7th Cir. 1995).

2. In determining whether the child would suffer "severe emotional trauma" if required to testify before the defendant, must the trial judge personally question the child witness (either in or outside the courtroom) in the defendant's presence? Additionally, before using the one-way television procedure, must the trial court determine whether the child would suffer "severe emotional distress" if he or she were to testify by two-way closed circuit television? The Supreme Court in *Craig* answered both of these questions in the negative. The Court stated:

> Although we think such evidentiary requirements could strengthen the grounds for use of protective measures, we decline to establish, as a matter of federal constitutional law, any such categorical evidentiary prerequisites for the use of the one-way television procedure. The trial court in this case, for example, could well have found on the basis of the expert testimony before it, that testimony by the child witnesses in the courtroom in the defendant's presence "will result in [each] child suffering serious emotional distress such that the child cannot reasonably communicate." [Citations omitted.] So long as a trial court makes such a case-specific finding of necessity, the Confrontation Clause does not prohibit a State from using a one-way closed circuit television procedure for the receipt of testimony by a child witness in a child abuse case.

Craig, 497 U.S. at 860. Do you agree?

3. Is it error for the trial court to base its case-specific finding of necessity on a medical expert's general testimony about the trauma a child may experience from testifying in court in the defendant's presence? *See United States v. Garcia*, 7 F.3d 885, 889 (9th Cir. 1993) ("Hearing an expert's general testimony on this subject is not prohibited by *Craig*, so long as the testimony is not the sole basis for finding that an individual child would suffer emotional trauma from testifying in the presence of a defendant.").

4. The Court in *Craig* stated that the trial court must find that the emotional distress suffered by the child witness in the presence of the defendant is more than *de minimis*, i.e., more than "mere nervousness or excitement or some reluctance to testify," *Craig*, 497 U.S. at 855–56, but it noted that the requirement is satisfied "at least" by a showing that "such trauma would impair the child's ability to communicate." *Id.* at 857. Is the Court's "more than *de minimis* trauma" requirement satisfied based upon a showing that the child would be traumatized from testifying in the defendant's presence without a finding that the child would be unable to communicate? *See United States v. Carrier*, 9 F.3d 867, 869 n.2 (10th Cir. 1993) (stating that the issue remains an open question); *but see Thomas v. People*, 803 P.2d 144, 150 n.13 (Colo. 1990) (suggesting that *Craig*'s holding would apply even where serious trauma suffered by child would not impair child's ability to communicate).

5. Additionally, "[t]he trial court must also find the child witness would be traumatized, not by the courtroom generally, but by the presence of the defendant." *Craig*, 497 U.S. at 855–56 (citations omitted). Thus, if the specific finding of necessity is merely based on the general trauma a child would suffer from testifying in the courtroom, videotaped testimony is not permitted. *See United States v. Boyles*, 57 F.3d 535, 546 (7th Cir. 1995) ("It is clear that a court cannot rest its findings on merely the general trauma a child may face in court, but rather, must find that the child would be traumatized by the presence of the defendant himself."); *Hoversten v. Iowa*, 998 F.2d 614, 616–17 (8th Cir. 1993) (affirming district court's grant of writ of habeas corpus where Iowa trial court's finding of necessity was based upon the "traumatic experience of testifying in open court," rather than her specific need for protection from the experience of testifying in front of defendant); *United States v. Farley*, 992 F.2d 1122, 1124 (10th Cir. 1993) ("General trauma experienced by retelling the events or because of the intimidating atmosphere of a courtroom will not justify use of closed circuit procedures.").

6. The majority in *Craig* posited that "[t]he central concern of the Confrontation Clause is to ensure the reliability of the evidence against a criminal defendant by subjecting it to rigorous testing in the context of an adversary proceeding before the trier of fact." *Craig*, 497 U.S. at 845. In the absence of a face-to-face confrontation with the child witness, what assurances of reliability are afforded the defendant under the Maryland statute? *See id.* at 845, 851; *see also Thomas v. Gunter*, 962 F.2d 1477, 1483 (10th Cir. 1992) (discussing factors considered to determine reliability of child witness' testimony); *Spigarolo v. Meachum*, 934 F.2d 19, 23 (2d Cir. 1991) (same).

Other exceptions to an absolute right to physically confront witnesses have been recognized by the Supreme Court. *Craig*, 497 U.S. at 846–49 (citing *Mattox v. United States*, 156 U.S. 237, 243 (1895) (former testimony of unavailable witness); *Crawford v. Washington*, 541 U.S. 36 (2004) (nontestimonial hearsay statements) *Bourjaily v. United States*, 483 U.S. 171 (1987) (hearsay statements of nontestifying co-conspirators); *Illinois v. Allen*, 397 U.S. 337 (1970) (trial judge may remove a defendant from the courtroom for disruptive behavior). Are the statements in *Craig* as reliable as the hearsay statements permitted under these other exceptions?

7. In a dissenting opinion, Justice Scalia harshly criticized the majority's finding that face-to-face confrontation with witnesses appearing at trial is not an indispensable element of the Sixth Amendment's guarantee of the right to confront one's accusers. He restated the reasoning of the majority as follows:

> The Confrontation Clause guarantees not only what it explicitly provides for — "face-to-face" confrontation — but also implied and collateral rights such as cross-examination, oath, and observation of demeanor (TRUE); the purpose of this entire cluster of rights is to ensure the reliability of evidence (TRUE); the Maryland procedure preserves the implied and collateral rights (TRUE), which adequately ensure the reliability of evidence (perhaps TRUE); therefore the Confrontation Clause is not violated by denying what it explicitly provides for — "face-to-face" confrontation (unquestionably FALSE).

Craig, 497 U.S. at 862 (Scalia, dissenting). Do you agree with Justice Scalia's statement of the majority's reasoning? Where does Scalia's characterization of the reasoning of the majority break down?

8. Following *Craig*, Congress passed the Child Victims' and Child Witnesses' rights statute, 18 U.S.C. § 3509, which authorizes federal courts to order two-way closed circuit testimony in child abuse cases "if the court finds that the child is unable to testify in open court in the presence of the defendant, for any of the following reasons:

(i)   The child is unable to testify because of fear.

(ii)   There is substantial likelihood, established by expert testimony, that the child would suffer emotional trauma from testifying.

(iii)   The child suffers a mental or other infirmity.

(iv)   Conduct by the defendant or defense counsel causes the child to be unable to continue testifying."

18 U.S.C. § 3509(b)(1)(B).

Do the findings required by Section 3509(b)(1)(B) satisfy the constitutional lines drawn by the Supreme Court in *Craig*? *See United States v. Carrier*, 9 F.3d 867, 871 (10th Cir. 1993) (failing to decide the issue because the district court's findings satisfied both § 3509(b)(1)(B) and the constitutional requirements of *Craig*); *United States v. Garcia*, 7 F.3d 885, 888 (9th Cir. 1993) (holding that the language of the statute that requires that the court find "the child is unable to testify in open court in the presence of the defendant" before ordering testimony via closed-circuit television is consistent with the standard approved in *Craig*); *United States v. Farley*, 992 F.2d 1122, 1124 (10th Cir. 1993) (holding that the district court's finding that the child witness would be unable to testify because of fear and she would likely suffer trauma if she did testify in the defendant's presence, both listed as requisite findings in 18 U.S.C. § 3509(b)(1)(B)(i) and (ii), satisfied the constitutional parameters set forth in *Craig*); *see also Thomas v. Gunter*, 962 F.2d 1477, 1481–82 (10th Cir. 1992) (holding that Colorado's videotaping statute authorizing a child witness to testify out of the presence of the defendant upon a finding by the trial judge that the child is "medically unavailable," satisfied requirements of *Craig*).

PROBLEM

Problem 9-1. *Craig Hearing.* The defendant is being prosecuted for child sexual abuse for allegedly molesting his seven-year-old stepdaughter, Amy. The trial court orders a *Craig* hearing in which the judge hears the testimony of Dr. Barnes, the child psychologist who examined Amy on several occasions. Dr. Barnes testifies that Amy would be deeply traumatized if forced to testify. However, he concludes that the traumatization would not only be due to the defendant's presence but also to Amy's fear of the courtroom. When pressed on this point, Dr. Barnes states that Amy's traumatization would equally be caused by the defendant's presence and her general fear of the courtroom. Additionally, Dr. Barnes testifies that Amy would suffer substantial emotional distress as a result of testifying, though he is uncertain whether this emotional distress would impair her ability to reasonably communicate. Under *Craig*, should the district court permit Amy to testify via two-way closed circuit television? Does your opinion change if the request is made under 18 U.S.C. § 3509?

D. SPECIFIC TYPES OF STATEMENTS

[1]   Former Testimony — The Use of Grand Jury and Preliminary Hearing Testimony

[a]   Introduction

Federal Rule of Evidence 804(b)(1)[30] creates a hearsay exception for former testimony by an unavailable declarant where the declarant made the statement under oath while testifying "as a witness" in a "proceeding" and the party against whom the statement is offered had an "opportunity" and "similar motive" to "develop" the declarant's testimony by direct, cross, or redirect examination at the former proceeding. The exception is limited and only authorizes admission of the testimony given in the prior proceeding. To be admitted, two conditions must be satisfied. First, the declarant must be unavailable. Second, the party against whom the prior testimony is offered must have had a similar, not necessarily an identical, motive to develop the testimony in the prior proceeding. The traditional formulation of the similar motive requirement is that the two proceedings must reflect a "substantial identity of issues."[31] "Identity of issues ensures that the opposing party had a meaningful opportunity to develop testimony when it was first offered."[32]

The hearsay exception is justified by the traditional policies of necessity and trustworthiness. Necessity is established by the unavailability of the witness at trial. The statement is deemed trustworthy because, by definition, the declarant was under oath and subject to direct and cross-examination at the former proceeding.

The exception for former testimony reaches only statements given in a "hearing or proceeding" or a deposition taken "in the course of a proceeding." The term "proceeding" has been broadly construed to include a trial, preliminary hearing, grand jury hearing, suppression hearing, or other inquiry conducted in a manner authorized by law, such as a foreign deposition authorized by Fed. R. Crim. Proc. 15. The term "testimony" reaches statements that are "sworn, subject to penalty of perjury, made in response to questions on the record (transcribed stenographically or electronically), all pursuant to legally authorized routine."[33] The exception, however, does not embrace affidavits, even though prepared for use in proceedings, since the party opponent did not have an opportunity to challenge the affiant's statements "by direct, cross, or redirect examination."

Clearly the government cannot invoke Rule 804(b)(1) to offer prior grand jury testimony because the defendant has no right to attend the grand jury proceedings or

---

[30] Rule 804(b)(1) provides, in relevant part:

(b) Hearsay exceptions. The following are not excluded by the hearsay rule if the declarant is unavailable as a witness:

(1) Former testimony. Testimony given as a witness at another hearing of the same or a different proceeding, or in a deposition taken in compliance with law in the course of the same or another proceeding, if the party against whom the testimony is now offered, or, in a civil action or proceeding, a predecessor in interest, had an opportunity and similar motive to develop the testimony by direct, cross, or redirect examination.

[31] *United States v. Taplin*, 954 F.2d 1256, 1259 (6th Cir. 1992); *see also* 8 JAMES W. MOORE et al., MOORE'S FEDERAL PRACTICE § 804.04[3] (2d ed. 1989).

[32] *Id.*

[33] MUELLER & KIRKPATRICK, EVIDENCE § 8.58, at 1016 (1995).

question the witness. Thus, the defendant did not have an opportunity to develop the testimony by cross-examination. On the other hand, whether the defendant can offer grand jury testimony in a criminal case is a different matter. Since the function of the grand jury is merely to determine probable cause that the accused committed the crimes alleged in the indictment, the prosecutor generally will not have the same motive to develop testimony in grand jury proceedings as he does at trial. The prosecutor is not necessarily motivated to rigorously examine the witness's credibility in the grand jury proceeding to the same extent he would at trial. Furthermore, because the grand jury is an investigative body, a prosecutor may not know, prior to indictment, which issues will have importance at trial and thus may fail to effectively develop the grand jury testimony. Additionally, if the prosecution did not fully test the witness's testimony in the grand jury proceeding, it is highly questionable whether the prior testimony is sufficiently reliable and trustworthy to justify admission as an exception to the hearsay rule.

A similar problem arises during a preliminary hearing. The purpose of the preliminary hearing is to determine whether there is sufficient evidence to require the defendant to stand trial, not whether the defendant is guilty of the criminal charges beyond a reasonable doubt. Usually, the defense strategy is not to impeach the credibility of government witnesses, since questions of credibility raise jury questions. Instead, the wiser strategy is often to examine witnesses for the limited purpose of discovering useful information to be used later at trial. Thus, the question arises whether the defendant had a "similar motive" at the preliminary hearing to develop the testimony by cross-examination. Assuming unavailability, should the witness's preliminary hearing testimony be admitted against the defendant? The issue of "similar motive" within the context of grand jury and preliminary hearing proceedings will be addressed later in this section.

[b]   Grand Jury Testimony Offered Against the Government — The Problem of Motivation to Develop Testimony

UNITED STATES v. SALERNO
505 U.S. 317 (1992)

JUSTICE THOMAS delivered the opinion of the Court.

Federal Rule of Evidence 804(b)(1) states an exception to the hearsay rule that allows a court, in certain instances, to admit the former testimony of an unavailable witness. We must decide in this case whether the Rule permits a criminal defendant to introduce the grand jury testimony of a witness who asserts the Fifth Amendment privilege at trial.

The seven respondents, Anthony Salerno, Vincent DiNapoli, Louis DiNapoli, Nicholas Auletta, Edward Halloran, Alvin O. Chattin, and Aniello Migliore, allegedly took part in the activities of a criminal organization known as the Genovese Family of La Cosa Nostra (Family) in New York City. In 1987, a federal grand jury in the Southern District of New York indicted the respondents and four others on the basis of these activities. The indictment charged the respondents with a variety of federal offenses, including 41 acts constituting a "pattern of illegal activity" in violation of the Racketeer Influenced and Corrupt Organizations Act (RICO), 18 U.S.C. § 1962(b).

Sixteen of the alleged acts involved fraud in the New York construction industry in the 1980's. According to the indictment and evidence later admitted at trial, the Family used its influence over labor unions and its control over the supply of concrete to rig bidding on large construction projects in Manhattan. The Family purportedly allocated contracts for these projects among a so-called "Club" of six concrete companies in exchange for a share of the proceeds.

Much of the case concerned the affairs of the Cedar Park Concrete Construction Corporation (Cedar Park). Two of the owners of this firm, Frederick DeMatteis and Pasquale Bruno, testified before the grand jury under a grant of immunity. In response to questions by the United States, they repeatedly stated that neither they nor Cedar Park had participated in the Club. At trial, however, the United States attempted to show that Cedar Park, in fact, had belonged to the Club by calling two contractors who had taken part in the scheme and by presenting intercepted conversations among the respondents. The United States also introduced documents indicating that the Family had an ownership interest in Cedar Park.

To counter the United States' evidence, the respondents subpoenaed DeMatteis and Bruno as witnesses in the hope that they would provide the same exculpatory testimony that they had presented to the grand jury. When both witnesses invoked their Fifth Amendment privilege against self-incrimination and refused to testify, the respondents asked the District Court to admit the transcripts of their grand jury testimony. Although this testimony constituted hearsay, *see* Rule 801(c), the respondents argued that it fell within the hearsay exception in Rule 804(b)(1) for former testimony of unavailable witnesses.

The District Court refused to admit the grand jury testimony. It observed that Rule 804(b)(1) permits admission of former testimony against a party at trial only when that party had a "similar motive to develop the testimony by direct, cross, or redirect examination." The District Court held that the United States did not have this motive, stating that the "motive of a prosecutor in questioning a witness before the grand jury in the investigatory stages of a case is far different from the motive of a prosecutor in conducting the trial." A jury subsequently convicted the respondents of the RICO counts and other federal offenses.

The United States Court of Appeals for the Second Circuit reversed, holding that the District Court had erred in excluding DeMatteis' and Bruno's grand jury testimony. 937 F.2d 797 (1991). Although the Court of Appeals recognized that "the government may have had no motive . . . to impeach . . . Bruno or DeMatteis" before the grand jury, it concluded that "the government's motive in examining the witnesses . . . was irrelevant." *Id.*, at 806. The Court of Appeals decided that, in order to maintain "adversarial fairness," Rule 804(b)(1)'s similar motive element should "evaporat[e]" when the Government obtains immunized testimony in a grand jury proceeding from a witness who refuses to testify at trial. *Ibid.* We granted certiorari and now reverse and remand.

II.

The hearsay rule prohibits admission of certain statements made by a declarant other than while testifying at trial. *See* Rule 801(c) (hearsay definition), 802 (hearsay rule). The parties acknowledge that the hearsay rule, standing by itself, would have blocked introduction at trial of DeMatteis' and Bruno's grand jury testimony. Rule

804(b)(1), however, establishes an exception to the hearsay rule for former testimony. This exception provides:

> "The following are not excluded by the hearsay rule if the declarant is unavailable as a witness:

> "(1) Former Testimony. — Testimony given as a witness at another hearing . . . if the party against whom the testimony is now offered . . . had an opportunity and similar motive to develop the testimony by direct, cross, or redirect examination."

We must decide whether the Court of Appeals properly interpreted Rule 804(b)(1) in this case.

The parties agree that DeMatteis and Bruno were "unavailable" to the defense as witnesses, provided that they properly invoked the Fifth Amendment privilege and refused to testify. *See* Rule 804(a)(1). They also agree that DeMatteis' and Bruno's grand jury testimony constituted "testimony given as . . . witness[es] at another hearing." They disagree, however, about whether the "similar motive" requirement in the final clause of Rule 804(b)(1) should have prevented admission of the testimony in this case.

A.

Nothing in the language of Rule 804(b)(1) suggests that a court may admit former testimony absent satisfaction of each of the Rule's elements. The United States thus asserts that, unless it had a "similar motive," we must conclude that the District Court properly excluded DeMatteis' and Bruno's testimony as hearsay. The respondents, in contrast, urge us not to read Rule 804(b)(1) in a "slavishly literal fashion." Brief for Respondents 31. They contend that "adversarial fairness" prevents the United States from relying on the similar motive requirement in this case. We agree with the United States.

When Congress enacted the prohibition against admission of hearsay in Rule 802, it placed 24 exceptions in Rule 803 and 5 additional exceptions in Rule 804. Congress thus presumably made a careful judgment as to what hearsay may come into evidence and what may not. To respect its determination, we must enforce the words that it enacted. The respondents, as a result, had no right to introduce DeMatteis' and Bruno's former testimony under Rule 804(b)(1) without showing a "similar motive." This Court cannot alter evidentiary rules merely because litigants might prefer different rules in a particular class of cases. *See Green v. Bock Laundry Machine Co.*, 490 U.S. 504, 524 (1989).

The respondents' argument for a different result takes several forms. They first assert that adversarial fairness requires us to infer that Rule 804(b)(1) contains implicit limitations. They observe, for example, that the Advisory Committee Note to Rule 804 makes clear that the former testimony exception applies only to statements made under oath or affirmation, even though the Rule does not state this restriction explicitly. The respondents maintain that we likewise may hold that Rule 804(b)(1) does not require a showing of similar motive in all instances.

The respondents' example does not persuade us to change our reading of Rule 804(b)(1). If the Rule applies only to sworn statements, it does so not because adversarial fairness implies a limitation, but simply because the word "testimony" refers only to statements made under oath or affirmation. *See* Black's Law Dictionary 1476 (6th ed. 1990). We see no way to interpret the text of Rule 804(b)(1) to mean that defendants sometimes do not have to show "similar motive."

The respondents also assert that courts often depart from the Rules of Evidence to prevent litigants from presenting only part of the truth. For example, citing *United States v. Miller*, 600 F.2d 498 (CA5 1979), the respondents maintain that, although parties may enjoy various testimonial privileges, they can forfeit these privileges by "opening the door" to certain subjects. In the respondents' view, the United States is attempting to use the hearsay rule like a privilege to keep DeMatteis' and Bruno's grand jury testimony away from the jury. They contend, however, that adversarial fairness requires us to conclude that the United States forfeited its right to object to admission of the testimony when it introduced contradictory evidence about Cedar Park.

This argument also fails. Even assuming that we should treat the hearsay rule like the rules governing testimonial privileges, we would not conclude that a forfeiture occurred here. Parties may forfeit a privilege by exposing privileged evidence, but do not forfeit one merely by taking a position that the evidence might contradict. *See* 8 J. Wigmore, Evidence § 2327, p. 636 (McNaughton rev. 1961); M. Larkin, Federal Testimonial Privileges § 2.06, pp. 2-103, 2-104, 2-120 (1991). In *Miller*, for example, the court held that a litigant, "after giving the jury his version of a privileged communication, [could not] prevent the cross-examiner from utilizing *the communication itself* to get at the truth." 600 F.2d, at 501 (emphasis added). In this case, by contrast, the United States never presented to the jury any version of what DeMatteis and Bruno had said in the grand jury proceedings. Instead, it attempted to show Cedar Park's participation in the Club solely through other evidence available to the respondents. The United States never exposed the jury to anything analogous to a "privileged communication." The respondents' argument, accordingly, fails on its own terms.

The respondents finally argue that adversarial fairness may prohibit suppression of exculpatory evidence produced in grand jury proceedings. They note that, when this Court required disclosure of a grand jury transcript in *Dennis v. United States*, 384 U.S. 855 (1966), it stated that "it is rarely justifiable for the prosecution to have exclusive access" to relevant facts. *Id.*, at 873. They allege that the United States nevertheless uses the following tactics to develop evidence in a one-sided manner: If a witness inculpates a defendant during the grand jury proceedings, the United States immunizes him and calls him at trial; however, if the witness exculpates the defendant, as Bruno and DeMatteis each did here, the United States refuses to immunize him and attempts to exclude the testimony as hearsay. The respondents assert that dispensing with the "similar motive" requirement would limit these tactics.

We again fail to see how we may create an exception to Rule 804(b)(1). The *Dennis* case, unlike this one, did not involve a question about the admissibility of evidence. Rather, it concerned only the need to disclose a transcript to the defendants. Moreover, in *Dennis*, we did not hold that adversarial fairness required the United States to make the grand jury transcript available. Instead, we ordered disclosure under the specific language of Federal Rule of Criminal Procedure 6(e). In this case, the language of Rule 804(b)(1) does not support the respondents. Indeed, the respondents specifically ask us to ignore it. Neither *Dennis* nor anything else that the respondents have cited provides us with this authority.

B.

The question remains whether the United States had a "similar motive" in this case. The United States asserts that the District Court specifically found that it did not and that we should not review its factual determinations. It also argues that a prosecutor generally will not have the same motive to develop testimony in grand jury proceedings as he does at trial. A prosecutor, it explains, must maintain secrecy during the investigatory stages of the criminal process and therefore may not desire to confront grand jury witnesses with contradictory evidence. It further states that a prosecutor may not know, prior to indictment, which issues will have importance at trial and accordingly may fail to develop grand jury testimony effectively.

The respondents disagree with both of the United States' arguments. They characterize the District Court's ruling as one of law, rather than fact, because the District Court essentially ruled that a prosecutor's motives at trial always differ from his motives in grand jury proceedings. The respondents contend further that the grand jury transcripts in this case actually show that the United States thoroughly attempted to impeach DeMatteis and Bruno. They add that, despite the United States' stated concern about maintaining secrecy, the United States revealed to DeMatteis and Bruno the identity of the major witnesses who testified against them at trial.

The Court of Appeals, as noted, erroneously concluded that the respondents did not have to demonstrate a similar motive in this case to make use of Rule 804(b)(1). It therefore declined to consider fully the arguments now presented by the parties about whether the United States had such a motive. Rather than to address this issue here in the first instance, we think it prudent to remand the case for further consideration.

[JUSTICE BLACKMUN's concurring opinion omitted].

JUSTICE STEVENS, dissenting.

Because I believe that the Government clearly had an "opportunity and similar motive" to develop by direct or cross-examination the grand jury testimony of Pasquale Bruno and Frederick DeMatteis, I would affirm the judgment of the Court of Appeals on the ground that the transcript of their grand jury testimony was admissible under the plain language of Federal Rule of Evidence 804(b)(1). As the Court explains, *ante*, at 2505–2506, the grand jury testimony of Bruno and DeMatteis was totally inconsistent with the Government's theory of the alleged RICO conspiracy to rig bids on large construction projects in Manhattan. Bruno and DeMatteis were principals in Cedar Park Construction Corporation (Cedar Park), which, according to the Government, was a member of the so-called "Club" of concrete companies that submitted rigged bids on construction projects in accordance with the orders of the Genovese Family of La Cosa Nostra. But notwithstanding the fact that they had been given grants of immunity, Bruno and DeMatteis repeatedly testified before the grand jury that they had not participated in either the Club or the alleged bid-rigging conspiracy. As the Court of Appeals explained, Cedar Park was "one of the largest contractors in the metropolitan New York City concrete industry," and it is arguable that without Cedar Park's participation, "there could be no 'club' of concrete contractors." 937 F.2d 797, 808 (CA2 1991). And without the "Club," the allegations of fraud in the construction industry — which "formed the core of the RICO charges" — "simply dissolv[e]." *Ibid.*

It is therefore clear that before the grand jury the Government had precisely the same interest in establishing that Bruno's and DeMatteis' testimony was false as it had at trial. Thus, when the prosecutors doubted Bruno's and DeMatteis' veracity before the grand jury — as they most assuredly did — they unquestionably had an "opportunity and similar motive to develop the testimony by direct, cross, or redirect examination" within the meaning of Rule 804(b)(1).

. . . .

Of course, the party might decide — for tactical reasons or otherwise — not to engage in a rigorous cross-examination, or even in any cross-examination at all. In such a case, however, I do not believe that it is accurate to say that the party lacked a similar motive to cross-examine the witness' instead, it is more accurate to say that the party had a similar motive to cross-examine the witness (i.e., to undermine the false or misleading testimony) but chose not to act on that motive. Although the Rules of Evidence allow a party to make that choice about whether to engage in cross-examination, they also provide that she must accept the consequences of that decision — including the possibility that the testimony might be introduced against her in a subsequent proceeding.

. . . .

NOTES AND QUESTIONS

1. The Supreme Court held that the Court of Appeals erroneously concluded that respondents did not have to demonstrate a similar motive to make use of Rule 804(b)(1), and remanded the case to determine whether the United States had such a motive. How should the court rule on remand?

2. In *Salerno*, the Government maintained that the issues before the grand jury are quite different from those at trial. Thus, the United States did not have a "similar motive" as required by Rule 804(b)(1). *Salerno*, 505 U.S. at 324–25. In contrast, Justice Stevens, in his dissenting opinion, asserted "that before the grand jury the Government had precisely the same interest in establishing that Bruno's and DeMatteis' testimony was false as it had at trial." *Id.* at 327. Do you agree with the Government or Justice Stevens? Does this come down to a case-by-case analysis? *See United States v. Miller*, 904 F.2d 65, 68 (D.C. Cir. 1990) (finding that the government had the same motive and opportunity to question witness when it brought him before the grand jury as it did at trial).

3. The Government also argued that the prosecutor must maintain secrecy during the investigatory stages of the criminal process and therefore may not desire to confront grand jury witnesses with contradictory evidence. Additionally, the government stated that a prosecutor may not know, prior to indictment which issues will have importance at trial and thus may fail to effectively develop the grand jury testimony? On remand, what weight should be given these arguments?

4. Do you agree with Justice Stevens that if the party against whom the testimony is now offered had a "similar motive" but chose not to act on that motive, for whatever reason, the testimony may nonetheless be introduced against him in a subsequent proceeding? *Salerno*, 505 U.S., at 329–30. In other words, is opportunity enough, so that prior testimony should not be excluded merely because the objecting party did not take advantage of the opportunity to develop the testimony? *See* Fed. R. Evid. 804(b)(1), Advisory Committee's Notes ("If the party against whom [the testimony is] now offered is the one against whom the testimony was offered previously, no unfairness is apparent in requiring him to accept his own prior conduct of cross-examination or decision not to cross-examine."). Does this construction of Rule 804(b)(1) undermine the rationale for admitting prior testimony? Is former testimony sufficiently trustworthy even though the party against whom the testimony is being offered did not rigorously examine the witness to test the witness's credibility and veracity?

[c]   Preliminary Hearing Testimony

STATE v. HOWELL
868 S.W.2d 238 (Tenn. 1993)

ANDERSON, JUSTICE.

In this capital case, the defendant, Michael Wayne Howell, was found guilty of grand larceny and the first-degree felony murder of Alvin Kennedy, but found not guilty of premeditated first-degree murder. . . .

On appeal, the defendant raises numerous issues for our review, involving alleged errors occurring at trial in the guilt phase. We have carefully considered the defendant's contentions and have decided that none has merit. We, therefore, affirm the defendant's conviction in the guilt phase.

. . . .

On Saturday, October 31, 1987, between 10:00 a.m. and 1:00 p.m., the defendant and his girlfriend, Mona Lisa Watson, walked to the house of his brother's girlfriend, Cheri Goff. After arriving, the defendant showed Goff a set of keys to the Lynn Whitsett Corporation property in Memphis where he had previously worked, and announced that "he was going to go get him a truck." The defendant also said "he was going down hard this time, and he was going to take some people with him." After making these statements, Goff said the defendant used her telephone to call someone about getting a gun for him. Goff also testified that she had previously seen the defendant carrying a silver handgun with a white, or bone, handle.

Later that same night, sometime after 8:00 p.m., Terry Lee Ellis drove Howell and Watson to Raines Road and left them at the Ryder Truck Terminal near the Lynn Whitsett property. Earlier, around 7:30 p.m., the defendant and Watson had stopped by the home of Robert Brink, the husband of one of Watson's friends. Brink said Howell asked to borrow some money and used the telephone, but did not stay long.

Around 2:30 a.m. on Sunday, November 1, 1987, the defendant and Watson purchased a candy bar at the Quick-Shop Food Store on Macon in Memphis. Cassandra Henderson, the clerk on duty testified that the defendant was driving a white pickup truck with writing on the door and a workman's rack on the back, which he had parked on the blind side of the store. Henderson also said that as Howell was leaving the store, he bumped into another customer, Rodney Graves, who was entering the store, and a fight broke out between the two men. After the fight, Henderson said she saw the defendant in the store parking lot with a silver pistol. Rodney Graves testified that after the fight, Howell went outside and returned to the front door of the store carrying a silver gun with bone handle, but nothing happened and the defendant left the premises.

Later that day, sometime in the evening of November 1, 1987, the defendant and Watson drove the Whitsett truck to Stanley Johnson's house. Johnson testified that Howell was waving around a nickel-plated.38 caliber pistol with a bone handle, which the defendant referred to as "Jesus Christ." In addition, Johnson said Howell told him that "anybody messes with us, I'll introduce them to Jesus Christ." Thereafter, between 9:00 and 10:00 p.m., Cheri Goff said she was returning home from a movie with some friends when she saw the defendant driving a white truck with a Lynn Whitsett logo on the side and red sideboards on the back.

At 11:05 p.m. on November 1, 1987, Tennessee Highway Patrol Officer Aaron Chism said he stopped by Loeb's 7-Eleven Market on Whitten Road off Interstate 40 in Shelby County, and saw the victim, Alvin Kennedy, working at his job on the midnight shift. Between 12:20 and 12:40 a.m. that same night, Brian Moser said he came into the Loeb's store to purchase a six-pack of beer, but there was no clerk in the store. As a result, after waiting a few minutes, Moser said he decided to go across the street to the Southland 7-Eleven and purchase his beer.

At 12:45 a.m., Charles Allen stopped at Loeb's 7-Eleven to purchase some gasoline. When he went to pay for his gas, Allen found Kennedy's body lying behind the counter in a pool of blood, the cash register drawer open, and all of the paper money missing. As a result, Allen said he ran across the street to the Southland 7-Eleven and asked the clerk to call the police.

Upon investigation, it was discovered that Kennedy had been shot once from close range in the upper right forehead. The wound had immediately rendered him unconscious, and he had died within a short time. It was also discovered that $111.16 was missing from the store. The tape from the cash register indicated that the last transaction had occurred at 12:24 a.m.

Susan Bauer, the clerk at the Southland 7-Eleven across the street from the Loeb's store, testified that she remembered Watson and the defendant purchasing beer and a candy bar at her store around 12:20 a.m., approximately 20 minutes before Allen came in asking her to call the police. She said she remembered when they came in because they parked the Whitsett truck on the blind side of the store, which she thought was suspicious for that time of night.

Later that day, Monday, November 2, 1987, at approximately 9:00 p.m., Charlene Calhoun was shot in the parking lot of her apartment complex near Interstate 40 in Dell City, Oklahoma, and her 1987 Toyota Tercel was stolen. A witness who heard the shooting said he saw a man and a woman get into a light-colored Toyota hatchback and drive away after the shots were fired. The Lynn Whitsett truck was found only 125 feet from the scene of the shooting, with its interior on fire, and the defendant's left palm prints on the truck's fenders. . . .

. . . .

Almost a month later, on November 29, 1987, the defendant and Watson were arrested in Panama City, Florida, after a shoot-out with police and a high-speed chase. They were driving the stolen Toyota from Oklahoma, but had replaced the Oklahoma tags with Tennessee plates from another vehicle. Florida police found a nickel-plated Smith & Wesson.38 revolver with a bone handle on the floorboard of the passenger's side where the defendant had been seated. Ballistics tests indicated that the bullet that had killed Alvin Kennedy had been fired from this gun, as had the bullet taken from the body of Charlene Calhoun in Oklahoma.

The last evidence introduced by the State was the redacted testimony of co-defendant Mona Lisa Watson given in April of 1988 at the defendant's Oklahoma preliminary hearing for the murder of Charlene Calhoun. Watson agreed to testify against the defendant in return for a life sentence. Although she later decided not to testify at both the Tennessee trial and the Oklahoma trial, Watson was questioned on direct examination by the prosecutors at the Oklahoma preliminary hearing. She testified that she and the defendant had driven Interstate 40 from Memphis to Oklahoma in the Lynn Whitsett truck on November 1 and 2, 1987. Watson said they drank beer and shot cocaine on the trip, and when they got to Dell City, Oklahoma, she said they got off the interstate and stopped at an apartment complex to walk around. After walking around for a few minutes, Watson said Howell shot Charlene Calhoun, the two of them took her car, and they set fire to the Lynn Whitsett truck by igniting lighter fluid she had thrown on the front seat. Then, Watson said she and the defendant drove back to Memphis in Calhoun's car, and thereafter to Florida on November 3, 1987.

On cross-examination during the Oklahoma preliminary hearing, the Oklahoma public defender representing Howell asked Watson questions about a shooting in Memphis prior to their trip to Oklahoma. Watson testified that before going to Oklahoma, she and the defendant had gone into a convenience store in Memphis to purchase a six-pack of beer. After Howell handed her the beer and told her to go to the car, Watson said the defendant pulled a gun and shot the clerk in the head, and that it was the same gun Howell had shown her earlier.

Later, at the Tennessee trial, Howell's defense counsel tried to impeach the preliminary hearing testimony of Watson. He attempted to introduce testimony from Watson's Oklahoma lawyer and the defendant's Oklahoma lawyer that Watson later stated that she had lied during the preliminary hearing in order to escape the death penalty herself. The Memphis trial judge, however, sustained the State's objection that the evidence was hearsay and self-serving, and ruled the evidence inadmissible. Except for this attempt to impeach Watson's former testimony, the defendant presented no testimony on his behalf at the guilt phase of the trial.

Based upon this evidence, the jury found the defendant guilty of first-degree murder in the perpetration of a felony and grand larceny, but not guilty of premeditated first-degree murder. . . .

D. *Oklahoma Preliminary Hearing Testimony*

We next consider whether the trial court erred in admitting the testimony of co-defendant, Mona Lisa Watson, given at the defendant's preliminary hearing in Oklahoma on the charges against him in that state for the murder of Charlene Calhoun. The trial court admitted this testimony under the former testimony exception to the hearsay rule. . . .

*   *   *

The defendant . . . contends that although he had an opportunity to cross examine Watson at the Oklahoma preliminary hearing, he did not have a similar motive to develop her testimony because the preliminary hearing involved separate charges in another state. He also argues that he was represented by a different lawyer in those proceedings, who had no real motive to inquire into or develop the facts relevant to the killing of Alvin Kennedy in Tennessee. As a result, the defendant asserts that admission of the former testimony violated the hearsay rule and his right to confrontation under the Sixth and Fourteenth Amendments to the U.S. Constitution, and Article I, § 9 of the Tennessee Constitution.

The Sixth Amendment to the U.S. Constitution, which is applicable to the states through the Fourteenth Amendment, *see Pointer v. Texas*, 380 U.S. 400 (1965), provides that "[i]n all criminal prosecutions, the accused shall enjoy the right to be confronted with the witnesses against him." The corresponding provision of the Tennessee Constitution provides "[t]hat in all criminal prosecutions, the accused hath the right . . . to meet the witnesses face to face." Tenn. Const. art. I, § 9. This Court has previously held that the former testimony exception to the hearsay rule has sufficient "indicia of reliability" so that admission of evidence thereunder comports with the right of confrontation. Accordingly, if Watson's Oklahoma preliminary hearing testimony met the requirements of the former testimony hearsay exception, it would also satisfy the right of confrontation.

In *State v. Causby, supra*, a first-degree murder case, this Court held that the trial court properly admitted a co-defendant's former testimony from a juvenile transfer hearing under the former testimony exception to the hearsay rule because the defendants had a full opportunity and similar motive to develop the prior testimony. Several factors were considered in reaching that conclusion, but the most emphasis was placed on the fact that at both the transfer hearing and the subsequent trial, the testimony was addressed to the same issue of "[w]hether or not the defendants had committed the offense" charged. *Causby*, 706 S.W.2d at 632.

Complete identity of the issues is not necessary. Other courts considering what constitutes a similar motive have concluded that if the issues in both cases are sufficiently similar, the requirement of similar motive is satisfied. *United States v. Licavoli*, 725 F.2d 1040, 1048 (6th Cir. 1984); *United States v. Pizarro*, 717 F.2d 336, 349 (7th Cir. 1983). . . . This conclusion comports with the Advisory Committee Note to Rule 804 that observes: "The common law . . . did require identity of issues as a means of insuring that the former handling of the witness was the equivalent of what would now be done if the opportunity were presented. Modern decisions reduce the requirement to 'substantial' identity." 28 U.S.C.A. at 447, subd. (b), except. (1).

The defendant's identity as the killer of Alvin Kennedy and Charlene Calhoun was an issue in both the Oklahoma hearing and the Tennessee trial. The testimony identifying the defendant as the killer of Alvin Kennedy circumstantially established the defendant's identity as the killer of Charlene Calhoun, since Kennedy and Calhoun were shot with the same gun. Likewise, Watson's testimony identifying the defendant as the person who shot Charlene Calhoun circumstantially established the defendant's identity as the thief of the Whitsett truck and killer of Alvin Kennedy. Consequently, the defendant had a similar motive to explore the identification issues at the Oklahoma preliminary hearing. In fact, the defendant has failed to point to any matter that would have been developed in cross-examination that was not raised in the prior proceedings. Therefore, we conclude that a similar motive existed to develop Watson's preliminary hearing testimony with respect to the killings of both Charlene Calhoun, and Alvin Kennedy in Tennessee.

It is true that the defendant was not represented by the same counsel in the Oklahoma hearing and the Tennessee trial. However, the rule requires only that the party against whom the testimony is offered have an opportunity and similar motive. An identity of lawyers is not necessary. [Cohen, Paine & Sheppeard, Tennessee Law of Evidence § 804(b)(1).2, at 460 (2d ed. 1990)]. Moreover, the facts relating to the murder of Alvin Kennedy were brought out on Watson's cross-examination by the defendant's Oklahoma counsel. If the party against whom [the testimony] is now offered is the one against whom the testimony was offered previously, no unfairness is apparent in requiring him to accept his own prior conduct of cross-examination. . . ." Fed. R. Evid. 804, advisory committee note, 28 U.S.C.A. at 447, subd. (b), except. (1).

Moreover, a party, for tactical reasons, may decide "not to engage in a rigorous cross-examination, or even in any cross-examination at all." [*United States v. Salerno*, 505 U.S. 317, 329 (1992)] (Stevens, J., dissenting). The party may have a similar motive, but simply choose not to act on it. *Id.*

> [A]s long as the party had a similar motive to develop the testimony in the prior proceeding, *there is no unfairness in requiring the party against whom the testimony is now offered to accept her prior decision to develop or not develop the testimony fully.*

United States v. Salerno, 505 U.S. at 329 n.6 (Stevens, J., dissenting) (emphasis added).

As a result of the foregoing, we conclude that defendant's Oklahoma counsel had a similar motive to defendant's Tennessee counsel to develop Watson's testimony about Alvin Kennedy's murder at the preliminary hearing in Oklahoma. Accordingly, we conclude that the admission of Watson's Oklahoma preliminary hearing testimony with respect to the murder of Alvin Kennedy in Memphis did not violate the hearsay rule nor the defendant's confrontation rights under the Sixth and Fourteenth Amendments to the U.S. Constitution, and Article I, § 9 of the Tennessee Constitution.

*   *   *

We therefore affirm the conviction of first-degree murder. . . .

NOTES AND QUESTIONS

1. The purpose of the preliminary hearing conducted in Oklahoma was to determine if the defendant should be tried for the murder of Charlene Calhoun. In contrast, the purpose of the Tennessee preliminary hearing was to determine whether the defendant should be tried for the murder of Alvin Kennedy. The defendant maintained that it was error to admit Watson's Oklahoma preliminary hearing testimony at the trial in Tennessee for the murder of Alvin Kennedy. The Oklahoma public defender had no real motive to inquire into or develop the facts relevant to the killing of Kennedy in Tennessee. Do you agree? The court reasoned that the defendant's identity as the killer of Alvin Kennedy and Charlene Calhoun was at issue in both the Oklahoma hearing and the Tennessee trial. Do you agree?

2. What is the test applied by the court for determining "similar motive"? *See United States v. Lombard*, 72 F.3d 170, 188 (1st Cir. 1995) ("The party against whom the prior testimony is offered must have had a similar, not necessarily an identical, motive to develop the adverse testimony in the prior proceeding."); *United States v. Koon*, 34 F.3d 1416, 1428 (9th Cir. 1994) (same); *United States v. Taplin*, 954 F.2d 1256, 1259 (6th Cir. 1992) (articulating the traditional formulation of the similar motive requirement).

3. To admit prior testimony under Rule 804(b)(1), does it matter whether the defendant was represented by the same counsel in both proceedings? The courts have consistently held that the rule requires only that the party against whom the testimony is offered have an opportunity and similar motive. "An identity of lawyers is not necessary." *State v. Howell*, 868 S.W.2d 238, 251 (Tenn. 1993); *see also United States v. Tannehill*, 49 F.3d 1049, 1057 (5th Cir. 1995) (holding that defendant's motive for cross-examination was not sufficiently different to preclude admission of the testimony under

Rule 804(b)(1) merely because different counsel with different defense theories conducted the cross-examination at the prior proceeding).

4. In *Cardenas v. State*, 811 P.2d 989, 992–93 (Wyo. 1991), the Wyoming Supreme Court expressly rejected appellant's argument that his motives to cross-examine the victim at the preliminary hearing were different from his motives to cross-examine her at trial:

> Appellant contends that his motives were different because the purpose of a preliminary hearing (the determination of probable cause) is different than the purpose of a trial (the determination of guilt). He asserts that during the preliminary hearing, his counsel was not motivated to go beyond attempting to rebut a finding of probable cause since a more extensive cross-examination would have forced him to reveal his theory of defense. That argument demonstrates that Appellant's cross-examination of the victim at the preliminary hearing may have been limited by a tactical decision, but it does not indicate that his motive to cross-examine the victim at the preliminary hearing was not similar to his motive to cross-examine her at trial. As in *Rodriguez*, where the defendant's motive in both proceedings was to discredit the witness' testimony, Appellant's motives were sufficiently similar to warrant the admissibility of the victim's preliminary hearing testimony under W.R.E. 804(b)(1).

Do you agree? Did the Wyoming Supreme Court adopt Justice Stevens's position in his dissenting opinion in *Salerno*?

5. In *Howell*, the court stated that "if Watson's Oklahoma preliminary hearing testimony met the requirements of the former testimony hearsay exception, it would also satisfy the confrontation clause." In *Crawford v. Washington*, 541 U.S. 36 (2004), the Supreme Court rejected the "indicia of reliability" test enunciated in *Ohio v. Roberts*, 448 U.S. 56 (1980). The Court held that where testimonial statements are at issue, the Sixth Amendment. demands unavailability and a prior opportunity for cross-examination. *Crawford*, 541 U.S. at 68. In other words, hearsay statements that are testimonial in nature are barred by the Confrontation Clause absent proof that the declarant is unavailable and the defendant had a prior opportunity to cross-examine the witness. Does admission of Watson's Oklahoma preliminary hearing testimony violate the Sixth Amendment right of confrontation as interpreted by the Supreme Court in *Crawford?*

PROBLEM

Problem 9-2. *Opportunity and Similar Motive.* Defendants Taplin and Bailey conspired to transport cocaine from Houston, Texas to Nashville, Tennessee. This business venture ended when both were charged with possession with intent to distribute cocaine and aiding and abetting, in violation of 21 U.S.C. § 841(a)(1) and 18 U.S.C. § 2, and conspiracy to possess with intent to distribute in violation of 21 U.S.C. § 846. Taplin filed a motion to suppress evidence, which Bailey joined. Bailey subsequently took the stand in support of his own motion, where he discussed the conspiracy to transport cocaine, and the recorded telephone calls that induced him to visit Jackson, Tennessee, and the circumstances of his own arrest. The purpose of Bailey's testimony was to demonstrate his standing to join Taplin's motion. Taplin's attorney was in the courtroom during Bailey's suppression testimony and was asked by the presiding judge if he had any questions. Bailey's motion was subsequently denied for lack of standing.

Bailey elected not to testify during Taplin's separate trial, invoking his Fifth Amendment privilege against self-incrimination. The government moved to admit portions of Bailey's testimony at the suppression hearing, arguing that it satisfies the requirements of Rule 804(b)(1). How should the district court rule on the government's motion? *See United States v. Taplin*, 954 F.2d 1256 (6th Cir. 1992).

[d]   Foreign Depositions Offered Against the Defendant

UNITED STATES v. SALIM
855 F.2d 944 (2d Cir. 1988)

PIERCE, CIRCUIT JUDGE:

In order to obtain evidence for use in domestic trials, litigants are apt to find it increasingly necessary to conduct depositions in foreign countries. However, foreign laws do not always permit witnesses to be deposed in the manner to which American courts and lawyers are accustomed. In certain cases, the use of unconventional foreign methods of examination may exceed the limits of accepted American standards of fairness and reliability, such as underlie the confrontation clause and the rule against hearsay. Concerns of this type are addressed best on a case-by-case basis.

This appeal requires us to determine the extent to which the deposition of a government witness, taken abroad in a manner different from that which would be required of a deposition taken in the United States, may be admitted in evidence and used against a defendant in a criminal prosecution. Mohamed Salim was convicted by a jury in the United States District Court for the Eastern District of New York on charges of conspiracy to distribute and to possess with intent to distribute heroin, in violation of 21 U.S.C. §§ 841(a), 846, and of offering a bribe to an officer of the United States Customs Service, in violation of 18 U.S.C. § 201(b). [T]he district court, Jack B. Weinstein, Judge, held that a witness' deposition, taken in France pursuant to French law, was properly admitted pursuant to Fed. R. Crim. P. 15 and Fed. R. Evid. 804(b)(1), and did not violate Salim's rights under the confrontation clause of the Constitution, U.S. Const. amend. VI, cl. 4. For the reasons that follow, we agree with the district court and therefore affirm the conviction.

In November 1986, Bebe Soraia Rouhani arrived at Orly Airport in Paris, France, en route from Karachi, Pakistan, to John F. Kennedy Airport in New York. A routine inspection by French customs officials revealed that she was carrying nine pounds of heroin in the lining of her suitcases. She told French officials that the suitcases had been given to her in Karachi and that she was supposed to deliver them at Kennedy Airport to a man named "Qazi," whose description she provided. French authorities gave this information to United States Customs agents in Paris, who relayed it to New York. Defendant Mohamed Salim was identified at Kennedy Airport by his description, and was arrested after fleeing across the lobby of the International Arrival Terminal when an undercover agent addressed him as "Qazi" and asked if he were meeting "Bebe." At the time of his arrest, Salim had in his possession a photocopy of Rouhani's passport, containing her description and photograph. While being taken from the airport to the Metropolitan Correctional Center, Salim offered a customs agent $20,000 to allow him to escape.

Prior to trial, the government sought permission from the district court to take Rouhani's deposition in France since she was being held in custody by French police while awaiting her own trial for drug smuggling. The district court concluded that Rouhani's testimony would be important to the trial of appellant, but since she was unlikely to be able to appear at his trial here to give live testimony, the court issued a Request for Judicial Assistance to the Republic of France, and arrangements were made for Rouhani to be deposed before the Honorable Evelyne Verleene-Thomas, Examining Magistrate of the trial court (Juge d'Instruction du Tribunal de Grande Instance) in Bobigny, France (the "magistrate"). Appellant was in federal custody in New York pending trial but could not be transported to France to attend the deposition because the United States Marshals Service lacked authority to keep him in custody in France. Consequently, efforts were made to have two open telephone lines available between the court in France and the courthouse in the United States to enable Salim to hear Rouhani's deposition testimony on one line and to consult privately with his attorney on the other line. Additionally, the government sought permission to record the deposition on audio or video tape. Both proposals were rejected by the French court as contrary to French law. However, the French magistrate did permit a court reporter from the court in the Eastern District of New York, who had traveled to France together with the Assistant United States Attorney and Salim's attorney, to be present and to transcribe portions of the proceedings, even though French practice required the examining magistrate to keep a written summary of her own.

On the day of the deposition, contrary to expectations, the magistrate required the American prosecutor and defense attorney to submit their questions in writing since French law only permits a judge to question witnesses. Magistrate Verleene-Thomas also informed counsel that French law prohibited appellant's attorney from being present in the room while Rouhani testified. Confronted with this situation, the Assistant United States Attorney, who would have been allowed to be present, voluntarily agreed to absent himself from the room as well in order to avoid any appearance of unfair advantage.

Over objections by defendant's counsel, the deposition then occurred in the following manner in the magistrate's chambers: the government submitted direct examination questions to the magistrate in English and French, and defense counsel submitted cross-questions in English. At the magistrate's direction, copies of the questions were provided to the witness' attorney, as apparently is required by French law. The questions were posed by the magistrate in French and translated into Farsi for Rouhani, whose responses were then translated into French and back into English and recorded by the court reporter. Upon the conclusion of this segment of the examination, the witness left the room and the English translations of Rouhani's responses were read back to the attorneys by the court reporter. Defense counsel then submitted further cross-questions, and the procedure was repeated; another round of cross-examination followed thereafter, and the witness again answered the questions posed. Appellant, in the United States, was accessible by telephone during this entire period, but defense counsel made no effort to contact him.

According to the court reporter's testimony at trial, some conversations were not recorded in the transcript because they occurred in French between Rouhani and her lawyer; additionally, the transcript shows that Rouhani's lawyer made some statements in French to the magistrate that were not officially translated, but instead were summarized by the magistrate, and those summations were translated for the record. All statements that were made in or translated into English are reflected in the transcript, which, except for the absence of the conversations between Rouhani and her lawyer, appears to constitute a complete record of the proceedings.

The attorneys agreed with the magistrate to interrupt taking the deposition for one week. The American participants flew back to New York, the court reporter prepared a transcript of the first round of proceedings, and defense counsel reviewed that transcript with his client. The attorneys and the reporter thereafter returned to Paris, and a new round of cross-questioning occurred. The new portions of the proceedings were read back as before, except that this time, they were also read to the defendant by telephone with the aid of yet another interpreter in New York. After further questioning by the defense and redirect examination by the prosecutor, defense counsel again conferred by telephone with his client. Both attorneys then indicated that they had no further questions, and the taking of the deposition was concluded.

During the taking of the deposition, and in accordance with French procedure, there were a few instances in which Rouhani's attorney answered on her behalf or prevented her from answering because of her rights under French law. There were also a few instances in which, with the consent of the American attorneys, the magistrate supplemented the questions submitted by counsel with some of her own in order to elicit more complete responses from the witness. From a reading of the transcript, it is apparent that the questions submitted by the American attorneys were asked by the magistrate and answered by the witness.

At appellant's trial, various portions of the deposition transcript were read into evidence over defendant's objections. The court instructed the jury that the defendant had not been present at the taking of the deposition and the court emphatically cautioned the jurors as to the difficulty of assessing Rouhani's credibility, particularly given the absence of demeanor evidence. The court also informed them about the possible incentive of the witness to curry favor with the French court because of her own forthcoming trial. However, in order to aid the jury in determining what weight to accord the deposition testimony, Judge Weinstein permitted the reporter who transcribed the deposition to testify both as to the procedures used and as to Rouhani's distraught demeanor during the examination. Following four days of trial, the jury convicted appellant on all counts.

DISCUSSION

The use of depositions in criminal cases is governed by Fed. R. Crim. P. 15, which permits a party in "exceptional circumstances" to depose its own witness in order to preserve the witness' testimony, particularly if that witness is likely to be unavailable to testify at trial. The district court determined that Rouhani would be unavailable to testify at Salim's trial in the United States given her imprisonment in France pending her own trial there, and that because her testimony was central to the case, "exceptional circumstances" existed sufficient to permit the government to depose her abroad. The court therefore exercised its discretion to issue letters rogatory to the French government, requesting its assistance in deposing Rouhani in France. . . .

On appeal, Salim challenges the taking and admission of the deposition testimony on various grounds, asserting in particular that the deposition . . . did not meet the criteria of Fed. R. Evid. 804(b)(1) for admission of former testimony. . . .

* * *

B. *Federal Rule of Evidence 804*

The district court determined and Salim does not contest that Rouhani was an unavailable declarant for purposes of Fed. R. Evid. 804(a). However, Salim vigorously challenges the court's ruling that Rouhani's deposition constituted former testimony for purposes of Fed. R. Evid. 804(b)(1). Under Rule 804(b)(1), an unavailable declarant's former testimony is admissible as an exception to the hearsay rule so long as the witness' former testimony was given "in a deposition taken in compliance with law in the course of the same . . . proceeding, if the party against whom the testimony is now offered . . . had an opportunity and similar motive to develop the testimony by direct, cross, or redirect examination." We agree with Judge Weinstein that Rouhani's testimony meets this test.

Although Salim complains that Rouhani's statements were not given under oath and that the transcript does not represent a verbatim translation and recording of all that occurred in the French magistrate's chambers, we are satisfied that her statements nevertheless qualify as "testimony given as a witness." While Rouhani was not under oath to tell the truth because French law does not permit an accused to take an oath, Rouhani nevertheless satisfied the affirmation requirement applicable to witnesses under Fed. R. Evid. 603. Under that rule, all that is required of a witness is an "affirmation administered in a form calculated to awaken the witness' conscience and impress the witness' mind with the duty to [testify truthfully]." The French judge took pains to impress upon Rouhani the need to answer truthfully, and the witness promised that she would do so. That is essentially all that Rule 603 requires. Moreover, it is noteworthy that the rule governing depositions taken pursuant to letters rogatory which, as discussed above, applies in criminal as well as civil cases, specifies that "[e]vidence obtained in response to a letter rogatory need not be excluded merely for the reason . . . that the testimony was not taken under oath." Fed. R. Civ. P. 28(b).

Furthermore, the interpreters who translated between English, French and Farsi were certified experts of the French court, sworn pursuant to French law to aid in the administration of justice. Although French legal custom apparently permits court interpreters to summarize or rephrase testimony as they translate, "[e]vidence obtained in response to a letter rogatory need not be excluded merely for the reason that it is not a verbatim transcript," Fed. R. Civ. P. 28(b). In any event, both of the interpreters in this case represented to the French judge on the record that they were making verbatim translations, thereby satisfying Fed. R. Evid. 604. Consequently, the transcript of the deposition reflects "[t]estimony given [by Rouhani] as a witness" for purposes of Fed. R. Evid. 804(b)(1).

We are also satisfied that the deposition was taken "in compliance with law," as required by Rule 804(b)(1). The "law" to which this provision refers is the law governing the taking of depositions: in this case, Fed. R. Crim. P. 15, and by incorporation, Fed. R. Civ. P. 28 and 31. Rule 28, as noted earlier, was specifically designed to permit depositions to be taken in the manner provided by the law of the foreign country in which the deposition is conducted, *see* Fed. R. Civ. P. 28 advisory committee note (1963) ("courts of other countries may be expected to follow their customary procedure for taking testimony"), and the drafters evidently contemplated the particular type of deposition that occurred in this case, *see id.* Thus, a deposition taken abroad pursuant to foreign law, but in conformity with Rule 28, would appear to be taken "in compliance with law" for purposes of the former testimony exception to the rule against hearsay, Fed. R. Evid. 804(b)(1).

Moreover, this approach is consistent with principles of comity in international relations, which instruct us "to demonstrate due respect . . . for any sovereign interest expressed by a foreign state," *Societe Nationale Industrielle Aerospatiale v. United States Dist. Court, S.D. Iowa*, 107 S. Ct. 2542, 2557 (1987), so long as that interest is compatible with our own sovereign interests, *see id.*, 107 S. Ct. at 2555 nn.27–28. In order to take Rouhani's deposition, the American court actively sought the aid of the French government and invoked the mechanisms provided by the French judiciary for the taking of testimony. We therefore must be willing to acquiesce in the insistence of the French court that French law be applied to the taking of the Rouhani deposition unless the application of such law is incompatible with those essential elements of our law that represent our "sovereign interests" and that cannot yield to foreign law. In short, unless the manner of examination required by the law of the host nation is so incompatible with our fundamental principles of fairness or so prone to inaccuracy or bias as to render the testimony inherently unreliable (or, in the words of the advisory notes to Rule 28, are "so devoid of substance or probative value as to warrant its exclusion altogether"), a deposition taken pursuant to letter rogatory in accordance with the law of the host nation is taken "in compliance with law" for purposes of Rule 804(b)(1). We do not find the Rouhani deposition to be so lacking in probative value or so inherently unreliable as to require its exclusion.

Rule 804(b)(1) also requires as a prerequisite to admitting former testimony that the party against whom the testimony is offered have had the opportunity to examine or cross-examine the declarant at the time the out-of-court statement was made. We reject Salim's assertion that his attorney did not have an adequate opportunity to cross-examine Rouhani at her deposition because he could not view the witness' demeanor and could not develop a spontaneous line of inquiry. Although defense counsel's task was undoubtedly made more difficult by the need to submit questions in writing, the cross-examination was not thereby rendered ineffective. A criminal defendant is entitled to "an *opportunity* for effective cross-examination, not cross-examination that is effective in whatever way, and to whatever extent, the defense might wish." *Delaware v. Fensterer*, 474 U.S. 15, 20 (1985) (per curiam) (emphasis in original). That opportunity "is generally satisfied when the defense is given a full and fair opportunity to probe and expose [the] infirmities [of testimony] through cross-examination, thereby calling to the attention of the factfinder the reasons for giving scant weight to the witness' testimony." *Delaware v. Fensterer*, 474 U.S. at 22. In this case, "[c]ounsel's questioning clearly partook of cross-examination as a matter of *form*. His presentation was replete with leading questions, the principal tool and hallmark of cross-examination. In addition, counsel's questioning comported with the principal *purpose* of cross-examination: to challenge whether the declarant was sincerely telling what [she] believed to be the truth, whether the declarant accurately perceived and remembered the matter [she] related, and whether the declarant's intended meaning is adequately conveyed by the language [she] employed." *Ohio v. Roberts*, 448 U.S. 56, 70–71 (1980) (footnote and quotation omitted; emphasis in original).

The lack of spontaneity inherent in a deposition on written questions, where the attorney cannot ask immediate follow-up questions, was adequately compensated for in this case by the ample opportunity to pose new questions to the witness after reviewing her responses to the earlier ones. The veracity of her responses can be discerned in part from the transcript itself and from the American court reporter's comments about the witness' demeanor. Additionally, although defense counsel chose not to consult with his client during the first round of examination, Salim could have been contacted very readily by telephone had it been necessary for his attorney to discuss some aspect of

Rouhani's testimony before proceeding with further cross-examination. Indeed, the one-week interval between the beginning and the conclusion of the deposition enabled counsel to analyze the transcript line by line personally with Salim to search for misstatements or inaccuracies that could be brought out upon counsel's return to France and during the next round of cross-examination. And on the last day of the taking of the deposition, counsel did in fact telephone Salim to discuss Rouhani's testimony before the deposition was concluded. These opportunities were sufficient to compensate both for the defendant's physical absence and for the disadvantages of conducting the deposition in the manner required by the French court.

In short, the record shows that despite the obstacles imposed by the French court and despite the need to conduct the deposition in a disadvantageous manner, counsel was accorded what was essentially a full and fair opportunity to cross-examine the witness to ensure that she was telling the truth. Under these circumstances, the deposition transcript was admissible under Rule 804(b)(1) because it "bore sufficient 'indicia of reliability' and afforded " 'the trier of fact a satisfactory basis for evaluating the truth of the prior statement." ' " *Ohio v. Roberts*, 448 U.S. at 73 (quoting *Mancusi v. Stubbs*, 408 U.S. 204, 216 (1972)).

*   *   *

The judgment of the district court is affirmed.

NOTES AND QUESTIONS

1. Under Fed. R. Evid. 804(b)(1), an unavailable declarant's former testimony is admissible as an exception to the hearsay rule so long as the witness' former testimony was given "in a deposition taken in compliance with law in the course of the same . . . proceeding, if the party against whom the testimony is now offered . . . had an opportunity and similar motive to develop the testimony by direct, cross, or redirect examination." In *Salim* the court held that even though Rouhani's statements were not given under oath, her statements nevertheless qualified as "testimony given as a witness." 855 F.2d at 952. What is the justification or authority for not requiring that the former testimony be under oath? Since the witness was not under oath, he apparently is not subject to prosecution for perjury in the event that he makes materially false statements. Doesn't the absence of an oath requirement undermine the reliability of the former testimony? Shouldn't the party against whom the former testimony is being offered be permitted to advise the jury that the witness was not under oath to tell the truth?

2. The court in *Salim* stated:

> [U]nless the manner of examination required by the law of the host nation is so incompatible with our fundamental principles of fairness or so prone to inaccuracy or bias as to render the testimony inherently unreliable. . . , a deposition taken pursuant to letter rogatory in accordance with the law of the host nation is taken 'in compliance with law' for purposes of Rule 804(b)(1).

Id. at 953. Applying this standard, the court concluded that Rouhani's deposition was not so inherently unreliable as to require its exclusion. Do you agree? What circumstances surrounding Rouhani's deposition "render the testimony inherently unreliable?"

3. The court rejected Salim's assertion that his attorney did not have an adequate opportunity to cross-examine Rouhani at her deposition because he could not view the witness' demeanor or develop a spontaneous line of inquiry as he was only permitted to submit his questions to the presiding French magistrate who then posed these questions to the witness without the attorney being present. Do you agree with the court's conclusion?

In *United States v. Kelly*, 892 F.2d 255, 263 (3d Cir. 1989), the Third Circuit held that the admissibility of a videotape deposition did not violate Rule 804(b)(1) or the defendant's right of confrontation because he was not physically present to consult with his attorney. The facts in *Kelly*, however, are distinguishable from those in *Salim*. In *Kelly*, the witnesses were under oath and the attorneys for the defendants were permitted to personally cross-examine them.

4. To be admissible under Rule 804(b)(1), the deposition must be taken "in compliance with law." What "law" does this provision refer to? Is this requirement satisfied if the deposition complies with the law of the place in which the deposition was taken? What domestic federal law governs the taking of foreign depositions? Was the deposition in *Salim* taken in compliance with United States law?

5. Federal Rule of Civil Procedure 28 permits depositions to be taken in the manner provided by the law of the foreign country in which the deposition is conducted, *see* Rule 28 advisory committee note (1963) ("courts of other countries may be expected to follow their customary procedure for taking testimony"). Were the procedures followed by the French magistrate consistent with United States law? How do they differ?

6. *Sixth Amendment Confrontation Clause*. The admission of the Rouhani's deposition testimony implicates important Sixth Amendment Confrontation Clause concerns. In *Coy v. Iowa*, 487 U.S. 1012(1988), the Supreme Court observed that "the Confrontation Clause guarantees the defendant a face-to-face meeting with witnesses appearing before the trier of fact." *Id.* at 1016. However, in *Maryland v. Craig*, 497 U.S. 836 (1990), the Court held that the Confrontation Clause does not guarantee criminal defendants the *absolute* right to a face-to-face meeting with witnesses against them at trial. *See* discussion *supra*, at p. 727. The Court held that a defendant's right to confront the witnesses against him may be satisfied absent a physical, face-to-face confrontation at trial where denial of such confrontation is necessary to further an important public policy and where the reliability of the testimony is otherwise assured. *Id.* Did the absence of face-to-face confrontation at the deposition and trial violate Salim's right to confrontation as articulated by the Supreme Court in *Maryland v. Craig*? In *Crawford v. Washington*, 541 U.S. 36 (2004), the Court held the admission of *testimonial* statements is barred by the Sixth Amendment Confrontation Clause absent proof of unavailability of the declarant and a prior opportunity for cross-examination. *Id.* at 68. The Court further held that depositions fall within the "core class" of testimonial statements. *Id.* at 51-52. Did the admission of Rouhani's deposition testimony violate the Confrontation Clause as construed by the Court in *Crawford*? Rohani was in custody in France awaiting trial for drug smuggling and thus was unavailable to testify. However, was Salim afforded an adequate opportunity for cross-examination?

PROBLEM

Problem 9-3. *Foreign Depositions.* Assume the facts in *Salim*, except for the following alterations. First, in addition to applying French rules of procedure, which only permit questions to be submitted in writing to the presiding magistrate, the court applied the French rules of evidence, which permit the admission of hearsay evidence. Second, pursuant to the French rules of procedure, the magistrate exercised discretion in excluding some of the questions submitted in writing by the parties, which the French court deemed to be irrelevant or in violation of French law. Third, the magistrate permitted the deposition to be videotaped, and the videotape deposition was introduced at the defendant's trial in the United States. Do the first two conditions, in addition to the other *Salim* facts, preclude admission under the former testimony exception? If inadmissible under Rule 804(b)(1), might the deposition still be admissible under the catchall hearsay exception found in Rule 804(b)(5)? Does the fact that the foreign deposition was videotaped weigh in favor of admissibility?

[2]   Dying Declaration

Federal Rule of Evidence 804(b)(2) exempts from the hearsay rule statements traditionally known as "dying declarations." The exception for deathbed statements, which has its origin in the common law, "was originally held to rest on the religious belief 'that the dying declarant, knowing that he is about to die would be unwilling to go to his maker with a lie on his lips.' "[34] Thus, it was presumed that persons making dying declarations were highly unlikely to lie. In modern times, however, this rationale and the reliability of deathbed statements has been placed into question. It just as easily follows that statements made under a belief of impending death may be motivated by revenge or a desire for self-exoneration or to protect one's loved ones, and are therefore not trustworthy. Furthermore, psychological stress and physical pain may cause flaws in the witness's perception and memory.

At the same time, a second justification has been advanced for exempting dying declarations from the hearsay rule. Statements made under a belief of impending death "are received from the necessitations of the case and to prevent an entire failure of justice, as it frequently happens that no other witnesses to the homicide are present."[35] Should necessity rather than reliability determine the admissibility of an out-of-court declaration?

To admit an out-of-court statement under Rule 804(b)(2), the prosecution must prove that at the time the statement was made the declarant subjectively believed that his or her death was imminent. Additionally, statements admitted under Rule 804(b)(2) must concern the cause or circumstances of what the declarant believed to be his impending death.

[a]   The Confrontation Clause Dilemma — Are Dying Declarations "Testimonial" Statements?

STATE v. LEWIS
235 S.W.3d 136 (Tenn. 2007)

On July 13, 2001, Gary Dean Finchum ("the victim") was shot during a robbery of his antiques store. He later died from his injuries. For her role in the crimes, Sabrina Renee Lewis ("the Defendant"), who was originally charged with felony murder and especially aggravated robbery, was convicted by a jury of criminally negligent homicide and facilitation of attempted especially aggravated robbery.

---

[34] JACK B. WEINSTEIN & MARGARET A. BERGER, WEINSTEIN'S EVIDENCE 804(b)(2)(01), at 804-124 to 804-125 (1994).

[35] *Carver v. United States*, 164 U.S. 694, 697 (1897).

FACTUAL AND PROCEDURAL BACKGROUND

The victim and his wife, Linda Finchum ("Finchum"), owned and operated Always Antiques in Madison. Some three weeks before the shooting, the Defendant stopped at the store seeking an estimate of value for two vases that she wanted to sell. Because the victim, who had left for the day, was responsible for the appraisals, Finchum asked the Defendant to come back later. The Defendant returned in two weeks, purportedly looking for a gift for her mother who lived in New York. The Finchums offered to travel to the Defendant's residence to examine the vases but she declined, explaining that she would return with the vases later in the day. Finchum did not see the Defendant again that day, but at approximately 10:00 a.m. on the day of the shooting, the victim telephoned her and before ending the conversation remarked, "I believe the woman with the vases is coming in."

One hour later, at approximately 11:00 a.m., Brenda Farmer and Judy Summers, who worked at Pugh's Pharmacy, heard several loud crashes coming from the direction of the antiques store located next door. Summers saw someone enter the front passenger's side of an older, gray, "long" vehicle which was parked outside the back door with the motor running. After a few minutes, the two women walked to the antiques store to investigate the noises. As they entered, the victim called out for help and asked them to "call 911," explaining that he had been "shot in the heart." Farmer ran back to the pharmacy, informed the other employees of the situation, and directed them to call 911. When she returned, the victim informed Farmer that "they" tried to rob him and that "a black man in blue jeans" had shot him. Summers, who also noticed a bullet wound in the victim's arm, observed the victim's shallow breathing and believed that he would likely die before the ambulance arrived.

Detective Mike Chastain of the Metro Police Department Armed Robbery unit arrived at the scene prior to the paramedics and observed the victim lying on the floor at the rear of the store. The victim, who was in "obvious pain" and "blood[-]soaked," identified himself to the detective and when asked if he had been robbed, responded, "[H]e tried to." He described his assailant as a "young male black" and showed the detective a blue, "floppy" hat that he had left behind. When the paramedics arrived and initiated treatment, the victim pointed with both of his hands and said, "[O]fficer, officer, the lady's information is on the desk." When asked about what "lady" to whom he was referring, the victim responded, "[T]he lady with the vases." On further questioning about whether the "lady" was connected to the robbery and shooting, the victim stated, "I know she is." Another detective found a piece of paper on the counter bearing the name "Sabrina Lewis," what appeared to be a driver's license number, and the words "two vases."

Detective Norris Tarkington discovered an address for "Sabrina Lewis," drove to her residence, and knocked on the door. Several minutes later, the Defendant answered the door and agreed to travel to the police station to provide a statement. The police also determined that the Defendant had a gray, late 1980s model vehicle registered in her name.

In a videotaped statement, the Defendant admitted to the police that she was in the antiques store on the date of the shooting, explaining that she had spoken with the victim, had negotiated a $125 price for the vases, and had given the victim her contact information. She claimed that she left the antiques store in a car that she had borrowed from her ex-boyfriend, dropped it off at Vanderbilt University Medical Center, and then visited at her mother's house for a few hours before returning to her own residence. The Defendant told the police that she gave $100 of the sale proceeds to her son and kept the remainder. . . .

THE CONFRONTATION CLAUSE

Initially, the resolution of two of the issues in this case depends in great measure upon recent decisions by the United States Supreme Court interpreting the Confrontation Clause found in the Sixth Amendment of the United States Constitution. The clause provides that "[i]n all criminal prosecutions, the accused shall enjoy the right . . . to be confronted with the witnesses against him." U.S. Const. amend. VI. Traditionally, this Court has interpreted the provision as affording "two types of protection for criminal defendants: the right to physically face the witnesses who testify against the defendant, and the right to cross-examine witnesses." *State v. Williams*, 913 S.W.2d 462, 465 (Tenn.1996) (citing *Pennsylvania v. Ritchie*, 480 U.S. 39, 51 (1987)). The Confrontation Clause is designed "to ensure the reliability of the evidence against a criminal defendant by subjecting it to rigorous testing in the context of an adversary proceeding before the trier of fact." *Maryland v. Craig*, 497 U.S. 836, 845 (1990). For years, Sixth Amendment challenges to out of court statements have been considered under the guidelines established by the United States Supreme Court in *Ohio v. Roberts*, 448 U.S. 56 (1980). In *Roberts*, the Court held that "when a hearsay declarant is not present for cross-examination at trial, the Confrontation Clause normally requires a showing that he is unavailable," *id.* at 66, and even when there is a showing of unavailability, the hearsay statement "is admissible only if it bears adequate 'indicia of reliability.' " *Id.* . . .

In *Crawford v. Washington*, 541 U.S. 36 (2004), however, the Supreme Court departed from its ruling in *Roberts* and established a new standard for the admissibility of hearsay statements under the Confrontation Clause. The Court concluded that "testimonial" hearsay is admissible only where the declarant is unavailable and there was "a prior opportunity for cross-examination." *Id.* at 68. "Where nontestimonial hearsay is at issue, it is wholly consistent with the Framers' design to afford the States flexibility in their development of hearsay law-as does *Roberts*, and as would an approach that exempted such statements from Confrontation Clause scrutiny altogether." *Id.* The Court left "for another day any effort to spell out a comprehensive definition of 'testimonial.' " *Id.*

We first considered the application of the *Crawford* ruling in *Maclin*, holding that "[a]fter *Crawford*, the threshold question in any Confrontation Clause case is whether a challenged statement is testimonial or nontestimonial." *Maclin*, 183 S.W.3d at 345. "If it is testimonial, the statement is inadmissible unless (1) the declarant is unavailable and (2) the accused had a prior opportunity to cross-examine the declarant." *Id.*. . . . In addition, we adopted a non-exhaustive list of factors to aid in the determination of whether a particular statement is testimonial:

(1) whether the declarant was a victim or an observer; (2) whether contact was initiated by the declarant or by law-enforcement officials; (3) the degree of formality attending the circumstances in which the statement was made; (4) whether the statement was given in response to questioning, whether the questioning was structured, and the scope of such questioning; (5) whether the statement was recorded (either in writing or by electronic means); (6) the declarant's purpose in making the statements; (7) the officer's purpose in

speaking with the declarant; and (8) whether an objective declarant under the circumstances would believe that the statements would be used at a trial.

Id. at 349. We described this standard as objective in nature. In essence, the factors were designed to determine "whether the statement was made 'under circumstances which would lead an objective witness reasonably to believe that the statement would be available for use at a later trial.' " *Id.* at 354.

Since our decision in *Maclin*, the United States Supreme Court has issued two opinions interpreting *Crawford*. In the first of those cases, *Davis v. Washington*, 547 U.S. 813 (2006), and its companion case, *Hammon v. Indiana*, 547 U.S. 813 (2006), the Court departed further from *Roberts*, concluding that only testimonial statements "cause the declarant to be a 'witness' within the meaning of the Confrontation Clause" and determining that "[i]t is the testimonial character of the statement that separates it from other hearsay that, while subject to traditional limitations upon hearsay evidence, is not subject to the Confrontation Clause." *Davis*, 126 S.Ct. at 2273. Thus, the ruling in *Davis* that the Confrontation Clause is inapplicable to nontestimonial hearsay conflicts with our interpretation in *Maclin* that the *Roberts* test should be used to determine the admissibility of nontestimonial hearsay. The Supreme Court distinguished testimonial and nontestimonial hearsay as follows:

> Statements are nontestimonial when made in the course of police interrogation under circumstances objectively indicating that the primary purpose of the interrogation is to enable police assistance to meet an ongoing emergency. They are testimonial when the circumstances objectively indicate that there is no such ongoing emergency, and that the primary purpose of the interrogation is to establish or prove past events potentially relevant to later criminal prosecution.

Id. at 2273–74. With this guidance, the Court established precedents for the treatment of 911 calls and statements made to officers at a crime scene. In *Davis*, the Court determined that the content of a call describing an ongoing physical attack was nontestimonial, while, in *Hammon*, the statements made by the victim in response to police questions shortly after she was attacked by her husband were deemed testimonial.

In the second case, *Whorton v. Bockting*, 127 S.Ct. 1173 (2007), the Court declined to apply *Crawford* retroactively and reiterated its holding that nontestimonial hearsay is not subject to challenge under the Confrontation Clause:

> Under *Roberts*, an out-of-court nontestimonial statement not subject to prior cross-examination could not be admitted without a judicial determination regarding reliability. Under *Crawford*, on the other hand, the Confrontation Clause has no application to such statements and therefore permits their admission even if they lack indicia of reliability.

Id. at 1183. The Court observed that "*Roberts* potentially excluded too much testimony because it imposed Confrontation Clause restrictions on nontestimonial hearsay." *Id.* at 1179. . . .

* * *

II. THE VICTIM'S STATEMENTS

Our next consideration is whether the admission of the victim's statement to Detective Chastain that he "knew" the "lady with the vases" was involved in the offenses qualifies as a dying declaration and, if so, is admissible in the context of the right of confrontation. The Defendant argues that the statement was merely an opinion and should not have been permitted as a dying declaration. . . .

As indicated, the general rule established in *Crawford* bars the admission of testimonial hearsay absent a showing of unavailability and a prior opportunity for cross-examination. So our first step is to determine the nature of the statement. In *Davis*, the Court held that a description of past events to the investigating law enforcement officers is testimonial. *Davis*, 126 S.Ct. at 2273. Statements are nontestimonial, however, when circumstances indicate that they are designed to "enable police assistance to meet an ongoing emergency." *Id.* In *Davis*, the evidence at issue was an audiotape of the victim's telephone call to 911. During the call, the victim stated that she was being attacked by Davis. The Court classified the statements as nontestimonial and contrasted them with the statements at issue in *Crawford:*

> [The victim in *Davis*] was speaking about events *as they were actually happening*, rather than "describ[ing] past events." Sylvia Crawford's interrogation, on the other hand, took place hours after the events she described had occurred. Moreover, any reasonable listener would recognize that [the victim] (unlike Sylvia Crawford) was facing an ongoing emergency. Although one *might* call 911 to provide a narrative report of a crime absent any imminent danger, [the victim's] call was plainly a call for help against bona fide physical threat. Third, the nature of what was asked and answered . . . again viewed objectively, was such that the elicited statements were necessary to be able to *resolve* the present emergency, rather than simply to learn (as in *Crawford*) what had happened in the past. . . . And finally, the difference in the level of formality between the two interviews is striking. Crawford was responding calmly . . . to a series of questions, with the officer-interrogator taping and making notes of her answers. . . .

Id. at 2276–77 (citations omitted). . . .

* * *

It is our view that the victim's statement to Detective Chastain, that he "knew" that "the lady with the vases" was involved in the offenses, qualifies as testimonial. The assailant had left the store. The victim had talked to Summers and Farmer who were first to arrive at the scene. The 911 call had already been made. In *Davis*, the Court pointed out that "the fact that [statements were] given at an alleged crime scene and were 'initial inquiries' is immaterial." *Id.* While the victim's statements here took place at the crime scene, they were responses to inquiries by the investigating officers. Even though the victim was in a state of distress from his wounds, his comments did not describe an "ongoing emergency," as defined in *Crawford*, and were instead descriptions of recent, but past, criminal activity as in *Hammon*. Because the statements were testimonial, we must next consider whether they should have been excluded under the rule in *Crawford* which not only requires the unavailability of the declarant, which was obviously satisfied, but the opportunity for cross-examination, which was not.

As indicated, the trial court admitted the victim's statements under the dying declaration exception to the hearsay rule. In *Crawford*, the Court included a footnote, describing the dying declaration as historically unique in the prosecution of homicide and hinting at the admissibility of such statements, even if testimonial:

The one deviation we have found involves dying declarations. The existence of that exception as a general rule of criminal hearsay law cannot be disputed. *Although many dying declarations may not be testimonial, there is authority for admitting even those that clearly are.* We need not decide in this case whether the Sixth Amendment incorporates an exception for testimonial dying declarations. If this exception must be accepted on historical grounds, it is *sui generis.*

Crawford, 541 U.S. at 56 n. 6 (citations omitted) (emphasis added). Since *Crawford*, we found no jurisdiction that has excluded a testimonial dying declaration. Several states have specifically allowed the declaration as an exception to the rule in *Crawford. See, e.g., Wallace v. State*, 836 N.E.2d 985, 992–96 (Ind.Ct.App.2005); *State v. Young*, 710 N.W.2d 272, 283–84 (Minn.2006).

Because the admissibility of the dying declaration is also deeply entrenched in the legal history of this state, it is also our view that this single hearsay exception survives the mandate of *Crawford* regardless of its testimonial nature. . . .

Rule 804(b)(2) of the Tennessee Rules of Evidence, effective January 1, 1990, is the common law embodiment of the dying declaration:

> Statement Under Belief of Impending Death.-In a prosecution for homicide, a statement made by the victim while believing that the declarant's death was imminent and concerning the cause or circumstances of what the declarant believed to be impending death.

Tenn. R. Evid. 804(b)(2) (2007). The Advisory Commission Comments to the rule confirm that "[t]he rule retains Tennessee's common law limitations. The trial must be for homicide of the declarant, and the declaration is limited to circumstances surrounding the declarant's death." *Id.*, Advisory Comm'n Cmts. "The traditional underlying theory is that a person who knows that he or she is facing imminent death will be truthful, for the eternal consequences of dying 'with a lie on one's lips' are too monumental to risk." Cohen, et al., *supra*, § 8.35[2][a] at 8-155. Indeed, the awareness of impending death has been deemed "equivalent to the sanction of an oath." *Anthony*, 19 Tenn. at 278 (citation and internal quotation marks omitted). Long ago, this Court more specifically addressed the reason behind the rule:

> [W]hen the party is at the point of death, and when every hope of this world is gone, when every motive to falsehood is silenced, and the mind is induced by the most powerful consideration to speak the truth, a situation, so solemn and so awful, is considered by the law as creating an obligation equal to that which is imposed by a positive oath administered in a court of justice.

Smith v. State, 28 Tenn. (9 Hum.) 9, 19 (1848) (citation and internal quotation marks omitted). This time-honored dying declaration exception to the rule against hearsay has five elements:

(1) The declarant must be dead at the time of the trial;

(2) the statement is admissible only in the prosecution of a criminal homicide;

(3) the declarant must be the victim of the homicide;

(4) the statement must concern the cause or the circumstances of the death; and

(5) the declarant must have made the statement under the belief that death was imminent.[9]

The Defendant concedes that these five conditions have been satisfied but argues that the victim's statement should have been excluded because it is an opinion rather than an assertion of fact. The Court of Criminal Appeals, relying on *Baxter v. State*, 83 Tenn. 657 (1885), held that "[b]ecause opinion evidence by a lay witness is not generally admissible, the declarant's expression of an opinion . . . is not generally admissible in evidence as a dying declaration." Our opinion, however, is that "[t]he lay opinion rule should be relaxed somewhat here, as was the case under prior law." Cohen et al. *supra*, § 8.35[2][e] at 8-156 (citing *Sherman v. State*, 140 S.W. 209, 215 (1911)). We believe that the common law supports that conclusion.

*　　*　　*

The traditional authorities have recognized that the general rule, which allows a statement of fact but precludes a mere opinion, often created confusion in the effort to separate one from the other. [T]he prevailing standard at common law permitted an opinion or conclusion "as to the identity of the assailant . . . where it was determined that such a statement was reasonable in view of the surrounding circumstances." 86 A.L.R.2d 905 at § 2. In contrast, an expression of opinion as to identity has been excluded when the circumstances established that the victim "could not have known whether [the defendant] fired the fatal shots." *Stevens v. Commonwealth*, 298 S.W. 678, 679 (1927).

Because a dying declaration is essentially a substitute for the testimony of the victim, the admissible evidence is limited to that to which the victim could have testified if present. Applying this reasoning, lay opinion should not be allowed simply because it is in the form of a dying declaration but it must not be unduly restricted when reasonably based. This historical perspective comports with Rule 701 of the Tennessee Rules of Evidence, which specifically governs the admission of opinion evidence by a lay witness:

> If a witness is not testifying as an expert, the witness's testimony in the form of opinions or inferences is limited to those opinions or inferences which are
>
> (1) rationally based on the perception of the witness and
>
> (2) helpful to a clear understanding of the witness's testimony or the determination of a fact in issue.

Tenn. R. Evid. 701(a). Here, the record suggests that the victim's identification of the Defendant is "rationally based upon the perception" of the victim. That is in compliance with the evidentiary rule. If the victim had lived, he would have been permitted to offer this testimony at trial. Under these circumstances, it is our view that the statement, while an expression of opinion and testimonial in nature, was admissible as a dying

---

[9] Cohen et al., *supra*, § 8.35[2][b]-[f] at 8– 156; *see also State v. Hampton*, 24 S.W.3d 823, 828–29 (Tenn. Crim. App. 2000). In *Dickason v. State*, 139 Tenn. 601, 202 S.W. 922, 923 (1918), a gunshot wound to the abdomen resulting in little chance of survival was deemed a sufficient basis for the victim to believe death was imminent. *See also State v. Keels*, 753 S.W.2d 140, 144 (Tenn.Crim.App.1988). Conversations between the declarant and a physician or a family member about physical condition may be important indicators. *See, e.g., Crittendon v. State*, 157 Tenn. 403, 8 S.W.2d 371 (1928). The "primary requirement of such proof is that the victim had a certain belief that rapid death was inevitable." David Lewis Raybin, *Tennessee Criminal Practice and Procedure* § 27.305 (1985). The declarant must have a "fixed and solemn belief that death is inevitable and near at hand." 41 C.J.S. *Homicide* § 274 (1991). . . .

declaration, an evidentiary rule which has thus far survived *Crawford* and its progeny. . . .

Accordingly, the judgments of the trial court and the Court of Criminal Appeals are affirmed.

NOTES AND QUESTIONS

(1) *Testimonial Statements.* Are dying declarations always testimonial? Such statements generally describe past events and are likely to be used in future prosecutions for homicide. Does it matter whether the hearsay statement was made to a police officer? An emergency medical technician providing the victim medical treatment at the scene? A bystander who found the victim on the street shortly before he died? If dying declarations are always testimonial in nature, is admission of such statements prohibited under the Confrontation Clause unless exempted from the rule in *Crawford*?

(2) *Relevant Factors.* In *Lewis*, the court adopted a non-exhaustive list of factors to aid in determining whether a particular statement is testimonial. *Lewis*, 235 S.W.3d at 143. Are these factors still relevant after *Davis* or post-*Davis* is the only consideration whether the police officer's primary purpose in eliciting the statements was to respond to an ongoing emergency? Are the *Lewis* factors relevant to determining whether the statement was made "under circumstances which would lead an objective witness reasonably to believe that the statement would be available for use at a later trial." *United States v. Crawford*, 541 U.S. 36, 52 (2004).

(3) *Belief of Impending Death.* Courts have considered numerous factors in determining whether the declarant believed that death was impending. *See Carver v. United States*, 164 U.S. 694, 695–96 (1897) (fact that victim received sacrament of last rights tended to show knowledge she was dying); *Mattox v. United States*, 156 U.S. 237, 251 (1895) (holding that a declarant's sense of impending death may be inferred "from the nature and extent of the wounds inflicted being obviously such that he must have felt or known he could not survive"); *United States v. Barnes*, 464 F.2d 828, 831 (D.C. Cir. 1972) (knowledge of impending death could be inferred from nature of injuries); *United States v. Mobley*, 421 F.2d 345, 347 (5th Cir. 1970) (same); *see also State v. Henderson*, 672 So.2d 1085, 1089 (La. App. 1996) (evidence of wounds that were mortal in nature coupled with statement by deceased inquiring whether she was going to die was sufficient to infer that declarant believed that death was impending); *State v. Scott*, 894 S.W.2d 810, 812 (Tex. App. 1994) ("Circumstances to be considered in evaluating a potential dying declaration include: (1) the express language of the declarant; (2) the nature of the injury; (3) any medical opinion provided to the declarant; and (4) the conduct of the declarant."). What other factors may be relevant to establish the declarant's knowledge of impending death?

(4) Must the declarant's belief that he is dying be expressed contemporaneously with the identification? *See Webb v. Lane*, 922 F.2d 390, 395–96 (7th Cir. 1991) ("Although the declarant must believe that death is imminent at the time he makes the statement, it is not true . . . that the declarant's expression of his impending death must coincide with the statement.").

PROBLEM

Problem 9-4. *Dying Declarations Limited to Homicide Prosecutions.* Suppose that the declarant suffers a brutal sexual assault, but survives the attack. The victim makes a statement to the paramedics while they are administering medical treatment, implicating the defendant as her attacker. The declarant then slips into a coma and, thus, is unavailable as defined in Rule 804(a)(4). The defendant is subsequently prosecuted for aggravated sexual assault. Should admissibility of the out-of-court statement made under belief of impending death turn on the nature of the criminal prosecution, that is, whether the defendant is prosecuted for homicide or some lesser crime? Is the statement any less reliable when the declaration was made under belief of impending death but the declarant actually survived? If the victim is not expected to recover from the coma, isn't there a compelling necessity for admission of the statement? On the other hand, if the victim ultimately dies from the injuries sustained, the same statement would be admissible as a dying declaration. Should the requirement under Rule 804(b)(2) that the dying declaration be admitted only in a homicide prosecution, be eliminated?

[b]   The Cause or Circumstances of Death

STATE v. SATTERFIELD
457 S.E.2d 440 (W. Va. 1995)

McHugh, Justice.

This case is before this Court upon the appeal of Shawn Satterfield from the October 7, 1993 order of the Circuit Court of Ritchie County which sentenced him to life imprisonment with eligibility for parole after a jury found him guilty of first degree murder with a recommendation of mercy. For reasons set forth below, we affirm the order of the circuit court.

The appellant and his half-brother, Brian Vincent, were charged with murdering Billy Harper, a retired public school bus driver, during the late night hours of January 22, 1993. The facts surrounding the murder are contradictory and unclear.

The strongest evidence against the appellant was provided by Glen Thomas and Bucky Moore, who were initially questioned by the police after witnesses stated that they saw Glen Thomas' car in the vicinity of the victim's home on the night of the murder. Thomas and Moore agreed to tell the police everything they knew about the murder if they would be granted immunity from prosecution for their involvement in the crime. Eventually, the trial court did grant immunity to Moore and Thomas for their testimony at trial.

At trial, Moore and Thomas testified that they gave the appellant and Brian Vincent a ride to the vicinity of the victim's home. The appellant or Brian Vincent indicated that they were planning to rob the victim and anticipated having to hit the victim on the head during the robbery. When the appellant and Brian Vincent got out of the car, they had an ax handle with them. The ax handle had originally belonged to Thomas, but Thomas alleged that the ax handle was removed from his car by Brian Vincent prior to the incident. Moore and Thomas maintained that they were to return to pick up the appellant and Brian Vincent later in the evening.

When Moore and Thomas returned to pick up the appellant and Brian Vincent, they were unable to locate them. Subsequently, Moore and Thomas alleged that when they saw the appellant and Brian Vincent, the two admitted that when robbing the victim, Brian Vincent had told the victim the appellant's name. Therefore, the appellant and Brian Vincent took turns striking the victim with the ax handle until he died. The appellant and Brian Vincent also allegedly told Moore and Thomas that they took the victim's billfold, which was never recovered, and a.22 rifle, which they hid behind a school bus stop in the vicinity. Evidently, the billfold was burned in the appellant's father's wood stove.

During a search of the area after the murder, the ax handle, which was wrapped in the victim's plaid flannel jacket, and the.22 rifle, were recovered. Forensic reports state that the hair on the ax handle was consistent with the victim's hair.

Moore's and Thomas' testimony further indicates that a couple of days after the murder the appellant and Brian Vincent stated that they needed a ride to Paul Greene's house, who is a friend of theirs, so that they could ask him to provide an alibi. The appellant and Brian Vincent were concerned with the disposal of their bloodied clothes.

Paul Greene testified that the appellant and Brian Vincent came to his home and requested that he provide an alibi. Though Mr. Greene refused to provide one, he did not ask for a reason for the request. However, Paul Greene did describe a black garbage bag that the appellant had brought with him. The black garbage bag allegedly contained the bloodied clothes of the appellant and Brian Vincent.

The appellant evidently took the bag with him when he and Brian Vincent left Mr. Greene's house and went to Don Vincent's house to stay the night. Don Vincent, who is co-defendant Brian Vincent's brother and appellant's half- brother, testified that he saw Brian Vincent retrieve the black garbage bag from a wood pile in his driveway. Brian Vincent and the appellant then disappeared into the woods with the black garbage bag and returned about thirty minutes later without it.

Several witnesses testified that they saw two people walking along the highway in the vicinity of the victim's house on the night of the murder. The witnesses provided different descriptions of the two people and different descriptions of what they were wearing.

* * *

Moreover, Moore testified that after he and Thomas could not find the appellant and Brian Vincent when they returned to pick them up on the night of the murder, he went to Del Vincent's house (Del Vincent is Brian Vincent's brother and appellant's half-brother) where he stayed the night.

Additionally, the only identifiable fingerprints at the crime scene were those of the victim. The expert testimony regarding the blood test results was contradictory. There was also testimony which indicates that all four men, the appellant, Brian Vincent, Thomas, and Moore, were smoking marihuana on the evening of the murder.

During the trial the appellant's attorney aggressively cross-examined Moore and even suggested that Moore may have committed the murder. In fact, the appellant's attorney implied that Moore had told people that he struck the first blow on the victim during the murder. After recross-examination, Moore concluded his testimony, but was subject to recall by the State. Before the trial court reconvened the next day, Moore committed suicide. The appellant's attorney stated that he would not be calling witnesses to testify that Moore stated that he struck the first blow. However, subsequent to the suicide, Del Vincent testified that Moore did not come by his place on that night. Additionally, pursuant to the appellant's questioning, Del Vincent testified that Moore asked him to provide an alibi, and that on previous occasions Moore had bragged that he was going to kill people.

Because of the appellant's attack on the credibility of Moore after his death and because the appellant suggested that Moore had committed the murders, the trial judge permitted the State to introduce a suicide note left by Moore which stated: "I didn't kill Harper and I won't do time for something that I didn't do. I'm sorry but I just can't take the presure [sic] of going through a trial. Good-by [sic]. [Signed] Bucky Moore. Tell Teresa [Bucky Moore's girlfriend] I loved he [sic] more than any thing in the world." The jury convicted the appellant of first degree murder with a recommendation of mercy based on the above evidence.

II.

The first issue before us is whether the trial judge erred by admitting into evidence the suicide note of Moore pursuant to the dying declaration exception to the hearsay rule found in the West Virginia Rules of Evidence 804(b)(2).

Even before the adoption of the rules of evidence, hearsay was generally not permitted in trials. *See* 29 Am. Jur. 2d Evidence § 658 (1994). The rationale for this rule is that out of court statements

> lack the conventional indicia of reliability: they are usually not made under oath or under circumstances that impress the declarant with the solemnity of his or her statements; the declarant's word is not subject to cross- examination; and the declarant is not available so that his or her demeanor and credibility may be assessed by the jury.

Id. (footnote omitted). Nevertheless, several exceptions to the hearsay rule have been recognized.

One of the exceptions is known as the dying declaration:

> The exception for dying declarations — which antedates the development of the hearsay rule and the adoption of the Constitution was originally held to rest on the religious belief "that the dying declarant, knowing that he is about to die would be unwilling to go to his maker with a lie on his lips."

4 Jack B. Weinstein & Margaret A. Berger, Weinstein's Evidence 804(b)(2)[01] at 804-124 to 804-125 (1994) (footnotes omitted and quote from Quick, *Some Reflections on Dying Declarations*, 6 Howard L.J. 109, 111 (1960)). Although in modern times the rationale for the dying declaration exception to the hearsay rule is not necessarily religious, scholars continue to recognize the trustworthiness of a statement of a dying person since a dying person will not personally benefit from lying. *See* 29A Am. Jur. 2d Evidence § 829 (1994) ("The dying declaration exception to the general rule prohibiting the admission of hearsay statements at trial is based on the belief that persons making dying declarations are highly unlikely to lie." (footnote omitted)). *See also* 2 Franklin D. Cleckley, Handbook on Evidence for West Virginia Lawyers § 8-4(B)(2) at 274 (3d 1994) ("The principle upon which the dying declaration is admitted . . . is that it has been made after the declarant . . . has presently approached so near upon the verge of death that he can see . . . no possible expectation, by anything he may do or say, of any personal benefit

or advantage to himself in any of the material affairs of the outside world[.]") *But see* 4 Weinstein, *supra* at ¶ 804(b)(2)[01] at 804-125 ("[T]he lack of inherent reliability of deathbed statements has often been pointed out: experience indicates that the desire for revenge or self-exoneration or to protect one's loved ones may continue until the moment of death.").

At common law the dying declaration exception only applied when the declarant was the murder victim. However, the adoption of the rules of evidence has broadened the common law:

> (b) Hearsay Exceptions. — The following are not excluded by the hearsay rule if the declarant is unavailable as a witness:
>
> *   *   *
>
> (2) Statement under Belief of Impending Death. — In a prosecution for homicide or in a civil action or proceeding, a statement made by a declarant while believing that his or her death was imminent, concerning the cause or circumstances of what the declarant believed to be impending death.

W. Va. R. Evid. 804(b)(2). The rules of evidence have obviously extended the dying declaration exception to civil cases and do not state that the declarant must be a murder victim.

Under the rules of evidence, the focus is not on who made the statement when determining whether the dying declaration is admissible. Instead, courts focus on the circumstances giving rise to the dying declaration:

> What is required for a dying declaration to be admissible is that the declarant have such a belief that he is facing death as to remove ordinary worldly motives for misstatement. In that regard, the court may consider the totality of the circumstances of motive to falsify and the manner in which the statement was volunteered or elicited.

Syl. pt. 3, *State v. Young*, 273 S.E.2d 592 (W. Va. 1980), *holding modified on a different ground by State v. Julius*, 408 S.E.2d 1 (W. Va. 1991).

In the case before us, the dying declaration was in the form of a suicide note. Few courts have addressed whether a suicide note would ever fall into the dying declaration exception to the hearsay rule. Common sense dictates, however, that just as the rules of evidence have broadened the common law to include declarants who are not murder victims, the rules of evidence would also contemplate situations in which a dying declaration could be contained in a suicide note.

Accordingly, we hold that a suicide note may be admissible pursuant to W. Va. R. Evid. 804(b)(2) as a dying declaration exception to the hearsay rule. In order for a statement found in a suicide note to be admissible as a dying declaration the following must occur: the statement must have been made when the declarant was under the belief that his death was imminent, and the dying declaration must concern the cause or circumstances of what the declarant believes to be his impending death.

However, even if a trial judge finds that a suicide note is a dying declaration, that does not necessarily mean that the suicide note is admissible. The trial judge must additionally analyze whether the suicide note is relevant pursuant to W. Va. R. Evid. 401 and, if so, thereby admissible pursuant to W. Va. R. Evid. 402. However, if the probative value of the evidence "is substantially outweighed by the danger of unfair prejudice,"

then, although relevant, the evidence may be excluded pursuant to W. Va. R. Evid.
403. . . .

Applying a 403 analysis to the hearsay exception is not a new concept. In Weinstein's
text the following discussion regarding the admissibility of a dying declaration appears:

> The true test of admissibility is whether admission of the [dying declaration]
> statement will help the jury in its task, i.e., whether it is sufficiently reliable and
> relevant to withstand exclusion because its probative value is substantially
> outweighed by the danger of prejudice to the party against whom it is offered.

4 Weinstein, *supra* at ¶ 804(b)(2)[01] at 804-131. . . .

We caution a trial judge to be mindful that evidence may not be excluded under W.
Va. R. Evid. 403 merely because he or she does not find the evidence to be credible,
although the trial judge may consider the probative value of the evidence when
undertaking the required balancing test pursuant to W. Va. R. Evid. 403. After all, it is
fundamental that credibility determinations are for the jury.

Thus, we hold that once a trial judge determines that a statement falls within the
dying declaration exception to the hearsay rule found in W. Va. R. Evid. 804(b)(2), then
it must be determined whether the evidence is relevant pursuant to W. Va. R. Evid. 401
and 402 and, if so, whether its probative value is substantially outweighed by unfair
prejudice pursuant to W. Va. R. Evid. 403. The statement is admissible only after the
trial judge determines that its probative value is not substantially outweighed by unfair
prejudice.

Applying the analysis we set forth above to this case poses two questions: (1) is
Moore's suicide note a dying declaration and (2) if so, is it relevant and is its probative
value substantially outweighed by unfair prejudice pursuant to W. Va. R. Evid. 401, 402
and 403.

Is Moore's suicide note a dying declaration? Clearly, there was evidence that Moore
wrote the suicide note with the belief that he was facing imminent death because he
killed himself soon after writing the note. Additionally, the suicide note explained why
Moore killed himself thereby explaining the causes or circumstances which led to his
death. Therefore, Moore's suicide note falls within the dying declaration exception to the
hearsay rule.

Is Moore's suicide note relevant and, if so, is its probative value substantially
outweighed by unfair prejudice to the appellant? Though the trial judge in the case
before us did not use this analysis, our review of the record reveals that Moore's suicide
note is relevant and its probative value is not substantially outweighed by any unfair
prejudice.

In summary, we hold that Moore's suicide note falls within the dying declaration
exception to the hearsay rule. We further conclude that the application of W. Va. R.
Evid. 401, 402, and 403 to the facts in this case demonstrates that the probative value of
the suicide note is not substantially outweighed by any unfair prejudice. Therefore, it
was not error for the trial judge to admit Moore's suicide note into evidence.

*   *   *

Affirmed.

NEELY, CHIEF JUSTICE, dissenting.

Treating a self-serving suicide note as the equivalent of a spontaneous declaration made in anticipation of imminent death lacks basic common sense. The dying declaration exception to the hearsay rule is used when the declarant is unavailable as a witness to admit "(2) Statement[s] under Belief of Impending Death. In a prosecution for homicide or in a civil action or proceeding, a statement made by a declarant while believing that his death is imminent, concerning the cause or circumstances of what he believed to be his impending death." Rule 804(b)(2), W.V.R.E.

At common law, the dying declaration was used to allow the admission of statements by murder victims who, with awareness of their impending demise, used their dying breath to identify their assailant. Accordingly, justice was served by preventing a murderer from evading justice by virtue of his success in killing the victim. As noted by the majority, this exception has since been expanded to include civil actions, and does not require that the declarant be the subject of the litigation seeking to introduce the statement. In this case Mr. Moore was a prosecution witness who was present at trial and subjected to direct, cross, and recross before his self-inflicted death.

Mr. Moore was in complete control of the timing and circumstances of his death. The majority fails to distinguish the difference between Mr. Moore's suicide note, and a statement made by a person facing inevitable death due to circumstances beyond his control. If ever there is a time to put one's best face forward, it would be in a note that will literally stand for all eternity as one's last testament. A suicide note is the perfect opportunity to rewrite one's own history in a way calculated to impress one's final audience.

My objection is not intended to imply Mr. Moore was lying: rather, the idea that suicide notes should be viewed as admissible evidence under the dying declaration exception to the hearsay rule is misguided.

In addition, Mr. Moore's note did not make reference to the cause or circumstances of his death, as required by Rule 804(b)(2), W.V.R.E. Another unsolved mystery is when he actually wrote the suicide note. Although it was found in the room with his body, it was not dated. How can the majority infer that the undated note was actually crafted under the belief of impending death?

The majority has employed a number of assumptions as a matter of law, and clothed them with an indicia of reliability that are totally unwarranted. A suicide note is a product of a controlled act accompanied by a planned statement. It is simply not analogous to a statement made under the belief of impending death by a person with a total lack of control over the timing and causation of his death. Denying this difference is absurd. It's like comparing the image captured by a photojournalist covering a war, to a staged photograph of a battlefield reenactment.

NOTES AND QUESTIONS

1. Do you agree with the *Satterfield* court's application of the dying declaration exception to the hearsay rule? Do self-serving hearsay statements, such as Moore's exculpatory statement denying responsibility for Harper's death, possess sufficient indicia of reliability? Do you agree with Chief Justice Neely's statement in his dissenting opinion that "[a] suicide note is the perfect opportunity to rewrite one's own history in a way calculated to impress one's final audience"? *Satterfield*, 457 S.E.2d at 455. Should Fed. R. Evid. 804(b)(2) be construed to exclude self-serving statements?

2. In his dissent, Chief Justice Neely stated that Moore's suicide note did not make reference to the "cause or circumstances" of his death. Do you agree? At the very least, Moore's statement concerned two separate but related matters. First, Moore's statement is compelling evidence that he committed suicide. Thus, his statement "concern[ed] the cause or circumstances of what the declarant believed to be impending death," i.e., his impending suicide. Second, Moore's suicide note concerned another matter, responsibility for Harper's death. Should the court have redacted Moore's statement in such a way as to exclude any reference to Harper's death as not concerning the cause or circumstances of Moore's death? In other words, should the requirement under Rule 804(b)(2) that the statement relate to the cause or circumstances of impending death be limited to statements identifying the person who inflicted the mortal wound, or describing the accident, assault or catastrophe that caused the fatal injury? *See United States v. Lemonakis*, 485 F.2d 941, 956 n.24 (D.C. Cir. 1973) (excluding third party suicide note tending to exculpate defendant by accepting responsibility for robberies as not related to cause or circumstances of impending death).

3. Does the admission of Moore's suicide violate the Sixth Amendment Confrontation Clause? Is the suicide note a testimonial statement under either *Crawford v. Washington*, 541 U.S. 36 (2004) or *Davis v. Washington*, 547 U.S. 813 (2006)?

[3]   Statements Against the Penal Interest of the Unavailable Declarant — The Problem of the Accomplice Who "Takes the Rap" or Implicates the Defendant

Under Fed. R. Evid. 804(b)(3),[36] a statement is not excluded as hearsay if the declarant is unavailable and the statement was against the declarant's penal interest. In *Williamson v. United States*, 512 U.S. 599 (1994), the Supreme Court articulated the principle behind the Rule: "Rule 804(b)(3) is founded on the commonsense notion that reasonable people, even reasonable people who are not especially honest, tend not to make self-inculpatory statements unless they believe them to be true." Thus, "[t]he question under Rule 804(b)(3) is always whether the statement was sufficiently against the declarant's penal interest 'that a reasonable person in the declarant's position would not have made the statement unless believing it to be true.' " *Id.* at 603–04.

Admission of third-party statements under Rule 804(b)(3) arises in two different contexts. First, a statement against penal interest may be offered by the prosecution to implicate the defendant. Second, a third-party statement may be introduced by the defendant to exculpate. In either case, the admission of out-of-court statements by an unavailable declarant requires careful thought. Depending upon the circumstances in which it is made, a particular statement that appears disserving may in fact be self-

---

[36] Rule 804 states, in relevant part:

(b) Hearsay exceptions. The following are not excluded by the hearsay rule if the declarant is unavailable as a witness:

*   *   *

(3) Statement against interest. A statement which was at the time of its making so far contrary to the declarant's pecuniary or proprietary interest, or so far tended to subject the declarant to civil or criminal liability, or to render invalid a claim by the declarant against another, that a reasonable person in the declarant's position would not have made the statement unless believing it to be true. A statement tending to expose the declarant to criminal liability and offered to exculpate the accused is not admissible unless corroborating circumstances clearly indicate the trustworthiness of the statement.

serving and motivated by a desire to minimize personal culpability by implicating others. Likewise, a third-party statement exculpating the accused may be fabricated to protect the defendant. For example, suppose a husband and wife are arrested and the husband confesses and states that his wife had "nothing to do with it." While the statement seems against the husband's interest (he "takes the rap"), his motive to protect his wife may override the penal interest of the statement. Thus, as a general rule there are three requirements that must be met before evidence is admissible as a declaration against penal interest: "(1) the declarant is unavailable, (2) the statement is genuinely adverse to the declarant's penal interest, and (3) 'corroborating circumstances clearly indicate the trustworthiness of the statement.' "[37] While Rule 804(b)(3) does not expressly require corroboration of statements inculpating the accused as a precondition to admissibility, many courts have imposed this requirement. Moreover, the party offering the statement bears the "formidable burden" of meeting the requirements of Rule 804(b)(3), and the court's decision on its admissibility is reviewed for abuse of discretion.[38]

When the statement is offered by the defendant, the requirement of corroborating circumstances was designed to protect against the possibility that the statement was fabricated to exculpate the accused. The Advisory Committee explained the requirement of corroborating circumstances as follows:

> [O]ne senses in the decisions a distrust of evidence of confessions by third persons offered to exculpate the accused arising from suspicions of fabrications either of the fact of the making of the confession or in its contents, enhanced in either instance by the required unavailability of the declarant.

Fed. R. Evid. 804(b)(3), Advisory Committee Notes. At the same time, the corroborating circumstances need not "remove all doubt with respect to the hearsay statement."[39]

When the proffered statement contains both self-inculpatory and non-self-inculpatory parts, is the entire statement admissible as a declaration against interest? In other words, does the rationale for the admission of declarations against penal interest that reasonable people tend not to make self-inculpatory statements unless they believe them to be true extend to a confession's non-self-inculpatory parts or to collateral statements that are neutral as to interest? This is the issue that the Supreme Court confronted in *Williamson v. United States*, below.

[a]   Third-Party Statements Offered Against the Defendant

WILLIAMSON v. UNITED STATES
512 U.S. 594 (1994)

JUSTICE O'CONNOR delivered the opinion of the Court, except as to Part II-C.

In this case we clarify the scope of the hearsay exception for statements against penal interest. Fed. Rule Evid. 804(b)(3).

A deputy sheriff stopped the rental car driven by Reginald Harris for weaving on the highway. Harris consented to a search of the car, which revealed 19 kilograms of

---

[37] *United States v. Bumpass*, 60 F.3d 1099, 1101 (4th Cir. 1995).

[38] *Id.*

[39] *Id.* at 1102.

cocaine in two suitcases in the trunk. Harris was promptly arrested.

Shortly after Harris' arrest, Special Agent Donald Walton of the Drug Enforcement Administration (DEA) interviewed him by telephone. During that conversation, Harris said that he got the cocaine from an unidentified Cuban in Fort Lauderdale; that the cocaine belonged to petitioner Williamson; and that it was to be delivered that night to a particular dumpster. Williamson was also connected to Harris by physical evidence: The luggage bore the initials of Williamson's sister, Williamson was listed as an additional driver on the car rental agreement, and an envelope addressed to Williamson and a receipt with Williamson's girlfriend's address were found in the glove compartment.

Several hours later, Agent Walton spoke to Harris in person. During that interview, Harris said he had rented the car a few days earlier and had driven it to Fort Lauderdale to meet Williamson. According to Harris, he had gotten the cocaine from a Cuban who was Williamson's acquaintance, and the Cuban had put the cocaine in the car with a note telling Harris how to deliver the drugs. Harris repeated that he had been instructed to leave the drugs in a certain dumpster, to return to his car, and to leave without waiting for anyone to pick up the drugs.

Agent Walton then took steps to arrange a controlled delivery of the cocaine. But as Walton was preparing to leave the interview room, Harris "got out of [his] chair . . . and . . . took a half step toward [Walton] . . . and . . . said, . . . 'I can't let you do that,' threw his hands up and said 'that's not true, I can't let you go up there for no reason.' " App. 40. Harris told Walton he had lied about the Cuban, the note, and the dumpster. The real story, Harris said, was that he was transporting the cocaine to Atlanta for Williamson, and that Williamson was traveling in front of him in another rental car. Harris added that after his car was stopped, Williamson turned around and drove past the location of the stop, where he could see Harris' car with its trunk open. Because Williamson had apparently seen the police searching the car, Harris explained that it would be impossible to make a controlled delivery.

Harris told Walton that he had lied about the source of the drugs because he was afraid of Williamson. Though Harris freely implicated himself, he did not want his story to be recorded, and he refused to sign a written version of the statement. Walton testified that he had promised to report any cooperation by Harris to the Assistant United States Attorney. Walton said Harris was not promised any reward or other benefit for cooperating.

Williamson was eventually convicted of possessing cocaine with intent to distribute, conspiring to possess cocaine with intent to distribute, and traveling interstate to promote the distribution of cocaine, 21 U.S.C. §§ 841(a)(1), 846; 18 U.S.C. § 1952. When called to testify at Williamson's trial, Harris refused, even though the prosecution gave him use immunity and the court ordered him to testify and eventually held him in contempt. The District Court then ruled that, under Rule 804(b)(3), Agent Walton could relate what Harris had said to him:

> "The ruling of the Court is that the statements . . . are admissible under [Rule 804(b)(3)], which deals with statements against interest.

> "First, defendant Harris' statements clearly implicated himself, and therefore, are against his penal interest.

> "Second, defendant Harris, the declarant, is unavailable.

"And third, as I found yesterday, there are sufficient corroborating circumstances in this case to ensure the trustworthiness of his testimony. Therefore, under [*United States v. Harrell*, 788 F.2d 1524 (CA11 1986)], these statements by defendant Harris implicating [Williamson] are admissible." App. 51–52.

Williamson appealed his conviction, claiming that the admission of Harris' statements violated Rule 804(b)(3) and the Confrontation Clause of the Sixth Amendment. The Court of Appeals for the Eleventh Circuit affirmed without opinion, and we granted certiorari.

II.

A.

The hearsay rule, Fed. Rule Evid. 802, is premised on the theory that out-of-court statements are subject to particular hazards. The declarant might be lying; he might have misperceived the events which he relates; he might have faulty memory; his words might be misunderstood or taken out of context by the listener. And the ways in which these dangers are minimized for in-court statements — the oath, the witness' awareness of the gravity of the proceedings, the jury's ability to observe the witness' demeanor, and, most importantly, the right of the opponent to cross-examine — are generally absent for things said out of court.

Nonetheless, the Federal Rules of Evidence also recognize that some kinds of out-of-court statements are less subject to these hearsay dangers, and therefore except them from the general rule that hearsay is inadmissible. One such category covers statements that are against the declarant's interest:

"statement[s] which . . . at the time of [their] making . . . so far tended to subject the declarant to . . . criminal liability . . . that a reasonable person in the declarant's position would not have made the statement[s] unless believing [them] to be true." Fed. Rule Evid. 804(b)(3).

To decide whether Harris' confession is made admissible by Rule 804(b)(3), we must first determine what the Rule means by "statement," which Federal Rule of Evidence 801(a)(1) defines as "an oral or written assertion." One possible meaning, "a report or narrative," Webster's Third New International Dictionary 2229, defn. 2(a) (1961), connotes an extended declaration. Under this reading, Harris' entire confession — even if it contains both self-inculpatory and non-self-inculpatory parts — would be admissible so long as in the aggregate the confession sufficiently inculpates him. Another meaning of "statement," "a single declaration or remark," *ibid.*, defn. 2(b), would make Rule 804(b)(3) cover only those declarations or remarks within the confession that are individually self-inculpatory. *See also id.*, at 131 (defining "assertion" as a "declaration"); *id.*, at 586 (defining "declaration" as a "statement").

Although the text of the Rule does not directly resolve the matter, the principle behind the Rule, so far as it is discernible from the text, points clearly to the narrower reading. Rule 804(b)(3) is founded on the commonsense notion that reasonable people, even reasonable people who are not especially honest, tend not to make self-inculpatory statements unless they believe them to be true. This notion simply does not extend to the broader definition of "statement." The fact that a person is making a broadly self-inculpatory confession does not make more credible the confession's non-self-inculpatory parts. One of the most effective ways to lie is to mix falsehood with truth, especially truth that seems particularly persuasive because of its self-inculpatory nature.

In this respect, it is telling that the non-self-inculpatory things Harris said in his first statement actually proved to be false, as Harris himself admitted during the second interrogation. And when part of the confession is actually self-exculpatory, the generalization on which Rule 804(b)(3) is founded becomes even less applicable. Self-exculpatory statements are exactly the ones which people are most likely to make even when they are false; and mere proximity to other, self-inculpatory, statements does not increase the plausibility of the self-exculpatory statements.

We therefore cannot agree with JUSTICE KENNEDY's suggestion that the Rule can be read as expressing a policy that collateral statements — even ones that are not in any way against the declarant's interest — are admissible. *Post*, at 614. Nothing in the text of Rule 804(b)(3) or the general theory of the hearsay Rules suggests that admissibility should turn on whether a statement is collateral to a self-inculpatory statement. The fact that a statement is self-inculpatory does make it more reliable; but the fact that a statement is collateral to a self-inculpatory statement says nothing at all about the collateral statement's reliability. We see no reason why collateral statements, even ones that are neutral as to interest, *post*, at 617–19, should be treated any differently from other hearsay statements that are generally excluded.

Congress certainly could, subject to the constraints of the Confrontation Clause, make statements admissible based on their proximity to self-inculpatory statements. But we will not lightly assume that the ambiguous language means anything so inconsistent with the Rule's underlying theory. In our view, the most faithful reading of Rule 804(b)(3) is that it does not allow admission of non-self-inculpatory statements, even if they are made within a broader narrative that is generally self-inculpatory. The district court may not just assume for purposes of Rule 804(b)(3) that a statement is self-inculpatory because it is part of a fuller confession, and this is especially true when the statement implicates someone else. "[T]he arrest statements of a codefendant have traditionally been viewed with special suspicion. Due to his strong motivation to implicate the defendant and to exonerate himself, a codefendant's statements about what the defendant said or did are less credible than ordinary hearsay evidence." *Lee v. Illinois*, 476 U.S. 530, 541 (1986) (internal quotation marks omitted); *see also Bruton v. United States*, 391 U.S. 123, 136 (1968); *Dutton v. Evans*, 400 U.S. 74, 98 (1970) (Harlan, J., concurring in result).

JUSTICE KENNEDY suggests that the Advisory Committee Notes to Rule 804(b)(3) should be read as endorsing the position we reject — that an entire narrative, including non-self-inculpatory parts (but excluding the clearly self-serving parts, *post*, at 620), may be admissible if it is in the aggregate self-inculpatory. *See post*, at 614–15. The Notes read, in relevant part:

> "[T]he third-party confession . . . may include statements implicating [the accused], and under the general theory of declarations against interest they would be admissible as related statements. . . . [*Douglas v. Alabama*, 380 U.S. 415 (1965), and *Bruton v. United States*, 391 U.S. 123 (1968)] . . . by no means require that all statements implicating another person be excluded from the category of declarations against interest. Whether a statement is in fact against interest must be determined from the circumstances of each case. Thus a statement admitting guilt and implicating another person, made while in custody, may well be motivated by a desire to curry favor with the authorities

and hence fail to qualify as against interest. . . . On the other hand, the same words spoken under different circumstances, *e.g.*, to an acquaintance, would have no difficulty in qualifying. . . . The balancing of self-serving against dissenting [sic] aspects of a declaration is discussed in McCormick § 256." 28 U.S.C. App., p. 790.

This language, however, is not particularly clear, and some of it — especially the Advisory Committee's endorsement of the position taken by Dean McCormick's treatise — points the other way:

> "A certain latitude as to contextual statements, neutral as to interest, giving meaning to the declaration against interest seems defensible, but bringing in self-serving statements contextually seems questionable
>
> . . . .
>
> [A]dmit[ting] the disserving parts of the declaration, and exclud[ing] the self-serving parts . . . seems the most realistic method of adjusting admissibility to trustworthiness, where the serving and disserving parts can be severed."
> *See* C. McCormick, Law of Evidence § 256, pp. 551–553 (1954) (footnotes omitted).

Without deciding exactly how much weight to give the Notes in this particular situation, . . . we conclude that the policy expressed in the statutory text points clearly enough in one direction that it outweighs whatever force the Notes may have. And though JUSTICE KENNEDY believes that the text can fairly be read as expressing a policy of admitting collateral statements, *post*, at 614, for the reasons given above we disagree.

B.

We also do not share JUSTICE KENNEDY's fears that our reading of the Rule "eviscerate[s] the against penal interest exception," *post*, at 616 (internal quotation marks omitted), or makes it lack "meaningful effect," *ibid.* There are many circumstances in which Rule 804(b)(3) does allow the admission of statements that inculpate a criminal defendant. Even the confessions of arrested accomplices may be admissible if they are truly self-inculpatory, rather than merely attempts to shift blame or curry favor.

For instance, a declarant's squarely self-inculpatory confession — "yes, I killed X" — will likely be admissible under Rule 804(b)(3) against accomplices of his who are being tried under a co-conspirator liability theory. *See Pinkerton v. United States*, 328 U.S. 640, 647 (1946). Likewise, by showing that the declarant knew something, a self-inculpatory statement can in some situations help the jury infer that his confederates knew it as well. And when seen with other evidence, an accomplice's self-inculpatory statement can inculpate the defendant directly: "I was robbing the bank on Friday morning," coupled with someone's testimony that the declarant and the defendant drove off together Friday morning, is evidence that the defendant also participated in the robbery.

Moreover, whether a statement is self-inculpatory or not can only be determined by viewing it in context. Even statements that are on their face neutral may actually be against the declarant's interest. "I hid the gun in Joe's apartment" may not be a confession of a crime; but if it is likely to help the police find the murder weapon, then it is certainly self-inculpatory. "Sam and I went to Joe's house" might be against the declarant's interest if a reasonable person in the declarant's shoes would realize that being linked to Joe and Sam would implicate the declarant in Joe and Sam's conspiracy. And other statements that give the police significant details about the crime may also, depending on the situation, be against the declarant's interest. The question under Rule 804(b)(3) is always whether the statement was sufficiently against the declarant's penal interest "that a reasonable person in the declarant's position would not have made the statement unless believing it to be true," and this question can only be answered in light of all the surrounding circumstances.

C.

In this case, however, we cannot conclude that all that Harris said was properly admitted. Some of Harris' confession would clearly have been admissible under Rule 804(b)(3); for instance, when he said he knew there was cocaine in the suitcase, he essentially forfeited his only possible defense to a charge of cocaine possession, lack of knowledge. But other parts of his confession, especially the parts that implicated Williamson, did little to subject Harris himself to criminal liability. A reasonable person in Harris' position might even think that implicating someone else would decrease his practical exposure to criminal liability, at least so far as sentencing goes. Small fish in a big conspiracy often get shorter sentences than people who are running the whole show, . . . especially if the small fish are willing to help the authorities catch the big ones. . . .

Nothing in the record shows that the District Court or the Court of Appeals inquired whether each of the statements in Harris' confession was truly self-inculpatory. As we explained above, this can be a fact-intensive inquiry, which would require careful examination of all the circumstances surrounding the criminal activity involved; we therefore remand to the Court of Appeals to conduct this inquiry in the first instance.

In light of this disposition, we need not address Williamson's claim that the statements were also made inadmissible by the Confrontation Clause, and in particular we need not decide whether the hearsay exception for declarations against interest is "firmly rooted" for Confrontation Clause purposes. . . . The judgment of the Court of Appeals is vacated, and the case is remanded for further proceedings.

So Ordered.

NOTES AND QUESTIONS

1. In *Williamson*, the Supreme Court held that the hearsay exception for statements against penal interest "does not allow admission of non-self-inculpatory statements, even if they are made within a broader narrative that is generally self-inculpatory." *Williamson, supra*, 512 U.S. at 600–01. Thus, only those statements that inculpate the declarant are admissible under the Fed. R. Evid. Rule 804(b)(3) as statements against penal interest. Additionally, the Court stated that this is a "fact-intensive inquiry," and remanded the case to the Court of Appeals to conduct this inquiry in the first instance. *Id.* at 605. On remand, which of Harris' post-arrest statements, if any, are likely to qualify as statements against penal interest?

2. In a separate concurring opinion, Justice Kennedy, joined by Chief Justice Rehnquist and Justice Thomas, observed that there has been a long-running debate among commentators over the admissibility of collateral statements. Justice Kennedy outlined three contrasting views:

Dean Wigmore took the strongest position in favor of admissibility, arguing that "the statement may be accepted, not merely as to the specific fact against interest, but also as to every fact contained in the same statement." 5 J. Wigmore, Evidence § 1465, p. 271 (3d ed. 1940) (emphasis deleted); *see also* 5 J. Wigmore, Evidence § 1465, p. 339 (J. Chadbourn rev. 1974); *Higham v. Ridgway*, 10 East. 109, 103 Eng. Rep. 717 (K.B. 1808). According to Wigmore, because "the statement is made under circumstances fairly indicating the declarant's sincerity and accuracy," the entire statement should be admitted. 5 J. Wigmore § 1465, p. 271 (3d ed. 1940). Dean McCormick's approach regarding collateral statements was more guarded. He argued for the admissibility of collateral statements of a neutral character, and for the exclusion of collateral statements of self-serving character. For example, in the statement "John and I robbed the bank," the words "John and" are neutral (save for the possibility of conspiracy charges). On the other hand, the statement "John, not I, shot the bank teller" is to some extent self-serving and therefore might be inadmissible. *See* C. McCormick, Law of Evidence § 256, pp. 552–553 (1954) (hereinafter McCormick). Professor Jefferson took the narrowest approach, arguing that the reliability of a statement against interest stems only from the disserving fact stated and so should be confined "to the proof of the fact which is against interest." Jefferson, *Declarations Against Interest: An Exception to the Hearsay Rule*, 58 Harv. L. Rev. 1, 62–63 (1944). Under the Jefferson approach, neither collateral neutral nor collateral self-serving statements would be admissible.

Williamson, supra, 512 U.S. at 611–12.

Justice Kennedy rejected each of these distinct approaches, opting instead for a different standard. He would admit all statements related to the precise statement against penal interest, subject to two limits. First, the court should exclude a collateral statement that is so self-serving as to render it unreliable. Justice Kennedy cites, for example, a statement that shifts blame to someone else for a crime the defendant could have committed. Second, the entire statement should be excluded in cases where the statement was made under circumstances where it is likely that the declarant had a significant motive to obtain favorable treatment. For instance, Justice Kennedy maintains that when the government makes an explicit offer of leniency in exchange for the declarant's admission of guilt, any subsequent statement should be inadmissible. 512 U.S. at 618–19. Do you agree with the position of Justice Kennedy, Dean Wigmore, Dean McCormick, or Professor Jefferson? Which is the better approach? Applying each of these different standards to Harris' post-arrest statements, which statements would be admissible as declarations against interest?

3. Justice Kennedy opined that the majority's reading of the Rule "eviscerate[s] the against penal interest exception," or makes it lack "meaningful effect." 512 U.S. at 616. He stated that the majority's reading of Rule 804(b)(3) would exclude third-party statements that inculpate a criminal defendant. Do you agree? Under what circumstances would Rule 804(b)(3) allow the admission of statements that are self-inculpatory and, at the same time, incriminate the accused? *See United States v. Mathews*, 20 F.3d 538, 546 (2d Cir. 1994) (declarant's out-of-court statement to his girlfriend implicating himself, as well as defendant, in all aspects of the robbery was properly admitted); *but see United States v. Mendoza*, 85 F.3d 1347 (8th Cir. 1996) (applying the standards set forth in *Williamson*, declarant's statement that defendant delivered the methamphetamine was not sufficiently against her penal interest to warrant admission under Rule

804(b)(3)); *United States v. Hazlett*, 32 F.3d 1313, 1316 (8th Cir. 1994) (declarant's statements incriminating defendant were inadmissible under Rule 804(b)(3) inasmuch as "she had nothing to lose by confessing, and she certainly had nothing to lose by implicating another person particularly someone more culpable").

Should the relevant test be whether the part of the statement implicating defendant is "integral" to the part implicating the declarant? In other words, should the statement be admissible if "[t]he fact adverse to the defendant and the fact adverse to the speaker had a direct logical bearing in an appraisal of the speaker's culpability"? MUELLER & KIRKPATRICK, EVIDENCE § 8.64, at 1051 (1995).

4. What factors should be considered in determining whether the declarant's statement is sufficiently against his penal interest? The mere fact that the declarant invoked his Fifth Amendment privilege against self-incrimination does not make the statement against penal interest. *See United States v. Thomas*, 62 F.3d 1332, 1338 (11th Cir. 1995). On the other hand, statements against penal interest are not limited to direct confessions. *See United States v. Slaughter*, 891 F.2d 691, 698 (9th Cir. 1989). Moreover, it is well settled that the self-inculpatory statement need not by itself prove the declarant guilty. The proffered statement need only be a "a brick in the wall" of proving the declarant's guilt. *United States v. Thomas*, 571 F.2d 285, 288 (5th Cir. 1978); *see also United States v. Nagib*, 56 F.3d 798, 804 (7th Cir. 1995) ("A statement may satisfy this requirement if it would be probative at trial against the declarant.").

5. In a concurring opinion, Justice Ginsburg, with whom Justices Blackmun, Stevens, and Souter joined, maintained that none of Harris' post-arrest statements to federal law enforcement officers fit within the hearsay exception for statements against penal interest. Justice Ginsburg reasoned that "Harris' arguably inculpatory statements are too closely intertwined with his self-serving declarations to be ranked as trustworthy," *Williamson, supra*, 512 U.S. at 608, and further stated:

> To the extent some of these statements tended to incriminate Harris, they provide only marginal or cumulative evidence of his guilt. They project an image of a person striving mightily to shift principal responsibility to someone else. . . . For these reasons, I would hold that none of Harris' hearsay statements were admissible under Rule 804(b)(3).

Id. at 609–10. Do you agree? Are any of Harris' hearsay statements sufficiently reliable to be admissible as declarations against penal interest? Can a custodial statement to law enforcement that shifts blame to an accomplice ever be sufficiently reliable to be admissible under Rule 804(b)(3)?

6. To what extent must the declarant's statement be against his penal interest? Fed. R. Evid. 804(b)(3) renders admissible a "statement which . . . at the time of its making . . . so far *tended to subject* the declarant to . . . criminal liability . . . that a reasonable person in the declarant's position would not have made . . . unless believing it to be true." (Emphasis added.) Should the phrase "tended to subject" be construed to include a broad scope of inculpatory statements? Consider the following problem.

7. In *Williamson*, the Supreme Court left open the question of whether the admission of Harris' statements violated the Sixth Amendment Confrontation Clause. However, *Williamson* was decided prior to the Supreme Court's ruling in *Crawford v. Washington*, 541 U.S. 36 (2004) (testimonial statements are inadmissible under the Confrontation Clause unless the declarant is unavailable and the defendant had an opportunity for cross-examination) and *Davis v. Washington*, 547 U.S. 813 (2006) (out-of-court statements made in response to police questioning are testimonial and inadmissible under the Confrontation Clause unless such statements were elicited in response to an ongoing emergency). After *Crawford* and *Davis*, what is the legal significance of *Williamson*? Do *Crawford* and *Davis* effectively trump *Williamson*, rendering it irrelevant? Stated another way, does *Williamson* retain legal viability post-*Crawford*? Can you envision a scenario where statements made against the declarant's penal interest are nontestimonial under *Crawford* and *Davis*, and therefore not barred by the Confrontation Clause, but nonetheless rendered inadmissible under *Williamson*? Does *Williamson* continue to impose a meaningful limitation on the admissibility of hearsay statements offered for admission under Rule 804(b)(3)?

PROBLEM

Problem 9-5. *Statements Creating Only a Risk of Prosecution.* The police conducted a search of an apartment where they observed three males asleep in the living room; one of the subjects was the defendant Butler. Officer Figueroa roused Butler from the couch. On the couch, directly under where Butler was sleeping, the officer found a .25 caliber semiautomatic pistol with an obliterated serial number wrapped in a stocking cap. Knowing that Butler was a convicted felon, the officer placed him under arrest for possession of a firearm. At the defendant's trial for being a felon in possession of a firearm, he offered an out-of-court statement by a witness who was present in the apartment but not charged with a crime. The witness stated that it was he — not Butler — who was lying down in the living room when the police arrived, while Butler was in the bedroom. Officers found two guns in the living room; no guns were found in the bedroom. The statement was also exculpatory as to Butler because the witness claimed that after the police had them up against the wall, he heard an officer exclaim that he had found guns and that they should give them to the felons.

By exculpating the defendant and placing himself in the room where the gun was found, the witness's statement creates a risk or possibility that he may be charged with firearms violations. Is a statement which only presents a risk of criminal prosecution sufficiently against the declarant's penal interest to be admissible under Rule 804(b)(3)? *See United States v. Butler*, 71 F.3d 243 (7th Cir. 1995); *United States v. Fowlie*, 24 F.3d 1059, 1068 (9th Cir. 1994) (a statement made by declarant while out of the country and facing no threat of punishment would not be against penal interest).

UNITED STATES v. JORDAN
509 F.3d 191 (4th Cir. 2007)

* * *

I.

This case arose from the "brutal murder" of Dwayne Tabon. On September 14, 2001, during a drug transaction in an apartment in Richmond, Virginia, Gordon and Jordan forcibly abducted Tabon, took him to another location, and set him on fire. Suffering from burns over ninety percent of his body, Tabon died ten days later.

On September 7, 2004, a grand jury sitting in the Eastern District of Virginia returned an indictment against Gordon and Jordan, charging both men with murder while engaged in a conspiracy to distribute and to possess with intent to distribute 50 or more grams of crack cocaine (Count One); conspiracy to use and carry a firearm during and in relation to the same crack cocaine conspiracy (Count Two); and possession of a firearm in furtherance of the crack cocaine conspiracy (Count Three). The indictment also charged Jordan with conspiracy to distribute crack cocaine and heroin from 1999 until June 17, 2004. Counts One, Two, and Three alleged that the offenses occurred on or about September 14, 2001.

*   *   *

Gordon's and Jordan's trial began on October 27, 2005. At trial, the Government sought to introduce statements made by a deceased alleged co-conspirator, Octavia Brown, to her friend Paul Adams. Gordon and Jordan objected to the admission of the statements, arguing that, under *Crawford v. Washington*, 541 U.S. 36 (2004), the statements were "testimonial" and thus barred by the Sixth Amendment's Confrontation Clause. They also argued that the statements were inadmissible hearsay. The district court rejected these arguments and admitted the statements, concluding that the statements were non-testimonial and admissible under Federal Rule of Evidence 804(b)(3) as statements against interest.

At the close of the Government's case-in-chief, Gordon and Jordan moved for a judgment of acquittal. The district court denied both motions. Gordon and Jordan renewed their motions at the close of all the evidence, and the district court again denied both motions.

Ultimately, the jury convicted Gordon and Jordan on all counts, and each was sentenced to life imprisonment. Gordon renewed his motion for judgment of acquittal or, alternatively, for a new trial, but the district court again denied the motion. Both defendants timely appealed. We have jurisdiction over this appeal pursuant to 28 U.S.C.A. § 1291 (West 2006).

*   *   *

III.

We . . . must turn to Jordan's contention that the admission of certain statements at trial, which were never "test[ed] in the crucible of cross-examination," *Crawford*, 541 U.S. at 61, deprived him of his Sixth Amendment Confrontation rights or, alternatively, that the statements constituted inadmissible hearsay under the Federal Rules of Evidence. We review the district court's decision to admit the testimony for an abuse of discretion.

The statements at issue were made by Octavia Brown, an alleged co-conspirator of Gordon and Jordan, to her friend Paul Adams. Adams picked up Brown on the night of Tabon's murder after receiving her frantic phone call. Several days after the murder, Brown began to stay at Adams's apartment. Brown eventually related to Adams "[i]n bits and pieces" what happened on the night that she frantically called him. Brown's statements to Adams included her admissions that she participated in the planning of a drug transaction; that she called the source of the drugs; that she witnessed the arrival of the drug courier (Tabon); that she was directed to the bedroom; that when she emerged from the bedroom, she saw Gordon and Jordan with guns pointed at the drug courier, who was taped up; that she was ordered to go outside and downstairs to direct the source to come up and settle a discrepancy; and that the source started toward the apartment but ran when he saw the number of people inside. Brown was incarcerated on matters unrelated to this case and committed suicide in 2002.

Noting that the critical issue was whether Brown reasonably believed the statements would later be used at trial at the time she made them, the district court ruled that Brown's statements to Adams were non-testimonial and thus did not implicate the Sixth Amendment's Confrontation Clause. The district court also concluded that Brown's statements, although hearsay, were admissible as statements against penal interest under Rule 804(b)(3).

In *Crawford*, the Supreme Court divided out-of-court statements into two categories: those that are "testimonial" and those that are not. *Crawford*, 541 U.S. at 60-69. The Court stated that testimonial hearsay is the "primary" concern of the Confrontation Clause. *Id.* at 53. The Confrontation Clause bars the use of testimonial statements unless the declarant is unavailable and the defendant has had a prior opportunity to cross-examine the declarant. *Crawford*, 541 U.S. at 53-54. The *Crawford* Court gave a non-exclusive list of three examples of "testimonial" statements: "*ex parte* in-court testimony or its functional equivalent-that is, material such as affidavits, custodial examinations, prior testimony that the defendant was unable to cross-examine, or similar pretrial statements that declarants would reasonably expect to be used prosecutorially;" "extrajudicial statements . . . contained in formalized testimonial materials, such as affidavits, depositions, prior testimony, or confessions;" and "statements that were made under circumstances which would lead an objective witness reasonably to believe that the statement would be available for use at a later trial." *Id.* at 51-52 (internal quotation marks omitted).

To our knowledge, no court has extended *Crawford* to statements made by a declarant to friends or associates. *See United States v. Franklin*, 415 F.3d 537, 545 (6th Cir. 2005) (concluding that statements were non-testimonial where witness "was privy to [Declarant]'s statements only as his friend and confidant"); *United States v. Saget*, 377 F.3d 223, 229 (2d Cir. 2004) ("Thus, we conclude that a declarant's statements to a confidential informant, whose true status is unknown to the declarant, do not constitute testimony within the meaning of *Crawford*."); *United States v. Manfre*, 368 F.3d 832, 838 n. 1 (8th Cir. 2004) ("[Declarant]'s comments were made to loved ones or acquaintances and are not the kind of memorialized, judicial-process-created evidence of which *Crawford* speaks."). Even assuming that statements to friends or associates may be considered testimonial in the rare case, the district court correctly concluded that "[t]he critical *Crawford* issue here is whether Ms. Brown, at the time she made her statements to Mr. Adams, reasonably believed these statements would be later used at trial." *Jordan II*, 399 F. Supp.2d at 708. As the district court found, "there was no indication Ms. Brown was aware that she would be called upon to testify until she was interviewed" by the Richmond City Police Department. *Id.* at 710. Brown's statements, made to a friend rather than to law enforcement personnel, "appear[ed] to flow more from atonement and contrition" than from an attempt to record past events or shift blame to others with the knowledge that the statements would later be used in court. *Id.* at 710. There is simply no evidence-only Jordan's conjecture-to suggest that Brown knew that her statements to her friend Adams would later be used at trial. We therefore conclude that the statements were non-testimonial and thus do not need to resort to *Crawford* and its Sixth Amendment principles.

Jordan alternatively contends that, even if Brown's statements to Adams are non-testimonial, they are inadmissible hearsay under Federal Rule of Evidence 802. The district court found that the statements fell within Rule 804(b)(3), the hearsay exception for statements against penal interest. Under Rule 804(b)(3), if the declarant is unavailable as a witness, "[a] statement which . . . at the time of its making . . . so far tended to subject the declarant to . . . criminal liability . . . that a reasonable person in the declarant's position would not have made the statement unless believing it to be true" is not excluded by the hearsay rule.[6]Fed. R. Evid. 804(b)(3).

Because of Brown's unavailability to testify, the sole question under Rule 804(b)(3) is whether Brown's statements to Adams, at the time they were made, exposed her to criminal liability such that a reasonable person in her shoes would not have made the statements unless believing them to be true. Brown's statements to Adams related to her involvement in a plan to lure a drug dealer to an apartment and described her observations and actions after she emerged from the bedroom on the night of Tabon's murder. She admitted that she called the dealer to order drugs, that she knew the group planned to rob the dealer, and that she further participated in the conspiracy by trying to lure another individual into the apartment. As a co-conspirator, Brown was legally responsible for all reasonably foreseeable acts her co-conspirators undertook in furtherance of the conspiracy. *See Pinkerton v. United States*, 328 U.S. 640, 646-48 (1946) (noting that conspirators who have not affirmatively withdrawn are liable for reasonably foreseeable overt acts of co-conspirators); *United States v. Cummings*, 937 F.2d 941, 944 (4th Cir. 1991) (same). Brown's statements thus no doubt subjected her to criminal liability so that a reasonable person would not have made them had they been untrue.

Jordan counters that Brown's statements were not entirely self-inculpatory, i.e., that they were given in bits and pieces as part of a narrative consisting of both self-inculpatory and non-self-inculpatory parts. Of course, the self-inculpatory nature of a statement can only be determined "by viewing [the statement] in context." *Williamson v. United States*, 512 U.S. 594, 603 (1994). In *Williamson*, the Supreme Court instructed that "statement" should be defined narrowly because "[t]he fact that a person is making a broadly self-inculpatory confession does not make more credible the confession's non-self-inculpatory parts." *Id.* at 599. But the Court noted that "confessions of arrested accomplices may be admissible if they are truly self-inculpatory, rather than merely attempts to shift blame or curry favor." *Id.* at 603.

Here, although Brown's statements to Adams inculpated Jordan, they also subjected *her* to criminal liability for a drug conspiracy and, by extension, for Tabon's murder. Brown made the statements to a friend in an effort to relieve herself of guilt, not to law enforcement in an effort to minimize culpability or criminal exposure. We thus conclude that Brown's statements to Adams were admissible under Rule 804(b)(3) and that the district court did not abuse its discretion in admitting them into evidence.

IV.

Based on the foregoing . . . we reject Jordan's Sixth Amendment and evidentiary challenges to his convictions. Accordingly, we . . . affirm Jordan's convictions.

---

[6] The district court, citing *United States v. Lowe*, 65 F.3d 1137, 1145 (4th Cir. 1995), stated that for Brown's statements to be admissible as statements against penal interest, the Fourth Circuit requires "corroborating circumstances clearly indicat[ing] the trustworthiness of the statement." *United States v. Jordan*, 399 F. Supp.2d 706, 709 (E.D.Va.2005). As Rule 804(b)(3) makes clear, however, corroborating circumstances are only required if the statement is "offered to exculpate the accused." Fed. R. Evid. 804(b)(3). *Lowe* involved evidence offered to exculpate the accused. Here, it is plain that Brown's statements were in no way offered to exculpate Gordon or Jordan. Thus, the district court need not have discussed whether "corroborating circumstances" existed.

NOTES AND QUESTIONS

(1) *Testimonial Statements.* In *Jordan,* the court held that Brown's statements were non-testimonial. Why? What is the reasoning of the court?

(2) *Lilly v. Virginia.* In *Lilly v. Virginia,* 527 U.S. 116 (1999), a plurality decision authored by Justice Stevens, the Supreme Court held that statements inculpating a defendant made by a co-conspirator to police after an arrest are inadmissible as against penal interest on Confrontation Clause grounds. Applying the test enunciated in *Ohio v. Roberts,* 448 U.S. 56 (1980), the plurality found that the out-of-court confession implicating both the declarant and the petitioner did not fall within a "firmly rooted exception" to the hearsay rule, and were not sufficiently trustworthy to satisfy the demands of the Confrontation Clause. In *Crawford v. Washington,* 541 U.S. 36 (2004), the Supreme Court overruled *Roberts.* Did *Crawford* overrule *Lilly*? Following the reasoning in *Crawford,* would the admission of out-of-court statements by a third-party that inculpate the defendant in criminal activity violate the Confrontation Clause? Are such statements always testimonial?

(3) *Self-Serving Statements.* Are Brown's statements both self-inculpatory and non-self-inculpatory? Which statements are non-self-inculpatory? Brown stated that she saw Gordon and Jordan with guns pointed at the drug courier, who was taped up. Are these statements against Brown's penal interest or do they merely shift blame to Gordon and Jordan for kidnaping and murdering the drug courier? Are Brown's non-self-inculpatory statements as reliable as her self-inculpatory ones? In support of its holding that Brown's statements were admissible under Rule 804(b)(3), the *Jordan* court relied on the following statement from *Williamson:* " 'confessions of arrested accomplices may be admissible if they are truly self-inculpatory, rather than merely attempts to shift blame or curry favor.' " *Jordan,* 509 F.3d at 202-03 (*quoting Williamson v. United States,* 512 U.S. at 603). Is this statement from *Williamson* taken out of context? Is the court's ruling in *Jordan* inconsistent with the holding in *Williamson*?

(4) *Corroborating Circumstances Indicating the Trustworthiness of the Statement.* To be admissible as a statement against penal interest, some courts apply a three-part test:

> (1) the declarant must be unavailable as a witness, (2) the statement must so far tend to subject the declarant to criminal liability that a reasonable person in the defendant's position would not have made the statement unless he or she believed it to be true, and (3) corroborating circumstances clearly indicate the trustworthiness of the statement.

United States v. Honken, 541 F.3d 1146, 1161 (8th Cir. 2008). *See also United States v. Lowe,* 65 F.3d 1137, 1145 (4th Cir. 1995). Is a finding of corroborating circumstances indicating the trustworthiness of the statements required by Rule 804(b)(3)? In *Jordan,* were there corroborating circumstances indicating the trustworthiness of Brown's statements?

[b] Third-Party Statements Offered by the Accused to Exculpate

UNITED STATES v. GARCIA
986 F.2d 1135 (7th Cir. 1993)

KANNE, CIRCUIT JUDGE.

Juan Garcia and Wilfredo Torres were arrested when police discovered two hundred and sixty pounds of marijuana in their truck's cab. Mr. Torres gave a full confession and told police that Mr. Garcia was ignorant of the marijuana's presence in the truck and Mr. Torres' plan to distribute it. Mr. Garcia also maintained his innocence. At trial, the district court excluded Mr. Torres' statements which exculpated Mr. Garcia, concluding that the requirements of Fed. R. Evid. 804(b)(3) were not satisfied. We find that the rule's requirements were met and reverse Mr. Garcia's conviction.

On January 24, 1991, Illinois State Trooper Jeff Gaither stopped a semi-truck headed north on I-55 near Bloomington, Illinois. Trooper Gaither stopped the tractor-trailer for a violation of the Motor Carrier Safety Code. Once stopped, Juan Garcia, the driver, got out of the truck to meet the officer. Trooper Gaither requested Mr. Garcia's driver's license as well as his logbook and bills of lading. Mr. Garcia produced a license but did not have a logbook or bills of lading. After Mr. Garcia told Trooper Gaither that he had a co-driver, he was instructed to return to the cab of the truck. When Mr. Garcia opened the door to get back in the truck, Trooper Gaither noticed a heavy scent of air freshener coming from the cab. At that time, the officer asked Wilfredo Torres, the co-driver, for his license and logbook; Mr. Torres produced both items. Trooper Gaither then directed Mr. Garcia out of the truck and into his squad car, informing Mr. Garcia that he was going to perform a motor carrier safety inspection. He asked for consent to search the truck's cab for Mr. Garcia's logbook. Mr. Garcia consented.

During this exchange, Trooper Percy arrived to assist. As instructed, Mr. Torres got out of the truck. Trooper Percy watched the two men while Trooper Gaither entered the truck's cab to perform the inspection and look for Mr. Garcia's logbook. Upon entering the cab, Trooper Gaither smelled a strong odor of marijuana. He summoned Trooper Percy, who also smelled the odor once he was inside the cab. The two officers observed four brown suitcases in the "sleeper" area of the cab. One suitcase's side pocket was slightly unzipped. Trooper Gaither could see duct tape through the opening, and when he squeezed the bag he felt "brick-like" objects which he believed were marijuana.

Following this discovery, Mr. Garcia and Mr. Torres were arrested and handcuffed. A K-9 unit was called to the scene, and performed a search of the cab that indicated the presence of an illegal substance. After this positive result, Trooper Gaither performed a full-scale search of the cab. In addition to the marijuana found in the suitcases, Trooper Gaither also discovered marijuana packages behind the bunks in the sleeping area. No evidence of personal marijuana use was found in the cab or the bunk area.

Special Agent Gerald Glowacki arrived at the scene, read Mr. Garcia his *Miranda* rights and took him to headquarters for questioning. Mr. Garcia told Agent Glowacki that he had been employed by the Tex-Mex trucking company, a Wisconsin based business, for about six months. He stated that two days earlier his truck had needed repairs in Milwaukee and that the company instructed him in the interim to join Mr.

Torres in Chicago as a co-driver on Mr. Torres' assigned run. Mr. Garcia understood from Mr. Torres that they were delivering a load of cheese to Dallas, Texas. Mr. Garcia also told Agent Glowacki that once they got to Dallas, Mr. Torres got them a hotel room and they went to dinner. During the meal, Mr. Torres left Mr. Garcia alone in the restaurant for about forty minutes. Both men then returned to the hotel; shortly thereafter, Mr. Torres left again. After his return, Mr. Torres acted disgusted with the company and told Mr. Garcia that they had to leave immediately to take the cheese to St. Louis, Missouri.

Mr. Garcia told Agent Glowacki that they soon left for Missouri, sharing the driving. Mr. Garcia stated that Mr. Torres took over the driving near the Missouri state line and that Mr. Garcia had slept through the rest of the trip until the men had reached Illinois. When Mr. Garcia awoke, he was told by Mr. Torres that they had delivered the cheese in St. Louis and were heading back to Wisconsin. At this time, Mr. Garcia started driving and shortly afterward was stopped by Trooper Gaither. Mr. Garcia admitted he had never seen the load of cheese or the bill of lading for the cheese during the trip. Mr. Garcia denied any knowledge that the truck contained marijuana and denied ever using marijuana.

Mr. Torres was also questioned following his arrest. He told Trooper Percy that the marijuana was his and that Mr. Garcia had nothing to do with the drugs. Next, Mr. Torres spoke with Agent Glowacki. After signing a waiver of his right to remain silent, Mr. Torres told Agent Glowacki that he had purchased the marijuana in Dallas and planned to sell it himself in Milwaukee. Mr. Torres stated: "I wanted to get rich quick. I took a chance and lost. Now I got to do the time, and I'm prepared to do it." Mr. Torres also told the agent that he had a six-year old conviction for drug sales in Milwaukee. Mr. Torres stated that his only drug associates were his brothers, and that Mr. Garcia was unaware of the marijuana. In a subsequent interview with Special Agent John Schaefer, Mr. Torres again maintained that Mr. Garcia did not know about the drugs in the truck. Mr. Torres also revealed that there had never been any cheese in the truck and thus no delivery in St. Louis.

Both Mr. Torres and Mr. Garcia were charged with knowingly and intentionally possessing over 100 kilograms of marijuana with the intent to distribute in violation of 21 U.S.C. §§ 841(a)(1) and 846. Prior to trial, both defendants moved to have the evidence seized from the truck suppressed as the fruit of an illegal search. Following a hearing, the district court ruled that the evidence was admissible and not the result of an unconstitutional search. After this adverse ruling, Mr. Torres pled guilty, reserving his right to appeal the legality of the search. Mr. Garcia proceeded to trial.

The day after Mr. Torres pled guilty, the government moved to suppress the portion of Mr. Torres' statements that exculpated Mr. Garcia. Following a hearing, the trial judge granted the government's motion. Preserving his objection, Mr. Garcia agreed to a stipulated statement to be read to the jury regarding Mr. Torres' confession. At trial, the jury was told that Torres had pled guilty to a charge that "he knowingly and intentionally possessed approximately 260 pounds of marijuana which he intended to distribute to others." The jury was also told that Mr. Torres "said that he was going to sell the marijuana in Milwaukee." However, the jury was not permitted to hear Mr. Torres' assertion that Mr. Garcia was not involved in the drug deal and unaware the truck contained marijuana.

At trial, the government's theory of the case was that Mr. Garcia was aware that he was transporting drugs for primarily two reasons: (1) Mr. Garcia must have known no cheese was ever carried or delivered because the trailer was empty, and (2) Mr. Garcia must have smelled marijuana in the cab because the police immediately noticed a strong odor of the drug. The government presented evidence consistent with the foregoing description of the stop and subsequent search of the truck. Government witnesses testified that a trucker would have known whether a trailer was empty or full merely by pulling it, and that a trucker would always have knowledge of his bills of lading since that is how he is paid. The government also introduced the marijuana found in the truck and displayed it to the jury. Despite defense counsel's objection, containers of marijuana remained open in the courtroom throughout the defendant's case-in- chief.

Mr. Garcia took the stand on his own behalf and denied any knowledge of the marijuana. He testified that he had worked for Tex-Mex for approximately six months and before that had driven a truck for his stepbrother in Texas. He stated that he had never used drugs or alcohol. Mr. Garcia also stated that he had passed a drug test when he acquired his chauffeur's license in 1989. He testified that he walked away from any group he knew was using marijuana and denied ever smelling marijuana.

Mr. Garcia also testified to the events of his trip with Mr. Torres. According to Mr. Garcia, he did not find the change in travel plans odd since Tex-Mex had changed his travel plans in the past. Further, he claimed that he did not see the contents of the trailer or the shipping papers because he was only the relief driver and the primary driver usually handles those aspects of trips. Mr. Garcia testified that, in his work experience, employees who questioned their superiors often lost their jobs; therefore, he kept quiet.

Mr. Garcia also testified that he had noticed the smell of air freshener in the cab, but did not find it peculiar since it was not unusually strong and many truckers use some type of freshener in their cabs. Mr. Garcia stated that he never smelled anything else "funny" in the cab, and that although he moved the suitcases off a bunk to sleep, he never opened them. Nor did he ask Mr. Torres about their contents since many truckers carry bags on long trips and he believed it was none of his business.

At the close of the trial, Mr. Garcia was convicted of possession with intent to distribute over 100 kilograms of marijuana in violation of 21 U.S.C. §§ 841(a)(1) and 846. The district judge refused to give Mr. Garcia a downward departure for being a minor or minimal participant and sentenced him to five years' imprisonment. This timely appeal followed.

On appeal, Mr. Garcia argues that the district court erred in excluding Mr. Torres' statements exculpating him. Because we believe it was error for the district court to refuse to admit the statements of Mr. Torres which exculpated Mr. Garcia, we reverse Mr. Garcia's conviction.

II.

As outlined above, following his arrest Mr. Torres made several statements to police admitting his involvement and stating that Mr. Garcia had no knowledge of the marijuana found in the truck. The trial court excluded these statements as hearsay not within any established exception. Mr. Garcia argues, as he did before the trial judge, that these statements fall under the "statements against interest" exception to hearsay, and thus are admissible evidence. Fed. R. Evid. 804(b)(3).

*   *   *

Federal Rule of Evidence 804(b)(3) permits certain testimony to be admitted at trial if the declarant is unavailable as a witness. . . . Mr. Garcia can prevail only if he satisfies the following three-part test: (1) Mr. Torres must have been unavailable as a witness, (2) Mr. Torres' statements exculpating Mr. Garcia must have been against Mr. Torres' penal interest, and (3) there must have been corroborating circumstances which clearly indicate the trustworthiness of Mr. Torres' statements. [*United States v. Garcia*, 897 F.2d 1413, 1420 (7th Cir. 1990)].

Both parties agree that the first two prongs of the test are satisfied. Mr. Torres invoked his Fifth Amendment privilege and refused to testify because his appeal regarding the constitutionality of the truck's search was pending. *See id.* (witness' refusal to testify makes him an unavailable witness). In addition, Mr. Torres' statements admitting the marijuana was his and stating that Mr. Garcia knew nothing about it clearly exposed him to criminal liability and were against his penal interest. Thus, the primary dispute is whether corroborating circumstances exist which clearly indicate the trustworthiness of Mr. Torres' statements exculpating Mr. Garcia.

Although Rule 804(b)(3) does not describe exactly what type of corroborating circumstances clearly indicate trustworthiness, the case law identifies some circumstances particularly relevant to our inquiry. In *United States v. Silverstein*, 732 F.2d 1338, 1346 (7th Cir. 1984), *cert. denied*, 469 U.S. 1111 (1985), we looked at the relationship between the confessing party and the exculpated party and concluded that it was likely that the confessor was fabricating his story for the benefit of a friend. Thus, if the two involved parties do not have a close relationship, one important corroborating circumstance exists.

In *Garcia*, we identified two additional factors which supported the trustworthiness of the testimony: (1) the confessor made a voluntary statement after being advised of his *Miranda* rights, and (2) there was no evidence that his statement was made in order to curry favor with authorities. 897 F.2d at 1421.

A review of the record reveals that these same factors are present in the instant case. There was no evidence that Mr. Torres and Mr. Garcia were friends. In fact, from the record it appears that the two men had only spoken briefly at work on a few occasions. Further, Mr. Torres voluntarily made the statements inculpating himself and exculpating Mr. Garcia shortly after being advised of his *Miranda* rights. Nothing in the record suggests that his statements were made to curry favor with authorities. Finally, we note that Mr. Torres repeated the exculpatory statements on several occasions and inculpated *only himself* when he pled guilty, under oath, before the trial judge. *Cf. United States v. Moore*, 936 F.2d 1508, 1517 (7th Cir.), *cert. denied*, 112 S. Ct. 607 (1991) (requisite corroborating circumstances were not present since the declarant recanted much of his unsworn post-arrest statement under oath during a court proceeding).

Despite the fact that this case mirrors others where we have held that the requisite circumstances were present, the government contends that Rule 804(b)(3) has not been satisfied. The government argues that Mr. Torres' statements to police, when viewed as a whole, contain several inconsistencies that cast doubt on their veracity. The government claims these inconsistencies demonstrate that Mr. Torres was protecting his drug source, and thus was probably protecting Mr. Garcia as well. We do not find this argument convincing. The inconsistencies relate to the provider and purchase price of the marijuana and are relatively minor.

The government's real complaint is that Mr. Torres would not identify his drug source. This is a very different matter from exculpating Mr. Garcia. Mr. Torres could have several reasons for refusing to reveal his source — in fact, one of his statements indicated that he was afraid he would be killed if he told the police from whom he obtained the marijuana. Moreover, the fact that Mr. Torres protected his source, who may have been a friend, does not mean that he was protecting Mr. Garcia, a virtual stranger.

The government points to another statement by Mr. Torres in an attempt to demonstrate that the requisite circumstances were not present. In addition to telling police that Mr. Garcia had nothing to do with the marijuana, Mr. Torres also said that Mr. Garcia had to know something was "wrong," referring to the presence of the marijuana-laden suitcases in the cab. We believe this statement only strengthens the trustworthiness of Mr. Torres' other statements. The fact that, in Mr. Torres' opinion, Mr. Garcia should have known something was "wrong" shows that Mr. Torres did not tell Mr. Garcia about the drugs in the truck. Therefore, we do not believe that this statement detracts from the circumstances which support the reliability of Mr. Torres' statements exculpating Mr. Garcia.

After examining the government's arguments we are left with the impression that the government misconstrues the requirements of Fed. R. Evid. 804(b)(3). In its brief, the government argued that Mr. Torres' statements exculpating Mr. Garcia were not clearly corroborated. Rule 804(b)(3) does not require that the statements themselves be clearly corroborated. Rather, the rule requires "corroborating circumstances [that] clearly indicate the trustworthiness of the statements." Fed. R. Evid. 804(b)(3). Moreover, the corroboration requirement of 804(b)(3) is a preliminary question as to the admissibility of evidence, not an ultimate determination as to the weight to be given such evidence. The district judge does not need to be completely convinced that exculpatory statements are true prior to their admission. Such a high burden was not intended by the corroboration requirement of 804(b)(3). The district court must find only that sufficient corroborating circumstances exist and then permit the jury to make the ultimate determination concerning the truth of the statements.

As described above, sufficient corroborating circumstances exist to clearly indicate the reliability of Mr. Torres' statements exculpating Mr. Garcia. There is no indication that Mr. Torres had any motive to fabricate the statements, a prospect the corroboration requirement was designed to prevent. "The requirement of corroboration should be construed in such a manner as to effectuate its purpose of circumventing fabrication." Fed. R. Evid. 804 advisory committee's note. Therefore, we hold that the requisite corroborating circumstances exist in this case and that the trial court's exclusion of Mr. Torres' statements exculpating Mr. Garcia was clearly erroneous.

* * *

III.

Because the trial court erred in granting the government's Motion to Suppress Mr. Torres' statements exculpating Mr. Garcia, Mr. Garcia's conviction is REVERSED and the case is REMANDED to the district court.

NOTES AND QUESTIONS

1. Under Fed. R. Evid. 804(b)(3), statements offered to exculpate the defendant require "corroborating circumstances [that] clearly indicate the trustworthiness of the statements." Does this require that the statements themselves be independently corroborated? In other words, in the absence of corroborating evidence, are statements offered to exculpate the accused nonetheless admissible if the surrounding circumstances establish their trustworthiness? *See United States v. Bumpass*, 60 F.3d 1099, 1102 (4th Cir. 1995) ("The rule requires not a determination that the declarant is credible, but a finding that the circumstances clearly indicate that the statement was not fabricated."). In *United States v. Garcia*, what facts or surrounding circumstances establish that Torres' statements exculpating Garcia were sufficiently trustworthy?

2. The courts have identified several factors that are relevant in determining whether sufficient corroboration exists to justify admitting a statement under the rule. In *Bumpass*, 60 F.3d at 1102, the court considered the following factors:

(1) whether the declarant had at the time of making the statement pled guilty or was still exposed to prosecution for making the statement, (2) the declarant's motive in making the statement and whether there was a reason for the declarant to lie, (3) whether the declarant repeated the statement and did so consistently, (4) the party or parties to whom the statement was made, (5) the relationship of the declarant with the accused, and (6) the nature and strength of independent evidence relevant to the conduct in question.

See also United States v. Noel, 938 F.2d 685, 688 (6th Cir. 1991); *United States v. Slaughter*, 891 F.2d 691, 698 (9th Cir. 1989).

[4]   Forfeiture by Wrongdoing

At common law, a defendant who by his own wrongful conduct prevented a witness from testifying at trial forfeited the right of confrontation. *See Reynolds v. United States*, 98 U.S. 145 (1878). According to the Supreme Court: "[T]he common-law authorities justified the wrongful-procurement rule by invoking the maxim that a defendant should not be permitted to benefit from his own wrong." *Giles v. California*, 128 S. Ct. 2678, 2686 (2008). *See also* G. GILBERT LAW OF EVIDENCE 140–41 (1756) (if a witness was prevented from testifying by the defendant's wrongdoing, the witness's out-of-court statements would be admitted into evidence because a defendant "shall never be admitted to shelter himself by such evil Practices on the Witness, that being to give him Advantage of his own Wrong"). Forfeiture by wrongdoing is essentially an equitable doctrine that prevents a defendant from benefitting from his wrongful acts. The common-law forfeiture rule "was aimed at removing the otherwise powerful incentive for defendants to intimidate, bribe, and kill witnesses against them-in other words, it is grounded in 'the ability of courts to protect the integrity of their proceedings.' " *Giles v. California*, 128 S. Ct. at 2691 (*quoting Davis v. Washington*, 547 U.S. 813, 834 (2006)).

In *Crawford v. Washington*, 541 U.S. 36 (2004), the Supreme Court declared that statements made by an out-of-court declarant whose absence was caused by the defendant's wrongful conduct are admissible as an exception to the Sixth Amendment right of confrontation. *Id.* at 62 ("the rule of forfeiture by wrongdoing (which we accept) extinguishes confrontation claims on essentially equitable grounds"). *See also Davis v. Washington*, 547 U.S. at 833 ("one who obtains the absence of a witness by wrongdoing forfeits the constitutional right to confrontation"). Forfeiture by wrongdoing is codified in Rule 804(b)(6) of the Federal Rules of Evidence, which excludes from the hearsay rule "[a] statement offered against a party that has engaged or acquiesced in wrongdoing that was intended to, and did, procure the unavailability of the declarant as a witness." FRE 804(b)(6). However, in order to fall within the exception to the Sixth

Amendment's Confrontation Clause is it sufficient to merely show that the defendant wrongfully caused the absence of a witness or must the proponent of the statement further prove that the defendant intended to prevent the witness from testifying at trial? Stated another way, is forfeiture by wrongdoing properly invoked only when the defendant caused the witness's absence and did so with the specific intent of preventing her from testifying at trial? This precise issue was the subject of litigation in *Giles v. California*, 128 S. Ct. 2678 (2008).

GILES v. CALIFORNIA
128 S. Ct. 2678 (2008)

JUSTICE SCALIA delivered the opinion of the Court, except as to Part II-D-2.

We consider whether a defendant forfeits his Sixth Amendment right to confront a witness against him when a judge determines that a wrongful act by the defendant made the witness unavailable to testify at trial.

I.

On September 29, 2002, petitioner Dwayne Giles shot his ex-girlfriend, Brenda Avie, outside the garage of his grandmother's house. No witness saw the shooting, but Giles' niece heard what transpired from inside the house. She heard Giles and Avie speaking in conversational tones. Avie then yelled "Granny" several times and a series of gunshots sounded. Giles' niece and grandmother ran outside and saw Giles standing near Avie with a gun in his hand. Avie, who had not been carrying a weapon, had been shot six times. One wound was consistent with Avie's holding her hand up at the time she was shot, another was consistent with her having turned to her side, and a third was consistent with her having been shot while lying on the ground. Giles fled the scene after the shooting. He was apprehended by police about two weeks later and charged with murder.

At trial, Giles testified that he had acted in self-defense. Giles described Avie as jealous, and said he knew that she had once shot a man, that he had seen her threaten people with a knife, and that she had vandalized his home and car on prior occasions. He said that on the day of the shooting, Avie came to his grandmother's house and threatened to kill him and his new girlfriend, who had been at the house earlier. He said that Avie had also threatened to kill his new girlfriend when Giles and Avie spoke on the phone earlier that day. Giles testified that after Avie threatened him at the house, he went into the garage and retrieved a gun, took the safety off, and started walking toward the back door of the house. He said that Avie charged at him, and that he was afraid she had something in her hand. According to Giles, he closed his eyes and fired several shots, but did not intend to kill Avie.

Prosecutors sought to introduce statements that Avie had made to a police officer responding to a domestic-violence report about three weeks before the shooting. Avie, who was crying when she spoke, told the officer that Giles had accused her of having an affair, and that after the two began to argue, Giles grabbed her by the shirt, lifted her off the floor, and began to choke her. According to Avie, when she broke free and fell to the floor, Giles punched her in the face and head, and after she broke free again, he opened a folding knife, held it about three feet away from her, and threatened to kill her if he found her cheating on him. Over Giles' objection, the trial court admitted these statements into evidence under a provision of California law that permits admission of out-of-court statements describing the infliction or threat of physical injury on a declarant when the declarant is unavailable to testify at trial and the prior statements are deemed trustworthy. Cal. Evid.Code Ann. § 1370 (West Supp.2008).

A jury convicted Giles of first-degree murder. He appealed. While his appeal was pending, this Court decided in *Crawford v. Washington*, 541 U.S. 36, 53–54 (2004), that the Confrontation Clause requires that a defendant have the opportunity to confront the witnesses who give testimony against him, except in cases where an exception to the confrontation right was recognized at the time of the founding. The California Court of Appeal held that the admission of Avie's unconfronted statements at Giles' trial did not violate the Confrontation Clause as construed by *Crawford* because *Crawford* recognized a doctrine of forfeiture by wrongdoing. It concluded that Giles had forfeited his right to confront Avie because he had committed the murder for which he was on trial, and because his intentional criminal act made Avie unavailable to testify. The California Supreme Court affirmed on the same ground. We granted certiorari.

II.

The Sixth Amendment provides that "[i]n all criminal prosecutions, the accused shall enjoy the right . . . to be confronted with the witnesses against him." The Amendment contemplates that a witness who makes testimonial statements admitted against a defendant will ordinarily be present at trial for cross-examination, and that if the witness is unavailable, his prior testimony will be introduced only if the defendant had a prior opportunity to cross-examine him. The State does not dispute here, and we accept without deciding, that Avie's statements accusing Giles of assault were testimonial. But it maintains (as did the California Supreme Court) that the Sixth Amendment did not prohibit prosecutors from introducing the statements because an exception to the confrontation guarantee permits the use of a witness's unconfronted testimony if a judge finds, as the judge did in this case, that the defendant committed a wrongful act that rendered the witness unavailable to testify at trial. We held in *Crawford* that the Confrontation Clause is "most naturally read as a reference to the right of confrontation at common law, admitting only those exceptions established at the time of the founding." *Id.*, at 54. We therefore ask whether the theory of forfeiture by wrongdoing accepted by the California Supreme Court is a founding-era exception to the confrontation right.

A.

We have previously acknowledged that two forms of testimonial statements were admitted at common law even though they were unconfronted. The first of these were declarations made by a speaker who was both on the brink of death and aware that he was dying. *See, e.g., King v. Woodcock*, 1 Leach 500, 501–504, 168 Eng. Rep. 352, 353–354 (1789); *State v. Moody*, 3 N.C. 31 (Super. L. & Eq. 1798); *United States v. Veitch*, 28 F. Cas. 367, 367–368 (No. 16,614) (CC DC 1803); *King v. Commonwealth*, 4 Va. 78, 80–81 (Gen.Ct.1817). Avie did not make the unconfronted statements admitted at Giles' trial when she was dying, so her statements do not fall within this historic exception.

A second common-law doctrine, which we will refer to as forfeiture by wrongdoing, permitted the introduction of statements of a witness who was "detained" or "kept away" by the "means or procurement" of the defendant. [citations omitted]. The doctrine has roots in the 1666 decision in *Lord Morley's Case*, at which judges concluded that a witness's having been "detained by the means or procurement of the prisoner," provided a basis to read testimony previously given at a coroner's inquest. 6 How. St. Tr., at 770–771. Courts and commentators also concluded that wrongful procurement of a witness's absence was among the grounds for admission of statements made at bail and committal hearings conducted under the Marian statutes, which directed justices of the peace to take the statements of felony suspects and the persons bringing the suspects before the magistrate, and to certify those statements to the court. This class of confronted statements was also admissible if the witness who made them was dead or unable to travel.

The terms used to define the scope of the forfeiture rule suggest that the exception applied only when the defendant engaged in conduct *designed* to prevent the witness from testifying. The rule required the witness to have been "kept back" or "detained" by "means or procurement" of the defendant. Although there are definitions of "procure" and "procurement" that would merely require that a defendant have caused the witness's absence, other definitions would limit the causality to one that was *designed* to bring about the result "procured." *See* 2 N. Webster, An American Dictionary of the English Language (1828) (defining "procure" as "to *contrive* and effect" (emphasis added)); *ibid.* (defining "procure" as "to get; to gain; to obtain; as by request, loan, effort, labor or purchase"); 12 Oxford English Dictionary 559 (2d ed.1989) (def.I(3)) (defining "procure" as "[t]o contrive or devise with care (an action or proceeding); to endeavour to cause or bring about (mostly something evil) *to* or *for* a person"). Similarly, while the term "means" could sweep in all cases in which a defendant caused a witness to fail to appear, it can also connote that a defendant forfeits confrontation rights when he uses an intermediary for the purpose of making a witness absent. *See* 9 *id.*, at 516 ("[A] person who intercedes for another or uses influence in order to bring about a desired result"); N. Webster, An American Dictionary of the English Language 822 (1869) ("That through which, or by the help of which, an end is attained").

Cases and treatises of the time indicate that a purpose-based definition of these terms governed. A number of them said that prior testimony was admissible when a witness was kept away by the defendant's "means and contrivance." *See* 1 J. Chitty, A Practical Treatise on the Criminal Law 81 (1816) ("kept away by the means and contrivance of the prisoner"); S. Phillipps, A Treatise on the Law of Evidence 165 (1814) ("kept out of the way by the means and contrivance of the prisoner"); *Drayton v. Wells*, 10 S.C.L. 409, 411 (S.C. 1819) ("kept away by the contrivance of the opposite party"). This phrase requires that the defendant have schemed to bring about the absence from trial that he "contrived." Contrivance is commonly defined as the act of "inventing, devising or planning," 1 Webster, *supra*, at 47, "ingeniously endeavoring the accomplishment of anything," "the bringing to pass by planning, scheming, or stratagem," or "[a]daption of means to an end; design, intention," 3 Oxford English Dictionary, *supra*, at 850.

An 1858 treatise made the purpose requirement more explicit still, stating that the forfeiture rule applied when a witness "had been kept out of the way by the prisoner, or by some one on the prisoner's behalf, *in order to prevent him from giving evidence against him.*" E. Powell, The Practice of the Law of Evidence 166 (1st ed. 1858) (emphasis added). The wrongful-procurement exception was invoked in a manner consistent with this definition. We are aware of no case in which the exception was invoked although the defendant had not engaged in conduct designed to prevent a witness from testifying, such as offering a bribe.

B.

The manner in which the rule was applied makes plain that unconfronted testimony would *not* be admitted without a showing that the defendant intended to prevent a witness from testifying. In cases where the evidence suggested that the defendant had caused a person to be absent, but had not done so to prevent the person from testifying- as in the typical murder case involving accusatorial statements by the victim-the testimony was excluded unless it was confronted or fell within the dying-declaration exception. Prosecutors do not appear to have even *argued* that the judge could admit the unconfronted statements because the defendant committed the murder for which he was on trial.

Consider *King v. Woodcock*. William Woodcock was accused of killing his wife, Silvia, who had been beaten and left near death. A Magistrate took Silvia Woodcock's account of the crime, under oath, and she died about 48 hours later. The judge stated that "[g]reat as a crime of this nature must always appear to be, yet the inquiry into it must proceed upon the rules of evidence." 1 Leach, at 500. Aside from testimony given at trial in the presence of the prisoner, the judge said, there were "two other species which are admitted by law: The one is the dying declaration of a person who has received a fatal blow; the other is the examination of a prisoner, and the depositions of the witnesses who may be produced against him" taken under the Marian bail and committal statutes. *Id.*, at 501. (footnote omitted). Silvia Woodcock's statement could not be admitted pursuant to the Marian statutes because it was unconfronted-the defendant had not been brought before the examining Magistrate and "the prisoner therefore had no opportunity of contradicting the facts it contains." *Id.*, at 502. Thus, the statements were admissible only if the witness "apprehended that she was in such a state of mortality as would inevitably oblige her soon to answer before her Maker for the truth or falsehood of her assertions." *Id.*, at 503. (footnote omitted). Depending on the account one credits, the court either instructed the jury to consider the statements only if Woodcock was "in fact under the apprehension of death," *id.*, at 504, or determined for itself that Woodcock was "quietly resigned and submitting to her fate" and admitted her statements into evidence, 1 E. East, Pleas of the Crown 356 (1803).

King v. Dingler, 2 Leach 561 (1791), applied the same test to exclude unconfronted statements by a murder victim. George Dingler was charged with killing his wife Jane, who suffered multiple stab wounds that left her in the hospital for 12 days before she died. The day after the stabbing, a Magistrate took Jane Dingler's deposition-as in *Woodcock*, under oath-"of the facts and circumstances which had attended the outrage committed upon her." 2 Leach, at 561. George Dingler's attorney argued that the statements did not qualify as dying declarations and were not admissible Marian examinations because they were not taken in the presence of the prisoner, with the result that the defendant did not "have, as he is entitled to have, the benefit of cross-examination." *Id.*, at 562. The prosecutor agreed, but argued the deposition should still be admitted because "it was the best evidence that the nature of the case would afford." *Id.*, at 563. Relying on *Woodcock*, the court "refused to receive the examination into evidence." *Id.*, at 563.

Many other cases excluded victims' statements when there was insufficient evidence that the witness was aware he was about to die. *See Thomas John's Case*, 1 East 357, 358 (P.C. 1790); *Welbourn's Case*, 1 East 358, 360 (P.C. 1792); *United States v. Woods*, 28 F. Cas. 762, 763 (No. 16,760) (CC DC 1834); *Lewis v. State*, 17 Miss. 115, 120 (1847); *Montgomery v. State*, 11 Ohio 424, 425–426 (1842); *Nelson v. State*, 26 Tenn. 542, 543 (1847); *Smith v. State*, 28 Tenn. 9, 23 (1848). Courts in all these cases did not even consider admitting the statements on the ground that the defendant's crime was to blame for the witness's absence-even when the evidence establishing that was overwhelming. . . .

*   *   *

The State and the dissent note that common-law authorities justified the wrongful-procurement rule by invoking the maxim that a defendant should not be permitted to benefit from his own wrong. *See, e.g.*, G. Gilbert, Law of Evidence 140–141 (1756) (if a witness was "detained and kept back from appearing by the means and procurement" testimony would be read because a defendant "shall never be admitted to shelter himself by such evil Practices on the Witness, that being to give him Advantage of his own Wrong"). But as the evidence amply shows, the "wrong" and the "evil Practices" to which these statements referred was conduct *designed* to prevent a witness from testifying. The absence of a forfeiture rule covering this sort of conduct would create an intolerable incentive for defendants to bribe, intimidate, or even kill witnesses against them. There is nothing mysterious about courts' refusal to carry the rationale further. The notion that judges may strip the defendant of a right that the Constitution deems essential to a fair trial, on the basis of a prior *judicial* assessment that the defendant is guilty as charged, does not sit well with the right to trial by jury.

It is akin, one might say, to "dispensing with jury trial because a defendant is obviously guilty." *Crawford*, 541 U.S., at 62.

C.

Not only was the State's proposed exception to the right of confrontation plainly not an "exceptio[n] established at the time of the founding," *id.*, at 54, it is not established in American jurisprudence *since* the founding. American courts never-prior to 1985-invoked forfeiture outside the context of deliberate witness tampering.

This Court first addressed forfeiture in *Reynolds v. United States*, 98 U.S. 145 (1879), where, after hearing testimony that suggested the defendant had kept his wife away from home so that she could not be subpoenaed to testify, the trial court permitted the government to introduce testimony of the defendant's wife from the defendant's prior trial. *See id.*, at 148–150. On appeal, the Court held that admission of the statements did not violate the right of the defendant to confront witnesses at trial, because when a witness is absent by the defendant's "wrongful procurement," the defendant "is in no condition to assert that his constitutional rights have been violated" if "their evidence is supplied in some lawful way." *Id.*, at 158. *Reynolds* invoked broad forfeiture principles to explain its holding. The decision stated, for example, that "[t]he Constitution does not guarantee an accused person against the legitimate consequences of his own wrongful acts," *ibid.*, and that the wrongful-procurement rule "has its foundation" in the principle that no one should be permitted to take advantage of his wrong, and is "the outgrowth of a maxim based on the principles of common honesty," *id.*, at 159.

Reynolds relied on these maxims (as the common-law authorities had done) to be sure. But it relied on them (as the common-law authorities had done) to admit prior testimony in a case where the defendant had engaged in wrongful conduct designed to prevent a witness's testimony. The Court's opinion indicated that it was adopting the common-law rule. It cited leading common-law cases-*Lord Morley's Case, Harrison's Case*, and *Scaife*-described itself as "content with" the "long-established usage" of the forfeiture principle, and admitted prior confronted statements under circumstances where admissibility was open to no doubt under *Lord Morley's Case.*

*   *   *

In 1997, this Court approved a Federal Rule of Evidence, entitled "Forfeiture by wrongdoing," which applies only when the defendant "engaged or acquiesced in wrongdoing that was intended to, and did, procure the unavailability of the declarant as a witness." Fed. Rule of Evid. 804(b)(6). We have described this as a rule "which codifies the forfeiture doctrine." *Davis v. Washington*, 547 U.S. 813, 833 (2006). Every commentator we are aware of has concluded the requirement of intent "means that the exception applies only if the defendant has in mind the particular purpose of making the witness unavailable." 5 C. Mueller & L. Kirkpatrick, Federal Evidence § 8:134, p. 235 (3d ed.2007); 5 J. Weinstein & M. Berger, Weinstein's Federal Evidence § 804.03 [7][b], p. 804-32 (J. McLaughlin ed., 2d ed.2008); 2 S. Brown, McCormick on Evidence 176 (6th ed.2006). The commentators come out this way because the dissent's claim that knowledge is sufficient to show intent is emphatically *not* the modern view. *See* 1 W. LaFave, Substantive Criminal Law § 5.2, p. 340 (2d ed.2003).

In sum, our interpretation of the common-law forfeiture rule is supported by (1) the most natural reading of the language used at common law; (2) the absence of common-law cases *admitting* prior statements on a forfeiture theory when the defendant had not engaged in conduct designed to prevent a witness from testifying; (3) the common law's uniform exclusion of unconfronted inculpatory testimony by murder victims (except testimony given with awareness of impending death) in the innumerable cases in which the defendant was on trial for killing the victim, but was not shown to have done so for the purpose of preventing testimony; (4) a subsequent history in which the dissent's broad forfeiture theory has not been applied. The first two and the last are highly persuasive; the third is in our view conclusive.

*   *   *

The state courts in this case did not consider the intent of the defendant because they found that irrelevant to application of the forfeiture doctrine. This view of the law was error, but the court is free to consider evidence of the defendant's intent on remand.

*   *   *

We decline to approve an exception to the Confrontation Clause unheard of at the time of the founding or for 200 years thereafter. The judgment of the California Supreme Court is vacated, and the case is remanded for further proceedings not inconsistent with this opinion.

NOTES AND QUESTIONS

(1) *The Scope of Application of Forfeiture by Wrongdoing.* Should forfeiture by wrongdoing be applied narrowly or broadly? In *Giles*, the majority contends that the wrongful-procurement rule should apply only where the defendant caused the declarant's absence *and* did so with the intent to prevent the witness from testifying at trial, reasoning that the forfeiture rule should be construed consistent with its common law application. In support of a narrow application of the rule, the majority opines: "It is not the role of courts to extrapolate from the words of the Sixth Amendment to the values behind it, and then to enforce its guarantees only to the extent they serve (in the courts' views) those underlying values." *Giles v. California*, 128 S. Ct., at 2692. The dissent argues, on the other hand, that the forfeiture exception should reach every case

in which a defendant committed wrongful acts that caused the victim's absence. *Id.* at 2698–99 (Breyer, J., dissenting, joined by Stevens and Kennedy, JJ.). In the dissent's view, a narrow application of the forfeiture rule permits the defendant to take advantage of his wrongful acts, where he caused the victim's absence, but the government is unable to prove that he was motivated by the intent to prevent the declarant from testifying at trial. If H, by killing W, is able to keep W's testimony out of court, hasn't H successfully "take[n] advantage of his own wrong." *Reynolds v. United States*, 98 U.S., 145, 159 (1979). Who has the better argument, the majority or the dissent?

(2) ***Related Areas of Law.*** The dissent argues that related areas of law prohibit the defendant from benefitting from his wrongful acts. For example, under the common law, a life insurance beneficiary who feloniously murders the insured, irrespective of the purpose, is prohibited from recovering under the policy. *Giles v. California*, 128 S. Ct., at 2697. Similarly, a beneficiary of a will who murders the testator is prohibited from inheriting under the will. *Id.* Do you find the dissent's argument compelling? Are the examples cited by the dissent distinguisable from the case at hand, where the defendant has a constitutionally protected right to effective cross examination of the witnesses against him?

(3) ***Justice Scalia's Textualist Argument.*** Do you agree with Justice Scalia's argument that the word "procurement" implies purpose or motive? *See Giles v. California*, 128 S. Ct., at 2683–84. The dissent argues that although a person may "procure" a result purposefully, a person may also "procure" a result by causing it, as the word "procure" can mean "cause," "bring about," and "effect," all words that do not require a particular motive or purpose. *Id.* at 2701 (Breyer, J., dissenting, joined by Stevens and Kennedy, JJ.).

(4) ***Process for Determining the Defendant's Motive.*** Assuming that the victim's statements are testimonial in nature, what is the process for determining whether such out-of-court declarations fall within the forfeiture by wrongdoing exception to the Sixth Amendment right of confrontation? Does the process involve a mini-trial on the merits, requiring the trial judge to find that the defendant procured the victim's absence (he killed her) with the intent to thwart the judicial process (to prevent her from testifying against him)? Is motive, rather than intent the dispositive factor? Does the majority's ruling create serious practical evidentiary problems? Are these concerns alleviated somewhat by application of a standard of proof by a preponderance of the evidence, rather than proof beyond a reasonable doubt? Federal Rule of Evidence 104(a) permits district courts to resolve preliminary questions regarding the admissibility of evidence by a preponderance of the evidence. *See Bourjaily v. United States*, 483 U.S. 171, 175–76 (1987) (holding that preliminary questions under Federal Rule of Evidence 801(d)(2)(E) may be resolved by preponderance of the evidence).

(5) ***Rebuttable Presumption.*** Should the law recognize a rebuttable presumption that the defendant acted with the "purpose" of preventing the victim from testifying based on evidence of a history of domestic abuse and violence?

(6) ***Testimonial Statements.*** In *Giles*, the majority stated that "[t]he State does not dispute here, and we accept without deciding, that Avie's statements accusing Giles of assault were testimonial." *Giles v. California*, 128 S. Ct., at 2682. The Confrontation Clause does not apply to out-of-court statements unless they are the equivalent of statements made at trial by a witness. Are Avie's disputed statements testimonial in

nature? If not, admission of such statements does not offend the Sixth Amendment Confrontation Clause.

(7) ***Prior Confronted Statements.*** The dissent maintains that the forfeiture rule applies only to confronted testimony. As a general proposition, aren't prior confronted statements by witnesses who are unavailable at trial admissible whether or not the defendant was responsible for their unavailability? *See Giles v. California*, 128 S. Ct., at 2691 (Breyer, J., dissenting, joined by Stevens and Kennedy, JJ.). *Crawford* bars the admission of testimonial statements only when the defendant did not have a prior opportunity for confrontation and the declarant is unavailable to testify. *Crawford v. Washington*, 541 U.S. 36, 68 (2004).

Chapter 10

IMPEACHMENT

A. INTRODUCTION: BOLSTERING, IMPEACHMENT AND REHABILITATION IN A CRIMINAL CASE[1]

One of the most important issues an attorney faces in the courtroom is how witnesses will be perceived by the jury. Because a large part of the evidence in a criminal trial is testimonial, the credibility of witnesses will most certainly be called into question. Accordingly, attorneys strive to enhance the credibility of their witnesses and diminish the credibility of their opponents' witnesses. Credibility evidence can, however, distract the jury from the central issues in a criminal case. Realizing this danger, courts have developed a number of restrictions on evidence that is offered solely to increase or decrease a witnesses' credibility in the eyes of the jurors. This chapter is an examination of the regulation of credibility evidence in criminal cases.

The process of enhancing and diminishing a witness' credibility occurs in recognizable stages. In chronological order, these stages are bolstering, impeachment, and rehabilitation. Evidentiary rules and restrictions have developed to govern credibility evidence at each of these stages. Bolstering, which is the first stage of credibility analysis, involves an attempt by the proponent of the witness to increase the credibility of his or her witness *before the witness' credibility is ever attacked*. The second stage, impeachment, is an attack on a witness in order to discredit the witness and/or the witness' testimony. The final stage is rehabilitation. Rehabilitation is an attempt by the proponent of a witness to repair his or her witness' credibility *after the witness' credibility has been attacked*.

The materials that follow focus on recurring problems with credibility evidence at each of these three stages. The examination begins with bolstering in a situation not uncommon in criminal cases: the calling of a plea bargain witness by the prosecution.

B. BOLSTERING THE CREDIBILITY OF THE PROSECUTION'S WITNESS

[1] The Plea Bargain Witness

The common law rule (and the rule that is still followed in most situations) is that bolstering is not allowed. *See* CHARLES T. MCCORMICK, 1 MCCORMICK ON EVIDENCE § 47 n.1, at 188 (John W. Strong, ed., 5th ed. 1999). The rationale is that it would be a waste of time to support a witness who has not yet been (and who may never be) impeached. The Federal Rules of Evidence address bolstering evidence in Rule 608:

(a) *Opinion and reputation evidence of character.* The credibility of a witness may be attacked or supported by evidence in the form of opinion or reputation,

---

[1] *See generally* 1 COURTROOM CRIMINAL EVIDENCE §§ 701–721, at 267–333 (4th ed. 2005).

but subject to these limitations: (1) the evidence may refer only to character for truthfulness or untruthfulness, and (2) *evidence of truthful character is admissible only after the character of the witness for truthfulness has been attacked* by opinion or reputation evidence or otherwise. (Emphasis added).

Rule 608 mirrors the just-mentioned common law prohibition on bolstering, but Rule 608 only applies to opinion or reputation evidence that bolsters the witness' character. Since there are ways of bolstering a witness' credibility without calling a reputation or opinion witness, Rule 608 does not respond to all situations where a party may attempt to bolster the credibility of his or her witness. To illustrate, consider the following hypothetical. Assume that three men are arrested and charged with a crime. Because the case is weak and there are no eyewitnesses, the police and the prosecutor fear that they will not be able to convict any of the three unless one of them testifies and admits his guilt while implicating the others. The problem, of course, is that none of them will testify. To "persuade" one to testify the prosecution enters into an agreement. The agreement provides that in return for truthful testimony, and the defendant passing a polygraph examination, the prosecution agrees to not prosecute the accused for crimes committed. Further, the agreement provides that if the accused provides false testimony he can be charged with perjury and have the original charges against him reinstated.

The prosecution knows that the defense, at trial, will try to impeach their plea bargain witness by suggesting that his testimony is nothing more than what the prosecution wanted him to say — coerced by the promise of not being prosecuted. To blunt this attack, can the prosecution bolster its witness, i.e., ask their plea bargain witness — on direct examination — if he has taken and passed a lie detector test? If not, can the prosecution at least ask the witness if he is receiving immunity from prosecution in return for "truthful" testimony, and that he faces reinstatement of charges for lying? If so, how does this comport with the general ban on bolstering?

UNITED STATES v. COSENTINO
844 F.2d 30 (2d Cir. 1988)

MESKILL, CIRCUIT JUDGE:

This is an appeal from a judgment of conviction entered in the United States District Court for the Southern District of New York, Kram, J., following a jury trial. Defendant-appellant Louis Cosentino was convicted of extortion . . . and use of the mails to facilitate bribery. . . . Cosentino challenges the admission of witness cooperation agreements during direct testimony of government witnesses. . . . For reasons that follow, we affirm.

Defendant-appellant Cosentino was a Project Superintendent for the New York City Housing Authority. As a superintendent, he had limited authority to purchase materials not available through the Housing Authority by placing "certificate for payment" orders with private vendors. Although Authority rules prohibited superintendents from placing more than $500 in such orders with any single vendor, Cosentino allegedly evaded this limitation by splitting orders among multiple companies owned by each vendor. He allegedly employed the same stratagem to circumvent another Authority rule that proscribed placement of more than one order with any single vendor in any thirty day period. According to the government, Cosentino solicited and received kickbacks from the vendors with whom he placed certificate for payment orders.

At trial, the government's case rested almost exclusively on the testimony of Alan Rappaport and Irving Eisenberg, two vendors who had dealt with Cosentino. They testified about the kickback scheme, explaining that Authority superintendents in general and Cosentino in particular placed orders only with vendors who kicked back a percentage of each order to the superintendent. There was also testimony that Cosentino received a $1,000 loan that he "worked off" by placing $10,000 worth of certificate for payment orders without demanding his usual ten percent kickback.

Cosentino took the stand on his own behalf to explain that he had split orders only in order to obtain necessary supplies that could not readily be procured through the Authority. He had evaded the rules, he said, to provide better service to the projects under his supervision. He also explained that he had paid the loan back out of his own pocket and emphatically denied soliciting or accepting bribes.

Because the case against Cosentino depended so heavily on the testimony of Rappaport and Eisenberg, their credibility was the central battleground of the trial. As participants in the kickback scheme who had agreed to testify in return for guilty pleas on reduced charges, they were especially vulnerable to impeachment. As a result, both the prosecuting Assistant United States Attorney (AUSA) and Cosentino's counsel highlighted credibility issues in their respective opening statements to the jury.

In opening, the prosecutor outlined the case against Cosentino, alluding specifically to the witnesses' background and cooperation agreements as follows:

> I will tell you now about Rappaport and Eisenberg, the two vendors you will hear testify in this trial. They were not innocent victims. They acknowledge their participation in corrupt and criminal [a]ctivity. They pleaded guilty to felony charges and have been sentenced, but before they pled guilty they entered into a cooperation agreement with the U.S. Attorney's Office, an agreement to [sic] which the U.S. Attorney's office agreed to accept their pleas and in return they agreed to testify.

> Remember, people who engage in conspiracy don't act in the open, and, as the evidence in this case will show, they tried not to keep records of their dealings. They acted in secret.

> So for us to be able to show you what happened at Highbridge Houses [where Cosentino was superintendent], it's necessary that we bring people right from out of the muck to testify before you today.

> Because Rappaport and Eisenberg participated in corrupt activities and because they have an agreement with the government, the government asks you to scrutinize their testimony very carefully. You may not like a lot of the things they have done, but, remember, they are not on trial here today. Only Louis Cosentino is on trial, so when Alan Rappaport and Irving Eisenberg testify, you should be asking yourself one question: Are they telling you the truth today or tomorrow?

> Listen closely to what they say and see if what they say doesn't make sense in light of all the evidence in this case.

Cosentino's counsel made a brief opening statement devoted almost entirely to the credibility issues. He focused on specific aspects of the cooperation deals that Rappaport and Eisenberg had struck with the government.

The only evidence they [i.e., the government] are going to give you are the words of Alan Rappaport and Irving Eisenberg, and, as [prosecuting AUSA] Mr. Richman says to you, they are raised up from the muck.

The government says criminals will be testifying against the innocent man sitting at the defense table, Mr. Louis Cosentino. You will find out that they are men who received large amounts of money from the New York City Housing Authority. You will find out that these are men who are convicted felons; both pled guilty in the court to felonies.

Cooperation agreements, they made deals with the government. A deal basically means: You give us what we want and we'll give you what you want. What the government wants is a conviction. So what are they going to do but come here and try to give the government what they want in exchange for which they will get lesser charges than originally exposed to, and, more importantly, their back is scratched by the government in a letter sent to the judge later on.

Mr. Eisenberg has already been sentenced, but if it were found out he did not give the government what the government wanted here in contradiction to what he said earlier, he leaves himself open to all the rest of the charges that he could have been charged with, and the government will go after him.

During the direct testimony of both Rappaport and Eisenberg, the government offered the full text of their written cooperation agreements. The district court admitted them over defense objection. The jury requested both agreements, in addition to other exhibits and testimony, during its deliberations leading to Cosentino's conviction on both counts.

On appeal, Cosentino principally argues that the admission of the cooperation agreements during direct examination constituted impermissible bolstering of the witnesses' credibility. He also argues that the agreements were misleadingly incomplete and that a limiting instruction should have been given. Finally, he contends that certain questions and statements by the AUSA constituted prosecutorial misconduct. We reject these contentions and affirm Cosentino's convictions.

DISCUSSION

I.

This appeal requires us to define the circumstances in which witness cooperation agreements may properly be admitted into evidence during the direct testimony of government witnesses. The existence and contents of such agreements are inevitably of considerable interest to both prosecution and defense. They tend to support witnesses' credibility by setting out promises to testify truthfully as well as penalties for failure to do so, such as prosecution for perjury and reinstatement of any charges dropped pursuant to the deal. The agreements can impeach, however, by revealing the witnesses' criminal background. Defense counsel can also argue that such witnesses cannot be believed because they are under pressure to deliver convictions and correspondingly tempted to twist facts to do so.

Cooperation agreements accordingly demand careful treatment under principles governing attack on and rehabilitation of witnesses' credibility. It is well settled that absent an attack, no evidence may be admitted to support a witness' credibility. We have invoked this rule in considering the admissibility of cooperation agreements because of their tendency to support or bolster credibility. *See, e.g.*, *United States v. Edwards*, 631 F.2d 1049, 1051 (2d Cir. 1980).

A witness' credibility is often tested by a sequence of attack on cross-examination followed by rehabilitation on redirect. It may sometimes be useful, however, to develop impeaching matter in direct examination of a "friendly" witness in order to deprive an adversary of the psychological advantage of revealing it to the jury for the first time during cross-examination. We have accordingly held that impeaching aspects of cooperation agreements may be brought out in the government's direct examination of a witness who testifies pursuant to such an agreement. Even in the absence of a prior attack on credibility, "the elicitation of the fact of the agreement and the witness' understanding of it, as a motivation for the witness to testify for the Government, should be permitted on direct examination in order to anticipate cross-examination by the defendant which might give the jury the unjustified impression that the Government was concealing this relevant fact." *Edwards*, 631 F.2d at 1052.

Because of the bolstering potential of cooperation agreements, however, we have permitted such agreements to be admitted in their entirety only after the credibility of the witness has been attacked. This restriction proceeds from our view that "the *entire* cooperation agreement bolsters more than it impeaches." *Edwards*, 631 F.2d at 1052. Thus, although the prosecutor may inquire into impeaching aspects of cooperation agreements on direct, bolstering aspects such as promises to testify truthfully or penalties for failure to do so may only be developed to rehabilitate the witness after a defense attack on credibility.[1]

Such an attack may come in a defendant's opening statement. If the opening sufficiently implicates the credibility of a government witness, we have held that testimonial evidence of bolstering aspects of a cooperation agreement may be introduced for rehabilitative purposes during direct examination. In such a situation the "rehabilitation" stage has already been reached on direct.

As a threshold matter, we must first decide whether the government's opening statement permissibly referred to the agreements in this case. Consistent with the foregoing principles, a prosecutor may refer to a witness cooperation agreement in opening only to the extent he or she could develop the same matter in direct questioning of a witness whose credibility has not been attacked. The prosecutor thus may advert to the existence of the agreement and related impeaching facts such as the witness' criminal background, but may not raise bolstering aspects of the agreement such as truth telling provisions, charge reinstatement conditions or penalties of perjury clauses. Because the witness alone can testify to his or her understanding of the agreement, the prosecutor also cannot discuss this aspect in opening. The excerpt from the record set forth above makes plain that the government in this case properly restricted its opening to appropriate matters.

It is also plain that Cosentino's counsel sufficiently raised matters of credibility in opening that the government could develop the whole cooperation agreements on direct. Cosentino's counsel made representations about reduction of charges and government intervention on behalf of the witnesses in the sentencing process, as well as the

---

[1] Other courts, apparently less concerned with the precise balance between impeaching and bolstering aspects, have declined to impose comparable conditions on admission of evidence of agreements that include bolstering provisions. Were we writing on a blank slate, we might have followed the other circuits that avoid the distinctions we have required judges and lawyers to make during the heat of trial.

possibility of prosecution for charges dropped in exchange for testimony in the event the witnesses failed to deliver convictions. These references clearly opened the door to rehabilitation on direct by evidence of bolstering aspects of the cooperation agreements.

We thus arrive at the central issue in this appeal: if *evidence* of the whole agreement was admissible during direct examination, was it error to admit the agreement itself? We have not before squarely confronted a situation involving introduction of a whole cooperation agreement on direct following a sufficient attack on credibility in the defense's opening. Cosentino argues that our prior decisions establish a rule that cooperation agreements can be admitted in their entirety only on redirect, thus controlling the outcome of this case. We do not read those decisions so mechanically. It is true that some cases have addressed only the admission of testimony of bolstering aspects on direct examination. It is also true that in summarizing these cases and others, we stated . . . that a prosecutor may "elicit *testimony* on the truth-telling portions . . . on direct," and may "introduce the *entire agreement* . . . on redirect examination to rehabilitate the witness." [*United States v. Smith*,] 778 F.2d [925,] 928 [(2d Cir. 1985) (emphasis added). But the result in these cases is not, as Cosentino argues, the product of a distinction between direct and redirect examination. Rather, the event that renders the bolstering aspects of cooperation agreements admissible, on direct or redirect, is the attack on credibility that gives the bolstering evidence a rehabilitative purpose.

We hold that the written text of a cooperation agreement may be admitted during a witness' direct testimony whenever a defense attack on credibility in opening has made evidence of the whole agreement admissible. We see no reason to distinguish between the written text of the agreement and testimony about it if the rehabilitation stage has otherwise been reached by the time direct examination of the witness begins. The decision about the form evidence of the agreement should take lies within the trial judge's discretion under Fed. R. Evid. 403. In the exercise of that discretion, it may sometimes be appropriate to redact the agreement to eliminate potentially prejudicial, confusing or misleading matter. *See, e.g.,* [*United States v.*] *Arroyo-Angulo*, 580 F.2d [1137,] 1145 & n.9 [(2d Cir. 1978) (deleting references to protective custody afforded witness' family); *United States v. Koss*, 506 F.2d 1103, 1112–13 & n.8 (2d Cir. 1974) (deleting references to organized crime and threats against witness' life on account of testifying), *cert. denied*, 421 U.S. 911, 95 S. Ct. 1565, 43 L. Ed. 2d 776 (1975). No such redaction was necessary in this case. We conclude that there was no abuse of discretion in the district court's decision to admit the entire witness cooperation agreements during the direct testimony of the government witnesses.

II.

Cosentino's two remaining claims relating to the cooperation agreements merit only brief discussion. First, he argues that the agreements were misleadingly incomplete in that they omitted elements of the deals that would have undermined the witnesses' credibility. Specifically, Cosentino points out that each agreement stated that "[n]o additional promises, agreements and conditions have been entered into other than those set forth in this letter and none will be entered into unless in writing and signed by all parties," but neither agreement specified the charges dropped or mentioned that the witnesses were promised a choice among sentencing judges.

In general, there is little danger that significant terms will be omitted from cooperation agreements: the government and the defendant have considerable interest in seeing to it that the agreement spells out all terms of the bargain. Even though some minor details may occasionally be left out, the probative value of individual agreements, including their completeness, can most efficiently be evaluated by the trial judge in the exercise of discretion under Fed. R. Evid. 403. In the instant case, nothing suggests that that discretion was abused. Although the agreements apparently omitted some incidental matters, they contained the essential impeaching and bolstering information that Rappaport and Eisenberg had committed crimes, pled guilty and struck deals under which the government traded a degree of conditional prosecutorial lenience for "truthful" testimony. In any event, defense counsel brought out every one of the omitted matters on cross-examination and discussed them further in summation. Revelation of the other details in written form would have given Cosentino little added leverage in attempting to raise doubts in the jurors' minds about the witnesses' credibility. Under these circumstances, the decision to admit the full agreements had no adverse effect on Cosentino's defense and fell well within the ambit of sound discretion.

Second, Cosentino argues that a limiting instruction should have been given on the truth telling portions of the agreements. He seeks an instruction under which the jury could use the impeaching motive or bias aspects of the agreements to undercut credibility, but could not use the bolstering portions as support for credibility.

No request for such an instruction was made below, so we review only for plain error. We discern no error of any kind in this respect. The proposed instruction would have been fundamentally at odds with the distinctions we have drawn between the impeachment and bolstering aspects of cooperation agreements. Although we have required a prior attack on credibility so that the whole agreement serves a rehabilitative function, we have never restricted use of an agreement to support credibility once that condition is satisfied. Our view presupposes that the agreement may and will be used to support credibility. The district court's treatment of the cooperation agreements was fully consistent with these principles.

* * *

CONCLUSION

For the foregoing reasons, Cosentino's conviction is affirmed.

NOTES

1. *Majority View — Bolstering By Mentioning Plea Agreement Permitted On Direct.* In footnote 1 of its opinion in *Cosentino* the Second Circuit notes that other circuits are not as precise in distinguishing between impeaching and bolstering aspects of a plea agreement. Indeed the majority rule appears to be that a prosecutor may inquire into both impeaching and bolstering aspects of such agreements on direct examination. *See, e.g., United States v. Spriggs,* 996 F.2d 320, 323–24 (D.C. Cir. 1993); *United States v. Lord,* 907 F.2d 1028, 1031 (10th Cir. 1990); *United States v. Drews,* 877 F.2d 10, 12 (8th Cir. 1989); *United States v. Machi,* 811 F.2d 991, 1003 (7th Cir. 1987); *United States v. Townsend,* 796 F.2d 158, 162–63 (6th Cir. 1986); *United States v. Binker,* 795 F.2d 1218, 1223 (5th Cir. 1986); *United States v. Oxman,* 740 F.2d 1298, 1302–03 (3d Cir. 1984), *vacated on other grounds* by *United States v. Pflaumer,* 473 U.S. 922 (1985); *United States v. McNeill,* 728 F.2d 5, 14 (1st Cir. 1984); *United States v. Henderson,* 717 F.2d 135, 137–38 (4th Cir. 1983). *But see United States v. Hilton,* 772 F.2d 783, 787 (11th Cir. 1985) (requiring attack on credibility before admission of bolstering aspects). *See also* COURTROOM CRIMINAL EVIDENCE § 702, at 269 n.3 (4th ed.

2005) (courts split, but many courts hold that it is premature bolstering for the prosecutor to elicit truthfulness provisions in a plea agreement on direct examination before defense has had an opportunity to impeach); CHRISTOPHER B. MUELLER & LAIRD C. KIRKPATRICK, 3 FEDERAL EVIDENCE § 6:79 at 533–34, 533 n.11 (3d ed. 2007).

    2. *Impeaching Aspects Of Plea Agreement Brought Out On Direct.* Note that the impeaching aspects of a plea agreement can present problems of prejudicing the defendant if the government witness was, prior to entering into the plea agreement, a codefendant of the defendant who is on trial:

> At trial, Von Ende, the coconspirator referred to above, testified for the government. At the conclusion of his testimony, to support his credibility and to blunt the impact of cross-examination, the government elicited from Von Ende testimony revealing that he had pled guilty himself and that, in exchange for his plea, charges against his wife had been dismissed. Melton [the defendant] argues that it was improper for the trial judge to deny his motion for a mistrial based on the admission of this evidence. *See United States v. Vaughn*, 546 F.2d 47 (5th Cir. 1977) (should not advise jury of codefendant's guilty plea). Although it is true that a codefendant's guilty plea cannot be admitted as evidence of the defendant's guilt, it can be admitted for other, proper purposes. This case is factually similar to *United States v. Veltre*, 591 F.2d 347 (5th Cir. 1979). In that case, the government also informed the jury that the codefendant, who testified at trial, had pled guilty to the crime. The court stated:

> Defense counsel's expected defense on this theory was merely brought out in advance by the government to blunt adverse impact on the jury and to minimize the impression that the government was trying to conceal Ms. Leone's guilty plea. Where, as here, the codefendant is a witness at trial, subject to the rigors of cross-examination, disclosure of the guilty plea to blunt the impact of attacks on her credibility serves a legitimate purpose and is permissible.

Id. at 349. Furthermore, in this case, the trial judge cautioned the jury that the guilty plea could not be used as substantive evidence of Melton's guilt, and the record demonstrates that the government did not unduly emphasize the plea during closing argument. *United States v. Melton*, 739 F.2d 576, 578–79 (11th Cir. 1984).

    3. *Exceptions — Fresh Complaint And Pretrial Identification.* In most jurisdictions a complaining witness in a sex offense case is permitted to testify about making a complaint to authorities or third parties during direct examination to bolster or corroborate the witness' testimony that a sexual assault occurred. *Battle v. United States*, 630 A.2d 211, 222 (D.C. 1993).

    Similarly, most jurisdictions allow a witness to testify about a pretrial identification of a defendant to bolster an in-court identification. *Hill v. State*, 500 P.2d 1075, 1078 (Okla. Crim. App. 1972); 1 COURTROOM CRIMINAL EVIDENCE § 702, at 272–73 (4th ed. 2005).

    4. *Corroboration Prior To Impeachment.* Another exception to the general ban on bolstering is corroboration. Corroboration involves calling a second witness to corroborate the first witness' version of the facts. Where the general rule against bolstering could prevent extrinsic evidence (such as a plea agreement, or testimony from the second witness that the first is a truthful person) prior to the first witness being impeached, most courts allow a corroboration witness to testify. *See Laughlin v. United States*, 385 F.2d 287, 293 (D.C. Cir. 1967). Limits on offering corroboration evidence is discussed in the material that follows.

[2]   Expert Testimony of Modus Operandi

Next consider the situation where government witnesses testify about criminal activity that might appear unusual to a lay juror and which may not be corroborated by any other fact witness. May the government call an expert witness to corroborate its fact witnesses by testifying that, typically, criminals operate in the fashion described by the government witnesses?

UNITED STATES v. CRUZ
981 F.2d 659 (2d Cir. 1992)

WINTER, CIRCUIT JUDGE:

Maximino Bonifacio appeals from his conviction by a jury . . . for conspiracy to possess cocaine with the intent to distribute, and for possession of cocaine with the intent to distribute and for distribution. . . . We reverse on the ground that expert testimony was improperly admitted. This testimony concerned the behavior of drug dealers from the Albany area seeking drugs from the Washington Heights area of New York City, and the modus operandi of drug trafficking rings in that area, including the role of a "broker" and the ethnicity of the area. Because the testimony was designed to bolster the credibility of a government fact-witness by mirroring his version of events . . . we reverse.

The government sought to prove that Bonifacio had acted as a "broker" between Domingo LaBoy, a drug dealer in the Albany area, styled by the parties as the "Capital District," and suppliers located in the Washington Heights area of Manhattan. The government's case was based largely upon the testimony of Juan Baez, a government informant, and LaBoy. Baez testified that, on November 13, 1990, he bought two ounces of cocaine from LaBoy in Albany and that, approximately one week later, he accompanied LaBoy to "the Dominican's house" where the three of them discussed the purchase of seven or eight ounces of cocaine. Bonifacio asked Baez if he wanted to go to New York, but Baez declined. Bonifacio then made a call on a pay phone and reported back that "everything was ready in New York." The following day, Baez again met LaBoy and purchased seven ounces of cocaine. Baez did not learn the identity of "the Dominican" until trial, when he identified Bonifacio. (During Baez's testimony, both he and the prosecutor referred to Bonifacio as "the Dominican.")

LaBoy testified that, subsequent to Baez's first approach, he and Bonifacio traveled to New York to purchase cocaine on five occasions. Each transaction was conducted in a similar manner. According to LaBoy, he and Bonifacio would travel to West 184th Street in Manhattan to meet a person known to Bonifacio. This person would take them upstairs to an apartment where two others would be waiting. Bonifacio would tell them the quantity of drugs they were seeking, and one of the men would then leave the apartment, returning approximately fifteen minutes later with cocaine. Generally, Bonifacio would check the cocaine and help count the money. After returning to the Capital District, LaBoy would meet alone with Baez to transfer the drugs.

The last witness for the prosecution was Special Agent Marano. Marano testified both as a fact-witness (regarding Bonifacio's arrest) and as an expert witness. Marano's expert testimony described typical drug trafficking operations in the Washington Heights area and the function of a broker in drug trafficking between Washington Heights and the Capital District. Bonifacio's trial counsel objected to the testimony as irrelevant. We quote the pertinent portions of Marano's direct testimony at some length:

Q: Let me ask you this, Special Agent Marano: Have you ever worked in New York City?

A: I spent ten years working in the New York City Office of the DEA.

Q: And are you familiar with 184th and St. Nicholas Avenue in Manhattan?

A: I am.

Q: What particular neighborhood is that?

A: It's a neighborhood that is surrounded by high-rise multi-family dwellings. It is what I would describe, especially to someone from the Capital District, as a tremendously overpopulated neighborhood.

Q: Does it have a name?

A: Washington Heights, Fort Washington area. Washington Heights area. It's just north of the George Washington Bridge. And as of the last five to ten years, it has become inundated with drug dealing.

                              *   *   *

Q: In the course of your work, have you been involved in a number of investigations, even recently, into the way drug selling or cocaine selling operations are run in New York City, particularly in the Washington Heights or Fort Washington area?

A: Yes, I have. It's a much more complex procedure. In that particular area, which does have a very high Hispanic population — by Hispanic, I mean people from Spanish speaking countries or territories, Puerto Rican people, Colombian people, Dominican, Nicaraguan, Honduran, for example. Cocaine entrepreneurs from all over the state, people who want to make a buck in cocaine, will be brought to a dealer in Manhattan by what we call a broker or middleman. So, for example, an entrepreneur or dealer from Troy or Schenectady would travel to the New York City area, particularly the area under discussion, the Washington Heights, discuss and meet a wholesaler. A cocaine wholesaler. They negotiate a deal. When the deal is struck, the wholesaler will have someone bring the cocaine to that individual and that individual will bring the cocaine back up to the Capital District. Now the person from the Capital District very often will never go to the exact locations, the apartment, where the cocaine is being kept. It is a very complex series of steps to get the cocaine from where it is being hidden to the customer. Because these dealers have learned over many years and over many arrests that the more difficult, the more complex they make it for the police to find the cocaine, the longer they can keep the cocaine in their possession and away from the police. So the cocaine may be stored in one of a thousand apartments in a multi-apartment complex scenario. . . .

Q: When the person from the Capital District is brought to an apartment in this particular area, could you tell us how that person comes into — makes the exchange of money for drugs?

A: The individual that comes down from the Capital District is usually brought down by a broker, as I've said. The broker will beep that someone, the wholesale cocaine dealer, by calling up that man's beeper. That man, the cocaine dealer, will then call back the broker at a telephone number that is programmed into his beeper. They will arrange a location at which to meet and there the negotiations will transpire. Most of the time the people involved, even though they may have been dealing this way for a number of months, even years, will not actually know the other individual's identity. They may know each other under pseudo names or street names like Gotco or Sneakers or Curly or something like that. This is so they can better insulate themselves from arrest.

In summation, the government relied upon the quoted testimony. We quote the pertinent portions of that summation:

Where does Mr. Bonifacio, the defendant here, come into this case? And that's the obvious question and that's the question that you have to answer. You heard Special Agent Marano testify about how drug operations are run in this particular area, our area here in the Capital District. The people will go down to New York, they will obtain various quantities of cocaine and then it will be packaged in amounts that allow them to either resell to other dealers or sell to users. . . . The cocaine is obtained in New York City, and Special Agent Marano described for you the way that the cocaine dealing operations work in the northern section of Manhattan, Washington Heights, Fort Washington area, that would include the vicinity of 184th Street and St. Nicholas Avenue. And he described how people are brought by a broker from this area down to the area, because the person from up here does not know the people in New York. The people in New York are only going to, obviously, deal with people they know. The person they know brings the customer from up here to an apartment where the person sits, where the transaction is negotiated. The people leave the apartment, go to an intermediate location, as Special Agent Marano described it, obtain the cocaine where it's hidden — or they go to the area where it is stashed, bring it to the location where the buyer is, where they only have to give the buyer the amount he is buying. So if there is police involvement, they're insulated. Their main stash is insulated. The buyer is sitting in the apartment, he or she does not know where the person has gone from the apartment in order to get the cocaine from the stash. And that is precisely what Domingo LaBoy described to you as what Mr. Bonifacio was doing with respect to him. Domingo LaBoy. There is no proof he had any connection in New York City. He was brought to the city by Mr. Bonifacio, he was taken to 184th Street, he was taken up to a fourth floor apartment. They sat in the apartment, the person left the apartment, came back with the cocaine, money was paid, Mr. Bonifacio and the other guy weighed it, looked at it to check it out to make sure it was okay, good stuff, the money was counted and they left with the cocaine and went back to Troy and sold it. And that is precisely what Mr. Bonifacio's role is in this case. It's just how Special Agent Marano described how the operations work. If you use your common sense and think about it, it is a perfectly logical way for a person to run a business like that in order to insulate themselves. . . .

Bonifacio took the stand and testified that he never had discussions with LaBoy or Baez concerning the buying or selling of cocaine. He stated that LaBoy was an auto mechanic and their meetings concerned automobile repairs, specifically the replacement of his car's brakes. Bonifacio testified that he had traveled with LaBoy to New York City only once, in separate cars, because LaBoy and Tomas Santos asked Bonifacio to follow them because they were worried about car trouble. Bonifacio testified that on that occasion he left the others at 191st Street and Riverside Drive, from which LaBoy and Santos continued on to an unknown destination.

DISCUSSION

Although the evidence was legally sufficient to convict Bonifacio, the government's case to the jury was heavily dependent upon the credibility of LaBoy's testimony concerning trips to New York with Bonifacio.

Fed. R. Evid. 702 provides:

> If scientific, technical, or other specialized knowledge will assist the trier of fact to understand the evidence or to determine a fact in issue, a witness qualified as an expert by knowledge, skill, experience, training, or education, may testify thereto in the form of an opinion or otherwise.

Because the district court has broad discretion regarding the admission or exclusion of expert testimony, we may overturn the exercise of that discretion only where the decision is "manifestly erroneous." We find such error here.

On appeal, the government argues that Marano's testimony was necessary to assist the jury because LaBoy's testimony as to the use of intermediaries or brokers was "beyond the knowledge or understanding of an average juror from the Capital District." We find that a doubtful proposition. That drug traffickers may seek to conceal their identities by using intermediaries would seem evident to the average juror from movies, television crime dramas, and news stories. Indeed, in telling slips of the tongue, the government's summation stated that it was "obvious []" that drug suppliers would not deal with unknown persons, in this case LaBoy, and that it was "common sense" and "logical" that they would use a known intermediary, in this case Bonifacio.

Moreover, at no time did the defense attempt to cast doubt on LaBoy's testimony on the ground that the trips to Washington Heights or events occurring there were improbable descriptions of drug transactions. Nor did the defense suggest that Bonifacio's presence at the drug transactions had an innocent explanation. Rather, the defense was that Bonifacio was not present at the drug transactions and that LaBoy had falsely accused Bonifacio as a means of bargaining with the government for a lenient disposition of his own case. Given the evidence and contentions of the parties, the dispositive factual issue was whether Bonifacio was present at the drug transactions. If so, his guilt would follow as night follows day. The role of a broker, therefore, however obvious or not to the average juror, was simply not an issue that the parties disputed.

Of course, one might speculate that the jury would, without prompting by the defense, find Bonifacio's alleged role confusing. If that concern were realistic, it would have been within the district court's discretion to admit expert testimony explaining that drug wholesalers often use intermediaries and make deliveries away from the actual locus of the drugs as means of avoiding identification and arrest. Had Marano's testimony been limited to that dry explanation of the concerns and defenses of drug traffickers, we might be inclined to affirm despite our doubts as to the need for such an explanation. The testimony, however, went into matters beyond explaining the role of a broker and had another use that was both impermissible and prejudicial.

The government's principal use of Marano's expert testimony was, as pressed in summation, to bolster LaBoy's version of events: travel by a Hispanic drug dealer and Hispanic middleman from the Capital District to Washington Heights, an area that is inhabited by Hispanics in thousands of apartments and is a source of drugs; Bonifacio acting as broker for LaBoy; a meeting with anonymous intermediaries for the wholesaler; and the exchange of drugs for money in an apartment in which the drugs were not located. In summation, the prosecutor was thus able to argue that Marano's "testi[mony] about how drug operations are run in this particular area . . . is precisely what Domingo LaBoy described to you as what Mr. Bonafacio [sic] was doing. . . ."

Such reasoning, however, is . . . "impermissible". . . . We reaffirm here the principle that the credibility of a fact-witness may not be bolstered by arguing that the witness's version of events is consistent with an expert's description of patterns of criminal conduct, at least where the witness's version is not attacked as improbable or ambiguous evidence of such conduct. First, . . . guilt may not be inferred from the conduct of unrelated persons. Second, although such expert testimony logically adds nothing to the believability of a witness's account (again absent a suggestion of implausibility), it strongly suggests to the jury that a law enforcement specialist — here an arresting officer — believes the government's witness [] to be credible and the defendant to be guilty, suggestions we have previously condemned.

This case is thus distinguishable from *United States v. Brown*, 776 F.2d 397 (2d Cir. 1985), *cert. denied*, 475 U.S. 1141 (1986). In *Brown*, we held that a police officer was permitted to describe a typical drug buy in Harlem, including the role of the "steerer," where the accused's defense was that he was on the scene but unaware of any drug transaction. In this case, Bonifacio's defense is that he was not present at the alleged drug buys. Indeed, with the exception of one trip, he denies even being in New York City at the pertinent times. In the present situation, as noted, if the jury believed the testimony of the prosecution witnesses that Bonifacio participated in the drug buys in New York City, a conviction was inevitable. His precise role in the transaction, therefore, was not in dispute.

The prejudicial effect of Marano's testimony is not seriously denied by the government. The testimony was thus relied upon heavily in the government's summation, which emphasized the similarities between LaBoy's testimony and Marano's description of typical drug transactions, to bolster the credibility of LaBoy's testimony.

*   *   *

Our ruling in no way retreats from the proposition "that the operations of narcotics dealers are a proper subject for expert testimony under Fed. R. Evid. 702." We hold only that the operations in question must have esoteric aspects reasonably perceived as beyond the ken of the jury and that expert testimony cannot be used solely to bolster the credibility of the government's fact-witnesses by mirroring their version of events.

Nor do we hold that expert testimony may not be used on some occasions to explain even non-esoteric matters, when the defense seeks to discredit the government's version of events as improbable criminal behavior. Where appropriate, the government may seek an agreement that such a defense will not be raised. *Cf. United States v. Figueroa*, 618 F.2d 934, 939–42 (2d Cir. 1980) (Before evidence of similar crimes may be offered to prove knowledge or intent, trial judge must "determine whether the issue sought to be proved by the evidence is really in dispute. . . . When the Government offers prior act evidence to prove an issue, counsel must express a decision not to dispute that issue with sufficient clarity that the trial court will be justified . . . in sustaining objection to any subsequent cross-examination or jury argument that seeks to raise the issue. . . .")

We reverse. The government may, of course, seek a retrial.

QUESTION

Would the outcome of the *Cruz* case have been any different if it were being tried before a jury in a rural area of upstate New York?

PROBLEM

Problem 10-1. An undercover police officer, Officer Johnson, as part of a "bust and buy" operation, went to the Washington Heights area of New York City where he believed it would be easy to buy cocaine. Officer Johnson was approached by a man named Fernandez who offered him cocaine. After some discussion Officer Johnson was told to go to a nearby apartment where he would be sold cocaine. At the apartment Officer Johnson bought cocaine and tried to leave. Officer Johnson states that Fernandez blocked his way and pointed to his (Fernandez's) waistband where Officer Johnson observed a pistol. Fernandez put his hand on the pistol and ordered Officer Johnson to snort cocaine before he would allow him to leave. After Officer Johnson snorted cocaine Fernandez said, "he's okay," and Officer Johnson was allowed to leave. Shortly thereafter Fernandez was arrested. A thorough search of Fernandez and the apartment failed to produce any pistol.

Fernandez is charged with distributing cocaine *and carrying a firearm in relation to a drug trafficking offense*. At trial Officer Johnson testifies to seeing Fernandez with a pistol and being ordered to snort cocaine. The government's next witness was Detective Hector Santiago, who testified as an expert on the methods of New York City drug dealers. Detective Santiago testifies that the practice of forcing customers to snort cocaine at gunpoint had begun in the fall of 1988 and that it was "becoming more and more popular among the drug dealers in the Washington Heights area," as a means of flushing out undercover officers. The technique was, he testified, "used to protect [the dealers] from police officers making undercover buys." When asked how the dealer would use a gun when instructing prospective buyers to snort cocaine, Santiago testified that one common way was to "have a gun in their waistband, and they will put their hand on the handle."

Fernandez is convicted on both counts and appeals, asserting that the expert testimony was improper bolstering of the testimony of Officer Johnson that a gun had been used in a drug trafficking offense. Was such testimony properly admitted?

(A) On appeal, what is Fernandez's strongest argument that the expert testimony of Detective Santiago was improper?

(B) What is the government's strongest argument to support such testimony? *See United States v. Castillo*, 924 F.2d 1227, 1233–34 (2d Cir. 1991).

C.   IMPEACHMENT

[1]   Introduction

[a]   Methods

Impeachment, the second stage in credibility analysis, is an attempt by the opponent of a witness to discredit the witness or the witness' testimony. Often the testimony given by a witness appears credible. In such cases impeachment may ignore the actual content of the testimony and attack the believability of the witness. This is not uncommon in criminal cases where witnesses often are people with criminal records. Such attacks are referred to as *ad hominem* attacks. An *ad hominem* attack may focus on the witness' character, physical or mental deficiencies, or biases (but not the testimony itself) that may make the witness less believable. Regardless of the specific type of *ad hominem* attack, the primary focus is on problems with the witness as opposed to problems with the testimony. The attorney impeaching a witness with an *ad hominem* attack is hoping that the jury will discount the testimony (the message) because of problems with the witness (the messenger).

On the other hand, sometimes it is simply not appropriate to attack the witness. In such cases the impeachment will focus not on the character, biases or physical or mental deficiencies of the witness but, rather, on the witness' testimony. Here the attacking attorney will be highlighting inconsistencies and contradictions in the testimony itself to suggest that what the witness says should not be believed.

Of course there is no reason that the witness' character for truthfulness and the testimony could not both be attacked in the proper circumstances. For example, one could offer evidence that a witness had been recently convicted of perjury to suggest that the witness is predisposed to lie, and also offer evidence of a prior inconsistent statement made by the witness to cast doubt on the credibility of a particular fact related in the witness' testimony.

There are five recognized means of impeachment:[2] (1) evidence of the witness' character or disposition for untruthfulness; (2) evidence of defects in the witness' ability to perceive, recollect or recount; (3) evidence of the witness' bias for or against a party; (4) prior inconsistent statements made by the witness; and (5) evidence that contradicts the witness. The materials that follow will examine the application of each of these types of impeachment in a criminal case.

[b]   Impeaching One's Own Witness[3]

Before looking at *how* the methods are applied, one should consider *who* can impeach. All of the above methods of impeachment are typically used by an opponent to attack the credibility of his adversary's witness. There are, however, some occasions where the *proponent* of a witness will want to impeach his own witness.

As a general rule, the common law prohibited the impeachment of one's own witness; this prohibition is commonly referred to as the "voucher rule." Under the voucher rule, the proponent of a witness may not *directly* attack the credibility of his own witness,

---

[2] *See* Christopher B. Mueller & Laird C. Kirkpatrick, 3 Federal Evidence §6:26, at 151–53 (3d ed. 2007).

[3] *See generally* Christopher B. Mueller & Laird C. Kirkpatrick, 3 Federal Evidence § 6:25, at 148–51 (3d ed. 2007); 1 Courtroom Criminal Evidence § 705, at 274–78 (4th ed. 2005).

but instead must introduce extrinsic evidence that contradicts his witness' testimony. Because courts and legislatures grew increasingly dissatisfied with the voucher rule, numerous exceptions to the voucher rule were created that allowed a more direct attack on the credibility of one's own witness.

The first exception allows the proponent to impeach a witness who has become indispensable, either by law or by the facts of the case. This method is commonly used in cases where there is only one eyewitness to a crime. The second exception to the voucher rule allows the proponent to impeach a witness who, to the surprise of the proponent, gives testimony that is damaging to the proponent's case. A limitation on this exception is that the proponent must first show that the testimony of the witness is both surprising and damaging. Further, this exception will not apply if the witness merely fails to give favorable testimony.

Even with these exceptions, the modern trend is toward the abolition of the voucher rule in its entirety. Indeed, Federal Rule of Evidence 607 contains language to this effect. Rule 607 states that "[t]he credibility of a witness may be attacked by any party, including the party calling him." The abolition of the voucher rule would have a threefold effect. First, a proponent would not be bound by the testimony that he offers; second, a proponent would have more freedom to offer prior statements made by his own witness; and third, standard impeachment methods could be used to impeach any witness.

[2]   Methods that are Attacks on the Witness (*AD HOMINEM* ATTACKS)

[a]   Showing that the Witness is Predisposed to Lie: Character for Untruthfulness

When a litigant suggests that a witness is predisposed to lie, the actual content of the witness' testimony is not the primary focus of the attack. In fact, the content of the testimony may not be raised. Rather, the witness' adversary is suggesting that the jury should disregard what the witness says because the witness has a propensity to be dishonest and, therefore, is probably lying. In short, the assertion is that the witness is a liar. Three principal methods are used in such an attack.

First, an opponent can offer evidence showing that the witness has, at some recent time, been convicted of a crime. Federal Rule of Evidence 609 addresses this method of impeachment and regulates the admission of both felony and misdemeanor convictions offered for this purpose.

Second, an opponent may cross-examine the witness while the witness is still on the witness stand about conduct that did not result in a criminal conviction, but which is probative of a witness' untruthfulness. This method of suggesting a predisposition to lie is the subject of Federal Rule of Evidence 608(b). The theory behind Rule 608(b) is that a propensity to engage in untruthful conduct indicates a propensity to lie.

Third, a second witness, referred to as a "character witness," can be called to the witness stand to give his or her opinion of the first ("principal") witness' character for untruthfulness or to tell the jury the community reputation of the principal witness for untruthfulness. Federal Rule of Evidence 608(a) regulates this form of impeachment.

The materials that follow in this subsection examine problems with the application of the three methods that attack a witness' character or disposition for truthfulness just described. The focus here is the same as it is throughout this text: the criminal case.

[i]   Conviction of a crime

EDWARD J. IMWINKELRIED, PAUL C. GIANNELLI, FRANCIS A. GILLIGAN & FREDRIC I. LEDERER, 1 COURTROOM CRIMINAL EVIDENCE § 708, at 282–94 (4th ed. 2005)[*]

§ 708. Prior Conviction.

The common-law rule that a natural person previously convicted of treason, a felony, or a misdemeanor involving dishonesty is incompetent to testify has been modified by the modern courts and legislatures. However, the idea that a person with a criminal record is less credible remains ingrained in the law in the form of the rule that a witness, including a defendant, may be impeached by showing that he or she has suffered a valid, final conviction for certain types of offenses. (A few states have carved out an exception to this general rule, prohibiting inquiry into the defendant's criminal record unless the defendant places his or her character in issue.)

Because the purpose of the impeachment use of a prior conviction is to decrease the witness' credibility, asking the witness about the defendant's prior criminal record is improper if the defendant has not taken the stand. Until the defendant does so, his or her credibility does not become a fact of consequence in the case under Rule 401. However, as soon as any witness, including the defendant, takes the stand, his credibility becomes a target for impeachment.

(A) What May the Opponent Prove? The opponent may prove that the witness has suffered a valid, final, recent conviction for certain types of offenses.

(1) *"Valid."* The requirement that the conviction be valid is especially important if the conviction was obtained in violation of due process of law or the witness' right to counsel under the sixth amendment. However, most courts limit the attack on a prior conviction used for impeachment to evidence of the denial of a right affecting the fairness of the trial, especially the sixth amendment right to counsel. These courts will not sustain collateral attacks based on the fact that otherwise reliable evidence supporting the conviction was obtained in violation of the fourth amendment.

(2) *"Final."* The general view is that so long as the trial court has entered a final judgment, the conviction may be used for impeachment purposes. In some states the sentence must be imposed in order to have a final judgment of conviction. Other courts have held that even absent a sentence or formal judgment, a final verdict can be used to impeach. At the very least, the jury must have returned a guilty verdict, or the judge must have finally accepted the defendant's guilty plea.

It is immaterial that a motion for a new trial or an appeal is pending. Although to rehabilitate the witness, the proponent may show that the motion for new trial has been made or that the appeal is pending, this showing does not preclude the use of the conviction. However, if the conviction has been reversed on appeal, it certainly may not be used for impeachment. In contrast, a pardon will usually not prevent the conviction's use for impeachment; a pardon can be granted for reasons other than innocence. Similarly, other courts have indicated that the imposition of probation as a sentence does not preclude the conviction's use for impeachment purposes.

Although there is consensus on the propositions stated in the preceding two paragraphs, a conflict exists over whether a judgment based on a plea of *nolo contendere* may be used to impeach a witness. Rule 410 of the Federal Rules of Evidence provides that a plea of *nolo contendere* which is later withdrawn may not be used. By negative implication, this rule suggests that if the plea is not withdrawn, a judgment based on the plea may be used.

(3) *"Recent."* Generally, admitting the conviction is discretionary with the trial judge, who must weigh the conviction's probative value against its prejudicial effects. In part, the conviction's probative value depends on its recency. The federal rule, 609, expressly singles out as discretionary the admissibility of a conviction which occurred more than ten years before the trial in question. The conviction is remote in time and admissible only if the judge determines that its probative value "substantially" outweighs its prejudicial effect and if advance written notice is given of the intent to use the prior conviction for impeachment. This notice grants the adverse party a better opportunity to ascertain if the conviction is valid and final.

(4) *"Conviction."* As previously stated, there must be a conviction. An arrest, indictment, or information may not be used for impeachment. However, . . . employing a different impeachment technique, codified in Rule 608(b), many jurisdictions allow a witness or defendant to be asked if he or she is actually guilty of a crime that has not resulted in a conviction.

Generally, a juvenile adjudication may not be used for impeachment. Nevertheless, the trial court may permit the use of a witness' juvenile adjudication to attack the credibility of that witness when in the words of Rule 609(d), evidence of the juvenile adjudication "is necessary to a fair determination of the issue of guilt or innocence." The offense must have been of the type that if committed by an adult would affect truthfulness or manifest moral turpitude.

(5) *"For Certain Types of Offenses."* There is a three-way split of authority over the type of offense that may be used for impeachment. In many states, the admissibility of a conviction for impeachment turns on the potential or actual sentence. Hence, some jurisdictions limit the admissible convictions to felonies.

In other jurisdictions, the conviction's admissibility depends on the nature of the underlying offense. For example, impeachment may be limited to convictions of "infamous crimes," of "felonies and misdemeanors involving moral turpitude," or of "felonies and misdemeanors in the nature of ' *crimen falsi.*' " Some courts require that all crimes used to impeach involve dishonesty.

The Federal Rules adopt a third, compromise position: If the crime is punishable by death or by imprisonment in excess of one year (Rule 609(a)(1)) *or* if the crime entails false statement or dishonesty, regardless of the punishment (Rule 609(a)(2)), the conviction may be used for impeachment. Rule 609(a)(2) has proven troublesome for the courts. The Advisory Committee Note indicates that Rule 609(a)(2) includes such crimes as fraud, embezzlement, and deceit. The cases construing Rule 609(a)(2) have held that crimes such as perjury, subornation of perjury, and income tax evasion involve an element of false statement. The cases split on the question of whether offenses such as larceny and robbery qualify under Rule 609(a)(2). The majority of the courts exclude such convictions when proffered under (a)(2); in effect, they have read the word "dishonesty" out of the statute. The 1990 amendment to Rule 609(a) strengthens the argument that such offenses do not fall within 609(a)(2). The tenth paragraph of the Advisory Committee Note accompanying the amendment states that some cases "take an unduly broad view of 'dishonesty,' admitting convictions such as for bank robbery or bank larceny."

(B) Which Methods May the Opponent Use to Prove the Fact of the Conviction? The minority view is that the best evidence rule prevents cross-examining the witness about the prior conviction; thus the questioner must introduce a properly authenticated copy of the judgment of conviction into evidence. However, in most jurisdictions the conviction may be shown either by cross-examination or by independent evidence of the conviction. Some jurisdictions allowing either cross-examination or independent evidence hold that when a witness denies a conviction, the cross-examination must be terminated and the impeachment continued only with independent evidence, that is, the introduction of the copy of the judgment.

In many jurisdictions permitting cross-examination the questioner may ask about such details of the prior conviction as the site of the conviction, the general nature of the crime, and the sentence imposed. In contrast, some courts, applying the old common-law rule, limit the examiner to the mere fact of the conviction.

(C) If the Proffered Evidence of a Conviction Is Otherwise Proper, Does the Trial Judge Have Discretion to Exclude It? In some jurisdictions no discretion is left to the trial judge. Congress has passed a statute depriving District of Columbia trial court judges of discretion to exclude convictions. However, the prevailing common-law rule in the United States is that allowing impeachment by prior conviction is discretionary with the trial judge, who must weigh its probative value against its prejudicial effect on the defendant. In applying this discretionary test, a number of factors must be considered — for example, how remote the conviction is in time; how directly the offense relates to credibility; how similar it is to the crime charged; how crucial the witness' testimony is; how time consuming the impeachment will be; and whether the witness will suffer undue humiliation or prejudice. Even if a consideration of these factors does not persuade the judge to altogether exclude evidence of the conviction, the judge might "sanitize" the evidence; while admitting evidence that the witness has suffered "a felony conviction," the judge could bar evidence of the identity of the offense.

Federal Rule of Evidence 609(a)(2) deprives federal trial judges of the power to exclude convictions involving false statement. Unlike Rule 609(a)(1), Rule 609(a)(2) makes no mention of the possibility of excluding the evidence by balancing probative value against probative danger. Under the earlier version of Rule 609, it could be argued that the judge may resort to Rule 403 and bar the conviction when its probative value is substantially outweighed by the incidental probative dangers. However, even prior to the 1990 amendment to Rule 609, most courts concluded that the omission of any reference to balancing in Rule 609(a)(2) manifests a congressional intent that convictions falling within 609(a)(2) be automatically admissible. The impetus for the amendment was the Supreme Court's 1989 decision in *Green v. Bock Laundry Machine Co.* In *Green*, the Court construed Rule 609(a)(2). The Court held that when a conviction falls under Rule 609(a)(2), the trial judge has no discretion to exclude the conviction under either Rule 609 or Rule 403. The Court added that as then worded, the balancing provision in Rule 609(a)(1) protected only the criminal accused. The defense could invoke the provision to restrict the impeachment of the accused or a defense witness when there is potential prejudice to the accused. However, as Rule 609 was then worded, the prosecution could not invoke either the 609 balancing provision or the protection of Rule 403 to limit the impeachment of a government witness.

In part in response to *Green*, Rule 609 was amended. As amended, Rule 609 reads:

(a) *General rule.* For the purpose of attacking the credibility of a witness,

(1) evidence that a witness other than an accused has been convicted of a crime shall be admitted, subject to Rule 403, if the crime was punishable by death or imprisonment in excess of one year under the law under which the witness was convicted, and evidence that an accused has been convicted of such a crime shall be admitted if the court determines that the probative value of admitting this evidence outweighs the prejudicial effect to the accused; and

(2) evidence that any witness has been convicted of a crime shall be admitted if it involved dishonesty or false statement, regardless of the punishment.

The accompanying Advisory Committee Note indicates that under the amendment, "the general balancing test of Rule 403" applies to government witnesses and defense witnesses other than the defendant. In these cases, the party opposing the admission of the evidence will have the burden of convincing the trial judge that the probative dangers incidental to admitting the evidence will significantly outweigh its probative value. The amendment applies a special balancing test when the prosecution offers a conviction to impeach an accused. Under that test, the proponent, namely the prosecution, bears the burden.

Given the widespread common law view that the trial judge has discretion to exclude an otherwise admissible conviction, some defense counsel have contended that legislation depriving the judge of discretion violates the principle of separation of powers and is unconstitutional. The courts have rejected these arguments and sustained the legislation.

QUESTIONS

1. Does Fed. R. Evid. 609 permit the admission of evidence of criminal convictions of the defendant if the defendant does not testify?

2. If a defendant is not found guilty by a jury but instead pleads guilty, may the defendant, at a subsequent trial, be impeached with that conviction pursuant to Rule 609?

3. If the defendant is convicted of a crime but the conviction is being appealed, may he or she be impeached with the conviction prior to the appellate court ruling on the appeal?

4. Under what circumstances, if any, may a defendant be impeached, under Rule 609 with a conviction that is more than ten years old?

5. May the *defendant* be impeached pursuant to Rule 609 with a juvenile adjudication? May a witness that is called by the prosecution?

6. What information, in addition to the fact of the conviction, may be put into evidence under Rule 609?

7. What convictions are automatically admissible to impeach under Rule 609? What convictions are admissible only after a balancing test under Rule 609? What types of convictions are never admissible to impeach under Rule 609?

Allowing the introduction of prior convictions to impeach is, arguably, the most difficult rule of impeachment faced by a criminal defendant. The evidentiary proposition that the prosecution wants the jury to accept is that, since the defendant (or the defendant's witness) has been convicted of a crime, he or she is a criminal; criminals are probably liars; since the defendant is a criminal he or she is probably a liar, and is probably lying right now on the witness stand.[4] Unfortunately, however, an alternative inference exists: because the defendant has committed other crimes, he or she is predisposed to commit crimes in general and, therefore, probably committed the one for which he or she is currently on trial.

The problem, of course, is that Rule 609(a), and its state counterparts, have a chilling effect on the defendant's right to testify in his or her own behalf. Since Rule 609(a) is a rule of impeachment, a defendant's convictions can only be used (pursuant to Rule 609(a)) if the defendant testifies. Therefore, by not testifying the defendant may be able to keep his or her criminal record from the jury and avoid the jury assuming that the defendant has a propensity to commit crimes and convicting the defendant on this occasion for past crimes.

Rule 609(a) can also present a "guilt by association" difficulty for the criminal defendant who does not take the witness stand. For example, if the defendant calls a witness with a criminal record, that witness may have his or her criminal convictions brought to the jury's attention pursuant to Rule 609(a). There may then be a "spillover" effect from the witness to the defendant resulting in the jury viewing the defendant as a criminal or one who associates with criminals.

Federal Rule of Evidence 609(a) recognizes the dangers just described and requires the court to balance probativeness against prejudice prior to admitting evidence of felony convictions that do not involve dishonesty or false statement. The *Jackson* case that follows is a state case from Maryland that explores such a balancing test in the context of the prosecution attempting, under Maryland's version of Federal Rule 609, to offer evidence of a conviction for the same offense for which the defendant is currently being tried.

JACKSON v. STATE
668 A.2d 8 (Md. 1995)

RAKER, JUDGE.

In this case we must determine whether the trial court abused its discretion by admitting a prior theft conviction to impeach the credibility of a defendant on trial for theft. We shall hold that the decision to permit same-crime impeachment was within the

---

[4] In EVIDENCE IN THE NINETIES, Professors Carlson, Imwinkelried and Kionka explained the relevance of a felony conviction to untruthful disposition as follows:

> The logical relevance of a witness' conviction is undeniable. The fact of the conviction is some evidence of the witness' willingness to disregard social norms. The prohibition of perjury is another social norm. Thus, evidence of the prior conviction is relevant under Federal Rule of Evidence 401; the evidence of the prior conviction increases the probability that at the time of trial, the witness will once again violate a social norm and testify untruthfully. The conviction is circumstantial proof of the witness' present perjury.

RONALD L. CARLSON, EDWARD J. IMWINKELRIED & EDWARD J. KIONKA, EVIDENCE IN THE NINETIES, 396–97 (3d ed. 1991).

trial court's discretion, and that prior convictions for offenses that are similar or identical to the charged crime are not per se inadmissible.

On January 28 and February 1, 1994, the Appellant, Robert M. Jackson, was tried by a jury in the Circuit Court for Baltimore City for theft of $300 or more in violation of Maryland Code Article 27, § 342. At the trial, he elected to testify and denied any involvement in the crime. He was convicted and sentenced to five years' imprisonment. . . .

On the morning of October 11, 1993, Neil McCabe, a supervisor in Lombard Hall at the University of Maryland at Baltimore, learned that a computer had been stolen from that building. The Appellant, a student at Morgan State University who had worked for McCabe the preceding summer, was charged with the theft.

*   *   *

Before trial, Appellant filed a motion in limine to exclude evidence of his involvement in two prior thefts in 1991. In the first case, Appellant received a probation before judgment disposition. In the second case, Appellant was convicted of three counts of theft arising from the same incident: theft of $300 or more, theft under $300, and conspiracy to commit theft. Defense counsel argued that a probation before judgment disposition is inadmissible for impeachment purposes because it is not a criminal conviction. Defense counsel also argued that the prior conviction was unduly prejudicial because it was for theft, the same crime as the charge before the court. He contended that allowing the State to impeach Jackson with a prior conviction for the same crime as the charged offense would lead the jury to infer improperly that because Appellant had previously been convicted of theft, he must be guilty in the present case.

The trial judge granted the motion in limine with respect to the probation before judgment disposition but denied the motion with respect to the theft conviction. She ruled that if Appellant elected to testify at trial, the prior theft conviction would be admissible for impeachment purposes under Maryland Rule 5-609, because the probative value outweighed the prejudicial effect.

Appellant was tried before a jury on January 28 and February 1, 1994. He denied guilt and presented an alibi defense supported by two corroborating witnesses. . . .

Appellant also testified. According to his testimony, on the evening of October 8, he attended a lecture at Johns Hopkins University, arriving at approximately 7:30 p.m. and returning home at 9:00 p.m. When he arrived at home, he saw that his clothes were strewn around his apartment and concluded that someone had broken in while he was gone. Because the window in his bedroom had been broken, he spent the night at the apartment of his neighbor, Ms. Jenkins. . . .

On cross-examination, the State asked Appellant whether he had previously been convicted of a crime involving dishonesty. Appellant admitted a prior conviction but denied knowing the name of the offense. The State then offered a certified copy of the docket entry from the Circuit Court for Prince George's County as proof of the 1991 theft conviction. Appellant was convicted and sentenced to five years' imprisonment.

II.

Maryland Rule 5-609 governs the admissibility of prior convictions to impeach a witness. The Rule provides in pertinent part:[1]

(a) *Generally*. For the purpose of attacking the credibility of a witness, evidence that the witness has been convicted of a crime shall be admitted if elicited from the witness or established by public record during examination of the witness, but only if (1) the crime was an infamous crime or other crime relevant to the witness's credibility and (2) the court determines that the probative value of admitting this evidence outweighs the danger of unfair prejudice to the witness or the objecting party.

Appellant argues that the trial court abused its discretion in admitting evidence of his prior theft conviction to impeach him because the prejudice outweighed the probative value. He contends that the similarity of the prior crime to the charged offense rendered the prior conviction so prejudicial as to outweigh any probative value that it may have had. We disagree. Under Rule 5-609, prior convictions for the same or similar offenses as the charged offense are not automatically excluded. The similarity between the prior conviction and the current charge is only one factor the trial court should consider in determining whether to admit the conviction.

In rejecting a rigid approach to the use of prior convictions, we follow the trend toward increasing flexibility that has marked the historical development of Rule 5-609. At common law, a person who had been convicted of an infamous crime or a crime involving dishonesty was incompetent to testify at any trial. The Legislature removed this disqualification by enacting Chapter 109 of the Acts of 1864, which permitted a person who had been convicted of an infamous crime to testify, but provided that the prior conviction could be admitted to impeach that person's credibility. This statute is now found in [the] Maryland Code. . . . While ameliorating the harsh common law rule disqualifying a person from testifying, "rather than allow these witnesses to testify free from the taint of their prior infamous convictions, the legislature chose to make these convictions admissible for impeachment purposes."

Rule 5-609 now governs the admissibility of impeachment by evidence of conviction of a crime.[4] The Rule creates a three-part test for determining whether a conviction is admissible for impeachment purposes. First, a conviction must fall within the eligible universe to be admissible. This universe consists of two categories: (1) infamous crimes, and (2) other crimes relevant to the witness's credibility. Md. Rule 5-609(a). Second, if the crime falls within one of these two categories, the proponent must establish that the conviction is less than fifteen years old. Md. Rule 5-609(b). Finally, the trial court must

---

[1] The Rule also includes several other limitations:

(b) *Time Limit*. — Evidence of a conviction is not admissible under this Rule if a period of more than 15 years has elapsed since the date of the conviction.

(c) *Other Limitations*. — Evidence of a conviction otherwise admissible under section (a) of this Rule shall be excluded if:

(1) the conviction has been reversed or vacated;

(2) the conviction has been the subject of a pardon; or

(3) an appeal or application for leave to appeal from the judgment of conviction is pending, or the time for noting an appeal or filing an application for leave to appeal has not expired.

Md. Rule 5-609(b) & (c).

[4] Maryland Rule 5-609, adopted July 1, 1994, was derived from Federal Rule of Evidence 609 and Maryland Rule 1-502. . . .

weigh the probative value of the impeaching evidence against the danger of unfair prejudice to the defendant. Md. Rule 5-609(c).

We are concerned here only with the third step — the trial court's exercise of its discretionary power and the weighing of the evidence — because Appellant concedes that the other two prongs of the test for admissibility are satisfied. First, the offense of theft falls within the eligible universe of admissible crimes because it is the "embodiment of deceitfulness," and thus bears on credibility. Second, with respect to timeliness, the 1991 theft conviction is sufficiently recent to satisfy the Rule's fifteen-year time limit. Appellant specifically complains that he was unfairly prejudiced because he was on trial for theft, and he was impeached with prior convictions for theft. In essence, he proposes mandatory exclusion of all prior convictions where those convictions are for the same type of crime as the offense that is charged.

We begin our discussion of the admissibility of a prior conviction for impeachment purposes . . . by "recognizing that in our system of criminal justice every defendant has the right to testify in his own defense." The State also has the right to impeach a defendant by presenting evidence of past convictions. This right is premised on the proposition that such evidence will assist the factfinder in measuring the credibility of the witness. The difficulty arises in balancing these two rights.

The current rule governing impeachment by evidence of conviction of a crime requires the trial judge to weigh the probative value against the unfair prejudice for all convictions used to impeach credibility. . . .

. . . [W]e reject a rigid approach to the use of prior crimes for impeachment. Thus, we conclude that a prior conviction that is the same as or similar to the crime charged is not *per se inadmissible*, but is subject to the probative-prejudice weighing process under Rule 5-609. The balancing prong of the rule contains no language prohibiting the use of similar prior crimes. Furthermore, we believe a per se rule barring same-crime impeachment would deny trial judges needed flexibility. Establishing such a per se rule would have the additional undesirable effect of shielding a defendant who specializes in a particular crime from cross-examination regarding his specialty crimes. We therefore reject Appellant's contention that same-crime impeachment evidence is per se inadmissible.

While impeachment of a witness by prior conviction has long been a part of Maryland law, we have also recognized the danger in admitting such evidence and particularly its potential to discourage defendants from testifying in their own behalf.[5] [*See*] *Gordon v. United States*, 383 F.2d 936, 940 (D.C. Cir. 1967). In *Ricketts* [*v. State*, 436 A.2d 906 (1981)], Judge Cole, writing for the Court, noted:

> The danger in admitting prior convictions as evidence to impeach the defendant stems from the risk of prejudice. The jury may improperly infer that the defendant has a history of criminal activity and therefore is not entitled to a favorable verdict. Such evidence may detract from careful attention to the facts, despite instructions from the Court, influencing the jury to conclude that if the defendant is wrongfully found guilty no real harm is done. Where the crime for which the defendant is on trial is identical or similar to the crime for

---

[5] To minimize some of the negative effects of impeachment through use of prior convictions, several courts have allowed the use of the prior conviction to attack credibility without permitting disclosure of the specific offense, a procedure sometimes referred to as "sanitization." *See, e.g.*, *State v. Brunson*, 625 A.2d 1085 (1993); *State v. Rutchik*, 341 N.W.2d 639 (1984); *Harmon v. Commonwealth*, 185 S.E.2d 48 (1971).

which he has been previously convicted the danger is greater, as the jury may conclude that because he did it *before* he most likely has done it *again*. The net effect of such evidence is often to discourage the defendant from taking the stand. Thus, the role of the trial judge takes on added importance. It becomes his function to admit only those prior convictions which will assist the jury in assessing the credibility of the defendant. The trial judge must weigh the probative value of the convictions against the prejudice to the defendant in asserting his defense.

Ricketts, 436 A.2d at 907–08.

We adopted Rule 5-609 to minimize this danger of prejudice. The Rule is designed to prevent a jury from convicting a defendant based on his past criminal record, or because the jury thinks the defendant is a bad person. *See Gordon*, 383 F.2d at 940. The Rule therefore imposes limitations on the use of past convictions in an effort to discriminate between the informative use of past convictions to test credibility, and the pretextual use of past convictions where the convictions are not probative of credibility but instead merely create a negative impression of the defendant.

This risk of prejudice is particularly great where the crime for which the defendant is on trial is identical or similar to the crime of which he has previously been convicted. . . . Rule 5-609 therefore requires the trial judge to perform his or her duty of weighing the legitimate probative value of the cross-examination against the illegitimate tendency to prejudice.

Maryland Rule 5-609 was derived from Federal Rule 609 and Maryland Rule 1-502. Although the Maryland Rule differs from the Federal Rule in some material ways,[6] both rules impose the same requirement that the trial court engage in a balancing process to determine whether the probative value outweighs the prejudicial effect.[7] Therefore we will look to federal cases interpreting the federal rule for guidance in interpreting the balancing prong of our state rule. While "the very nature of judicial discretion precludes rigid standards for its exercise," *Gordon*, 383 F.2d at 941, the federal courts have developed a number of factors to guide trial judges in this endeavor. *See id.* at 940.

Numerous courts around the country have established guidelines to be considered in weighing the probative value of a past conviction against the prejudicial effect. *See, e.g., id.; United States v. Mahone*, 537 F.2d 922, 929 (7th Cir. 1976). These factors are (1) the impeachment value of the prior crime; (2) the point in time of the conviction and the defendant's subsequent history; (3) the similarity between the past crime and the charged crime; (4) the importance of the defendant's testimony; and (5) the centrality of the defendant's credibility. *Mahone*, 537 F.2d at 929. While these factors should not be considered mechanically or exclusively, we believe they may be a useful aid to trial courts in performing the balancing exercise mandated by the Rule.

Although trial judges are not obliged to detail every step of their logic, we urge trial judges when discharging this duty to place the specific circumstances and factors critical

---

[6] Under Federal Rule 609, prior convictions of crimes involving dishonesty or false statement are per se admissible, Fed. R. Evid. 609(a)(2), while prior convictions of felonies are admissible only if the probative value outweighs the prejudicial effect. Fed. R. Evid. 609(a)(1).

[7] *See, e.g., United States v. Cook*, 608 F.2d 1175, 1185 (1979) (Federal Rule 609(a)(1) requires the trial judge to weigh the probative value of the impeaching conviction against the prejudice to the defendant).

to the decision on the record. In *Mahone*, the court set forth the following recommended procedure:

> In the future, to avoid the unnecessary raising of the issue of whether the judge has meaningfully invoked his discretion under Rule 609, we urge trial judges to make such determinations after a hearing on the record, as the trial judge did in the instant case, and to explicitly find that the prejudicial effect of the evidence to the defendant will be outweighed by its probative value. When such a hearing on the record is held and such an explicit finding is made, the appellate court easily will be able to determine whether the judge followed the strictures of Rule 609 in reaching his decision. The hearing need not be extensive. Bearing in mind that Rule 609 places the burden of proof on the government,[8] the judge should require a brief recital by the government of the circumstances surrounding the admission of the evidence, and a statement of the date, nature and place of the conviction. The defendant should be permitted to rebut the government's presentation, pointing out to the court the possible prejudicial effect to the defendant if the evidence is admitted.

537 F.2d at 929 (footnote added) (citations omitted).

In sum, we hold that the similarity of the prior conviction to the offense charged does not, absent other considerations, require exclusion. Evidence of a prior conviction for a crime that is similar or identical to the charged crime is subject to the balancing of its probativeness against its potential for unfair prejudice. Although the *Mahone* guidelines include a factor related to the degree of similarity between the prior conviction and the charged offense, this is only one consideration and should not be viewed in isolation.

The approach we adopt today appears to be in line with the view of the majority of state and federal courts in this country. Courts have been particularly inclined to allow same-crime impeachment where the defendant has presented an alibi, rendering his credibility particularly important, or where the defendant has attempted to present himself to the jury as someone "of stellar character."

III.

In the present case, we find that the trial judge's decision reflects a proper exercise of the discretion vested in her under Rule 5-609. We find that the trial court properly balanced the various factors in this case and did not abuse its discretion in admitting the Appellant's prior conviction for theft. When the trial court exercises its discretion in these matters, we will give great deference to the court's opinion. Consistent with our prior cases, this court will not disturb that discretion unless it is clearly abused.

*   *   *

Applying the *Mahone* factors to this case, four of the five factors weighed in favor of admitting the prior theft conviction. First, the offense of theft, because of its inherent deceitfulness, is universally recognized as conduct which reflects adversely on a witness's honesty. Second, Appellant's prior theft conviction was less than three years old. The trial judge noted that if it had been more remote in time, she might have excluded the conviction. As discussed above, however, the third factor, similarity of the

---

[8] In determining whether a prior conviction should be admitted for impeachment, the burden of persuasion is on the proponent of the evidence. In this case, therefore, the State had the burden of showing that the probative value of the prior conviction outweighed the prejudice.

prior conviction to the charged offense, weighs against admission.

In applying the fourth and fifth factors in the *Mahone* analysis — the importance of the defendant's testimony and the centrality of the defendant's credibility — we recognize that they differ from the first three, because these two factors can be interpreted to weigh either for or against admitting prior convictions. Factors four and five are restatements of the considerations that underlie the Rule: balancing the defendant's right to testify against the State's right to impeach the witness on cross-examination. Where credibility is the central issue, the probative value of the impeachment is great, and thus weighs heavily against the danger of unfair prejudice. The Appellant's credibility clearly was central to this case; therefore, it was important for the State to be able to present evidence bearing on credibility. Thus, we resolve the balance between the two factors in favor of admitting the Appellant's prior theft conviction.

In the present case, the Appellant portrayed himself as a college student, a member of the United States Navy Reserves, and a summer employee of the University of Maryland entrusted with responsibilities for payroll, job site management, and supervision of approximately 30 high school students. It would be patently unfair to permit the Appellant to present this "stellar" picture to the jury but to preclude the State from presenting evidence which would contradict this image. Moreover, the State did not overemphasize Appellant's prior convictions and, notably, never even mentioned the prior theft conviction in its closing argument. In addition, the trial court limited any prejudicial effect by instructing the jury to consider the evidence only in evaluating Jackson's credibility and for no other purpose.

We are unable to say that the trial court abused its discretion in permitting the state to impeach Appellant with evidence of his prior conviction for theft. Even though the prior felony conviction was for the same crime as the charged offense, the prejudice did not thereby outweigh the probative value.

Judgment of the Circuit Court for Baltimore City Affirmed.

NOTES

1. *Federal Rule 609(a)and Weighing Prejudice.* Federal Rule 609(a)(1) deals with impeachment by felony convictions and provides *two standards* for a court to use relative to balancing prejudice against probativeness when a felony conviction not involving dishonesty or false statement is offered to impeach under Rule 609. One standard favors admissibility while the other is more protective of the defendant.

(A) The Defendant's Standard. If the defendant testifies the court must determine that "the probative value of admitting the evidence outweighs the prejudicial effect to the accused." Accordingly, if the probative value of admitting evidence of a felony conviction and prejudice to the defendant are equal, the evidence is not admitted. The probative value must "*outweigh*" the prejudice to gain admissibility.

(B) The Standard for Government Witnesses and Witnesses Called by the Defendant. For all witnesses other than the defendant, admissibility is favored since the evidence is to be admitted even when prejudice outweighs probative value. For other witnesses the court is to use the balancing test provided in Federal Rule 403, which mandates admissibility unless the unfair prejudice "*substantially outweigh[s]*" the probative value of admitting the felony conviction to impeach. Accordingly, if the defendant calls a witness with a criminal record, evidence of that witness' felony

convictions may be admitted to impeach even if the prejudicial effect of such evidence slightly outweighs its probative value.

(C) Two Prongs of Rule 609(a). It should be remembered that Rule 609(a) has two parts, and the second part does not have a balancing test; it provides for mandatory admissibility. The first part, Rule 609(a)(1) concerns felony convictions that do not involve "dishonesty or false statement." Rule 609(a)(2) concerns admitting evidence of the conviction of a crime (any crime — felony or misdemeanor) that involves "dishonesty or false statement." Rule 609(a)(2) gives the trial court no discretion to exclude crimes that involve dishonesty or false statement; accordingly there is no balancing test applicable to the defendant or any other witness prior to admitting such evidence.

It is important, therefore, to determine whether a crime involves dishonesty or false statement. The advisory committee note to the 1990 amendment to Rule 609 stated that "[b]y the phrase 'dishonesty and false statement,' the conference means crimes such as perjury, subornation of perjury, false statement, criminal fraud, embezzlement, or false pretense, or any other crime in the nature of *crimen falsi*, commission of which involves some element of deceit, untruthfulness, or falsification bearing on the accused's propensity to testify truthfully."

2.*"Pulling The Sting."* It is not at all unusual for the calling party to anticipate impeachment by a prior conviction and ask the witness on direct about convictions that would be admissible to impeach under Federal Rule 609 (or one of its state counterparts). In fact the advisory committee note to the 1990 amendment to Rule 609 states that "[i]t is common for witnesses to reveal on direct examination their convictions to 'remove the sting' of the impeachment." *See, e.g., United States v. Handly,* 591 F.2d 1125, 1128 (5th Cir. 1979); *United States v. Apuzzo,* 555 F.2d 306, 307 (2d Cir. 1977).

The theory behind "pulling the sting" is that it will lessen the impact of the impeachment to admit it on direct rather than to appear to have been "hiding" the information from the jury. This is consistent with Federal Rule of Evidence 607, which allows a party to impeach a witness whom he or she called. Note that the prohibition on bolstering would bar a lawyer from asking a witness on direct about the witness' not having been convicted of a crime. *United States v. Hicks,* 748 F.2d 854, 859 (4th Cir. 1984).

3. *Other Uses Of Convictions.* Rule 609 and its state counterparts only address the admissibility of convictions to impeach under Rule 609, i.e., to show a predisposition to lie. Accordingly, Rule 609 has no application when convictions are offered to show bias, or for some other purpose. *See Davis v. Alaska,* 415 U.S. 308 (1974) (prior juvenile adjudication admissible to prove bias, not to show a past violation of the law); Christopher B. Mueller & Laird C. Kirkpatrick, 3 Federal Evidence §6:42, at 277–78 (3d ed. 2007). Similarly, Rule 609 has no application to offering convictions under Fed. R. Evid. 404(b) to prove other aspects of character.

4. *The Time Of The Attack.* Federal Rule 609 does not require that a witness be impeached by prior convictions while he or she is testifying. Arguably, however, a court could require the impeachment while the witness is testifying pursuant to its authority to control the "mode and order" of interrogation contained in Rule 611(a). If impeached while testifying, the defendant is usually allowed an opportunity to briefly explain. *See* Christopher B. Mueller & Laird C. Kirkpatrick, 3 Federal Evidence §6:43, at 303 (3d ed. 2007).

QUESTIONS

1. What kind of felonies do not involve "dishonesty or false statement" and also are probative of untruthful character? *See Gordon v. United States*, 383 F.2d 936, 940 (D.C. Cir. 1967).

2. If Jackson were being tried in federal court, where Fed. R. Evid. 609 applies, would the balancing test of Rule 609(a)(1) apply, or would the prior convictions for theft be automatically admitted under Rule 609(a)(2) as offenses involving "dishonesty or false statement"? *See United States v. Mejia-Alarcon*, 995 F.2d 982, 989 (10th Cir. 1993); *United States v. Sellers*, 906 F.2d 597, 603 (11th Cir. 1990). *But see United States v. Carden*, 529 F.2d 443, 446 (5th Cir. 1976).

PROBLEM

Problem 10-2. Federal DEA agents went to the home of John Breck after receiving a tip that he was selling marijuana. When they arrived at his home and announced their presence, Breck pointed a pistol at the DEA agents. When he was ordered to drop the pistol Breck complied and was arrested. In his home DEA agents found large quantities of marijuana.

Breck was charged in state court, with possession of a controlled substance with the intent to distribute. Breck was also charged in federal court, with using a firearm in the course of a felony. Both charges are felonies. The state charges went to trial first and Breck was convicted.

Breck is now on trial in federal court for using a firearm in the course of a felony. Breck testifies in his federal trial. On cross-examination the prosecutor asks him if he has ever been convicted of a felony. When Breck answers "no" the prosecutor asks if he was convicted in state court of possession of a controlled substance with the intent to distribute. Over objection, the federal prosecutor is allowed to prove the conviction.

(A) Is the state felony conviction, arising out of the same facts as the crime for which a defendant is on trial in federal court, admissible to impeach under Federal Rule 609?

(B) If so, does the probative value of admitting the conviction outweigh the prejudice to the defendant? *See United States v. Breckenridge*, 782 F.2d 1317, 1323 (5th Cir. 1986); *United States v. Burkhead*, 646 F.2d 1283, 1285 (8th Cir. 1981); Christopher B. Mueller & Laird C. Kirkpatrick, 3 Federal Evidence § 6:43, at 304–06 (3d ed. 2007).

(C) What if the felony conviction used to impeach occurred *after* the incidents for which the defendant is on trial? If Breck were released on bail and before being tried on either charge is arrested and convicted of income tax evasion, could he be asked at either of the two trials if he had ever been convicted of the felony of income tax evasion? *See United States v. Bogers*, 635 F.2d 749, 750 (8th Cir. 1980).

Next consider the question of what qualifies as a "conviction" that may be used under Federal Rule of Evidence 609. Specifically, if a defendant is convicted and his or her conviction is overturned on appeal for a violation of the defendant's constitutional rights (and not as a result of a determination that the defendant did not commit the crime charged), may the conviction be used to impeach?

UNITED STATES v. PENTA
475 F.2d 92 (1st Cir. 1973)

COFFIN, CHIEF JUDGE.

In June, 1970, appellant Penta was convicted of fraudulently possessing and transferring counterfeit Federal Reserve Notes in violation of 18 U.S.C. §§ 472 and 473. His sole defense was that he was entrapped by an alleged government agent. We affirmed the conviction in December, 1970, in an unpublished memorandum and order. Subsequently, in May, 1972, in a post-conviction collateral proceeding, the Massachusetts Supreme Judicial Court reversed earlier state court convictions of appellant in the mid-1960's for concealing stolen motor vehicles, on the basis that some of the evidence introduced resulted from an illegal search and seizure. *Commonwealth v. Penta*, 282 N.E.2d 674.[1] Since these convictions had been used in the 1970 federal trial to impeach appellant's credibility, he moved for a new trial and appeals from the denial thereof.

Initially we are met with the government's contention, superficially appealing, that appellant may not be heard to complain about the use of the state convictions by the prosecutor on cross-examination since his own trial counsel elicited admissions of these convictions from him on direct examination. While there is some authority for the view that a defendant who first raises the issue of his prior convictions cannot complain of prosecutorial reference thereto, that rule is based upon the premise that the convictions were properly admissible in the first place to impeach the defendant's credibility and might have been inquired into by the prosecutor in the face of a defendant's silence on direct examination. That is a far cry from what we take to be the claim here: that while the state convictions may have been properly admissible at the time of the federal trial, their subsequent reversal requires a new federal trial. Moreover, we cannot fault appellant's trial counsel who, apparently acting in good faith, introduced into evidence appellant's prior state convictions, so as to prevent the prosecutor, on cross-examination, from stunning the jury by being first to bring these skeletons out of what otherwise might have been viewed as the defendant's deceptively clean closet. We thus address appellant's argument.

Appellant does not deny that he committed the act in question, but rather argues that he was entrapped by one O'Connell, a former business associate acting as a government agent. His story is that O'Connell owed him several thousand dollars, which O'Connell said could be paid only if appellant helped him, as a middleman, to sell counterfeit money. O'Connell supposedly approached appellant on December 3, 1969, with this request which was allegedly consistently refused until December 10, the morning of the sale. From the testimony of government agent Hurley it appears that O'Connell first told Hurley on December 9 that an unnamed friend of his wished to sell counterfeit money. At that time Hurley told O'Connell that he "would see what [he] could do for [O'Connell]" on account of his help.[3] Late at night, after viewing samples of the counterfeit money, Hurley instructed O'Connell how to continue dealing with appellant and set up a meeting preceding the sale. Appellant's name was never revealed to Hurley, despite his continual questioning, until one hour before the meeting on December 10.

---

[1] The search warrants involved did not comply with Mass. Gen. Laws ch. 276, § 2B, which, as it has not been contended otherwise, we take to furnish constitutional minima.

[3] O'Connell, who did not testify in this case, subsequently received a reward of $2000.

At the conclusion of appellant's testimony his trial counsel asked him about his prior convictions and parole status, all of which he openly admitted. Assuming *arguendo* that after O'Connell's December 9 visits with Hurley he could be said to have become a government agent — an issue sent to the jury — only then would appellant's credibility be crucial to his defense of entrapment. In that situation, appellant alleges — and we will assume so at this juncture — that the evidence of prior convictions must have affected the jury's view of his veracity. Consequently we must determine if the subsequent reversal of those convictions requires a new trial on the counterfeiting charge.

It has recently been decided that if a conviction is based, in part, on the use of prior convictions which are constitutionally invalid due to lack of counsel and which were introduced to impeach a defendant's credibility, it must be set aside if there is no harmless error. *Loper v. Beto*, 405 U.S. 473 (1972). While the Supreme Court had before it in *Loper* the broad question "Does the use of prior, void convictions for impeachment purposes deprive a criminal defendant of due process of law where their use might well have influenced the outcome of the case," in its resolution of that issue in the particular fact situation before it, the Court drew exclusively upon the rationale behind the rule in *Gideon v. Wainwright*, 372 U.S. 335 (1963), which "goes to 'the very integrity of the fact-finding process' in criminal trials" and recognizes that convictions of uncounseled defendant lack reliability. *Loper, supra,* 405 U.S. at 484. . . .

. . . We agree that the use of evidence obtained from an unlawful search and seizure has a definite influence on the fact-finding process, but in a very different way from deprivation of counsel. Such evidence tends to make the resulting conviction more, not less trustworthy. There is no lack of reliability as there was in *Loper*.

If the use of appellant's prior state convictions, subsequently found to suffer from a constitutional defect, require that his federal conviction be vacated absent harmless error, it is only because the fruits of the poisonous tree now contain this additional genus. But an examination of the roots of that tree and recent actions to limit its growth require rejection of appellant's claim. The exclusionary rule has been called a deterrent against future illegal police conduct. "Its purpose is to deter — to compel respect for the constitutional guaranty in the only effectively available way — by removing the incentive to disregard it." *Elkins v. United States*, 364 U.S. 206 (1960). And long ago, *Weeks v. United States*, 232 U.S. 383 (1914), established the rule as a remedy for violations of the offender's Fourth Amendment rights.

*   *   *

If the exclusionary rule's application in these circumstances is sought to be justified as a remedy for violation of appellant's Fourth Amendment rights many years ago by Massachusetts police, we think that the suggested cure is worse than the disease. First, appellant has already received a remedy which is the most appropriate — his prior convictions were reversed. But more fundamentally, at the time of the federal trial the Massachusetts Supreme Judicial Court had already affirmed appellant's state convictions. There was not the least hint or suggestion that those convictions were invalid. The situation is far different from cases like *Loper* where a trial judge could rather easily resolve a deprivation of counsel claim by reference to a defendant's sworn statements and trial court records of prior convictions. It would play havoc with our court system to require a judge to conduct side-trials into the allegedly invalid prior convictions to determine the legality of a search or seizure. We do not think that the theoretical possibilities regarding additional police deterrence or the need to effectively remedy violations of Fourth Amendment rights can serve as the justification for imposing such heavy burdens on our courts.

Nothing we have said so far is meant to suggest that we would condone introduction of the state convictions had they been overturned, on the basis of the illegal search, prior to the time of the federal trial. . . . No case has gone so far to suggest that the prosecution might introduce what has already been determined to be illegally obtained evidence from prior unrelated acts or convictions to impeach generally a defendant's credibility. . . . We only go so far as to hold that a conviction which may have been influenced by the use, for general impeachment purposes, of prior convictions, which have been subsequently overturned on constitutional grounds relating to an illegal search or seizure, may properly stand.

To the extent that we may be incorrect in reading the recent Supreme Court holdings as requiring rejection of appellant's claim, we still believe that the use of the prior convictions constituted harmless error beyond a reasonable doubt. First, appellant's credibility on his entrapment defense was greatly harmed by evidence relevant to predisposition that he had been charged with possession of burglar tools in the past. Second, his story was contradicted directly in part by government agents who testified to appellant's suede coat being dry — though he alleged having walked some three blocks in a rainstorm to the place of the sale — and to his having stated, after being warned of his right to remain silent, that he had been sent out with some money to obtain some bread and had returned with neither money nor bread — a fact appellant denied at trial. Though appellant may have been incorrect in his testimony on these points and still may have been capable of being believed as to his story of entrapment in the main, we think that the use of the convictions when considered in this context added no more than minimally to the enormous damage already done to his credibility.

Affirmed.

QUESTIONS

1. According to the First Circuit in *Penta*, when is it that an invalid conviction may not be used to impeach?

2. Assume that defendant is convicted of robbery but his conviction is overturned on appeal and a new trial ordered because evidence admitted at his trial was unconstitutionally seized. If the defendant faces trial on unrelated charges, cocaine possession, before he is retried on the overturned robbery conviction, may the robbery conviction be used to impeach the defendant if he testifies in his cocaine possession trial?

[ii]   Misconduct Not Resulting in Conviction that Shows a Predisposition to Lie

EDWARD J. IMWINKELRIED, PAUL C. GIANNELLI, FRANCIS A. GILLIGAN & FREDRIC I. LEDERER, 1 COURTROOM CRIMINAL EVIDENCE § 709, at 294–300 (4th ed. 2005)[*]

§ 709. Misconduct Not Resulting in Conviction.

In this area little uniformity exists in the rules of the various jurisdictions. There is a three-way split of authority over this impeachment technique.

View # 1. At one extreme, a minority of courts allow the cross-examiner to impeach the witness by questioning about any illegal or immoral act; the act need not relate to untruthfulness or veracity.

View # 2. The federal rule, Rule 608(b), follows the majority view. Rule 608(b) allows the judge discretion to permit cross-examination concerning misconduct which is "probative of untruthfulness." This impeachment technique is available against witness, including the defendant or the alleged victim. Effective December 1, 2003, the wording of Rule 608(b) was amended. The amendment strikes the prior term "credibility" from the statutory text and substitutes "character for truthfulness." One court attempted to define the scope of the provision by in effect analogizing to Rule 609(a)(2) governing convicting impeachment. The cross-examiner may inquire about prior acts of perjury or deceit.

Unless the opponent has an alternative theory of admissibility such as uncharged misconduct. . . , he or she is limited to the witness's answer and may not prove the act by extrinsic evidence. If the witness perjuriously denies the act of misconduct, the cross-examiner must "take the answer;" the cross-examiner may not call another witness to prove the prior witness's act of misconduct. For that matter, the opponent may not ask the question at all unless he or she has a good-faith belief that the witness committed the act. The Advisory Committee Note accompanying the 2003 amendment to Rule 608(b) explains that "[t]he Rule has been amended to clarify that the sole reason for proffering that evidence is to attack or support the witness' character for truthfulness. On occasion the Rule's use of the overbroad term 'credibility' has been read 'to bar extrinsic evidence for bias, competency, and contradiction impeachment since they too deal with credibility.'" However, the Note added "the extrinsic evidence prohibition of Rule 608(b) bars any reference to the consequences that a witness might have suffered as a result of the alleged bad acts. For example, Rule 608(b) prohibits counsel from mentioning that a witness was suspended or disciplined for the conduct that is the subject of impeachment. . . . ."

View # 3. At the other extreme, another minority of jurisdictions generally prohibit cross-examination about specific acts of misconduct which have not resulted in a conviction.

However, even some of these jurisdictions recognize one or both of two "exceptions" to this prohibition. First, the opponent may prove acts of misconduct directly related to the case — for example, attempted subornation of perjury by a witness in the case. In this situation, the evidence is also relevant to the historical merits as proof of consciousness of guilt. That relevance beings Rule 404(b) into play, and extrinsic evidence is admissible under Rule 404(b).

Second, if on direct-examination the witness makes a sweeping claim disavowing any misconduct, the opponent may question him or her regarding specific acts. The sweeping claim triggers another impeachment technique, specific contradiction. Thus, if a defendant on direct examination stated that he or she had "never" possessed drugs, the prosecutor could impeach the defendant's statements; the trial judge would permit the prosecutor to conduct cross-examination and introduce independent evidence of the defendant's possession of drugs on prior occasions. At one time, most courts assumed that the sweeping denial doctrine applied only if the defendant made the denial on direct examination. The Supreme Court has, however, indicated that a denial solicited on cross-examination by the prosecutor will suffice. In reality, neither of these doctrines is a true "exception" to the general rule. In the case of this "exception" as in the first, there is an alternative theory of logical relevance — specific contradiction. . . . These doctrines are not exceptions to the general rule limiting an opponent using this impeachment technique to cross-examination; they are simply cases in which the evidence is also logically relevant on another theory.

* * *

As the excerpt from COURTROOM CRIMINAL EVIDENCE suggests, a primary problem with applying Rule 608(b) is determining whether a specific instance of conduct is or is not probative of truthfulness. For example, in the context of a criminal case it is not unusual for the defendant or other witnesses to have been arrested or to have used drugs. Is evidence that a witness has used drugs or been arrested admissible under Rule 608(b) to impeach? The three cases that follow examine these issues, among others.

UNITED STATES v. BEROS
833 F.2d 455 (3d Cir. 1987)

A. LEON HIGGINBOTHAM, JR., CIRCUIT JUDGE.

On this appeal from a final judgment of conviction and sentence, the appellant presents four grounds for this Court's review. He argues . . . [among other things] that the district court abused its discretion by admitting a sworn statement previously made by appellant on an application for a marriage license, falsely stating that his marital status was single. . . .

* * *

Appellant James M. Beros, an officer of the Teamsters Joint Council 40 and a trustee of the Western Pennsylvania Teamsters and Employees Pension Fund ("Pension Fund"), was indicted on a sixteen count indictment. In its several counts, the indictment alleged that on separate occasions Beros was guilty of "embezzling, stealing, abstracting or converting to his own use" funds of the Teamsters Joint Council 40 and of the Pension Fund, in violation of 29 U.S.C. § 501(c) (1982) and 18 U.S.C. § 664 (1982), and that Beros was guilty of conspiring with another person to commit those offenses.

Beros was tried by jury and convicted on seven of the charged counts. He was fined $20,000 and was placed on probation for a period of five years. On appeal, Beros challenges these convictions and sentences. . . .

* * *

III.

. . . [The appellant] next argues that the district court abused its discretion by allowing cross-examination of himself and other defense witnesses regarding a false statement previously made by Beros to a sworn statement. The statement in question was made in May 1981, when Beros, who was in fact married, lied about his marital status on a Nevada marriage license, and thereby attested that he was legally competent to marry Christine Molitoris, with whom he had had an affair and who had accompanied him on several of the trips named in the indictment. Beros sought to have this evidence excluded from his trial. He argued that it was unduly prejudicial because it was inflammatory and because its use was calculated to arouse moral indignation by demonstrating that he had attempted to commit bigamy.[5] The district court denied Beros's motion and allowed the government to use evidence of this false statement to impeach Beros's character in its cross-examination of him and to examine his character witnesses regarding their knowledge of the incident.

The propriety of the district court's exercise of discretion in this matter is too evident to merit much discussion. The Federal Rules of Evidence clearly provide that evidence regarding specific instances of conduct relevant to a defendant's character is permissible on cross-examination where the defendant has put his or her character in question by his or her testimony or through that of a witness presented by the defendant, or where the issue of his credibility is an essential element of the charged offense. See Federal Rules of Evidence 608(b) and 405(b).

It cannot be disputed that Beros's character and honesty were central issues to his case. Further, when he took the stand, he subjected his credibility to scrutiny as do all witnesses. The evidence in question was therefore certainly admissible, subject only to a discretionary decision by the district court to exclude it.

Beros correctly notes that a proper limit upon the admission of relevant character evidence is imposed in instances where the probative value of the evidence is outweighed by its prejudicial impact. See Fed. R. Evid. 403. This case, however, does not present such an instance.

The evidence in question may well have tended to demonstrate Beros's capacity for untruthfulness, but that is the legitimate purpose for which it was offered. We are aware that the detriment to his credibility that Beros suffered as the result of the admission of this evidence may have been great, given the magnitude of his attempted falsehood. We are unpersuaded, however, that because of this significance the evidence should have been excluded. We agree with the district court that there was no genuine potential for unfair prejudice to Beros as the result of the admission of the evidence.

The correctness of our conclusion appears more certain in light of the fact that evidence of Beros's adultery with Molitoris had already been admitted without challenge. Moreover, the district court sufficiently mitigated any potential for unfair prejudicial effect that the evidence might have had, by preventing the government from suggesting in any way that Beros had in fact committed bigamy. Accordingly, we find no abuse of discretion. . . .

---

[5] There is no indication in the record or in the briefs that the appellant denies the veracity of the accusation.

UNITED STATES v. CLEMONS

32 F.3d 1504 (11th Cir. 1994)

KRAVITCH, CIRCUIT JUDGE:

Eugene Clemons and Dedrick Smith were convicted of murdering a federal agent engaged in the performance of his official duties in violation of 18 U.S.C. §§ 1111 and 1114.

George Douglas Althouse was a Special Agent of the U.S. Drug Enforcement Administration (DEA) assigned to the Birmingham, Alabama office. As part of his duties, Althouse worked on an investigation with Sergeant Mark Hobbs of the Hoover, Alabama Police Department. Hobbs and Althouse planned to meet on the evening of Thursday, May 28, 1992 between 10:00 and 11:00 p.m. to discuss search warrants to be executed the following day. Jefferson County Sheriff's Deputy Naylor Braswell, Althouse's housemate, agreed to accompany Althouse to the meeting with Hobbs. Braswell and Althouse left for the meeting shortly before 10:00 p.m. in Braswell's undercover automobile, a black Model Z-28 Camaro. En route, they stopped at a Chevron service station. Braswell went into the station to obtain the telephone number for a pizza delivery source. Althouse remained in the car. . . . While inside the service station, Braswell suddenly observed an individual sitting in the driver's seat of the Camaro and pointing a gun to Althouse's head. Moments later Braswell heard several shots and saw Althouse exit the car. Althouse fired his weapon at the Camaro as it sped away. Althouse died shortly thereafter from gunshot wounds.

Testimony offered at trial revealed that prior to the murder Dedrick Smith had told several individuals, including Clemons, that he needed an engine for his Z-28 Camaro. On the evening of the murder, Smith, Clemons and a third individual, Kenny Reed, drove to a shopping center looking for a suitable car for Smith. Failing to find such a vehicle, they proceeded onto the highway. When Clemons spotted a Z-28 Camaro in a Chevron service station, they stopped and Clemons, carrying a gun, exited the car. Smith and Reed were driving to a nearby parking lot to wait for Clemons when they heard several gunshots and observed Clemons, driving the Camaro, pull out of the Chevron station at high speed. Clemons drove to the house of a friend, Herman Shannon. After examining the contents of the car, Clemons and Shannon concluded that it was likely a police vehicle. Both Clemons and Smith subsequently left town. Clemons was arrested in Cleveland, Ohio on June 6. Smith was arrested in Birmingham several days later. Both were convicted by a jury of murdering Agent Althouse.

*   *   *

Smith contends that the court erred in . . . permitting him to be cross-examined by Clemons regarding irrelevant and prejudicial matters [among other things].

*   *   *

IV.

Smith . . . argues that the court erred in allowing Clemons to cross-examine him concerning prior conduct involving drug use, ownership of a pistol and assault of a police officer. Although the court expressly prohibited the government from inquiring into Smith's prior conduct, each defendant was given wide latitude in cross-examining his codefendant. Smith testified on cross-examination by both the government and by

Clemons that he had not witnessed people selling crack cocaine at Herman Shannon's house during the time he lived there, and that he had moved out of the house in the second week of January 1992. Clemons sought to impeach Smith's credibility by asking him whether he personally had ever used or sold crack cocaine. . . .

Fed. R. Evid. 608(b) provides that specific instances of conduct, if probative of truthfulness or untruthfulness, may be inquired into on cross-examination of a witness. The court is given broad discretion in assessing the propriety of this mode of inquiry. In this instance, questions pertaining to Smith's knowledge of possible drug transactions taking place at Shannon's house were raised for the first time on cross-examination. The relevance of this line of questioning was never demonstrated, and cannot be gleaned by this court. The government suggests that Clemons's inquiry was probative of Smith's credibility as "a witness who had been implicated by other witnesses who were at Shannon's house at the time of Agent Althouse's murder." We do not agree that the question whether Smith ever used or sold drugs was probative of his credibility as a witness. This circuit has long adhered to the proposition that a witness's use of drugs may not be used to attack his general credibility, but only his ability to perceive the underlying events and to testify lucidly at trial. Neither Clemons nor the government contended at trial that Smith was unable to comprehend the events that transpired on the evening of Agent Althouse's murder due to the influence of crack-cocaine, nor did either party attempt to show that Smith was using drugs during the trial. The question of Smith's possible drug use was neither probative of his truthfulness or his capacity to testify nor relevant to discovering the facts of this case.

*   *   *

Even where an abuse of discretion is shown, however, nonconstitutional evidentiary errors are not grounds for reversal absent a reasonable likelihood that the defendant's substantial rights were affected. Here, Smith denied having used or sold crack-cocaine, and the matter was not only dropped entirely by Clemons's counsel, but was never raised again by any party for the remainder of the trial. It is difficult to discern what prejudice may have inured to Smith from this extremely limited foray into his personal drug habits. By the same token, even removing from consideration the inadmissible question concerning drug use, the totality of the evidence against Smith was weighty. . . . We conclude that the evidentiary error identified by this court does not merit a reversal of Smith's conviction.

Accordingly, the convictions of Clemons and Smith are each affirmed.

UNITED STATES v. DENNIS
625 F.2d 782 (8th Cir. 1980)

McMILLIAN, CIRCUIT JUDGE.

Willie H. Dennis appeals his conviction on twelve counts of an eighteen-count indictment charging seventeen violations of the Extortionate Credit Transactions Act (ECT). . . . We affirm.

From September 10, 1962, through October 2, 1978, Dennis was employed by the General Motors Assembly Division in St. Louis, Missouri. Beginning at least as early as 1970, Dennis started lending money to fellow plant workers and others at twenty-five percent a week interest, a practice which he continued until at least March 10, 1978. On Thursday, which is payday for the nightshift employees, Dennis customarily lent to and collected from nightshift employees in the plant cafeteria. On Friday, which is payday for the dayshift employees, Dennis made loans and collections in front of the guard shack at the plant entrance. Occasionally, other individuals made collections on behalf of Dennis; and, when a payment was long overdue, Dennis searched out the debtor at locations away from the plant. Documents taken from Dennis in the contested searches identified his debtors by name, amount of loan, interest paid and interest collected. These records revealed the following facts about Dennis's operation: (1) from December 22, 1977, through March 10, 1978, the total amount collected was $31,777.00, of which $22,701.00 was interest; (2) the usual rate of interest was twenty-five percent a week or thirteen hundred percent a year; and (3) there were 133 accounts as of March 10, 1978, with a total balance outstanding of $52,956.00.

* * *

Dennis contends that the trial court erred in restricting his cross-examination of a key witness whom he wished to impeach with character evidence under Rule 608 Fed. R. Evid. and evidence of convictions under Rule 609 Fed. R. Evid. We find no error in this regard.

James Louis was an important witness for the government. Not only was he the complaining witness for counts thirteen, fourteen and fifteen, but also he was the only witness to testify about Dennis's contacts with other victims. He testified that Dennis talked about having a gun and that he had seen Dennis with a gun. He was the only borrower who kept written records of his loan transactions. On direct examination, the prosecutor brought out two felony convictions, including one twenty-two year old conviction, and one instance of employment as a paid informant for the Drug Enforcement Agency. Dennis claims that, once the prosecutor opened the subject of Louis's background on direct, Dennis should have been allowed to develop the full background by a wide-ranging cross-examination.

Where the testimony of one witness is critical to the government's case, the defendant has a right to attack that witness's credibility by a wide-ranging cross-examination. The Federal Rules of Evidence, however, place certain limitations on such impeachment. Under Rule 608(b), the court in its discretion may allow impeachment of a witness by cross-examination concerning specific instances of conduct not resulting in conviction if the conduct relates to the witness's character for truthfulness or untruthfulness. The court balances a question's relevance to honesty and veracity with its prejudicial impact. Rule 609(a) provides that in a criminal case the prior conviction of a prosecution witness may be used to impeach his credibility if it (1) was a felony and the court in its discretion determines that its probative value outweighs its prejudicial effect, or (2) involved dishonesty or false statement. . . . Rule 609(b) limits evidence of convictions to those within ten years or with special probative value. . . .

The court rejected Dennis's attempts to put in four types of evidence for impeachment. First, Dennis wanted to cross-examine Louis about convictions that ranged from twenty-six to thirty-five years old. All of the offenses were remote in time, older even than the twenty-two year old conviction brought out on direct; and none of the convictions related to offenses that were especially probative of truthfulness. Therefore, the trial court did not abuse its discretion in rejecting them under Rule 609. Second, Dennis wanted to cross-examine Louis about an arrest for tax problems, which did not result in a conviction. Although cross-examination about arrests without convictions is precluded, Rule 608(b) would permit inquiry into the specific acts that may have led to the arrest if those acts related to *crimen falsi*, e.g., perjury, suborning of perjury, false statement, embezzlement, false pretenses. The trial court did not err in precluding evidence of the arrest for tax problems. . . . Third, Dennis wanted to cross-examine Louis extensively about his activities as a paid informant. Dennis was permitted to question Louis about his being paid as an informant for the Drug Enforcement Agency but was barred from asking about the specific financial arrangements. The court's ruling noted that Louis was before the court as "a victim of extortion not as an accomplice or informant." Cross-examination about specific instances of conduct should be limited to an elicitation of the basic facts. There was no error in excluding excessive and irrelevant details of Louis's acknowledged work as an informant. . . .

* * *

Accordingly, the judgment of the district court is affirmed.

NOTES

1. *False Statements.* The *Beros* case is typical of cases which hold that making a false statement is admissible to impeach under Rule 608(b). It is important to remember that the untruthful conduct need not create criminal liability or result in a conviction. *United States v. Bagaric,* 706 F.2d 42, 65 (2d Cir. 1983) (statement before immigration judge found to be false by the immigration judge). For other examples of untruthful statements admitted under Rule 608(b), see *United States v. Williams,* 986 F.2d 86, 89 (4th Cir. 1993) (using fake driver's license to cash checks); *United States v. Jones,* 900 F.2d 512, 520–21 (2d Cir. 1990) (using false statements on employment application). *See generally* CHRISTOPHER B. MUELLER & LAIRD C. KIRKPATRICK, 3 FEDERAL EVIDENCE § 6:33, at 208–12 (3d ed. 2007); 1 COURTROOM CRIMINAL EVIDENCE § 709, at 294 n.108 (4th ed. 2005).

2. *Misconduct That Is Not Admissible.* As the *Clemons* and *Dennis* cases indicate, questions about drug usage and arrests are not admissible under Rule 608(b). In addition to excluding arrests, courts uniformly consider the fact of being charged or indicted to be inadmissible under Rule 608(b). *United States v. Abadie,* 879 F.2d 1260, 1267 (5th Cir. 1989). As to arrests, it is important to note that it is proper to ask about the behavior itself that led to an arrest. *United States v. Kirk,* 496 F.2d 947, 949–50 (8th Cir. 1974).

3. *Acquittals.* If a defendant is charged with a theft but is acquitted, may he or she be asked in a subsequent trial for a different offense, whether he or she committed the acts that were the subject of the acquittal? First, it is important to keep in mind that the questioner must have a good faith belief that the witness actually committed the act prior to asking about it. *United States v. Cardarella,* 570 F.2d 264, 267–68 (8th Cir. 1978). *See generally* 1 COURTROOM CRIMINAL EVIDENCE §709, at 298 (4th ed. 2005). In *Dowling v. United States,* 493 U.S. 342 (1990), the United States Supreme Court held that it did not violate due process or collateral estoppel to offer evidence of bad acts under Rule 404(b) even though the defendant had been tried and acquitted. Of course, since conviction requires proof beyond a reasonable doubt, and admission under Rule 608(b) requires a lesser degree of proof, it is possible to argue that the defendant committed the acts for Rule 608(b) purposes notwithstanding the acquittal. However, there may not be much utility in asking about such acts since the witness is likely to deny committing the acts and point out that he or she was acquitted. Finally, Rule 608(b) does not allow extrinsic evidence to establish that the act was in fact committed.

4. *Self-Incrimination.* The last sentence of Rule 608(b) makes clear that the witness does not have to answer questions about misconduct if to do so would violate the witness' privilege against self-incrimination and the question goes only to the witness' credibility.

PROBLEMS

Problem 10-3. Defendant is on trial for sexually abusing two children aged 9 and 7, respectively. He attempts to introduce evidence showing that the children have made false accusations in the past. The accusations do not, however, involve false accusations of sexual misconduct. The evidence is a statement given to the defendant's attorney by a police officer that indicates that one year ago, the children falsely accused a person of theft. The statement also indicates that the police officer investigated the allegations and found them to be untrue.

Assume that you are representing defendant and the case is being tried in a federal court, or in a state that has a rule of evidence identical to Federal Rule 608(b).

(A) Would evidence of the false accusations be admissible: If so, to show what?

(B) If admissible, how would you prove the false accusations were made: ask the children about them when they testify, or offer the statement of the police officer (or the officer's live testimony)? Does it matter which method you choose? *See State v. Goldenstein*, 505 N.W.2d 332, 340 (Minn. App. 1993; *Spivey v. State*, 397 S.E.2d 588 (Ga. 1990).

Problem 10-4. Assume that police officers are trained in how to interrogate suspects. One method of interrogation involves telling lies to the suspect to induce a confession. For example, if a person is arrested and suspected of having shot someone the police officer may tell the suspect that the shooting victim is being treated at the hospital and is not seriously hurt, when in fact the victim has died. Another typical, "lie" occurs in "date rape" cases. The police officer may tell the suspect (falsely) that he (the police officer) has himself done the same thing and it is not particularly serious, in an effort to get the accused to confess.

Assume that a police officer routinely lies to suspects in order to get them to confess in the manner described above, and that this police officer is testifying in a murder case *where he did no interrogation* but did investigate the crime scene. Would it be permissible to ask him if he routinely lies to suspects? If so, under what theory would such a question be admissible?

[iii]   The Character Witness: Opinion and Reputation Evidence of a Witness' Character for Untruthfulness

EDWARD J. IMWINKELRIED, PAUL C. GIANNELLI, FRANCIS A. GILLIGAN & FREDRIC I. LEDERER, 1 COURTROOM CRIMINAL EVIDENCE § 707, at 278–82 (4th ed. 2005)*

§ 707. Character Trait for Untruthfulness.

As soon as a witness testifies, his or her credibility becomes an issue in the case. One method of impeachment is an attack on the witness' character trait of truthfulness. . . . In brief, the opponent may introduce timely reputation or opinion evidence about the witness' character trait of untruthfulness.

(a) *"Reputation or Opinion Evidence."* There are two permissible types of character evidence. Evidence of an individual's reputation among members of the community is called reputation evidence. Evidence consisting of a witness' personal opinion is called opinion evidence.

At common law and still under the minority view today, only reputation evidence is admissible to impeach credibility. The character witness is not permitted to give a personal opinion despite the fact that opinion evidence may be more persuasive. The modern trend, however, is to permit both opinion and reputation evidence. The Federal Rules allow both. In truth, even traditional courts that have a rule barring opinion evidence often admit it disguised as reputation evidence. Since the controlling federal provision, Rule 608(a), generically refers to "Opinion," both lay and expert opinion are seemingly admissible.

To lay a proper foundation for reputation evidence, the proponent must show that the character witness (1) is a resident of the same community as the witness and (2) has lived in that community long enough to have become familiar with the witness' reputation in that community. While the courts originally insisted that the community be residential, the trend is to admit a reputation arising within any large social group likely to be familiar with the witness. A large corporation, church congregation, or university student body can qualify as a "community" in the broad, contemporary sense of the term. If the witness is imprisoned in a penal institute, the inmate population can constitute the relevant "community."

In the jurisdictions admitting opinion evidence, a proper foundation requires the character witness to (1) know the witness personally and (2) be well enough acquainted to have had an opportunity to form a reliable opinion of the witness' character trait for truthfulness. When the opinion takes the form of expert testimony, the testimony must also comply with the foundational requirements [for expert testimony].

The courts have resisted attempts to circumvent these restrictions on reputation and opinion evidence. In one case, the defense attempted to introduce testimony that the complainant had a reputation for telling a particular type of lie. The court upheld the trial judge's exclusion of the testimony. The court acknowledged that the defendant has the right to introduce reputation testimony about the witness' character trait of untruthfulness. However, the court reasoned that, in effect, the defense was attempting to suggest to the jury that on specific past occasions, the complainant had told similar lies. The court commented that . . . "[e]vidence of specific instances of conduct is not a permissible method of proving character as circumstantial evidence of conduct on direct examination." Nor may the party attacking the witness' credibility ask another witness whether the earlier witness lied or whether the witness believed the earlier witness' testimony. An answer to either question would represent improper opinion. The only permissible opinion is one directly related to the witness' character trait for untruthfulness.

(b) *"About the Witness' Character Trait of Untruthfulness."* The majority view is that only the witness' specific character trait for truthfulness is in issue. This view has been phrased differently in various jurisdictions without a change in result; some courts refer to the character trait for truthfulness and veracity, others to truth and honesty, and still others to integrity or mendacity. It is unclear whether the differing standards have led to differing results; whatever phrasing the state opts for, the results in the jurisdiction limiting proof to the character trait of truthfulness are relatively uniform.

The minority view is that in addition to the specific character trait of truthfulness, the witness' general moral character is in issue. The Federal Rules specifically reject this minority view for the reason that the minority approach results in unfair surprise, waste of time, and confusion for the fact finders. Under both the minority and majority approaches, even an opinion witness is precluded from opining that the other witness lied.

* * *

(c) *"Timely."* We are interested in the witness' credibility at the time of trial. The question is whether the witness is lying now. The evidence introduced must consist of a reputation arising or an opinion formed near the time of the trial. . . .

QUESTIONS

1. What are the two permissible types of evidence of a witness' character for truthfulness? Are both types permitted under the Federal Rules?

2. What foundation is necessary prior to offering *reputation* evidence from a character witness relative to truthfulness?

3. What foundation is necessary prior to offering *opinion* evidence from a character witness relative to truthfulness?

4. May a character witness, called pursuant to Fed. R. Evid. 608(a), be asked if he or she believes the principal witness?

5. May a character witness describe specific conduct of the principal witness that led the character witness to form the opinion that the principal witness was not truthful?

UNITED STATES v. MELTON
739 F.2d 576 (11th Cir. 1984)

JAMES C. HILL, CIRCUIT JUDGE:

Jerry T. Melton was tried in the district court and convicted on one count of conspiracy, 18 U.S.C. § 371, and seven counts of wire fraud, 18 U.S.C. § 1343. The evidence at trial showed that Melton contacted by telephone a large number of persons who had advertised expensive automobiles for sale in local newspapers. Melton informed the persons that he owned a precious gem collection and that he wished to barter gems for their cars. Melton offered various rationales to support his offers: that he wanted to obtain a car for his son, that he needed cash, or that he wished to consummate the transaction by barter for tax reasons. The government produced evidence at trial demonstrating that the "gems" offered by Melton (and accepted by some persons) in exchange for the cars were worthless and that Melton and several other persons had planned the scheme in order to obtain the cars by fraud. Melton appeals to this court, requesting that we set aside his conviction on various grounds including insufficiency of the evidence. We affirm.

* * *

At trial, Melton testified in his own behalf. In rebuttal, the government produced five witnesses who testified that they were familiar with Melton's reputation for truthfulness and honesty and that they would not believe Melton under oath. Melton contends that the trial court should not have allowed the government to use the testimony of five witnesses. We reject this contention. By choosing to testify, Melton placed his credibility in issue as does any other witness. Thus, the government could properly demonstrate that Melton's credibility was suspect. Melton's contention that it was unduly prejudicial to allow as many as five rebuttal witnesses to testify is governed by Rule 403 of the Federal Rules of Evidence. Thus, we will reverse Melton's conviction only upon a showing of abuse of discretion by the trial judge. We perceive no abuse in this case; indeed, if Melton was able to convince individuals to trade expensive cars for worthless gems, the trial judge could well have concluded that the government should be allowed to call five witnesses to counteract any effect Melton's obviously believable personality might have on the jury.

* * *

The judgment of the district court is Affirmed.

UNITED STATES v. DOTSON
799 F.2d 189 (5th Cir. 1986)

CLARK, CHIEF JUDGE:

Appellant Leon Frederick Dotson appeals his conviction on three counts of receiving firearms in violation of 18 U.S.C. §§ 922(h) and 922(a). Finding that the district court erred in allowing government agents to testify as to their opinions of the truth and veracity of Dotson and Dotson's witnesses without offering an adequate predicate upon which they based their opinions, we reverse.

Dotson was convicted in 1977 and 1978 of state and federal felonies for the possession of marijuana. In 1982 he was released from federal detention and placed on parole. As a result of his status as a convicted felon on parole, federal law prohibited Dotson from knowingly receiving firearms. 18 U.S.C. § 922(h).

The three handguns that were the subject of the charges against Dotson included a Colt.38 revolver, a Colt.45 pistol, and a.9 mm Walther pistol. As part of his defense of necessity, Dotson took the stand himself and called various witnesses to explain how and why he had obtained the handguns.

The essence of Dotson's defense is his contention that he was faced with serious and repeated threats to his physical safety shortly after his release and return home. On one occasion, an Officer Charles Kirk of the Greenville, Mississippi police was called to investigate an alleged attack in which 30 bullets were fired into Dotson's house. Kirk testified at trial that he advised Dotson to obtain a weapon for protection.

Dotson testified that he had purchased the Colt.38 before his earlier convictions, and that he had left the handgun with others during his incarceration and before the attack. He testified that, after his talk with Kirk, he reclaimed the weapon for his protection. Both Dotson and his mother, Erma Dotson, testified that he had received the Colt.45 as part of his father's estate. Finally, both Dotson and his friend, Reginald Owens, testified that the.9 mm Walther was obtained in pawn for a gambling loan, and that Owens had kept the pistol until Dotson needed it for his protection. In addition, Dotson's girlfriend, Crystal Johnson, offered testimony corroborating Dotson's version of how he acquired the handguns; her testimony also bolstered Dotson's claims of serious threats, as did the testimony of Kirk, Owens, and Erma Dotson.

As part of its rebuttal to Dotson's defense of necessity, the government called four government agents to testify that, in their opinion, Dotson and one or more of his witnesses were not of truthful character and not to be believed under oath.

The government first called FBI agent John Canale, who testified as follows:

Q: Have you had occasion to conduct an investigation into the activities of the defendant, Fred Dotson, and his associates?

A: Yes, sir, I have.

Q: As a result of this investigation and what you have learned and all that you have seen in this case, have you formed an opinion as to the truthfulness of the defendant, Frederick Leon Dotson?

A: Yes, sir, I have.

Q: Is that opinion of his truthfulness good or bad?

A: Bad.

Q: Would you believe Frederick Leon Dotson under oath?

A: No, sir, I would not.

The prosecutor then asked Canale the same questions with regard to Dotson's girlfriend, Crystal Johnson. After Canale stated his opinion, defense counsel objected as follows:

If the court please, I object to that your honor. I don't believe that an adequate predicate has been laid. He knows her and general reputation in the community that he lives —

The court interrupted at this point and overruled the objection.

Thereupon the prosecutor proceeded in similar fashion to elicit opinions from Canale as to Owens and Kirk. Three more government agents were called — another FBI agent, a state narcotics agent, and an Internal Revenue Services agent — to offer their opinions on the truthfulness of Dotson and his witnesses. The form of questioning and the opinions elicited did not differ materially from the example offered above, with two exceptions. The Mississippi narcotics agent testified that she had known Dotson for six or seven years and Owens "[w]ithin the last year"; otherwise, she also based her opinion of Dotson, Owens and two more of his witnesses on her investigation of this case. The IRS agent limited his opinion testimony to the truthfulness of Erma Dotson, whom he had investigated on a separate occasion.

The jury returned verdicts of guilty on all three counts of receiving firearms. Dotson was convicted and sentenced to a total of five years.

On appeal, Dotson challenges the admission of the government agents' opinion testimony based solely on their conduct of an investigation. . . .

II.

Federal Rule of Evidence 608(a) reads in relevant part:

> The credibility of a witness may be attacked or supported by evidence in the form of opinion or reputation . . . for truthfulness or untruthfulness. . . .

Prior to the adoption of Rule 608(a), there had been confusion and conflict among courts and commentators as to the propriety of offering opinion evidence to impeach the credibility of a witness. It had been common practice for counsel to ask witnesses whether, based upon their knowledge of the principal witness's reputation in the community for truth and veracity, they would believe him under oath. Recognizing that "witnesses who testify to reputation often seem in fact to be giving their opinions, disguised somewhat misleadingly as reputation," Advisory Committee's Note, Fed. R. Evid. 608(a), Rule 608(a) makes clear that witnesses may state their opinions directly.

In *United States v. Lollar*, 606 F.2d 587 (5th Cir. 1979), a case in which a challenge was made only to the impeachment of the defendant, this Circuit stated that Rule 608(a) imposes no requirement that "counsel first ask the impeaching witness about his knowledge of the defendant's reputation for truth and veracity, and whether based on that knowledge he would believe the defendant under oath. . . ." *Id.* at 589. The *Lollar* decision quotes Judge Weinstein at length:

> Witnesses may now be asked directly to state their opinion of the principal witness's character for truthfulness and they may answer for example, "I think X is a liar." The rule imposes no prerequisite conditioned upon long acquaintance or recent information about the witness. . . .

Id. (citing 3 Weinstein's Evidence para. 608[04], at 608–20 (1978)).

In the case before us on review, Dotson does not challenge the form of the evidence at issue. Rather he asserts that there are limits to the introduction of opinion testimony. In particular, he refers to Federal Rules of Evidence 403 and 701, which operate to exclude opinions (1) whose probative value is outweighed by the danger of confusion and prejudice and (2) that are not helpful to the trier of fact.

Federal Rule of Evidence 403 provides that relevant "evidence may be excluded if its probative value is substantially outweighed by the danger of unfair prejudice, confusion of the issues, or misleading the jury. . . ." We do not decide here whether or not such considerations may be sufficient to exclude the impeachment testimony of government agents in certain cases. No objection was made which required a Rule 403 balancing. We therefore decline to address this issue on appeal.

* * *

Although Rule 608(a) clarifies the older, more confusing approach to eliciting an impeaching witness's opinion, we do not construe it to abandon all limits on the reliability and relevance of opinion evidence. Judge Weinstein, in explaining Rule 608(a)'s liberalized approach (which *Lollar* quotes above) qualifies the admissibility of such testimony thus: "If the court finds the witness lacks sufficient information to have formed a reliable opinion, [the judge] can exclude relying on Rules 403 and 602." 3 Weinstein's Evidence para. 608 [04], at 608–20 (1985). In addition, Rule 701 explicitly limits opinion evidence:

> If the witness is not testifying as an expert, his testimony in the form of opinions or inferences is limited to those opinions or inferences which are (a) rationally based on the perception of the witness and (b) helpful to a clear understanding of . . . the determination of a fact in issue.

The Rule 701(a) limitation is characterized by the committee as the "familiar requirement of first-hand knowledge or observation," Advisory Committee's Note, Fed. R. Evid. 701(a). The second limitation, (b), requires that opinion testimony be helpful in resolving issues. The Advisory Committee warns that "[i]f . . . attempts are made to introduce meaningless assertions which amount to little more than choosing up sides, exclusion for lack of helpfulness is called for by the rule." Advisory Committee's Note, Fed. R. Evid. 701(b).

An opinion, or indeed any form of testimony, without the underlying facts, may be excluded if it amounts to no more than a conclusory observation. . . .

The only basis offered by three of the four government agents who testified at Dotson's trial that Dotson and his witnesses were not to be believed under oath was the fact that they took part in a criminal investigation of Dotson. The two FBI agents merely stated that they had taken part in an investigation of Dotson. No other testimony was elicited with respect to how long the agents had known Dotson, or in what way they had acted to form their opinions of his veracity. Each agent offered his opinion of not only Dotson's character for truthfulness, but also the veracity of his girlfriend Johnson, his friend Owens, and Officer Kirk. The state narcotics agent stated that she had known Dotson for six or seven years and had gotten to know Owens within the last year. No further basis for opinion was offered outside of the fact that she took part in an investigation. She also testified as to the character of Johnson and Kirk. On the other hand, IRS agent Alvin Patton's testimony on the truthfulness of Erma Dotson did in fact evidence a sufficient basis. For example, Patton stated that he interviewed Erma Dotson four times, that he investigated her tax returns and financial information, and that he studied her testimony before the grand jury. He also limited his opinion to Erma Dotson's truthfulness with respect to the financial aspects of her son's case. Patton was entitled to express his opinion that Erma Dotson was not to be believed under oath. Of all the agents who testified, only Patton provided a predicate upon which the court could have determined that the opinion was reliable and helpful.

In the absence of some underlying basis to demonstrate that the opinions were more than bare assertions that the defendant and his witnesses were persons not to be believed, the opinion evidence should not have been admitted.

When and by whom the basis for such opinion must be developed is a question initially committed to the sound discretion of the trial court. That court has the responsibility for determining the order of proof, but the determination should be made deliberately and in the exercise of a considered discretion. Here, no account was taken of the value to the jury of the opinion expressed or of the possible prejudice to the defendant from the brusque branding of his testimony as lies. The record should reflect some indication that the court did not merely let down the bars to the expression of any opinions the prosecutor's witnesses wanted to voice.

As Judge Weinstein has noted, cross examination is available to test opinions. In some cases, cross-examination may suffice to protect a defendant who raises no objection to an opinion witness's testimony. Where, however, the defendant in a criminal case objects to the lack of a basis for a government agent's unsupported assertion that the defendant and his witnesses are unworthy of belief, the court should require that the witness identify the basis or source of the opinion. Unless that basis or source demonstrates that the opinion is rationally based on the perception of the witness and would be helpful to the jury in determining the fact of credibility, it should not become a part of the proof in the case.

We do not hold that government agents may never testify as to the truthfulness of a defendant or defense witnesses. Nor do we hold that a government agent's opinion of a witness's character may never be based exclusively on what the agent learned on an official investigation. But the fact that one has conducted an investigation of the defendant, has known the defendant, or has had minimal contact with defendant's witnesses is not a sufficiently reliable basis under Rules 608(a) and 701 for that witness, over objection, to put before the jury the opinion that they are liars.

The vice of this procedure was heightened in the case at bar by the use made of the opinions. The prosecutor, in closing argument, referred to this opinion testimony in the following manner:

> Another fact that you can consider is what the people, the good solid people in this community; narcotics officers, police officers, the FBI, what they think about [the defendant] and his associates. His associates, such as — if you believe his defense, you have to believe Reginald Owens, Frederick Dotson, Frederick Dotson's latest girlfriend.

If this is permitted, the government's agents and attorney could move from presenting factual proof of incrimination to suggesting to the jury that the "good people" of the community ought to put the "bad people" behind bars. This is but a variation on the theme of attempts to convict, not for the criminal act charged, but by showing the defendant to be a "bad person" through proof about other crimes. A prosecutor errs if he goes outside the record to express a personal opinion to the jury that the defendant's testimony is incredible. If his witnesses may state such opinions without providing basis in fact, and the prosecutor sums them up as fact, the same vice inheres.

The government observes that the agents who testified were not technically "case agents" in the case for which Dotson was on trial. This is not determinative. As we stated above, we do not hold that government agents may not ever express opinion about witnesses in their cases. They may do so on the same basis as any other witness. Indeed, we hold that admitting Patton's testimony was not error. The error as to the others lay in admitting, over objection, opinion proof without predicate facts showing its reliability and helpfulness. With the exception of Patton's testimony, the admission of the investigators' opinions was reversible error.

* * *

Because the testimony of the government agents should not have been admitted absent evidence of the underlying facts upon which it was based, the judgment of conviction is Reversed.

NOTES

1. *Cross-Examination Of The Character Witness.* When a character witness takes the witness stand and attacks the credibility of the principal or target witness by offering reputation or opinion testimony, the character witness is subject to cross-examination. Federal Rule of Evidence 608(b)(2) provides for the testing of the basis of the character witness' testimony by asking about specific instances of conduct of the principal witness. Extrinsic evidence of conduct is not allowed; rather character witnesses are asked if "they have heard" of instances where the target witness did *truthful* things. The theory is that it is proper to show the jury that the character witness does not know enough about the activities of the target witness (or the target witness' reputation) to have a credible opinion that the target witness is untruthful. Of course, such questions have the additional effect of putting good conduct of the target witness before the jury.

2. *The Criminal Defendant Who Testifies.* When the defendant takes the witness stand the prosecution may attack the defendant's character for truthfulness even if the defendant did not put any pertinent character trait specifically into evidence. *See United States v. Augello*, 452 F.2d 1135, 1139 (2d Cir. 1971). Accordingly, if the defendant testifies, the prosecution may be able to offer evidence of the defendant's convictions, misconduct that did not result in a conviction, and testimony from character witnesses to suggest that the defendant has a predisposition to lie.

PROBLEM

Problem 10-5. Defendant is on trial for murder. The government calls as a witness against the defendant a former cellmate of the defendant. The cellmate, named Bill McPhee, testifies that the defendant told him that he (the defendant) had committed the murder.

On cross-examination the cellmate admits that he has on several occasions been involuntarily committed to mental institutions. After the prosecution rests, the defense calls a psychiatrist, Dr. Phillips, who is prepared to testify that he has treated Bill McPhee for several years and that in his opinion Bill McPhee is a pathological liar.

(A) Is the testimony of Dr. Phillips admissible?

Assume that the prosecution objects that no foundation has been laid for Dr. Phillips' opinion. In response, the jury is excused and the defense elicits the following testimony from Dr. Phillips:

> My examinations of Bill McPhee have resulted in my diagnosing him as suffering from a recognized mental disorder known as "pseudologia fantastica." Pseudologia fantastica is a variant of lying, often characterized as an extreme form of pathological lying, and is sometimes referred to as Munchausen's

Disease, named after Baron von Munchausen — a German storyteller who wandered the countryside spinning tall tales.

This condition causes McPhee to spin out webs of lies which are ordinarily self-aggrandizing and serve to place him in the center of attention. Put otherwise, coping for Mr. McPhee, given his personality structure, entails seeking attention, tailoring his words to the audience, creating fantasies in which he is the central figure, and through which he attempts to enlist his audience. . . . Mr. McPhee's stories are an attempt to draw others into his fantasy world in order to meet the interpersonal needs which were not met during his childhood.

(B) Is the testimony of Dr. Phillips admissible? If so, what should he be allowed to say? *See United States v. Shay*, 57 F.3d 126, 131–34 (1st Cir. 1995); Christopher B. Mueller & Laird C. Kirkpatrick, 3 Federal Evidence § 263, at 149–52 (2d ed. 1994).

(C) If Dr. Phillips had never examined Bill McPhee but had observed him in the courtroom, could he testify that Bill McPhee is a "pathological liar" based upon his observations of his body movements and mannerisms while testifying? *See United States v. Riley*, 657 F.2d 1377, 1387 (8th Cir. 1981).

[b]   Sensory or Mental Deficiencies that Limit the Ability to Perceive, Remember, or Relate

An *ad hominem* attack on a witness that does not directly implicate character for truthfulness involves an attack on the witness' *capacity* to perceive, remember, or relate. Here one is not suggesting that the witness is a liar, but rather that the witness has a mental or physical incapacity that makes the testimony suspect.

The appropriateness of such an attack is not controversial when it concerns sensory deficiencies such as poor eyesight or poor hearing; the relevance to the jury that an eyewitness had poor eyesight is apparent. A more controversial method of attack involves presenting evidence that the witness is a drug addict, alcoholic, or has a history of mental illness.

UNITED STATES v. LOVE
329 F.3d 981 (8th Cir. 2003)

Deon Love was convicted of a federal firearm violation and was sentenced to 120 months' incarceration. He argues that his Sixth Amendment right of confrontation was violated when the district court impermissibly restricted his cross-examination of three government witnesses. William Craig Thomas, Tommy Cummings, and Chris Davis. More specifically, Love urges that the district court's limit on his examination of Thomas is of "particular significance." We agree.. The district court's constraints on Love's cross-examination of Thomas-a crucial adverse witness-violated the Confrontation Clause of the United States Constitution. Accordingly, we reverse Love's conviction and remand for new trial.

I.

BACKGROUND

On January 23, 2002, a two-count indictment was returned charging Love with being a felon and drug user in possession of a firearm and selling a stolen firearm. After trial, on May 21, 2002, a jury acquitted Love on the selling charge, but concluded that he was guilty of illegally possessing a firearm.

In support of the government's claim that Love-an undisputed felon-illegally "possessed" a firearm, the jury heard from only one witness who actually observed Love with a firearm. Thomas testified that on April 27, 2001, he saw Love with a "rifle" or "shotgun" and a "little revolver." Thomas stated that Love offered to sell him these weapons because Love was a felon and could not legally possess them. According to Thomas, he declined Love's offer, and Love maintained possession of the firearms.

In response to this testimony, Love attempted to cross-examine Thomas about his mental disability. The district court sustained the government's objection to any inquiry into Thomas's mental disability. Love proffered evidence[FN5] to the court that Thomas had been diagnosed with schizophrenia and a short- and long-term memory impairment. Love argued that Thomas's mental illness-specifically his impaired memory-was relevant to his ability to competently recall and recount events more than a year after they allegedly occurred.

FN5. The precise proffer is as follows:

> What I wanted to question him on is statements or an opinion that Dr. Novelus who submitted a report in favor of his mental disability, and Mr. Thomas did receive that disability, Your Honor, Dr. Novelus determined that Mr. Craig Thomas has-his short-term memory and long-term memory are impaired. He has severe mental impairments and he could also be an intrinsic schizophreni[c], which I can see where that possibly may or may not be as relevant, but, Your Honor, I certainly wanted to be able to question him regarding his mental ability and his impairments. I think it went-it goes directly to his ability to be a competent witness relating facts over a year old. Appellant's Br., at 16.

On appeal Love acknowledges that Thomas's schizophrenia diagnosis is of questionable relevance and instead concentrates his argument on Thomas's disabled memory. Similarly, our analysis is limited to whether the district court too narrowly limited Love's cross-examination of Thomas's impaired memory.

II.

DISCUSSION

The Sixth Amendment guarantees a defendant an opportunity for effective cross-examination of witnesses. However, courts "retain wide latitude insofar as the Confrontation Clause is concerned to impose reasonable limits on such cross-examination based on concerns about, among other things, harassment, prejudice, confusion of the issues, the witness'[s] safety, or interrogation that is repetitive or only marginally relevant." *Delaware v. Van Arsdall*, 475 U.S. 673, 679 (1986). A Confrontation Clause violation is shown when a defendant demonstrates that a reasonable jury might have received a significantly different impression of a witness's credibility had counsel been permitted to pursue the proposed line of cross-examination. A trial court's decision to limit cross-examination will not be reversed unless there has been a clear abuse of discretion and a showing of prejudice to defendant.

Accordingly, we begin with a consideration of Love's right to challenge the accuracy of Thomas's testimony with evidence that Thomas might have a mental defect. As the Fifth Circuit has noted, "a defendant has 'the right to attempt to challenge [a witness's] credibility with competent or relevant evidence of any mental defect or treatment at a time probatively related to the time period about which he was attempting to testify.'" *United States v. Jimenez*, 256 F.3d 330, 343 (5th Cir.2001) (quoting *United States v. Partin*, 493 F.2d 750, 763 (5th Cir.1974)). However, "[to] be relevant, the mental health records must evince an 'impairment' of the witness's 'ability to comprehend, know, and correctly relate the truth.'" *Jimenez*, 256 F.3d at 343 (quoting *Partin*, 493 F.2d at 762). Factors which district courts should consider before permitting such cross-examination include: 1) the nature of the psychological problems; 2) whether the witness suffered from the condition at the time of the events to which the witness will testify; 3) the temporal recency or remoteness of the condition. *See Boggs v. Collins*, 226 F.3d 728, 742 (6th Cir.2000).

The government urges us to affirm because "the district court had ample opportunity to observe Thomas's demeanor[,] to conclude that Thomas was not then suffering from the defect[,] and was able to competently recall events from the past." However, the government's argument misunderstands the role of the district court-it is to determine the *relevance* of a witness's reported mental defect. We do not expect the district court to assume the role of a mental-health expert, and we recognize that the existence of a mental condition, which bears on competence, may not be discernible from a witness's demeanor.

In this case, upon Love's inquiry into Thomas's disability, Thomas answered "diabetes" and then promptly objected to any further questioning. The district court sustained the objection without hearing any evidence of the witness's malady. Evidence of Thomas's impaired memory diagnosis was first introduced during Love's proffer. After becoming aware of the witness's alleged long- and short-term memory affliction, the district court again sustained the objection and offered no comment on the matter.

We are convinced that the district court violated Love's right of confrontation when it sustained Thomas's objection. First, we examine the nature of the psychological problems. *Collins*, 226 F.3d at 742. Here the nature of the psychological problem in question is memory loss-a condition that implicates Thomas's ability "to comprehend, know and correctly relate the truth." *Jimenez*, 256 F.3d at 343 (citations omitted). Second, we look to whether the witness suffered from the condition at the time of the events to which the witness will testify. Thomas has suffered from this condition since at least 1996. He testified in May of 2002 about events that took place in April 2001-six years *after* receiving a diagnosis of impaired memory. Finally, we consider the temporal recency or remoteness of the condition. Here the temporal gulf-five years-between Thomas's diagnosis and the events that he observed is not of sufficient duration to eclipse the relevancy of the inquiry. Accordingly, we conclude that the district court violated Love's right of confrontation by limiting his cross-examination regarding Thomas's mental defect.

Despite finding error below, our inquiry is not complete. We must now consider whether the record shows "beyond a doubt that the error complained of did not contribute to the verdict obtained." *Van Arsdall*, 475 U.S. at 678–79. In *United States v. Caldwell*, 88 F.3d 522, 524 (8th Cir.1996), we held that when a trial court's decision to limit cross-examination violates the Confrontation Clause, a determination must be made as to whether "the error was harmless in the context of the trial as a whole." The Supreme Court has held that "[t]he harmless error doctrine recognizes the principle that the central purpose of a criminal trial is to decide the factual question of the defendant's guilt or innocence . . . and promotes public respect for the criminal process by focusing on the underlying fairness of the trial rather than on the virtually inevitable presence of immaterial error." *Van Arsdall*, 475 U.S. at 681 (internal citation omitted). In assessing whether the error was harmless, we consider "multiple factors, including the importance of the [witness's] testimony to the overall case against [the defendant]; whether it was cumulative, the presence of corroborating or contradicting evidence, the extent of cross-examination otherwise permitted, and the overall strength of the government's case." *Caldwell*, 88 F.3d at 525Considering these factors, it is impossible for us to conclude that the error in limiting the cross-examination of Thomas was "harmless beyond a reasonable doubt." *Van Arsdall*, 475 U.S. at 684. First, in relation to importance of the witness's testimony to the overall case against defendant, we note that Thomas was the sole witness to see Love with a firearm in his *possession*. Second, because Thomas was the *only* witness to observe Love with a firearm, it cannot be said that his testimony was cumulative. Third, the record is void of any other examination regarding Thomas's recall capacity-it was neither permitted nor attempted. The final factor-the overall strength of the government's case-is fatal for the government's contention that any error was harmless.

The government argues that "even if the testimony of Thomas was disregarded in its entirety, [the] . . . case against Love was strong." We are not so convinced. The other witnesses-offered to support the selling charge of which Love was acquitted-testified that at no time during the alleged sale did they observe a firearm in Love's possession. Thus, if the testimony of Thomas was disregarded, then the government is left with less than overwhelming evidence of Love's guilt, and we are unable to say that the court's error was "harmless beyond a reasonable doubt." *Caldwell*, 88 F.3d at 525.

III.

CONCLUSION

In conclusion, only one witness-Thomas-stated that he actually observed Love possess a firearm. Love was barred from pursuing a line of questioning into this critical witness's impaired memory diagnosis. This limitation denied Love his constitutionally-guaranteed right to effectively cross-examine Thomas, and we cannot definitively state "that this denial did not contribute to the verdict obtained." *Van Arsdall*, 475 U.S. at 678–79. We reverse and remand for new trial.

NOTES AND QUESTIONS

1. *Mental Illness.* A witness' psychological history may be relevant if the mental illness adversely affects the witness' ability to perceive or relate. In *United States v. Jimenez*, 256 F.3d 330 (5th Cir. 2001), the court stated that the mental impairment evidence must be relevant to the witness' " 'ability to comprehend, know, and correctly relate the truth.' " *Id.* at 343 (internal citations omitted). The *Jimenez* court further posited:

[T]he decisions of this and other circuits stand for the general principle that a diagnosis of schizophrenia or a psychosis will be relevant, unless the diagnosis is too remote in time from the events alleged in the indictment. *Compare Partin*, 493 F.2d at 764 (witness diagnosed with schizophrenia six months prior to defendants' Hobbs Act violations); *Greene v. Wainwright*, 634 F.2d 272, 274, 276 (5th Cir. 1981) (witness was allegedly involved in "certain bizarre criminal actions . . . such as shooting out windows of a bar," during the "same general time period as the [defendant's] marijuana sale"); *United States v. Society of Indep. Gasoline Marketers*, 624 F.2d 461, 467 (4th Cir. 1979) (witness hospitalized for schizophrenia, manic depression, and delusions during the time of defendants' Sherman Act violations); and *United States v. Lindstrom*, 698 F.2d 1154, 1164–67 (11th Cir. 1983) (witness diagnosed with paranoia and schizophrenia during the time of defendants' conspiracy) *with United States v. Diecidue*, 603 F.2d 535, 551 (5th Cir. 1979) (witness committed twelve years prior to defendants' conspiracy, but never again treated for mental illness).

For witnesses whose mental history is less severe, district courts are permitted greater latitude in excluding records and limiting cross-examination. *See United States v. Sasso*, 59 F.3d 341, 347–48 (2d Cir. 1995) (affirming limit on cross-examination of witness who was depressed and took Prozac and Elovil shortly before the time of the defendants' firearms smuggling conspiracy); *United States v. Butt*, 955 F.2d 77, 83 (1st Cir. 1992) (affirming exclusion of records and expert testimony, and limit on cross-examination of a witness who once attempted suicide, but was never diagnosed with a mental illness); *United States v. Moore*, 923 F.2d 910, 913 (1st Cir. 1991) (affirming limit on cross-examination of witness who saw a therapist after the death of her child, and ten years prior to the embezzlement conspiracy). Moreover, none of the cited cases involve adolescent witnesses, among whom depression and suicidal tendencies may be less indicative of severe mental incapacity. *Id.* at 343–44.

Applying the three-part test articulated in *Love*, should evidence that a crucial government witness has suffered from clinical depression, taken prescription medication to treat his mental illness, and once attempted suicide be admitted to impeach his testimony identifying the defendant as the perpetrator of a violent crime?

2. ***Probative Factors.*** What factors are probative in determining whether evidence of mental illness may be admitted for impeachment purposes? In *United States v. Love*, the court applied a three-part test. First, the court examined the nature of the psychological problems and whether the witness' mental condition affected his ability to comprehend and correctly relate the truth. *Id.* at 985 Second, the court looked to whether the witness suffered from the mental condition at the time of the events to which the witness will testify. *Id.* Finally, the court considered whether the mental condition was recent or remote in time. *Id.*

In *United States v. Sasso*, 59 F.3d 341 (2d Cir. 1995), the Second Circuit found the following factors probative on the issue of impeachment:

Evidence of a witness's psychological history may be admissible when it goes to her credibility. In assessing the probative value of such evidence, the court should consider such factors as the nature of the psychological problem, *see, e.g., Chnapkova v. Koh*, 985 F.2d 79, 81 (2d Cir. 1993) (paranoid and delusional condition likely to be probative), the temporal recency or remoteness of the history, *see, e.g., id.* at 81–82 (paranoid delusions five years earlier not too remote); *United States v. Bari*, 750 F.2d 1169, 1179 (2d Cir. 1984) (more than 10 years too remote); *United States v. Glover*, 588 F.2d 876, 878 (2d Cir. 1978) (12 years too remote), and whether the witness suffered from the problem at the time of the events to which she is to testify, so that it may have affected her "ability to perceive or to recall events or to testify accurately," *United States v. Butt*, 955 F.2d 77, 82 (1st Cir. 1992) (internal quotes omitted).

The trial court has discretion to limit such evidence if it determines that the probative value of the evidence is outweighed by its potential for unfair prejudice, confusion of the issues, or waste of time. *See* Fed. R. Evid. 403. Its decisions on these questions will not be overturned in the absence of an abuse of discretion. *Id.* at 348.

3. Drug Use. Evidence of drug use is admissible for the purpose of attacking, not the addict's general credibility, but his ability to observe and recall the events in question. *See United States v. Leonard*, 494 F.2d 955 (D.C. Cir. 1974). In *United States v. Sampol*, 636 F.2d 621 (D.C. Cir. 1980), the D.C. Circuit elaborated on when evidence of drug addiction is admissible for impeachment:

> Counsel for Ignacio Novo informed the trial court that Canete's father had said that the witness was addicted to drugs. Counsel had previously told the court that Canete's father considered his son to be mentally incompetent and that Canete had alienated his entire family by his persistent involvement in legal troubles. Without conducting a hearing, the judge barred all inquiry into Canete's drug use.

> We have recognized that it is proper to explore the drug addiction of a witness in order to attack his credibility and capacity to observe the events in question. *United States v. Leonard*, 494 F.2d [955], 971 [(D.C. Cir. 1974)] at 971. . . .

> Although the narcotics addiction of a witness is relevant to his capacity to observe, a trial judge must deal with an allegation of drug use with some sensitivity because of the highly inflammatory nature of such a charge. The possibility that exploration of a witness's addiction will generate unwarranted prejudice demands that the judge exercise discretion to keep the scope of such examination within proper bounds. Accordingly, before the court will permit a witness to be questioned before the jury about his use of narcotics, counsel must establish a foundation showing either that the witness was using drugs at the time he observed the events in dispute, *United States v. Leonard, supra*, 494 F.2d at 971, or that he is under the influence of narcotics while testifying. Thus in the *Leonard* case we upheld a ruling by the trial court foreclosing any further inquiry into a witness's drug use after he testified that he had taken drugs neither on the day he observed the crime nor during the previous several months.

> Applying these principles to the facts in this case, we discern no error in the trial court's ruling. To justify exploration of this particularly sensitive area, defense counsel proffered only that the witness's father, who openly disapproved of his son, had informed counsel of Canete's addiction to drugs. No offer was made to prove that Canete was influenced by narcotics during his testimony or at the time of the events which were the subject of his testimony. Counsel had previously attempted without success to show that Canete was mentally incompetent and immoral, and his effort to present the witness's unusual

religious beliefs to the jury had also failed. Furthermore, the fact that Canete was not the government's principal witness weakens the argument of the appellants.

Appellants stress that the judge prohibited any questioning of the witness even outside the presence of the jury, where there would have been no danger of prejudice. It is true that normally the better practice in this situation is to permit counsel to establish a foundation by examining the witness outside the hearing of the jurors. [S] ee *United States v. Leonard, supra.* On the other hand, we by no means favor, and do not intend to establish, a general rule requiring a factual proffer as a precondition for cross-examination into uncharted areas. Defense counsel often cannot foresee what new information a particular line of questioning will divulge, and inquiry is usually permissible when counsel has merely a reasonable basis for suspecting that a circumstance is true.

In this case, however, given the dubious basis of counsel's proffer, the fact that Canete was not the key witness for the government, and the sensitive nature of the subject matter, we cannot say that the trial judge exceeded the boundaries of his discretion.

Id. at 666–67. *See also United States v. Womack*, 496 F.3d 791 (7th Cir. 2007) (drug use was only relevant to impeach the witness' ability to perceive the underlying events and testify lucidly at trial).

4. *Alcoholism.* Clearly, evidence that a witness was intoxicated at the time he or she observed an event is relevant to impeach. On the other hand, evidence that the witness is an alcoholic, without establishing that the witness was intoxicated at the time events were observed, is generally excluded. *See United States v. Spano*, 421 F.3d 599 (7th Cir. 2005) (admission of evidence that cooperating coconspirator was an alcoholic and a marijuana user was not warranted absent evidence that the witness was high or drunk while testifying, or alcohol or marijuana use impaired his memory or prevented him from understanding the events about which he testified); *United States v. DiPaolo*, 804 F.2d 225, 229–30 (2d Cir. 1986); 1 COURTROOM CRIMINAL EVIDENCE § 710, at 303 (4th ed. 2005).

5. *Extrinsic Evidence Generally Available.* Most courts view evidence of a witness' sensory or mental capacity to always be relevant, and to permit extrinsic evidence showing the deficiency. *See generally* 1 COURTROOM CRIMINAL EVIDENCE § 710, at 300 (4th ed. 2005); CHRISTOPHER B. MUELLER & LAIRD C. KIRKPATRICK, 3 FEDERAL EVIDENCE § 6:80, at 538–40 (3d ed. 2007).

[c]   Bias

A traditional form of impeachment is to show that a witness has a bias that favors either the state or the defendant. There are several ways to show bias that seldom raise issues as to appropriateness. For example, courts routinely allow evidence that a witness is related to the defendant, or has a monetary interest in providing testimony. Other facts that are generally accepted as relevant to show bias include: a personal relationship (common memberships in clubs or organizations, sexual relationship, etc.), an employment relationship between the witness and a party, showing that the witness has been "coached" by trial counsel, or is subject to civil or criminal liability for testifying in a certain way, among other things. *See generally* CHRISTOPHER B. MUELLER & LAIRD C. KIRKPATRICK, 3 FEDERAL EVIDENCE § 6:77, at 517-25 (3d ed. 2007).

What are the outer boundaries of such testimony? That is, how far may a defendant go in suggesting that a witness is biased? If the defendant is African-American, would it be appropriate for him or her to ask the investigating police officer if the officer has ever used racial slurs? In *Olden v. Kentucky*, the United States Supreme Court discussed the balance between harassment, prejudicial impeachment for bias, and a defendant's Sixth Amendment right "to be confronted with the witnesses against him."

OLDEN v. KENTUCKY
488 U.S. 227 (1988)

PER CURIAM.

Petitioner James Olden and his friend Charlie Ray Harris, both of whom are black, were indicted for kidnaping, rape, and forcible sodomy. The victim of the alleged crimes, Starla Matthews, a young white woman, gave the following account at trial: She and a friend, Regina Patton, had driven to Princeton, Kentucky, to exchange Christmas gifts with Bill Russell, petitioner's half brother. After meeting Russell at a local car wash and exchanging presents with him, Matthews and Patton stopped in J.R.'s, a "boot-legging joint" serving a predominantly black clientele, to use the restroom. Matthews consumed several glasses of beer. . . . As time passed . . . Matthews lost track of Patton and became somewhat intoxicated. When petitioner told her that Patton had departed and had been in a car accident, she left the bar with petitioner and Harris to find out what had happened. She was driven in Harris' car to another location, where, threatening her with a knife, petitioner raped and sodomized her. Harris assisted by holding her arms. Later, she was driven to a dump, where two other men joined the group. There, petitioner raped her once again. At her request, the men then dropped her off in the vicinity of Bill Russell's house.

On cross-examination, petitioner's counsel focused on a number of inconsistencies in Matthews' various accounts of the alleged crime. Matthews originally told the police that she had been raped by four men. Later, she claimed that she had been raped by only petitioner and Harris. At trial, she contended that petitioner was the sole rapist. Further, while Matthews testified at trial that petitioner had threatened her with a knife, she had not previously alleged that petitioner had been armed.

Russell, who also appeared as a State's witness, testified that on the evening in question he heard a noise outside his home and, when he went out to investigate, saw Matthews get out of Harris' car. Matthews immediately told Russell that she had just been raped by petitioner and Harris.

Petitioner and Harris asserted a defense of consent. According to their testimony, Matthews propositioned petitioner as he was about to leave the bar, and the two engaged in sexual acts behind the tavern. Afterwards, on Matthews' suggestion, Matthews, petitioner, and Harris left in Harris' car in search of cocaine. When they discovered that the seller was not at home, Matthews asked Harris to drive to a local dump so that she and petitioner could have sex once again. Harris complied. . . . [T]he men . . . then dropped Matthews off, at her request, in the vicinity of Bill Russell's home.

*   *   *

Although Matthews and Russell were both married to and living with other people at the time of the incident, they were apparently involved in an extramarital relationship. By the time of trial the two were living together, having separated from their respective spouses. Petitioner's theory of the case was that Matthews concocted the rape story to protect her relationship with Russell, who would have grown suspicious upon seeing her disembark from Harris' car. In order to demonstrate Matthews' motive to lie, it was crucial, petitioner contended, that he be allowed to introduce evidence of Matthews' and Russell's current cohabitation. Over petitioner's vehement objections, the trial court nonetheless granted the prosecutor's motion in limine to keep all evidence of Matthews' and Russell's living arrangement from the jury. Moreover, when the defense attempted to cross-examine Matthews about her living arrangements, after she had claimed during direct examination that she was living with her mother, the trial court sustained the prosecutor's objection.

Based on the evidence admitted at trial, the jury acquitted Harris of being either a principal or an accomplice to any of the charged offenses. Petitioner was likewise acquitted of kidnaping and rape. However, in a somewhat puzzling turn of events, the jury convicted petitioner alone of forcible sodomy. He was sentenced to 10 years' imprisonment.

Petitioner appealed, asserting, *inter alia*, that the trial court's refusal to allow him to impeach Matthews' testimony by introducing evidence supporting a motive to lie deprived him of his Sixth Amendment right to confront witnesses against him. The Kentucky Court of Appeals upheld the conviction. The court specifically held that evidence that Matthews and Russell were living together at the time of trial was not barred by the State's rape shield law. Moreover, it acknowledged that the evidence in question was relevant to petitioner's theory of the case. But it held, nonetheless, that the evidence was properly excluded as "its probative value [was] outweighed by its possibility for prejudice." By way of explanation, the court stated: "[T]here were the undisputed facts of race; Matthews was white and Russell was black. For the trial court to have admitted into evidence testimony that Matthews and Russell were living together at the time of the trial may have created extreme prejudice against Matthews." . . .

The Kentucky Court of Appeals failed to accord proper weight to petitioner's Sixth Amendment right "to be confronted with the witnesses against him." That right, incorporated in the Fourteenth Amendment and therefore available in state proceedings, includes the right to conduct reasonable cross-examination.

In *Davis v. Alaska*, [415 U.S. 308 (1974)] we observed that, subject to "the broad discretion of a trial judge to preclude repetitive and unduly harassing interrogation. . . , the cross-examiner has traditionally been allowed to impeach, i.e., discredit, the witness." *Id.*, at 316. We emphasized that "the exposure of a witness' motivation in testifying is a proper and important function of the constitutionally protected right of cross-examination." *Id.*, at 316–317, *citing Greene v. McElroy*, 360 U.S. 474, 496 (1959). Recently, in *Delaware v. Van Arsdall*, 475 U.S. 673 (1986), we reaffirmed *Davis*, and held that "a criminal defendant states a violation of the Confrontation Clause by showing that he was prohibited from engaging in otherwise appropriate cross-examination designed to show a prototypical form of bias on the part of the witness, and thereby 'to expose to the jury the facts from which jurors . . . could appropriately draw inferences relating to the reliability of the witness.'" 475 U.S., at 680, *quoting Davis, supra*, 415 U.S., at 318.

In the instant case, petitioner has consistently asserted that he and Matthews engaged in consensual sexual acts and that Matthews — out of fear of jeopardizing her relationship with Russell — lied when she told Russell she had been raped and has continued to lie since. It is plain to us that "[a] reasonable jury might have received a significantly different impression of [the witness'] credibility had [defense counsel] been permitted to pursue his proposed line of cross-examination." *Delaware v. Van Arsdall, supra*, 475 U.S., at 680.

The Kentucky Court of Appeals did not dispute, and indeed acknowledged, the relevance of the impeachment evidence. Nonetheless, without acknowledging the significance of, or even adverting to, petitioner's constitutional right to confrontation, the court held that petitioner's right to effective cross-examination was outweighed by the danger that revealing Matthews' interracial relationship would prejudice the jury against her. While a trial court may, of course, impose reasonable limits on defense counsel's inquiry into the potential bias of a prosecution witness, to take account of such factors as "harassment, prejudice, confusion of the issues, the witness' safety, or interrogation that [would be] repetitive or only marginally relevant," *Delaware v. Van Arsdall, supra*, at 679, the limitation here was beyond reason. Speculation as to the effect of jurors' racial biases cannot justify exclusion of cross-examination with such strong potential to demonstrate the falsity of Matthews' testimony.

In *Delaware v. Van Arsdall, supra*, we held that "the constitutionally improper denial of a defendant's opportunity to impeach a witness for bias, like other Confrontation Clause errors, is subject to *Chapman* [*v. California*, 386 U.S. 18 (1967)] harmless-error analysis." *Id.*, 475 U.S., at 684. Thus we stated: "The correct inquiry is whether, assuming that the damaging potential of the cross-examination were fully realized, a reviewing court might nonetheless say that the error was harmless beyond a reasonable doubt. Whether such an error is harmless in a particular case depends upon a host of factors, all readily accessible to reviewing courts. These factors include the importance of the witness' testimony in the prosecution's case, whether the testimony was cumulative, the presence or absence of evidence corroborating or contradicting the testimony of the witness on material points, the extent of cross-examination otherwise permitted, and, of course, the overall strength of the prosecution's case." Here, Matthews' testimony was central, indeed crucial, to the prosecution's case. Her story, which was directly contradicted by that of petitioner and Harris, was corroborated only by the largely derivative testimony of Russell, whose impartiality would also have been somewhat impugned by revelation of his relationship with Matthews. Finally, as demonstrated graphically by the jury's verdicts, which cannot be squared with the State's theory of the alleged crime, . . . the State's case against petitioner was far from overwhelming. In sum, considering the relevant *Van Arsdall* factors within the context of this case, we find it impossible to conclude "beyond a reasonable doubt" that the restriction on petitioner's right to confrontation was harmless.

The . . . the judgment of the Kentucky Court of Appeals is reversed, and the case is remanded for further proceedings not inconsistent with this opinion.

It is so ordered.

NOTES AND QUESTIONS

1. *Limits on Right to Cross-Examine to Show Bias.* The defendant's constitutional right to show bias described in *Olden, supra*, does have limits. The Sixth Amendment right of confrontation guarantees effective, not limitless, cross-examination. Courts balance the effectiveness of the cross-examination against concerns of harassment, prejudice, confusion of the issues, the witness' safety and the repetitiveness or marginally relevant nature of the interrogation. *United States v. Muhammad*, 928 F.2d

1461, 1466–67 (7th Cir. 1991). The Seventh Circuit described when a court may properly limit a defendant's cross-examination:

> Limitations on cross-examination do not interfere with the defendant's Sixth Amendment rights provided that cross-examination was sufficient to enable a jury to evaluate the defendant's theory of defense and to make a discriminating appraisal of the witness' motives and bias.

Id. at 1467. *See also United States v. Stewart*, 433 F.3d 273 (2d Cir. 2006) ("In determining whether a trial judge has abused his discretion in the curtailment of cross-examination of government witnesses, the test is whether the jury was already in possession of sufficient information to make a discriminating appraisal of the particular witnesses's possible motives for testifying falsely in favor of the government."); *United States v. Smith*, 308 F.3d 726 (7th Cir. 2002) ("So long as the accused is given the opportunity to expose bias, further cross examination is at the discretion of the district court."); *United States v. Zaccaria*, 240 F.3d 75 (1st Cir. 2001) ("So long as a reasonably complete picture of the witness' veracity, bias, and motivation is developed, the judge enjoys power and discretion to set appropriate boundaries.") (citations omitted); *United States v. Boggs*, 226 F.3d 728 (6th Cir. 2000) ("First, a reviewing court must assess whether the jury had enough information, despite the limits paced on otherwise permitted cross-examination, to assess the defense theory of bias or improper motive. Second, if this is not the case, and there is indeed a denial or significant diminution of cross-examination that implicates the Confrontation Clause, the Court applies a balancing test, weighing the violation against the competing interests at stake.") (citations omitted).

2. Appellate Review. A trial court's ruling limiting a defendant's cross-examination is usually reviewed on an abuse of discretion standard. *See United States v. Saunders*, 973 F.2d 1354, 1358 (7th Cir. 1992); *United States v. Robinson*, 956 F.2d 1388, 1397 (7th Cir. 1992). When, however, a constitutional right is implicated, *some* appellate courts review rulings limiting cross-examination *de novo. United States v. Neely*, 980 F.2d 1074, 1080 (7th Cir. 1992); *United States v. Saunders, supra*, 973 F.2d at 1358. *Cf. United States v. Alexius*, 76 F.3d 642, 644 (5th Cir. 1996) (restriction of defendant's right of cross-examination is reviewed on an abuse of discretion standard; evidentiary rulings only constitute reversible error when they implicate "substantial rights").

Accordingly, an appellate court will attempt to determine if the trial court's limitation of cross-examination implicated the Confrontation Clause in determining what standard of review to use and whether to uphold a trial court's ruling.

3. Harmless Error. In *Olden*, the Supreme Court posited that Sixth Amendment Confrontation Clause errors are subject to harmless-error analysis. What is the legal standard for determining whether a trial court's restriction on cross-examination constituted harmless error? What factors are relevant in determining whether the Confrontation Clause violation constituted harmless or prejudicial error? Why did the *Olden* Court find that the restriction on petitioner's right to confrontation was not merely harmless error?

4. Bringing Out Bias on Direct. Courts are receptive to the prosecution eliciting on direct, the fact that its witness may have a bias against the defendant. For example, courts generally allow the prosecution to bring out the fact that a witness has entered into a plea agreement, including portions of the plea agreement that may bolster the witness' credibility. *See* Section B[1] of this chapter, *supra.* Other examples include questioning a witness about compensation or entering into witness protection programs.

See generally CHRISTOPHER B. MUELLER & LAIRD C. KIRKPATRICK, 3 FEDERAL EVIDENCE §§ 6:78 & 6:79, at 526–30 & 530–38 (3d ed. 2007).

PROBLEMS

Problem 10-6. Defendant is charged with conspiracy to defraud insurance companies by faking automobile accidents. Allegations against defendant were that in 1990 and 1991 he would walk in front of a car of an accomplice and then fall to the ground screaming — pretending to have been injured. The defendant would then go to another accomplice, Dr. Long, who would write a medical report substantiating a faked back injury.

At trial the prosecution called Dr. Long to testify. Defendant wished to question Dr. Long about Dr. Long's arrest in 1980 for possessing with intent to sell 90 pounds of marijuana. The trial court refused to allow defendant to cross-examine Dr. Long about the marijuana sales. Defendant was convicted and appealed.

On appeal defendant claims that his Sixth Amendment right to confront witnesses was violated by the trial court's ruling limiting his cross-examination of Dr. Long. Specifically, he argues that his theory of defense was that Dr. Long was the architect of the scheme because he was in severe financial straits. The cross-examination into the specifics of the drug sales would have shown the jury that Dr. Long would do anything to get money — even sell drugs. Without the details of the drug sales, defendant argues, "you make him look like a saint and take all the stink out of it."

(A) Does defendant have a constitutional right to cross-examine Dr. Long about his 1980 marijuana possession charges?

(B) What standard of review should the court of appeals use? *See United States v. Neely,* 980 F.2d 1074, 1080–81 (7th Cir. 1992); *Dorsey v. Parke,* 872 F.2d 163, 165–68 (6th Cir. 1989).

Problem 10-7. Defendant is on trial for kidnapping. The principal witness against him, a man named Smith, testifies on direct examination that defendant recruited him to assist in the kidnapping scheme. On cross-examination the defendant's attorney asks Smith if he is a homosexual, and if he ever made a homosexual advance to defendant that was rebuffed (defendant and Smith are both males). The trial court refuses to allow such cross-examination.

Defendant is convicted and on appeal claims that his Sixth Amendment right to confront witnesses against him was violated by the trial court ruling. Should such questioning have been permitted? If so, was it reversible error to prohibit it? *See United States v. Jones,* 766 F.2d 412, 414 (9th Cir. 1985); *United States v. Nuccio,* 373 F.2d 168, 171 (2d Cir. 1967).

[3]   Methods that Attack the Witness' Testimony

[a]   Prior Inconsistent Statement or Act

Offering evidence of a prior statement that is inconsistent with the testimony given by a witness is a proper method of impeaching a witness. The theory behind this method is that the prior contradictory statement suggests that the witness changed positions, is unsure, or speaks "out of both sides of his or her mouth." Accordingly, doubts are raised about the accuracy of both the testimony given on the witness stand *and* the prior statement.

Since prior statements made by a witness can raise hearsay problems, it is important to remember that when using a prior statement to *impeach*, the prior statement is not being offered as true; rather, the significance of the prior inconsistent statement is simply that it was made. The mere fact that the witness has told more than one version of the same event casts doubt as to the veracity of both the prior statement and the testimony from the witness stand. Therefore, since the prior statement is not "offered for the truth of the matter asserted" the hearsay rule is not implicated.

A problem area with the use of prior inconsistent statements in criminal cases involves the potential for abuse that exists when a prosecutor calls a witness knowing the witness will give unfavorable testimony, and then impeaches the witness by offering a prior inconsistent statement that inculpates the defendant.[5] After a brief examination of how the prior inconsistent statement method is used, and what constitutes an *inconsistent* statement, the materials below return to the abuse problem just mentioned.

[i] Mechanics

EDWARD J. IMWINKELRIED, PAUL C. GIANNELLI, FRANCIS A. GILLIGAN & FREDRIC I. LEDERER, 1 COURTROOM CRIMINAL EVIDENCE § 711, at 305-09 (4th ed. 2005)[*]

§ 711. Prior Inconsistent Statement.

. . . [W]hat does "inconsistent" mean in this context? A few jurisdictions strictly require a flat contradiction between the pretrial statement and the trial testimony. The trial judge has discretion in determining whether there is a requisite inconsistency. However, the majority view is that any significant variance between the testimony and the previous statement is sufficient. Generally, if the witness' pretrial statement omits a material fact which he or she would not reasonably have done or if the witness alters a significant fact in his or her testimony, the pretrial statement is sufficiently inconsistent. Suppose that the witness claims to have no memory about the statement. The trial judge need not accept the claim at face value. If the judge finds that in fact the witness is being evasive, the claim is an implied denial and sufficiently inconsistent. However, if the judge finds the witness to be truly amnesiac, the judge may exclude the allegedly inconsistent statement. It is consistent to believe that a currently genuinely amnesiac person would have made an earlier statement.

Cross-Examination About the Statement

When an inconsistent statement is in written form, the question arises whether the cross-examiner must show the writing to the witness before questioning the witness about the writing. The early common law required the cross-examiner to do so. However, Rule 613(a) reads: "In examining a witness concerning a prior [written] statement made by the witness. . . , the statement need not be shown . . . to the

---

[5] Recall that Fed. R. Evid. 607 (and its state counterparts) allows a party to impeach its own witness. *See* Section C.1.b of this chapter, *supra*.

witness at that time, but on request the same shall be shown . . . to opposing counsel." That language appears to abolish the common law requirement. One court has held, though, that the trial judge retains discretion to require the cross-examiner to submit the writing to the witness.[137] When the cross-examiner satisfies the above requirements, he or she has a right to question about the inconsistent statement, even when under Rule 607 the prosecutor has already elicited the witness's admission of the statement on direct examination.

Extrinsic Evidence of the Statement

In addition to cross-examining the witness about the prior inconsistent statement, the opponent may sometimes use extrinsic evidence to prove the statement. For example, the opponent may call another witness to the stand to testify to the prior witness' prior inconsistent statement. Extrinsic evidence is permissible when the following conditions are satisfied: (1) The opponent has laid a proper foundation on cross-examination; (2) the witness has denied making the inconsistent statement; and (3) the statement relates to a material fact in the case rather than a collateral fact.

Condition #1: a foundation on cross. The first condition, the requirement for a proper foundation on cross-examination, relates back to the 1820 English opinion, *Queen Caroline's Case.* The jurisdictions following this case require that the opponent name the place of the statement, the time, and the person to whom the statement was made. The witness is given an opportunity to explain or to deny the statement.

A second group of jurisdictions do not require that the witness be told the details of the prior statement as a prerequisite to cross-examination. The courts in this second group permit the opponent to ask general questions about the prior inconsistent statement such as, "Have you ever told anyone that you saw the defendant around before stepping into the alley?"

A third group of jurisdictions completely dispense with the requirement for a foundation in certain circumstances. For instance, some permit the opponent to omit the foundation on cross so long as the witness to be impeached is excused subject to recall. The proponent could then recall the witness to explain away or deny the inconsistent statement. There is a division of sentiment over the proper interpretation of the pertinent federal provision, Rule 613(b); but under the literal wording of the rule, it arguably suffices if the witness to be impeached simply remains in the courtroom until the time when the opponent offers the extrinsic evidence to impeach the witness. While the literal text requires that "the witness [be] afforded an opportunity to explain or deny the" allegedly inconsistent statement, the statute does not describe the opportunity as "prior" or demand that the opportunity be afforded "before" the presentation of the extrinsic testimony about the statement. So long as the witness remains, the witness can retake the stand to deny or explain the statement. Yet, a fair reading of the recent cases suggests that it is still a widespread practice for trial judges to exercise discretion to require a prior opportunity.

Condition #2: a denial on cross. The second condition is that on cross, the witness deny the prior inconsistent statement. This condition is clearly satisfied if the witness

---

[137] *United States v. Marks*, 816 F.2d 1207, 1211 (7th Cir. 1987) (A defense attorney cross-examined prosecution witnesses about the content of FBI interview reports, commonly known as "302s"; "since a statement appearing in an interview report could easily be garbled, yet seem authoritative when read from a paper that the jury would infer was an official FBI document, the judge was reasonable in insisting that the witness be allowed to examine his purported statement before being impeached by it."). . . .

makes an outright denial that he or she ever made the inconsistent statement. The condition can also be satisfied when the witness claims that he or she cannot remember making such a statement. As previously noted, if the judge believes the witness is trying to be evasive, the judge can disbelieve the claim and find an implied denial. If the witness admits making the statement, the trial judge will usually not permit extrinsic evidence.

When the witness fully admits the statement, there is little or no need for the extrinsic evidence. Rule 403 comes into play. However, the minority view is that even if the witness admits the statement, it is provable through extrinsic proof.

Condition #3: compliance with the collateral fact rule. The third condition of admissibility of extrinsic evidence is that the statement must not relate to a collateral fact. This condition is merely an application of the general collateral fact rule. . . .

UNITED STATES v. STROTHER
49 F.3d 869 (2d Cir. 1995)

ALTIMARI, CIRCUIT JUDGE:

Defendant-appellant Richard T. Strother ("Strother") appeals from a judgment of conviction . . . following a jury trial, on one count of knowingly executing a scheme or artifice to defraud a financial institution by means of false representations, in violation of 18 U.S.C. § 1344. The thrust of the government's case was that Strother, an attorney and businessman, induced Christine Wollschleager, an employee of Connecticut Bank and Trust ("CBT"), to authorize payment of a single CBT check despite insufficient funds in his account by falsely representing that he would provide funds to cover the check. Strother's principal contention on appeal is that the district court committed reversible error in excluding two internal bank memoranda and statements contained in a third that he claims should have been admitted as . . . prior inconsistent statements of Wollschleager, the government's chief witness. For the reasons set forth below, we reverse the judgment of the district court and remand for a new trial.

The single check at issue was written for $82,500 on June 5, 1989 by Strother on an account at CBT in the name of Strother Film Partners I (the "CBT account"). The check was payable to Wall Street Clearing Co., a clearinghouse for Strother's brokerage firm, A.T. Brod ("Brod"). In mid-May 1989, Strother purchased $1,000,000 face value of bonds issued by Western Savings and Loan Association ("Western"), for $82,500. At that time, he also held $1,266,000 face value of Western bonds that he had purchased previously through Brod. On June 5, Strother received a telegram from Wall Street Clearing Co. demanding that Strother either pay the $82,500 by the following day or face liquidation of his Western bonds.

To pay for the Western bonds, Strother sent a check for $82,500 drawn on the CBT account (the "CBT check"), although that account held only $610. The following day, Strother wrote a second check for $82,500 drawn on his personal account at Citibank (the "Citibank account"), payable to Strother Film Partners. The government alleged that Strother was aware that neither the CBT account nor the Citibank account had adequate funds to cover either check.

On June 9, 1989, Strother called Wollschleager, the interim manager at the Saybrook branch of CBT. Wollschleager testified that she was familiar with Strother, who "[a]lways kept very, very high balances" and was an "[e]xcellent customer." When asked about the phone conversation, she testified at trial that Strother "said that he had written a check for $82,500, he asked me to pay the check, and said he was wiring me money" from his available funds. She also stated that she believed the wire would arrive shortly, and that Strother never asked her to "hold" the check, which would have been impossible and contrary to bank regulations.

Strother did not wire any funds to CBT. On June 12, however, the Citibank check was deposited at the CBT branch in Saybrook, although the funds were unavailable at that time. On the same day, the CBT check was presented for payment to CBT. Because the CBT account lacked sufficient funds to cover the check, it appeared on CBT's overdraft list prepared on the morning of June 13. The list indicated that $82,500 in unavailable funds had been deposited. Although Wollschleager was aware that the CBT account contained insufficient funds, she authorized payment on the CBT check. She testified that she did so because of Strother's request on June 9 and his assurance that he would wire funds to CBT. Wollschleager testified that she knew that Strother had not wired the funds, but was not concerned because she assumed that Strother simply deposited the funds. Had Strother wired the funds, she testified, they would have been available for deposit and the CBT check would not have appeared on the overdraft list. Wollschleager ordered payment on the CBT check even though she knew she was authorized to pay only up to $5000 on accounts with insufficient funds.

Several days later, Citibank refused to honor the Citibank check because Strother had insufficient funds in that account. . . .

. . . On June 20, Strother, Wollschleager, and Rose Sbalcio, the new branch manager at Saybrook, met to discuss the CBT check. . . . According to Sbalcio, Strother stated that he planned on covering the check with a large interest payment that was scheduled on the Western bonds on June 15. Those interest payments were never made, however, because on June 14 federal regulators seized Western, which was insolvent. . . . Strother never covered the CBT check, and CBT thereby incurred a loss of $82,500.

At trial, [the government produced evidence] of the June 9 phone conversation and surrounding events. . . . Strother sought to introduce three internal bank memoranda as . . . prior inconsistent statements. The district court excluded two of the memoranda, and admitted the third as a business record, but redacted most of the relevant portions. Strother, who did not testify or present any witnesses, was convicted after a three-day trial on the single count in the indictment. He was sentenced principally to twelve months' imprisonment, and now appeals.

DISCUSSION

1. *Exclusion of Memoranda*

Strother's principal contention on appeal is that the district court erroneously excluded from evidence two internal bank memoranda and statements from a third that were essential to his defense. He contends that each should have been admitted as . . . a prior inconsistent statement of Wollschleager. Through these memoranda, Strother sought to establish: that Wollschleager's testimony regarding the phone call was unreliable; that Strother never expressly or impliedly requested that CBT make payment on the check; and that Wollschleager authorized payment not based on Strother's assurances, but instead because of her own mistaken belief that sufficient funds had been wired into the CBT account. As the government conceded at oral argument, had Strother merely asked Wollschleager to hold, rather than pay, the check, no crime would have occurred. We will first review each of the memoranda, and then consider whether the district court erred in its rulings.

Wollschleager Memorandum

Wollschleager prepared a memorandum at Sbalcio's direction, which was dated June 22, 1989, thirteen days after her phone conversation with Strother (the "Wollschleager Memorandum"). . . . The Wollschleager Memorandum provided in relevant part that Strother called,

> stating he expected a check to hit his account, but he was having a deposit wired in — the deposit was credited 6/12/89 and at the same time a check was presented in the amount of $82,500.00, the account showed that it was using unavailable funds. Because of the phone call, and Richard Strother being a known customer, and the deposit being made the check was paid and charged.

The memorandum did not make any reference to a request by Strother that Wollschleager pay the CBT check.

Probation Memorandum

CBT placed Wollschleager on probation because she failed to follow bank policy when approving payment on the CBT check. Sbalcio prepared a memorandum dated August 29, 1989 (the "Probation Memorandum") recounting the incident, which Wollschleager signed, confirming that she "discussed this memo to my file." The memorandum states that Strother

> told Christine that he was wiring funds into his account . . . to cover a check that was to be presented for payment on that day. . . . On June 13, 1989, the morning overdraft report showed that one item was submitted for payment of $82,500 against unavailable funds of $82,500. Mr. Strother had not wired the funds to CBT but had deposited a check drawn on Citibank, N.A. *Since Christine was unaware of this transaction, she approved payment of the overdraft.* (Emphasis added).

Like the Wollschleager Memorandum, the Probation Memorandum did not expressly note that Strother had requested payment on the CBT check. Moreover, the Probation Memorandum contradicted Wollschleager's trial testimony that she knew that Strother had deposited a check rather than wired funds. . . .

Charge-Off Memorandum

The last memorandum at issue, which was prepared by Sbalcio on December 14, 1989, requested that the CBT accounting department "charge off" the $82,500 as a loss (the "Charge-Off Memorandum"). Such memoranda were routinely prepared whenever an obligation to CBT was charged off as a loss. Sbalcio testified that she included "[a]s much [information] as possible" in the document, some of which she learned from discussions with Wollschleager. Although the Charge-Off Memorandum was admitted as a business record, the district court redacted all statements in the document attributable to Wollschleager. Like the other excluded documents, the Charge-Off Memorandum omitted any mention of an explicit request by Strother for the bank to pay the check. It also stated that

> On June 14, 1989 Christine discovered that a confirmation to approve use of unavailable funds had not been requested from the Area Manager. . . . Christine told the area office that the deposit would clear because the funds had been wired in. On June 16, 1989, Return Items informed Christine that a deposited item had been returned due to the unavailability of funds. Christine was told that the deposit of June 12, 1989 was a check and not a wire.

Governing Law

*   *   *

Strother . . . sought to introduce the three memoranda as prior inconsistent statements of Wollschleager in an effort to impeach her credibility. A witness's prior statement may be offered to impeach that witness's credibility if (1) the statement is inconsistent with the witness's trial testimony, (2) the witness is afforded an opportunity to deny or explain the same, and (3) the opposing party is afforded the opportunity to cross-examine the witness thereon. *See* Fed. R. Evid. 613(b). Under certain circumstances, a witness's prior silence regarding critical facts may constitute a prior inconsistent statement where "failure to mention those matters . . . conflict[s] with that which is later recalled. Where the belatedly recollected facts merely augment that which was originally described, the prior silence is often simply too ambiguous to have any probative force. . . ." At the same time, "statements need not be diametrically opposed to be inconsistent." We review a district court's determination of whether statements are inconsistent with each other for an abuse of discretion.

Application

The district court excluded the Wollschleager Memorandum on the grounds that it was [not] a prior inconsistent statement. We conclude that the district court abused its discretion by not admitting the Wollschleager Memorandum as a prior inconsistent statement. Wollschleager testified at trial that Strother specifically asked her to make payment on the check. By contrast, the memorandum she prepared shortly after the incident omits any reference to such a request, although it does mention that Strother said he was wiring in funds to cover a check that he had written. It would have been "natural" for Wollschleager to include Strother's request in her earlier statement.

Highlighting this inconsistency was essential to Strother's defense, which was that he never asked Wollschleager to pay the check, but instead asked her to hold it pending the wire of funds. As noted above, the government conceded at oral argument that if Strother had asked Wollschleager to hold the check rather than to pay it, no crime would have occurred. Moreover, in rebuttal summation, the government stressed that Wollschleager's recollection of the June 9 conversation "went virtually unchallenged," including her recollection that Strother asked her to pay the check. Accordingly, the district court should have admitted the Wollschleager Memorandum as a prior inconsistent statement to allow Strother to impeach Wollschleager's recollection of the phone conversation.

The district court also concluded that the Probation Memorandum was [not] a prior inconsistent statement. We believe, however, that the Probation Memorandum should have been admitted as a prior inconsistent statement. Like the Wollschleager Memorandum, this memorandum did not include any mention of a request for payment by Strother. More significantly, at trial, Wollschleager testified that she was aware that Strother had not wired in funds, but had made a deposit by check instead. By contrast, the Probation Memorandum states that Wollschleager was unaware that Strother had deposited a check rather than wired funds. These inconsistencies clearly would have supported Strother's claim that Wollschleager authorized payment on the CBT check because of her own mistake, rather than because of Strother's alleged request.

*   *   *

The district court admitted the Charge-Off Memorandum as a business record, but redacted the hearsay statements attributable to Wollschleager. The memorandum was inconsistent with Wollschleager's trial testimony much like the Probation Memorandum. Unlike either the Wollschleager or Probation Memoranda, however, the Charge-Off Memorandum was not Wollschleager's statement. Sbalcio prepared the document, and the record does not suggest that Wollschleager adopted the statement as her own. Accordingly, the district court did not err in declining to admit the document as a prior inconsistent statement.

Nor did the district court err in declining to admit the excluded portions of the Charge-Off Memorandum as a business record, in view of the fact that this memorandum was made six months after the relevant events and contained narrative statements based on multiple hearsay, rather than entries relied on by a functioning entity as a record of its transactions. The timeliness with which a report is prepared with relation to the events recorded therein is important " 'to assure a fairly accurate recollection of the matter . . . [and] because any trustworthy habit of making regular business records will ordinarily involve the making of the record *contemporaneously.*' " *Seattle-First Nat'l Bank v. Randall*, 532 F.2d 1291, 1296 (9th Cir. 1976) (quoting 5 Wigmore, Evidence 1526) (emphasis in original).

In summary, we conclude that the district court erred in failing to admit the Wollschleager and Probation Memoranda into evidence as prior inconsistent statements. Moreover, we reject the government's claim that, because Strother was permitted to cross examine Wollschleager as to the two documents, the district court errors were harmless. Extrinsic evidence of a prior inconsistent statement is more persuasive to a jury than a witness's acknowledgement of inconsistencies in a prior statement. Because of the exclusion of the Wollschleager and Probation Memoranda, Strother was restricted from effectively presenting his defense that Wollschleager authorized payment of the CBT check not based on Strother's assurances and request for payment, but based on her mistaken belief that sufficient funds had been wired into Strother's account. . . .

*   *   *

CONCLUSION

Based on the foregoing, we reverse the judgment of the district court and remand for a new trial.

NOTE

Inconsistency. To be used for impeachment purposes, a prior statement must, of course, be inconsistent with the witness' trial testimony. A statement that is completely contradictory is obviously inconsistent. There is no requirement, however, of complete contradiction; the requirement is *inconsistency*, which is something less than a complete contradiction.

(A) Details Added in Trial Testimony. The *Strother* case presents a scenario where a detail added at trial is inconsistent with a prior statement that omitted the detail. As the *Strother* court noted, courts look to see if it would have been "natural" for the detail given at trial to have been included in the prior statement if indeed the detail had occurred. *United States v. Meserve*, 271 F.3d 314 (1st Cir. 2001) (the test "is an elastic one, because the 'naturalness' of a witness's decision not to include certain information in an earlier statement may depend on the 'nuances of the prior statement's context, as well as [the witness's] own loquacity' ") (citations omitted).

In criminal cases where the defendant takes the witness stand, it is not uncommon for the defendant to have refused to make a statement before trial after receiving his or her *Miranda* warnings. It is well settled that in such a situation the prosecution cannot impeach a defendant with his failure to make a statement even though a denial would have been "natural." *Doyle v. Ohio*, 426 U.S. 610, 619 (1976).

(B) Trial Testimony of "I Don't Recall." If a witness gives a statement before trial, but at trial testifies that he or she has no memory of events recounted in the pretrial statement, is the earlier statement inconsistent with the trial testimony? It is possible for both the pretrial statement and the trial statement to be accurate (and therefore consistent): people can forget what they once knew. The impeachment problem is to determine whether the claimed lack of memory is merely evasive (and inconsistent) or honest (and consistent). This is a decision for the trial judge. *See United States v. Thompson*, 708 F.2d 1294, 1299 (8th Cir. 1983) (judge may disbelieve claim); *United States v. Rogers*, 549 F.2d 490 495–96 (8th Cir. 1976) ("The trial judge must be accorded reasonable discretion in determining whether a claim of faulty memory is inconsistent with statements previously given."). *See also United States v. DeSimone*, 488 F.3d 561 (1st Cir. 2007) (Corrado's testimony that he did not recall whether Corley had called him about the Williams payment was not necessarily inconsistent with Corley's proffered testimony about the conversation).

Admitting evidence of the prior statement to impeach is troublesome when the statement is not admissible substantively. Recall that under the Federal Rules, only prior inconsistent statements that were given at trial or hearing under oath and subject to cross-examination are admissible as substantive evidence. *See* Fed. R. Evid. 801(d)(1). Accordingly (assuming there is no other exception to the hearsay rule that applies), most prior inconsistent statements are admissible only to impeach. There is a great danger that the jury will consider the prior inconsistent statement as true rather than merely casting doubt on the witness' trial testimony. Therefore, courts must balance the probativeness of the prior statement on the impeachment issue with the dangers recited in Fed R. Evid. 403. *See generally* CHRISTOPHER B. MUELLER & LAIRD C. KIRKPATRICK, 3 FEDERAL EVIDENCE § 6:99, at 660-61 (3d ed. 2007). This problem is examined further in the subsection that follows.

QUESTIONS

1. What statements contained in the "Wollschleager Memorandum" and the "Probation Memorandum" were inconsistent with the testimony given at trial by Christine Wollschleager? If no statements were inconsistent, why did the Second Circuit consider them to be prior inconsistent statements?

2. On retrial, can Strother's attorney ask Christine Wollschleager about her statements contained in the "Wollschleager Memorandum" and the "Probation Memorandum" without showing her either of the two documents?

3. On retrial, if Christine Wollschleager's trial testimony remains the same, and if on cross-examination she admits that the "Wollschleager Memorandum" and the "Probation Memorandum" omit any reference to her being asked to pay the $82,500 CBT check, can the two documents be admitted into evidence? Under Fed. R. Evid. 613, what foundation must be laid prior to the admission of extrinsic evidence of a prior inconsistent statement? *See United States v. Soundingsides*, 820 F.2d 1232, 1240–41 (10th Cir. 1981); *cf.* CHRISTOPHER B. MUELLER & LAIRD C. KIRKPATRICK, 3 FEDERAL EVIDENCE § 6:101, at 677–78 (3d ed. 2007).

PROBLEM

Problem 10-8. Assume that defendant is charged with stealing farm equipment. A neighbor of the defendant gives a statement to the police indicating that he purchased some stolen farm equipment from the defendant. Police agree not to prosecute the neighbor in return for his testimony identifying defendant as the person who sold him his equipment.

At trial the neighbor is called to the witness stand. After first establishing that the farm equipment on the neighbor's farm was stolen, the prosecutor asks the neighbor where he purchased the equipment. The neighbor states, "I do not recall." The neighbor is then shown a copy of the police report containing his out-of-court statement identifying the defendant as the person who sold him the equipment. The prosecutor asks, "Does this refresh your memory?" The neighbor says, "No."

The prosecutor then seeks to impeach the neighbor with the statement in the police report identifying defendant as the person who sold the neighbor the equipment. The defendant objects, stating, "there is nothing inconsistent between 'I do not recall' and the statement in the police report, so impeachment by prior inconsistent statement is improper."

Should the impeachment be permitted? *See United States v. Rogers*, 549 F.2d 490, 496 (8th Cir. 1976). If so, may the prosecutor offer the police report containing the neighbor's statement into evidence as a prior inconsistent statement?

[ii]   Preventing Abuse

The use of prior inconsistent statements creates a unique opportunity for abuse. That problem concerns calling a witness to testify that either the prosecution or defense knows will give unfavorable testimony to their case, but who has, in the past, given a statement that helps their case. The prior statement is inadmissible hearsay. Accordingly, the only way the favorable testimony can be heard by the jury is if the witness is impeached with it. Can either the prosecutor or defendant call a witness solely to get otherwise inadmissible hearsay before the jury? Put another way, can a witness be called solely for impeachment? Does the admissibility of the prior statement depend on the intent of the party calling the witness to be impeached? Some court have adopted a "primary purpose" test, which looks to whether a party set up the introduction of a prior inconsistent statement by calling a witness, knowing that he will offer adverse testimony. Other courts apply a Rule 403 balancing inquiry. Under Rule 403, the proper test is whether, irrespective of the calling party's motive, the probative value of a statement for impeaching the credibility of a witness is substantially outweighed by the danger of unfair prejudice. Finally, does it matter whether the prosecution or defense is seeking to introduce a prior inconsistent statement to impeach its own witness?

UNITED STATES v. BUFFALO
358 F.3d 519 (8th Cir. 2004)

Karsten Buffalo appeals his jury conviction of one count of assault with a dangerous weapon in violation of 18 U.S.C. §§ 1153 and 113(a)(3) and one count of assault resulting in serious bodily injury in violation of 18 U.S.C. §§ 1153 and 113(a)(6). Buffalo claims, among other points of contention, that the district court erred by refusing to allow testimony that someone else confessed to the crime and that the district court should have allowed him to question the victim about prior fights. For the reasons stated below, we affirm in part, reverse in part, and remand for a new trial.

I. FACTUAL BACKGROUND

On the night of November 2, 2001, Jules Uses Many shot the defendant, Karsten Buffalo, with a BB gun after an argument. The following night, when Uses Many was walking home alone from a bar on the Cherry Creek Indian Reservation, he was assaulted with a baseball bat by four or five people and suffered serious injuries. He identified Buffalo as his assailant, and the government charged Buffalo with the assault, proceeding to trial on the theory that the attack was motivated by Buffalo's desire to exact revenge on Uses Many for the previous night's BB gun shooting.

Buffalo, however, denied any involvement in the attack and, at trial, attempted to prove an alibi defense. To bolster this defense, he sought to show that someone else was responsible for the beating-namely, Rodney "Rocky" Hayes. Like Buffalo, Hayes had been involved in past altercations with Uses Many. According to Buffalo, while he was detained awaiting trial on the charges in this case, two of his cell mates (Chastyn Waloke and Justin Romero) independently told him that Hayes had confessed to them that he attacked Uses Many on the night in question. Buffalo sought to introduce this testimony, but the government objected to its admission on the ground that it was inadmissible hearsay. Moreover, because several people were involved in the assault on Uses Many, the government took the position that, even if Hayes had confessed, his participation in the assault did nothing to exonerate Buffalo.

* * *

By the following morning, Hayes had been located, and Buffalo called him to testify in spite of the court's peremptory ruling that, if Buffalo called Hayes, he would not be permitted to call Waloke and Romero as impeachment witnesses. In the court's view, Buffalo would only have been permitted to call Waloke and Romero to testify about Hayes's alleged confession if the government, and not Buffalo, had called Hayes. The court commented that permitting Buffalo to call Hayes only to impeach him with

Waloke's and Romero's testimony would be nothing more than an attempt to set up a strawman to circumvent the rule against hearsay under the guise of impeachment.

On the stand, Hayes admitted that he told Waloke and Romero that he wished he had been the one to assault Uses Many, but he denied having said that he had anything to do with the assault. Uses Many also took the stand and testified that he was certain Buffalo attacked him, despite defense counsel's attempt to highlight the physical similarities between Buffalo and Hayes. Neither Waloke nor Romero testified, and the jury returned a verdict of guilty on two counts. The district court sentenced him to two concurrent terms of seventy months imprisonment. This appeal followed.

II. DISCUSSION

B. Admissibility of Hayes's Confession for Impeachment Purposes

If offered merely "to prove the truth of the matter asserted," Fed. R. Evid. 801(c), Waloke's and Romero's testimony that Hayes confessed to them would have constituted excludable hearsay under the Federal Rules of Evidence. The district court's exclusion of the testimony, therefore, was correct insofar as the court ruled that Buffalo could not introduce Waloke's and Romero's testimony to prove that Hayes indeed confessed. However, testimony oftentimes serves more than one purpose, and while it may be inadmissible for one purpose, it may be admissible for another. Such is the case here. The testimony that Hayes confessed should have been admitted to impeach Hayes's testimony as a prior inconsistent statement under Federal Rule of Evidence 613(b).

The trial court ruled that it would not permit Buffalo to call Hayes and then to impeach him with Waloke's and Romero's testimony about the confession because to do so would simply be a pretext to get before the jury otherwise inadmissible hearsay testimony. The trial court's ruling appears, in part, to have arisen out of the traditional rule against impeaching one's own witness. This rule, however, was abandoned with the adoption of Federal Rule of Evidence 607, which provides: "The credibility of a witness may be attacked by any party, including the party calling the witness." Fed. R. Evid. 607.

This case requires us to consider the interplay between the ability of parties to impeach their own witnesses, embodied in Rule 607, and Rule 613(b), which allows the admission of prior inconsistent statements of a witness under limited circumstances. Specifically, Rule 613(b) provides:

> Extrinsic evidence of a prior inconsistent statement by a witness is not admissible unless the witness is afforded an opportunity to explain or deny the same and the opposite party is afforded an opportunity to interrogate the witness thereon, or the interests of justice otherwise require. Fed. R. Evid. 613(b).

1. The Danger of Admitting Prior Inconsistent Statements

When a party is allowed to impeach its own witness with a prior inconsistent statement, the underlying problems associated with the introduction of out-of-court statements surface. This is so because "the power to impeach one's own witness can be abused." *See* 27 Charles Alan Wright & Victor James Gold, *Federal Practice and Procedure: Evidence* § 6093 (1990). Calling a witness only to impeach him or her with a prior inconsistent statement can have the effect of undermining the rule against hearsay. *Id.*

Many courts, including our own, have recognized this potential for abuse in impeaching one's own witness with prior inconsistent statements. *See United States v. Fay*, 668 F.2d 375, 379 (8th Cir.1981) (holding trial court did not abuse discretion in excluding testimony where defendant sought to call witness knowing she would deny hearsay within hearsay statement and intending to call another witness to impeach that testimony where exception to hearsay rule did not excuse second layer of hearsay). The danger, which the district court recognized in Buffalo's case, is that a party will call a witness, knowing him or her to be adverse, merely to make an end-run around the rule against hearsay by impeaching the witness with a prior inconsistent statement that the jury would not otherwise have been allowed to hear. We are concerned under these circumstances that, despite any limiting instruction, the jury will misuse the inconsistent statement as substantive evidence, rather than consider it only on the issue of a witness's credibility.

2. Managing the Prejudicial Effect of Prior Inconsistent Statements

To address this concern, some circuits have adopted a "primary purpose" test, which has its genesis in a 1975 Fourth Circuit case, *United States v. Morlang*, 531 F.2d 183, 190 (4th Cir.1975). The court in *Morlang* held that a party may not intentionally set up the introduction of a prior inconsistent statement by calling a witness who the party knows will offer adverse testimony. *Id.* at 190. In *Morlang*, the government called a prisoner in a bribery prosecution, knowing that the prisoner would deny that he made a statement to another prisoner implicating the defendant. *Id.* The government then called the second prisoner to testify that the first prisoner indeed made such a statement to him. *Id.* The Fourth Circuit reversed the defendant's conviction, reasoning that the government had used the rule allowing impeachment with prior inconsistent statements to put inadmissible evidence before the jury. *Id.*

The test announced in *Morlang* requires courts to determine the calling party's intent. The *Morlang* court's "primary purpose" test looks to a party's intent in calling a witness and prohibits impeachment of that witness with a prior inconsistent statement "where employed as a mere subterfuge to get before the jury evidence not otherwise admissible." *Id.; see also United States v. Kane*, 944 F.2d 1406 (7th Cir.1991) ("Impeachment of one's own witness cannot be permitted where employed as a mere subterfuge to present to the jury evidence not otherwise admissible."); *United States v. Peterman*, 841 F.2d 1474, 1479 (10th Cir.1988) (holding that government may not "use impeachment as a guise for submitting to the jury substantive evidence that is otherwise unavailable") (citation and quotation omitted); *Whitehurst v. Wright*, 592 F.2d 834, 839 (5th Cir.1979) (upholding district court's refusal to allow impeachment where plaintiff called a witness, whose testimony she knew would be unhelpful, for the purpose of impeaching him with a helpful prior inconsistent statement that was inadmissible for substantive purposes on hearsay grounds).

In *United States v. Logan*, 121 F.3d 1172 (8th Cir.1997), this court commented on the potential for abusing the ability to impeach one's own witnesses with prior inconsistent statements. We noted that " '[c]ourts must be watchful that impeachment is not used as a subterfuge to place otherwise inadmissible hearsay before the jury,' " *id.* at 1175 (quoting *United States v. Rogers*, 549 F.2d 490, 497 (8th Cir.1976)), but we disavowed adherence to any rule that would require trial courts to inquire into the state of mind of the party calling the witness to be impeached. *Logan*, 121 F.3d at 1175. In *Logan*, we cited a collection of cases that focus on determining the government's true motive in impeaching one of its own witnesses with a prior inconsistent statement, and we stated that "the relevant question is simply whether the evidence is admissible under Fed. R. Ev. 403." *Id.*

Indeed, even the Fourth Circuit, which formulated the primary purpose rule in *Morlang*, has stated that "[f]ederal evidence law does *not* ask the judge, either at trial or upon appellate review, to crawl inside the prosecutor's head to divine his or her true motivation." *United States v. Ince*, 21 F.3d 576, 580 (4th Cir.1994). Instead, to determine whether testimony of a prior inconsistent statement is a "mere subterfuge" to get before the jury otherwise inadmissible hearsay, "the proper inquiry is whether, as an objective matter and irrespective of the [calling party's] motive, the probative value of a statement for impeaching the credibility of a witness is 'substantially outweighed by the danger of unfair prejudice, confusion of the issues, or misleading the jury, or by considerations of undue delay, waste of time, or needless presentation of cumulative evidence,' *see* Fed. R. Ev. 403." *Logan*, 121 F.3d at 1175.

3. Rule 613(b)

Thus, we must examine Waloke's and Romero's testimony in light of Rule 403's balancing test. However, before turning to the Rule 403 analysis in this case, we must first determine whether Buffalo met the foundational requirements of a Rule 613(b) prior inconsistent statement. Under Rule 613(b), a party seeking to introduce a prior inconsistent statement must ordinarily confront the witness with the prior inconsistent statement and afford him or her an opportunity to explain or deny the inconsistency. *United States v. Roulette*, 75 F.3d 418, 423 (8th Cir.1996); *accord United States v. Schnapp*, 322 F.3d 564, 571 (8th Cir.2003) ("[E]xtrinsic evidence of a prior inconsistent statement by a witness is not admissible unless: (1) the witness is afforded an opportunity to explain or deny the statement and the opposing party is afforded an opportunity to interrogate the witness about the statement or (2) the interests of justice otherwise require."). In addition, "under Rule 613(b) a witness may not be impeached on a collateral matter by use of extrinsic evidence of prior inconsistent statements. Contradiction of a witness by prior inconsistent statements may be shown only on a matter material to the substantive issues of the trial." *Id.* (internal citations omitted).

In Buffalo's case, Hayes's statement to Waloke and Romero involved matters that were material to the charges against the defendant, and Buffalo squarely confronted Hayes with his inconsistent statements during direct examination. Hayes denied having confessed or having played any role in the Uses Many attack. Instead, he testified that he stated to Waloke and Romero that he wished he had assaulted Uses Many. The government could have pursued Hayes's alleged prior statement during its cross-examination of him, but the prosecutor chose not to. In short, Buffalo established the proper Rule 613(b) foundation of Hayes's prior inconsistent statements. We, therefore, must consider whether Rule 403 allows Waloke's and Romero's testimony because, as noted above, when a prior inconsistent statement is offered to impeach the calling party's own witness, "the relevant question is simply whether the evidence is admissible under Fed. R. Ev. 403." *Logan*, 121 F.3d at 1175.

4. Rule 403 Balancing Inquiry

Rule 403 provides that even relevant evidence should be excluded when "its probative value is substantially outweighed by the danger of unfair prejudice, confusion of the issues, or misleading the jury, or by consideration of undue delay, waste of time, or needless presentation of cumulative evidence." Fed. R. Evid. 403. The vast majority of cases on the issue of impeaching one's own witness with a prior inconsistent statement speak to the government's use of the statements to impeach its witnesses where the statements inculpate the defendant. For example, in *United States v. Ince*, 21 F.3d 576 (4th Cir.1994), within a few hours of a shooting, a witness for the prosecution told police that the defendant admitted to her that he fired the shots in question. In the defendant's trial for assault with a dangerous weapon, that same witness testified that she could not remember what the defendant told her. *Id.* at 578. After unsuccessfully attempting to refresh her memory with a copy of her statement to the police, the government called the police officer who interviewed her. *Id.* at 579. He testified that she told him that the defendant had confessed to firing the gun. *Id.* Reversing the defendant's conviction, the court articulated the danger of admitting this sort of testimony in a criminal trial:

> When the prosecution attempts to introduce a prior inconsistent statement to impeach its own witness, the statement's likely prejudicial impact often substantially outweighs its probative value for impeachment purposes because the jury may ignore the judge's limiting instructions and consider the "impeachment" testimony for substantive purposes. . . . That risk is multiplied when the statement offered as impeachment testimony contains the defendant's alleged admission of guilt. Thus, a trial judge should rarely, if ever, permit the Government to "impeach" its own witness by presenting what would otherwise be inadmissible hearsay if that hearsay contains an alleged confession to the crime for which the defendant is being tried.

Id. at 581.

When the defendant seeks to introduce a prior inconsistent statement for impeachment purposes, the dangers identified above are not implicated. Simply put, the prejudicial impact of the statement does not endanger the defendant's liberty by risking a conviction based on out-of-court statements that are not subject to confrontation by way of cross-examination. Under the unique circumstances of this case, the value to Buffalo in calling Hayes to the stand was to bolster Buffalo's alibi defense by demonstrating to the jury the striking physical similarities between Buffalo, who Uses Many positively identified as his assailant, and Hayes, who admittedly wished he had been able to "get his hands on" Uses Many. While Waloke's and Romero's testimony of Hayes's confession poses the obvious risk of being misused by the jury as substantive evidence, a limiting instruction could have minimized this risk, especially in light of the government's theory that Hayes's confession was not necessarily exculpatory because several people assaulted Uses Many. Moreover, while not directly pertinent to the conventional Rule 403 balancing test, Buffalo offered significant corroboration of Waloke's and Romero's testimony, such as Waloke's observation of blood on Hayes's shoes after the assault and his identification of the vehicle that he said Hayes arrived in when he confessed to Waloke, which was the same type and color as the vehicle an eye witness observed at the scene of the crime.

* * *

In our view, the testimony should have been allowed at Buffalo's trial, and the district court abused its discretion by failing to conduct a Rule 403 inquiry. Eighth Circuit case law clearly provides that the probative value of a Rule 613(b) prior inconsistent statement must be weighed against the prejudicial effect of its admission, but the district court flatly rejected the proffered testimony as being a "strawman" issue without giving any consideration to Rules 403, 607, or 613(b). We cannot say that the court's failure to conduct a Rule 403 inquiry and its categorical exclusion of Waloke's and Romero's testimony was harmless error. *See United States v. Wilcox*, 50 F.3d 600, 603 (8th Cir.1995) (citation omitted) ("An error is harmless if the reviewing court, after reviewing the entire record, determines that no substantial rights of the defendant were affected, and that the error did not influence or had only a very slight influence on the verdict."). We, therefore, reverse and remand for a new trial.

NOTES AND QUESTIONS

1. *The "Primary Purpose Test."* To avoid the problem where a party calls a witness, knowing he will testify adversely, merely to impeach the witness with a prior inconsistent statement that would otherwise be inadmissible, some courts have adopted a "primary purpose" test. The test, which has its genesis in *United States v. Morlang*, 531 F.2d 183, 190 (4th Cir. 1975), looks at the primary purpose for calling a witness. If the government calls a witness for the primary purpose of getting an otherwise inadmissible prior inconsistent statement before the jury the impeachment will not be allowed.

In the case of *United States v. Webster*, 734 F.2d 1191 (7th Cir. 1984), Judge Posner, writing for the Seventh Circuit, explained the primary purpose test:

> [I]t would be an abuse of [Federal Rule of Evidence 607], in a criminal case, for the prosecution to call a witness that it knew would not give it useful evidence, just so it could introduce hearsay evidence against the defendant in the hope that the jury would miss the subtle distinction between impeachment and substantive evidence — or, if it didn't miss it, would ignore it. The purpose would not be to impeach the witness but to put in hearsay as substantive evidence against the defendant, which Rule 607 does not contemplate or authorize.

Id. at 1192. *See also United States v. Giles*, 246 F.3d 966 (7th Cir. 2001) (defendant could not call individual in witness protection program to testify "because it is clear that a party may not call a witness for the sole purpose of impeaching him") *(quoting United States v. Webster*, 734 F.2d 1191 (7th Cir. 1984)).

2. *Rule 403 Balancing.* There is some authority applying the primary purpose test to exclude defense impeachment. *See, e.g., United States v. Grooms*, 978 F.2d 425, 429 (8th Cir. 1992) (citing *Morlang* in excluding defendant's prior inconsistent statement impeachment of a witness); *United States v. Sebetich*, 776 F.2d 412, 428–29 (3d Cir. 1985) (no error to exclude defense impeachment when defendant called witness expecting witness to deny making a prior statement); CHRISTOPHER B. MUELLER & LAIRD C. KIRKPATRICK, 3 FEDERAL EVIDENCE § 6:28, at 165 n.5 (3d ed. 2007). However, the Eighth Circuit in *Buffalo* rejected the primary purpose test in favor of a Rule 403 balancing inquiry. The court stated that "the proper inquiry is whether, as an objective matter and irrespective of the [calling party's] motive, the probative value of a statement for impeaching the credibility of a witness is 'substantially outweighed by the danger of unfair prejudice, confusion of the issues, or misleading the jury, or by considerations of undue delay, waste of time, or needless presentation of cumulative evidence.' Fed. R. Evid. 403." *United States v. Buffalo*, 358 F.3d at 524. Which is the better test? Should the admissibility of a prior inconsistent statement offered to impeach a party's own witness be determined by application of the "primary purpose" test or Rule 403 balancing?

3. *The "Bad Faith Rule."* In *United States v. Billue*, 994 F.2d 1152 (11th Cir. 1993), the court calls the primary purpose test the "bad faith rule," suggesting that a prosecutor acts in bad faith if he or she calls a witness knowing that the witness' testimony will be useless and intending to impeach the witness with a prior inconsistent statement. According to *Billue*, however, the prosecutor acts in good faith when he or she calls a witness for other purposes.

4. *The "Essential Witness Exception."* The exception to the rule forbidding the prosecution to impeach its own witnesses with prior inconsistent statements is commonly referred to as the "essential witness exception." The name of the exception comes from a passage in *United States v. DeLillo*, 620 F.2d 939 (2d Cir. 1980), which states:

> Beyond doubt, Monahan was not called to the stand by the government as a subterfuge with the primary aim of getting to the jury a statement impeaching him. Monahan's corroborating testimony was *essential* in many areas of the government's case. Once there, the government had the right to question him, and to attempt to impeach him, about those aspects of his testimony which conflicted with Gorman's account of the same events. *Morlang* itself explicitly recognizes the propriety of impeachment where it is "necessary to alleviate the harshness of subjecting a party to the mercy of a witness who is recalcitrant or may have been unscrupulously tampered with." 531 F.2d at 190. To the extent that defendants rely on *Morlang* for the principle that a witness cannot be put on the stand if the side calling him knows that he will give testimony that it will have to impeach, it seems clear to us that the effect of Fed. R. Evid. 607, codifying the right to impeach one's own witnesses without special restriction, is to nullify the plausibility of such a reading.

United States v. DeLillo, 620 F.2d 939, 946–47 (2d Cir. 1980) (emphasis added).

The essential witness exception requires the court to look at the witness' testimony as a whole. If part of the testimony is essential to establishing a fact of consequence in the litigation, the witness may be impeached with a prior inconsistent statement. *See generally* CHRISTOPHER B. MUELLER & LAIRD C. KIRKPPATRICK, 3 FEDERAL EVIDENCE § 6:28, at 167–71 (3d ed. 2007); 1 McCORMICK ON EVIDENCE § 38 (Kenneth S. Broun ed., 6th ed. 2006).

PROBLEM

Problem 10-9. Defendant Bob Carter is on trial for conspiring to sell cocaine. The government has called several witnesses to testify that they and defendant Carter are members of a gang known as "Third World Crips" (TWC). The testimony from these witnesses is that defendant Carter was the leader of the gang, and that the members would sell cocaine Carter gave to them and then give most of the profits to Carter.

The government calls another member of the TWC, Cedric Scott. Scott testifies that he is a member of the TWC, that he is in the cocaine business and that he knows the defendant, Bob Carter. He then testifies that he has been offered a one-year prison sentence in return for truthful testimony against defendant Bob Carter and the cocaine conspiracy. When asked about the defendant's involvement in selling cocaine, Scott says he was not aware that Carter was in the TWC and denies that Carter had any involvement in cocaine sales or that Carter had ever given him (Scott) any cocaine to sell. The prosecutor shows Scott a police officer's report containing a statement attributed to him. The statement in the report indicates that defendant Carter is a member of the TWC, is involved in the cocaine conspiracy, and that he (Carter) supplied Scott with cocaine. Scott says that seeing the statement does not refresh his memory, and the statements in it are false.

The jury is excused and an FBI agent is called to the witness stand. The FBI agent testifies that he interviewed Scott one week before trial, and Scott admitted receiving a phone call from defendant Carter's brother who promised Scott a job with the TWC when he (Scott) got out of jail. The agent also testifies that Scott told him he was afraid of defendant Carter's brother because he saw him tie a person to a telephone pole and set him on fire. Finally, the agent testifies that Scott told him his statement was true but he was afraid and not going to testify. The FBI agent states that he told all of this to the government prosecutor one week ago.

When the jury returns, the trial court allows the government to call the police officer who took Scott's statement. She testifies to all of Scott's statements in the police report that contradict his courtroom testimony, and the statement itself is shown to the jury as evidence of impeachment by prior inconsistent statement.

Defendant Carter is convicted and on appeal argues that it was error for the government to impeach its own witness (Scott) with the prior inconsistent statement.

(A) What are the strongest arguments the defendant can make that the impeachment was improper?

(B) How should the appellate court rule? *See United States v. Carter*, 973 F.2d 1509, 1512–13 (10th Cir. 1992).

(C) Would it make any difference if, instead of being afraid to testify for fear of retaliation, the witness (Scott) merely recanted and said that his first statement was false, and so notified the government one week before trial? *See United States v. Gomez-Gallardo*, 915 F.2d 553, 555–56 (9th Cir. 1990).

[b]   Contradiction

The fifth means of impeachment is contradiction. Offering contradictory evidence has two effects. First, evidence that contradicts what a witness said on direct, if believed, may have the effect of convincing the trier of fact that the specific fact testified to is incorrect. Second, by being shown that the witness was wrong on one point, the trier of fact may be persuaded to doubt the witness' credibility on other points.

Subject only to limitations imposed by the collateral fact rule (and its modern code counterpart, Fed. R. Evid. 403), virtually anything testified to may be subjected to contradictory testimony to suggest that the witness is not truthful. The next three cases demonstrate how matters may become the subject of counterproof that contradicts.

WALDER v. UNITED STATES
347 U.S. 62 (1954)

Mr. Justice Frankfurter delivered the opinion of the Court.

In May 1950, petitioner was indicted in the United States District Court for the Western District of Missouri for purchasing and possessing one grain of heroin. Claiming that the heroin capsule had been obtained through an unlawful search and seizure, petitioner moved to suppress it. The motion was granted, and shortly thereafter, on the Government's motion, the case against petitioner was dismissed.

In January of 1952, petitioner was again indicted, this time for four other illicit transactions in narcotics. The Government's case consisted principally of the testimony of two drug addicts who claimed to have procured the illicit stuff from petitioner under the direction of federal agents. The only witness for the defense was the defendant himself, petitioner here. He denied any narcotics dealings with the two Government informers and attributed the testimony against him to personal hostility.

Early on his direct examination petitioner testified as follows:

Q: Now, first, Mr. Walder, before we go further in your testimony, I want to you (sic) tell the Court and jury whether, not referring to these informers in this case, but whether you have ever sold any narcotics to anyone.

A: I have never sold any narcotics to anyone in my life.

Q: Have you ever had any narcotics in your possession, other than what may have been given to you by a physician for an ailment?

A: No.

Q: Now, I will ask you one more thing. Have you ever handed or given any narcotics to anyone as a gift or in any other manner without the receipt of any money or any other compensation?

A: I have not.

Q: Have you ever even acted as, say, have you acted as a conduit for the purpose of handling what you knew to be a narcotic from one person to another?

A: No, Sir.

On cross-examination, in response to a question by Government counsel making reference to this direct testimony, petitioner reiterated his assertion that he had never purchased, sold or possessed any narcotics. Over the defendant's objection, the Government then questioned him about the heroin capsule unlawfully seized from his home in his presence back in February 1950. The defendant stoutly denied that any narcotics were taken from him at that time. The Government then put on the stand one of the officers who had participated in the unlawful search and seizure and also the chemist who had analyzed the heroin capsule there seized. The trial judge admitted this evidence, but carefully charged the jury that it was not to be used to determine whether the defendant had committed the crimes here charged, but solely for the purpose of impeaching the defendant's credibility. The defendant was convicted and the Court of Appeals for the Eighth Circuit affirmed, one judge dissenting. The question which divided that court, and the sole issue here, is whether the defendant's assertion on direct examination that he had never possessed any narcotics opened the door, solely for the purpose of attacking the defendant's credibility, to evidence of the heroin unlawfully seized in connection with the earlier proceeding. Because this question presents a novel aspect of the scope of the doctrine of *Weeks v. United States*, 232 U.S. 383, we granted certiorari.

The Government cannot violate the Fourth Amendment[2] — in the only way in which the Government can do anything, namely through its agents — and use the fruits of such unlawful conduct to secure a conviction. *Weeks v. United States, supra.* Nor can the Government make indirect use of such evidence for its case, or support a conviction on evidence obtained through leads from the unlawfully obtained evidence. All these methods are outlawed, and convictions obtained by means of them are invalidated, because they encourage the kind of society that is obnoxious to free men.

It is one thing to say that the Government cannot make an affirmative use of evidence unlawfully obtained. It is quite another to say that the defendant can turn the illegal method by which evidence in the Government's possession was obtained to his own advantage, and provide himself with a shield against contradiction of his untruths. Such an extension of the *Weeks* doctrine would be a perversion of the Fourth Amendment.

Take the present situation. Of his own accord, the defendant went beyond a mere denial of complicity in the crimes of which he was charged and made the sweeping claim that he had never dealt in or possessed any narcotics. Of course, the Constitution guarantees a defendant the fullest opportunity to meet the accusation against him. He must be free to deny all the elements of the case against him without thereby giving leave to the Government to introduce by way of rebuttal evidence illegally secured by it, and therefore not available for its case in chief. Beyond that, however, there is hardly justification for letting the defendant affirmatively resort to perjurious testimony in reliance on the Government's disability to challenge his credibility.

The situation here involved is to be sharply contrasted with that presented by *Agnello v. United States*, 269 U.S. 20. There the Government, after having failed in its efforts to introduce the tainted evidence in its case in chief, tried to smuggle it in on cross-examination by asking the accused the broad question "Did you ever see narcotics before?" After eliciting the expected denial, it sought to introduce evidence of narcotics located in the defendant's home by means of an unlawful search and seizure, in order to discredit the defendant. In holding that the Government could no more work in this evidence on cross-examination than it could in its case in chief, the Court foreshadowed, perhaps unwittingly, the result we reach today:

> And the contention that the evidence of the search and seizure was admissible in rebuttal is without merit. In his direct examination, Agnello was not asked and did not testify concerning the can of cocaine. In cross-examination, in answer to a question permitted over his objection, he said he had never seen it. He did nothing to waive his constitutional protection or to justify cross-examination in respect of the evidence claimed to have been obtained by the search. . . . 269 U.S. at page 35.

The judgment is affirmed.

---

[2] "The right of the people to be secure in their persons, houses, papers, and effects, against unreasonable searches and seizures, shall not be violated. . . ."

UNITED STATES v. CONTRERAS
602 F.2d 1237 (5th Cir. 1979)

PER CURIAM:

Lonjinos Ramos Contreras was convicted after trial by jury on both counts of a two-count indictment charging unlawful distribution of heroin, in violation of 21 U.S.C. § 841(a)(1). We affirm.

* * *

As his final assignment of error, Contreras contends that the trial court erroneously allowed the government to question defense witness Alvaredo about alleged statements made to a DEA agent concerning purchases of large quantities of cocaine. Appellant argues that these statements involved criminal activity on the part of Alvaredo which did not result in a conviction, and therefore constitute improper impeachment under Rule 608(b) of the Federal Rules of Evidence.[5]

Alvaredo testified on direct examination that he observed the DEA agent lift a "coke" spoon to his nose, and that he knew it was a "coke" spoon "because I have seen a bunch of them in Playboys and this and that."

On cross-examination, the prosecutor inquired into Alvaredo's knowledge of cocaine and related paraphernalia, at one point asking whether Alvaredo had discussed with a DEA agent "going to Ft. Stockton to purchase large quantities of cocaine."[6] Alvaredo denied the discussion, and the court properly overruled the defense's objection to the inquiry.

Contrary to appellant's assertions, Rule 608 of the Federal Rules of Evidence is not applicable to this situation. This is not a case where specific instances of misconduct, totally unrelated to the witness' substantive testimony, were used in an attempt to impeach. Alvaredo's direct testimony revealed the alleged basis for his knowledge that the spoon he observed was a "coke" spoon. The government was entitled to test the credibility and factual foundation of that statement.

The trial court has broad discretion concerning the scope of cross-examination. Furthermore, the scope of the direct examination may be exceeded on cross-examination in an effort to test the truthfulness of the witness. The questioning of

---

[5] Rule 608(b), Federal Rules of Evidence, provides that:

Specific instances of the conduct of a witness, for the purpose of attacking or supporting his credibility, other than conviction of a crime as provided in rule 609, may not be proved by extrinsic evidence. They may, however, in the discretion of the court, if probative of truthfulness or untruthfulness, be inquired into on cross-examination of the witness (1) concerning his character for truthfulness or untruthfulness, or (2) concerning the character for truthfulness or untruthfulness of another witness as to which character the witness being cross-examined has testified.

[6] The controverted cross-examination of Alvaredo developed as follows:

Q: You recognized it as a coke spoon, is that right?
A: That is right.
Q: How did you recognize it as a cocaine spoon?
A: Because I have seen it in a bunch of books.
Q: Isn't it a fact that you know a little bit about cocaine?
A: No, I don't, at all.
Q: Isn't it a fact that you discussed with Special Agent Hernandez on many occasions going to Ft. Stockton to purchase large quantities of cocaine?
A: No.

Alvaredo was properly within the scope of cross-examination and did not constitute reversible error.

Affirmed.

NOTES

1. ***The Collateral Fact Rule AndFederal Rule Of Evidence 403.*** The collateral fact rule bars the use of *extrinsic evidence* to impeach a witness. Accordingly, if an attorney is using a recognized means of impeachment that is applicable in the circumstances of the case, he or she may always cross-examine the witness about the matter (use intrinsic evidence). The theory behind the collateral fact rule is that extrinsic evidence about collateral credibility issues raises serious problems about unfair prejudice, confusion, waste of time and misleading the jury by emphasizing credibility issues over the substantive issues in the case. The impact of the collateral fact rule is that, when it applies, a cross-examiner must take the answer the witness gives (whether true, false or incomplete) and cannot call another witness or offer documentary evidence to further the impeachment. *See generally* 1 COURTROOM CRIMINAL EVIDENCE § 715, at 317–22 (4th ed. 2005); CHARLES T. MCCORMICK, 1 MCCORMICK ON EVIDENCE § 49, (Kenneth S. Broun ed., 6th ed. 2006). Since this can be a rather severe limitation, it is important to know when the collateral fact rule applies and when it does not.

(A) Impeachment Techniques Implicated. The rule applies to only three techniques: (1) specific instances of misconduct that have not resulted in a conviction *when offered to show character for truthfulness* (Fed. R. Evid 608(b)); (2) prior inconsistent statement (Fed. R. Evid. 613)); and (3) contradiction.

The rule does not apply to certain impeachment techniques that necessarily, or by definition, require or permit the introduction of extrinsic evidence. For example, conviction of a crime (Fed. R. Evid. 609) can be shown extrinsically by offering a public record of conviction. Likewise, opinion and reputation of character for truthfulness (Fed. R. Evid. 608(a)) necessarily requires calling a reputation and/or opinion witness. Similarly, courts permit the use of extrinsic evidence when showing bias or mental or sensory incapacity, holding that these matters are not collateral. *See generally* 1 COURTROOM CRIMINAL EVIDENCE § 715, at 318 (4th ed. 2005).

(B) Defining "Collateral Fact." There are three categories of facts that may be considered not collateral. First, matters are not collateral if they are relevant to establish a fact of consequence in the litigation. *See United States v. Grooms*, 978 F.2d 425, 429 (8th Cir. 1992) ("matter material to the substantive issues in the case"); *State v. Watkins*, 419 N.W.2d 660, 665 (Neb. 1988) (matter that the party could prove independently of the contradiction).

Second, certain credibility issues are never considered collateral. Bias, mental or sensory defect, opinion and reputation when offered to show character for truthfulness, and conviction of a crime when offered to show character for truthfulness, fall into this category.

Third, sometimes a witness's testimony about a particular fact appears collateral, however, if the witness were mistaken about the apparently collateral fact his or her testimony on the historical merits of the case are called into question. This is sometimes referred to as the "linchpin fact test." *See* CHARLES T. MCCORMICK, 1 MCCORMICK ON EVIDENCE § 49, at 203 (Kenneth S. Broun ed., 6th ed. 2006) ("[T]he extrinsic evidence is non-collateral and . . . admissible when it relates to a so-called "linchpin" fact. [F]or purposes of impeachment a part of the witness's story may be attacked where as a matter of human experience, he could not be mistaken about that fact if the thrust of his testimony on the historical merits was true."); 1 COURTROOM CRIMINAL EVIDENCE § 715, at 319 (4th ed. 2005).

(C)Federal Rule Of Evidence 403. The collateral fact rule was developed at common law and there is no modern rule of evidence specifically dealing with collateral matters in this context. Federal Rule of Evidence 403 (and its state counterparts), however, gives the trial court the option of excluding evidence for reasons that comport with the concerns addressed by the collateral fact rule. When a court with a modern evidence code permits or excludes extrinsic evidence of matters that would have been considered under the collateral fact rule at common law, it is balancing the probativeness of the extrinsic evidence on the issue of credibility with the dangers cited in Fed. R. Evid. 403. *See United States v. Grooms*, 978 F.2d 425, 429 (8th Cir. 1992) (after discussing the collateral fact rule court excluded evidence under Rule 403); *but see United States v. Kozinski*, 16 F.3d 795, 805–06 (7th Cir. 1994) (court excludes testimony as extrinsic testimony on collateral matter without mentioning Rule 403).

2. *Federal Rule Of Evidence 608(b) and Contradiction.* Rule 608(b) contains a complete ban on offering extrinsic evidence of specific instances of conduct *when offered to show character for truthfulness.* Rule 608(b) does not regulate impeachment by contradiction. Accordingly, a specific instance of conduct may be brought up on cross-examination of a witness to *contradict* a matter testified to on direct. If the witness denies the specific instance of conduct on cross-examination, extrinsic evidence of the specific instance of conduct may be offered if the court finds that the collateral evidence rule, and Fed. R. Evid. 403, are not contravened. CHRISTOPHER B. MUELLER & LAIRD C. KIRKPATRICK, 3 FEDERAL EVIDENCE. §§6:37 & 6:85, at 244–50 & 562-64 (3d ed. 2007). In *United States v. Costillo*, 181 F.3d 1129 (9th Cir. 1999), court explained the distinction between evidence governed by Rule 608(b) and evidence offered to impeach by contradiction. The court stated:

> Rule 608(b) prohibits the use of extrinsic evidence of conduct to impeach a witness' credibility in terms of his general veracity. In contrast, the concept of impeachment by contradiction permits courts to admit extrinsic evidence that specific testimony is false, because contradicted by other evidence:
>
>> [D]irect-examination testimony containing a broad disclaimer of misconduct sometimes can open the door for extrinsic evidence to contradict even though the contradictory evidence is otherwise inadmissible under Rules 404 and 608(b) and is, thus, collateral. This approach has been justified on the grounds that the witness should not be permitted to engage in perjury, mislead the trier of fact, and then shield himself from impeachment by asserting the collateral-fact doctrine.

2A CHARLES A. WRIGHT & VICTOR J. GOLD, FEDERAL PRACTICE AND PROCEDURE, § 6119 at 116-17.

QUESTIONS

1. In the two preceding cases, did the impeachment involve collateral matters?

2. If the impeachment in the two preceding cases involved collateral matters, was the impeachment consistent with the collateral fact rule? Explain.

PROBLEMS

Problem 10-10. Defendant is on trial for robbing a drug store with a knife. After the prosecution rests, the defendant takes the stand and states only that he did not commit the crime and that he was in another state at the time the robbery was committed. On cross-examination the prosecution asks defendant if he had committed any other robberies with a knife in the last five years. Defendant, answers "no." The prosecution is then allowed to call an FBI agent to testify. The FBI agent testifies that when the agent was working undercover last year the defendant told him that he (the defendant) had committed a robbery of a liquor store with a knife.

Was the testimony of the FBI agent properly admitted? If so, to show what? *See United States v. Pisari*, 636 F.2d 855, 856–59 (1st Cir. 1981); *Walder v. United States*, 347 U.S. 62, 66 (1954); CHRISTOPHER B. MUELLER & LAIRD C. KIRKPATRICK, 3 FEDERAL EVIDENCE § 6 :90, at 606-09 (3d ed. 2007).

Problem 10-11. Defendant Riggs is charged with arson. The government claims he was hired by the owner of a car dealership to set fire to the dealership so the owner could collect insurance money.

At trial the defendant Riggs takes the witness stand. He testifies on direct that "he never set fire to anything in his life." On cross-examination the prosecuting attorney asks Riggs about several fires to property he owned and for which the defendant collected insurance money. Defendant was never charged with a crime in any of the fires. Defendant denies that he ever set fire to any property he owned. The prosecutor then calls a neighbor of Riggs to the witness stand to testify that he saw Riggs set fire to his (Rigg's) garage three years ago.

Defendant is convicted and appeals. He argues that it was improper for the prosecution to ask about other fires since it violates Rule 404(b)'s ban against offering evidence of other bad acts to show a propensity to commit such acts. Defendant also urges that it violates Rule 608(b), since that rule does not permit extrinsic evidence of bad acts and since arson is not conduct that shows a character for untruthfulness. What result on appeal? *See United States v. Riggio*, 70 F.3d 336, 339 (5th Cir. 1995).

Problem 10-12. Defendant is on trial for conspiracy to sell cocaine. At trial, Bill Bass, the person whom the government alleges was the drug "kingpin" in the area, testifies for the government against the defendant. Bass testifies at length about his drug dealings with the defendant. On cross-examination, Bass testifies that a man named Maury owed him $3,000 from a gambling debt but never paid him.

Defendant wishes to call Maury to the witness stand to contradict Bass and to testify that he (Maury) did pay Bass the $3,000. Should the defendant be allowed to call Maury for this purpose? *See United States v. Kozinski*, 16 F.3d 795, 805–06 (7th Cir. 1994).

D.   REHABILITATION

As mentioned at the beginning of this chapter, the process of enhancing and diminishing credibility usually occurs in recognizable stages. The third and last stage (following bolstering and impeachment) is rehabilitation. Like the other stages, evidentiary rules and restrictions exist to regulate the way an attorney may rehabilitate a witness who has had his or her credibility attacked by one of the impeachment methods.

There are two overriding principles that regulate rehabilitation. The first principle was encountered at the outset of this chapter when the concept of bolstering was examined — there may be no attempt to enhance a witness' credibility until the witness' credibility has been attacked. The second principle is that the method used to repair credibility must respond to the method of attack with relative directness. Put another way, a "wall attacked at one point may not be fortified at another, distinct point." CHARLES T. MCCORMICK, 1 MCCORMICK ON EVIDENCE § 47, at 190 (Kenneth S. Broun ed., 6th ed. 2006).

There are three methods most commonly used to repair a witness' credibility.[6] First, a witness who has been attacked on cross-examination will be given an opportunity to respond, deny or attempt to explain away the facts that have been used to attack credibility. For example, assume that a witness is attacked during cross-examination with questions that show bias toward a party. On re-direct the witness will be allowed to explain that the witness and the party are, in reality, on good terms and that there is no bias; or, perhaps, the witness might explain that while they may not be on good terms, the witness' testimony nevertheless is not slanted for or against the party. *See generally* 1 COURTROOM CRIMINAL EVIDENCE § 717, at 323–24 (4th ed. 2005); CHRISTOPHER B. MUELLER & LAIRD C. KIRKPATRICK, 3 FEDERAL EVIDENCE §§ 6 :77 & 6:102, at 514–15 & 684–85 (3d ed. 2007).

Affording the witness an opportunity to respond to an attack by offering an explanation or denial is within the court's sound discretion and is not particularly controversial. In fact, the concept of allowing the witness an opportunity to respond and explain is reflected in Fed. R. Evid. 613 (extrinsic evidence of a prior inconsistent statement by a witness is not admissible unless the witness is given an opportunity to explain or deny the statement).

The second and third methods of repairing credibility are; offering evidence of good character for truthfulness and offering prior statements of the witness who has been attacked that are consistent with the witness' trial testimony. Unlike affording the witness an opportunity to explain or deny, these methods can generate controversy. The principal controversy involved with using character evidence and prior consistent statements to repair credibility concerns the second overriding principle recited above — the method of repair must respond to the method of attack.

[1] Evidence of Truthful Character to Rehabilitate

Federal Rule of Evidence 608 allows a witness' credibility to be supported by extrinsic opinion or reputation evidence but imposes two qualifications on the admissibility of such evidence. First, the opinion and reputation evidence offered to support the witness may refer only to "character for *truthfulness*." Second, opinion and reputation evidence of truthful character is admissible *only* after the witness' *character* for truthfulness has been attacked "*by opinion or reputation evidence or otherwise.*"

It is the second of Rule 608's two qualifications that sometimes presents problems. Which of the methods of attacking a witness' credibility constitutes an attack on *character* within the meaning of Rule 608? There are seven recognized methods of attack. Three are, by definition, attacks on character (conviction of a crime, misconduct not resulting in conviction, and opinion and reputation for truthfulness). The other four

---

[6] In *Courtroom Criminal Evidence*, five methods of rehabilitation are mentioned. In addition to the three methods discussed in this text, the authors of *Courtroom Criminal Evidence* identify the offer of corroborative evidence and expert testimony as methods that are available, in the proper circumstances, to rehabilitate. 1 COURTROOM CRIMINAL EVIDENCE §§ 718 & 721, at 334 & 332–33 (4th ed. 2005).

methods either may or may not be construed as an "otherwise" attack on character (bias, mental or sensory incapacity, prior inconsistent statement, and contradiction). The advisory committee note to Rule 608(a) provides some clarification:

> Opinion or reputation that the witness is untruthful specifically qualifies as an attack under the rule, and evidence of misconduct, including conviction of a crime, and of corruption also fall within this category. Evidence of bias or interest does not. Whether evidence in the form of contradiction is an attack on the character of the witness must depend on the circumstances.

In *United States v. Dring*, the Ninth Circuit had occasion to explore these issues.

UNITED STATES v. DRING
930 F.2d 687 (9th Cir. 1991)

Choy, Circuit Judge:

Alan J. Dring was convicted of importing marijuana, possession with intent to distribute, and related conspiracy charges. On appeal, Dring alleges that the district court erred by (1) barring presentation of evidence regarding his truthful character among other things. . . . We AFFIRM.

FACTUAL AND PROCEDURAL BACKGROUND

At approximately 2:30 a.m. on May 22, 1986, a fishing boat carrying 13,000 pounds of marijuana, docked at Pier 3 in San Francisco Harbor. The marijuana had been transferred to the fishing boat a few miles offshore from a larger vessel, the Panamco II.

*   *   *

Stationed aboard the fishing boat and on the pier were undercover United States Customs agents, who witnessed the unloading of the marijuana. The agents saw an unidentified white male step out of a blue pickup truck parked on the pier. He opened the back of a large tractor-trailer and spoke broken Spanish to the occupants, eleven illegal aliens from Mexico. He supervised the transfer of the marijuana from the boat to the trailer.

During the unloading, Mark Lawrence, the caretaker of a tugboat docked at Pier 3, went over to investigate the early morning events. He talked for a moment with the man from the blue pickup truck and then left. After the unloading had been completed, the agents followed the tractor-trailer and apprehended its driver, Michael Thompson, as well as the eleven illegal aliens. . . .

*   *   *

At trial, the Government presented considerable circumstantial evidence and five eyewitnesses who placed Dring at the pier that night. All five witnesses — the three agents, Thompson, and Leroy Ludahl, the captain of the fishing boat — had identified Dring from photographic arrays in late 1988 or early 1989. . . .

Dring presented a defense of mistaken identity. Mark Lawrence, the tugboat caretaker who lived on Pier 3, testified that Dring was not the man he had spoken to on the pier. Two alibi witnesses testified that Dring had spent the night in question at his home in Napa Valley. Finally, Dring took the stand and denied any involvement in the drug-smuggling operation.

The Government attacked Dring's defense with contradiction evidence and one rebuttal witness. The district court precluded Dring from introducing character evidence of his veracity. . . .

I. *Evidence of Dring's Truthful Character*

Dring argues that the district court erred by barring the introduction of evidence as to his truthful character. The question before this court is a mixed question of law and fact, wherein matters of law predominate. We review it *de novo*.

Federal Rule of Evidence 608(a)(2) provides that "[e]vidence of truthful character is admissible only after the character of the witness for truthfulness has been attacked by opinion or reputation evidence or otherwise." Dring concedes that the Government did not use opinion or reputation evidence against him, but still maintains that the Government "otherwise" attacked his character for truthfulness.[1]

The first exchange cited by Dring was the response of a Government witness to cross-examination by Dring's counsel. We hold that defense-initiated "attacks" on the character of a defense witness do not trigger rehabilitative testimony under Rule 608(a). To hold otherwise would enable defense attorneys to manufacture attacks on the truthful character of their own witnesses.

The other statements cited by Dring are also insufficient to trigger rehabilitative testimony. The purpose of Rule 608(a)(2) is to encourage direct attacks on a witness's

---

[1] Dring argues that the following exchanges constituted Government attacks on his character for truthfulness:

Q: [by defense counsel]: But since Mr. Dring was offering this as an explanation of his whereabouts on May 21, you certainly wanted to talk to . . . Chilly George to confirm it, didn't you?

A: [by Agent MacKenzie]: I felt that in the future, that if we wanted to talk to Mr. Chilly George, we could probably chase him down by asking Mr. Dring, but at that time I thought he was not telling us the truth. I did not pursue it. . . .

A: [by prosecution to Dring]: Now, when Mr. MacKenzie and Mr. Landry spoke to you about the evening of May 21st and the morning of May 22nd, 1986, you did not tell them the truth, did you? . . .

Q: [by prosecution]: If I understand your testimony, the six people that testified in court and identified you as being on Pier 3, they're all mistaken, is that correct?

A: [by Dring]: Yes, sir.

Q: It wasn't you?

A: No, sir, it was not me. . . .

Q: [by prosecution]: In January 1986, did you tell Mr. Borgen that you might be in some trouble and might need an alibi?

A: [by Dring]: I told him what was happening to me.

Q: Well, did you tell him in '86 that you might be in trouble and might need an alibi?

A: I told him what was happening to me.

Dring also argues that the Government attacked his character for truthfulness in its closing and rebuttal arguments:

> And I submit the evidence is clear and convincing that the defendant lied. Not just about a little thing, he lied about a lot. . . .

*   *   *

> I'll tell you what it adds up to. . . . A man who will put up a false and perjured defense. Now, I guess it was bad form of me, according to Mr. Goldstein, to suggest that Mr. Dring was not telling the truth. Well, that's what criminal trials are all about, they're a search for the truth.

The Government attorney concluded by saying that Dring had presented "a false alibi."

veracity in the instant case and to discourage peripheral attacks on a witness's general character for truthfulness.[2] To this end, the Rule prohibits rehabilitation by character evidence of truthfulness after direct attacks on a witness's veracity in the instant case. However, the Rule permits rehabilitation after indirect attacks on a witness's general character for truthfulness.

The Advisory Committee's Note to Rule 608(a) provides that "[o]pinion or reputation that the witness is untruthful specifically qualifies as an attack under the rule, and evidence of misconduct, including conviction of crime, and of corruption[3] also fall within this category. Evidence of bias or interest does not. *Whether evidence in the form of contradiction is an attack upon the character of the witness must depend upon the circumstances.* (emphasis added).

Thus, evidence of a witness's bias for or against a party in the instant case, or evidence of a witness's interest in the outcome of the instant case, constitutes a direct attack that does not trigger rehabilitation under Rule 608(a). For example, it would be permissible to imply that, because of bias due to family relationship, a father is lying to protect his son. Such evidence directly undermines the veracity and credibility of the witness in the instant case, without implicating the witness as a liar in general. By way of contrast, indirect attacks on truthfulness include opinion evidence, reputation evidence, and evidence of corruption, which require the jury to infer that the witness is lying at present, simply because he has lied often in the past.[4]

It is for the trial court, exercising its discretion, to determine whether given conduct constitutes a direct or indirect attack on a witness's character for truthfulness. On the one hand, the presentation of contradiction evidence, in the form of contravening testimony by other witnesses, does not trigger rehabilitation.[5] Vigorous cross-examination, including close questioning of a witness about his version of the facts and pointing out inconsistencies with the testimony of other witnesses, does not necessarily trigger rehabilitation. Nor is rehabilitation in order when an attorney maintains in her closing argument that a witness's testimony is not credible, given inconsistencies with other witnesses' testimony.

On the other hand, "[a] slashing cross-examination may carry strong accusations of misconduct and bad character, which the witness's denial will not remove from the jury's mind. If the judge considers that fairness requires it, he may permit evidence of good

---

[2] The Advisory Committee's Note to Rule 608(a) states that "[c]haracter evidence in support of credibility is admissible under the rule only after the witness' character has first been attacked, as has been the case at common law. The enormous needless consumption of time which a contrary practice would entail justifies the limitation." Analogously, by admitting character evidence only pertaining to truthfulness, "the result [of Rule 608(a)] is to sharpen relevancy, to reduce surprise, waste of time, and confusion, and to make the lot of the witness somewhat less unattractive."

[3] "Evidence of corruption," refers to evidence of prior corrupt conduct including but not limited to forgery, fraud, perjury, bribery, false pretenses, cheating, and embezzlement.

[4] On occasion, a single piece of evidence may serve a dual purpose, both as evidence of bias and corruption. [*See*] *People v. Ah Fat*, 48 Cal. 61, 64 (1874) (evidence that state's witness had offered to identify killer "if there was any coin in it"). . . . We need not decide whether evidence of this dual nature triggers rehabilitation under Rule 608(a).

[5] By calling the jury's attention to inconsistencies in testimony, the attorney may simply intend to question the ability of the witness to perceive or recall certain facts due to excitement, fatigue, poor eyesight, poor lighting, great distance from the event in question, or fading memory affected by the passage of time. Even where an attorney points out inconsistencies to attack a witness's truthfulness, the attack is direct and relevant because it focuses on the credibility of the witness in the present case without relying on prior acts of corruption or bad character.

character, a mild palliative for the rankle of insinuation by such cross-examination."
McCormick § 49 at 117 [(3d ed. 1984)].

Thus, vigorous cross-examination or the presentation of contradiction evidence can
and should trigger rehabilitation where such evidence amounts to the kind of indirect
attack on truthfulness embodied by "evidence of bad reputation, bad opinion of
character for truthfulness, conviction of crime, or eliciting from the witness on
cross-examination acknowledgment of misconduct which has not resulted in conviction."
McCormick § 49 at 116–17.

In this light, the statements cited by Dring constituted direct attacks on Dring's
credibility in the instant case. The Government did not introduce opinion or reputation
testimony to attack Dring's general character for truthfulness.[6] Nor did it present
evidence of prior misconduct or corruption. The Government merely emphasized
inconsistencies between Dring's testimony and that of other witnesses. It observed that
Dring, a criminal defendant testifying on his own behalf, had a distinct pro-defense bias
and a compelling interest in the outcome of the case. Therefore, the district court's
denial of rehabilitative testimony was proper.

*   *   *

Affirmed.

NOTES

1. **What a Supporting Character Witness Can Say.** Once the principal witness'
character has been attacked, a supporting character witness may be called. The
supporting character witness may testify as to the principal witness' reputation for
truthfulness or may offer an opinion that the principal witness has a truthful character.
Specifically, the supporting character witness may *not* testify about specific instances of
conduct by the principal witness that show truthful character. Such testimony, coming
from the character witness, would constitute extrinsic evidence of specific instances of
conduct. See *United States v. Melia*, 691 F.2d 672, 674–75 (4th Cir. 1982).

2. **Cross-Examination of the Rehabilitation Character Witness.** Note that the
supportive, or rehabilitation, character witness may be cross-examined and asked about
specific instances of conduct by the principal witness that show *untruthfulness*. FED. R.
EVID. 608(b). The purpose of such questioning is not to establish that the principal
witness committed the particular acts but, rather, to test the supportive character
witness' knowledge of the principal witness or of the principal witness' reputation in the
community in an effort to discredit the character witness' testimony. In *United States
v. Skelton*, 514 F.3d 433, 444 (5th Cir. 2008), the court stated that "[o]nce a witness has
testified concerning a defendant's good character, it is permissible during cross-
examination to attempt to undermine his credibility by asking him whether he has
heard of prior misconduct of the defendant which is inconsistent with the witness' direct
testimony." (internal citations omitted). See also *United States v. Monteleone*, 77 F.3d
1086, 1089 (8th Cir. 1996). A major treatise on evidence further elaborates on the
proper impeachment of a character witness:

---

[6] . . . [I]t is not merely attacks on *truthfulness* which trigger rehabilitation, but rather attacks on a
witness's prior history or general *character for truthfulness*. Far from attempting to prove that Dring was
generally a liar, the Government merely suggested that Dring was lying in the instant case about his degree
of involvement in the crime. The Government placed Dring's veracity in the instant case at issue, but not his
reputation for veracity.

The character witness may be asked not only concerning the specific acts of the principal witness probative of truthfulness or untruthfulness, but may be cross-examined concerning familiarity with convictions as well as arrests, rumors, reports, indictments, etc., of the principal witness. Such facts have a natural bearing upon the reputation of the principal witness. Lack of familiarity with such facts is relevant to an assessment of the basis for the character witness' testimony. Familiarity with such matters explores the character witness' standard of "truthfulness" or "untruthfulness." Whatever the form of the question, the cross-examiner mut, of course, have a good faith basis supporting his inquiry.

HANDBOOK OF FEDERAL EVIDENCE § 608.5, at 622–35.

Finally, when the supportive character witness is cross-examined on specific instances of conduct of the principal witness, the specific instances must be of a type that people would consider in forming an opinion or developing a reputation for truthfulness. *Id.* at 1089–90 (error to cross-examine defendant's reputation character witness concerning whether he knew defendant had lied before a federal grand jury, since grand jury testimony is secret and was not likely to have become a matter of general knowledge in the community).

QUESTIONS

1. According to the court in *Dring*, what methods or kinds of attacks on credibility constitute an attack on character and justify the admission of supportive character evidence to rehabilitate?

2. According to the court in *Dring*, what methods or kinds of attacks on credibility do *not* constitute an attack on character and do *not* justify the admission of supportive character evidence to rehabilitate? *See United States v. Drury*, 396 F.3d 1303, 1315 (11th Cir. 2004) ("An 'attack' that consists only of 'Government counsel pointing out inconsistencies in testimony and arguing that the accused's testimony is not credible does not constitute an attack on the accused's reputation for truthfulness within the meaning of Rule 608.") (internal citations omitted)).

3. When does "vigorous cross-examination" constitute an attack on character for truthfulness?

PROBLEMS

Problem 10-13. Defendant is on trial for murder and testifies that he did not commit the crime and was in another state at the time of the homicide. On cross-examination the prosecution offers evidence showing that defendant had been convicted of the felony of robbery two years ago.

(A) May the defendant call a witness to testify that, in the witness' opinion, the defendant has a good character for truthfulness?

(B) If so, could the defendant call a person who had administered a polygraph test to the defendant shortly before trial to testify that, based upon a review of the test results, the witness is of the opinion that defendant is a truthful person? *See United States v. Thomas*, 768 F.2d 611, 618–19 (5th Cir. 1985).

Problem 10-14. Defendant is on trial for murder. He has pled not guilty by reason of insanity. Defendant's psychiatrist has examined defendant several times. He testifies in support of defendant's insanity plea. On cross-examination of defendant's psychiatrist the government suggests that the psychiatrist's diagnosis depends largely on interviews with defendant, and that if defendant lied in those interviews the diagnosis would be false.

(A) After the cross-examination of the psychiatrist, may the defendant call a witness to give opinion and reputation testimony that defendant (not the psychiatrist) has a truthful character? *See United States v. Lechoco*, 542 F.2d 84, 86–89 (D.C. Cir. 1976).

(B) Does it make any difference whether defendant did or did not take the witness stand? *See id.*

[2] Evidence of a Prior Consistent Statement to Rehabilitate

To begin with, one may not rehabilitate a witness with a prior consistent statement if the witness' *character for truthfulness* has been attacked. The principle that demands that the method used to repair credibility must meet the method used to attack credibility blocks prior consistent statements to rehabilitate in this situation. *See United States v. Tome*, 513 U.S. 150, 115 S. Ct. 696, 701 (1995) (a consistent statement has little rebuttal force when impeachment is by a method other than a charge of recent fabrication or improper influence or motive); 1 COURTROOM CRIMINAL EVIDENCE § 720, at 327–28 (4th ed. 2005). Accordingly, if the attack consists of offering a prior conviction, bad opinion or reputation for truthfulness, or untruthful misconduct that did not result in conviction, the witness cannot be supported by showing that the witness has made statements consistent with his or her courtroom testimony in the past. *Id.*

Whether a prior consistent statement may be used to rehabilitate after an impeachment using other methods depends upon two factors: (1) the nature of the attack, and (2) when the prior consistent statement was made. First, the attack must be construed as one that charges recent fabrication or improper influence or motive. Second, the prior consistent statement must have been *before* the improper influence or motive, or recent fabrication, arose. A prior consistent statement is not deemed relevant to rehabilitate in the absence of these two conditions. The same conditions apply when offering prior consistent statements to rehabilitate after an impeachment by prior inconsistent statement. The prior inconsistent statement must be accompanied by or construed as a charge of recent fabrication or improper influence or motive that arose prior to the fabrication or improper influence or motive. *See generally* CHRISTOPHER B. MUELLER & LAIRD C. KIRKPATRICK, 3 FEDERAL EVIDENCE § 6:102, at 684–85 (3d ed. 2007); *United States v. Tome*, 513 U.S. 150, 115 S. Ct. 696, 705 (1995) (Fed. R. Evid. 801(d)(1)(B) permits the introduction of prior consistent statements to rebut a charge of recent fabrication or improper influence or motive only when those statements were made before the charged recent fabrication or improper influence or motive.).

To illustrate, consider the example of a person charged with a crime who is offered and accepts a reduced sentence in return for a guilty plea and testimony against a co-defendant. At trial the co-defendant could question the witness about the plea agreement and argue that the witness' testimony was the product of undue influence or bias motivated by receiving the plea agreement from the government. If so, the government could then offer prior consistent statements made by the witness *before* the witness entered into the plea agreement to rehabilitate. Statements consistent with the witness' testimony made *after* the plea agreement would be irrelevant and just as tainted by improper motive or undue influence as the trial testimony.

The following case, *United States v. Quinto*, discusses the use of prior consistent statements used to rehabilitate at common law and as codified by the Federal Rules of Evidence. Note also *Quinto*'s discussion about how the Federal Rules have significantly changed the rules governing the admissibility of prior consistent statements as *substantive* evidence.

UNITED STATES v. QUINTO
582 F.2d 224 (2d Cir. 1978)

WATERMAN, CIRCUIT JUDGE:

While it is superfluous to say that the intent of a tax evader is to try "to screw the government out of some cash if (he can)," what makes this contested tax evasion case remarkable is that, according to the government, Quinto, the alleged tax evader here, was gracious enough to acknowledge to two Internal Revenue Service agents when interviewed by them that that is precisely what he was hoping to accomplish by failing to report approximately $15,000 of income over a two-year period. Not surprisingly, though, Quinto's recollection of his interview with the IRS agents, as developed during his testimony in his own defense at his trial . . . on two charges of tax evasion (26 U.S.C. § 7201) and two charges of willfully subscribing false income tax returns (26 U.S.C. § 7206(1)), is somewhat different.

* * *

Inasmuch as the defense acknowledged that Quinto had failed to report . . . $15,700 received . . . during 1974 and 1975, the government's proof at trial was directed at establishing that at the time he had failed to report the income Quinto had had the willful intent that must exist for a defendant to be convicted of tax evasion (§ 7201) and of willfully subscribing false income tax returns (§ 7206(1)). To establish the willfulness of Quinto's failure to report income, the government relied upon the testimony of James Wallwork, a Special Agent in the Intelligence Division of the Internal Revenue Service. The crucial portion of the agent's testimony concerned an interview with Quinto conducted by Wallwork, Peter Fuhrman, another IRS Special Agent, and two Assistant United States Attorneys. Several days prior to August 20, 1976, the date on which the interview was conducted, a federal prosecutor had called Quinto and asked him to appear for the interview at the prosecutor's office in the United States Courthouse in Brooklyn. At the time the invitation was extended, the agents and the prosecutor were fully aware that Quinto had not reported the $15,700 he had received . . . during 1974 and 1975. Unaccompanied by counsel, Quinto appeared at the scheduled time and was ushered into the prosecutor's office. Wallwork testified at trial that, prior to the start of the interrogation, one of the two prosecutors who was present advised Quinto that he was a target of a grand jury investigation and that he was also a subject of a criminal investigation by the Internal Revenue Service. *Miranda* warnings were also given, and these were repeated several times during the course of the interview. After the initial warnings had been given, Quinto claimed to understand his rights and expressed his desire to proceed with the discussion. Quinto was eventually asked why he had not reported the money he had received . . . during 1974 and 1975, and according to Wallwork, Quinto, after some abortive attempts to extricate himself from his obvious predicament, blurted out: "Okay, I was trying to screw the government out of some cash if I could."

Defense counsel conducted a vigorous cross-examination of Wallwork which was designed to show that the meeting of August 20 had been more of an inquisition than an interview. . . .

. . . [T]he prosecution on redirect examination elicited from Wallwork that the agents had prepared a memorandum following the August 20 "interview" with Quinto. The document, consisting of eight single-spaced, typed pages, purported to describe exactly what had happened at Quinto's session with the agents. It disclosed, among other things, that Quinto had been read the rights to which Wallwork had previously referred in his direct testimony and, in what was portrayed as a verbatim quotation of Quinto's remarks, that Quinto had confessed that his purpose in failing to report the income was "to screw the government out of some cash if [he] could." Arguing that there had been "a general attack on the agent's credibility," the government attempted to introduce the memorandum as a prior consistent statement usable not only to corroborate Wallwork's in-court direct testimony but also usable under Fed. R. Evid. 801(d)(1)(B) as "substantive evidence" to prove that Quinto had made the fatal admission the IRS agents claim he made. The defense objected to the admission of the document, and, although the judge sustained the objection, he expressly left open the possibility that he might permit the document to be admitted later in the trial "if there [were] a challenge to its credibility, even the form of a contradiction."

Quinto testified in his own defense. . . . [H]is recollection of what had transpired at his interview conducted by the IRS agents and the federal prosecutors differed materially from the version of that incident conveyed to the jury through Agent Wallwork's testimony and, importantly, the version which would eventually be conveyed to the jury through the later-admitted IRS memorandum of that interview as well. Quinto, claiming that he had been lured to the interview on the pretext that the discussions there would involve certain land condemnation procedures, stated that the interview had been conducted in inquisitorial fashion, his inquisitors "badgering" and "goading" him and calling him a "liar" at several points during the interview. Quinto stated that he had not been informed at the start of the interview that he was a target, and that he had no recollection of having been informed that he had the right to leave the room at any time, or that he could refuse to answer questions. As to the supposed admission that he was trying "to screw the government out of some cash," Quinto testified that Agent Wallwork had distorted what Quinto had actually said:

When they were goading me and goading me, I just said, "Do you think for one moment I would try to screw the Government out of a few dollars?" That's what I said, in just that tone, with a question mark on the end of it.

* * *

After the defense had rested, the judge, of his own accord, reopened the question of the admissibility of the IRS memorandum:

The Court: A little earlier this morning, Mr. Marcus, you offered in evidence the statement of the revenue agent. . . .

Mr. Marcus: Yes, your Honor.

The Court: I sustained the objection at the time and I have been thinking about it further, and have wondered whether you were now taking the position that the implied attack upon Mr. Wallwork's credibility as to recent fabrication or improper motive or influence or something, had been sufficiently established to warrant its admission.

Mr. Marcus: That in fact, is the basis for the offer at that time. It would seem to me that at this point, we have had almost a day of Mr. Quinto, in essence, saying that Special Agent Wallwork lied in connection with saying "He was not given his rights," saying he was or was not told he was a target, etc.

The Court: I know what he said. Just when you made the offer, you didn't say anything that rang the bell that you were reasserting the argument, which you had previously made, *and which I expressly left open in the event the contradictions should occur.* You did intend to reassert that —

Mr. Marcus: That is correct, your Honor.

The Court: I will reflect on the matter over lunch. I will give you my ruling after lunch. (emphasis supplied).

After lunch, the judge did exactly that, ruling that "I have decided that I will admit [the memorandum] into evidence under 801(d)(1)(2) [sic], I believe it is." Thereafter, the prosecutor distributed the memorandum, now an exhibit in the case, to the jurors and it was taken by them into the jury room when they retired to deliberate Quinto's fate.

Quinto's principal argument on appeal is that the district court committed reversible error by admitting the IRS memorandum into evidence as a prior consistent statement under Fed. R. Evid. 801(d)(1)(B). We agree, and we hold that the memorandum should have been excluded regardless of whether it was offered for the truth of the matters asserted therein or merely for the more limited purpose of rehabilitating the in-court testimony of Agent Wallwork of the Internal Revenue Service.

For nearly 200 years last past, the courts have enforced, except in certain very limited circumstances, a general prohibition against the use of prior consistent statements. While it is true that the use of such statements to prove the truth of the matters asserted has always been clearly barred by the hearsay rule, the courts have also generally prohibited the use of such evidence even when the proponent of the prior consistent statement was simply offering it for the more limited purpose of bolstering the witness's damaged credibility. The rationale for excluding most, but not all, prior consistent statements being offered to establish the witness's credibility is one of relevancy. "The witness is not helped by [the prior consistent statement;] even if it is an improbable or untrustworthy story, it is not made more probable or more trustworthy by any number of repetitions of it." 4 Wigmore, Evidence § 1123, at 255 (Chadbourn rev. 1972). There have been situations, however, in which courts traditionally have felt that it is indeed relevant to the issue of whether the witness's in-court testimony should be believed that on prior occasions the witness has uttered statements which are consistent with his in-court testimony. "Prior consistent statements traditionally have been admissible to rebut charges of recent fabrication or improper influence or motive." Note to Rule 801, Notes of the Advisory Committee on the Proposed Rules of Evidence [hereinafter " Advisory Committee Notes"], 56 F.R.D. 183, 296 (1972). But the prior consistent statements have been so admissible only when the statements were made prior to the time the supposed motive to falsify arose. Only then was the prior consistent statement "relevant" on the issue of credibility; that is, it tended to make the trustworthiness of the witness's in-court testimony more probable, after that testimony had been assailed, inasmuch as the consistency of the prior statement with the witness's testimony at trial made it "appear that the statement in the form now uttered was independent of the [alleged] discrediting influence." 4 Wigmore, Evidence § 1128, at 268 (Chadbourn rev. 1972).

To the extent that a prior consistent statement is used for rehabilitative purposes, the Federal Rules of Evidence have apparently not altered prior law. . . . While credibility is always an issue of consequence and while "testimony which aids in the jury's determination of a [witness's] credibility and veracity [is always relevant]," it is well-recognized, as we have already explained, that only some well-defined classes of prior consistent statements can really so assist the jury. Therefore, it has been only those particular categories of prior consistent statements which have been able to withstand the objection that the prior consistent statement is irrelevant to the issue of the witness's credibility.

In one very significant respect, though, the Federal Rules of Evidence, through the adoption of Fed. R. Evid. 801(d)(1)(B), have altered the preexisting evidentiary law on the use of prior consistent statements. Fed. R. Evid. 801(d)(1)(B) provides, in pertinent part:

> (d) *Statements which are not hearsay.* A statement is not hearsay if —
>
> (1) Prior statement by witness. The declarant testifies at the trial or hearing and is subject to cross-examination concerning the statement, and the statement is . . . (B) consistent with his testimony and is offered to rebut an express or implied charge against him of recent fabrication or improper influence or motive. . . .

As can be seen, Fed. R. Evid. 801(d)(1)(B) does not, in and of itself, purport to allow the introduction of any prior consistent statements, but it does insure that any prior consistent statement which satisfies its requirements will not be regarded as "hearsay" and thus inadmissible under Fed. R. Evid. 802. In other words, prior consistent statements which satisfy the conditions set forth in Fed. R. Evid. 801(d)(1)(B) can now be used, in contrast to the restricted permissible uses under preexisting law, as "substantive evidence," Note to Rule 801, Advisory Committee Notes, *supra*, 56 F.R.D. at 296, to prove the truth of the matters asserted therein. It is of greatest importance, however, that, inasmuch as the drafters of the proposed Federal Rules of Evidence intended that prior consistent statements could be used as substantive evidence only in those "situations in which rehabilitation through consistency would formerly have been allowed," the standards for determining whether prior consistent statements can now be admitted as substantive evidence are precisely the same as the traditional standards and, as explained above, continue to be the standards used under the new rules of evidence for determining which varieties of prior consistent statements can be admitted for the more limited purpose of rehabilitation.

It is clear, therefore, that to avoid having the prior consistent statement found irrelevant under Fed. R. Evid. 402 or incapable of satisfying the requirements of Fed. R. Evid. 801(d)(1)(B), the proponent must demonstrate three things. First, he must show that the prior consistent statement is "consistent with (the witness's in-court) testimony." Fed. R. Evid. 801(d)(1)(B). Second, the party offering the prior consistent statement must establish that the statement is being "offered to rebut an express or implied charge against (the witness) of recent fabrication or improper influence or motive." *Id.* Finally, it is necessary that, as was the situation under the law of evidence prior to the adoption of the Federal Rules of Evidence, the proponent must demonstrate that the prior consistent statement was made prior to the time that the supposed motive to falsify arose.

Here, during oral argument before us, in response to pointed questioning from the bench the government has failed to satisfy this third requirement. The various improper motives[5] the defense vigorously asserted the IRS agent might have had for lying on the witness stand, motives reducible essentially to a claim that, regardless of Quinto's actual guilt or innocence, throughout the entire investigation the government agents were ruthlessly seeking a conviction, presumably to enhance their own professional advancement and aggrandizement would have been as operative at the time the IRS agents compiled the memorandum summarizing their interview with Quinto as those motives were at the time the IRS agents testified at trial. Indeed, Quinto's testimony attempted to show that the "interview" had been more in the nature of a trap and an inquisition and that, even at the time of the interview, the IRS agents and the prosecutors were, in common parlance, out "to get" him. Thus, the deeply rooted prejudice which Quinto claims was motivating the agents' actions existed both at the time the memorandum was compiled and at the time of Quinto's trial.

Moreover, while the admissibility of the memorandum was being debated at trial, at no time during his extended remarks on the subject did the prosecutor apparently point out to Judge Pratt exactly what improper motives might have existed at trial that did not also exist at the time of the compilation of the memorandum. Indeed, restricting his argument advocating the document's admission to the ground that there had been "a general attack on the agent's credibility," indeed, a "broad based attack on motive, intent, integrity of not only this agent, but the Internal Revenue Service in the preparation and prosecution of this case," the prosecutor seemingly thought the memorandum admissible regardless of the time when the alleged motive to falsify might have arisen. Judge Pratt also mistakenly assumed that, regardless of the time when any motive to falsify might have arisen, the memorandum was admissible as soon as there had been a clear "challenge to [the agent's] credibility, even [in] the form of a contradiction," or "contradictory testimony by someone else." Although the district judge refused to admit the document during the redirect examination of Agent Wallwork, he did permit it to be introduced after Wallwork's testimony had been "contradicted" by Quinto and several other witnesses. The judge's apparent reasons for allowing the document to be admitted are not, and historically have not been, a sufficient basis for admitting prior consistent statements for rehabilitative purposes. A former consistent statement helps in no respect to remove such discredit as may arise from a contradiction by other witnesses. When B is produced to swear to the contrary of what A has asserted on the stand, it cannot help us, in deciding between them, to know that A has asserted the same thing many times previously. If that were an argument, then the witness who had repeated his story to the greatest number of people would be the most credible.

We therefore conclude that the memorandum was irrelevant for the rehabilitative purpose of bolstering Agent Wallwork's challenged credibility and, to the extent that it was used or could be used as substantive evidence to prove the truth of the matters asserted in the memorandum, it did not satisfy the requirements of Fed. R. Evid. 801(d)(1)(B) and it therefore was not excluded from the definition of hearsay contained

---

[5] The prosecutor did not claim that Agent Wallwork's testimony was being attacked as a "recent fabrication," but instead claimed that the testimony was being assailed on the ground that it was based on "improper motive, bias." *Id.*

in Fed. R. Evid. 801(c). . . . We therefore hold that the district court erred in admitting the IRS memorandum against Quinto.

* * *

Judgment order reversed and case remanded for a new trial on all counts of the indictment.

The next case, *United States v. Stuart*, examines the use of prior consistent statements to rehabilitate when the impeachment was by prior inconsistent statement. The situation in *Stuart* is one that is not uncommon in criminal cases: impeachment of a government witness who was given a plea agreement in exchange for testimony against an accomplice in crime.

UNITED STATES v. STUART
718 F.2d 931 (9th Cir. 1983)

CHOY, CIRCUIT JUDGE:

A jury found Kathleen Gayle Stuart guilty of conspiring to misapply, and misapplying, funds of a savings and loan institution, and of making false entries in the records of a savings and loan association. On appeal, Stuart contends that the district court erred in . . . (3) admitting a prior consistent statement of a key government witness in the absence of a charge of recent fabrication [among other things]. [W]e affirm.

In July of 1980, Kathleen Stuart and John Van de Water discussed the possibility of illegally withdrawing funds from Gibraltar Savings and Loan Association ("Gibraltar"). Shortly thereafter, Van de Water obtained a position at Gibraltar's Laguna Hills branch, and Stuart obtained a position at Gibraltar's Santa Monica branch for the purpose of facilitating an illegal interbranch withdrawal of funds from a Gibraltar "jumbo account," an account with a balance in excess of $100,000. Van de Water used the computer terminal at the bank to locate various jumbo accounts and targeted an account located in the Laguna branch belonging to one Roper. A $40,000 withdrawal from the Roper account through the Santa Monica branch was planned. The money was to be used in the preparation of a cashier's check which, in turn, was to be used to purchase gold coins.

. . . Van de Water appeared at Gibraltar's Santa Monica branch and obtained from Stuart a $40,000 cashier's check [prepared from funds Stuart had withdrawn from Roper's account.]

On May 13, 1982, [Stuart was charged in] a three-count indictment. . . . Van de Water entered into a plea agreement with the Government by which he agreed to plead guilty to one count of aiding and abetting Stuart's misapplication [of funds] and to testify truthfully at Stuart's trial.

* * *

At trial, Stuart . . . call[ed] as a witness an FBI agent who interviewed Van de Water on the day after his arrest. The purpose of calling the agent was to impeach the testimony given by Van de Water during the Government's case in chief by introducing through the agent's testimony an alleged prior inconsistent statement made by Van de

Water during his interview. However, Stuart also requested the district court to preclude the Government from eliciting on cross-examination of the agent various prior consistent statements by Van de Water to the agent during the interview. The district court ruled that, in the event defense counsel called the agent and questioned him regarding an alleged prior inconsistent statement made to the agent by Van de Water during the interview, the Government would be permitted to question the agent regarding prior consistent statements made by Van de Water during the same interview.

On June 29, 1982, the jury returned a verdict of guilty on all three counts. Stuart was sentenced to 5 years' probation and 500 hours of community service. The sentences imposed as to all three counts were to run concurrently.

II. DISCUSSION

*   *   *

C. Introduction of Prior Consistent Statements

At the trial, Stuart elicited from an FBI agent on direct examination a prior inconsistent statement Van de Water had made to the agent. . . . The Government then elicited from the agent some prior consistent statements Van de Water had made during the same interview implicating Stuart in the crime involving Gibraltar. On appeal, Stuart contends that the introduction of prior consistent statements was improper simply because there was no charge of recent fabrication. Stuart's argument . . . is . . . unmeritorious.

Rule 801(d)(1)(B), Fed. R. Evid., permits introduction of prior consistent statements that are offered to rebut a charge of improper influence or motive, as well as of recent fabrication. The record in this case reveals that, prior to the agent's testimony, Stuart had vigorously cross-examined Van de Water regarding his plea agreement with the Government, thereby calling into question Van de Water's motive in testifying. Therefore, the introduction of prior consistent statements made prior to the plea agreement was proper. *United States v. Allen*, 579 F.2d 531, 532–33 (9th Cir. 1978) (prior consistent statements of a declarant made to an agent may be elicited from the agent under Rule 801(d)(1)(B) where defendant had sharply attacked the credibility of the declarant and implied that the declarant was testifying out of a motive to avoid criminal prosecution).

*   *   *

The judgment of the district court is Affirmed.

NOTES

1. ***Rehabilitating the Government Plea Bargain Witness.*** As the *Stuart* case indicates, sometimes a government witness cooperates with the government in return for a favor, such as a plea agreement or immunity from prosecution. If the plea agreement is raised as a credibility attack by the opponent charging recent fabrication, improper motive or undue influence it would be proper for the government to offer a prior consistent statement, *made before the government entered into the plea agreement* or grant of immunity to rehabilitate. *See United States v. Washington*, 462

F.3d 1124, 1135 (9th Cir. 2006) (court did not abuse its discretion by admitting prior consistent statements, where defense counsel alleged that a motive to lie and improper influence arose at the time that witnesses entered into plea agreements and were presented with an opportunity to collude with each other, and prior consistent statements pre-dated this alleged motive to lie and improper influence); *United States v. Stoecker*, 215 F.3d 788 (7th Cir. 2000) (district court did not abuse its discretion by admitting prior consistent statement of government witness, where during voir dire, defendant asked witness if he knew the implications of his trial testimony under the plea agreement, specifically, that any reduction of sentence was up to the government, suggesting recent fabrication, and where the statements in question were made approximately four years before the original indictment and five years before the plea agreement).

What if, however, there is no prior consistent statement to offer? In such situations, to support its witness after attack based upon undue influence or improper motive, the government often asks its plea bargain witness about the results of other cases where the witness has helped the government. The suggestion is that the government witness is supplying truthful information (and not fabricating to please the government) because the other cases resulted in guilty pleas or convictions. *United States v. Penny*, 60 F.3d 1257, 1264 (7th Cir. 1995) ("evidence of cooperation on other matters is admissible to justify a cooperation agreement *and to rebut allegations of bias*") (emphasis added). Furthermore, since the other evidence of cooperation is offered to rebut a bias attack, and not as evidence of truthful character under Fed. R. Evid. 608, extrinsic evidence is permitted. *Id.* (government permitted to call case agent to testify about other cases the government's witness had worked on to rebut allegations of bias against the government's main witness).

2. *Claims of Failed or Faulty Memory.* If a prior inconsistent statement is used to impeach and the thrust of the attack is that the witness has a faulty memory, courts usually allow rehabilitation by a prior consistent statement if the consistent statement was made when the event testified about was fresh in the memory of the witness. *See United States v. Coleman*, 631 F.2d 908, 913–14 (D.C. Cir. 1980) (charge was one of fabrication; court notes, however, that claim of inaccurate memory could justify admission of prior consistent statement); 1 COURTROOM CRIMINAL EVIDENCE § 720, at 328–29 (4th ed. 2005).

Federal Rule of Evidence 801(d)(1)(B) does not list a charge of faulty memory as a charge that can be rebutted by offering prior consistent statements. The Rule does, of course, list a charge of "recent fabrication" as a charge that would permit the use of a prior consistent statement in rebuttal. It is arguable that a charge of faulty memory is, by implication, a charge of recent fabrication.

3. *Trial Court Discretion.* It is the trial court that determines if the attacking party's impeachment has raised a charge of recent fabrication or improper influence or motive, and whether the prior statement was made before the fabrication, influence or motive arose. *See United States v. Dennis*, 625 F.2d 782, 797–98 (8th Cir. 1980).

PROBLEMS

Problem 10-15. Police Officer Bill Walton is charged with criminal assault for beating a man in the course of making an arrest.

Walton claims that the victim, Larry Ganes, approached him as he was making an arrest (of a different person) on a city street and refused to move on. When informed that if he did not move away he would be arrested, Ganes pulled a knife from his belt and lunged at Walton. Walton struck Ganes, took the knife from him and arrested him.

Ganes' story is different. Ganes claims that Officer Walton told him to move on and Ganes replied, "I'm on a public street I don't have to." At that point without warning, according to Ganes, Walton attacked him and took a work knife he was carrying in a holster from him.

At trial the defendant, Officer Walton, testifies. After his testimony he is cross-examined by the prosecution attorney. The prosecutor first asks Walton the difference between the crimes of "carrying a deadly weapon" and "possession of a prohibited weapon." Walton replies (correctly) that "possession" implies an intent to use, and "carrying" does not. The prosecutor then asks what crime, if any, Ganes was charged with. Walton replies (again correctly), "carrying a deadly weapon." The prosecutor then asks how the decision to charge Ganes with "carrying a deadly weapon" was made. Officer Walton replied, "the district attorney made the decision based upon his interview with me the next day." The prosecutor then asks, "isn't it true that at no point did Mr. Ganes ever seek to use his knife against you"? Officer Walton replies, "no, that is not true."

After these questions, Officer Walton's attorney offers into evidence the police report filed by Officer Walton that night, before he (Officer Walton) was charged with assaulting Larry Ganes, and before he (Officer Walton)spoke with the district attorney the next day. The police report clearly states that Ganes made an assault on Officer Walton, and is offered as a prior consistent statement. The trial court refuses to admit the report, stating,

> the prosecutor merely attempted to show an inconsistency in Walton's testi-
> mony; that he did not say the same thing the day after the incident that he did
> at trial. That is not charging Officer Walton with making a fabrication.

Officer Walton is convicted and appeals, claiming that it was error not to allow him to offer his police report as a prior consistent statement for rehabilitation. What result? *See Gaines v. Walker*, 986 F.2d 1438, 1444–45 (D.C. Cir. 1993).

Problem 10-16. Defendant is on trial for importing large quantities of marijuana. One of his largest customers was Faber. Faber would buy several thousand pounds of marijuana at a time from defendant and sell it on the street. Faber has been arrested and has agreed to testify against defendant and several other marijuana dealers in return for immunity.

At trial Faber testifies on direct that he bought several thousand pounds of marijuana from defendant and has observed defendant make deals to purchase marijuana. On cross-examination Faber is questioned about his grant of immunity from the government that shielded him from prosecution for various drug offenses. The government, on re-direct, then asks Faber if he had cooperated with the government on *other* major drug investigations not involving the defendant, and if his cooperation had led to convictions. Over defendant's objection (which was overruled), Faber answers "yes" to both questions.

In closing argument defendant's counsel told the jury that Faber's grant of immunity gave him a "powerful reason to lie." Defense counsel continued and accused Faber of lying and manufacturing evidence. He concluded his closing argument by saying that

Faber, for the grant of immunity, "would do anything the government asked." Defendant was convicted.

On appeal defendant argues that evidence of cooperation and the resultant convictions procured by Faber *on other cases* was improper rehabilitation. What result? *See United States v. Lochmondy*, 890 F.2d 817, 821–22 (6th Cir. 1989).

Chapter 11

PHOTOGRAPHS, VIDEOTAPES, AUDIO RECORDINGS AND DEMONSTRATIONS

A. INTRODUCTION

The use of photographs, videotapes, and audio recordings is commonplace in criminal trials. For example, in virtually every homicide prosecution the government introduces into evidence autopsy photographs of the victim, as well as photographs depicting the crime scene. The photographs are offered to prove the identity of the victim, the manner of death, or an element of the crime, or to demonstrate the type of murder weapon utilized in committing the homicide.

Video recordings also play a prominent role in criminal cases. In some areas, police routinely videotape lineups to show that the procedures employed were not unduly suggestive. Police officers also videotape confessions to demonstrate that the defendant's statements were voluntarily given. Additionally, law enforcement officers frequently videotape undercover sting operations. At the same time, video cameras are often installed by commercial businesses as a security measure. For example, bank security officers install surveillance cameras at ATM machines in order to detect fraudulent or unauthorized cash transactions. Video cameras are also frequently installed at convenience stores that have become a favorite target of armed robbers. A video recording depicting the defendant engaged in criminal activity is powerfully incriminating evidence.

In narcotics trafficking investigations, law enforcement officers frequently tape record conversations of undercover meetings. In many cases, undercover officers involved in controlled drug purchases are equipped with a so-called "wire," or electronic monitoring device. In other cases, telephone conversations discussing drug transactions are surreptitiously recorded pursuant to a court-ordered wiretap or by consent of one of the parties to the conversation. The defendant's incriminating statements captured on audiotape can likewise provide compelling evidence of guilt.

The admission of video and audio recordings, as well as still photographs, poses unique evidentiary problems. For example, autopsy photographs can be extremely prejudicial to the defendant. Often depicting gruesome injuries and bloody crime scenes, the admission of such evidence may unfairly prejudice the defendant by inflaming the passions of the jury. At the same time, when video and audio recordings are introduced into evidence, issues of authentication rather than unfair prejudice often determine admissibility. For example, if electronic equipment is used to record criminal activity, the authenticity of the proffered evidence may turn on whether the equipment was capable of accurately taping the conversation or meeting, and whether the operator was competent to operate the device. Furthermore, when portions of such recordings are inaudible or unintelligible this may implicate concerns about the evidence's trustworthiness and reliability.

At trial, the tape recordings as well as written transcripts of the recorded conversations are presented to the jury. As a general rule, the tapes themselves are the primary evidence and the transcripts are only admitted as an aid to the jury. However, when faced with a taped conversation in a foreign language, this rule makes little sense and the English translation should be accorded greater evidentiary weight.

Federal Rule of Evidence 901(a) requires authentication as a precondition to the admissibility of evidence. Under this rule, authentication is satisfied by evidence sufficient to support a finding that "the matter is what its proponent claims."[1] Rule 901(b) sets forth by way of illustration a non-exhaustive list of methods by which evidence may be authenticated. Several of those methods are particularly relevant to establishing the authenticity of photographs, video and audio recordings.[2]

Finally, courtroom demonstrations, which purport to show the jury what presumably occurred at the scene of the crime, can be highly persuasive evidence and leave a particularly potent image in the minds of the jurors. Thus, the court must take special care to ensure that conditions of the courtroom demonstration fairly depict the events at issue. The party introducing the demonstrative evidence must demonstrate a substantial similarity of conditions. The critical issue here is whether strict adherence to this standard should be required in a criminal prosecution.

This chapter examines issues of unfair prejudice and authentication as they relate to the admissibility of photographs, video and audio recordings within the context of a criminal prosecution. Additionally, the threshold requirements for the admission of demonstrative evidence — in particular courtroom reenactments of the crime — are considered.

---

[1] Rule 901(a) provides in relevant part:

> The requirement of authentication or identification as a condition precedent to admissibility is satisfied by evidence sufficient to support a finding that the matter in question is what its proponent claims.

[2] Rule 901(b) provides in relevant part:

> By way of illustration only, and not by way of limitation, the following are examples of authentication or identification conforming with the requirements of this rule:
>
> (1) *Testimony of witness with knowledge.* Testimony that a matter is what it is claimed to be.
>
> *   *   *
>
> (3) *Comparison by trier or expert witness.* Comparison by the trier of fact or by expert witnesses with specimens which have been authenticated.
>
> (4) *Distinctive characteristics and the like.* Appearance, contents, substance, internal patterns, or other distinctive characteristics, taken in conjunction with circumstances.
>
> (5) *Voice identification.* Identification of a voice, whether heard firsthand or through mechanical or electronic transmission or recording, by opinion based upon hearing the voice at any time under circumstances connecting it with the alleged speaker.
>
> (6) *Telephone conversations.* Telephone conversations, by evidence that a call was made to the number assigned at the time by the telephone company to a particular person or business, if (A) in the case of a person, circumstances, including self-identification, show the person answering to be the one called. . . .
>
> *   *   *
>
> (9) *Process or system.* Evidence describing a process or system used to produce a result and showing that the process or system produces an accurate result.

B. PHOTOGRAPHS AND VIDEOTAPES

[1]   Photographs of Homicide Victims

UNITED STATES v. YAHWEH
792 F. Supp. 104 (S.D. Fla. 1992)

ROETTGER, CHIEF JUDGE.

Violent crime cases are the exception in federal courts. The instant case is arguably the most violent case ever tried in a federal court: the indictment charges the sixteen defendants on trial with 14 murders by means such as beheading, stabbing, occasionally by pistol shots, plus severing of body parts such as ears to prove the worthiness of the killer. Plus, they are charged with arson of a slumbering neighborhood by molotov cocktails with the perpetrators under orders to wait outside the innocent victims' homes wearing ski masks and brandishing machetes to deter the victims from fleeing the flames.

In the course of the trial, the Government sought to introduce into evidence medical examiners' photographs of the victims. Defendants objected to the admission of these photographs into evidence on the grounds that the photographs were not relevant pursuant to Fed. R. Evid. 401 and prejudicial in effect pursuant to Fed. R. Evid. 403. Specifically, the Defendants contend that the size of the photographs, which are roughly 30 × 40 inches, were designed to inflame the passions of the jury.

The relevance of these photographs is without question. Photographs of homicide victims are relevant in showing the identity of the victim, the manner of death, the murder weapon, or any other element of the crime. In addition to identifying the victims and the means of death, the photographs in this case corroborate the testimony of witnesses, Lloyd Clark, Ricardo Woodside and Robert Rozier, whose credibility is central to the government's case.

With reference to the beating of Aston Green, Lloyd Clark testified that he "saw somebody jump on his [Aston Green's] chest." (transcript II. 385). Further, Ricardo Woodside testified that there were "people jumping up and down on his chest. . . ." (transcript II. 1633). Government Exhibit 7 shows the outline of a footprint on the chest of Aston Green. Dr. Charles Wetli, the medical examiner who performed the autopsy on Aston Green, stated that this injury was consistent with someone jumping on the deceased's chest.

Ricardo Woodside testified concerning the decapitation of Aston Green. He estimated that he heard approximately fifteen to thirty "chops" as if a knife was coming down on flesh. He also heard the attention-riveting statement: "Damn. This blade is dull." (transcript II. 1642). This testimony at first seemed incredible. However, it was corroborated by Government Exhibit 9. This exhibit clearly shows that a number of "chops" were necessary for the decapitation.

Prior to the admission of exhibits 7 & 9 in the enlarged size, this court reviewed the same photographs in the 8" × 10" size. The latter did not show the detail necessary to corroborate the witnesses' testimony. The footprint could not be seen clearly on the 8" × 10" of Exhibit 7 and the number of lacerations on the top of Aston Green's torso were not clearly visible on the 8" × 10" of Exhibit 9. Discussing the enlargements of Aston Green, Dr. Wetli testified, and the court concurs, that 8" × 10" photographs did not reveal the contusions on the deceased's face, the machete marks on the neck or the footprint on the chest. The enlarged photographs clearly show the footprint and that numerous "chops" were necessary for the decapitation.

Relevant evidence can be excluded pursuant to Fed. R. Evid. 403 if "its probative value is substantially outweighed by the danger of unfair prejudice. . . ." The subject matter of the photographs in question — decapitation, slit throat, removed ears, repeated stabbing, and gun shot wounds — is both difficult to view as well as disturbing and distasteful. However, so were the crimes alleged. Murder, particularly "murder most foul" by methods such as decapitation or stabbing and the removal of body parts, is inherently offensive. However, these exhibits are not flagrantly or deliberately gruesome depictions of the crimes.

After careful review of the exhibits and the medical examiners' testimony and objections, the court found no distortion, exercised its discretion and overruled the objections.

In *United States v. McRae*, 593 F.2d 700 (5th Cir. 1979), the Fifth Circuit held that:

> Relevant evidence is inherently prejudicial; but it is only unfair prejudice, substantially outweighing probative value, which permits exclusion of relevant matter under Rule 403. Unless trials are to be conducted on scenarios, on unreal facts tailored and sanitized for the occasion, the application of Rule 403 must be cautious and sparing. . . . It is not designed to permit the court to "even out" the weight of evidence, to mitigate a crime. . . . *id.* at 707.

Defendants argue that the gruesome or prejudicial effect of the photographs [is] heightened by the size of the photographs. The Eleventh Circuit cases dealing with photographs make no mention as to any value or prejudicial effect produced by the size of the photograph. In *United States v. Thompson*, 744 F.2d 1065 (4th Cir. 1984), a blown up black and white autopsy photograph of a four month old boy who died of meningitis complicated by malnutrition and starvation was admitted into evidence to illustrate the testimony of the medical examiner.

As the offense of murder is usually the domain of state court,[3] the issue of admission into evidence of enlarged photographs of murder victims has been addressed at greater length in state courts. Courts in Alabama, Florida, and Georgia have permitted admission of blown up color photographs into evidence.

In *Bankhead v. State*, 585 So. 2d 112 (Ala. 1991), the Supreme Court of Alabama held that projection of color photographic slides on a large screen in front of the jury was permissible as this procedure did not distort the victim's wounds or mislead the jury. In *Bombailey v. State*, 580 So. 2d 41 (Ala. Crim. App. 1990), the Court of Criminal Appeals of Alabama held that the fact that the photographs of a child abuse victim were in color and were enlarged is of no particular significance as long as there was no distortion of the depiction of the injuries.

In *Jones v. State*, 293 S.E.2d 708 (Ga. 1982), the Supreme Court of Georgia held that enlarged photographs are admissible in evidence provided there is no distortion or enlargement of the objects in the pictures. In *Wilson v. State*, 262 S.E.2d 810 (Ga. 1980), the Supreme Court of Georgia held that enlarged color photographs were admissible despite contentions that there was no issue as to how the person died or which wounds could have caused death.

---

[3] Murder becomes a part of this cause as a racketeering act defined by 18 U.S.C. § 1961(1).

In *Gopaul v. State*, 536 So. 2d 296 (Fla. App., 3d Dist. 1988), the Court of Appeals held that enlarged colored photographs of an infant's pelvic area were relevant to the jury's understanding of the expert testimony concerning the victim's injury. In *Brown v. State*, 532 So. 2d 1326 (Fla. App., 3d Dist. 1988), the Court of Appeals held that a color photograph of the crime scene, 2 feet by 3 feet in size, of the deceased lying on the bed where she was shot with large amounts of blood on the body, bed and floor was admissible despite the admission of the crime scene sketch.

This court adopted the procedure of examining each photograph by having the medical examiners explain the need for a photograph on the basis of contents and size. The photographs at issue here are not as gruesome as the crime scene photograph discussed in *Brown*. All the photographs in this case which were introduced by the government at the 30" × 40" size were autopsy photographs. Photographs of the victims at the scene of the crime were all in the 8" × 10" size. The photographs were very clinical in nature establishing the location and nature of the wounds. There was very little blood. Those which might be considered more offensive[5] were used by the medical examiner's pathologists for illustration of their testimony, but the court required the government to reduce those exhibits to 16" × 20" size which, after examination by the court, were admitted into evidence and will be the ones, with the other 300 plus exhibits, provided the jury for their deliberations. Dr. Wetli, who has testified in 250 murder cases at the state level and has seen and used blow ups of this size in state court, characterized their use as occasional but not rare.

Each medical examiner selected the photographs necessary to illustrate his or her testimony to the jury. Dr. Barnhart stated "[t]hey were ones which I think could be looked at by a lay person and one could understand location and nature of the wounds from the photographs." (transcript II. 4686). Defense counsel argued that an analytical chart could show specifically where injuries occurred and the extent of the injuries. In comparing the utility of an enlarged photograph as opposed to a chart, Dr. Wetli responded "[b]ecause the picture is much better than a diagram and my words. . . . [It] just depicts exactly what it is, what is there. . . . If you want a jury to have a tr ue understanding of what I saw and how it matches up, not just with those marks but other photographs as well as what I presume will be other evidence entered, therefore the complete picture that is going to be given, then the pictures are extremely helpful." (transcript II. 2220–2221). Further, he stated "diagrams will misstate the issue in that there is no blood and instruments and so forth; but the truth is the truth and the injuries are there." (transcript II. 2255). *Brown v. State, supra*, also rejects defendants' contentions about preemptive use of the charts only.

Dr. Rao also selected the photographs to illustrate her testimony. When questioned about the necessity of enlarged photographs and whether the same thing could be shown by an 8" × 10", Dr. Rao replied that a projector would be necessary. All the medical examiners' pictures were slides made into photographic exhibits. The court can take judicial notice that at a usual distance the image of slides (transparencies) projected onto a screen would be larger than the size of the 30" × 40" pictures used as an aid to the medical examiner's testimony.

---

[5] These were Government Exhibit 6 (the decapitated head of Aston Green placed above the body — which, in this court's opinion, is fairly benign considering the decapitation and far more benign than a front picture of the headless torso would be), Government Exhibit 9 (back view of the headless torso of Aston Green), Government Exhibit 195 (severed throat of Clair Walters), and Government Exhibit 197 (side view of Clair Walters' head from which ear had been removed).

The court specifically instructed the jury that no weight should be given to the differing sizes of the photographs and cautioned the jury that some of the photographs might be disturbing. However, unlike the *Thompson* case where a juror informed the court that he could not be objective after viewing the enlarged autopsy photograph of the abused child, the jurors in this case have not expressed any such views. The court carefully observed the jurors and their reactions to the photographs. After the brief initial reaction to seeing the first autopsy photograph — not intense, but apparently from recognition they would see photos of homicide victims — the jurors showed no signs of being disturbed by the exhibits.

Displaying an enlarged photograph while the medical examiner testified to facts illustrated in the photograph enabled all members of the jury simultaneously to follow the witness' testimony. Having seen many juries in trials struggle with a witness' presentation when 8" × 10" photographs are used, it is clearly easier for the jury to capture the substance of the testimony without straining to view the photograph. For twenty years, this court has stood by the jury box to observe as witnesses testified in front of the jury box concerning exhibits being published to the jury there. In this court's view the larger 30" × 40" pictures were the right size to illustrate and clarify the witness' testimony; in fact, even the 16" × 20" size was inadequately small by comparison.

The probative value of the enlarged autopsy photographs substantially outweighs the danger of unfair prejudice and therefore the objections to the photographs are overruled. Although enlargements may magnify certain wounds, they have by no means distorted the nature of the wounds in this case. This court has attempted to keep the photographs to about life-size. However, in certain instances larger blow ups have been permitted as necessary to illustrate the medical examiner's testimony, such as with reference to severed ears and a severed trachea and carotid artery. Even with an enlargement larger than life size, the court found the enlargement did not distort the subject. Additionally, arguments as to size cut both ways. Photographs many times smaller than life size do minimize the wounds inflicted, but, as was the case with the footprint in Exhibit 7, may not accurately reflect injuries which were present.

NOTES AND QUESTIONS

1. *Relevance.* In *Yahweh*, the court overruled defendants' objections to the admission of enlarged autopsy photographs depicting murders by decapitation, stabbing and severing of body parts. The court found admissible Government Exhibit 6 (the decapitated head of one of the murder victims placed above the body), Government Exhibit 9 (the back view of the headless torso of the murder victim), and Government Exhibit 195 (the severed throat of a second murder victim). The court held that these particularly gruesome photographs were relevant under Fed. R. Evid. 401. Were the autopsy photographs necessary to establish the identity of the victims? Were the photographs offered to prove an element of the crime? What was the stated relevance of these autopsy photographs? How would you characterize their probative value — highly, moderately or minimally probative? Do you agree with the court's ruling on admissibility? For cases upholding the admission of crime scene and autopsy photographs *see United States v. Fields*, 483 F.3d 313, 355 (5th Cir. 2007) (photos showing victim's body decomposing were highly probative); *United States v. Brown*, 441 F.3d 1330, 1361–63 (11th Cir. 2006) (district court did not abuse its discretion by admitting color photographs of victim's body, which had been stabbed multiple times; photos were probative on the number and nature of stab wounds, and presence of aggravating factor of heinous and cruel manner of offense, and were not cumulative);

United States v. Sarracino, 340 F.3d 1148 (10th Cir. 2003) (autopsy photos admissible to assist medical expert in describing murder victim's injuries, despite defendant's claim that towel around victim's head made it look as if victim had been decapitated); United *States v. Ortiz*, 315 F.3d 873, 897 (8th Cir. 2002) (photographs of murder victim were relevant to corroborate testimony of government's key witness, establishing that victim had been bound with duct tape and beaten before his murder); *United States v. Velasquez*, 246 F.3d 204 (2d Cir. 2001) (autopsy photos relevant to showing the extent of inmate's injuries, establishing that cruel and unusual punishment had occurred); *United States v. Ingle*, 157 F.3d 1147 (8th Cir. 1998) (photos taken at crime scene and during the autopsy corroborated the testimony of government witnesses and assisted the jury in understanding the medical examiner's testimony).

2. *Rule 403 Balancing.* The court in *Yahweh* reaffirmed the fundamental principle of evidence codified in Fed. R. Evid. 403 that relevant evidence can be excluded if "its probative value is substantially outweighed by the danger of unfair prejudice. . . ." However, the court held that the exhibits were not "flagrantly or deliberately gruesome depictions of the crimes," and therefore not unfairly prejudicial. The court appeared to minimize the prejudicial effect of the autopsy photographs on the jury. The court characterized the subject matter of the photographs in question — decapitation, slit throat, removed ears, repeated stabbing, and gun shot wounds — as merely "disturbing and distasteful." *Yahweh*, 792 F. Supp. at 106. Is this a fair characterization of the evidence? Several of the photographs were enlarged to roughly 30 × 40 inches. Are these photographs likely to arouse the passions of the jury?

3. *Standard of Review.* The admission of photographs of homicide victims is reviewed on appeal only for an abuse of discretion. " 'The trial judge's exercise of discretion in balancing the prejudicial effect and probative value of photographic evidence . . . is rarely disturbed.' " *United States v. Sides*, 944 F.2d 1554, 1562 (10th Cir. 1991) (citations omitted). *See, e.g., United States v. Moore*, 38 F.3d 977, 981 (8th Cir. 1994) (autopsy photographs which admittedly "added little, if anything, to the government's case" were nonetheless admitted to show the trajectory of the bullet); *United States v. Treas-Wilson*, 3 F.3d 1406, 1410 (10th Cir. 1993) ("gruesomeness alone does not make photographs inadmissible"; photographs graphically depicted the nature of the fatal wound and were probative of defendant's state of mind); *United States v. De Parias*, 805 F.2d 1447, 1454 (11th Cir. 1986) (photographs of homicide victims were admissible to identify the victim as well as the means of death; Rule 403 is to be sparingly used). Did the district court abuse its discretion in admitting the autopsy photographs?

4. Defense counsel argued that an analytical chart should be admitted in evidence in place of the autopsy photographs. *Yahweh*, 792 F. Supp. at 107–08. Counsel maintained that an analytical chart could be used to demonstrate the location and extent of the injuries without inflaming the jury. *Id.* The court, however, rejected defendant's proposal. Why isn't a diagram depicting the murder victim sufficient to aid the medical examiner in explaining his testimony? What if defendants stipulated to the manner of death? Must the prosecutor accept the stipulation? Does this fact minimize the probative value of the autopsy photographs? In other words, if the defendants are willing to stipulate that the victims were killed in the manner represented by the Government, what then is the justification for admitting the photographs? In this case, would the probative value be substantially outweighed by the risk of unfair prejudice?

5. *Authentication.* Even though a photograph is relevant under Rule 401, and not unfairly prejudicial pursuant to Rule 403, the photograph's authenticity must still be established. Federal Rule of Evidence 901 governs this requirement:

> The requirement of authentication or identification as a condition precedent to admissibility is satisfied by evidence sufficient to support a finding that the matter in question is what its proponent claims.

In the case of autopsy or crime scene photographs, authentication is shown by the testimony of a witness with knowledge. The proponent of the exhibits simply calls to the witness stand the person who took the photograph or some other person with personal knowledge who can testify "that a matter is what it is claimed to be." FED. R. EVID. 901(b)(1). *See United States v. Salcido*, 506 F.3d 729, 732–33 (9th Cir. 2007) (government properly authenticated child pornography videos and images under Rule 901 by presenting detailed evidence as to the chain of custody and how the images were retrieved from the defendant's computer); *United States v. Goldin*, 311 F.3d 191, 197 (3d Cir. 2002) ("Because the tape was authenticated at trial by a person with knowledge — the camera operator-the trial court did not abuse its discretion when it admitted the tape."). Authenticity may also be established by circumstantial evidence. *See United States v. Englebrecht*, 917 F.2d 376, 378 (8th Cir. 1990) (authenticity of photograph found during search of defendant's residence showing him standing in front of a marijuana crop established by circumstantial evidence).

[2] Video Recordings — The "Silent Witness" Theory

UNITED STATES v. REMBERT
863 F.2d 1023 (D.C. Cir. 1988)

SENTELLE, CIRCUIT JUDGE.

Reginald T. Rembert ("Rembert" or "appellant") appeals from his conviction under all counts of a six-count indictment, charging two counts each of kidnapping, 18 U.S.C. § 1201(a)(1) (1982); interstate transportation of a stolen vehicle, 18 U.S.C. §§ 2312 & 2 (1982); and armed robbery, D.C. Code §§ 22-2901, -3202 (1981). His sole assignment of error relates to the admission into evidence of photographs taken by a bank surveillance camera. Rembert contends that there was not a sufficient evidentiary foundation for the admission of the photos. We disagree and affirm.

Rembert's convictions arise from crime sprees occurring on July 7 and 26, 1987. On July 7, according to the testimony of victim witness Mary Simon, she drove to a Signet Bank in Falls Church, Virginia, at approximately 10:30 p.m. As she attempted to use her bank card in the automatic teller machine ("ATM"), a man armed with a knife reached into the open window of her car, grabbed her by the neck, and threatened to kill her if she did not give him her ATM code number. At trial she positively identified appellant as being this man. A second man, referred to in the record as "Washington," joined them at her car. She gave the two men her ATM number. They used the number and her bank card to extract $150 from her account. The two men forced Simon to accompany them in her car, driven by appellant, to a park in Washington, D.C. They made multiple stops and robbed Simon of her jewelry before leaving her in her vehicle, still in Washington.

A second victim witness, Andrea McGee, testified that on Sunday, July 26, 1987, in the midafternoon, she drove her automobile to an ATM machine in Washington, D.C. After she discovered the machine was out of order, she accidentally drove her car into the wall of the bank, where it became stuck. Two men, one of whom she later identified at a line-up and in court as appellant, and a third man not further involved in the incident, assisted in freeing her vehicle. The men identified as appellant and his companion then told her that they had missed their bus while helping her, and asked her to drive them to a bus stop. However, once in the car and under way, one of them threatened her with a butcher's knife and told her to drive to Virginia. The other man, identified as appellant, rifled through her purse. Once in Virginia, the assailants ordered her to stop at a bank, where appellant's companion took her bank card and demanded her code number in order to obtain money. With some difficulty, he extracted $10 from the machine. Appellant's companion then took over the driving, and the two forced her to accompany them to another bank. At that bank they spotted a male customer, later identified as John Lynn, attempting to use the ATM machine. Appellant jumped from the car with the knife and began stabbing Lynn. Appellant's companion demanded and obtained Lynn's wallet, keys, and card code. After unsuccessfully attempting to steal Lynn's car, the assailants fled the scene in McGee's car, appellant driving, and forced her to accompany them to a Seat Pleasant, Maryland, branch of Sovran Bank, where they unsuccessfully attempted to use Lynn's ATM card. After taking her purse, they finally returned McGee to Washington, D.C., where they abandoned her and her vehicle near the point of her abduction.

In addition to positive eyewitness identifications of Rembert by the two women victims and Lynn, the prosecution offered at trial evidence that each had identified Rembert in line-ups and that Simon had identified appellant in a series of photographs taken by a closed-circuit surveillance video camera at the Seat Pleasant bank where the two assailants took McGee. These photographs were received into evidence.

*   *   *

II. ANALYSIS

As noted above, appellant's sole assignment of error concerns the admission of the photographic evidence from the video recorder at the Sovran Bank in Seat Pleasant, Maryland. The sole authenticating witness for the photos was Katie Wohlfarth, a supervisor in the loss control division of the bank, who testified that she was in charge of investigating questioned activities through the ATM machines. She testified that the machine-maintained records at the Seat Pleasant branch showed an unusual pattern of use associated with John Lynn's ATM card on July 26, 1987, at approximately 8:00 p.m. The machine's records indicated that the card had been entered ten times on that occasion and was retained by the machine on the tenth attempt. She further testified that video cameras are maintained at each of the three ATM machines at the Seat Pleasant location. A video recorder taped the view from each camera in sequence, rotating to the next camera, taking a photograph every three seconds. This videotaping process imprints the date and time at which the pictures were made on the resultant photographs. She then identified a strip of pictures which was admitted into evidence over Rembert's objection. She further testified that she had viewed the original videotape and the resultant photographs and that the photographs were fair and accurate depictions of what was on the videotape. The imprinted date and times on the photographs ranged from 8:04:22 p.m. until 8:13:30 p.m. on July 26, 1987. On cross examination, she testified that she had no personal knowledge of the events that transpired at the Seat Pleasant location on that date, and could not say from her own knowledge whether the photographs fairly and accurately depicted the scene and events at that time and place or not.

Appellant argues that photographs are admitted under two theories of authentication, and that the foundation offered by the prosecution in the present case meets neither theory. He first presents the classic model of illustrative or "pictorial testimony" use of photographs as evidence. Under this theory, a sponsoring witness (whether or not he is the photographer) who has personal knowledge of the scene depicted testifies that the photograph fairly and accurately portrays that scene. . . . Obviously this model was not followed in Rembert's trial.

Appellant next argues that the only other basis for the introduction of photographic evidence is the "silent witness" model, under which the admissibility of a photograph is based on the reliability of the process by which it is made. This model is most often associated with the introduction of x-rays, where obviously no witness has viewed the scene portrayed. Appellant persuasively contends that the foundational evidence of the witness Wohlfarth does not meet that description. Her testimony did not really speak to the reliability of the process. She testified rather as a custodian of the records without supplying evidence as to the type of camera used, its general reliability, the quality of its product, the purpose of its employment, the process by which it is focused, or the general reliability of the entire system.

Appellant is undoubtedly correct that the evidence in this case does not meet either of those two models. He is further correct that those models are adopted in the Federal Rules of Evidence under the Authentication and Identification heading of Rule 901. Fed. R. Evid. 901(b)(1) (testimony that a matter is what it is claimed to be); 901(b)(9) (evidence describing a process or system used to produce a result and showing that the process or system produces an accurate result). But this does not close our inquiry. Rule 901 expressly prefaces the two subsections set forth above by the language that they function "[b]y way of illustration only, and not by way of limitation," thereby leaving room for the general application of Rule 901(a). That general provision states that "[t]he requirement of authentication or identification as a condition precedent to admissibility is satisfied by evidence sufficient to support a finding that the matter in question is what its proponent claims."

As we have already held in a case also dealing with photographic evidence, "[a]uthentication and identification are specialized aspects of relevancy that are necessary conditions precedent to admissibility." *United States v. Blackwell*, 694 F.2d 1325, 1330 (D.C. Cir. 1982) (citations omitted). The *Blackwell* case involved a prosecution for unlawful possession of firearms. The photographs in question depicted the defendant holding a firearm, apparently the same as one of the guns seized at the time of his arrest. The prosecution had obtained the photographs as the result of a search of the same room in which the firearms were found. No witness could testify as to when the photographs were made, where they were made, by what process, or whether they fairly and accurately depicted any particular scene on any particular date. The detective who conducted the search did testify that the details of the pictured weapon and the background interior were similar to the details of the weapon and room in question. We applied the same authentication and identification analysis as we would have with reference to the contents of any documentary evidence. That is, we required only that "the proponent of documentary evidence make a showing sufficient to permit a reasonable juror to find that the evidence is what its proponent claims." 694 F.2d at 1330 (citation omitted). We further held that under Rule 901, "[t]he sufficiency of a showing of a document's authenticity rests within the sound discretion of the trial judge," and that "[t]he trial court's determination regarding admissibility will not be overturned absent a clear abuse of discretion."

These same principles apply to the photographic evidence in the instant case. Appellant correctly states the two traditional bases for the admission of the photographic evidence, but the uses of photography have not stood still and neither should the law. Nor has the law on the use of photographic evidence remained unaffected by the changes in society. For example, in *United States v. Stearns*, 550 F.2d 1167 (9th Cir. 1977), Judge (now Justice) Kennedy wrote for the Ninth Circuit in a case in which the trial court had admitted certain photographs of a boat taken on the open seas. The defendants in that case were charged with stealing a boat named the Sea Wind. As part of a factually involved trial, the defendants contended that they had taken Sea Wind only to protect the vessel and at a time when their own vessel, the Iola, was disabled. Details within the photograph showed the rigging of the Sea Wind in the foreground (as if the photograph were taken from that vessel) and the Iola under full sail in the background. Other details in companion photographs provided circumstantial evidence of the date of the taking of the photographs as being after the time of the alleged disability of the Iola. In upholding the trial court's admission of the evidence, Judge Kennedy wrote: "Even if direct testimony as to foundation matters is absent . . . the contents of a photograph itself, together with such other circumstantial or indirect evidence as bears upon the issue, may serve to explain and authenticate a photograph sufficiently to justify its admission into evidence." *Id.* at 1171.

Other courts, both federal and state, have likewise modernized their standards for admissibility of photographic evidence. In *United States v. Taylor*, 530 F.2d 639 (5th Cir. 1976), for example, the trial court had admitted into evidence in a bank robbery trial contact prints made from a film taken by the bank camera after the victim bank employees had been locked in a vault. The bank camera was in the business area of the bank so that none of the witnesses could testify as to the accuracy of the scene depicted at the time of the taking of the prints. The only foundational evidence was introduced by government witnesses not present at the time of the robbery, who testified as to the manner in which the film was installed in the camera, how the camera was activated, the removal of the film immediately after the robbery, the chain of possession, and the method of development. The Fifth Circuit held that admission of that evidence on that foundation was within the discretion of the district court and that the district court did not abuse its discretion. *Id.* at 641–42. . . .

Consistent with our decision in *Blackwell* and the teachings of our sister circuits and the courts of the several states, we conclude that the contents of photographic evidence to be admitted into evidence need not be merely illustrative, but can be admitted as evidence independent of the testimony of any witness as to the events depicted, upon a foundation sufficient to meet the requirements of Federal Rule of Evidence 901(a). In this case the circumstantial evidence provided by the victim witnesses as to the occurrences at the ATM machines, together with the testimony of Wohlfarth as to the loading of the cameras and the security of the film, coupled with the internal indicia of date, place, and event depicted in the evidence itself provide ample support for the District Court's exercise of its discretion. Just as the Ninth Circuit held that the contents alone provided sufficient circumstantial evidence for the authentication of the photographs in *Stearns*, so do the contents of the photos in the instant case supply any further need for authentication that the contact prints from the ATM machine may require on the present record.

*   *   *

III. CONCLUSION

. . . [T]he role of photography in technology and society at large is a changing one, and the courts must change with it. For the reasons set forth above, we conclude that our precedent in *Blackwell* and the reasoning of the other authorities collected above persuasively show that the evidence herein was properly admitted. The judgment of the District Court is without error and is therefore

Affirmed.

NOTES AND QUESTIONS

1. The court in *Rembert* relaxed the requirements for authenticating videotape evidence. The court held that " 'the contents of a photograph itself, together with such other circumstantial or indirect evidence as bears upon the issue, may serve to explain and authenticate a photograph sufficiently to justify its admission into evidence.' " *Rembert, supra*, 863 F.2d at 1027 (quoting *United States v. Stearns*, 550 F.2d 1167, 1171 (9th Cir. 1977)). This view stands in contrast to the position adopted in *United States v. McMillan*, 508 F.2d 101, 104 (8th Cir. 1974), where the court recited seven foundational guidelines for admission of electronic tape recordings: (1) the recording device was capable of recording the events offered in evidence; (2) the operator was competent to operate the device; (3) the recording is authentic and correct; (4) changes, additions or deletions have not been made in the recording; (5) the recording has been preserved in a manner that is shown to the court; (6) the speakers on the tape are identified; and (7) the conversation elicited was made voluntarily and in good faith, without any kind of inducement. *See also United States v. Biggins*, 551 F.2d 64, 66 (5th Cir. 1977) (requiring the government to demonstrate: (1) the operator's competency; (2) the fidelity of the recording equipment; (3) the absence of material alterations; and (4) the identification of relevant sounds or voices).

The current trend is towards a more flexible standard. The courts have not required strict compliance with the *McMillan* and *Biggins* factors. *See United States v. Oslund*, 453 F.3d 1048, 1054-55 (8th Cir. 2006) ("[I]t is worth noting that the technology related to recording devices has greatly advanced since *McMillan* was decided, a fact that supports the premise that the *McMillan* factors are guidelines to be viewed in light of specific circumstances, not a rigid set of tests to be satisfied."); *United States v. Buchanan*, 70 F.3d 818, 827 (5th Cir. 1995) ("Although compliance with the *Biggins* requirements is the 'preferred method' of proceeding, strict compliance is not required."); *United States v. Clark*, 986 F.2d 65, 68 (4th Cir. 1993) (stating that "[i]n *McMillan*, the court did not require strict compliance with the guidelines, and it admitted a tape because its substance and the circumstances under which it was obtained were sufficient proof of its reliability.").

2. What is the justification for the multi-factor standard for authentication? One court has opined that the *McMillan* criteria have "particular application to government usage of recording equipment, where special concerns may arise regarding the competence and reliability of inculpatory evidence." *United States v. O'Connell*, 841 F.2d 1408, 1420 (8th Cir.1988). In other words, where the recording is produced by law enforcement authorities in an adversarial setting, legitimate questions of reliability may arise. However, when the facts demonstrate that the recording was found in the defendant's possession, should the evidence be subject to the same authentication requirements as applicable when a government agent or informant initiates a conversation knowing that it is going to be recorded? In *United States v. Kandiel*, 865

F.2d 967, 974 (8th Cir. 1989), the court answered the question in the negative, stating that under such circumstances mechanical or wooden application of the *McMillan* factors is unnecessary. When the tape recording was produced by someone other than the government, the government is not in a position to determine the competency of the operator or fidelity of the recording equipment. In *Kandiel*, the court posited that authenticity of tape recordings found in the defendant's possession is satisfied if the government offers sufficient circumstantial evidence to identify the speakers and demonstrate the accuracy of the tapes. *Id.*

3. In *Rembert*, appellant argued that photographs are admissible under two theories of authentication, and that the foundation offered by the prosecution satisfied neither theory. *Rembert, supra*, 863 F.2d at 1027. How is authenticity established under the "pictorial testimony" theory? What is the basis for establishing authenticity under the "silent witness" theory? *See United States v. Fadayini*, 28 F.3d 1236, 1241 (D.C. Cir. 1994). How do these two theories of authentication differ? Is appellant correct that the evidence in *Rembert* failed to meet either of these two models? What kind of foundation is required for the admission of a surveillance tape that has been digitally enhanced? *See United States v. Seifert*, 445 F.3d 1043 (8th Cir. 2006) (in arson prosecution, government laid proper foundation for tape, through expert video analyst's testimony about each step of the digital enhancement process, and enhanced tape remained accurate reproduction of original security tape, with adjustments to brightness and speed).

4. Under the "pictorial testimony" and "silent witness" theories is the evidence admitted for purely illustrative purposes, i.e., to illustrate the testimony of the witnesses, or as substantive evidence of the facts depicted? Was the photographic evidence in *Rembert* admitted for illustrative purposes or as independent probative evidence of what it shows? *See State v. Berky*, 447 S.E.2d 147, 148 (Ga. App. 1994), *superseded by statute*, Ga. Code Ann., § 24-4-48 (1996), *as recognized in Phagan v. State*, 486 S.E.2d 876, 883 (Ga. 1997) ("Under the silent witness theory, a videotape constitutes independent probative evidence of what it shows."). A substantial majority of jurisdictions have adopted the silent witness theory. *See Berky*, 447 S.E.2d at 148-149, and the federal and state cases cited therein.

5. When portions of the sound recording accompanying the video recording are either inaudible or unintelligible, should the videotape be excluded on the basis of a Fed. R. Evid. 403 objection that the poor audio recording renders the tape more prejudicial than probative? The district court has wide discretion to determine the potential for prejudice presented by the admission of any video or audio recording, and the standard of review on appeal is abuse of discretion. Recordings may be admitted so long as the inaudible or unintelligible portions are not so substantial as to render the recording as a whole untrustworthy. *See United States v. Polk*, 56 F.3d 613, 631-32 (5th Cir. 1995) (quality of the recordings was not so poor as to constitute prejudicial error by their admission); *United States v. Roach*, 28 F.3d 729, 733 (8th Cir. 1994) (poor audio recording did not render the videotape unduly prejudicial).

6. The process of authenticating still photographs is rather simple. The proponent of the photograph has the exhibit marked for identification and then hands it to the witness. The witness next identifies the object or scene depicted and explains the basis of his of her knowledge. The witness need not be the person who took the photograph, nor does the witness need to have been present when it was taken. *See* 1 COURTROOM CRIMINAL EVIDENCE § 410, at 123 (3d ed. 1998).

C. AUDIO RECORDINGS AND THE USE OF TRANSCRIPTS

UNITED STATES v. STONE
960 F.2d 426 (5th Cir. 1992)

GARWOOD, CIRCUIT JUDGE.

Defendants-appellants Louis Elton Stone (Stone) and Denise Sienhausen (Sienhausen) were convicted of conspiring to manufacture, and attempting to manufacture, in excess of one hundred grams of methamphetamine. They both appeal, raising various challenges to their convictions. We affirm.

In July 1989, Stone entered the Scientific Chemical Company in Harris County, Texas and attempted to purchase three pounds of ephedrine, which is used as a precursor chemical in the manufacture of methamphetamine, but was not itself a controlled substance at that time. Scientific Chemical was out of ephedrine, so the salesman took $350 from Stone, told him that he would order the ephedrine, and asked Stone to get back in touch with him in a few days. The salesman also recorded Stone's name, driver's license number, and address, and in accordance with the company's practice of cooperating with the Drug Enforcement Administration (DEA) by reporting purchases of certain chemicals, called Agent Norris Rogers at the DEA office in Houston with this information. After running some checks on Stone, Rogers called the Scientific Chemical salesman back and gave him his pager number, with instructions to give the number to Stone and tell Stone he could call the number to reach someone who could procure ephedrine for him.

Several days later, Stone called Rogers' pager number and told him that he was looking for someone who could provide him with ephedrine. Rogers arranged a meeting with Stone for the following day. At that meeting, on July 21, 1989, Rogers posed as a black market chemical salesman. Stone said that he had customers waiting for methamphetamine, and that he was anxious to supply it because he was in debt to his attorney for representation on a prior arrest for methamphetamine manufacturing. Rogers said that he was making a decent living as a black market chemical salesman, but that his real aspiration was to expand into the more lucrative area of methamphetamine manufacturing, and that he would supply the ephedrine only if Stone would teach him how to cook methamphetamine. Stone agreed. They worked out an arrangement in which Rogers would sell Stone a pound and a half of ephedrine for the $350 Stone had left with Scientific Chemical, and would give Stone another pound and a half in exchange for Stone's teaching him how to cook methamphetamine. Stone told Rogers that, at the suggestion of his girlfriend, he was operating a methamphetamine lab in the attic of her parents' house. Rogers asked him if he had all of the other chemicals and equipment necessary for manufacturing methamphetamine, and Stone said that he did. Stone and Rogers agreed to meet again three days later.

On July 24, they met outside a restaurant in Houston. Rogers was wearing a concealed transmitter in order to record their conversations. Stone told Rogers that there had been a change in plans; he was there to pick up his girlfriend's mother, who was going to be at home that afternoon, making the house unavailable for methamphetamine manufacturing. Stone told Rogers to go to a pay phone and wait for Stone to page him with further instructions. Rogers did so, and a few minutes later Stone called him and told him to meet him at a convenience store. Rogers went there, and Stone arrived shortly thereafter with a woman he introduced as his girlfriend

Denise. This woman was later determined to be the defendant Sienhausen. In the back seat of Rogers' car, Stone and Sienhausen began talking about how badly they needed the ephedrine in order to sell some methamphetamine and alleviate their financial problems. They told Rogers that the house would not be available until later that night, after Sienhausen's mother went to bed, but they asked Rogers to go ahead and give them the ephedrine. Stone then suggested that he and Sienhausen leave and conduct the manufacturing on their own, and bring Rogers back part of the finished product. Suspecting that they were trying to cut him out of the operation altogether and would not return with the finished product, Rogers rejected their requests. Stone and Sienhausen therefore agreed to drive him to Sienhausen's parents' house several blocks away.

They arrived at the house and all three entered the garage. Stone and Sienhausen again tried to persuade Rogers to leave the ephedrine with them, but Rogers said that he would not do that until he had seen some lab equipment, so that he could be sure they actually knew how to manufacture methamphetamine. Stone or Sienhausen said that the lab equipment was under Sienhausen's bed and was inaccessible as long as her mother was up and moving around the house. Rogers then suggested that if Stone would at least write down the formula for manufacturing methamphetamine as proof that he knew how to do it, Rogers would leave and wait until later that night to return. Stone did so, discussing some of the steps as he wrote. During this time, Sienhausen mentioned that both she and Stone knew how to "cook," and that they never stored the lab equipment in one place, so that if either got arrested, the other would be able to continue operations and make some money to get the first one out of jail. Rogers took the recipe written by Stone and gave them about a pound of ephedrine. He left with Stone's promise that they would call him on the pager when they started the manufacturing.

After Rogers left, surveillance agents saw Stone and Sienhausen leave the house. Stone and Sienhausen never called Rogers, and they did not return to the house during the next several days. Two days later, on July 26, the police executed a search warrant on the house. They found no methamphetamine, ephedrine, or lab equipment. On July 27, surveillance was conducted at Stone's residence in Houston. A red truck arrived at the residence, and the officers searched the vehicle and detained the driver, a man named Gary Mock (Mock). In the truck they found Freon and sodium hydroxide, both of which are used in the methamphetamine manufacturing process. On July 31, after learning that a warrant had been issued for their arrest, Stone and Sienhausen turned themselves in.

On August 23, 1989, a two-count indictment was returned against Stone and Sienhausen, charging them with conspiring with each other to manufacture, and aiding and abetting each other in the attempt to manufacture, in excess of 100 grams of methamphetamine, in violation of 21 U.S.C. §§ 841(a)(1), 841(b)(1)(A), 846, and 18 U.S.C. § 2. A jury found Stone and Sienhausen guilty of both counts. . . . Stone and Sienhausen both appeal their convictions.

DISCUSSION

* * *

VII. *Admission of Audio Tapes and Use of Written Transcripts*

During the investigation, the government made five tapes of Rogers' conversations with Stone or with Stone and Sienhausen together. The first three were taped from telephone conversations and were clear recordings. The fourth and fifth tapes were made on July 24, when Rogers wore a concealed transmitter to his meetings with Stone and Sienhausen. The tapes were made by a second DEA agent, Alton Lewis (Lewis), who carried the receiver in his vehicle and followed Rogers from the restaurant to the convenience store and then to Sienhausen's parents' house. A heavy thunderstorm during this time interfered with the reception, and large portions of the tapes are very difficult to understand. Rogers prepared written transcripts of the fourth and fifth tapes.

Prior to trial, the defendants contended that the fourth and fifth tapes were unintelligible, and that to allow the jury to consider typed transcripts of the tapes would constitute unauthorized bolstering of the evidence contained on the tapes. The defendants objected to use of the transcripts for this reason, and in a separate motion asked that the district court conduct a hearing outside the jury's presence prior to admitting any transcripts in order to determine their accuracy. At a pretrial hearing, the court ruled that the transcripts could not be admitted into evidence or taken to the jury room during deliberations, but could merely be used as a potential guide for the jury while the tapes were being played. The court found no need to rule on defendants' further request that it hold a hearing to determine the accuracy of the transcripts, because that motion merely requested such a hearing before the transcripts were admitted into evidence. The defendants then promptly filed written motions requesting that the government be prohibited from using the transcripts before the jury at all.

Immediately prior to trial, the district court indicated that it had listened to one tape and reviewed the transcript, and that the defendants' objection to use of the transcript as a potential guide for the jury was overruled. During the same conference, counsel for the government notified the court that it had that morning submitted revised versions of the transcripts for the fourth and fifth tapes, which were essentially the same but contained some typographical corrections. Defense counsel did not renew its motion that the court compare the tapes to the new transcripts.

At the end of the first day of trial, the district court admitted the tapes into evidence over defendants' objection that they were of such poor quality that they would mislead the jury. On the second day of trial, the district court allowed the government to play the fourth and fifth tapes for the jury and to submit the transcripts to the jury to be used as potential guides while the tapes were playing. The defendants renewed their objection to use of the transcripts, and the court again overruled the objection, noting that from its review it had concluded that the tape was not so unintelligible that someone familiar with the conversation could not make an accurate transcript. The court instructed the jury that the transcripts had been prepared by the government's agent, and cautioned the jury as follows:

> "Now, this [transcript] is only for your general guidance. You are directed and ordered by this Court to make your own interpretation of what you hear from that tape. This is only what the Government believes on this tape. And if you feel it's unintelligible, then you are to disregard anything that you feel is unintelligible, notwithstanding what the Government has down as to what its position is on that tape.

> "So, in effect, I will let you consider this just as — well, just as a transcript as far as the Government's version is concerned. The defense in no way adopts

this version. . . . However, it's my decision to allow you to use it for whatever weight, if any, you desire to give to it. If you feel that tape is unintelligible, then disregard what the Government thinks is on that tape. And if you listen and you hear it differently from what is down here, you ought to consider what you hear as best you can from the tape."

The court further stated: "It [the transcript] is not evidence in this case. The tape is the evidence."

In this appeal, Stone and Sienhausen make three distinct challenges regarding the tapes and transcripts: (1) that the government failed to establish the predicate for admission of the tapes; (2) that the tapes' unintelligibility rendered the district court's admission of the tapes an abuse of discretion; and (3) that the district court compounded its error by wrongfully allowing use of the transcripts and restricting cross-examination of Rogers about the transcripts.

On Stone and Sienhausen's first point, the guiding principles for this Circuit were set forth in *United States v. Biggins*, 551 F.2d 64 (1977). There the Court held that when seeking to introduce a recording in a criminal prosecution, the government bears the burden of "going forward with foundation evidence demonstrating that the recording as played is an accurate reproduction of relevant sounds previously audited by a witness," which generally requires the government to demonstrate (1) the competency of the operator, (2) the fidelity of the recording equipment, (3) the absence of material deletions, additions, or alterations, and (4) the identification of the relevant speakers. *Id.* at 66. The *Biggins* Court further held that although strict compliance with the government's particularized burden is "the preferred method of proceeding," even in the absence of such compliance, the trial judge retains broad discretion to independently determine that the recording accurately reproduces the auditory experience. *Id.* at 66–67.

In the present case, prior to admission of the tapes, Rogers testified that they were the tapes of his conversations with Stone and Sienhausen, that they had been recorded by Lewis while Rogers was talking with the defendants and wearing a hidden transmitter, that they had been kept in a secure place from the time they were made, and that no alterations had been made. Later, after the tapes had been played for the jury, Lewis testified and went into a little more detail about the recording equipment and its capabilities. He admitted that the thunderstorm reduced the transmitter's effective range, and that at times he had not been able to stay close enough to Rogers to make an intelligible recording.

We conclude that the government adequately laid a foundation for the tapes under *Biggins*. Although not all of the *Biggins* factors were thoroughly covered before the tapes were played, the *Biggins* decision indicates that the list is not meant to command "formalistic adherence" at the expense of the district court's discretion. *Id.* at 67. We perceive no abuse of that discretion here, particularly since the essence of the defendants' opposition to the tapes at trial was not really an authentication issue. The defendants did not contend that the government had not adequately established the content of the tapes to make them admissible, i.e., the defendants did not challenge the means by which the tapes were prepared or suggest alteration or distortion of the tapes, but instead simply questioned the usefulness of the final product (and did this for the first time during the trial itself).

On the defendants' second contention regarding the tapes, this Court has consistently held that poor quality and partial unintelligibility do not render tapes inadmissible unless the unintelligible portions are so substantial as to render the recording as a whole untrustworthy, and that this determination is left to the sound discretion of the trial judge. . . . We find no abuse of discretion in the admission of the tapes here, particularly given the precautions taken by the court when they were played.

Finally, on Stone and Sienhausen's third point, this Circuit's guidelines for use of transcripts were set out in *United States v. Onori*, 535 F.2d 938, 946–49 (5th Cir. 1976). In *Onori*, this Court held that transcripts given to the jury are evidence, admitted for a limited purpose, and that therefore a determination of the transcript's accuracy is typically a jury function rather than a judicial one constituting a precondition to admission. The *Onori* Court indicated that the preferred procedure was to have the parties arrive at a "stipulated" transcript to be given to the jury; if the parties cannot agree on all portions of the transcript, then the transcript may contain both versions of the disputed portions, or the court may give two transcripts to the jury. *Id.* at 948–49. The *Onori* Court, consistent with its classification of the accuracy of a transcript as basically a factual determination, held that the defendants in that case, having been offered the opportunity to present their own version of the transcript and to have their expert witness testify as to errors in the government's, had not shown reversible error in the district court's refusal to rule on the accuracy of the government's transcript before giving it to the jury. We have likewise held that when a defendant challenges the government's translation of a foreign-language conversation for the jury, but fails to offer his own translation, the district court is under no obligation to pass on the transcript's accuracy.

The situation of Stone and Sienhausen was in some ways distinct from the situation contemplated in *Onori*. *Onori* described an instance in which the defendants alleged specific errors in the government's transcript. Almost by necessity, a challenge to a translation by the government will similarly concern specific defects. In the present case, however, the defendants' contention was that so much of the tape was unintelligible that no reliable transcript could be made. To place upon them the burden of coming forward with their own transcript would be to require of them what they contended could not be done. Therefore, *Onori* alone would not provide authority for admission of the transcript in this case without a finding of the transcript's accuracy.

However, the district court in this case went considerably beyond the minimum procedure set forth in *Onori*. At the beginning of trial, the district court had before it the defendants' motion to make an *in camera* determination of the accuracy of the government's transcripts, and, if it found them to be inaccurate, to suppress them. In the conference immediately prior to the beginning of trial, the judge informed counsel that he had listened to the tape given him and had read the transcript, and that he was denying the motion to suppress the transcript. He indicated, though, that the jury would receive a thorough instruction as to the weight to give the transcript. On the second day of trial, when the defendants renewed their objection as the tapes were about to be played, the district court stated: "I listened to the tape myself, compared it to the transcript, and it was my determination that it is not so unintelligible that someone familiar with the transaction could not have made a transcript that was just for the jury's consideration." The defendants did not request a more specific finding as to the accuracy of the transcript.

We conclude that the district court's handling of the situation was within its discretion. Its finding that a reliable transcript could have been made by someone familiar with the conversation was a direct consideration and rejection of the objection raised by the defendants, and put the case back into the posture contemplated in *Onori*:

it was the province of the jury to decide whether the government's transcript was accurate, and the obligation of the defendants to raise specific challenges to the transcript before the jury. Moreover, the district court gave a thorough limiting instruction to the jury, which the *Onori* decision indicates is "the key to protecting a defendant's rights in this situation." *Onori*, 535 F.2d at 949. The defendants argue to this Court that the district court listened to only one of the two disputed tapes and never made any specific findings about accuracy. However, the trial transcript reveals no request by the defendants for either of these steps.

*　　*　　*

CONCLUSION

Because we find no reversible error presented by any of Stone and Sienhausen's contentions, the judgment of the district court is Affirmed.

NOTES AND QUESTIONS

1. *Authentication of Tape Recordings.* In *Stone*, defendants raised several legal challenges to the admissibility of the tape recordings and use of the transcripts. First, defendants claimed that the government had failed to properly authenticate the recordings. In rejecting this argument, the court stated that while compliance with the factors articulated in *Biggins* is "the preferred method" for authenticating a recording, strict compliance is not required, and the trial court retains broad discretion to independently determine that the recording accurately reproduces the auditory experience. *United States v. Stone*, 960 F.2d 426, 436 (5th Cir. 1992). *See* discussion of *United States v. Biggins*, 551 F.2d 64 (5th Cir. 1977), by the court in *Stone, supra*. Despite the fact that the government failed to satisfy all of the *Biggins* factors, the court found no abuse of the district court's discretion. In the absence of formal adherence to *Biggins*, what was the basis for the court's ruling that the government adequately laid a proper foundation for admitting the tapes?

2. The court in *Stone* posited that "the essence of defendants' opposition to the tapes was not really an authentication issue." What did the court mean by this statement? Is *Stone* an authentication case? If not, then what is the real basis for defendants' legal challenge to the admissibility of the tape recordings?

3. *Unintelligibility of Tape Recordings.* Defendants' second contention was directed at the poor quality and partial unintelligibility of the tapes. Defendants claimed that because certain portions of the tapes are unintelligible the tapes should be excluded. What is the legal standard enunciated by the court for determining when tapes that are partially inaudible or unintelligible should be rendered inadmissible? In other words, when should tapes be excluded that are partially unintelligible? *See United States v. Segines*, 17 F.3d 847, 854 (6th Cir. 1994) (setting forth the relevant standard); *United States v. Degaglia*, 913 F.2d 372, 378 (7th Cir. 1990) (same).

4. *Transcripts.* Defendants' third challenge was directed at the use of the transcripts. What is the proper procedure to be followed when the defendants allege specific errors in the government's transcript? The *Stone* court stated that the accuracy of a transcript is basically a factual determination to be made by the trier of fact. Thus, the jury is ultimately to resolve any disputes on the accuracy of the transcript. *See United States v. Onori*, 535 F.2d 938, 946–49 (5th Cir. 1976) (setting forth the procedure for resolving inaccuracies in the government's transcript).

5. *English Translation Transcripts.* As a general rule, tape recordings are played to the jury and received as substantive evidence in the case. The transcripts, on the other hand, are admitted only as an aid to the jury. In *Stone*, the District Court instructed the jury accordingly: "It [the transcript], is not evidence is this case. The tape is the evidence." *Stone*, 960 F.2d at 435; *see also United States v. Fuentes-Montijo*, 68 F.3d 352, 353 (9th Cir. 1995) ("the tapes themselves are the primary evidence"); *United States v. Cruz*, 765 F.2d 1020, 1023 (11th Cir. 1985) ("What was said at the time it was recorded is what the real evidence is, the transcripts are not. They are merely to help you identify."). Does this approach make sense when the taped conversation is in a foreign language? In this situation, the foreign language tapes are unintelligible to the jury. When the tape recorded conversation is in a foreign language, shouldn't the English-translated transcript be considered by the jury as substantive evidence? In *United States v. Fuentes-Montijo*, 68 F.3d 352, 353–54 (9th Cir. 1995), the court answered this question in the affirmative and upheld the following jury instruction by the district court:

> I previously instructed you that the recordings, and not the transcripts, are the evidence. I want to correct that at this time. The transcripts have been certified by a federally certified court interpreter. While in a case involving English conversations which have been recorded, the jury is routinely instructed that they are not bound by the transcript, that is because every juror is just as capable as the person preparing the transcript to tell what is being said on the recording. This is not so with the recorded Spanish conversations that have been introduced in this case. Accordingly, I am now instructing you that the transcripts are guides prepared for you so that you can understand the Spanish language recordings. You are not free to reject the accuracy of the interpretation of the tape recordings differently than the interpretation given by the certified court interpreter in the transcripts.

In sustaining the district court's instruction to the jury, the Ninth Circuit opined:

> When faced with a taped conversation in a language other than English and a disputed English translation transcript, the usual admonition that the tape is the evidence and the transcript only a guide is not only nonsensical, it has the potential for harm where the jury includes bilingual jurors. As the Second Circuit said in *Bahadar*, it is "hard to imagine any other proper and effective handling of this evidence." (citations omitted). The district court's actions and instructions here were well within its discretion.

Id. at 355–56 (quoting *United States v. Bahadar*, 954 F.2d 821, 830 (2d Cir. 1992)).

What is the potential "harm" referenced by the court where the jury includes bilingual jurors?

6. *Accuracy of English Translation Transcripts.* What if there is a dispute as to the accuracy of the government's English translation transcript? Because the taped conversation is in a foreign language, the jury is not able to listen to the tape and make a factual determination whether the transcript accurately reflects what was said on the tape. How is the jury supposed to resolve the conflict? Must the defendant offer into evidence an alternative translated transcript? Must the jury then decide between the two versions offered? *See United States v. Font-Ramirez*, 944 F.2d 42, 48 (1st Cir. 1991) ("Because [appellant] did not offer an alternative transcript and did not point out any specific inaccuracies in the government's transcript, the district court was within its discretion in allowing its use.").

7. *Standard of Proof.* While Fed. R. Evid. 901(a) requires that the party requesting admission must provide proof "sufficient to support a finding that the matter is what its proponent claims," the rule fails to set forth the relevant standard of proof. Several courts require proof by clear and convincing evidence. For example, the Seventh Circuit holds:

> The Government must prove, by clear and convincing evidence, that the proffered tape is a true, accurate and authentic recording of the conversation between the parties. . . . [T]he Government may meet this burden by establishing the tape's chain of custody or by establishing otherwise a foundation as to the trustworthiness and accuracy of the evidence . . .

United States v. Westmoreland, 312 F.3d 302, 311 (7th Cir. 2002) (citations omitted). *See also United States v. Hamilton*, 334 F.3f 170, 186–87 (2d Cir. 2003); *United States v. Starks*, 515 F.2d 112, 121 (3d Cir. 1975). What is the justification for requiring the heightened standard of clear and convincing evidence rather than the lower standard of preponderance of the evidence?

8. *Voice Identification.* Federal Rule of Evidence 901(b)(5) permits voice identification to be made "by opinion based upon hearing the voice at any time under circumstances connecting it with the alleged speaker. As long as the basic requirement of familiarity is met, lay opinion testimony is an acceptable means for establishing the speaker's identity." *United States v. Degaglia*, 913 F.2d 372, 375–76 (7th Cir. 1990) (citations omitted). The standard requires a low threshold showing. " 'Minimal familiarity [with the defendant's voice] is sufficient for admissibility purposes.' " *Id.* (quoting *United States v. Cerone*, 830 F.2d 938, 949 (8th Cir. 1987)). Recorded conversations have been properly admitted where the witness spoke with the defendant on two or three separate occasions for a total of two hours or less. *See, e.g., United States v. Khorrami*, 895 F.2d 1186, 1194 (7th Cir. 1988); *United States v. Carrasco*, 887 F.2d 794, 804 & n.17 (7th Cir. 1989); *United States v. Shukitis*, 877 F.2d 1322, 1328 (7th Cir. 1989); *United States v. Vega*, 860 F.2d 779, 788 (7th Cir. 1988). Furthermore, any claims that the identification procedures were impermissibly suggestive and unreliable go to the weight the jury accords the evidence, not to its admissibility. *See United States v. Degaglia*, 913 F.2d 372, 376 (7th Cir. 1990); *United States v. Alvarez*, 860 F.2d 801, 809 (7th Cir. 1988).

9. *Telephone Conversations.* Federal Rule of Evidence 901(b)(6) permits identification of persons who are parties to a telephone conversation

> by evidence that a call was made to the number assigned at the time by the telephone company to a particular person or business, if (A) in the case of a person, circumstances, including self-identification, show the person answering to be the one called, or (B) in the case of a business, the call was made to a place of business and the conversation related to business reasonably transacted over the telephone.

Mere assertion of identity by a person talking on the telephone is not in itself sufficient to authenticate that person's identity. *See United States v. Khan*, 53 F.3d 507, 516 (2d Cir. 1995). Some additional evidence, which "need not fall in[to] any set pattern," may provide the necessary foundation. FED. R. EVID. 901(b)(6) advisory committee note. "[S]elf-identification of *the person called* at a place where he reasonably could be expected to be has long been regarded as sufficient" for authentication purposes. *Khan, supra*, 53 F.3d at 516 (citations omitted). At the same time, self-identification by a person making a telephone call, without more, is insufficient to establish the identity of the caller. *Id.; see also Noriega v. United States*, 437 F.2d 435, 436 (9th Cir. 1971) (call made by defendant properly authenticated where defendant provided witness with a number, witness left message for defendant and defendant returned the call).

D.   DEMONSTRATIONS AND COURTROOM REENACTMENTS

UNITED STATES v. GASKELL
985 F.2d 1056 (11th Cir. 1993)

BIRCH, CIRCUIT JUDGE:

The defendant, Robert Gaskell, was convicted of involuntary manslaughter of his infant daughter in violation of 18 U.S.C. § 1112. He appeals his conviction, arguing that a government witness was allowed to conduct an unscientific and prejudicial demonstration of "shaken baby syndrome," using a model of an infant. Gaskell also contends that the district court improperly excluded the testimony of a defense expert witness and erroneously instructed the jury on the required elements of proof for involuntary manslaughter. We REVERSE Gaskell's conviction.

Robert Gaskell was the father of Kristen Gaskell, who was born on July 7, 1989. Beginning in September, 1989, Kristen had a series of problems with her health, including fevers and vomiting. On at least four occasions prior to her death, Kristen was treated for recurring vomiting, either in an emergency room or after admission as a hospital patient.

On February 10, 1990, Kristen vomited again and was cleaned up by Gaskell and Kristen's mother, Diane Gaskell. Shortly thereafter, Diane left to go shopping, leaving Kristen in Gaskell's care. That day, at approximately 4:55 p.m., the Gaskells' neighbors, Janet and Scott Young, returned home from the circus. Both Janet and Scott were certified as emergency medical technicians. Scott testified that as they arrived home, Gaskell ran out of his open door yelling that Kristen was not breathing. Janet and Scott attempted to revive Kristen. Both testified that Kristen appeared pale, with the blue skin tint associated with a lack of oxygen. Both testified that there was vomit on the rug and in Kristen's mouth and nose, and that the odor of a baby's vomit was discernable around Kristen. Janet removed a small amount of white, milky fluid from Kristen's mouth using a turkey baster. Using procedures modified for infants, Janet and Scott performed cardiopulmonary resuscitation ("CPR") on Kristen. Shortly thereafter, emergency medical technicians arrived and continued the attempt to revive Kristen. Kristen was pronounced dead at approximately 6:01 p.m. on February 10th.

At trial, both the government and the defense presented expert medical testimony regarding the cause of Kristen's death. Dr. Robert John Nelms, the Medical Examiner for Monroe County, Florida, performed an autopsy on Kristen on the day following her death. Dr. Nelms testified that Kristen did not die of asphyxiation. He observed what he characterized as a "ligature" mark on Kristen's neck as well as signs of internal trauma indicating a head injury. He concluded that Kristen had died either as the result of strangulation or from being struck on the head with some object. Dr. Roger Mittleman of the Dade County Medical Examiner's Office also testified for the government. Dr. Mittleman disagreed with some of Dr. Nelms's conclusions. He testified that the "ligature" mark was merely a skin rash and that Kristen most likely had died of "shaken baby syndrome," a category of internal head trauma. Dr. Mittleman testified that forcefully shaking an infant can result in fatal injury because of the delicacy of an infant's brain and the inability of the undeveloped muscles in an infant's neck to restrain the movement of its head.

Over the objection of defense counsel, Dr. Mittleman was allowed to conduct a demonstration of shaken baby syndrome by manipulating a rubber infant mannequin used to practice infant CPR techniques. Dr. Mittleman forcefully shook the doll before the jury so that the head repeatedly swung back against the doll's back and then forward onto the doll's chest. He testified that the neck of the CPR doll was stiffer than an infant's and, thus, greater force was required to produce the head movement associated with shaken baby syndrome. Dr. Mittleman added that the degree of force required was "above and beyond what we consider child care. We are all taught to support the baby's head." R6-23.

Dr. Glenn Wagner, the Assistant Armed Forces Medical Examiner at the Armed Forces Institute of Pathology and a specialist in pediatric pathology, testified for the defense. Dr. Wagner concluded that Kristen did not asphyxiate as a result of vomiting, but had died of internal head trauma suggestive of shaken baby syndrome. He added that the injuries could have been inflicted if Gaskell had panicked, reached down into the playpen and quickly lifted Kristen by her arms. On cross-examination, he stated that Kristen's injuries would require forceful shaking, but that he could not determine whether the injuries resulted from a panicked attempt to revive Kristen or from deliberate child abuse. Dr. Bruce McIntosh, a pediatrician at St. Vincent Medical Center in Jacksonville, Florida, also testified for the defense. He concluded that Kristen had been shaken in a misguided attempt to revive her and that her injuries were consistent with shaken baby syndrome.

*   *   *

The jury acquitted Gaskell of second-degree murder and voluntary manslaughter, but found him guilty of involuntary manslaughter. Gaskell appeals his conviction.

II. *Evidentiary Rulings*

A. *The Demonstration by Dr. Mittleman*

Gaskell argues that Dr. Mittleman's demonstration of shaken baby syndrome using a rubber infant mannequin was irrelevant and unfairly prejudicial. "As a general rule, the district court has wide discretion to admit evidence of experiments conducted under substantially similar conditions." *Barnes v. General Motors Corp.*, 547 F.2d 275, 277 (5th Cir. 1977). The burden is on the party offering a courtroom demonstration or experiment to lay a proper foundation establishing a similarity of circumstances and conditions. Although the conditions of the demonstration need not be identical to the event at issue, "they must be so nearly the same in substantial particulars as to afford a fair comparison in respect to the particular issue to which the test is directed." *Id.* (quoting *Illinois Central Gulf R.R. Co. v. Ishee, Mississippi*, 317 So. 2d 923, 926 (Miss. 1975)).[1] Further, experimental or demonstrative evidence, like any evidence offered at trial, should be excluded "if its probative value is substantially outweighed by the danger of unfair prejudice, confusion of the issues, or misleading the jury." Fed. R. Evid. 403.

---

[1] *Accord Jackson v. Fletcher*, 647 F.2d 1020, 1027 (10th Cir. 1981) ("[T]he party introducing the evidence [of an experiment] has a burden of demonstrating substantial similarity of conditions. They may not be identical but they ought to be sufficiently similar so as to provide a fair comparison.").

In the presence of the jury, the government proposed that Dr. Mittleman should use the doll "to demonstrate the amount of force which would be necessary to cause [Kristen's] injuries[.]" R6-24. Moreover, the demonstration was conducted during a segment of Dr. Mittleman's testimony concerning the degree of force required to produce the fatal injuries. The conditions of the demonstration, offered for this purpose, were not sufficiently similar to the alleged actions of the defendant to allow a fair comparison. As noted by defense counsel in her objection, due to differences in the weight of the doll's head as well as the flexibility and length of the doll's neck, a considerably greater degree of force was required in order to produce the head movement characteristic of shaken baby syndrome. As the party offering the evidence, the burden was on the government to show that the conditions of Dr. Mittleman's demonstration were sufficiently similar to the circumstances of Kristen's death to afford a fair comparison. Based on the differences enumerated by defense counsel, the government failed to meet this burden. Dr. Mittleman admitted that the doll's neck was stiffer than that of a seven-month-old infant and that this would affect the degree of force necessary to move the head in the required fashion. Dr. Mittleman explained that his presentation was based on a demonstration of shaken baby syndrome by a police officer whose knowledge was derived from the confession of a father in an unrelated case. Although an expert may rely upon hearsay as the basis for his or her opinion if the out of court statements are "of a type reasonably relied upon by experts in the particular field," the government did not establish that Dr. Mittleman's hearsay knowledge of this unrelated case provided any reliable or accurate basis upon which to draw conclusions regarding Kristen's death. See Fed. R. Evid. 703. Further, although Dr. Mittleman repeatedly shook the doll before the jury, he was unable to state the number of oscillations required to produce Kristen's injuries. The conditions of the demonstration were thus substantially dissimilar; the government failed to establish that either the degree of force or the number of oscillations bore any relationship to the defendant's actions. Although the presentation did illustrate the path of movement of an infant's head during shaken baby syndrome, this phenomenon could have been demonstrated with equal effectiveness by a direct manipulation of the doll's head, as suggested by defense counsel at sidebar.

Whatever slight probative value that inhered in the demonstration was overwhelmed by its unfairly prejudicial effects. The sight of an adult male repeatedly shaking a representation of an infant with the degree of force necessary to manipulate the doll's head in the required fashion was likely to form a strong impression upon the jury. This prejudicial effect was magnified by the fact that the outcome of this trial hinged upon whether the jury believed that the degree of injury suffered by Kristen could support Gaskell's testimony that he inflicted the fatal injuries in a panicked attempt to revive her. By displaying a greater degree of force than the level required to produce shaken baby syndrome in a seventh-month-old infant and by arbitrarily selecting a number of oscillations, the demonstration tended to implant a vision of Gaskell's actions in the jurors' minds that was not supported by any factual basis for the demonstration. We are thus persuaded that, under Rule 403, the unfairly prejudicial nature of the demonstration outweighed any probative value.

The government argues, and the trial judge ruled, that the court's cautionary instructions to the jury and Gaskell's ability to point out the differences between the doll and a seven-month-old infant on cross-examination negated any prejudice resulting from the display. Under the circumstances of this case, we cannot agree. The demonstration was presented to the jury as an illustration of the amount of force required to produce Kristen's injuries. The trial court's instruction to the jury to assess the demonstration "in light of the statements and testimony you have heard" failed to highlight the dissimilarities of the demonstration with the events at issue. R6–26. Further, Dr. Mittleman's admission that the doll's neck was "a bit stiffer" than Kristen's was unlikely to erase the image of Dr. Mittleman violently and repeatedly shaking the doll. R6-29. The demonstration could not illuminate either the degree of force or the number of oscillations required to injure Kristen. Neither the cautionary instruction nor Dr. Mittleman's answers on cross-examination provided any scale of comparison from which the jury might have been able to infer from the demonstration the amount of force applied to Kristen. The ability to cross-examine is not a substitute for the offering party's burden of showing that a proffered demonstration or experiment offers a fair comparison to the contested events. Particularly where the demonstration unfairly tended to prejudice the jury on the one genuinely contested issue, without providing any significantly probative testimony, neither the cautionary instruction nor the ability to cross-examine was sufficient to cure the error. The verdict turned on whether the jury believed that the manner in which Gaskell handled Kristen was consistent with a frightened attempt to revive her. By unfairly prejudicing the jury upon this pivotal issue, it is likely that the error affected his substantial rights, warranting reversal. . . .

. . . The cumulative effect of these errors requires the reversal of Gaskell's conviction.

Reversed.

NOTES AND QUESTIONS

1. *Rule 403 Balancing.* In *Gaskell*, what was the purpose of the courtroom demonstration? To what issue in the case was the evidence relevant? Based on the conditions of the demonstration, was there any probative value whatsoever to Dr. Mittleman's demonstration? The court stated that, like any evidence offered at trial, experimental or demonstrative evidence should be excluded if its probative value is substantially outweighed by the danger of unfair prejudice. Fed. R. Evid. 403. Why did the court find that the probative value of the demonstration was substantially outweighed by the risk of unfair prejudice? What are the important differences between the conditions of the demonstration and the alleged actions of the defendant and circumstances of the baby's death?

2. *Laying a Proper Foundation.* The party offering evidence in the form of a courtroom demonstration or experiment must lay a proper foundation for admission of the evidence. What is the threshold requirement for admission of experimental evidence? Must the conditions of the demonstration be identical or nearly identical to the event at issue? *See United States v. Wanoskia*, 800 F.2d 235, 237–38 (10th Cir. 1986) (setting forth the relevant test and upholding the admission of the experiment offered to demonstrate that the victim could not have committed suicide because she could not have held the gun at the distance required to be consistent with the physical evidence).

3. *Dissimilarities Between Experimental and Actual Conditions.* Should any dissimilarities between experimental and actual conditions go to the weight to be accorded the evidence by the jury, rather than its admissibility? *See Szeliga v. General Motors Corp.*, 728 F.2d 566, 567 (1st Cir. 1984) ("Dissimilarities between experimental and actual conditions affect the weight of the evidence, not its admissibility."); *Renfro Hosiery Mills Co. v. National Cash Register Co.*, 552 F.2d 1061, 1065 (4th Cir. 1977) ("If there is substantial similarity, the differences between the test and the actual occurrence ordinarily are regarded as affecting the weight of the evidence rather than its admissibility.").

4. Several circuits have recognized that courtroom demonstrations tend to leave a particularly potent image in the juror's minds. *See Gaskell, supra*, 985 F.2d at 1061 n.2; *United States v. Wanoskia*, 800 F.2d 235, 237–38 (10th Cir. 1986); *Carson v. Polley*, 689 F.2d 562, 579 (5th Cir. 1982). In *Wanoskia*, the court observed:

> Demonstrative evidence, and in particular, reenactments of events, can be highly persuasive. The opportunity for the jury to see what supposedly happened can accomplish in seconds what might otherwise take days of testimony. By conveying a visual image of what allegedly occurred, one side can imprint on the jury's mind its version of the facts. Thus the court must take special care to ensure that the demonstration fairly depicts the events at issue.

Wanoskia, supra, 800 F.2d at 237–38 (citations omitted).

In *Wanoskia*, the district court first viewed the demonstration outside the presence of the jury to ensure that the demonstration did not unfairly prejudice defendant, and later instructed the jury to disregard the demonstration if it determined that the testimony lacked an adequate foundation. Should the procedures employed in *Wanoskia* be required for admission of demonstration evidence, or merely encouraged?

5. ***Computer Generated Evidence.*** Computer generated evidence is increasingly proffered in criminal cases. If the purpose of the computer evidence is to illustrate and explain a witness's testimony, courts refer to such evidence as animation. In contrast, if the purpose is to re-create an event, such evidence is classified as simulation evidence. *See Hinkle v. City of Clarksburg*, 81 F.3d 416, 425 (4th Cir. 1996); *State v. Sayles*, 662 N.W.2d 1, 9 (Iowa 2003); *People v. Cauley*, 32 P.3d 602, 606–07 (Colo. Ct. App. 2001). According to the court in *State v. Sayles*, "a simulation is based on scientific or physical principles and data entered into a computer, which is programmed to analyze the data and draw a conclusion from it, and courts generally require proof to show the validity of the science before the simulation evidence is admitted." *State v. Sayles*, 662 N.W.2d at 9. Thus, the classification of computer-generated evidence as a simulation or an animation may affect the evidentiary foundation required for its admission. *Id.*

APPENDIX A

IN THE MATTER OF AN INVESTIGATION OF THE W. VIRGINIA STATE POLICE CRIME LABORATORY, SEROLOGY DIVISION.
438 S.E.2d 501(W.Va. 1993)

MILLER, JUSTICE:

This case is an extraordinary proceeding arising from a petition filed with this Court on June 2, 1993, by William C. Forbes, Prosecuting Attorney for Kanawha County, requesting the appointment of a circuit judge to conduct an investigation into whether habeas corpus relief should be granted to prisoners whose convictions were obtained through the willful false testimony of Fred S. Zain, a former serologist with the Division of Public Safety. On June 3, 1993, in response to the petition, we entered an order appointing the Honorable James O. Holliday, a retired circuit judge, to supervise an investigation of the Serology Division at the West Virginia State Police Crime Laboratory. On November 4, 1993, after an extensive, five-month investigation, Judge Holliday filed his report with this Court, a copy of which is attached as an Appendix to this opinion.

The report chronicles the history of allegations of misconduct on the part of Trooper Zain, beginning with the wrongful conviction of Glen Dale Woodall, who was eventually released after DNA testing conclusively established his innocence. The report further discusses allegations of misconduct and incompetence by Trooper Zain's subordinates during his tenure with the Division of Public Safety. Finally, the report summarizes the findings of James McNamara, Laboratory Director of the Florida Department of Law Enforcement, and Ronald Linhart, Supervisor of Serology in the Crime Laboratory for the Los Angeles County Sheriff's Department, who were selected by Barry Fisher, Chairman of the Laboratory Accreditation Board of the American Society of Crime Laboratory Directors (ASCLD), to conduct an analysis of the policies, procedures, practices, and records of the Serology Division during Trooper Zain's tenure.

The ASCLD report and the deposition testimony of fellow officers in the Serology Division during Trooper Zain's tenure support the multiple findings of fact by Judge Holliday regarding Trooper Zain's long history of falsifying evidence in criminal prosecutions. Specifically, the report states:

"The acts of misconduct on the part of Zain included (1) overstating the strength of results; (2) overstating the frequency of genetic matches on individual pieces of evidence; (3) misreporting the frequency of genetic matches on multiple pieces of evidence; (4) reporting that multiple items had been tested, when only a single item had been tested; (5) reporting inconclusive results as conclusive; (6) repeatedly altering laboratory records; (7) grouping results to create the erroneous impression that genetic markers had been obtained from all samples tested; (8) failing to report conflicting results; (9) failing to conduct or to report conducting additional testing to resolve conflicting results; (10) implying a match with a suspect when testing supported only a match with the victim; and (11) reporting scientifically impossible or improbable results." (Footnote omitted).

The report by Judge Holliday further notes that the ASCLD team concluded that these irregularities were " 'the result of systematic practice rather than an occasional inadvertent error' " and discusses specific cases that were prosecuted in which Serology Division records indicate that scientifically inaccurate, invalid, or false testimony or reports were given by Trooper Zain.

In addition to investigating what occurred during Trooper Zain's tenure in the Serology Division, Judge Holliday also explored how these irregularities could have happened. The report notes that many of Trooper Zain's former supervisors and subordinates regarded him as "pro-prosecution." The report further states: "It appears that Zain was quite skillful in using his experience and position of authority to deflect criticism of his work by subordinates." Although admittedly beyond the scope of the investigation, the report by Judge Holliday notes that there was evidence that Trooper Zain's supervisors may have ignored or concealed complaints of his misconduct. Finally, the report discusses ASCLD criticisms of certain operating procedures during Trooper Zain's tenure, which the report concludes "undoubtedly contributed to an environment within which Zain's misconduct escaped detection." According to the report, these procedural deficiencies included:

> "(1) no written documentation of testing methodology; (2) no written quality assurance program; (3) no written internal or external auditing procedures; (4) no routine proficiency testing of laboratory technicians; (5) no technical review of work product; (6) no written documentation of instrument maintenance and calibration; (7) no written testing procedures manual; (8) failure to follow generally-accepted scientific testing standards with respect to certain tests; (9) inadequate record-keeping; and (10) failure to conduct collateral testing."

Judge Holliday's report correctly concludes that Trooper Zain's pattern and practice of misconduct completely undermined the validity and reliability of any forensic work he performed or reported, and thus constitutes newly discovered evidence. It further recognizes the appropriate standard of review in cases of newly discovered evidence as set forth by this Court most recently in Syllabus Point 1 of *State v. O'Donnell*, 433 S.E.2d 566 (1993):

> "A new trial will not be granted on the ground of newly-discovered evidence unless the case comes within the following rules: (1) The evidence must appear to have been discovered since the trial, and, from the affidavit of the new witness, what such evidence will be, or its absence satisfactorily explained. (2) It must appear from facts stated in his affidavit that [defendant] was diligent in ascertaining and securing his evidence, and that the new evidence is such that due diligence would not have secured it before the verdict. (3) Such evidence must be new and material, and not merely cumulative; and cumulative evidence is additional evidence of the same kind to the same point. (4) The evidence must be such as ought to produce an opposite result at a second trial on the merits. (5) And the new trial will generally be refused when the sole object of the new evidence is to discredit or impeach a witness on the opposite side."

Newly discovered evidence is not the only ground on which habeas relief can be afforded. It has long been recognized by the United States Supreme Court that it is a violation of due process for the State to convict a defendant based on false evidence.

Chief Justice Warren, writing for a unanimous court in *Napue v. Illinois*, 360 U.S. 264 (1959), summarized this principle:

> "*First*, it is established that a conviction obtained through use of false evidence, known to be such by representatives of the State, must fall under the Fourteenth Amendment. . . . The same result obtains when the State, although not soliciting false evidence, allows it to go uncorrected when it appears." (Emphasis in original; citations omitted).

In *Giglio v. United States*, 405 U.S. 150 (1972), a unanimous Court again concluded that the Government was responsible for false testimony on the part of one of its witnesses even though the prosecutor was unaware of its falsity. In *Giglio*, a Government witness was promised immunity if he would testify against the defendant. This promise was made by an assistant district attorney who was not involved in the *Giglio* trial. The trial prosecutor was unaware of the promise. On cross-examination, the witness denied that he received any promise of immunity. The Supreme Court in *Giglio* began by reaffirming *Napue's* principle:

> "In *Napue*. . . , we said, 'the same result obtains when the State, although not soliciting false evidence, allows it to go uncorrected when it appears.' [360 U.S.] at 269. Thereafter *Brady v. Maryland*, 373 U.S. [82], at 87 held that suppression of material evidence justifies a new trial irrespective of the good faith or bad faith of the prosecutor.'" 405 U.S. at 153–54.

It then made this observation as to responsibility of the prosecutor's office: "Moreover, whether the nondisclosure was a result of negligence or design, it is the responsibility of the prosecutor. The prosecutor's office is an entity and as such it is the spokesman for the Government." 405 U.S. at 154.

Thus, in this case, it matters not whether a prosecutor using Trooper Zain as his expert ever knew that Trooper Zain was falsifying the State's evidence. The State must bear the responsibility for the false evidence. The law forbids the State from obtaining a conviction based on false evidence.

It is also recognized that, although it is a violation of due process for the State to convict a defendant based on false evidence, such conviction will not be set aside unless it is shown that the false evidence had a material effect on the jury verdict. As explained in *United States ex rel. Wilson v. Warden Cannon*, 538 F.2d 1272, 1277 (1976), *citing Giglio*, 405 U.S. at 153–54:

> "'A finding of materiality of the evidence is required under *Brady* [v. Maryland, 373 U.S. 83(1963)]. A new trial is required if "the false testimony could . . . in any reasonable likelihood have affected the judgment of the jury . . ." *Napue* [v. Illinois, 360 U.S. 264] at 271."

There is some divergence of view among the federal courts of appeals as to the test to be used in determining what impact false testimony will have on the ultimate question of whether a criminal conviction should be set aside. For example, in *United States v. Langston*, 970 F.2d 692, 700 (10th Cir. 1992), the court made this statement with regard to ascertaining the impact of false testimony:

> "The test for materiality is the same as the test for harmless constitutional error. The test for harmless constitutional error is 'whether it appears "beyond a reasonable doubt that the error complained of did not contribute to the verdict obtained.'" *Yates v. Evatt*, 500 U.S. 391, [—] (1991) 'To say that an error did not

contribute to the verdict is, rather to find that error unimportant in relation to everything else the jury considered on the issue in question, as revealed by the record.' *Yates*, [500 U.S. at —]. *Yates* thus instructs us 'to make a judgment about the significance' of the tainted evidence relative to the remaining evidence."

A more general standard was announced in *United States v. Lopez*, 985 F.2d 520, 523 (11th Cir. 1993), where this cryptic test was given: "The standard of review is whether the prosecutor's failure to correct false evidence may have had an effect on the outcome of the trial." (Citations omitted).

Other jurisdictions have also adopted tests for determining the impact of false testimony. The Supreme Court of Illinois in *People v. Cornille*, 448 N.E.2d 857, 866 (1983), relying on its prior decisions, set this standard: "Once the defendant establishes the condemned use of false testimony, he is entitled to a new trial unless the State can establish beyond a reasonable doubt that the false testimony was immaterial in that it did not contribute to the conviction." (Citations omitted). Wisconsin's Supreme Court in *State v. Nerison*, 401 N.W.2d 1, 8 (1987), gave this standard: "Due process requires a new trial if the prosecutor in fact used false testimony which, in any reasonable likelihood, could have affected the judgment of the jury."

Where evidentiary error is concerned, however, the ultimate question is the impact on the verdict. . . . Our test for evi dentiary error is contained in Syllabus Point 2 of *State v. Atkins*, 261 S.E.2d 55 (1979):

> "Where improper evidence of a nonconstitutional nature is introduced by the State in a criminal trial, the test to determine if the error is harmless is: (1) the inadmissible evidence must be removed from the State's case and a determination made as to whether the remaining evidence is sufficient to convince impartial minds of the defendant's guilt beyond a reasonable doubt; (2) if the remaining evidence is found to be insufficient, the error is not harmless; (3) if the remaining evidence is sufficient to support the conviction, an analysis must then be made to determine whether the error had any prejudicial effect on the jury."

Judge Holliday's report concludes that, in light of the overwhelming evidence, further litigation of whether Trooper Zain's misconduct significantly tainted his participation in numerous criminal prosecutions is unwarranted. In this regard, the report states: "It is believed that, as a matter of law, any testimonial or documentary evidence offered by Zain at any time in any criminal prosecution should be deemed invalid, unreliable, and inadmissible in determining whether to award a new trial in any subsequent habeas corpus proceeding". . . .

We agree with Judge Holliday's recommendation that in any habeas corpus hearing involving Zain evidence, the only issue is whether the evidence presented at trial, independent of the forensic evidence presented by Trooper Zain, would have been sufficient to support the verdict. As we have earlier stated, once the use of false evidence is established, as here, such use constitutes a violation of due process. The only inquiry that remains is to analyze the other evidence in the case under the *Atkins* rule to determine if there is sufficient evidence to uphold the conviction.

In those cases in which Zain evidence was presented and a guilty plea was entered, the habeas court's task will require a different analysis. The issue then becomes whether the defendant should be allowed to withdraw the guilty plea. . . .

Ordinarily, at a guilty plea hearing there is no formal testimony given by the State to establish the defendant's guilt, although the defendant is generally called upon to provide a factual basis for the acceptance of the plea. The focus of such a hearing is to determine whether the plea is voluntary, whether the defendant understands the rights he is waiving by virtue of the plea and the nature of the charge against him, n4 and whether the court is satisfied that a factual basis exists for accepting the plea.

. . .

The matters brought before this Court by Judge Holliday are shocking and represent egregious violations of the right of a defendant to a fair trial. They stain our judicial system and mock the ideal of justice under law. We direct Prosecutor Forbes to pursue any violation of criminal law committed by Trooper Zain and urge that he consult with the United States District Attorney for the Southern District of West Virginia. We direct our Clerk to send all relevant papers to both of them. This conduct should not go unpunished.

This corruption of our legal system would not have occurred had there been adequate controls and procedures in the Serology Division. Judge Holliday's report is replete with the deficiencies and derelictions that existed and as were uncovered by the American Society of Crime Laboratory Directors whose team reviewed the forensic data.[6] To ensure that this event does not recur, we direct the Superintendent of the Division of Public Safety to file with the Clerk of this Court a report outlining the steps that are to be taken to obtain certification of the State Police forensic laboratory by the American Society of Crime Laboratory Directors. We direct that this report be filed within sixty days from the date of the entry of this opinion.

Finally, we wish to commend Judge Holliday for the thoroughness of his report and the quality of the investigation he conducted. . . . We adopt Judge Holliday's report and order its immediate implementation.

Implementation of report directed.

---

[6] Judge Holliday in note 7 of his report outlines the work of this organization:

"The American Society of Crime Laboratory Directors, a national association, has established a voluntary Crime Laboratory Accreditation Program in which any crime laboratory may participate in order to demonstrate that its management, operations, personnel, procedures, instruments, physical plant, security, and safety procedures meet certain standards. These standards, which are incorporated into an Accreditation Manual, represent the consensus of the members of ASCLD. For example, the two major requirements for ASCLD/LAB accreditation include (1) periodic, internal case report and case note review and (2) proficiency testing in which blind and/or open samples of which the 'true' results are unknown to the examiner prior to the analysis. State police laboratories which have received ASCLD/LAB accreditation include the Illinois State Police, the Arizona Department of Public Safety, the Washington State Patrol, the Missouri State Highway Patrol, the Michigan State Police, the Oregon State Police, the Texas Department of Public Safety, the North Carolina State Bureau of Investigation, the Virginia Bureau of Forensic Sciences, the Florida Department of Law Enforcement, the Wisconsin State Crime Laboratory, and the Indiana State Police."

IN THE MATTER OF AN INVESTIGATION OF THE WEST VIRGINIA STATE POLICE CRIME LABORATORY, SEROLOGY DIVISION

CIVIL ACTION NO. 93-MISC-402

REPORT

This report is filed pursuant to an administrative order by Chief Justice Margaret L. Workman directing an investigation of the policies, procedures, and records of the West Virginia State Police Crime Laboratory, Serology Division, and contains findings of fact, conclusions of law, and recommendations regarding actions to be taken in light of the investigation.[1]

PROCEDURAL HISTORY

In 1987, Glen Dale Woodall was convicted of multiple felonies, including two counts of sexual assault, and sentenced to a prison term of 203 to 335 years. *State v. Woodall*, 385 S.E.2d 253 (1989). At Woodall's trial, forensic testimony by West Virginia State Police Officer Fred S. Zain indicated that, based upon his scientific analysis of semen recovered from the victims, "The assailant's blood types . . . were identical to Mr. Woodall's." *Id.* at 260. Zain further testified that this combination of blood traits would statistically occur in only 6 of every 10,000 males in West Virginia. *Id.* Although Woodall's conviction was affirmed on appeal, DNA testing ordered by the Supreme Court of Appeals in a subsequent habeas corpus proceeding conclusively established that he Could not have been the perpetrator. In 1992, Woodall's conviction was overturned by the trial court, and he was awarded his freedom.

Following Woodall's release, he retained counsel to institute a suit against the State of West Virginia for false imprisonment. After conducting an investigation, including review Zain's work as Chief of Serology at the Division of Public Safety, the State's insurer recommended settlement for the policy limit of $1 million. Following consultation with the Colonel J.R. Buckalew, Superintendent of the Division of Public Safety, the State of West Virginia settled Woodall's case for $1 million.[2]

At the direction of Colonel Buckalew, an internal audit was conducted regarding Zain's work in the serology department. Later, a grand jury investigation of possible criminal conduct was instituted in the Circuit Court of Kanawha County. Finally, in response to questions regarding the propriety of the insurance settlement, the legislative Commission on Special Investigation initiated its own probe.

The internal audit, conducted by State Police Officers R.S. White and T.S. Smith, identified certain improprieties with respect to Zain's work, but concluded that no

---

[1] This report addresses only the effect of any irregularities in the serology division on the validity of convictions obtained pursuant to its involvement. The investigation did not address either the potential civil liability of the State or the criminal responsibility of former West Virginia Trooper Fred Zain as the result of any irregularities. Consideration is being given to a recommendation, *inter alia*, that the Supreme Court direct the Division of Public Safety to have its Criminal Identification Bureau accredited by the American Society of Crime Laboratory Directors. It is anticipated that a final report will be issued by early December addressing this recommendation.

[2] The chronology of events which resulted in the settlement is set forth in the Petition for Extraordinary Relief filed with the Supreme Court of Appeals on June 2, 1993, by William C. Forbes, Prosecuting Attorney for Kanawha County.

material inclusion or exclusion errors were made. . . ."[3] Colonel Buckalew summarized these findings to William C. Forbes, Prosecuting Attorney for Kanawha County, in a letter dated November 10, 1992, stating that, "Based on our review of those files, we concluded that there is no need to take any further action with respect to any of Fred Zain's cases." On April 6, 1993, however, shortly following Colonel Buckalew's resignation, his successor, Colonel T.L. Kirk, requested further investigation by Prosecutor Forbes.

On June 2, 1993, following such investigation, Prosecutor Forbes filed a petition for extraordinary relief with the Supreme Court of Appeals requesting (1) the appointment of a circuit judge to conduct an investigation into whether habeas corpus relief should be granted to prisoners whose convictions were obtained through questionable forensic evidence and (2) the appointment of an independent forensic expert to conduct a thorough investigation of the serology department at the Division of Public Safety. On June 3, 1993, Chief Justice Margaret L. Workman entered an administrative order recalling the undersigned to supervise an investigation of the serology department at the Division Of Public Safety.

On June 16, 1993, pursuant to the administrative order, Alexander Ross, Coordinator of the West Virginia Prosecuting Attorneys Association, was appointed special prosecutor to represent the State of West Virginia, and George Castelle, Chief Public Defender of Kanawha County, was appointed public defender to represent in this investigation prisoners whose convictions might be affected. An order was also entered directing the transfer of documents in the possession of the Commission on Special Investigation to the Clerk of the Supreme Court of Appeals. These documents consisted of original and photocopy records maintained in the serology department of the Division of Public Safety during the period in which Zain served as director.[4] A further order was entered placing these materials under seal, subject to inspection by the special prosecutor, the public defender, their designates, or any other person pursuant to subsequent order.

On June 17, 1993, it was determined that the records reflected 133 cases in which Zain had made positive identification Of either the suspect or the victim.[5] A list of these individuals was forwarded to Nicholas J. Hun, Commissioner of the Division of Corrections, with a request to conduct a comparison with his records. On June 22, 1993, Commissioner Hun responded, identifying 21 prisoners at the West Virginia Penitentiary, 7 prisoners at the Huttonsville Correctional Center, five prisoners at the Pruntytown Correctional Center, and 5 parolees, in whose cases serology department records indicated that Zain had made a positive identification. Commissioner Hun further identified 24 individuals for whom additional information was needed, such as a social security number, date of birth, or county of conviction, in order to complete his investigation. Later, after this information was secured, 1 additional prisoner at the

---

[3] In deposition testimony taken in connection with this investigation, Smith was asked whether this conclusion included the Woodall case. Smith replied that, in his view, the Woodall case was not an "inclusion/exclusion" problem because the serology evidence did not exclude him as a suspect. The only problem, in Smith's view, was that the strength of the serology evidence was significantly overstated.

[4] Initially, it was represented that Zain served as the director of serology from 1986-1989. Consequently, the records reviewed covered only this period. It later became evident, however, that Zain actually directed the operations of the serology department as early as 1979 and was involved in rendering his expert opinion in West Virginia criminal prosecutions after his departure in 1989.

[5] As previously noted, these cases were drawn from records of cases processed in the serology department during the period of 1986–1989.

West Virginia Penitentiary, 1 additional prisoner at the Huttonsville Correctional Center, and 2 additional parolees were identified. The attorney for one prisoner whose name did not appear on the original list submitted a letter noting that Zain had offered inculpatory testimony at trial. Finally, during his visit to the West Virginia Penitentiary, many other prisoners whose names were not on the original list indicated to the public defender that Zain participated in their prosecutions.[6]

On June 23, 1993, an order was entered appointing the American Society of Crime Laboratory Directors/Laboratory Accreditation Board [ASCLD],[7] and Barry Fisher, Chairman of the Laboratory Accreditation Board, to conduct a preliminary investigation, using such qualified personnel as it deemed appropriate under the circumstances. On July 19, 1993, James McNamara, Laboratory Director of the Florida Department of Law Enforcement, and Ronald Linhart, Supervisor of Serology in the Crime Laboratory for the Los Angeles County Sheriff's Department, began their investigation into the policies, procedures, practices, and records of the serology department during the period Zain served as its director. They were directed to focus their efforts on 36 cases involving individuals initially identified by the Division of Corrections and who are currently incarcerated. They examined the laboratory practices in the serology division, laboratory case files, laboratory records, and trial testimony by Zain in selected cases.

On July 23, 1993, the ASCLD team concluded its investigation and on August 6, 1993, filed its report. Following a meeting with the ASCLD team on July 23, 1993, an order was entered on July 29, 1993, directing the preservation of evidence in 70 cases in which Zain was alleged to have been involved. A copy of this order was sent to every circuit clerk in the State, with directions to forward a copy to every prosecuting attorney, court reporter, and law enforcement agency in the county. A further order was entered the same day, directing the preservation of all records of testing by the serology division of the state police crime laboratory by Zain or performed under his supervision. Later, orders were entered directing the preservation of evidence in another 64 cases in which Zain was alleged to have been involved, for a total of 134 cases.

After analyzing the ASCLD report, the special prosecutor and public defender were authorized to take depositions of former and current employees of the serology lab. On September 2, 1993, depositions were taken from Lynn C. Inman Moreland, employed in the serology lab from 1978 through 1986; Sabrina Gayle Midkiff, employed in the serology lab from 1978 through 1987; Howard Brent Myers, employed in the serology lab since 1986; and Jeffrey A. Bowles, employed in the serology lab since 1988. On

---

[6] n6 Additional prisoners continued to contact the public defender during the course of the investigation to indicate that Zain had been involved in their prosecutions.

[7] The American Society of Crime Laboratory Directors, a national association, has established a voluntary Crime Laboratory Accreditation Program in which any crime laboratory may participate in order to demonstrate that its management, operations, personnel, procedures, instruments, physical plant, security, and safety procedures meet certain standards. These standards, which are incorporated into an Accreditation Manual, represent the consensus of the members of ASCLD. For example, the two major requirements for ASCLD/LAB accreditation include (1) periodic, internal case report and case note review and (2) proficiency testing in which blind and/or open samples of which the "true" results are unknown to the examiner prior to the analysis. State police laboratories which have received ASCLD/LAB accreditation include the Illinois State Police, the Arizona Department of Public Safety, the Washington State Patrol, the Missouri State Highway Patrol, the Michigan State Police, the Oregon State Police, the Texas Department of Public Safety, the North Carolina State Bureau of Investigation, the Virginia Bureau of Forensic Sciences, the Florida Department of Law Enforcement, the Wisconsin State Crime Laboratory, and the Indiana State Police.

September 22, 1993, depositions were taken from Ted A. Smith, employed in the serology department since 1985 and its director since Zain's departure; Bernard Dale Humphreys, employed in the personnel department at Public Safety since 1985; Gary Allen Wick, employed as director of internal affairs at Public Safety since 1988; David L. Lemmon, employed in internal affairs from 1983 to 1987; Robert Scott White, founder of the serology division at the State Police Crime Laboratory in 1964 and director of the crime laboratory from 1990 to 1992, when he retired; Kenneth Wayne Blake, director of the State Police Criminal Identification Bureau, which encompassed the State Police Crime Laboratory, from 1985 to 1988; Larry Lee Herald, director of the State Police Criminal Identification Bureau, from 1977 to 1985; and Kevin H. McDowell, a State Police employee who conducted an internal investigation in 1985. Several invitations were extended to former State Police serologist Fred S. Zain to offer testimony regarding the allegations of misconduct. His attorney initially advised that although Zain would submit to an informal interview, he would not answer any questions under oath.[8] It was determined that unsworn testimony by Zain would not further the goal of the investigation to uncover the truth about his conduct during his tenure in the serology department.

Moreland and Midkiff testified that Zain became their supervisor in 1979 or in the early 1980s. They testified that during their employment, particularly in the later years, they observed Zain recording on his worksheet results from enzyme test plates which appeared to them and to other employees, including State Police Officer Blake, Zain's supervisor, to be blank. Midkiff estimated that she had observed at least 100 instances of such conduct, stating such occurrences became routine over the years and were known in the other divisions of the State Police crime lab. She could not, however, remember the identity of any specific case in which this occurred. Midkiff also testified that it appeared to her that the results found by Zain in such cases appeared to be consistent with results from tests of known samples from the suspect or the victim, thereby inculpating the suspect.[9] Both Moreland and Midkiff testified that they had written a letter reporting these incidents to Herold and Blake, but that no action was taken.[10] Moreland and Midkiff also testified that they showed the blank plates and Zain's worksheets to Zain's supervisors, but nothing was done.[11] Midkiff further attributed her transfer from the serology lab and demotion to the fact that she reported Zain for taking away hair samples she had been requested to test.[12]

Myers and Bowles testified that when they went to work in the serology lab, no one told them of any problems with Zain's work or with the reporting of results. Neither testified that they had ever seen Zain report results from a blank plate, although they agreed that he sometimes reported findings that they would not have. Both attributed these differences in opinion to the fact that Zain had more laboratory experience. Myers did testify that after Zain left the serology lab, he rewrote one of Zain's reports

---

[8] Later, in a letter dated September 17, 1993, Zain's attorney withdrew his offer to submit to an unsworn interview.

[9] This testimony is consistent with the observations of the ASCLD team that, when in doubt, Zain's findings would always inculpate the suspect.

[10] Officials at the Division of Public Safety testified that no such letter was ever received and neither Moreland or Midkiff could produce a copy.

[11] Although Moreland and Midkiff testified that Zain criticized them for being too conservative, both agreed that Zain never tried to force them to make false reports, never tried to override or change their reports, and never asked them to testify to results with which they disagreed.

[12] Midkiff testified that her personnel records reflect other reasons for her demotion and transfer.

because he disagreed with its conclusions. Myers also testified that after he had been unable to find blood on a murder suspect's jacket, it was sent to Texas, where Zain found a bloodstain which tested consistent with the blood of the victim. In addition, Bowles testified that at some point he began to have doubts about whether all of the tests for which results were reported by Zain had been actually performed, based primarily on his perception that a large number of tests appeared to have been done in a short period of time. Bowles also testified that at least twice after Zain left the lab, evidence on which Bowles had been unable to obtain genetic markers was subsequently sent to Texas for testing by Zain, who again was able to identify genetic markers.[13]

Smith, who became employed in the serology department after the departure of Moreland and Midkiff, testified that prior to his 1992 audit of Zain's work,[14] he was unaware of any complaints regarding misconduct on the part of Zain. He testified that Zain, as his supervisor, never requested him to report results with which be disagreed. He further testified that he was never asked to report that tests had been performed when they had not been performed. Smith did testify, however, that after Zain left the department, problems began to surface with Zain's work.[15] For example, after his departure to Texas, Zain was asked to retest evidence and would report findings inconsistent with those of the serology department.[16] In preparing for trial, serology department employees were occasionally unable to match Zain's reports to laboratory notes prepared when testing was performed. Smith testified that, eventually, the employees in the serology department became so concerned with the validity of Zain's reports, they refused to testify in the cases involved in those reports.[17] Despite these problems, Smith testified that he was deeply disturbed[18] when, as the result of the 1992 audit, he discovered evidence that Zain had falsely reported results on worksheets that could not be supported by data on the laboratory notes, including falsely reporting that testing had been performed on multiple items, when only a few had been tested, and falsely reporting that multiple genetic markers had been identified, when only a few had been identified.[19] Smith also discovered what appeared to be material alterations to laboratory notes by Zain. As with the ASCLD investigation, Smith

---

[13] Myers and Bowles testified that Zain never attempted to force them to change results or report results that they did not agree with, did not try to get them to testify falsely or contrary to their findings, and did not, as far as they knew, fabricate evidence.

[14] Smith testified that the audit was prompted by the Woodall settlement.

[15] Smith further testified that after he became director of the serology department, he changed several procedures in order to improve the quality of the testing being performed. For example, the department began quantifying the amount of seminal fluid tested, which Smith testified is helpful in interpreting serological observations. Smith did testify, however, that, to the best of his knowledge and belief, the testing procedures used in the serology department during Zain's tenure were in conformance with contemporary principles of forensic testing.

[16] After Zain left the serology department, in spite of concern regarding his work, he was requested to perform forensic analysis in cases in which he was not involved prior to his departure. One of the reasons this occurred, according to Smith's testimony, was that several prosecutors expressed dissatisfaction with the reports they were receiving from serology and specifically requested that the evidence be analyzed by Zain.

[17] Consequently, Zain continued to testify in cases in which he was involved prior to his departure.

[18] Specifically, Smith testified that, "I saw my whole world crumbling. That was just my first response, I thought, 'Gosh, I just can't believe this. I just can't believe it.' I would go into the Lieutenant's office, and I'd go in and I'd shake my head, 'I just can't believe it,' because I didn't see a reason for it."

[19] Although Smith admitted that it was theoretically possible that Zain had performed additional testing without anyone's knowledge to support Zain's reports that such testing had been performed or genetic markers had been identified, Smith testified that such testing would have ordinarily been documented in some fashion, which had not been done.

discovered improprieties in every case he reviewed in which Zain had been involved.

Humphreys testified that he could not locate the Moreland and Midkiff letter in Zain's personnel file.[20] He further testified, however, that it was possible that it had been retained by one of Zain's supervisors and that, because the matter was resolved without the superintendent's involvement, the letter was never placed in Zain's personnel file. Humphreys finally testified that, other than Zain himself in 1988, no one had reviewed Zain's personnel file for several years.

Lemmon testified that he was aware only of problems of a personal nature that Moreland and Midkiff had with Zain. Lemmon further testified that although the results of any internal investigation regarding Zain's misconduct or incompetence should have been on file and that he was aware that an internal investigation had been conducted, he could not explain why a file could not be located in internal affairs.

McDowell testified that the internal investigation he conducted at the direction of Blake, Zain's supervisor, was precipitated by emotional problems suffered by Midkiff, allegedly caused, in part, by her conflicts with Zain. McDowell stated that, as a part of the Midkiff investigation,[21] he contacted FBI officials, who indicated that Zain "apparently doesn't like to do things by the book."[22] Finally, McDowell's investigation, he noted, was primarily directed at Midkiff and not Zain.

Wick located a letter in the Midkiff investigation file from Blake, who was then Zain's supervisor, dated March 18, 1985, to Kenneth W. Nimmich, Assistant Section Chief, Federal Bureau of Investigation Academy, Quantico, Virginia, which stated:

> In regard to your telephone conversations with Trooper K.H. McDowell reference an internal investigation being conducted within our laboratory, I request any information such as grades, practical examinations, attitudes, abilities etc., that you can provide regarding T/Sergeant F. S. Zains attendance at the schools he attended at the FBI Academy.
>
> This is an internal investigation being conducted within our organization and any information obtained will only be used for an internal investigation of *allegations of misconduct and incompetence on one of the members assigned to the Serology section Of our laboratory.*
>
> F. S. Zain attended two (2) courses relating to serology on the following dates: (1) March 13–25, 1977, (2) October 22–November 4, 1978.
>
> Thank you for your cooperation.

(Emphasis supplied). Despite the existence of this letter in the Midkiff investigation file, however, Wick testified that he could locate no complaints or other evidence regarding any internal investigation of Zain during his tenure in the serology department. Wick further testified that he could not find a copy of the letter allegedly written by Moreland and Midkiff to Zain's supervisors regarding allegations of his misconduct.

---

[20] Teresa L. Sage, an assistant attorney general assigned to the West Virginia State Police, submitted a letter indicating that a search of the laboratory's general correspondence files also failed to disclose this letter.

[21] Unquestionably, the primary focus of McDowell's investigation was Midkiff. Only after Midkiff's allegations against Zain did McDowell pursue what can best be described as an inquiry into those allegations. It is fairly clear that at no time did anyone consider the focus of the investigation to be Zain.

[22] Specifically, in notes apparently taken by McDowell during telephone Conversations with FBI instructors, he recorded, "Jim Mudd & Jim Kearney found Fred amusing made comments like Fred does not do things by the book etc. don't see how you can work with him."

White testified that although he vaguely remembered both Moreland and Midkiff complaining that Zain was reporting results from tests they performed which varied from their interpretations, he could not remember any of the specifics. He further remembered conversations with Zain in which he accused Moreland and Midkiff of incompetence. White testified that he did not recall seeing a letter from Moreland and Midkiff complaining about Zain's misconduct and incompetence. White did remember, however, that an inquiry into Zain's work had been conducted and that White had been directed by Blake to contact the FBI instructor who had taught a serology course Zain attended. White further recalled being told by the FBI instructor that Zain "did well below the class average." With respect to this inquiry, White also recollected that the officer in charge had told him that he had recommended to Zain's supervisors that allegations of Zain's misconduct and incompetence should be pursued further. Other than this series of events, however, and other than general statements that Zain was "pro-prosecution" and complaints of a personal, as opposed to a professional, nature, White stated that until the 1992 audit commenced in the wake of the Woodall settlement, he could not recall other allegations of misconduct or incompetence.[23] Finally, White, who assisted Smith in conducting the 1992 audit, corroborated Smith's testimony regarding the results of the audit.[24]

Although he recalled their personal squabbling with Zain, Herald disputed Moreland and Midkiff's contention that they had complained to him that Zain was reporting results from blank plates. Herald also disputed Moreland and Midkiff's contention that they had sent a letter to Herald complaining about Zain's misconduct and incompetence. Herald testified that although, as director of the Criminal Identification Bureau, the serology department was under his supervision, he had no knowledge of the field of serology and stated that he relied on Blake to properly supervise the department.[25]

Blake, like Herald, recalled personal problems between Moreland, Midkiff, and Zain, but disputed that Moreland and Midkiff had complained to him that Zain was fabricating results. He further disputed their assertion that they had written a letter to him complaining about Zain's misconduct and incompetence. He stated, "If they had come to me . . . and said that there was somebody fabricating evidence, oh, Lord, I think the whole roof would have come off this building. . . . I assure you that if there had been a problem with evidence. . . . Zain would have been fired. . . ." Blake was unable to explain, however, why the investigation of Midkiff's emotional problems included contacting the FBI regarding Zain's integrity and professional competence. When asked about the FBI's response, Blake admitted that he recalled negative comments regarding

---

[23] In his deposition testimony, Smith also referred to Zain as "very pro-prosecution," and opined that part of the tension between Midkiff and Zain resulted from her more conservative approach to interpreting test results. For example, Smith stated, "There's always going to be test results that are weak and we have to decide whether we think they are acceptable to call. Typically, Gayle [Midkiff] would say, no, I think they are too weak. I'm not going to call them unless I can duplicate them, as Fred [Zain] may take the approach go ahead and call them[,] based On my experience, I think you can make the call."

[24] White also testified that, following the 1992 audit, Superintendent Buckalew instructed him to contact serologists outside West Virginia about conducting an additional investigation. White stated that although he contacted serologists in Florida, Indiana, and North Carolina, they were either unable or unwilling to conduct such investigation. This testimony was corroborated by Smith, who explained that one reason the issue of an outside investigation was not pursued further was due to Superintendent Buckalew's departure.

[25] In fact, Herald testified in response to a question regarding whether Moreland and Midkiff had shown him how Zain was reporting results from blank plates, "They [might as] well have shown me a page of Chinese arithmetic. I wouldn't have understood that anyway."

Zain's competence, but that he was later assured by another officer that Zain was competent.[26]

Although the testimony of the former and current employees of the Division of Public Safety and the serology department was conflicting, it generally supports the findings of the ASCLD report with respect to Zain's conduct. Without question, as Blake's letter to the FBI indicates, an investigation of another officer in serology was conducted in 1985 which included allegations of misconduct and incompetence on the part of Zain. Whether this inquiry into Zain was prompted by a letter or oral communication is irrelevant. It also appears from the testimony that Zain consistently interpreted marginal or nonexistent scientific evidence as inculpatory. It further appears, from the audit conducted by Smith and White, that serology department records conclusively establish that Zain falsely reported that testing had been performed when it had not been performed and falsely reported results stronger than those which testing had actually reflected.[27] Whether Zain reported findings from blank plates is unclear, but almost everyone who worked with him agreed that he often reported findings with which they disagreed and that those findings consistently inculpated the suspect.

It appears that Zain was quite skillful in using his experience and position of authority to deflect criticism of his work by his subordinates. Evidence regarding whether Zain's supervisors ignored or concealed complaints of his misconduct is conflicting and the issue beyond the scope of this investigation. For the purposes of this investigation, it is sufficient that the deposition testimony provides additional evidence of the allegations of misconduct on the part of Zain.

FINDINGS OF FACT

The ASCLD report identifies multiple incidents of misconduct on the part of former State Police serologist Fred Zain.[28] The deposition testimony of fellow officers in the

---

[26] With respect to its overall operation, Blake testified that, "We ran the laboratory on a shoestring budget, and we went through some very lean years." For example, although Blake wanted periodic proficiency testing of his technicians, he testified that his budget did not permit such testing as frequently as he would have liked.

[27] It further appears that Zain may have testified falsely concerning his academic credentials. In *State v. William E. Smith*, Raleigh County Criminal Action No. 85-F-43, Zain testified that, "My educational background is that I have a Bachelor of Science degree in Biology *with a minor in chemistry.*" [Emphasis supplied]. The undergraduate transcript which appears in his personnel file reflects a major in biology, but no entry appears under the designation "minor." The transcript further reflects that although Zain registered a total of nine times for chemistry courses, his academic record was less than stellar. He received an "F" in Organic Chemistry and only received a "D" when he later took the course. He received a "D" in Organic Chemistry Lab and, after withdrawing from an earlier course, received a "C" in General Chemistry. In addition to this grade of "C" in the three-hour General Chemistry course, Zain received a "B" in a two-hour chemistry course entitled "Qualitative Analysis," a "B" in a three-hour course entitled "General Chemistry Qualitative Analysis," and an "A" in a two-hour course entitled "Quantitative Analysis." Thus, it appears that Zain had only 10 hours of chemistry courses in which he received a grade of "C" or above. In addition to his rather poor performance in most of his chemistry courses, Zain's transcript reflects an "F" in Zoology, in which he later received a "C," a "D" in Botany, a "D" in College Algebra, and a "D" in Genetics.

[28] The qualifications of the members of the ASCLD team are excellent. James J. McNamara, with over 15 years forensic serology experience, has been Bureau Chief/Special Agent of the Florida Department of Law Enforcement, Orlando Regional Crime Laboratory, since 1988. In addition to a Master of Public Administration from the University of Central Florida, a Master of Science in Criminal Justice from Rollins College, and a Bachelor of Science in Forensic Science from the University of Central Florida, Mr. McNamara has attended many graduate courses and seminars in the field of forensic science, holds several memberships in state and national forensic science associations, and has testified in numerous trials at both the state and federal level

serology department during Zain's tenure lends additional support to the ASCLD findings.

The acts of misconduct on the part of Zain included (1) Overstating the strength of results; (2) Overstating the frequency of genetic matches on individual pieces of evidence; (3) misreporting the frequency of genetic matches on multiple pieces of evidence; (4) reporting that multiple items had been tested, when only a single item had been tested; (5) reporting inconclusive results as conclusive; (6) repeatedly altering laboratory records; (7) grouping results to create the erroneous impression that genetic markers had been obtained from all samples tested; (8) failing to report conflicting results; (9) failing to conduct or to report conducting additional testing to resolve conflicting results; (10) implying a match with a suspect when testing supported only a match with the victim; and (11) reporting scientifically impossible or improbable results. Moreover, the ASCLD team concluded that this misconduct was "the result of systematic practice rather than an occasional inadvertent error."[29]

Some of the ASCLD comments on specific cases reviewed are illustrative of the types of activity in which Zain engaged. They raise the distinct possibility that Zain's pattern of misconduct may have resulted in serious miscarriages of justice in cases in which he was involved. In *State v. Gerald Wayne Davis*, the report states, "The reported results showed an ABO type foreign to both victim and defendant. The remaining marker was identical to the victim. This would normally be interpreted as *excluding* defendant *as the* semen donor. The report incorrectly implied a match between the semen and the defendant. The ABO mismatch was dismissed as bacterial contamination by Mr. Zain. However, no satisfactory foundation for that opinion was found in the laboratory records nor the transcript of testimony. If the ABO result is discounted, the correct conclusion is no information regarding the semen donor." [Emphasis added]. In *State v. David McDonald*, the report states, "Many of the samples gave no results with some markers, but a result was listed on the worksheet. ABO types were listed for all samples on the worksheets. However, no ABO typing was found for this case in the data sheets." In *State v. Robert Parsons*, the report states, "The enzyme typing on blood on an orange towel . . . gave results consistent with the victim, excluding the defendant. This was run four times, as reflected on the data sheets, with equivalent results. The ABO type was run once and gave a result consistent with the defendant, excluding the victim. . . . The final report attributed the blood to the defendant based on ABO type only. The enzymes were not reported. This appears to be an incorrect attribution of donor of the blood on the towel." In *State v. Darrell Lee white*, the report states, "All items were listed together on the report of typing results implying, incorrectly, that all typing markers gave results for all items. No incorrect attribution appears to have been made, but the weight of the match was overstated." In *State v. Thomas Sayre*, the report states, "This was a sexual assault case in which the typing results were identical to the victim. The

---

in the State of Florida. Ronald R. Linhart, with over 20 years forensic science experience, has been Supervising Criminalist in the Los Angeles County Sheriff's Department since 1988. In addition to a Bachelor of Science in Chemistry from the University of California at Riverside, Mr. Linhart has attended graduate courses at UCLA and California State at Los Angeles, has participated in numerous training programs, including ones conducted by the Federal Bureau of Investigations, the American Medical Association, and the California Department of Justice, and has offered expert testimony in over 400 cases.

[29] The ASCLD team reported, "Irregularities were found in most of the cases reviewed in this investigation. . . ." Although the ASCLD team acknowledged, "The time available for this investigation prohibited an in depth review for most of the relatively large number of cases presented," it further stated, "We recommend a more thorough technical review of individual cases in which the irregularities may have had a significant impact on pleas or convictions."

reported conclusion was ambiguous but implied a match with the defendant. The report should have stated no information on the semen donor." In *State v. Dale S. O'Neil, the* report states, "Some samples critical to the final conclusion reflected a difference between the worksheet and the data sheet, with the data sheet reflecting the victim's type and the worksheet reflecting a mixture which included the defendant. The worksheet showed evidence of alteration." In *State v. Ronald Bennett, the* report states, "ABO grouping test results . . . indicated A, B, and O activity on a napkin . . . yet the result was reported as 'A.' Data sheets also showed one enzyme type . . . to be not callable on the napkin, yet it was reported. . . . Another enzyme . . . was shown in parentheses on the data sheets which usually meant inconclusive, yet it, too, was called. . . . The data in this case does not support the attribution of donor stated in the case report." In *State v. Micah D. Truitt, the* report states, "[The] data sheet showed 'O' activity on a knife . . . yet the report stated that ABO 'A' was found on the knife. It also showed '635 Jkt R Sleeve' with 'O' activity, but this was not reported at all. There appears to be an incorrect attribution of donor." In *State v. James E. Richardson*, the report states, "There was no evidence that Lewis testing was performed on the swab, but the report implies that it was. The conclusion did not include any frequency, but a transcript was reviewed to see how these results were explained in court by Mr. Zain. He incorrectly multiplied the non-secretor frequency . . . by 50% since the stain included semen (from males only) and finally by the PGM 1∓ frequency, even though there may have been masking by the victim's PGM type. That the semen could not have originated from a secretor based on the absence of any blood group factors is not a certainty as stated in his testimony. . . . The value of the serological testing was overstated in both the report and the testimony."

The ASCLD report also criticized certain operating procedures of the serology division during Zain's tenure, which undoubtedly contributed to an environment within which Zain's misconduct escaped detection. These procedural deficiencies included (1) no written documentation of testing methodology; (2) no written quality assurance program; (3) no written internal or external auditing procedures; (4) no routine proficiency testing of laboratory technicians; (5) no technical review of work product; (6) no written documentation of instrument maintenance and calibration; (7) no written testing procedures manual; (8) failure to follow generally-accepted scientific testing standards with respect to certain tests; (9) inadequate record-keeping; and (10) failure to conduct collateral testing. Although the ASCLD investigators have concluded that these procedural deficiencies appear to have been rectified and do not seriously undermine the validity of testing performed by other technicians in the serology department during Zain's tenure, they demonstrate the danger of relying on forensic evidence analyzed in a laboratory without a proper quality assurance program.[30]

The overwhelming evidence of a pattern and practice of misconduct by Zain completely undermines the validity and reliability of any forensic work he performed or reported during his tenure in the serology department of the state police crime laboratory. If the information which is now available concerning the pattern and practice of misconduct by Zain had been available during the prosecution of cases in which he was

---

[30] The ASCLD team has noted, in a letter submitted following submission of its report, these procedural deficiencies "limit the ability to assess the reliability of analytical results." A comprehensive quality assurance program, therefore, is not only critical to ensuring appropriate testing and reporting methodology, it is crucial to properly reviewing previous work to determine its reliability. In this regard, the ASCLD team further observed, however, that "many forensic laboratories in this Country developed and documented their quality assurance programs during the 1980s. West Virginia was undoubtedly not unique in not having such programs in place in the review period."

involved, the evidence regarding the results of serological testing would have been deemed inadmissible.

CONCLUSIONS OF LAW

The findings of fact made in this report constitute newly discovered evidence. In deciding whether newly discovered evidence in a criminal prosecution warrants the award of a new trial, five factors are considered: (1) whether the evidence was discovered since trial; (2) whether, through the exercise of due diligence by trial counsel, the evidence should have been discovered prior to the conclusion of trial; (3) whether the evidence is not merely cumulative, but provides insights not apparent from the evidence adduced at trial; (4) whether the evidence ought to produce a verdict of acquittal at a second trial; and (5) whether the evidence would merely serve to impeach a prosecution witness. Syl. pt. 1, *State v. O'Donnell*, 443 S.E.2d 566 (1993); Syl. pt. 1, *State v. King*, 313 S.E.2d 440 (1984); Syl., *State v. Frazier*, 253 S.E.2d 534 (1979); Syl. pt. 2, *State v. Stewart*, 239 S.E.2d 777 (1977); Syl. pt. 10, *State v. Hamric*, 151 S.E.2d 252 (1966); Syl., *State v. Farley*, 104 S.E.2d 265 (1958); *State v. Spradley*, 84 S.E.2d 156, 162 (1954) (collecting cases). Due to the nature of these factors, the Court has noted, " 'A new trial on the ground of after-discovered evidence or new discovered evidence is very seldom granted and the circumstances must be unusual or special.' Syllabus Point 9, *State v. Hamric*, 151 S.E.2d 252 (1966)." Syl. pt. 2, *State v. King. supra*. On occasion, however, it has awarded a new trial in a criminal case on the basis of newly discovered evidence. In *State v. O'Donnell, supra*, for example, the Court awarded a new trial based upon a letter to the defendant from the alleged victim of a sexual assault that recanted her story that the group sex which served as the foundation for the prosecution was involuntary. *Id.*at 571–72. In *State v. Stewart, supra*, involving allegations of police misconduct, the Court also awarded a new trial where an informant testified "that the reports from which [the trooper] derived his testimony were routinely altered and falsified." 239 S.E.2d at 785.

Although there is no authority in West Virginia directly involving false testimony by a prosecution expert, the issue has been addressed in other jurisdictions. As a general rule, courts have held that where newly [***62] discovered evidence indicates that an expert witness committed perjury or gave wilfully false testimony during the trial, a new trial will be awarded only where such evidence would probably produce a different result. *Perjury or Wilfully False Testimony of Expert Witness as Basis for New Trial on Ground of Newly Discovered Evidence*, 38 A.L.R.3d 812 (1971). In *State v. Coleman*, 228 N.W.2d 618, 619 (1975), for example, where the newly discovered evidence consisted of a showing that a prosecution expert had testified falsely regarding his academic qualifications, the Nebraska Supreme Court refused to award a new trial, concluding that the expert's background and training, excluding the questionable academic credentials, were sufficient to qualify him as an expert witness.[31] On the other hand, in

---

[31] Similarly, in *State v. Hamilton*, 791 S.W.2d 789, 794 (Mo. App. 1990), where the state's serological expert admitted subsequent to trial that his trial testimony that the defendant was within the 61% of the male population who could have committed a rape was incorrect, but that any male could have committed the crime, the court refused to award a new trial, stating that, "While the latter testimony is marginally in appellant's favor, the practical import of both is the same: neither test exonerates the appellant and neither test clearly implicates him." *See also People v. Lovitz*, 468 N.E.2d 1010 (Ill. App. 1984) (defendant not entitled to new trial due to revised opinion of prosecution's firearms expert after he discovered design defect in gun, because other significant evidence indicated guilt); *Trotter v. State*, 736 S.W.2d 536 (Mo. App. 1987) (defendant not entitled to a new trial where prosecution's firearms expert changed opinion subsequent to trial regarding the type of

State v. DeFronzo, 394 N.E.2d 1027, 1034 (1978), where the newly discovered evidence demonstrated that the prosecution's expert, a police laboratory technician, had falsified not only his academic credentials, but had also testified falsely regarding his training and experience in the fields of drug testing, firearm testing, and handwriting analysis; his performance of certain chemical tests on the drugs involved in the prosecution; and his performance of tests on a firearm involved in the prosecution, the court awarded a new trial.[32]

A careful review of the newly discovered evidence in this case reveals that four of the five elements for the award of a new trial are present. This evidence was obviously discovered since trial. Although some of this evidence could have been discovered by diligent trial counsel, much of it, particularly regarding misconduct by Zain, could not have been reasonably discovered.[33] The evidence is not cumulative, but would have injected a new element in the trial — the intentional falsification of evidence by the prosecution's expert forensic witness.[34] Finally, the evidence goes well beyond mere impeachment evidence, but strikes at the heart of the integrity of the State's case in every prosecution in which Zain was involved.[35] Only the fourth element — whether, excluding the serological evidence, the other evidence adduced at trial would have been sufficient to sustain a conviction beyond a reasonable doubt — remains in doubt.

In order to ascertain whether this newly discovered evidence regarding Zain's misconduct warrants the award of a new trial, the forensic evidence must be analyzed in light of the other evidence of guilt in each of the cases in which he was involved. For example, where the defendant admitted intercourse with the prosecutrix, but asserted that sexual relations were consensual, forensic evidence regarding the source of semen would ordinarily be collateral, and a new trial may not be warranted. On the other hand, where the prosecutrix was unable to identify the defendant as her assailant, but serological evidence identified the defendant as the source of semen found on the

---

Zgun used in the murder of a police officer where there was no attempt at trial to connect the defendant with the gun).

[32] Similarly, in Syl. pt. 1 of *State v. Caldwell*, 322 N.W.2d 574 (Minn. 1992), the Minnesota Supreme Court held, "Appellant is entitled to a new trial where the uncontroverted testimony of the state's fingerprint expert, which was the only significant evidence tending to establish where he was when the murders of which he was convicted were committed, is subsequently discovered to have been incorrect."

[33] In fact, one of the problems in the serology department at the state police crime laboratory during Trooper Zain's tenure as director was that his subordinates were discouraged or prevented from challenging his authority, and none of Trooper Zain's supervisors had the expertise to monitor his activities.

[34] In addition, the absence of comprehensive internal operating procedures in the serology division, a condition apparently inadequately explored by defense counsel in prosecutions in which serological evidence was a factor, could have influenced the weight given such evidence by a jury. As the Court recently noted, for example, in Syllabus Point 2 of *State v. Thomas*, 421 S.E.2d 227 (1992), "There is nothing inherently unreliable in statistical evidence based on blood-typing and enzyme tests. First, blood tests themselves are reliable *when properly conducted*, and these tests are valuable only when their results are placed in the context of statistical probabilities." Consequently, if blood tests are not properly conducted, any statistical conclusions drawn therefrom are inherently unreliable. Statistics can have the unfortunate quality of lending an appearance of legitimacy to questionable scientific conclusions or, as the Court stated in *Thomas, supra* at 691, 421 S.E.2d at 232, "Psuedo-science is eminently convincing because it is accompanied by all the mumbo-jumbo of real science."

[35] In *State v. DeFronzo*, 394 N.E.2d at 1033, the court stated, "The court can conceive of no infringement which is more serious than the lying of a police officer which substantially contributes to the conviction and loss of freedom of a defendant. . . . The court is perplexed as to why the State is satisfied to have the conviction stand under such circumstances. The State seems to fail to realize that its highest duty to the people of the State of Ohio is the participation in the system's quest for justice. The word justice is not synonymous with the word convictions."

victim's undergarments, and the defense was alibi, a new trial may be warranted. Accordingly, in order to determine whether a new trial should be granted to defendants in whose cases in which Zain rendered an inculpatory report or offered inculpatory testimony, it will be necessary to analyze the effect of such involvement in individual prosecutions.

RECOMMENDATIONS

Due to the undisputed nature of the overwhelming evidence of misconduct on the part of Zain, both the special prosecutor and public defender agree that it would not be in the interest of judicial economy to litigate whether his serological work should be subjected to scrutiny in individual cases. It is believed that, as a matter of law, any testimonial or documentary evidence offered by Zain at any time in any criminal prosecution should be deemed invalid, unreliable, and inadmissible in determining whether to award a new trial in any subsequent habeas corpus proceeding. The only issue in any habeas corpus proceeding would be whether the evidence presented at or prior to trial or prior to the entry of a guilty plea, independent of the forensic evidence presented by Zain, would have been sufficient to support the verdict or plea.

Due to many factors, including inadequate record-keeping by the serology department, it is impossible to ascertain, with any degree of certainty, the identity of every case in which Zain may have been involved. Therefore, it is recommended that the Division of Corrections be directed to inform all prisoners and parolees of their right to file a petition for post-conviction habeas corpus with the Supreme Court of Appeals if Zain was involved in their prosecution and rendered an inculpatory report or offered inculpatory testimony.[36] If the Supreme Court determines, through whatever procedure it deems appropriate, that Zain was involved in a petitioner's prosecution, the Court could then issue a rule to show cause returnable before the presiding judge or in the circuit court of the county of conviction. The circuit court could then appoint counsel to represent the petitioner to ascertain (1) whether Zain was involved in the petitioner's prosecution; (2) whether Zain rendered an inculpatory report or offered inculpatory testimony; and (3) whether, excluding the serological evidence, the other evidence adduced at trial would have been sufficient to sustain a conviction beyond a reasonable doubt.

As previously discussed, orders have been entered directing the preservation of evidence in 134 cases in which Zain was alleged to have been involved. Due to recent advances in field of DNA testing, scientifically reliable results can now be obtained from samples which have significantly deteriorated. It is recommended that, as a condition to any post-conviction habeas corpus proceeding, the petitioner be required to consent to DNA testing of any available serological evidence.[37] It is further recommended that an accredited laboratory be designated by the Court to conduct all such testing. If such testing conclusively establishes the guilt of the petitioner, then further habeas corpus proceedings would ordinarily be unnecessary. If such testing conclusively establishes

---

[36] A sample form is attached to this report as one method of allowing prisoners to pursue post-conviction habeas corpus relief due to the involvement of Zain.

[37] This DNA testing, of course, could have been requested by the prosecution even in the absence of this recommendation. Specific language has been included in the proposed post-conviction habeas corpus form to advise prisoners of the DNA testing requirement. Moreover, when an attorney is appointed for the petition when a case is returned to Circuit court, the attorney may advise the petitioner against submission to DNA testing and to voluntarily withdraw the petition.

the innocence of the petitioner, then an order granting his or her release should ordinarily be entered. Only where such testing proves inconclusive should the full post-conviction habeas corpus review be provided.[38]

Dated: November 4, 1993
JAMES O. HOLLIDAY
Senior Judge

---

[38] As a final matter, it is recommended that other than Midkiff's personnel file, Moreland's personnel file, and the McDowell investigation file, other than McDowell's notations regarding conversations with the FBI regarding Zain, the entire investigative file in this matter, including this report, the ASCLD report, correspondence, orders, transcripts, and other documents, should be made available for public inspection. It is further recommended that several copies of these materials should be made available to every correctional facility in which petitioners who seek habeas corpus review pursuant to this report are incarcerated.

Appendix B

Federal Rules of Evidence for United States Courts and Magistrates

ARTICLE I.   GENERAL PROVISIONS

Rule 101.   Scope

These rules govern proceedings in the courts of the United States and before United States bankruptcy judges and United States magistrate judges, to the extent and with the exceptions stated in rule 1101.

Rule 102.   Purpose and Construction

These rules shall be construed to secure fairness in administration, elimination of unjustifiable expense and delay, and promotion of growth and development of the law of evidence to the end that the truth may be ascertained and proceedings justly determined.

Rule 103.   Rulings on Evidence

(a)   **Effect of erroneous ruling.** Error may not be predicated upon a ruling which admits or excludes evidence unless a substantial right of the party is affected, and

(1)   Objection. In case the ruling is one admitting evidence, a timely objection or motion to strike appears of record, stating the specific ground of objection, if the specific ground was not apparent from the context; or

(2)   Offer of proof. In case the ruling is one excluding evidence, the substance of the evidence was made known to the court by offer or was apparent from the context within which questions were asked. Once the court, at or before trial, makes a definitive ruling on the record admitting or excluding evidence, a party need not renew an objection or offer of proof to preserve a claim of error for appeal. But if under the court's ruling there is a condition precedent to admission or exclusion, such as the introduction of certain testimony or the pursuit of a certain claim or defense, no claim of error may be predicated upon the ruling unless the condition precedent is satisfied.

(b)   **Record of offer and ruling.** The court may add any other or further statement which shows the character of the evidence, the form in which it was offered, the objection made, and the ruling thereon. It may direct the making of an offer in question and answer form.

(c)   **Hearing of jury.** In jury cases, proceedings shall be conducted, to the extent practicable, so as to prevent inadmissible evidence from being suggested to the jury by any means, such as making statements or offers of proof or asking questions in the hearing of the jury.

(d)   **Plain error.** Nothing in this rule precludes taking notice of plain errors affecting substantial rights although they were not brought to the attention of the court.

Rule 104.   Preliminary Questions

(a)   **Questions of admissibility generally.** Preliminary questions concerning the qualification of a person to be a witness, the existence of a privilege, or the admissibility of evidence shall be determined by the court, subject to the provisions of subdivision (b).

In making its determination it is not bound by the rules of evidence except those with respect to privileges.

(b) Relevancy conditioned on fact. When the relevancy of evidence depends upon the fulfillment of a condition of fact, the court shall admit it upon, or subject to, the introduction of evidence sufficient to support a finding of the fulfillment of the condition.

(c) Hearing of jury. Hearings on the admissibility of confessions shall in all cases be conducted out of the hearing of the jury. Hearings on other preliminary matters shall be so conducted when the interests of justice require, or when an accused is a witness and so requests.

(d) Testimony by accused. The accused does not, by testifying upon a preliminary matter, become subject to cross-examination as to other issues in the case.

(e) Weight and credibility. This rule does not limit the right of a party to introduce before the jury evidence relevant to weight or credibility.

Rule 105. Limited Admissibility

When evidence which is admissible as to one party or for one purpose but not admissible as to another party or for another purpose is admitted, the court, upon request, shall restrict the evidence to its proper scope and instruct the jury accordingly.

Rule 106. Remainder of or Related Writings or Recorded Statements

When a writing or recorded statement or part thereof is introduced by a party, an adverse party may require the introduction at that time of any other part or any other writing or recorded statement which ought in fairness to be considered contemporaneously with it.

ARTICLE II. JUDICIAL NOTICE

Rule 201. Judicial Notice of Adjudicative Facts

(a) Scope of rule. This rule governs only judicial notice of adjudicative facts.

(b) Kinds of facts. A judicially noticed fact must be one not subject to reasonable dispute in that it is either (1) generally known within the territorial jurisdiction of the trial court or (2) capable of accurate and ready determination by resort to sources whose accuracy cannot reasonably be questioned.

(c) When discretionary. A court may take judicial notice, whether requested or not.

(d) When mandatory. A court shall take judicial notice if requested by a party and supplied with the necessary information.

(e) Opportunity to be heard. A party is entitled upon timely request to an opportunity to be heard as to the propriety of taking judicial notice and the tenor of the matter noticed. In the absence of prior notification, the request may be made after judicial notice has been taken.

(f) Time of taking notice. Judicial notice may be taken at any stage of the proceeding.

(g) Instructing jury. In a civil action or proceeding, the court shall instruct the jury to accept as conclusive any fact judicially noticed. In a criminal case, the court shall instruct the jury that it may, but is not required to, accept as conclusive any fact judicially noticed.

ARTICLE III. PRESUMPTIONS IN CIVIL ACTIONS AND PROCEEDINGS

Rule 301. Presumptions in General in Civil Actions and Proceedings

In all civil actions and proceedings not otherwise provided for by Act of Congress or by these rules, a presumption imposes on the party against whom it is directed the burden of going forward with evidence to rebut or meet the presumption, but does not shift to such party the burden of proof in the sense of the risk of nonpersuasion, which remains throughout the trial upon the party on whom it was originally cast.

Rule 302. Applicability of State Law in Civil Actions and Proceedings

In civil actions and proceedings, the effect of a presumption respecting a fact which is an element of a claim or defense as to which State law supplies the rule of decision is determined in accordance with State law.

ARTICLE IV. RELEVANCY AND ITS LIMITS

Rule 401. Definition of "Relevant Evidence"

"Relevant evidence" means evidence having any tendency to make the existence of any fact that is of consequence to the determination of the action more probable or less probable than it would be without the evidence.

Rule 402. Relevant Evidence Generally Admissible; Irrelevant Evidence Inadmissible

All relevant evidence is admissible, except as otherwise provided by the Constitution of the United States, by Act of Congress, by these rules, or by other rules prescribed by the Supreme Court pursuant to statutory authority. Evidence which is not relevant is not admissible.

Rule 403. Exclusion of Relevant Evidence on Grounds of Prejudice, Confusion, or Waste of Time

Although relevant, evidence may be excluded if its probative value is substantially outweighed by the danger of unfair prejudice, confusion of the issues, or misleading the jury, or by considerations of undue delay, waste of time, or needless presentation of cumulative evidence.

Rule 404. Character Evidence Not Admissible to Prove Conduct; Exceptions; Other Crimes

(a) Character evidence generally. Evidence of a person's character or a trait of character is not admissible for the purpose of proving action in conformity therewith on a particular occasion, except:

(1) Character of accused. In a criminal case, evidence of a pertinent trait of character offered by an accused, or by the prosecution to rebut the same, or if evidence of a trait of character of the alleged victim of the crime is offered by an accused and admitted under Rule 404(a)(2), evidence of the same trait of character of the accused offered by the prosecution;

(2) Character of alleged victim. In a criminal case, and subject to the limitations imposed by Rule 412, evidence of a pertinent trait of character of the alleged victim of the crime offered by an accused, or by the prosecution to rebut the same, or evidence of

a character trait of peacefulness of the alleged victim offered by the prosecution in a homicide case to rebut evidence that the alleged victim was the first aggressor;

(3) Character of witness. Evidence of the character of a witness, as provided in rules 607, 608, and 609.

(b) Other crimes, wrongs, or acts. Evidence of other crimes, wrongs, or acts is not admissible to prove the character of a person in order to show action in conformity therewith. It may, however, be admissible for other purposes, such as proof of motive, opportunity, intent, preparation, plan, knowledge, identity, or absence of mistake or accident, provided that upon request by the accused, the prosecution in a criminal case shall provide reasonable notice in advance of trial, or during trial if the court excuses pretrial notice on good cause shown, of the general nature of any such evidence it intends to introduce at trial.

Rule 405. Methods of Proving Character

(a) Reputation or opinion. In all cases in which evidence of character or a trait of character of a person is admissible, proof may be made by testimony as to reputation or by testimony in the form of an opinion. On cross-examination, inquiry is allowable into relevant specific instances of conduct.

(b) Specific instances of conduct. In cases in which character or a trait of character of a person is an essential element of a charge, claim, or defense, proof may also be made of specific instances of that person's conduct.

Rule 406. Habit; Routine Practice

Evidence of the habit of a person or of the routine practice of an organization, whether corroborated or not and regardless of the presence of eyewitnesses, is relevant to prove that the conduct of the person or organization on a particular occasion was in conformity with the habit or routine practice.

Rule 407. Subsequent Remedial Measures

When, after an injury or harm allegedly caused by an event, measures are taken that, if taken previously, would have made the injury or harm less likely to occur, evidence of the subsequent measures is not admissible to prove negligence, culpable conduct, a defect in a product, a defect in a product's design, or a need for a warning or instruction. This rule does not require the exclusion of evidence of subsequent measures when offered for another purpose, such as proving ownership, control, or feasibility of precautionary measures, if controverted, or impeachment.

Rule 408. Compromise and Offers to Compromise

(a) Prohibited uses. Evidence of the following is not admissible on behalf of any party, when offered to prove liability for, invalidity of, or amount of a claim that was disputed as to validity or amount, or to impeach through a prior inconsistent statement or contradiction:

(1) furnishing or offering or promising to furnish — or accepting or offering or promising to accept — a valuable consideration in compromising or attempting to compromise a claim; and

(2) conduct or statements made in compromise negotiations regarding the claim, except when offered in a criminal case and the negotiations related to a claim by a public office or agency in the exercise of regulatory, investigative, or enforcement authority.

(B)   Permitted uses. This rule does not require the exclusion of the evidence is offered for purposes not prohibited by subdivision (a). Examples of permissible purposes include proving a witness's bias or prejudice; negating a contention of undue delay; and proving an effort to obstruct a criminal investigation or prosecution.

Rule 409.   Payment of Medical and Similar Expenses

Evidence of furnishing or offering or promising to pay medical, hospital, or similar expenses occasioned by an injury is not admissible to prove liability for the injury.

Rule 410.   Inadmissibility of Pleas, Offers of Pleas, Plea Discussions, and Related Statements

Except as otherwise provided in this rule, evidence of the following is not, in any civil or criminal proceeding, admissible against the defendant who made the plea or was a participant in the plea discussions:

(1) a plea of guilty which was later withdrawn;

(2) a plea of nolo contendere;

(3) any statement made in the course of any proceedings under Rule 11 of the Federal Rules of Criminal Procedure or comparable state procedure regarding either of the foregoing pleas; or

(4) any statement made in the course of plea discussions with an attorney for the prosecuting authority which do not result in a plea of guilty or which result in a plea of guilty later withdrawn.

However, such a statement is admissible (i) in any proceeding wherein another statement made in the course of the same plea or plea discussions has been introduced and the statement ought in fairness be considered contemporaneously with it, or (ii) in a criminal proceeding for perjury or false statement if the statement was made by the defendant under oath, on the record and in the presence of counsel.

Rule 411.   Liability Insurance

Evidence that a person was or was not insured against liability is not admissible upon the issue whether the person acted negligently or otherwise wrongfully. This rule does not require the exclusion of evidence of insurance against liability when offered for another purpose, such as proof of agency, ownership, or control, or bias or prejudice of a witness.

Rule 412.   Sex Offense Cases; Relevance of Alleged Victim's Past Sexual Behavior or Alleged Sexual Behavior Or Alleged Sexual Predisposition

(a)   Evidence generally inadmissible. The following evidence is not admissible in any civil or criminal proceeding involving alleged sexual misconduct except as provided in subdivisions (b) and (c):

(1) Evidence offered to prove that any alleged victim engaged in other sexual behavior.

(2) Evidence offered to prove any alleged victim's sexual predisposition.

(b)   Exceptions.

(1) In a criminal case, the following evidence is admissible, if otherwise admissible under these rules:

(**A**) evidence of specific instances of sexual behavior by the alleged victim offered to prove that a person other than the accused was the source of semen, injury or other physical evidence;

(**B**) evidence of specific instances of sexual behavior by the alleged victim with respect to the person accused of the sexual misconduct offered by the accused to prove consent or by the prosecution; and

(**C**) evidence the exclusion of which would violate the constitutional rights of the defendant.

(**2**) In a civil case, evidence offered to prove the sexual behavior or sexual predisposition of any alleged victim is admissible if it is otherwise admissible under these rules and its probative value substantially outweighs the danger of harm to any victim and of unfair prejudice to any party. Evidence of an alleged victim's reputation is admissible only if it has been placed in controversy by the alleged victim.

(**c**) **Procedure to determine admissibility.**

(**1**) A party intending to offer evidence under subdivision (b) must:

(**A**) file a written motion at least 14 days before trial specifically describing the evidence and stating the purpose for which it is offered unless the court, for good cause requires a different time for filing or permits filing during trial; and

(**B**) serve the motion on all parties and notify the alleged victim or, when appropriate, the alleged victim's guardian or representative.

(**2**) Before admitting evidence under this rule the court must conduct a hearing in camera and afford the victim and parties a right to attend and be heard. The motion, related papers, and the record of the hearing must be sealed unless the court orders otherwise.

Rule 413. Evidence of Similar Crimes in Sexual Assault Cases

(**a**) In a criminal case in which the defendant is accused of an offense of sexual assault, evidence of the defendant's commission of another offense or offenses of sexual assault is admissible, and may be considered for its bearing on any matter to which it is relevant.

(**b**) In a case in which the Government intends to offer evidence under this rule, the attorney for the Government shall disclose the evidence to the defendant, including statements of witnesses or a summary of the substance of any testimony that is expected to be offered, at least fifteen days before the scheduled date of trial or at such later time as the court may allow for good cause.

(**c**) This rule shall not be construed to limit the admission or consideration of evidence under any other rule.

(**d**) For purposes of this rule and Rule 415, "offense of sexual assault" means a crime under Federal law or the law of a State (as defined in section 513 of title 18, United States Code) that involved:

(**1**) any conduct proscribed by chapter 109A of title 18, United States Code;

(**2**) contact, without consent, between any part of the defendant's body or an object and the genitals or anus of another person;

(3) contact, without consent, between the genitals or anus of the defendant and any part of another person's body;

(4) deriving sexual pleasure or gratification from the infliction of death, bodily injury, or physical pain on another person; or

(5) an attempt or conspiracy to engage in conduct described in paragraphs (1)–(4).

Rule 414.   Evidence of Similar Crimes in Child Molestation Cases

(a) In a criminal case in which the defendant is accused of an offense of child molestation, evidence of the defendant's commission of another offense or offenses of child molestation is admissible, and may be considered for its bearing on any matter to which it is relevant.

(b) In a case in which the Government intends to offer evidence under this rule, the attorney for the Government shall disclose the evidence to the defendant, including statements of witnesses or a summary of the substance of any testimony that is expected to be offered, at least fifteen days before the scheduled date of trial or at such later time as the court may allow for good cause.

(c) This rule shall not be construed to limit the admission or consideration of evidence under any other rule.

(d) For purposes of this rule and Rule 415, "child" means a person below the age of fourteen, and "offense of child molestation" means a crime under Federal law or the law of a State (as defined in section 513 of title 18, United States Code) that involved:

(1) any conduct proscribed by chapter 109A of title 18, United States Code, that was committed in relation to a child;

(2) any conduct proscribed by chapter 110 of title 18, United States Code;

(3) contact between any part of the defendant's body or an object and the genitals or anus of a child;

(4) contact between the genitals or anus of the defendant and any part of the body of a child;

(5) deriving sexual pleasure or gratification from the infliction of death, bodily injury, or physical pain on a child;

(6) an attempt or conspiracy to engage in conduct described in paragraphs (1)–(5).

Rule 415.   Evidence of Similar Acts in Civil Cases Concerning Sexual Assault or Child Molestation

(a) In a civil case in which a claim for damages or other relief is predicated on a party's alleged commission of conduct constituting an offense of sexual assault or child molestation, evidence of that party's commission of another offense or offenses of sexual assault or child molestation is admissible and may be considered as provided in Rule 413 and Rule 414 of these rules.

(b) A party who intends to offer evidence under this Rule shall disclose the evidence to the party against whom it will be offered, including statements of witnesses or a summary of the substance of any testimony that is expected to be offered, at least fifteen days before the scheduled date of trial or at such later time as the court may allow for good cause.

(c) This rule shall not be construed to limit the admission or consideration of evidence under any other rule.

ARTICLE V.   PRIVILEGES

Rule 501.   General Rule

Except as otherwise required by the Constitution of the United States or provided by Act of Congress or in rules prescribed by the Supreme Court pursuant to statutory authority, the privilege of a witness, person, government, State, or political subdivision thereof shall be governed by the principles of the common law as they may be interpreted by the courts of the United States in the light of reason and experience. However, in civil actions and proceedings, with respect to an element of a claim or defense as to which State law supplies the rule of decision, the privilege of a witness, person, government, State, or political subdivision thereof shall be determined in accordance with State law.

Rule 502.   Attorney-Client Privilege and Work Product; Limitations on Waiver

The following provisions apply, in the circumstances set out, to disclosure of a communication or information covered by the attorney-client privilege or work-product protection.

(a)   Disclosure Made in a Federal Proceeding or to a Federal Office or Agency; Scope of a Waiver. When the disclosure is made in a Federal proceeding or to a Federal office or agency and waives the attorney-client privilege or work-product protection, the waiver extends to an undisclosed communication or information in a Federal or State proceeding only if:

the waiver is intentional;

the disclosed and undisclosed communications or information concern the same subject matter; and

they ought in fairness to be considered together.

(b)   Inadvertent disclosure When made in a Federal proceeding or to a Federal office or agency, the disclosure does not operate as a waiver in a Federal or State proceeding if:

the disclosure is inadvertent;

the holder of the privilege or protection took reasonable steps to prevent disclosure; and

the holder promptly took reasonable steps to rectify the error, including (if applicable) following Federal Rule of Civil Procedure 26(b)(5)(B).

(c)   Disclosure Made in a State Proceeding. When the disclosure is made in a State proceeding and is not the subject of a State-court order concerning waiver, the disclosure does not operate as a waiver in a Federal proceeding if the disclosure:

would not be a waiver under this rule if it had been made in a Federal proceeding; or

is not a waiver under the law of the State where the disclosure occurred.

(d)   Controlling effect of court orders. A Federal court may order that the privilege or protection is not waived by disclosure connected with the litigation pending before the court--in which event the disclosure is also not a waiver in any other Federal or State proceeding.

(e)   **Controlling Effect of a Party Agreement.**   An agreement on the effect of disclosure in a Federal proceeding is binding only on the parties to the agreement, unless it is incorporated into a court order.

(f)   **Controlling Effect of This Rule.**   Notwithstanding Rules 101 and 1101, this rule applies to State proceedings and to Federal court-annexed and Federal court-mandated arbitration proceedings, in the circumstances set out in the rule. And notwithstanding Rule 501, this rule applies even if State law provides the rule of decision.

(g)   **Definitions** — In this rule:

(1) "attorney-client privilege" means the protection that applicable law provides for confidential attorney-client communications; and

(2) "work-product protection" means the protection that applicable law provides for tangible material (or its intangible equivalent) prepared in anticipation of litigation or for trial.

ARTICLE VI.   WITNESSES

Rule 601.   General Rule of Competency

Every person is competent to be a witness except as otherwise provided in these rules. However, in civil actions and proceedings, with respect to an element of a claim or defense as to which State law supplies the rule of decision, the competency of a witness shall be determined in accordance with State law.

Rule 602.   Lack of Personal Knowledge

A witness may not testify to a matter unless evidence is introduced sufficient to support a finding that the witness has personal knowledge of the matter. Evidence to prove personal knowledge may, but need not, consist of the witness' own testimony. This rule is subject to the provisions of rule 703, relating to opinion testimony by expert witnesses.

Rule 603.   Oath or Affirmation

Before testifying, every witness shall be required to declare that the witness will testify truthfully, by oath or affirmation administered in a form calculated to awaken the witness' conscience and impress the witness' mind with the duty to do so.

Rule 604.   Interpreters

An interpreter is subject to the provisions of these rules relating to qualification as an expert and the administration of an oath or affirmation to make a true translation.

Rule 605.   Competency of Judge as Witness

The judge presiding at the trial may not testify in that trial as a witness. No objection need be made in order to preserve the point.

Rule 606.   Competency of Juror as Witness

(a)   **At the trial.** A member of the jury may not testify as a witness before that jury in the trial of the case in which the juror is sitting. If the juror is called so to testify, the opposing party shall be afforded an opportunity to object out of the presence of the jury.

(b) Inquiry into validity of verdict or indictment. Upon an inquiry into the validity of a verdict or indictment, a juror may not testify as to any matter or statement occurring during the course of the jury's deliberations or to the effect of anything upon that or any other juror's mind or emotions as influencing the juror to assent to or dissent from the verdict or indictment or concerning the juror's mental processes in connection therewith. But a juror may testify about (1) whether extraneous prejudicial information was improperly brought to the jury's attention, (2) whether any outside influence was improperly brought to bear upon any juror, or (3) whether the verdict reported is the result of a clerical mistake. A juror's affidavit or evidence of any statement by the juror may not be received on a matter about which the juror would be precluded from testifying.

Rule 607.   Who May Impeach

The credibility of a witness may be attacked by any party, including the party calling the witness.

Rule 608.   Evidence of Character and Conduct of Witness

(a) Opinion and reputation evidence of character. The credibility of a witness may be attacked or supported by evidence in the form of opinion or reputation, but subject to these limitations: (1) the evidence may refer only to character for truthfulness or untruthfulness, and (2) evidence of truthful character is admissible only after the character of the witness for truthfulness has been attacked by opinion or reputation evidence or otherwise.

(b) Specific instance of conduct. Specific instances of the conduct of a witness, for the purpose of attacking or supporting the witness' character for truthfulness, other than conviction of crime as provided in rule 609, may not be proved by extrinsic evidence. They may, however, in the discretion of the court, if probative of truthfulness or untruthfulness, be inquired into on cross-examination of the witness (1) concerning the witness' character for truthfulness or untruthfulness, or (2) concerning the character for truthfulness or untruthfulness of another witness as to which character the witness being cross-examined has testified.

The giving of testimony, whether by an accused or by any other witness, does not operate as a waiver of the accused's or the witness' privilege against self-incrimination when examined with respect to matters that relate only to character for truthfulness.

Rule 609.   Impeachment by Evidence of Conviction of Crime

(a) General rule. For the purpose of attacking the credibility of a witness,

(1) evidence that a witness other than an accused has been convicted of a crime shall be admitted, subject to Rule 403, if the crime was punishable by death or imprisonment in excess of one year under the law under which the witness was convicted, and evidence that an accused has been convicted of such a crime shall be admitted if the court determines that the probative value of admitting this evidence outweighs its prejudicial effect to the accused; and

(2) evidence that any witness has been convicted of a crime shall be admitted regardless of the punishment, if it readily can be determined that establishing the elements of the crime require proof or admission of an act of dishonesty or false statement by the witness.

(b) Time limit. Evidence of a conviction under this rule is not admissible if a period of more than ten years has elapsed since the date of the conviction or of the release of the witness from the confinement imposed for that conviction, whichever is the later date, unless the court determines, in the interests of justice, that the probative value of the conviction supported by specific facts and circumstances substantially outweighs its prejudicial effect. However, evidence of a conviction more than 10 years old as calculated herein, is not admissible unless the proponent gives to the adverse party sufficient advance written notice of intent to use such evidence to provide the adverse party with a fair opportunity to contest the use of such evidence.

(c) **Effect of pardon, annulment, or certificate of rehabilitation.** Evidence of a conviction is not admissible under this rule if (1) the conviction has been the subject of a pardon, annulment, certificate of rehabilitation, or other equivalent procedure based on a finding of the rehabilitation of the person convicted, and that person has not been convicted of a subsequent crime that was punishable by death or imprisonment in excess of one year, or (2) the conviction has been the subject of a pardon, annulment, or other equivalent procedure based on a finding of innocence.

(d) **Juvenile adjudications.** Evidence of juvenile adjudications is generally not admissible under this rule. The court may, however, in a criminal case allow evidence of a juvenile adjudication of a witness other than the accused if conviction of the offense would be admissible to attack the credibility of an adult and the court is satisfied that admission in evidence is necessary for a fair determination of the issue of guilt or innocence.

(e) **Pendency of appeal.** The pendency of an appeal therefrom does not render evidence of a conviction inadmissible. Evidence of the pendency of an appeal is admissible.

Rule 610.   Religious Beliefs or Opinions

Evidence of the beliefs or opinions of a witness on matters of religion is not admissible for the purpose of showing that by reason of their nature the witness' credibility is impaired or enhanced.

Rule 611.   Mode and Order of Interrogation and Presentation

(a) **Control by court.** The court shall exercise reasonable control over the mode and order of interrogating witnesses and presenting evidence so as to (1) make the interrogation and presentation effective for the ascertainment of the truth, (2) avoid needless consumption of time, and (3) protect witnesses from harassment or undue embarrassment.

(b) **Scope of cross-examination.** Cross-examination should be limited to the subject matter of the direct examination and matters affecting the credibility of the witness. The court may, in the exercise of discretion, permit inquiry into additional matters as if on direct examination.

(c) **Leading questions.** Leading questions should not be used on the direct examination of a witness except as may be necessary to develop the witness' testimony. Ordinarily leading questions should be permitted on cross-examination. When a party calls a hostile witness, an adverse party, or a witness identified with an adverse party, interrogation may be by leading questions.

Rule 612.   Writing Used to Refresh Memory

Except as otherwise provided in criminal proceedings by section 3500 of title 18, United States Code, if a witness uses a writing to refresh memory for the purpose of testifying, either:

(1) while testifying, or

(2) before testifying, if the court in its discretion determines it is necessary in the interests of justice,

an adverse party is entitled to have the writing produced at the hearing, to inspect it, to cross-examine the witness thereon, and to introduce in evidence those portions which relate to the testimony of the witness. If it is claimed that the writing contains matters not related to the subject matter of the testimony the court shall examine the writing in camera, excise any portions not so related, and order delivery of the remainder to the party entitled thereto. Any portion withheld over objections shall be preserved and made available to the appellate court in the event of an appeal. If a writing is not produced or delivered pursuant to order under this rule, the court shall make any order justice requires, except that in criminal cases when the prosecution elects not to comply, the order shall be one striking the testimony or, if the court in its discretion determines that the interests of justice so require, declaring a mistrial.

Rule 613.   Prior Statements of Witnesses

(a) **Examining witness concerning prior statement.** In examining a witness concerning a prior statement made by the witness, whether written or not, the statement need not be shown nor its contents disclosed to the witness at that time, but on request the same shall be shown or disclosed to opposing counsel.

(b) **Extrinsic evidence of prior inconsistent statement of witness.** Extrinsic evidence of a prior inconsistent statement by a witness is not admissible unless the witness is afforded an opportunity to explain or deny the same and the opposite party is afforded an opportunity to interrogate the witness thereon, or the interests of justice otherwise require. This provision does not apply to admissions of a party-opponent as defined in rule 801(d)(2).

Rule 614.   Calling and Interrogation of Witnesses by Court

(a) **Calling by court.** The court may, on its own motion or at the suggestion of a party, call witnesses, and all parties are entitled to cross-examine witnesses thus called.

(b) **Interrogation by court.** The court may interrogate witnesses, whether called by itself or by a party.

(c) **Objections.** Objections to the calling of witnesses by the court or to interrogation by it may be made at the time or at the next available opportunity when the jury is not present.

Rule 615.   Exclusion of Witnesses

At the request of a party the court shall order witnesses excluded so that they cannot hear the testimony of other witnesses, and it may make the order of its own motion. This rule does not authorize exclusion of (1) a party who is a natural person, or (2) an officer or employee of a party which is not a natural person designated as its representative by its attorney, or (3) a person whose presence is shown by a party to be essential to the presentation of the party's cause, or (4) a person authorized by statute to be present.

ARTICLE VII. OPINIONS AND EXPERT TESTIMONY

Rule 701. Opinion Testimony by Lay Witnesses

If the witness is not testifying as an expert, the witness' testimony in the form of opinions or inferences is limited to those opinions or inferences which are (a) rationally based on the perception of the witness, and (b) helpful to a clear understanding of the witness' testimony or the determination of a fact in issue, and (c) not based on scientific, technical or other specialized knowledge within the scope of Rule 702.

Rule 702. Testimony by Experts

If scientific, technical, or other specialized knowledge will assist the trier of fact to understand the evidence or to determine a fact in issue, a witness qualified as an expert by knowledge, skill, experience, training, or education, may testify thereto in the form of an opinion or otherwise, if (1) the testimony is based upon sufficient facts or data, (2) the testimony is the product of reliable principles and methods, and (3) the witness has applied the principles and methods reliably to the facts of the case.

Rule 703. Bases of Opinion Testimony by Experts

The facts or data in the particular case upon which an expert bases an opinion or inference may be those perceived by or made known to the expert at or before the hearing. If of a type reasonably relied upon by experts in the particular field in forming opinions or inferences upon the subject, the facts or data need not be admissible in evidence in order for the opinion or inference to be admitted. Facts or data that are otherwise inadmissible shall not be disclosed to the jury by the proponent of the opinion or inference unless the court determines that their probative value in assisting the jury substantially outweighs their prejudicial effect.

Rule 704. Opinion on Ultimate Issue

(a) Except as provided in subdivision (b), testimony in the form of an opinion or inference otherwise admissible is not objectionable because it embraces an ultimate issue to be decided by the trier of fact.

(b) No expert witness testifying with respect to the mental state or condition of a defendant in a criminal case may state an opinion or inference as to whether the defendant did or did not have the mental state or condition constituting an element of the crime charged or of a defense thereto. Such ultimate issues are matters for the trier of fact alone.

Rule 705. Disclosure of Facts or Data Underlying Expert Opinion

The expert may testify in terms of opinion or inference and give reasons therefor without first testifying to the underlying facts or data, unless the court requires otherwise. The expert may in any event be required to disclose the underlying facts or data on cross-examination.

Rule 706. Court Appointed Experts

(a) **Appointment.** The court may on its own motion or on the motion of any party enter an order to show cause why expert witnesses should not be appointed, and may request the parties to submit nominations. The court may appoint any expert witnesses agreed upon by the parties, and may appoint expert witnesses of its own selection. An expert witness shall not be appointed by the court unless the witness consents to act. A witness so appointed shall be informed of the witness' duties by the court in writing, a copy of which shall be filed with the clerk, or at a conference in which the parties shall have opportunity to participate. A witness so appointed shall advise the parties of the witness' findings, if any; the witness' deposition may be taken by any party; and the witness may be called to testify by the court or any party. The witness shall be subject to cross-examination by each party, including a party calling the witness.

(b) Compensation. Expert witnesses so appointed are entitled to reasonable compensation in whatever sum the court may allow. The compensation thus fixed is payable from funds which may be provided by law in criminal cases and civil actions and proceedings involving just compensation under the fifth amendment. In other civil actions and proceedings the compensation shall be paid by the parties in such proportion and at such time as the court directs, and thereafter charged in like manner as other costs.

(c) Disclosure of appointment. In the exercise of its discretion, the court may authorize disclosure to the jury of the fact that the court appointed the expert witness.

(d) Parties' experts of own selection. Nothing in this rule limits the parties in calling expert witnesses of their own selection.

ARTICLE VIII. HEARSAY

Rule 801. Definitions

The following definitions apply under this article:

(a) Statement. A "statement" is (1) an oral or written assertion or (2) nonverbal conduct of a person, if it is intended by the person as an assertion.

(b) Declarant. A "declarant" is a person who makes a statement.

(c) Hearsay. "Hearsay" is a statement, other than one made by the declarant while testifying at the trial or hearing, offered in evidence to prove the truth of the matter asserted.

(d) Statements which are not hearsay. A statement is not hearsay if —

(1) Prior statement by witness. The declarant testifies at the trial or hearing and is subject to cross-examination concerning the statement, and the statement is (A) inconsistent with the declarant's testimony, and was given under oath subject to the penalty of perjury at a trial, hearing, or other proceeding, or in a deposition, or (B) consistent with the declarant's testimony and is offered to rebut an express or implied charge against the declarant of recent fabrication or improper influence or motive, or (C) one of identification of a person made after perceiving the person; or

(2) Admission by party-opponent. The statement is offered against a party and is (A) the party's own statement, in either an individual or a representative capacity or (B) a statement of which the party has manifested an adoption or belief in its truth, or (C) a statement by a person authorized by the party to make a statement concerning the subject, or (D) a statement by the party's agent or servant concerning a matter within the scope of the agency or employment, made during the existence of the relationship, or (E) a statement by a coconspirator of a party during the course and in furtherance of the conspiracy. The contents of the statement shall be considered but are not alone sufficient to establish the declarant's authority under subdivision (C), the agency or employment relationship and scope thereof under subdivision (D), or the existence of the conspiracy and the participation therein of the declarant and the party against whom the statement is offered under subdivision (E).

Rule 802. Hearsay Rule

Hearsay is not admissible except as provided by these rules or by other rules prescribed by the Supreme Court pursuant to statutory authority or by Act of Congress.

Rule 803. Hearsay Exceptions; Availability of Declarant Immaterial

The following are not excluded by the hearsay rule, even though the declarant is available as a witness:

(1) Present sense impression. A statement describing or explaining an event or condition made while the declarant was perceiving the event or condition, or immediately thereafter.

(2) Excited utterance. A statement relating to a startling event or condition made while the declarant was under the stress of excitement caused by the event or condition.

(3) Then existing mental, emotional, or physical condition. A statement of the declarant's then existing state of mind, emotion, sensation, or physical condition (such as intent, plan, motive, design, mental feeling, pain, and bodily health), but not including a statement of memory or belief to prove the fact remembered or believed unless it relates to the execution, revocation, identification, or terms of declarant's will.

(4) Statements for purposes of medical diagnosis or treatment. Statements made for purposes of medical diagnosis or treatment and describing medical history, or past or present symptoms, pain, or sensations, or the inception or general character of the cause or external source thereof insofar as reasonably pertinent to diagnosis or treatment.

(5) Recorded recollection. A memorandum or record concerning a matter about which a witness once had knowledge but now has insufficient recollection to enable the witness to testify fully and accurately, shown to have been made or adopted by the witness when the matter was fresh in the witness' memory and to reflect that knowledge correctly. If admitted, the memorandum or record may be read into evidence but may not itself be received as an exhibit unless offered by an adverse party.

(6) Records of regularly conducted activity. A memorandum, report, record, or data compilation, in any form, of acts, events, conditions, opinions, or diagnoses, made at or near the time by, or from information transmitted by, a person with knowledge, if kept in the course of a regularly conducted business activity, and if it was the regular practice of that business activity to make the memorandum, report, record, or data compilation, all as shown by the testimony of the custodian or other qualified witness, or by certification that complies with Rule 902(11), Rule 902(12), or a statute permitting certification, unless the source of information or the method or circumstances of preparation indicate lack of trustworthiness. The term "business" as used in this paragraph includes business, institution, association, profession, occupation, and calling of every kind, whether or not conducted for profit.

(7) Absence of entry in records kept in accordance with the provisions of paragraph (6). Evidence that a matter is not included in the memoranda, reports, records, or data compilations, in any form, kept in accordance with the provisions of paragraph (6), to prove the nonoccurrence or nonexistence of the matter, if the matter was of a kind of which a memorandum, report, record, or data compilation was regularly made and preserved, unless the sources of information or other circumstances indicate lack of trustworthiness.

(8)   Public records and reports. Records, reports, statements, or data compilations, in any form, of public offices or agencies, setting forth (A) the activities of the office or agency, or (B) matters observed pursuant to duty imposed by law as to which matters there was a duty to report, excluding, however, in criminal cases matters observed by police officers and other law enforcement personnel, or (C) in civil actions and proceedings and against the Government in criminal cases, factual findings resulting from an investigation made pursuant to authority granted by law, unless the sources of information or other circumstances indicate lack of trustworthiness.

(9)   Records of vital statistics. Records or data compilations, in any form, of births, fetal deaths, deaths, or marriages, if the report thereof was made to a public office pursuant to requirements of law.

(10)   Absence of public record or entry. To prove the absence of a record, report, statement, or data compilation, in any form, or the nonoccurrence or nonexistence of a matter of which a record, report, statement, or data compilation, in any form, was regularly made and preserved by a public office or agency, evidence in the form of a certification in accordance with rule 902, or testimony, that diligent search failed to disclose the record, report, statement, or data compilation, or entry.

(11)   Records of religious organizations. Statement of births, marriages, divorces, deaths, legitimacy, ancestry, relationship by blood or marriage, or other similar facts of personal or family history, contained in a regularly kept record of a religious organization.

(12)   Marriage, baptismal, and similar certificates. Statements of fact contained in a certificate that the maker performed a marriage or other ceremony or administered a sacrament, made by a clergyman, public official, or other person authorized by the rules or practices of a religious organization or by law to perform the act certified, and purporting to have been issued at the time of the act or within a reasonable time thereafter.

(13)   Family records. Statements of fact concerning personal or family history contained in family Bibles, genealogies, charts, engravings on rings, inscriptions on family portraits, engravings on urns, crypts, or tombstones, or the like.

(14)   Records of documents affecting an interest in property. The record of a document purporting to establish or affect an interest in property, as proof of the content of the original recorded document and its execution and delivery by each person by whom it purports to have been executed, if the record is a record of a public office and an applicable statute authorizes the recording of documents of that kind in that office.

(15)   Statements in documents affecting an interest in property. A statement contained in a document purporting to establish or affect an interest in property if the matter stated was relevant to the purpose of the document, unless dealings with the property since the document was made have been inconsistent with the truth of the statement or the purport of the document.

(16)   Statements in ancient documents. Statements in a document in existence twenty years or more the authenticity of which is established.

(17)   Market reports, commercial publications. Market quotations, tabulations, lists, directories, or other published compilations, generally used and relied upon by the public or by persons in particular occupations.

(18)   ***Learned treatises.*** To the extent called to the attention of an expert witness upon cross-examination or relied upon by the expert witness in direct examination, statements contained in published treatises, periodicals, or pamphlets on a subject of history, medicine, or other science or art, established as a reliable authority by the testimony or admission of the witness or by other expert testimony or by judicial notice. If admitted, the statements may be read into evidence but may not be received as exhibits.

(19)   ***Reputation concerning personal or family history.*** Reputation among members of a person's family by blood, adoption, or marriage, or among a person's associates, or in the community, concerning a person's birth, adoption, marriage, divorce, death, legitimacy, relationship by blood, adoption, or marriage, ancestry, or other similar fact of personal or family history.

(20)   ***Reputation concerning boundaries or general history.*** Reputation in a community, arising before the controversy, as to boundaries of or customs affecting lands in the community, and reputation as to events of general history important to the community or State or nation in which located.

(21)   ***Reputation as to character.*** Reputation of a person's character among associates or in the community.

(22)   ***Judgment of previous conviction.*** Evidence of a final judgment, entered after a trial or upon a plea of guilty (but not upon a plea of nolo contendere), adjudging a person guilty of a crime punishable by death or imprisonment in excess of one year, to prove any fact essential to sustain the judgment, but not including, when offered by the Government in a criminal prosecution for purposes other than impeachment, judgments against persons other than the accused. The pendency of an appeal may be shown but does not affect admissibility.

(23)   ***Judgment as to personal, family, or general history, or boundaries.*** Judgments as proof of matters of personal, family or general history, or boundaries, essential to the judgment, if the same would be provable by evidence of reputation.

Rule 804.   Hearsay Exceptions; Declarant Unavailable

(a)   **Definition of unavailability.** "Unavailability as a witnes" includes situations in which the declarant —

(1) is exempted by ruling of the court on the ground of privilege from testifying concerning the subject matter of the declarant's statement; or

(2) persists in refusing to testify concerning the subject matter of the declarant's statement despite an order of the court to do so; or

(3) testifies to a lack of memory of the subject matter of the declarant's statement; or

(4) is unable to be present or to testify at the hearing because of death or then existing physical or mental illness or infirmity; or

(5) is absent from the hearing and the proponent of a statement has been unable to procure the declarant's attendance (or in the case of a hearsay exception under subdivision (b)(2), (3), or (4), the declarant's attendance or testimony) by process or other reasonable means.

A declarant is not unavailable as a witness if exemption, refusal, claim of lack of memory, inability, or absence is due to the procurement or wrongdoing of the proponent of a statement for the purpose of preventing the witness from attending or testifying.

(b) Hearsay exceptions. The following are not excluded by the hearsay rule if the declarant is unavailable as a witness:

(1) Former testimony. Testimony given as a witness at another hearing of the same or a different proceeding, or in a deposition taken in compliance with law in the course of the same or another proceeding, if the party against whom the testimony is now offered, or, in a civil action or proceeding, a predecessor in interest, had an opportunity and similar motive to develop the testimony by direct, cross, or redirect examination.

(2) Statement under belief of impending death. In a prosecution for homicide or in a civil action or proceeding, a statement made by a declarant while believing that the declarant's death was imminent, concerning the cause or circumstances of what the declarant believed to be impending death.

(3) Statement against interest. A statement which was at the time of its making so far contrary to the declarant's pecuniary or proprietary interest, or so far tended to subject the declarant to civil or criminal liability, or to render invalid a claim by the declarant against another, that a reasonable person in the declarant's position would not have made the statement unless believing it to be true. A statement tending to expose the declarant to criminal liability is not admissible in any criminal case unless corroborating circumstances clearly indicate the trustworthiness of the statement.

(4) Statement of personal or family history. (A) A statement concerning the declarant's own birth, adoption, marriage, divorce, legitimacy, relationship by blood, adoption, or marriage, ancestry, or other similar fact of personal or family history, even though declarant had no means of acquiring personal knowledge of the matter stated; or (B) a statement concerning the foregoing matters, and death also, of another person, if the declarant was related to the other by blood, adoption, or marriage or was so intimately associated with the other's family as to be likely to have accurate information concerning the matter declared.

(5) [Transferred to Rule 807]

(6) Forfeiture by wrongdoing. A statement offered against a party that has engaged or acquiesced in wrongdoing that was intended to, and did, procure the unavailability of the declarant as a witness.

Rule 805. Hearsay Within Hearsay

Hearsay included within hearsay is not excluded under the hearsay rule if each part of the combined statements conforms with an exception to the hearsay rule provided in these rules.

Rule 806. Attacking and Supporting Credibility of Declarant

When a hearsay statement, or a statement defined in Rule 801(d)(2), (C), (D), or (E), has been admitted in evidence, the credibility of the declarant may be attacked, and if attacked may be supported, by any evidence which would be admissible for those purposes if declarant had testified as a witness. Evidence of a statement or conduct by the declarant at any time, inconsistent with the declarant's hearsay statement, is not subject to any requirement that the declarant may have been afforded an opportunity to deny or explain. If the party against whom a hearsay statement has been admitted calls the declarant as a witness, the party is entitled to examine the declarant on the statement as if under cross-examination.

Rule 807. Residual Exception

A statement not specifically covered by Rule 803 or 804, but having equivalent circumstantial guarantees of trustworthiness, is not excluded by the hearsay rule if the court determines that (A) the statement is offered as evidence of a material fact; (B) the statement is more probative on the point for which it is offered than any other evidence which the proponent can procure through reasonable efforts; and (C) the general purposes of these rules and the interests of justice will best be served by admission of the statement into evidence. However, a statement may not be admitted under this exception unless the proponent of it makes known to the adverse party sufficiently in advance of the trial or hearing to provide the adverse party with a fair opportunity to prepare to meet it, the proponent's intention to offer the statement and the particulars of it, including the name and address of the declarant.

ARTICLE IX. AUTHENTICATION AND IDENTIFICATION

Rule 901. Requirement of Authentication or Identification

(a) **General provision.** The requirement of authentication or identification as a condition precedent to admissibility is satisfied by evidence sufficient to support a finding that the matter in question is what its proponent claims.

(b) **Illustrations.** By way of illustration only, and not by way of limitation, the following are examples of authentication or identification conforming with the requirements of this rule:

(1) *Testimony of witness with knowledge.* Testimony that a matter is what it is claimed to be.

(2) *Nonexpert opinion on handwriting.* Nonexpert opinion as to the genuineness of handwriting, based upon familiarity not acquired for purposes of the litigation.

(3) *Comparison by trier or expert witness.* Comparison by the trier of fact or by expert witnesses with specimens which have been authenticated.

(4) *Distinctive characteristics and the like.* Appearance, contents, substance, internal patterns, or other distinctive characteristics, taken in conjunction with circumstances.

(5) *Voice identification.* Identification of a voice, whether heard firsthand or through mechanical or electronic transmission or recording, by opinion based upon hearing the voice at any time under circumstances connecting it with the alleged speaker.

(6) *Telephone conversations.* Telephone conversations, by evidence that a call was made to the number assigned at the time by the telephone company to a particular person or business, if (A) in the case of a person, circumstances, including self-identification, show the person answering to be the one called, or (B) in the case of a business, the call was made to a place of business and the conversation related to business reasonably transacted over the telephone.

(7) *Public records or reports.* Evidence that a writing authorized by law to be recorded or filed and in fact recorded or filed in a public office, or a purported public

record, report, statement, or data compilation, in any form, is from the public office where items of this nature are kept.

(8) Ancient documents or data compilation. Evidence that a document or data compilation, in any form, (A) is in such condition as to create no suspicion concerning its authenticity, (B) was in a place where it, if authentic, would likely be, and (C) has been in existence 20 years or more at the time it is offered.

(9) Process or system. Evidence describing a process or system used to produce a result and showing that the process or system produces an accurate result.

(10) Methods provided by statute or rule. Any method of authentication or identification provided by Act of Congress or by other rules prescribed by the Supreme Court pursuant to statutory authority.

Rule 902. Self-Authentication

Extrinsic evidence of authenticity as a condition precedent to admissibility is not required with respect to the following:

(1) Domestic public documents under seal. A document bearing a seal purporting to be that of the United States, or of any State, district, Commonwealth, territory, or insular possession thereof, or the Panama Canal Zone, or the Trust Territory of the Pacific Islands, or of a political subdivision, department, officer, or agency thereof, and a signature purporting to be an attestation or execution.

(2) Domestic public documents not under seal. A document purporting to bear the signature in the official capacity of an officer or employee of any entity included in paragraph (1) hereof, having no seal, if a public officer having a seal and having official duties in the district or political subdivision of the officer or employee certifies under seal that the signer has the official capacity and that the signature is genuine.

(3) Foreign public documents. A document purporting to be executed or attested in an official capacity by a person authorized by the laws of a foreign country to make the execution or attestation, and accompanied by a final certification as to the genuineness of the signature and official position (A) of the executing or attesting person, or (B) of any foreign official whose certificate of genuineness of signature and official position relates to the execution or attestation or is in a chain of certificates of genuineness of signature and official position relating to the execution or attestation. A final certification may be made by a secretary of an embassy or legation, consul general, consul, vice consul, or consular agent of the United States, or a diplomatic or consular official of the foreign country assigned or accredited to the United States. If reasonable opportunity has been given to all parties to investigate the authenticity and accuracy of official documents, the court may, for good cause shown, order that they be treated as presumptively authentic without final certification or permit them to be evidenced by an attested summary with or without final certification.

(4) Certified copies of public records. A copy of an official record or report or entry therein, or of a document authorized by law to be recorded or filed and actually recorded or filed in a public office, including data compilations in any form, certified as correct by the custodian or other person authorized to make the certification, by certificate complying with paragraph (1), (2), or (3) of this rule or complying with any Act of Congress or rule prescribed by the Supreme Court pursuant to statutory authority.

(5) Official publications. Books, pamphlets, or other publications purporting to be issued by public authority.

(6) Newspapers and periodicals. Printed materials purporting to be newspapers or periodicals.

(7) Trade inscriptions and the like. Inscriptions, signs, tags, or labels purporting to have been affixed in the course of business and indicating ownership, control, or origin.

(8) Acknowledged documents. Documents accompanied by a certificate of acknowledgment executed in the manner provided by law by a notary public or other officer authorized by law to take acknowledgments.

(9) Commercial paper and related documents. Commercial paper, signatures thereon, and documents relating thereto to the extent provided by general commercial law.

(10) Presumptions under Acts of Congress. Any signature, document, or other matter declared by Act of Congress to be presumptively or prima facie genuine or authentic.

(11) Certified domestic records of regularly conducted activity. The original or a duplicate of a domestic record of regularly conducted activity that would be admissible under Rule 803(6) if accompanied by a written declaration of its custodian or other qualified person, in a manner complying with any Act of Congress or rule prescribed by the Supreme Court pursuant to statutory authority, certifying that the record —

(A) was made at or near the time of the occurrence of the matters set forth by, or from information transmitted by, a person with knowledge of those matters;

(B) was kept in the course of regularly conducted activity; and

(C) was made by the regularly conducted activity as a regular practice.

A party intending to offer a record into evidence under this paragraph must provide written notice of that intention to all adverse parties, and must make the record and declaration available for inspection sufficiently in advance of their offer into evidence to provide an adverse party with a fair opportunity to challenge them.

(12) Certified foreign records of regularly conducted activity. In a civil case, the original or duplicate of a foreign record of regularly conducted activity that would be admissible under Rule 803(6) if accompanied by a written declaration by its custodian or other qualified person certifying that the record —

(A) was made at or near the time of the occurrence of the matters set forth by, or from information transmitted by, a person with knowledge of those matters;

(B) was kept in the course of regularly conducted activity; and

(C) was made by the regularly conducted activity as a regular practice.

The declaration must be signed in a manner that, if falsely made, would subject the maker to criminal penalty under the laws of the country where the declaration is signed. A party intending to offer a record into evidence under this paragraph must provide written notice of that intention to all adverse parties, and must make the record and declaration available for inspection sufficiently in advance of their offer into evidence to provide an adverse party with a fair opportunity to challenge them.

Rule 903. Subscribing Witness' Testimony Unnecessary

The testimony of a subscribing witness is not necessary to authenticate a writing unless required by the laws of the jurisdiction whose laws govern the validity of the writing.

ARTICLE X. CONTENTS OF WRITINGS, RECORDINGS, AND PHOTO- GRAPHS

Rule 1001. Definitions

For purposes of this article the following definitions are applicable:

(1) ***Writings and recordings.*** "Writings" and "recordings" consist of letters, words, or numbers, or their equivalent, set down by handwriting, typewriting, printing, photostating, photographing, magnetic impulse, mechanical or electronic recording, or other form of data compilation.

(2) ***Photographs.*** "Photograph" include still photographs, X-ray films, video tapes, and motion pictures.

(3) ***Original.*** An "original" of a writing or recording is the writing or recording itself or any counterpart intended to have the same effect by a person executing or issuing it. An "original" of a photograph includes the negative or any print therefrom. If data are stored in a computer or similar device, any printout or other output readable by sight, shown to reflect the data accurately, is an "original."

(4) ***Duplicate.*** A "duplicate" is a counterpart produced by the same impression as the original, or from the same matrix, or by means of photography, including enlargements and miniatures, or by mechanical or electronic re-recording, or by chemical reproduction, or by other equivalent technique which accurately reproduces the original.

Rule 1002. Requirement of Original

To prove the content of a writing, recording, or photograph, the original writing, recording, or photograph is required, except as otherwise provided in these rules or by Act of Congress.

Rule 1003. Admissibility of Duplicates

A duplicate is admissible to the same extent as an original unless (1) a genuine question is raised as to the authenticity of the original or (2) in the circumstances it would be unfair to admit the duplicate in lieu of the original.

Rule 1004. Admissibility of Other Evidence of Contents

The original is not required, and other evidence of the contents of a writing, recording, or photograph is admissible if:

(1) ***Originals lost or destroyed.*** All originals are lost or have been destroyed, unless the proponent lost or destroyed them in bad faith; or

(2) ***Original not obtainable.*** No original can be obtained by any available judicial process or procedure; or

(3) ***Original in possession of opponent.*** At a time when an original was under the control of the party against whom offered, that party was put on notice, by the pleadings or otherwise, that the contents would be a subject of proof at the hearing, and that party does not produce the original at the hearing; or

(4) *Collateral matters.* The writing, recording, or photograph is not closely related to a controlling issue.

Rule 1005.   Public Records

The contents of an official record, or of a document authorized to be recorded or filed and actually recorded or filed, including data compilations in any form, if otherwise admissible, may be proved by copy, certified as correct in accordance with rule 902 or testified to be correct by a witness who has compared it with the original. If a copy which complies with the foregoing cannot be obtained by the exercise of reasonable diligence, then other evidence of the contents may be given.

Rule 1006.   Summaries

The contents of voluminous writings, recordings, or photographs which cannot conveniently be examined in court may be presented in the form of a chart, summary, or calculation. The originals, or duplicates, shall be made available for examination or copying, or both, by other parties at reasonable time and place. The court may order that they be produced in court.

Rule 1007.   Testimony or Written Admission of Party

Contents of writings, recordings, or photographs may be proved by the testimony or deposition of the party against whom offered or by that party's written admission, without accounting for the nonproduction of the original.

Rule 1008.   Functions of Court and Jury

When the admissibility of other evidence of contents of writings, recordings, or photographs under these rules depends upon the fulfillment of a condition of fact, the question whether the condition has been fulfilled is ordinarily for the court to determine in accordance with the provisions of rule 104. However, when an issue is raised (a) whether the asserted writing ever existed, or (b) whether another writing, recording, or photograph produced at the trial is the original, or (c) whether other evidence of contents correctly reflects the contents, the issue is for the trier of fact to determine as in the case of other issues of fact.

ARTICLE XI.   MISCELLANEOUS RULES

Rule 1101.   Applicability of Rules

(a)   Courts and magistrates. These rules apply to the United States district courts, the District Court of Guam, the District Court of the Virgin Islands, the District Court for the Northern Mariana Islands, the United States courts of appeals, the United States Claims Court, and to United States bankruptcy judges and United States magistrate judges, in the actions, cases, and proceedings and to the extent hereinafter set forth. The terms "judge" and "court" in these rules include United States bankruptcy judges and United States magistrate judges.

(b)   Proceedings generally. These rules apply generally to civil actions and proceedings, including admiralty and maritime cases, to criminal cases and proceedings, to contempt proceedings except those in which the court may act summarily, and to proceedings and cases under title 11, United States Code.

(c)   Rule of privilege. The rule with respect to privileges applies at all stages of all actions, cases, and proceedings.

(d)   Rules inapplicable. The rules (other than with respect to privileges) do not apply in the following situations:

(1) ***Preliminary questions of fact.*** The determination of questions of fact preliminary to admissibility of evidence when the issue is to be determined by the court under rule 104.

(2) ***Grand jury.*** Proceedings before grand juries.

(3) ***Miscellaneous proceedings.*** Proceedings for extradition or rendition; preliminary examinations in criminal cases; sentencing, or granting or revoking probation; issuance of warrants for arrest, criminal summonses, and search warrants; and proceedings with respect to release on bail or otherwise.

(e) Rules applicable in part. In the following proceedings these rules apply to the extent that matters of evidence are not provided for in the statutes which govern procedure therein or in other rules prescribed by the Supreme Court pursuant to statutory authority: the trial of misdemeanor and other petty offenses by United States magistrates; review of agency actions when the facts are subject to trial de novo under section 706(2)(F) of title 5, United States Code; review of orders of the Secretary of Agriculture under section 2 of the Act entitled "An Act to authorize association of producers of agricultural products" approved February 18, 1922 (7 U.S.C. 292), and under sections 6 and 7(c) of the Perishable Agricultural Commodities Act, 1930 (7 U.S.C. 499f, 499g(c)); naturalization and revocation of naturalization under sections 310–318 of the Immigration and Nationality Act (8 U.S.C. 1421–1429); prize proceedings in admiralty under sections 7651–7681 of title 10, United States Code; review of orders of the Secretary of the Interior under section 2 of the Act entitled "An Act authorizing associations of producers of aquatic products" approved June 25, 1934 (15 U.S.C. 522); review of orders of petroleum control boards under section 5 of the Act entitled "An Act to regulate interstate and foreign commerce in petroleum and its products by prohibiting the shipment in such commerce of petroleum and its products produced in violation of State law, and for other purposes," approved February 22, 1935 (15 U.S.C. 715d); actions for fines, penalties, or forfeitures under part V of title IV of the Tariff Act of 1930 (19 U.S.C. 1581–1624), or under the Anti-Smuggling Act (19 U.S.C. 1701–1711); criminal libel for condemnation, exclusion of imports, or other proceedings under the Federal Food, Drug, and Cosmetic Act (21 U.S.C. 301–392); disputes between seamen under sections 4079, 4080, and 4081 of the Revised Statutes (22 U.S.C. 256–258); habeas corpus under sections 2241–2254 of title 28, United States Code; motions to vacate, set aside or correct sentence under section 2255 of title 28, United States Code; actions for penalties for refusal to transport destitute seamen under section 4578 of the Revised Statutes (46 U.S.C. 679); actions against the United States under the Act entitled "An Act authorizing suits against the United States in admiralty for damage caused by and salvage service rendered to public vessels belonging to the United States, and for other purposes," approved March 3, 1925 (46 U.S.C. 781–790), as implemented by section 7730 of title 10, United States Code.

Rule 1102.   Amendments

Amendments to the Federal Rules of Evidence may be made as provided in section 2072 of title 28 of the United States Code.

Rule 1103.   Title

These rules may be known and cited as the Federal Rules of Evidence.

TABLE OF CASES

[References are to pages]

[References are to pages]

[References are to pages]

[References are to pages]

[References are to pages]

[References are to pages]

[References are to pages]

[References are to pages]

[References are to pages]

[References are to pages]

T

[References are to pages]

[References are to pages]

INDEX

* *

[References are to pages.]

A

[References are to pages.]